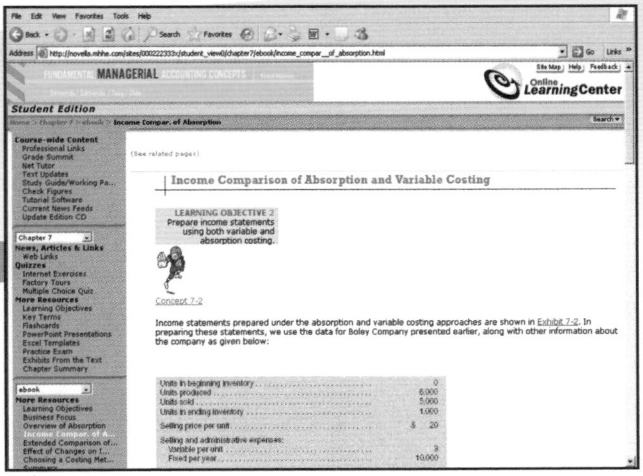

Interactive Online Version
of the Textbook

Online Learning Center

In addition to the textbook, students can rely on this online version of the text for a convenient way to study. The interactive content is integrated with Homework Manager to give students quick access to relevant content as they work through problems, exercises, and practice quizzes.

Features:

- online version of the text is integrated with Homework Manager
- students referred to sections of the online book as they tackle an assignment or take a practice quiz

McGraw-Hill's OnePass eliminates the frustration of remembering multiple access codes for different online resources. Now students can use the access code found on their OnePass card to register and create one password for access to their book's online resources. By having just one access code for everything, students can go back and forth between tutorials as they study. And instructors can use OnePass to integrate these supplements into a learning path that fits a specific teaching style.

ONEpass

Homework Manager helps you

McGraw-Hill's Homework Manager

Assign coursework online

Problems and exercises from the book as well as questions from the testbank have been integrated into Homework Manager to give you many options as you deliver assignments and quizzes to students online. You can choose from static or algorithmic questions and have graded results automatically stored in your gradebook.

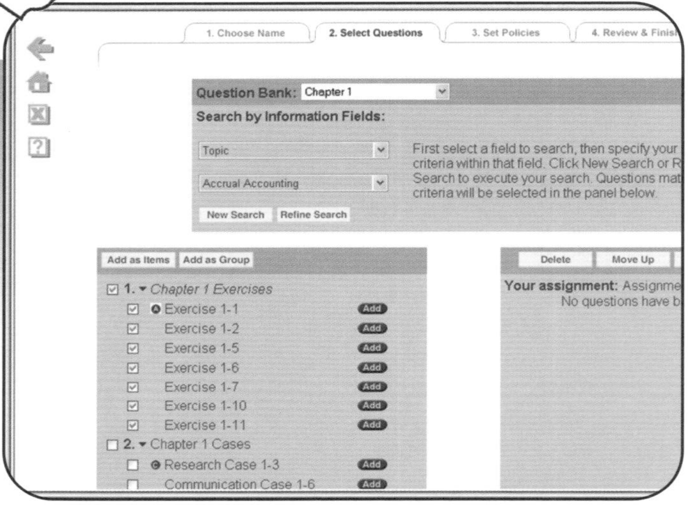

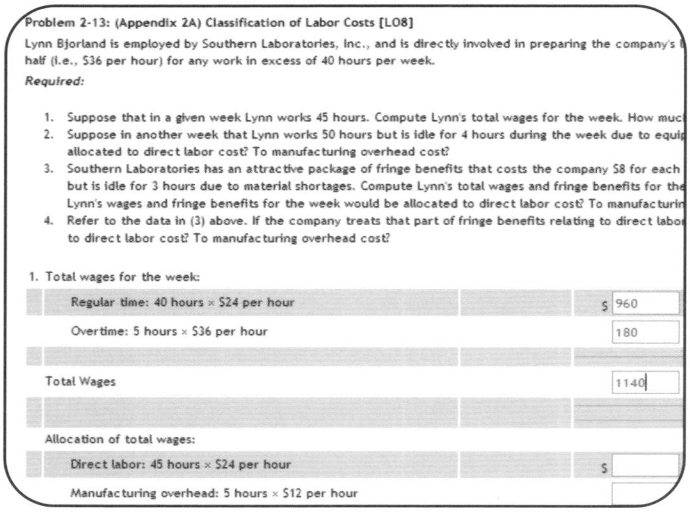

efficiently manage your class.

Control how content is presented.

Homework Manager gives you a flexible and easy way to present coursework to students. You determine which questions to ask and how much help students will receive as they work through assignments. For example, you can determine the number of attempts a student can make with each problem; provide hints and feedback with each question, including references to the online version of the text; and much more.

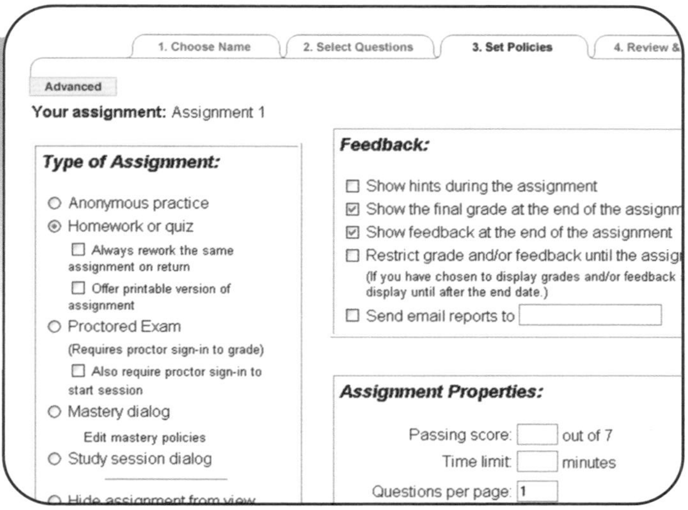

Track student progress.

Assignments are graded automatically, with the results stored in your private gradebook. Detailed results let you see at a glance how each student does on an assignment or an individual problem. You can even see how many attempts it took them to solve it. You can monitor how the whole class does on each problem, and even exactly where individual students might need extra help.

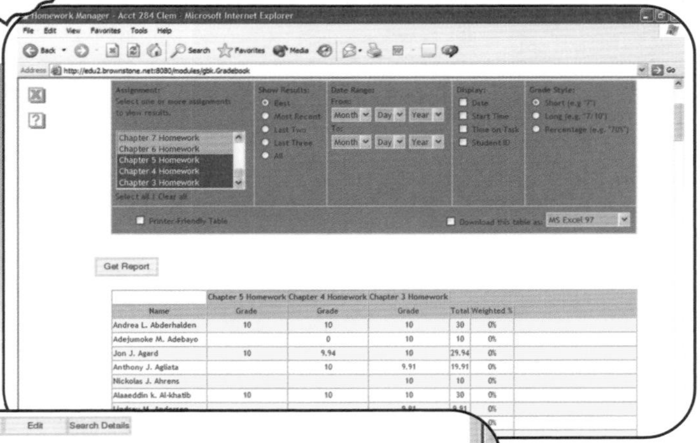

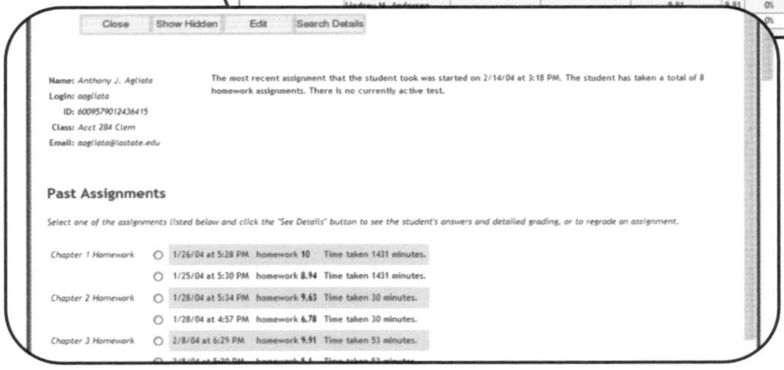

Professors can allow Homework Manager to give students helpful feedback.

Auto-grading and feedback.

Question 1: *Score 6.5/8*

Your response	Correct response

Your response

Exercise 2-1: Using Cost Terms [LO2, LO5, LO7]

Following are a number of cost terms introduced in the chapter:

Period cost	Fixed cost
Variable cost	Prime cost
Opportunity cost	Conversion cost
Product cost	Sunk cost

Choose the cost term or terms above that most appropriately describe the costs identified in each of the following situations. A cost term can be used more than once.

1. Crestline Books, Inc., prints a small book titled *The Pocket Speller*. The paper going into the manufacture of the book would be called direct materials and classified as a `Product cost` (6%). In terms of cost behavior, the paper could also be described as a `Product cost` (0%) with respect to the number of books printed.
2. Instead of compiling the words in the book, the author hired by the company could have earned considerable fees consulting with business organizations. The consulting fees forgone by the author would be called `Opportunity cost` (6%).
3. The paper and other materials used in the manufacture of the book, combined with the direct labor cost involved, would be called `Prime cost` (6%).
4. The salary of Crestline Books' president would be classified as a `Product cost` (0%), and the salary will appear on the income statement as an expense in the time period in which it is incurred.
5. Depreciation on the equipment used to print the book would be classified by Crestline Books as a `Product cost` (6%). However, depreciation on any equipment used by the company in selling and administrative activities would be classified as a `Period cost` (6%). In terms of cost behavior, depreciation would probably be classified as a `Fixed cost` (6%) with respect to the number of books printed.
6. A `Product cost` (6%) is also known as an inventoriable cost,

Correct response

Exercise 2-1: Using Cost Terms [LO2, LO5, LO7]

Following are a number of cost terms introduced in the chapter:

Period cost	Fixed cost
Variable cost	Prime cost
Opportunity cost	Conversion cost
Product cost	Sunk cost

Choose the cost term or terms above that most appropriately describe the costs identified in each of the following situations. A cost term can be used more than once.

1. Crestline Books, Inc., prints a small book titled *The Pocket Speller*. The paper going into the manufacture of the book would be called direct materials and classified as a `Product cost`. In terms of cost behavior, the paper could also be described as a `variable cost` with respect to the number of books printed.
2. Instead of compiling the words in the book, the author hired by the company could have earned considerable fees consulting with business organizations. The consulting fees forgone by the author would be called `Opportunity cost`.
3. The paper and other materials used in the manufacture of the book, combined with the direct labor cost involved, would be called `Prime cost`.
4. The salary of Crestline Books' president would be classified as a `Period cost`, and the salary will appear on the income statement as an expense in the time period in which it is incurred.
5. Depreciation on the equipment used to print the book would be classified by Crestline Books as a `Product cost`. However, depreciation on any equipment used by the company in selling and administrative activities would be classified as a `Period cost`. In terms of cost behavior, depreciation would probably be classified as a `Fixed cost` with respect to the number of books printed.
6. A `Product cost` is also known as an inventoriable cost, since

Immediately after finishing an assignment or quiz, students can compare their answers side by side with the detailed solutions. Students can try again with new numbers to see if they have mastered the concept.

Fundamental Managerial
ACCOUNTING
Concepts

THIRD EDITION

Fundamental Managerial ACCOUNTING Concepts

Thomas P. Edmonds
University of Alabama–Birmingham

Cindy D. Edmonds
University of Alabama–Birmingham

Bor-Yi Tsay
All of the University of Alabama–Birmingham

Philip R. Olds
Virginia Commonwealth University

Nancy W. Schneider
Lynchburg College

McGraw-Hill Irwin

Boston Burr Ridge, IL Dubuque, IA Madison, WI New York San Francisco St. Louis
Bangkok Bogotá Caracas Kuala Lumpur Lisbon London Madrid Mexico City
Milan Montreal New Delhi Santiago Seoul Singapore Sydney Taipei Toronto

This book is dedicated to our students whose questions have so frequently casued us to reevaluate our method of presentation that they have, in fact, become major contributors to the development of this text.

McGraw-Hill Irwin

FUNDAMENTAL MANAGERIAL ACCOUNTING CONCEPTS

Published by McGraw-Hill/Irwin, a business unit of The McGraw-Hill Companies, Inc., 1221 Avenue of the Americas, New York, NY, 10020.

Some ancillaries, including electronic and print components, may not be available to customers outside the United States.

This book is printed on acid-free paper.

2 3 4 5 6 7 8 9 0 VNH/VNH 0 9 8 7 6 5

ISBN 0-07-299105-4

Editorial director: *Brent Gordon*
Publisher: *Stewart Mattson*
Sponsoring editor: *Steve Schuetz*
Managing developmental editor: *Gail Korosa*
Marketing manager: *Richard Kolasa*
Media producer: *Elizabeth Mavetz*
Lead project manager: *Pat Frederickson*
Senior production supervisor: *Michael R. McCormick*
Senior designer: *Mary E. Kazak*
Photo research coordinator: *Jeremy Cheshareck*
Photo researcher: *David Tietz*
Supplement producer: *Matthew Perry*
Senior digital content specialist: *Brian Nacik*
Cover design: *Lodge Design*
Cover image: © *Joseph Sohmj ChromoSohm, Inc./Corbis*
Interior design: *Ellen Pettengell*
Typeface: *10/12 Times*
Compositor: *Cenveo*
Printer: *Von Hoffmann Corporation*

Library of Congress Cataloging-in-Publication Data

Fundamental managerial accounting concepts / Thomas P. Edmonds ... [et at.].-- 3rd ed.
p. cm.
Includes index.
ISBN 0-07-299105-4 (alk. paper)
1. Managerial accounting. I. Edmonds, Thomas P.
HF5657.4.E35 2006
658.15'11--dc22 2004042316

www.mhhe.com

"This is a good idea, and perhaps it would help with the major problem I think I encounter with managerial accounting—moving from a problem memorizing format to a problem analysis and decision format."
Marilyn P. Salter, University of Central Florida

"In general, Edmonds does a much better job of covering service and merchandising businesses than other textbooks do."
Nancy Ruhe, West Virginia University

"There is a world of difference teaching from Edmonds. It is now actually a pleasure teaching accounting to non-accounting majors. I feel they leave the course having the understanding of accounting."
Gary Reynolds, Ozark Technical Community College

NOTE FROM THE AUTHORS

Over the past 15 years, major changes in accounting education have impacted the way most college and university professors teach introductory accounting. We are gratified that our concepts approach has been so effective it has become a market leader in the change movement. We are confident our teaching approach offers students a more sound understanding of introductory managerial accounting than traditional methods.

Innovative traditionalists

We do not aim to radically transform accounting education, but instead to make it more effective. Recent trends require accounting educators to modify their teaching strategies. Technology and globalization have changed the business environment. The business environment has shifted toward service companies, especially in the United States. Traditional texts, however, emphasize accounting practices developed for manufacturing companies. This text serves the modern business environment by emphasizing decision-making concepts that apply to both service and manufacturing companies. We introduce such topics as operating leverage, cost-volume-profit analysis, relevance, and cost allocation early. Our budgeting chapter illustrates a retail company rather than a manufacturing company. Because we repeatedly emphasize decision-making concepts throughout the text, we include traditional topics like manufacturing cost flow, job-order and process costing, and recording procedures toward the end of the text.

Helping students develop critical thinking skills

Traditionally, skill development in introductory accounting has been focused at a relatively low level, concentrating primarily on comprehension and recall. Accounting education has traditionally emphasized content. Rigor has been measured by the quantity of content covered. Authors and educators have added more and more topics to the curricula and accounting textbooks have grown ever larger. This model provides little opportunity to help students develop the skills that the modern business environment they will face demands.

This text helps teachers move from the traditional educational paradigm more easily than you might imagine. The content focuses on essential concepts, reducing the amount of material you must cover. You have more time to work on skill development. The Instructors' Resource Manual provides step-by-step instructions for implementing innovative teaching methods such as active learning and group dynamics. It offers enticing short discovery learning cases which provide class-opening experiences that effectively stimulate student interest and help develop critical thinking skills. The text itself also includes many innovative features to better prepare students for the business challenges ahead in today's dynamic environment.

Tom Edmonds • Cindy Edmonds • Bor-Yi Tsay • Phil Olds • Nancy Schneider

ABOUT THE

Thomas P. Edmonds

Thomas P. Edmonds, Ph.D., holds the Friends and Alumni Professorship in the Department of Accounting at the University of Alabama at Birmingham (UAB). He has been actively involved in teaching accounting principles throughout his academic career. Dr. Edmonds has coordinated the accounting principles courses at the University of Houston and UAB. He currently teaches introductory accounting in mass sections that frequently contain more than 180 students. He has received five prestigious teaching awards including the UAB President's Excellence in Teaching Award and the distinguished Ellen Gregg Ingalls Award for excellence in classroom teaching. He has written numerous articles that have appeared in many publications including *Issues in Accounting*, the *Journal of Accounting Education*, *Advances in Accounting Education*, *Accounting Education: A Journal of Theory, Practice and Research,* the *Accounting Review*, *Advances in Accounting,* the *Journal of Accountancy*, *Management Accounting*, the *Journal of Commercial Bank Lending*, the *Banker's Magazine*, and the *Journal of Accounting, Auditing, and Finance*. Dr. Edmonds is a member of the editorial board for *Advances in Accounting: Teaching and Curriculum Innovations* and *Issues in Accounting Education.* He has published four textbooks, five practice problems (including two computerized problems), and a variety of supplemental materials including study guides, work papers, and solutions manuals. Dr. Edmonds' writing is influenced by a wide range of business experience. He is a successful entrepreneur. He has worked as a management accountant for Refrigerated Transport, a trucking company. Dr. Edmonds also worked in the not-for-profit sector as a commercial lending officer for the Federal Home Loan Bank. In addition, he has acted as a consultant to major corporations including First City Bank of Houston, AmSouth Bank in Birmingham, Texaco, and Cortland Chemicals. Dr. Edmonds began his academic training at Young Harris Community College in Young Harris, Georgia. He received a B.B.A. degree with a major in finance from Georgia State University in Atlanta, Georgia. He obtained an M.B.A. degree with a concentration in finance from St. Mary's University in San Antonio, Texas. His Ph.D. degree with a major in accounting was awarded by Georgia State University. Dr. Edmonds' work experience and academic training have enabled him to bring a unique user perspective to this textbook.

Cindy D. Edmonds

Cindy D. Edmonds, Ph.D., is an Associate Professor of Accounting at the University of Alabama at Birmingham. She serves as the coordinator of the introductory accounting courses at UAB. Dr. Edmonds received the 2001 Loudell Ellis Robinson Excellence in Teaching Award. Also, in 2000 and 2001 she was one of two School of Business faculty members nominated for the Ellen Gregg Ingalls Award for excellence in classroom teaching. She has written a variety of supplemental text materials including practice problems, a study guide, work papers, and test banks. Dr. Edmonds' articles appear in numerous publications including *Advances in Accounting Education*, *Journal of Education for Business*, *Journal of Accounting Regulation*, *Advances in Accounting*, *Management Accounting*, *CMA Journal*, *Disclosures*, and *Business & Professional Ethics Journal*. Her manuscript "Running a City on a Shoe String" received a certificate of merit award from the Institute of Management Accountants. The manuscript was used by the City of Vestavia in its application for Moody's Municipal Bond Rating. Dr. Edmonds is heavily involved in service activities. She is the 2001 president of the Birmingham Chapter of the American Society of Women Accountants. Dr. Edmonds has worked in the insurance industry, in a manufacturing company, and in a governmental agency. This work experience has enabled her to bring a real-world flavor to her writing. Dr. Edmonds holds a B.S. degree from Auburn University, an M.B.A degree from the University of Houston and a Ph.D. degree from the University of Alabama.

AUTHORS

Bor-Yi Tsay

Bor-Yi Tsay, Ph.D., CPA is a Professor of Accounting at the University of Alabama at Birmingham (UAB) where he has taught since 1986. He has taught principles of accounting courses at the University of Houston and UAB. Currently, he teaches an undergraduate cost accounting course and an MBA accounting analysis course. Dr. Tsay received the 1996 Loudell Ellis Robinson Excellence in Teaching Award. He has also received numerous awards for his writing and publications including John L. Rhoads Manuscripts Award, John Pugsley Manuscripts Award, Van Pelt Manuscripts Award, and three certificates of merits from the Institute of Management Accountants. His articles appeared in *Journal of Accounting Education, Management Accounting, Journal of Managerial Issues, CPA Journal, CMA Magazine, Journal of Systems Management,* and *Journal of Medical Systems.* He currently serves as a member of the board of the Birmingham Chapter, Institute of Management Accountants. He is also a member of the American Institute of Certified Public Accountants and Alabama Society of Certified Public Accountants. Dr. Tsay received a B.S. in agricultural economics from National Taiwan University, an M.B.A. with a concentration in Accounting from Eastern Washington University, and a Ph.D. in Accounting from the University of Houston.

Philip R. Olds

Professor Olds is Associate Professor of Accounting at Virginia Commonwealth University (VCU). He serves as the **coordinator of the introduction to accounting courses at VCU.** Professor Olds received his A.S. degree from Brunswick Junior College in Brunswick, Georgia (now Costal Georgia Community College). He received a B.B.A. in Accounting from Georgia Southern College (now Georgia Southern University) and his M.P.A. and Ph.D. degrees are from Georgia State University. After graduating from Georgia Southern, he worked as an auditor with the U.S. Department of Labor in Atlanta, Georgia. A CPA in Virginia, Professor Olds has published articles in various professional journals and presented papers at national and regional conferences. He also served as the faculty adviser to the VCU chapter of Beta Alpha Psi for five years. In 1989, he was recognized with an Outstanding Faculty Vice-President Award by the national Beta Alpha Psi organization.

Nancy Schneider

Professor Schneider is Associate Professor of Accounting at Lynchburg College in central Virginia where she has served for many years as the lead instructor for the accounting principles courses. Since attending graduate school she has participated in the writing, reviewing, editing, checking, and revising of college-level accounting and finance textbooks, textbook supplements, and related teaching materials. She has a deep personal commitment to student learning and to finding and sharing ways to improve college teaching. She is a recipient of the Sydnor Award for Teaching Excellence in Business at Lynchburg College and is frequently nominated by students for the College Excellence in Teaching Award. Professor Schneider initiated and organizes a highly popular annual symposium in which professors across all disciplines at the College exchange good teaching ideas. She has made numerous presentations at local and regional conferences, often related to teaching strategies, and is the coauthor of articles published in professional journals. Professor Schneider's professional activities also include active membership on the board of her local chapter of the Institute of Management Accountants where she regularly involves students in professional accounting educational meetings. Prior to teaching accounting, she was an auditor with an international public accounting firm in Atlanta and an internal auditor for a large integrated oil and gas company in Houston. Professor Schneider has maintained an active license to practice as a certified public accountant since 1980, and became a certified management accountant in 1992. She is a member of the American Institute of Certified Public Accountants and the Virginia Society of Certified Public Accountants. Professor Schneider received a Bachelor's degree in Mathematics Education with High Honors from the University of Florida in 1973, and a Master's degree in Professional Accountancy from Georgia State University in 1978.

HOW DOES THE BOOK HELP

STUDENTS SEE THE BIG PICTURE?

"I think Edmond's approach to introducing concepts, and his flow of topics is the best of any accounting textbook I have used. His approach allows me to emphasis a piece of the puzzle at a time building to the whole picture."
Gary Reynolds, Ozark Technical Community College

"I think students have benefit-ed from this approach because they see the concepts in action in decision making."
Julie A. Lockhart, Western Washington University

PRINCIPAL FEATURES

Isolating Concepts

How do you promote student understanding of concepts? We believe new concepts should be isolated and introduced individually in decision-making contexts. For example, we do not include a chapter covering cost terminology (usually Chapter 2 in traditional approaches). We believe introducing a plethora of detached cost terms in a single chapter is ineffective. Students have no conceptual framework for the new vocabulary.

Interrelationships between Concepts

Although introducing concepts in isolation enhances student comprehension of them, students must ultimately understand how business concepts interrelate. The text is designed to build knowledge progressively, leading students to integrate the concepts they have learned independently. For example, see how the concept of relevance is compared on page 138 of Chapter 4 to the concept of cost behavior (which is explained in Chapter 2) and how the definitions of direct costs are contrasted on page 186 of Chapter 5 with the earlier introduced concepts of cost behavior and cost relevance. Also, chapters 1 through 12 include a comprehensive problem designed to integrate concepts across chapters. The problem builds in each successive with the same company experiencing new conditions that require the application of across chapter concepts.

Context-Sensitive Nature of Terminology

Students can be confused when they discover the exact same cost can be classified as fixed, variable, direct, indirect, relevant, or not relevant. For example, the cost of a store manager's salary is fixed regardless of the number of customers that shop in the store. The cost of store manager salaries, however, is variable relative to the number of stores a company operates. The salary costs are directly traceable to particular stores but not to particular sales made in a store. The salary cost is relevant when deciding whether to eliminate a given store but not relevant to deciding whether to eliminate a department within a store. Students must learn to identify the circumstances that determine the classification of costs. The chapter material, exercises, and problems in this text are designed to encourage students to analyze the decision-making context rather than to memorize definitions. Exercise 2–1A in Chapter 2 illustrates how the text teaches students to interpret different decision-making environments.

EXERCISE 2–1A *Identifying Cost Behavior* **L.O. 1**

Hoover's Kitchen, a fast-food restaurant company, operates a chain of restaurants across the nation. Each restaurant employs eight people; one is a manager paid a salary plus a bonus equal to 3 percent of sales. Other employees, two cooks, one dishwasher, and four waitresses, are paid salaries. Each manager is budgeted $3,000 per month for advertising cost.

Required

Classify each of the following costs incurred by Hoover's Kitchen as fixed, variable, or mixed.

a. Manager's compensation relative to the number of customers.
b. Waitresses' salaries relative to the number of restaurants.
c. Advertising costs relative to the number of customers for a particular restaurant.
d. Rental costs relative to the number of restaurants.
e. Cooks' salaries at a particular location relative to the number of customers.
f. Cost of supplies (cups, plates, spoons, etc.) relative to the number of customers.

Managerial Orientation

The overall theme of the text is to introduce concepts in the context of decision making. In the first chapter, for example, we describe how product costing affects financing availability, management motivation, and income tax considerations. In Chapter 2, we illustrate how a fixed cost structure provides a competitive operating advantage to show the effect of cost behavior on operating leverage. In Chapter 8, we focus on interpreting variances as well as computing them. The practical usefulness of management accounting information is continually reinforced.

Information Overload

The table of contents reflects our efforts to address the information overload problem. We believe existing managerial textbooks include significantly more material than can be digested by the typical managerial accounting student. In contrast with traditional texts that normally have between 18 and 20 chapters, we have limited this text to 14 chapters.

Excel Spreadsheets

Spreadsheet applications are essential to contemporary accounting practice. Students must recognize the power of spreadsheet software and know how accounting data are presented in spreadsheets. We discuss Microsoft Excel spreadsheet applications where appropriate throughout the text. In most instances, the text illustrates actual spreadsheets. End-of-chapter materials include problems students can complete using spreadsheet software. A sample of the logo used to identify problems suitable for Excel spreadsheet solutions is shown here.

PROBLEM 2–18A *Cost Behavior and Averaging* **L.O. 1**

eXcel
www.mhhe.com/edmonds3e

Jenny Tang has decided to start Tang Cleaning, a residential housecleaning service company. She is able to rent cleaning equipment at a cost of $600 per month. Labor costs are expected to be $50 per house cleaned and supplies are expected to cost $5 per house.

Required

a. Determine the total expected cost of equipment rental and the average expected cost of equipment rental per house cleaned, assuming that Tang Cleaning cleans 10, 20, or 30 houses during one month. Is the cost of equipment a fixed or a variable cost?
b. Determine the total expected cost of labor and the average expected cost of labor per house cleaned, assuming that Tang Cleaning cleans 10, 20, or 30 houses during one month. Is the cost of labor a fixed or a variable cost?
c. Determine the total expected cost of supplies and the average expected cost of supplies per house cleaned, assuming that Tang Cleaning cleans 10, 20, or 30 houses during one month. Is the cost of supplies a fixed or a variable cost?

CHECK FIGURES
c. Total supplies cost for cleaning 30 houses: $150
d. Total cost for 20 houses: $1,700

WHAT'S NEW THIS EDITION?

" The new manuscript exhibits a more personal approach in its writing style. This makes a big difference in it being "readable". I believe that students will appreciate this new style as well. I compare it to the difference between reading a factual and informative textbook, to reading a personal letter or even an interesting novel. Kudos to Edmonds for departing from the usual and ordinary and expanding to his new vision of communicating with students."
Steve Muller,
Valencia Community College

Revisions for **Fundamental Managerial Accounting Concepts** are in response to extensive feedback from instructors and students. Through formal reviews, instructor and student suggestions, and focus groups, we have responded with constructive changes. Detailed revisions are summarized below. However, there are two significant features.

Comprehensive Problem to Integrate Concepts Across Chapters

Chapters 1 through 12 include a comprehensive problem designed to integrate concepts across chapters. Students often fail to understand the interrelationships between various accounting concepts because they fail to distinguish between new concepts and new contexts. By studying a problem series with the same company facing different accounting issues, students can focus on particular accounting concepts without the distraction of a new setting for each concept.

User-Friendly Writing Style

Every chapter of the text has been rewritten in an easy to read and comprehend writing style. Many students are not habitual or skilled readers. If complex concepts are not described in concrete terms with familiar vocabulary, students will sometimes give up and not read the textbook at all.

Overall revisions

- The presentation of material has been simplified.
- The text has been thoroughly updated to include all relevant changes in authoritative pronouncements.
- A logo representing the focus company of each chapter has been included to add realism to these fictitious companies.
- Real companies are highlighted in blue.
- The exercises and problems have been thoroughly revised.
- All real world data have been updated to reflect information contained in the companies' most recent annual reports.
- There is an ethics case in the *Analyze, Think, Communicate* section of the end-of-chapter materials for each chapter.
- Check figures have been added to Problems in Series A.
- New supplement to chapter 13 added on Annual Report and Financial Statement Analysis Projects.

COMPREHENSIVE PROBLEM

Use the same transaction data for Magnificant Modems, Inc. as was used in Chapter 1 (see page 00).

Required

a. Based on these data, identify each cost incurred by the company as (1) fixed versus variable relative to the number of units produced and sold; and (2) product versus general, selling, and administrative (G, S, & A). The solution for the first item is shown as an example.

Cost Item	Fixed	Variable	Product	G,S,&A
Depreciation on manufacturing equipment	X		X	
Direct materials				
Direct labor				
Production supplies				
Rent on manufacturing facility				
Sales commissions				
Depreciation on administrative equipment				
Administrative costs (rent and salaries)				

b. Replace the question marks in the following table to indicate the product cost per unit assuming levels of production of 5,000, 6,000, 7,000, and 8,000.

Cost of Goods Sold	$455,000	?	?	?
Divided by Number of Units	5,000	6,000	7,000	8,000
Cost Per Unit	$ 91	?	?	?

ame and Type of Company Used as Main Chapter Example

Chapter Title	Company Used as Main Chapter Example	Company Logo	Type of Company
Management Accounting: A Value-Added Discipline	Patillo Manufacturing Company		Manufactures wooden tables
Cost Behavior, Operating Leverage, and Profitability Analysis	Star Productions, Inc. (SPI)		Promotes rock concerts
Analysis of Cost, Volume, and Pricing to Increase Profitability	Bright Day Distributors		Sells nonprescription health food supplements
Relevant Information for Special Decisions	Premier Office Products		Manufactures printers
Cost Accumulation,Tracing, and Allocation	In Style, Inc. (ISI)		Retail clothing store
6. Cost Management in an Automated Business Environment: ABC, ABM, and TQM	Carver Soup Company (CSP)		Produces vegetable and tomato soup
7. Planning for Profit and Cost Control	Hampton Hams (HH)		Sells cured hams nationwide through retail outlets
8. Performance Evaluation	Melrose Manufacturing Company		Makes small, high-quality statues used in award ceremonies
9. Responsibility Accounting	Panther Holding Company		Furniture Manufacturing Division
Planning for Capital Investments	EZ Rentals		Rents computers, monitors, and projection equipment
Product Costing in Service and nufacturing Entities	Ventra Manufacturing Company		Constructs mahogany jewelry boxes
Job-Order, Process, and Hybrid Cost Systems	Benchmore Boat Company		Manufactures boats
	Janis Juice Company		Makes fruit juice

SUPPLEMENT

Annual Report and Financial Statement Analysis Projects

Annual Report Project for The Topps Company, Inc. (2003)

Management's Discussion and Analysis

The annual report for The Topps Company, Inc. opens with a letter to the stockholders that describes the company's mission, products and services, customers, past performance, and future prospects. The letter is followed by a section called "Management's Discussion and Analysis" in which management talks about financial results and trends, liquidity, risk factors, and other matters deemed necessary to provide adequate disclosure to users of the report. Read The Topps Company Stockholders' Letter and Management's Discussion and Analysis on pages 1 through 11 to answer questions 1–6.

1. What are the company's two reportable business segments?
2. What were company's goals for each segment in 2003? What specific achievements resulted from these goals?
3. What percentage of the company's total sales came from the Entertainment segment?
4. What effect has inflation had on the company's operations?
5. What is management's view of the company's liquidity status for the foreseeable future? How does the company plan to meet its cash needs?
6. What caused the changes between the company's fiscal year 2003 and 2002 net sales, gross margin, and selling, general and administrative expenses?

Income Statement—Vertical Analysis

7. Using Excel, compute common-size income statements for all three fiscal years. In common-size income statements, net sales is 100% and every other number is a percent-

Required

Assume that you are Dr. Sterling's accountant. Write a memo describing a pricing strategy that resolves the apparent problem of high costs during months of low volume. Recommend in your memo the price to charge per pet treated during the month of December.

ATC 2–5 ETHICAL DILEMMA *Profitability Versus Social Conscience (Effects of Cost Behavior)*

Advances in biological technology have enabled two research companies, Bio Labs, Inc. and Scientific Associates, to develop an insect-resistant corn seed. Neither company is financially strong enough to develop the distribution channels necessary to bring the product to world markets. World Agra Distributors, Inc., has negotiated contracts with both companies for the exclusive right to market their seed. Bio Labs signed an agreement to receive an annual royalty of $1,000,000. In contrast, Scientific Associates chose an agreement that provides for a royalty of $0.50 per pound of seed sold. Both agreements have a 10-year term. During 2004, World Agra sold approximately 1,600,000 pounds of the Bio Labs, Inc., seed and 2,400,000 pounds of the Scientific Associates seed. Both types of seed were sold for $1.25 per pound. By the end of 2004, it was apparent that the seed developed by Scientific Associates was superior. Although insect infestation was virtually nonexistent for both types of seed, the seed developed by Scientific Associates produced corn that was sweeter and had consistently higher yields.

World Agra Distributors' chief financial officer, Roger Weatherstone, recently retired. To the astonishment of the annual planning committee, Mr. Weatherstone's replacement, Ray Borrough, adamantly recommended that the marketing department develop a major advertising campaign to promote the seed developed by Bio Labs, Inc. The planning committee reluctantly approved the recommendation. A $100,000 ad campaign was launched; the ads emphasized the ability of the Bio Labs seed to avoid insect infestation. The campaign was silent with respect to taste or crop yield. It did not mention the seed developed by Scientific Associates. World Agra's sales staff was instructed to push the Bio Labs seed and to sell the Scientific Associates seed only on customer demand. Although total sales remained relatively constant during 2005, sales of the Scientific Associates seed fell to approximately 1,300,000 pounds while sales of the Bio Labs, Inc., seed rose to 2,700,000 pounds.

Required

a. Determine the amount of increase or decrease in profitability experienced by World Agra in 2006 as a result of promoting Bio Labs seed. Support your answer with appropriate commentary.

b. Did World Agra's customers in particular and society in general benefit or suffer from the decision to promote the Bio Labs seed?

c. Review the standards of ethical conduct in Exhibit 1–13 of Chapter 1 and comment on whether Mr. Borrough's recommendation violated any of the standards in the code of ethical conduct.

d. Comment on your belief regarding the adequacy of the Standards of Ethical Conduct for Managerial Accountants to direct the conduct of management accountants.

ATC 2–6 SPREADSHEET ASSIGNMENT *Using Excel*

Charlie Stork rented a truck for his business on two previous occasions. Since he will soon be renting a truck again, he would like to analyze his bills and determine how the rental fee is calculated. His two bills for truck rental show that on September 1, he drove 1,000 miles and the bill was $1,500, and on December 5, he drove 600 miles and the bill was $1,380.

HOW DOES THE BOOK

Real World Examples

The Edmonds' text provides a variety of thought-provoking, real-world examples of managerial accounting as an essential part of the management process.

The Curious Accountant

Each chapter opens with a short vignette that sets the stage and helps pique student interest. These vignettes pose a question about a real-world accounting issue related to the topic of the chapter. The answer to the question appears in a separate sidebar a few pages further into the chapter.

Focus on International Issues

These boxed inserts expose students to international issues in accounting.

Check Yourself

These short question/answer features occur at the end of each main topic and ask students to stop and think about the material just covered. The answer follows to provide immediate feedback before students go on to a new topic.

THE *curious* ACCOUNTANT

In the first course of accounting, you learned how retailers, such as Wal-Mart, account for the cost of equipment that lasts more than one year. Recall that the equipment was recorded as an asset when purchased, and then it was depreciated over its expected useful life. The depreciation charge reduced the company's assets and increased its expenses. This approach was justified under the matching principle, which seeks to recognize costs as expenses in the same period that the cost (resource) is used to generate revenue.

...cenario. Black & Decker ...trimmers, Black & ...ge trimmers. ...ment the same way Wal- ...ack & Decker account for ... page 17.)

...ranoid survive." ...res: ...y. I worry about factories ...ple, and I worry about

3

ANSWER TO *curious* ACCOUNTANT

As you have seen, accounting for depreciation related to manufacturing assets is different from accounting for depreciation for nonmanufacturing assets. Depreciation on the checkout equipment at Wal-Mart is recorded as depreciation expense. Depreciation on manufacturing equipment at Black & Decker is considered a product cost. It is included first as a part of the cost of inventory and eventually as a part of the expense, cost of goods sold. Recording depreciation on manufacturing equipment as an inventory cost is simply another example of the matching principle, because the cost does not become an expense until revenue from the product sale is recognized.

crime loses the opportunity for white-collar employment. Second chances are rarely granted. It is vital to learn to recognize and avoid the common features of ethical misconduct.

Upstream and Downstream Costs

Most companies incur product-related costs before and after, as well as during, the manufac- turing process. For ex... ment costs prior to ma... manufacturing process... manufacturing proces... advertising, sales com...

Distinguish product

Activity-Based Management

Simple changes in perspective can have dramatic results. For example, imagine how realizing the world is round instead of flat changed the nature of travel. A recent change in perspective developing in management accounting is the realization that an organization cannot manage *costs.* Instead, it manages the *activities* that cause costs to be incurred. **Activities** represent the measures an organization takes to accomplish its goals.

focus on INTERNATIONAL ISSUES

Where in the World Do New Managerial Accounting Practices Come From?

Many of the emerging practices in managerial accounting have their foundations in Asian companies. These companies established employee relationships that achieve continuous improvement by encouraging employees to participate in the design as well as the execution of their work. Employee empowerment through the practice known as *kaizen management* recognizes gradual, continuous improvement as the ultimate key to cost reduction and quality control. Employees are encouraged to identify and eliminate nonvalue-added activities, idle time, and waste. The response is overwhelming when employee suggestions are taken seriously. For example, the Toyota Motor Corporation reported the receipt of approximately two million employee suggestions in one year alone.

Source: Takao Tanaka, "Kaizen Budgeting: Toyota's Cost Control System Under TQC," *Journal of Cost Management,* Winter 1996, p. 62.

concerts are shown in Exhibit 2–21.

Exhibit 2–21 *Cost Behavior Relative to Number of Concerts*

Number of concerts (a)	1	2	3	4	
Cost per concert (b)	$48,000	$48,000	$ 48,000	$ 48,000	$ 4
Total cost (a × b)	$48,000	$96,000	$144,000	$192,000	$24

In this context, the total cost of hiring the band increases proportionately with the ... of concerts while cost per concert remains constant. The band cost is therefore varia... same cost can behave as either a fixed cost or a variable cost, depending on the **activ...** When identifying a cost as fixed or variable, first ask, fixed or variable *relative to what activity base?* The cost of the band is fixed relative to *the number of tickets sold for a specific concert;* it is variable relative to *the number of concerts produced.*

Check Yourself 2–4

Is the compensation cost for managers of Pizza Hut Restaurants a fixed cost or a variable cost?

Answer The answer depends on the context. For example, since a store manager's salary remains unchanged regardless of how many customers enter a particular restaurant, it can be classified as a fixed cost relative to the number of customers at a particular restaurant. However, the more restaurants that Pizza Hut operates, the higher the total managers' compensation cost will be. Accordingly, managers' salary cost would be classified as a variable cost relative to the number of restaurants opened.

MOTIVATE STUDENTS?

REALITY *bytes*

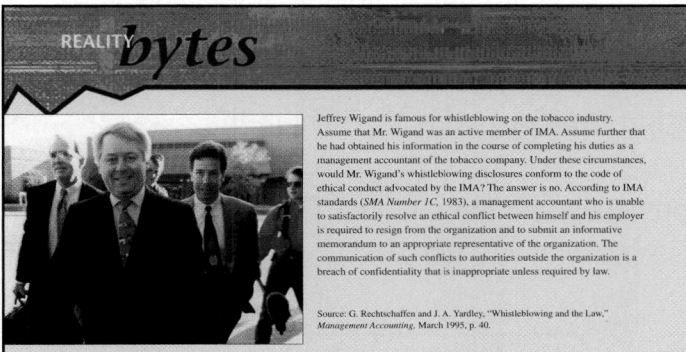

Jeffrey Wigand is famous for whistleblowing on the tobacco industry. Assume that Mr. Wigand was an active member of IMA. Assume further that he had obtained his information in the course of completing his duties as a management accountant of the tobacco company. Under these circumstances, would Mr. Wigand's whistleblowing disclosures conform to the code of ethical conduct advocated by the IMA? The answer is no. According to IMA standards (*SMA Number 1C*, 1983), a management accountant who is unable to satisfactorily resolve an ethical conflict between himself and his employer is required to resign from the organization and to submit an informative memorandum to an appropriate representative of the organization. The communication of such conflicts to authorities outside the organization is a breach of confidentiality that is inappropriate unless required by law.

Source: G. Rechtschaffen and J. A. Yardley, "Whistleblowing and the Law," *Management Accounting*, March 1995, p. 40.

Activity-Based Costing

A company that allocates indirect costs using **activity-based costing (ABC)** follows a two-stage process. In the first stage, costs are assigned to pools based on the activities that cause the costs to be incurred. In the second stage, the costs in the activity cost pools are allocated to products using a variety of cost drivers. The first step in developing an ABC system is to identify essential activities and the costs of performing those activities.

Topic Tackler PLUS 6–1

A business undertakes **activities** to accomplish its mission. Typical activities include acquiring raw materials, transforming raw materials into finished products, and delivering products to customers. These broadly defined activities can be divided into subcategories. For example, the activity of acquiring raw materials involves separate subcategory activities such as identifying suppliers, obtaining price quotations, evaluating materials specifications, completing purchase orders, and receiving purchased materials. Each of these subcategories can be subdivided into yet more detailed activities. For instance, identifying suppliers may include such activities as reviewing advertisements, searching Internet sites, and obtaining recommendations from business associates. Further subdivisions are possible. Companies perform thousands of activities.

***a look* back**

To plan and control business operations effectively, managers need to understand how different costs behave in relation to changes in the volume of activity. Total *fixed cost* remains constant when activity changes. Fixed cost per unit decreases with increases in activity and increases with decreases in activity. In contrast, total *variable cost* increases proportionately with increases in activity and decreases proportionately with decreases in activity. Variable cost per unit remains constant regardless of activity levels. The definitions of fixed and variable costs have meaning only within the context of a specified range of activity (the relevant range) for a defined period of time. In addition, cost behavior depends on the relevant volume measure (a store manager's salary is fixed relative to the number of customers visiting a particular store but is variable relative to the number of stores operated). A mixed cost has both fixed and variable cost components.

Fixed costs allow companies to take advantage of *operating leverage*. With operating leverage, each additional sale decreases the cost per unit. This principle allows a small percentage change in volume of revenue to cause a significantly larger percentage change in prof-

to determine net income. The contribution margin represents the amount available to pay fixed costs and provide a profit. Although not permitted by GAAP for external reporting, many companies use the contribution margin format for internal reporting purposes.

Cost per unit is an average cost that is easier to compute than the actual cost of each unit and is more relevant to decision making than actual cost. Accountants must use judgment when choosing the time span from which to draw data for computing the average cost per unit. Distortions can result from using either too long or too short a time span.

Fixed and variable costs can be estimated using such tools as the *high-low method* and *scattergraphs*. Both are easy to use and can be reasonably accurate.

***a look* forward**

The next chapter will show you how changes in cost, volume, and pricing affect profitability. You will learn to determine the number of units of product that must be produced and sold in order to break even (the number of units that will produce an amount of revenue that is exactly equal to total cost). You will learn to establish the price of a product using a cost-plus pricing approach and to establish the cost of a product using a target-pricing approach. Finally, the chapter will show you how to use a break-even chart to examine potential profitability over a

Reality Bytes

Real-world applications related to specific chapter topics are introduced through *Reality Bytes*. Reality Bytes may offer survey results, graphics, quotations from business leaders, and other supplemental topics that enhance opportunities for students to connect the text material to actual accounting practice.

Topic Tackler Plus

A logo indicates a topic explained on the Topic Tackler Plus DVD. The DVD includes two hard-to-learn topics for each chapter explained with video, PowerPoint, practice quizzes, self tests, and a demonstration, self-study problem walkthrough.

A Look Back/A Look Forward

Students need a roadmap to make sense of where the chapter topics fit into the "whole" picture. A Look Back reviews the chapter material and a Look Forward introduces students to what is to come.

"I thought the pedagogy was excellent in this book. Additionally, I was pleased with the "qualitative considerations" discussions in many of the chapters."
David McIntyre, Clemson University

HOW CAN TECHNOLOGY

Our technology resources help student and instructors focus on learning success. By using the Internet and multimedia students get book-specific help at their convenience. Compare our technology to those of any other book and we're confident you'll agree that **Fundamental Managerial Accounting Concepts** has the best in the market.

Teaching aids make in-class presentations easy and stimulating. These aids give you more power than ever to teach your class the way you want.

OnePass

McGraw-Hill/Irwin offers a complete range of technology to support and complement **Fundamental Managerial Accounting Concepts**. One Pass integrates all of the text's multimedia resources. With just one access code students can obtain state of the art study aids, including Homework Manager, NetTutor and an interactive online version of the text.

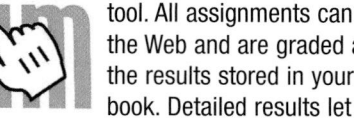

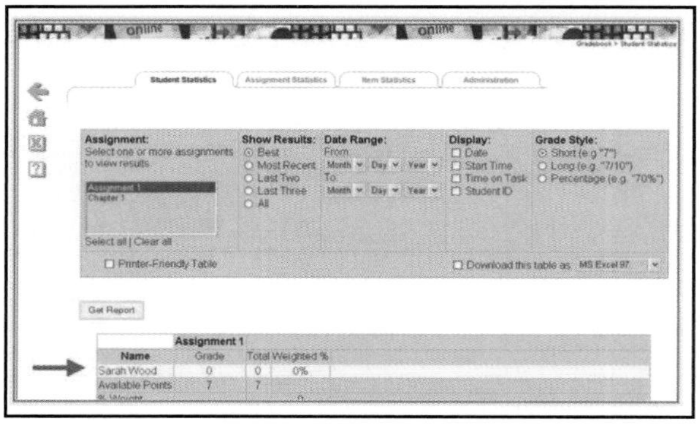

McGraw-Hill's Homework Manager

McGraw-Hill's Homework Manager is a Web-based supplement that duplicates problem structures directly from the end-of-chapter material in your textbook. It includes static problems and algorithms to provide a limitless supply of online self-graded practice for students, or assignments and tests with unique versions of every problem. Say goodbye to cheating in your classroom; say hello to the power and flexibility you've been waiting for in creating assignments. All Exercises and Problems in Series A are available with Homework Manager.

McGraw-Hill's Homework Manager is also a useful grading tool. All assignments can be delivered over the Web and are graded automatically with the results stored in your private grade book. Detailed results let you see at a glance how each student does on an assignment or an individual problem—you can even see how many tries it took them to solve it.

Students receive full access to McGraw-Hill's Homework Manager when they purchase OnePass, or they can order directly from your Homework Manager course web page.

HELP STUDENT SUCCESS?

Topic Tackler Plus DVD

This software is a complete tutorial focusing on areas in the course that give students the most trouble. It provides help on two key topics for each chapter by use of

- Video clips
- PowerPoint slide shows
- Interactive exercises
- Self-grading quizzes

A logo in the text marks the topic given further coverage in Topic Tackler Plus.

The DVD also includes for each chapter the Self-Study Review Problem presented in an audio-narrated PowerPoint slide presentation, as well as a short video

"I found the CD to be an excellent addition to the text. It contains some of the best material I have seen for this level of text."
Dan R. Ward, University of Louisiana, Lafayette

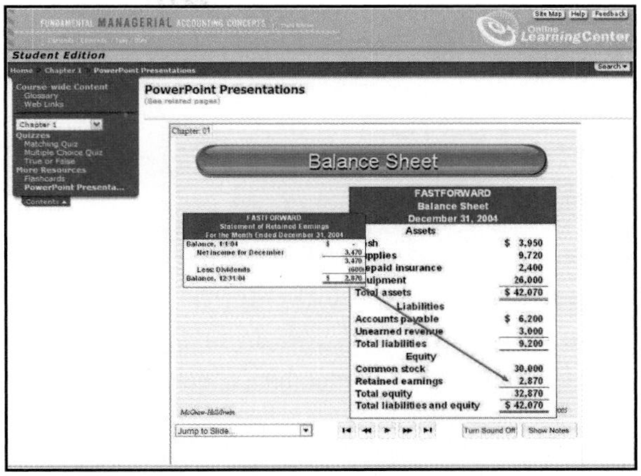

Online Learning Center (OLC)

www.mhhe.com/edmonds3e

More and more students are studying online. That's why we offer an Online Learning Center (OLC) that follows **Fundamental Managerial Accounting Concepts** chapter by chapter. The OLC includes the following:

- Excel Spreadsheets
- Spreadsheet Tips
- Text Updates
- Glossary
- Key Term Flashcards
- Chapter Learning Objectives
- Interactive Quizzes
- E Lectures (audio-narrated PowerPoints)
- Additional Check Figures
- Mobile Resources
- Topic Tackler Plus

For instructors, the book's secured OLC contains essential course materials. You can pull all of this material into your PageOut course syllabus or use it as part of another online course management system. It doesn't require any building or maintenance on your part. It's ready to go the moment you type in the URL.

- Instructor's Manual
- Solutions Manual
- Solutions to Excel Template Assignments
- Sample Syllabi
- All Text Exhibits
- Text Updates

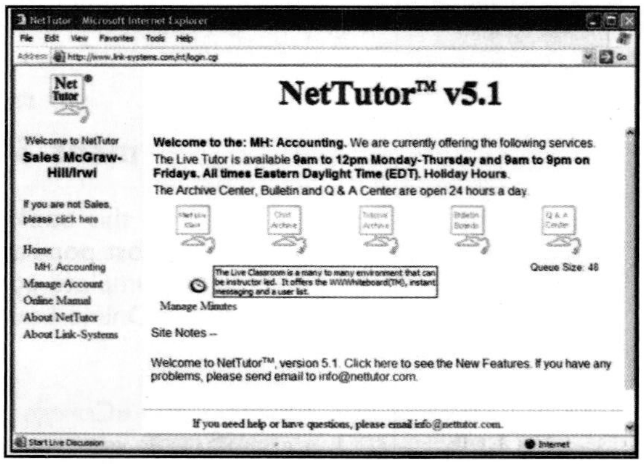

NetTutor

Many students work or have other commitments outside of class, making it difficult for them to get help with their questions during regular school hours. NetTutor is a breakthrough program that connects your students with qualified tutors online so they can get help at their convenience.

Students can communicate with tutors in a variety of ways:

- The Live Tutor Center, where students can view tutor-created spreadsheets, T-accounts, and instant responses to their questions
- The Q&A Center, which allows students to submit questions anytime and receive answers within 24 hours.
- The Archive Center that lets students browse for answers to previously asked questions. They can also search for questions pertinent to a particular topic.

With OnePass, students receive unlimited access to NetTutor for the length of the course.

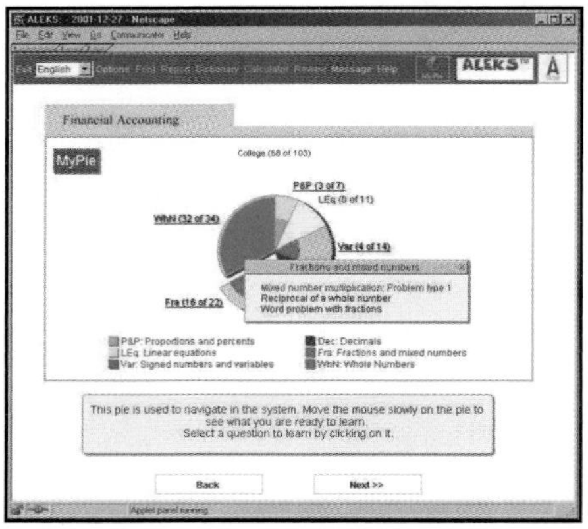

ALEKS

ALEKS for the Accounting Cycle

ALEKS (Assessment and Learning in Knowledge Spaces) provides precise assessment and individualized instruction in the fundamental skills your students need to succeed in accounting. ALEKS motivates your students because it can tell what a student knows, doesn't know, and is most ready to learn next. ALEKS uses an artificial intelligence engine to exactly identify a student's knowledge of accounting.

To learn more about adding ALEKS to your accounting course, visit *www.business.aleks.com*.

eInstruction®

CPS Classroom Performance System

This is a revolutionary system that brings ultimate interactivity to the classroom. CPS is a wireless response system that gives you immediate feedback from every student in the class. CPS units include easy-to-use software for creating and delivering questions and assessments to your class. With CPS you can ask subjective and objective questions. Then every student simply responds with their individual, wireless response pad, providing instant results. CPS is the perfect tool for engaging students while gathering important assessment data.

Instructor's Resource CD

This CD includes electronic versions of the Instructor's Manual, Solutions Manual, Test Bank, and Computerized Test Bank, as well as PowerPoint slides, video clips, and all exhibits in the text in a PowerPoint format.

Online Course Management WebCT, eCollege, and Blackboard

We offer **Fundamental Managerial Accounting Concepts** content for complete online courses. You can customize the Online Learning Center content and author your own course materials. No matter which online course solution you choose, you can count on the highest level of support. Our specialists offer free training and answer any question you have through the life of your adoption.

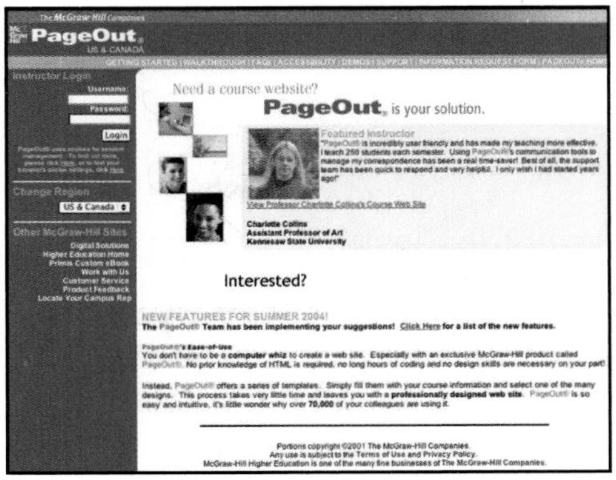

PageOut

McGraw-Hill's Course Management System
Pageout is the easiest way to create a Website for your accounting course. Just fill in a series of boxes with plain English and click on one of our professional designs. In no time your course is online with a Website that contains your syllabus. If you need help, our team of specialists is ready to take your course materials and build a custom website to your specifications. To learn more visit *www.pageout.net.*

Knowledge Gateway

Knowledge Gateway is an all-purpose service and resource center for instructors teaching online. While training programs from WebCT and Blackboard will help teach you their software, only McGraw-Hill/Irwin has services to help you actually manage and teach your online course, as well as run and maintain the software. To see how these platforms can assist your online course, visit *www.mhhe.com/solutions.*

HOW ARE CHAPTER

Regardless of the instructional approach, there is no shortcut to learning accounting. Students must practice to master basic accounting concepts. The text includes a prodigious supply of practice materials and exercises and problems.

Self-Study Review Problem

These representative example problems include a detailed, worked-out solution and provide another level of support for students before they work problems on their own. These review problems are included on the Topic Tackler Plus DVD in an animated audio presentation.

SELF-STUDY REVIEW PROBLEM

Mensa Mountaineering Company (MMC) provides guided mountain climbing expeditions in the Rocky Mountains. Its only major expense is guide salaries; it pays each guide $4,800 per climbing expedition. MMC charges its customers $1,500 per expedition and expects to take five climbers on each expedition.

Part 1

Base your answers on the preceding information.

Required

a. Determine the total cost of guide salaries and the cost of guide salaries per climber assuming that four, five, or six climbers are included in a trip. Relative to the number of climbers in a single expedition, is the cost of guides a fixed or a variable cost?
b. Relative to the number of expeditions, is the cost of guides a fixed or a variable cost?
c. Determine the profit of an expedition assuming that five climbers are included in the trip.
d. Determine the profit assuming a 20 percent increase (six climbers total) in expedition revenue. What is the percentage change in profitability?
e. Determine the profit assuming a 20 percent decrease (four climbers total) in expedition revenue. What is the percentage change in profitability?
f. Explain why a 20 percent shift in revenue produces more than a 20 percent shift in profitability. What term describes this phenomenon?

Part 2

Assume that the guides offer to make the climbs for a percentage of expedition fees. Specifically, MMC

Exercise Series A & B and Problem Series A & B

There are two sets of problems and exercises, Series A and B. Instructors can assign one set for homework and another set for class work.

• Check figures

The figures provide a quick reference for students to check on their progress in solving the problem. These are included for all problems in Series A.

• Excel

Many exercises and problems can be solved using the Excel™ spreadsheet templates contained on the text's Online Learning Center. A logo appears in the margins next to these exercises and problems for easy identification.

Bently Trust Corporation has two service departments, actuary and economic analysis. Bently also has three operating departments, annuity, fund management, and employee benefit services. The annual costs of operating the service departments are $720,000 for actuary and $960,000 for economic analysis. Bently uses the direct method to allocate service center costs to operating departments. Other relevant data follow.

	Operating Costs*	Revenue
Annuity	$1,000,000	$1,680,000
Fund management	1,800,000	2,520,000
Employee benefit services	1,200,000	2,200,000

*The operating costs are measured before allocating service center costs.

Required

a. Use operating costs as the cost driver for allocating service center costs to operating departments.
b. Use revenue as the cost driver for allocating service center costs to operating departments.

PROBLEMS—SERIES A

All Problems in Series A are available with McGraw-Hill's Homework Manager

L.O. 1, 2, 3, 4, 5 **PROBLEM 5–18A** *Cost Accumulation and Allocation*

excel
www.mhhe.com/edmonds3e

CHECK FIGURE
a. (2) $590,000

Belcher Manufacturing Company makes two different products, M and N. The company's two departments are named after the products; for example, Product M is made in Department M. Belcher's accountant has identified the following annual costs associated with these two products.

Financial data	
Salary of vice president of production division	$ 90,000
Salary of supervisor Department M	38,000
Salary of supervisor Department N	28,000
Direct materials cost Department M	150,000
Direct materials cost Department N	210,000
Direct labor cost Department M	120,000
Direct labor cost Department N	340,000
Direct utilities cost Department M	60,000
Direct utilities cost Department N	12,000
General factorywide utilities	18,000
Production supplies	18,000
Fringe benefits	69,000
Depreciation	360,000
Nonfinancial data	
Machine hours Department M	5,000
Machine hours Department N	1,000

Required

a. Identify the costs that are (1) direct costs of Department M, (2) direct costs of Department N, and (3) indirect costs.
b. Select the appropriate cost drivers for the indirect costs and allocate these costs to Departments M and N.
c. Determine the total estimated cost of the products made in Departments M and N. Assume that Belcher produced 2,000 units of Product M and 4,000 units of Product N during the year. If Belcher prices its products at cost plus 30 percent of cost, what price per unit must it charge for Product M and for Product N?

L.O. 1, 3, 4 **PROBLEM 5–19A** *Selecting an Appropriate Cost Driver (What Is the Base?)*

"I'm glad to see that so many of them involve service, rather than manufacturing businesses."
Nancy Ruhe,
West Virginia University

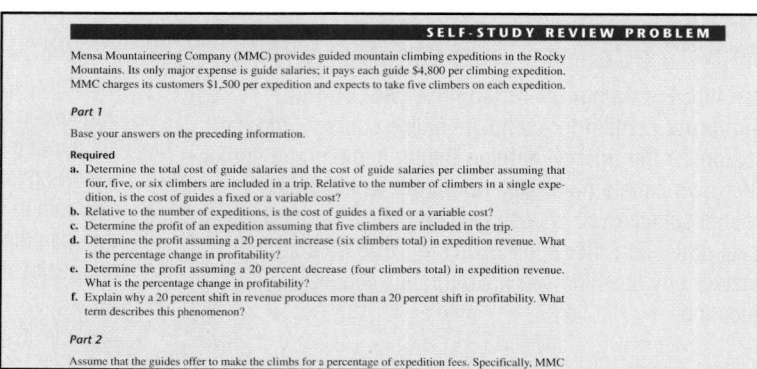

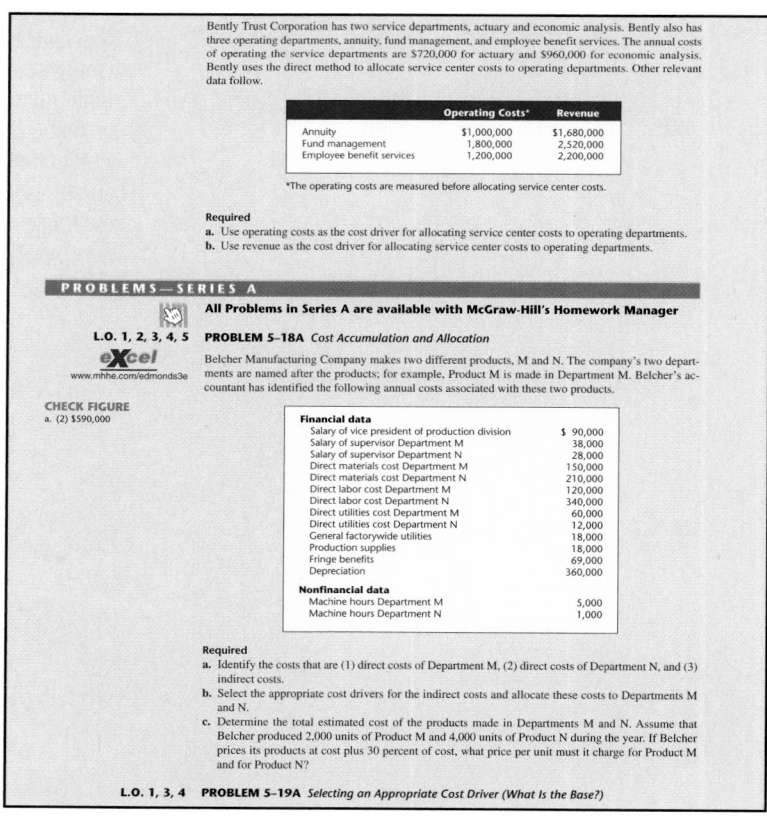

CONCEPTS REINFORCED?

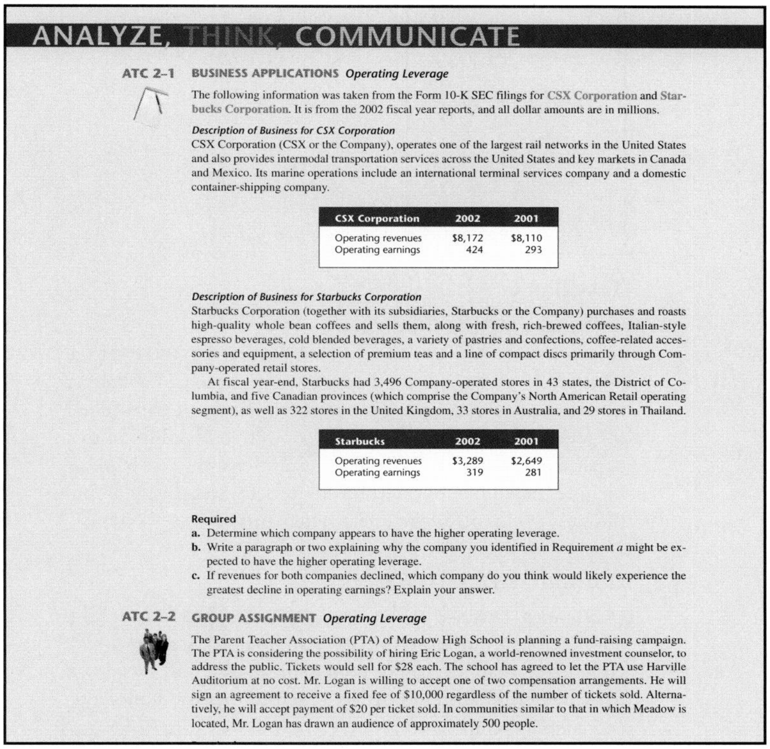

ANALYZE, THINK, COMMUNICATE

ATC 2-1 **BUSINESS APPLICATIONS** *Operating Leverage*

The following information was taken from the Form 10-K SEC filings for CSX Corporation and Starbucks Corporation. It is from the 2002 fiscal year reports, and all dollar amounts are in millions.

Description of Business for CSX Corporation

CSX Corporation (CSX or the Company), operates one of the largest rail networks in the United States and also provides intermodal transportation services across the United States and key markets in Canada and Mexico. Its marine operations include an international terminal services company and a domestic container-shipping company.

CSX Corporation	2002	2001
Operating revenues	$8,172	$8,110
Operating earnings	424	293

Description of Business for Starbucks Corporation

Starbucks Corporation (together with its subsidiaries, Starbucks or the Company) purchases and roasts high-quality whole bean coffees and sells them, along with fresh, rich-brewed coffees, Italian-style espresso beverages, cold blended beverages, a variety of pastries and confections, coffee-related accessories and equipment, a selection of premium teas and a line of compact discs primarily through Company-operated retail stores.

At fiscal year-end, Starbucks had 3,496 Company-operated stores in 43 states, the District of Columbia, and five Canadian provinces (which comprise the Company's North American Retail operating segment), as well as 322 stores in the United Kingdom, 33 stores in Australia, and 29 stores in Thailand.

Starbucks	2002	2001
Operating revenues	$3,289	$2,649
Operating earnings	319	281

Required

a. Determine which company appears to have the higher operating leverage.
b. Write a paragraph or two explaining why the company you identified in Requirement *a* might be expected to have the higher operating leverage.
c. If revenues for both companies declined, which company do you think would likely experience the greatest decline in operating earnings? Explain your answer.

ATC 2-2 **GROUP ASSIGNMENT** *Operating Leverage*

The Parent Teacher Association (PTA) of Meadow High School is planning a fund-raising campaign. The PTA is considering the possibility of hiring Eric Logan, a world-renowned investment counselor, to address the public. Tickets would sell for $28 each. The school has agreed to let the PTA use Harville Auditorium at no cost. Mr. Logan is willing to accept one of two compensation arrangements. He will sign an agreement to receive a fixed fee of $10,000 regardless of the number of tickets sold. Alternatively, he will accept payment of $20 per ticket sold. In communities similar to that in which Meadow is located, Mr. Logan has drawn an audience of approximately 500 people.

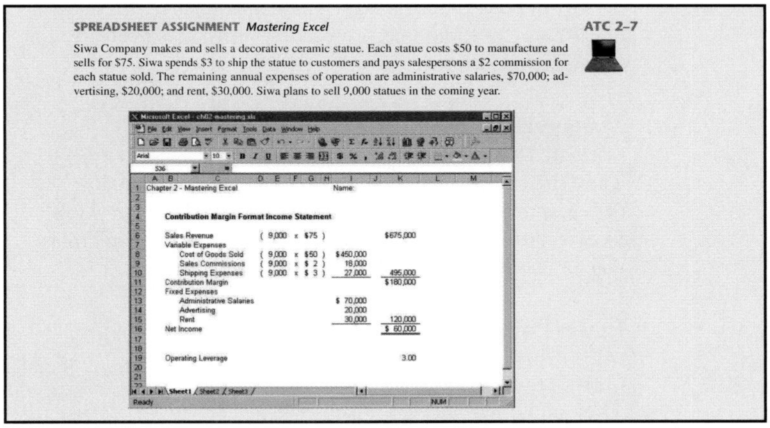

SPREADSHEET ASSIGNMENT *Mastering Excel* ATC 2-7

Siwa Company makes and sells a decorative ceramic statue. Each statue costs $50 to manufacture and sells for $75. Siwa spends $3 to ship the statue to customers and pays salespersons a $2 commission for each statue sold. The remaining annual expenses of operation are administrative salaries, $70,000; advertising, $20,000; and rent, $30,000. Siwa plans to sell 9,000 statues in the coming year.

Chapter 2 - Mastering Excel Name:

Contribution Margin Format Income Statement

Sales Revenue	(9,000 x $75)		$675,000
Variable Expenses			
Cost of Goods Sold	(9,000 x $50)	$450,000	
Sales Commissions	(9,000 x $ 2)	18,000	
Shipping Expenses	(9,000 x $ 3)	27,000	495,000
Contribution Margin			$180,000
Fixed Expenses			
Administrative Salaries		$ 70,000	
Advertising		20,000	
Rent		30,000	120,000
Net Income			$ 60,000
Operating Leverage			3.00

Analyze, Think, Communicate (ATC)

Each chapter includes an innovative section entitled Analyze, Think, Communicate (ATC). This section contains:

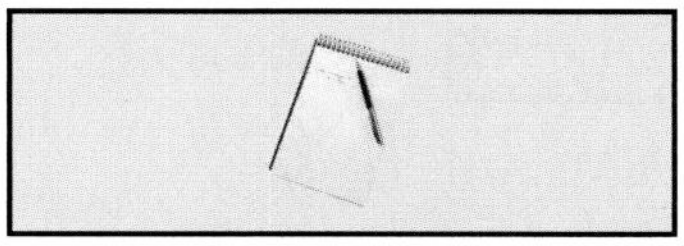

- Writing assignments

- Group exercises

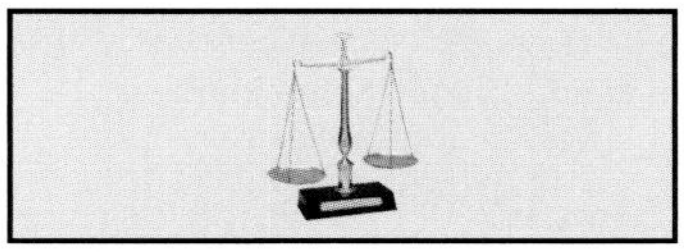

- Ethics cases

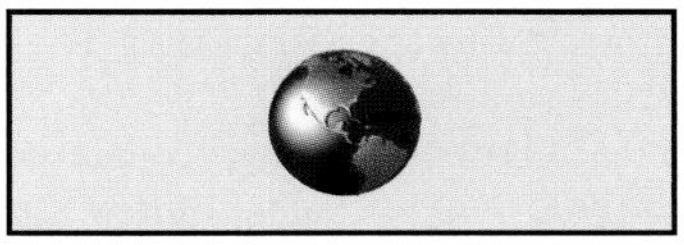

- Internet assignments

- Excel spreadsheet applications

Mastering Excel

The Excel applications are used to make students comfortable with this analytical tool and to show its use in accounting.

"The innovative end of chapter materials are especially on target as an aid to improving student critical thinking and writing skills. The Excel spreadsheet applications are also excellent real world activities."
Dan R. Ward,
University of Louisiana, Lafayette

SUPPLEMENTS for Instructors

Instructor's Manual

ISBN 0072991070

(Also available on the password-protected Instructor Online Learning Center (OLC) and Instructor's Resource CD.)

This comprehensive manual includes step-by-step, explicit instructions on how the text can be used to implement alternative teaching methods. It also provides guidance for instructors who use the traditional lecture method. The guide includes lesson plans and demonstration problems with student work papers, as well as solutions. It was prepared by Tom Edmonds and Nancy Schneider.

Solutions Manual

ISBN 0072991062

(Also available on the password-protected Instructor Online Learning Center (OLC) and Instructor Resource CD)

Prepared by the authors, the manual contains complete solutions to all the text's end-of-chapter exercises, problems, and cases.

Solutions Transparencies

ISBN 0072991100

Transparencies are prepared in easy-to-read 14-point bold type. They are mirror images of the answers provided in the solutions manual and are consistent with the forms contained in the working papers. This ensures congruence between your class presentations and the follow-up exposure that students attain when they view the solutions manual or use the working papers.

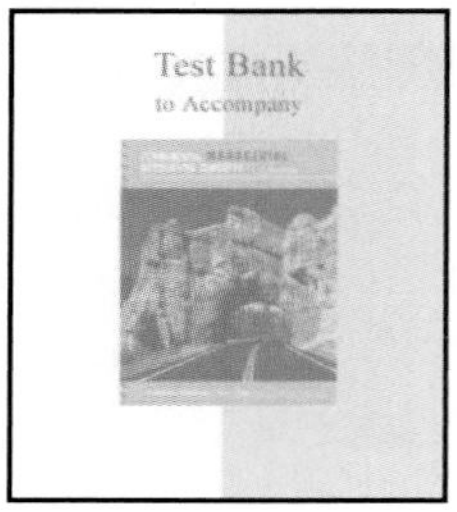

Test Bank

ISBN 0072991097

(Also available on the Instructor's Resource CD)

This test bank in Word™ format contains multiple-choice questions, essay, and short problems. Each test item is coded for level of difficulty and learning objective. In addition to an expansive array of traditional test questions, the test bank includes new types of questions that focus exclusively on how business events affect financial statements.

Computerized Test Bank

(Also available on the Instructor's Resource CD)

This test bank utilizes testing software to quickly create customized exams. It can be used to make different versions of the same test, change the answer order, edit and add questions, and conduct online testing.

Instructor's Resource CD-ROM

ISBN 0072991127

This CD includes electronic versions of the Instructor's Manual, Solutions Manual, Test Bank, computerized Test Bank, as well as PowerPoint slides, video clips, all exhibits in the text in PowerPoint, and spreadsheet templates with solutions. This CD-ROM makes it easy for instructors to create multimedia presentations.

Managerial Accounting Video Library

ISBN 0072376171

These short videos, developed by Dallas County Community College, provide an impetus for class discussion. These provide a focus on the preparation, analysis, and use of accounting information for business decision making.

PowerPoint Presentation

(Available on the Online Learning Center OLC and Instructor's Resource CD-ROM)

These audio-narrated slides can serve as interactive class discussions and were prepared by Jon A. Booker and Charles W. Caldwell of Tennessee Technological University and Susan Galbreath of David Lipscomb University.

SUPPLEMENTS for Students

OnePass

One Pass integrates all of the text's multimedia resources. With just one access code, students can obtain state of the art study aids, including Homework Manager, NetTutor and an online version of the text.

Homework Manager

This web-based software duplicates problem structures directly from the end-of-chapter material in the textbook. It uses algorithms to provide a limitless supply of self-graded practice for students. It shows students where they made errors. All Exercises and Problems in Series A are available with Homework Manager.

Study Guide

ISBN 0072991143

This proactive guide incorporates many of the accounting skills essential to student success. Each chapter contains. A review and explanation of the chapter's learning objectives, as well as multiple-choice problems and short exercises. Unique to this Study Guide is a series of articulation problems that require students to indicate how accounting events affect the elements of financial statements. The guide includes appropriate working papers and a complete set of solutions. It was prepared by Philip Olds.

Working Papers

ISBN 0072989440

Working papers are available to direct students in solving text assignments.

Computerized Practice Set

ISBN 0072536667

Ramblewood
Manufacturing, Inc.

Topic Tackler Plus DVD

This tutorial offers a virtual helping hand in understanding the most challenging topics in the managerial accounting course. Through a step-by-step sequence of video clips, PowerPoint slides, interactive practice exercises, and self tests, Topic Tackler Plus offers help on two key topics for each chapter. These topics are indicated by a logo in the text. Another component on the DVD takes the Self-Study Review Problem in the book and demonstrates how to solve it in an animated audio presentation.

www.mhhe.com/edmonds3e

Excel Templates

(Available on the Online Learning Center (OLC)

These templates allow students to develop spreadsheet skills to solve selected assignments identified by an icon in the end-of-chapter material.

PowerPoint Presentation

(Available on the Online Learning Center (OLC)

These PowerPoint slides cover key chapter topics in an audio-narrated presentation sure to help students learn. These were prepared by Jon A. Booker and Charles W. Caldwell of Tennessee Technological University and Susan Galbreath of David Lipscomb University.

ALEKS for the Accounting Cycle

ISBN 0072975326

Or check the ALEKS website at *www.business.aleks.com*

Online Learning Center (OLC)

www.mhhe.com/edmonds3e

See page xv for details

ACKNOWLEDGEMENTS

Special thanks to the talented people who prepared the supplements. These take a great deal of time and effort to write and we appreciate their efforts. Amelia Baldwin of the University of Alabama prepared the Test Bank. Tim Nygaard of Madisonville Community College developed the Self-Review Problem PowerPoint slides. Leonard Stokes of Siena College wrote the online quizzes. Linda Schain of Hofstra University developed the Topic Tackler Plus DVD. Jack Terry of ComSource Associates prepared the Excel templates. Jon Booker and Charles W. Caldwell both of Tennessee Technological University, and Susan C. Galbreath of David Lipscomb University did the PowerPoint presentation. We also thank our accuracy checkers for checking the text manuscript and solutions manual. They include Susan Pope of University of Akron and Linda Herrington at Community College of Allegheny County. A special thanks to Linda Bell of William Jewell College for her contribution to the Financial Statement Analysis material that appears in the Supplement to Chapter 13.

We are deeply indebted to our sponsoring editor, Steve Schuetz. His direction and guidance have added clarity and quality to the text. We especially appreciate the efforts of our developmental editor, Gail Korosa. Gail has coordinated the exchange of ideas among our class testers, reviewers, copy editor, and error checkers; she has done far more than simply pass along ideas. She has contributed numerous original suggestions that have enhanced the quality of the text. Our editors have certainly facilitated our efforts to prepare a book that will facilitate a meaningful understanding of accounting. Even so, their contributions are to no avail unless the text reaches its intended audience. We are most grateful to Rich Kolasa and Jackie Powers and the sales staff for providing the informative advertising that has so accurately communicated the unique features of the concepts approach to accounting educators. Many others at McGraw-Hill/Irwin at a moment's notice redirected their attention to focus their efforts on the development of this text. We extend our sincere appreciation to Pat Fredrickson, Elizabeth Mavetz, Michael McCormick, Mary Kazak, Jeremy Cheshareck, Matt Perry and Erwin Llereza. We deeply appreciate the long hours that you committed to the formation of a high-quality text.

Thomas P. Edmonds • Cindy D. Edmonds • Bor-Yi Tsay • Philip R. Olds • Nancy W. Schneider

We express our sincere thanks to the following individuals who provided extensive reviews for the third edition:

Reviewers

Daniel Benco, Southeastern Oklahoma University
Steve Buchheit, Texas Tech University
Dennis Caplan, Iowa State University
Julie Chenier, Louisiana State University
Robert Fahnestock, University of West Florida
John Goetz, University of Texas Arlington
Judith Harris, Nova Southeastern University
Sheila Johnston, University of Louisville, Louisville
Elliott Levy, Bentley College
Julie Lockhart, Western Washington University
Lois Mahoney, University of Central Florida
David McIntyre, Clemson University
John Moore, Virginia State University
Chei Paik, George Washington University
Emil Radosevich, Albuquerque TVI Community College
Celia Renner, Boise State University
Gary Reynolds, Ozark Technical Community College
Nancy Ruhe, West Virginia University, Morgantown
Marilyn Salter, University of Central Florida
Angela Sandberg, Jacksonville State University
John Shaver, Louisiana Tech University
Scott Steinkamp, College of Lake County
Michael VanBreda, Southern Methodist University
Dan Ward, University of Louisiana, Lafayette

Our appreciation to those who reviewed previous editions

Jed Ashley, Grossmont College

James Bates, Mountain Empire Community College

Frank Beigbeder, Rancho Santiago College

Dorcas Berg, Wingate College

Ashton Bishop, James Madison University

Amy Bourne, Tarrant County College

Eric Carlsen, Kean University

Sue Counte, Jefferson College

Jill D'Aquila, Iona College

Walt Doehring, Genesee Community College

Patricia Douglas, Loyola Marymount University

Dean Edmiston, Emporia State University

Robert Elmore, Tennessee Technological University

Jeffrey Galbreath, Greenfield Community College

William Geary, College of William and Mary

Dinah Gottschalk, James Madison University

Donald Gribbin, Southern Illinois University

Larry Hegstad, Pacific Lutheran University

Fred Jex, Macomb Community College

Robert Landry, Massassoit Community College

Mark Lawrence, University of Alabama at Birmingham

Bruce Lindsey, Genesee Community College

Philip Little, Western Carolina University

Pat McMahon, Palm Beach Community College

Irvin Nelson, Utah State University

Bruce Neumann, University of Colorado

Hossein Nouri, College of New Jersey

Ashton Oravetz, Tyler Junior College

Thomas Phillips, Louisiana Tech University

Marjorie Platt, Northeastern University

Jane Reimers, Florida State University

Diane Riordan, James Madison University

Tom Robinson, University of Alaska

Kathryn Savage, Northern Arizona University

Bob Smith, Florida State University

Suneel Udpa, St. Mary's College

Sean Wright, DeVry Institute of Technology, Phoenix

Allan Young, DeVry Institute of Technology, Atlanta

Many others have contributed directly or indirectly to the development of the text. Participants in workshops and focus groups have provided useful feedback. Colleagues and friends have extended encouragement and support. Among these individuals our sincere appreciation is extended to Lowell Broom, University of Alabama at Birmingham; Bill Schwartz and Ed Spede of Virginia Commonwealth University; Doug Cloud, Pepperdine University—Malibu; Charles Bailey, University of Central Florida; Bob Holtfreter, Central Washington University; Kimberly Temme, Maryville University; Beth Vogel, Mount Mary College; Robert Minnear, Emory University; Shirish Seth, California State University at Fullerton; Richard Emery, Linfield College; Gail Hoover, Rockhurst; Bruce Robertson, Lock Haven University; Jeannie Folk, College of Dupage; Marvelyn Burnette, Wichita State University; Ron Mannino, University of Massachusetts; John Reisch, Florida Atlantic University; Rosalie Hallbaurer, Florida International University; Lynne H. Shoaf, Belmont Abbey College; Jayne Maas, Towson University; Ahmed Goma, Manhattan College; John Rude, Bloomsburg University; Jack Paul, Lehigh University; Terri Gutierrez, University of Northern Colorado; Khondkar Karim, Monmouth University; Carol Lawrence, University of Richmond; Jeffrey Power, Saint Mary's University; Joanne Sheridan, Montana State University; and George Dow, Valencia Community College.

BRIEF CONTENTS

CONTENTS

Chapter 1 Management Accounting: A Value-Added Discipline 2

Chapter 2 Cost Behavior, Operating Leverage, and Profitability Analysis 48

Chapter 3 Analysis of Cost, Volume, and Pricing to Increase Profitability 94

Chapter 4 Relevant Information for Special Decisions 134

Chapter 5 Cost Accumulation, Tracing, and Allocation 182

Chapter 6 Cost Management in an Automated Business Environment: ABC, ABM, and TQM 228

Chapter 7 Planning for Profit and Cost Control 272

Chapter 10 Planning for Capital Investments 398

Chapter 11 Product Costing in Service and Manufacturing Entities 438

Chapter 12 Job-Order, Process, and Hybrid Cost Systems 482

Chapter 13 Financial Statement Analysis 530

Chapter 14 Statement of Cash Flows 588

Fundamental Managerial ACCOUNTING Concepts

CHAPTER *one*

MANAGEMENT ACCOUNTING

A VALUE-ADDED DISCIPLINE

LEARNING *objectives*

After you have mastered the material in this chapter, you will be able to:

1 Distinguish between managerial and financial accounting.

2 Identify the cost components of a product made by a manufacturing company: the cost of materials, labor, and overhead.

3 Explain the need for determining the average cost per unit of a product.

4 Distinguish between a cost and an expense.

5 Explain the effects on financial statements of product costs versus general, selling, and administrative costs.

6 Explain how cost classification affects financial statements and managerial decisions.

7 Identify the standards of ethical conduct and the features that motivate misconduct.

8 Distinguish product costs from upstream and downstream costs.

9 Explain how products provided by service companies differ from products made by manufacturing companies.

10 Explain how emerging trends such as activity-based management, value-added assessment, and just-in-time inventory are affecting the managerial accounting discipline.

THE *curious* ACCOUNTANT

In the first course of accounting, you learned how retailers, such as **Wal-Mart**, account for the cost of equipment that lasts more than one year. Recall that the equipment was recorded as an asset when purchased, and then it was depreciated over its expected useful life. The depreciation charge reduced the company's assets and increased its expenses. This approach was justified under the matching principle, which seeks to recognize costs as expenses in the same period that the cost (resource) is used to generate revenue.

In this course, the focus will often be on manufacturing entities, so consider the following scenario. Black & Decker manufactures cordless hedge trimmers that it sells to Wal-Mart. In order to produce the hedge trimmers, Black & Decker had to purchase a robotic machine that it expects can be used to produce 1 million hedge trimmers.

Do you think **Black & Decker** should account for depreciation on its manufacturing equipment the same way Wal-Mart accounts for depreciation on its registers at the checkout counters? If not, how should Black & Decker account for its depreciation? Remember the matching principle when thinking of your answer. (Answer on page 17.)

CHAPTER *opening*

Andy Grove, president and CEO of ***Intel Corporation****, is credited with the motto "Only the paranoid survive." Mr. Grove describes a wide variety of concerns that make him paranoid. Specifically, he declares:*

> *I worry about products getting screwed up, and I worry about products getting introduced prematurely. I worry about factories not performing well, and I worry about having too many factories. I worry about hiring the right people, and I worry about*

morale slacking off. And, of course, I worry about competitors. I worry about other people figuring out how to do what we do better or cheaper, and displacing us with our customers.

Do Intel's historical-based financial statements contain the information Mr. Grove needs? No. ***Financial accounting*** *is not designed to satisfy all the information needs of business managers. Its scope is limited to the needs of external users such as investors and creditors. The field of accounting designed to meet the needs of internal users is called* ***managerial accounting.***

Differences Between Managerial and Financial Accounting

LO1 Distinguish between managerial and financial accounting.

While the information needs of internal and external users overlap, the needs of managers generally differ from those of investors or creditors. Some distinguishing characteristics are discussed in the following section.

Users and Types of Information

Financial accounting provides information used primarily by investors, creditors, and others *outside* a business. In contrast, managerial accounting focuses on information used by executives, managers, and employees who work *inside* the business. These two user groups need different types of information.

Internal users need information to *plan, direct,* and *control* business operations. The nature of information needed is related to an employee's job level. Lower level employees use nonfinancial information such as work schedules, store hours, and customer service policies. Moving up the organizational ladder, financial information becomes increasingly important. Middle managers use a blend of financial and nonfinancial information, while senior executives concentrate on financial data. To a lesser degree, senior executives also use general economic data and nonfinancial operating information. For example, an executive may consider the growth rate of the economy before deciding to expand the company's workforce.

External users (investors and creditors) have greater needs for general economic information than do internal users. For example, an investor debating whether to purchase stock versus bond securities might be more interested in government tax policy than financial statement data. Exhibit 1–1 summarizes the information needs of different user groups.

Level of Aggregation

External users generally desire *global information* that reflects the performance of a company as a whole. For example, an investor is not so much interested in the performance of a particular Sears store as she is in the performance of **Sears Roebuck Company** versus that of **JC Penney Company**. In contrast, internal users focus on detailed information about specific subunits of the company. To meet the needs of the different user groups financial accounting data are more aggregated than managerial accounting data.

Regulation

Financial accounting is designed to generate information for the general public. In an effort to protect the public interest, Congress established the **Securities and Exchange Commission**

Exhibit 1–1 *Relationship Between Type of User and Type of Information*

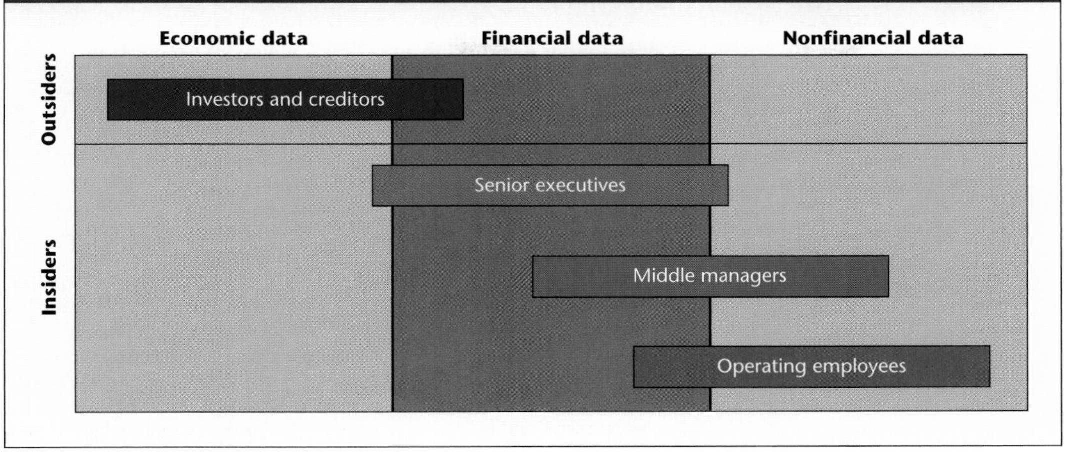

(SEC) and gave it authority to regulate public financial reporting practices. The SEC has delegated much of its authority for developing accounting rules to the private sector **Financial Accounting Standards Board (FASB),** thereby allowing the accounting profession considerable influence over financial accounting reports. The FASB supports a broad base of pronouncements and practices known as **generally accepted accounting principles (GAAP).** GAAP severely restricts the accounting procedures and practices permitted in published financial statements.

Around the turn of the century, a number of high-profile business failures raised questions about the effectiveness of self-regulation and the usefulness of audits to protect the public. The **Sarbanes-Oxley Act of 2002** was adopted to address these concerns. The act creates a five-member Public Company Accounting Oversight Board (PCAOB) with the authority to set and enforce auditing, attestation, quality control, and ethics standards for auditors of public companies. The PCAOB is empowered to impose disciplinary and remedial sanctions for violations of its rules, securities laws, and professional auditing and accounting standards. Public corporations operate in a complex regulatory environment that requires the services of attorneys and professional accountants.

Beyond financial statement data, much of the information generated by management accounting systems is proprietary information not available to the public. Since this information is not distributed to the public, it need not be regulated to protect the public interest. Management accounting is restricted only by the **value-added principle.** Management accountants are free to engage in any information gathering and reporting activity so long as the activity adds value in excess of its cost. For example, management accountants are free to provide forecasted information to internal users. In contrast, financial accounting as prescribed by GAAP does not permit forecasting.

Information Characteristics

While financial accounting is characterized by its objectivity, reliability, consistency, and historical nature, managerial accounting is more concerned with relevance and timeliness. Managerial accounting uses more estimates and fewer facts than financial accounting. Financial accounting reports what happened yesterday; managerial accounting reports what is expected to happen tomorrow.

Time Horizon and Reporting Frequency

Financial accounting information is reported periodically, normally at the end of a year. Management cannot wait until the end of the year to discover problems. Planning, controlling, and directing require immediate attention. Managerial accounting information is delivered on a continual basis.

Exhibit 1–2 summarizes significant differences between financial and managerial accounting.

Exhibit 1–2 *Comparative Features of Managerial Versus Financial Accounting Information*

Features	Managerial Accounting	Financial Accounting
Users	Insiders including executives, managers, and operators	Outsiders including investors, creditors, government agencies, analysts, and reporters
Information type	Economic and physical data as well as financial data	Financial data
Level of aggregation	Local information on subunits of the organization	Global information on the company as a whole
Regulation	No regulation, limited only by the value-added principle	Regulation by SEC, FASB, and other determinors of GAAP
Information characteristics	Estimates that promote relevance and enable timeliness	Factual information that is characterized by objectivity, reliability, consistency, and accuracy
Time horizon	Past, present, and future	Past only, historically based
Reporting frequency	Continuous reporting	Delayed with emphasis on annual reports

Product Costing

A major focus for managerial accountants is determining **product cost.**[1] Managers need to know the cost of their products for a variety of reasons. For example, **cost-plus pricing** is a common business practice.[2] **Product costing** is also used to control business operations. It is useful in answering questions such as: Are costs higher or lower than expected? Who is responsible for the variances between expected and actual costs? What action can be taken to control the variances?

Topic Tackler PLUS

1–1

Product Costs in Manufacturing Companies

LO2 Identify the cost components of a product made by a manufacturing company: the cost of materials, labor, and overhead.

The cost of making products includes the cost of materials, labor, and other resources (usually called **overhead**). To understand how these costs affect financial statements, consider the example of Tabor Manufacturing Company.

Tabor Manufacturing Company

Tabor Manufacturing Company makes wooden tables. The company spent $1,000 cash to build four tables: $390 for materials, $470 for a carpenter's labor, and $140 for tools used in making the tables. How much is Tabor's expense? The answer is zero. The $1,000 cash has been converted into products (four tables). The cash payments for materials, labor, and tools were *asset exchange* transactions. One asset (cash) decreased while another asset (tables) increased. Tabor will not recognize any expense until the tables are sold; in the meantime, the cost of the tables is held in an asset account called **Finished Goods** Inventory. Exhibit 1–3 illustrates how cash is transformed into inventory.

---

[1] This text uses the term *product* in a generic sense to mean both goods and services.

[2] Other pricing strategies will be introduced in subsequent chapters.

Exhibit 1–3 *Transforming the Asset Cash Into the Asset Finished Goods*

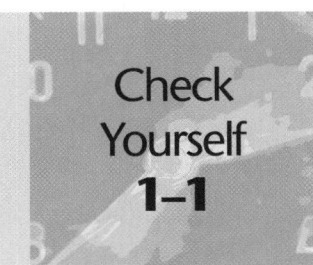

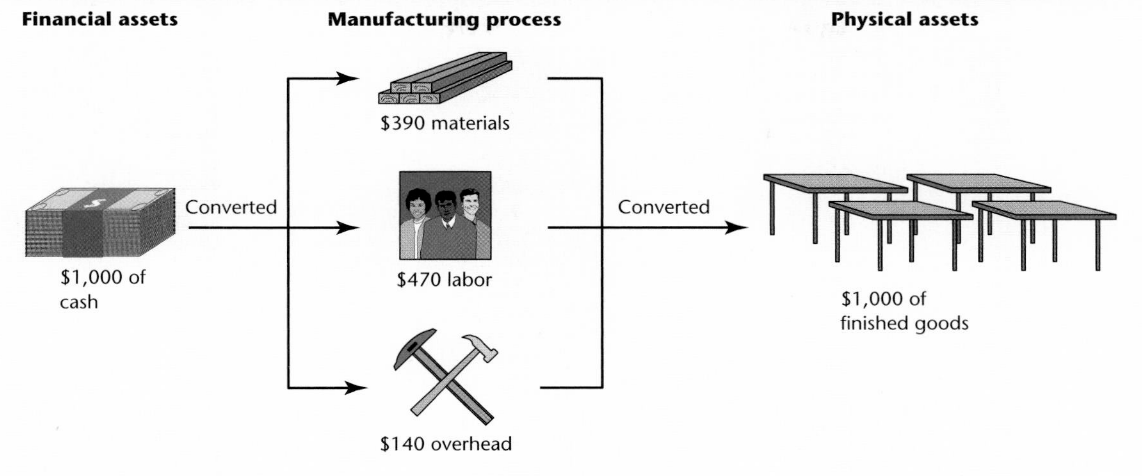

Average Cost per Unit

LO3 Explain the need for determining the average cost per unit of a product.

How much did each table made by Tabor cost? The *actual* cost of each of the four tables likely differs. The carpenter probably spent a little more time on some of the tables than others. Material and tool usage probably varied from table to table. Determining the exact cost of each table is virtually impossible. Minute details such as a second of labor time cannot be effectively measured. Even if Tabor could determine the exact cost of each table, the information would be of little use. Minor differences in the cost per table would make no difference in pricing or other decisions management needs to make. Accountants therefore normally calculate cost per unit as an *average.* In the case of Tabor Manufacturing, the **average cost** per table is $250 ($1,000 ÷ 4 units). Unless otherwise stated, assume *cost per unit* means *average cost per unit.*

Check Yourself 1–1

All boxes of General Mills' Total Raisin Bran cereal are priced at exactly the same amount in your local grocery store. Does this mean that the actual cost of making each box of cereal was exactly the same price?

Answer No, making each box would not cost exactly the same amount. For example, some boxes contain slightly more or less cereal than other boxes. Accordingly, some boxes cost slightly more or less to make than others do. General Mills uses average cost rather than actual cost to develop its pricing strategy.

Costs Can Be Assets or Expenses

LO4 Distinguish between a cost and an expense.

It might seem odd that wages earned by production workers are recorded as inventory instead of being expensed. Remember, however, that expenses are assets used in the process of *earning revenue*. The cash paid to production workers is not used to produce revenue. Instead, the cash is used to produce inventory. Revenue will be earned when the inventory is used (sold). So long as the inventory remains on hand, all product costs (materials, labor, and overhead) remain in an inventory account.

When a table is sold, the average cost of the table is transferred from the Inventory account to the Cost of Goods Sold (expense) account. If some tables remain unsold at the end of the accounting period, part of the *product costs* is reported as an asset (inventory) on the balance sheet while the other part is reported as an expense (cost of goods sold) on the income statement.

Exhibit 1–4 *Cost Classification for Tabor Manufacturing Company*

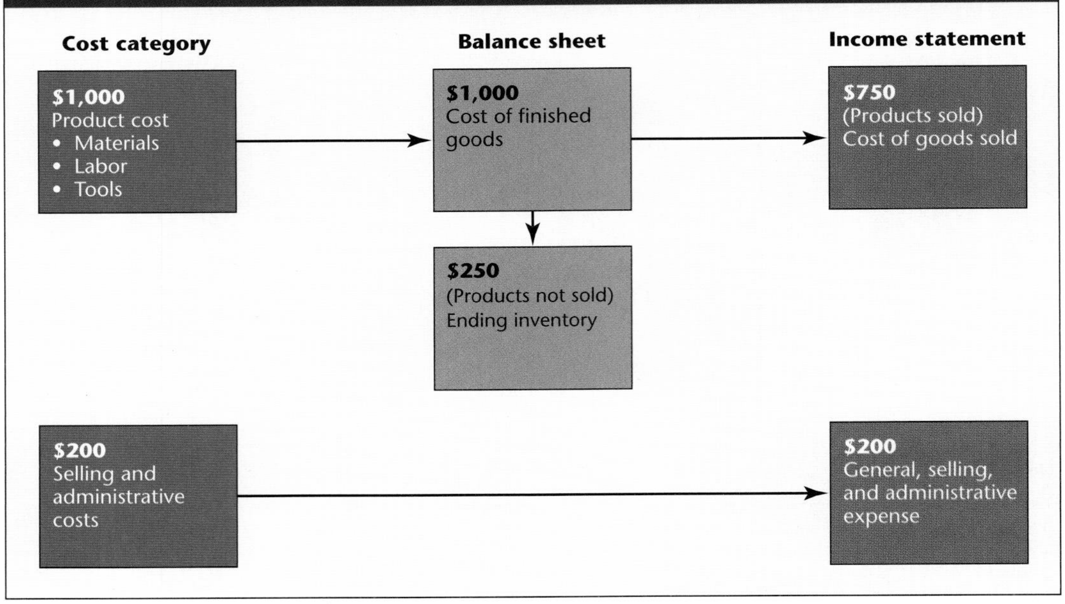

Costs that are not classified as product costs are normally expensed in the period in which they are incurred. These costs include *general operating costs, selling and administrative costs, interest costs,* and the *cost of income taxes.*

To illustrate, return to the Tabor Manufacturing example. Recall that Tabor made four tables at an average cost per unit of $250. Assume Tabor pays an employee who sells three of the tables a $200 sales commission. The sales commission is expensed immediately. The total product cost for the three tables (3 tables × $250 each = $750) is expensed on the income statement as cost of goods sold. The portion of the total product cost remaining in inventory is $250 (1 table × $250). Exhibit 1–4 shows the relationship between the costs incurred and the expenses recognized for Tabor Manufacturing Company.

Effect of Product Costs on Financial Statements

LO5 Explain the effects on financial statements of product costs versus general, selling, and administrative costs.

To illustrate accounting for product costs in manufacturing companies, assume Patillo Manufacturing Company was started on January 1, 2004. Patillo experienced the following accounting events during its first year of operations.[3] *Assume that all transactions are cash transactions.*

1. Acquired $15,000 cash by issuing common stock.
2. Paid $2,000 for materials that were used to make products. All products started were completed during the period.
3. Paid $1,200 for salaries of selling and administrative employees.
4. Paid $3,000 for wages of production workers.
5. Paid $2,800 for furniture used in selling and administrative offices.
6. Recognized depreciation on the office furniture purchased in Event 5. The furniture was acquired on January 1, had a $400 estimated salvage value, and a four-year useful life. The annual depreciation charge is $600 ([$2,800 − $400] ÷ 4).

[3] This illustration assumes that all inventory started during the period was completed during the period. Patillo therefore uses only one inventory account, Finished Goods Inventory. Many manufacturing companies normally have three categories of inventory on hand at the end of an accounting period: Raw Materials Inventory, Work in Process Inventory (inventory of partially completed units), and Finished Goods Inventory. Chapter 11 discusses these inventories in greater detail.

Exhibit 1–5 *Effect of Product Versus Selling and Administrative Costs on Financial Statements*

	Assets				Equity					
Event No.	**Cash**	**+ Inventory**	**+ Office Furn.***	**+ Manuf. Equip.***	**= Com. Stk.**	**+ Ret. Ear.**	**Rev.**	**− Exp.**	**= Net Inc.**	**Cash Flow†**
1	15,000				15,000					15,000 FA
2	(2,000)	2,000								(2,000) OA
3	(1,200)					(1,200)		− 1,200	(1,200)	(1,200) OA
4	(3,000)	3,000								(3,000) OA
5	(2,800)		2,800							(2,800) IA
6			(600)			(600)		− 600	(600)	
7	(4,500)			4,500						(4,500) IA
8		1,000		(1,000)						
9	7,500					7,500	7,500		7,500	7,500 OA
10		(4,000)				(4,000)		− 4,000	(4,000)	
Totals	9,000	+ 2,000	+ 2,200	+ 3,500	= 15,000	+ 1,700	7,500	− 5,800	= 1,700	9,000 NC

*Negative amounts in these columns represent accumulated depreciation.

†The letters in the far right-hand column of Exhibit 1–5 designate different types of cash flow activities. The letters FA represent financing activities, IA represents investing activities, and OA represents operating activities. The letters NC on the bottom row represent the net change in cash. If you have not studied the statement of cash flows, we recommend that you study the information in the Appendix at the end of this chapter prior to continuing your study. Alternatively, your instructor might prefer to cover cash flow effects later in the course. In this case, you can ignore the information in the Cash Flow column.

7. Paid $4,500 for manufacturing equipment.
8. Recognized depreciation on the equipment purchased in Event 7. The equipment was acquired on January 1, had a $1,500 estimated salvage value, and a three-year useful life. The annual depreciation charge is $1,000 ([$4,500 − $1,500) ÷ 3).
9. Sold inventory to customers for $7,500 cash.
10. The inventory sold in Event 9 cost $4,000 to make.

The effects of these transactions on the balance sheet, income statement, and statement of cash flows are shown in Exhibit 1–5. Study each row in this exhibit, paying particular attention to how similar costs such as salaries for selling and administrative personnel and wages for production workers have radically different effects on the financial statements. The example illustrates the three elements of product costs, materials (Event 2), labor (Event 4), and overhead (Event 8). These events are discussed in more detail below.

Materials Costs (Event 2)

Materials used to make products are usually called **raw materials.** The cost of raw materials is first recorded in an asset account (Inventory). The cost is then transferred from the Inventory account to the Cost of Goods Sold account at the time the goods are sold. Remember that materials cost is only one component of total manufacturing costs. When inventory is sold, the combined cost of materials, labor, and overhead is expensed as *cost of goods sold.* The costs of materials that can be easily and conveniently traced to products are called **direct raw materials** costs.

Labor Costs (Event 4)

The salaries paid to selling and administrative employees (Event 3) and the wages paid to production workers (Event 4) are accounted for differently. Salaries paid to selling and administrative employees are expensed immediately, but the cost of production wages is added to inventory. Production wages are expensed as part of cost of goods sold at the time the inventory is sold. Labor costs that can be easily and conveniently traced to products are called **direct labor** costs. The cost flow of wages for production employees versus salaries for selling and administrative personnel is shown in Exhibit 1–6.

Exhibit 1–6 *Flow of Labor Costs*

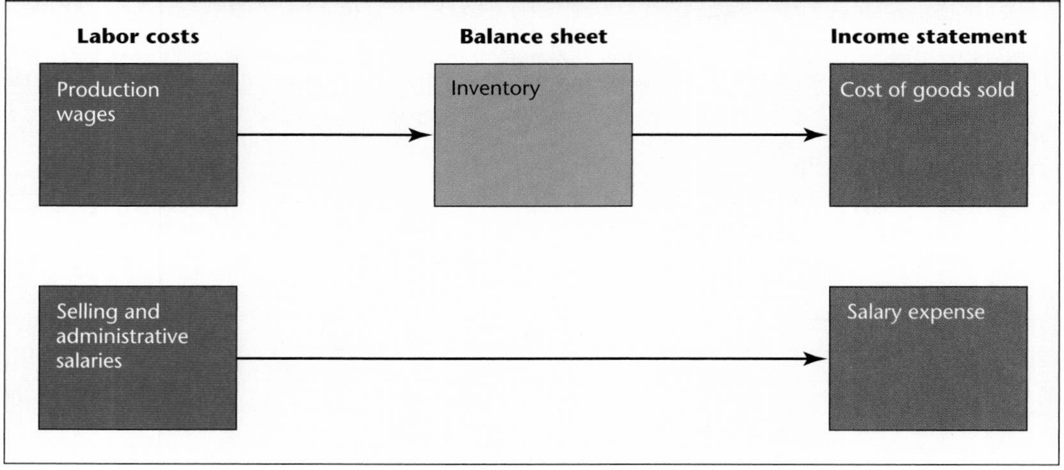

Overhead Costs (Event 8)

Although depreciation cost totaled $1,600 ($600 on office furniture and $1,000 on manufacturing equipment), only the $600 of depreciation on the office furniture is expensed directly on the income statement. The depreciation on the manufacturing equipment is split between the income statement (cost of goods sold) and the balance sheet (inventory). The depreciation cost flow for the manufacturing equipment versus the office furniture is shown in Exhibit 1–7.

Exhibit 1–7 *Flow of Depreciation Costs*

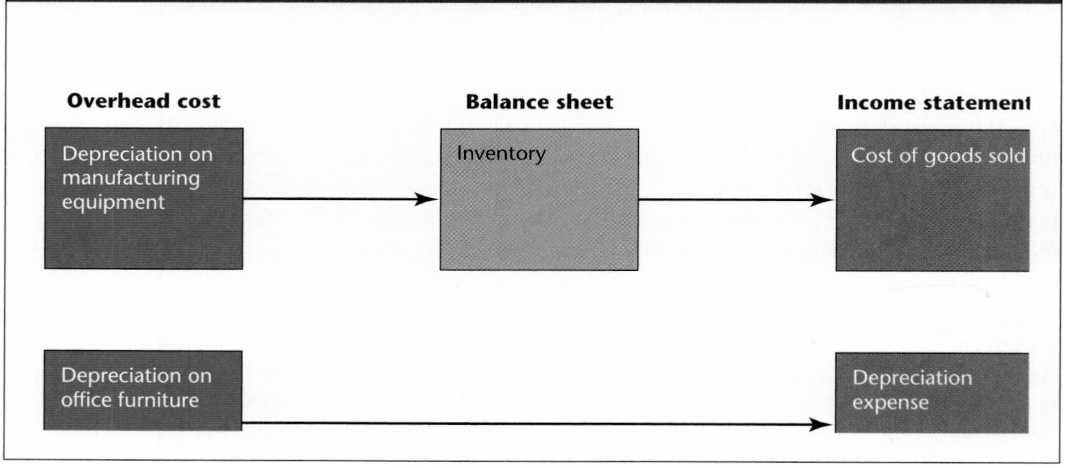

Total Product Cost. A summary of Patillo Manufacturing's total product cost is shown in Exhibit 1–8.

Exhibit 1–8 *Schedule of Inventory Costs*

Materials	$2,000
Labor	3,000
Manufacturing overhead*	1,000
Total product costs	6,000
Less: Cost of goods sold	(4,000)
Ending inventory balance	$2,000

*Depreciation ([$4,500 − $1,500] ÷ 3)

General, Selling, and Administrative Costs

General, selling, and administrative costs (G,S,&A) are normally expensed *in the period* in which they are incurred. Because of this recognition pattern, nonproduct expenses are sometimes called **period costs.** In Patillo's case, the salary expense for selling and administrative employees and the depreciation on office furniture are period costs reported directly on the income statement.

The income statement, balance sheet, and statement of cash flows for Patillo Manufacturing are displayed in Exhibit 1–9.

The $4,000 cost of goods sold reported on the income statement includes a portion of the materials, labor, and overhead costs incurred by Patillo during the year. Similarly, the $2,000 of finished goods inventory on the balance sheet includes materials, labor, and overhead costs. These product costs will be recognized as expense in the next accounting period when the goods are sold. Initially classifying a cost as a product cost delays, but does not eliminate, its recognition as an expense. All product costs are ultimately recognized as expense (cost of goods sold). Cost classification does not affect cash flow. Cash inflows and outflows are recognized in the period that cash is collected or paid regardless of whether the cost is recorded as an asset or expensed on the income statement.

Exhibit 1–9

PATILLO MANUFACTURING COMPANY
Financial Statements

Income Statement for 2004		
Sales Revenue		$7,500
Cost of Goods Sold		(4,000)
Gross Margin		3,500
G, S, & A Expenses		
Salaries Expense		(1,200)
Depreciation Expense—Office Furniture		(600)
Net Income		$1,700
Balance Sheet as of December 31, 2004		
Cash		$ 9,000
Finished Goods Inventory		2,000
Office Furniture	$2,800	
Accumulated Depreciation	(600)	
Book Value		2,200
Manufacturing Equipment	4,500	
Accumulated Depreciation	(1,000)	
Book Value		3,500
Total Assets		$16,700
Stockholders' Equity		
Common Stock		$15,000
Retained Earnings		1,700
Total Stockholders' Equity		$16,700
Statement of Cash Flows for 2004		
Operating Activities		
Inflow from Revenue		$7,500
Outflow for Inventory		(5,000)
Outflow for S&A Salaries		(1,200)
Net Inflow from Operating Activities		1,300
Investing Activities		
Outflow for Equipment and Furniture		(7,300)
Financing Activities		
Inflow from Capital Acquisitions		15,000
Net Change in Cash		9,000
Beginning Cash Balance		-0-
Ending Cash Balance		$9,000

Overhead Costs: A Closer Look

Costs such as depreciation on manufacturing equipment cannot be easily traced to products. Suppose that Patillo Manufacturing makes both tables and chairs. What part of the depreciation is caused by manufacturing tables versus manufacturing chairs? Similarly, suppose a production supervisor oversees employees who work on both tables and chairs. How much of the supervisor's salary relates to tables and how much to chairs? Likewise, the cost of glue used in the production department would be difficult to trace to tables versus chairs. You could count the drops of glue used on each product, but the information would not be useful enough to merit the time and money spent collecting the data.

Costs that cannot be traced to products and services in a *cost-effective* manner are called **indirect costs.** The indirect costs incurred to make products are called **manufacturing overhead.** Some of the items commonly included in manufacturing overhead are indirect materials, indirect labor, factory utilities, rent of manufacturing facilities, and depreciation on manufacturing assets.

Check Yourself 1–2

Lawson Manufacturing Company paid production workers wages of $100,000. It incurred materials costs of $120,000 and manufacturing overhead costs of $160,000. Selling and administrative salaries were $80,000. Lawson started and completed 1,000 units of product and sold 800 of these units. The company sets sales prices at $220 above the average per unit production cost. Based on this information alone, determine the amount of gross margin and net income. What is Lawson's pricing strategy called?

Answer Total product cost is $380,000 ($100,000 labor + $120,000 materials + $160,000 overhead). Cost per unit is $380 ($380,000 ÷ 1,000 units). The sales price per unit is $600 ($380 + $220). Cost of goods sold is $304,000 ($380 × 800 units). Sales revenue is $480,000 ($600 × 800 units). Gross margin is $176,000 ($480,000 revenue − $304,000 cost of goods sold). Net income is $96,000 ($176,000 gross margin − $80,000 selling and administrative salaries). Lawson's pricing strategy is called *cost-plus* pricing.

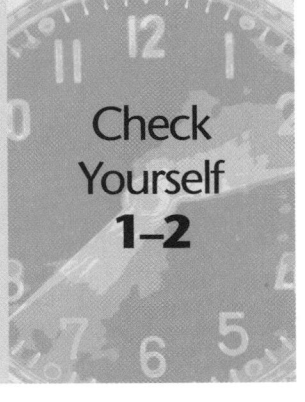

Exhibit 1–10 *Cost Allocation*

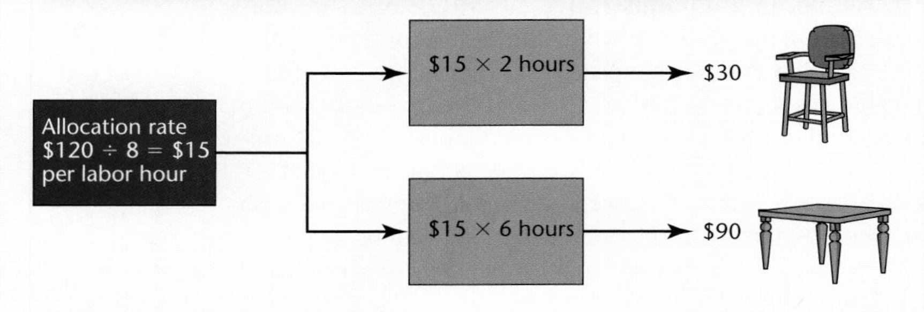

Since indirect costs cannot be effectively traced to products, they are normally assigned to products using **cost allocation,** a process of dividing a total cost into parts and assigning the parts to relevant cost objects. To illustrate, suppose that production workers spend an eight-hour day making a chair and a table. The chair requires two hours to complete and the table requires six hours. Now suppose that $120 of utilities cost is consumed during the day. How much of the $120 should be assigned to each piece of furniture? The utility cost cannot be directly traced to each specific piece of furniture, but the piece of furniture that required more labor also likely consumed more of the utility cost. Using this line of reasoning, it is rational to allocate the utility cost to the two pieces of furniture based on *direct labor hours* at a rate of $15 per hour ($120 ÷ 8 hours). The chair would be assigned $30 ($15 per hour × 2 hours) of the utility cost and the table would be assigned the remaining $90 ($15 × 6 hours) of utility cost. The allocation of the utility cost is shown in Exhibit 1–10.

We discuss the details of cost allocation in a later chapter. For now, recognize that overhead costs are normally allocated to products rather than traced directly to them.

Manufacturing Product Cost Summary

As explained, the cost of a product made by a manufacturing company is normally composed of three categories: direct materials, direct labor, and manufacturing overhead. Relevant information about these three cost components is summarized in Exhibit 1–11.

Exhibit 1–11 *Components of Manufacturing Product Cost*

Component 1—Direct Materials
Sometimes called *raw materials.* In addition to basic resources such as wood or metals, it can include manufactured parts. For example, engines, glass, and car tires can be considered as raw materials for an automotive manufacturer. If the amount of a material in a product is known, it can usually be classified as a direct material. The cost of direct materials can be easily traced to specific products.

Component 2—Direct Labor
The cost of wages paid to factory workers involved in hands-on contact with the products being manufactured. If the amount of time employees worked on a product can be determined, this cost can usually be classified as direct labor. Like direct materials, labor costs must be easily traced to a specific product in order to be classified as a direct cost.

Component 3—Manufacturing Overhead
Costs that cannot be easily traced to specific products. Accordingly, these costs are called *indirect costs.* They can include but are not limited to the following:

1. Indirect materials such as glue, nails, paper, and oil. Indeed, note that indirect materials used in the production process may not appear in the finished product. An example is a chemical solvent used to clean products during the production process but not a component material found in the final product.
2. Indirect labor such as the cost of salaries paid to production supervisors, inspectors, and maintenance personnel.
3. Rental cost for manufacturing facilities and equipment.
4. Utility costs.
5. Depreciation.
6. Security.
7. The cost of preparing equipment for the manufacturing process (i.e., setup costs).
8. Maintenance cost for the manufacturing facility and equipment.

Importance of Cost Classification

LO6 Explain how cost classification affects financial statements and managerial decisions.

What happens if an expense item is misclassified as an asset? Financial statements appear more favorable than the actual condition of the company. Specifically, the amount of total assets and net income are overstated. This condition may have significant consequences for management, investors, and the government. For example, managers who earn bonuses based on net income will benefit. Similarly, the inflated financial reports may be used to encourage investors to buy stock or lenders to make loans. On the negative side, the inflated earnings will result in the overpayment of income taxes.

Marion Manufacturing Company

To illustrate practical implications of cost classification, consider the events experienced by Marion Manufacturing Company (MMC) during its first year of operations. All transactions are cash transactions.

1. MMC was started when it acquired $12,000 from issuing common stock
2. MMC incurred $4,000 of costs to design its product and plan the manufacturing process.
3. MMC incurred specifically identifiable product costs (materials, labor, and overhead) of $8,000.
4. MMC made 1,000 units of product and sold 700 of the units for $18 each.

Exhibit 1–12 displays a set of financial statements that are prepared under the following two scenarios.

Exhibit 1–12 *Financial Statements Under Alternative Cost Classification Scenarios*

Income Statements	Scenario 1	Scenario 2
Sales Revenue (700 × $18)	$12,600	$12,600
Cost of Goods Sold	(5,600)	(8,400)
Gross Margin	7,000	4,200
Selling and Administrative Expense	(4,000)	0
Net Income	$3,000	$ 4,200
Balance Sheets		
Assets		
Cash	$12,600	$12,600
Inventory	2,400	3,600
Total Assets	$15,000	$16,200
Stockholders' Equity		
Common Stock	$12,000	$12,000
Retained Earnings	3,000	4,200
Total Stockholders' Equity	$15,000	$16,200
Statements of Cash Flows		
Operating Activities		
Inflow from Customers	$12,600	$12,600
Outflow for Inventory	(8,000)	(12,000)
Outflow for S&A	(4,000)	0
Net Inflow from Operating Activities	600	600
Investing Activities	0	0
Financing Activities		
Acquisition of Capital	12,000	12,000
Net Change in Cash	12,600	12,600
Beginning Cash Balance	0	0
Ending Cash Balance	$12,600	$12,600

Scenario 1: The $4,000 of design and planning costs are classified as selling and administrative expenses.

Scenario 2: The $4,000 of design and planning costs are classified as product costs, meaning they are first accumulated in the Inventory account and then expensed when the goods are sold. Given that MMC made 1,000 units and sold 700 units of inventory, 70% (700 ÷ 1,000) of the design cost has passed through the Inventory account into the Cost of Goods Sold account, leaving 30% (300 ÷ 1,000) remaining in the Inventory account.

Statement Differences

Comparing the financial statements prepared under Scenario 1 with those prepared under Scenario 2 reveals the following.

1. There are no selling and administrative expenses under Scenario 2. The design cost was treated as a product cost and placed into the Inventory account rather than being expensed.
2. Cost of goods sold is $2,800 ($4,000 design cost × .70) higher under Scenario 2.
3. Net income is $1,200 higher under Scenario 2 ($4,000 understated expense − $2,800 overstated cost of goods sold).
4. Ending inventory is $1,200 ($4,000 design cost × .30) higher under Scenario 2.

While the Scenario 2 income statement and balance sheet are overstated, cash flow is not affected by the alternative cost classifications. Regardless of how the design cost is classified, the same amount of cash was collected and paid. This explains why financial analysts consider the statement of cash flows to be a critical source of information.

Practical Implications

The financial statement differences shown in Exhibit 1–12 are *timing differences.* When MMC sells the remaining 300 units of inventory, the $1,200 of design and planning costs included in inventory under Scenario 2 will be expensed through cost of goods sold. In other words, once the entire inventory is sold, total expenses and retained earnings will be the same under both scenarios. Initially recording cost in an inventory account only delays eventual expense recognition. However, the temporary effects on the financial statements can influence the (1) availability of financing, (2) motivations of management, and (3) timing of income tax payments.

Availability of Financing

The willingness of creditors and investors to provide capital to a business is influenced by their expectations of the business's future financial performance. In general, more favorable financial statements enhance a company's ability to obtain financing from creditors or investors.

Management Motivation

Financial statement results might affect executive compensation. For example, assume that Marion Manufacturing adopted a management incentive plan that provides a bonus pool equal to 10 percent of net income. In Scenario 1, managers would receive $300 ($3,000 × 0.10). In Scenario 2, however, managers would receive $420 ($4,200 × 0.10). Do not be deceived by the small numbers used for convenience in the example. We could illustrate with millions of dollars just as well as with hundreds of dollars. Managers would clearly favor Scenario 2. In fact, managers might be tempted to misclassify costs to manipulate the content of financial statements.

Income Tax Considerations

Since income tax expense is calculated as a designated percentage of taxable income, managers seek to minimize taxes by reporting the minimum amount of taxable income. Scenario

1 in Exhibit 1–12 depicts the most favorable tax condition. In other words, with respect to taxes, managers prefer to classify costs as expenses rather than assets. The Internal Revenue Service is responsible for enforcing the proper classification of costs. Disagreements between the Internal Revenue Service and taxpayers are ultimately settled in federal courts.

Topic Tackler PLUS 1–2

Ethical Considerations

LO7 Identify the standards of ethical conduct and the features that motivate misconduct.

The preceding discussion provides some insight into conflicts of interest management accountants might face. It is tempting to misclassify a cost if doing so will significantly increase a manager's bonus. Management accountants must be prepared not only to make difficult choices between legitimate alternatives but also to face conflicts of a more troubling nature, such as pressure to:

1. Undertake duties they have not been trained to perform competently.
2. Disclose confidential information.
3. Compromise their integrity through falsification, embezzlement, bribery, and so on.
4. Issue biased, misleading, or incomplete reports.

Yielding to such temptations can have disastrous consequences. The primary job of a management accountant is to provide information useful in making decisions. Information is worthless if its provider cannot be trusted. Accountants have an obligation to themselves, their organizations, and the public to maintain high standards of ethical conduct. In recognition of this obligation, the Institute of Management Accountants (IMA) has issued *Standards of Ethical Conduct for Management Accountants,* which are summarized in Exhibit 1–13. Management accountants are also frequently required to abide by organizational codes of ethics. Failure to adhere to professional and organizational ethical standards can lead to personal disgrace and loss of employment.

Exhibit 1–13 *Standards of Ethical Conduct for Management Accountants*

Competence Management accountants have a responsibility to
- Maintain an appropriate level of professional competence by ongoing development of their knowledge and skills.
- Perform their professional duties in accordance with relevant laws, regulations, and technical standards.
- Prepare complete and clear reports and recommendations after appropriate analysis of relevant and reliable information.

Confidentiality Management accountants have a responsibility to
- Refrain from disclosing confidential information acquired in the course of their work except when authorized, unless legally obligated to do so.
- Inform subordinates as appropriate regarding the confidentiality of information acquired in the course of their work and monitor their activities to ensure the maintenance of the confidentiality.
- Refrain from using or appearing to use confidential information acquired in the course of their work for unethical or illegal advantage either personally or through third parties.

Integrity Management accountants have a responsibility to
- Avoid actual or apparent conflicts of interest and advise all appropriate parties of any potential conflict.
- Refrain from engaging in any activity that would prejudice their ability to carry out their duties ethically.
- Refuse any gift, favor, or hospitality that would influence or would appear to influence their actions.
- Refrain from either actively or passively subverting the attainment of the organization's legitimate and ethical objectives.
- Recognize and communicate professional limitations or other constraints that would preclude responsible judgment or successful performance of an activity.
- Communicate unfavorable as well as favorable information and professional judgments or opinions.
- Refrain from engaging in or supporting any activity that would discredit the profession.

Objectivity Management accountants have a responsibility to
- Communicate information fairly and objectively.
- Disclose fully all relevant information that could reasonably be expected to influence an intended user's understanding of the reports, comments, and recommendations presented.

REALITY *bytes*

Jeffrey Wigand is famous for whistleblowing on the tobacco industry. Assume that Mr. Wigand was an active member of IMA. Assume further that he had obtained his information in the course of completing his duties as a management accountant of the tobacco company. Under these circumstances, would Mr. Wigand's whistleblowing disclosures conform to the code of ethical conduct advocated by the IMA? The answer is no. According to IMA standards (*SMA Number 1C,* 1983), a management accountant who is unable to satisfactorily resolve an ethical conflict between himself and his employer is required to resign from the organization and to submit an informative memorandum to an appropriate representative of the organization. The communication of such conflicts to authorities outside the organization is a breach of confidentiality that is inappropriate unless required by law.

Source: G. Rechtschaffen and J. A. Yardley, "Whistleblowing and the Law," *Management Accounting,* March 1995, p. 40.

Common Features of Criminal and Ethical Misconduct

People who engage in unethical or criminal behavior usually do so unexpectedly. They start with small indiscretions that evolve gradually into more serious violations of trust. A key element in avoiding unethical or illegal conduct is *awareness*. In an effort to increase awareness, Donald Cressey studied hundreds of criminal cases to identify the primary factors that lead to trust violations.[4] He found three factors common to all cases:

1. The existence of a secret problem.
2. The presence of an opportunity.
3. The capacity for rationalization.

Individuals differ about what they think must be kept secret. Consider an owner's reaction to the likelihood of an imminent business failure. One owner might feel so ashamed she cannot discuss the problem with anyone. Another person in the same situation might want to talk to anyone, even a stranger, in the hope of getting help. Cressey's findings suggest that the person who is inclined toward secrecy is more likely to accept an unethical or illegal solution. In other words, secrecy increases vulnerability.

Companies have a responsibility to minimize opportunities for unethical or criminal activity. Most companies establish policies and procedures, commonly called *internal controls,* specifically for this purpose.

Few individuals think of themselves as evil. They develop rationalizations to justify their misconduct. Cressey found a significant number of embezzlers who contended that they were only "borrowing" the money even after they were convicted and sentenced to jail. Common rationalizations involve peer pressure, loyalty to unscrupulous superiors, family needs, revenge, and personal vices such as drug addiction, gambling, and promiscuity. To avoid ethical misconduct, accountants must develop a strong sense of personal responsibility. They cannot allow themselves to blame other people or unfair circumstances for their problems.

For professional accountants, ethical misconduct is a particularly serious offense. In this arena, a single mistake can jeopardize an accountant's career. A person guilty of white-collar

[4] D. R. Cressey, *Other People's Money* (Montclair, NJ: Patterson Smith, 1973).

ANSWER TO *curious* ACCOUNTANT

As you have seen, accounting for depreciation related to manufacturing assets is different from accounting for depreciation for nonmanufacturing assets. Depreciation on the checkout equipment at Wal-Mart is recorded as depreciation expense. Depreciation on manufacturing equipment at Black & Decker is considered a product cost. It is included first as a part of the cost of inventory and eventually as a part of the expense, cost of goods sold. Recording depreciation on manufacturing equipment as an inventory cost is simply another example of the matching principle, because the cost does not become an expense until revenue from the product sale is recognized.

crime loses the opportunity for white-collar employment. Second chances are rarely granted. It is vital to learn to recognize and avoid the common features of ethical misconduct.

Upstream and Downstream Costs

LO8 Distinguish product costs from upstream and downstream costs.

Most companies incur product-related costs before and after, as well as during, the manufacturing process. For example, Ford Motor Company incurs significant research and development costs prior to mass producing a new car model. These **upstream costs** occur before the manufacturing process begins. Similarly, companies normally incur significant costs after the manufacturing process is complete. Examples of **downstream costs** include transportation, advertising, sales commissions, and bad debts. While upstream and downstream costs are not considered to be product costs for financial reporting purposes, profitability analysis requires that they be considered in cost-plus pricing decisions. To be profitable, a company must recover the total cost of developing, producing, and delivering its products to customers.

Product Costs in Service Companies

LO9 Explain how products provided by service companies differ from products made by manufacturing companies.

Service businesses, such as doctors' offices, chimney sweeps, and real estate agencies, differ from manufacturing companies in that they provide assistance rather than goods to their customers. *Nevertheless, service companies, like manufacturing companies, incur materials, labor, and overhead costs* in the process of providing services. For example, a hospital providing medical service to a patient incurs costs for medical supplies (materials), salaries of doctors and nurses (labor), and depreciation, utilities, insurance, and so on (overhead).

The primary difference between manufacturing entities and service companies is that the products provided by service companies are consumed immediately. In contrast, products made by manufacturing companies can be held in the form of inventory until they are sold to customers. Managers of service companies are expected to control costs, improve quality, and increase productivity. Product costing information is useful in achieving these goals regardless of whether a company's product is consumed immediately or later. Although service companies might not report product costs as inventory in their financial statements, they certainly segregate and analyze product costs for internal decision making.

Check Yourself 1–3

The cost of making a Burger King hamburger includes the cost of materials, labor, and overhead. Does this mean that Burger King is a manufacturing company?

Answer No, Burger King is not a manufacturing company. It is a service company because its products are consumed immediately. In contrast, there may be a considerable delay between the time the product of a manufacturing company is made and the time it is consumed. For example, it could be several months between the time Ford Motor Company makes an Explorer and the time the Explorer is ultimately sold to a customer. The primary difference between service and manufacturing companies is that manufacturing companies have inventories of products and service companies do not.

Emerging Trends in Managerial Accounting

LO10 Explain how emerging trends such as activity-based management, value-added assessment, and just-in-time inventory are affecting the managerial accounting discipline.

Global competition has forced many companies to reengineer their production and delivery systems to eliminate waste, reduce errors, and minimize costs. A key ingredient of successful **reengineering** is benchmarking. **Benchmarking** involves identifying the **best practices** used by world-class competitors. By studying and mimicking these practices, a company uses benchmarking to implement highly effective and efficient operating methods. Best practices employed by world-class companies include total quality management (TQM), activity-based management (ABM), value-added assessment, and just-in-time inventory (JIT).

Total Quality Management

To promote effective and efficient operations, many companies practice **total quality management (TQM)**. TQM is a two-dimensional management philosophy using (1) a systematic problem-solving philosophy that encourages front-line workers to achieve *zero defects* and (2) an organizational commitment to achieving *customer satisfaction.* A key component of TQM is **continuous improvement,** an ongoing process through which employees strive to eliminate waste, reduce response time, minimize defects, and simplify the design and delivery of products and services to customers.

Activity-Based Management

Simple changes in perspective can have dramatic results. For example, imagine how realizing the world is round instead of flat changed the nature of travel. A recent change in perspective developing in management accounting is the realization that an organization cannot manage *costs.* Instead, it manages the *activities* that cause costs to be incurred. **Activities** represent the measures an organization takes to accomplish its goals.

focus on INTERNATIONAL ISSUES

Where in the World Do New Managerial Accounting Practices Come From?

Many of the emerging practices in managerial accounting have their foundations in Asian companies. These companies established employee relationships that achieve continuous improvement by encouraging employees to participate in the design as well as the execution of their work. Employee empowerment through the practice known as *kaizen management* recognizes gradual, continuous improvement as the ultimate key to cost reduction and quality control. Employees are encouraged to identify and eliminate nonvalue-added activities, idle time, and waste. The response is overwhelming when employee suggestions are taken seriously. For example, the **Toyota Motor Corporation** reported the receipt of approximately two million employee suggestions in one year alone.

Source: Takao Tanaka, "Kaizen Budgeting: Toyota's Cost Control System Under TQC," *Journal of Cost Management,* Winter 1996, p. 62.

Exhibit 1–14 *Value Chain*

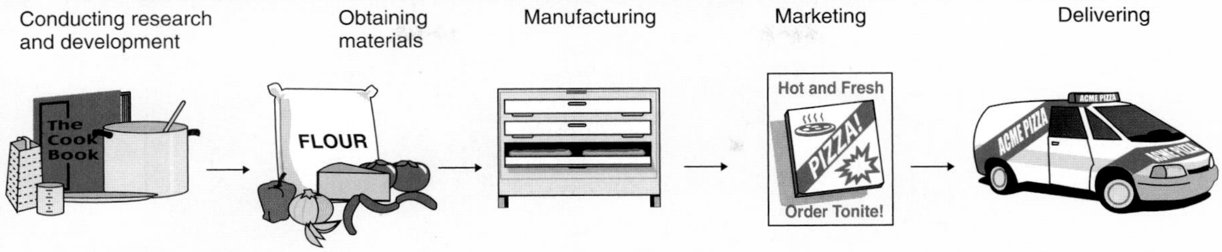

The primary goal of all organizations is to provide products (goods and services) their customers *value*. The sequence of activities used to provide products is called a **value chain. Activity-based management** assesses the value chain to create new or refine existing **value-added activities** and to eliminate or reduce *nonvalue-added activities.* A value-added activity is any unit of work that contributes to a product's ability to satisfy customer needs. For example, cooking is an activity that adds value to food served to a hungry customer. **Nonvalue-added** activities are tasks undertaken that do not contribute to a product's ability to satisfy customer needs. Waiting for the oven to preheat so that food can be cooked does not add value. Most customers value cooked food, but they do not value waiting for it.

To illustrate, consider the value-added activities undertaken by a pizza restaurant. Begin with a customer who is hungry for pizza; certain activities must occur to satisfy that hunger. These activities are pictured in Exhibit 1–14. At a minimum, the restaurant must conduct research and development (devise a recipe), obtain raw materials (acquire the ingredients), manufacture the product (combine and bake the ingredients), market the product (advertise its availability), and deliver the product (transfer the pizza to the customer).

Businesses gain competitive advantages by adding activities that satisfy customer needs. For example, Domino's Pizza grew briskly by recognizing the value customers placed on the convenience of home pizza delivery. Alternatively, Little Caesar's has been highly successful by satisfying customers who value low prices. Other restaurants capitalize on customer values pertaining to taste, ambiance, or location. Businesses can also gain competitive advantages by identifying and eliminating nonvalue-added activities, providing products of comparable quality at lower cost than competitors. Some of the more common nonvalue-added activities and approaches taken to eliminate them are discussed next.

Just-in-Time Inventory

A common nonvalue-added activity found in many business organizations is maintaining excess amounts of inventory. Consumers want products to be available when requested, but they do not benefit when businesses maintain more inventory than necessary to meet demand. In fact, customers could suffer if businesses hold excessive inventory because inventory holding costs must be passed on in the form of higher prices.

Many **inventory holding costs** are obvious: financing, warehouse space, supervision, theft, damage, and obsolescence. Other costs are hidden: diminished motivation, sloppy work, inattentive attitudes, and increased production time. Many managers work closely with their suppliers to minimize the amount of inventory they carry. They may guarantee the supplier a steady stream of purchases and prompt payment. In exchange, the supplier grants **most-favored customer status** that ensures priority treatment over other customers when shortages exist. Assured priority delivery from a reliable supplier enables a company to minimize the amount of inventory it carries and thereby reduces inventory holding cost.

Many businesses have been able to simultaneously reduce their inventory holding costs and increase customer satisfaction by making products available **just in time (JIT)** for customer consumption. For example, hamburgers that are cooked to order are fresher and more

At Ford Motor Company's plant in Valencia, Spain, suppliers feed parts such as these bumpers just in time and in the right order directly to the assembly line.

individualized than those that are prepared in advance and stored until a customer orders one. Many fast-food restaurants have discovered that JIT systems lead not only to greater customer satisfaction but also to lower costs through reduced waste.

Check Yourself 1–4

A strike at a General Motors brake plant caused an almost immediate shutdown of many of the company's assembly plants. What could have caused such a rapid and widespread shutdown?

Answer A rapid and widespread shutdown could have occurred because General Motors uses a just-in-time inventory system. With a just-in-time inventory system, there is no stockpile of inventory to draw on when strikes or other forces disrupt inventory deliveries. This illustrates a potential negative effect of using a just-in-time inventory system.

Just-in-Time Illustration

To illustrate the benefits of a JIT system, consider Paula Elliot, a student at a large urban university. She helps support herself by selling flowers. Three days each week, Paula drives to a florist, purchases 25 single stem roses, returns to the school, and sells the flowers to individuals from a location on a local street corner. She pays $2 per rose and sells each one for $3. Some days she does not have enough flowers to meet customer demand. Other days, she must discard one or two unsold flowers; she believes quality is important and refuses to sell flowers that are not fresh. During May, she purchased 300 roses and sold 280. She calculated her driving cost to be $45. Exhibit 1–15 displays Paula's May income statement.

Exhibit 1–15 *Income Statement*

Sales Revenue (280 units × $3 per unit)	$840
Cost of Goods Sold (300 units × $2 per unit)	(600)
Gross Margin	240
Driving Expense	(45)
Net Income	$195

After studying just-in-time inventory systems in her managerial accounting class, Paula decided to apply the concepts to her small business. She *reengineered* her distribution system by purchasing her flowers from a florist within walking distance of her sales location. She had considered purchasing from this florist earlier but had rejected the idea because the florist's regular selling price of $2.25 per rose was too high. After learning about *most-favored customer status,* she developed a strategy to get a price reduction. By guaranteeing that she would buy at least 30 roses per week, she was able to convince the local florist to match her current cost of $2.00 per rose. The local florist agreed that she could make purchases in batches of any size so long as the total amounted to at least 30 per week. Under this arrangement, Paula was able to buy roses *just in time* to meet customer demand. Each day she purchased a small number of flowers. When she ran out, she simply returned to the florist for additional ones.

The JIT system also enabled Paula to eliminate the cost of the *nonvalue-added activity* of driving to her former florist. Customer satisfaction actually improved because no one was ever turned away because of the lack of inventory. In June, Paula was able to buy and sell 310 roses with no waste and no driving expense. The June income statement is shown in Exhibit 1–16.

Exhibit 1–16 *Income Statement*

Sales Revenue (310 units × $3 per unit)	$930
Cost of Goods Sold (310 units × $2 per unit)	(620)
Gross Margin	310
Driving Expense	0
Net Income	$310

Paula was ecstatic about her $115 increase in profitability ($310 in June − $195 in May = $115 increase), but she was puzzled about the exact reasons for the change. She had saved $40 (20 flowers × $2 each) by avoiding waste and eliminated $45 of driving expenses. These two factors explained only $85 ($40 waste + $45 driving expense) of the $115 increase. What had caused the remaining $30 ($115 − $85) increase in profitability? Paula asked her accounting professor to help her identify the remaining $30 difference.

The professor explained that May sales had suffered from *lost opportunities.* Recall that under the earlier inventory system, Paula had to turn away some prospective customers because she sold out of flowers before all customers were served. Sales increased from 280 roses in May to 310 roses in June. A likely explanation for the 30 unit difference (310 − 280) is that customers who would have purchased flowers in May were unable to do so because of a lack of availability. May's sales suffered from the lost opportunity to earn a gross margin of $1 per flower on 30 roses, a $30 **opportunity cost.** This opportunity cost is the missing link in explaining the profitability difference between May and June. The total $115 difference consists of (1) $40 savings from waste elimination, (2) $45 savings from eliminating driving expense, and (3) opportunity cost of $30. The subject of opportunity cost has widespread application and is discussed in more depth in subsequent chapters of the text.

Value Chain Analysis Across Companies

Comprehensive value chain analysis extends from obtaining raw materials to the ultimate disposition of finished products. It encompasses the activities performed not only by a particular organization but also by that organization's suppliers and those who service its finished products. For example, PepsiCo must be concerned with the activities of the company that supplies the containers for its soft drinks as well as the retail companies that sell its products. If cans of Pepsi fail to open properly, the customer is more likely to blame PepsiCo than the supplier of the cans. Comprehensive value chain analysis can lead to identifying and eliminating nonvalue-added activities that occur between companies. For example, container producers could be encouraged to build manufacturing facilities near Pepsi's bottling factories, eliminating the nonvalue-added activity of transporting empty containers from the manufacturer to the bottling facility. The resulting cost savings benefits customers by reducing costs without affecting quality.

a look back

Managerial accounting focuses on the information needs of *internal* users, while *financial accounting* focuses on the information needs of *external* users. Managerial accounting uses economic, operating, and nonfinancial, as well as financial, data. Managerial accounting information is local (pertains to the company's subunits), is limited by cost/benefit considerations, is more concerned with relevance and timeliness, and is future oriented. Financial accounting information, on the other hand, is more global than managerial accounting information. It supplies information that applies to the whole company. Financial accounting is regulated by numerous authorities, is characterized by objectivity, is focused on reliability and accuracy, and is historical in nature.

Both managerial and financial accounting are concerned with product costing. Financial accountants need product cost information to determine the amount of inventory reported on the balance sheet and the amount of cost of goods sold reported on the income statement. Managerial accountants need to know the cost of products for pricing decisions and for control and evaluation purposes. When determining unit product costs, managers use the average cost per unit. The actual cost of each product requires an unreasonable amount of time and record keeping and makes no difference in product pricing and product cost control decisions.

Product costs are the costs incurred to make products: the costs of direct materials, direct labor, and overhead. *Overhead costs* are product costs that cannot be cost effectively traced to a product; therefore, they are assigned to products using *cost allocation.* Overhead costs include indirect materials, indirect labor, depreciation, rent, and utilities for manufacturing facilities. Product costs are first accumulated in an asset account (Inventory). They are expensed as cost of goods sold in the period the inventory is sold. The difference between sales revenue and cost of goods sold is called *gross margin.*

General, selling, and administrative costs are classified separately from product costs. They are subtracted from gross margin to determine net income. General, selling, and administrative costs can be divided into two categories. Costs incurred before the manufacturing process begins (research and development costs) are *upstream costs.* Costs incurred after manufacturing is complete (transportation) are *downstream costs.* Service companies, like manufacturing companies, incur materials, labor, and overhead costs, but the products provided by service companies are consumed immediately. Therefore, service company product costs are not accumulated in an Inventory account. A *code of ethical conduct* is needed in the accounting profession because accountants hold positions of trust and face conflicts of interest. In recognition of the temptations that accountants face, the IMA has issued *Standards of Ethical Conduct for Management Accountants,* which provides accountants guidance in resisting temptations and in making difficult decisions.

Emerging trends such as *just-in-time inventory* and *activity-based management* are methods that many companies have used to reengineer their production and delivery systems to eliminate waste, reduce errors, and minimize costs. Activity-based management seeks to eliminate or reduce *nonvalue-added activities* and to create new *value-added activities.* Just-in-time inventory seeks to reduce inventory holding costs and to lower prices for customers by making inventory available just in time for customer consumption.

a look forward

In addition to distinguishing costs by product versus G, S, & A classification, other classifications can be used to facilitate managerial decision making. In the next chapter, costs are classified according to the *behavior* they exhibit when the number of units of product increases or decreases (volume of activity changes). You will learn to distinguish between costs that vary with activity volume changes versus costs that remain fixed with activity volume changes. You will learn not only to recognize *cost behavior* but also how to use such recognition to evaluate business risk and opportunity.

APPENDIX

The **statement of cash flows** explains how a company obtained and used *cash* during the accounting period (usually one year). The sources of cash are called *cash inflows,* and the uses are known as *cash outflows.* The statement classifies cash receipts (inflows) and payments (outflows) into three categories: operating activities, investing activities, and financing activities. The **operating activities** section of the statement of cash flows reports the cash received from revenue and the cash paid for expenses.

The **investing activities** section of the statement of cash flows includes cash received from the sales of or the amount paid for productive assets. **Productive assets** are assets used to operate the business. They are sometimes called *long-term* assets because they are normally used for more than one accounting period. For example, cash outflows for the purchase of land or cash inflows from the sale of a building would be reported in the investing activities section of the statement of cash flows. In contrast, cash spent for the purchase of supplies would be reported in the operating activities section because supplies represent short-term assets that would generally be consumed within a single accounting period.

The **financing activities** section of the statement of cash flows reports the cash transactions associated with the resource providers (owners and creditors). More specifically, financing activities include cash obtained from or paid to owners, including dividends. Also, cash borrowed from or principal repaid to creditors would be reported in the financing activities section. However, note that interest paid to creditors is treated as an expense and is reported in the operating activities section of the statement of cash flows. The primary cash inflows and outflows associated with each type of business activity are shown in Exhibit 1–1A; the list of items in the exhibit is not comprehensive. More detailed coverage of the statement of cash flows is presented in Chapter 14.

Exhibit 1–1A *Classification Scheme: Statement of Cash Flows*

Cash flows from operating activities:
- Cash receipts (inflows) from revenue
- Cash payments (outflows) for expenses (including interest)

Cash flows from investing activities:
- Cash receipts (inflows) from the sale of long-term assets
- Cash payments (outflows) for the purchase of long-term assets

Cash flows from financing activities:
- Cash receipts (inflows) from borrowed funds
- Cash receipts (inflows) from issuing common stock
- Cash payments (outflows) to repay borrowed funds
- Cash payments (outflows) for dividends

SELF-STUDY REVIEW PROBLEM

Tuscan Manufacturing Company makes a unique headset for use with mobile phones. During 2003, its first year of operations, Tuscan experienced the following accounting events. Other than the adjusting entries for depreciation, assume that all transactions are cash transactions.

1. Acquired $850,000 cash from the issue of common stock.
2. Paid $50,000 of research and development costs to develop the headset.
3. Paid $140,000 for the materials used to make headsets, all of which were started and completed during the year.
4. Paid salaries of $82,200 to selling and administrative employees.
5. Paid wages of $224,000 to production workers.
6. Paid $48,000 to purchase furniture used in selling and administrative offices.
7. Recognized depreciation on the office furniture. The furniture, acquired January 1, had an $8,000 estimated salvage value and a four-year useful life. The amount of depreciation is computed as ([cost − salvage] ÷ useful life). Specifically, ([$48,000 − $8,000] ÷ 4 = $10,000).
8. Paid $65,000 to purchase manufacturing equipment.
9. Recognized depreciation on the manufacturing equipment. The equipment, acquired January 1, had a $5,000 estimated salvage value and a three-year useful life. The amount of depreciation is computed as ([cost − salvage] ÷ useful life). Specifically, ([$65,000 − $5,000] ÷ 3 = $20,000).
10. Paid $136,000 for rent and utility costs on the manufacturing facility.
11. Paid $41,000 for inventory holding expenses for completed headsets (rental of warehouse space, salaries of warehouse personnel, and other general storage costs).
12. Tuscan started and completed 20,000 headset units during 2003. The company sold 18,400 headsets at a price of $38 per unit.
13. Compute the average product cost per unit and recognize the appropriate amount of cost of goods sold.

Required

a. Show how these events affect the balance sheet, income statement, and statement of cash flows by recording them in a horizontal financial statements model.
b. Explain why Tuscan's recognition of cost of goods sold expense had no impact on cash flow.
c. Prepare a formal income statement for the year.
d. Distinguish between the product costs and the upstream and downstream costs that Tuscan incurred.
e. The company president believes that Tuscan could save money by buying the inventory that it currently makes. The warehouse supervisor said that would not be possible because the purchase price of $27 per unit was above the $26 average cost per unit of making the product. Assuming that the

purchased inventory would be available on demand, explain how the company president could be correct and why the warehouse supervisor could be biased in his assessment of the option to buy the inventory.

Solution to Requirement a

Event No.	Assets: Cash	+ Inventory	+ Office Furn.*	+ Manuf. Equip.*	= Equity: Com. Stk.	+ Ret. Ear.	Rev.	− Exp.	= Net Inc.	Cash Flow
1	850,000				850,000					850,000 FA
2	(50,000)					(50,000)		− 50,000	(50,000)	(50,000) OA
3	(140,000)	140,000								(140,000) OA
4	(82,200)					(82,200)		− 82,200	(82,200)	(82,200) OA
5	(224,000)	(224,000)								(224,000) OA
6	(48,000)		48,000							(48,000) IA
7			(10,000)			(10,000)		− 10,000	(10,000)	
8	(65,000)			65,000						(65,000) IA
9		20,000		(20,000)						
10	(136,000)	136,000								(136,000) OA
11	(41,000)					(41,000)		− 41,000	(41,000)	(41,000) OA
12	699,200					699,200	699,200		699,200	699,200 OA
13		(478,400)				(478,400)		− 478,400	(478,400)	
Totals	763,000 +	41,600 +	38,000 +	45,000	= 850,000 +	37,600	699,200	− 661,660	= 37,600	763,200 NC

*Negative amounts in these columns represent accumulated depreciation.

The average cost per unit of product is determined by dividing the total product cost by the number of headsets produced. Specifically, ($140,000 + $224,000 + $20,000 + $136,000) ÷ 20,000 = $26. Cost of goods sold is $478,400 ($26 × 18,400).

Solution to Requirement b

The impact on cash flow occurs when Tuscan pays for various product costs. In this case, cash outflows occurred when Tuscan paid for materials, labor, and overhead. The cash flow consequences of these transactions were recognized before the cost of goods sold expense was recognized.

Solution to Requirement c

TUSCAN MANUFACTURING COMPANY
Income Statement
For the Year Ended December 31, 2003

Sales Revenue (18,400 units × $38)	$699,200
Cost of Goods Sold (18,400 × $26)	(478,400)
Gross Margin	220,800
R & D Expenses	(50,000)
Selling and Admin. Salary Expense	(82,200)
Admin. Depreciation Expense	(10,000)
Inventory Holding Expense	(41,000)
Net Income	$ 37,600

Solution to Requirement d

Inventory product costs for manufacturing companies focus on the costs necessary to make the product. The cost of research and development (Event 2) occurs before the inventory is made and is therefore an upstream cost, not an inventory (product) cost. The inventory holding costs (Event 11) are incurred after the inventory has been made and are therefore downstream costs, not product costs. Selling costs (included in Events 4 and 7) are normally incurred after products have been made and are therefore usually classified as downstream costs. Administrative costs (also included in Events 4 and 7) are not related to making products and are therefore not classified as product costs. Administrative costs may be incurred before, during, or after products are made, so they may be classified as either upstream or downstream costs. Only the costs of materials, labor, and overhead that are actually incurred for the purpose of making goods (Events 3, 5, 9, and 10) are classified as product costs.

Solution to Requirement e

Since the merchandise would be available on demand, Tuscan could operate a just-in-time inventory system thereby eliminating the inventory holding expense. Since the additional cost to purchase is $1 per unit ($27 − $26), it would cost Tuscan an additional $20,000 ($1 × 20,000 units) to purchase its product. However, the company would save $41,000 of inventory holding expense. The warehouse supervisor could be biased by the fact that his job would be lost if the company purchased its products and thereby could eliminate the need for warehousing inventory. If Tuscan does not maintain inventory, it would not need a warehouse supervisor.

KEY TERMS

Activities *18*
Activity-based management (ABM) *19*
Average cost *7*
Benchmarking *18*
Best practices *18*
Continuous improvement *18*
Cost allocation *12*
Cost-plus pricing *6*
Direct labor *9*
Direct raw materials *9*
Downstream costs *17*
Financial accounting *4*
Financial Accounting Standards Board (FASB) *5*
Financing activities *23*
Finished goods *6*
General, selling, and administrative costs *11*
Generally accepted accounting principles (GAAP) *5*
Indirect costs *11*
Inventory holding costs *19*
Investing activities *23*
Just in time (JIT) *19*
Managerial accounting *4*
Manufacturing overhead *11*
Most-favored customer status *19*
Nonvalue-added activities *19*
Operating activities *22*
Opportunity cost *21*
Overhead *6*
Period costs *11*
Product costs *6*
Product costing *6*
Productive assets *23*
Raw materials *9*
Reengineering *18*
Sarbanes-Oxley Act of 2002 *5*
Securities and Exchange Commission (SEC) *4*
Statement of cash flows *22*
Total quality management (TQM) *18*
Upstream costs *17*
Value-added activity *19*
Value-added principle *5*
Value chain *19*

QUESTIONS

1. What are some differences between financial and managerial accounting?
2. What does the value-added principle mean as it applies to managerial accounting information? Give an example of value-added information that may be included in managerial accounting reports but is not shown in publicly reported financial statements.
3. What are the two dimensions of a total quality management (TQM) program? Why is TQM being used in business practice?
4. How does product costing used in financial accounting differ from product costing used in managerial accounting?
5. What does the statement "costs can be assets or expenses" mean?
6. Why are the salaries of production workers accumulated in an inventory account instead of being expensed on the income statement?
7. How do product costs affect the financial statements? How does the classification of product cost (as an asset vs. an expense) affect net income?
8. What is an indirect cost? Provide examples of product costs that would be classified as indirect.
9. How does a product cost differ from a general, selling, and administrative cost? Give examples of each.
10. Why is cost classification important to managers?
11. What does the term *reengineering* mean? Name some reengineering practices.
12. What is cost allocation? Give an example of a cost that needs to be allocated.
13. How has the Institute of Management Accountants responded to the need for high standards of ethical conduct in the accounting profession?
14. What are some of the common ethical conflicts that accountants encounter?
15. What costs should be considered in determining the sales price of a product?
16. What does the term *activity-based management* mean?
17. What is a value chain?
18. What do the terms *value-added activity* and *nonvalue-added activity* mean? Provide an example of each type of activity.
19. What is a just-in-time (JIT) inventory system? Name some inventory costs that can be eliminated or reduced by its use.

EXERCISES—SERIES A

All Exercises in Series A are available with McGraw-Hill's Homework Manager

L.O. 1 **EXERCISE 1–1A** *Identifying Financial Versus Managerial Accounting Items*

Required

Indicate whether each of the following items is representative of managerial or of financial accounting.

a. Information is historically based and usually reported annually.
b. Information is local and pertains to subunits of the organization.
c. Information includes economic and nonfinancial data as well as financial data.
d. Information is global and pertains to the company as a whole.
e. Information is provided to insiders including executives, managers, and operators.
f. Information is factual and is characterized by objectivity, reliability, consistency, and accuracy.
g. Information is reported continuously and has a current or future orientation.
h. Information is provided to outsiders including investors, creditors, government agencies, analysts, and reporters.
i. Information is regulated by the SEC, FASB, and other sources of GAAP.
j. Information is based on estimates that are bounded by relevance and timeliness.

L.O. 5 **EXERCISE 1–2A** *Identifying Product Versus General, Selling, and Administrative Costs*

Required

Indicate whether each of the following costs should be classified as a product cost or as a general, selling, and administrative cost.

a. Indirect labor used to manufacture inventory.
b. Attorney's fees paid to protect the company from frivolous lawsuits.
c. Research and development costs incurred to create new drugs for a pharmaceutical company.
d. The cost of secretarial supplies used in a doctor's office.
e. Depreciation on the office furniture of the company president.
f. Direct materials used in a manufacturing company.
g. Indirect materials used in a manufacturing company.
h. Salaries of employees working in the accounting department.
i. Commissions paid to sales staff.
j. Interest on the mortgage for the company's corporate headquarters.

L.O. 5 **EXERCISE 1–3A** *Classifying Costs: Product or GS&A/Asset or Expense*

Required

Use the following format to classify each cost as a product cost or a general, selling, and administrative (G, S, & A) cost. Also indicate whether the cost would be recorded as an asset or an expense. The first item is shown as an example.

Cost Category	Product/ G, S, & A	Asset/ Expense
Wages of production workers	Product	Asset
Advertising costs		
Promotion costs		
Production supplies		
Depreciation on administration building		
Depreciation on manufacturing equipment		
Research and development costs		
Cost to set up manufacturing equipment		
Utilities used in factory		
Cars for sales staff		
Distributions to stockholders		
General office supplies		
Raw materials used in the manufacturing process		
Cost to rest office equipment		

EXERCISE 1–4A *Identifying Effect of Product Versus General, Selling, and Administrative Costs on Financial Statements* L.O. 5

Required

Cadeshia Industries recognized accrued compensation cost. Use the following model to show how this event would affect the company's financial statement under the following two assumptions: (1) the compensation is for office personnel and (2) the compensation is for production workers. Use pluses or minuses to show the effect on each element. If an element is not affected, indicate so by placing the letters NA under the appropriate heading.

	Assets = Liab. + Equity	Rev. − Exp. = Net Inc.	Cash Flow
1.			
2.			

EXERCISE 1–5A *Identify Effect of Product Versus General, Selling, and Administrative Costs on Financial Statements* L.O. 5

Required

Chappell Industries recognized the annual cost of depreciation on December 31, 2007. Using the following horizontal financial statement model, indicate how this event affected the company's financial statements under the following two assumptions: (1) the depreciation was on office furniture and (2) the depreciation was on manufacturing equipment. Indicate whether the event increases (I), decreases (D), or has no affect (NA) on each element of the financial statements. Also, in the Cash column, indicate whether the cash flow is associated with operating activities (OA), investing activities (IA), or financing activities (FA). (Note: Show accumulated depreciation as a decrease in the book value of the appropriate asset account.)

Event No.	Assets				Equity			
	Cash +	Inventory +	Manuf. Equip. +	Office Furn. =	Com. Stk. +	Ret. Ear.	Rev. − Exp. = Net Inc.	Cash Flow
1.								
2.								

EXERCISE 1–6A *Identifying Product Costs in a Manufacturing Company* L.O. 2

Andrea Pomare was talking to another accounting student, Don Cantrell. Upon discovering that the accounting department offered an upper-level course in cost measurement, Andrea remarked to Don, "How difficult can it be? My parents own a toy store. All you have to do to figure out how much something costs is look at the invoice. Surely you don't need an entire course to teach you how to read an invoice."

Required

a. Identify the three main components of product cost for a manufacturing entity.

b. Explain why measuring product cost for a manufacturing entity is more complex than measuring product cost for a retail toy store.

c. Assume that Andrea's parents rent a store for $8,000 per month. Different types of toys use different amounts of store space. For example, displaying a bicycle requires more store space than displaying a deck of cards. Also, some toys remain on the shelf longer than others. Fad toys sell rapidly, but traditional toys sell more slowly. Under these circumstances, how would you determine the amount of rental cost required to display each type of toy? Identify two other costs incurred by a toy store that may be difficult to allocate to individual toys.

EXERCISE 1–7A *Identifying Product Versus General, Selling, and Administrative Costs* L.O. 5

A review of the accounting records of Zammon Manufacturing indicated that the company incurred the following payroll costs during the month of August.

1. Salary of the company president—$75,000.
2. Salary of the vice president of manufacturing—$50,000.
3. Salary of the chief financial officer—$40,000.
4. Salary of the vice president of marketing—$35,000.

5. Salaries of middle managers (department heads, production supervisors) in manufacturing plant—$75,000.
6. Wages of production workers—$540,000.
7. Salaries of administrative secretaries—$78,000.
8. Salaries of engineers and other personnel responsible for maintaining production equipment—$135,000.
9. Commissions paid to sales staff—$128,000.

Required

a. What amount of payroll cost would be classified as general, selling, and administrative expense?
b. Assuming that Zammon made 4,000 units of product and sold 3,600 of them during the month of June, determine the amount of payroll cost that would be included in cost of goods sold.

L.O. 2, 4, 5

EXERCISE 1–8A *Recording Product Versus General, Selling, and Administrative Costs in a Financial Statements Model*

Trammell Manufacturing experienced the following events during its first accounting period.

1. Recognized depreciation on manufacturing equipment.
2. Recognized depreciation on office furniture.
3. Recognized revenue from cash sale of products.
4. Recognized cost of goods sold from sale referenced in Event 3.
5. Acquired cash by issuing common stock.
6. Paid cash to purchase raw materials that were used to make products.
7. Paid wages to production workers.
8. Paid salaries to administrative staff.

Required

Use the following horizontal financial statements model to show how each event affects the balance sheet, income statement, and statement of cash flows. Indicate whether the event increases (I), decreases (D), or has no effect (NA) on each element of the financial statements. In the Cash Flow column, indicate whether the cash flow is associated with operating activities (OA), investing activities (IA), or financing activities (FA). The first transaction has been recorded as an example. (*Note:* Show accumulated depreciation as a decrease in the book value of the appropriate asset account.)

	Assets					Equity											
Event No.	Cash	+	Inventory	+	Manuf. Equip.	+	Office Furn.	=	Com. Stk.	+	Ret. Ear.	Rev.	−	Exp.	=	Net Inc.	Cash Flow
1.	NA		I		D		NA		NA		NA	NA		NA		NA	NA

L.O. 2, 3, 4

EXERCISE 1–9A *Allocating Product Costs Between Ending Inventory and Cost of Goods Sold*

Kasey Manufacturing Company began operations on January 1. During the year, it started and completed 4,000 units of product. The company incurred the following costs.

1. Raw materials purchased and used—$6,000.
2. Wages of production workers—$9,000.
3. Salaries of administrative and sales personnel—$3,600.
4. Depreciation on manufacturing equipment—$10,800.
5. Depreciation on administrative equipment—$4,000.

Kasey sold 3,000 units of product.

Required

a. Determine the total product cost for the year.
b. Determine the total cost of the ending inventory.
c. Determine the total of cost of goods sold.

L.O. 4, 5

EXERCISE 1–10A *Financial Statement Effects for Manufacturing Versus Service Organizations*

The following financial statements model shows the effects of recognizing depreciation in two different circumstances. One circumstance represents recognizing depreciation on a machine used in a factory. The other circumstance recognizes depreciation on computers used in a consulting firm. The effects of each event have been recorded using the letter (I) to represent increase, (D) for decrease, and (NA) for no effect.

Event No.	Assets				Equity						
	Cash +	Inventory +	Equip. =	Com. Stk. +	Ret. Ear.	Rev. −	Exp. =	Net Inc.	Cash Flow
1	NA	NA	D	NA	D	NA	I	D	NA
2	NA	I	D	NA	NA	NA	NA	NA	NA

Required

a. Identify the event that represents depreciation on the computers.

b. Explain why recognizing depreciation on equipment used in a manufacturing company affects financial statements differently from recognizing depreciation on equipment used in a service organization.

EXERCISE 1–11A *Identifying the Effect of Product Versus General, Selling, and Administrative Cost on the Income Statement and Statement of Cash Flows* L.O. 5

Required

Each of the following events describes acquiring an asset that requires a year-end adjusting entry. Explain how acquiring the asset and making the adjusting entry affect the amount of net income and the cash flow shown on the year-end financial statements. Also, in the Cash Flow column, indicate whether the cash flow is associated with operating activities (OA), investing activities (IA), or financing activities (FA). Use (NA) for no effect. Assume a December 31 annual closing date. The first event has been recorded as an example. Assume that any products that have been made have not been sold.

	Net Income	Cash Flow
Event No.	Amount of Change	Amount of Change
1. Purchase of printers	NA	(4,000)
1. Make adjusting entry	(1,000)	NA

1. Paid $4,000 cash on January 1 to purchase printers to be used for administrative purposes. The printers had an estimated expected useful life of three years and a $1,000 salvage value.
2. Paid $4,000 cash on January 1 to purchase manufacturing equipment. The equipment had an estimated expected useful life of three years and a $1,000 salvage value.
3. Paid $5,400 cash in advance on May 1 for a one-year rental contract on administrative offices.
4. Paid $5,400 cash in advance on May 1 for a one-year rental contract on manufacturing facilities.
5. Paid $1,000 cash to purchase supplies to be used by the marketing department. At the end of the year, $50 of supplies was still on hand.
6. Paid $1,000 cash to purchase supplies to be used in the manufacturing process. At the end of the year, $50 of supplies was still on hand.

EXERCISE 1–12A *Upstream and Downstream Costs* L.O. 8

During 2008, Wake Manufacturing Company incurred $9,000,000 of research and development (R&D) costs to create a long-life battery to use in computers. In accordance with FASB standards, the entire R&D cost was recognized as an expense in 2008. Manufacturing costs (direct materials, direct labor, and overhead) are expected to be $26 per unit. Packaging, shipping, and sales commissions are expected to be $5 per unit. Wake expects to sell 200,000 batteries before new research renders the battery design technologically obsolete. During 2008, Wake made 22,000 batteries and sold 20,000 of them.

Required

a. Identify the upstream and downstream costs.

b. Determine the 2008 amount of cost of goods sold and the ending inventory balance.

c. Determine the sales price assuming that Wake desires to earn a profit margin that is equal to 25 percent of the *total cost* of developing, making, and distributing the batteries.

d. Prepare an income statement for 2008. Use the sales price developed in Requirement *c*.

e. Why would Wake price the batteries at a level that would generate a loss for the 2008 accounting period?

L.O. 10 EXERCISE 1–13A *Value Chain Analysis*

Autosound Company manufactures and sells high-quality audio speakers. The speakers are encased in solid walnut cabinets supplied by Garrison Cabinet, Inc. Garrison packages the speakers in durable moisture-proof boxes and ships them by truck to Autosound's manufacturing facility, which is located 50 miles from the cabinet factory.

Required

Identify the nonvalue-added activities that occur between the companies described in the preceding scenario. Provide a logical explanation as to how these nonvalue-added activities could be eliminated.

L.O. 10 EXERCISE 1–14A *Identify the Effect of a Just-in-Time Inventory System on Financial Statements*

After reviewing the financial statements of Baird Company, Tim Hanson concluded that the company was a service company. Mr. Hanson based his conclusion on the fact that Baird's financial statements displayed no inventory accounts.

Required

Explain how Baird's implementation of a 100 percent effective just-in-time inventory system could have led Mr. Hanson to a false conclusion regarding the nature of Baird's business.

L.O. 10 EXERCISE 1–15A *Using JIT to Minimize Waste and Lost Opportunity*

Lucy Quinn, a teacher at Grove Middle School, is in charge of ordering the T-shirts to be sold for the school's annual fund-raising project. The T-shirts are printed with a special Grove School logo. In some years, the supply of T-shirts has been insufficient to satisfy the number of sales orders. In other years, T-shirts have been left over. Excess T-shirts are normally donated to some charitable organization. T-shirts cost the school $4 each and are normally sold for $6 each. Ms. Quinn has decided to order 800 shirts.

Required

a. If the school receives actual sales orders for 750 shirts, what amount of profit will the school earn? What is the cost of waste due to excess inventory?

b. If the school receives actual sales orders for 850 shirts, what amount of profit will the school earn? What amount of opportunity cost will the school incur?

c. Explain how a JIT inventory system could maximize profitability by eliminating waste and opportunity cost.

L.O. 10 EXERCISE 1–16A *Using JIT to Minimize Holding Costs*

Jay's Pet Supplies purchases its inventory from a variety of suppliers, some of which require a six-week lead time before delivering the goods. To ensure that she has a sufficient supply of goods on hand, Ms. Lane, the owner, must maintain a large supply of inventory. The cost of this inventory averages $40,000. She usually finances the purchase of inventory and pays a 10 percent annual finance charge. Ms. Lane's accountant has suggested that she establish a relationship with a single large distributor who can satisfy all of her orders within a two-week time period. Given this quick turnaround time, she will be able to reduce her average inventory balance to $10,000. Ms. Lane also believes that she could save $6,000 per year by reducing phone bills, insurance, and warehouse rental space costs associated with ordering and maintaining the larger level of inventory.

Required

a. Is the new inventory system available to Ms. Lane a pure or approximate just-in-time system?

b. Based on the information provided, how much of Ms. Lane's inventory holding cost could be eliminated by taking the accountant's advice?

PROBLEMS—SERIES A

All Problems in Series A are available with McGraw-Hill's Homework Manager

L.O. 2, 3, 4, 5, 6 PROBLEM 1–17A *Product Versus General, Selling, and Administrative Costs*

CHECK FIGURES
a. Average Cost per Unit: $8.40
f. $90,400

Reavis Manufacturing Company was started on January 1, 2006, when it acquired $90,000 cash by issuing common stock. Reavis immediately purchased office furniture and manufacturing equipment costing $10,000 and $28,000, respectively. The office furniture had a five-year useful life and a zero salvage value. The manufacturing equipment had a $4,000 salvage value and an expected useful life of three years. The company paid $12,000 for salaries of administrative personnel and $16,000 for wages to production personnel. Finally, the company paid $18,000 for raw materials that were used to make inventory. All inventory was started and completed during the year. Reavis completed production on 5,000 units of product and sold 4,000 units at a price of $12 each in 2006. (Assume that all transactions are cash transactions.)

Required

a. Determine the total product cost and the average cost per unit of the inventory produced in 2006.
b. Determine the amount of cost of goods sold that would appear on the 2006 income statement.
c. Determine the amount of the ending inventory balance that would appear on the December 31, 2006, balance sheet.
d. Determine the amount of net income that would appear on the 2006 income statement.
e. Determine the amount of retained earnings that would appear on the December 31, 2006, balance sheet.
f. Determine the amount of total assets that would appear on the December 31, 2006 balance sheet.
g. Determine the amount of net cash flow from operating activities that would appear on the 2006 statement of cash flows.
h. Determine the amount of net cash flow from investing activities that would appear on the 2006 statement of cash flows.

PROBLEM 1–18A *Effect of Product Versus Period Costs on Financial Statements*

L.O. 2, 4, 5

www.mhhe.com/edmonds3e

CHECK FIGURES
Cash balance: $47,400
Net income: $10,700

Chateau Manufacturing Company experienced the following accounting events during its first year of operation. With the exception of the adjusting entries for depreciation, assume that all transactions are cash transactions.

1. Acquired $67,000 cash by issuing common stock.
2. Paid $9,500 for the materials used to make its products, all of which were started and completed during the year.
3. Paid salaries of $5,300 to selling and administrative employees.
4. Paid wages of $6,200 to production workers.
5. Paid $9,600 for furniture used in selling and administrative offices. The furniture was acquired on January 1. It had a $1,600 estimated salvage value and a four-year useful life.
6. Paid $27,000 for manufacturing equipment. The equipment was acquired on January 1. It had a $8,000 estimated salvage value and a three-year useful life.
7. Sold inventory to customers for $38,000 that had cost $20,000 to make.

Required

Explain how these events would affect the balance sheet, income statement, and statement of cash flows by recording them in a horizontal financial statements model as indicated here. The first event is recorded as an example. In the Cash Flow column, indicate whether the amounts represent financing activities (FA), investing activities (IA), or operating activities (OA).

Financial Statements Model

	Assets								Equity								
Event No.	**Cash**	+	**Inventory**	+	**Manuf. Equip.***	+	**Office Furn.***	=	**Com. Stk.**	+	**Ret. Ear.**	**Rev.**	−	**Exp.**	=	**Net Inc.**	**Cash Flow**
1	67,000								67,000								67,000 FA

*Record accumulated depreciation as negative amounts in these columns.

PROBLEM 1–19A *Product Versus General, Selling, and Administrative Costs*

L.O. 2, 3, 4, 5

CHECK FIGURES
Net income: $540
Total assets: $3,540

The following transactions pertain to 2007, the first year operations of Lakeview Company. All inventory was started and completed during 2007. Assume that all transactions are cash transactions.

1. Acquired $3,000 cash by issuing common stock.
2. Paid $600 for materials used to produce inventory.
3. Paid $900 to production workers.
4. Paid $300 rental fee for production equipment.
5. Paid $240 to administrative employees.

6. Paid $120 rental fee for administrative office equipment.
7. Produced 300 units of inventory of which 200 units were sold at a price of $10.50 each.

Required

Prepare an income statement, balance sheet, and statement of cash flows.

L.O. 2, 3, 4, 5

excel

www.mhhe.com/edmonds3e

PROBLEM 1–20A *Service Versus Manufacturing Companies*

Savoy Company began operations on January 1, 2006, by issuing common stock for $36,000 cash. During 2006, Savoy received $48,000 cash from revenue and incurred costs that required $72,000 of cash payments.

Required

Prepare an income statement, balance sheet, and statement of cash flows for Savoy Company for 2006, under each of the following independent scenarios.

CHECK FIGURES

a. Net loss: $24,000
b. Total assets: $66,000
c. Net income: $13,200

a. Savoy is a promoter of rock concerts. The $72,000 was paid to provide a rock concert that produced the revenue.
b. Savoy is in the car rental business. The $72,000 was paid to purchase automobiles. The automobiles were purchased on January 1, 2006, have four-year useful lives, with no expected salvage value. Savoy uses straight-line depreciation. The revenue was generated by leasing the automobiles.
c. Savoy is a manufacturing company. The $72,000 was paid to purchase the following items:
   (1) Paid $9,600 cash to purchase materials that were used to make products during the year.
   (2) Paid $24,000 cash for wages of factory workers who made products during the year.
   (3) Paid $2,400 cash for salaries of sales and administrative employees.
   (4) Paid $36,000 cash to purchase manufacturing equipment. The equipment was used solely to make products. It had a three-year life and a $7,200 salvage value. The company uses straight-line depreciation.
   (5) During 2005, Savoy started and completed 2,000 units of product. The revenue was earned when Savoy sold 1,500 units of product to its customers.
d. Refer to Requirement *c*. Could Savoy determine the actual cost of making the 500th unit of product? How likely is it that the actual cost of the 500th product was exactly the same as the cost of producing the 501st unit of product? Explain why management may be more interested in average cost than in actual cost.

L.O. 2, 3, 4, 5, 6

PROBLEM 1–21A *Importance of Cost Classification*

Dextron Manufacturing Company (DMC) was started when it acquired $60,000 by issuing common stock. During the first year of operations, the company incurred specifically identifiable product costs (materials, labor, and overhead) amounting to $30,000. DMC also incurred $20,000 of engineering design and planning costs. There was a debate regarding how the design and planning costs should be classified. Advocates of Option 1 believe that the costs should be classified as general, selling, and administrative costs. Advocates of Option 2 believe it is more appropriate to classify the design and planning costs as product costs. During the year, DMC made 4,000 units of product and sold 3,000 units at a price of $18 each. All transactions were cash transactions.

CHECK FIGURE

a. Option 1: NI = $11,500
   Option 2: Total Assets = $76,500

Required

a. Prepare an income statement, balance sheet, and statement of cash flows under each of the two options.
b. Identify the option that results in financial statements that are more likely to leave a favorable impression on investors and creditors.
c. Assume that DMC provides an incentive bonus to the company president equal to 10 percent of net income. Compute the amount of the bonus under each of the two options. Identify the option that provides the president with the higher bonus.
d. Assume a 35 percent income tax rate. Determine the amount of income tax expense under each of the two options. Identify the option that minimizes the amount of the company's income tax expense.
e. Comment on the conflict of interest between the company president as determined in Requirement *c* and the owners of the company as indicated in Requirement *d*. Describe an incentive compensation plan that would avoid a conflict of interest between the president and the owners.

L.O. 10

PROBLEM 1–22A *Value Chain Analysis*

Hacienda Company invented a new process for manufacturing ice cream. The ingredients are mixed in high-tech machinery that forms the product into small round beads. Like a bag of balls, the ice cream beads are surrounded by air pockets in packages. This design has numerous advantages. First, each bite of ice cream melts rapidly when placed in a person's mouth, creating a more flavorful sensation when compared to ordinary ice cream. Also, the air pockets mean that a typical serving includes a smaller amount of ice cream. This not only reduces materials cost but also provides the consumer with a low-calorie snack. A cup appears full of ice cream, but it is really half full of air. The consumer eats only half the ingredients that are contained in a typical cup of blended ice cream. Finally, the texture of the ice cream makes scooping it out of a large container a very easy task. The frustration of trying to get a spoon into a rock-solid package of blended ice cream has been eliminated. Hacienda Company named the new product Sonic Cream.

Like many other ice cream producers, Hacienda Company purchases its raw materials from a food wholesaler. The ingredients are mixed in Hacienda's manufacturing plant. The packages of finished product are distributed to privately owned franchise ice cream shops that sell Sonic Cream directly to the public.

Hacienda provides national advertising and is responsible for all research and development costs associated with making new flavors of Sonic Cream.

Required

a. Based on the information provided, draw a comprehensive value chain for Hacienda Company that includes its suppliers and customers.

b. Identify the place in the chain where Hacienda Company is exercising its opportunity to create added value beyond that currently being provided by its competitors.

PROBLEM 1–23A *Using JIT to Reduce Inventory Holding Costs*

L.O. 10

CHECK FIGURE
a. $360,000

Levis Manufacturing Company obtains its raw materials from a variety of suppliers. Levis's strategy is to obtain the best price by letting the suppliers know that it buys from the lowest bidder. Approximately four years ago, unexpected increased demand resulted in materials shortages. Levis was unable to find the materials it needed even though it was willing to pay premium prices. Because of the lack of raw materials, Levis was forced to close its manufacturing facility for two weeks. Its president vowed that her company would never again be at the mercy of its suppliers. She immediately ordered her purchasing agent to perpetually maintain a one-month supply of raw materials. Compliance with the president's orders resulted in a raw materials inventory amounting to approximately $2,000,000. Warehouse rental and personnel costs to maintain the inventory amounted to $10,000 per month. Levis has a line of credit with a local bank that calls for a 12 percent annual rate of interest. Assume that Levis finances the raw materials inventory with the line of credit.

Required

a. Based on the information provided, determine the annual holding cost of the raw materials inventory.

b. Explain how a JIT system could reduce Levis's inventory holding cost.

c. Explain how most-favored customer status could enable Levis to establish a JIT inventory system without risking the raw materials shortages experienced in the past.

PROBLEM 1–24A *Using JIT to Minimize Waste and Lost Opportunity*

L.O. 10

excel
www.mhhe.com/edmonds3e

CHECK FIGURES
a. $900
b. $3,700

Pass CPA, Inc., provides review courses twice each year for students studying to take the CPA exam. The cost of textbooks is included in the registration fee. Text material requires constant updating and is useful for only one course. To minimize printing costs and ensure availability of books on the first day of class, Pass CPA has books printed and delivered to its offices two weeks in advance of the first class. To ensure that enough books are available, Pass CPA normally orders 10 percent more than expected enrollment. Usually there is an oversupply of books that is thrown away. However, demand occasionally exceeds expectations by more than 10 percent and there are too few books available for student use. Pass CPA had been forced to turn away students because of a lack of textbooks. Pass CPA expects to enroll approximately 100 students per course. The tuition fee is $800 per student. The cost of teachers is $25,000 per course, textbooks cost $60 each, and other operating expenses are estimated to be $35,000 per course.

Required

a. Prepare an income statement, assuming that 95 students enroll in a course. Determine the cost of waste associated with unused books.

b. Prepare an income statement, assuming that 115 students attempt to enroll in the course. Note that five students are turned away because of too few textbooks. Determine the amount of lost profit resulting from the inability to serve the five additional students.

c. Suppose that textbooks can be produced through a high-speed copying process that permits delivery *just in time* for class to start. The cost of books made using this process, however, is $65 each. Assume that all books must be made using the same production process. In other words, Pass CPA cannot order some of the books using the regular copy process and the rest using the high-speed process. Prepare an income statement under the JIT system assuming that 95 students enroll in a course. Compare the income statement under JIT with the income statement prepared in Requirement *a.* Comment on how the JIT system would affect profitability.

d. Assume the same facts as in Requirement *c* with respect to a JIT system that enables immediate delivery of books at a cost of $65 each. Prepare an income statement under the JIT system, assuming that 115 students enroll in a course. Compare the income statement under JIT with the income statement prepared in Requirement *b.* Comment on how the JIT system would affect profitability.

e. Discuss the possible effect of the JIT system on the level of customer satisfaction.

EXERCISES—SERIES B

L.O. 1

EXERCISE 1–1B *Financial Versus Managerial Accounting Items*

Required

Indicate whether each of the following items is representative of financial or managerial accounting.

a. Monthly sales reports used by the vice president of marketing to help allocate funds.
b. Divisional profit reports used by the company president to determine bonuses for divisional vice presidents.
c. Financial results used by stockbrokers to evaluate a company's profitability.
d. Quarterly budgets used by management to determine future borrowing needs.
e. Financial statements prepared in accordance with generally accepted accounting principles.
f. Annual financial reports submitted to the SEC in compliance with federal securities laws.
g. Projected budget information used to make logistical decisions.
h. Condensed financial information sent to current investors at the end of each quarter.
i. Audited financial statements submitted to bankers when applying for a line of credit.
j. A weekly cash budget used by the treasurer to determine whether cash on hand is excessive.

L.O. 5

EXERCISE 1–2B *Identifying Product Versus General, Selling, and Administrative Costs*

Required

Indicate whether each of the following costs should be classified as a product cost or as a general, selling, and administrative cost.

a. The fabric used in making a customized sofa for a customer.
b. The salary of an engineer who maintains all manufacturing plant equipment.
c. Wages paid to workers in a manufacturing plant.
d. The salary of the receptionist working in the sales department.
e. Supplies used in the sales department.
f. Wages of janitors who clean the factory floor.
g. The salary of the company president.
h. The salary of the cell phone manufacturing plant manager.
i. The depreciation on administrative buildings.
j. The depreciation on the company treasurer's computer.

L.O. 5

EXERCISE 1–3B *Classifying Costs: Product or Period/Asset or Expense*

Required

Use the following format to classify each cost as a product cost or a general, selling, and administrative (G,S,&A) cost. Also indicate whether the cost would be recorded as an asset or an expense. The first cost item is shown as an example.

Cost Category	Product/ G, S, & A	Asset/ Expense
Raw material used to make products	Product	Asset
Lubricant used to maintain factory equipment		
Cost of a delivery truck		
Cash dividend to stockholders		
Cost of merchandise shipped to customers		

continued

Cost Category	Product/ G, S, & A	Asset/ Expense
Depreciation on vehicles used by salespeople		
Wages of administrative building security guards		
Supplies used in the plant manager's office		
Computers for the accounting department		
Depreciation on computers used in factory		
Natural gas used in the factory		
Cost of television commercials		
Wages of factory workers		
Paper and ink cartridges used in the cashier's office		

EXERCISE 1–4B *Effect of Product Versus General, Selling, and Administrative Costs on Financial Statements* L.O. 5

Required

Ashton Plastics Company accrued a tax liability for $2,500. Use the following horizontal financial statements model to show the effect of this accrual under the following two assumptions: (1) the tax is on administrative buildings or (2) the tax is on production equipment. Use plus signs and/or minus signs to show the effect on each element. If an element is not affected, indicate so by placing the letters NA under the appropriate heading.

	Assets	=	Liab.	+	Equity	Rev.	−	Exp.	=	Net Inc.	Cash Flow
1.											
2.											

EXERCISE 1–5B *Effect of Product Versus General, Selling, and Administrative Cost on Financial Statements* L.O. 5

Required

Seffner Corporation recognized the annual expiration of insurance on December 31, 2008. Using the following horizontal financial statements model shown, indicate how this event affected the company's financial statements under the following two assumptions: (1) the insurance was for office equipment or (2) the insurance was for manufacturing equipment. Indicate whether the event increases (I), decreases (D), or does not affect (NA) each element of the financial statements. In the Cash Flow column, indicate whether the cash flow is associated with operating activities (OA), investing activities (IA), or financing activities (FA).

	Assets						Equity								
Event No.	Cash	+	Prepaid Insurance	+	Inventory	=	Com. Stk.	+	Ret. Ear.	Rev.	−	Exp.	=	Net Inc.	Cash Flow
1.															
2.															

EXERCISE 1–6B *Product Costs in a Manufacturing Company* L.O. 2

Because friends and neighbors frequently praise her baking skills, Susan Spann plans to start a new business baking cakes for customers. She wonders how to determine the cost of her cakes.

Required

a. Identify and give examples of the three components of product cost incurred in producing cakes.

b. Explain why measuring product cost for a bakery is more complex than measuring product cost for a retail store.

c. Assume that Susan decides to bake cakes for her customers at her home. Consequently, she will avoid the cost of renting a bakery. However, her home utility bills will increase. She also plans to offer different types of cakes for which baking time will vary. Cakes mixed with ice cream will require freezing, and other cakes will need refrigeration. Some can cool at room temperature. Under these circumstances, how can Susan estimate the amount of utility cost required to produce a given cake? Identify two costs other than utility cost that she will incur that could be difficult to measure.

L.O. 5

EXERCISE 1–7B *Product Versus General, Selling, and Administrative Costs*

In reviewing Desoto Company's September accounting records, Don Albani, the chief accountant, noted the following depreciation costs.

1. Factory buildings—$30,000.
2. Computers used in manufacturing—$4,800.
3. A building used to display finished products—$9,600.
4. Trucks used to deliver merchandise to customers—$16,800.
5. Forklifts used in the factory—$26,400.
6. Furniture used in the president's office—$10,800.
7. Elevators in administrative buildings—$7,200.
8. Factory machinery—$10,800.

Required

a. What amount of depreciation cost would be classified as general, selling, and administrative expense?
b. Assume that Desoto manufactured 4,500 units of product and sold 3,000 units of product during the month of September. Determine the amount of depreciation cost that would be included in cost of goods sold.

L.O. 2, 4, 5

EXERCISE 1–8B *Recording Product Versus General, Selling, and Administrative Costs in a Financial Statements Model*

Upton Electronics Company experienced the following events during its first accounting period.

1. Received $200,000 cash by issuing common stock.
2. Paid $30,000 cash for wages to production workers.
3. Paid $20,000 for salaries to administrative staff.
4. Purchased for cash and used $18,000 of raw materials.
5. Recognized $2,000 of depreciation on administrative offices.
6. Recognized $3,000 of depreciation on manufacturing equipment.
7. Recognized $96,000 of sales revenue from cash sales of products.
8. Recognized $60,000 of cost of goods sold from the sale referenced in Event 7.

Required

Use a horizontal financial statements model to show how each event affects the balance sheet, income statement, and statement of cash flows. Indicate whether the event increases (I), decreases (D), or does not affect (NA) each element of the financial statements. In the Cash Flow column, indicate whether the cash flow is associated with operating activities (OA), investing activities (IA), or financing activities (FA). The first transaction is shown as an example. (*Note:* Show accumulated depreciation as a decrease in the book value of the appropriate asset account.)

	Assets									Equity							
Event No.	**Cash**	+	**Inventory**	+	**Manuf. Equip.**	+	**Adm. Offices**	=	**Com. Stk.**	+	**Ret. Ear.**	**Rev.**	–	**Exp.**	=	**Net Inc.**	**Cash Flow**
1	I		NA		NA		NA		I		NA	NA		NA		NA	I FA

L.O. 2, 3, 4

EXERCISE 1–9B *Allocating Product Costs Between Ending Inventory and Cost of Goods Sold*

Tanaka Manufacturing Company began operations on January 1. During January, it started and completed 2,000 units of product. The company incurred the following costs:

1. Raw materials purchased and used—$2,000.
2. Wages of production workers—$1,600.
3. Salaries of administrative and sales personnel—$800.
4. Depreciation on manufacturing equipment—$1,200.
5. Depreciation on administrative equipment—$960.

Tanaka sold 1,600 units of product.

Required

a. Determine the total product cost.
b. Determine the total cost of the ending inventory.
c. Determine the total of cost of goods sold.

EXERCISE 1–10B *Financial Statement Effects for Manufacturing Versus Service Organizations*

L.O. 4 & 5

The following horizontal financial statements model shows the effects of recording the expiration of insurance in two different circumstances. One circumstance represents the expiration of insurance on a factory building. The other circumstance represents the expiration of insurance on an administrative building. The cash flow effects are shown using (I) for increase, (D) for decrease, and (NA) for no effect.

	Assets							Equity								
Event No.	**Cash**	**+**	**Prepaid Insurance**	**+**	**Inventory**	**=**	**Com. Stk.**	**+**	**Ret. Ear.**	**Rev.**	**−**	**Exp.**	**=**	**Net Inc.**	**Cash Flow**
1	NA		D		I		NA		NA	NA		NA		NA	NA
2.	NA		D		NA		NA		D	NA		I		D	NA

Required

a. Identify the event that represents the expiration of insurance on the factory building.

b. Explain why recognizing the expiration of insurance on a factory building affects financial statements differently than recognizing the expiration of insurance on an administrative building.

EXERCISE 1–11B *Effect of Product Versus General, Selling, and Administrative Cost on the Income Statement and Statement of Cash Flows*

L.O. 5

Each of the following asset acquisitions requires a year-end adjusting entry.

	Net Income	Cash Flow
Event No.	**Amount of Change**	**Amount of Change**
1. Purchased franchise	NA	(75,000) IA
1. Adjusting Entry	(7,500)	NA

1. Paid $75,000 cash on January 1 to purchase a hamburger franchise that had an estimated expected useful life of 10 years and no salvage value.
2. Paid $75,000 cash on January 1 to purchase a patent to manufacture a special product. The patent had an estimated expected useful life of 10 years.
3. Paid $4,800 cash on April 1 for a one-year insurance policy on the administrative building.
4. Paid $4,800 cash on April 1 for a one-year insurance policy on the manufacturing building.
5. Paid $2,500 cash to purchase office supplies for the accounting department. At the end of the year, $600 of office supplies was still on hand.
6. Paid $2,500 cash to purchase factory supplies. At the end of the year, $600 of factory supplies was still on hand.

Required

Explain how both acquiring the asset and recording the adjusting entry affect the amount of net income and the cash flow reported in the annual financial statements. In the Cash Flow Column, indicate whether the cash flow is associated with operating activities (OA), investing activities (IA), financing activities (FA). Assume a December 31 annual closing date. The first event is shown as an example. Assume that any products that have been made have not been sold.

EXERCISE 1–12B *Upstream and Downstream Costs*

L.O. 8

During 2007 Troy Pharmaceutical Company incurred $10,000,000 of research and development (R&D) costs to develop a new hay fever drug called Allergone. In accordance with FASB standards, the entire R&D cost was recognized as expense in 2007. Manufacturing costs (direct materials, direct labor, and overhead) to produce Allergone are expected to be $40 per unit. Packaging, shipping, and sales commissions are expected to be $5 per unit. Troy expects to sell 1,000,000 units of Allergone before developing a new drug to replace it in the market. During 2007, Troy produced 160,000 units of Allergone and sold 100,000 of them.

Required

a. Identify the upstream and downstream costs.

b. Determine the 2007 amount of cost of goods sold and the December 31, 2007, ending inventory balance.

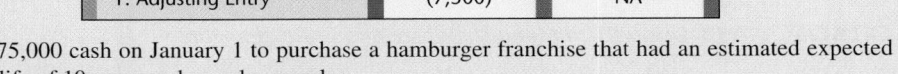

c. Determine the unit sales price Troy should establish assuming it desires to earn a profit margin equal to 40 percent of the *total cost* of developing, manufacturing, and distributing Allergone.
d. Prepare an income statement for 2007 using the sales price from Requirement *c*.
e. Why would Jocelyn price Allergone at a level that would generate a loss for 2007?

L.O. 10 EXERCISE 1–13B *Value Chain Analysis*

Fastidious Vincent washed his hair at home and then went to a barbershop for a haircut. The barber explained that shop policy is to shampoo each customer's hair before cutting, regardless of how recently it had been washed. Somewhat annoyed, Vincent submitted to the shampoo, after which the barber cut his hair with great skill. After the haircut, the barber dried his hair and complimented Vincent on his appearance. He added, "That will be $18, $3 for the shampoo and $15 for the cut and dry." Vincent did not tip the barber.

Required
Identify the nonvalue-added activity described. How could the barber modify this nonvalue-added activity?

L.O. 10 EXERCISE 1–14B *Effect of a Just-in-Time Inventory System on Financial Statements*

In reviewing Kelowna Company's financial statements for the past two years, Sylvia Peters, a bank loan officer, noticed that the company's inventory level had increased significantly while sales revenue had remained constant. Such a trend typically indicates increasing inventory carrying costs and slowing cash inflows. Ms. Peters concluded that the bank should deny Kelowna's credit line application.

Required
Explain how implementing an effective just-in-time inventory system would affect Kelowna's financial statements and possibly reverse Ms. Peters's decision about its credit line application.

L.O. 10 EXERCISE 1–15B *Using JIT to Minimize Waste and Lost Opportunity*

Dawn Choi is the editor-in-chief of her school's yearbook. The school has 800 students and 60 faculty and staff members. The firm engaged to print copies of the yearbook charges the school $15 per book and requires a 10-day lead time for delivery. Dawn and her editors plan to order 700 copies to sell at the school fair for $24 each.

Required
a. If the school sells 600 yearbooks, what amount of profit will it earn? What is the cost of waste due to excess inventory?
b. If 100 buyers are turned away after all yearbooks have been sold, what amount of profit will the school earn? What amount of opportunity cost will the school incur?
c. How could Pedro use a JIT inventory system to maximize profits by eliminating waste and opportunity cost?

L.O. 10 EXERCISE 1–16B *Using JIT to Minimize Holding Costs*

Angie's Beauty Salon purchases inventory supplies from a variety of vendors, some of which require a four-week lead time before delivering inventory purchases. To ensure that she will not run out of supplies, Angie Hammond, the owner, maintains a large inventory. The average cost of inventory on hand is $9,000. Ms. Hammond usually finances inventory purchases with a line of credit that has a 12 percent annual interest charge. Her accountant has suggested that she purchase all inventory from a single large distributor that can satisfy all of her orders within a three-day period. With such prompt delivery, Ms. Hammond would be able to reduce her average inventory balance to $2,000. She also believes that she could save $1,000 per year through reduced phone bills, insurance costs, and warehouse rental costs associated with ordering and maintaining the higher level of inventory.

Required
a. Is the inventory system the accountant suggested to Ms. Hammond a pure or approximate just-in-time system?
b. Based on the information provided, how much inventory holding cost could Ms. Hammond eliminate by taking the accountant's advice?

PROBLEMS—SERIES B

PROBLEM 1–17B *Product Versus General, Selling, and Administrative Costs*

L.O. 2, 3, 4, 5, 6

Looney Manufacturing Company was started on January 1, 2007, when it acquired $167,500 cash by issuing common stock. Looney immediately purchased office furniture and manufacturing equipment costing $25,000 and $47,500, respectively. The office furniture had a four-year useful life and a zero salvage value. The manufacturing equipment had a $5,500 salvage value and an expected useful life of six years. The company paid $17,500 for salaries of administrative personnel and $22,500 for wages of production personnel. Finally, the company paid $30,500 for raw materials that were used to make inventory. All inventory was started and completed during the year. Looney completed production on 6,000 units of product and sold 5,600 units at a price of $17.50 each in 2007. (Assume that all transactions are cash transactions.)

Required

a. Determine the total product cost and the average cost per unit of the inventory produced in 2007.
b. Determine the amount of cost of goods sold that would appear on the 2007 income statement.
c. Determine the amount of the ending inventory balance that would appear on the December 31, 2007, balance sheet.
d. Determine the amount of net income that would appear on the 2007 income statement.
e. Determine the amount of retained earnings that would appear on the December 31, 2007, balance sheet.
f. Determine the amount of total assets that would appear on the December 31, 2007, balance sheet.
g. Determine the amount of net cash flow from operating activities that would appear on the 2007 statement of cash flows.
h. Determine the amount of net cash flow from investing activities that would appear on the 2007 statement of cash flows.

PROBLEM 1–18B *Effect of Product Versus General, Selling, and Administrative Costs on Financial Statements*

L.O. 2, 4, 5

Watson Company experienced the following accounting events during its first year of operation. With the exception of the adjusting entries for depreciation, all transactions were cash transactions.

1. Acquired $99,000 cash by issuing common stock.
2. Paid $18,750 for the materials used to make its products. All products started were completed during the period.
3. Paid salaries of $7,500 to selling and administrative employees.
4. Paid wages of $11,250 to production workers.
5. Paid $15,000 for furniture used in selling and administrative offices. The furniture was acquired on January 1. It had a $1,875 estimated salvage value and a seven-year useful life.
6. Paid $27,500 for manufacturing equipment. The equipment was acquired on January 1. It had a $2,500 estimated salvage value and a five-year useful life.
7. Sold inventory to customers for $53,750 that had cost $31,250 to make.

Required

Explain how these events would affect the balance sheet, income statement, and statement of cash flows by recording them in a horizontal financial statements model as indicated here. The first event is recorded as an example. In the Cash Flow column, indicate whether the amounts represent financing activities (FA), investing activities (IA), or operating activities (OA).

Financial Statements Model

	Assets								Equity									
Event No.	Cash	+	Inventory	+	Manuf. Equip.*	+	Office Furn.*	=	Com. Stk.	+	Ret. Ear.	Rev.	−	Exp.	=	Net Inc.	Cash Flow
1	99,000								99,000								99,000 FA

*Record accumulated depreciation as negative amounts in these columns.

PROBLEM 1–19B *Product Versus General, Selling, and Administrative Costs*

L.O. 2, 3, 4, 5

The following transactions pertain to 2008, the first year of operations of Womack Company. All inventory was started and completed during the accounting period. All transactions were cash transactions.

1. Acquired $44,800 of contributed capital from its owners.
2. Paid $7,680 for materials used to produce inventory.
3. Paid $3,520 to production workers.
4. Paid $4,000 rental fee for production equipment.
5. Paid $1,200 to administrative employees.
6. Paid $2,560 rental fee for administrative office equipment.
7. Produced 1,900 units of inventory of which 1,500 units were sold at a price of $13.92 each.

Required
Prepare an income statement, balance sheet, and statement of cash flows.

L.O. 2, 3, 4, 5

PROBLEM 1–20B *Service Versus Manufacturing Companies*

Hague Company began operations on January 1, 2006, by issuing common stock for $75,200 cash. During 2006, Hague received $61,600 cash from revenue and incurred costs that required $72,000 of cash payments.

Required
Prepare an income statement, balance sheet, and statement of cash flows for Hague Company for 2006, under each of the following independent scenarios.

a. Hague is an employment agency. The $72,000 was paid for employee salaries and advertising.
b. Hague is a trucking company. The $72,000 was paid to purchase two trucks. The trucks were purchased on January 1, 2006, had five-year useful lives and no expected salvage value. Hague uses straight-line depreciation.
c. Hague is a manufacturing company. The $72,000 was paid to purchase the following items:
   (1) Paid $14,400 cash to purchase materials used to make products during the year.
   (2) Paid $22,400 cash for wages to production workers who make products during the year.
   (3) Paid $3,200 cash for salaries of sales and administrative employees.
   (4) Paid $32,000 cash to purchase manufacturing equipment. The equipment was used solely for the purpose of making products. It had a six-year life and a $3,200 salvage value. The company uses straight-line depreciation.
   (5) During 2006, Hague started and completed 2,600 units of product. The revenue was earned when Hague sold 2,200 units of product to its customers.
d. Refer to Requirement *c.* Could Hague determine the actual cost of making the 500th unit of product? How likely is it that the actual cost of the 500th unit of product was exactly the same as the cost of producing the 501st unit of product? Explain why management may be more interested in average cost than in actual cost.

L.O. 2, 3, 4, 5, 6

PROBLEM 1–21B *Importance of Cost Classification*

Addison Company was started when it acquired $84,000 by issuing common stock. During the first year of operations, the company incurred specifically identifiable product costs (materials, labor, and overhead) amounting to $48,000. Addison also incurred $24,000 of product development costs. There was a debate regarding how the product development costs should be classified. Advocates of Option 1 believed that the costs should be included in the general, selling, and administrative cost category. Advocates of Option 2 believed it would be more appropriate to classify the product development costs as product costs. During the first year, Addison made 10,000 units of product and sold 8,000 units at a price of $16.80 each. All transactions were cash transactions.

Required
a. Prepare an income statement, balance sheet, and statement of cash flows under each of the two options.
b. Identify the option that results in financial statements that are more likely to leave a favorable impression on investors and creditors.
c. Assume that Addison provides an incentive bonus to the company president that is equal to 8 percent of net income. Compute the amount of the bonus under each of the two options. Identify the option that provides the president with the higher bonus.
d. Assume a 35 percent income tax rate. Determine the amount of income tax expense under each of the two options. Identify the option that minimizes the amount of the company's income tax expense.
e. Comment on the conflict of interest between the company president as determined in Requirement *c* and the stockholders of the company as indicated in Requirement *d.* Describe an incentive compensation plan that would avoid conflicts between the interests of the president and the owners.

PROBLEM 1–22B *Value Chain Analysis*

L.O. 10

Kelly Doss visited her personal physician for treatment of flu symptoms. She was greeted by the receptionist, who gave her personal history and insurance forms to complete. She needed no instructions; she completed these same forms every time she visited the doctor. After completing the forms, Ms. Doss waited for 30 minutes before being ushered into the patient room. After waiting there for an additional 15 minutes, Dr. Brannon entered the room. The doctor ushered Ms. Doss into the hallway where he weighed her and called her weight out to the nurse for recording. Ms. Doss had gained 10 pounds since her last visit, and the doctor suggested that she consider going on a diet. Dr. Brannon then took her temperature and asked her to return to the patient room. Ten minutes later, he returned to take a throat culture and draw blood. She waited another 15 minutes for the test results. Finally, the doctor returned and told Ms. Doss that she had strep throat and bronchitis. Dr. Brannon prescribed an antibiotic and told her to get at least two days of bed rest. Ms. Doss was then ushered to the accounting department to settle her bill. The accounting clerk asked her several questions; the answers to most of them were on the forms that she had completed when she first arrived at the office. Finally, Ms. Doss paid her required copayment and left the office. Three weeks later, she received a bill indicating that she had not paid the copayment. She called the accounting department, and, after a search of the records, the clerk verified that the bill had, in fact, been paid. The clerk apologized for the inconvenience and inquired as to whether Ms. Doss's health had improved.

Required

a. Identify at least three value-added and three nonvalue-added activities suggested in this scenario.
b. Provide logical suggestions for how to eliminate the nonvalue-added activities.

PROBLEM 1–23B *Using JIT to Reduce Inventory Holding Costs*

L.O. 10

McCoy Automobile Dealership, Inc. (MAD), buys and sells a variety of cars made by Saig Motor Corporation. MAD maintains about 30 new cars in its parking lot for customers' selection; the cost of this inventory is approximately $320,000. Additionally, MAD hires security guards to protect the inventory from theft and a maintenance crew to keep the facilities attractive. The total payroll cost for the guards and maintenance crew amounts to $80,000 per year. MAD has a line of credit with a local bank that calls for a 15 percent annual rate of interest. Recently, David Mazur, the president of MAD, learned that a competitor in town, Wade Dealership, has been attracting some of MAD's usual customers because Wade could offer them lower prices. Mr. Mazur also discovered that Wade carries no inventory at all but shows customers a catalog of cars as well as pertinent information from on-line computer databases. Wade promises to deliver any car that a customer identifies within three working days.

Required

a. Based on the information provided, determine MAD's annual inventory holding cost.
b. Name the inventory system that Wade uses and explain how the system enables Wade to sell at reduced prices.

PROBLEM 1–24B *Using JIT to Minimize Waste and Lost Opportunity*

L.O. 10

Donna's Hamburger is a small fast-food shop in a busy shopping center that operates only during lunch hours. Donna Hudson, the owner and manager of the shop, is confused. On some days, she does not have enough hamburgers to satisfy customer demand. On other days, she has more hamburgers than she can sell. When she has excess hamburgers, she has no choice but to dump them. Usually, Ms. Hudson prepares about 160 hamburgers before the busy lunch hour. The product cost per hamburger is approximately $0.75; the sales price is $2.50 each. Ms. Hudson pays general, selling, and administrative expenses that include daily rent of $50 and daily wages of $40.

Required

a. Prepare an income statement based on sales of 100 hamburgers per day. Determine the cost of wasted hamburgers if 160 hamburgers were prepared in advance.
b. Prepare an income statement assuming that 200 customers attempt to buy a hamburger. Since Ms. Hudson has prepared only 160 hamburgers, she must reject 40 customer orders because of insufficient supply. Determine the amount of lost profit.
c. Suppose that hamburgers can be prepared quickly after each customer orders. However, Ms. Hudson must hire an additional part-time employee at a cost of approximately $20 per day. The per unit cost of each hamburger remains at $0.75. Prepare an income statement under the JIT system assuming that 100 hamburgers are sold. Compare the income statement under JIT with the income statement prepared in Requirement *a*. Comment on how the JIT system would affect profitability.

d. Assume the same facts as in Requirement *c* with respect to a JIT system that requires additional labor costing $20 per day. Prepare an income statement under the JIT system, assuming that 200 hamburgers are sold. Compare the income statement under JIT with the income statement prepared in Requirement *b*. Comment on how the JIT system would affect profitability.

e. Explain how the JIT system might be able to improve customer satisfaction as well as profitability.

ANALYZE, THINK, COMMUNICATE

ATC 1–1 BUSINESS APPLICATIONS CASE *Financial Versus Managerial Accounting*

In the July 20, 1998, edition of *Business Week* magazine, Harold Ruttenberg, founder and CEO of Just For Feet, Inc., referred to some information that highlighted his company's success. When comparing his "big box stores" to his mall-based rivals, he noted that the size of a typical Just For Feet store is between 15,000 and 25,000 square feet, while rival stores such as Foot Locker and Footaction USA, Inc., average between 4,000 and 6,000. Ruttenberg noted that the larger size lets Just For Feet buy in bulk and negotiate discounts of between 15 percent and 20 percent. These discounts are passed on to customers in each store's Combat Zone, where discounts can reach 70 percent. Such discounting has enabled Just For Feet to retain a highly competitive pricing advantage. Ruttenberg also highlighted the company's selection and training programs that have produced employees whose performance far outpaces the competition. The average Just For Feet store produces sales of $650 per square foot; the typical mall store produces only $250 per square foot. On the down side, Ruttenberg noted that Just For Feet experienced a sharp increase in inventory holding costs until an information system was installed to help bring the inventory stock level down. It fell 22 percent, from $152 of inventory per square foot in 1996 to $119 of inventory per square foot in 1997.

Required

a. Indicate whether the information described in this narrative would be best described as financial or managerial accounting information. Support your answer with appropriate commentary.

b. Provide some additional examples of managerial and financial accounting information that could apply to Just For Feet, Inc.

c. Explain why the manager of a Just For Feet store needs different kinds of information than investors or creditors need. Give an example of information that would be useful to a store manager but irrelevant to an investor or creditor.

ATC 1–2 GROUP ASSIGNMENT *Product Versus Upstream and Downstream Costs*

Victor Holt, the accounting manager of Sexton Inc., gathered the following information for 2006. Some of it can be used to construct an income statement for 2006. Ignore items that do not appear on an income statement. Some computation may be required. For example, the cost of manufacturing equipment would not appear on the income statement. However, the cost of manufacturing equipment is needed to compute the amount of depreciation. All units of product were started and completed in 2006.

1. Issued $864,000 of common stock.
2. Paid engineers in the product design department $10,000 for salaries that were accrued at the end of the previous year.
3. Incurred advertising expenses of $70,000.
4. Paid $720,000 for materials used to manufacture the company's product.

Department	Square Footage
Research and development	10,000
Manufacturing	60,000
Selling and administrative	30,000
Total	100,000

5. Incurred utility costs of $160,000. These costs were allocated to different departments on the basis of square footage of floor space. Mr. Holt identified three departments and determined the square footage of floor space for each department to be as shown in the table to the right.
6. Paid $880,000 for wages of production workers.
7. Paid cash of $658,000 for salaries of administrative personnel. There was $16,000 of accrued salaries owed to administrative personnel at the end of 2006. There was no beginning balance in the Salaries Payable account for administrative personnel.

8. Purchased manufacturing equipment two years ago at a cost of $10,000,000. The equipment had an eight-year useful life and a $2,000,000 salvage value.
9. Paid $390,000 cash to engineers in the product design department.
10. Paid a $258,000 cash dividend to owners.
11. Paid $80,000 to set up manufacturing equipment for production.
12. Paid a one-time $186,000 restructuring cost to redesign the production process to implement a just-in-time inventory system.
13. Prepaid the premium on a new insurance policy covering nonmanufacturing employees. The policy cost $72,000 and had a one-year term with an effective starting date of May 1. Four employees work in the research and development department and eight employees in the selling and administrative department. Assume a December 31 closing date.
14. Made 69,400 units of product and sold 60,000 units at a price of $70 each.

Required

a. Divide the class into groups of four or five students per group, and then organize the groups into three sections. Assign Task 1 to the first section of groups, Task 2 to the second section of groups, and Task 3 to the third section of groups.

Group Tasks

(1) Identify the items that are classified as product costs and determine the amount of cost of goods sold reported on the 2006 income statement.

(2) Identify the items that are classified as upstream costs and determine the amount of upstream cost expensed on the 2006 income statement.

(3) Identify the items that are classified as downstream costs and determine the amount of downstream cost expensed on the 2006 income statement.

b. Have the class construct an income statement in the following manner. Select a member of one of the groups assigned the first group task identifying the product costs. Have that person go to the board and list the costs included in the determination of cost of goods sold. Anyone in the other groups who disagrees with one of the classifications provided by the person at the board should voice an objection and explain why the item should be classified differently. The instructor should lead the class to a consensus on the disputed items. After the amount of cost of goods sold is determined, the student at the board constructs the part of the income statement showing the determination of gross margin. The exercise continues in a similar fashion with representatives from the other sections explaining the composition of the upstream and downstream costs. These items are added to the income statement started by the first group representative. The final result is a completed income statement.

RESEARCH ASSIGNMENT *Skills Needed by Managerial Accountants* ATC 1–3

The September 1999 issue of *Strategic Finance* contains the article "Counting More, Counting Less: Transformations in the Management Accounting Profession," written by Keith Russell, Gary Siegel, and C. S. Kuleszo. It appears on pages 38 to 44. This article reviews findings from a survey of managerial accountants conducted by the Institute of Management Accountants (IMA). Read this article and complete the following requirements.

Required

a. What skills did the management accountants identify as being most important for their success?

b. Did the respondents see their work as being most closely associated with the accounting or finance function?

c. Like all business professionals, management accountants must continuously update their skills. What were the five most important skills the respondents said they had acquired in the five years prior to the survey?

d. Non-accountants often view accountants as persons who work alone sitting at a desk. What percentage of the respondents to the IMA survey said they work on cross-functional teams?

WRITING ASSIGNMENT *Emerging Practices in Managerial Accounting* ATC 1–4

The 1998 annual report of the Maytag Corporation contained the following excerpt:

> *During the first quarter of 1996, the Company announced the restructuring of its major appliance operations in an effort to strengthen its position in the industry and to deliver improved performance to both customers and shareowners. This included the consolidation of two separate organizational units into a single operation responsible for all activities associated with the manufacture and distribution of the Company's brands of major appliances and the closing of a cooking products plant in Indianapolis, Indiana, with transfer of that production to an existing plant in Cleveland, Tennessee.*

The restructuring cost Maytag $40 million and disrupted the lives of many of the company's employees.

Required

Assume that you are Maytag's vice president of human relations. Write a letter to the employees who are affected by the restructuring. The letter should explain why it was necessary for the company to undertake the restructuring. Your explanation should refer to the ideas discussed in the section "Emerging Trends in Managerial Accounting" of this chapter.

ATC 1–5 ETHICAL DILEMMA *Product Cost Versus Selling and Administrative Expense*

Eddie Emerson is a proud woman with a problem. Her daughter has been accepted into a prestigious law school. While Ms. Emerson beams with pride, she is worried sick about how to pay for the school; she is a single parent who has worked hard to support herself and her three children. She had to go heavily into debt to finance her own education. Even though she now has a good job, family needs have continued to outpace her income and her debt burden is staggering. She knows she will be unable to borrow the money needed for her daughter's law school.

Ms. Emerson is the controller of a small manufacturing company. She has just accepted a new job offer. Indeed, she has not yet told her employer that she will be leaving in a month. She is concerned that her year-end incentive bonus may be affected if her boss learns of her plans to leave. She plans to inform the company immediately after receiving the bonus. She knows her behavior is less than honorable, but she believes that she has been underpaid for a long time. Her boss, a relative of the company's owner, makes twice what she makes and does half the work. Why should she care about leaving with a little extra cash? Indeed, she is considering an opportunity to boost the bonus.

Ms. Emerson's bonus is based on a percentage of net income. Her company recently introduced a new product line that required substantial production start-up costs. Ms. Emerson is fully aware that GAAP requires these costs to be expensed in the current accounting period, but no one else in the company has the technical expertise to know exactly how the costs should be treated. She is considering misclassifying the start-up costs as product costs. If the costs are misclassified, net income will be significantly higher, resulting in a nice boost in her incentive bonus. By the time the auditors discover the misclassification, Ms. Emerson will have moved on to her new job. If the matter is brought to the attention of her new employer, she will simply plead ignorance. Considering her daughter's needs, Ms. Emerson decides to classify the start-up costs as product costs.

Required

a. Based on this information, indicate whether Ms. Emerson believes the number of units of product sold will be equal to, less than, or greater than, the number of units made. Write a brief paragraph explaining the logic that supports your answer.

b. Explain how the misclassification could mislead an investor or creditor regarding the company's financial condition.

c. Explain how the misclassification could affect income taxes.

d. Identify the factors that contributed to the breach of ethical conduct. When constructing your answer, you may want to refer to the section "Common Features of Criminal and Ethical Misconduct" of this chapter.

e. Review the standards of ethical conduct shown in Exhibit 1–13 and identify at least two standards that Ms. Emerson's misclassification of the start-up costs violated.

ATC 1–6 SPREADSHEET ASSIGNMENT *Using Excel*

The following transactions pertain to 2006, the first year operations of the Barlett Company. All inventory was started and completed during 2006. Assume that all transactions are cash transactions.

1. Acquired $2,000 cash by issuing common stock.
2. Paid $400 for materials used to produce inventory.
3. Paid $600 to production workers.
4. Paid $200 rental fee for production equipment.
5. Paid $160 to administrative employees.
6. Paid $80 rental fee for administrative office equipment.
7. Produced 300 units of inventory of which 200 units were sold at a price of $7.00 each.

Required

Construct a spreadsheet that includes the income statement, balance sheet, and statement of cash flows.

SPREADSHEET ASSIGNMENT *Mastering Excel*

ATC 1–7

Mantooth Manufacturing Company experienced the following accounting events during its first year of operation. With the exception of the adjusting entries for depreciation, assume that all transactions are cash transactions.

1. Acquired $50,000 by issuing common stock.
2. Paid $8,000 for the materials used to make its products, all of which were started and completed during the year.
3. Paid salaries of $4,400 to selling and administrative employees.
4. Paid wages of $7,000 to production workers.
5. Paid $9,600 for furniture used in selling and administrative offices. The furniture was acquired on January 1. It had a $1,600 estimated salvage value and a four-year useful life.
6. Paid $13,000 for manufacturing equipment. The equipment was acquired on January 1. It had a $1,000 estimated salvage value and a three-year useful life.
7. Sold inventory to customers for $25,000 that had cost $14,000 to make.

Construct a spreadsheet of the financial statements model as shown here:

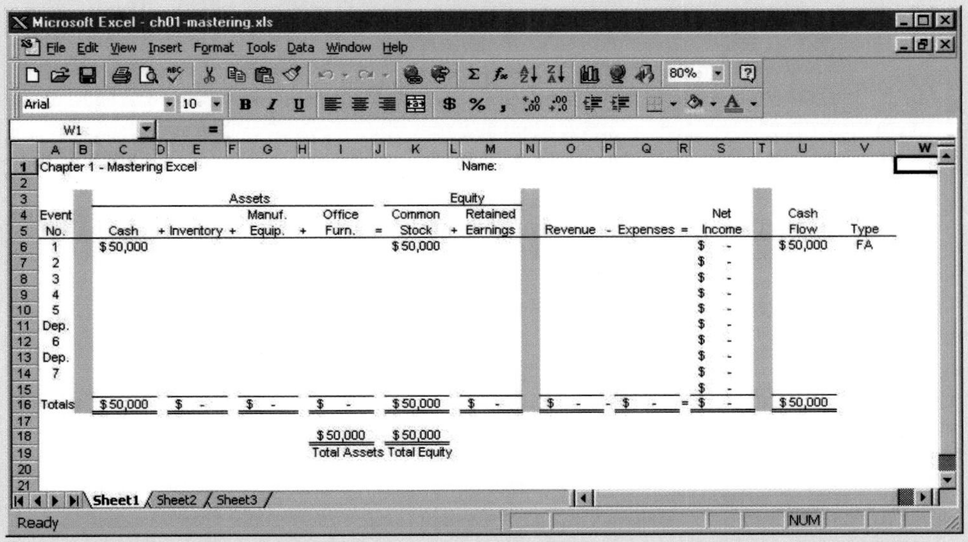
Microsoft Excel - ch01-mastering.xls

Chapter 1 - Mastering Excel   Name:

Event No.	Cash	+ Inventory +	Manuf. Equip. +	Office Furn. =	Common Stock +	Retained Earnings	Revenue –	Expenses =	Net Income	Cash Flow	Type
1	$50,000				$50,000				$ -	$50,000	FA
2									$ -		
3									$ -		
4									$ -		
5									$ -		
Dep.									$ -		
6									$ -		
Dep.									$ -		
7									$ -		
									$ -		
Totals	$50,000	$ -	$ -	$ -	$50,000	$ -	$ -	$ -	$ -	$50,000	
				$50,000 Total Assets	$50,000 Total Equity						

Required

Place formulas in row 16 to automatically add the columns. Also add formulas in column S to calculate net income after each event, and add formulas in row 18 to compute total assets and equity. Notice that you must enter the events since only the first one is shown as an example.

Spreadsheet Tips

1. The column widths are set by choosing Format, then Column, and then Width.
2. The shading in columns B, N, and T is added by highlighting a column and choosing Format, then Cells, and then clicking on the tab titled Patterns and choosing a color.
3. The sum function is an easy way to add a column or row. For example, the formula in cell C16 is =SUM(C6:C15).
4. As an example of the formulas in column S (net income), the formula in cell S7 is =S6+O7−Q7.
5. If you find that some of the columns are too far to the right to appear on your screen, you can set the zoom level to show the entire spreadsheet. The zoom is set by choosing View, then Zoom, and then clicking on Custom and typing 100 percent in the box. The shortcut method to set the zoom is to click in the box on the right side of the top tool bar that appears immediately below the menu.

COMPREHENSIVE PROBLEM

Magnificent Modems, Inc. makes modem cards that are used in notebook computers. The company completed the following transactions during 2006. All purchases and sales were made with cash.

1. Acquired $750,000 of cash from the owners.
2. Purchased $270,000 of manufacturing equipment. The equipment has a $30,000 salvage value and a four-year useful life. Label the purchase of the equipment as **Event 2a** and the recognition of depreciation as **Event 2b.**
3. The company started and completed 5,000 modems. Direct materials purchased and used amounted to $40 per unit.
4. Direct labor costs amounted to $25 per unit.
5. The cost of manufacturing supplies used amounted to $4 per unit.
6. The company paid $50,000 to rent the manufacturing facility.
7. Magnificent sold all 5,000 units at a cash price of $120 per unit. Label the recognition of the sale as **Event 7a** and the cost of goods sold as **Event 7b.** (Hint: It will be necessary to determine the manufacturing costs in order to record the cost of goods sold.)
8. The sales staff was paid a $6 per unit sales commission.
9. Paid $39,000 to purchase equipment for administrative offices. The equipment was expected to have a $3,000 salvage value and a three-year useful life. Label the purchase of the equipment as **Event 9a** and the recognition of depreciation as **Event 9b.**
10. Administrative expenses consisting of office rental and salaries amounted to $71,950.

Required:

a. Record the transaction data for Magnificent Modems, Inc. in the financial statements like the one shown below. In the cash flow column, use parentheses to indicate cash outflows. Indicate whether each cash flow item is a financing activity (FA), investing activity (IA), or operating activity (OA). The first transaction is recorded as an example.

	Assets				=	Equity						
Event No.	**Cash**	**+ Inventory**	**+ Manuf. Equip.***	**+ Office Equip.***	**=**	**C. Stock**	**+ Ret. Ear.**	**Rev.**	**– Exp.**	**= Net Inc.**	**Cash Flow**	
1	750,000					750,000					750,000	FA
Ck. Fig.	544,050	+ 0	+ 210,000	+ 27,000	=	750,000	+ 31,050	600,000	– 568,950	= 31,050	544,050	NC

*Negative amounts in these columns represent accumulated depreciation.

b. Use the following forms to prepare an income statement and balance sheet.

MAGNIFICENT MODEMS, INC. Income Statement For the Period Ended December 31, 2006	
Sales	
Cost of Goods Sold	
Gross Margin	
Sales Commission	
Depreciation Expense	
Administrative Expense	
Net Income	$31,050

MAGNIFICENT MODEMS, INC. Balance Sheet As of December 31, 2006	
Assets:	
Cash	
Manufacturing Equipment, Net of Acc. Depreciation	
Administrative Equipment, Net of Acc. Depreciation	
Finished Goods Inventory	
Total Assets	$781,050
Equity	
Common Stock	
Retained Earnings	
Total Stockholder's Equity	$781,050

CHAPTER *two*

COST BEHAVIOR, OPERATING LEVERAGE, AND PROFITABILITY ANALYSIS

LEARNING *objectives*

After you have mastered the material in this chapter, you will be able to:

1. Distinguish between fixed and variable cost behavior.
2. Demonstrate the effects of operating leverage on profitability.
3. Show how cost behavior affects profitability.
4. Prepare an income statement using the contribution margin approach.
5. Calculate the magnitude of operating leverage.
6. Use cost behavior to create a competitive operating advantage.
7. Demonstrate how the relevant range and the decision-making context affect cost behavior.
8. Select an appropriate time period for calculating the average cost per unit.
9. Define the term *mixed costs.*
10. Use the high-low method and scattergraphs to estimate fixed and variable costs.

THE *curious* ACCOUNTANT

News flash! On October 20, 2003, **Southwest Airlines** announced that its third-quarter earnings would be up *41 percent* over the same quarter of 2002, yet its revenues were up only 12 percent. On October 15, 2003, Nissan announced that it expected an increase in revenue of 8 percent to cause earnings to rise *15 percent.* In January 2003 **Intel** announced that its fourth-quarter revenue was up 2.5 percent, while its earnings were up *128 percent.*

Can you explain why such small changes in these companies' revenues resulted in such relatively large changes in their earnings? In other words, if a company's sales increase 10 percent, why do its earnings not also increase 10 percent? (Answer on page 54.)

CHAPTER *opening*

Three college students are planning a vacation. One of them suggests inviting a fourth person along, remarking that four can travel for the same cost as three. Certainly, some costs will be the same whether three or four people go on the trip. For example, the hotel room costs $800 per week, regardless of whether three or four people stay in the room. In accounting terms the cost of the hotel room is a fixed cost. *The* total *amount of a fixed cost does not change when volume changes. The total hotel room cost is $800 whether 1, 2, 3, or 4 people use the room. In contrast, some costs vary in direct proportion with changes in volume. When volume increases,* total *variable cost increases; when volume decreases,* total *variable cost decreases. For example, the cost of tickets to a theme park is a* ***variable cost.***

The total cost of tickets increases proportionately with each vacationer who goes to the theme park. Cost behavior (fixed versus variable) can significantly impact profitability. This chapter explains cost behavior and ways it can be used to increase profitability.

Topic Tackler PLUS 2–1

Fixed Cost Behavior

LO1 Distinguish between fixed and variable cost behavior.

How much more will it cost to send one additional employee to a sales meeting? If more people buy our products, can we charge less? If sales increase by 10 percent, how will profits be affected? Managers seeking answers to such questions must consider cost behavior. Knowing how costs behave relative to the level of business activity enables managers to more effectively plan and control costs. To illustrate, consider the entertainment company Star Productions, Inc. (SPI).

SPI specializes in promoting rock concerts. It is considering paying a band $48,000 to play a concert. Obviously, SPI must sell enough tickets to cover this cost. In this example, the relevant activity base is the number of tickets sold. The cost of the band is a **fixed cost** because it does not change regardless of the number of tickets sold. Exhibit 2–1 illustrates the fixed cost behavior pattern, showing the *total cost* and the *cost per unit* at three different levels of activity.

Exhibit 2–1 *Fixed Cost Behavior*

Number of tickets sold (a)	2,700	3,000	3,300
Total cost of band (b)	$48,000	$48,000	$48,000
Cost per ticket sold (b ÷ a)	$17.78	$16.00	$14.55

Total versus *per unit* fixed costs behave differently. The total cost for the band remains constant (fixed) at $48,000. In contrast, fixed cost per unit decreases as volume (number of tickets sold) increases. The term *fixed cost* is consistent with the behavior of *total cost.* Total fixed cost remains constant (fixed) when activity changes. However, there is a contradiction between the term *fixed cost per unit* and the *per unit behavior pattern of a fixed cost.* Fixed cost per unit is *not* fixed. It changes with the number of tickets sold. This contradiction in terminology can cause untold confusion. Study carefully the fixed cost behavior patterns in Exhibit 2–2.

Exhibit 2–2 *Fixed Cost Behavior*

When Activity	Increases	Decreases
Total fixed cost	Remains constant	Remains constant
Fixed cost **per unit**	Decreases	Increases

The fixed cost data in Exhibit 2–1 help SPI's management decide whether to sponsor the concert. For example, the information influences potential pricing choices. The per unit costs represent the minimum ticket prices required to cover the fixed cost at various levels of activity. SPI could compare these per unit costs to the prices of competing entertainment events (such as the prices of movies, sporting events, or theater tickets). If the price is not competitive, tickets will not sell and the concert will lose money. Management must also consider the number of tickets to be sold. The volume data in Exhibit 2–1 can be compared to the band's track record of ticket sales at previous concerts. A proper analysis of these data can reduce the risk of undertaking an unprofitable venture.

Topic Tackler PLUS 2–2

Operating Leverage

LO2 Demonstrate the effects of operating leverage on profitability.

Heavy objects can be moved with little effort using *physical* leverage. Business managers apply **operating leverage** to magnify small changes in revenue into dramatic changes in

REALITY bytes

Who cares if costs exhibit fixed or variable behavior? Andrew Farkas cares. Mr. Farkas has used the concept of fixed cost to establish a successful real estate property management company, Insignia Financial Group. Mr. Farkas's stake in Insignia is reported to be worth approximately $160 million. Property management companies existed before Mr. Farkas started Insignia, but the property management business was considered to have a relatively low profit potential because the costs of operating such companies were high relative to the level of revenue they were able to generate. Mr. Farkas spent millions of dollars to develop a standardized computer management process. The investment was substantial, and the cost was basically fixed. When Mr. Farkas implemented an aggressive plan to expand Insignia's client base, revenues soared but costs remained relatively stable. The result was a highly profitable business that earned Mr. Farkas recognition as the "first new real-estate mogul in a decade."

Source: Fred Vogelstein, "A Real-Estate Tycoon for the '90s," *U.S. News & World Report,* May 19, 1997, p. 52.

profitability. The *lever* managers use to achieve disproportionate changes between revenue and profitability is fixed costs. The leverage relationships between revenue, fixed costs, and profitability are displayed in Exhibit 2–3.

When all costs are fixed, every sales dollar contributes one dollar toward the potential profitability of a project. Once sales dollars cover fixed costs, each additional sales dollar represents pure profit. As a result, a small change in sales volume can significantly affect profitability. To illustrate, assume SPI estimates it will sell 3,000 tickets for $18 each. A 10 percent difference in actual sales volume will produce a 90 percent difference in profitability. Examine the data in Exhibit 2–4 to verify this result.

Exhibit 2–3 *Operating Leverage*

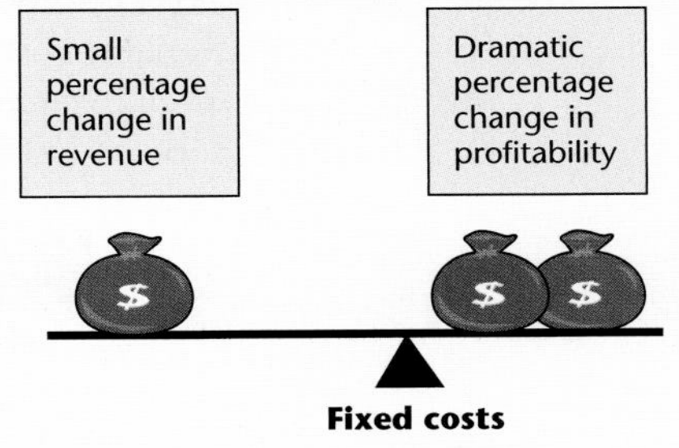

Exhibit 2–4 *Effect of Operating Leverage on Profitability*

Number of tickets sold	2,700	⇐ −10% ⇐	3,000	⇒ +10% ⇒	3,300
Sales revenue ($18 per ticket)	$48,600		$54,000		$59,400
Cost of band (fixed cost)	(48,000)		(48,000)		(48,000)
Gross margin	$ 600	⇐ −90% ⇐	$ 6,000	⇒+90% ⇒	$11,400

Calculating Percentage Change

The percentages in Exhibit 2–4 are computed as follows:

$$[(\text{Alternative measure} - \text{Base measure}) \div \text{Base measure}] \times 100 = \%\ \text{change}$$

The base measure is the starting point. To illustrate, compute the percentage change in gross margin when moving from 3,000 units (base measure) to 3,300 units (the alternative measure).

$$[(\text{Alternative measure} - \text{Base measure}) \div \text{Base measure}] \times 100 = \%\ \text{change}$$
$$[(\$11{,}400 - \$6{,}000) \div \$6{,}000] \times 100 = 90\%$$

The percentage *decline* in profitability is similarly computed:

$$[(\text{Alternative measure} - \text{Base measure}) \div \text{Base measure}] \times 100 = \%\ \text{change}$$
$$[(600 - \$6{,}000) \div \$6{,}000] \times 100 = (90\%)$$

Risk and Reward Assessment

Risk refers to the possibility that sacrifices may exceed benefits. A fixed cost represents a commitment to an economic sacrifice. It represents the ultimate risk of undertaking a particular business project. If SPI pays the band but nobody buys a ticket, the company will lose $48,000. SPI can avoid this risk by substituting *variable costs* for the *fixed cost.*

Variable Cost Behavior

LO2 Demonstrate the effects of operating leverage on profitability.

To illustrate variable cost behavior, assume SPI arranges to pay the band $16 per ticket sold instead of a fixed $48,000. Exhibit 2–5 shows the total cost of the band and the cost per ticket sold at three different levels of activity.

Exhibit 2–5 *Variable Cost Behavior*

Number of tickets sold (a)	2,700	3,000	3,300
Total cost of band (b)	$43,200	$48,000	$52,800
Cost per ticket sold (b ÷ a)	$16	$16	$16

Since SPI will pay the band $16 for each ticket sold, the *total* variable cost increases in direct proportion to the number of tickets sold. If SPI sells one ticket, total band cost will be $16 (1 × $16); if SPI sells two tickets, total band cost will be $32 (2 × $16); and so on. The total cost of the band increases proportionately as ticket sales move from 2,700 to 3,000 to 3,300. The variable cost *per ticket* remains $16, however, regardless of whether the number of tickets sold is 1, 2, 3, or 3,000. The behavior of variable cost *per unit* is contradictory to the word *variable.* Variable cost per unit remains *constant* regardless of how many tickets are sold. Study carefully the variable cost behavior patterns in Exhibit 2–6.

Exhibit 2–6 *Variable Cost Behavior*

When Activity	**Increases**	**Decreases**
Total variable cost	Increases proportionately	Decreases proportionately
Variable cost **per unit**	Remains constant	Remains constant

Shifting the cost structure from fixed to variable enables SPI to avoid the fixed cost risk. If no one buys a ticket, SPI loses nothing because it incurs no cost. If only one person buys a ticket at an $18 ticket price, SPI earns a $2 profit ($18 sales revenue − $16 cost of band). Should managers therefore avoid fixed costs whenever possible? Not necessarily.

Shifting the cost structure from fixed to variable reduces not only the level of risk but also the potential for profits. Managers cannot avoid the risk of fixed costs without also sacrificing the benefits. Variable costs do not offer operating leverage. Exhibit 2–7 shows that a variable cost structure produces a proportional relationship between sales and profitability. A 10 percent increase or decrease in sales results in a corresponding 10 percent increase or decrease in profitability.

Exhibit 2–7 *Variable Cost Eliminates Operating Leverage*

Number of tickets sold	2,700	⇐ −10% ⇐	3,000	⇒ +10% ⇒	3,300
Sales revenue ($18 per ticket)	$48,600		$54,000		$59,400
Cost of band (variable cost)	(43,200)		(48,000)		(52,800)
Gross margin	$ 5,400	⇐ −10% ⇐	$ 6,000	⇒ +10% ⇒	$ 6,600

Check Yourself 2-1

Suppose that you are sponsoring a political rally at which Ralph Nader will speak. You estimate that approximately 2,000 people will buy tickets to hear Mr. Nader's speech. The tickets are expected to be priced at $12 each. Would you prefer a contract that agrees to pay Mr. Nader $10,000 or one that agrees to pay him $5 per ticket purchased?

Answer Your answer would depend on how certain you are that 2,000 people will purchase tickets. If it were likely that many more than 2,000 tickets would be sold, you would be better off with a fixed cost structure, agreeing to pay Mr. Nader a flat fee of $10,000. If attendance numbers are highly uncertain, you would be better off with a variable cost structure thereby guaranteeing a lower cost if fewer people buy tickets.

Relationship Between Cost Behavior and Revenue

LO1 Distinguish between fixed and variable cost behavior.

Exhibit 2–8 compares the relationship between revenue and total fixed cost with the relationship between revenue and total variable cost. A pure fixed cost structure offers greater risk and higher potential rewards. A company will incur losses unless it generates enough revenue to cover its fixed cost. Thereafter, every dollar of revenue represents pure profit. As volume increases, income becomes disproportionately greater than total costs. In contrast, a pure variable cost structure offers the security of earning a profit at any level of sales. But since costs increase proportionately with increases in revenue, there is no operating leverage benefit.

Exhibit 2–8 *Cost Behavior and Revenue Relationships*

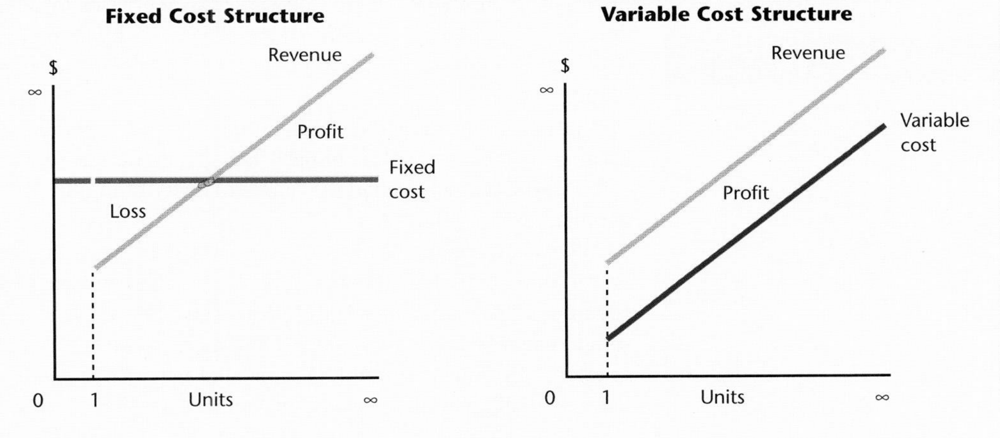

Effect of Cost Structure on Profit Stability

LO3 Show how cost behavior affects profitability.

The preceding discussion suggests that companies with higher levels of fixed costs are more likely to experience earnings volatility. To illustrate, suppose three companies produce and sell the same product. Each company sells 10 units for $10 each. Furthermore, each company incurs costs of $60 in the process of making and selling its products. However, the companies operate under radically different **cost structures.** The entire $60 of cost incurred by Company A is fixed. Company B incurs $30 of fixed cost and $30 of variable cost ($3 per unit). All $60 of cost incurred by Company C is variable ($6 per unit). Exhibit 2–9 displays income statements for the three companies.

Exhibit 2–9 *Income Statements*

	Company Name		
	A	B	C
Variable Cost per Unit (a)	$ 0	$ 3	$ 6
Sales Revenue (10 units × $10)	$100	$100	$100
Variable Cost (10 units × a)	0	(30)	(60)
Fixed Cost	(60)	(30)	0
Net Income	$ 40	$ 40	$ 40

ANSWERS TO THE *curious* ACCOUNTANT . . .

The explanation for how a company's earnings can rise faster, as a percentage, than its revenue rises is operating leverage, and operating leverage is due entirely to fixed costs. As the chapter explained, when a company's output goes up, its fixed cost per unit goes down. As long as it can keep prices about the same, this lower unit cost will result in higher profit per unit sold. In real world companies, the relationship between changing sales levels and changing earnings levels can be very complex, but the existence of fixed costs helps to explain why an 8 percent rise in revenue can cause a 15 percent rise in net earnings. Chapter 3 will investigate the relationships among an entity's cost structure, output level, pricing strategy, and profits earned in more depth.

Exhibit 2–10 *Income Statements*

	Company Name		
	A	**B**	**C**
Variable Cost per Unit (a)	$ 0	$ 3	$ 6
Sales Revenue (11 units × $10)	$110	$110	$110
Variable Cost (11 units × a)	0	(33)	(66)
Fixed Cost	(60)	(30)	0
Net Income	$ 50	$ 47	$ 44

Exhibit 2–11 *Income Statements*

	Company Name		
	A	**B**	**C**
Variable Cost per Unit (a)	$ 0	$ 3	$ 6
Sales Revenue (9 units × $10)	$90	$90	$90
Variable Cost (9 units × a)	0	(27)	(54)
Fixed Cost	(60)	(30)	0
Net Income	$30	$33	$36

When sales change, the amount of the corresponding change in net income is directly influenced by the company's cost structure. The more fixed cost, the greater the fluctuation in net income. To illustrate, assume sales increase by one unit; the resulting income statements are displayed in Exhibit 2–10.

Company A, with the highest level of fixed costs, experienced a $10 ($50 − $40) increase in profitability; Company C, with the lowest level of fixed cost (zero), had only a $4 ($44 − $40) increase in profitability. Company B, with a 50/50 mix of fixed and variable cost, had a mid-range $7 ($47 − $40) increase in net income. The effect of fixed cost on volatility applies to decreases as well as increases in sales volume. To illustrate, assume sales decrease by one unit (from 10 to 9 units). The resulting income statements are displayed in Exhibit 2–11.

Company A again experiences the largest variance in earnings ($10 decrease). Company B had a moderate decline of $7, and Company C had the least volatility with only a $4 decline.

What cost structure is the best? Should a manager use fixed or variable costs? The answer depends on sales volume expectations. A manager who expects revenues to increase should use a fixed cost structure. On the other hand, if future sales growth is uncertain or if the manager believes revenue is likely to decline, a variable cost structure makes more sense.

Check Yourself 2–2

If both Kroger Food Stores and Delta Airlines were to experience a 5 percent increase in revenues, which company would be more likely to experience a higher percentage increase in net income?

Answer Delta would be more likely to experience a higher percentage increase in net income because a large portion of its cost (e.g., employee salaries and depreciation) is fixed cost, while a large portion of Kroger's cost is variable (e.g., cost of goods sold).

An Income Statement under the Contribution Margin Approach

LO4 Prepare an income statement using the contribution margin approach.

The impact of cost structure on profitability is so significant that managerial accountants frequently construct income statements that classify costs according to their behavior patterns.

Such income statements first subtract variable costs from revenue; the resulting subtotal is called the **contribution margin.** The contribution margin represents the amount available to cover fixed expenses and thereafter to provide company profits. Net income is computed by subtracting the fixed costs from the contribution margin. A contribution margin style income statement cannot be used for public reporting (GAAP prohibits its use in external financial reports), but it is widely used for internal reporting purposes. Exhibit 2–12 illustrates income statements prepared using the contribution margin approach.

Exhibit 2–12 *Income Statements*

	Company Name	
	Bragg	**Biltmore**
Variable Cost per Unit (a)	\$ 6	\$ 12
Sales Revenue (10 units × \$20)	\$200	\$200
Variable Cost (10 units × a)	(60)	(120)
Contribution Margin	140	80
Fixed Cost	(120)	(60)
Net Income	\$ 20	\$ 20

Measuring Operating Leverage Using Contribution Margin

LO5 Calculate the magnitude of operating leverage.

A contribution margin income statement allows managers to easily measure operating leverage. The magnitude of operating leverage can be determined as follows:

$$\text{Magnitude of operating leverage} = \frac{\text{Contribution margin}}{\text{Net income}}$$

Applying this formula to the income statement data reported for Bragg Company and Biltmore Company in Exhibit 2–12 produces the following measures.

Bragg Company:

$$\text{Magnitude of operating leverage} = \frac{140}{20} = 7$$

Biltmore Company:

$$\text{Magnitude of operating leverage} = \frac{80}{20} = 4$$

The computations show that Bragg is more highly leveraged than Biltmore. Bragg's change in profitability will be seven times greater than a given percentage change in revenue. In contrast, Biltmore's profits change by only four times the percentage change in revenue. For example, a 10 percent increase in revenue produces a 70 percent increase (10 percent × 7) in profitability for Bragg Company and a 40 percent increase (10 percent × 4) in profitability for Biltmore Company. The income statements in Exhibits 2–13 and 2–14 confirm these expectations.

Operating leverage itself is neither good nor bad; it represents a strategy that can work to a company's advantage or disadvantage, depending on how it is used. The next section explains how managers can use operating leverage to create a competitive business advantage.

Exhibit 2–13 *Comparative Income Statements for Bragg Company*

Units (a)	**10**		**11**
Sales Revenue (\$20 × a)	\$200	⇒ +10% ⇒	\$220
Variable Cost (\$6 × a)	(60)		(66)
Contribution Margin	140		154
Fixed Cost	(120)		(120)
Net Income	\$ 20	⇒ +70% ⇒	\$ 34

Exhibit 2–14 *Comparative Income Statements for Biltmore Company*

Units (a)	**10**		**11**
Sales Revenue (\$20 × a)	\$200	⇒ +10% ⇒	\$220
Variable Cost (\$12 × a)	(120)		(132)
Contribution Margin	80		88
Fixed Cost	(60)		(60)
Net Income	\$ 20	⇒ +40% ⇒	\$ 28

Check Yourself 2–3

Boeing Company's 2001 10K annual report filed with the Securities and Exchange Commission refers to "higher commercial airlines segment margins." Is Boeing referring to gross margins or contribution margins?

Answer Since the data come from the company's external annual report, the reference must be to gross margins (revenue − cost of goods sold), a product cost measure. The contribution margin (revenue − variable cost) is a measure used in internal reporting.

Using Fixed Cost to Provide a Competitive Operating Advantage

LO6 Use cost behavior to create a competitive operating advantage.

Mary MaHall and John Strike have established tutoring companies to support themselves while they attend college. Both Ms. MaHall and Mr. Strike function as owner/managers; they each hire other students to actually provide the tutoring services. Ms. MaHall pays her tutors salaries; her labor costs are fixed at $16,000 per year regardless of the number of hours of tutoring performed. Mr. Strike pays his employees $8 per hour; his labor is therefore a variable cost. Both businesses currently provide 2,000 hours of tutoring services at a price of $11 per hour. As shown in Exhibit 2–15, both companies currently produce the same profit.

Exhibit 2–15 *Comparative Profitability at 2,000 Hours of Tutoring*

		MaHall		Strike
Number of hours of tutoring provided		2,000		2,000
Service revenue ($11 per hour)		$22,000		$22,000
Cost of tutors	Fixed	(16,000)	Variable ($8 × 2,000)	(16,000)
Net income		$ 6,000		$ 6,000

Suppose Ms. MaHall adopts a strategy to win over Mr. Strike's customers by reducing the price of tutoring services from $11 per hour to $7 per hour. If Ms. MaHall succeeds, her company's income will double as shown in Exhibit 2–16. Mr. Strike is in a vulnerable position because if he matches MaHall's price cut he will lose $1 ($7 new per hour price − $8 cost per hour for tutor) for each hour of tutoring service that his company provides.

Exhibit 2–16 *MaHall's Profitability at 4,000 Hours of Tutoring*

		MaHall
Number of hours of tutoring provided		4,000
Service revenue ($7 per hour)		$28,000
Cost of tutors	Fixed	(16,000)
Net income (loss)		$12,000

Is Mr. Strike's business doomed? Not necessarily; Ms. MaHall's operating leverage strategy only works if volume increases. If Mr. Strike matches Ms. MaHall's price, thereby maintaining the existing sales volume levels between the two companies, both companies incur losses. Exhibit 2–17 verifies this conclusion. Under these circumstances, Ms. MaHall would be forced to raise her price or to face the same negative consequences that she is attempting to force on Mr. Strike.

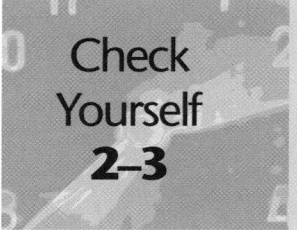

Exhibit 2–17 *Comparative Profitability at 2,000 Hours of Tutoring*

		MaHall		Strike
Number of hours of tutoring provided		2,000		2,000
Service revenue ($7 per hour)		$14,000		$14,000
Cost of tutors	Fixed	(16,000)	Variable ($8 × 2,000)	(16,000)
Net income (loss)		$(2,000)		$(2,000)

Cost Behavior Summarized

LO1 Distinguish between fixed and variable cost behavior.

The term *fixed* refers to the behavior of *total* fixed cost. The cost *per unit* of a fixed cost *varies inversely* with changes in the level of activity. As activity increases, fixed cost per unit decreases. As activity decreases, fixed cost per unit increases. These relationships are graphed in Exhibit 2–18.

Exhibit 2–18 *Graphical Presentation of Fixed Cost Behavior*

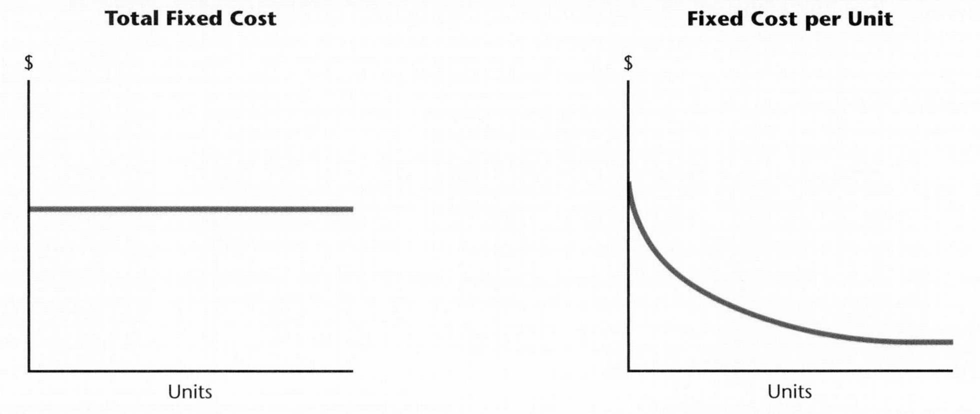

The term *variable* refers to the behavior of *total* variable cost. Total variable cost increases or decreases proportionately with changes in the volume of activity. In contrast, variable cost *per unit* remains *fixed* at all levels of activity. These relationships are graphed in Exhibit 2–19.

Exhibit 2–19 *Graphical Presentation of Variable Cost Behavior*

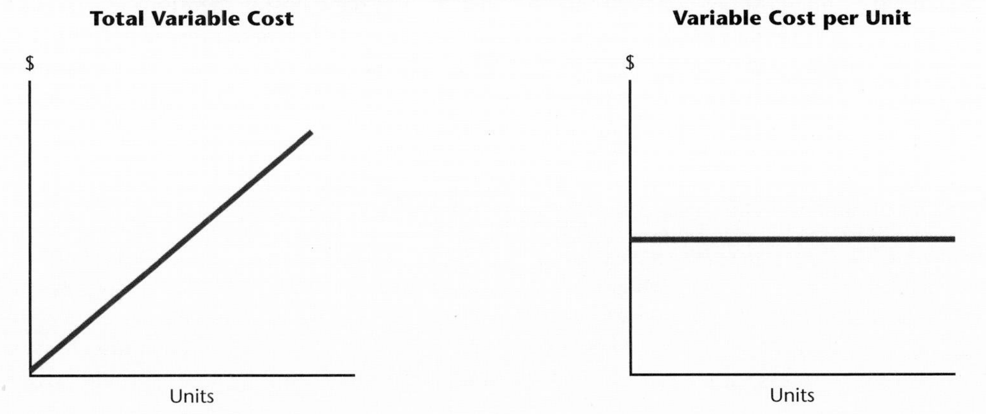

The relationships between fixed and variable costs are summarized in the chart in Exhibit 2–20. Study these relationships thoroughly.

Exhibit 2–20 *Fixed and Variable Cost Behavior*

When Activity Level Changes	Total Cost	Cost per Unit
Fixed costs	Remains constant	Changes *inversely*
Variable costs	Changes in direct proportion	Remains constant

The Relevant Range

LO7 Demonstrate how the relevant range and the decision-making context affect cost behavior.

Suppose SPI, the rock concert promoter mentioned earlier, must pay $5,000 to rent a concert hall with a seating capacity of 4,000 people. Is the cost of the concert hall fixed or variable? Since total cost remains unchanged regardless of whether one ticket, 4,000 tickets, or any number in between is sold, the cost is fixed relative to ticket sales. However, what if demand for tickets is significantly more than 4,000? In that case, SPI might rent a larger concert hall at a higher cost. In other words, *the cost is fixed only for a designated range of activity (1 to 4,000).*

A similar circumstance affects many variable costs. For example, a supplier may offer a volume discount to buyers who purchase more than a specified number of products. The point is that descriptions of cost behavior pertain to a specified range of activity. The range of activity over which the definitions of fixed and variable costs are valid is commonly called the **relevant range.**

Context-Sensitive Definitions of Fixed and Variable

The behavior pattern of a particular cost may be either fixed or variable, depending on the context. For example, the cost of the band was fixed at $48,000 when SPI was considering hiring it to play a single concert. Regardless of how many tickets SPI sold, the total band cost was $48,000. However, the band cost becomes variable if SPI decides to hire it to perform at a series of concerts. The total cost and the cost per concert for one, two, three, four, or five concerts are shown in Exhibit 2–21.

Exhibit 2–21 *Cost Behavior Relative to Number of Concerts*

Number of concerts (a)	1	2	3	4	5
Cost per concert (b)	$48,000	$48,000	$ 48,000	$ 48,000	$ 48,000
Total cost (a × b)	$48,000	$96,000	$144,000	$192,000	$240,000

In this context, the total cost of hiring the band increases proportionately with the number of concerts while cost per concert remains constant. The band cost is therefore variable. The same cost can behave as either a fixed cost or a variable cost, depending on the **activity base.** When identifying a cost as fixed or variable, first ask, fixed or variable *relative to what activity base?* The cost of the band is fixed relative to *the number of tickets sold for a specific concert;* it is variable relative to *the number of concerts produced.*

Check Yourself 2–4

Is the compensation cost for managers of Pizza Hut Restaurants a fixed cost or a variable cost?

Answer The answer depends on the context. For example, since a store manager's salary remains unchanged regardless of how many customers enter a particular restaurant, it can be classified as a fixed cost relative to the number of customers at a particular restaurant. However, the more restaurants that Pizza Hut operates, the higher the total managers' compensation cost will be. Accordingly, managers' salary cost would be classified as a variable cost relative to the number of restaurants opened.

REALITY *bytes*

Stella is a business student who works part time at **Costco Wholesale, Inc.** to help pay for her college expenses. She is currently taking a managerial accounting course, and has heard her instructor refer to depreciation as a fixed cost. However, as a requirement for her first accounting course, Stella reviewed Costco's financial statements for 2000, 2001, and 2002. The depreciation expense increased about 34 percent over these three years. She is not sure why depreciation expense would be considered a fixed cost.

Stella's accounting instructor reminded her that when an accountant says a cost is fixed, he or she means the cost is fixed in relation to one particular factor. A cost that is fixed in relation to one factor can be variable when compared to some other factor. For example, the depreciation for a retailer may be fixed relative to the number of customers who visit a particular store, but variable relative to the number of stores the company opens. In fact, Costco's depreciation increased from 2000 to 2002 mainly because the company built and opened additional stores.

Stella's instructor suggested that Costco's depreciation expense would be more stable if analyzed on a per store basis, rather than in total. Being curious, Stella prepared the following table, where costs are in thousands. Over the three years, she noted that total depreciation expense increased 34.3 percent, while depreciation per store increased only 12.4 percent. Although the costs on a per store basis were more stable than the total depreciation costs, they still were not fixed, so she asked her instructor for further explanation.

Fiscal year	Total Depreciation Expense	Average Depreciation Expense per Store
2000	$254,397	$812.8
2001	301,297	873.3
2002	341,781	913.9

The instructor suggested Costco's average per store depreciation costs were increasing because the equipment and buildings purchased for the new stores (opened from 2000 to 2002) probably cost more than those purchased for the older stores. This would raise the average depreciation expense per store. The instructor also reminded her that in the real world very few costs are perfectly fixed or perfectly variable.

Cost Averaging

LO8 Select an appropriate time period for calculating the average cost per unit.

Lake Resorts, Inc. (LRI), offers water skiing lessons for guests. Since the demand for lessons is seasonal (guests buy more lessons in July than in December), LRI has chosen to rent (rather than own) the necessary equipment (boat, skis, ropes, life jackets) only when it is needed. LRI's accountant has collected the following data pertaining to providing ski lessons:

1. The daily fee to rent equipment is $80.
2. Instructors are paid $15 per lesson hour.
3. Fuel costs are $2 per lesson hour.
4. Lessons take one hour each.
5. LRI can provide up to ten lessons in one day.

Management wants to know the cost per lesson if 2, 5, or 10 lessons are provided per day. The cost is computed in Exhibit 2–22.

Exhibit 2–22 *Analysis of Total and Unit Cost*

Number of Lessons (a)	2	5	10
Cost of equipment rental	$ 80	$ 80	$ 80
Cost of instruction (a × $15)	30	75	150
Cost of fuel (a × $2)	4	10	20
Total cost (b)	$114	$165	$250
Cost per lesson (b ÷ a)	$ 57	$ 33	$ 25

The cost per lesson in Exhibit 2–22 is an *average* cost. Accountants focus on average costs because they are relatively easy to compute and are frequently more relevant to decision making than are actual costs. Imagine the difficulties of trying to determine the actual cost of each individual lesson. Because the equipment rental cost covers any number of lessons within the relevant range, it cannot be identified as an actual cost of any particular lesson. Towing heavier skiers behind the boat uses more gas than towing lighter ones. Wind conditions, water currents, the number of times a skier falls, and the presence of other boats affect cost factors such as fuel consumption and the actual time required to conduct a lesson. Determining the exact cost for each lesson is impossible.

Even if LRI could compute the actual cost per lesson, the information would be of little value. Of what use is knowing that on a given day the fifth lesson cost a little more or less to provide than the sixth? Customers expect standardized pricing. They do not want pricing that depends on which way the wind is blowing, even if the wind affects the actual cost of a ski lesson. Also, customers prefer price data in advance to help them decide whether to take a lesson. They do not want to wait until after the lesson for someone to determine the exact cost. Average cost data may be more useful than actual cost information for pricing decisions.

Average cost data can help managers evaluate employee performance and control costs. Knowing an instructor spent a few minutes more or less on a particular lesson is of little use. Knowing, however, that an instructor averages 10 extra minutes per lesson signals the need for correction action. Knowing what happens *on average* is more useful than knowing what happened in a particular instance.

Computing the average cost per unit requires choosing the time span over which to average costs. Suppose the following: On a single day in 2007 an instructor conducted 10 lessons for a total cost of $250. During the 2006 season, LRI provided a total of 589 lessons for a cost of $19,437. During the last five seasons, LRI provided 2,500 lessons for a total cost of $55,000. Exhibit 2–23 shows the average cost per lesson for the day, the year, and the five-year period.

If management decides to price individual ski lessons at average cost plus $5, should the price be $30 ($25 + $5), $38 ($33 + $5) or $27 ($22 + $5)?[1] The shortest time interval (one day) represents the most current information, but it may also be the least relevant. Suppose the one-day average reflects costs on a Sunday when demand for ski lessons was extremely high. The fixed cost of equipment rental is spread over a large number of lessons, resulting in a low cost per lesson. However, the Sunday average has little relevance to setting Monday's prices when customer demand drops sharply as many weekend vacationers return to work.

Distortions can also result from using time spans that are too long. For example, averaging costs over the previous five seasons may not reflect current costs or recent changes in customer demand. Equipment rental cost was probably less five years ago than it is today.

In this case a one-year average is probably most appropriate. If last year's season is a good predictor of this year's demand, pricing lessons at $38 provides a return that approximates management's $5 per lesson target profit. On days when demand is high, cost per unit will be low, and LRI will earn more than $5 per lesson. On days when demand is low, it will earn less than $5. However, on average, it will earn the desired return. Selecting the most appropriate

Exhibit 2–23 *Cost per Lesson*

	Span of Time		
	One Day	**One Year**	**Five Years**
Total cost of lessons (a)	$250	$19,437	$55,000
Number of lessons (b)	10	589	2,500
Cost per lesson (a ÷ b)	$ 25	$ 33	$ 22

[1] The cost plus method is only one of several possible pricing strategies. Other pricing practices are discussed in subsequent chapters.

time span requires considerable accounting judgment. *A professional management accountant provides much more than number crunching.*

Use of Estimates in Real-World Problems

LO9 Define the term *mixed costs.*

Imagine trying to classify as fixed or variable all the different costs incurred by a large company such as Delta Airlines. Record keeping would be horrendous. Further complications would arise because some costs have both fixed and variable components. Consider the cost Delta incurs to use airport facilities. An airport may charge Delta a flat annual rental fee for terminal space plus a charge each time a plane takes off or lands. The flat rental fee is a fixed cost while the charge per flight is variable. The total facilities cost is mixed. Such costs are called **mixed costs** or **semivariable costs.**

To minimize the record keeping difficulties involved in identifying actual fixed and variable costs, many companies make decisions using estimated rather than actual costs. Several techniques exist to divide total cost into estimated fixed and variable components.

High-Low Method of Estimating Fixed and Variable Costs

LO10 Use the high-low method and scattergraphs to estimate fixed and variable costs.

The management of Rainy Day Books (RDB) wants to expand operations. To help evaluate risks involved in opening an additional store, the company president wants to know the amount of fixed cost a new store will likely incur. Suppose RDB's accountant decides to use the **high-low method** to supply the president with the requested information. The estimated amount of fixed cost for the new store would be developed in the following four steps.

Step 1 ***Assemble sales volume and cost history for an existing store.*** Assuming the new store would operate with roughly the same cost structure, the accountant can use the historical data to estimate the fixed cost likely to be incurred by the new store. To illustrate, assume the accounting data set for the existing store is displayed in Exhibit 2–24.

Exhibit 2–24 *Cost Data*

Month	Units Sold	Total Cost
January	30,000	$450,000
February	14,000	300,000
March	12,000	150,000
April	25,000	440,000
May	10,000	180,000
June	11,000	240,000
July	20,000	350,000
August	18,000	400,000
September	17,000	360,000
October	16,000	320,000
November	27,000	490,000
December	34,000	540,000

Step 2 ***Select the high and low points in the data set.*** In this example, the month with the lowest number of units sold does not correspond to the month with the lowest total cost. The lowest point in units sold occurred in May; the lowest total cost occurred in March. Because the total cost depends on the *number of units sold,* May should be classified as the low point. The high point in sales volume occurred in December. The units sold and cost data for the December and May high and low points follow:

	Units Sold	Total Cost
High (December)	34,000	$540,000
Low (May)	10,000	$180,000

Step 3 ***Determine the estimated variable cost per unit.*** The variable cost per unit is determined by dividing the difference in the total cost by the difference in the number of units sold. In this case, the variable cost per unit is as follows:

$$\text{Variable cost per unit} = \frac{\text{Difference in total cost}}{\text{Difference in volume}} = \frac{(\$540{,}000 - \$180{,}000)}{(34{,}000 - 10{,}000)} = \frac{\$360{,}000}{24{,}000} = \$15$$

Step 4 ***Determine the estimated total fixed costs.*** The total fixed cost can now be determined by subtracting the variable cost from the total cost using either the high point or the low point. Either point yields the same result. Computations using the high point follow:

$$\text{Fixed Cost} + \text{Variable Cost} = \text{Total Cost}$$
$$\text{Fixed Cost} = \text{Total Cost} - \text{Variable Cost}$$
$$\text{Fixed Cost} = \$540{,}000 - (\$15 \times 34{,}000 \text{ units})$$
$$\text{Fixed Cost} = \$30{,}000$$

Although 12 data points are available, the high-low method uses only 2 of them to estimate the amounts of fixed and variable costs. If either or both of these points is not representative of the true relationship between fixed and variable costs, the estimates produced by the high-low method will be inaccurate. *The chief advantage of the high-low method is its simplicity; the chief disadvantage is its vulnerability to inaccuracy.* RDB's accountant decides to test the accuracy of the high-low method results.

Scattergraph Method of Estimating Fixed and Variable Costs

LO10 Use the high-low method and scattergraphs to estimate fixed and variable costs.

Scattergraphs are sometimes used as an estimation technique for dividing total cost into fixed and variable cost components. To assess the accuracy of the high-low estimate of fixed cost, RDB's accountant constructs a **scattergraph.** The horizontal axis is labeled with the number of books sold and the vertical axis with total costs. The 12 data points are plotted on the graph, and a line is drawn through the high and low points in the data set. The result is shown in Exhibit 2–25.

After studying the scattergraph in Exhibit 2–25, the accountant is certain that the high and low points are not representative of the data set. Most of the data points are above the high-low line. As shown in the second scattergraph in Exhibit 2–26, the line should be shifted upward to reflect the influence of the other data points.

The graph in Exhibit 2–26 is identical to the graph in Exhibit 2–25 except the straight line is plotted through the center of the entire data set rather than just the high and low points. The new line, a **visual fit line,** is drawn to visually minimize the total distance between the data points and the line. Usually, half of the data points are above and half below a visual fit line.

Exhibit 2–25 *Scattergraph Depicting High-Low Estimate*

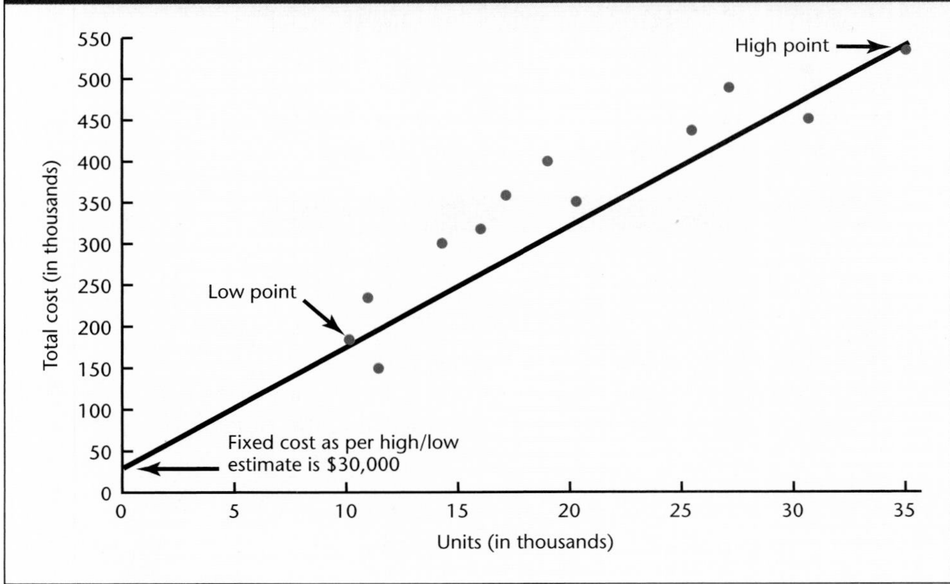

Exhibit 2–26 *Scattergraph Depicting Line Drawn by Visual Inspection*

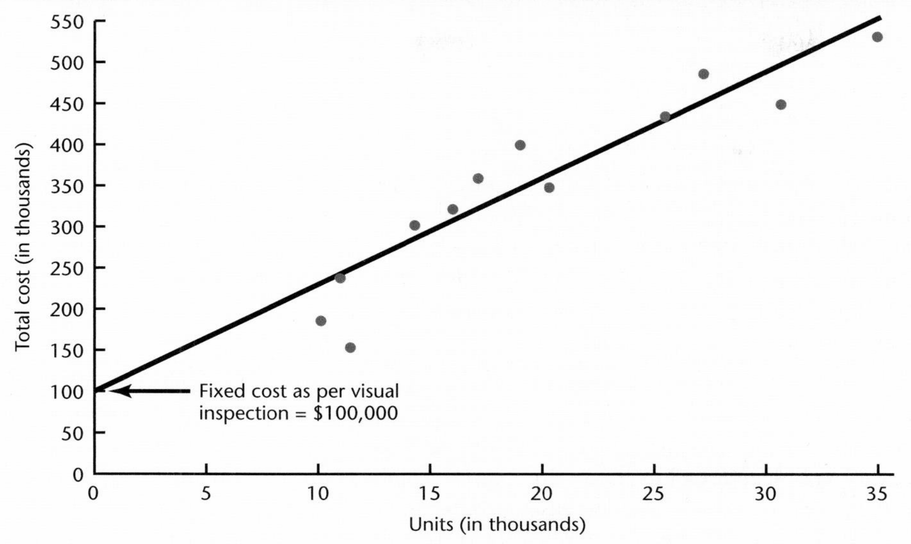

The estimated variable cost per unit is measured by the slope (steepness) of the visual fit line. The fixed cost is the point (the *intercept*) where the visual fit line intersects the vertical axis (the total cost line).

The intercept in Exhibit 2–26 provides a fixed cost estimate of $100,000. Although RDB's president had only asked for the amount of fixed cost, the variable cost can be easily determined

focus on INTERNATIONAL ISSUES

Another Reason Fixed Costs Aren't Always Fixed

Suppose that a company is renting a facility at an annual rental rate that does not change for the next five years *no matter what.* Is this a fixed cost? By now, you are aware that the proper response is to ask fixed in relation to what? Is the rental cost of this facility fixed in relation to the activity at this facility? The answer seems to be yes, but it might be "not necessarily."

Consider the **Exxon Mobil Corporation**. If Exxon Mobil rents facilities in a country in the eastern hemisphere, Malaysia for example, the annual rental fee may be stated and paid in the local currency. In Malaysia, this is the ringgit. Even though Exxon Mobil may be paying the same number of ringgit in rent each year, Exxon Mobil's rental cost in U.S. dollars could vary greatly over time. Such potential foreign currency exchange fluctuations cause companies to enter very complex hedging arrangements to add stability to transactions that must be paid in foreign currencies.

Exxon Mobil was founded and has its headquarters in the United States. It does much business in the United States. Furthermore, it is listed on the New York Stock Exchange and prepares its financial statements in U.S. dollars. However, it does much more business and has many more assets in countries outside the United States. Consider the following table from Exxon Mobil's 2002 financial statements. Before a multinational company can determine whether a cost is fixed, it must determine the applicable currency.

Geographical Area	Earnings*	Percentage of Total	Long-Term Assets*	Percentage of Total
United States	$2,131	28%	$34,138	36%
Non-United States	5,444	72	60,802	64
Totals	$7,575	100%	$94,940	100%

*Amounts in millions.

by subtracting the fixed cost from the total cost at any point along the visual fit line. For example, at 15,000 units, total cost is $300,000. Variable cost is determined as follows:

$$\text{Fixed Cost} + \text{Variable Cost} = \text{Total Cost}$$
$$\text{Variable Cost} = \text{Total Cost} - \text{Fixed Cost}$$
$$\text{Variable Cost} = \$300{,}000 - \$100{,}000$$
$$\text{Variable Cost} = \$200{,}000$$

Variable cost per unit is $13.33, calculated by dividing the total variable cost by the number of units ($200,000 ÷ 15,000 units = $13.33 per unit).

Statistical tools like least-squares regression can improve the accuracy of fitting a line through the data points. While such tools are beyond the scope of this text, you may have the opportunity to study them in more advanced courses.

a look back

To plan and control business operations effectively, managers need to understand how different costs behave in relation to changes in the volume of activity. Total *fixed cost* remains constant when activity changes. Fixed cost per unit decreases with increases in activity and increases with decreases in activity. In contrast, total *variable cost* increases proportionately with increases in activity and decreases proportionately with decreases in activity. Variable cost per unit remains constant regardless of activity levels. The definitions of fixed and variable costs have meaning only within the context of a specified range of activity (the relevant range) for a defined period of time. In addition, cost behavior depends on the relevant volume measure (a store manager's salary is fixed relative to the number of customers visiting a particular store but is variable relative to the number of stores operated). A mixed cost has both fixed and variable cost components.

Fixed costs allow companies to take advantage of *operating leverage.* With operating leverage, each additional sale decreases the cost per unit. This principle allows a small percentage change in volume of revenue to cause a significantly larger percentage change in profits. The *magnitude of operating leverage* can be determined by dividing the contribution margin by net income. When all costs are fixed and revenues have covered fixed costs, each additional dollar of revenue represents pure profit. Having a fixed cost structure (employing operating leverage) offers a company both risks and rewards. If sales volume increases, costs do not increase, allowing profits to soar. Alternatively, if sales volume decreases, costs do not decrease and profits decline significantly more than revenues. Companies with high variable costs in relation to fixed costs do not experience as great a level of operating leverage. Their costs increase or decrease in proportion to changes in revenue. These companies face less risk but fail to reap disproportionately higher profits when volume soars.

Under the contribution margin approach, variable costs are subtracted from revenue to determine the *contribution margin.* Fixed costs are then subtracted from the contribution margin to determine net income. The contribution margin represents the amount available to pay fixed costs and provide a profit. Although not permitted by GAAP for external reporting, many companies use the contribution margin format for internal reporting purposes.

Cost per unit is an average cost that is easier to compute than the actual cost of each unit and is more relevant to decision making than actual cost. Accountants must use judgment when choosing the time span from which to draw data for computing the average cost per unit. Distortions can result from using either too long or too short a time span.

Fixed and variable costs can be estimated using such tools as the *high-low method* and *scattergraphs.* Both are easy to use and can be reasonably accurate.

a look forward

The next chapter will show you how changes in cost, volume, and pricing affect profitability. You will learn to determine the number of units of product that must be produced and sold in order to break even (the number of units that will produce an amount of revenue that is exactly equal to total cost). You will learn to establish the price of a product using a cost-plus pricing approach and to establish the cost of a product using a target-pricing approach. Finally, the chapter will show you how to use a break-even chart to examine potential profitability over a range of operating activity and how to use a technique known as *sensitivity analysis* to examine how simultaneous changes in sales price, volume, fixed costs, and variable costs affect profitability.

SELF-STUDY REVIEW PROBLEM

Mensa Mountaineering Company (MMC) provides guided mountain climbing expeditions in the Rocky Mountains. Its only major expense is guide salaries; it pays each guide $4,800 per climbing expedition. MMC charges its customers $1,500 per expedition and expects to take five climbers on each expedition.

Part 1

Base your answers on the preceding information.

Required

a. Determine the total cost of guide salaries and the cost of guide salaries per climber assuming that four, five, or six climbers are included in a trip. Relative to the number of climbers in a single expedition, is the cost of guides a fixed or a variable cost?

b. Relative to the number of expeditions, is the cost of guides a fixed or a variable cost?

c. Determine the profit of an expedition assuming that five climbers are included in the trip.

d. Determine the profit assuming a 20 percent increase (six climbers total) in expedition revenue. What is the percentage change in profitability?

e. Determine the profit assuming a 20 percent decrease (four climbers total) in expedition revenue. What is the percentage change in profitability?

f. Explain why a 20 percent shift in revenue produces more than a 20 percent shift in profitability. What term describes this phenomenon?

Part 2

Assume that the guides offer to make the climbs for a percentage of expedition fees. Specifically, MMC will pay guides $960 per climber on the expedition. Assume also that the expedition fee charged to climbers remains at $1,500 per climber.

Required

g. Determine the total cost of guide salaries and the cost of guide salaries per climber assuming that four, five, or six climbers are included in a trip. Relative to the number of climbers in a single expedition, is the cost of guides a fixed or a variable cost?

h. Relative to the number of expeditions, is the cost of guides a fixed or a variable cost?

i. Determine the profit of an expedition assuming that five climbers are included in the trip.

j. Determine the profit assuming a 20 percent increase (six climbers total) in expedition revenue. What is the percentage change in profitability?

k. Determine the profit assuming a 20 percent decrease (four climbers total) in expedition revenue. What is the percentage change in profitability?

l. Explain why a 20 percent shift in revenue does not produce more than a 20 percent shift in profitability.

Solution to Part 1, Requirement a

Number of climbers (a)	4	5	6
Total cost of guide salaries (b)	$4,800	$4,800	$4,800
Cost per climber (b ÷ a)	1,200	960	800

Since the total cost remains constant (fixed) regardless of the number of climbers on a particular expedition, the cost is classified as fixed. Note that the cost per climber decreases as the number of climbers increases. This is the *per unit* behavior pattern of a fixed cost.

Solution to Part 1, Requirement b

Since the total cost of guide salaries changes proportionately each time the number of expeditions increases or decreases, the cost of salaries is variable relative to the number of expeditions.

Solution to Part 1, Requirements c, d, and e

Number of Climbers	4	Percentage Change	5	Percentage Change	6
Revenue ($1,500 per climber)	$6,000	⇐ (20%) ⇐	$7,500	⇒ +20% ⇒	$9,000
Cost of guide salaries (fixed)	4,800		4,800		4,800
Profit	$1,200	⇐ (55.6%) ⇐	$2,700	⇒+55.6% ⇒	$4,200

Percentage change in revenue: ±$1,500 ÷ $7,500 = ±20%
Percentage change in profit: ±$1,500 ÷ $2,700 = ±55.6%

Solution to Part 1, Requirement f
Since the cost of guide salaries remains fixed while volume (number of climbers) changes, the change in net income, measured in absolute dollars, exactly matches the change in revenue. More specifically, each time MMC increases the number of climbers by one, revenue and net income increase by $1,500. Since the base figure for net income ($2,700) is lower than the base figure for revenue ($7,500), the percentage change in net income ($1,500 ÷ $2,700 = 55.6%) is higher than percentage change in revenue ($1,500 ÷ $7,500). This phenomenon is called *operating leverage.*

Solution for Part 2, Requirement g

Number of climbers (a)	4	5	6
Per climber cost of guide salaries (b)	$ 960	$ 960	$ 960
Cost per climber (b × a)	3,840	4,800	5,760

Since the total cost changes in proportion to changes in the number of climbers, the cost is classified as variable. Note that the cost per climber remains constant (stays the same) as the number of climbers increases or decreases. This is the *per unit* behavior pattern of a variable cost.

Solution for Part 2, Requirement h
Since the total cost of guide salaries changes proportionately with changes in the number of expeditions, the cost of salaries is also variable relative to the number of expeditions.

Solution for Part 2, Requirements i, j, and k

Number of Climbers	4	Percentage Change	5	Percentage Change	6
Revenue ($1,500 per climber)	$6,000	⇐ (20%) ⇐	$7,500	⇒ +20% ⇒	$9,000
Cost of guide salaries (variable)	3,840		4,800		5,760
Profit	$2,160	⇐ (20%) ⇐	$2,700	⇒ +20% ⇒	$3,240

Percentage change in revenue: ±$1,500 ÷ $7,500 = ±20%
Percentage change in profit: ±$540 ÷ $2,700 = ±20%

Solution for Part 2, Requirement l
Since the cost of guide salaries changes when volume (number of climbers) changes, the change in net income is proportionate to the change in revenue. More specifically, each time the number of climbers increases by one, revenue increases by $1,500 and net income increases by $540 ($1,500 − $960). Accordingly, the percentage change in net income will always equal the percentage change in revenue. This means that there is no operating leverage when all costs are variable.

KEY TERMS

Activity base *58*
Contribution margin *55*
Cost averaging *59*
Cost behavior *57*
Cost structure *53*
Fixed cost *50*
High-low method *61*
Mixed costs (semivariable costs) *61*
Operating leverage *50*
Relevant range *58*
Scattergraph *62*
Variable cost *49*
Visual fit line *62*

QUESTIONS

1. Define *fixed cost* and *variable cost* and give an example of each.
2. How can knowing cost behavior relative to volume fluctuations affect decision making?
3. Define the term *operating leverage* and explain how it affects profits.
4. How is operating leverage calculated?
5. Explain the limitations of using operating leverage to predict profitability.
6. If volume is increasing, would a company benefit more from a pure variable or a pure fixed cost structure? Which cost structure would be advantageous if volume is decreasing?
7. When are economies of scale possible? In what types of businesses would you most likely find economies of scale?
8. Explain the risk and rewards to a company that result from having fixed costs.
9. Are companies with predominately fixed cost structures likely to be most profitable?
10. How is the relevant range of activity related to fixed and variable cost? Give an example of how the definitions of these costs become invalid when volume is outside the relevant range.
11. Sam's Garage is trying to determine the cost of providing an oil change. Why would the average cost of this service be more relevant information than the actual cost for each customer?
12. When would the high-low method be appropriate for estimating variable and fixed costs? When would least-squares regression be the most desirable?
13. Which cost structure has the greater risk? Explain.
14. The president of Bright Corporation tells you that he sees a dim future for his company. He feels that his hands are tied because fixed costs are too high. He says that fixed costs do not change and therefore the situation is hopeless. Do you agree? Explain.
15. All costs are variable because if a business ceases operations, its costs fall to zero. Do you agree with the statement? Explain.
16. Because of seasonal fluctuations, Norel Corporation has a problem determining the unit cost of the products it produces. For example, high heating costs during the winter months causes per unit cost to be higher than per unit cost in the summer months even when the same number of units of product is produced. Suggest several ways that Norel can improve the computation of per unit costs.
17. Verna Salsbury tells you that she thinks the terms fixed cost and variable cost are confusing. She notes that fixed cost per unit changes when the number of units changes. Furthermore, variable cost per unit remains fixed regardless of how many units are produced. She concludes that the terminology seems to be backward. Explain why the terminology appears to be contradictory.

EXERCISES—SERIES A

All Exercises in Series A are available with McGraw-Hill's Homework Manager

EXERCISE 2–1A *Identifying Cost Behavior*

L.O. 1

Hoover's Kitchen, a fast-food restaurant company, operates a chain of restaurants across the nation. Each restaurant employs eight people; one is a manager paid a salary plus a bonus equal to 3 percent of sales. Other employees, two cooks, one dishwasher, and four waitresses, are paid salaries. Each manager is budgeted $3,000 per month for advertising cost.

Required

Classify each of the following costs incurred by Hoover's Kitchen as fixed, variable, or mixed.

a. Manager's compensation relative to the number of customers.
b. Waitresses' salaries relative to the number of restaurants.
c. Advertising costs relative to the number of customers for a particular restaurant.
d. Rental costs relative to the number of restaurants.
e. Cooks' salaries at a particular location relative to the number of customers.
f. Cost of supplies (cups, plates, spoons, etc.) relative to the number of customers.

L.O. 1

EXERCISE 2–2A *Identifying Cost Behavior*

At the various activity levels shown, Taylor Company incurred the following costs.

	Units sold	20	40	60	80	100
a.	Total salary cost	$1,200.00	$1,600.00	$2,000.00	$2,400.00	$2,800.00
b.	Total cost of goods sold	1,800.00	3,600.00	5,400.00	7,200.00	9,000.00
c.	Depreciation cost per unit	240.00	120.00	80.00	60.00	48.00
d.	Total rent cost	3,200.00	3,200.00	3,200.00	3,200.00	3,200.00
e.	Total cost of shopping bags	2.00	4.00	6.00	8.00	10.00
f.	Cost per unit of merchandise sold	90.00	90.00	90.00	90.00	90.00
g.	Rental cost per unit of merchandise sold	36.00	18.00	12.00	9.00	7.20
h.	Total phone expense	80.00	100.00	120.00	140.00	160.00
i.	Cost per unit of supplies	1.00	1.00	1.00	1.00	1.00
j.	Total insurance cost	480.00	480.00	480.00	480.00	480.00

Required
Identify each of these costs as fixed, variable, or mixed.

L.O. 1

EXERCISE 2–3A *Determining Fixed Cost per Unit*

Simon Corporation incurs the following annual fixed costs:

Item	Cost
Depreciation	$ 30,000
Officers' salaries	100,000
Long-term lease	40,000
Property taxes	10,000

Required
Determine the total fixed cost per unit of production, assuming that Simon produces 4,000, 4,500, or 5,000 units.

L.O. 1

EXERCISE 2–4A *Determining Total Variable Cost*

The following variable production costs apply to goods made by Keller Manufacturing Corporation.

Item	Cost per Unit
Materials	$5.00
Labor	2.80
Variable overhead	0.40
Total	$8.20

Required
Determine the total variable production cost, assuming that Keller makes 10,000, 15,000, or 20,000 units.

EXERCISE 2–5A *Fixed Versus Variable Cost Behavior*

L.O. 1

Whaley Company's cost and production data for two recent months included the following:

	January	February
Production (units)	100	200
Rent	$2,000	$2,000
Utilities	$ 500	$1,000

Required

a. Separately calculate the rental cost per unit and the utilities cost per unit for both January and February.

b. Based on both total and per unit amounts, identify which cost is variable and which is fixed. Explain your answer.

EXERCISE 2–6A *Fixed Versus Variable Cost Behavior*

L.O. 1

Hernadez Trophies makes and sells trophies it distributes to little league ballplayers. The company normally produces and sells between 10,000 and 13,000 trophies per year. The following cost data apply to various activity levels.

Number of trophies	10,000	11,000	12,000	13,000
Total costs incurred				
Fixed	$ 60,000			
Variable	50,000			
Total costs	$110,000			
Cost per unit				
Fixed	$ 6.00			
Variable	5.00			
Total cost per trophy	$11.00			

Required

a. Complete the preceding table by filling in the missing amounts for the levels of activity shown in the first row of the table. Round all cost per unit figures to the nearest whole penny.

b. Explain why the total cost per trophy decreases as the number of trophies increases.

EXERCISE 2–7A *Fixed Versus Variable Cost Behavior*

L.O. 1

Barlow Entertainment sponsors rock concerts. The company is considering a contract to hire a band at a cost of $50,000 per concert.

Required

a. What are the total band cost and the cost per person if concert attendance is 2,000, 2,500, 3,000, 3,500, or 4,000?

b. Is the cost of hiring the band a fixed or a variable cost?

c. Draw a graph and plot total cost and cost per unit if attendance is 2,000, 2,500, 3,000, 3,500, or 4,000.

d. Identify Barlow's major business risks and explain how they can be minimized.

EXERCISE 2–8A *Fixed Versus Variable Cost Behavior*

L.O. 1

Barlow Entertainment sells souvenir T-shirts at each rock concert that it sponsors. The shirts cost $8 each. Any excess shirts can be returned to the manufacturer for a full refund of the purchase price. The sales price is $12 per shirt.

Required

a. What are the total cost of shirts and cost per shirt if sales amount to 2,000, 2,500, 3,000, 3,500, or 4,000?

b. Is the cost of T-shirts a fixed or a variable cost?
c. Draw a graph and plot total cost and cost per shirt if sales amount to 2,000, 2,500, 3,000, 3,500, or 4,000.
d. Comment on Barlow's likelihood of incurring a loss due to its operating activities.

L.O. 1

EXERCISE 2–9A *Graphing Fixed Cost Behavior*

The following graphs depict the dollar amount of fixed cost on the vertical axes and the level of activity on the horizontal axes.

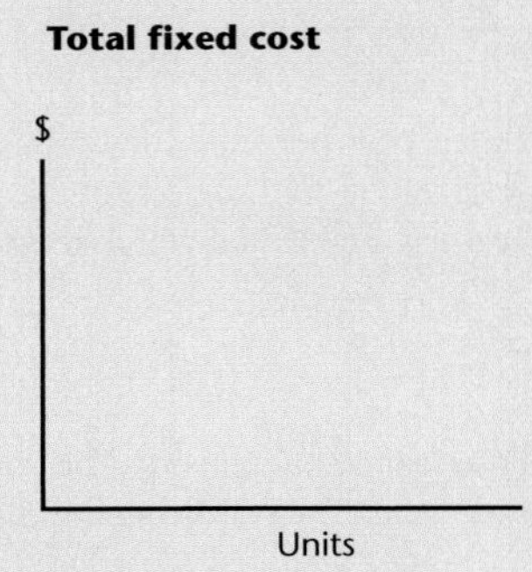

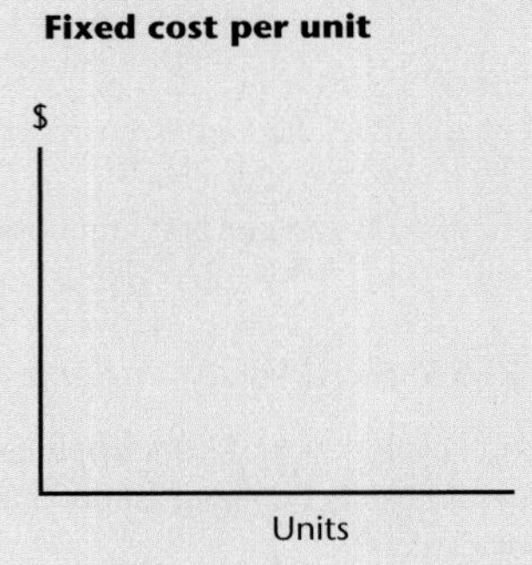

Required
a. Draw a line that depicts the relationship between total fixed cost and the level of activity.
b. Draw a line that depicts the relationship between fixed cost per unit and the level of activity.

L.O. 1

EXERCISE 2–10A *Graphing Variable Cost Behavior*

The following graphs depict the dollar amount of variable cost on the vertical axes and the level of activity on the horizontal axes.

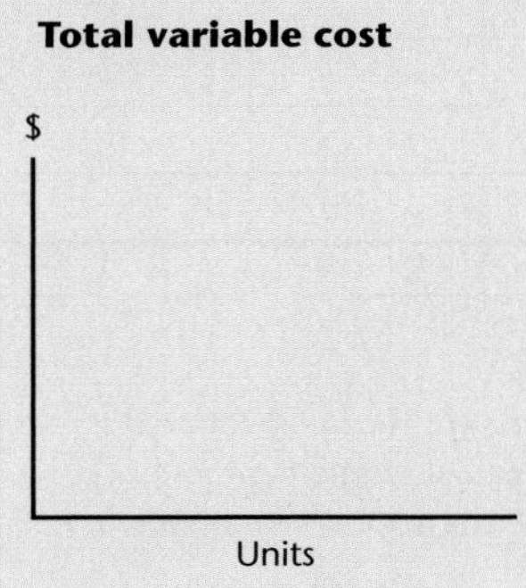

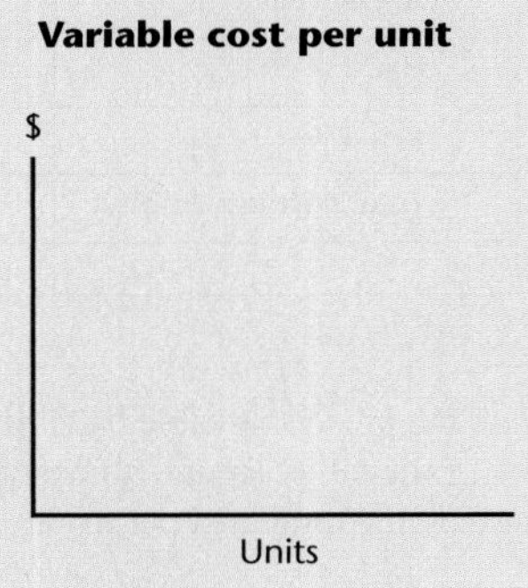

Required
a. Draw a line that depicts the relationship between total variable cost and the level of activity.
b. Draw a line that depicts the relationship between variable cost per unit and the level of activity.

L.O. 1

EXERCISE 2–11A *Mixed Cost at Different Levels of Activity*

Damon Corporation paid one of its sales representatives $5,000 during the month of March. The rep is paid a base salary plus $15 per unit of product sold. During March, the rep sold 200 units.

Required
Calculate the total monthly cost of the sales representative's salary for each of the following months.

Month	April	May	June	July
Number of units sold	240	160	250	160
Total variable cost				
Total fixed cost				
Total salary cost				

EXERCISE 2–12A *Using Fixed Cost as a Competitive Business Strategy*

L.O. 1, 2, 3, 6

The following income statements illustrate different cost structures for two competing companies.

Income Statements	Company Name	
	Keef	Reef
Number of Customers (a)	80	80
Sales Revenue (a × $250)	$20,000	$20,000
Variable Cost (a × $200)	N/A	(16,000)
Variable Cost (a × $0)	0	N/A
Contribution Margin	20,000	4,000
Fixed Cost	(16,000)	0
Net Income	$ 4,000	$ 4,000

Required

a. Reconstruct Keef's income statement, assuming that it serves 160 customers when it lures 80 customers away from Reef by lowering the sales price to $150 per customer.

b. Reconstruct Reef's income statement, assuming that it serves 160 customers when it lures 80 customers away from Keef by lowering the sales price to $150 per customer.

c. Explain why the price-cutting strategy increased Keef Company's profits but caused a net loss for Reef Company.

EXERCISE 2–13A *Using Contribution Margin Format Income Statement to Measure the Magnitude of Operating Leverage*

L.O. 4, 5

The following income statement was drawn from the records of Mantooth Company, a merchandising firm.

MANTOOTH COMPANY Income Statement For the Year Ended December 31, 2006	
Sales Revenue (3,500 units × $120)	$420,000
Cost of Goods Sold (3,500 units × $64)	(224,000)
Gross Margin	196,000
Sales Commissions (10% of sales)	(42,000)
Administrative Salaries Expense	(60,000)
Advertising Expense	(20,000)
Depreciation Expense	(25,000)
Shipping and Handling Expenses (3,500 units × $4.00)	(14,000)
Net Income	$ 35,000

Required

a. Reconstruct the income statement using the contribution margin format.

b. Calculate the magnitude of operating leverage.

c. Use the measure of operating leverage to determine the amount of net income Mantooth will earn if sales increase by 10 percent.

L.O. 5 EXERCISE 2–14A *Assessing the Magnitude of Operating Leverage*

The following income statement applies to Lyons Company for the current year:

Income Statement	
Sales Revenue (400 units × $25)	$10,000
Variable Cost (400 units × $10)	(4,000)
Contribution Margin	6,000
Fixed Costs	(3,500)
Net Income	$ 2,500

Required

a. Use the contribution margin approach to calculate the magnitude of operating leverage.

b. Use the operating leverage measure computed in Requirement *a* to determine the amount of net income that Lyons Company will earn if it experiences a 20 percent increase in revenue. The sales price per unit is not affected.

c. Verify your answer to Requirement *b* by constructing an income statement based on a 20 percent increase in sales revenue. The sales price is not affected. Calculate the percentage change in net income for the two income statements.

L.O. 8 EXERCISE 2–15A *Averaging Costs*

Mallory Camps, Inc., leases the land on which it builds camp sites. Mallory is considering opening a new site on land that requires $2,500 of rental payment per month. The variable cost of providing service is expected to be $4 per camper. The following chart shows the number of campers Mallory expects for the first year of operation of the new site.

Jan.	Feb.	Mar.	Apr.	May	June	July	Aug.	Sept.	Oct.	Nov.	Dec.	Total
150	100	250	250	350	500	700	700	400	250	100	250	4,000

Required

Assuming that Mallory wants to earn $8 per camper, determine the price it should charge for a camp site in February and August.

L.O. 10 EXERCISE 2–16A *Estimating Fixed and Variable Costs Using the High-Low Method*

Petrosky Boat Company makes inexpensive aluminum fishing boats. Production is seasonal, with considerable activity occurring in the spring and summer. Sales and production tend to decline in the fall and winter months. During 2007, the high point in activity occurred in June when it produced 300 boats at a total cost of $175,000. The low point in production occurred in January when it produced 140 boats at a total cost of $111,000.

Required

Use the high-low method to estimate the amount of fixed cost incurred each month by Petrosky Boat Company.

PROBLEMS—SERIES A

All Problems in Series A are available with McGraw-Hill's Homework Manager

L.O. 1 PROBLEM 2–17A *Identifying Cost Behavior*

Required

Identify the following costs as fixed or variable.

Costs related to plane trips between San Diego, California, and Orlando, Florida, follow. Pilots are paid on a per trip basis.

a. Pilots' salaries relative to the number of trips flown.
b. Depreciation relative to the number of planes in service.
c. Cost of refreshments relative to the number of passengers.
d. Pilots' salaries relative to the number of passengers on a particular trip.
e. Cost of a maintenance check relative to the number of passengers on a particular trip.
f. Fuel costs relative to the number of trips.

National Union Bank operates several branch offices in grocery stores. Each branch employs a supervisor and two tellers.

g. Tellers' salaries relative to the number of tellers in a particular district.
h. Supplies cost relative to the number of transactions processed in a particular branch.
i. Tellers' salaries relative to the number of customers served at a particular branch.
j. Supervisors' salaries relative to the number of branches operated.
k. Supervisors' salaries relative to the number of customers served in a particular branch.
l. Facility rental costs relative to the size of customer deposits.

Costs related to operating a fast-food restaurant follow.

m. Depreciation of equipment relative to the number of restaurants.
n. Building rental cost relative to the number of customers served in a particular restaurant.
o. Manager's salary of a particular store relative to the number of employees.
p. Food cost relative to the number of customers.
q. Utility cost relative to the number of restaurants in operation.
r. Company president's salary relative to the number of restaurants in operation.
s. Land costs relative to the number of hamburgers sold at a particular restaurant.
t. Depreciation of equipment relative to the number of customers served at a particular restaurant.

PROBLEM 2–18A *Cost Behavior and Averaging*

L.O. 1

excel
www.mhhe.com/edmonds3e

CHECK FIGURES
c. Total supplies cost for cleaning 30 houses: $150
d. Total cost for 20 houses: $1,700

Jenny Tang has decided to start Tang Cleaning, a residential housecleaning service company. She is able to rent cleaning equipment at a cost of $600 per month. Labor costs are expected to be $50 per house cleaned and supplies are expected to cost $5 per house.

Required

a. Determine the total expected cost of equipment rental and the average expected cost of equipment rental per house cleaned, assuming that Tang Cleaning cleans 10, 20, or 30 houses during one month. Is the cost of equipment a fixed or a variable cost?
b. Determine the total expected cost of labor and the average expected cost of labor per house cleaned, assuming that Tang Cleaning cleans 10, 20, or 30 houses during one month. Is the cost of labor a fixed or a variable cost?
c. Determine the total expected cost of supplies and the average expected cost of supplies per house cleaned, assuming that Tang Cleaning cleans 10, 20, or 30 houses during one month. Is the cost of supplies a fixed or a variable cost?
d. Determine the total expected cost of cleaning houses, assuming that Tang Cleaning cleans 10, 20, or 30 houses during one month.
e. Determine the average expected cost per house, assuming that Tang Cleaning cleans 10, 20, or 30 houses during one month. Why does the cost per unit decrease as the number of houses increases?
f. If Ms. Tang tells you that she prices her services at 25 percent above cost, would you assume that she means average or actual cost? Why?

PROBLEM 2–19A *Context-Sensitive Nature of Cost Behavior Classifications*

L.O. 1

CHECK FIGURE
b. Average teller cost for 60,000 transactions: $1.33

Citizens Bank's start-up division establishes new branch banks. Each branch opens with three tellers. Total teller cost per branch is $80,000 per year. The three tellers combined can process up to 80,000 customer transactions per year. If a branch does not attain a volume of at least 50,000 transactions during its first year of operations, it is closed. If the demand for services exceeds 80,000 transactions, an additional teller is hired, and the branch is transferred from the start-up division to regular operations.
b. Average cost at 80K transactions: $1.00

Required

a. What is the relevant range of activity for new branch banks?
b. Determine the amount of teller cost in total and the average teller cost per transaction for a branch that processes 50,000, 60,000, 70,000, or 80,000 transactions. In this case (the activity base is the number of transactions for a specific branch), is the teller cost a fixed or a variable cost?

c. Determine the amount of teller cost in total and the average teller cost per branch for Citizens Bank, assuming that the start-up division operates 10, 15, 20, or 25 branches. In this case (the activity base is the number of branches), is the teller cost a fixed or a variable cost?

L.O. 1

excel

www.mhhe.com/edmonds3e

CHECK FIGURES

a. Average cost at 300 units: $225

b. Average price at 150 units: $310

PROBLEM 2–20A *Context-Sensitive Nature of Cost Behavior Classifications*

Adriane Dawkins operates a sales booth in computer software trade shows, selling an accounting software package, *Accountech.* She purchases the package from a software manufacturer for $200 each. Booth space at the convention hall costs $7,500 per show.

Required

a. Sales at past trade shows have ranged between 100 and 300 software packages per show. Determine the average cost of sales per unit if Ms. Dawkins sells 100, 150, 200, 250, or 300 units of *Accountech* at a trade show. Use the following chart to organize your answer. Is the cost of booth space fixed or variable?

	Sales Volume in Units (a)				
	100	150	200	250	300
Total cost of software (a × $200)	$20,000				
Total cost of booth rental	7,500				
Total cost of sales (b)	$27,500				
Average cost per unit (b ÷ a)	$275.00				

b. If Ms. Dawkins wants to earn a $60 profit on each package of software she sells at a trade show, what price must she charge at sales volumes of 100, 150, 200, 250, or 300 units?

c. Record the total cost of booth space if Ms. Dawkins attends one, two, three, four, or five trade shows. Record your answers in the following chart. Is the cost of booth space fixed or variable relative to the number of shows attended?

	Number of Trade Shows Attended				
	1	2	3	4	5
Total cost of booth rental	$7,500				

d. Ms. Dawkins provides decorative shopping bags to customers who purchase software packages. Some customers take the bags; others do not. Some customers stuff more than one software package into a single bag. The number of bags varies in relation to the number of units sold, but the relationship is not proportional. Assume that Ms. Dawkins uses $40 of bags for every 50 software packages sold. What is the additional cost per unit sold? Is the cost fixed or variable?

L.O. 2

CHECK FIGURES

Part 1, b: $3,200

Part 2, c: 10%

Part 3, a: cost per student for 22 students: $20

PROBLEM 2–21A *Effects of Operating Leverage on Profitability*

Smartt Training Services (STS) provides instruction on the use of computer software for the employees of its corporate clients. It offers courses in the clients' offices on the clients' equipment. The only major expense STS incurs is instructor salaries; it pays instructors $4,000 per course taught. STS recently agreed to offer a course of instruction to the employees of Cartee Incorporated at a price of $360 per student. Cartee estimated that 20 students would attend the course.

Base your answer on the preceding information.

Part 1:

Required

a. Relative to the number of students in a single course, is the cost of instruction a fixed or a variable cost?

b. Determine the profit, assuming that 20 students attend the course.

c. Determine the profit, assuming a 10 percent increase in enrollment (i.e., enrollment increases to 22 students). What is the percentage change in profitability?

d. Determine the profit, assuming a 10 percent decrease in enrollment (i.e., enrollment decreases to 18 students). What is the percentage change in profitability?
e. Explain why a 10 percent shift in enrollment produces more than a 10 percent shift in profitability. Use the term that identifies this phenomenon.

Part 2:
The instructor has offered to teach the course for a percentage of tuition fees. Specifically, she wants $200 per person attending the class. Assume that the tuition fee remains at $360 per student.

Required
a. Is the cost of instruction a fixed or a variable cost?
b. Determine the profit, assuming that 20 students take the course.
c. Determine the profit, assuming a 10 percent increase in enrollment (i.e., enrollment increases to 22 students). What is the percentage change in profitability?
d. Determine the profit, assuming a 10 percent decrease in enrollment (i.e., enrollment decreases to 18 students). What is the percentage change in profitability?
e. Explain why a 10 percent shift in enrollment produces a proportional 10 percent shift in profitability.

Part 3:
STS sells a workbook with printed material unique to each course to each student who attends the course. Any workbooks that are not sold must be destroyed. Prior to the first class, STS printed 20 copies of the books based on the client's estimate of the number of people who would attend the course. Each workbook costs $20 and is sold to course participants for $32. This cost includes a royalty fee paid to the author and the cost of duplication.

Required
a. Calculate the workbook cost in total and per student, assuming that 18, 20, or 22 students attempt to attend the course.
b. Classify the cost of workbooks as fixed or variable relative to the number of students attending the course.
c. Discuss the risk of holding inventory as it applies to the workbooks.
d. Explain how a just-in-time inventory system can reduce the cost and risk of holding inventory.

PROBLEM 2–22A *Effects of Fixed and Variable Cost Behavior on the Risk and Rewards of Business Opportunities*

L.O. 2, 3, 6

Autumn and Zogby Universities offer executive training courses to corporate clients. Autumn pays its instructors $6,000 per course taught. Zogby pays its instructors $300 per student enrolled in the class. Both universities charge executives a $360 tuition fee per course attended.

CHECK FIGURES
a. Zogby NI: $1,200
b. NI: $2,000

Required
a. Prepare income statements for Autumn and Zogby, assuming that 25 students attend a course.
b. Autumn University embarks on a strategy to entice students from Zogby University by lowering its tuition to $200 per course. Prepare an income statement for Autumn, assuming that the university is successful and enrolls 40 students in its course.
c. Zogby University embarks on a strategy to entice students from Autumn University by lowering its tuition to $200 per course. Prepare an income statement for Zogby, assuming that the university is successful and enrolls 40 students in its course.
d. Explain why the strategy described in Part *b* produced a profit but the same strategy described in Part *c* produced a loss.
e. Prepare income statements for Autumn and Zogby Universities, assuming that 15 students attend a course, assuming that both universities charge executives a $360 tuition fee per course attended.
f. It is always better to have fixed than variable cost. Explain why this statement is false.
g. It is always better to have variable than fixed cost. Explain why this statement is false.

PROBLEM 2–23A *Analyzing Operating Leverage*

L.O. 5

eXcel
www.mhhe.com/edmonds3e

Norm Champion is a venture capitalist facing two alternative investment opportunities. He intends to invest $500,000 in a start-up firm. He is nervous, however, about future economic volatility. He asks you to analyze the following financial data for the past year's operations of the two firms he is considering and give him some business advice.

	Company Name	
	Morton	Bailey
Variable Cost per Unit (a)	$18	$9
Sales Revenue (10,000 units × $24)	$240,000	$240,000
Variable Cost (10,000 units × a)	(180,000)	(90,000)
Contribution Margin	$60,000	$150,000
Fixed Cost	(30,000)	(120,000)
Net Income	$ 30,000	$ 30,000

CHECK FIGURES
b. % of change for Bailey: 50
c. % of change for Morton: (20)

Required

a. Use the contribution margin approach to compute the operating leverage for each firm.

b. If the economy expands in coming years, Morton and Bailey will both enjoy a 10 percent per year increase in sales, assuming that the selling price remains unchanged. Compute the change in net income for each firm in dollar amount and in percentage. (*Note:* Since the number of units increases, both revenue and variable cost will increase.)

c. If the economy contracts in coming years, Morton and Bailey will both suffer a 10 percent decrease in sales volume, assuming that the selling price remains unchanged. Compute the change in net income for each firm in dollar amount and in percentage. (*Note:* Since the number of units decreases, both total revenue and total variable cost will decrease.)

d. Write a memo to Norm Champion with your analyses and advice.

L.O. 8 PROBLEM 2–24A *Selecting the Appropriate Time Period for Cost Averaging*

CHECK FIGURES
a. Monday: $3.20
b. Friday: $4.60

Fernandez Cinemas is considering a contract to rent a movie for $1,600 per day. The contract requires a minimum one-week rental period. Estimated attendance is as follows:

Monday	Tuesday	Wednesday	Thursday	Friday	Saturday	Sunday
500	400	100	500	900	1,000	600

Required

a. Determine the average cost per person of the movie rental contract separately for each day.

b. Suppose that Fernandez chooses to price movie tickets at cost as computed in Part *a* plus $3.00. What price would it charge per ticket on each day of the week?

c. Use weekly averaging to determine a reasonable price to charge for movie tickets.

d. Comment on why weekly averaging may be more useful to business managers than daily averaging.

L.O. 8 PROBLEM 2–25A *Identifying Relevant Issues for Cost Averaging*

Mountaintop, Inc., offers mountain-climbing expeditions for its customers, providing food, equipment, and guides. Climbs normally require one week to complete. The company's accountant is reviewing historical cost data to establish a pricing strategy for the coming year. The accountant has prepared the following table showing cost data for the most recent climb, the company's average cost per year, and the five-year average cost.

	Span of Time		
	Recent Climb	One Year	Five Years
Total cost of climbs (a)	$9,000	$524,800	$1,550,000
Number of climbers (b)	12	640	2,500
Cost per climber (a ÷ b)	$750	$820	$620

Required

Write a memo that explains the potential advantages and disadvantages of using each of the per unit cost figures as a basis for establishing a price to charge climbers during the coming year. What other factors must be considered in developing a pricing strategy?

PROBLEM 2–26A *Estimating Fixed and Variable Cost*

L.O. 10

CHECK FIGURE
b. FC = $1,540

Dorough Computer Services, Inc., has been in business for six months. The following are basic operating data for that period.

	Month					
	July	**Aug.**	**Sept.**	**Oct.**	**Nov.**	**Dec.**
Service hours	120	136	260	420	320	330
Revenue	$6,000	$6,800	$13,000	$21,000	$16,000	$16,500
Operating costs	$4,300	$5,300	$ 7,100	$11,200	$ 9,100	$10,600

Required

a. What is the average service revenue per hour for the six-month time period?
b. Use the high-low method to estimate the total monthly fixed cost and the variable cost per hour.
c. Determine the average contribution margin per hour.
d. Use the scattergraph method to estimate the total monthly fixed cost and the variable cost per hour.
e. Compare the results of the two methods and comment on the difference.

PROBLEM 2–27A *Estimating Fixed and Variable Cost*

L.O. 10

CHECK FIGURE
c. VC/unit: $5

Zassoda Handcrafts, Inc. manufactures "antique" wooden cabinets to house modern radio and CD players. ZHI began operations in January of last year. Marie Lamb, the owner, asks for your assistance. She believes that she needs to better understand the cost of the cabinets for pricing purposes. You have collected the following data concerning actual production over the past year:

Month	Number of Cabinets Produced	Total Cost
January	800	$22,000
February	3,600	33,500
March	1,960	30,500
April	600	19,600
May	1,600	30,000
June	1,300	28,000
July	1,100	26,600
August	1,800	32,000
September	2,280	33,000
October	2,940	32,500
November	3,280	33,000
December	400	17,500

Required

a. To understand the department's cost behavior, you decide to plot the points on graph paper and sketch a total cost line.
  (1) Enter the number of units and their costs in increasing order.
  (2) Plot the points on the graph.
  (3) Sketch a graph so the line "splits" all of the points (half of the points appear above and half below the line).
b. Using the line you just sketched, visually estimate the total cost to produce 2,000 units.
c. Using the high-low method, compute the total cost equation for the preceding data.
  (1) Compute the variable cost per unit.
  (2) Compute total fixed costs.
  (3) Assemble the total cost equation.
  (4) Sketch a line between the high and low points on your graph.
d. Using the high-low method, estimate the total cost to produce 2,000 units.
e. After discussing the results with your teammates, decide which method you believe is better.

EXERCISES—SERIES B

L.O. 1 **EXERCISE 2–1B** ***Identifying Cost Behavior***

Zulu Copies, Inc., provides professional copying services to customers through the 15 copy stores it operates in the southwestern United States. Each store employs a manager and four assistants. The manager earns $4,000 per month plus a bonus of 3 percent of sales. The assistants earn hourly wages. Each copy store costs $3,000 per month to lease. The company spends $5,000 per month on corporate-level advertising and promotion.

Required
Classify each of the following costs incurred by Zulu Copies as fixed, variable, or mixed.

a. Store manager's salary relative to the number of copies made for customers.
b. Cost of paper relative to the number of copies made for customers.
c. Lease cost relative to the number of stores.
d. Advertising and promotion costs relative to the number of copies a particular store makes.
e. Lease cost relative to the number of copies made for customers.
f. Assistants' wages relative to the number of copies made for customers.

L.O. 1 **EXERCISE 2–2B** ***Identifying Cost Behavior***

At the various sales levels shown, Attala Company incurred the following costs.

	Units sold	50	100	150	200	250
a.	Total shipping cost	$ 40.00	$ 80.00	$ 120.00	$ 160.00	$ 200.00
b.	Rent cost per unit of merchandise sold	12.00	6.00	4.00	3.00	2.40
c.	Total utility cost	200.00	300.00	400.00	500.00	600.00
d.	Supplies cost per unit	4.00	4.00	4.00	4.00	4.00
e.	Total insurance cost	500.00	500.00	500.00	500.00	500.00
f.	Total salary cost	1,500.00	2,000.00	2,500.00	3,000.00	3,500.00
g.	Cost per unit of merchandise sold	8.00	8.00	8.00	8.00	8.00
h.	Total cost of goods sold	4,000.00	8,000.00	12,000.00	16,000.00	20,000.00
i.	Depreciation cost per unit	30.00	15.00	10.00	7.50	6.00
j.	Total rent cost	600.00	600.00	600.00	600.00	600.00

Required
Identify each of these costs as fixed, variable, or mixed.

L.O. 1 **EXERCISE 2–3B** ***Determining Fixed Cost per Unit***

Bali Corporation incurs the following annual fixed production costs:

Item	Cost
Insurance cost	$ 80,000
Patent amortization cost	1,500,000
Depreciation cost	750,000
Property tax cost	100,000

Required
Determine the total fixed production cost per unit if Bali produces 10,000, 20,000, or 50,000 units

L.O. 1 **EXERCISE 2–4B** ***Determining Total Variable Cost***

The following variable manufacturing costs apply to goods produced by Orlando Manufacturing Corporation.

Item	Cost per Unit
Materials	$3.00
Labor	2.00
Variable overhead	1.00
Total	$6.00

Required

Determine the total variable manufacturing cost if Orlando produces 4,000, 6,000, or 8,000 units.

EXERCISE 2–5B *Fixed Versus Variable Cost Behavior*

L.O. 1

Larose Company's production and total cost data for two recent months follow.

	January	February
Units produced	400	800
Total depreciation cost	$4,000	$4,000
Total factory supplies cost	$2,000	$4,000

Required

a. Separately calculate the depreciation cost per unit and the factory supplies cost per unit for both January and February.

b. Based on total and per unit amounts, identify which cost is variable and which is fixed. Explain your answer.

EXERCISE 2–6B *Fixed Versus Variable Cost Behavior*

L.O. 1

Professional Chairs Corporation produces ergonomically designed chairs favored by architects. The company normally produces and sells from 5,000 to 8,000 chairs per year. The following cost data apply to various production activity levels.

Number of Chairs	5,000	6,000	7,000	8,000
Total costs incurred				
Fixed	$ 84,000			
Variable	60,000			
Total costs	$144,000			
Per unit chair cost				
Fixed	$ 16.80			
Variable	12.00			
Total cost per chair	$ 28.80			

Required

a. Complete the preceding table by filling in the missing amounts for the levels of activity shown in the first row of the table.

b. Explain why the total cost per chair decreases as the number of chairs increases.

EXERCISE 2–7B *Fixed Versus Variable Cost Behavior*

L.O. 1

Bo Shuttler needs extra money quickly because his mother's sudden hospitalization has resulted in unexpected medical bills. Mr. Shuttler has learned fortune-telling skills through his long friendship with Frank Lopez, who tells fortunes during the day at the city market. Mr. Lopez has agreed to let Mr. Shuttler use his booth to tell fortunes during the evening for a rent of $50 per night.

Required

a. What is the booth rental cost both in total and per customer if the number of customers is 5, 10, 15, 20, or 25?

b. Is the cost of renting the fortune-telling booth fixed or variable relative to the number of customers?

c. Draw two graphs. On one, plot total booth rental cost for 5, 10, 15, 20, and 25 customers; on the other, plot booth rental cost per customer for 5, 10, 15, 20, or 25 customers.

d. Mr. Shuttler has little money. What major business risks would he take by renting the fortune-telling booth? How could he minimize those risks?

L.O. 1

EXERCISE 2–8B *Fixed Versus Variable Cost Behavior*

In the evenings, Bo Shuttler works telling fortunes using his friend Frank Lopez's booth at the city market. Mr. Lopez pays the booth rental, so Mr. Shuttler has no rental cost. As a courtesy, Mr. Shuttler provides each customer a soft drink. The drinks cost him $0.50 per customer.

Required

a. What is the soft drink cost both in total and per customer if the number of customers is 5, 10, 15, 20, or 25?

b. Is the soft drink cost fixed or variable?

c. Draw two graphs. On one, plot total soft drink cost for 5, 10, 15, 20, and 25 customers; on the other, plot soft drink cost per customer for 5, 10, 15, 20, and 25 customers.

d. Comment on the likelihood that Mr. Shuttler will incur a loss on this business venture.

L.O. 1

EXERCISE 2–9B *Graphing Fixed Cost Behavior*

Rudolf Computers leases space in a mall at a monthly rental cost of $3,000. The following graphs depict rental cost on the vertical axes and activity level on the horizontal axes.

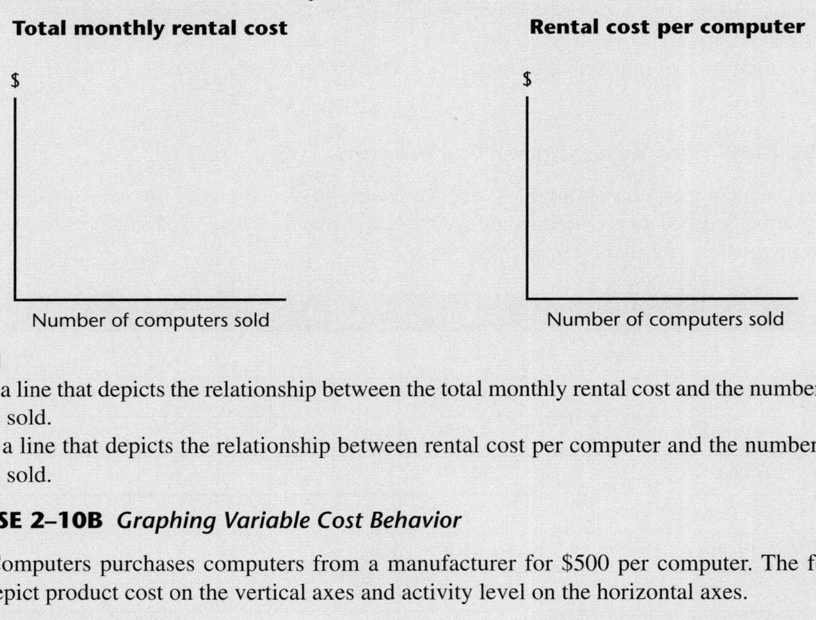

Required

a. Draw a line that depicts the relationship between the total monthly rental cost and the number of computers sold.

b. Draw a line that depicts the relationship between rental cost per computer and the number of computers sold.

L.O. 1

EXERCISE 2–10B *Graphing Variable Cost Behavior*

Larsen Computers purchases computers from a manufacturer for $500 per computer. The following graphs depict product cost on the vertical axes and activity level on the horizontal axes.

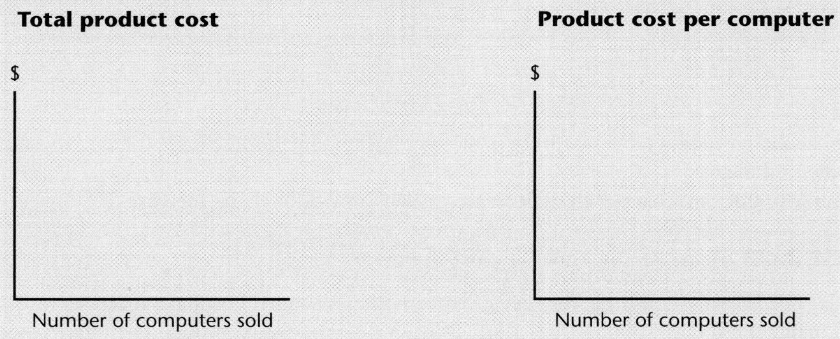

Required

a. Draw a line that depicts the relationship between total product cost and the number of computers sold.

b. Draw a line that depicts the relationship between cost per computer and the number of computers sold.

EXERCISE 2–11B *Mixed Cost at Different Levels of Activity*

L.O. 1

Lebron Hats Corporation uses workers in Philippines to manually weave straw hats. The company pays the workers a daily base wage plus $0.20 per completed hat. On Monday, workers produced 100 hats for which the company paid wages of $30.

Required

Calculate the total cost of the workers' wages for each of the following days.

Day	Monday	Tuesday	Wednesday	Thursday
Number of hats woven	100	120	160	80
Total variable cost				
Total fixed cost				
Total wages cost				

EXERCISE 2–12B *Effect of Cost Structure on Projected Profits*

L.O. 1, 2, 3, 6

Logan and Martin compete in the same market. The following budgeted income statements illustrate their cost structures.

Income Statements		
	Company	
	Logan	Martin
Number of Customers (a)	80	80
Sales Revenue (a × $125)	$10,000	$10,000
Variable Cost (a × $80)	NA	(6,400)
Contribution Margin	10,000	3,600
Fixed Costs	(6,400)	NA, 0
Net Income	$ 3,600	$ 3,600

Required

a. Assume that Logan can lure all 80 customers away from Martin by lowering its sales price to $75 per customer. Reconstruct Logan's income statement based on 160 customers.

b. Assume that Martin can lure all 80 customers away from Logan by lowering its sales price to $90 per customer. Reconstruct Martin's income statement based on 160 customers.

c. Why does the price-cutting strategy increase Logan's profits but result in a net loss for Millenium?

EXERCISE 2–13B *Using a Contribution Margin Format Income Statement to Measure the Magnitude of Operating Leverage*

L.O. 4, 5

Dothan Company, a merchandising firm, reported the following operating results.

Income Statement	
Sales Revenue (7,500 units × $80)	$600,000
Cost of Goods Sold (7,500 units × $48)	(360,000)
Gross Margin	240,000
Sales Commissions (10% of sales revenue)	(60,000)
Administrative Salaries Expense	(67,000)
Advertising Expense	(20,000)
Depreciation Expense	(41,000)
Shipping and Handling Expense (7,500 units × $1.60)	(12,000)
Net Income	$ 40,000

Required

a. Reconstruct the income statement using the contribution margin format.

b. Calculate the magnitude of operating leverage.
c. Use the measure of operating leverage to determine the amount of net income that Dothan will earn if sales revenue increases by 10 percent.

L.O. 5

EXERCISE 2–14B *Assessing the Magnitude of Operating Leverage*

The following budgeted income statement applies to Hope Company:

Income Statement	
Sales Revenue (600 units × $90)	$54,000
Variable Cost (600 units × $50)	(30,000)
Contribution Margin	24,000
Fixed Costs	(16,000)
Net Income	$ 8,000

Required
a. Use the contribution margin approach to calculate the magnitude of operating leverage.
b. Use the operating leverage measure computed in Requirement *a* to determine the amount of net income that Hope Company will earn if sales volume increases by 10 percent. Assume the sales price per unit remains unchanged at $90.
c. Verify your answer to Requirement *b* by constructing an alternative income statement based on a 10 percent increase in sales volume. The sales price per unit remains unchanged at $90. Calculate the percentage change in net income for the two income statements.

L.O. 8

EXERCISE 2–15B *Averaging Costs*

Nassar Entertainment, Inc., operates a movie theater that has monthly fixed expenses of $9,000. In addition, the company pays film distributors $1.50 per ticket sold. The following chart shows the number of tickets Nassar expects to sell in the coming year:

Jan.	Feb.	Mar.	Apr.	May	June	July	Aug.	Sept.	Oct.	Nov.	Dec.	Total
2,600	1,400	3,000	3,600	4,000	4,800	6,000	5,400	4,200	3,000	3,800	3,200	45,000

Required
Assume that Nassar wants to earn $2.50 per movie patron. What price should it charge for a ticket in January and in September?

L.O. 10

EXERCISE 2–16B *Estimating Fixed and Variable Costs Using the High-Low Method*

Carmichael Ice Cream Company produces various ice cream products for which demand is highly seasonal. The company sells more ice cream in warmer months and less in colder ones. Last year, the high point in production activity occurred in August when Carmichael produced 45,000 gallons of ice cream at a total cost of $36,000. The low point in production activity occurred in February when the company produced 21,000 gallons of ice cream at a total cost of $30,000.

Required
Use the high-low method to estimate the amount of fixed cost per month incurred by Carmichael Ice Cream Company.

PROBLEMS—SERIES B

L.O. 1

PROBLEM 2–17B *Identifying Cost Behavior*

Required
Identify the following costs as fixed or variable.

Costs related to operating a retail gasoline company.

a. The company's cost of national TV commercials relative to the number of stations in operation.
b. Depreciation of equipment relative to the number of customers served at a station.
c. Property and real estate taxes relative to the amount of gasoline sold at a particular station.
d. Depreciation of equipment relative to the number of stations.
e. Cashiers' wages relative to the number of customers served in a station.
f. Salary of a manager of a particular station relative to the number of employees.
g. Gasoline cost relative to the number of customers.
h. Utility cost relative to the number of stations in operation.

Costs related to shuttle bus trips between Chicago's O'Hare Intercontinental Airport and downtown Chicago. Each bus driver receives a specific salary per month. A manager schedules bus trips and supervises drivers, and a secretary receives phone calls.

i. Fuel costs relative to the number of passengers on a particular trip.
j. Drivers' salaries relative to the number of trips driven.
k. Office staff salaries relative to the number of passengers on a particular trip.
l. Depreciation relative to the number of buses in service.
m. A driver's salary relative to the number of passengers on a particular trip.
n. Fuel costs relative to the number of trips.

Janet's Barbershop operates several stores in shopping centers. Each store employs a supervisor and three barbers. Each barber receives a specific salary per month plus a 10 percent commission based on the service revenues he or she has generated.

o. Store rental costs relative to the number of customers.
p. Barbers' commissions relative to the number of customers.
q. Supervisory salaries relative to the number of customers served in a particular store.
r. Barbers' salaries relative to the number of barbers in a particular district.
s. Supplies cost relative to the number of hair services provided in a particular store.
t. Barbers' salaries relative to the number of customers served at a particular store.

PROBLEM 2–18B *Cost Behavior and Averaging* — L.O. 1

Gene Solarz asks you to analyze the operating cost of his lawn services business. He has bought the needed equipment with a cash payment of $27,000. Upon your recommendation, he agrees to adopt straight-line depreciation. The equipment has an expected life of three years and no salvage value. Mr. Solarz pays his workers $30 per lawn service. Material costs, including fertilizer, pesticide, and supplies, are expected to be $6 per lawn service.

Required

a. Determine the total cost of equipment depreciation and the average cost of equipment depreciation per lawn service, assuming that Mr. Solarz provides 20, 25, or 30 lawn services during one month. Is the cost of equipment a fixed or a variable cost?
b. Determine the total expected cost of labor and the average expected cost of labor per lawn service, assuming that Mr. Solarz provides 20, 25, or 30 lawn services during one month. Is the cost of labor a fixed or a variable cost?
c. Determine the total expected cost of materials and the average expected cost of materials per lawn service, assuming that Mr. Solarz provides 20, 25, or 30 lawn services during one month. Is the cost of fertilizer, pesticide, and supplies a fixed or a variable cost?
d. Determine the total expected cost per lawn service, assuming that Mr. Solarz provides 20, 25, or 30 lawn services during one month.
e. Determine the average expected cost per lawn service, assuming that Mr. Solarz provides 20, 25, or 30 lawn services during one month. Why does the cost per unit decrease as the number of lawn services increases?
f. If Mr. Solarz tells you that he prices his services at 30 percent above cost, would you assume that he means average or actual cost? Why?

PROBLEM 2–19B *Context-Sensitive Nature of Cost Behavior Classifications* — L.O. 1

Sanchez and Adams Tax Services' Development Department is responsible for establishing new community branches. Each branch opens with two tax accountants. Total cost of payroll per branch is $75,000 per year. Together the two accountants can process up to 2,500 simple tax returns per year. The firm's policy requires closing branches that do not reach the quota of 1,500 tax returns per year. On the other hand, the firm hires an additional accountant for a branch and elevates it to the status of a regular operation if the customer demand for services exceeds 2,500 tax returns.

Required

a. What is the relevant range of activity for a new branch established by the Development Department?

b. Determine the amount of payroll cost in total and the average payroll cost per transaction for a branch that processes 1,500, 2,000, or 2,500 tax returns. In this case (the activity base is the number of tax returns for a specific branch), is the payroll cost a fixed or a variable cost?

c. Determine the amount of payroll cost in total and the average payroll cost per branch for Sanchez and Adams Tax Services, assuming that the Development Department operates 20, 30, or 40 branches. In this case (the activity base is the number of branches), is the payroll cost a fixed or a variable cost?

L.O. 1

PROBLEM 2–20B *Context-Sensitive Nature of Cost Behavior Classifications*

Bill Lankey sells a newly developed camera, Superb Image. He purchases the cameras from the manufacturer for $150 each and rents a store in a shopping mall for $5,000 per month.

Required

a. Determine the average cost of sales per unit if Mr. Lankey sells 100, 200, 300, 400, or 500 units of Superb Image per month. Use the following chart to organize your answer.

	Sales Volume in Units (a)				
	100	200	300	400	500
Total cost of cameras (a × $150)	$15,000				
Total cost of store rental	5,000				
Total cost of sales (b)	$20,000				
Average cost per unit (b ÷ a)	$200.00				

b. If Mr. Lankey wants to make a gross profit of $20 on each camera he sells, what price should he charge at sales volumes of 100, 200, 300, 400, or 500 units?

c. Record the total cost of store rental if Mr. Lankey opens a camera store at one, two, three, four, or five shopping malls. Record your answers in the following chart. Is the cost of store rental fixed or variable relative to the number of stores opened?

	Shopping Malls				
	1	2	3	4	5
Total cost of store rental	$5,000				

d. Mr. Lankey provides decorative ornaments to customers who purchase cameras. Some customers take the ornaments, others do not, and some take more than one. The number of ornaments varies in relation to the number of cameras sold, but the relationship is not proportional. Assume that, on average, Mr. Lankey gives away $150 worth of ornaments for every 100 cameras sold. What is the additional cost per camera sold? Is the cost fixed or variable?

L.O. 2

PROBLEM 2–21B *Effects of Operating Leverage on Profitability*

Successful CPA, Inc., conducts CPA review courses. Public universities that permit free use of a classroom support the classes. The only major expense incurred by Successful CPA is the salary of instructors, which is $10,000 per course taught. The company recently planned to offer a review course in Boston for $500 per candidate; it estimated that 60 candidates would attend the course.
Complete these requirements based on the preceding information.

Part 1:
Required

a. Relative to the number of CPA candidates in a single course, is the cost of instruction a fixed or a variable cost?

b. Determine the profit, assuming that 60 candidates attend the course.

c. Determine the profit, assuming a 10 percent increase in enrollment (i.e., enrollment increases to 66 students). What is the percentage change in profitability?
d. Determine the profit, assuming a 10 percent decrease in enrollment (i.e., enrollment decreases to 54 students). What is the percentage change in profitability?
e. Explain why a 10 percent shift in enrollment produces more than a 10 percent shift in profitability. Use the term that identifies this phenomenon.

Part 2:
The instructor has offered to teach the course for a percentage of tuition fees. Specifically, he wants $250 per candidate attending the class. Assume that the tuition fee remains at $500 per candidate.

Required
f. Is the cost of instruction a fixed or a variable cost?
g. Determine the profit, assuming that 60 candidates take the course.
h. Determine the profit, assuming a 10 percent increase in enrollment (i.e., enrollment increases to 66 students). What is the percentage change in profitability?
i. Determine the profit, assuming a 10 percent decrease in enrollment (i.e., enrollment decreases to 54 students). What is the percentage change in profitability?
j. Explain why a 10 percent shift in enrollment produces a proportional 10 percent shift in profitability.

Part 3:
Successful CPA sells a workbook to each student who attends the course. The workbook contains printed material unique to each course. Workbooks that are not sold must be destroyed. Prior to the first class, Successful CPA printed 60 copies of the books based on the estimated number of people who would attend the course. Each workbook costs $40 and is sold for $50. This cost includes a royalty fee paid to the author and the cost of duplication.

Required
k. Calculate the total cost and the cost per candidate of the workbooks, assuming that 54, 60, or 66 candidates attempt to attend the course.
l. Classify the cost of workbooks as fixed or variable relative to the number of candidates attending the course.
m. Discuss the risk of holding inventory as it applies to the workbooks.
n. Explain how a just-in-time inventory system can reduce the cost and risk of holding inventory.

PROBLEM 2–22B *Effects of Fixed and Variable Cost Behavior on the Risk and Rewards of Business Opportunities*

L.O. 2, 3, 6

Hoover Club and Beaver Club are competing health and recreation clubs in Seattle. They both offer tennis training clinics to adults. Hoover pays its coaches $6,000 per season. Beaver pays its coaches $200 per student enrolled in the clinic per season. Both clubs charge a tuition fee of $300 per season.

Required
a. Prepare income statements for Hoover and Beaver, assuming that 30 students per season attend each clinic.
b. The ambitious new director of Hoover Club tries to increase his market share by reducing the club's tuition per student to $180 per clinic. Prepare an income statement for Hoover, assuming that the club attracts all of Beaver's customers and therefore is able to enroll 60 students in its clinics.
c. Independent of Part *b,* Beaver Club tries to lure Hoover's students by lowering its price to $180 per student. Prepare an income statement for Beaver, assuming that the club succeeds in enrolling 60 students in its clinics.
d. Explain why the strategy described in Part *b* produced a profit while the same strategy described in Part *c* produced a loss.
e. Prepare an income statement for Hoover Club and Beaver Club, assuming that 18 students attend a clinic at the original $300 tuition price.
f. It is always better to have fixed rather than variable cost. Explain why this statement is false.
g. It is always better to have variable rather than fixed cost. Explain why this statement is false.

PROBLEM 2–23B *Analysis of Operating Leverage*

L.O. 7, 8

Wendy Ludman has invested in two start-up companies. At the end of the first year, she asks you to evaluate their operating performance. The following operating data apply to the first year.

	Company Name	
	Nanya	Tatung
Variable cost per unit (a)	$30	$15
Sales revenue (20,000 units × $45)	$900,000	$900,000
Variable cost (20,000 units × a)	(600,000	(300,000)
Contribution margin	300,000	600,000
Fixed cost	(150,000)	(450,000)
Net income	$150,000	$150,000

Required

a. Use the contribution margin approach to compute the operating leverage for each firm.

b. If the economy expands in the coming year, Nanya and Tatung will both enjoy a 10 percent per year increase in sales volume, assuming that the selling price remains unchanged. (*Note:* Since the number of units increases, both revenue and variable cost will increase.) Compute the change in net income for each firm in dollar amount and in percentage.

c. If the economy contracts in the following year, Nanya and Tatung will both suffer a 10 percent decrease in sales volume, assuming that the selling price remains unchanged. (*Note:* Since the number of units decreases, both revenue and variable cost decrease.) Compute the change in net income for each firm in both dollar amount and percentage.

d. Write a memo to Wendy Ludman with your evaluation and recommendations.

L.O. 8 PROBLEM 2–24B *Selecting the Appropriate Time Period for Cost Averaging*

The Greenland Amusement Park is considering signing a contract to hire a circus at a cost of $2,700 per day. The contract requires a minimum performance period of one week. Estimated circus attendance is as follows:

Monday	Tuesday	Wednesday	Thursday	Friday	Saturday	Sunday
600	500	450	700	960	1,450	1,340

Required

a. For each day, determine the average cost of the circus contract per person attending.

b. Suppose that the park prices circus tickets at cost as computed in Part *a* plus $1.80. What would be the price per ticket charged on each day of the week?

c. Use weekly averaging to determine a reasonable price to charge for the circus tickets.

d. Comment on why weekly averaging may be more useful to business managers than daily averaging.

L.O. 7 PROBLEM 2–25B *Identifying Relevant Issues for Cost Averaging*

Arizona Tours, Inc., organizes adventure tours for people interested in visiting a desert environment. A desert tour generally lasts three days. Arizona provides food, equipment, and guides. Victor Vladmyer, the president of Arizona Tours, needs to set prices for the coming year. He has available the company's past cost data in the following table.

	Span of Time		
	Recent Tour	One Year	Ten Years
Total cost of tours (a)	$8,100	$456,000	$3,150,000
Number of tourists (b)	30	1,600	14,000
Cost per tourist (a ÷ b)	$ 270	$ 285	$ 225

Required

Write a memo to Mr. Vladmyer explaining the potential advantages and disadvantages of using each of the different per tourist cost figures as a basis for establishing a price to charge tourists during the coming year. What other factors must Mr. Vladmyer consider in developing a pricing strategy?

PROBLEM 2–26B *Estimating Fixed and Variable Costs*

L.O. 10

Chapman Legal Services provides legal advice to clients. The following data apply to the first six months of operation.

	Month					
	Jan.	Feb.	Mar.	Apr.	May	June
Service hours	50	80	125	140	170	195
Revenue	$4,000	$6,400	$10,000	$11,200	$13,600	$15,600
Operating costs	6,200	7,100	8,380	8,500	8,761	9,680

Required

a. What is the average service revenue per hour for the six-month time period?
b. Use the high-low method to estimate the total monthly fixed cost and the variable cost per hour.
c. Determine the average contribution margin per hour.
d. Use the scattergraph method to estimate the total monthly fixed cost and the variable cost per hour.
e. Compare the results of the two methods and comment on any differences.

PROBLEM 2–27B *Estimating Fixed and Variable Cost*

L.O. 10

Pretty Frames, Inc. (PFI), which manufactures ornate frames for original art work, began operations in January 2003. Justin Jamail, the owner, asks for your assistance. He believes that he needs to better understand the cost of the frames for pricing purposes. You have collected the following data concerning actual production over the past year:

Month	Number of Frames Produced	Total Cost
January	1,600	$42,000
February	7,200	65,000
March	3,920	59,000
April	1,200	37,200
May	3,200	58,000
June	2,600	54,000
July	2,200	51,200
August	3,600	62,000
September	4,560	64,000
October	5,880	63,000
November	6,560	64,000
December	800	33,000

Required

a. To understand the department's cost behavior, you decide to plot the points on graph paper and sketch a total cost line.
 (1) Enter the number of units and their costs in increasing order.
 (2) Plot the points on the graph.
 (3) Sketch a graph so the line "splits" all of the points (half of the points appear above and half appear below the line).
b. Using the line you just sketched, visually estimate the total cost to produce 4,000 units.
c. Using the high-low method, compute the total cost equation for the preceding data.
 (1) Compute the variable cost per unit.
 (2) Compute total fixed costs.
 (3) Assemble the total cost equation.
 (4) Sketch a line between the high and low points on your graph.
d. Using the high-low method, estimate the total cost to produce 4,000 units.
e. After discussing the results with your teammates, decide which method you believe is better.

ANALYZE, THINK, COMMUNICATE

ATC 2–1 BUSINESS APPLICATIONS *Operating Leverage*

The following information was taken from the Form 10-K SEC filings for CSX Corporation and Starbucks Corporation. It is from the 2002 fiscal year reports, and all dollar amounts are in millions.

Description of Business for CSX Corporation

CSX Corporation (CSX or the Company), operates one of the largest rail networks in the United States and also provides intermodal transportation services across the United States and key markets in Canada and Mexico. Its marine operations include an international terminal services company and a domestic container-shipping company.

CSX Corporation	2002	2001
Operating revenues	$8,172	$8,110
Operating earnings	424	293

Description of Business for Starbucks Corporation

Starbucks Corporation (together with its subsidiaries, Starbucks or the Company) purchases and roasts high-quality whole bean coffees and sells them, along with fresh, rich-brewed coffees, Italian-style espresso beverages, cold blended beverages, a variety of pastries and confections, coffee-related accessories and equipment, a selection of premium teas and a line of compact discs primarily through Company-operated retail stores.

At fiscal year-end, Starbucks had 3,496 Company-operated stores in 43 states, the District of Columbia, and five Canadian provinces (which comprise the Company's North American Retail operating segment), as well as 322 stores in the United Kingdom, 33 stores in Australia, and 29 stores in Thailand.

Starbucks	2002	2001
Operating revenues	$3,289	$2,649
Operating earnings	319	281

Required

a. Determine which company appears to have the higher operating leverage.

b. Write a paragraph or two explaining why the company you identified in Requirement *a* might be expected to have the higher operating leverage.

c. If revenues for both companies declined, which company do you think would likely experience the greatest decline in operating earnings? Explain your answer.

ATC 2–2 GROUP ASSIGNMENT *Operating Leverage*

The Parent Teacher Association (PTA) of Meadow High School is planning a fund-raising campaign. The PTA is considering the possibility of hiring Eric Logan, a world-renowned investment counselor, to address the public. Tickets would sell for $28 each. The school has agreed to let the PTA use Harville Auditorium at no cost. Mr. Logan is willing to accept one of two compensation arrangements. He will sign an agreement to receive a fixed fee of $10,000 regardless of the number of tickets sold. Alternatively, he will accept payment of $20 per ticket sold. In communities similar to that in which Meadow is located, Mr. Logan has drawn an audience of approximately 500 people.

Required

a. In front of the class, present a statement showing the expected net income assuming 500 people buy tickets.

b. The instructor will divide the class into groups and then organize the groups into four sections. The instructor will assign one of the following tasks to each section of groups.

Group Tasks

(1) Assume the PTA pays Mr. Logan a fixed fee of $10,000. Determine the amount of net income that the PTA will earn if ticket sales are 10 percent higher than expected. Calculate the percentage change in net income.

(2) Assume that the PTA pays Mr. Logan a fixed fee of $10,000. Determine the amount of net income that the PTA will earn if ticket sales are 10 percent lower than expected. Calculate the percentage change in net income.
(3) Assume that the PTA pays Mr. Logan $20 per ticket sold. Determine the amount of net income that the PTA will earn if ticket sales are 10 percent higher than expected. Calculate the percentage change in net income.
(4) Assume that the PTA pays Mr. Logan $20 per ticket sold. Determine the amount of net income that the PTA will earn if ticket sales are 10 percent lower than expected. Calculate the percentage change in net income.

c. Have each group select a spokesperson. Have one of the spokespersons in each section of groups go to the board and present the results of the analysis conducted in Part *b*. Resolve any discrepancies in the computations presented at the board and those developed by the other groups.

d. Draw conclusions regarding the risks and rewards associated with operating leverage. At a minimum, answer the following questions.
(1) Which type of cost structure (fixed or variable) produces the higher growth potential in profitability for a company?
(2) Which type of cost structure (fixed or variable) faces the higher risk of declining profitability for a company?
(3) Under what circumstances should a company seek to establish a fixed cost structure?
(4) Under what circumstances should a company seek to establish a variable cost structure?

RESEARCH ASSIGNMENT *Fixed Versus Variable Cost* — ATC 2–3

The March 8, 2004 edition of *BusinessWeek* contained an article titled "Courting the Mass Affluent" (see page 68). The article discusses the efforts of **Charles Schwab Corp.** to attract a bigger share of investors who have $100,000 to $1 million to invest. Read this article and complete the following requirements.

Required

a. Schwab increased its marketing budget during the first quarter of 2004. What was the amount of the increase? Is this cost fixed or variable relative to the number of new customers that the company attracts.

b. Assume that Schwab acquires a significant number of new customers. Name several costs that are likely to remain fixed as revenue increases.

c. Assume that Schwab acquires a significant number of new customers. Name several costs that are likely to vary with increasing revenue.

d. Consider the cost of establishing a new customer account. Describe a set of circumstances under which this would be a fixed cost and a different set of circumstances under which this would be a variable cost.

WRITING ASSIGNMENT *Cost Averaging* — ATC 2–4

Candice Sterling is a veterinarian. She has always been concerned for the pets of low-income families. These families love their pets but frequently do not have the means to provide them proper veterinary care. Dr. Sterling decides to open a part-time veterinary practice in a low-income neighborhood. She plans to volunteer her services free of charge two days per week. Clients will be charged only for the actual costs of materials and overhead. Dr. Sterling leases a small space for $300 per month. Utilities and other miscellaneous costs are expected to be approximately $180 per month. She estimates the variable cost of materials to be approximately $10 per pet served. A friend of Dr. Sterling who runs a similar type of clinic in another area of town indicates that she should expect to treat the following number of pets during her first year of operation.

Jan.	Feb.	Mar.	Apr.	May	June	July	Aug.	Sept.	Oct.	Nov.	Dec.
18	26	28	36	42	54	63	82	42	24	20	15

Dr. Sterling's friend has noticed that visits increase significantly in the summer because children who are out of school tend to bring their pets to the vet more often. Business tapers off during the winter and reaches a low point in December when people spend what little money they have on Christmas presents for their children. After looking at the data, Dr. Sterling becomes concerned that the people in the neighborhood will not be able to afford pet care during some months of operation even if it is offered at cost. For example, the cost of providing services in December would be approximately $42 per pet treated ($480 overhead ÷ 15 pets = $32 per pet, plus $10 materials cost). She is willing to provide her services free of charge, but she realizes that she cannot afford to subsidize the practice further by personally paying for the costs of materials and overhead in the months of low activity. She decides to discuss the matter with her accountant to find a way to cut costs even more. Her accountant tells her that her problem is cost *measurement* rather than cost *cutting*.

Required

Assume that you are Dr. Sterling's accountant. Write a memo describing a pricing strategy that resolves the apparent problem of high costs during months of low volume. Recommend in your memo the price to charge per pet treated during the month of December.

ATC 2–5 ETHICAL DILEMMA *Profitability Versus Social Conscience (Effects of Cost Behavior)*

Advances in biological technology have enabled two research companies, Bio Labs, Inc. and Scientific Associates, to develop an insect-resistant corn seed. Neither company is financially strong enough to develop the distribution channels necessary to bring the product to world markets. World Agra Distributors, Inc., has negotiated contracts with both companies for the exclusive right to market their seed. Bio Labs signed an agreement to receive an annual royalty of $1,000,000. In contrast, Scientific Associates chose an agreement that provides for a royalty of $0.50 per pound of seed sold. Both agreements have a 10-year term. During 2004, World Agra sold approximately 1,600,000 pounds of the Bio Labs, Inc., seed and 2,400,000 pounds of the Scientific Associates seed. Both types of seed were sold for $1.25 per pound. By the end of 2004, it was apparent that the seed developed by Scientific Associates was superior. Although insect infestation was virtually nonexistent for both types of seed, the seed developed by Scientific Associates produced corn that was sweeter and had consistently higher yields.

World Agra Distributors' chief financial officer, Roger Weatherstone, recently retired. To the astonishment of the annual planning committee, Mr. Weatherstone's replacement, Ray Borrough, adamantly recommended that the marketing department develop a major advertising campaign to promote the seed developed by Bio Labs, Inc. The planning committee reluctantly approved the recommendation. A $100,000 ad campaign was launched; the ads emphasized the ability of the Bio Labs seed to avoid insect infestation. The campaign was silent with respect to taste or crop yield. It did not mention the seed developed by Scientific Associates. World Agra's sales staff was instructed to push the Bio Labs seed and to sell the Scientific Associates seed only on customer demand. Although total sales remained relatively constant during 2005, sales of the Scientific Associates seed fell to approximately 1,300,000 pounds while sales of the Bio Labs, Inc., seed rose to 2,700,000 pounds.

Required

a. Determine the amount of increase or decrease in profitability experienced by World Agra in 2006 as a result of promoting Bio Labs seed. Support your answer with appropriate commentary.

b. Did World Agra's customers in particular and society in general benefit or suffer from the decision to promote the Bio Labs seed?

c. Review the standards of ethical conduct in Exhibit 1–13 of Chapter 1 and comment on whether Mr. Borrough's recommendation violated any of the standards in the code of ethical conduct.

d. Comment on your belief regarding the adequacy of the Standards of Ethical Conduct for Managerial Accountants to direct the conduct of management accountants.

ATC 2–6 SPREADSHEET ASSIGNMENT *Using Excel*

Charlie Stork rented a truck for his business on two previous occasions. Since he will soon be renting a truck again, he would like to analyze his bills and determine how the rental fee is calculated. His two bills for truck rental show that on September 1, he drove 1,000 miles and the bill was $1,500, and on December 5, he drove 600 miles and the bill was $1,380.

Required

Construct a spreadsheet to calculate the variable and fixed costs of this mixed cost that will allow Mr. Stork to predict his cost if he drives the truck 700 miles. The cells that show as numbers should all be formulas except C5, C6, E5, E6, and C18. Constructing the spreadsheet in this manner will allow you to change numbers in these five cells to recalculate variable cost, fixed cost, or predicted total cost.

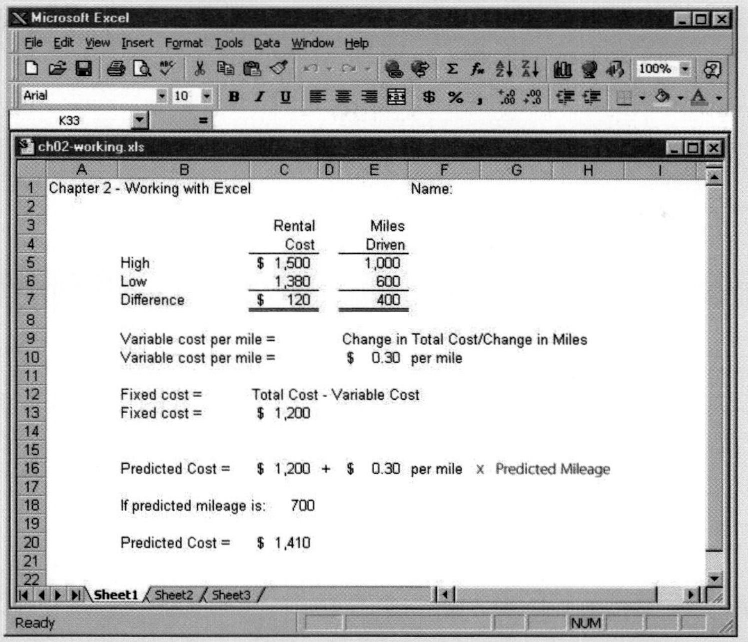

Spreadsheet Tip

1. To format cells to show dollar signs, commas, or both, choose Format, then Cells, then click on the tab titled Numbers, and choose Accounting.

SPREADSHEET ASSIGNMENT *Mastering Excel*

ATC 2–7

Siwa Company makes and sells a decorative ceramic statue. Each statue costs $50 to manufacture and sells for $75. Siwa spends $3 to ship the statue to customers and pays salespersons a $2 commission for each statue sold. The remaining annual expenses of operation are administrative salaries, $70,000; advertising, $20,000; and rent, $30,000. Siwa plans to sell 9,000 statues in the coming year.

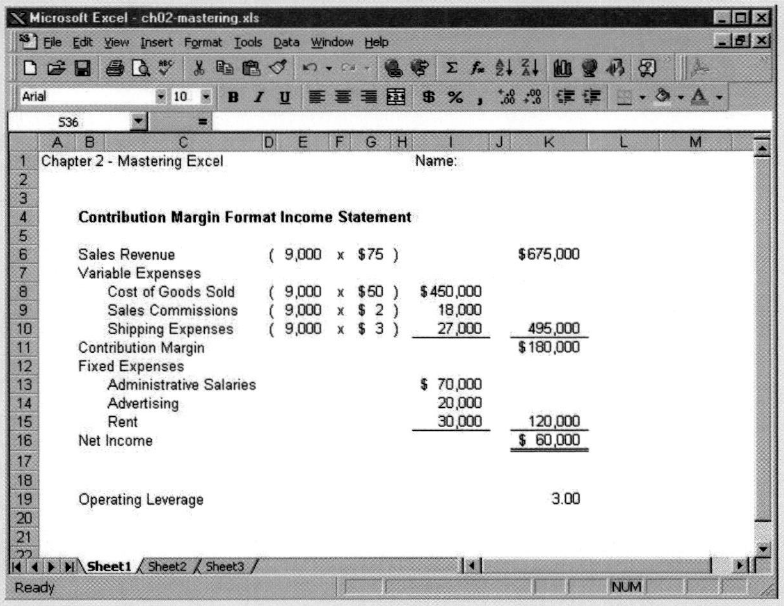

Required

Construct a spreadsheet that shows a contribution margin format income statement and that calculates operating leverage. Place formulas in the spreadsheet to allow changes to any of the preceding information to be automatically reflected in the income statement and operating leverage.

COMPREHENSIVE PROBLEM

Use the same transaction data for Magnificant Modems, Inc. as was used in Chapter 1 (see page 00).

Required

a. Based on these data, identify each cost incurred by the company as (1) fixed versus variable relative to the number of units produced and sold; and (2) product versus general, selling, and administrative (G, S, & A). The solution for the first item is shown as an example.

Cost Item	Fixed	Variable	Product	G,S,&A
Depreciation on manufacturing equipment	X		X	
Direct materials				
Direct labor				
Production supplies				
Rent on manufacturing facility				
Sales commissions				
Depreciation on administrative equipment				
Administrative costs (rent and salaries)				

b. Replace the question marks in the following table to indicate the product cost per unit assuming levels of production of 5,000, 6,000, 7,000, and 8,000.

Cost of Goods Sold	$455,000	?	?	?
Divided by Number of Units	5,000	6,000	7,000	8,000
Cost Per Unit	$ 91	?	?	?

CHAPTER *three*

ANALYSIS OF COST, VOLUME, AND PRICING TO INCREASE PROFITABILITY

LEARNING *objectives*

After you have mastered the material in this chapter, you will be able to:

1 Determine the sales price of a product using a cost-plus pricing approach.

2 Use the contribution per unit approach to calculate the break-even point.

3 Use the contribution per unit approach to calculate the sales volume required to realize a target profit.

4 Use the contribution per unit approach to conduct cost-volume-profit analysis.

5 Use target pricing to reengineer a product.

6 Draw and interpret a cost-volume-profit graph.

7 Calculate the margin of safety in units, dollars, and percentage.

8 Explain how spreadsheet software can be used to conduct sensitivity analysis for cost-volume-profit relationships.

9 Use the contribution margin ratio and the equation method to conduct cost-volume-profit analysis.

10 Identify the limitations of cost-volume-profit analysis.

11 Perform multiple-product break-even analysis. (Appendix)

THE *curious* ACCOUNTANT

In August 2002, **American Airlines** announced several changes in its way of doing business. These changes included eliminating all of the first-class seats on some routes.

In February 2003, **Circuit City** laid off 3,900 sales personnel throughout its more than 600 stores in the United States. What makes this action unusual is that many of those fired were among the most productive salespeople in the company.

Why would American Airlines eliminate some of its highest priced seats at a time when airline traffic was already down around the globe? Why would Circuit City fire its best salespeople and replace them with less experienced, less proven employees? (Answers on page 101.)

CHAPTER *opening*

The president of Bright Day Distributors recently completed a managerial accounting course. He was particularly struck by the operating leverage *concept. His instructor had demonstrated how a small percentage increase in sales volume could produce a significantly higher percentage increase in profitability. Unfortunately, the discussion had been limited to the effects of changes in sales volume. In practice, changes in sales volume are often related to changes in sales price. For example, reducing selling prices often leads to increases in sales volume. Sales volume may also change in response to cost changes such as increasing the advertising budget. Furthermore, significant changes in sales volume could redefine the relevant range, changing the fixed and variable costs. Bright Day's president realized that understanding operating leverage was only one piece of understanding how to manage a business. He also needed to understand how changes in prices, costs, and volume affect profitability. Bright Day's president is interested in* ***cost-volume-profit (CVP) analysis.***

3–1

Determining the Contribution Margin per Unit

LO1 Determine the sales price of a product using a cost-plus pricing approach.

Analyzing relationships among the CVP variables is simplified by using an income statement organized using the contribution margin format. Recall that the *contribution margin* is the difference between sales revenue and variable costs. It measures the amount available to cover fixed costs and thereafter to provide enterprise profits. Consider the following illustration.

Bright Day Distributors sells nonprescription health food supplements including vitamins, herbs, and natural hormones in the northwestern United States. Bright Day recently obtained the rights to distribute the new herb mixture Delatine. Recent scientific research found that Delatine delayed aging in laboratory animals. The researchers hypothesized that the substance would have a similar effect on humans. Their theory could not be confirmed because of the relatively long human life span. The news media reported the research findings; as stories turned up on television and radio news, talk shows, and in magazines, demand for Delatine increased.

Delatine costs $24 per bottle. Bright Day uses a **cost-plus pricing strategy;** it sets prices at cost plus a markup equal to 50 percent of cost. A bottle of Delatine is priced at $36 per bottle ($24 + [0.50 × $24]). The **contribution margin per unit** is:

Sales revenue per unit	$36
Variable cost per unit	24
Contribution margin per unit	$12

For every bottle of Delatine it sells, Bright Day earns a $12 contribution margin. Bright Day's first concern is whether it can sell enough units for total contribution margin to cover fixed costs. The president made this position clear when he said, "We don't want to lose money on this product. We have to sell enough units to pay our fixed costs." Bright Day can use the per unit contribution margin to determine the quantity of sales that is necessary to break even.

Determining the Break-Even Point

LO2 Use the contribution per unit approach to calculate the break-even point.

Bright Day's management team suspects that enthusiasm for Delatine will abate quickly as the news media shift to other subjects. To attract customers immediately, the product managers consider television advertising. The marketing manager suggests running a campaign of several hundred cable channel ads at an estimated cost of $60,000. The company president asks, "How many bottles of Delatine would we have to sell to *break even?*"

The **break-even point** is the point where *total revenue equals total costs.* The cost of the advertising campaign is $60,000 regardless of the number of bottles of Delatine sold. It is a *fixed cost.* Given Bright Day's expected contribution margin of $12 per bottle, the break-even point measured in units is:

$$\text{Break-even volume in units} = \frac{\text{Fixed costs}}{\text{Contribution margin per unit}}$$

$$= \frac{\$60{,}000}{\$12} = 5{,}000 \text{ units}$$

The break-even point measured in *sales dollars* is the number of units that must be sold to break even multiplied by the sales price per unit. For Delatine, the break-even point in sales dollars is $180,000 (5,000 units × $36). The following income statement confirms these results.

Sales Revenue (5,000 units × $36)	$180,000
Total Variable Expenses (5,000 units × $24)	(120,000)
Total Contribution Margin (5,000 units × $12)	60,000
Fixed Expenses	(60,000)
Net Income	$ 0

Once fixed costs have been covered (5,000 units have been sold), net income will increase by $12 (*per unit contribution margin*) for each additional bottle sold. Similarly, profitability will decrease by $12 for each per unit decrease in sales volume. Study the effect of the per unit contribution margin on profitability by comparing the following income statements.

	Number of Units Sold (a)				
	4,998	4,999	5,000	5,001	5,002
Sales Revenue ($36 per unit × a)	$179,928	$179,964	$180,000	$180,036	$180,072
Total Variable Expenses ($24 per unit × a)	(119,952)	(119,976)	(120,000)	(120,024)	(120,048)
Total Contribution Margin ($12 per unit × a)	$ 59,976	$ 59,988	$ 60,000	$ 60,012	$ 60,024
Fixed Expenses	(60,000)	(60,000)	(60,000)	(60,000)	(60,000)
Net Income	$ (24)	$ (12)	$ 0	$ 12	$ 24

As sales increase from 5,000 to 5,001, net income increases from zero to $12. When sales increase by one additional unit, net income again rises by $12 (moves from $12 to $24). Income increases by the $12 per unit contribution margin with each additional unit sold. The effect of an increase or decrease in sales volume on net income can be computed by multiplying the amount of the change in sales volume by the contribution margin per unit. Suppose sales increase from 5,400 to 5,600 units. This increase will affect profitability by $2,400 ([5,600 − 5,400] × $12). The following comparative income statements confirm this result.

	Number of Units Sold		200 Unit Difference
	5,400	5,600	
Sales Revenue ($36 per unit)	$194,400	$201,600	$7,200
Total Variable Expenses ($24 per unit)	(129,600)	(134,400)	(4,800)
Total Contribution Margin ($12 per unit)	64,800	67,200	2,400
Fixed Expenses	(60,000)	(60,000)	0
Net Income	$ 4,800	$ 7,200	$2,400

Using the Contribution Approach to Estimate the Sales Volume Necessary to Reach a Target Profit

LO3 Use the contribution per unit approach to calculate the sales volume required to realize a target profit.

Bright Day's president decides the ad campaign should produce a $40,000 profit. He asks the accountant to determine the sales volume that is required to achieve this level of profitability. For this result, the contribution margin must be sufficient to cover the fixed costs and to provide the desired profit. The required sales volume in units can be computed as shown here:

$$\text{Sales volume in units} = \frac{\text{Fixed costs} + \text{Desired profit}}{\text{Contribution margin per unit}}$$

$$= \frac{\$60{,}000 + \$40{,}000}{\$12} = 8{,}333.33 \text{ units}$$

The required volume in sales dollars is this number of units multiplied by the sales price per unit (8,333.33 units × \$36 = \$300,000). The following income statement confirms this result; all amounts are rounded to the nearest whole dollar.

Sales Revenue (8,333.33 units × \$36)	\$300,000
Total Variable Expenses (8,333.33 units × \$24)	(200,000)
Total Contribution Margin (8,333.33 units × \$12)	100,000
Fixed Expenses	(60,000)
Net Income	\$ 40,000

In practice, the company will not sell partial bottles of Delatine. The accountant rounds 8,333.33 bottles to whole units. For planning and decision making, managers frequently make decisions using approximate data. Accuracy is desirable, but it is not as important as relevance. Do not be concerned when computations do not produce whole numbers. Rounding and approximation are common characteristics of managerial accounting data.

Check Yourself 3–1

VolTech Company manufactures small engines that it sells for \$130 each. Variable costs are \$70 per unit. Fixed costs are expected to be \$100,000. The management team has established a target profit of \$188,000. How many engines must VolTech sell to attain the target profit?

Answer

$$\text{Sales volume in units} = \frac{\text{Fixed costs} + \text{Desired profit}}{\text{Contribution margin per unit}} = \frac{\$100{,}000 + \$188{,}000}{\$130 - \$70} = 4{,}800 \text{ units}$$

Using the Contribution Approach to Estimate the Effects of Changes in Sales Price

LO4 Use the contribution per unit approach to conduct cost-volume-profit analysis.

After reviewing the accountant's computations, the president asks the marketing manager, "What are our chances of reaching a sales volume of 8,334 units?" The manager replies, "Slim to none." She observes that no Bright Day product has ever sold more than 4,000 bottles when initially offered. Also, market research revealed that customers are resistant to paying \$36. Based on prices for competing products, the marketing manager believes customers would pay \$28 per bottle for Delatine. The company president asks how changing the projected sales price will affect the sales volume required to produce the \$40,000 target profit.

Reducing the sales price from \$36 to \$28 will significantly decrease the contribution margin. If the sales price is \$28 per bottle, the new contribution margin becomes a mere \$4 (\$28 − \$24) per unit. As shown here, the significant drop in contribution margin per unit (from \$12 to \$4) will cause a dramatic increase in the sales volume necessary to attain the target profit:

$$\text{Sales volume in units} = \frac{\text{Fixed costs} + \text{Desired profit}}{\text{Contribution margin per unit}}$$

$$= \frac{\$60{,}000 + \$40{,}000}{\$4} = 25{,}000 \text{ units}$$

The required sales volume *in dollars* is $700,000 (25,000 units × $28 per bottle). The following income statement confirms these results.

Sales Revenue (25,000 units × $28)	$700,000
Total Variable Expenses (25,000 units × $24)	(600,000)
Total Contribution Margin (25,000 units × $4)	100,000
Fixed Expenses	(60,000)
Net Income	$ 40,000

Target Pricing

LO5 Use target pricing to reengineer a product.

The marketing manager concludes it would be impossible to sell 25,000 bottles of Delatine at any price. She suggests that the company drop its cost-plus pricing strategy and replace it with *target pricing.* **Target pricing** begins by determining the *market price* at which a product will sell. This becomes the target price. The focus then shifts to developing the product at a *cost* that will enable the company to be profitable selling the product at the *target price.* Since the target price leads to a target cost, this market-based pricing strategy is also called *target costing.*

Target pricing focuses on the design stage of product development. With respect to Delatine the target price is $28 per bottle. Bright Day must design the product *at a cost* that will support this price and provide the desired profit of $40,000. Fortunately, the marketing manager had some suggestions.

Using the Contribution Approach to Estimate the Effects of Changes in Variable Costs

LO4 Use the contribution per unit approach to conduct cost-volume-profit analysis.

The previously discussed $24 cost is for a bottle of 100 capsules, each containing 90 milligrams (mg) of pure Delatine. The manufacturer is willing to provide Delatine to Bright Day in two alternative package sizes: (1) a bottle costing $12 that contains 100 capsules of 30 mg strength pure Delatine and (2) a bottle costing $3 that contains 100 capsules containing 5 mg of Delatine mixed with a vitamin C compound. The 5 mg dosage is the minimum required to permit a package label to indicate the product contains Delatine. The marketing manager observes that either option would enable Bright Day to sell Delatine at a price customers would be willing to pay.

The president vehemently rejected the second option, calling it a blatant attempt to deceive customers by suggesting they were buying Delatine when in fact they were getting vitamin C. *He considered the idea unethical and dangerous.* He vowed that he would not be seen on the six o'clock news trying to defend a fast buck scheme while his company's reputation went up in smoke. After calming down, he agreed that the first option had merit. The appropriate dosage for Delatine was uncertain; customers who wanted 90 mg per day could take three capsules instead of one. He asked the accountant, "What's the effect on the bottom line?"

The variable cost changes from $24 to $12 per bottle. The contribution margin per unit increases from $4 per bottle ($28 sales price − $24 variable cost per bottle) to $16 per bottle ($28 sales price − $12 variable cost per bottle). The significant increase in contribution margin per unit dramatically decreases the sales volume necessary to attain the target profit. The computations follow:

$$\text{Sales volume in units} = \frac{\text{Fixed costs} + \text{Desired profit}}{\text{Contribution margin per unit}}$$

$$= \frac{\$60{,}000 + \$40{,}000}{\$16} = 6{,}250 \text{ units}$$

REALITY *bytes*

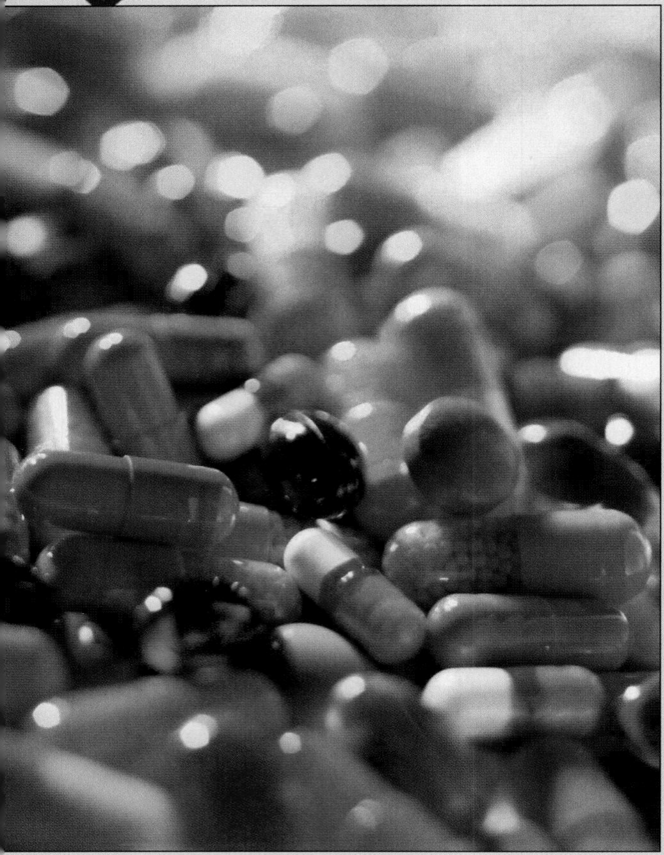

Healthy people or healthy profits? If you were president of a major drug manufacturing company, which would you choose? Long-term studies for the treatment of high blood pressure suggest that the cheapest medications available (beta blockers and diuretics) are more effective and safer than more expensive ones. Even so, a survey of drug ads in the *New England Journal of Medicine* reveals an advertising program that advocates the use of more expensive medications (calcium-channel blockers and ACE inhibitors). The most aggressively marketed are the high-priced, high-profit calcium-channel blockers. This marketing effort persists despite the fact that studies have linked these drugs to an increased risk of heart attack, cancer, and suicide. Why are the drug companies interested in selling these drugs? Could it have something to do with the fact that calcium-channel blockers have a price of more than three times that of diuretics? The marketing campaign appears to be working. Between 1992 and 1995, sales of calcium-channel blockers increased by approximately 15 percent while that of diuretics dropped by 50 percent. One study suggests that the shift to the more expensive drugs is adding approximately $3 billion in unnecessary expenditures to the national medical bill. Healthy people, or healthy profits? Practicing high ethical standards in business is not always an easy task. Keep in mind, however, that shortcuts to high profitability are filled with booby traps. A class action lawsuit could easily wipe out any benefit attained by unscrupulous business practices. The demise of the silicone breast implant industry stands as a clear example.

Source: Catherine Arnst, "Is Good Marketing Bad Medicine?" *Business Week,* April 13, 1998, p. 62. The opinions regarding the ethical implications are those of the authors of this text.

The required sales volume in sales dollars is $175,000 (6,250 units × $28 per bottle). The following income statement confirms these amounts.

Sales Revenue (6,250 units × $28)	$175,000
Total Variable Expenses (6,250 units × $12)	(75,000)
Total Contribution Margin (6,250 units × $16)	100,000
Fixed Expenses	(60,000)
Net Income	$ 40,000

Although the drop in required sales from 25,000 units to 6,250 was significant, the marketing manager was still uneasy about the company's ability to sell 6,250 bottles of Delatine. She observed again that no other Bright Day product had produced sales of that magnitude. The accountant suggested reducing projected fixed costs by advertising on radio rather than television. While gathering cost data for the potential television ad campaign, the accountant had consulted radio ad executives who had assured him radio ads could equal the TV audience exposure at about half the cost. Even though the TV ads would likely be more effective, he argued that since radio advertising costs would be half those of TV, the desired profit could be attained at a significantly lower volume of sales. The company president was impressed with the possibilities. He asked the accountant to determine the required sales volume if advertising costs were $30,000 instead of $60,000.

ANSWERS TO THE *curious* ACCOUNTANT . . .

American Airlines eliminated some first-class seats in order to increase its operating efficiency, even if it meant forgoing some revenue. To accomplish this, the company decided to reduce the number of flights it operated per day, and to reduce the number of different types of airplanes it uses. By reducing the number of flights, the occupancy level of each flight was increased. Since airlines have a significant amount of fixed costs for each flight operated, higher occupancy rates reduce the cost per passenger, and this should increase profits per flight. By reducing the number of different types of airplanes used, the company could reduce the costs of maintenance, since each type of plane requires its own inventory of replacement parts and special training for maintenance personnel.

Circuit City fired many of its most productive salespeople to reduce operating costs. These sales personnel were paid in part on a commission basis, so the more they sold, the greater Circuit City's selling expenses were. The company's main rival, **Best Buy**, was paying its sales personnel an hourly wage only rather than commissions. Although sales commissions motivate employees to be more aggressive in selling the company's goods, the sales commission is paid on *all* sales made, and not just on the additional sales that result from motivation of the commission. Circuit City decided that the higher sales generated by the most successful members of the sales staff were not sufficient to justify their higher costs, so they were laid off.

Neither American Airlines nor Circuit City made their decisions by focusing only on revenues or only on costs. Rather, their decisions were based on an analysis of the interactions of costs, revenues, and the volume of sales that would be generated as cost and pricing strategies were altered.

Using the Contribution Approach to Estimate the Effects of Changes in Fixed Costs

LO4 Use the contribution per unit approach to conduct cost-volume-profit analysis.

Since the contribution margin will cover a smaller amount of fixed costs, changing the fixed costs from \$60,000 to \$30,000 will dramatically reduce the sales level required to earn the target profit. The computations follow:

$$\text{Sales volume in units} = \frac{\text{Fixed costs + Desired profit}}{\text{Contribution margin per unit}}$$

$$= \frac{\$30{,}000 + \$40{,}000}{\$16} = 4{,}375 \text{ units}$$

The required sales volume in sales dollars is \$122,500 (4,375 units × \$28). The following income statement confirms these amounts.

Sales Revenue (4,375 units × \$28)	\$122,500
Total Variable Expenses (4,375 units × \$12)	(52,500)
Total Contribution Margin (4,375 units × \$16)	70,000
Fixed Expenses	(30,000)
Net Income	\$ 40,000

The marketing manager supported using radio instead of television ads. Obviously, she could not guarantee any specific sales volume, but she felt confident that sales projections within a range of 4,000 to 5,000 units were reasonable.

Using the Cost-Volume Profit Graph

LO6 Draw and interpret a cost-volume-profit graph.

To visually analyze the revised projections, Bright Day's accountant prepared a cost-volume-profit (CVP) chart that pictured CVP relationships over a range of sales activity from zero to 6,000 units. The accountant followed the steps below to produce the CVP graph (sometimes called a *break-even chart*) shown in Exhibit 3–1. The graph is drawn under the following assumptions:

- The contribution margin is $16 (sales price $28 − variable cost $12 per bottle).
- The fixed cost is $30,000.
- The desired profit is $40,000.

Procedures for Drawing the CVP Graph

1. *Draw and label the axes:* The horizontal axis represents activity (expressed in units) and the vertical axis represents dollars.
2. *Draw the fixed cost line:* Total fixed costs are constant for all levels of activity. Draw a horizontal line representing the amount of fixed costs across the graph at $30,000, the fixed-cost level.
3. *Draw the total cost line:* The total cost line representing the combination of fixed and variable costs is a diagonal line that rises as it moves from left to right. To draw the line, plot one point of the total cost line at the intersection of the fixed-cost line and the vertical axis. In this case, plot the first point at the zero level of activity and $30,000 (fixed cost). Next, select an arbitrary activity level. In this case we assume 6,000 units. At this volume, the total cost is $102,000 ([6,000 units × $12] + $30,000 fixed cost). Plot a point at the coordinates of 6,000 units and $102,000. Draw a straight line through these two points.
4. *Draw the sales line:* Draw the revenue line using a procedure similar to that described for drawing the total cost line. Select some arbitrary level of activity and multiply that volume by the sales price per unit. Plot the result on the graph and draw a line from the origin (zero units, zero revenue) through this point. For example, at a volume of 6,000 units, the revenue is $168,000 (6,000 units × $28). Plot a point at the coordinates of 6,000 units and $168,000. Draw a line from the origin through the plotted point.

Trace these steps to the graph in Exhibit 3–1.

Calculating the Margin of Safety

LO7 Calculate the margin of safety in units, dollars, and percentage.

The final meeting of Bright Day's management team focused on the reliability of the data used to construct the CVP chart. The accountant called attention to the sales volume figures in the area of profitability. Recall that Bright Day must sell 4,375 bottles of Delatine to earn the

Exhibit 3–1 *Cost-Volume-Profit Graph*

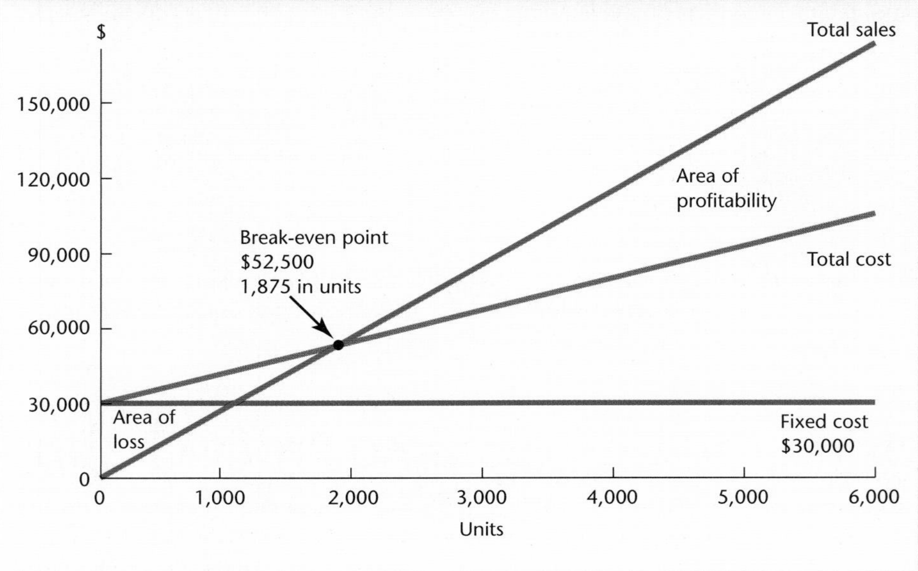

The relationship among the costs to produce a company's goods, the volume of goods it produces, the price it can charge for those goods, and the profit it earns is relevant to all industries, but perhaps no industry demonstrates the effects of these relationships more dramatically than automobile manufacturing. First, the automobile industry is globally competitive, and companies in the United States are often at a cost disadvantage. Some of this cost disadvantage comes from obvious sources, such as having to pay higher wages than do companies in countries such as South Korea. Other cost disadvantages are not so obvious. For example, according to *The Wall Street Journal**, the cost of providing health care insurance to workers adds around $1,000 to the cost of each car produced in the United States. In some countries, the government provides health care to workers.

Domestic automakers cannot simply charge more for their goods to cover their higher costs, because more consumers would buy cars from foreign manufacturers. What if domestic manufacturers decide to charge more for their cars and accept that they will sell fewer cars? Then the average cost to make each car will increase because much of these costs are fixed. Remember, as activity (volume) decreases, cost per unit increases.

As a result of these conflicts, for the past several years, carmakers have tried to keep their sales volume high by using rebates to reduce the price of their cars. This has led to its own problem. Car buyers have come to expect these rebates, so they do not want to buy domestic cars until sufficient rebates are offered. Of course, the lower selling price means the manufacturers' profits are lower.

How can car manufacturers in the United States escape this cycle of higher costs, lower prices, and lower profits? One strategy has been to introduce new models. The hope is that if a new model is attractive enough to consumers, and no equivalent foreign model exists at a lower price, customers will buy the car without being offered a rebate. Consider that Chevrolet introduced a completely redesigned Corvette for the 2005 model year. This $50,000 car is expected to sell at its full sticker price, or more. Meanwhile, if you want to buy one of Chevrolet's more expensive SUVs, there is a good chance you can get a rebate.

*(June 5, 2003, pp. A-1, A-12)

desired profit. In dollars, budgeted sales are $122,500 (4,375 bottles × $28 per bottle). The accountant highlighted the large gap between these budgeted sales and break-even sales. The amount of this gap, called the *margin of safety,* can be measured in units or in sales dollars as shown here:

	In Units	In Dollars
Budgeted sales	4,375	$122,500
Break-even sales	(1,875)	(52,500)
Margin of safety	2,500	$ 70,000

Recap of Delatine Decision Process

Management considers a new product named Delatine. Delatine has a projected sales price of $36 and variable cost of $24 per bottle. Fixed cost is projected to be $60,000. The break-even point is 5,000 units ($60,000 ÷ [$36 – $24] = 5,000).

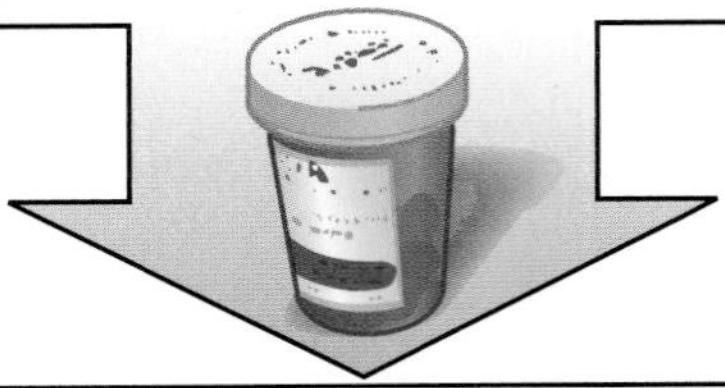

Management desires to earn a $40,000 profit on Delatine. The sales volume required to earn the desired profit is 8,334 units ([$60,000 + $40,000] ÷ [$36 – $24] = 8,334).

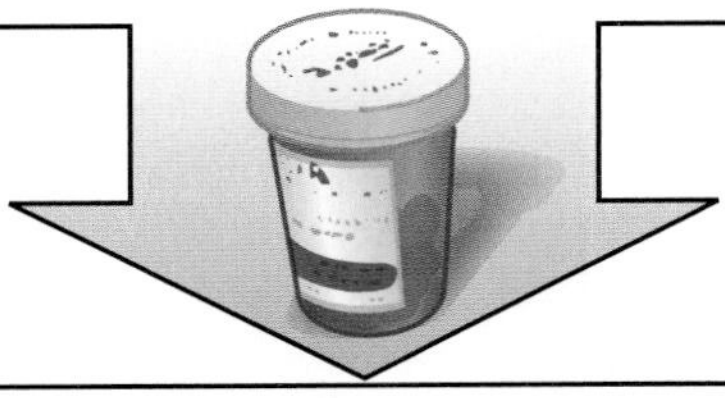

The marketing manager advocates a target pricing approach that lowers the proposed selling price to $28 per bottle. The sales volume required to earn a $40,000 profit increases to 25,000 units ([$60,000 + $40,000] ÷ [$28 – $24] = 25,000).

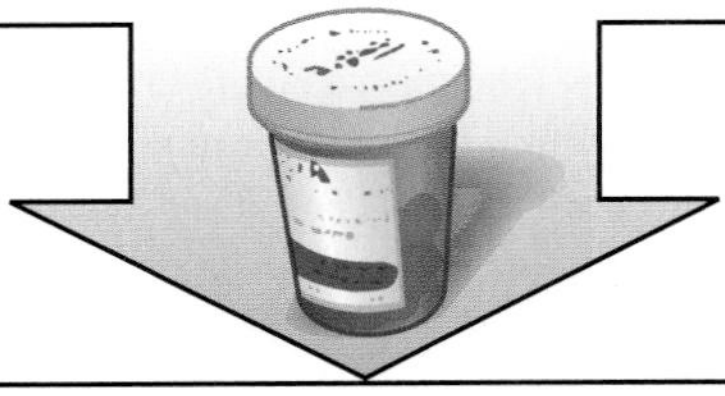

Target costing is employed to reengineer the product, thereby reducing variable cost to $12 per bottle. The sales volume required to earn a $40,000 profit decreases to 6,250 units ([$60,000 + $40,000] ÷ [$28 – $12] = 6,250).

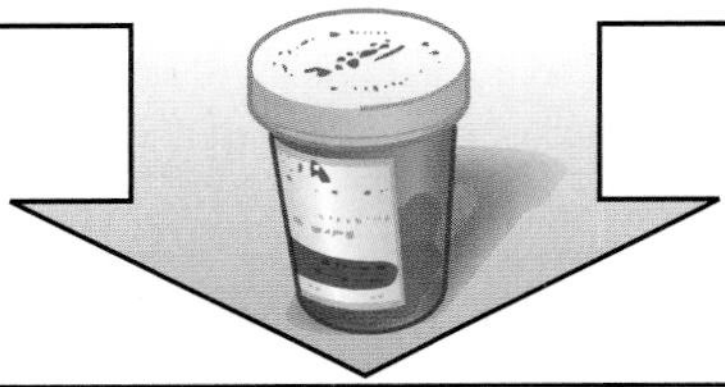

Target costing is applied further to reduce fixed cost to $30,000. The sales volume required to earn a $40,000 profit decreases to 4,375 units ([$30,000 + $40,000] ÷ [$28 – $12] = 4,375). The new break-even point is 1,875 units ($30,000 ÷ [$28 – $12] = 1,875).

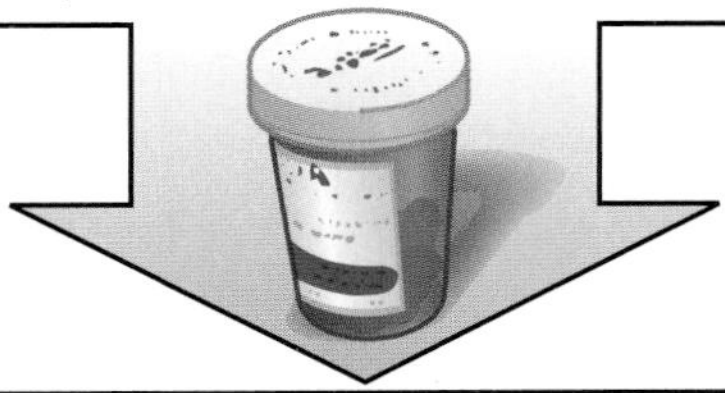

In view of a 57.14% margin of safety ([4,375 – 1,875] ÷ 4,375 = .5714) , management decides to add Delatine to its product line.

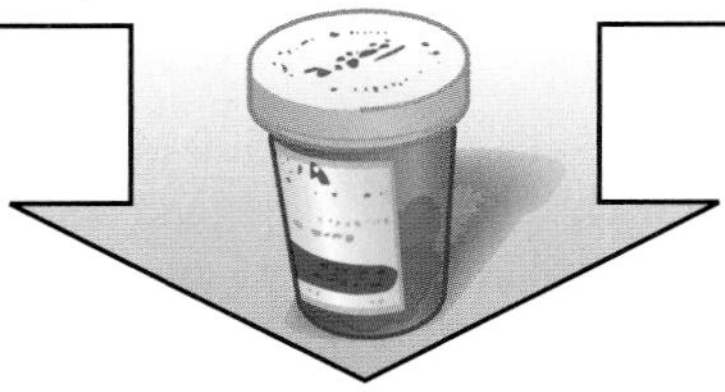

The **margin of safety** measures the cushion between budgeted sales and the break-even point. It quantifies the amount by which actual sales can fall short of expectations before the company will begin to incur losses.

To help compare diverse products or companies of different sizes, the margin of safety can be expressed as a percentage. Divide the margin of safety by the budgeted sales volume[1] as shown here:

$$\text{Margin of safety} = \frac{\text{Budgeted sales} - \text{Break-even sales}}{\text{Budgeted sales}}$$

$$\text{Margin of safety} = \frac{\$122{,}500 - \$52{,}500}{\$122{,}500} \times 100 = 57.14\%$$

This analysis suggests actual sales would have to fall short of expected sales by more than 57 percent before Bright Day would experience a loss on Delatine. The large margin of safety suggests the proposed radio advertising program to market bottles of 30mg Delatine capsules has minimal risk.

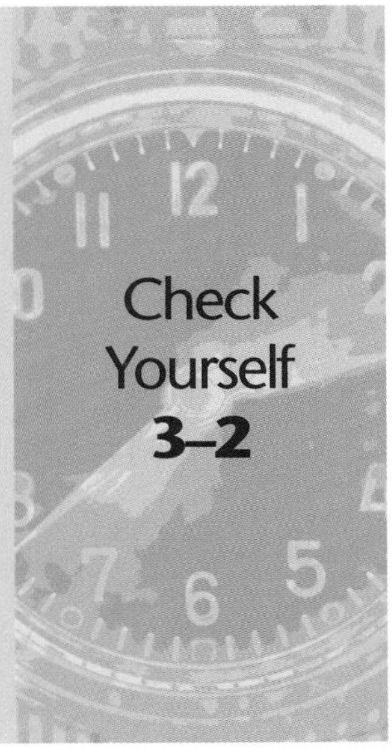

Suppose that Bright Day is considering the possibility of selling a protein supplement that will cost Bright Day $5 per bottle. Bright Day believes that it can sell 4,000 bottles of the supplement for $25 per bottle. Fixed costs associated with selling the supplement are expected to be $42,000. Does the supplement have a wider margin of safety than Delatine?

Answer Calculate the break-even point for the protein supplement.

$$\text{Break-even volume in units} = \frac{\text{Fixed costs}}{\text{Contribution margin per unit}} = \frac{\$42{,}000}{\$25 - \$5} = 2{,}100 \text{ units}$$

Calculate the margin of safety. Note that the margin of safety expressed as a percentage can be calculated using the number of units or sales dollars. Using either units or dollars yields the same percentage.

$$\text{Margin of safety} = \frac{\text{Budgeted sales} - \text{Break-even sales}}{\text{Budgeted sales}} = \frac{4{,}000 - 2{,}100}{4{,}000} = \; = 47.5\%$$

The margin of safety for Delatine (57.14 percent) exceeds that for the protein supplement (47.5 percent). This suggests that Bright Day is less likely to incur losses selling Delatine than selling the supplement.

Performing Sensitivity Analysis Using Spreadsheet Software

LO8 Explain how spreadsheet software can be used to conduct sensitivity analysis for cost-volume-profit relationships.

While useful, the margin of safety offers only a one dimensional measure of risk—change in sales volume. Profitability is affected by multidimensional forces. Fixed or variable costs, as well as sales volume, could differ from expectations. Exhibit 3–2 uses data pertaining to Bright Day's proposed project for marketing Delatine to illustrate an Excel spreadsheet showing the sensitivity of profits to simultaneous changes in fixed cost, variable cost, and sales volume. Recall the accountant estimated the radio ad campaign would cost $30,000. The spreadsheet projects profitability if advertising costs are as low as $20,000 or as high as $40,000. The effects of potential simultaneous changes in variable cost and sales volume are similarly projected.

[1] The margin of safety percentage can be based on actual as well as budgeted sales. For example, an analyst could compare the margins of safety of two companies under current operating conditions by substituting actual sales for budgeted sales in the computation, as follows: ([Actual sales − Break-even sales] ÷ Actual sales).

Exhibit 3–2 *Spreadsheet Report to Facilitate "What-If" Analysis*

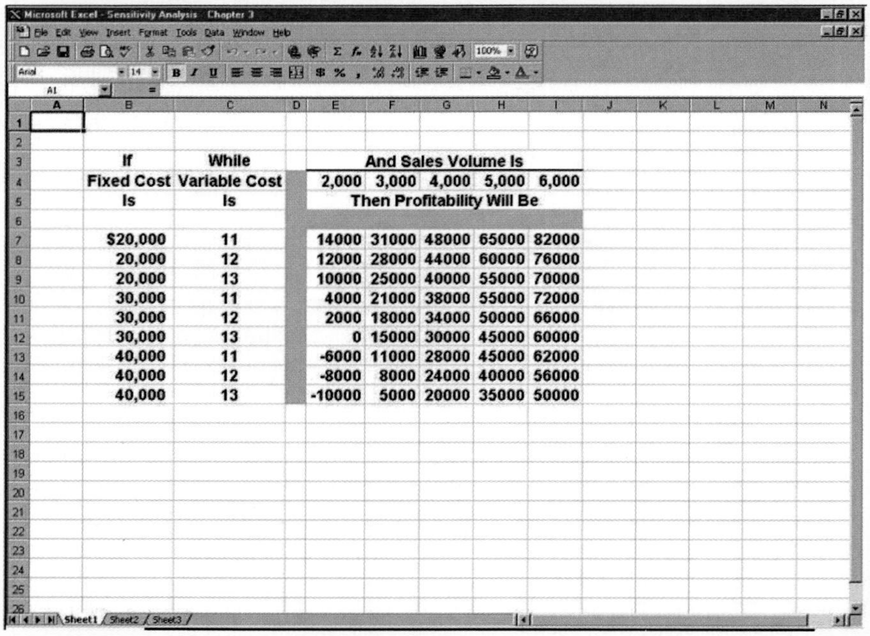

If Fixed Cost Is	While Variable Cost Is	And Sales Volume Is 2,000	3,000	4,000	5,000	6,000
		Then Profitability Will Be				
$20,000	11	14000	31000	48000	65000	82000
20,000	12	12000	28000	44000	60000	76000
20,000	13	10000	25000	40000	55000	70000
30,000	11	4000	21000	38000	55000	72000
30,000	12	2000	18000	34000	50000	66000
30,000	13	0	15000	30000	45000	60000
40,000	11	-6000	11000	28000	45000	62000
40,000	12	-8000	8000	24000	40000	56000
40,000	13	-10000	5000	20000	35000	50000

The range of scenarios illustrated in the spreadsheet represents only a few of the many alternatives management can analyze with a few quick keystrokes. The spreadsheet program recalculates profitability figures instantly when one of the variables changes. If the president asks what would happen if Bright Day sold 10,000 units, the accountant merely substitutes the new number for one of the existing sales volume figures, and revised profitability numbers are instantly available. By changing the variables, management can get a real feel for the sensitivity of profits to changes in cost and volume. Investigating a multitude of what-if possibilities involving simultaneous changes in fixed cost, variable cost, and volume is called **sensitivity analysis.**

Assessing the Pricing Strategy

After reviewing the spreadsheet analysis, Bright Day's management team is convinced it should undertake radio advertising for Delatine. Only under the most dire circumstances (if actual sales are significantly below expectations while costs are well above expectations) will the company incur a loss. In fact, the president feels uneasy because the projections seem too good to be true. If Bright Day pays $12 per bottle for Delatine and sells it for $28 per bottle as projected, the effective markup on cost would be 133 percent ([$28 - $12] ÷ $12). Recall the company's normal markup is only 50 percent of cost. The president asks the marketing manager, "Are you sure people will buy this stuff at that price?"

The marketing manager explains she is advocating a pricing strategy known as **prestige pricing.** Many people will pay a premium to be the first to use a new product, especially when it receives widespread news media attention, as is the case with Delatine. Similarly, people will pay more for a product with a prestigious brand name. As news coverage of Delatine fades, competitors begin to offer alternatives, and customer interest wanes, the time will come to reduce prices. The marketing manager is confident the product will sell initially at the proposed price.

Exhibit 3–3 *Budgeted Income Statement*

Sales Revenue (4,375 units × $28 sale price)	$122,500
Total Variable Expenses (4,375 units × $12 cost per bottle)	(52,500)
Total Contribution Margin (4,375 units × $16)	70,000
Fixed Expenses	(30,000)
Net Income	$ 40,000

Using the Contribution Approach to Assess the Effect of Simultaneous Changes in CVP Variables

LO4 Use the contribution per unit approach to conduct cost-volume-profit analysis.

The contribution approach previously illustrated to analyze one dimensional CVP relationships easily adapts to studying the effects of simultaneous changes in CVP variables. To illustrate several possible scenarios, assume Bright Day has developed the budgeted income statement in Exhibit 3–3.

A Decrease in Sales Price Accompanied by an Increase in Sales Volume

The marketing manager believes reducing the sales price per bottle to $25 will increase sales volume by 625 units. The per unit contribution margin would drop to $13 ($25 sales price − $12 cost per bottle). The expected sales volume would become 5,000 (4,375 + 625). Should Bright Day reduce the price? Compare the projected profit without these changes ($40,000) with the projected profit if the sales price is $25, computed as follows:

$$\text{Profit} = \text{Contribution margin} - \text{Fixed cost}$$
$$\text{Profit} = (5{,}000 \times \$13) - \$30{,}000 = \$35{,}000$$

Since budgeted income falls from $40,000 to $35,000, Bright Day should not reduce the sales price.

An Increase in Fixed Cost Accompanied by an Increase in Sales Volume

Return to the budgeted income statement in Exhibit 3–3. If the company buys an additional $12,000 of advertising, management believes sales can increase to 6,000 units. The contribution margin per unit will remain $16 ($28 − $12). Should Bright Day incur the additional advertising cost, increasing fixed costs to $42,000? The expected profit would be:

$$\text{Profit} = \text{Contribution margin} - \text{Fixed cost}$$
$$\text{Profit} = (6{,}000 \times \$16) - \$42{,}000 = \$54{,}000$$

Since budgeted income increases from $40,000 to $54,000, Bright Day should seek to increase sales through additional advertising.

A Simultaneous Reduction in Sales Price, Fixed Costs, Variable Costs, and Sales Volume

Return again to the budgeted income statement in Exhibit 3–3. Suppose Bright Day negotiates a $4 reduction in the cost of a bottle of Delatine. The management team considers passing some of the savings on to customers by reducing the sales price to $25 per bottle. Furthermore, the team believes it could reduce advertising costs by $8,000 and still achieve sales of 4,200 units. Should Bright Day adopt this plan to reduce prices and advertising costs?

The contribution margin would increase to $17 per bottle ($25 revised selling price − $8 revised variable cost per bottle) and fixed cost would fall to $22,000 ($30,000 − $8,000). Based on a sales volume of 4,200 units, the expected profit is:

Profit = Contribution margin − Fixed cost
Profit = (4,200 × $17) − $22,000 = $49,400

Because budgeted income increases from $40,000 to $49,400, Bright Day should proceed with the revised operating strategy.

Many other possible scenarios could be considered. The contribution approach can be used to analyze independent or simultaneous changes in the CVP variables.

Performing Cost-Volume-Profit (CVP) Analysis Using the Contribution Margin Ratio

LO9 Use the contribution margin ratio and the equation method to conduct cost-volume-profit analysis.

The **contribution margin ratio** is the contribution margin divided by sales, computed using either total figures or per unit figures. The contribution margin *ratio* can be used in CVP analysis as an alternative to using the *per unit* contribution margin. To illustrate, assume Bright Day is considering selling a new product called Multi Minerals. The expected sales price, variable cost, and contribution margin per unit for Multi Minerals are:

Sales revenue per unit	$20
Variable cost per unit	12
Contribution margin per unit	$ 8

Based on these data, the *contribution margin ratio* for Multi Minerals is 40 percent ($8 ÷ $20). This ratio means every dollar of sales provides 40 cents ($1.00 × 0.40) to cover fixed costs. After fixed costs have been covered, each dollar of sales provides 40 cents of profit.

While the *per unit contribution margin* approach produces results measured in units, the *contribution margin ratio* approach produces results expressed in dollars. The two approaches merely represent different ways to reach the same conclusion. To illustrate, the two alternative approaches to calculate the break-even point are shown here, assuming Bright Day expects to incur $24,000 of fixed expenses to market Multi Minerals:

Per Unit Contribution Approach Break-even in Units	Contribution Ratio Approach Break-even in Dollars
$\frac{\text{Fixed costs}}{\text{Contribution margin per unit}} = \text{Units}$	$\frac{\text{Fixed costs}}{\text{Contribution margin ratio}} = \text{Dollars}$
$\frac{\$24,000}{\$8} = 3,000 \text{ units}$	$\frac{\$24,000}{40\%} = \$60,000$

Recall the break-even point in units can be converted to sales dollars by multiplying the number of units to break even by the sales price per unit (3,000 units × $20 per unit = $60,000). Alternatively, the break-even point in sales dollars can be converted to units by dividing ($60,000 ÷ $20 = 3,000). The two approaches represent different views of the same data. The relationship between the two approaches holds when other CVP variables are added or changed. For example, either approach can provide the sales volume necessary to reach a target profit of $8,000, as follows:

Per Unit Contribution Approach Sales Volume in Units	Contribution Ratio Approach Sales Volume in Dollars
$\frac{\text{Fixed costs} + \text{Desired profit}}{\text{Contribution margin per unit}} = \text{Units}$	$\frac{\text{Fixed costs} + \text{Desired profit}}{\text{Contribution margin ratio}} = \text{Dollars}$
$\frac{\$24{,}000 + \$8{,}000}{\$8} = 4{,}000 \text{ units}$	$\frac{\$24{,}000 + \$8{,}000}{40\%} = \$80{,}000$

Once again, multiplying the $20 sales price by the sales volume expressed in units equals the sales volume in dollars ($20 × 4,000 = $80,000).

Topic Tackler PLUS

3–2

Performing Cost-Volume-Profit Analysis Using the Equation Method

LO9 Use the contribution margin ratio and the equation method to conduct cost-volume-profit analysis.

A third way to analyze CVP relationships uses the **equation method.** Begin with expressing the break-even point as an algebraic equation, as shown here.[2]

$$\text{Sales} = \text{Variable cost} + \text{Fixed cost}$$

Expanding the equation provides the basis for computing the break-even point in number of units, as shown here:

$$\begin{matrix}\text{Selling price per unit} \\ \times \\ \text{Number of units sold}\end{matrix} = \begin{matrix}\text{Variable cost per unit} \\ \times \\ \text{Number of units sold}\end{matrix} + \text{Fixed cost}$$

Using the Multi Minerals $20 sales price, $12 variable cost, and $24,000 fixed cost, the *break-even point in units* is:

$$\begin{aligned}\$20 \times \text{Units} &= \$12 \times \text{Units} + \$24{,}000 \\ \$8 \times \text{Units} &= \$24{,}000 \\ \text{Units} &= 3{,}000\end{aligned}$$

As before, the break-even sales volume in *units* can be converted into break-even sales volume in *dollars* by multiplying the sales price per unit by the number of units sold. The *break-even point* for Multi Minerals expressed in *dollars* is:

$$\begin{matrix}\text{Selling price per unit} & \times & \text{Number of units sold} & = & \text{Sales volume in dollars} \\ \$20 & \times & 3{,}000 & = & \$60{,}000\end{matrix}$$

The equation method can also be used to analyze additional CVP relationships. For example, the equation to determine the sales volume necessary to attain a target profit of $8,000 is:

$$\begin{matrix}\text{Selling price per unit} \\ \times \\ \text{Number of units sold}\end{matrix} = \begin{matrix}\text{Variable cost per unit} \\ \times \\ \text{Number of units sold}\end{matrix} + \text{Fixed cost} + \text{Desired profit}$$

---

[2] The equation method results in the same computation as the per unit contribution margin approach. Consider the following. Using the per unit contribution margin approach, the break-even point is determined as follows (X is the break-even point in units):

$$X = \text{Fixed cost} \div \text{Per unit contribution margin}$$

Using the equation method, the break-even point is determined as follows (X is the break-even point in units):

$$\begin{aligned}&\text{Unit sales price } (X) = \text{Variable cost per unit } (X) + \text{Fixed cost} \\ &(\text{Unit sales price} - \text{Variable cost per unit})\ (X) = \text{Fixed cost} \\ &\text{Per unit contribution margin } (X) = \text{Fixed cost} \\ &X = \text{Fixed cost} \div \text{Per unit contribution margin}\end{aligned}$$

The computations are:

$$\$20 \times \text{Units} = \$12 \times \text{Units} + \$24{,}000 + \$8{,}000$$
$$\$8 \times \text{Units} = \$32{,}000$$
$$\text{Units} = 4{,}000$$

Comparing these results with those determined using the per unit contribution approach and the contribution margin ratio approach demonstrates that the equation method is simply another way to achieve the same result. The method to use depends on personal and management preferences.

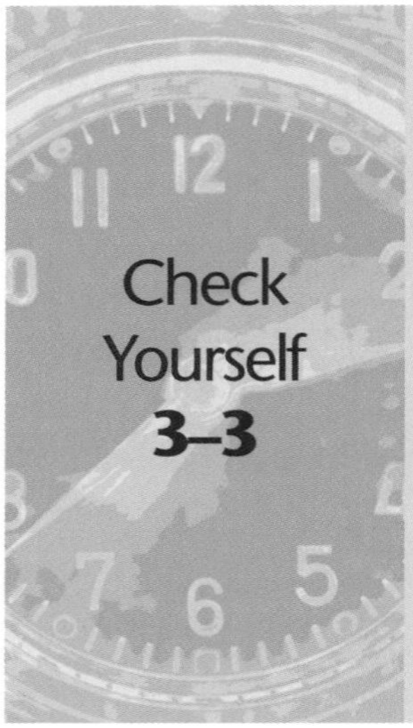

Recall the information presented in Check Yourself 3–1. VolTech Company manufactures small engines that it sells for $130 each, with variable costs of $70 per unit, expected fixed costs of $100,000, and a target profit of $188,000. Use the equation method to calculate the number of engines VolTech must sell to attain the target profit.

Answer

$$\begin{matrix}\text{Selling price per unit} \\ \times \\ \text{Number of units sold}\end{matrix} = \begin{matrix}\text{Variable cost per unit} \\ \times \\ \text{Number of units sold}\end{matrix} + \text{Fixed cost} + \text{Desired profit}$$

$$\$130 \times \text{Units} = \$70 \times \text{Units} + \$100{,}000 + \$188{,}000$$
$$\$60 \times \text{Units} = \$288{,}000$$
$$\text{Units} = 4{,}800$$

This is the same result determined in the Check Yourself 3–1 exercise. The only difference is in the method used to make the computation.

Cost-Volume-Profit Limitations

LO10 Identify the limitations of cost-volume-profit analysis.

Because cost-volume-profit analysis presumes strictly linear behavior among the variables, its accuracy is limited. Actual CVP variables rarely behave with true linearity. Suppose, for example, a business receives volume discounts on materials purchases: the more material purchased, the lower the cost per unit. The total cost varies but not in direct proportion to the amount of material purchased. Similarly, fixed costs can change. A supervisor's fixed salary may change if the supervisor receives a raise. Likewise, the cost of telephone service, rent, insurance, taxes, and so on may increase or decrease. In practice, fixed costs frequently fluctuate. Furthermore, sales prices may vary as a result of promotions or other factors. None of the CVP variables is likely to behave with strict linearity.

Finally, CVP analysis presumes inventory levels remain constant during the period. In other words, sales and production are assumed to be equal. CVP formulas provide the estimated number of units that must be *produced and sold* to break even or to achieve some designated target profit. Manufacturing or acquiring, but not selling, inventory generates costs without producing corresponding revenue. Changes in inventory levels undoubtedly affect CVP relationships. The assumptions underlying CVP analysis are rarely entirely valid in business practice. Within the relevant range of activity, however, deviations from the basic assumptions are normally insignificant. A prudent business manager who exercises good judgment will find the projections generated by cost-volume-profit analysis useful regardless of these limitations.

a look back

Profitability is affected by changes in sale price, costs, and the volume of activity. The relationship among these variables is examined using *cost-volume-profit (CVP) analysis.* The *contribution margin,* determined by subtracting variable costs from the sales price, is a useful variable in CVP analysis. The *contribution margin per unit* is the amount each unit sold provides to cover fixed costs. Once fixed costs have been covered, each additional unit sold increases net income by the amount of the per unit contribution margin.

The *break-even point* (the point where total revenue equals total cost) in units can be determined by dividing fixed costs by the contribution margin per unit. The break-even point in sales dollars can be determined by multiplying the number of break-even units by the sales price per unit. To determine sales in units to obtain a designated profit, the sum of fixed costs and desired profit is divided by the contribution margin per unit. The contribution margin per unit can also be used to assess the effects on the company's profitability of changes in sales price, variable costs, and fixed costs.

Many methods are available to determine the prices at which products should sell. In *cost-plus pricing,* the sales price per unit is determined by adding a percentage markup to the cost per unit. In contrast, *target pricing* (*target costing*) begins with an estimated market price customers would be willing to pay for the product and then develops the product at a cost that will enable the company to earn its desired profit.

A *break-even graph* can depict cost-volume-profit relationships for a product over a range of sales activity. The horizontal axis represents volume of activity and the vertical axis represents dollars. Lines for fixed costs, total costs, and sales are drawn based on the sales price per unit, variable cost per unit, and fixed costs. The graph can be used to determine the break-even point in units and sales dollars.

The *margin of safety* is the number of units or the amount of sales dollars by which actual sales can fall below expected sales before a loss is incurred. The margin of safety can also be expressed as a percentage to permit comparing different size companies. The margin of safety can be computed as a percentage by dividing the difference between budgeted sales and break-even sales by the amount of budgeted sales.

Spreadsheet software as well as the contribution margin approach can be used to conduct sensitivity analysis of cost-volume-profit relationships. *Sensitivity analysis* predicts the effect on profitability of different scenarios of fixed costs, variable costs, and sales volumes. The effects of simultaneous changes in all three variables can be assessed. A *contribution margin ratio* can be used to determine the break-even point in sales dollars. The ratio is a percentage determined by dividing the contribution margin per unit by the sales price per unit. Using the contribution margin ratio, the break-even volume in dollars can be determined by dividing the total fixed costs by the ratio. Cost-volume-profit relationships can also be examined using this algebraic equation:

$$\text{Sales} = \text{Variable cost} + \text{Fixed cost}$$

Cost-volume-profit analysis is built upon certain simplifying assumptions. The analysis assumes true linearity among the CVP variables and a constant level of inventory. Although these assumptions are not literally valid in actual practice, CVP analysis nevertheless provides managers with helpful insights for decision-making.

a look forward

The next chapter introduces the concept of *cost relevance.* Applying the concepts you have learned to real-world business problems can be challenging. Frequently, so much data is available that it is difficult to distinguish important from useless information. The next chapter will help you learn to identify information that is relevant in a variety of short-term decision-making scenarios including special offers, outsourcing, segment elimination, and asset replacement.

APPENDIX

LO11 Perform multiple-product break-even analysis.

Multiple-Product Break-Even Analysis

When a company analyzes CVP relationships for multiple products that sell simultaneously, the break-even point can be affected by the relative number (sales mix) of the products sold. For example, suppose Bright Day decides to run a special sale on its two leading antioxidants, vitamins C and E. The income statements at the break-even point are presented in Exhibit 3–4.

Recall that the break-even point is the point where total sales equal total costs. Net income is zero at that point. The data in Exhibit 3–4 indicate that the budgeted break-even sales volume for the antioxidant special is 2,700 bottles of vitamins with a sales mix of 2,000 bottles of vitamin C and 700 bottles of vitamin E. What happens if the relative sales mix changes? Exhibit 3–5 depicts the expected condition if total sales remain at 2,700 units but the sales mix changes to 2,100 bottles of vitamin C and 600 bottles of vitamin E.

Although the total number of bottles sold remains at 2,700 units, profitability shifts from breaking even to a $280 loss because of the change in the sales mix of the two products, that is, selling more vitamin C than expected and less vitamin E. Because vitamin C has a lower contribution margin ($1.20 per bottle) than vitamin E ($4.00 per bottle), selling more of C and less of E reduces profitability. The opposite impact occurs if Bright Day sells more E and less C. Exhibit 3–6 depicts the expected condition if total sales remain at 2,700 units but the sales mix changes to 1,350 bottles each of vitamin C and vitamin E.

Companies must consider sales mix when conducting break-even analysis for multiproduct business ventures. The multiple product break-even point can be determined using the per unit contribution margin approach. However, it is necessary to use a weighted average to determine the per unit contribution margin. The contribution margin of each product must be weighted by its proportionate share of units

Exhibit 3–4 *Budgeted Data for Antioxidant Special*

	Vitamin C					Vitamin E					Total	
	Budgeted Number		Per Unit		Budgeted Amount	Budgeted Number		Per Unit		Budgeted Amount	Budgeted Number	Budgeted Amount
Sales	2,000	@	$7.20	=	$14,400	700	@	$11.00	=	$7,700	2,700	$22,100
Variable cost	2,000	@	6.00	=	(12,000)	700	@	7.00	=	(4,900)	2,700	(16,900)
Contribution margin	2,000	@	1.20	=	2,400	700	@	4.00	=	2,800	2,700	5,200
Fixed cost					(2,400)					(2,800)		(5,200)
Net income					$ 0					$ 0		$ 0

Exhibit 3–5 *Budgeted Data for Antioxidant Special*

	Vitamin C					Vitamin E					Total	
	Budgeted Number		Per Unit		Budgeted Amount	Budgeted Number		Per Unit		Budgeted Amount	Budgeted Number	Budgeted Amount
Sales	2,100	@	$7.20	=	$15,120	600	@	$11.00	=	$6,600	2,700	$21,720
Variable cost	2,100	@	6.00	=	(12,600)	600	@	7.00	=	(4,200)	2,700	(16,800)
Contribution margin	2,100	@	1.20	=	2,520	600	@	4.00	=	2,400	2,700	4,920
Fixed cost					(2,400)					(2,800)		(5,200)
Net income					$ 120					$ (400)		$ (280)

Exhibit 3–6 *Budgeted Data for Antioxidant Special*

	Vitamin C					Vitamin E					Total	
	Budgeted Number		Per Unit		Budgeted Amount	Budgeted Number		Per Unit		Budgeted Amount	Budgeted Number	Budgeted Amount
Sales	1,350	@	$7.20	=	$9,720	1,350	@	$11.00	=	$14,850	2,700	$24,570
Variable cost	1,350	@	6.00	=	(8,100)	1,350	@	7.00	=	(9,450)	2,700	(17,550)
Contribution margin	1,350	@	1.20	=	1,620	1,350	@	4.00	=	5,400	2,700	7,020
Fixed cost					(2,400)					(2,800)		(5,200)
Net income					$ (780)					$ 2,600		$ 1,820

sold. For example, in the preceding case, the relative sales mix between the two products is one half (1,350 units ÷ 2,700 units = 50 percent). What is the break-even point given a relative sales mix of one-half for each product? To answer this question, the companies must first determine the weighted average per unit contribution margin by multiplying the contribution margin of each product by 50 percent. The required computation is shown here.

Weighted Average Contribution Margin	
Vitamin C ($1.20 × 0.50)	$0.60
Vitamin E ($4.00 × 0.50)	2.00
Weighted average per unit contribution margin	$2.60

The break-even point in total units at a 50/50 sales mix is computed as follows.

Break-even point = Fixed costs ÷ Weighted average per unit contribution margin
Break-even point = $5,200 ÷ $2.60 = 2,000 total units

Next divide the total units to break even in proportion to the relative sales mix. In other words, the break-even point occurs at 1,000 bottles of Vitamin C (50 percent of 2,000) and 1,000 bottles of Vitamin E (50 percent of 2,000). The income statements presented in Exhibit 3–7 illustrate these results:

Exhibit 3–7 *Budgeted Data for Antioxidant Special*

	Vitamin C			Vitamin E			Total	
	Budgeted Number	Per Unit	Budgeted Amount	Budgeted Number	Per Unit	Budgeted Amount	Budgeted Number	Budgeted Amount
Sales	1,000	@ $7.20 =	$ 7,200	1,000	@ $11.00 =	$11,000	2,000	$18,200
Variable cost	1,000	@ 6.00 =	(6,000)	1,000	@ 7.00 =	(7,000)	2,000	(13,000)
Contribution margin	1,000	@ 1.20 =	1,200	1,000	@ 4.00 =	4,000	2,000	5,200
Fixed cost			(2,400)			(2,800)		(5,200)
Net income			$(1,200)			$ 1,200		$ 0

SELF-STUDY REVIEW PROBLEM

Sharp Company makes and sells pencil sharpeners. The variable cost of each sharpener is $20. The sharpeners are sold for $30 each. Fixed operating expenses amount to $40,000.

Required

a. Determine the break-even point in units and sales dollars.
b. Determine the sales volume in units and dollars that is required to attain a profit of $12,000. Verify your answer by preparing an income statement using the contribution margin format.
c. Determine the margin of safety between sales required to attain a profit of $12,000 and break-even sales.
d. Prepare a break-even graph using the cost and price assumptions outlined above.

Solution to Requirement a

Formula for Computing Break-even Point in Units

$$\frac{\text{Fixed cost + Target profit}}{\text{Contribution margin per unit}} = \frac{\$40{,}000 + \$0}{\$30 - \$20} = 4{,}000 \text{ Units}$$

Break-even Point in Sales Dollars	
Sales price	$ 30
Times number of units	4,000
Sales volume in dollars	$120,000

Solution to Requirement b

Formula for Computing Unit Sales Required to Attain Desired Profit
$\dfrac{\text{Fixed cost} + \text{Target profit}}{\text{Contribution margin per unit}} = \dfrac{\$40{,}000 + \$12{,}000}{\$30 - \$20} = 5{,}200 \text{ units}$

Sales Dollars Required to Attain Desired Profit	
Sales price	$ 30
Times number of units	5,200
Sales volume in dollars	$156,000

Income Statement	
Sales Volume in Units (a)	5,200
Sales Revenue (a × $30)	$156,000
Variable Costs (a × $20)	(104,000)
Contribution Margin	52,000
Fixed Costs	(40,000)
Net Income	$ 12,000

Solution to Requirement c

Margin of Safety Computations	Units	Dollars
Budgeted sales	5,200	$156,000
Break-even sales	(4,000)	(120,000)
Margin of safety	1,200	$ 36,000

Percentage Computation
$\dfrac{\text{Margin of safety in \$}}{\text{Budgeted sales}} = \dfrac{\$36{,}000}{\$156{,}000} = 23.08\%$

Solution to Requirement d

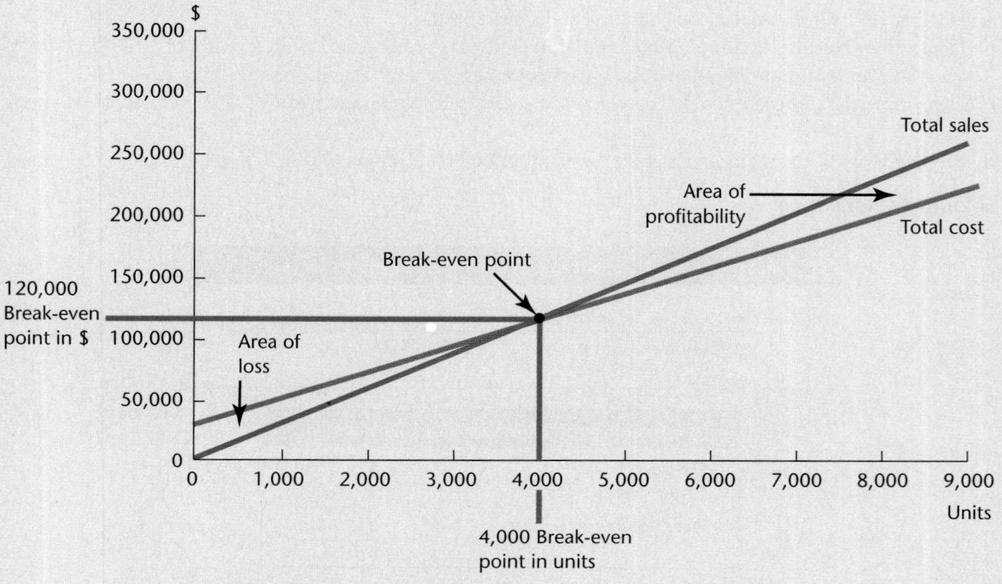

KEY TERMS

Break-even point *96*
Contribution margin per unit *96*
Contribution margin ratio *108*
Cost-plus pricing strategy *96*
Cost-volume-profit (CVP) analysis *96*
Equation method *109*
Margin of safety *105*
Prestige pricing *106*
Sensitivity analysis *106*
Target pricing (target costing) *99*

QUESTIONS

1. What does the term *break-even point* mean? Name the two ways it can be measured.
2. How does a contribution margin income statement differ from the income statement used in financial reporting?
3. In what three ways can the contribution margin be useful in cost-volume-profit analysis?
4. If Company A has a projected margin of safety of 22 percent while Company B has a margin of safety of 52 percent, which company is at greater risk when actual sales are less than budgeted?
5. What variables affect profitability? Name two methods for determining profitability when simultaneous changes occur in these variables.
6. When would the customer be willing to pay a premium price for a product or service? What pricing strategy would be appropriate under these circumstances?
7. What are three alternative approaches to determine the break-even point? What do the results of these approaches show?
8. What is the equation method for determining the break-even point? Explain how the results of this method differ from those of the contribution margin approach.
9. If a company is trying to find the break-even point for multiple products that sell simultaneously, what consideration must be taken into account?
10. What assumptions are inherent in cost-volume-profit analysis? Since these assumptions are usually not wholly valid, why do managers still use the analysis in decision making?
11. Mary Hartwell and Jane Jamail, college roommates, are considering the joint purchase of a computer that they can share to prepare class assignments. Ms. Hartwell wants a particular model that costs $2,000; Ms. Jamail prefers a more economical model that costs $1,500. In fact, Ms. Jamail is adamant about her position, refusing to contribute more than $750 toward the purchase. If Ms. Hartwell is also adamant about her position, should she accept Ms. Jamail's $750 offer and apply that amount toward the purchase of the more expensive computer?
12. How would the algebraic formula used to compute the break-even point under the equation method be changed to solve for a desired target profit?
13. Setting the sales price is easy: Enter cost information and desired profit data into one of the cost-volume-profit formulas, and the appropriate sales price can be computed mathematically. Do you agree with this line of reasoning? Explain.
14. What is the relationship between cost-volume-profit analysis and the relevant range?

EXERCISES—SERIES A

All Exercises in Series A are available with McGraw-Hill's Homework Manager

EXERCISE 3–1A *Per Unit Contribution Margin Approach*

L.O. 2

Thorpe Corporation sells products for $15 each that have variable costs of $10 per unit. Thorpe's annual fixed cost is $300,000.

Required
Use the per unit contribution margin approach to determine the break-even point in units and dollars.

EXERCISE 3–2A *Equation Method*

L.O. 2

Moreno Corporation produces products that it sells for $7 each. Variable costs per unit are $4, and annual fixed costs are $81,000.

Required
Use the equation method to determine the break-even point in units and dollars.

L.O. 3 **EXERCISE 3–3A** ***Contribution Margin Ratio***

Jaffe Company incurs annual fixed costs of $60,000. Variable costs for Jaffe's product are $7.50 per unit, and the sales price is $12.50 per unit. Jaffe desires to earn an annual profit of $40,000.

Required
Use the contribution margin ratio approach to determine the sales volume in dollars and units required to earn the desired profit.

L.O. 3 **EXERCISE 3–4A** ***Equation Method***

Crespo Company produces a product that sells for $21 per unit and has a variable cost of $15 per unit. Crespo incurs annual fixed costs of $230,000. It desires to earn a profit of $70,000.

Required
Use the equation method to determine the sales volume in units and dollars required to earn the desired profit.

L.O. 3 **EXERCISE 3–5A** ***Determining Fixed and Variable Cost per Unit***

Vidal Corporation produced and sold 24,000 units of product during October. It earned a contribution margin of $72,000 on sales of $336,000 and determined that cost per unit of product was $18.50.

Required
Based on this information, determine the variable and fixed cost per unit of product.

L.O. 3 **EXERCISE 3–6A** ***Determining Variable Cost from Incomplete Cost Data***

Amaya Corporation produced 150,000 watches that it sold for $24 each during 2006. The company determined that fixed manufacturing cost per unit was $6 per watch. The company reported a $600,000 gross margin on its 2006 financial statements.

Required
Determine the total variable cost, the variable cost per unit, and the total contribution margin.

L.O. 2, 3 **EXERCISE 3–7A** ***Contribution Margin per Unit Approach for Break-even and Desired Profit***

Information concerning a product produced by Cheung Company appears here.

Sales price per unit	$160
Variable cost per unit	$35
Total annual fixed manufacturing and operating costs	$900,000

Required
Determine the following:
a. Contribution margin per unit.
b. Number of units that Cheung must sell to break even.
c. Sales level in units that Cheung must reach to earn a profit of $360,000.

L.O. 4 **EXERCISE 3–8A** ***Changing Sales Price***

Dansby Company produces a product that has a variable cost of $6 per unit; the product sells for $13 per unit. The company's annual fixed costs total $350,000; it had net income of $70,000 in the previous year. In an effort to increase the company's market share, management is considering lowering the selling price to $11.60 per unit.

Required
If Dansby desires to maintain net income of $70,000, how many additional units must it sell to justify the price decline?

L.O. 4 **EXERCISE 3–9A** ***Simultaneous Change in Sales Price and Desired Profit***

Use the cost data presented in Exercise 3–8A but assume that in addition to increasing its market share by lowering its selling price to $11.60, Dansby desires to increase its net income by $14,000

Required
Determine the number of units the company must sell to earn the desired income.

EXERCISE 3–10A *Components of Break-even Graph* **L.O. 2, 3, 6**

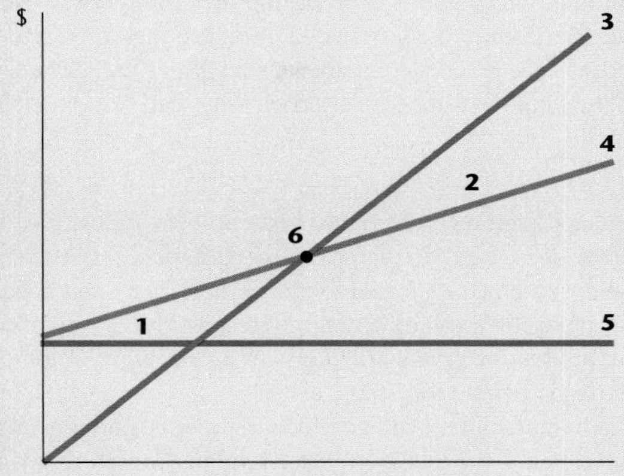

Required

Match the numbers shown in the graph with the following items.

a. Fixed cost line
b. Total cost line
c. Break-even point
d. Area of profit
e. Revenue line
f. Area of loss

EXERCISE 3–11A *Evaluating Simultaneous Changes in Fixed and Variable Costs* **L.O. 4**

Dennis Company currently produces and sells 7,500 units annually of a product that has a variable cost of $12 per unit and annual fixed costs of $200,000. The company currently earns a $70,000 annual profit. Assume that Dennis has the opportunity to invest in new labor-saving production equipment that will enable the company to reduce variable costs to $9 per unit. The investment would cause fixed costs to increase by $20,000 because of additional depreciation cost.

Required

a. Use the equation method to determine the sales price per unit under existing conditions (current equipment is used).
b. Prepare a contribution margin income statement, assuming that Dennis invests in the new production equipment. Recommend whether Dennis should invest in the new equipment.

EXERCISE 3–12A *Margin of Safety* **L.O. 7**

Bates Company makes a product that sells for $18 per unit. The company pays $8 per unit for the variable costs of the product and incurs annual fixed costs of $150,000. Bates expects to sell 24,000 units of product.

Required

Determine Bates' margin of safety expressed as a percentage.

EXERCISE 3–13A *Cost-Volume-Profit Relationship* **L.O. 2, 3, 4**

Clemmons, Inc., is a manufacturing company that makes small electric motors it sells for $72 per unit. The variable costs of production are $48 per motor, and annual fixed costs of production are $144,000.

Required

a. How many units of product must Clemmons make and sell to break even?
b. How many units of product must Clemmons make and sell to earn a $36,000 profit?
c. The marketing manager believes that sales would increase dramatically if the price were reduced to $68 per unit. How many units of product must Clemmons make and sell to earn a $36,000 profit, if the sales price is set at $68 per unit?

EXERCISE 3–14A *Understanding of the Global Economy through CVP Relationships* **L.O. 4**

An article published in the December 8, 1997, issue of *U.S. News & World Report* summarized several factors likely to support a continuing decline in the rate of inflation over the next decade. Specifically, the article stated that "global competition has. . . fostered an environment of cheap labor, cost cutting, and increased efficiency." The article notes that these developments in the global economy have led to a condition in which "the production of goods is outpacing the number of consumers able to buy them." Even so, the level of production is not likely to decline because factories have been built in developing countries where labor is cheap. The recent decline in the strength of the Asian economies is likely to have a snowballing effect so that within the foreseeable future, there will "be too many goods chasing too few buyers."

Required

a. Identify the production cost factor(s) referred to that exhibit variable cost behavior. Has (have) the cost factor(s) increased or decreased? Explain why the variable costs have increased or decreased.
b. Identify the production cost factor(s) referred to that exhibit fixed cost behavior. Has (have) the cost factor(s) increased or decreased? Explain why the fixed costs have increased or decreased.
c. The article implies that production levels are likely to remain high even though demand is expected to be weak. Explain the logic behind this implication.
d. The article suggests that manufacturers will continue to produce goods even though they may have to sell goods at a price that is below the total cost of production. Considering what you know about fixed and variable costs, speculate on how low manufacturers would permit prices to drop before they would stop production.

L.O. 5

EXERCISE 3–15A *Target Costing*

The marketing manager of Cline Corporation has determined that a market exists for a telephone with a sales price of $43 per unit. The production manager estimates the annual fixed costs of producing between 20,000 and 40,000 telephones would be $450,000.

Required

Assume that Cline desires to earn a $150,000 profit from the phone sales. How much can Cline afford to spend on variable cost per unit if production and sales equal 30,000 phones?

Appendix A

L.O. 11

EXERCISE 3–16A *Multiple Product Break-even Analysis*

Roberts Company manufactures two products. The budgeted per unit contribution margin for each product follows.

	Ascend	Advance
Sales price	$85	$98
Variable cost per unit	(45)	(38)
Contribution margin per unit	$40	$60

Roberts expects to incur annual fixed costs of $90,000. The relative sales mix of the products is 75 percent for Ascend and 25 percent for Advance.

Required

a. Determine the total number of products (units of Ascend and Advance combined) Roberts must sell to break even.
b. How many units each of Ascend and Advance must Roberts sell to break even?

PROBLEMS—SERIES A

All Problems in Series A are available with McGraw-Hill's Homework Manager

L.O. 2

excel

www.mhhe.com/edmonds3e

PROBLEM 3–17A *Determining the Break-even Point and Preparing a Contribution Margin Income Statement*

Dester Manufacturing Company makes a product that it sells for $50 per unit. The company incurs variable manufacturing costs of $20 per unit. Variable selling expenses are $5 per unit, annual fixed manufacturing costs are $187,000, and fixed selling and administrative costs are $113,000 per year.

Required
Determine the break-even point in units and dollars using each of the following approaches.

CHECK FIGURE
a. 12,000 units

a. Contribution margin per unit.
b. Equation method.
c. Contribution margin ratio.
d. Confirm your results by preparing a contribution margin income statement for the break-even sales volume.

PROBLEM 3–18A ***Determining the Break-even Point and Preparing a Break-even Graph*** **L.O. 2, 6**

Steinmetz Company is considering the production of a new product. The expected variable cost is $45 per unit. Annual fixed costs are expected to be $570,000. The anticipated sales price is $60 each.

CHECK FIGURE
a. $2,280,000

Required
Determine the break-even point in units and dollars using each of the following.

a. Contribution margin per unit approach.
b. Equation method.
c. Contribution margin ratio approach.
d. Prepare a break-even graph to illustrate the cost-volume-profit relationships.

PROBLEM 3–19A ***Effect of Converting Variable to Fixed Costs*** **L.O. 2, 3, 4**

Pinkerton Manufacturing Company reported the following data regarding a product it manufactures and sells. The sales price is $27.

CHECK FIGURE
b. 30,000 units

Variable costs	
Manufacturing	$10 per unit
Selling	6 per unit
Fixed costs:	
Manufacturing	$190,000 per year
Selling and administrative	85,000 per year

Required
a. Use the per unit contribution margin approach to determine the break-even point in units and dollars.
b. Use the per unit contribution margin approach to determine the level of sales in units and dollars required to obtain a profit of $55,000.
c. Suppose that variable selling costs could be eliminated by employing a salaried sales force. If the company could sell 45,000 units, how much could it pay in salaries for salespeople and still have a profit of $95,000? (*Hint:* Use the equation method.)

PROBLEM 3–20A ***Analyzing Change in Sales Price Using the Contribution Margin Ratio*** **L.O. 2, 3, 4**

Aliant Company reported the following data regarding the product it sells.

CHECK FIGURE
c. 37,500 units

Sales price	$32
Contribution margin ratio	20%
Fixed costs	$540,000

Required
Use the contribution margin ratio approach and consider each requirement separately.

a. What is the break-even point in dollars? In units?
b. To obtain a profit of $80,000, what must the sales be in dollars? In units?
c. If the sales price increases to $40 and variable costs do not change, what is the new break-even point in dollars? In units?

PROBLEM 3–21A ***Analyzing Sales Price and Fixed Cost Using the Equation Method*** **L.O. 2, 3, 4**

excel
www.mhhe.com/edmonds3e

Kruse Company is considering adding a new product. The cost accountant has provided the following data.

Expected variable cost of manufacturing	$41 per unit
Expected annual fixed manufacturing costs	$69,000

CHECK FIGURE
a. 8,000 units

The administrative vice president has provided the following estimates.

Expected sales commission	$4 per unit
Expected annual fixed administrative costs	$31,000

The manager has decided that any new product must at least break even in the first year.

Required

Use the equation method and consider each requirement separately.

a. If the sales price is set at $57.50, how many units must Kruse sell to break even?

b. Kruse estimates that sales will probably be 10,000 units. What sales price per unit will allow the company to break even?

c. Kruse has decided to advertise the product heavily and has set the sales price at $60. If sales are 9,000 units, how much can the company spend on advertising and still break even?

L.O. 7

PROBLEM 3–22A *Margin of Safety and Operating Leverage*

Musso Company is considering the addition of a new product to its cosmetics line. The company has three distinctly different options: a skin cream, a bath oil, or a hair coloring gel. Relevant information and budgeted annual income statements for each of the products follow.

CHECK FIGURES

b. NI:

Skin Cream $102,000

Bath Oil $88,000

Color Gel $90,000

	Relevant Information		
	Skin Cream	**Bath Oil**	**Color Gel**
Budgeted Sales in Units (a)	70,000	120,000	40,000
Expected Sales Price (b)	$8	$3	$12
Variable Costs Per Unit (c)	$5	$1	$ 7
Income Statements			
Sales Revenue (a × b)	$560,000	$360,000	$480,000
Variable Costs (a × c)	(350,000)	(120,000)	(280,000)
Contribution Margin	210,000	240,000	200,000
Fixed Costs	(150,000)	(200,000)	(150,000)
Net Income	$ 60,000	$ 40,000	$ 50,000

Required

a. Determine the margin of safety as a percentage for each product.

b. Prepare revised income statements for each product, assuming a 20 percent increase in the budgeted sales volume.

c. For each product, determine the percentage change in net income that results from the 20 percent increase in sales. Which product has the highest operating leverage?

d. Assuming that management is pessimistic and risk averse, which product should the company add to its cosmetic line? Explain your answer.

e. Assuming that management is optimistic and risk aggressive, which product should the company add to its cosmetics line? Explain your answer.

L.O. 2, 3, 4, 6, 7

PROBLEM 3–23A *Comprehensive CVP Analysis*

CHECK FIGURES

b. 1,600 units

c. 2,000 units

e. 3,200 units

Weissman Company makes and sells products with variable costs of $50 each. Weissman incurs annual fixed costs of $32,000. The current sales price is $70.

Required

The following requirements are interdependent. For example, the $8,000 desired profit introduced in Requirement *c* also applies to subsequent requirements. Likewise, the $60 sales price introduced in Requirement *d* applies to the subsequent requirements.

a. Determine the contribution margin per unit.

b. Determine the break-even point in units and in dollars. Confirm your answer by preparing an income statement using the contribution margin format.

c. Suppose that Weissman desires to earn an $8,000 profit. Determine the sales volume in units and dollars required to earn the desired profit. Confirm your answer by preparing an income statement using the contribution margin format.
d. If the sales price drops to $60 per unit, what level of sales is required to earn the desired profit? Express your answer in units and dollars. Confirm your answer by preparing an income statement using the contribution margin format.
e. If fixed costs drop to $24,000, what level of sales is required to earn the desired profit? Express your answer in units and dollars. Confirm your answer by preparing an income statement using the contribution margin format.
f. If variable cost drops to $40 per unit, what level of sales is required to earn the desired profit? Express your answer in units and dollars. Confirm your answer by preparing an income statement using the contribution margin format.
g. Assume that Weissman concludes that it can sell 1,600 units of product for $60 each. Recall that variable costs are $40 each and fixed costs are $24,000. Compute the margin of safety in units and dollars and as a percentage.
h. Draw a break-even graph using the cost and price assumptions described in Requirement *g*.

PROBLEM 3–24A *Assessing Simultaneous Changes in CVP Relationships*

L.O. 2, 3, 4, 6, 7

CHECK FIGURES
a. $750,000
c. 6,750 units

Green Shades, Inc. (GSI), sells hammocks; variable costs are $75 each, and the hammocks are sold for $125 each. GSI incurs $250,000 of fixed operating expenses annually.

Required

a. Determine the sales volume in units and dollars required to attain a $50,000 profit. Verify your answer by preparing an income statement using the contribution margin format.
b. GSI is considering implementing a quality improvement program. The program will require a $10 increase in the variable cost per unit. To inform its customers of the quality improvements, the company plans to spend an additional $20,000 for advertising. Assuming that the improvement program will increase sales to a level that is 3,000 units above the amount computed in Requirement a, should GSI proceed with plans to improve product quality? Support your answer by preparing a budgeted income statement.
c. Determine the new break-even point in units and sales dollars as well as the margin of safety percentage, assuming that the quality improvement program is implemented.
d. Prepare a break-even graph using the cost and price assumptions outlined in Requirement *b*.

Appendix A

PROBLEM 3–25A *Determining the Break-even Point and Margin of Safety for a Company with Multiple Products*

L.O. 11

excel
www.mhhe.com/edmonds3e

Pinson Company produces two products. Budgeted annual income statements for the two products are provided here.

	Power					Lite					Total	
	Budgeted Number		Per Unit		Budgeted Amount	Budgeted Number		Per Unit		Budgeted Amount	Budgeted Number	Budgeted Amount
Sales	160	@	$500	=	$80,000	640	@	$450	=	$288,000	800	$368,000
Variable Cost	160	@	320	=	(51,200)	640	@	330	=	(211,200)	800	(262,400)
Contribution Margin	160	@	180	=	28,800	640	@	120	=	76,800	800	105,600
Fixed Costs					(12,000)					(54,000)		(66,000)
Net Income					$16,800					$ 22,800		$ 39,600

Required

CHECK FIGURES
d. Power: 100 units
Lite: 400 units

a. Based on budgeted sales, determine the relative sales mix between the two products.
b. Determine the weighted-average contribution margin per unit.
c. Calculate the break-even point in total number of units.
d. Determine the number of units of each product Pinson must sell to break even.
e. Verify the break-even point by preparing an income statement for each product as well as an income statement for the combined products.
f. Determine the margin of safety based on the combined sales of the two products.

EXERCISES—SERIES B

L.O. 2 **EXERCISE 3–1B** *Per Unit Contribution Margin Approach*

Sloan Corporation manufactures products that have variable costs of $10 per unit. Its fixed cost amounts to $81,000. It sells the produce for $13 each.

Required
Use the per unit contribution margin approach to determine the break-even point in units and dollars.

L.O. 2 **EXERCISE 3–2B** *Equation Method*

Rapaka Corporation manufactures products that it sells for $29 each. Variable costs are $20 per unit, and annual fixed costs are $450,000.

Required
Use the equation method to determine the break-even point in units and dollars.

L.O. 3 **EXERCISE 3–3B** *Contribution Margin Ratio*

Hooten Company incurs annual fixed costs of $310,000. Variable costs for Hooten's product are $18 per unit, and the sales price is $24 per unit. Hooten desires to earn a profit of $50,000.

Required
Use the contribution margin ratio approach to determine the sales volume in dollars and units required to earn the desired profit.

L.O. 3 **EXERCISE 3–4B** *Equation Method*

Lundy Company manufactures a product that sells for $71 per unit. It incurs fixed costs of $390,000. Variable cost for its product is $50 per unit. Lundy desires to earn a target profit is $240,000.

Required
Use the equation method to determine the sales volume in units and dollars required to earn the desired profit.

L.O. 3 **EXERCISE 3–5B** *Fixed and Variable Cost per Unit*

Nall Corporation broke even by producing and selling 37,000 units of product during 2005. It earned a contribution margin of $111,000 on sales of $740,000. The company determined that cost per unit of product was $27.

Required
Based on this information, determine the variable and fixed cost per unit of product.

L.O. 3 **EXERCISE 3–6B** *Determining Variable Cost From Incomplete Data*

Johnston Corporation produced 75,000 tires and sold them for $60 each during 2007. The company determined that fixed manufacturing cost per unit was $16 per tire. The company reported gross profit of $900,000 on its 2007 financial statements.

Required
Determine the total variable cost, the variable cost per unit, and the total contribution margin.

L.O. 2, 3 **EXERCISE 3–7B** *Contribution Margin per Unit Approach for Break-even and Desired Profit*

Information concerning a product produced by Odess Company appears here:

Sales price per unit	$786
Variable cost per unit	426
Total fixed manufacturing and operating costs	$450,000

Required
Determine the following:

a. Contribution margin per unit.
b. Number of units Odess must sell to break even.
c. Sales level in units that Odess must reach in order to earn a profit of $90,000.

EXERCISE 3–8B *Change in Sales Price*

L.O. 4

Belcher Company manufactures a product that has a variable cost of $13 per unit. The company's fixed costs total $280,000. Belcher had net income of $80,000 in the previous year. Its product sells for $25 per unit. In an effort to increase the company's market share, management is considering lowering the product's selling price to $23 per unit.

Required
If Belcher desires to maintain net income of $80,000, how many additional units must it sell in order to justify the price decline?

EXERCISE 3–9B *Simultaneous Change in Sales Price and Desired Profit*

L.O. 4

Use the cost data presented in Exercise 3–8B, but assume that in addition to increasing its market share by lowering its selling price to $23, Belcher desires to increase its net income by $40,000.

Required
Determine the number of units that Belcher must sell to earn the desired income.

EXERCISE 3–10B *Components of Break-even Graph*

L.O. 2, 3, 6

Austin, a 10-year-old boy, wants to sell lemonade on a hot summer day. He hopes to make enough money to buy a new Game Boy. Mark, his elder brother, tries to help him compute his prospect of doing so. The following is the relevant information:

Variable costs	
Lemonade	$0.30 per cup
Paper cup	$0.10 per cup
Fixed costs	
Table and chair	$36.00
Price	$1.00 per cup

The following graph depicts the dollar amount of cost or revenue on the vertical axis and the number of lemonade cups sold on the horizontal axis.

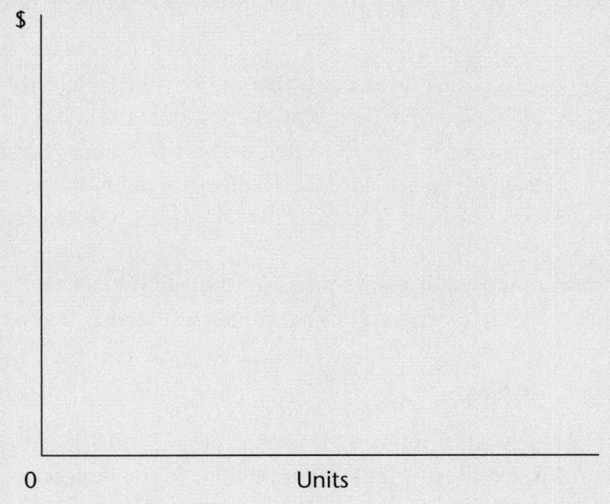

Required
a. Draw a line that depicts the total cost.
b. Draw a line that depicts the total revenue.
c. Identify the break-even point.
d. Identify the area representing profit.
e. Identify the area representing loss.

EXERCISE 3–11B *Evaluating Simultaneous Changes in Fixed and Variable Costs*

L.O. 4

Crenshaw Company currently produces and sells 10,000 units of a telephone per year that has a variable cost of $10 per unit and a fixed cost of $275,000. The company currently earns a $125,000 annual profit. Assume that Crenshaw has the opportunity to invest in a new machine that will enable the company to reduce variable costs to $7 per unit. The investment would cause fixed costs to increase by $18,000.

Required

a. Use the equation method to determine the sales price per unit under existing conditions (current machine is used).

b. Prepare a contribution margin income statement assuming Crenshaw invests in the new technology. Recommend whether Crenshaw should invest in the new technology.

L.O. 7 EXERCISE 3–12B *Margin of Safety*

Suarez Company manufactures scanners that sell for $135 each. The company pays $55 per unit for the variable costs of the product and incurs fixed costs of $1,600,000. Suarez expects to sell 36,000 scanners.

Required

Determine Suarez's margin of safety expressed as a percentage.

L.O. 2, 3, 4 EXERCISE 3–13B *Cost-Volume-Profit Relationship*

Plutchak Corporation manufactures faucets. The variable costs of production are $9 per faucet. Fixed costs of production are $94,500. Plutchak sells the faucets for a price of $30 per unit.

Required

a. How many faucets must Plutchak make and sell to break even?

b. How many faucets must Plutchak make and sell to earn a $21,000 profit?

c. The marketing manager believes that sales would increase dramatically if the price were reduced to $29 per unit. How many faucets must Plutchak make and sell to earn a $21,000 profit, assuming the sales price is set at $29 per unit?

L.O. 4 EXERCISE 3–14B *Understanding the Global Economy Through CVP Relationships*

An article published in the April 2, 2001 issue of *BusinessWeek* summarized several factors that had contributed to the economic slowdown that started in the fourth quarter of 2000. Specifically, the article stated, "When companies lowered their demand forecasts, they concluded that they didn't have just a little excess capacity—they had massive excessive capacity,. . ." The article continues to argue that companies with too much capacity have no desire to invest, no matter how low interest rates are.

Required

a. Identify the production cost factor(s) referred to that exhibit variable cost behavior. Has (have) the cost factor(s) increased or decreased? Explain why the variable costs have increased or decreased.

b. Identify the production cost factor(s) referred to that exhibit fixed cost behavior. Has (have) the cost factor(s) increased or decreased? Explain why the fixed costs have increased or decreased.

c. The article argues that new investments in production facilities will decrease. Explain the logic behind this argument.

d. In an economic downturn, manufacturers are pressured to sell their product at low prices. Comment on how low a manufacturer's prices can go before management decides to quit production.

L.O. 5 EXERCISE 3–15B *Target Costing*

After substantial marketing research, Traynor Corporation management believes that it can make and sell a new battery with a prolonged life for laptop computers. Management expects the market demand for its new battery to be 10,000 units per year if the battery is priced at $150 per unit. A team of engineers and accountants determines that the fixed costs of producing 8,000 units to 16,000 units is $450,000.

Required

Assume that Traynor desires to earn a $300,000 profit from the battery sales. How much can it afford to spend on variable cost per unit if production and sales equal 10,000 batteries?

Appendix A

L.O. 11 EXERCISE 3–16B *Multiple Product Break-even Analysis*

Cain Company makes two products. The budgeted per unit contribution margin for each product follows:

	Product M	Product N
Sales price	$48	$75
Variable cost per unit	33	40
Contribution margin per unit	$15	$35

Cain expects to incur fixed costs of $115,000. The relative sales mix of the products is 60 percent for Product M and 40 percent for Product N.

Required

a. Determine the total number of products (units of M and N combined) Cain must sell to break even.
b. How many units each of Product M and Product N must Cain sell to break even?

PROBLEMS—SERIES B

PROBLEM 3–17B *Determining the Break-even Point and Preparing a Contribution Margin Income Statement* L. O. 2

Perkins Company manufactures radio and cassette players and sells them for $360 each. According to the company's records, the variable costs, including direct labor and direct materials, are $240. Factory depreciation and other fixed manufacturing costs are $292,000 per year. Perkins pays its salespeople a commission of $30 per unit. Annual fixed selling and administrative costs are $158,000.

Required

Determine the break-even point in units and dollars, using each of the following.

a. Contribution margin per unit approach.
b. Equation method.
c. Contribution margin ratio approach.
d. Confirm your results by preparing a contribution margin income statement for the break-even point sales volume.

PROBLEM 3–18B *Determining the Break-even Point and Preparing a Break-even Graph* L. O. 2, 6

Executive officers of Rosenthal Company are assessing the profitability of a potential new product. They expect that the variable cost of making the product will be $36 per unit and fixed manufacturing cost will be $480,000. The executive officers plan to sell the product for $60 per unit.

Required

Determine the break-even point in units and dollars using each of the following approaches.

a. Contribution margin per unit.
b. Equation method.
c. Contribution margin ratio.
d. Prepare a break-even graph to illustrate the cost-volume-profit relationships.

PROBLEM 3–19B *Effect of Converting Variable to Fixed Costs* L. O. 2, 3, 4

Hollis Company manufactures and sells its own brand of cameras. It sells each camera for $78. The company's accountant prepared the following data:

Manufacturing costs	
Variable	$18 per unit
Fixed	$150,000 per year
Selling and administrative expenses	
Variable	$6 per unit
Fixed	$66,000 per year

Required

a. Use the per unit contribution margin approach to determine the break-even point in units and dollars.
b. Use the per unit contribution margin approach to determine the level of sales in units and dollars required to obtain a $270,000 profit.

c. Suppose that variable selling and administrative costs could be eliminated by employing a salaried sales force. If the company could sell 9,500 units, how much could it pay in salaries for the salespeople and still have a profit of $270,000? (*Hint:* Use the equation method.)

L. O. 2, 3, 4

PROBLEM 3–20B *Analyzing Change in Sales Price Using the Contribution Margin Ratio*

Milby Company reported the following data regarding the one product it sells.

Sales price	$80
Contribution margin ratio	20%
Fixed costs	$160,000 per year

Required

Use the contribution margin ratio approach and consider each requirement separately.

a. What is the break-even point in dollars? In units?
b. To obtain a $80,000 profit, what must the sales be in dollars? In units?
c. If the sales price increases to $84 and variable costs do not change, what is the new break-even point in units? In dollars?

L. O. 2, 3, 4

PROBLEM 3–21B *Analyzing Sales Price and Fixed Cost Using the Equation Method*

Berger Company is analyzing whether its new product will be profitable. The following data are provided for analysis.

Expected variable cost of manufacturing	$39 per unit
Expected fixed manufacturing costs	$65,000 per year
Expected sales commission	$9 per unit
Expected fixed administrative costs	$16,000 per year

The company has decided that any new product must at least break even in the first year.

Required

Use the equation method and consider each requirement separately.

a. If the sales price is set at $75, how many units must Berger sell to break even?
b. Berger estimates that sales will probably be 4,000 units. What sales price per unit will allow the company to break even?
c. Berger has decided to advertise the product heavily and has set the sales price at $80. If sales are 3,500 units, how much can the company spend on advertising and still break even?

L. O. 7

PROBLEM 3–22B *Margin of Safety and Operating Leverage*

Fine Company has three distinctly different options available as it considers adding a new product to its automotive division: engine oil, coolant, or windshield washer. Relevant information and budgeted annual income statements for each product follow.

	Relevant Information		
	Engine Oil	Coolant	Windshield Washer
Budgeted Sales in Units (a)	20,000	30,000	125,000
Expected Sales Price (b)	$2.40	$2.85	$1.15
Variable Costs Per Unit (c)	$1.00	$1.25	$0.35
Income Statements			
Sales Revenue (a × b)	$48,000	$85,500	$143,750
Variable Costs (a × c)	(20,000)	(37,500)	(43,750)
Contribution Margin	28,000	48,000	100,000
Fixed Costs	(21,000)	(32,000)	(50,000)
Net Income	$ 7,000	$ 16,000	$ 50,000

Required

a. Determine the margin of safety as a percentage for each product.
b. Prepare revised income statements for each product, assuming 20 percent growth in the budgeted sales volume.
c. For each product, determine the percentage change in net income that results from the 20 percent increase in sales. Which product has the highest operating leverage?
d. Assuming that management is pessimistic and risk averse, which product should the company add? Explain your answer.
e. Assuming that management is optimistic and risk aggressive, which product should the company add? Explain your answer.

PROBLEM 3–23B *Comprehensive CVP Analysis*

L. O. 2, 3, 4, 6, 7

Mahdi Company makes a product that it sells for $75. Mahdi incurs annual fixed costs of $80,000 and variable costs of $50 per unit.

Required

The following requirements are interdependent. For example, the $20,000 desired profit introduced in Requirement *c* also applies to subsequent requirements. Likewise, the $70 sales price introduced in Requirement *d* applies to the subsequent requirements.

a. Determine the contribution margin per unit.
b. Determine the break-even point in units and in dollars. Confirm your answer by preparing an income statement using the contribution margin format.
c. Suppose that Mahdi desires to earn a $20,000 profit. Determine the sales volume in units and dollars required to earn the desired profit. Confirm your answer by preparing an income statement using the contribution margin format.
d. If the sales price drops to $70 per unit, what level of sales is required to earn the desired profit? Express your answer in units and dollars. Confirm your answer by preparing an income statement using the contribution margin format.
e. If fixed costs drop to $70,000, what level of sales is required to earn the desired profit? Express your answer in units and dollars. Confirm your answer by preparing an income statement using the contribution margin format.
f. If variable costs drop to $40 per unit, what level of sales is required to earn the desired profit? Express your answer in units and dollars. Confirm your answer by preparing an income statement using the contribution margin format.
g. Assume that Mahdi concludes that it can sell 4,800 units of product for $68 each. Recall that variable costs are $40 each and fixed costs are $70,000. Compute the margin of safety in units and dollars and as a percentage.
h. Draw a break-even graph using the cost and price assumptions described in Requirement *g*.

PROBLEM 3–24B *Assessing Simultaneous Changes in CVP Relationships*

L. O. 2, 3, 4, 6, 7

Sarris Company sells tennis racquets; variable costs for each are $75, and each is sold for $105. Sarris incurs $270,000 of fixed operating expenses annually.

Required

a. Determine the sales volume in units and dollars required to attain a $120,000 profit. Verify your answer by preparing an income statement using the contribution margin format.
b. Sarris is considering establishing a quality improvement program that will require a $10 increase in the variable cost per unit. To inform its customers of the quality improvements, the company plans to spend an additional $60,000 for advertising. Assuming that the improvement program will increase sales to a level that is 5,000 units above the amount computed in Requirement *a,* should Sarris proceed with plans to improve product quality? Support your answer by preparing a budgeted income statement.
c. Determine the new break-even point and the margin of safety percentage, assuming Sarris adopts the quality improvement program.
d. Prepare a break-even graph using the cost and price assumptions outlined in Requirement *b*.

Appendix A

L. O. 11

PROBLEM 3–25B *Determining the Break-even Point and Margin of Safety for a Company with Multiple Products*

Executive officers of Witt Company have prepared the annual budgets for its two products, Washer and Dryer, as follows.

	Washer			Dryer			Total	
	Budgeted Quantity	Per Unit	Budgeted Amount	Budgeted Quantity	Per Unit	Budgeted Amount	Budgeted Quantity	Budgeted Amount
Sales	400	@ $540 =	$216,000	1,200	@ $300 =	$360,000	1,600	$576,000
Variable Cost	400	@ 300 =	(120,000)	1,200	@ 180 =	(216,000)	1,600	(336,000)
Contribution Margin	400	@ 240 =	96,000	1,200	@ 120 =	144,000	1,600	240,000
Fixed Costs			(34,000)			(44,000)		(78,000)
Net Income			$ 62,000			$100,000		$162,000

Required

a. Based on the number of units budgeted to be sold, determine the relative sales mix between the two products.

b. Determine the weighted-average contribution margin per unit.

c. Calculate the break-even point in total number of units.

d. Determine the number of units of each product Witt must sell to break even.

e. Verify the break-even point by preparing an income statement for each product as well as an income statement for the combined products.

f. Determine the margin of safety based on the combined sales of the two products.

ANALYZE, THINK, COMMUNICATE

ACT 3–1

BUSINESS APPLICATIONS CASE *Effect of Costs Changes*

An article in the January 26, 2004, issue of *BusinessWeek* explains how automobile manufacturers in the United States are beginning to adopt a practice already prevalent among Japanese manufacturers. Specifically, rather than build each model of vehicle on its own unique chassis, or platform, the same basic platform is being used as the foundation for several very different models. For example, Honda uses the platform designed for the Civic as the platform for the CR-V, Element, and Acura R-SX.

Required

Read the article, "Detroit Tries It the Japanese Way," *BusinessWeek,* January 26, 2004, pp. 76–77. Based on the information in the article, prepare a memorandum that identifies as many reasons as you can think of to explain how using the same platform to produce several different models will reduce automobile manufacturers' costs. Be specific, and consider not only the concepts introduced in this chapter but also those from Chapters 1 and 2. For each reason you identify, provide a brief explanation about how this factor will help reduce the companies' costs. Also, explain which type of cost, fixed or variable, would be affected the most by the use of one platform to produce multiple models.

ATC 3–2

GROUP ASSIGNMENT *Effect of Changes in Fixed and Variable Cost on Profitability*

In a month when it sold 200 units of product, Queen Manufacturing Company (QMC) produced the following internal income statement.

Revenue	$8,000
Variable Costs	(4,800)
Contribution Margin	3,200
Fixed Costs	(2,400)
Net Income	$ 800

QMC has the opportunity to alter its operations in one of the following ways:

1. Increasing fixed advertising costs by $1,600, thereby increasing sales by 120 units.

2. Lowering commissions paid to the sales staff by $8 per unit, thereby reducing sales by 10 units.
3. Decreasing fixed inventory holding cost by $800, thereby decreasing sales by 20 units.

Required

a. The instructor will divide the class into groups and then organize the groups into two sections. For a large class (12 or more groups), four sections may be necessary. At least three groups in each section are needed. Having more groups in one section than another section is acceptable because offsetting advantages and disadvantages exist. Having more groups is advantageous because more people will work on the task but is disadvantageous because having more people complicates communication.

Group Task

The sections are to compete with each other to see which section can identify the most profitable alternative in the shortest period of time. No instruction is provided regarding how the sections are to proceed with the task. In other words, each section is required to organize itself with respect to how to accomplish the task of selecting the best alternative. A total quality management (TQM) constraint is imposed that requires zero defects. A section that turns in a wrong answer is disqualified. Once an answer has been submitted to the instructor, it cannot be changed. Sections continue to turn in answers until all sections have submitted a response. The first section to submit the correct answer wins the competition.

b. If any section submits a wrong answer, the instructor or a spokesperson from the winning group should explain how the right answer was determined.

c. Discuss the dynamics of group interaction. How was the work organized? How was leadership established?

RESEARCH ASSIGNMENT *Accuracy Versus Relevance*

ATC 3–3

Frequently, actual fixed and variable cost data are not available. Managerial accountants are required to estimate these costs to facilitate decision making. In the article "Three Significant Digits" in the Winter 1997 edition of the *Journal of Cost Management,* Alfred M. King charged that too many accountants overemphasize reliability and accuracy at the expense of relevance. Read this article and complete the following requirements.

Required

a. The following excerpt is from the King article. "Many management accountants complain that while they are treated as professionals in their chosen field of accounting, they are not invited to sit at the management table when major business decisions are being studied and debated. In short, accountants are not starting players on the management team." Summarize Mr. King's explanation of why this condition exists.

b. Answer the following questions.
   (1) Mr. King notes that "it is better to be approximately right than precisely wrong." He suggests that these words of wisdom are more relevant to managerial accountants than to financial accountants. Explain why Mr. King makes this argument.
   (2) Mr. King charges that the current educational environment leads students to the erroneous conclusion that (1) there is such a thing as the "true" cost of a product and (2) this one "true" cost can be determined accurately and precisely. Why does Mr. King believe this to be an erroneous conclusion?

c. What is the primary weakness associated with the use of the high-low method of estimating cost behavior? What alternative methods can be used to overcome this weakness? (The high-low method is explained in Chapter 2.)

WRITING ASSIGNMENT *Operating Leverage, Margin of Safety, and Cost Behavior*

ATC 3–4

The article "Up Front: More Condensing at the Digest?" in the October 19, 1998, issue of *BusinessWeek* reported that Thomas Ryder, CEO of **Reader's Digest Association**, was considering a spin-off of Reader's Digest's direct-marketing operations into a joint venture with **Time Warner**. The article's author, Robert McNatt, noted that the direct marketing of books, music, and videos is a far larger part of the Reader's Digest business than is its namesake magazine. Furthermore, the article stated that 1998 direct-marketing sales of $1.6 billion were down 11 percent from 1997. The decline in revenue caused the division's operating profits to decline 58 percent. The article stated that the contemplated alliance with Time Warner could provide some fast help. Gerald Levin, Time Warner chairman, has said that his company's operations provide customer service and product fulfillment far better than other Web sellers do because of Time Warner's established 250 Web sites.

Required

a. Write a memo explaining how an 11 percent decrease in sales could result in a 58 percent decline in operating profits.

b. Explain briefly how the decline in revenue will affect the company's margin of safety.

c. Explain why a joint venture between Reader's Digest's direct-marketing division and Time Warner could work to the advantage of both companies. (*Hint:* Consider the effects of fixed-cost behavior in formulating your response.)

ATC 3–5 ETHICAL DILEMMA *Manipulating Reported Earnings*

The article "Garbage In, Garbage Out" (*Fortune,* May 25, 1998, pp. 130–38) describes a litany of questionable accounting practices that ultimately led to the demise of **Waste Management, Inc.** Under pressure to retain its reputation on Wall Street as a growth company, Waste Management extended its estimates of the lives of its garbage trucks two to four years beyond the standard used in the industry. It also began to use a $25,000 expected salvage value on each truck when the industry standard was to recognize a zero salvage value. Because Waste Management owned approximately 20,000 trucks, these moves had a significant impact on the company's earnings. Extended lives and exaggerated salvage values were also applied to the company's 1.5 million steel dumpsters and its landfill facilities. These accounting practices boosted reported earnings by approximately $110 million per year. The long-term effect on real earnings was disastrous, however; maintenance costs began to soar and the company was forced to spend millions to keep broken-down trucks on the road. Overvalued assets failed to generate expected revenues. The failure to maintain earnings growth ultimately led to the replacement of management. When the new managers discovered the misstated accounting numbers, the company was forced to recognize a pretax charge of $3.54 billion in its 1997 income statement. The stock price plummeted, and the company was ultimately merged out of existence.

Required

a. Did Waste Management manipulate the recognition of fixed or variable costs?

b. Explain how extending the life estimate of an asset increases earnings and the book value of assets.

c. Explain how inflating the salvage value of an asset increases earnings and the book value of assets.

d. Speculate as to what motive would cause executives to manipulate earnings.

e. Review the standards of ethical conduct shown in Exhibit 1–13 of Chapter 1 and comment on whether Waste Management's accounting practices violated any standards.

ACT 3–6 SPREADSHEET ASSIGNMENT *Using Excel*

Bishop Company has provided the estimated data that appear in rows 4 to 8 of the following spreadsheet.

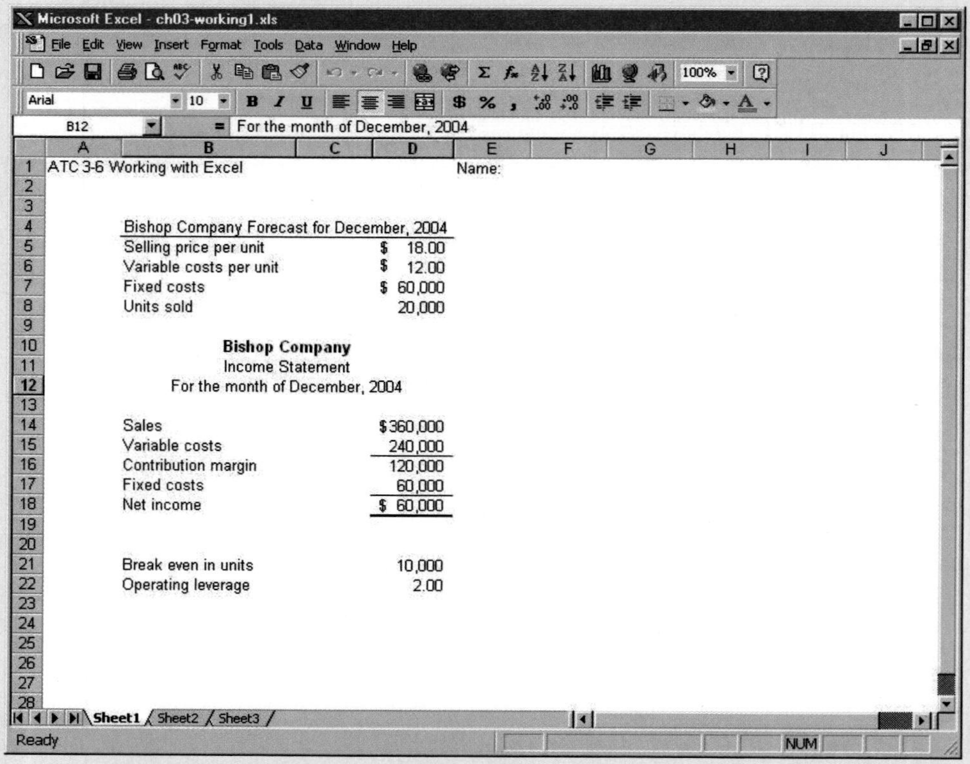

Row	A	B	C	D	E
1	ATC 3-6 Working with Excel				Name:
4		Bishop Company Forecast for December, 2004			
5		Selling price per unit		$ 18.00	
6		Variable costs per unit		$ 12.00	
7		Fixed costs		$ 60,000	
8		Units sold		20,000	
10		**Bishop Company**			
11		Income Statement			
12		For the month of December, 2004			
14		Sales		$360,000	
15		Variable costs		240,000	
16		Contribution margin		120,000	
17		Fixed costs		60,000	
18		Net income		$ 60,000	
21		Break even in units		10,000	
22		Operating leverage		2.00	

Required

Construct a spreadsheet as follows that would allow you to determine net income, breakeven in units, and operating leverage for the estimates at the top of the spreadsheet, and to see the effects of changes to the estimates. Set up this spreadsheet so that any change in the estimates will automatically be reflected in the calculation of net income, breakeven, and operating leverage.

Spreadsheet Tip

1. To center a heading across several columns, such as the Income Statement title, highlight the area to be centered (Columns B, C, and D), choose Format, then choose Cells, and click on the tab titled Alignment. Near the bottom of the alignment window, place a check mark in the box titled Merge cells. The shortcut method to merge cells is to click on the icon near the middle of the top icons that contains an *a* in a box.

SPREADSHEET ASSIGNMENT *Mastering Excel*

ATC 3–7

Required

Build the spreadsheet pictured in Exhibit 3–2. Be sure to use formulas that will automatically calculate profitability if fixed cost, variable cost, or sales volume is changed.

Spreadsheet Tip

1. The shading in column D and in row 6 can be inserted by first highlighting a section to be shaded, choosing Format from the main menu, then Cells, and then clicking on the tab titled Patterns, and then choosing a color for the shading. The shortcut method to accomplish the shading is to click on the fill color icon (it looks like a tipped bucket and is in the upper right area of the screen).

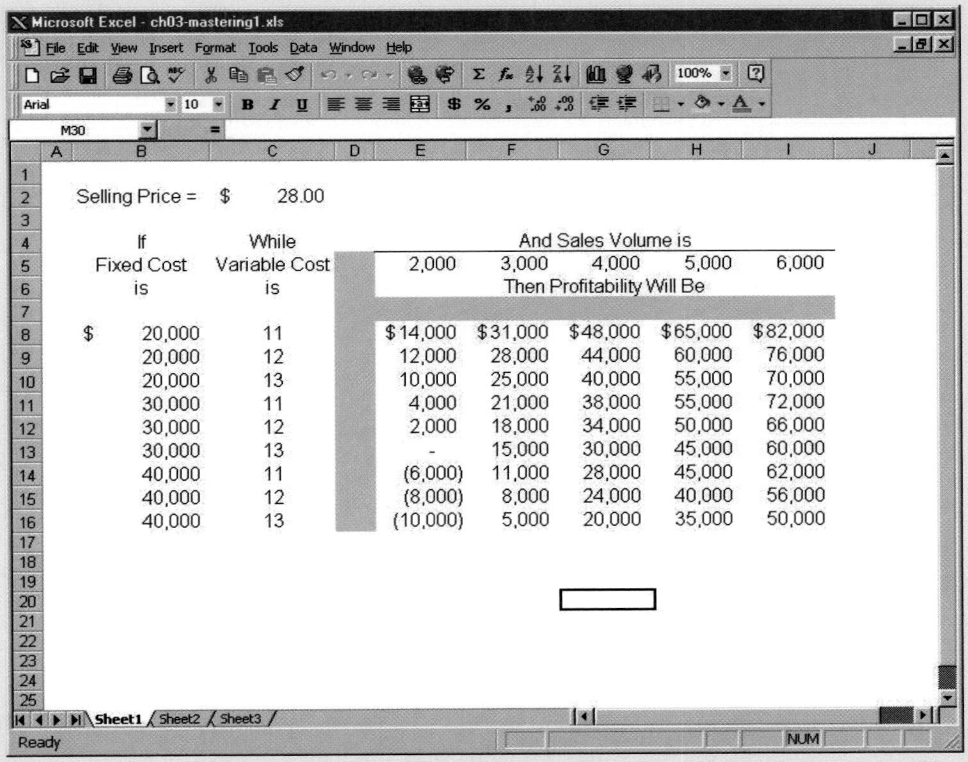

Microsoft Excel - ch03-mastering1.xls

	A	B	C	D	E	F	G	H	I
1									
2		Selling Price =	$ 28.00						
3									
4		If	While				And Sales Volume is		
5		Fixed Cost	Variable Cost		2,000	3,000	4,000	5,000	6,000
6		is	is				Then Profitability Will Be		
7									
8	$	20,000	11		$14,000	$31,000	$48,000	$65,000	$82,000
9		20,000	12		12,000	28,000	44,000	60,000	76,000
10		20,000	13		10,000	25,000	40,000	55,000	70,000
11		30,000	11		4,000	21,000	38,000	55,000	72,000
12		30,000	12		2,000	18,000	34,000	50,000	66,000
13		30,000	13		-	15,000	30,000	45,000	60,000
14		40,000	11		(6,000)	11,000	28,000	45,000	62,000
15		40,000	12		(8,000)	8,000	24,000	40,000	56,000
16		40,000	13		(10,000)	5,000	20,000	35,000	50,000

2. Similar to basic math rules, the order of calculation within a formula is multiplication and division before addition and subtraction. Therefore, if you wish to subtract variable cost from selling price and multiply the difference by units sold, the formula must be = (28 − C8)*E5.
3. The quickest way to get the correct formulas in the area of E8 to I16 is to place the proper formula in cell E8 and then copy this formula to the entire block of E8:I16. However, the formulas must use the $ around the cell addresses to lock either the row or the column, or both. For example, the formula = 2*B8 can be copied to any other cell and the cell reference will remain B8 because the $ symbol locks the row and column. Likewise, $B8 indicates that only the column is locked, and B$8 indicates that only the row is locked.

COMPREHENSIVE PROBLEM

Use the same transaction data for Magnificant Modems, Inc. as was used in Chapter 1. (See page 00.)

Required

a. Use the following partially completed form to prepare an income statement using the contribution margin format.

Sales Revenue	$600,000
Variable Costs:	
Contribution Margin	225,000
Fixed costs	
Net Income	$31,050

b. Determine the break-even point in units and in dollars.

c. Assume that next year's sales are budgeted to be the same as the current year's sales. Determine the margin of safety expressed as a percentage.

CHAPTER *four*

RELEVANT INFORMATION FOR SPECIAL DECISIONS

LEARNING *objectives*

After you have mastered the material in this chapter, you will be able to:

1. Identify the characteristics of relevant information.
2. Recognize sunk costs and explain why they are not relevant in decision making.
3. Distinguish between unit-level, batch-level, product-level, and facility-level costs and understand how these costs affect decision making.
4. Identify opportunity costs and explain why they are relevant in decision making.
5. Distinguish between quantitative and qualitative characteristics of decision making.
6. Make appropriate special order decisions by analyzing relevant information.
7. Make appropriate outsourcing decisions by analyzing relevant information.
8. Make appropriate segment elimination decisions by analyzing relevant information.
9. Make appropriate asset replacement decisions by analyzing relevant information.
10. Explain the conflict between short- and long-term profitability. (Appendix)
11. Make decisions about allocating scarce resources by analyzing relevant information. (Appendix)

THE *curious* ACCOUNTANT

In February 2003 *The Wall Street Journal* ran an article about the difference between prescription drug prices in the United States and Canada. The article showed the Canadian prices for 10 popular prescription drugs, such as **Celebrex** and **Zocor**, were only 38 percent of prices charged in the United States.

Major pharmaceutical companies have *earnings before tax* that average around 25 percent of sales, indicating that their costs average around 75 percent of the prices they charge. In other words, it cost approximately 75 cents to generate one dollar of revenue. Given that drugs are sold in Canada for 38 percent of the U.S. sales price, a drug that is sold in the U.S. for a dollar would be sold in Canada for only 38 cents.

How can drugs be sold in Canada for less (38 cents) than cost (75 cents)? (Answer on page 142.)

CHAPTER *opening*

Mary Daniels is a partner in a small investment company. Her research indicates that Secor, Inc., is a likely takeover target of a multinational corporation. Ms. Daniels wants to buy some Secor stock because she is certain its price will appreciate significantly in the immediate future. Unfortunately, she is short of cash. She wishes she had known about Secor last week when she bought 1,000 shares of Telstar Communications, Inc., at $24 per share. Telstar had recently launched a series of satellites designed to make worldwide phone service feasible and convenient. With a small device not much larger than a thick credit card, customers could send and receive phone calls anywhere in the world. The day after Ms. Daniels bought the stock, Telstar announced technical difficulties with the satellites, and its stock price *dropped to $20 per share. She told herself that Telstar stock is going nowhere, but if she sold it now, she'd take a $4,000 loss ([$24 cost − $20 market] × 1,000 shares). Ms. Daniels decided to hold the Telstar stock instead of selling it and buying Secor. The Secor stock seemed like a sure thing, but she didn't want to incur a loss. Did Ms. Daniels make the right decision?*

The Decision Environment

Business decision makers cope with enormous challenges. They frequently must make decisions with incomplete information, yet are also faced with an overabundance of useless information. Highly successful executives may seem to have an uncanny knack for distinguishing between relevant and irrelevant data. Success, however, is not a matter of luck. The keys to effective decision making are discussed in the following pages.

Relevant Information

LO1 Identify the characteristics of relevant information

Two primary characteristics distinguish relevant from useless information. First, **relevant information** *differs* among the alternatives under consideration. Suppose you are deciding between two job offers. Both jobs offer the same salary. Salary, therefore, is not *relevant* to the decision-making process. Although salary is important in choosing a job, it is not relevant in choosing between these two job offers. If you receive a third job offer that pays a different salary, salary then becomes relevant because you could differentiate the third offer from the other two. *Relevant information* differs *among the alternatives under consideration.*

A second characteristic of relevant information is that it is *future oriented.* "Don't cry over spilled milk." "It's water over the dam." These aphorisms remind people they cannot change the past. With regard to business decisions, the principle means *you cannot avoid a cost that has already been incurred.*

To illustrate, return to the segment at the opening of this chapter. Recall that Mary Daniels had purchased 1,000 shares of Telstar stock at $24 per share. She had an opportunity to sell the Telstar stock at $20 per share and invest the proceeds in Secor shares, which were expected to increase in value because Secor was rumored to be the target of a takeover attempt. Ms. Daniels decided to keep her investment in Telstar because she did not want to incur a loss. Did she make the right choice?

Whether Ms. Daniels will make more money by holding the Telstar stock instead of selling it and buying Secor is unknown. The stock price of either company could go up or down. However, she based the decision on *irrelevant* data. Ms. Daniels incurred a loss *when the price of Telstar dropped.* She cannot *avoid* a loss that already exists. Past mistakes should not affect current decisions. Owning the Telstar stock is equivalent to having $20,000 cash today. The relevant question is whether to invest the $20,000 in Telstar or Secor. If Secor is the better alternative, Ms. Daniels should sell the Telstar stock and buy Secor stock.

Sunk Cost

LO2 Recognize sunk costs and explain why they are not relevant in decision making.

Ms. Daniels' Telstar stock investment is an example of a *sunk cost.* A **sunk cost** has been incurred in a past transaction. *Since* sunk costs *have been incurred in past transactions and cannot be changed, they are not relevant for making current decisions.*

Why even bother to collect historical information if it is not relevant? Historical information may be useful in predicting the future. A company that earned $5,000,000 last year is more likely to earn $5,000,000 this year than a company that earned $5,000 last year. The predictive capacity is relevant because it provides insight into the future.

Relevant (Differential) Revenues

LO1 Identify the characteristics of relevant information.

As indicated, relevant revenues must (1) be future oriented and (2) differ for the alternatives under consideration. Since relevant revenues differ between the alternatives, they are sometimes called **differential revenues.** For example, suppose that Pecks Department Stores sells men's, women's, and children's clothing and is considering eliminating the children's line. The revenue generated by the children's department is *differential (relevant) revenue* because Pecks' total revenue would be different if the department were eliminated.

Relevant (Avoidable) Costs

LO1 Identify the characteristics of relevant information.

Businesses seek to minimize cost. Managers *avoid* costs whenever possible. In fact, **relevant costs** are frequently called **avoidable costs.** Avoidable (relevant) costs are the costs managers can eliminate by making specific choices. Return to the Pecks Department Stores example. Costs management could avoid by eliminating the children's department include: merchandise cost; the salaries of buyers and sales staff; interest on debt used to finance the inventory; packaging and transportation; insurance; lost, damaged, and stolen merchandise; bad debts; shopping bags; sales slips; price tags; and other supplies. Many other costs could *not* be avoided. For example, the company president's salary cannot be avoided by closing down the children's line. Pecks will pay the president her salary whether or not it closes the children's department. Other costs that cannot be avoided include depreciation on the buildings, rent, property taxes, general advertising, and storewide utilities. If a cost is the same (does not *differ*) for two alternatives, it cannot be avoided by selecting one of the alternatives. In other words, *avoidable costs differ between the alternatives.*

Topic Tackler PLUS 4–1

Relationship of Cost Avoidance to a Cost Hierarchy

LO3 Distinguish between unit-level, batch-level, product-level, and facility-level costs and understand how these costs affect decision making.

Classifying costs into one of four hierarchical levels helps identify avoidable costs.[1]

1. *Unit-level costs.* Costs incurred each time a company generates one unit of product are **unit-level costs.**[2] Examples include the cost of direct materials, direct labor, inspections, packaging, shipping, and handling. Incremental (additional) unit-level costs increase *with each additional unit of product generated. Unit-level costs can be avoided by eliminating the production of a single unit of product.*

---

[1] R. Cooper and R. S. Kaplan, *The Design of Cost Management Systems* (Englewood Cliffs, NJ: Prentice-Hall, 1991). Our classifications are broader than those typically presented. They encompass service and merchandising companies as well as manufacturing businesses. The original cost hierarchy was developed as a platform for activity-based costing, a topic introduced later. These classifications are equally useful as a tool for identifying avoidable costs.

[2] Recall that we use the term *product* in a generic sense to represent producing goods or services.

2. *Batch-level costs.* Many products are generated in batches rather than individual units. For example, a heating and air conditioning technician may service a batch of air conditioners in an apartment complex. Some of the job costs apply only to individual units, and other costs relate to the entire batch. For instance, the labor to service each air conditioner is a unit-level cost, but the cost of driving to the site is a **batch-level cost.**

   Classifying costs as unit- versus batch-level frequently depends on the context rather than the type of cost. For example, shipping and handling costs to send 200 computers to a university are batch-level costs. In contrast, the shipping and handling cost to deliver a single computer to each of a number of individual customers is a unit-level cost. Eliminating a batch of work avoids both batch-level and unit-level costs. Similarly, adding a batch of work increases batch-level and unit-level costs. Increasing the number of units in a particular batch increases unit-level but not batch-level costs. Decreasing the number of units in a batch reduces unit-level costs but not batch-level costs.
3. *Product-level costs.* Costs incurred to support specific products or services are called **product-level costs.** Product-level costs include quality inspection costs, engineering design costs, the costs of obtaining and defending patents, the costs of regulatory compliance, and inventory holding costs such as interest, insurance, maintenance, and storage. *Product-level costs can be avoided by discontinuing a product line.* For example, suppose the Snapper Company makes the engines used in its lawn mowers. Buying engines from an outside supplier instead of making them would allow Snapper to avoid the product-level costs such as legal fees for patents, manufacturing supervisory costs of producing the engines, and the maintenance and inventory costs of holding engine parts.
4. *Facility-level costs.* **Facility-level costs** are incurred to support the entire company. They are not related to any specific product, batch, or unit of product. Because these costs maintain the facility as a whole, they are frequently called *facility-sustaining costs.* Facility-level costs include building rent or depreciation, personnel administration and training, property and real estate taxes, insurance, maintenance, administrative salaries, general selling costs, landscaping, utilities, and security. Total facility-level costs cannot be avoided unless the entire company is dissolved. However, eliminating a business segment (such as a division, department, or office) may enable a company to avoid some facility-level costs. For example, if a bank eliminates one of its branches, it can avoid the costs of renting, maintaining, and insuring that particular branch building. In general, *segment-level* facility costs can be avoided when a segment is eliminated. In contrast, *corporate-level* facility costs cannot be avoided unless the corporation is eliminated.

Precise distinctions between the various categories are often difficult to draw. One company may incur sales staff salaries as a facility-level cost while another company may pay sales commissions traceable to product lines or even specific units of a product line. Cost classifications cannot be memorized. Classifying specific cost items into the appropriate categories requires thoughtful judgment.

Relevance Is an Independent Concept

The concept of relevance is independent from the concept of cost behavior. In a given circumstance, relevant costs could be either fixed or variable. Consider the following illustration. Executives of Better Bakery Products are debating whether to add a new product, either cakes or pies, to the company's line. Projected costs for the two options follow.

Cost of Cakes		Cost of Pies	
Materials (per unit)	$ 1.50	Materials (per unit)	$ 2.00
Direct labor (per unit)	1.00	Direct labor (per unit)	1.00
Supervisor's salary*	25,000.00	Supervisor's salary*	25,000.00
Franchise fee†	50,000.00	Advertising‡	40,000.00

*It will be necessary to hire a new production supervisor at a cost of $25,000 per year.

†Cakes will be distributed under a nationally advertised label. Better Bakery pays an annual franchise fee for the right to use the product label. Because of the established brand name, Better Bakery will not be required to advertise the product.

‡Better Bakery will market the pies under its own name and will advertise the product in the local market in which the product sells.

LO1 Identify the characteristics of relevant information.

Which costs are relevant? Fifty cents per unit of the materials can be avoided by choosing cakes instead of pies. A portion of the materials cost is therefore relevant. Labor costs will be one dollar per unit whether Better Bakery makes cakes or pies. Labor cost is therefore not relevant. Although both materials and direct labor are variable costs, one is relevant but the other is not.

Since Better Bakery must hire a supervisor under either alternative, the supervisor's salary is not relevant. The franchise fee can be avoided if Better Bakery makes pies and advertising costs can be avoided if it makes cakes. All three of these costs are fixed, but only two are relevant. Finally, all the costs (whether fixed or variable) could be avoided if Better Bakery rejects both products. Whether a cost is fixed or variable has no bearing on its relevance.

Relevance of Opportunity Costs

LO4 Identify opportunity costs and explain why they are relevant in decision making.

Suppose you pay $50 for a highly sought-after ticket to an Olympic event. Just outside the stadium, someone offers to buy your ticket for $500. If you decline the offer, how much does attending the event cost you? From a decision-making perspective, the cost is $500. If you enter the stadium, you give up the *opportunity* to obtain $500 cash. The relevant cost is $500. The $50 original purchase price is an irrelevant *sunk cost.* The sacrifice represented by a lost opportunity is an **opportunity cost.** Opportunity costs that are (1) future oriented and (2) differ between the alternatives are relevant for decision-making purposes.

Suppose a few minutes after you turn down the offer to sell your ticket for $500, another person offers you $600 for the ticket. If you decline the second offer, has your opportunity cost risen to $1,100 (the first $500 offer plus the second $600 offer)? No; opportunity costs are not cumulative. If you had accepted the first offer, you could not have accepted the second. You may have many opportunities, but accepting one alternative eliminates the possibility of accepting any others. Accountants normally measure opportunity cost as the highest value of the available alternative courses of action. In this case, the opportunity cost of attending the Olympic event is $600.

Opportunity costs are not recorded in financial accounting records and are not reported in financial statements. You would not report the above described $600 opportunity cost as an expense on the income statement, but it will certainly affect your decision about whether to attend the Olympic event. *Opportunity costs are relevant costs.*

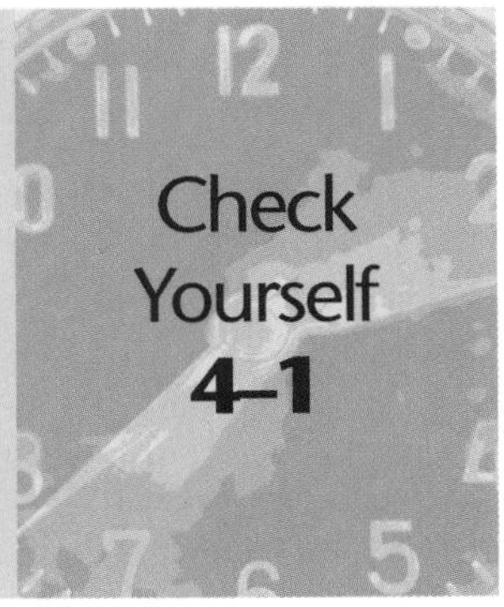

Aqua, Inc., makes statues for use in fountains. On January 1, 2003, the company paid $13,500 for a mold to make a particular type of statue. The mold had an expected useful life of four years and a salvage value of $1,500. On January 1, 2005, the mold had a market value of $3,000 and a salvage value of $1,200. The expected useful life did not change. What is the relevant cost of using the mold during 2005?

Answer The relevant cost of using the mold in 2005 is the opportunity cost ([market value − salvage value] ÷ remaining useful life), in this case, ($3,000 − $1,200) ÷ 2 = $900. The book value of the asset and associated depreciation is based on a sunk cost that cannot be avoided because it has already been incurred and therefore is not relevant to current decisions. In contrast, Aqua could avoid the opportunity cost (market value) by selling the mold.

REALITY *bytes*

Determining what price to charge for their company's goods or services is one of the most difficult decisions that business managers make. Charge too much and customers will go elsewhere. Charge less than customers are willing to pay and lose the opportunity to earn profits. This problem is especially difficult when managers are deciding if they should reduce (mark down) the price of aging inventory—for example, flowers that are beginning to wilt, fruit that is beginning to overripen, or clothing that is going out of season.

At first managers may be reluctant to mark down the inventory below its cost because this would cause the company to take a loss on the aging inventory. However, the concept of sunk cost applies here. Since the existing inventory has already been paid for, its cost is sunk. Since the cost is sunk it is not relevant to the decision. Does this mean the merchandise should be sold for any price? Not necessarily. The concept of opportunity cost must also be considered.

If the goods are marked down too far, too quickly, they may be sold for less than is possible. The lost potential revenue is an opportunity cost. To minimize the opportunity cost, the amount of a markdown must be the smallest amount necessary to sell the merchandise. The decision is further complicated by qualitative considerations. If a business develops a reputation for repeated markdowns, customers may hesitate to buy goods, thinking that the price will fall further if they only wait a while. The result is a dilemma as to when and how much to mark down aging inventories.

How do managers address this dilemma? Part of the answer has been the use of technology. For years airlines have used computerized mathematical models to help them decide how many seats on a particular flight should be sold at a discount. More recently, retailers have used this same type of modeling software. Such software allows retailers to take fewer markdowns at more appropriate times, thereby resulting in higher overall gross profit margins.

(For a more complete discussion of this topic, see *The Wall Street Journal*, August 7, 2001, pp. A-1, A-6.)

Relevance Is Context-Sensitive

LO1 Identify the characteristics of relevant information.

A particular cost that is relevant in one context may be irrelevant in another. Consider a store that carries men's, women's, and children's clothing. The store manager's salary could not be avoided by eliminating the children's department, but it could be avoided if the entire store were closed. The salary is not relevant to deciding whether to eliminate the children's department but is relevant with respect to deciding to close a store. In one context, the salary is not relevant. In the other context, it is relevant.

Relationship Between Relevance and Accuracy

LO1 Identify the characteristics of relevant information.

Information need not be exact to be relevant. You may decide to delay purchasing a laptop computer you want if you know its price is going to drop even if you don't know exactly how much the price decrease will be. You know part of the cost can be avoided by waiting; you are just not sure of the amount.

The most useful information is both relevant and precise. Totally inaccurate information is useless. Likewise, irrelevant information is useless regardless of its accuracy.

Quantitative Versus Qualitative Characteristics of Decision Making

LO5 Distinguish between quantitative and qualitative characteristics of decision making.

Relevant information can have both **quantitative** and **qualitative characteristics.** The previous examples focused on quantitative data. Now consider qualitative issues. Suppose you are deciding which of two laptop computers to purchase. Computer A costs $300 more than Computer B. Both computers satisfy your technical requirements; however, Computer A has a more attractive appearance. From a quantitative standpoint, you would select Computer B because you could avoid $300 of cost. However, if the laptop will be used in circumstances when clients need to be impressed, appearance—a qualitative characteristic—may be more important than minimizing cost. You might purchase Computer A even though quantitative factors favor Computer B. Both qualitative and quantitative data are relevant to decision making.

As with quantitative data, qualitative features must *differ* between the alternatives to be relevant. If the two computers were identical in appearance, attractiveness would not be relevant to making the decision.

Topic Tackler PLUS 4–2

Relevant Information and Special Decisions

LO6 Make appropriate special order decisions by analyzing relevant information.

Five types of special decisions are frequently encountered in business practice: (1) special order, (2) outsourcing, (3) segment elimination, (4) asset replacement, and (5) scarce resource allocation. The following sections discuss using relevant information in making the first four types of special decisions. The Appendix to this chapter discusses scarce resource decisions.

Special Order Decisions

Occasionally, a company receives an offer to sell its goods at a price significantly below its normal selling price. The company must make a **special order decision** to accept or reject the offer.

Quantitative Analysis

Assume Premier Office Products manufactures printers. Premier expects to make and sell 2,000 printers in 10 batches of 200 units per batch during the coming year. Expected production costs are summarized in Exhibit 4–1.

Adding its normal markup to the total cost per unit, Premier set the selling price at $360 per printer.

Suppose Premier receives a *special order* from a new customer for 200 printers. If Premier accepts the order, its expected sales would increase from 2,000 units to 2,200 units. But the special order customer is willing to pay only $250 per printer. This price is well below not only Premier's normal selling price of $360 but also the company's expected per unit cost of $329.25. Should Premier accept or reject the special order? At first glance, it seems Premier should reject the special order because the customer's offer is below the expected cost per unit. Analyzing relevant costs and revenue leads, however, to a different conclusion.

The quantitative analysis follows in three steps.

Exhibit 4–1 *Budgeted Cost for Expected Production of 2,000 Printers*

Unit-level costs		
Materials costs (2,000 units × $90)	$180,000	
Labor costs (2,000 units × $82.50)	165,000	
Overhead (2,000 units × $7.50)	15,000	
Total unit-level costs (2,000 × $180)		$360,000
Batch-level costs		
Assembly setup (10 batches × $1,700)	17,000	
Materials handling (10 batches × $500)	5,000	
Total batch-level costs (10 batches × $2,200)		22,000
Product-level costs		
Engineering design	14,000	
Production manager salary	63,300	
Total product-level costs		77,300
Facility level costs		
Segment-level costs		
Division manager's salary	85,000	
Administrative costs	12,700	
Corporate-level costs		
Company president's salary	43,200	
Depreciation	27,300	
General expenses	31,000	
Total facility-level costs		199,200
Total expected cost		$658,500
Cost per unit: $658,500 ÷ 2,000 = $329.25		

Step 1 Determine the amount of the relevant (differential) revenue Premier will earn by accepting the special

ANSWERS TO THE *curious* ACCOUNTANT

There are several factors that enable drug companies to reduce their prices to certain customers. One significant factor is the issue of relevant cost. Pharmaceutical manufacturers have a substantial amount of fixed cost, such as research and development. For example, in 2002 **Pfizer, Inc.** had research and development expenses that were 16 percent of sales, while its cost of goods sold expense was only 12.5 percent of sales. With respect to a special order decision, the research and development costs would not change and therefore would not be relevant. In contrast, the unit-level cost of goods sold would increase and therefore would be relevant. Clearly, relevant costs are significantly less than the total cost. If Canadian prices are based on relevant costs, that is, if drug companies view Canadian sales as a special order opportunity, the lower prices may provide a contribution to profitability even though they are significantly less than the prices charged in the United States.

order. Premier's alternatives are (1) to accept or (2) to reject the special order. If Premier accepts the special order, additional revenue will be $50,000 ($250 x 200 units). If Premier rejects the special order, additional revenue will be zero. Since the amount of revenue differs between the alternatives, the $50,000 is relevant.

Step 2 **Determine the amount of the relevant (differential) cost Premier will incur by accepting the special order.** Examine the costs in Exhibit 4–1. If Premier accepts the special order, it will incur additional unit-level costs (materials, labor, and overhead). It will also incur the cost of one additional 200-unit batch. The unit- and batch-level costs are relevant because Premier could avoid them by rejecting the special order. The other costs in Exhibit 4–1 are not relevant because Premier will incur them whether it accepts or rejects the special order.

Step 3 **Accept the special order if the relevant revenue exceeds the relevant (avoidable) cost. Reject the order if relevant cost exceeds relevant revenue.** Exhibit 4–2 summarizes the relevant figures. Since the relevant revenue exceeds the relevant cost, Premier should accept the special order because profitability will increase by $11,800.

Exhibit 4–2 *Relevant Information for Special Order of 200 Printers*

Differential revenue ($250 × 200 units)	$50,000
Avoidable unit-level costs ($180 × 200 units)	(36,000)
Avoidable batch-level costs ($2,200 × 1 batch)	(2,200)
Contribution to income	$11,800

Opportunity Costs

Premier can consider the special order because it has enough excess productive capacity to make the additional units. Suppose Premier has the opportunity to lease its excess capacity (currently unused building and equipment) for $15,000. If Premier uses the excess capacity to make the additional printers, it must forgo the opportunity to lease the excess capacity to a third party. Sacrificing the potential leasing income represents an opportunity cost of accepting the special order. Adding this opportunity cost to the other relevant costs increases the cost of accepting the special order to $53,200 ($38,200 unit-level and batch-level costs + $15,000 opportunity cost). The avoidable costs would then exceed the differential revenue, resulting in a projected loss of $3,200 ($50,000 differential revenue − $53,200 avoidable costs). Under these circumstances Premier would be better off rejecting the special order and leasing the excess capacity.

Relevance and the Decision Context

Assume Premier does not have the opportunity to lease its excess capacity. Recall the original analysis indicated the company could earn an $11,800 contribution to profit by accepting a special order to sell 200 printers at $250 per unit (see Exhibit 4–2). Because Premier can earn a contribution to profit by selling printers for $250 each, can the company reduce its normal

Exhibit 4–3 *Projections Based on 2,200 Printers at a Sales Price of $250 per Unit*

Revenue ($250 × 2,200 units)		$ 550,000
Unit-level supplies and inspection ($180 × 2,200 units)	$396,000	
Batch-level costs ($2,200 × 11 batches)	24,200	
Product-level costs	77,300	
Facility-level costs	199,200	
Total cost		(696,700)
Projected loss		$(146,700)

selling price (price charged to existing customers) to $250? The answer is no, as illustrated in Exhibit 4–3.

If a company is to be profitable, it must ultimately generate revenue in excess of total costs. Although the facility-level and product-level costs are not relevant to the special order decision, they are relevant to the operation of the business as a whole.

Qualitative Characteristics

Should a company ever reject a special order if the relevant revenues exceed the relevant costs? Qualitative characteristics may be even more important than quantitative ones. If Premier's regular customers learn the company sold printers to another buyer at $250 per unit, they may demand reduced prices on future purchases. Exhibit 4–3 shows Premier cannot reduce the price for all customers. Special order customers should therefore come from outside Premier's normal sales territory. In addition, special order customers should be advised that the special price does not apply to repeat business. Cutting off a special order customer who has been permitted to establish a continuing relationship is likely to lead to ill-feelings and harsh words. A business's reputation can depend on how management handles such relationships. Finally, at full capacity, Premier should reject any special orders at reduced prices because filling those orders reduces its ability to satisfy customers who pay full price.

LO7 Make appropriate outsourcing decisions by analyzing relevant information.

Outsourcing Decisions

Companies can sometimes purchase products they need for less than it would cost to make them. This circumstance explains why automobile manufacturers purchase rather than make many of the parts in their cars or why a caterer might buy gourmet desserts from a specialty company. Buying goods and services from other companies rather than producing them internally is commonly called **outsourcing.**

That test was so easy. How did you score so bad?
I outsourced my homework.

Quantitative Analysis

Assume Premier Office Products is considering whether to outsource production of the printers it currently makes. A supplier has offered to sell an unlimited supply of printers to Premier for $240 each. The estimated cost of making the printers is $329.25 per unit (see Exhibit 4–1). The data suggest that Premier could save money by outsourcing. Analyzing relevant costs proves this presumption wrong.

A two-step quantitative analysis for the outsourcing decision follows:

Step 1 **Determine the production costs Premier can avoid if it outsources printer production.** A review of Exhibit 4–1 discloses the costs Premier could avoid by outsourcing. If Premier purchases the printers, it can avoid the unit-level costs (materials, labor, overhead), assembly setup costs, and materials handling costs. It can also avoid the product-level costs (engineering design costs and production manager salary). Deciding to outsource will not, however, affect the facility-level costs. Because Premier will incur them whether or not it

Exhibit 4–4 *Relevant Cost for Expected Production for Outsourcing 2,000 Printers*

Unit-level costs ($180 × 2,000 units)	$360,000
Batch-level costs ($2,200 × 10 batches)	22,000
Product-level costs	77,300
Total relevant cost	$459,300

Cost per unit: $459,300 ÷ 2,000 = $229.65

outsources printer production, the facility-level costs are not relevant to the outsourcing decision. Exhibit 4–4 shows the avoidable (relevant) costs of outsourcing.

Step 2 **Compare the avoidable (relevant) production costs with the cost of buying the product and select the lower-cost option.** Because the relevant production cost is less than the purchase price of the printers ($229.65 per unit versus $240.00), the quantitative analysis suggests that Premier should continue to make the printers. Profitability would decline by $20,700 ($459,300 − [$240 × 2,000]) if printer production were outsourced.

Opportunity Costs

Suppose Premier's accountant determines that the space Premier currently uses to manufacture printers could be converted to warehouse space for storing finished goods. Using this space for warehouse storage would save Premier the $40,000 per year it currently spends to rent warehouse space. By using the space to manufacture printers, Premier is *forgoing the opportunity* to save $40,000 in warehouse costs. Because this *opportunity cost* can be avoided by purchasing the printers, it is relevant to the outsourcing decision. After adding the opportunity cost to the other relevant costs, the total relevant cost increases to $499,300 ($459,300 + $40,000) and the relevant cost per unit becomes $249.65 ($499,300 ÷ 2,000). Since Premier can purchase printers for $240, it should outsource printer production. It would be better off buying the printers and using the warehouse space to store finished goods than to continue producing the printers.

Evaluating the Effect of Growth on the Level of Production

The decision to outsource would change if expected production increased from 2,000 to 3,000 units. Because some of the avoidable costs are fixed relative to the level of production, cost per unit decreases as volume increases. For example, the product-level costs (engineering design, production manager's salary, and opportunity cost) are fixed relative to the level of production. Exhibit 4–5 shows the relevant cost per unit if Premier expects to produce 3,000 printers.

At 3,000 units of production, the relevant cost of making printers is less than the cost of outsourcing ($230.10 versus $240.00). If management believes the company is likely to experience growth in the near future, it should reject the outsourcing option. Managers must consider potential growth when making outsourcing decisions.

Exhibit 4–5 *Relevant Cost for Expected Production for Outsourcing 3,000 Printers*

Unit-level costs ($180 × 3,000 units)	$540,000
Batch-level costs ($2,200 × 15 batches)	33,000
Product-level costs	77,300
Opportunity cost	40,000
Total relevant cost	$690,300

Cost per unit: $690,300 ÷ 3,000 units = $230.10

Qualitative Features

A company that uses **vertical integration** controls the full range of activities from acquiring raw materials to distributing goods and services. Outsourcing reduces the level of vertical integration, passing some of a company's control over its products to outside suppliers. The reliability of the supplier is critical to an outsourcing decision. An unscrupulous supplier may lure an unsuspecting manufacturer into an outsourcing decision using **low-ball pricing.** Once the manufacturer is dependent on the supplier, the supplier raises prices. If a price sounds too good to be true, it probably is too good to be true. Other potential problems include product quality and delivery commitments. If the printers do not work properly or are not delivered on time, Premier's customers will be dissatisfied with Premier, not the supplier. Outsourcing requires that Premier depend on the supplier to deliver quality products at designated prices according to a specified schedule. Any supplier failures will become Premier's failures.

To protect themselves from unscrupulous or incompetent suppliers, many companies establish a select list of reliable **certified suppliers.** These companies seek to become the preferred customers of the suppliers by offering incentives such as guaranteed volume purchases with prompt payments. These incentives motivate the suppliers to ship high quality products on a timely basis. The purchasing companies recognize that prices ultimately depend on the suppliers' ability to control costs, so the buyers and suppliers work together to minimize costs. For example, buyers may share confidential information about their production plans with suppliers if such information would enable the suppliers to more effectively control costs.

Companies must approach outsourcing decisions cautiously even when relationships with reliable suppliers are ensured. Outsourcing has both internal and external effects. It usually displaces employees. If the supplier experiences difficulties, reestablishing internal production capacity is expensive once a trained workforce has been released. Loyalty and trust are difficult to build but easy to destroy. In fact, companies must consider not only the employees who will be discharged but also the morale of those who remain. Cost reductions achieved through outsourcing are of little benefit if they are acquired at the expense of low morale and reduced productivity.

focus on INTERNATIONAL ISSUES

Outsourcing—How Do They Do It in Japan?

Many outsourcing opportunities suffer from a lack of long-term commitment. For example, a supplier may be able to attain economic efficiencies by redesigning its facilities to produce a product needed by a special order customer. Unfortunately, the redesign cost cannot be recovered on a small order quantity. The supplier needs assurances of a long-term relationship to justify a significant investment in the supply relationship. Japanese businesses have resolved this condition through what is sometimes called *obligational contract relationships.* While these contracts are renewable annually, most suppliers expect to form a supply relationship that will last more than five years. Indeed, Japanese custom establishes a commitment between the supplier and the buyer that includes the exchange of sensitive cost information. If deficiencies in price, delivery, or quality conformance occur, the buyer is likely to send production engineers to the offices of the supplier. The buyer's engineers will study the facilities of the supplier and give detailed advice as to how to achieve improved results. In the process of analyzing the supplier's operations, the buyer obtains detailed information regarding the supplier's costs. This information is used to negotiate prices that ensure reasonable rather than excessive profits for the supplier.

Accordingly, costs are controlled for not only the supplier but also the buyer.

Source: Miles B. Gietzmann, "Emerging Practices in Cost Accounting," *Management Accounting* (UK), January 1995, pp. 24–25.

In spite of potential pitfalls outsourcing entails, the vast majority of U.S. businesses engage in some form of it. Such widespread acceptance suggests that most companies believe the benefits achieved through outsourcing exceed the potential shortcomings.

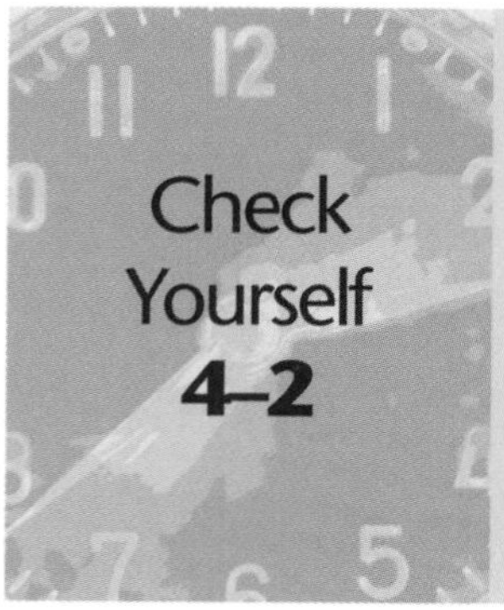

Addison Manufacturing Company pays a production supervisor a salary of $48,000 per year. The supervisor manages the production of sprinkler heads that are used in water irrigation systems. Should the production supervisor's salary be considered a relevant cost to a special order decision? Should the production supervisor's salary be considered a relevant cost to an outsourcing decision?

Answer The production supervisor's salary is not a relevant cost to a special order decision because Addison would pay the salary regardless of whether it accepts or rejects a special order. Since the cost does not differ for the alternatives, it is not relevant. In contrast, the supervisor's salary would be relevant to an outsourcing decision. Addison could dismiss the supervisor if it purchased the sprinkler heads instead of making them. Since the salary could be avoided by purchasing heads instead of making them, the salary is relevant to an outsourcing decision.

Segment Elimination Decisions

LO8 Make appropriate segment elimination decisions by analyzing relevant information.

Businesses frequently organize operating results into subcomponents called **segments.** Segment data are used to make comparisons among different products, departments, or divisions. For example, in addition to the companywide income statement provided for external users, JCPenney may prepare separate income statements for each retail store for internal users. Executives can then evaluate managerial performance by comparing profitability measures among stores. *Segment reports* can be prepared for products, services, departments, branches, centers, offices, or divisions. These reports normally show segment revenues and costs. The primary objective of segment analysis is to determine whether relevant revenues exceed relevant costs.

Quantitative Analysis

Assume Premier Office Products makes copy equipment and computers as well as printers. Each product line is made in a separate division of the company. Division (segment) operating results for the most recent year are shown in Exhibit 4–6. Initial review of the results suggests the copier division should be eliminated because it is operating at a loss. However, analyzing the relevant revenues and expenses leads to a different conclusion.

A three-step quantitative analysis for the segment elimination decision follows:

Step 1 **Determine the amount of relevant (differential) revenue that pertains to eliminating the copier division.** The alternatives are (1) to eliminate or (2) to continue to operate the copier division. If Premier eliminates the copier line it will lose the $550,000 of revenue the copier division currently produces. If the division continues to operate Premier will earn the revenue. Since the revenue differs between the alternatives, it is relevant.

Step 2 **Determine the amount of cost Premier can avoid if it eliminates the copier division.** If it eliminates copiers, Premier can avoid the unit-level, batch-level, product-level, and segment-level facility-sustaining costs. The relevant revenue and the avoidable costs are shown in Exhibit 4–7.

Premier will incur the corporate-level facility-sustaining costs whether it eliminates the copier segment or continues to operate it. Since these costs do not differ between the alternatives, they are not relevant to the elimination decision. These indirect costs have been *allocated* to the three segments. The subject of *allocation* will be fully discussed in Chapters 5 and 6. At this point, it is sufficient to note that the term means to divide a total into parts and to assign those parts to certain objects (in this case, to

Exhibit 4–6 *Projected Revenues and Costs by Segment*

	Copiers	Computers	Printers	Total
Projected revenue	$550,000	$850,000	$780,000	$2,180,000
Projected costs				
Unit-level costs				
Materials costs	(120,000)	(178,000)	(180,000)	(478,000)
Labor costs	(160,000)	(202,000)	(165,000)	(527,000)
Overhead	(30,800)	(20,000)	(15,000)	(65,800)
Batch-level costs				
Assembly setup	(15,000)	(26,000)	(17,000)	(58,000)
Materials handling	(6,000)	(8,000)	(5,000)	(19,000)
Product-level costs				
Engineering design	(10,000)	(12,000)	(14,000)	(36,000)
Production manager salary	(52,000)	(55,800)	(63,300)	(171,100)
Facility-level costs				
Segment level				
Division manager salary	(82,000)	(92,000)	(85,000)	(259,000)
Administrative costs	(12,200)	(13,200)	(12,700)	(38,100)
Allocated—corporate level				
Company president salary	(34,000)	(46,000)	(43,200)	(123,200)
Building rental	(19,250)	(29,750)	(27,300)	(76,300)
General facility expenses	(31,000)	(31,000)	(31,000)	(93,000)
Projected profit (loss)	$(22,250)	$136,250	$121,500	$ 235,500

the three segments). For example, the total $93,000 of general corporate-level facility expenses has been allocated equally among the three segments, $31,000 to each. This $93,000 of costs will be incurred even if Premier eliminates the copier segment. The other two corporate-level facility costs (president's salary and building rental) have not been allocated equally among the three segments. A total cost can be allocated among segments in many ways. Discussion of these alternatives is provided in subsequent chapters. Regardless of the allocation, the total cost is unchanged before and after the segment elimination. These and other allocated costs are not relevant.

Exhibit 4–7 *Relevant Revenue and Cost Data for Copier Segment*

Projected revenue	$550,000
Projected costs	
Unit-level costs	
Materials costs	(120,000)
Labor costs	(160,000)
Overhead	(30,800)
Batch-level costs	
Assembly setup	(15,000)
Materials handling	(6,000)
Product-level costs	
Engineering design	(10,000)
Production manager salary	(52,000)
Facility-level costs	
Segment level	
Division manager salary	(82,000)
Administrative costs	(12,200)
Projected profit (loss)	$ 62,000

Step 3 **If the relevant revenue is less than the avoidable cost, eliminate the segment (division). If not, continue to operate it.** Because operating the segment is contributing $62,000 per year to company profitability (see Exhibit 4–7), Premier should not eliminate the copiers division. Exhibit 4–8 shows Premier's estimated revenues and costs if the computers and printers divisions were operated without the copiers division. Projected company profit declines by $62,000 ($235,500 − $173,500) without the copiers segment, confirming that eliminating it would be detrimental to Premier's profitability.

Qualitative Considerations in Decisions to Eliminate Segments

As with other special decisions, management should consider qualitative factors when determining whether to eliminate segments. Employee lives will be disrupted; some employees may be reassigned elsewhere in the company, but others will be discharged. As with outsourcing decisions, reestablishing internal production capacity is difficult once a trained workforce has been released. Furthermore, employees in other segments, suppliers, customers, and investors may believe that the elimination of a segment implies the company as a whole is experiencing financial difficulty. These individuals may lose confidence in the company and seek business contacts with other companies they perceive to be more stable.

Exhibit 4–8 *Projected Revenues and Costs Without Copier Division*

	Computers	Printers	Total
Projected revenue	$850,000	$780,000	$1,630,000
Projected costs			
Unit-level costs			
Materials costs	(178,000)	(180,000)	(358,000)
Labor costs	(202,000)	(165,000)	(367,000)
Overhead	(20,000)	(15,000)	(35,000)
Batch-level costs			
Assembly setup	(26,000)	(17,000)	(43,000)
Materials handling	(8,000)	(5,000)	(13,000)
Product-level costs			
Engineering design	(12,000)	(14,000)	(26,000)
Production manager salary	(55,800)	(63,300)	(119,100)
Facility-level costs			
Segment level			
Division manager salary	(92,000)	(85,000)	(177,000)
Administrative costs	(13,200)	(12,700)	(25,900)
Allocated—corporate level*			
Company president salary	(63,000)	(60,200)	(123,200)
Depreciation	(39,375)	(36,925)	(76,300)
General facility expenses	(46,500)	(46,500)	(93,000)
Projected profit (loss)	$ 94,125	$ 79,375	$ 173,500

*The corporate-level facility costs that were previously *allocated* to the copier division have been reassigned on the basis of one-half to the computer division and one-half to the printer division.

Management must also consider the fact that sales of different product lines are frequently interdependent. Some customers prefer one-stop shopping; they want to buy all their office equipment from one supplier. If Premier no longer sells copiers, customers may stop buying its computers and printers. Eliminating one segment may reduce sales of other segments.

What will happen to the space Premier used to make the copiers? Suppose Premier decides to make telephone systems in the space it previously used for copiers. The contribution to profit of the telephone business would be an *opportunity cost* of operating the copier segment. As demonstrated in previous examples, adding the opportunity cost to the avoidable costs of operating the copier segment could change the decision.

As with outsourcing, volume changes can affect elimination decisions. Because many costs of operating a segment are fixed, the cost per unit decreases as production increases. Growth can transform a segment that is currently producing real losses into a segment that produces real profits. Managers must consider growth potential when making elimination decisions.

Check Yourself 4–3

Capital Corporation is considering eliminating one of its operating segments. Capital employed a real estate broker to determine the marketability of the building that houses the segment. The broker obtained three bids for the building: $250,000, $262,000, and $264,000. The book value of the building is $275,000. Based on this information alone, what is the relevant cost of the building?

Answer The book value of the building is a sunk cost that is not relevant. There are three bids for the building, but only one is relevant because Capital could sell the building only once. The relevant cost of the building is the highest opportunity cost, which in this case is $264,000.

Summary of Relationships Between Avoidable Costs and the Hierarchy of Business Activity

LO3 Distinguish between unit-level, batch-level, product-level, and facility-level costs and understand how these costs affect decision making.

A relationship exists between the cost hierarchy and the different types of special decisions just discussed. A special order involves making additional units of an existing product. Deciding to accept a special order affects unit-level and possibly batch-level costs. In contrast,

Exhibit 4–9 *Relationship Between Decision Type and Level of Cost Hierarchy*

Decision Type	Unit level	Batch level	Product level	Facility level
Special order	X	X		
Outsourcing	X	X	X	
Elimination	X	X	X	X

outsourcing a product stops the production of that product. Outsourcing can avoid many product-level as well as unit- and batch-level costs. Finally, if a company eliminates an entire business segment, it can avoid some of the facility-level costs. The more complex the decision level, the more opportunities there are to avoid costs. Moving to a higher category does not mean, however, that all costs at the higher level of activity are avoidable. For example, all product-level costs may not be avoidable if a company chooses to outsource a product. The company may still incur inventory holding costs or advertising costs whether it makes or buys the product. Understanding the relationship between decision type and level of cost hierarchy helps when identifying avoidable costs. The relationships are summarized in Exhibit 4–9. For each type of decision, look for avoidable costs in the categories marked with an X. Remember also that sunk costs cannot be avoided.

Equipment Replacement Decisions

LO9 Make appropriate asset replacement decisions by analyzing relevant information.

Equipment may become technologically obsolete long before it fails physically. Managers should base **equipment replacement decisions** on profitability analysis rather than physical deterioration. Assume Premier Office Products is considering replacing an existing machine with a new one. The following table summarizes pertinent information about the two machines:

Old Machine		New Machine	
Original cost	$90,000	Cost of the new machine	$29,000
Accumulated depreciation	(33,000)	Salvage value (in 5 years)	4,000
Book value	$57,000	Operating expense ($4,500 × 5 years)	22,500
Market value (now)	$14,000		
Salvage value (in 5 years)	2,000		
Annual depreciation expense	11,000		
Operating expenses ($9,000 × 5 years)	45,000		

Quantitative Analysis

First determine what relevant costs Premier will incur if it keeps the *old machine.*

1. The *original cost* ($90,000), *current book value* ($57,000), *accumulated depreciation* ($33,000), and *annual depreciation expense* ($11,000) are different measures of a cost that was incurred in a prior period. They represent irrelevant sunk costs.
2. The $14,000 market value represents the current sacrifice Premier must make if it keeps using the existing machine. In other words, if Premier does not keep the machine, it can sell it for $14,000. In economic terms, *forgoing the opportunity* to sell the machine costs as much as buying it. The *opportunity cost* is therefore relevant to the replacement decision.
3. The salvage value of the old machine reduces the opportunity cost. Premier can sell the old machine now for $14,000 or use it for five more years and then sell it for $2,000. The opportunity cost of using the old machine for five more years is therefore $12,000 ($14,000 − $2,000).
4. Because the $45,000 ($9,000 × 5) of operating expenses will be incurred if the old machine is used but can be avoided if it is replaced, the operating expenses are relevant costs.

Next, determine what relevant costs will be incurred if Premier purchases and uses the *new machine.*

1. The cost of the new machine represents a future economic sacrifice Premier must incur if it buys the new machine. It is a relevant cost.
2. The salvage value reduces the cost of purchasing the new machine. Part ($4,000) of the $29,000 cost of the new machine will be recovered at the end of five years. The relevant cost of purchasing the new machine is $25,000 ($29,000 − $4,000).
3. The $22,500 ($4,500 × 5) of operating expenses will be incurred if the new machine is purchased; it can be avoided if the new machine is not purchased. The operating expenses are relevant costs.

The relevant costs for the two machines are summarized here:

Old Machine		New Machine	
Opportunity cost	$14,000	Cost of the new machine	$29,000
Salvage value	(2,000)	Salvage value	(4,000)
Operating expenses	45,000	Operating expenses	22,500
Total	$57,000	Total	$47,500

The analysis suggests that Premier should acquire the new machine because buying it produces the lower relevant cost. The $57,000 cost of using the old machine can be *avoided* by incurring the $47,500 cost of acquiring and using the new machine. Over the five-year period, Premier would save $9,500 ($57,000 − $47,500) by purchasing the new machine. One caution: this analysis ignores income tax effects and the time value of money, which are explained later. The discussion in this chapter focuses on identifying and using relevant costs in decision making.

a look back

Decision making requires managers to choose from alternative courses of action. Successful decision making depends on a manager's ability to identify *relevant information.* Information that is relevant for decision making differs among the alternatives and is future oriented. Relevant revenues are sometimes called *differential revenues* because they differ among the alternatives. Relevant costs are sometimes called *avoidable costs* because they can be eliminated or avoided by choosing a specific course of action.

Costs that do not differ among the alternatives are not avoidable and therefore not relevant. *Sunk costs* are not relevant in decision making because they have been incurred in past transactions and therefore cannot be avoided. *Opportunity costs* are relevant because they represent potential benefits that may or may not be realized, depending on the decision maker's choice. In other words, future benefits that differ among the alternatives are relevant. Opportunity costs are not recorded in the financial accounting records.

Classifying costs into one of four hierarchical levels facilitates identifying relevant costs. *Unit-level costs* such as materials and labor are incurred each time a single unit of product is made. These costs can be avoided by eliminating the production of a single unit of product. *Batch-level costs* are associated with producing a group of products. Examples include setup costs and inspection costs related to a batch (group) of work rather than a single unit. Eliminating a batch would avoid both batch-level costs and unit-level costs. *Product-level costs* are incurred to support specific products or services (design and regulatory compliance costs). Product-level costs can be avoided by discontinuing a product line. *Facility-level costs,* like the president's salary, are incurred on behalf of the whole company or a segment of the company. In segment elimination decisions, the facility-level costs related to a particular segment being considered for elimination are relevant and avoidable. Those applying to the company as a whole are not avoidable.

Cost behavior (fixed or variable) is independent from the concept of relevance. Furthermore, a cost that is relevant in one decision context may be irrelevant in another context. Decision making depends on qualitative as well as quantitative information. *Quantitative information refers to information that can be measured using numbers. Qualitative information* is nonquantitative information such as personal preferences or opportunities.

Four types of special decisions that are frequently encountered in business are (1) *special orders,* (2) *outsourcing,* (3) *elimination decisions,* and (4) *asset replacement.* The relevant costs in a special order decision are the unit-level and batch-level costs that will be incurred if the special order is accepted. If the differential revenues from the special order exceed the relevant costs, the order should be accepted. Outsourcing decisions determine whether goods and services should be purchased from other companies. The relevant costs are the unit-level, batch-level, and product-level costs that could be avoided if the company outsources the product or service. If these costs are more than the cost to buy and the qualitative characteristics are satisfactory, the company should outsource. Segment-related unit-level, batch-level, product-level, and facility-level costs that can be avoided when a segment is eliminated are relevant. If the segment's avoidable costs exceed its differential revenues, it should be eliminated, assuming favorable qualitative factors. Asset replacement decisions compare the relevant costs of existing equipment with the relevant costs of new equipment to determine whether replacing the old equipment would be profitable.

a look forward

The next chapter begins a two-chapter investigation of cost measurement. Accountants seek to determine the cost of certain objects. A cost object may be a product, a service, a department, a customer, or any other thing for which the cost is being determined. Some costs can be directly traced to a cost object, while others are difficult to trace. Costs that are difficult to trace to cost objects are called *indirect costs,* or *overhead.* Indirect costs are assigned to cost objects through a process known as *cost allocation.* The next chapter introduces the basic concepts and procedures of cost allocation.

APPENDIX

Short-Term Versus Long-Term Goals

LO10 Explain the conflict between short- and long-term profitability.

To examine conflicts between short-term versus long-term goals, we return to the equipment replacement decision made by the management team of Premier Office Products (see page 000 for details). Suppose that the final equipment replacement decision is made by a departmental supervisor who is under significant pressure to maximize profitability. She is told that if profitability declines, she will lose her job. Under these circumstances, the supervisor may choose to keep the old machine even though it is to the company's advantage to purchase the new one. This occurs because the beneficial impact of the new machine is realized in the second through fifth years. Indeed, replacing the equipment will result in more expense/loss recognition in the first year. To illustrate, study the following information.

Year	First	Second	Third	Fourth	Fifth	Totals
Keep old machine						
Depreciation expense*	$11,000	$11,000	$11,000	$11,000	$11,000	$ 55,000
Operating expense	9,000	9,000	9,000	9,000	9,000	45,000
Total	$20,000	$20,000	$20,000	$20,000	$20,000	$100,000
Replace old machine						
Loss on disposal†	$43,000	$ 0	$ 0	$ 0	$ 0	$43,000
Depreciation expense‡	5,000	5,000	5,000	5,000	5,000	25,000
Operating expense	4,500	4,500	4,500	4,500	4,500	22,500
Total	$52,500	$ 9,500	$ 9,500	$ 9,500	$ 9,500	$90,500

*($57,000 book value − $2,000 salvage) ÷ 5 years = $11,000

†($57,000 book value − $14,000 market value) = $43,000

‡($29,000 cost − $4,000 salvage) ÷ 5 years = $5,000

This analysis verifies that total cost at the end of the five-year period is $9,500 less if the equipment is replaced ($100,000 − $90,500). Notice, however, that total costs at the end of the first year are higher by $32,500 ($52,500 − $20,000) if the old machine is replaced. A decision maker under significant pressure to report higher profitability may be willing to sacrifice tomorrow's profits to look better today. By emphasizing short-term profitability, she may secure a promotion before the long-term effects of her decision become apparent. Even if she stays in the same position, her boss may be replaced by someone not so demanding in terms of reported profitability. The department supervisor's intent is to survive the moment and let the future take care of itself. Misguided reward systems can be as detrimental as threats of punishment. For example, a manager may choose short-term profitability to obtain a bonus that is based on reported profitability. It is the responsibility of upper-level management to establish policies and procedures that motivate subordinates to perform in ways that maximize the company's long-term profitability.

LO11 Make decisions about allocating scarce resources by analyzing relevant information.

Decisions Regarding the Allocation of Scarce Resources

Suppose that Premier Office Products makes two types of computers: a high-end network server and an inexpensive personal computer. The relevant sales and variable cost data for each unit follow.

Network Server		Personal Computer	
Sales price	$4,000	Sales price	$1,500
Less: Variable cost	(3,760)	Less: Variable cost	(1,370)
Contribution margin	$ 240	Contribution margin	$ 130

In many circumstances, variable costs act as proxies for *avoidable costs.* For example, by definition, unit-level costs increase and decrease in direct proportion with the number of units of product made and sold. As previously indicated, unit-level costs are avoidable with respect to many special decision scenarios. To the extent that variable costs are proxies for avoidable costs, the contribution margin can be used as a measure of profitability. Other things being equal, higher contribution margins translate into more profitable products. If Premier could sell 1,000 computers, the company would certainly prefer that they be network servers. The contribution to profitability on those machines is almost double the contribution margin on the personal computer.

Even though the contribution margin is higher for network servers, selling personal computers may be more profitable. Why? If Premier can sell considerably more of the personal computers, the volume of activity will make up for the lower margin. In other words, selling three personal computers produces more total margin (3 × $130 = $390) than selling one network server (1 × $240). Many factors could limit the sales of one or both of the products. Factors that limit a business's ability to satisfy the demand for its product are called **constraints.** Suppose that warehouse space is limited (i.e., the warehouse is a scarce resource that constrains sales). Accordingly, Premier cannot warehouse all of the computers that it needs to satisfy its customer orders. If a network server requires considerably more warehouse space than a personal computer, stocking and selling personal computers may be more profitable than stocking and selling network servers. To illustrate, assume that it requires 5 square feet of warehouse space for a network server and 2 square feet for a personal computer. If only 2,100 square feet of warehouse space are available, which computer should Premier stock and sell?

In this case, the warehouse space is considered a scarce resource. The computer that produces the highest contribution margin per unit of scarce resource (i.e., per square foot) is the more profitable product. The per unit computations for each product are shown here.

	Network Server	Personal Computer
Contribution margin per unit (a)	$ 240	$ 130
Divide by warehouse space needed to store one unit (b)	5 sq. ft.	2 sq. ft.
Contribution margin per unit of scarce resource (a ÷ b)	$ 48	$ 65

The data suggest that Premier should focus on the personal computer. Even though the personal computer produces a lower contribution margin per product, its contribution margin per scarce resource is higher. The effect on total profitability is shown as follows.

	Network Server	Personal Computer
Amount of available warehouse space (a)	2,100	2,100
Divide by warehouse space needed to store one unit (b)	5 sq. ft.	2 sq. ft.
Warehouse capacity in number of units (a ÷ b) = (c)	420	1,050
Times contribution margin per unit (d)	$ 240	$ 130
Total profit potential (c × d)	$100,800	$136,500

Although the quantitative data suggest that Premier will maximize profitability by limiting its inventory to personal computers, qualitative considerations may force the company to maintain a reasonable sales mix between the two products. For example, a business that buys several personal computers may also need a network server. A customer who cannot obtain both products from Premier may choose to buy nothing at all. Instead, the customer will find a supplier who will satisfy all of his needs. In other words, Premier may still need to stock some servers to offer a competitive product line.

The chairman of the board of directors asked Premier's president why company sales had remained level while the company's chief competitor had experienced significant increases. The president replied, "You cannot sell what you do not have. Our warehouse is too small. We stop production when we fill up the warehouse. The products sell out rapidly, and then we have to wait around for the next batch of computers to be made. When we are out of stock, our customers turn to the competition. We are constrained by the size of the warehouse." In business terms, the warehouse is a **bottleneck.** Its size is limiting the company's ability to sell its products.

Many businesses use a management practice known as the **theory of constraints (TOC)** to increase profitability by managing bottlenecks or constrained resources. TOC's primary objective is to identify the bottlenecks restricting the operations of the business and then to open those bottlenecks through a practice known as **relaxing the constraints.** The effect of applying TOC to the Premier case is apparent via contribution margin analysis. According to the preceding computations, a new server and a new personal computer produce a contribution margin of $48 and $65 per square foot of storage space, respectively. So long as additional warehouse space can be purchased for less than these amounts, Premier can increase its profitability by acquiring the space.

SELF-STUDY REVIEW PROBLEM

Flying High, Inc. (FHI), is a division of The Master Toy Company. FHI makes remote-controlled airplanes. During 2004, FHI incurred the following costs in the process of making 5,000 planes.

Unit-level materials costs (5,000 units @ $80)	$ 400,000
Unit-level labor costs (5,000 units @ $90)	450,000
Unit-level overhead costs (5,000 @ $70)	350,000
Depreciation cost on manufacturing equipment*	50,000
Other manufacturing overhead†	140,000
Inventory holding costs	240,000
Allocated portion of The Master Toy Company's facility-level costs	600,000
Total costs	$2,230,000

*The manufacturing equipment, which originally cost $250,000, has a book value of $200,000, a remaining useful life of four years, and a zero salvage value. If the equipment is not used in the production process, it can be leased for $30,000 per year.

†Includes supervisors' salaries and rent for the manufacturing building.

Required:

a. FHI uses a cost-plus pricing strategy. FHI sets its price at product cost plus $100. Determine the price that FHI should charge for its remote-controlled airplanes.

b. Assume that a potential customer that operates a chain of high-end toy stores has approached FHI. A buyer for this chain has offered to purchase 1,000 planes from FHI at a price of $275 each. Ignoring qualitative considerations, should FHI accept or reject the order?

c. FHI has the opportunity to purchase the planes from Arland Manufacturing Company for $325 each. Arland maintains adequate inventories so that it can supply its customers with planes on demand. Should FHI accept the opportunity to outsource the making of its planes?

d. Use the contribution margin format to prepare an income statement based on historical cost data. Prepare a second income statement that reflects the relevant cost data that Master Toy should consider in a segment elimination decision. Based on a comparison of these two statements, indicate whether Master Toy should eliminate the FHI division.

e. FHI is considering replacing the equipment it currently uses to manufacture its planes. It could purchase replacement equipment for $480,000 that has an expected useful life of four years and a salvage value of $40,000. The new equipment would increase productivity substantially, reducing unit-level labor costs by 20 percent. Assume that FHI would maintain its production and sales at 5,000 planes per year. Prepare a schedule that shows the relevant costs of operating the old equipment versus the costs of operating the new equipment. Should FHI replace the equipment?

Solution to Requirement a.

Product Cost for Remote-Controlled Airplanes	
Unit-level materials costs (5,000 units × $80)	$ 400,000
Unit-level labor costs (5,000 units × $90)	450,000
Unit-level overhead costs (5,000 units × $70)	350,000
Depreciation cost on manufacturing equipment	50,000
Other manufacturing overhead	140,000
Total product cost	$1,390,000

The cost per unit is $278 ($1,390,000 ÷ 5,000 units). The sales price per unit is $378 ($278 + $100). Depreciation expense is included because cost-plus pricing is usually based on historical cost rather than relevant cost. To be profitable in the long run, a company must ultimately recover the amount it paid for the equipment (the historical cost of the equipment).

Solution to Requirement b.
The incremental (relevant) cost of making 1,000 additional airplanes follows. The depreciation expense is not relevant because it represents a sunk cost. The other manufacturing overhead costs are not relevant because they will be incurred regardless of whether FHI makes the additional planes.

Per Unit Relevant Product Cost for Airplanes	
Unit-level materials costs	$ 80
Unit-level labor costs	90
Unit-level overhead costs	70
Total relevant product cost	$240

Since the relevant (incremental) cost of making the planes is less than the incremental revenue, FHI should accept the special order. Accepting the order will increase profits by $35,000 ([$275 incremental revenue − $240 incremental cost] × 1,000 units).

Solution to Requirement c.
Distinguish this decision from the special order opportunity discussed in Requirement *b*. That special order (Requirement *b*) decision hinged on the cost of making additional units with the existing production process. In contrast, a make-or-buy decision compares current production with the possibility of making zero units (closing down the entire manufacturing process). If the manufacturing process were shut down, FHI could avoid the unit-level costs, the cost of the lost opportunity to lease the equipment, the other manufacturing overhead costs, and the inventory holding costs. Since the planes can be purchased on demand, there is no need to maintain any inventory. The allocated portion of the facility-level costs is not relevant because it would be incurred regardless of whether FHI manufactured the planes. The relevant cost of making the planes follows.

Relevant Manufacturing Cost for Airplanes	
Unit-level materials costs (5,000 units × $80)	$ 400,000
Unit-level labor costs (5,000 units × $90)	450,000
Unit-level overhead costs (5,000 units × $70)	350,000
Opportunity cost of leasing the equipment	30,000
Other manufacturing overhead costs	140,000
Inventory holding cost	240,000
Total product cost	$1,610,000

The relevant cost per unit is $322 ($1,610,000 ÷ 5,000 units). Since the relevant cost of making the planes ($322) is less than the cost of purchasing them ($325), FHI should continue to make the planes.

Solution to Requirement d.

Income Statements	Historical Cost Data	Relevant Cost Data
Revenue (5,000 units × $378)	$1,890,000	$1,890,000
Less variable costs:		
Unit-level materials costs (5,000 units × $80)	(400,000)	(400,000)
Unit-level labor costs (5,000 units × $90)	(450,000)	(450,000)
Unit-level overhead costs (5,000 units × $70)	(350,000)	(350,000)
Contribution Margin	690,000	690,000
Depreciation cost on manufacturing equipment	(50,000)	
Opportunity cost of leasing manufacturing equipment		(30,000)
Other manufacturing overhead costs	(140,000)	(140,000)
Inventory holding costs	(240,000)	(240,000)
Allocated facility-level administrative costs	(600,000)	
Net Loss	$ (340,000)	
Contribution to Master Toy's Profitability		$ 280,000

Master Toy should not eliminate the segment (FHI). Although it appears to be incurring a loss, the allocated facility-level administrative costs are not relevant because Master Toy would incur these costs regardless of whether it eliminated FHI. Also, the depreciation cost on the manufacturing equipment is not relevant because it is a sunk cost. However, since the company could lease the equipment if the segment were eliminated, the $30,000 potential rental fee represents a relevant opportunity cost. The relevant revenue and cost data show that FHI is contributing $280,000 to the profitability of The Master Toy Company.

Solution to Requirement e.

The relevant costs of using the old equipment versus the new equipment are the costs that differ for the two alternatives. In this case relevant costs include the purchase price of the new equipment, the opportunity cost of the old equipment, and the labor costs. These items are summarized in the following table. The data show the total cost over the four-year useful life of the replacement equipment.

Relevant Cost Comparison	Old Equipment	New Equipment
Opportunity to lease the old equipment ($30,000 × 4 years)	$ 120,000	
Cost of new equipment ($480,000 − $40,000)		$ 440,000
Unit-level labor costs (5,000 units × $90 × 4 years)	1,800,000	
Unit-level labor costs (5,000 units × $90 × 4 years × .80)		1,440,000
Total relevant costs	$1,920,000	$1,880,000

Since the relevant cost of operating the new equipment is less than the cost of operating the old equipment, FHI should replace the equipment.

KEY TERMS

Avoidable costs *137*
Batch-level costs *138*
Bottleneck (Appendix) *153*
Certified suppliers *145*
Constraints (Appendix) *152*
Differential revenues *137*
Equipment replacement decisions *149*
Facility-level costs *138*
Low-ball pricing *145*
Opportunity costs *139*
Outsourcing *143*
Product-level costs *138*
Qualitative characteristics *140*
Quantitative characteristics *140*
Relaxing the constraints (Appendix) *153*
Relevant costs *137*
Relevant information *136*
Segment *146*
Special order decisions *141*
Sunk costs *136*
Theory of constraints (TOC) (Appendix) *153*
Unit-level costs *137*
Vertical integration *144*

QUESTIONS

1. Identify the primary qualities of revenues and costs that are relevant for decision making.
2. Are variable costs always relevant? Explain.
3. Identify the four hierarchical levels used to classify costs. When can each of these levels of costs be avoided?
4. Describe the relationship between relevance and accuracy.
5. "It all comes down to the bottom line. The numbers never lie." Do you agree with this conclusion? Explain your position.
6. Carmon Company invested $300,000 in the equity securities of Mann Corporation. The current market value of Carmon's investment in Mann is $250,000. Carmon currently needs funds for operating purposes. Although interest rates are high, Carmon's president has decided to borrow the needed funds instead of selling the investment in Mann. He explains that his company cannot afford to take a $50,000 loss on the Mann stock. Evaluate the president's decision based on this information.
7. What is an opportunity cost? How does it differ from a sunk cost?
8. A local bank advertises that it offers a free noninterest-bearing checking account if the depositor maintains a $500 minimum balance in the account. Is the checking account truly free?
9. A manager is faced with deciding whether to replace machine A or machine B. The original cost of machine A was $20,000 and that of machine B was $30,000. Because the two cost figures differ, they are relevant to the manager's decision. Do you agree? Explain your position.
10. Are all fixed costs unavoidable?
11. Identify two qualitative considerations that could be associated with special order decisions.
12. Which of the following would not be relevant to a make-or-buy decision?
    - **(a)** Allocated portion of depreciation expense on existing facilities.
    - **(b)** Variable cost of labor used to produce products currently purchased from suppliers.
    - **(c)** Warehousing costs for inventory of completed products (inventory levels will be constant regardless of whether products are purchased or produced).
    - **(d)** Cost of materials used to produce the items currently purchased from suppliers.
    - **(e)** Property taxes on the factory building.
13. What two factors should be considered in deciding how to allocate shelf space in a retail establishment?
14. What level(s) of costs is(are) relevant in special order decisions?
15. Why would a company consider outsourcing products or services?
16. Chris Sutter, the production manager of Satellite Computers, insists that the floppy drives used in the company's upper-end computers be outsourced since they can be purchased from a supplier at a lower cost per unit than the company is presently incurring to produce the drives. Jane Meyers, his assistant, insists that if sales growth continues at the current levels, the company will be able to produce the drives in the near future at a lower cost because of the company's predominately fixed cost structure. Does Ms. Meyers have a legitimate argument? Explain.
17. Identify some qualitative factors that should be considered in addition to quantitative costs in deciding whether to outsource.
18. The managers of Wilcox, Inc., are suggesting that the company president eliminate one of the company's segments that is operating at a loss. Why may this be a hasty decision?
19. Why would a supervisor choose to continue using a more costly old machine instead of replacing it with a less costly new machine?
20. Identify some of the constraints that limit a business's ability to satisfy the demand for its products or services.

EXERCISES—SERIES A

All Exercises in Series A are available with McGraw-Hill's Homework Manager

L.O. 1 **EXERCISE 4–1A** *Distinction Between Relevance and Cost Behavior*

Lucy Taylor is trying to decide which of two different kinds of candy to sell in her retail candy store. One type is a name brand candy that will practically sell itself. The other candy is cheaper to purchase but does not carry an identifiable brand name. Ms. Taylor believes that she will have to incur significant advertising costs to sell this candy. Several cost items for the two types of candy are as follows:

Brandless Candy		Name Brand Candy	
Cost per box	$ 4.00	Cost per box	$ 6.00
Sales commissions per box	0.50	Sales commissions per box	1.00
Rent of display space	1,500.00	Rent of display space	1,500.00
Advertising	3,000.00	Advertising	2,000.00

Required
Identify each cost as being relevant or irrelevant to Ms. Taylor's decision and indicate whether it is fixed or variable relative to the number of boxes sold.

EXERCISE 4–2A *Distinction Between Relevance and Cost Behavior*

L.O. 1, 2

Bron Company makes and sells a single product. Bron incurred the following costs in its most recent fiscal year.

Cost Items Appearing on the Income Statement	
Materials Cost ($7 per unit)	Sales Commissions (2% of sales)
Company President's Salary	Salaries of Administrative Personnel
Depreciation on Manufacturing Equipment	Shipping and Handling ($0.25 per unit)
Customer Billing Costs (1% of sales)	Depreciation on Office Furniture
Rental Cost of Manufacturing Facility	Manufacturing Supplies ($0.25 per unit)
Advertising Costs ($250,000 per year)	Production Supervisor's Salary
Labor Cost ($5 per unit)	

Bron could purchase the products that it currently makes. If it purchased the items, the company would continue to sell them using its own logo, advertising program, and sales staff.

Required
Identify each cost as relevant or irrelevant to the outsourcing decision and indicate whether the cost is fixed or variable relative to the number of products manufactured and sold.

EXERCISE 4–3A *Distinction Between Avoidable Costs and Cost Behavior*

L.O. 1

Elegance Company makes fine jewelry that it sells to department stores throughout the United States. Elegance is trying to decide which of two bracelets to manufacture. Elegance has a labor contract that prohibits the company from laying off workers freely. Cost data pertaining to the two choices follow.

	Bracelet A	Bracelet B
Cost of materials per unit	$ 30	$ 50
Cost of labor per unit	40	40
Advertising cost per year	8,000	6,000
Annual depreciation on existing equip.	5,000	4,000

Required
a. Identify the fixed costs and determine the amount of fixed cost for each product.
b. Identify the variable costs and determine the amount of variable cost per unit for each product.
c. Identify the avoidable costs and determine the amount of avoidable cost for each product.

EXERCISE 4–4A *Special Order Decision*

L.O. 1, 2, 6

Solid Concrete Company pours concrete slabs for single-family dwellings. Russell Construction Company, which operates outside Solid's normal sales territory, asks Solid to pour 40 slabs for Russell's new development of homes. Solid has the capacity to build 300 slabs and is presently working on 250 of them. Russell is willing to pay only $3,000 per slab. Solid estimates the cost of a typical job to include unit-level materials, $1,500; unit-level labor, $1,000; and an allocated portion of facility-level overhead, $700.

Required
Should Solid accept or reject the special order to pour 40 slabs for $3,000 each? Support your answer with appropriate computations.

L.O. 1, 2, 6

EXERCISE 4–5A *Special Order Decision*

Lance Company manufactures a personal computer designed for use in schools and markets it under its own label. Lance has the capacity to produce 20,000 units a year but is currently producing and selling only 15,000 units a year. The computer's normal selling price is $1,600 per unit with no volume discounts. The unit-level costs of the computer's production are $600 for direct materials, $200 for direct labor, and $250 for indirect unit-level manufacturing costs. The total product- and facility-level costs incurred by Lance during the year are expected to be $2,000,000 and $800,000, respectively. Assume that Lance receives a special order to produce and sell 4,000 computers at $1,200 each.

Required
Should Lance accept or reject the special order? Support your answer with appropriate computations.

L.O. 5

EXERCISE 4–6A *Identifying Qualitative Factors for a Special Order Decision*

Required
Describe the qualitative factors that Lance should consider before accepting the special order described in Exercise 4–5A.

L.O. 6

EXERCISE 4–7A *Using the Contribution Margin Approach for a Special Order Decision*

Shane Company, which produces and sells a small digital clock, bases its pricing strategy on a 30 percent markup on total cost. Based on annual production costs for 15,000 units of product, computations for the sales price per clock follow.

Unit-level costs	$180,000
Fixed costs	60,000
Total cost (a)	240,000
Markup (a × 0.30)	72,000
Total sales (b)	$312,000
Sales price per unit (b ÷ 15,000)	$ 20.80

Required

a. Shane has excess capacity and receives a special order for 6,000 clocks for $15 each. Calculate the contribution margin per unit; based on it, should Shane accept the special order?

b. Support your answer by preparing a contribution margin income statement for the special order.

L.O. 7

EXERCISE 4–8A *Outsourcing Decision*

Rider Bicycle Manufacturing Company currently produces the handlebars used in manufacturing its bicycles, which are high-quality racing bikes with limited sales. Rider produces and sells only 5,000 bikes each year. Due to the low volume of activity, Rider is unable to obtain the economies of scale that larger producers achieve. For example, Rider could buy the handlebars for $30 each; they cost $34 each to make. The following is a detailed breakdown of current production costs.

Item	Unit Cost	Total
Unit-level costs		
Materials	$14	$ 70,000
Labor	11	55,000
Overhead	4	20,000
Allocated facility-level costs	5	25,000
Total	$34	$170,000

After seeing these figures, Rider's president remarked that it would be foolish for the company to continue to produce the handlebars at $34 each when it can buy them for $30 each.

Required
Do you agree with the president's conclusion? Support your answer with appropriate computations.

L.O. 7

EXERCISE 4–9A *Establishing Price for an Outsourcing Decision*

Easy Cut, Inc., makes and sells lawn mowers for which it currently makes the engines. It has an opportunity to purchase the engines from a reliable manufacturer. The annual costs of making the engines are shown here.

Cost of materials (20,000 Units × $20)	$ 400,000
Labor (20,000 Units × $25)	500,000
Depreciation on manufacturing equipment*	45,000
Salary of supervisor of engine production	180,000
Rental cost of equipment used to make engines	120,000
Allocated portion of corporate-level facility-sustaining costs	45,000
Total cost to make 20,000 engines	$1,290,000

*The equipment has a book value of $72,000 but its market value is zero.

Required

a. Determine the maximum price per unit that Easy Cut would be willing to pay for the engines.

b. Would the price computed in Requirement a change if production increased to 25,000 units? Support your answer with appropriate computations.

EXERCISE 4–10A *Outsourcing Decision with Qualitative Factors*

L.O. 5, 7

Surround Sound, Inc. (SSI), which makes and sells 80,000 radios annually, currently purchases the radio speakers it uses for $8 each. Each radio uses one speaker. The company has idle capacity and is considering the possibility of making the speakers that it needs. SSI estimates that the cost of materials and labor needed to make speakers would be a total of $7 for each speaker. In addition, the costs of supervisory salaries, rent, and other manufacturing costs would be $160,000. Allocated facility-level costs would be $96,000.

Required

a. Determine the change in net income SSI would experience if it decides to make the speakers.

b. Discuss the qualitative factors that SSI should consider.

EXERCISE 4–11A *Outsourcing Decision Affected by Opportunity Costs*

L.O. 4, 7

Sertoma Electronics currently produces the shipping containers it uses to deliver the electronics products it sells. The monthly cost of producing 9,000 containers follows.

Unit-level materials	$ 4,500
Unit-level labor	6,000
Unit-level overhead	3,900
Product-level costs*	9,000
Allocated facility-level costs	22,500

*One-third of these costs can be avoided by purchasing the containers.

Loehman Container Company has offered to sell comparable containers to Sertoma for $2.25 each.

Required

a. Should Sertoma continue to make the containers? Support your answer with appropriate computations.

b. Sertoma could lease the space it currently uses in the manufacturing process. If leasing would produce $9,000 per month, would your answer to Requirement *a* be different? Explain.

EXERCISE 4–12A *Opportunity Cost*

L.O. 4

Swift Truck Lines, Inc., owns a truck that cost $80,000. Currently, the truck's book value is $48,000, and its expected remaining useful life is four years. Swift has the opportunity to purchase for $60,000 a replacement truck that is extremely fuel efficient. Fuel cost for the old truck is expected to be $8,000 per year more than fuel cost for the new truck. The old truck is paid for but, in spite of being in good condition, can be sold for only $32,000.

Required

Should Swift Truck Lines replace the old truck with the new fuel-efficient model, or should it continue to use the old truck until it wears out? Explain.

EXERCISE 4–13A *Opportunity Costs*

L.O. 4, 5

Tim Kozlowski owns his own taxi, for which he bought a $20,000 permit to operate two years ago. Mr. Kozlowski earns $37,000 a year operating as an independent but has the opportunity to sell the taxi and permit for $75,000 and take a position as dispatcher for Trenton Taxi Co. The dispatcher position pays $31,000 a year for a 40-hour week. Driving his own taxi, Mr. Kozlowski works approximately 55 hours per week. If he sells his business, he will invest the $75,000 and can earn a 10 percent return.

Required

a. Determine the opportunity cost of owning and operating the independent business.
b. Based solely on financial considerations, should Mr. Kozlowski sell the taxi and accept the position as dispatcher?
c. Discuss the qualitative as well as quantitative factors that Mr. Kozlowski should consider.

L.O. 8

EXERCISE 4–14A *Segment Elimination Decision*

Quell Company operates three segments. Income statements for the segments imply that profitability could be improved if Segment A were eliminated.

QUELL COMPANY
Income Statements For the Year 2009

Segment	A	B	C
Sales	$196,000	$260,000	$345,000
Cost of Goods Sold	(143,000)	(98,000)	(190,000)
Sales Commissions	(20,000)	(38,000)	(22,000)
Contribution Margin	33,000	124,000	133,000
General Fixed Oper. Exp. (allocation of president's salary)	(44,000)	(52,000)	(44,000)
Advertising Expense (specific to individual divisions)	(3,000)	(10,000)	0
Net Income	$ (14,000)	$ 62,000	$ 89,000

Required

a. Explain the effect on profitability if segment A is eliminated.
b. Prepare comparative income statements for the company as a whole under two alternatives: (1) the retention of Segment A and (2) the elimination of Segment A.

L.O. 8

EXERCISE 4–15A *Segment Elimination Decision*

Moreno Transport Company divides its operations into four divisions. A recent income statement for Hess Division follows.

MORENO TRANSPORT COMPANY
Hess Division
Income Statement For the Year 2005

Revenue	$ 650,000
Salaries for Drivers	(420,000)
Fuel Expenses	(80,000)
Insurance	(110,000)
Division-Level Facility-Sustaining Costs	(60,000)
Companywide Facility-Sustaining Costs	(130,000)
Net Loss	$(150,000)

Required

a. Should Hess Division be eliminated? Support your answer by explaining how the division's elimination would affect the net income of the company as a whole. By how much would companywide income increase or decrease?
b. Assume that Hess Division is able to increase its revenue to $700,000 by raising its prices. Would this change the decision you made in Requirement *a?* Determine the amount of the increase or decrease that would occur in companywide net income if the segment were eliminated if revenue were $700,000.
c. What is the minimum amount of revenue required to justify continuing the operation of Hess Division?

L.O. 8

EXERCISE 4–16A *Identifying Avoidable Cost of a Segment*

Howell Corporation is considering the elimination of one of its segments. The segment incurs the following fixed costs. If the segment is eliminated, the building it uses will be sold.

Advertising expense	$ 97,000
Supervisory salaries	159,000
Allocation of companywide facility-level costs	45,000
Original cost of building	100,000
Book value of building	60,000
Market value of building	70,000
Maintenance costs on equipment	50,000
Real estate taxes on building	7,000

Required
Based on this information, determine the amount of avoidable cost associated with the segment.

EXERCISE 4–17A *Asset Replacement Decision* — L.O. 9

A machine purchased three years ago for $200,000 has a current book value using straight-line depreciation of $120,000; its operating expenses are $30,000 per year. A replacement machine would cost $250,000, have a useful life of nine years, and would require $14,000 per year in operating expenses. It has an expected salvage value of $66,000 after nine years. The current disposal value of the old machine is $60,000; if it is kept nine more years, its residual value would be $10,000.

Required
Based on this information, should the old machine be replaced? Support your answer.

EXERCISE 4–18A *Asset Replacement Decision* — L.O. 9

McKee Company is considering replacement of some of its manufacturing equipment. Information regarding the existing equipment and the potential replacement equipment follows.

Existing Equipment		Replacement Equipment	
Cost	$ 90,000	Cost	$ 95,000
Operating expenses*	105,000	Operating expenses*	20,000
Salvage value	10,000	Salvage value	14,000
Market value	60,000	Useful life	8 years
Book value	32,000		
Remaining useful life	8 years		

*The amounts shown for operating expenses are the cumulative total of all such expected expenses to be incurred over the useful life of the equipment.

Required
Based on this information, recommend whether to replace the equipment. Support your recommendation with appropriate computations.

EXERCISE 4–19A *Asset Replacement Decision* — L.O. 9

Pendorric Company paid $72,000 to purchase a machine on January 1, 2006. During 2008, a technological breakthrough resulted in the development of a new machine that costs $125,000. The old machine costs $40,000 per year to operate, but the new machine could be operated for only $12,000 per year. The new machine, which will be available for delivery on January 1, 2009, has an expected useful life of four years. The old machine is more durable and is expected to have a remaining useful life of four years. The current market value of the old machine is $20,000. The expected salvage value of both machines is zero.

Required
Based on this information, recommend whether to replace the machine. Support your recommendation with appropriate computations.

EXERCISE 4–20A *Annual Versus Cumulative Data for Replacement Decision* — L.O. 4, 9

Because of rapidly advancing technology, Sayre Publications, Inc., is considering replacing its existing typesetting machine with leased equipment. The old machine, purchased two years ago, has an expected useful life of six years and is in good condition. Apparently, it will continue to perform as expected for the remaining four years of its expected useful life. A four-year lease for equipment with comparable productivity can be obtained for $15,000 per year. The following data apply to the old machine.

Original cost	$180,000
Accumulated depreciation	60,000
Current market value	77,500
Estimated salvage value	7,500

Required

a. Determine the annual opportunity cost of using the old machine. Based on your computations, recommend whether to replace it.

b. Determine the total cost of the lease over the four-year contract. Based on your computations, recommend whether to replace the old machine.

Appendix

L.O. 11 **EXERCISE 4–21A** *Scarce Resource Decision*

Ensor Funtime Novelties has the capacity to produce either 25,000 corncob pipes or 12,000 cornhusk dolls per year. The pipes cost $3 each to produce and sell for $6 each. The dolls sell for $10 each and cost $4 to produce.

Required

Assuming that Ensor Funtime Novelties can sell all it produces of either product, should it produce the corncob pipes or the cornhusk dolls? Show computations to support your answer.

PROBLEMS—SERIES A

All Problems in Series A are available with McGraw-Hill's Homework Manager

L.O. 1 **PROBLEM 4–22A** *Context-Sensitive Relevance*

Required

Respond to each requirement independently.

a. Describe two decision-making contexts, one in which unit-level materials costs are avoidable, and the other in which they are unavoidable.

b. Describe two decision-making contexts, one in which batch-level setup costs are avoidable, and the other in which they are unavoidable.

c. Describe two decision-making contexts, one in which advertising costs are avoidable, and the other in which they are unavoidable.

d. Describe two decision-making contexts, one in which rent paid for a building is avoidable, and the other in which it is unavoidable.

e. Describe two decision-making contexts, one in which depreciation on manufacturing equipment is avoidable, and the other in which it is unavoidable.

L.O. 1 **PROBLEM 4–23A** *Context-Sensitive Relevance*

CHECK FIGURES
a. Contribution to profit for Job A: $168,000
b. Contribution to profit: $(1,000)

Myl Construction Company is a building contractor specializing in small commercial buildings. The company has the opportunity to accept one of two jobs; it cannot accept both because they must be performed at the same time and Myl does not have the necessary labor force for both jobs. Indeed, it will be necessary to hire a new supervisor if either job is accepted. Furthermore, additional insurance will be required if either job is accepted. The revenue and costs associated with each job follow.

Cost Category	Job A	Job B
Contract price	$700,000	$600,000
Unit-level materials	250,000	220,000
Unit-level labor	240,000	243,000
Unit-level overhead	17,000	14,000
Supervisor's salary	80,000	80,000
Rental equipment costs	25,000	28,000
Depreciation on tools (zero market value)	20,000	20,000
Allocated portion of companywide facility-sustaining costs	9,000	8,000
Insurance cost for job	16,000	16,000

Required

a. Assume that Myl has decided to accept one of the two jobs. Identify the information relevant to selecting one job versus the other. Recommend which job to accept and support your answer with appropriate computations.

b. Assume that Job Ais no longer available. Myl's choice is to accept or reject Job B alone. Identify the information relevant to this decision. Recommend whether to accept or reject Job B. Support your answer with appropriate computations.

PROBLEM 4–24A *Effect of Order Quantity on Special Order Decision*

L.O. 3, 5, 6

CHECK FIGURE
a. Relevant cost per unit: $56

Bogati Quilting Company makes blankets that it markets through a variety of department stores. It makes the blankets in batches of 1,000 units. Bogati made 20,000 blankets during the prior accounting period. The cost of producing the blankets is summarized here.

Materials cost ($20 per unit × 20,000)	$ 400,000
Labor cost ($25 per unit × 20,000)	500,000
Manufacturing supplies ($3 × 20,000)	60,000
Batch-level costs (20 batches at $4,000 per batch)	80,000
Product-level costs	140,000
Facility-level costs	300,000
Total costs	$1,480,000
Cost per unit = $1,480,000 ÷ 20,000 = $74	

Required

a. Quality Motels has offered to buy a batch of 500 blankets for $55 each. Bogati's normal selling price is $90 per unit. Based on the preceding quantitative data, should Bogati accept the special order? Support your answer with appropriate computations.

b. Would your answer to Requirement *a* change if Quality offered to buy a batch of 1,000 blankets for $55 per unit? Support your answer with appropriate computations.

c. Describe the qualitative factors that Bogati Quilting Company should consider before accepting a special order to sell blankets to Quality Motels.

PROBLEM 4–25A *Effects of the Level of Production on an Outsourcing Decision*

L.O. 5, 6

CHECK FIGURE
a. Total relevant cost: $75,000

Vaida Chemical Company makes a variety of cosmetic products, one of which is a skin cream designed to reduce the signs of aging. Vaida produces a relatively small amount (15,000 units) of the cream and is considering the purchase of the product from an outside supplier for $4.50 each. If Vaida purchases from the outside supplier, it would continue to sell and distribute the cream under its own brand name. Vaida's accountant constructed the following profitability analysis.

Revenue (15,000 units × $10)	$150,000
Unit-level materials costs (15,000 units × $1.40)	(21,000)
Unit-level labor costs (15,000 units × $0.50)	(7,500)
Unit-level overhead costs (15,000 × $0.10)	(1,500)
Unit-level selling expenses (15,000 × $0.25)	(3,750)
Contribution margin	116,250
Skin cream production supervisor's salary	(45,000)
Allocated portion of facility-level costs	(11,250)
Product-level advertising cost	(36,000)
Contribution to companywide income	$ 24,000

Required

a. Identify the cost items relevant to the make-or-outsource decision.

b. Should Vaida continue to make the product or buy it from the supplier? Support your answer by determining the change in net income if Vaida buys the cream instead of making it.

c. Suppose that Vaida is able to increase sales by 10,000 units (sales will increase to 25,000 units). At this level of production, should Vaida make or buy the cream? Support your answer by explaining how the increase in production affects the cost per unit.

d. Discuss the qualitative factors that Vaida should consider before deciding to outsource the skin cream. How can Vaida minimize the risk of establishing a relationship with an unreliable supplier?

L.O. 5, 7, 9

CHECK FIGURES
a. Avoidable cost per unit: $119
b. Avoidable cost per unit with new equipment: $31

PROBLEM 4–26A *Outsourcing Decision Affected by Equipment Replacement*

Grant Bike Company (GBC) makes the frames used to build its bicycles. During 2006, GBC made 20,000 frames; the costs incurred follow.

Unit-level materials costs (20,000 units × $40)	$ 800,000
Unit-level labor costs (20,000 units × $50)	1,000,000
Unit-level overhead costs (20,000 × $10)	200,000
Depreciation on manufacturing equipment	100,000
Bike frame production supervisor's salary	80,000
Inventory holding costs	300,000
Allocated portion of facility-level costs	500,000
Total costs	$2,980,000

Grant has an opportunity to purchase frames for $102 each.

Additional Information

1. The manufacturing equipment, which originally cost $500,000, has a book value of $400,000, a remaining useful life of four years, and a zero salvage value. If the equipment is not used to produce bicycle frames, it can be leased for $60,000 per year.
2. GBC has the opportunity to purchase for $960,000 new manufacturing equipment that will have an expected useful life of four years and a salvage value of $80,000. This equipment will increase productivity substantially, reducing unit-level labor costs by 60 percent. Assume that GBC will continue to produce and sell 20,000 frames per year in the future.
3. If GBC outsources the frames, the company can eliminate 80 percent of the inventory holding costs.

Required

a. Determine the avoidable cost per unit of making the bike frames, assuming that GBC is considering the alternatives between making the product using the existing equipment and outsourcing the product to the independent contractor. Based on the quantitative data, should GBC outsource the bike frames? Support your answer with appropriate computations.

b. Assuming that GBC is considering whether to replace the old equipment with the new equipment, determine the avoidable cost per unit to produce the bike frames using the new equipment and the avoidable cost per unit to produce the bike frames using the old equipment. Calculate the impact on profitability if the bike frames were made using the old equipment versus the new equipment.

c. Assuming that GBC is considering to either purchase the new equipment or outsource the bike frame, calculate the impact on profitability between the two alternatives.

d. Discuss the qualitative factors that GBC should consider before making a decision to outsource the bike frame. How can GBC minimize the risk of establishing a relationship with an unreliable supplier?

L.O. 8

excel
www.mhhe.com/edmonds3e

CHECK FIGURE
a. Contribution to profit: $12,000

PROBLEM 4–27A *Eliminating a Segment*

Lackey Boot Co. sells men's, women's, and children's boots. For each type of boot sold, it operates a separate department that has its own manager. The manager of the men's department has a sales staff of nine employees, the manager of the women's department has six employees, and the manager of the children's department has three employees. All departments are housed in a single store. In recent years, the children's department has operated at a net loss and is expected to continue to do so. Last year's income statements follow.

	Men's Department	Women's Department	Children's Department
Sales	$580,000	$430,000	$165,000
Cost of Goods Sold	(260,000)	(180,000)	(103,000)
Gross Margin	320,000	250,000	62,000
Department Manager's Salary	(50,000)	(40,000)	(20,000)
Sales Commissions	(106,000)	(82,000)	(30,000)
Rent on Store Lease	(20,000)	(20,000)	(20,000)
Store Utilities	(5,000)	(5,000)	(5,000)
Net Income (loss)	$139,000	$103,000	$ (13,000)

Required

a. Determine whether to eliminate the children's department.

b. Confirm the conclusion you reached in Requirement *a* by preparing income statements for the company as a whole with and without the children's department.

c. Eliminating the children's department would increase space available to display men's and women's boots. Suppose management estimates that a wider selection of adult boots would increase the store's net earnings by $32,000. Would this information affect the decision that you made in Requirement *a?* Explain your answer.

PROBLEM 4–28A *Effect of Activity Level and Opportunity Cost on Segment Elimination Decision*

L.O. 4, 8

CHECK FIGURE
a. Contribution to profit: $(40,000)

Partlow Manufacturing Co. produces and sells specialized equipment used in the petroleum industry. The company is organized into three separate operating branches: Division A, which manufactures and sells heavy equipment; Division B, which manufactures and sells hand tools; and Division C, which makes and sells electric motors. Each division is housed in a separate manufacturing facility. Company headquarters is located in a separate building. In recent years, Division B has been operating at a net loss and is expected to continue to do so. Income statements for the three divisions for 2008 follow.

	Division A	Division B	Division C
Sales	$3,200,000	$ 750,000	$4,000,000
Less: Cost of Goods Sold			
Unit-Level Manufacturing Costs	(1,900,000)	(450,000)	(2,400,000)
Rent on Manufacturing Facility	(400,000)	(220,000)	(300,000)
Gross Margin	900,000	80,000	1,300,000
Less: Operating Expenses			
Unit-Level Selling and Admin. Expenses	(200,000)	(35,000)	(250,000)
Division-Level Fixed Selling and Admin. Expenses	(250,000)	(85,000)	(300,000)
Headquarters Facility-Level Costs	(150,000)	(150,000)	(150,000)
Net Income (loss)	$ 300,000	$(190,000)	$ 600,000

Required

a. Based on the preceding information, recommend whether to eliminate Division B. Support your answer by preparing companywide income statements before and after eliminating Division B.

b. During 2008, Division B produced and sold 20,000 units of hand tools. Would your recommendation in response to Requirement *a* change if sales and production increase to 30,000 units in 2009? Support your answer by comparing differential revenue and avoidable cost for Division B, assuming that it sells 30,000 units.

c. Suppose that Partlow could sublease Division B's manufacturing facility for $320,000. Would you operate the division at a production and sales volume of 30,000 units, or would you close it? Support your answer with appropriate computations.

PROBLEM 4–29A *Comprehensive Problem Including Special Order, Outsourcing, and Segment Elimination Decisions*

L.O. 6, 7, 8

excel
www.mhhe.com/edmonds3e

CHECK FIGURE
a. CM: $7,500

Weems, Inc., makes and sells state-of-the-art electronics products. One of its segments produces The Math Machine, an inexpensive four-function calculator. The company's chief accountant recently prepared the following income statement showing annual revenues and expenses associated with the segment's operating activities. The relevant range for the production and sale of the calculators is between 30,000 and 60,000 units per year.

Revenue (40,000 units × $16)	$640,000
Unit-Level Variable Costs	
Materials Cost (40,000 × $4)	(160,000)
Labor Cost (40,000 × $2)	(80,000)
Manufacturing Overhead (40,000 × $1)	(40,000)
Shipping and Handling (40,000 × $0.50)	(20,000)
Sales Commissions (40,000 × $2)	(80,000)
Contribution Margin	260,000
Fixed Expenses	
Advertising Costs	(40,000)
Salary of Production Supervisor	(120,000)
Allocated Companywide Facility-Level Expenses	(160,000)
Net Loss	$ (60,000)

Required (Consider each of the requirements independently.)

a. A large discount store has approached the owner of Weems about buying 5,000 calculators. It would replace The Math Machine's label with its own logo to avoid affecting Weems' existing customers. Because the offer was made directly to the owner, no sales commissions on the transaction would be involved, but the discount store is willing to pay only $9.00 per calculator. Based on quantitative factors alone, should Weems accept the special order? Support your answer with appropriate computations. Specifically, by what amount would the special order increase or decrease profitability?

b. Weems has an opportunity to buy the 40,000 calculators it currently makes from a reliable competing manufacturer for $9.80 each. The product meets Weems' quality standards. Weems could continue to use its own logo, advertising program, and sales force to distribute the products. Should Weems buy the calculators or continue to make them? Support your answer with appropriate computations. Specifically, how much more or less would it cost to buy the calculators than to make them? Would your answer change if the volume of sales were increased to 60,000 units?

c. Because the calculator division is currently operating at a loss, should it be eliminated from the company's operations? Support your answer with appropriate computations. Specifically, by what amount would the segment's elimination increase or decrease profitability?

Appendix

L.O. 11

PROBLEM 4–30A *Allocating Scarce Resources*

CHECK FIGURES
a. Contribution to margin per hour: $2 for A and $1.50 for B

The following information applies to the products of Hardaway Company.

	Product A	Product B
Selling price per unit	$26	$24
Variable cost per unit	22	18

Required

Identify the product that should be produced or sold under each of the following constraints. Consider each constraint separately.

a. One unit of Product A requires 2 hours of labor to produce, and one unit of Product B requires 4 hours of labor to produce. Due to labor constraints, demand is higher than the company's capacity to make both products.

b. The products are sold to the public in retail stores. The company has limited floor space and cannot stock as many products as it would like. Display space is available for only one of the two products. Expected sales of Product A are 10,000 units and of Product B are 8,000 units.

c. The maximum number of machine hours available is 40,000. Product A uses 2 machine hours, and Product B uses 5 machine hours. The company can sell all the products it produces.

L.O. 10

PROBLEM 4–31A *Conflict Between Short-Term Versus Long-Term Performance*

excel
www.mhhe.com/edmonds3e

CHECK FIGURE
a. Relevant costs: $560,000 for keeping the old machine

Bill Oakes manages the cutting department of Rancont Timber Company. He purchased a tree-cutting machine on January 1, 2006, for $400,000. The machine had an estimated useful life of five years and zero salvage value, and the cost to operate it is $90,000 per year. Technological developments resulted in the development of a more advanced machine available for purchase on January 1, 2007, that would allow a 25 percent reduction in operating costs. The new machine would cost $240,000 and have a four-year useful life and zero salvage value. The current market value of the old machine on January 1, 2007, is $200,000, and its book value is $320,000 on that date. Straight-line depreciation is used for both machines. The company expects to generate $224,000 of revenue per year from the use of either machine.

Required

a. Recommend whether to replace the old machine on January 1, 2007. Support your answer with appropriate computations.

b. Prepare income statements for four years (2007 through 2010) assuming that the old machine is retained.

c. Prepare income statements for four years (2007 through 2010) assuming that the old machine is replaced.

d. Discuss the potential ethical conflicts that could result from the timing of the loss and expense recognition reported in the two income statements.

EXERCISES—SERIES B

EXERCISE 4–1B *Distinction Between Relevance and Cost Behavior* **L.O. 1**

Ken Griffith is planning to rent a small shop for a new business. He can sell either sandwiches or donuts. The following costs pertain to the two products.

Sandwiches		Donuts	
Cost per sandwich	$ 2.00	Cost per dozen donuts	$ 1.45
Sales commissions per sandwich	0.05	Sales commissions per dozen donuts	0.07
Monthly shop rental cost	1,000.00	Monthly shop rental cost	1,000.00
Monthly advertising cost	500.00	Monthly advertising cost	300.00

Required

Identify each cost as relevant or irrelevant to Mr. Griffith's product decision and indicate whether the cost is fixed or variable relative to the number of units sold.

EXERCISE 4–2B *Distinction Between Relevance and Cost Behavior* **L.O. 1, 2**

Rhodes Company makes and sells a toy plane. Rhodes incurred the following costs in its most recent fiscal year:

Cost Items Reported on Income Statement
Costs of TV Commercials
Labor Costs ($3 per unit)
Sales Commissions (1% of sales)
Sales Manager's Salary
Shipping and Handling Costs ($0.75 per unit)
Cost of Renting the Administrative Building
Utility Costs for the Manufacturing Plant ($0.25 per unit produced)
Manufacturing Plant Manager's Salary
Materials Costs ($4 per unit produced)
Real Estate Taxes on the Manufacturing Plant
Depreciation on Manufacturing Equipment
Packaging Cost ($1 per unit produced)
Wages of the Plant Security Guard

Rhodes could purchase the toy planes from a supplier. If it did, the company would continue to sell them using its own logo, advertising program, and sales staff.

Required

Identify each cost as relevant or irrelevant to the outsourcing decision and indicate whether the cost is fixed or variable relative to the number of toy planes manufactured and sold.

EXERCISE 4–3B *Distinction Between Avoidable Costs and Cost Behavior* **L.O. 1**

Dublar Phones, Inc., makes telephones that it sells to department stores throughout the United States. Dublar is trying to decide which of two telephone models to manufacture. The company could produce either telephone with its existing machinery. Cost data pertaining to the two choices follow:

	Model 90	Model 30
Materials cost per unit	$ 36	$ 36
Labor cost per unit	40	24
Product design cost	12,000	7,000
Depreciation on existing manufacturing machinery	3,000	3,000

Required

a. Identify the fixed costs and determine the amount of fixed cost for each model.
b. Identify the variable costs and determine the amount of variable cost for each model.
c. Identify the avoidable costs.

EXERCISE 4–4B *Special Order Decision* **L.O. 1, 2, 6**

Mai Textile Company manufactures high-quality bed sheets and sells them in sets to a well-known retail company for $40 a set. Mai has sufficient capacity to produce 100,000 sets of sheets annually;

the retail company currently purchases 80,000 sets each year. Mai's unit-level cost is $25 per set and its fixed cost is $800,000 per year. A motel chain has offered to purchase 10,000 sheet sets from Mai for $32 per set. If Mai accepts the order, the contract will prohibit the motel chain from reselling the bed sheets.

Required
Should Mai accept or reject the special order? Support your answer with appropriate computations.

L.O. 1, 2, 6

EXERCISE 4–5B *Special Order Decision*

Estrada Automotive Company manufactures an engine designed for motorcycles and markets the product using its own brand name. Although Estrada has the capacity to produce 28,000 engines annually, it currently produces and sells only 25,000 units per year. The engine normally sells for $650 per unit, with no quantity discounts. The unit-level costs to produce the engine are $200 for direct materials, $150 for direct labor, and $60 for indirect manufacturing costs. Estrada expects total annual product- and facility-level costs to be $500,000 and $750,000, respectively. Assume Estrada receives a special order from a new customer seeking to buy 1,000 engines for $460 each.

Required
Should Estrada accept or reject the special order? Support your answer with appropriate computations.

L.O. 5

EXERCISE 4–6B *Identifying Qualitative Factors for a Special Order Decision*

Required
Describe the qualitative factors that Estrada should consider before accepting the special order described in Exercise 4–5B.

L.O. 6

EXERCISE 4–7B *Using the Contribution Margin Approach for a Special Order Decision*

Merkel Company produces and sells a food processor that it prices at a 25 percent markup on total cost. Based on data pertaining to producing and selling 30,000 food processors, Merkel computes the sales price per food processor as follows.

Unit-level costs	$ 600,000
Fixed costs	480,000
Total cost (a)	1,080,000
Markup (a × .25)	270,000
Total sales revenue (b)	$1,350,000
Sales price per unit (b ÷ 30,000)	$45.00

Required

a. Merkel receives a special order for 7,000 food processors for $19 each. Merkel has excess capacity. Calculate the contribution margin per unit for the special order. Based on the contribution margin per unit, should Merkel accept the special order?

b. Support your answer by preparing a contribution margin income statement for the special order.

L.O. 7

EXERCISE 4–8B *Making an Outsourcing Decision*

Boutwell Boats Company currently produces a battery used in manufacturing its boats. The company annually manufactures and sells 2,000 units of a particular model of fishing boat. Because of the low volume of activity, Boutwell is unable to obtain the economies of scale that larger producers achieve. For example, the costs associated with producing the batteries it uses are almost 30 percent more than the cost of purchasing comparable batteries. Boutwell could buy batteries for $75 each; it costs $100 each to make them. A detailed breakdown of current production costs for the batteries follows:

Item	Unit Cost	Total
Unit-level costs:		
Materials	$ 30	$ 60,000
Labor	25	50,000
Overhead	5	10,000
Allocated facility-level costs	40	80,000
Total	$100	$200,000

Based on these figures, Boutwell's president asserted that it would be foolish for the company to continue to produce the batteries at $100 each when it can buy them for $75 each.

Required
Do you agree with the president's conclusion? Support your answer with appropriate computations.

EXERCISE 4–9B *Establishing a Price for an Outsourcing Decision* L.O. 7

Smiles, Inc., makes and sells skateboards. Smiles currently makes the 60,000 wheels used annually in its skateboards but has an opportunity to purchase the wheels from a reliable manufacturer. The costs of making the wheels follow.

Annual Costs Associated with Manufacturing Skateboard Wheels	
Materials (60,000 units × $4.50)	$270,000
Labor (60,000 units × $2.50)	150,000
Depreciation on manufacturing equipment*	30,000
Salary of wheel production supervisor	65,000
Rental cost of equipment used to make wheels	55,000
Allocated portion of corporate-level facility-sustaining costs	40,000
Total cost to make 60,000 wheels	$610,000

*The equipment has a book value of $74,000 but its market value is zero.

Required
a. Determine the maximum price per unit that Smiles would be willing to pay for the wheels.
b. Would the price computed in Requirement *a* change if production were increased to 80,000 units? Support your answer with appropriate computations.

EXERCISE 4–10B *Making an Outsourcing Decision with Qualitative Factors Considered* L.O. 5, 7

Cox Computers currently purchases for $15 each keyboard it uses in the 50,000 computers it makes and sells annually. Each computer uses one keyboard. The company has idle capacity and is considering whether to make the keyboards that it needs. Cox estimates that materials and labor costs for making keyboards would be $9 each. In addition, supervisory salaries, rent, and other manufacturing costs would be $400,000. Allocated facility-level costs would amount to $70,000.

Required
a. Determine the change in net income that Cox would experience if it decides to make the keyboards.
b. Discuss the qualitative factors that Cox should consider.

EXERCISE 4–11B *Outsourcing Decision Affected by Opportunity Costs* L.O. 4, 7

Kwang Doors Company currently produces the doorknobs for the doors it makes and sells. The monthly cost of producing 3,000 doorknobs is as follows:

Unit-level materials	$2,700
Unit-level labor	2,400
Unit-level overhead	1,800
Product-level costs*	3,000
Allocated facility-level costs	9,600

*Twenty percent of these costs can be avoided if the doorknobs are purchased.

Nash Company has offered to sell comparable doorknobs to Kwang for $3 each.

Required
a. Should Kwang continue to make the doorknobs? Support you answer with appropriate computations.
b. For $3,000 per month, Kwang could lease the manufacturing space to another company. Would this potential cash inflow affect your response to Requirement *a?* Explain.

EXERCISE 4–12B *Opportunity Cost* L.O. 4

Bester Fishing Tours, Inc., owns a boat that originally cost $98,000. Currently, the boat's net book value is $25,000, and its expected remaining useful life is four years. Bester has an opportunity to purchase for

$72,000 a replacement boat that is extremely fuel efficient. Fuel costs for the old boat are expected to be $12,000 per year more than fuel costs would be for the replacement boat. Bester could sell the old boat, which is fully paid for and in good condition, for only $32,000.

Required

Should Bester replace the old boat with the new fuel-efficient model, or should it continue to use the old one until it wears out? Explain.

L.O. 4, 5

EXERCISE 4–13B *Opportunity Costs*

Two years ago, Patrick Hale bought a truck for $28,000 to offer delivery service. Patrick earns $35,000 a year operating as an independent trucker. He has an opportunity to sell his truck for $15,000 and take a position as an instructor in a truck driving school. The instructor position pays $28,000 a year for working 40 hours per week. Driving his truck, Patrick works approximately 60 hours per week. If Patrick sells his truck, he will invest the proceeds of the sale in bonds that pay a 12 percent return.

Required

a. Determine the opportunity cost of owning and operating the independent delivery business.
b. Based solely on financial considerations, should Patrick sell his truck and accept the instructor position?
c. Discuss the qualitative as well as quantitative characteristics that Patrick should consider.

L.O. 8

EXERCISE 4–14B *Segment Elimination Decision*

The Mosley Company operates three segments. Income statements for the segments imply that Mosley could improve profitability if Segment A were eliminated.

THE MOSLEY COMPANY
Income Statement
For the Year 2009

Segment	X	Y	Z
Sales	$ 58,000	$140,000	$132,000
Cost of Goods Sold	(44,000)	(55,000)	(56,000)
Sales Commissions	(4,000)	(14,000)	(13,000)
Contribution Margin	10,000	75,000	63,000
General Fixed Oper. Exp. (allocation of president's salary)	(10,000)	(10,000)	(10,000)
Advertising Expense (specific to individual segments)	(6,000)	(7,000)	0
Net Income	$ (26,000)	$ 30,000	$ 27,000

Required

a. Explain the effect on Mosley's profitability if segment X is eliminated.
b. Prepare comparative income statements for the company as a whole under the two alternatives: (1) Segment X is retained or (2) Segment X is eliminated.

L.O. 8

EXERCISE 4–15B *Segment Elimination Decision*

Hanson Company divides its operations into six divisions. A recent income statement for the Clairmont Division follows:

Income Statement	
Revenue	$ 800,000
Salaries for Employees	(550,000)
Operating Expenses	(145,000)
Insurance	(48,000)
Division-Level Facility-Sustaining Costs	(98,000)
Companywide Facility-Sustaining Costs	(60,000)
Net Loss	$(101,000)

Required

a. Should Hanson eliminate the Clairmont Division? Support your answer by explaining how the division's elimination would affect the net income of the company as a whole. By how much would companywide income increase or decrease?

b. Assume that the Clairmont Division could increase its revenue to $850,000 by raising prices. Would this change the decision you made in response to Requirement *a?* Assuming Hanson's revenue becomes $850,000, determine the amount of the increase or decrease that would occur in companywide net income if the segment were eliminated.

c. What is the minimum amount of revenue the Clairmont Division must generate to justify its continued operation?

EXERCISE 4–16B *Identifying Avoidable Cost of a Segment*

L.O. 8

The Ohldin Corporation is considering the elimination of one of its segments. The following fixed costs pertain to the segment. If the segment is eliminated, the building it uses will be sold.

Annual advertising expense	$169,000
Market value of the building	48,000
Annual depreciation on the building	18,000
Annual maintenance costs on equipment	26,000
Annual real estate taxes on the building	8,000
Annual supervisory salaries	72,000
Annual allocation of companywide facility-level costs	30,000
Original cost of the building	75,000
Current book value of the building	54,000

Required

Based on this information, determine the amount of avoidable cost associated with the segment.

EXERCISE 4–17B *Asset Replacement Decision*

L.O. 9

Tench Electronics purchased a manufacturing plant four years ago for $8,000,000. The plant costs $2,000,000 per year to operate. Its current book value using straight-line depreciation is $6,000,000. Tench could purchase a replacement plant for $12,000,000 that would have a useful life of 10 years. Because of new technology, the replacement plant would require only $500,000 per year in operating expenses. It would have an expected salvage value of $1,000,000 after 10 years. The current disposal value of the old plant is $1,400,000, and if Tench keeps it 10 more years, its residual value would be $500,000.

Required

Based on this information, should Tench replace the old plant? Support your answer with appropriate computations.

EXERCISE 4–18B *Asset Replacement Decision*

L.O. 9

Calder Company is considering whether to replace some of its manufacturing equipment. Information pertaining to the existing equipment and the potential replacement equipment follows:

Existing Equipment		Replacement Equipment	
Cost	$60,000	Cost	$45,000
Operating expenses*	50,000	Operating expenses*	10,000
Salvage value	12,000	Salvage value	10,000
Market value	20,000	Useful life	10 years
Book value	30,000		
Remaining useful life	10 years		

*The amounts shown for operating expenses are the cumulative total of all such expenses expected to be incurred over the useful life of the equipment.

Required

Based on this information, recommend whether to replace the equipment. Support your recommendation with appropriate computations.

EXERCISE 4–19B *Asset Replacement Decision*

L.O. 9

Kase Company, a Texas-based corporation, paid $65,000 to purchase an air conditioner on January 1, 1995. During 2005, surging energy costs prompted management to consider replacing the air conditioner with a more energy-efficient model. The new air conditioner would cost $90,000. Electricity for the existing air conditioner costs the company $35,000 per year; the new model would cost only $24,000 per year. The new model, which has an expected useful life of 10 years, would be installed on January 1, 2006. Because the old air conditioner is more durable, Kase estimates it still has a remaining useful life of 10 years even though it has been used. The current market value of the old air conditioner is $30,000. The expected salvage value of both air conditioners is zero.

Required
Based on this information, recommend whether to replace the equipment. Support your recommendation with appropriate computations.

L.O. 4, 9

EXERCISE 4–20B *Annual Versus Cumulative Data for Replacement Decision*

Because their three adult children have all at last left home, Dan and Alberta Quaker recently moved to a smaller house. Dan owns a riding lawnmower he bought three years ago to take care of the former house's huge yard; it should last another five years. With the new house's smaller yard, Dan thinks he could hire someone to cut his grass for $350 per year. He wonders if this option is financially sound. Relevant information follows.

Riding Lawn Mower	Amount
Original cost	$1,800
Accumulated depreciation	720
Current market value	1,000
Estimated salvage value	0

Required
a. What is the annual opportunity cost of using the riding mower? Based on your computations, recommend whether Dan should sell it and hire a lawn service.
b. Determine the total cost of hiring a lawn service for the next five years. Based on your computations, recommend whether Dan should sell the mower and hire a lawn service.

Appendix

L.O. 11

EXERCISE 4–21B *Scarce Resource Decision*

Centech has the capacity to annually produce either 50,000 desktop computers or 28,000 laptop computers. Relevant data for each product follow:

	Desktop	Laptop
Sales price	$1,000	$1,800
Variable costs	400	650

Required
Assuming that Centech can sell all it produces of either product, should the company produce the desktop computers or the laptop computers? Provide computations to support your answer.

PROBLEMS–SERIES B

L.O. 1

PROBLEM 4–22B *Context-Sensitive Relevance*

Required
Respond to each requirement independently.

a. Describe two decision-making contexts, one in which unit-level labor costs are avoidable, and the other in which they are unavoidable.
b. Describe two decision-making contexts, one in which batch-level shipping costs are avoidable, and the other in which they are unavoidable.
c. Describe two decision-making contexts, one in which administrative costs are avoidable, and the other in which they are unavoidable.
d. Describe two decision-making contexts, one in which the insurance premium paid on a building is avoidable, and the other in which it is unavoidable.
e. Describe two decision-making contexts, one in which amortization of a product patent is avoidable, and the other in which it is unavoidable.

L.O. 1

PROBLEM 4–23B *Context-Sensitive Relevance*

Reeves Machines Company is evaluating two customer orders from which it can accept only one because of capacity limitations. The data associated with each order follow.

Cost Category	Order A	Order B
Contract price	$940,000	$860,000
Unit-level materials	350,000	306,000
Unit-level labor	330,000	304,800
Unit-level overhead	106,000	98,000
Supervisor's salary	80,000	80,000
Rental equipment costs	20,000	24,000
Depreciation on tools (zero market value)	28,000	28,000
Allocated portion of companywide facility-sustaining costs	8,000	7,200
Insurance coverage	54,000	54,000

Required

a. Assume that Reeves has decided to accept one of the two orders. Identify the information relevant to selecting one order versus the other. Recommend which job to accept, and support your answer with appropriate computations.

b. The customer presenting Order A has withdrawn it because of its financial hardship. Under this circumstance, Reeves' choice is to accept or reject Order B alone. Identify the information relevant to this decision. Recommend whether to accept or reject Order B. Support your answer with appropriate computations.

PROBLEM 4–24B *Effect of Order Quantity on Special Order Decision*

L.O. 3, 5, 6

Wayland Company made 100,000 electric drills in batches of 1,000 units each during the prior accounting period. Normally, Wayland markets its products through a variety of hardware stores. The following is the summarized cost to produce electric drills.

Materials cost ($5.00 per unit × 100,000)	$ 500,000
Labor cost ($4.00 per unit × 100,000)	400,000
Manufacturing supplies ($0.50 × 100,000)	50,000
Batch-level costs (100 batches at $2,000 per batch)	200,000
Product-level costs	150,000
Facility-level costs	180,000
Total costs	$1,480,000
Cost per unit = $1,480,000 ÷ 100,000 = $14.80	

Required

a. Bypassing Wayland's regular distribution channel, Good Home Repair and Maintenance, Inc., has offered to buy a batch of 500 electric drills for $12.50 each directly from Wayland. Wayland's normal selling price is $20 per unit. Based on the preceding quantitative data, should Wayland accept the special order? Support your answer with appropriate computations.

b. Would your answer to Requirement *a* change if Good Home Repair and Maintenance offered to buy a batch of 1,000 electric drills for $11.60 each? Support your answer with appropriate computations.

c. Describe the qualitative factors that Weyland Company should consider before accepting a special order to sell electric drills to Good Home Repair and Maintenance.

PROBLEM 4–25B *Effects of the Level of Production on an Outsourcing Decision*

L.O. 5, 6

One of Aree Company's major products is a fuel additive designed to improve fuel efficiency and keep engines clean. Aree, a petrolchemical firm, makes and sells 200,000 units of the fuel additive per year. Its management is evaluating the possibility of having an outside supplier manufacture the product for Aree for $1.28 each. Aree would continue to sell and distribute the fuel additive under its own brand name for either alternative. Aree's accountant constructed the following profitability analysis.

Revenue (200,000 units × $2.50)	$500,000
Unit-level materials costs (200,000 units × $0.50)	(100,000)
Unit-level labor costs (200,000 units × $0.10)	(20,000)
Unit-level overhead costs (200,000 × $0.25)	(50,000)
Unit-level selling expenses (200,000 × $0.15)	(30,000)
Contribution margin	300,000
Fuel additive production supervisor's salary	(100,000)
Allocated portion of facility-level costs	(40,000)
Product-level advertising cost	(60,000)
Contribution to companywide income	$100,000

Required

a. Identify the cost items relevant to the make-or-outsource decision.

b. Should Aree continue to make the fuel additive or buy it from the supplier? Support your answer by determining the change in net income if Aree buys the fuel additive instead of making it.

c. Suppose that Aree is able to increase sales by 200,000 units (sales will increase to 400,000 units). At this level of sales, should Aree make or buy the fuel additive? Support your answer by explaining how the increase in production affects the cost per unit.

d. Discuss the qualitative factors that Aree should consider before deciding to outsource the fuel additive. How can Aree minimize the risk of establishing a relationship with an unreliable supplier?

L.O. 5, 7, 9

PROBLEM 4–26B *Outsourcing Decision Affected by Equipment Replacement*

During 2007, K-Bee Toy Company made 15,000 units of Model T, the costs of which follow.

Unit-level materials costs (15,000 units × $6)	$ 90,000
Unit-level labor costs (15,000 units × $20)	300,000
Unit-level overhead costs (15,000 × $8)	120,000
Depreciation on manufacturing equipment	48,000
Model T production supervisor's salary	42,000
Inventory holding costs	108,000
Allocated portion of facility-level costs	72,000
Total costs	$780,000

An independent contractor has offered to make the same product for K-Bee for $42 each.

Additional Information:

1. The manufacturing equipment originally cost $420,000 and has a book value of $240,000, a remaining useful life of four years, and a zero salvage value. If the equipment is not used to produce Model T in the production process, it can be leased for $36,000 per year.
2. K-Bee has the opportunity to purchase for $200,000 new manufacturing equipment that will have an expected useful life of four years and a salvage value of $80,000. This equipment will increase productivity substantially, thereby reducing unit-level labor costs by 20 percent.
3. If K-Bee discontinues the production of Model T, the company can eliminate 50 percent of its inventory holding cost.

Required

a. Determine the avoidable cost per unit to produce Model T assuming that K-Bee is considering the alternatives between making the product using the existing equipment and outsourcing the product to the independent contractor. Based on the quantitative data, should K-Bee outsource Model T? Support your answer with appropriate computations.

b. Assuming that K-Bee is considering whether to replace the old equipment with the new equipment, determine the avoidable cost per unit to produce Model T using the new equipment and the avoidable cost per unit to produce Model T using the old equipment. Calculate the impact on profitability if Model T were made using the old equipment versus the new equipment.

c. Assuming that K-Bee is considering either to produce the new equipment or to outsource Model T, calculate the impact on profitability between the two alternatives.

d. Discuss the qualitative factors that K-Bee should consider before making a decision to outsource Model T. How can K-Bee minimize the risk of establishing a relationship with an unreliable supplier?

L.O. 8

PROBLEM 4–27B *Eliminating a Segment*

Howell's Grocery Store has three departments, meat, canned food, and produce, each of which has its own manager. All departments are housed in a single store. Recently, the produce department has been suffering a net loss and is expected to continue doing so. Last year's income statements follow.

	Meat Department	Canned Food Department	Produce Department
Sales	$650,000	$580,000	$420,000
Cost of Goods Sold	(270,000)	(330,000)	(260,000)
Gross Margin	380,000	250,000	160,000
Departmental Manager's Salary	(42,000)	(30,000)	(35,000)
Rent on Store Lease	(80,000)	(80,000)	(80,000)
Store Utilities	(20,000)	(20,000)	(20,000)
Other General Expenses	(98,000)	(98,000)	(98,000)
Net Income (loss)	$140,000	$ 22,000	$(73,000)

Required

a. Determine whether to eliminate the produce department.

b. Confirm the conclusion you reached in Requirement *a* by preparing a before and an after income statement, assuming that the produce department is eliminated.

c. Eliminating the produce department would allow the meat department to expand. It could add seafood to its products. Suppose that management estimates that offering seafood would increase the store's net earnings by $160,000. Would this information affect the decision that you made in Requirement *a?* Explain your answer.

PROBLEM 4–28B ***Effect of Activity Level and Opportunity Cost on Segment Elimination Decision*** **L.O. 4, 8**

Ozaydin Company has three separate operating branches: Division X, which manufactures utensils; Division Y, which makes plates; and Division Z, which makes cooking pots. Each division operates its own facility. The company's administrative offices are located in a separate building. In recent years, Division Z has experienced a net loss and is expected to continue to do so. Income statements for 2008 follow.

	Division X	Division Y	Division Z
Sales	$2,000,000	$1,600,000	$1,710,000
Less: Cost of Goods Sold			
Unit-Level Manufacturing Costs	(1,100,000)	(580,000)	(900,000)
Rent on Manufacturing Facility	(240,000)	(220,000)	(450,000)
Gross Margin	660,000	800,000	360,000
Less: Operating Expenses			
Unit-Level Selling and Admin. Expenses	(60,000)	(45,000)	(150,000)
Division-Level Fixed Selling and Admin. Expenses	(140,000)	(125,000)	(240,000)
Administrative Facility-Level Costs	(80,000)	(80,000)	(80,000)
Net Income (loss)	$ 200,000	$ 370,000	$ (110,000)

Required

a. Based on the preceding information, recommend whether to eliminate Division Z. Support your answer by preparing companywide income statements before and after eliminating Division Z.

b. During 2008, Division Z produced and sold 30,000 units of product. Would your recommendation in Requirement a change if sales and production increase to 45,000 units in 2009? Support your answer by comparing differential revenue and avoidable cost for Division Z, assuming that 45,000 units are sold.

c. Suppose that Ozaydin could sublease Division Z's manufacturing facility for $910,000. Would you operate the division at a production and sales volume of 45,000 units, or would you close it? Support your answer with appropriate computations.

PROBLEM 4–29B ***Comprehensive Problem Including Special Order, Outsourcing, and Segment Elimination Decisions*** **L.O. 6, 7, 8**

Yelton Company's electronics division produces a radio/cassette player. The vice president in charge of the division is evaluating the income statement showing annual revenues and expenses associated with the division's operating activities. The relevant range for the production and sale of the radio/cassette player is between 40,000 and 120,000 units per year.

Income Statement	
Revenue (50,000 units × $40)	$2,000,000
Unit-Level Variable Costs	
Materials Cost (50,000 × $18)	(900,000)
Labor Cost (50,000 × $10)	(500,000)
Manufacturing Overhead (50,000 × $2)	(100,000)
Shipping and Handling (50,000 × $1)	(50,000)
Sales Commissions (50,000 × $3)	(150,000)
Contribution Margin	300,000
Fixed Expenses	
Advertising Costs Related to the Division	(40,000)
Salary of Production Supervisor	(150,000)
Allocated Companywide Facility-Level Expenses	(220,000)
Net Loss	$ (110,000)

Required (Consider each of the requirements independently.)

a. An international trading firm has approached top management about buying 30,000 radio/cassette players for $33 each. It would sell the product in a foreign country, so that Yelton's existing customers would not be affected. Because the offer was made directly to top management, no sales commissions on the transaction would be involved. Based on quantitative features alone, should Yelton accept the special order? Support your answer with appropriate computations. Specifically, by what amount would profitability increase or decrease if the special order is accepted?

b. Yelton has an opportunity to buy the 50,000 radio/cassette players it currently makes from a foreign manufacturer for $32 each. The manufacturer has a good reputation for reliability and quality, and Yelton could continue to use its own logo, advertising program, and sales force to distribute the products. Should Yelton buy the radio/cassette players or continue to make them? Support your answer with appropriate computations. Specifically, how much more or less would it cost to buy the radio/cassette players than to make them? Would your answer change if the volume of sales were increased to 120,000 units?

c. Because the electronics division is currently operating at a loss, should it be eliminated from the company's operations? Support your answer with appropriate computations. Specifically, by what amount would the segment's elimination increase or decrease profitability?

Appendix

L.O. 11

PROBLEM 4–30B *Allocating Scarce Resources*

Deen Company makes two products, M and N. Product information follows.

	Product M	Product N
Selling price per unit	$75	$90
Variable cost per unit	48	55

Required

Identify the product that should be produced or sold under each of the following constraints. Consider each constraint separately.

a. One unit of Product M requires 3 hours of labor to produce, and one unit of Product N requires 5 hours of labor to produce. Due to labor constraints, demand is higher than the company's capacity to make both products.

b. The products are sold to the public in retail stores. The company has limited floor space and cannot stock as many products as it would like. Display space is available for only one of the two products. Expected sales of Product M are 8,000 units, and expected sales of Product N are 7,000 units.

c. The maximum number of machine hours available is 36,000. Product M uses 6 machine hours, and Product N uses 10 machine hours. The company can sell all the products it produces.

L.O. 10

PROBLEM 4–31B *Conflict Between Short-Term Versus Long-Term Performance*

Curtis Construction Components, Inc., purchased a machine on January 1, 2003, for $480,000. The chief engineer estimated the machine's useful life to be six years and its salvage value to be zero. The operating cost of this machine is $240,000 per year. By January 1, 2005, a new machine that requires 30 percent less operating cost than the existing machine has become available for $360,000; it would have a four-year useful life with zero salvage. The current market value of the old machine on January 1, 2005, is $200,000, and its book value is $320,000 on that date. Straight-line depreciation is used for both machines. The company expects to generate $640,000 of revenue per year from the use of either machine.

Required

a. Recommend whether to replace the old machine on January 1, 2005. Support your answer with appropriate computations.

b. Prepare income statements for four years (2005 through 2008) assuming that the old machine is retained.

c. Prepare income statements for four years (2005 through 2008) assuming that the old machine is replaced.

d. Discuss the potential ethical conflicts that could result from the timing of the loss and expense recognition reported in the two income statements.

ANALYZE, THINK, COMMUNICATE

BUSINESS APPLICATION CASE *Elimination of a Product Line*

ATC 4–1

The following excerpts were drawn from the article entitled "The Scottish Shogun," published in *U.S. News & World Report,* May 19, 1997, on pages 44 and 45.

The Japanese car maker [Mazda Motor Company] has accumulated nearly a billion dollars in operating losses in three years. Its market share in Japan fell from nearly 8 percent to below 5 percent in the first half of the decade, and its overall car production dropped by a stunning 46 percent. In fact, Mazda has been fighting for its life. To salvage the company, Ford Motor Co., Mazda's biggest shareholder, gambled $430 million [in 1996] and raised its equity stake in Mazda to 33.4 percent, which in practice gave it operating control. The U.S. car maker chose Henry Wallace, a Ford man for 25 years, to spearhead a turnaround. Mr. Wallace is the first foreigner to lead a big Japanese company. In this case, Mr. Wallace has been warmly embraced by the Japanese—both inside and outside Mazda. Wallace's first move was to retrench—cut product lines, consolidate sales channels, reduce inventory, and in the United States, halt unprofitable fleet and car-rental sales. Wallace also took action to instill a profit motive among the board of directors. Wallace observed, "I don't think previously there was a strong profit motive within the company." Instead, Mazda was a club of engineers who turned out wonderful niche cars—some with exotic styling, others with superb performance—that few consumers wanted to buy. When drivers developed a taste for sport utility vehicles, Mazda's beautiful sedans collected dust on the lots.

Required

a. The article indicated that one action Mr. Wallace took was to cut product lines. Explain which levels (unit, batch, product, and/or facility) of costs could be avoided by eliminating product lines. What sacrifices will Mazda likely have to make to obtain the cost savings associated with eliminating product lines?

b. Suppose that the cost data on the table below apply to three sales channels that were eliminated through the consolidation program.

Additional Information

(1) Sales are expected to drop by 10 percent because of the consolidation program. The remaining sales volume was absorbed by other sales channels.

(2) Half of the sales staff accepted transfers that placed them in positions in other sales channels. The other half left the company.

(3) The supervisor of Channel 1 accepted a job transfer. The other two supervisors left the company.

Annual Costs of Operating Each Sales Channel	Channel 1	Channel 2	Channel 3
Unit-level selling costs:			
Selling supplies	$ 32,000	$ 22,000	$ 40,000
Sales commissions	355,000	225,000	425,000
Shipping and handling	40,000	24,000	49,000
Miscellaneous	20,000	17,000	29,000
Facility-level selling costs:			
Rent	245,000	236,000	240,000
Utilities	40,000	48,000	50,000
Staff salaries	900,000	855,000	1,088,000
Supervisory salaries	150,000	100,000	170,000
Depreciation on equipment	300,000	307,000	303,000
Allocated companywide expenses	100,000	100,000	100,000

(4) The combined equipment, with an expected remaining useful life of four years and a $700,000 salvage value, had a market value of $625,000.

(5) The offices operated by the eliminated channels were closed.

Determine the amount of annual costs saved by consolidating the sales channels.

c. How will reducing inventory save costs?

d. Although the cost-cutting measures are impressive, Mr. Wallace was quoted as saying, "Obviously no one is going to succeed in our business just by reducing costs." Speculate as to some other measures that Mr. Wallace could take to improve Mazda's profitability.

ATC 4–2 GROUP ASSIGNMENT *Relevance and Cost Behavior*

Maccoa Soft, a division of Zayer Software Company, produces and distributes an automated payroll software system. A contribution margin format income statement for Maccoa Soft for the past year follows.

Revenue (12,000 units × $1,200)	$14,400,000
Unit-Level Variable Costs	
Product Materials Cost (12,000 × $60)	(720,000)
Installation Labor Cost (12,000 × $200)	(2,400,000)
Manufacturing Overhead (12,000 × $2)	(24,000)
Shipping and Handling (12,000 × $25)	(300,000)
Sales Commissions (12,000 × $300)	(3,600,000)
Nonmanufacturing Miscellaneous Costs (12,000 × $5)	(60,000)
Contribution Margin (12,000 × $608)	7,296,000
Fixed Costs	
Research and Development	(2,700,000)
Legal Fees to Ensure Product Protection	(780,000)
Advertising Costs	(1,200,000)
Rental Cost of Manufacturing Facility	(600,000)
Depreciation on Production Equipment (zero market value)	(300,000)
Other Manufacturing Costs (salaries, utilities, etc.)	(744,000)
Division-Level Facility Sustaining Costs	(1,730,000)
Allocated Companywide Facility-Level Costs	(1,650,000)
Net Loss	$ (2,408,000)

a. Divide the class into groups and then organize the groups into three sections. Assign Task 1 to the first section, Task 2 to the second section, and Task 3 to the third section. Each task should be considered independently of the others.

Group Tasks

(1) Assume that Maccoa has excess capacity. The sales staff has identified a large franchise company with 200 outlets that is interested in Maccoa's software system but is willing to pay only $800 for each system. Ignoring qualitative considerations, should Maccoa accept the special order?

(2) Maccoa has the opportunity to purchase a comparable payroll system from a competing vendor for $600 per system. Ignoring qualitative considerations, should Maccoa outsource producing the software? Maccoa would continue to sell and install the software if the manufacturing activities were outsourced.

(3) Given that Maccoa is generating a loss, should Zayer eliminate it? Would your answer change if Maccoa could increase sales by 1,000 units?

b. Have a representative from each section explain its respective conclusions. Discuss the following:

(1) Representatives from Section 1 should respond to the following: The analysis related to the special order (Task 1) suggests that all variable costs are always relevant. Is this conclusion valid? Explain your answer.

(2) Representatives from Section 2 should respond to the following: With respect to the outsourcing decision, identify a relevant fixed cost and a nonrelevant fixed cost. Discuss the criteria for determining whether a cost is or is not relevant.

(3) Representatives from Section 3 should respond to the following: Why did the segment elimination decision change when the volume of production and sales increased?

ATC 4–3 RESEARCH ASSIGNMENT *Systems Replacement Decision*

The April 2003, issue if *Strategic Finance* contains an article "Why Automate Payables and Receivables? Electronic Are More Accurate and Less Costly," written by Suzanne Hurt. It appears on pages 33 to 35. This article notes that while financial resource management (FRM) software is available to automate processing transactions such as receivables and payables, 86 percent of these transactions are still paper based. In the article, the author explains some of the reasons companies should consider switching to an Internet-based FRM system and gives some examples of the costs savings that companies such as General Electric have realized by adopting such software. Read this article and complete the following requirements.

Required

a. Identify the relevant costs a company should consider when considering the switch from a manual system to an Internet-based FRM system of accounting for receivables and payables. Think carefully. The article does not specifically all of these costs.

b. The article notes that one advantage of an Internet-based FRM system is that it allows companies to get money from receivables collected and deposited into the bank more quickly. What type of cost does this represent for a company that continues to use a manual system rather than adopt an automated system?

c. The author identifies what she thinks is the biggest challenge facing a company trying to switch to an Internet-based FRM system. What is this challenge?

WRITING ASSIGNMENT *Relevant Versus Full Cost*

ATC 4–4

State law permits the State Department of Revenue to collect taxes for municipal governments that operate within the state's jurisdiction and allows private companies to collect taxes for municipalities. To promote fairness and to ensure the financial well-being of the state, the law dictates that the Department of Revenue must charge municipalities a fee for collection services that is above the cost of providing such services but does not define the term *cost*. Until recently, Department of Revenue officials have included a proportionate share of all departmental costs such as depreciation on buildings and equipment, supervisory salaries, and other facility-level overhead costs when determining the cost of providing collection services, a measurement approach known as *full costing*. The full costing approach has led to a pricing structure that places the Department of Revenue at a competitive disadvantage relative to private collection companies. Indeed, highly efficient private companies have been able to consistently underbid the Revenue Department for municipal customers. As a result, it has lost 30 percent of its municipal collection business over the last two years. The inability to be price competitive led the revenue commissioner to hire a consulting firm to evaluate the current practice of determining the cost to provide collection services.

The consulting firm concluded that the cost to provide collection services should be limited to the relevant costs associated with providing those services, defined as the difference between the costs that would be incurred if the services were provided and the costs that would be incurred if the services were not provided. According to this definition, the costs of depreciation, supervisory salaries, and other facility-level overhead costs are not included because they are the same regardless of whether the Department of Revenue provides collection services to municipalities. The Revenue Department adopted the relevant cost approach and immediately reduced the price it charges municipalities to collect their taxes and rapidly recovered the collection business it had lost. Indeed, several of the private collection companies were forced into bankruptcy. The private companies joined together and filed suit against the Revenue Department, charging that the new definition of cost violates the intent of the law.

Required

a. Assume that you are an accountant hired as a consultant for the private companies. Write a brief memo explaining why it is inappropriate to limit the definition of the costs of providing collection services to relevant costs.

b. Assume that you are an accountant hired as a consultant for the Department of Revenue. Write a brief memo explaining why it is appropriate to limit the definition of the costs of providing collection services to relevant costs.

c. Speculate on how the matter will be resolved.

ETHICAL DILEMMA *Asset Replacement Clouded by Self-Interest*

ATC 4–5

John Dillworth is in charge of buying property used as building sites for branch offices of the National Bank of Commerce. Mr. Dillworth recently paid $110,000 for a site located in a growing section of the city. Shortly after purchasing this lot, Mr. Dillworth had the opportunity to purchase a more desirable lot at a significantly lower price. The traffic count at the new site is virtually twice that of the old site, but the price of the lot is only $80,000. It was immediately apparent that he had overpaid for the previous purchase. The current market value of the purchased property is only $75,000. Mr. Dillworth believes that it would be in the bank's best interest to buy the new lot, but he does not want to report a loss to his boss, Kelly Fullerton. He knows that Ms. Fullerton will severely reprimand him, even though she has made her share of mistakes. In fact, he is aware of a significant bad loan that Ms. Fullerton recently approved. When confronted with the bad debt by the senior vice president in charge of commercial lending, Ms. Fullerton blamed the decision on one of her former subordinates, Ira Sacks. Ms. Fullerton implied that Mr. Sacks had been dismissed for reckless lending decisions when, in fact, he had been an excellent loan officer with an uncanny ability to assess the creditworthiness of his customers. Indeed, Mr. Sacks had voluntarily resigned to accept a better position.

Required

a. Determine the amount of the loss that would be recognized on the sale of the existing branch site.

b. Identify the type of cost represented by the $110,000 original purchase price of the land. Also identify the type of cost represented by its current market value of $75,000. Indicate which cost is relevant to a decision as to whether the original site should be replaced with the new site.

c. Is Mr. Dillworth's conclusion that the old site should be replaced supported by quantitative analysis? If not, what facts do justify his conclusion?

d. Assuming that Mr. Dillworth is a certified management accountant (CMA), do you believe the failure to replace the land violates any of the standards of ethical conduct in Exhibit 1–13 in Chapter 1? If so, which standards would be violated?

e. Discuss the ethical dilemma that Mr. Dillworth faces within the context of Donald Cressey's common features of ethical misconduct that were outlined in Chapter 1.

ATC 4–6 SPREADSHEET ASSIGNMENT *Using Excel*

Dorina Company makes cases of canned dog food in batches of 1,000 cases and sells each case for $15. The plant capacity is 50,000 cases; the company currently makes 40,000 cases. DoggieMart has offered to buy 1,500 cases for $12 per case. Because product-level and facility-level costs are unaffected by a special order, they are omitted.

Required

a. Prepare a spreadsheet like the following one to calculate the contribution to income if the special order is accepted. Construct formulas so that the number of cases or the price could be changed and the new contribution would be automatically calculated.

b. Try different order sizes (such as 2,000) or different prices to see the effect on contribution to profit.

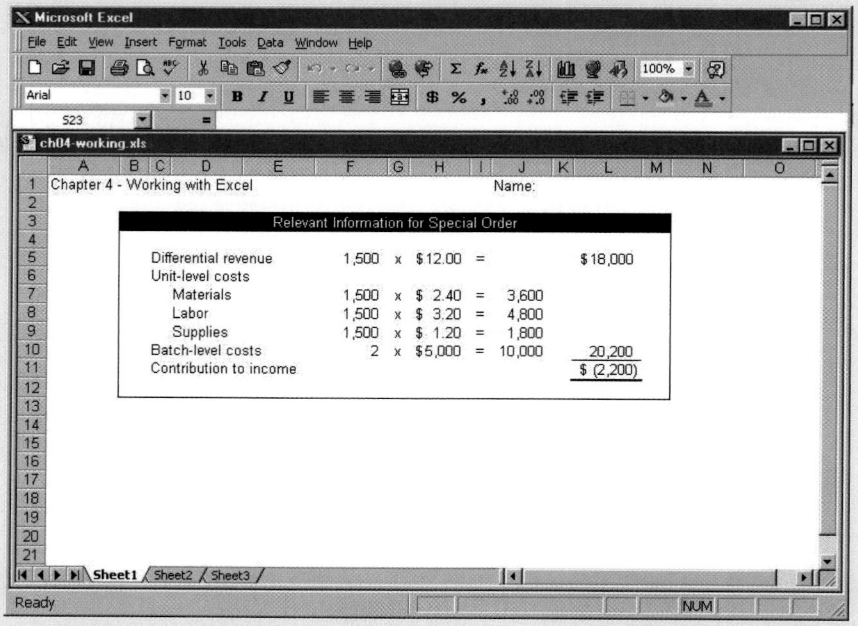

Chapter 4 - Working with Excel						Name:	
Relevant Information for Special Order							
Differential revenue	1,500	x	$12.00	=		$18,000	
Unit-level costs							
Materials	1,500	x	$ 2.40	=	3,600		
Labor	1,500	x	$ 3.20	=	4,800		
Supplies	1,500	x	$ 1.20	=	1,800		
Batch-level costs	2	x	$5,000	=	10,000	20,200	
Contribution to income						$ (2,200)	

Spreadsheet Tips

1. The numbers in cells F7 to F9 should be formulas that refer to F5. This allows the number of cases to be changed in cell F5 with the other cells changing automatically.
2. The formula in cell F10 uses a function named ROUNDUP to calculate the even number of batches. The formula should be = ROUNDUP(F5/1000,0) where the zero refers to rounding up to the nearest whole number.

ATC 4–7 SPREADSHEET ASSIGNMENT *Mastering Excel*

Refer to Problem 4–30A.

Required

a. Prepare a spreadsheet to solve Requirements *a, b,* and *c* in Problem 4–30A.

b. While constructing formulas for Requirement *a* of Problem 4–30A, include a formula to calculate contribution margin per labor hour.

c. While constructing formulas for Requirement *b* of Problem 4–30A, include formulas to calculate total contribution margin for each product.

d. While constructing formulas for Requirement *c* of Problem 4–30A, include formulas to calculate contribution margin per machine hour and total contribution margin for each product.

COMPREHENSIVE PROBLEM

Use the same transaction data for Magnificent Modems, Inc. as was used in Chapter 1. (See page 00.)

Required

a. One of Magnificent Modems' sales representatives receives a special offer to sell 1,000 modems at a price of $72 each. Should the offer be accepted?

b. Magnificent Modems has the opportunity to purchase the modems that it currently makes. The modems can be purchased at a price of $76 each. Assuming the manufacturing equipment has a zero market value, should Magnificent buy the modems?

c. Assume that Magnificent Modems expects production and sales to grow to 10,000. At this volume of production, should Magnificent buy the modems?

CHAPTER *five*

COST ACCUMULATION, TRACING, AND ALLOCATION

LEARNING *objectives*

After you have mastered the material in this chapter, you will be able to:

1. Describe the relationships among cost objects, cost drivers, and cost accumulation.
2. Distinguish direct costs from indirect costs.
3. Use basic mathematics to compute indirect cost allocations.
4. Select appropriate cost drivers for allocating indirect costs in a variety of different circumstances.
5. Use allocation to solve problems that emerge in the process of making cost-plus pricing decisions.
6. Explain why companies establish indirect cost pools.
7. Explain the nature and allocation of joint product and by-product common costs.
8. Recognize human motivation as a key variable in the allocation process.
9. Understand how to allocate service center costs to operating departments using the direct and step methods. (Appendix)

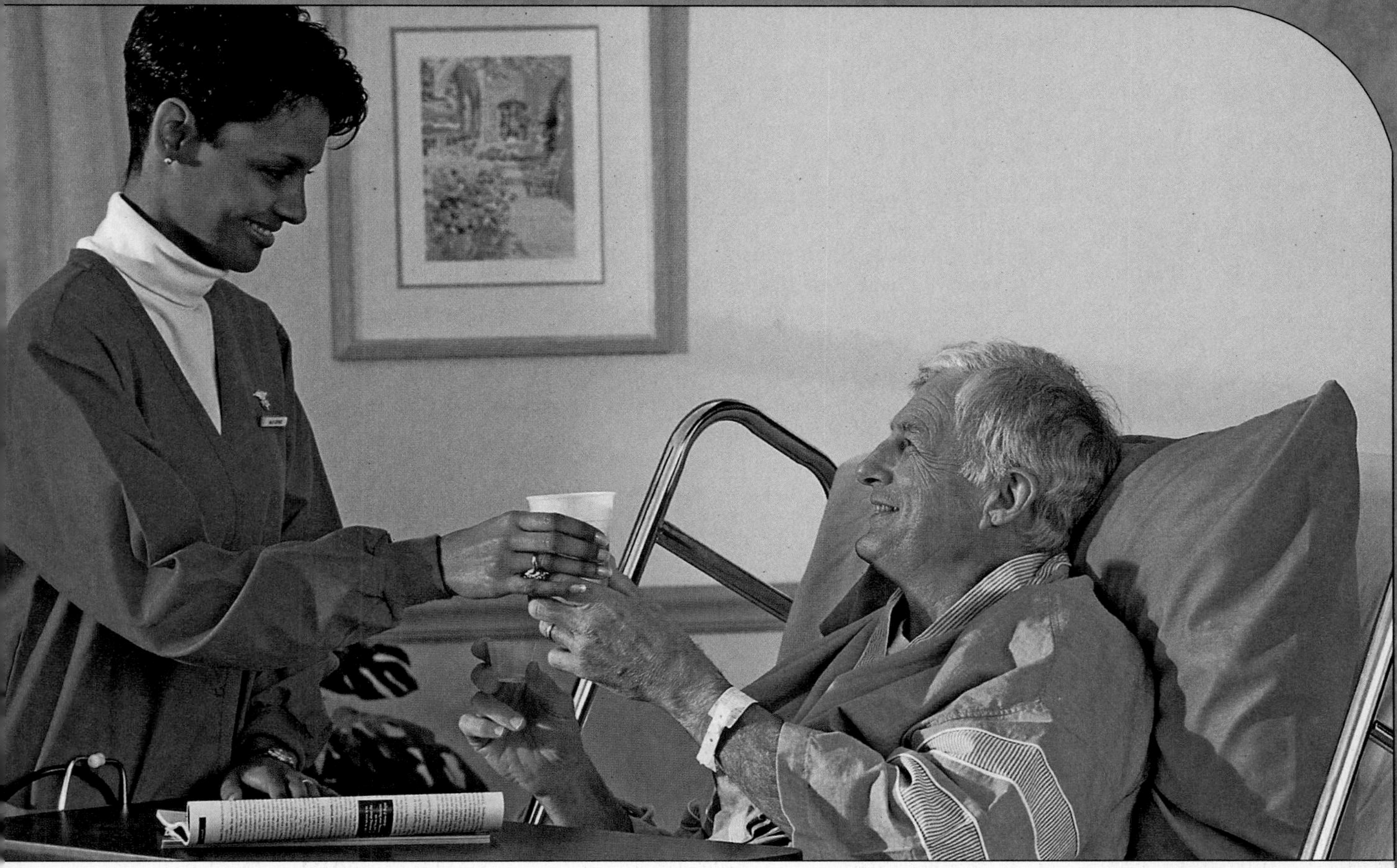

THE *curious* ACCOUNTANT

A former patient of a California hospital complained about being charged $7 for a single aspirin tablet. After all, an entire bottle of 100 aspirins can be purchased at the local grocery store for around $2.

Can you think of any reasons, other than shameless profiteering, that a hospital would need to charge $7 for an aspirin? Remember that the hospital is not just selling the aspirin; it is also delivering it to the patient. (Answer on page 190.)

CHAPTER *opening*

What does it cost? This is one of the questions most frequently asked by business managers. Managers must have reliable cost estimates to price products, evaluate performance, control operations, and prepare financial statements. As this discussion implies, managers need to know the cost of many different things. The things we are trying to determine the cost of are commonly called ***cost objects****. For example, if we are trying to determine the cost of operating a department, that department is the cost object. Cost objects may be products, processes, departments, services, activities, and so on. This chapter explains techniques managerial accountants use to determine the cost of a variety of cost objects.*

Use of Cost Drivers to Accumulate Costs

LO1 Describe the relationships among cost objects, cost drivers, and cost accumulation.

Accountants use **cost accumulation** to determine the cost of a particular object. Suppose the Atlanta Braves advertising manager wants to promote a Tuesday night ball game by offering free baseball caps to all children who attend. What would the promotion cost? The team's accountant must *accumulate* many individual costs and add them together. For simplicity consider only three cost components: (1) the cost of the caps, (2) the cost of advertising the promotion, and (3) the cost of an employee to work on the promotion.

Cost accumulation begins with identifying the cost objects. The primary cost object is the cost of the promotion. Three secondary cost objects are (1) the cost of caps, (2) the cost of advertising, and (3) the cost of labor. The costs of the secondary cost objects are combined to determine the cost of the primary cost object.

Determining the costs of the secondary cost objects requires identifying what *drives* those costs. A **cost driver** has a *cause-and-effect* relationship with a cost object. For example, the *number of caps* (cost driver) has an effect on the *cost of caps* (cost object). The *number of advertisements* is a cost driver for the *advertising cost* (cost object); the *number of labor hours* worked is a cost driver for the *labor cost* (cost object). Using the following assumptions about unit costs and cost drivers, the accumulated cost of the primary cost object (cost of the cap promotion) is:

Cost Object	Cost Per Unit	×	Cost Driver	=	Total Cost of Object
Cost of Caps	$2.50	×	4,000 Caps	=	$10,000
Cost of Advertising	$100.00	×	50 Advertisements	=	5,000
Cost of Labor	$8.00	×	100 Hours	=	800
Cost of Cap Promotion					$15,800

The Atlanta Braves should run the promotion if management expects it to produce additional revenues exceeding $15,800.

Estimated Versus Actual Cost

The accumulated cost of the promotion—$15,800—is an *estimate.* Management cannot know *actual* costs and revenues until after running the promotion. While actual information is more accurate, it is not relevant for deciding whether to run the promotion because the decision must be made before the actual cost is known. Managers must accept a degree of inaccuracy in exchange for the relevance of timely information. Many business decisions are based on estimated rather than actual costs.

Managers use cost estimates to set prices, bid on contracts, evaluate proposals, distribute resources, plan production, and set goals. Certain circumstances, however, require actual cost data. For example, published financial reports and managerial performance evaluations use actual cost data. Managers frequently accumulate both estimated and actual cost data for the same cost object. For example, companies use cost estimates to establish goals and use actual costs to evaluate management performance in meeting those goals. The following discussion provides a number of business examples that use estimated data, actual data, or a combination of both.

Assignment of Cost to Objects in a Retail Business

Exhibit 5–1 displays the January income statement for In Style, Inc. (ISI), a retail clothing store. ISI subdivides its operations into women's, men's, and children's departments. To encourage the departmental managers to maximize sales, ISI began paying the manager of each department a bonus based on a percentage of departmental sales revenue.

Although the bonus incentive increased sales revenue, it also provoked negative consequences. The departmental managers began to argue over floor space; each manager wanted more space to display merchandise. The managers reduced prices; they increased sales commissions. In the drive to maximize sales, the managers ignored the need to control costs. To improve the situation, the store manager decided to base future bonuses on each department's contribution to profitability rather than its sales revenue.

Exhibit 5–1 *Income Statement*

IN STYLE, INC.
Income Statement
For the Month Ended January 31

Sales	$360,000
Cost of goods sold	(216,000)
Gross margin	144,000
Sales commissions	(18,000)
Dept. managers' salaries	(12,000)
Store manager's salary	(9,360)
Depreciation	(16,000)
Rental fee for store	(18,400)
Utilities	(2,300)
Advertising	(7,200)
Supplies	(900)
Net income	$ 59,840

Identifying Direct Versus Indirect Costs

LO2 Distinguish direct costs from indirect costs.

The new bonus strategy requires determining the cost of operating each department. Each department is a separate *cost object.* Assigning costs to the departments (cost objects) requires **cost tracing** and **cost allocation.** *Direct costs* can be easily traced to a cost object. *Indirect costs* cannot be easily traced to a cost object. Whether or not a cost is easily traceable requires *cost/benefit analysis.*

Some of ISI's costs can be easily traced to the cost objects (specific departments). The cost of goods sold is an example of an easily traced cost. Price tags on merchandise can be coded so cash register scanners capture the departmental code for each sale. The cost of goods sold is not only easily traceable but also very useful information. Companies need cost of goods sold information for financial reporting (income statement and balance sheet) and for management decisions (determining inventory reorder points, pricing strategies, and cost control). Because the cost of tracing *cost of goods sold* is small relative to the benefits obtained, cost of goods sold is a *direct cost.*

In contrast, the cost of supplies (shopping bags, sales slips, pens, staples, price tags) used by each department is much more difficult to trace. How could the number of staples used to seal shopping bags be traced to any particular department? The sales staff could count the number of staples used, but doing so would be silly for the benefits obtained. Although tracing the cost of supplies to each department may be possible, it is not worth the effort of doing so. The cost of supplies is therefore an *indirect cost.* Indirect costs are also called **overhead costs.**

Direct and indirect costs can be described as follows:

> **Direct costs** can be traced to cost objects in a *cost-effective* manner.
> **Indirect costs** cannot be traced to objects in a *cost-effective* manner.

By analyzing the accounting records, ISI's accountant classified the costs from the income statement in Exhibit 5–1 as direct or indirect, as shown in Exhibit 5–2. The next paragraph explains the classifications.

All figures represent January costs. Items 1 though 4 are direct costs, traceable to the cost objects in a cost-effective manner. Cost of goods sold is traced to departments at the point of sale using cash register scanners. Sales commissions are based on a percentage of departmental sales and are therefore easy to trace to the departments. Departmental managers' salaries are also easily traceable to the departments. Equipment, furniture, and fixtures are tagged with department codes that permit tracing depreciation charges directly to specific departments.

Exhibit 5–2 *Income Statement Classification of Costs*

Cost Item	Direct Costs: Women's	Direct Costs: Men's	Direct Costs: Children's	Indirect Costs
1. Cost of goods sold—$216,000	$120,000	$58,000	$38,000	
2. Sales commissions—$18,000	9,500	5,500	3,000	
3. Dept. managers' salaries—$12,000	5,000	4,200	2,800	
4. Depreciation—$16,000	7,000	5,000	4,000	
5. Store manager's salary				$ 9,360
6. Rental fee for store				18,400
7. Utilities				2,300
8. Advertising				7,200
9. Supplies				900
Totals	$141,500	$72,700	$47,800	$38,160

Items 5 through 8 are incurred on behalf of the company as a whole and are therefore not directly traceable to a specific department. Although Item 9 could be traced to specific departments, the cost of doing so would exceed the benefits. The cost of supplies is therefore also classified as indirect.

Cost Classifications—Independent and Context Sensitive

Whether a cost is direct or indirect is independent of whether it is fixed or variable. In the ISI example, both cost of goods sold and the cost of supplies vary relative to sales volume (both are variable costs), but cost of goods sold is direct and the cost of supplies is indirect. Furthermore, the cost of rent and the cost of depreciation are both fixed relative to sales volume, but the cost of rent is indirect and the cost of depreciation is direct. In fact, the very same cost can be classified as direct or indirect, depending on the cost object. The store manager's salary is not directly traceable to a specific department, but it is traceable to a particular store.

Similarly, identifying costs as direct or indirect is independent of whether the costs are relevant to a given decision. ISI could avoid both cost of goods sold and the cost of supplies for a particular department if that department were eliminated. Both costs are relevant to a segment elimination decision, yet one is direct, and the other is indirect. You cannot memorize costs as direct or indirect, fixed or variable, relevant or not relevant. When trying to identify costs as to type or behavior, you must consider the context in which the costs occur.

Topic Tackler PLUS 5–1

LO3 Use basic mathematics to compute indirect cost allocations.

Allocating Indirect Costs to Objects

Cost **allocation** involves dividing a total cost into parts and assigning the parts to designated cost objects. How should ISI allocate the $38,160 of indirect costs to each of the three departments? First, identify a cost driver for each cost to be allocated. For example, there is a cause and effect relationship between store size and rent cost; the larger the building, the higher the rent cost. This relationship suggests that the more floor space a department occupies, the more rent cost that department should bear. To illustrate, assume ISI's store capacity is 23,000 square feet and the women's, men's, and children's departments occupy 12,000, 7,000, and 4,000 square feet, respectively. ISI can achieve a rational allocation of the rent cost using the following two-step process.[1]

[1] Other mathematical approaches achieve the same result. This text consistently uses the two-step method described here. Specifically, the text determines allocations by (1) computing a *rate* and (2) multiplying the *rate* by the *weight of the base* (cost driver).

REALITY *bytes*

How does Southwest Airlines know the cost of flying a passenger from Houston, Texas, to Los Angeles, California? The fact is that Southwest does not know the actual cost of flying particular passengers anywhere. There are many indirect costs associated with flying passengers. Some of these include the cost of planes, fuel, pilots, office buildings, and ground personnel. Indeed, besides insignificant food and beverage costs, there are few costs that could be traced directly to customers. Southwest and other airlines are forced to use allocation and averaging to determine the estimated cost of providing transportation services to customers. Estimated rather than actual cost is used for decision-making purposes.

Step 1. Compute the *allocation rate* by dividing the *total cost to be allocated* ($18,400 rental fee) by the *cost driver* (23,000 square feet of store space). *The cost driver is also called the* **allocation base.** This computation produces the **allocation rate**, as follows:

Total cost to be allocated	÷	Cost driver (allocation base)	=	Allocation rate
$18,400 rental fee	÷	23,000 square feet	=	$0.80 per square foot

Step 2. Multiply the *allocation rate* by the *weight of the cost driver* (weight of the base) to determine the allocation *per cost object,* as follows:

Cost Object	Allocation Rate	×	Number of Square Feet	=	Allocation per Cost Object
Women's department	$0.80	×	12,000	=	$ 9,600
Men's department	0.80	×	7,000	=	5,600
Children's department	0.80	×	4,000	=	3,200
Total			23,000		$18,400

It is also plausible to presume utilities cost is related to the amount of floor space a department occupies. Larger departments will consume more heating, lighting, air conditioning, and so on than smaller departments. Floor space is a reasonable cost driver for utility cost. Based on square footage, ISI can allocate utility cost to each department as follows:

Step 1. Compute the allocation rate by dividing the total cost to be allocated ($2,300 utility cost) by the cost driver (23,000 square feet of store space):

Total cost to be allocated	÷	Cost driver	=	Allocation rate
$2,300 utility cost	÷	23,000 square feet	=	$0.10 per square foot

Step 2. Multiply the *allocation rate* by the *weight of the cost driver* to determine the allocation *per cost object:*

Cost Object	Allocation Rate	×	Number of Square Feet	=	Allocation per Cost Object
Women's department	$0.10	×	12,000	=	$1,200
Men's department	0.10	×	7,000	=	700
Children's department	0.10	×	4,000	=	400
Total			23,000		$2,300

Check Yourself 5–1

HealthCare, Inc., wants to estimate the cost of operating the three departments (Dermatology, Gynecology, and Pediatrics) that serve patients in its Health Center. Each department performed the following number of patient treatments during the most recent year of operation: Dermatology, 2,600; Gynecology, 3,500; and Pediatrics, 6,200. The annual salary of the Health Center's program administrator is $172,200. How much of the salary cost should HealthCare allocate to the Pediatrics Department?

Answer

Step 1 Compute the *allocation rate.*

Total cost to be allocated	÷	Cost driver (patient treatments) =	Allocation rate
$172,200 salary cost	÷	(2,600 + 3,500 + 6,200)	= $14 per patient treatment

Step 2 Multiply the *allocation rate* by the *weight of the cost driver* (weight of the base) to determine the allocation per *cost object.*

Cost Object	Allocation Rate	×	No. of Treatments	=	Allocation per Cost Object
Pediatrics department	$14	×	6,200	=	$86,800

Selecting a Cost Driver

Topic Tackler PLUS 5–2

LO4 Select appropriate cost drivers for allocating indirect costs in a variety of different circumstances.

Companies can frequently identify more than one cost driver for a particular indirect cost. For example, ISI's shopping bag cost is related to both the *number of sales transactions* and the *volume of sales dollars.* As either of these potential cost drivers increases, shopping bag usage also increases. The most useful cost driver is the one with the strongest cause-and-effect relationship.

Consider shopping bag usage for T-shirts sold in the children's department versus T-shirts sold in the men's department. Assume ISI studied T-shirt sales during the first week of June and found the following:

Department	Children's	Men's
Number of sales transactions	120	92
Volume of sales dollars	$1,440	$1,612

Given that every sales transaction uses a shopping bag, the children's department uses far more shopping bags than the men's department even though it has a lower volume of sales dollars. A reasonable explanation for this circumstance is that children's T-shirts sell for less than men's T-shirts. The number of sales transactions is the better cost driver because it has a stronger cause and effect relationship with shopping bag usage than does the volume of sales dollars. Should ISI therefore use the number of sales transactions to allocate supply cost to the departments? Not necessarily.

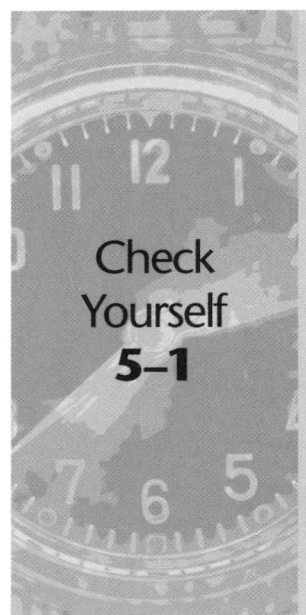

The *availability of information* also influences cost driver selection. While the number of sales transactions is the more accurate cost driver, ISI could not use this allocation base unless it maintains records of the number of sales transactions per department. If the store tracks the volume of sales dollars but not the number of transactions, it must use dollar volume even if the number of transactions is the better cost driver. For ISI, sales volume in dollars appears to be the best *available* cost driver for allocating supply cost.

Assuming that sales volume for the women's, men's, and children's departments was $190,000, $110,000, and $60,000, respectively, ISI can allocate the supplies cost as follows:

Step 1. Compute the allocation rate by dividing the total cost to be allocated ($900 supplies cost) by the cost driver ($360,000 total sales volume):

Total cost to be allocated	÷	Cost driver	=	Allocation rate
$900 supplies cost	÷	$360,000 sales volume	=	$0.0025 per sales dollar

Step 2. Multiply the allocation rate by the weight of the cost driver to determine the allocation per cost object:

Cost Object	Allocation Rate	×	Sales Volume	=	Allocation per Cost Object
Women's department	$0.0025	×	$190,000	=	$475
Men's department	0.0025	×	110,000	=	275
Children's department	0.0025	×	60,000	=	150
Total			$360,000		$900

ISI believes sales volume is also the appropriate allocation base for advertising cost. The sales generated in each department were likely influenced by the general advertising campaign. ISI can allocate advertising cost as follows:

Step 1. Compute the allocation rate by dividing the total cost to be allocated ($7,200 advertising cost) by the cost driver ($360,000 total sales volume):

Total cost to be allocated	÷	Cost driver	=	Allocation rate
$7,200 advertising cost	÷	$360,000 sales volume	=	$0.02 per sales dollar

Step 2. Multiply the allocation rate by the weight of the cost driver to determine the allocation per cost object:

Cost Object	Allocation Rate	×	Sales Volume	=	Allocation per Cost Object
Women's department	$0.02	×	$190,000	=	$3,800
Men's department	0.02	×	110,000	=	2,200
Children's department	0.02	×	60,000	=	1,200
Total			$360,000		$7,200

There is no strong cause-and-effect relationship between the store manager's salary and the departments. ISI pays the store manager the same salary regardless of sales level, square footage of store space, number of labor hours, or any other identifiable variable. Because no plausible cost driver exists, ISI must allocate the store manager's salary arbitrarily. Here the manager's salary is simply divided equally among the departments as follows:

Step 1. Compute the allocation rate by dividing the total cost to be allocated ($9,360 manager's monthly salary) by the allocation base (number of departments):

Total cost to be allocated	÷	Cost driver	=	Allocation rate
$9,360 store manager's salary	÷	3 departments	=	$3,120 per department

ANSWERS TO THE *curious* ACCOUNTANT

When we compare the cost that a hospital charges for an aspirin to the price we pay for an aspirin, we are probably not considering the full cost that we incur to purchase aspirin. If someone asks you what you pay for an aspirin, you would probably take the price of a bottle, say $2, and divide it by the number of pills in the bottle, say 100. This would suggest their cost is $.02 each. Now, consider what it cost to buy the aspirins when all costs are considered. First, there is your time to drive to the store; what do you get paid per hour? Then, there is the cost of operating your automobile. You get the idea; in reality, the cost of an aspirin, from a business perspective, is much more than just the cost of the pills themselves.

Exhibit 5–3 shows the income statement of Tenent Healthcare Corporation for three recent years. Tenent Healthcare claims to be "... the second largest investor-owned health care services company in the United States." In 2002 it operated 114 hospitals with 27,870 beds in 16 states. As you can see, while it generated over $11 billion in revenue, it also incurred a lot of expenses. Look at its first two expense categories. Although it incurred $1.6 billion in supplies expenses, it incurred three times this amount in compensation expense. In other words, it cost a lot more to have someone deliver the aspirin to your bed than the aspirin itself costs.

In 2002 Tenent earned $302 million from its $11.4 billion in sales. This is a return on sales percentage of 2.6 percent ($302 ÷ $11,414). Therefore, on a $7 aspirin, Tenent would earn 19 cents of profit, which is still not a bad profit for selling one aspirin. As a comparison, in 2002, Kroger's return on sales was 2.3 percent, which is not much different than Tenent's.

Exhibit 5–3

TENENT HEALTHCARE CORPORATION
Consolidated Statements of Income
(Dollars in Millions)

	Years ended May 31		
	2000	**2001**	**2002**
Net operating revenues	$11,414	$12,053	$13,913
Operating expenses:			
Salaries and benefits	4,508	4,680	5,346
Supplies	1,595	1,677	1,960
Provision for doubtful accounts	851	849	986
Other operating expenses	2,525	2,603	2,824
Depreciation	411	428	472
Goodwill amortization	94	99	101
Other amortization	28	27	31
Impairment of goodwill and long-lived assets and restructuring charges	355	143	99
Loss from early extinguishment of debt	—	56	383
Operating income	1,047	1,491	1,711
Interest expense	(479)	(456)	(327)
Investment earnings	22	37	32
Minority interests	(21)	(14)	(38)
Net gains on sales of facilities and long-term investments	49	28	—
Income before income taxes	618	1,086	1,378
Income taxes	(278)	(443)	(593)
Income from continuing operations, before discontinued operations and cumulative effect of accounting change	340	643	785
Discontinued operations, net of taxes	(19)	—	—
Cumulative effect of accounting change, net of taxes	(19)	—	—
Net income	$ 302	$ 643	$ 785

Exhibit 5–4 *Profit Analysis by Department*

	Department			
	Women's	**Men's**	**Children's**	**Total**
Sales	$190,000	$110,000	$60,000	$360,000
Cost of goods sold	(120,000)	(58,000)	(38,000)	(216,000)
Sales commissions	(9,500)	(5,500)	(3,000)	(18,000)
Dept. managers' salary	(5,000)	(4,200)	(2,800)	(12,000)
Depreciation	(7,000)	(5,000)	(4,000)	(16,000)
Store manager's salary	(3,120)	(3,120)	(3,120)	(9,360)
Rental fee for store	(9,600)	(5,600)	(3,200)	(18,400)
Utilities	(1,200)	(700)	(400)	(2,300)
Advertising	(3,800)	(2,200)	(1,200)	(7,200)
Supplies	(475)	(275)	(150)	(900)
Departmental profit	$ 30,305	$ 25,405	$ 4,130	$ 59,840

Step 2. Multiply the allocation rate by the weight of the cost driver to determine the allocation per cost object:

Cost Object	Allocation Rate	×	Number of Departments	=	Allocation per Cost Object
Women's department	$3,120	×	1	=	$3,120
Men's department	3,120	×	1	=	3,120
Children's department	3,120	×	1	=	3,120
Total			3		$9,360

As the allocation of the store manager's salary demonstrates, many allocations are arbitrary or based on a weak relationship between the allocated cost and the allocation base (cost driver). Managers must use care when making decisions using allocated costs.

Behavioral Implications

Using the indirect cost allocations just discussed, Exhibit 5–4 shows the profit each department generated in January. ISI paid the three departmental managers bonuses based on each department's contribution to profitability. The store manager noticed an immediate change in the behavior of the departmental managers. For example, the manager of the women's department offered to give up 1,000 square feet of floor space because she believed reducing the selection of available products would not reduce sales significantly. Customers would simply buy different brands. Although sales would not decline dramatically, rent and utility cost allocations to the women's department would decline, increasing the profitability of the department.

In contrast, the manager of the children's department wanted the extra space. He believed the children's department was losing sales because it did not have enough floor space to display a competitive variety of merchandise. Customers came to the store to shop at the women's department, but they did not come specifically for children's wear. With additional space, the children's department could carry items that would draw customers to the store specifically to buy children's clothing. He believed the extra space would increase sales enough to cover the additional rent and utility cost allocations.

The store manager was pleased with the emphasis on profitability that resulted from tracing and assigning costs to specific departments.

Effects of Cost Behavior on Selecting the Most Appropriate Cost Driver

LO4 Select appropriate cost drivers for allocating indirect costs in a variety of different circumstances.

As previously mentioned, indirect costs may exhibit variable or fixed cost behavior patterns. Failing to consider the effects of cost behavior when allocating indirect costs can lead to significant distortions in product cost measurement. We examine the critical relationships between cost behavior and cost allocation in the next section of the text.

Using Volume Measures to Allocate Variable Overhead Costs

A *causal relationship* exists between variable overhead product costs (indirect materials, indirect labor, inspection costs, utilities, etc.) and the volume of production. For example, the cost of indirect materials such as glue, staples, screws, nails, and varnish will increase or decrease in proportion to the number of desks a furniture manufacturing company makes. *Volume measures are good cost drivers* for allocating variable overhead costs.

Volume can be expressed by such measures as the number of units produced, the number of labor hours worked, or the amount of *direct* materials used in production. Given the variety of possible volume measures, how does management identify the most appropriate cost driver (allocation base) for assigning particular overhead costs? Consider the case of Filmier Furniture Company.

Using Units as the Cost Driver

During the most recent year, Filmier Furniture Company produced 4,000 chairs and 1,000 desks. It incurred $60,000 of *indirect materials* cost during the period. How much of this cost should Filmier allocate to chairs versus desks? Using number of units as the cost driver produces the following allocation.

Step 1. Compute the allocation rate.

Total cost to be allocated	÷	Cost driver	=	Allocation rate
$60,000 indirect materials cost	÷	5,000 units	=	$12 per unit

Step 2. Multiply the allocation rate by the weight of the cost driver to determine the allocation per cost object.

Product	Allocation Rate	×	Number of Units Produced	=	Allocated Cost
Desks	$12	×	1,000	=	$12,000
Chairs	12	×	4,000	=	48,000
Total			5,000	=	$60,000

Using Direct Labor Hours as the Cost Driver

Using the number of units as the cost driver assigns an *equal amount* ($12) of indirect materials cost to each piece of furniture. However, if Filmier uses more indirect materials to make a desk than to make a chair, assigning the same amount of indirect materials cost to each is inaccurate. Assume Filmier incurs the following direct costs to make chairs and desks:

	Desks	Chairs	Total
Direct labor hours	3,500 hrs.	2,500 hrs.	6,000 hrs.
Direct materials cost	$1,000,000	$500,000	$1,500,000

Both direct labor hours and direct materials cost are volume measures that indicate Filmier uses more indirect materials to make a desk than a chair. It makes sense that the amount of direct labor used is related to the amount of indirect materials used. Because production workers use materials to make furniture, it is plausible to assume that the more hours they work, the more materials they use. Using this reasoning, Filmier could assign the indirect materials cost to the chairs and desks as follows:

Step 1. Compute the allocation rate.

Total cost to be allocated	÷	Cost driver	=	Allocation rate
$60,000 indirect materials cost	÷	6,000 hours	=	$10 per hour

Step 2. Multiply the allocation rate by the weight of the cost driver.

Product	Allocation Rate	×	Number of Labor Hours	=	Allocated Cost
Desks	$10.00	×	3,500	=	$35,000
Chairs	10.00	×	2,500	=	25,000
Total			6,000	=	$60,000

Basing the allocation on labor hours rather than number of units assigns a significantly larger portion of the indirect materials cost to desks ($35,000 versus $12,000). Is this allocation more accurate? Suppose the desks, but not the chairs, require elaborate, labor-intensive carvings. A significant portion of the labor is then not related to consuming indirect materials (glue, staples, screws, nails, and varnish). It would therefore be inappropriate to allocate the indirect materials cost based on direct labor hours.

Using Direct Material Dollars as the Cost Driver

If labor hours is an inappropriate allocation base, Filmier can consider direct material usage, measured in material dollars, as the allocation base. It is likely that the more lumber (direct material) Filmier uses, the more glue, nails, and so forth (indirect materials) it uses. It is reasonable to presume direct materials usage drives indirect materials usage. Using direct materials dollars as the cost driver for indirect materials produces the following allocation:

Step 1. Compute the allocation rate.

Total cost to be allocated	÷	Cost driver	=	Allocation rate
$60,000 indirect materials cost	÷	$1,500,000 direct material dollars	=	$0.04 per direct material dollar

Step 2. Multiply the allocation rate by the weight of the cost driver.

Product	Allocation Rate	×	Number of Direct Material Dollars	=	Allocated Cost
Desks	$0.04	×	$1,000,000	=	$40,000
Chairs	0.04	×	500,000	=	20,000
Total			$1,500,000	=	$60,000

One candy bar, two kids—Now that is a serious allocation problem.
I should get more because I'm bigger.
You don't need more; you're too big as it is. I should get more.
Choosing the right allocation base. Now that's a serious problem.

Selecting the Best Cost Driver

Which of the three volume-based cost drivers (units, labor hours, or direct material dollars) results in the most accurate allocation of the overhead cost? Management must use judgment to decide. In this case, direct material dollars appears to have the most convincing relationship to indirect materials usage. If the cost Filmier was allocating were fringe benefits, however, direct labor hours would be a more appropriate cost driver. If the cost Filmier was allocating were machine maintenance cost, a different volume-based cost driver, machine hours, would be an appropriate base. The most accurate allocations of indirect costs may actually require using multiple cost drivers.

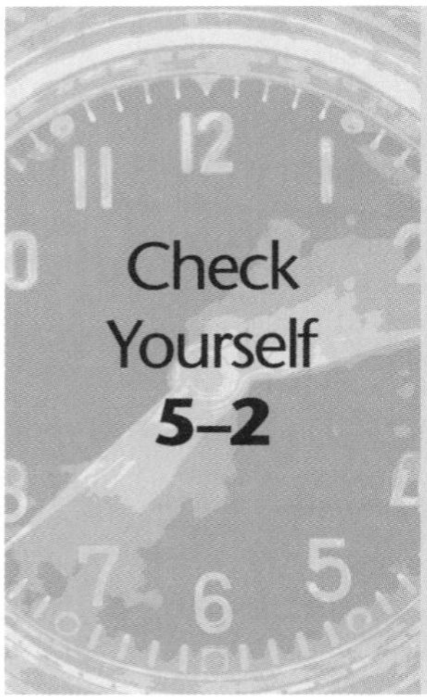

Boston Boat Company builds custom sailboats for customers. During the current accounting period, the company built five different size boats that ranged in cost from $35,000 to $185,000. The company's manufacturing overhead cost for the period was $118,000. Would you recommend using the number of units (boats) or direct labor hours as the base for allocating the overhead cost to the five boats? Why?

Answer Using the number of units as the allocation base would assign the same amount of overhead cost to each boat. Since larger boats require more overhead cost (supplies, utilities, equipment, etc.) than smaller boats, there is no logical link between the number of boats and the amount of overhead cost required to build a particular boat. In contrast, there is a logical link between direct labor hours used and overhead cost incurred. The more labor used, the more supplies, utilities, equipment, and so on used. Since larger boats require more direct labor than smaller boats, using direct labor hours as the allocation base would allocate more overhead cost to larger boats and less overhead cost to smaller boats, producing a logical overhead allocation. Therefore, Boston should use direct labor hours as the allocation base.

Allocating Fixed Overhead Costs

Fixed costs present a different cost allocation problem. By definition, the volume of production does not drive fixed costs. Suppose Lednicky Bottling Company rents its manufacturing facility for $28,000 per year. The rental cost is fixed regardless of how much product Lednicky bottles. However, Lednicky may still use a volume-based cost driver as the allocation base. The object of allocating fixed costs to products is to distribute a *rational share* of the overhead cost to each product. Selecting an allocation base that spreads total overhead cost equally over total production often produces a rational distribution. For example, assume Lednicky produced 2,000,000 bottles of apple juice during 2006. If it sold 1,800,000 bottles of the juice during 2006, how much of the $28,000 of rental cost should Lednicky allocate to ending inventory and how much to cost of goods sold? A rational allocation follows:

Step 1. Compute the allocation rate.

Total cost to be allocated	÷	Allocation base (cost driver)	=	Allocation rate
$28,000 rental cost	÷	2,000,000 units	=	$0.014 per bottle of juice

Because the base (number of units) used to allocate the cost does not drive the cost, it is sometimes called an *allocation base* instead of a *cost driver*. However, many managers use the term cost driver in conjunction with fixed cost even though that usage is technically inaccurate. The terms allocation base and cost driver are frequently used interchangeably.

Step 2. Multiply the allocation rate by the weight of the cost driver.

Financial Statement Item	Allocation Rate	×	Number of Bottles	=	Allocated Cost
Inventory	$0.014	×	200,000	=	$ 2,800
Cost of goods sold	0.014	×	1,800,000	=	25,200

Using number of units as the allocation base assigns equal amounts of the rental cost to each unit of product. Equal allocation is appropriate so long as the units are homogeneous. If the units are not identical, however, Lednicky may need to choose a different allocation base to rationally distribute the rental cost. For example, if some of the bottles are significantly larger than others, Lednicky may find using some physical measure, like liters of direct material used, to be a more appropriate allocation base. Whether an indirect cost is fixed or variable, selecting the most appropriate allocation base requires sound reasoning and judgment.

Allocating Costs to Solve Timing Problems

LO5 Use allocation to solve problems that emerge in the process of making cost-plus pricing decisions.

Monthly fluctuations in production volume complicate fixed cost allocations. To illustrate, assume Grave Manufacturing pays its production supervisor a monthly salary of $3,000. Furthermore, assume Grave makes 800 units of product in January and 1,875 in February. How much salary cost should Grave assign to the products made in January and February, respectively? The allocation seems simple. Just divide the $3,000 monthly salary cost by the number of units of product made each month as follows:

January	**$3,000**	**÷**	**800 units**	**=**	**$3.75 cost per unit**
February	**$3,000**	**÷**	**1,875 units**	**=**	**$1.60 cost per unit**

If Grave Manufacturing based a cost-plus pricing decision on these results, it would price products made in January significantly higher than products made in February. It is likely such price fluctuations would puzzle and drive away customers. Grave needs an allocation base that will spread the annual salary cost evenly over annual production. A timing problem exists, however, because Grave must allocate the salary cost before the end of the year. In order to price its products, Grave needs to know the allocated amount before the actual cost information is available. Grave can manage the timing problem by using estimated rather than actual costs.

Grave Manufacturing can *estimate* the annual cost of the supervisor's salary (indirect labor) as $36,000 ($3,000 × 12 months). The *actual* cost of indirect labor may differ because the supervisor might receive a pay raise or be replaced with a person who earns less. Based on current information, however, $36,000 is a reasonable estimate of the annual indirect labor cost. Grave must also estimate total annual production volume. Suppose Grave produced 18,000 units last year and expects no significant change in the current year. It can allocate indirect labor cost for January and February as follows:

Step 1. Compute the allocation rate.

Total cost to be allocated	**÷**	**Allocation base (cost driver)**	**=**	**Allocation rate**
$36,000	**÷**	**18,000 units**	**=**	**$2.00 per unit**

Step 2. Multiply the rate by the weight of the base (number of units per month) to determine how much of the salary cost to allocate to each month's production.

Month	Allocation Rate	×	Number of Units Produced	=	Allocation per Month
January	$2.00	×	800	=	$1,600
February	2.00	×	1,875	=	3,750

Grave Manufacturing will add these indirect cost allocations to other product costs to determine the total estimated product cost to use in cost-plus pricing or other managerial decisions.

Because the overhead allocation rate is determined *before* actual cost and volume data are available, it is called the **predetermined overhead rate.** Companies use predetermined overhead rates for product costing estimates and pricing decisions during a year, but they must use actual costs in published year-end financial statements. If necessary, companies adjust their accounting records at year-end when they have used estimated data on an interim basis. The procedures for making such adjustments are discussed in a later chapter.

Establishing Cost Pools

LO6 Explain why companies establish indirect cost pools.

Allocating *individually* every single indirect cost a company incurs would be tedious and not particularly useful relative to the benefit obtained. Instead, companies frequently accumulate many individual costs into a single **cost pool.** The *total* of the pooled costs is then allocated to the cost objects. For example, a company may accumulate costs for gas, water, electricity, and telephone service into a single *utilities* cost pool. It would then allocate the total cost in the utilities cost pool to the cost objects rather than individually allocating each of the four types of utility cost.

How far should pooling costs go? Why not pool utility costs with fringe benefit costs? The most accurate cost information comes from pooling costs with common cost drivers. To obtain rational allocations of various indirect costs to cost objects, companies must use different allocation bases (cost drivers). They should therefore limit pooling to costs with common cost drivers.

Allocating Joint Costs

LO7 Explain the nature and allocation of joint product and by-product common costs.

Joint costs are common costs incurred in the process of making two or more **joint products.** The cost of raw milk is a joint cost of producing the joint products cream, whole milk, 2 percent milk, and skim milk. Joint costs include not only materials costs but also the labor and overhead costs of converting the materials into separate products. The point in the production process at which products become separate and identifiable is the **split-off point.** For financial reporting of inventory and cost of goods sold, companies must allocate the joint costs to the separate joint products. Some joint products require additional processing after the split-off point. Any additional materials, labor, or overhead costs incurred after the split-off point are assigned to the specific products to which they relate.

To illustrate, assume Westar Chemical Company produces from common raw materials the joint products Compound AK and Compound AL. Compound AL requires further processing before Westar can sell it. The diagram in Exhibit 5–5 illustrates the joint product costs.

Exhibit 5–5 *Allocation of Joint Cost*

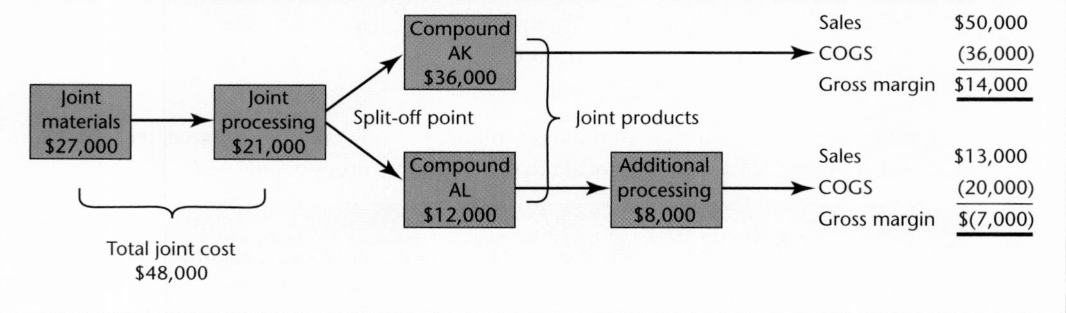

The joint cost of producing a batch of the two compounds is $48,000, representing $27,000 of materials cost and $21,000 of processing cost. A batch results in 3,000 gallons of Compound AK and 1,000 gallons of Compound AL. Westar allocates joint costs to the products based on the number of gallons produced, as follows:

Step 1. Compute the allocation rate.

Total cost to be allocated ÷ Allocation base = Allocation rate
$48,000 joint cost ÷ 4,000 gallons = $12 per gallon

Step 2. Multiply the allocation rate by the weight of the base.

Joint Product	Allocation Rate	×	Number of Gallons Produced	=	Allocated Cost
Compound AK	$12	×	3,000	=	$36,000
Compound AL	12	×	1,000	=	12,000

Westar sells 3,000 gallons of Compound AK for $50,000, and 1,000 gallons of Compound AL for $13,000. Exhibit 5–5 shows the gross margins for each product using the joint cost allocations computed above.

Joint Costs and the Issue of Relevance

Because Compound AL shows a $7,000 loss, a manager might mistakenly conclude that Westar should not incur $8,000 of additional processing costs to bring this product to market. However, the allocated joint cost ($12,000) is *not relevant* to deciding whether to further process Compound AL. Westar will incur the joint cost regardless. The allocated cost does not differ between the alternatives (process further versus not process further). Compound AL is actually contributing $5,000 ($13,000 sales revenue − $8,000 additional processing cost) to Westar's overall profitability, as the following table shows.

	With Additional Processing	Without Additional Processing
Sales	$63,000	$50,000
Cost of goods sold	(56,000)	(48,000)
Gross margin	$ 7,000	$ 2,000

If Compound AL is processed beyond the split-off point, Westar will earn sales revenue from both Compound AK and Compound AL ($50,000 + $13,000 = $63,000). Cost of goods sold is the joint cost plus the cost of additional processing ($48,000 + $8,000 = $56,000). If Compound AL is not processed further it has no market value. Westar would earn sales revenue from Compound AK ($50,000) only, and cost of goods sold is the joint cost ($48,000) only.

Relative Sales Value as the Allocation Base

To avoid the appearance that a product such as Compound AL is producing losses, many companies allocate joint costs to products based on the relative sales value of each product at the split-off point. Westar Chemical would allocate all of the joint cost to Compound AK because Compound AL has no market value at the split-off point. The resulting gross margins follow.

	Compound AK	Compound AL
Sales	$50,000	$13,000
Cost of goods sold	(48,000)	(8,000)
Gross margin	$ 2,000	$ 5,000

Westar's total profit on the joint products is $7,000 whether it allocates the joint costs using gallons or relative market value. However, using market value as the allocation base produces a positive gross margin for both products, reducing the likelihood that a manager will mistakenly eliminate a product that is contributing to profitability.

Check Yourself 5-3

What are some logical split-off points for a meat processing company engaged in butchering beef?

Answer The first logical split-off point occurs when processing separates the hide (used to produce leather) from the carcass. Other split-off points occur as further processing produces different cuts of meat (T-bone and New York strip steaks, various roasts, chops, ground chuck, etc.).

By-Product Costs

Like joint products, **by-products** share common materials, labor, and overhead costs. Unlike joint products, by-products have a relatively insignificant market value. For example, sawdust is a by-product of producing lumber. Although accounting for by-products is not discussed in this text, be aware that the common costs of producing them are not relevant to further processing decisions.

Cost Allocation: The Human Factor

LO8 Recognize human motivation as a key variable in the allocation process.

Cost allocations significantly affect individuals. They may influence managers' performance evaluations and compensation. They may dictate the amount of resources various departments, divisions, and other organizational subunits receive. Control over resources usually offers managers prestige and influence over organization operations. The following scenario illustrates the emotional impact and perceptions of fairness of cost allocation decisions.

Using Cost Allocations in a Budgeting Decision

Sharon Southport, dean of the School of Business at a major state university, is in dire need of a budgeting plan. Because of cuts in state funding, the money available to the School of Business for copying costs next year will be reduced substantially. Dean Southport supervises four departments: management, marketing, finance, and accounting. The Dean knows the individual department chairpersons will be unhappy and frustrated with the deep cuts they face.

Using Cost Drivers to Make Allocations

To address the allocation of copying resources, Dean Southport decided to meet with the department chairs. She explained that the total budgeted for copying costs will be $36,000. Based on past usage, department allocations would be as follows: $12,000 for management, $10,000 for accounting, $8,000 for finance, and $6,000 for marketing.

Dr. Bill Thompson, the management department chair, immediately protested that his department could not operate on a $12,000 budget for copy costs. Management has more faculty members than any other department. Dr. Thompson argued that copy costs are directly related to the number of faculty members, so copy funds should be allocated based on the number of faculty members. Dr. Thompson suggested that number of faculty members rather than past usage should be used as the allocation base.

Since the School of Business has 72 faculty members (29 in management, 16 in accounting, 12 in finance, and 15 in marketing), the allocation should be as follows:

Step 1. Compute the allocation rate.

Total cost to be allocated	÷	Cost driver	=	Allocation rate
$36,000	÷	72	=	$500 per faculty member

Step 2. Multiply the rate by the weight of the driver (the number of faculty per department) to determine the allocation per object (department).

Department	Allocation Rate	×	Number of Faculty	=	Allocation per Department	Allocation Based on Past Usage
Management	$500	×	29		$14,500	$12,000
Accounting	500	×	16		8,000	10,000
Finance	500	×	12		6,000	8,000
Marketing	500	×	15		7,500	6,000
Total					$36,000	$36,000

Seeing these figures, Dr. Bob Smethers, chair of the accounting department, questioned the accuracy of using the number of faculty members as the cost driver. Dr. Smethers suggested the number of *students* rather than the number of *faculty members* drives the cost of copying. He argued that most copying results from duplicating syllabi, exams, and handouts. The accounting department teaches mass sections of introductory accounting that have extremely high student/teacher ratios. Because his department teaches more students, it spends more on copying costs even though it has fewer faculty members. Dr. Smethers recomputed the copy cost allocation as follows.

Step 1. Compute the allocation rate based on number of students. University records indicate that the School of Business taught 1,200 students during the most recent academic year. The allocation rate (copy cost per student) follows.

Total cost to be allocated	÷	Cost driver	=	Allocation rate
$36,000	÷	1,200	=	$30 per student

Step 2. Multiply the rate by the weight of the driver (number of students taught by each department) to determine the allocation per object (department).

Department	Allocation Rate	×	Number of Students	=	Allocation per Department	Allocation Based on Past Usage
Management	$30	×	330		$ 9,900	$12,000
Accounting	30	×	360		10,800	10,000
Finance	30	×	290		8,700	8,000
Marketing	30	×	220		6,600	6,000
Total					$36,000	$36,000

Choosing the Best Cost Driver

Dr. Thompson objected vigorously to using the number of students as the cost driver. He continued to argue that the size of the faculty is a more appropriate allocation base. The chair of the finance department sided with Dr. Smethers, the chair of the marketing department kept quiet, and the dean had to settle the dispute.

Dean Southport recognized that the views of the chairpersons were influenced by self-interest. The allocation base affects the amount of resources available to each department. Furthermore, the dean recognized that the size of the faculty does drive some of the copying costs. For example, the cost of copying manuscripts that faculty submit for publication relates to faculty size. The more articles faculty submit, the higher the copying cost. Nevertheless, the dean decided the number of students has the most significant impact on copying costs. She also wanted to encourage faculty members to minimize the impact of funding cuts on student services. Dean Southport therefore decided to allocate copying costs based on the number of students taught by each department. Dr. Thompson stormed angrily out of the meeting. The dean developed a budget by assigning the available funds to each department using the number of students as the allocation base.

Controlling Emotions

Dr. Thompson's behavior may relieve his frustration but it doesn't indicate clear thinking. Dean Southport recognized that Dr. Thompson's contention that copy costs were related to faculty size had some merit. Had Dr. Thompson offered a compromise rather than an emotional outburst, he might have increased his department's share of the funds. Perhaps a portion of the allocation could have been based on the number of faculty members with the balance allocated based on the number of students. Had Dr. Thompson controlled his anger, the others might have agreed to compromise. Technical expertise in computing numbers is of little use without the interpersonal skills to persuade others. Accountants may provide numerical measurements, but they should never forget the impact of their reports on the people in the organization.

a look back

Managers need to know the costs of products, processes, departments, activities, and so on. The target for which accountants attempt to determine cost is a *cost object.* Knowing the cost of specific objects enables management to control costs, evaluate performance, and price products. *Direct costs* can be cost-effectively traced to a cost object. *Indirect costs* cannot be easily traced to designated cost objects.

The same cost can be direct or indirect, depending on the cost object to which it is traced. For example, the salary of a Burger King restaurant manager can be directly traced to a particular store but cannot be traced to particular food items made and sold in the store. Classifying a cost as direct or indirect is independent of whether the cost behaves as fixed or variable; it is also independent of whether the cost is relevant to a given decision. A direct cost could be either fixed or variable or either relevant or irrelevant, depending on the context and the designated cost object.

Indirect costs are assigned to cost objects using *cost allocation.* Allocation divides an indirect cost into parts and distributes the parts among the relevant cost objects. Companies frequently allocate costs to cost objects in proportion to the *cost drivers* that cause the cost to be incurred. The first step in allocating an indirect cost is to determine the allocation rate by dividing the total cost to be allocated by the chosen cost driver. The next step is to multiply the allocation rate by the amount of the cost driver for a particular object. The result is the amount of indirect cost to assign to the cost object.

A particular indirect cost may be related to more than one driver. The best cost driver is the one that most accurately reflects the amount of the resource used by the cost object. Objects that consume the most resources should be allocated a proportionately greater share of the costs. If no suitable cost driver exists, companies may use arbitrary allocations such as dividing a total cost equally among cost objects.

Cost allocations have behavioral implications. Using inappropriate cost drivers can distort allocations and lead managers to make choices that are detrimental to the company's profitability.

To avoid the inefficiency of allocating every individual indirect cost, managers accumulate many indirect costs into *cost pools.* The costs combined in a pool should have a common cost driver. A single allocation can then be made of the cost pool total.

The joint costs incurred in the process of making two or more products are allocated among the products at the *split-off point,* the point at which products become separate and identifiable. The allocation base can be the products' relative sales values or some quantity measure of the amount of each product made. If one of the joint products requires additional processing costs to bring it to market, only these additional processing costs are relevant to a decision about whether to undertake further processing. The allocated joint costs are not relevant because they will be incurred whether or not the joint product is processed after the split-off point. By-products share common costs with other products but have an insignificant market value relative to their joint products.

a look forward

The failure to accurately allocate indirect costs to cost objects can result in misinformation that impairs decision making. The next chapter explains how increased use of automation in production has caused allocations determined using traditional approaches to be distorted. The chapter introduces allocating indirect costs using more recently developed *activity-based costing* and explains how *activity-based management* can improve efficiency and productivity. Finally, the chapter introduces *total quality management,* a strategy that seeks to minimize the costs of conforming to a designated standard of quality.

APPENDIX

Allocating Service Center Costs

LO9 Understand how to allocate service center costs to operating departments using the direct and step methods.

Most organizations establish departments responsible for accomplishing specific tasks. Departments that are assigned tasks leading to the accomplishment of the primary objectives of the organization are called **operating departments.** Those that provide support to operating departments are called **service departments.** For example, the department of accounting at a university is classified as an operating department because its faculty perform the university's primary functions of teaching, research, and service. In contrast, the maintenance department is classified as a service department because its employees provide janitorial services that support primary university functions. Professors are more likely to be motivated to perform university functions when facilities are clean, but the university's primary purpose is not to clean buildings. Similarly, the lending department in a bank is an operating department and the personnel department is a service department. The bank is in the business of making loans. Hiring employees is a secondary function that assists the lending activity.

The costs to produce a product (or a service) include both operating and service department costs. Therefore, service department costs must somehow be allocated to the products produced (or services provided). Service department costs are frequently distributed to products through a two-stage allocation process. First-stage allocations involve the distribution of costs from service center cost pools to operating department cost pools. In the second stage, costs in the operating cost pools are allocated to products. Three different approaches can be used to allocate costs in the first stage of the two-stage costing process: the *direct method,* the *step method,* and the *reciprocal method.*

Direct Method

The **direct method** is the simplest allocation approach. It allocates service department costs directly to operating department cost pools. To illustrate, assume that Candler & Associates is a law firm that desires to determine the cost of handling each case. The firm has two operating departments, one that represents clients in civil suits and the other that defends clients in criminal cases. The two operating departments are supported by two service departments, personnel and secretarial support. Candler uses a two-stage allocation system to allocate the service centers' costs to the firm's legal cases. In the first stage, the costs to operate each service department are accumulated in separate cost pools. For example, the costs to operate the personnel department are \$80,000 in salary, \$18,000 in office rental, \$12,000 in depreciation, \$3,000 in supplies, and \$4,000 in miscellaneous costs. These costs are added together in a single services department cost pool amounting to \$117,000. Similarly, the costs incurred by the secretarial department are accumulated in a cost pool. We assume that this cost pool contains \$156,800 of accumulated costs. The amounts in these cost pools are then allocated to the operating departments' cost pools. The appropriate allocations are described in the following paragraphs.

Assume that Candler's accountant decides that the number of attorneys working in the two operating departments constitutes a rational cost driver for the allocation of the personnel department cost pool and that the number of request forms submitted to the secretarial department constitutes a rational cost driver for the allocation of costs accumulated in the secretarial department cost pool. The total number of attorneys working in the two operating departments is 18, 11 in the civil department and 7 in the criminal department. The secretarial department received 980 work request forms with 380 from the civil department and 600 from the criminal department. Using these cost drivers as the allocation bases, the accountant made the following first-stage allocations.

Determination of Allocation Rates

$$\text{Allocation rate for personnel department cost pool} = \frac{\$117{,}000}{18} = \$6{,}500 \text{ per attorney}$$

$$\text{Allocation rate for secretarial department cost pool} = \frac{\$156{,}800}{980} = \$160 \text{ per request form}$$

The accountant then multiplied these rates by the weight of the base to determine the amount of each service cost pool to allocate to each operating department cost pool. The appropriate computations are shown in Exhibit 5–1A.

As indicated, the allocated service department costs are pooled with other operating department overhead costs to form the operating department cost pools. In the second stage of the costing process, the costs in the operating department cost pools are allocated to the firm's products (cases). To illustrate second-stage allocations, assume that Candler allocates the operating department overhead cost pools on the basis of billable hours. Furthermore, assume that the civil department expects to bill 30,580 hours to its clients and the criminal department expects to bill 25,262 hours. Based on this information, the following predetermined overhead rates are used to allocate operating department cost pools to particular cases.

$$\text{Predetermined overhead rate for the civil department} = \frac{\$917{,}400}{30{,}580} = \$30 \text{ per billable hour}$$

$$\text{Predetermined overhead rate for the criminal department} = \frac{\$606{,}288}{25{,}262} = \$24 \text{ per billable hour}$$

Exhibit 5–1A *First-Stage Allocations for Candler & Associates—Direct Method*

Allocated Service Department Overhead	Allocation Rate	×	Weight of Base	=	Civil Department	Criminal Department	Total Service Department Cost Pool
Personnel	\$6,500	×	11 attorneys	=	\$ 71,500		
	6,500	×	7 attorneys	=		\$ 45,500	
Total cost of personnel department							\$117,000
Secretarial	160	×	380 requests	=	60,800		
	160	×	600 requests	=		96,000	
Total cost of secretarial department							156,800
Total of cost pools after allocation				=	132,300	141,500	\$273,800
Other operating department overhead costs				=	785,100	464,788	
Total of operating department overhead cost pools				=	\$917,400	\$606,288	

These rates are used to calculate the amount of operating department cost pools to include in the determination of the cost to litigate specific cases. For example, a case in the civil department that required 300 billable hours of legal service is allocated $9,000 (300 hours × $30 predetermined overhead rate) of overhead cost. Assuming that the direct costs to litigate the case amounted to $25,000, the total cost of this particular case is $34,000 ($25,000 direct cost + $9,000 allocated overhead). This accumulated cost figure could be used as a guide to determine the charge to the client or the profitability of the case.

Step Method

The direct method of allocating service center costs fails to consider the fact that service departments render assistance to other service departments. A service that is performed by one service department for the benefit of another service department is called an **interdepartmental service.** To illustrate this, we return to the case of Candler & Associates. Suppose that Candler's personnel department works with the employees in the secretarial department as well as the attorneys in the civil and criminal operating departments. Under these circumstances, Candler needs a cost approach that recognizes the interdepartmental service activity. One such approach is known as the **step method.** The primary difference between the direct method and the step method is depicted graphically in Exhibit 5–2A. Focus your attention on the first stage of the allocation process. Notice that the step method includes one additional allocation, specifically from the personnel department cost pool to the secretarial department cost pool. The direct method ignores this interdepartmental service cost allocation. Indeed, the direct method derives its name from the fact that it allocates costs only from service cost pools to operating cost pools.

The fact that the direct method ignores the effect of interdepartmental services may cause distortions in the measurement of cost objects. The primary purpose of the step method is to avoid such distortions, thereby improving the accuracy of product costing. To illustrate this point, consider Candler & Associates. First, note that the interdepartmental portion of the personnel department cost is, in fact, a cost of providing secretarial services. In other words, the personnel service costs could be reduced if the personnel department did not provide service to the secretarial staff. Accordingly, the cost of providing personnel support to the secretarial staff should be included in the secretarial cost pool. Under the direct method, however, the interdepartmental service cost is allocated between the civil and criminal operating departments. This is not a problem in and of itself because the cost of secretarial service is also allocated between the civil and criminal operating departments. Unfortunately, the base used to allocate personnel costs to the operating departments (i.e., number of attorneys) distributes more cost to the civil department than to the criminal department. This is unfortunate because the criminal department uses more secretarial service than the civil department does. In other words, more secretarial cost (i.e., interdepartmental personnel cost) is being allocated to the civil department although the criminal department uses more secretarial services. This means that ultimately the cost to litigate civil cases will be overstated and the cost to litigate criminal cases will be understated.

The step method corrects this distortion by distributing the interdepartmental personnel department cost to the secretarial department cost pool before it is allocated to the operating departments. Because the secretarial cost pool is allocated on the basis of requests for secretarial service, more of the interdepartmental cost will be allocated to the criminal operating deparment. To validate this result, assume that

Exhibit 5–2A *Comparison of Direct and Step Allocation Methods*

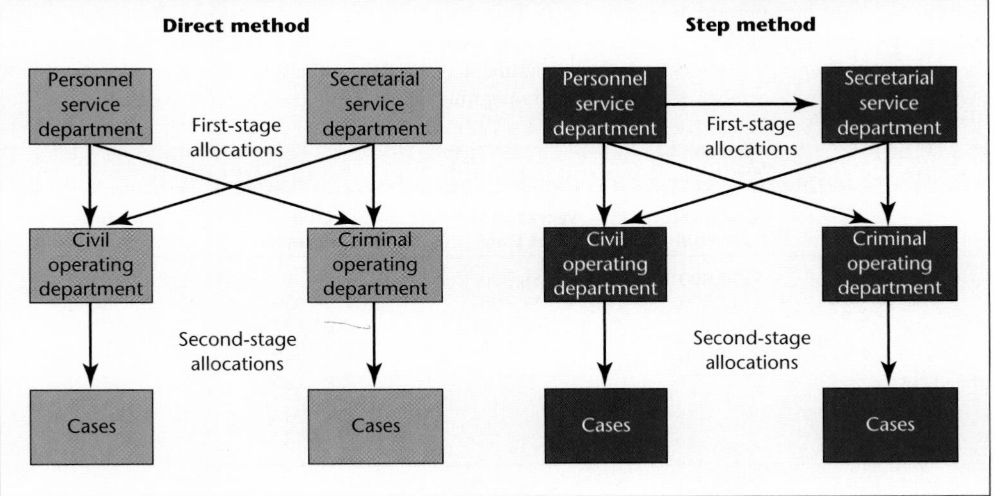

the personnel department cost pool is allocated to the secretarial department cost pool and the two operating department cost pools on the basis of the number of employees in each department. In addition to the 18 attorneys in the firm, assume that two employees work in the secretarial department. Accordingly, the allocation rate for the personnel cost pool is calculated as follows.

$$\text{Allocation rate for personnel department cost pool} = \frac{\$117,000}{20} = \$5,850 \text{ per employee}$$

Based on this rate, the first step in the allocation process distributes the personnel department cost pool as indicated here.

Personnel Cost Pool Allocated to	Allocation Rate		Weight of Base		Allocated Cost
Secretarial	$5,850	×	2 employees	=	$ 11,700
Civil	5,850	×	11 employees	=	64,350
Criminal	5,850	×	7 employees	=	40,950
Total			20 employees		$117,000

The result of the distribution of personnel department costs is shown as the Step 1 allocation in Exhibit 5–3A. The $11,700 interdepartmental personnel department cost allocated to the secretarial department cost pool is added to the $156,800 existing balance in that cost pool (See Exhibit 5–3A). The result is the accumulation of secretarial cost of $168,500. The second step in the costing process allocates this cost pool to the operating departments. Recall that the secretarial cost pool is allocated on the basis of number of work request forms submitted. Furthermore, recall that 980 request forms were submitted to the secretarial department (380 from the civil department and 600 from the criminal department). Accordingly, the allocation rate for the secretarial department cost pool is computed as follows.

$$\text{Allocation rate for secretarial department cost pool} = \frac{\$168,500}{980} = \$171.93878 \text{ per request form}$$

Based on this rate, the second step in the allocation process distributes the secretarial cost pool as indicated here.

Secretarial Cost Pool Allocated to	Allocation Rate		Weight of Base		Allocated Cost
Civil	$171.93878	×	380 requests	=	$ 65,337
Criminal	171.93878	×	600 requests	=	103,163
Total		×	980 requests		$168,500

The result of this allocation is shown as the Step 2 allocation in Exhibit 5–3A. Notice that the final cost pools for the operating departments reflect the expected shift in the cost distribution between the two departments. Specifically, the cost pool in the criminal department is higher and the cost pool in the civil department is lower than the comparable cost pool amounts computed under the direct method (see Exhibit 5–3A for the appropriate comparison). This distribution of cost is consistent with the fact that more of the interdepartmental service cost should be assigned to the criminal department because it uses more secretarial services than does the civil department. Accordingly, the step method of allocation more accurately reflects the manner in which the two operating departments consume resources.

Exhibit 5–3A *First-Stage Allocations for Candler & Associates—Step Method*

	Personnel Cost Pool		Secretarial Cost Pool		Civil Department		Criminal Department
Cost to be allocated	$117,000		$156,800				
Step 1 allocation	(117,000)	=	11,700	+	$ 64,350	+	$ 40,950
Step 2 allocation			(168,500)	=	65,337	+	103,163
Total in cost pool after allocation	$ 0		$ 0		129,687		144,113
Other operating department overhead costs					785,100		464,788
Total of operating department overhead cost pool					$914,787		$608,901

The preceding illustration considered a simple two-stage allocation process with only two service departments and two operating departments. In large organizations, the costing process may be significantly more complex. Interdepartmental cost allocations may involve several service departments. For example, a personnel department may provide service to a secretarial department that provides service to an engineering department that provides service to the accounting department that provides service to several operating departments. In addition, general overhead costs may be allocated to both service and operating departments before costs are allocated from service to operating departments. For example, general utility costs may be pooled together and allocated to service and operating departments on the basis of square footage of floor space. These allocated utility costs are then redistributed to other service departments and to operating departments in a sequence of step-down allocations. The step-down process usually begins with the cost pool that represents resources used by the largest number of departments. This constitutes the first step in the costing process. The second step proceeds with allocations from the cost pool that represents resources used by the second largest number of departments and so on, until all overhead costs have been allocated to the operating departments. Accordingly, the first stage of a two-stage costing process may include many allocations (steps) before all costs have been distributed to the operating departments. Regardless of how many allocations are included in the first stage, the second stage begins when costs are allocated from the operating departments to the organizations' products.

Reciprocal Method

Note that the step method is limited to one-way interdepartmental relationships. In practice, many departments have two-way working relationships. For example, the personnel department may provide services to the secretarial department and receive services from it. Two-way associations in which departments provide and receive services from one another are called **reciprocal relationships.** Allocations that recognize reciprocal relationships require complex mathematical manipulation involving the use of simultaneous linear equations. The resultant cost distributions are difficult to interpret. Furthermore, the results attained with the **reciprocal method** are not significantly different from those attained through the step method. As a result, the reciprocal method is rarely used in practice.

SELF-STUDY REVIEW PROBLEM

New budget constraints have pressured Body Perfect Gym to control costs. The owner of the gym has notified division managers that their job performance evaluations will be highly influenced by their ability to minimize costs. The gym has three divisions, weight lifting, aerobics, and spinning. The owner has formulated a report showing how much it cost to operate each of the three divisions last year. In preparing the report, Mr. Ripple identified several indirect costs that must be allocated among the divisions. These indirect costs are $4,200 of laundry expense, $48,000 of gym supplies, $350,000 of office rent, $50,000 of janitorial services, and $120,000 for administrative salaries. To provide a reasonably accurate cost allocation, Mr. Ripple has identified several potential cost drivers. These drivers and their association with each division follow.

Cost Driver	Weight Lifting	Aerobics	Spinning	Total
Number of participants	26	16	14	56
Number of instructors	10	8	6	24
Square feet of gym space	12,000	6,000	7,000	25,000
Number of staff	2	2	1	5

Required

a. Identify the appropriate cost objects.

b. Identify the most appropriate cost driver for each indirect cost, and compute the allocation rate for assigning each indirect cost to the cost objects.

c. Determine the amount of supplies expense that should be allocated to each of the three divisions.

d. The spinning manager wants to use the number of staff rather than the number of instructors as the allocation base for the supplies expense. Explain why the spinning manager would take this position.

e. Identify two cost drivers other than your choice for Requirement *b* that could be used to allocate the cost of the administrative salaries to the three divisions.

Solution to Requirement a
The objective is to determine the cost of operating each division. Therefore, the cost objects are the three divisions (weight lifting, aerobics, and spinning).

Solution to Requirement b
The costs, appropriate cost drivers, and allocation rates for assigning the costs to the departments follow:

Cost	Base	Computation	Allocation Rate
Laundry expense	Number of participants	$ 4,200 ÷ 56	$75 per participant
Supplies expense	Number of instructors	48,000 ÷ 24	$2,000 per instructor
Office rent	Square feet	350,000 ÷ 25,000	$14 per square foot
Janitorial service	Square feet	50,000 ÷ 25,000	$2 per square foot
Administrative salaries	Number of divisions	120,000 ÷ 3	$40,000 per division

There are other logical cost drivers. For example, supplies expense could be allocated based on the number of staff. It is also logical to use a combination of cost drivers. For example, the allocation of supplies expense could be based on the combined number of instructors and staff. For this problem, we assumed that Mr. Ripple chose the number of instructors as the base for allocating supplies expense.

Solution to Requirement c

Department	Cost to Be Allocated	Allocation Rate	×	Weight of Base	=	Amount Allocated
Weight lifting	Supplies expense	$2,000	×	10	=	$20,000
Aerobics	Supplies expense	2,000	×	8	=	16,000
Spinning	Supplies expense	2,000	×	6	=	12,000
Total						$48,000

Solution to Requirement d
If the number of staff were used as the allocation base, the allocation rate for supplies expense would be as follows:

$48,000 ÷ 5 staff = $9,600 per staff member

Using this rate, the total supplies expense would be allocated among the three divisions as follows:

Department	Cost to Be Allocated	Allocation Rate	×	Weight of Base	=	Amount Allocated
Weight lifting	Supplies expense	$9,600	×	2	=	$19,200
Aerobics	Supplies expense	9,600	×	2	=	19,200
Spinning	Supplies expense	9,600	×	1	=	9,600
Total						$48,000

By using the number of staff as the allocation base instead of the number of instructors, the amount of overhead cost allocated to the spinning division falls from $12,000 to $9,600. Since managers are evaluated based on minimizing costs, it is clearly in the spinning manager's self-interest to use the number of staff as the allocation base.

Solution to Requirement e
Among other possibilities, bases for allocating the administrative salaries include the number of participants, the number of lessons, or the number of instructors.

KEY TERMS

Allocation *186*
Allocation base *187*
Allocation rate *187*
By-products *198*
Cost accumulation *184*
Cost allocation *185*
Cost driver *184*
Cost objects *183*
Cost pool *196*
Cost tracing *185*
Direct cost *185*
Direct method (Appendix) *202*
Indirect cost *185*
Interdepartmental service (Appendix) *203*
Joint costs *196*

Joint products *196*
Operating departments (Appendix) *201*
Overhead costs *185*
Predetermined overhead rate *196*
Reciprocal method (Appendix) *205*
Reciprocal relationships (Appendix) *205*
Service departments (Appendix) *201*
Split-off point *196*
Step method (Appendix) *203*

QUESTIONS

1. What is a cost object? Identify four different cost objects in which an accountant would be interested.
2. Why is cost accumulation imprecise?
3. If the cost object is a manufactured product, what are the three major cost categories to accumulate?
4. What is a direct cost? What criteria are used to determine whether a cost is a direct cost?
5. Why are the terms *direct cost* and *indirect cost* independent of the terms *fixed cost* and *variable cost?* Give an example to illustrate.
6. Give an example of why the statement, "All direct costs are avoidable," is incorrect.
7. What are the important factors in determining the appropriate cost driver to use in allocating a cost?
8. How is an allocation rate determined? How is an allocation made?
9. In a manufacturing environment, which costs are direct and which are indirect in product costing?
10. Why are some manufacturing costs not directly traceable to products?
11. What is the objective of allocating indirect manufacturing overhead costs to the product?
12. On January 31, the managers of Integra, Inc., seek to determine the cost of producing their product during January for product pricing and control purposes. The company can easily determine the costs of direct materials and direct labor used in January production, but many fixed indirect costs are not affected by the level of production activity and have not yet been incurred. The managers can reasonably estimate the overhead costs for the year based on the fixed indirect costs incurred in past periods. Assume the managers decide to allocate an equal amount of these estimated costs to the products produced each month. Explain why this practice may not provide a reasonable estimate of product costs in January.
13. Respond to the following statement: "The allocation base chosen is unimportant. What is important in product costing is that overhead costs be assigned to production in a specific period by an allocation process."
14. Larry Kwang insists that the costs of his school's fund-raising project should be determined after the project is complete. He argues that only after the project is complete can its costs be determined accurately and that it is a waste of time to try to estimate future costs. Georgia Sundum counters that waiting until the project is complete will not provide timely information for planning expenditures. How would you arbitrate this discussion? Explain the trade-offs between accuracy and timeliness.
15. Define the term *cost pool.* How are cost pools important in allocating costs?
16. What are the three methods used for allocating service center costs? How do the methods differ?
17. What is the difference between a joint product and a by-product?

EXERCISES—SERIES A

All Exercises in Series A are available with McGraw-Hill's Homework Manager

EXERCISE 5–1A *Allocating Costs Between Divisions*

L.O. 1, 3

Loftis Services Company (LSC) has 50 employees, 36 of whom are assigned to Division A and 14 to Division B. LSC incurred $360,000 of fringe benefits cost during 2006.

Required

Determine the amount of the fringe benefits cost to be allocated to Division A and to Division B.

EXERCISE 5–2A *Direct Versus Indirect Costs*

L.O. 2

Burr Ridge Construction Company is composed of two divisions, (1) Home Construction and (2) Commercial Construction. The Home Construction Division is in the process of building 12 houses and the Commercial Construction Division is working on 3 projects. Cost items of the company follow:

Labor on a particular house
Salary of the supervisor of commercial construction projects

Supplies, such as glue and nails, used by the Home Construction Division
Cost of building permits
Materials used in commercial construction project
Depreciation on home building equipment (small tools such as hammers or saws)
Company president's salary
Depreciation on crane used in commercial construction
Depreciation on home office building
Salary of corporate office manager
Wages of workers assigned to a specific construction project
Supplies used by the Commercial Construction Division

Required

a. Identify each cost as being a direct or indirect cost assuming the cost objects are the individual products (houses or projects).
b. Identify each cost as being a direct or indirect cost, assuming the cost objects are the two divisions.
c. Identify each cost as being a direct or indirect cost assuming the cost object is Burr Ridge Construction Company as a whole.

L.O. 3, 4 **EXERCISE 5–3A** *Allocating Overhead Cost Among Products*

Donna Hats, Inc., manufactures three different models of hats, Vogue, Beauty, and Deluxe. Donna expects to incur $600,000 of overhead cost during the next fiscal year. Other budget information follows.

	Vogue	Beauty	Deluxe	Total
Direct labor hours	3,000	5,000	4,500	12,500
Machine hours	1,000	1,000	1,000	3,000

Required

a. Use direct labor hours as the cost driver to compute the allocation rate and the budgeted overhead cost for each product.
b. Use machine hours as the cost driver to compute the allocation rate and the budgeted overhead cost for each product.
c. Describe a set of circumstances where it would be more appropriate to use direct labor hours as the allocation base.
d. Describe a set of circumstances where it would be more appropriate to use machine hours as the allocation base.

L.O. 3, 4 **EXERCISE 5–4A** *Allocating Overhead Costs Among Products*

Ritchey Company makes three products in its factory: plastic cups, plastic tablecloths, and plastic bottles. The expected overhead costs for the next fiscal year include the following.

Factory manager's salary	$150,000
Factory utility costs	70,000
Factory supplies	30,000
Total overhead costs	$250,000

Ritchey uses machine hours as the cost driver to allocate overhead costs. Budgeted machine hours for the products are as follows.

Cups	500 Hours
Tablecloths	800
Bottles	1,200
Total machine hours	2,500

Required

a. Allocate the budgeted overhead costs to the products.
b. Provide a possible explanation as to why Ritchey chose machine hours, instead of labor hours, as allocation base.

EXERCISE 5–5A *Allocating Costs Among Products*

L.O. 3, 4

Sudderth Construction Company expects to build three new homes during a specific accounting period. The estimated direct materials and labor costs are as follows.

Expected Costs	Home 1	Home 2	Home 3
Direct labor	$120,000	$180,000	$340,000
Direct materials	180,000	260,000	360,000

Assume Sudderth needs to allocate two major overhead costs ($80,000 of employee fringe benefits and $40,000 of indirect materials costs) among the three jobs.

Required

Choose an appropriate cost driver for each of the overhead costs and determine the total cost of each house.

EXERCISE 5–6A *Allocating to Smooth Cost Over Varying Levels of Production*

L.O. 3, 5

Production workers for Bakari Manufacturing Company provided 320 hours of labor in January and 480 hours in February. Bakari expects to use 4,000 hours of labor during the year. The rental fee for the manufacturing facility is $7,200 per month.

Required

Explain why allocation is needed. Based on this information, how much of the rental cost should be allocated to the products made in January and to those made in February?

EXERCISE 5–7A *Allocating to Solve a Timing Problem*

L.O. 3, 5

Production workers for Poole Manufacturing Company provided 2,700 hours of labor in January and 1,800 hours in February. The company, whose operation is labor intensive, expects to use 36,000 hours of labor during the year. Poole paid a $45,000 annual premium on July 1 of the prior year for an insurance policy that covers the manufacturing facility for the following 12 months.

Required

Explain why allocation is needed. Based on this information, how much of the insurance cost should be allocated to the products made in January and to those made in February?

EXERCISE 5–8A *Allocating to Solve a Timing Problem*

L.O. 3, 5

Coastal Air is a large airline company that pays a customer relations representative $4,000 per month. The representative, who processed 1,000 customer complaints in January and 1,300 complaints in February, is expected to process 16,000 customer complaints during 2007.

Required

a. Determine the total cost of processing customer complaints in January and in February.

b. Explain why allocating the cost of the customer relations representative would or would not be relevant to decision making.

EXERCISE 5–9A *Allocating Overhead Cost to Accomplish Smoothing*

L.O. 3, 5

Mimosa Corporation expects to incur indirect overhead costs of $72,000 per month and direct manufacturing costs of $11 per unit. The expected production activity for the first four months of 2007 is as follows.

	January	February	March	April
Estimated production in units	4,000	7,000	3,000	6,000

Required

a. Calculate a predetermined overhead rate based on the number of units of product expected to be made during the first four months of the year.

b. Allocate overhead costs to each month using the overhead rate computed in Requirement *a.*

c. Calculate the total cost per unit for each month using the overhead allocated in Requirement *b.*

L.O. 3, 5

EXERCISE 5–10A *Allocating Overhead for Product Costing*

Seiko Manufacturing Company produced 1,200 units of inventory in January 2005. It expects to produce an additional 8,400 units during the remaining 11 months of the year. In other words, total production for 2005 is estimated to be 9,600 units. Direct materials and direct labor costs are $64 and $52 per unit, respectively. Seiko Company expects to incur the following manufacturing overhead costs during the 2005 accounting period.

Production supplies	$ 4,800
Supervisor salary	192,000
Depreciation on equipment	144,000
Utilities	36,000
Rental fee on manufacturing facilities	96,000
Total	$472,800

Required

a. Determine the cost of the 1,200 units of product made in January.

b. Is the cost computed in Requirement *a* actual or estimated? Could Seiko improve accuracy by waiting until December to determine the cost of products? Identify two reasons that a manager would want to know the cost of products in January. Discuss the relationship between accuracy and relevance as it pertains to this problem.

L.O. 3, 5

EXERCISE 5–11A *How the Allocation of Fixed Cost Affects a Pricing Decision*

Barnhart Manufacturing Co. expects to make 48,000 chairs during the 2006 accounting period. The company made 8,000 chairs in January. Materials and labor costs for January were $32,000 and $48,000, respectively. Barnhart produced 3,000 chairs in February. Material and labor costs for February were $12,000 and $18,000, respectively. The company paid the $240,000 annual rental fee on its manufacturing facility on January 1, 2006.

Required

Assuming that Barnhart desires to sell its chairs for cost plus 30 percent of cost, what price should be charged for the chairs produced in January and February?

L.O. 6

EXERCISE 5–12A *Cost Pools*

McLaurin Department Stores, Inc. has three departments: women's, men's, and children's. The following are the indirect costs related to its operations:

Payroll taxes
Paper rolls for cash registers
Medical insurance
Salaries of secretaries
Water bill
Vacation pay
Sewer bill
Staples
Natural gas bill
Pens
Ink cartridges

Required

a. Organize the costs in the following three pools: indirect materials, indirect labor, and indirect utilities, assuming that each department is a cost object.

b. Identify an appropriate cost driver for each pool.

c. Explain why accountants use cost pools.

L.O. 3, 7

EXERCISE 5–13A *Allocating Joint Product Cost*

Mistrot Chemical Company makes three products, B217, K360, and X639, which are joint products from the same materials. In a standard batch of 150,000 pounds of raw materials, the company generates 35,000 pounds of B217, 75,000 pounds of K360, and 40,000 pounds of X639. A standard batch costs $1,800,000 to produce. The sales prices per pound are $8.00, $19.20, and $32.00 for B217, K360, and X639, respectively.

Required

a. Allocate the joint product cost among the three final products using weight as the allocation base.
b. Allocate the joint product cost among the three final products using market value as the allocation base.

Appendix

EXERCISE 5–14A *Human Factor*

L.O. 8

Brentwood Clinics provides medical care in three departments: internal medicine (IM), pediatrics (PD), and obstetrics gynecology (OB). The estimated costs to run each department follow:

	IM	PD	OB
Physicians	$400,000	$300,000	$200,000
Nurses	80,000	120,000	160,000

Brentwood expects to incur $360,000 of indirect (overhead) costs in the next fiscal year.

Required

a. Based on the information provided, name four allocation bases that could be used to assign the overhead cost to each department.
b. Assume the manager of each department is permitted to recommend how the overhead cost should be allocated to the departments. Which of the allocation bases named in Requirement *a* is the manager of OB most likely to recommend? Explain why. What argument may the manager of OB use to justify his choice of the allocation base?
c. Which of the allocation bases would result in the fairest allocation of the overhead cost from the perspective of the company president?
d. Explain how classifying overhead costs into separate pools could improve the fairness of the allocation of the overhead costs.

EXERCISE 5–15A *Allocating a Service Center Cost to Operating Departments*

L.O. 3, 9

Puya Corporation's computer services department assists two operating departments in using the company's information system effectively. The annual cost of computer services is $800,000. The production department employs 22 employees, and the sales department employs 18 employees. Puya uses the number of employees as the cost driver for allocating the cost of computer services to operating departments.

Required

Allocate the cost of computer services to operating departments.

EXERCISE 5–16A *Allocating Costs of Service Centers to Operating Departments—Step Method*

L.O. 3, 9

Nabors Health Care Center, Inc., has three clinics servicing the Birmingham metropolitan area. The company's legal services department supports the clinics. Moreover, its computer services department supports all of the clinics and the legal services department. The annual cost of operating the legal services department is $960,000. The annual cost of operating the computer services department is $480,000. The company uses the number of patients served as the cost driver for allocating the cost of legal services and the number of computer workstations as the cost driver for allocating the cost of computer services. Other relevant information follows.

	Number of Patients	Number of Workstations
Hoover clinic	6,000	15
Eastwood clinic	4,200	16
Gardendale clinic	5,800	12
Legal services		7
Computer services		10

Required

a. Allocate the cost of computer services to all of the clinics and the legal services department.
b. After allocating the cost of computer services, allocate the cost of legal services to the three clinics.
c. Compute the total allocated cost of service centers for each clinic.

L.O. 3, 9

EXERCISE 5–17A *Allocating Costs of Service Centers to Operating Departments—Direct Method*

Bently Trust Corporation has two service departments, actuary and economic analysis. Bently also has three operating departments, annuity, fund management, and employee benefit services. The annual costs of operating the service departments are $720,000 for actuary and $960,000 for economic analysis. Bently uses the direct method to allocate service center costs to operating departments. Other relevant data follow.

	Operating Costs*	Revenue
Annuity	$1,000,000	$1,680,000
Fund management	1,800,000	2,520,000
Employee benefit services	1,200,000	2,200,000

*The operating costs are measured before allocating service center costs.

Required

a. Use operating costs as the cost driver for allocating service center costs to operating departments.
b. Use revenue as the cost driver for allocating service center costs to operating departments.

PROBLEMS—SERIES A

All Problems in Series A are available with McGraw-Hill's Homework Manager

L.O. 1, 2, 3, 4, 5

excel www.mhhe.com/edmonds3e

CHECK FIGURE
a. (2) $590,000

PROBLEM 5–18A *Cost Accumulation and Allocation*

Belcher Manufacturing Company makes two different products, M and N. The company's two departments are named after the products; for example, Product M is made in Department M. Belcher's accountant has identified the following annual costs associated with these two products.

Financial data	
Salary of vice president of production division	$ 90,000
Salary of supervisor Department M	38,000
Salary of supervisor Department N	28,000
Direct materials cost Department M	150,000
Direct materials cost Department N	210,000
Direct labor cost Department M	120,000
Direct labor cost Department N	340,000
Direct utilities cost Department M	60,000
Direct utilities cost Department N	12,000
General factorywide utilities	18,000
Production supplies	18,000
Fringe benefits	69,000
Depreciation	360,000
Nonfinancial data	
Machine hours Department M	5,000
Machine hours Department N	1,000

Required

a. Identify the costs that are (1) direct costs of Department M, (2) direct costs of Department N, and (3) indirect costs.
b. Select the appropriate cost drivers for the indirect costs and allocate these costs to Departments M and N.
c. Determine the total estimated cost of the products made in Departments M and N. Assume that Belcher produced 2,000 units of Product M and 4,000 units of Product N during the year. If Belcher prices its products at cost plus 30 percent of cost, what price per unit must it charge for Product M and for Product N?

L.O. 1, 3, 4

PROBLEM 5–19A *Selecting an Appropriate Cost Driver (What Is the Base?)*

The Newman School of Vocational Technology has organized the school training programs into three departments. Each department provides training in a different area as follows: nursing assistant, dental hygiene, and office technology. The school's owner, Lucy Newman, wants to know how much it costs to operate each of the three departments. To accumulate the total cost for each department, the accountant has identified several indirect costs that must be allocated to each. These costs are $15,750 of phone expense, $3,360 of office supplies, $864,000 of office rent, $96,000 of janitorial services, and $72,000 of salary paid to the dean of students. To provide a reasonably accurate allocation of costs, the accountant has identified several possible cost drivers. These drivers and their association with each department follow.

Cost Driver	Department 1	Department 2	Department 3
Number of telephones	28	16	19
Number of faculty members	20	16	12
Square footage of office space	24,000	14,000	10,000
Number of secretaries	2	2	2

Required

a. Identify the appropriate cost objects.
b. Identify the appropriate cost driver for each indirect cost and compute the allocation rate for assigning each indirect cost to the cost objects.
c. Determine the amount of telephone expense that should be allocated to each of the three departments.
d. Determine the amount of supplies expense that should be allocated to Department 3.
e. Determine the amount of office rent that should be allocated to Department 2.
f. Determine the amount of janitorial services cost that should be allocated to Department 1.
g. Identify two cost drivers not listed here that could be used to allocate the cost of the dean's salary to the three departments.

L.O. 1, 2

PROBLEM 5–20A *Cost Allocation in a Service Industry*

CHECK FIGURES
b. To SF: $1,114;
To Chi: $546

Eagle Airlines is a small airline that occasionally carries overload shipments for the overnight delivery company Never-Fail, Inc. Never-Fail is a multimillion-dollar company started by Peter Never immediately after he failed to finish his first accounting course. The company's motto is "We Never-Fail to Deliver Your Package on Time." When Never-Fail has more freight than it can deliver, it pays Eagle to carry the excess. Eagle contracts with independent pilots to fly its planes on a per trip basis. Eagle recently purchased an airplane that cost the company $6,000,000. The plane has an estimated useful life of 100,000,000 miles and a zero salvage value. During the first week in January, Eagle flew two trips. The first trip was a round trip flight from Chicago to San Francisco, for which Eagle paid $500 for the pilot and $350 for fuel. The second flight was a round trip from Chicago to New York. For this trip, it paid $300 for the pilot and $150 for fuel. The round trip between Chicago and San Francisco is approximately 4,400 miles and the round trip between Chicago and New York is 1,600 miles.

Required

a. Identify the direct and indirect costs that Eagle incurs for each trip.
b. Determine the total cost of each trip.
c. In addition to depreciation, identify three other indirect costs that may need to be allocated to determine the cost of each trip.

L.O. 1, 3, 4

PROBLEM 5–21A *Cost Allocation in a Manufacturing Company*

McCord Manufacturing Company makes tents that it sells directly to camping enthusiasts through a mail-order marketing program. The company pays a quality control expert $75,000 per year to inspect completed tents before they are shipped to customers. Assume that the company completed 1,600 tents in January and 1,200 tents in February. For the entire year, the company expects to produce 15,000 tents.

CHECK FIGURES
d. Jan.: $8,000
Feb.: $6,000

Required

a. Explain how changes in the cost driver (number of tents inspected) affect the total amount of fixed inspection cost.
b. Explain how changes in the cost driver (number of tents inspected) affect the amount of fixed inspection cost per unit.
c. If the cost objective is to determine the cost per tent, is the expert's salary a direct or an indirect cost?
d. How much of the expert's salary should be allocated to tents produced in January and February?

L.O. 1, 4, 8

excel
www.mhhe.com/edmonds3e

PROBLEM 5–22A *Fairness in the Allocation Process*

Foreman Manufacturing Company uses two departments to make its products. Department I is a cutting department that is machine intensive and uses very few employees. Machines cut and form parts and then place the finished parts on a conveyor belt that carries them to Department II where they are assembled into finished goods. The assembly department is labor intensive and requires many workers to assemble parts into finished goods. The company's manufacturing facility incurs two significant overhead costs, employee fringe benefits and utility costs. The annual costs of fringe benefits are $504,000 and utility costs are $360,000. The typical consumption patterns for the two departments are as follows.

	Department I	Department II	Total
Machine hours used	16,000	4,000	20,000
Direct labor hours used	5,000	13,000	18,000

The supervisor of each department receives a bonus based on how well the department controls costs. The company's current policy requires using a single activity base (machine hours or labor hours) to allocate the total overhead cost of $864,000.

Required

a. Assume that you are the supervisor of Department I. Choose the allocation base that would minimize your department's share of the total overhead cost. Calculate the amount of overhead that would be allocated to both departments using the base that you selected.

b. Assume that you are the supervisor of Department II. Choose the allocation base that would minimize your department's share of the total overhead cost. Calculate the amount of overhead that would be allocated to both departments using the base that you selected.

c. Assume that you are the plant manager and have the authority to change the company's overhead allocation policy. Formulate an overhead allocation policy that would be fair to the supervisors of both Department I and Department II. Compute the overhead allocations for each department using your policy.

L.O. 1, 3, 5

PROBLEM 5–23A *Allocation to Accomplish Smoothing*

CHECK FIGURES
a. $5.60
c. March: $59.20

Roddick Corporation estimated its overhead costs would be $36,000 per month except for January when it pays the $72,000 annual insurance premium on the manufacturing facility. Accordingly, the January overhead costs were expected to be $108,000 ($72,000 + $36,000). The company expected to use 7,000 direct labor hours per month except during July, August, and September when the company expected 9,000 hours of direct labor each month to build inventories for high demand that normally occurs during the Christmas season. The company's actual direct labor hours were the same as the estimated hours. The company made 3,500 units of product in each month except July, August, and September in which it produced 4,500 units each month. Direct labor costs were $29 per unit, and direct materials costs were $19 per unit.

Required

a. Calculate a predetermined overhead rate based on direct labor hours.

b. Determine the total allocated overhead cost for January, March, and August.

c. Determine the cost per unit of product for January, March, and August.

d. Determine the selling price for the product, assuming that the company desires to earn a gross margin of $20 per unit.

L.O. 1, 3, 5

PROBLEM 5–24A *Allocating Indirect Costs Between Products*

CHECK FIGURES
a. Cost/unit for EZRecords: $225
b. Cost/unit for ProOffice: $230

Dana Helton is considering expanding her business. She plans to hire a salesperson to cover trade shows. Because of compensation, travel expenses, and booth rental, fixed costs for a trade show are expected to be $15,000. The booth will be open 30 hours during the trade show. Ms. Helton also plans to add a new product line, ProOffice, which will cost $180 per package. She will continue to sell the existing product, EZRecords, which costs $100 per package. Ms. Helton believes that the salesperson will spend approximately 20 hours selling EZRecords and 10 hours marketing ProOffice.

Required

a. Determine the estimated total cost and cost per unit of each product, assuming that the salesperson is able to sell 80 units of EZRecords and 50 units of ProOffice.

b. Determine the estimated total cost and cost per unit of each product, assuming that the salesperson is able to sell 200 units of EZRecords and 100 units of ProOffice.

c. Explain why the cost per unit figures calculated in Requirement *a* are different from the amounts calculated in Requirement *b.* Also explain how the differences in estimated cost per unit will affect pricing decisions.

PROBLEM 5–25A *Allocating Joint Product Cost*

L.O. 3, 7

CHECK FIGURES
a. GM for drumsticks: $(980)
b. Total cost of breasts: $7,087.50

Merkle Chicken, Inc., processes and packages chicken for grocery stores. It purchases chickens from farmers and processes them into two different products: chicken drumsticks and chicken steak. From a standard batch of 12,000 pounds of raw chicken that costs $7,000, the company produces two parts: 2,800 pounds of drumsticks and 4,200 pounds of breast for a processing cost of $2,450. The chicken breast is further processed into 3,200 pounds of steak for a processing cost of $2,000. The market price of drumsticks per pound is $1.00 and the market price per pound of chicken steak is $3.40. If Merkle decided to sell chicken breast instead of steak, the price per pound would be $2.00.

Required

a. Allocate the joint cost to the joint products, drumsticks and breasts, using weight as the allocation base. Calculate the net income for each product. Since the drumsticks are producing a net loss, should that product line be eliminated?

b. Reallocate the joint cost to the joint products, drumsticks and breasts, using relative market values as the allocation base. Calculate the net income for each product. Compare the total net income (drumsticks + breasts) computed in Requirement *b* with that computed in Requirement *a* above. Explain why the total amount is the same. Comment on which allocation base (weight or market value) is more appropriate.

c. Should you further process chicken breasts into chicken steak?

Appendix

PROBLEM 5–26A *Allocating Service Center Costs—Step Method and Direct Method*

L.O. 3, 9

excel
www.mhhe.com/edmonds3e

CHECK FIGURES
a. Allocated cost from Billing to Retail: $567,300
b. Allocated cost from HR to LS: $192,000

Logan Information Services, Inc., has two service departments, human resources and billing. Logan's operating departments, organized according to the special industry each department serves, are health care, retail, and legal services. The billing department supports only the three operating departments, but the human resources department supports all operating departments and the billing department. Other relevant information follows.

	Human Resources	Billing	Health Care	Retail	Legal Services
Number of employees	30	60	120	100	80
Annual cost*	$720,000	$1,710,000	$6,000,000	$4,800,000	$2,800,000
Annual revenue	—	—	$9,000,000	$6,200,000	$4,800,000

*This is the operating cost before allocating service department costs.

Required

a. Allocate service department costs to operating departments, assuming that Logan adopts the step method. The company uses the number of employees as the base for allocating human resources department costs and department annual revenue as the base for allocating the billing department costs.

b. Allocate service department costs to operating departments, assuming that Logan adopts the direct method. The company uses the number of employees as the base for allocating the human resources department costs and department annual revenue as the base for allocating the billing department costs.

c. Compute the total allocated cost of service centers for each operating department using each allocation method.

EXERCISES—SERIES B

EXERCISE 5–1B *Allocating Costs Between Divisions*

L.O. 1, 3

Thornton and Hart, LLP, has three departments: auditing, tax, and information systems. The departments occupy 2,500 square feet, 1,500 square feet, and 1,000 square feet of office space, respectively. The firm pays $9,000 per month to rent its offices.

Required

How much monthly rent cost should Thornton and Hart allocate to each department?

L.O. 2

EXERCISE 5–2B *Direct Versus Indirect Costs*

Kackle and Associates LLP is an accounting firm that provides two major types of professional services: (1) tax services as provided by the tax department and (2) auditing services as provided by the audit department. Each department has numerous clients. Engagement with each individual client is a separate service (i.e., product) and each department has several engagements in each period. Cost items of the firm follow.

Salary of the partner in charge of the audit department
Salary of the managing partner of the firm
Cost of office supplies such as paper, pencils, erasers, etc.
Depreciation of computers used in the tax department
License fees of the firm
Professional labor of a tax engagement
Secretarial labor supporting both departments
Professional labor of an audit engagement
Depreciation of computers used in the audit department
Salary of the partner in charge of the tax department
Travel expenditures of an audit engagement

Required

a. Identify each cost as being a direct or indirect cost assuming the cost objects are the individual engagements (audit engagements or tax engagements).
b. Identify each cost as being a direct or indirect cost assuming the cost objects are the two departments.
c. Identify each cost as being a direct or indirect cost assuming the cost object is Kackle and Associates LLP as a whole.

L.O. 3, 5

EXERCISE 5–3B *Allocating Overhead Costs Among Products*

Ager, Inc., manufactures three different sizes of automobile sunscreens, large, medium, and small. Ager expects to incur $720,000 of overhead costs during the next fiscal year. Other budget information for the coming year follows:

	Large	Medium	Small	Total
Direct labor hours	2,500	5,000	4,500	12,000
Machine hours	700	1,300	1,000	3,000

Required

a. Use direct labor hours as the cost driver to compute the allocation rate and the budgeted overhead cost for each product.
b. Use machine hours as the cost driver to compute the allocation rate and the budgeted overhead cost for each product.
c. Describe a set of circumstances where it would be more appropriate to use direct labor hours as the allocation base.
d. Describe a set of circumstances where it would be more appropriate to use machine hours as the allocation base.

L.O. 3, 4

EXERCISE 5–4B *Allocating Overhead Costs Among Products*

Fraser Company makes three models of computer disks in its factory, Zip100, Zip250, and Zip40. The expected overhead costs for the next fiscal year are as follows:

Payroll for factory managers	$270,000
Factory maintenance costs	110,000
Factory insurance	40,000
Total overhead costs	$420,000

Fraser uses labor hours as the cost driver to allocate overhead cost. Budgeted labor hours for the products are as follows:

Zip100	2,000 hours
Zip250	1,300
Zip40	900
Total labor hours	4,200

Required

a. Allocate the budgeted overhead costs to the products.

b. Provide a possible explanation as to why Fraser chose labor hours, instead of machine hours, as allocation base.

EXERCISE 5–5B *Allocating Costs Among Products*

L.O. 3, 4

Pillson Company makes household plastic bags in three different sizes, Snack, Sandwich, and Storage. The estimated direct materials and direct labor costs are as follows.

Expected Costs	Snack	Sandwich	Storage
Direct materials	$140,000	$235,000	$375,000
Direct labor	60,000	120,000	240,000

Pillson allocates two major overhead costs among the three products: $72,000 of indirect labor cost for workers who move various materials and products to different stations in the factory and $126,000 of employee pension costs.

Required

Determine the total cost of each product.

EXERCISE 5–6B *Allocating Indirect Cost Over Varying Levels of Production*

L.O. 3, 5

Malone Company's annual factory depreciation is $18,000. Malone estimated it would operate the factory a total of 2,400 hours this year. The factory operated 200 hours in November and 150 hours in December.

Required

Why would Malone need to allocate factory depreciation cost? How much depreciation cost should Malone allocate to products made in November and those made in December?

EXERCISE 5–7B *Allocating Indirect Cost Over Varying Levels of Production*

L.O. 3, 5

On January 1, Kinzey Corporation paid the annual royalty of $810,000 for rights to use patented technology to make batteries for laptop computers. Kinzey plans to use the patented technology to produce five different models of batteries. Kinzey uses machine hours as a common cost driver and plans to operate its machines 54,000 hours in the coming year. The company used 3,000 machine hours in June and 3,600 hours in July.

Required

Why would Kinzey need to allocate the annual royalty payment rather than simply assign it in total to January production? How much of the royalty cost should Kinzey allocate to products made in June and those made in July?

EXERCISE 5–8B *Allocating a Fixed Cost*

L.O. 3, 5

Last year, Hermit Nassar bought an automobile for $29,000 to use in his taxi business. He expected to drive the vehicle for 150,000 miles before disposing of it for $2,000. Hermit drove 3,200 miles this week and 2,800 miles last week.

Required

a. Determine the total cost of vehicle depreciation this week and last week.

b. Explain why allocating the vehicle cost would or would not be relevant to decision making.

EXERCISE 5–9B *Allocating Overhead Cost to Accomplish Smoothing*

L.O. 3, 5

In 2007, Harris Corporation incurred direct manufacturing costs of $30 per unit and manufacturing overhead costs of $270,000. The production activity for the four quarters of 2007 follows:

	1st Quarter	2nd Quarter	3rd Quarter	4th Quarter
Number of units produced	3,300	2,700	4,500	2,000

Required

a. Calculate a predetermined overhead rate based on the number of units produced during the year.

b. Allocate overhead costs to each quarter using the overhead rate computed in Requirement *a.*

c. Using the overhead allocation determined in Requirement *b,* calculate the total cost per unit for each quarter.

L.O. 3, 5

EXERCISE 5–10B *Allocating Overhead for Product Costing*

Tricon Manufacturing Company produced 500 units of inventory in January 2006. The company expects to produce an additional 5,900 units of inventory during the remaining 11 months of the year, for total estimated production of 6,400 units in 2006. Direct materials and direct labor costs are $74 and $84 per unit, respectively. Tricon expects to incur the following manufacturing overhead costs during the 2006 accounting period:

Indirect materials	$ 6,800
Depreciation on equipment	104,000
Utilities cost	29,200
Salaries of plant manager and staff	304,000
Rental fee on manufacturing facilities	84,000
Total	$528,000

Required

a. Determine the estimated cost of the 500 units of product made in January.

b. Is the cost computed in Requirement *a* actual or estimated? Could Tricon improve accuracy by waiting until December to determine the cost of products? Identify two reasons that a manager would want to know the cost of products in January. Discuss the relationship between accuracy and relevance as it pertains to this problem.

L.O. 3, 5

EXERCISE 5–11B *How Fixed Cost Allocation Affects a Pricing Decision*

Sonola Manufacturing Company expects to make 45,000 travel sewing kits during 2005. In January, the company made 1,800 kits. Materials and labor costs for January were $7,200 and $9,000, respectively. In February, Sonola produced 2,200 kits. Material and labor costs for February were $8,800 and $11,000, respectively. The company paid $54,000 for annual factory insurance on January 10, 2005. Ignore other manufacturing overhead costs.

Required

Assuming that Sonola desires to sell its sewing kits for cost plus 25 percent of cost, what price should it charge for the kits produced in January and February?

L.O. 6

EXERCISE 5–12B *Cost Pools*

Wilson Furniture Company incurred the following costs in the process of making tables and chairs.

Glue	Paint
Supervisor salaries	Water bill
Gas bill	Vacation pay
Payroll taxes	Sewer bill
Cost of nails	Staples
Medical insurance	Electric bill

Required

a. Organize the costs in the following three pools: indirect materials, indirect labor, and indirect utilities.

b. Identify an appropriate cost driver for each pool.

c. Explain why accountants use cost pools.

L.O. 3, 7

EXERCISE 5–13B *Allocating Joint Product Cost*

Bailey Food Corporation makes two products from soybeans, cooking oil and cattle feed. From a standard batch of 100,000 pounds of soybeans, Bailey produces 20,000 pounds of cooking oil and 80,000 pounds of cattle feed. Producing a standard batch costs $12,000. The sales prices per pound are $1.20 for cooking oil and $0.90 for cattle feed.

Required

a. Allocate the joint product cost to the two products using weight as the allocation base.
b. Allocate the joint product cost to the two products using market value as the allocation base.

Appendix

EXERCISE 5–14B *Human Factor* L.O. 8

Kramer Company builds custom sailboats. Kramer currently has three boats under construction. The estimated costs to complete each boat are shown below.

	Boat 1	Boat 2	Boat 3
Direct materials	$25,000	$32,000	$12,000
Direct labor	22,000	20,000	14,000

Kramer expects to incur $36,000 of indirect (overhead) costs in the process of making the boats.

Required

a. Based on the information provided, name four allocation bases that could be used to assign the overhead costs to each boat.
b. Assume that the production manager of each boat is permitted to recommend how the overhead costs should be allocated to the boats. Which of the allocation bases named in Requirement *a* is the manager of Boat 2 most likely to recommend? Explain why. What argument may the manager of Boat 2 use to justify his choice of the allocation base?
c. Which of the allocation bases would result in the fairer allocation of the overhead costs from the perspective of the company president?
d. Explain how classifying overhead costs into separate pools could improve the fairness of the allocation of the overhead costs.

EXERCISE 5–15B *Allocating a Service Center Cost to Operating Departments* L.O. 3, 9

The administrative department of Steeler Consulting, LLC, provides office administration and professional support to its two operating departments. Annual administrative costs are $900,000. In 2008, the hours chargeable to clients generated by the information services department and the financial planning department were 24,000 and 36,000, respectively. Steeler uses chargeable hours as the cost driver for allocating administrative costs to operating departments.

Required

Allocate the administrative costs to the two operating departments.

EXERCISE 5–16B *Allocating Service Centers' Costs to Operating Departments—Step Method* L.O. 3, 9

Bearden Consulting, LLP, has three operating departments: tax, estate planning, and small business. The company's internal accounting and maintenance departments support the operating departments. Moreover, the maintenance department also supports the internal accounting department. Other relevant information follows:

	Annual Cost*	Square Feet	Operating Revenue
Tax	$4,800,000	8,000	$8,500,000
Estate planning	2,300,000	2,000	3,500,000
Small business	3,000,000	4,000	6,000,000
Internal accounting	690,000	1,000	0
Maintenance	450,000	1,000	0

*The annual cost figures do not include costs allocated from service departments.

Bearden allocates its maintenance cost based on the square footage of each department's office space. The firm allocates the internal accounting cost based on each department's operating revenue.

Required

a. Allocate the maintenance cost to the operating and internal accounting departments.

b. After allocating the maintenance cost, allocate the internal accounting cost to the three operating departments.
c. Compute the total allocated cost of the service departments for each operating department.

L.O. 3, 9

EXERCISE 5–17B *Allocating Service Centers' Costs to Operating Departments—Direct Method*

Wang Corporation, a book publisher, has two service departments, editing and typesetting. Wang also has three operating departments, children's fiction, youth fiction, and adult fiction. The annual costs of operating the editing department are $240,000 and of operating the typesetting department are $420,000. Wang uses the direct method to allocate service center costs to operating departments. Other relevant data follow.

	Number of Pages	Number of Hours
Children	14,000	5,000
Youth	10,000	8,000
Adult	16,000	7,000

Required
a. Allocate the service center costs to the operating departments using the number of pages as the cost driver.
b. Allocate the service center costs to the operating departments using the number of hours as the cost driver.

PROBLEMS—SERIES B

L.O. 1, 2, 3, 4, 5

PROBLEM 5–18B *Cost Accumulation and Allocation*

Ridgewood Tools Company has two production departments in its manufacturing facilities. Home tools specializes in hand tools for individual home users, and professional tools makes sophisticated tools for professional maintenance workers. Ridgewood's accountant has identified the following annual costs associated with these two products:

Financial data	
Salary of vice president of production	$180,000
Salary of manager, home tools	54,000
Salary of manager, professional tools	43,500
Direct materials cost, home tools	300,000
Direct materials cost, professional tools	375,000
Direct labor cost, home tools	336,000
Direct labor cost, professional tools	414,000
Direct utilities cost, home tools	75,000
Direct utilities cost, professional tools	30,000
General factorywide utilities	31,500
Production supplies	40,500
Fringe benefits	112,500
Depreciation	360,000
Nonfinancial data	
Machine hours, home tools	4,000
Machine hours, professional tools	2,000

Required
a. Identify the costs that are the (1) direct costs of home tools, (2) direct costs of professional tools, and (3) indirect costs.
b. Select the appropriate cost drivers and allocate the indirect costs to home tools and to professional tools.
c. Assume that each department makes only a single product. Home tools produces its Deluxe Drill for home use, and professional tools produces the Professional Drill. The company made 30,000 units of Deluxe Drill and 40,000 units of Professional Drill during the year. Determine the total estimated cost of the products made in each department. If Ridgewood prices its products at cost plus 30 percent of cost, what price per unit must it charge for the Deluxe Drill and the Professional Drill?

PROBLEM 5–19B *Selecting an Appropriate Cost Driver (What Is the Base?)* **L.O. 1, 3, 4**

Perrion Research Institute has three departments, biology, chemistry, and physics. The institute's controller wants to estimate the cost of operating each department. He has identified several indirect costs that must be allocated to each department including $22,400 of phone expense, $4,800 of office supplies, $2,240,000 of office rent, $280,000 of janitorial services, and $300,000 of salary paid to the director. To provide a reasonably accurate allocation of costs, the controller identified several possible cost drivers. These drivers and their association with each department follow.

Cost Driver	Biology	Chemistry	Physics
Number of telephones	20	28	32
Number of researchers	16	20	24
Square footage of office space	8,000	8,000	12,000
Number of secretaries	1	1	1

Required

a. Identify the appropriate cost objects.
b. Identify the appropriate cost driver for each indirect cost, and compute the allocation rate for assigning each indirect cost to the cost objects.
c. Determine the amount of telephone expense that should be allocated to each of the three departments.
d. Determine the amount of supplies expense that should be allocated to the physics department.
e. Determine the amount of office rent cost that should be allocated to the chemistry department.
f. Determine the amount of janitorial services cost that should be allocated to the biology department.
g. Identify two cost drivers not listed here that could be used to allocate the cost of the director's salary to the three departments.

PROBLEM 5–20B *Cost Allocation in a Service Industry* **L.O. 1, 2**

Solarz, Adams, and Associates provides legal services for its local community. In addition to its regular attorneys, the firm hires some part-time attorneys to handle small cases. Two secretaries assist all part-time attorneys exclusively. In 2009, the firm paid $48,000 for the two secretaries who worked a total of 3,200 hours. Moreover, the firm paid Sue Rivera $60 per hour and Tim Gasden $50 per hour for their part-time legal services.

In August 2009, Ms. Rivera completed a case that took her 60 hours. Mr. Gasden finished a case on which he worked 20 hours. The firm also paid a private investigator to uncover relevant facts. The investigation fees cost $1,000 for Ms. Rivera's case and $750 for Mr. Gasden's case. Ms. Rivera used 30 hours of secretarial assistance, and Mr. Gasden used 40 hours.

Required

a. Identify the direct and indirect costs incurred in each case completed in August 2009.
b. Determine the total cost of each case.
c. In addition to secretaries' salaries, identify three other indirect costs that may need to be allocated to determine the cost of the cases.

PROBLEM 5–21B *Cost Allocation in a Manufacturing Company* **L.O. 1, 3, 4**

Calla's Doors, Inc., makes a particular type of door. The labor cost is $120 per door and the material cost is $200 per door. Calla's rents a factory building for $84,000 a month. Calla's plans to produce 24,000 doors annually. In March and April, it made 2,000 and 3,000 doors, respectively.

Required

a. Explain how changes in the cost driver (number of doors made) affect the total amount of fixed rental cost.
b. Explain how changes in the cost driver (number of doors made) affect the fixed rental cost per unit.
c. If the cost objective is to determine the cost per door, is the factory rent a direct or an indirect cost?
d. How much of the factory rent should be allocated to doors produced in March and April?

PROBLEM 5–22B *Fairness in the Allocation Process* **L.O. 1, 4, 8**

Hillshire Furniture Company has two production departments. The parts department uses automated machinery to make parts; as a result, it uses very few employees. The assembly department is labor intensive because workers manually assemble parts into finished furniture. Employee fringe benefits and utility costs are the two major overhead costs of the company's production division. The fringe benefits and utility costs for the year are $600,000 and $288,000, respectively. The typical consumption patterns for the two departments follow.

	Parts	Assembly	Total
Machine hours used	52,000	8,000	60,000
Direct labor hours used	3,500	20,500	24,000

The supervisor of each department receives a bonus based on how well the department controls costs. The company's current policy requires using a single activity base (machine hours or labor hours) to allocate the total overhead cost of $888,000.

Required

a. Assume that you are the parts department supervisor. Choose the allocation base that would minimize your department's share of the total overhead cost. Calculate the amount of overhead to allocate to both departments using the base that you selected.

b. Assume that you are the assembly department supervisor. Choose the allocation base that would minimize your department's share of the total overhead cost. Calculate the amount of overhead to allocate to both departments using the base that you selected.

c. Assume that you are the plant manager and that you have the authority to change the company's overhead allocation policy. Formulate an overhead allocation policy that would be fair to the supervisors of both the parts and assembly departments. Compute the overhead allocation for each department using your policy.

L.O. 1, 3, 5

PROBLEM 5–23B *Allocation to Accomplish Smoothing*

Zivago Corporation's overhead costs are usually $48,000 per month. However, the company pays $108,000 of real estate tax on the factory facility in March. Thus, the overhead costs for March increase to $156,000. The company normally uses 5,000 direct labor hours per month except for August, September, and October, in which the company requires 9,000 hours of direct labor per month to build inventories for high demand in the Christmas season. Last year, the company's actual direct labor hours were the same as usual. The company made 5,000 units of product in each month except August, September, and October in which it produced 9,000 units per month. Direct labor costs were $16 per unit; direct materials costs were $14 per unit.

Required

a. Calculate a predetermined overhead rate based on direct labor hours.

b. Determine the total allocated overhead cost for the months of March, August, and December.

c. Determine the cost per unit of product for the months of March, August, and December.

d. Determine the selling price for the product, assuming that the company desires to earn a gross margin of $10 per unit.

L.O. 1, 3, 5

PROBLEM 5–24B *Allocating Indirect Cost Between Products*

Darcy Corporation has hired a marketing representative to sell the company's two products, Marvelous and Wonderful. The representative's total salary and fringe benefits are $8,000 monthly. The product cost is $90 per unit for Marvelous and $144 per unit for Wonderful. Darey expects the representative to spend 48 hours per month marketing Marvelous and 112 hours promoting Wonderful.

Required

a. Determine the estimated total cost and cost per unit, assuming that the representative is able to sell 100 units of Marvelous and 70 units of Wonderful in a month. Allocate indirect cost on the basis of labor hours.

b. Determine the estimated total cost and cost per unit, assuming that the representative is able to sell 250 units of Marvelous and 140 units of Wonderful. Allocate indirect cost on the basis of labor hours.

c. Explain why the cost per unit figures calculated in Requirement *a* differ from the amounts calculated in Requirement *b*. Also explain how the differences in estimated cost per unit will affect pricing decisions.

L.O. 3, 9

PROBLEM 5–25B *Allocating Joint Product Cost*

Yu-San Tea Co. makes two products: a high-grade tea branded Wulong and a low-grade tea branded San Tea for the Asian market. Yu-San purchases tea leaves from tea firms in mountainous villages of Taiwan and processes the tea leaves into a high-quality product. The tea leaves are dried and baked in the manufacturing process. Yu-San pays farmers $600 for 900 kilograms of tea leaves. For 900 kilograms of green leaves, the company can produce 100 kilograms of Wulong and 200 kilograms of tea fragments including dried leave stems and broken dried leaves. The cost of this process is $300 per batch. The tea fragments are packaged into San Tea. The market price for San Tea is $2.00 per kilogram. The market price is $20 per kilogram for Wulong. Yu-San has an option of taking an additional process to refine the 100 kilograms of Wulong into 30 kilograms of Donding, a prestigious brand. The market price of Donding is $100 per kilogram. The cost of the additional process is $250 per batch.

Required

a. Allocate the joint cost to the joint products, Wulong and San Tea, using weight as the allocation base. Calculate the net income for each product. Since the San Tea is sold at a loss, should that product line be eliminated?

b. Allocate the joint cost to the joint products, Wulong and San Tea, using relative market value as the allocation base. Calculate the net income for each product. Compare the total net income (Wulong + San Tea) computed in Requirement *b* with that computed in Requirement *a* above. Explain why the total amount is the same. Comment on which allocation base (weight or relative market value) is more appropriate.

c. Should you further process Wulong into Donding?

Appendix

PROBLEM 5–26B ***Allocating Service Center Costs—Step Method and Direct Method*** **L.O. 3, 9**

Alabaster Corporation has three production departments, forming, assembly, and packaging. The maintenance department supports only the production departments; the computer services department supports all departments including maintenance. Other relevant information follows.

	Forming	Assembly	Packaging	Maintenance	Computer Services
Machine hours	12,000	5,000	3,000	800	0
Number of computers	14	20	11	15	8
Annual cost*	$450,000	$800,000	$250,000	$100,000	$90,000

*This is the annual operating cost before allocating service department costs.

Required

a. Allocate service department costs to operating departments, assuming that Alabaster adopts the step method. The company uses the number of computers as the base for allocating the computer services costs and machine hours as the base for allocating the maintenance costs.

b. Use machine hours as the base for allocating maintenance department costs and the number of computers as the base for allocating computer services cost. Allocate service department costs to operating departments, assuming that Alabaster adopts the direct method.

c. Compute the total allocated cost of service centers for each operating department using each allocation method.

ANALYZE, THINK, COMMUNICATE

BUSINESS APPLICATIONS CASE ***Allocating Fixed Costs*** **ATC 5–1**

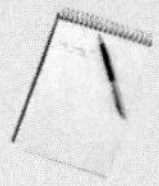

Peixoto Company pays $5,000 per month to rent its manufacturing facility. Peixoto estimates total production volume for 2006 to be 20,000 units of product. The company actually produced 1,500 units of product during January and 1,800 units in February.

Required

a. Indicate whether the rent charge is a

(1) Product or general, selling, and administrative (G,S&A) cost.

(2) Relevant cost with respect to a special order decision.

(3) Fixed or variable cost relative to the volume of production.

(4) Direct or indirect if the cost object is the cost of products made in January.

b. With respect to the rent charge, determine the total cost and the cost per unit of products made in January and February.

c. Assuming that actual production in 2006 is 21,000 units, indicate whether the cost of the January production determined in Requirement *b* is over- or understated.

d. Assume that the information computed in Requirement *b* was used to price Peixoto's product in 2006. Furthermore, assume that management used the price estimates to project income and that the income projections were used in public announcements to stock analysts. Finally, assume that actual production was 21,000 units. Indicate whether year-end net income is likely to be higher or lower than management forecasts. Describe the likely impact on Peixoto's stock price and executive stock option incentive program.

ATC 5–2 GROUP ASSIGNMENT *Selection of the Cost Driver*

Vulcan College School of Business is divided into three departments, accounting, marketing, and management. Relevant information for each of the departments follows.

Cost Driver	Accounting	Marketing	Management
Number of students	1,400	800	400
Number of classes per semester	64	36	28
Number of professors	20	24	10

Vulcan is a private school that expects each department to generate a profit. It rewards departments for profitability by assigning 20 percent of each department's profits back to that department. Departments have free rein as to how to use these funds. Some departments have used them to supply professors with computer technology. Others have expanded their travel budgets. The practice has been highly successful in motivating the faculty to control costs. The revenues and direct costs for the year 2004 follow.

	Accounting	Marketing	Management
Revenue	$29,600,000	$16,600,000	$8,300,000
Direct costs	24,600,000	13,800,000	6,600,000

Vulcan allocates to the School of Business $4,492,800 of indirect overhead costs such as administrative salaries and costs of operating the registrar's office and the bookstore.

Required

a. Divide the class into groups and organize the groups into three sections. Assign each section a department. For example, groups in Section 1 should represent the Accounting Department. Groups in Sections 2 and 3 should represent the Marketing Department and Management Department, respectively. Assume that the dean of the school is planning to assign an equal amount of the college overhead to each department. Have the students in each group prepare a response to the dean's plan. Each group should select a spokesperson who is prepared to answer the following questions.
(1) Is your group in favor of or opposed to the allocation plan suggested by the dean?
(2) Does the plan suggested by the dean provide a fair allocation? Why?
The instructor should lead a discussion designed to assess the appropriateness of the dean's proposed allocation plan.

b. Have each group select the cost driver (allocation base) that best serves the self-interest of the department it represents.

c. Consensus on Requirement *c* should be achieved before completing Requirement *d.* Each group should determine the amount of the indirect cost to be allocated to each department using the cost driver that best serves the self-interest of the department it represents. Have a spokesperson from each section go to the board and show the income statement that would result for each department.

d. Discuss the development of a cost driver(s) that would promote fairness rather than self-interest in allocating the indirect costs.

ATC 5–3 RESEARCH ASSIGNMENT *Cost Accounting Issues at Real-World Companies*

The July 2003 issue of *Strategic Finance* contains the article "Roles and Practices in Management Accounting Today: Results From the 2003 IMA-E&Y Survey" written by Ashish Garg, Debashis Ghosh,

James Hudick, and Chwen Nowacki. This article reviews findings from a survey of managerial accountants conducted by the Institute of Management Accountants (IMA). Read this article and complete the following requirements.

Required

a. The article notes that cost management is an important element for strategic decision making. Why did respondents to the survey believe this was the case?

b. The authors noted that decision makers were most interested in "actionable" cost information. What are the attributes of actionable cost information?

c. Ninety-eight percent of respondents to the survey said that factors exist that cause distortions of cost information. What factors were identified that are responsible for these distortions?

d. Considering the proliferation of "off the shelf" software that is available, many people believe only a minority of companies develop their own cost management systems. According to the article, what percentage of companies actually do develop their systems "in house," and what do you think are the implications of the in-house development for managerial accountants?

WRITING ASSIGNMENT *Selection of the Appropriate Cost Driver*

ATC 5–4

Bullions Enterprises, Inc. (BEI), makes gold, silver, and bronze medals used to recognize outstanding athletic performance in regional and national sporting events. The per unit direct costs of producing the medals follows.

	Gold	Silver	Bronze
Direct materials	$300	$130	$ 35
Labor	120	120	120

During 2002, BEI made 1,200 units of each type of medal for a total of 3,600 (1,200 × 3) medals. All medals are created through the same production process, and they are packaged and shipped in identical containers. Indirect overhead costs amounted to $324,000. BEI currently uses the number of units as the cost driver for the allocation of overhead cost. As a result, BEI allocated $90 ($324,000 ÷ 3,600 units) of overhead cost to each medal produced.

Required

The president of the company has questioned the wisdom of assigning the same amount of overhead to each type of medal. He believes that overhead should be assigned on the basis of the cost to produce the medals. In other words, more overhead should be charged to expensive gold medals, less to silver, and even less to bronze. Assume that you are BEI's chief financial officer. Write a memo responding to the president's suggestion.

ETHICAL DILEMMA *Allocation to Achieve Fairness*

ATC 5–5

The American Acupuncture Association offers continuing professional education courses for its members at its annual meeting. Instructors are paid a fee for each student attending their courses but are charged a fee for overhead costs that is deducted from their compensation. Overhead costs include fees paid to rent instructional equipment such as overhead projectors, provide supplies to participants, and offer refreshments during coffee breaks. The number of courses offered is used as the allocation base for determining the overhead charge. For example, if overhead costs amount to $5,000 and 25 courses are offered, each course is allocated an overhead charge of $200 ($5,000 ÷ 25 courses). Heidi McCarl, who taught one of the courses, received the following statement with her check in payment for her instructional services.

Instructional fees (20 students × $50 per student)	$1,000
Less: Overhead charge	(200)
Less: Charge of sign language assistant	(240)
Amount due instructor	$ 560

Although Ms. McCarl was well aware that one of her students was deaf and required a sign language assistant, she was surprised to find that she was required to absorb the cost of this service.

Required

a. Given that the Americans with Disabilities Act stipulates that the deaf student cannot be charged for the cost of providing sign language, who should be required to pay the cost of sign language services?

b. Explain how allocation can be used to promote fairness in distributing service costs to the disabled. Describe two ways to treat the $240 cost of providing sign language services that improve fairness.

ATC 5–6 SPREADSHEET ASSIGNMENT *Using Excel*

Brook Health Care Center, Inc., has three clinics servicing the Birmingham metropolitan area. The company's legal services department supports the clinics. Moreover, its computer services department supports all of the clinics and the legal services department. The company uses the number of computer workstations as the cost driver for allocating the cost of computer services and the number of patients as the cost driver for allocating cost of legal services. The annual cost of the Department of Legal Services was $340,000, and the annual cost of the Department of Computer Services was $250,000. Other relevant information follows.

	Number of Patients	Number of Workstations
Hoover Clinic	3,100	17
Eastwood Clinic	2,300	13
Gardendale Clinic	2,800	6
Legal Services	0	14

Required

a. Construct a spreadsheet like the following one to allocate the service costs using the step method.

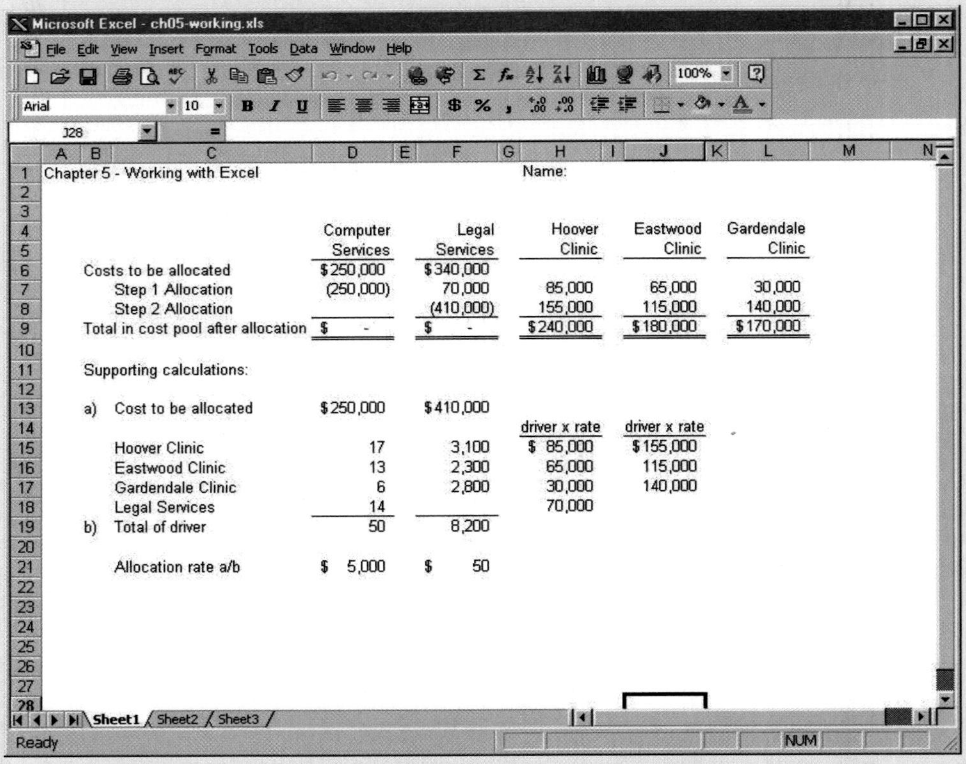

Row	C	D	F	H	J	L
1	Chapter 5 - Working with Excel			Name:		
4		Computer	Legal	Hoover	Eastwood	Gardendale
5		Services	Services	Clinic	Clinic	Clinic
6	Costs to be allocated	$250,000	$340,000			
7	Step 1 Allocation	(250,000)	70,000	85,000	65,000	30,000
8	Step 2 Allocation		(410,000)	155,000	115,000	140,000
9	Total in cost pool after allocation	$ -	$ -	$240,000	$180,000	$170,000
11	Supporting calculations:					
13	a) Cost to be allocated	$250,000	$410,000			
14				driver x rate	driver x rate	
15	Hoover Clinic	17	3,100	$ 85,000	$155,000	
16	Eastwood Clinic	13	2,300	65,000	115,000	
17	Gardendale Clinic	6	2,800	30,000	140,000	
18	Legal Services	14		70,000		
19	b) Total of driver	50	8,200			
21	Allocation rate a/b	$ 5,000	$ 50			

Spreadsheet Tips

1. The headings in rows 4 and 5 are right aligned. To right align text, choose Format, then Cells, and then click on the tab titled Alignment, and set the horizontal alignment to Right. The shortcut method to right align text is to click on the right align icon in the middle of the second tool bar.
2. The supporting calculation section must be completed simultaneously with the allocation table. However, most of the supporting calculations can be completed first. The exception is that the value in cell F13 refers to the sum of cells F6 and F7.

SPREADSHEET ASSIGNMENT ***Mastering Excel*** **ATC 5–7**

Phillips Paints manufactures three types of paint in a joint process: rubberized paint, rust-proofing paint, and aluminum paint. In a standard batch of 250,000 gallons of raw material, the outputs are 120,000 gallons of rubberized paint, 40,000 gallons of rust-proofing paint, and 90,000 gallons of aluminum paint. The production cost of a batch is $2,700,000. The sales prices per gallon are $15, $18, and $20 for rubberized, rust-proofing, and aluminum paint, respectively.

Required

a. Construct a spreadsheet to allocate joint costs to the three products using the number of gallons as the allocation base.

b. Include formulas in your spreadsheet to calculate the gross margin for each paint.

COMPREHENSIVE PROBLEM

Magnificent Modems has excess production capacity and is considering the possibility of making and selling paging equipment. The following estimates are based on a production and sales volume of 1,000 pagers.

Unit-level manufacturing costs are expected to be $20. Sales commissions will be established at $1 per unit. The current facility-level costs, including depreciation on manufacturing equipment ($60,000), rent on the manufacturing facility ($50,000), depreciation on the administrative equipment ($12,000), and other fixed administrative expenses ($71,950), will not be affected by the production of the pagers. The chief accountant has decided to allocate the facility-level costs to the existing product (modems) and to the new product (pagers) on the basis of the number of units of product made (i.e., 5,000 modems and 1,000 pagers).

Required

a. Determine the per-unit cost of making and selling 1,000 pagers.

b. Assuming the pagers could be sold at a price of $34 each, should Magnificent make the pagers?

c. Comment on the validity of using the number of units as an allocation base.

CHAPTER *six*

COST MANAGEMENT IN AN AUTOMATED BUSINESS ENVIRONMENT

ABC, ABM, AND TQM

LEARNING *objectives*

After you have mastered the material in this chapter you will be able to:

1 Explain the limitations of using direct labor hours as a single companywide overhead allocation base.

2 Explain how automation has affected the selection of cost drivers.

3 Distinguish between volume-based and activity-based cost drivers.

4 Identify and use activity cost centers and related cost drivers in an activity-based cost system.

5 Classify activities into one of four hierarchical categories: unit-level, batch-level, product-level, and facility-level activities.

6 Explain the effect of undercosting or overcosting on profitability.

7 Distinguish among manufacturing costs, upstream costs, and downstream costs.

8 Explain the relationships among the components of quality costs.

9 Prepare and interpret quality cost report information.

Need it there tomorrow?
EXPRESS MAIL
from $13.65
Get Express Mail® service.
Next day delivery or your money back. Guaranteed.
Consumer

THE *curious* ACCOUNTANT

A vendor's acceptance of credit and debit cards is expensive. Normally, the credit card company charges a fee by discounting the amount paid to the vendor for each charge. For example, suppose that the **U.S. Postal Service (USPS)** accepts a charge card as payment for $100 of stamps. When the USPS presents the credit card receipt to the credit card company for payment, the company pays USPS less than $100, perhaps $96. The actual discount rate depends on individual agreements between credit card companies and their customers. In this case, the USPS receives only $96 for $100 worth of stamps. Even so, the credit card customer must pay the bank $100. The $4 difference between the amount that the bank gave USPS and the amount that the customer paid the USPS is the fee that the bank charges for providing credit services. Incidentally, the credit card customer usually is required to pay the bank interest if the credit balance remains outstanding after the payment due date and may pay an annual fee. At a minimum, the USPS must pay a fee to enable its customers to pay for purchases with their charge cards.

Because the USPS has a virtual monopoly on regular delivery mail, why is it willing to pay fees to permit customers to use credit cards? Why doesn't the agency accept only cash or checks? (Answers on page 241.)

CHAPTER *opening*

Worldwide growth in capitalism has fostered an increasingly competitive global business environment. Companies have responded by using technology to increase productivity. Management accountants have worked with engineers to more accurately measure and control costs. They have eliminated many nonvalue-added activities and have employed quality control procedures that reduce costs and enhance customer satisfaction. These innovative business practices have enabled companies to eliminate unprofitable products and to promote products that maximize profitability. This chapter focuses on newer and emerging business practices employed by world-class companies.

Development of a Single Companywide Cost Driver

LO1 Explain the limitations of using direct labor hours as a single companywide overhead allocation base.

When accountants first developed cost systems, manufacturing processes were labor intensive. Indirect manufacturing costs were relatively minor and highly correlated with labor use; products that used large amounts of labor consumed large amounts of overhead. This link made the number of labor hours a suitable cost driver for allocating overhead costs.

To illustrate, suppose during an eight-hour day Friedman Company production employees worked on two jobs, Job 1 for two hours and Job 2 for six hours. Friedman consumed utilities of $120 during the day. How much of the $120 should the company assign to each job? Friedman cannot trace the utility cost directly to a specific job, but the job that required more labor likely consumed more of the utility cost. The longer employees work the more heat, lights, and water they use. Allocating the utility cost to the two jobs based on *direct labor hours* produces rational results. Friedman could allocate the utility cost at $15 per hour ($120 ÷ 8 hours). It could assign Job 1 $30 of the utility cost ($15 per hour × 2 hours), and Job 2 the remaining $90 ($15 × 6 hours).

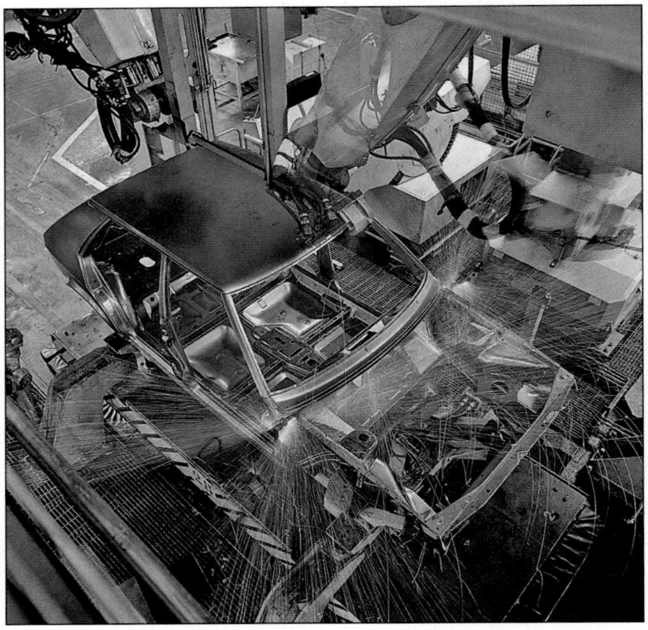

In addition to utilities, direct labor drives many other indirect costs. Consider the depreciation cost of tools employees use while working on production jobs. The more time employees work, the more they use the tools. Direct labor hours could be an effective cost driver (allocation base) for allocating tool depreciation costs. The same logic applies to supervisory salaries, production supplies, factory rent expense, and other overhead costs. Many companies applied this reasoning to justify using direct labor hours as the *sole base* for establishing a **companywide allocation rate.** These companies then allocated all overhead costs to their products or other cost objects using the single labor-based, companywide overhead rate. Even though using one base to allocate all overhead costs inaccurately measured some cost objects, in the labor intensive environment that spawned companywide allocation rates, overhead costs were relatively small compared to the costs of labor and materials. Allocation inaccuracies were relatively insignificant in amount.

Automation has changed the nature of manufacturing processes. The number of direct labor hours is no longer an effective allocation base in many modern manufacturing companies. Machines have replaced most human workers. Because they operate technically complex equipment, the remaining workers are highly skilled and not easily replaced. Companies resist laying off these trained workers when production declines. Neither do companies add employees when production increases. Adjusting production volume merely requires turning additional machines on or off. In such circumstances, direct labor is not related to production volume. Direct labor is therefore not an effective base for allocating overhead costs. Former labor-intensive companies that adopt automation usually must develop more sophisticated ways to allocate overhead costs.

When companies replace people with machines, overhead costs such as machinery depreciation and power usage become greater in proportion to total manufacturing costs. In highly automated companies, overhead costs may be greater than direct labor and direct materials costs combined. Although misallocating minor overhead amounts does little harm, misallocating major costs destroys the usefulness of accounting information and leads to poor decisions. Managers must consider how automation affects overhead cost allocation.

Effects of Automation on Selecting a Cost Driver

LO2 Explain how automation has affected the selection of cost drivers.

In an automated manufacturing environment, robots and sophisticated machinery, rather than human labor, transform raw materials into finished goods. To illustrate the effect of these changes on selecting a cost driver, return to the previous Friedman Company example. Suppose Friedman automates the production process for Job 2, replacing most labor with four hours of machine processing and reducing the number of direct labor hours required from six to one. Assume the new machinery acquired increases utility consumption and depreciation charges, raising daily overhead costs from \$120 to \$420. Because Job 1 requires two hours of direct labor and Job 2 now requires one hour of direct labor, Friedman's companywide allocation rate increases to \$140 per direct labor hour (\$420 ÷ 3 hours). The company would allocate \$280 (\$140 × 2 hours) of the total overhead cost to Job 1 and \$140 (\$140 × 1 hour) to Job 2. The pre- and post-automation allocations are compared here.

Product	Preautomation Cost Distribution	Postautomation Cost Distribution
Job 1	\$ 30	\$280
Job 2	90	140
Total	\$120	\$420

Using direct labor hours as the cost driver after automating production of Job 2 distorts the overhead cost allocation. Although Friedman did not change the production process for Job 1 at all, Job 1 received a \$250 (\$280 − \$30) increase in its share of allocated overhead cost. This increase should have been assigned to Job 2 because automating production of Job 2 caused overhead costs to increase. The decrease in direct labor hours for Job 2 causes the distortion. Prior to automation, Job 2 used six of eight total direct labor hours and was therefore allocated 75 percent (6 ÷ 8) of the overhead cost. After automation, Job 2 consumed only one of three total direct labor hours, reducing its overhead allocation to only 33 percent of the total. These changes in the allocation base, coupled with the increase in total overhead cost, caused the post automation overhead cost allocation for Job 1 to be significantly overstated and for Job 2 to be significantly understated.

One way to solve the misallocation problem is to find a more suitable volume-based cost driver. For example, Friedman could allocate utility costs using machine hours instead of direct labor hours. This text illustrated using different **volume-based cost drivers** (such as material dollars and direct labor hours) in Chapter 5. Unfortunately, automated production processes often generate costs which have no cause-and-effect relationship with volume-based cost drivers. Many companies have therefore adopted **activity-based cost drivers** to improve the accuracy of indirect cost allocations. To illustrate, consider the case of Carver Soup Company.

Activity-Based Cost Drivers

LO3 Distinguish between volume-based and activity-based cost drivers.

Carver Soup Company (CSC) produces batches of vegetable and tomato soup. Each time CSC switches production from vegetable soup to tomato soup or vice versa, it incurs certain costs.

For example, production workers must clean the mixing, blending, and cooking equipment. They must change settings on the equipment to the specifications for the particular soup to be processed. CSC must test each batch for quality to ensure the recipe has been correctly followed. Because these costs are incurred for each new batch, they are called **start-up,** or **setup, costs.** CSC plans to make 180 batches of each type of soup during the coming year. The following table summarizes expected production information:

	Vegetable	Tomato	Total
Number of cans	954,000	234,000	1,188,000
Number of setups	180	180	360

CSC expects each setup will cost \$264, for total expected setup costs of \$95,040 (\$264 × 360 setups). Using number of cans as the cost driver (volume-based driver) produces an allocation rate of \$0.08 per can (\$95,040 ÷ 1,188,000 cans). Multiplying the allocation rate by the weight of the base (number of cans) produces the following setup cost allocation:

Product	Allocation Rate	×	Number of Cans Produced	=	Allocated Product Cost
Vegetable	\$0.08	×	954,000	=	\$76,320
Tomato	0.08	×	234,000	=	18,720

As expected, the volume-based (number of cans) allocation rate assigns more cost to the high-volume vegetable soup product. However, assigning more setup cost to the vegetable soup makes little sense. Since both products require the *same number* of setups, the setup cost should be distributed equally between them. The volume-based cost driver *overcosts* the high-volume product (vegetable soup) and *undercosts* the low-volume product (tomato soup).

Setup costs are driven by the number of times CSC employees perform the setup activities. The more setups employees undertake, the greater the total setup cost. An *activity-based cost driver* (number of setups) provides a more accurate allocation base for setup costs. Using the allocation rate of \$264 (\$95,040 ÷ 360 setups) per setup assigns the same amount of setup cost to each product, as follows:

Product	Allocation Rate	×	Number of Setups	=	Allocated Product Cost
Vegetable	\$264	×	180	=	\$47,520
Tomato	264	×	180	=	47,520

Activity-Based Cost Drivers Enhance Relevance

The *activity-based cost driver* produces a better allocation because it distributes the *relevant* costs to the appropriate products. If CSC were to stop producing tomato soup, it could *avoid* spending \$47,520 for 180 setups (assuming CSC could eliminate labor, supplies, and other resources used in the setup process). *Avoidable costs are relevant* to decision making. The inaccurate volume-based product cost data could mislead a manager into making a poor decision. Suppose a company specializing in setup activities offered to provide CSC 180 tomato soup setups for \$40,000. A manager relying on the volume-based allocated cost of \$18,720 would reject the \$40,000 offer to outsource as too costly. In fact, CSC should accept the offer because it could avoid \$47,520 of cost if the outside company performs the setup activity. In a highly automated environment in which companies produce many different products at varying volume levels, it is little wonder that many companies have turned to activity-based costing to improve the accuracy of cost allocations and the effectiveness of decisions.

Check Yourself 6–1

Professional Training Services, Inc. (PTSI), offers professional exam review courses for both the certified public accountant (CPA) and the certified management accountant (CMA) exams. Many more students take the CPA review courses than the CMA review courses. PTSI uses the same size and number of classrooms to teach both courses; its CMA courses simply have more empty seats. PTSI is trying to determine the cost of offering the two courses. The company's accountant has decided to allocate classroom rental cost based on the number of students enrolled in the courses. Explain why this allocation base will likely result in an inappropriate assignment of cost to the two cost objects. Identify a more appropriate allocation base.

Answer Using the number of students as the allocation base will assign more of the rental cost to the CPA review courses because those courses have higher enrollments. This allocation is inappropriate because the number of classrooms, not the number of students, drives the amount of rental cost. Since both courses require the same number of classrooms, the rental cost should be allocated equally between them. Several allocation bases would produce an equal allocation, such as the number of classrooms, the number of courses, or a 50/50 percentage split.

Activity-Based Costing

Topic Tackler PLUS 6–1

A company that allocates indirect costs using **activity-based costing (ABC)** follows a two-stage process. In the first stage, costs are assigned to pools based on the activities that cause the costs to be incurred. In the second stage, the costs in the activity cost pools are allocated to products using a variety of cost drivers. The first step in developing an ABC system is to identify essential activities and the costs of performing those activities.

A business undertakes **activities** to accomplish its mission. Typical activities include acquiring raw materials, transforming raw materials into finished products, and delivering products to customers. These broadly defined activities can be divided into subcategories. For example, the activity of acquiring raw materials involves separate subcategory activities such as identifying suppliers, obtaining price quotations, evaluating materials specifications, completing purchase orders, and receiving purchased materials. Each of these subcategories can be subdivided into yet more detailed activities. For instance, identifying suppliers may include such activities as reviewing advertisements, searching Internet sites, and obtaining recommendations from business associates. Further subdivisions are possible. Companies perform thousands of activities.

Identifying Activity Centers

LO4 Identify and use activity cost centers and related cost drivers in an activity-based cost system.

Maintaining separate cost records for thousands of activities is expensive. To reduce record-keeping costs, companies group related activities into hubs called **activity centers.** The overhead costs of these related activities are combined into a cost pool for each activity center. Because the activities assigned to each center are related, a business can obtain rational cost allocations using a common cost driver for an entire cost pool. Determining the optimal number of activity centers requires *cost/benefit analysis.* Companies will incur the higher record-keeping costs for additional activity centers only to the extent that the additional accuracy improves decision making.

Comparing ABC with Traditional Two-Stage Cost Allocation

How do ABC systems differ from the traditional two-stage allocation systems discussed in the appendix to Chapter 5? Traditional two-stage allocation systems pool costs by departments, then allocate departmental cost pools to cost objects using volume-based cost drivers. In contrast, ABC systems pool costs by activity centers, then allocate activity center cost pools to

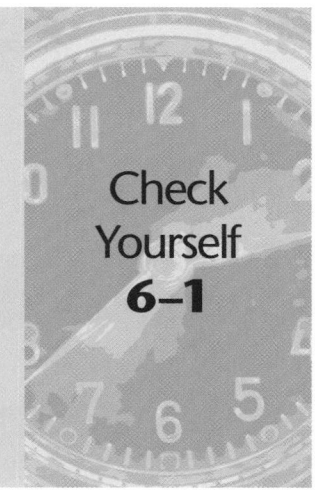

Exhibit 6–1

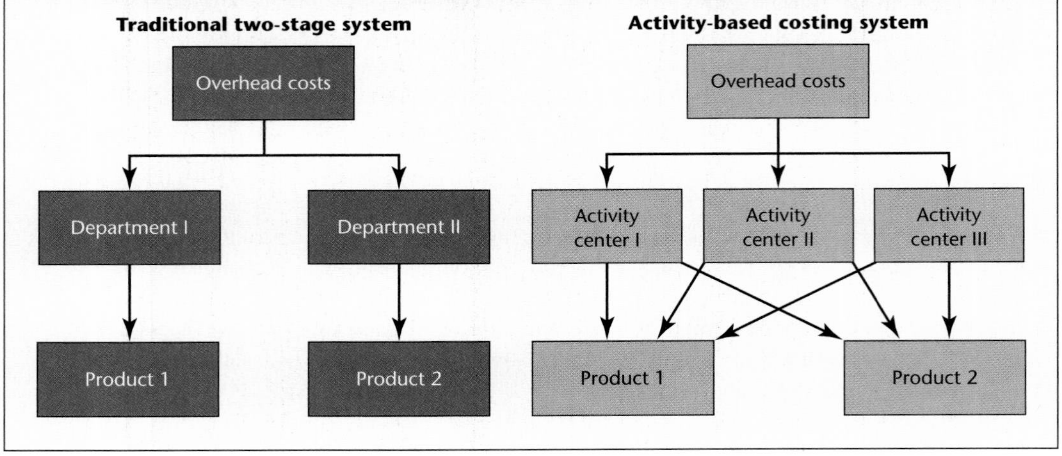

cost objects using a variety of volume- and activity-based cost drivers. ABC systems use many more activity centers than the number of departments in a traditional two-stage allocation system. As a result, ABC improves cost tracing by using more cause-and-effect relationships in assigning indirect costs to numerous activity centers. Exhibit 6–1 illustrates the primary differences between a traditional two-stage allocation system and an ABC system.

focus on INTERNATIONAL ISSUES

Eliminating Nonvalue-Added Activities in a Sushi Bar

Identifying and eliminating activities that do not add value can lead to increased customer satisfaction and profitability. An emerging trend in Japanese sushi bars validates this point. Sushi delivered via conveyor belt leads to significant cost savings that are passed on to customers. A moving belt, not a waiter, delivers sushi directly to the customers. Chefs fill the merry-go-round conveyor belt, instead of patron orders. The savings associated with the elimination of nonvalue-added activities such as taking orders, delivering food, and avoiding waste have enabled conveyor belt shops to offer customers quality sushi at economy prices—two pieces for $1 vs. $3 to $4 at standard sushi shops. Customers are so wowed by the deal that they are braving waits of up to an hour. Owners are benefiting, too, because diners get their fill and move on faster, thereby increasing turnover and sales volume. The increased volume produced is highly profitable because fixed costs are not affected by the soaring sales. When insights gained through activity-based costing (ABC) lead to changes in the way a business is managed, the process is known as *activity-based management* (ABM).

Source: Miki Tanikawa, "Sushi Bars: What Comes Around," *Business Week*, November 9, 1998, p. 8.

Types of Production Activities

LO5 Classify activities into one of four hierarchical categories: unit-level, batch-level, product-level, and facility-level activities.

Many companies organize activities into four hierarchical categories to improve cost tracing. These categories are (1) unit-level activities, (2) batch-level activities, (3) product-level activities, and (4) facility-level activities.[1] The overhead costs in each category are pooled and allocated to products based on how the products benefit from the activities. *The primary objective is to trace the cost of performing activities to the products that are causing the activities to be performed.* To illustrate, consider the overhead costs incurred by Unterman Shirt Company.

Unterman has two product lines, dress shirts and casual shirts. The company expects to incur overhead costs of $5,730,000 in the course of producing 680,000 dress shirts and 120,000 casual shirts during 2003. Currently, Unterman assigns an equal amount of overhead to each shirt, simply dividing the total expected overhead cost by the total expected production ($5,730,000 ÷ 800,000 units = $7.16 per shirt, rounded). Each type of shirt requires approximately the same amount of direct materials, $8.20 per shirt, and the same amount of direct labor, $6.80 per shirt. The total cost per shirt is $22.16 ($7.16 + $8.20 + $6.80). Unterman sells shirts for $31 each, yielding a gross margin of $8.84 per shirt ($31 − $22.16).

Bob Unterman, president and owner of the company, believes the direct materials and direct labor costs are reasonable, but the overhead costs must not be the same for both product lines. Mr. Unterman hired a consultant, Rebecca Lynch, to trace the overhead costs. Ms. Lynch decided to use an *activity-based cost* system. She identified the activities necessary to make shirts and classified them into the following four activity cost centers.

Unit-Level Activity Center

Unit-level activities occur each time a unit of product is made. For example, for every shirt made, Unterman incurs inspection costs, machine-related utility costs, and costs for production supplies. Total unit-level cost increases with every shirt made and decreases with reductions in production volume. Some costs behave so much like unit-level costs that they may be accounted for as unit-level even though they are not strictly unit-level. For example, suppose Unterman employees lubricate production machinery after every eight hours of continuous operation. Although Unterman does not incur lubrication cost for each shirt produced, the cost behavior pattern is so closely tied to production levels that it may be accounted for as a unit-level cost.

Ms. Lynch identified the following unit-level overhead costs: (1) $300,000 for machine-related utilities, (2) $50,000 for machine maintenance, (3) $450,000 for indirect labor and indirect materials, (4) $200,000 for inspection and quality control, and (5) $296,000 for miscellaneous unit-level costs. She assigned these costs into a single *unit-level activity center* overhead cost pool of $1,296,000. This assignment illustrates the first stage of the two-stage ABC allocation system. Of the total $5,730,000 overhead cost, Ms. Lynch has allocated $1,296,000 to one of the four activity centers. The remaining overhead cost is allocated among the three other activity centers.

The second-stage cost assignment involves allocating the $1,296,000 unit-level cost pool between the two product lines. Because unit-level costs are incurred each time a shirt is produced, they should be allocated using a base correlated to production levels. Ms. Lynch chose direct labor hours as the allocation base. Past performance indicates the dress shirts will require 272,000 direct labor hours and the casual shirts will require 48,000 direct labor hours. Based on this information, Ms. Lynch allocated the unit-level overhead costs and computed the cost per unit as shown in Exhibit 6–2.

The unit-level costs exhibit a variable cost behavior pattern. Total cost varies in direct proportion to the number of units produced. Cost per unit is constant. Because production volume

[1] The types of costs in each category were discussed in Chapter 4. Review the cost hierarchy before continuing in this chapter.

Exhibit 6–2 *Allocation of Unit-Level Overhead Costs*

	Product Lines		
	Dress Shirts	**Casual Shirts**	**Total**
Number of direct labor hours (a)	272,000	48,000	320,000
Cost per labor hour ($1,296,000 ÷ 320,000 hours) (b)	$4.05	$4.05	NA
Total allocated overhead cost (c = a × b)	$1,101,600	$194,400	$1,296,000
Number of shirts (d)	680,000	120,000	800,000
Cost per shirt (c ÷ d)	$1.62	$1.62	NA

does not affect the unit-level overhead cost, the pricing of shirts should not be affected by the fact that the company makes more dress shirts than casual shirts.

Batch-Level Activity Center

Batch-level activities relate to producing groups of products. Batch-level costs are fixed regardless of the number of units produced in a single batch. For example, the costs of setting up machinery to cut fabric for a certain size shirt remain unchanged regardless of the number of shirts cut at that particular machine setting. Similarly, the cost of a first-item batch test is the same whether 200 or 2,000 shirts are made in the batch. Materials handling costs are also commonly classified as batch-level because materials are usually transferred from one department to another in batches. For example, all of the size small casual shirts are cut in the sizing department, then the entire batch of cut fabric is transferred in one operation to the sewing department. The cost of materials handling is the same regardless of whether the batch load is large or small.

Because total batch costs depend on the number of batches produced, more batch costs should be allocated to products that require more batches. Ms. Lynch identified $690,000 of total batch-level overhead costs and assigned this amount to a batch-level cost pool.

For the second-stage allocation, Ms. Lynch determined that the casual shirt line requires considerably more setups than the dress-shirt line because the casual shirts are subject to frequent style changes. Because customers buy limited amounts of items with short shelf lives, Unterman must produce casual shirts in small batches. Ms. Lynch decided more of the batch-level costs should be allocated to the casual-shirt line than to the dress-shirt line. She chose number of setups as the most rational allocation base. Since casual shirts require 1,280 setups and dress shirts require 1,020 setups, Ms. Lynch allocated the batch-level costs as shown in Exhibit 6–3.

ABC demonstrates that the per shirt batch-level cost for casual shirts ($3.20 per shirt) is considerably more than for dress shirts ($0.45). One reason is that the casual-shirt line incurs more batch-level costs ($384,000 versus $306,000). The other is that Unterman produces far fewer casual shirts than dress shirts (120,000 units versus 680,000). Because batch-level costs are fixed relative to the number of units in a particular batch, the cost per unit is greater the smaller the batch. For example, if setup costs are $300, the setup cost per unit for a batch of 100 units is $3 ($300 ÷ 100 units). For a batch of only 10 units, however, the setup cost per unit is $30 ($300 ÷ 10 units). When batch-level costs are significant, companies should pursue high volume products. Low-volume products are more expensive to make because the fixed costs must be spread over fewer units. To the extent that cost affects pricing, Unterman should charge more for casual shirts than dress shirts.

Product-Level Activity Center

Product-level activities support specific products or product lines. Examples include raw materials inventory holding costs; engineering development costs; and legal fees for patents, copyrights, trademarks, and brand names. Unterman Shirt Company positions itself as a fashion leader. It incurs extensive design costs to ensure that it remains a trendsetter. The company

Exhibit 6–3 *Allocation of Batch-Level Overhead Costs*

	Product Lines		
	Dress Shirts	**Casual Shirts**	**Total**
Number of setups performed (a)	1,020	1,280	2,300
Cost per setup ($690,000 ÷ 2,300 setups) (b)	$300	$300	NA
Total allocated overhead cost (c = a × b)	$306,000	$384,000	$690,000
Number of shirts (d)	680,000	120,000	800,000
Cost per shirt (c ÷ d)	$0.45	$3.20	NA

Exhibit 6–4 *Allocation of Product-Level Overhead Costs*

	Product Lines		
	Dress Shirts	**Casual Shirts**	**Total**
Percent of product-level activity utilization (a)	30%	70%	100%
Total allocated overhead cost (b = a × $1,800,000)	$540,000	$1,260,000	$1,800,000
Total units produced (c)	680,000	120,000	800,000
Cost per unit (b ÷ c)	$0.79*	$10.50	NA

*Rounded to the nearest whole cent.

also incurs engineering costs to continually improve the quality of materials used in its shirts and legal fees to protect its brand names. After reviewing Unterman's operations, Ms. Lynch concluded she could trace $1,800,000 of the total overhead cost to the product-level activity center.

The second-stage allocation requires dividing these activities between the dress-shirt line and the casual-shirt line. Interviews with fashion design staff disclosed that they spend more time on casual shirts because of the frequent style changes. Similarly, the engineers spend more of their time developing new fabric, buttons, and zippers for casual shirts. The materials used in dress shirts are fairly stable. Although engineers spend some time improving the quality of dress shirt materials, they devote far more time to the more unusual materials used in the casual shirts. Similarly, the legal department spends more time developing and protecting patents, trademarks, and brand names for the casual-shirt line. Ms. Lynch concluded that 70 percent of the product-level cost pool applied to casual shirts and 30 percent to dress shirts. She allocated product-level costs to the two product lines as shown in Exhibit 6–4.

Product-level costs are frequently distributed unevenly among different product lines. Unterman Shirt Company incurs substantially more costs to sustain its casual shirt line than its dress shirt line. Using a single companywide overhead rate in such circumstances distorts cost measurements. Distorted product cost measurements can lead to negative consequences such as irrational pricing policies and rewards for inappropriate decisions. Activity-based costing reduces measurement distortions by more accurately tracing costs to the products that cause their incurrence.

Facility-Level Activity Center

Facility-level activities benefit the production process as a whole and are not related to any specific product, batch, or unit of production. For example, insuring the manufacturing facility against fire losses does not benefit any particular product or product line. Facility-level costs include depreciation on the manufacturing plant, security, landscaping, plant maintenance, general utilities, and property taxes. For Unterman Shirt Company, Ms. Lynch identified $1,944,000 of facility-level overhead costs. Because no cause and effect relationship exists between these facility-level manufacturing costs and the two product lines, she must allocate these costs arbitrarily. Basing the arbitrary allocation on the total number of units produced, Ms. Lynch allocated 85 percent (680,000 ÷ 800,000) of the facility-level cost pool to

Exhibit 6–5 *Allocation of Facility-Level Overhead Costs*

	Product Lines		
	Dress Shirts	**Casual Shirts**	**Total**
Percent of total units (a)	85%	15%	100%
Total allocated overhead cost (b = a × $1,944,000)	$1,652,400	$291,600	$1,944,000
Total units produced (c)	680,000	120,000	800,000
Cost per unit (b ÷ c)	$2.43	$2.43	NA

the dress shirt line and 15 percent (120,000 ÷ 800,000) to the casual shirt line as shown in Exhibit 6–5.

Classification of Activities Not Limited to Four Categories

The number of activity centers a business uses depends on cost/benefit analysis. The four categories illustrated for Unterman Shirt Company represent a useful starting point. Any of the four categories could be further subdivided into more detailed activity centers. Unterman could establish an activity cost center for unit-level labor-related activities and a different activity center for unit-level machine-related activities. Identifying all potential activity centers in a real-world company can be daunting. Paulette Bennett describes the process used in the Material Control Department at Compumotor, Inc., as follows:

> Recognizing that ordinarily the two biggest problems with an ABC project are knowing where to start and how deep to go, we began by analyzing the activities that take place in our procurement process. As the old saying goes, to find the biggest alligators you usually have to wade into the weeds; therefore, we started by writing down all the procurement activities. Creating a real world picture of costs by activity was our aim. But had we used our initial list we would have designed a spreadsheet so large that no human could ever have emerged alive at the other end.[2]

Ms. Bennett's abbreviated list still included 83 separate activities. The list represented the activity centers for only one department of a very large company. Although the Unterman example used only four categories, the real world equivalent is far more complex.

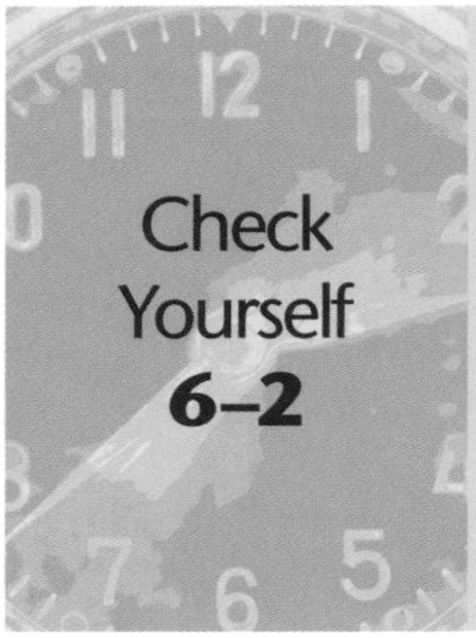

Under what circumstances would the number of units produced be an inappropriate allocation base for batch-level costs?

Answer Using the number of units produced as the allocation base would allocate more of the batch-level costs to high-volume products and less of the costs to low-volume products. Since batch-level costs are normally related to the number of batches rather than the number of units made in each batch, allocation of batch-level costs based on units produced would result in poor product cost estimates; the costing system would overcost high-volume products and undercost low-volume products. It would be appropriate to use the number of units produced only when each batch consists of the same number of product units. Even under these circumstances, the number of units merely serves as a proxy for the number of batches. It would still be more appropriate to use the number of batches to allocate batch-level costs.

Context-Sensitive Classification of Activities

Particular activities could fall into any of the four hierarchical categories. For example, inspecting each individual item produced is a unit-level activity. Inspecting the first item of each

[2] Paulette Bennett, "ABM and the Procurement Cost Model," *Management Accounting,* March 1996, pp. 28–32.

batch to ensure the setup was correct is a batch-level activity. Inspecting a specific product line is a product-level activity. Finally, inspecting the factory building is a facility-level activity. To properly classify activities, you must learn to analyze the context within which they occur.

Selecting Cost Drivers

Activity-based costing uses both *volume-based* cost drivers and *activity-based* cost drivers. Volume-based drivers are appropriate for indirect costs that increase or decrease relative to the volume of activity. Using cost drivers such as units, direct labor hours, or machine hours is appropriate for unit-level activities. The flaw in traditional costing systems is that they use a volume-based measure (usually direct labor hours) to allocate all indirect costs. In contrast, the more sophisticated ABC approach uses activity drivers such as number of setups or percentage of utilization for overhead costs that are not influenced by volume. ABC improves the accuracy of allocations by using a combination of volume- and activity-based cost drivers.

Using ABC Information to Trace Costs to Product Lines

Topic Tackler PLUS 6–2

Exhibit 6–6 summarizes the ABC allocations Ms. Lynch prepared. Mr. Unterman was shocked to learn that overhead costs for casual shirts are virtually three times those for dress shirts. Exhibit 6–7 compares the per unit gross margins for the two product lines using the traditional cost system and using the ABC system. Recall that direct materials and direct labor costs for

Exhibit 6–6 *ABC Overhead Cost Allocation*

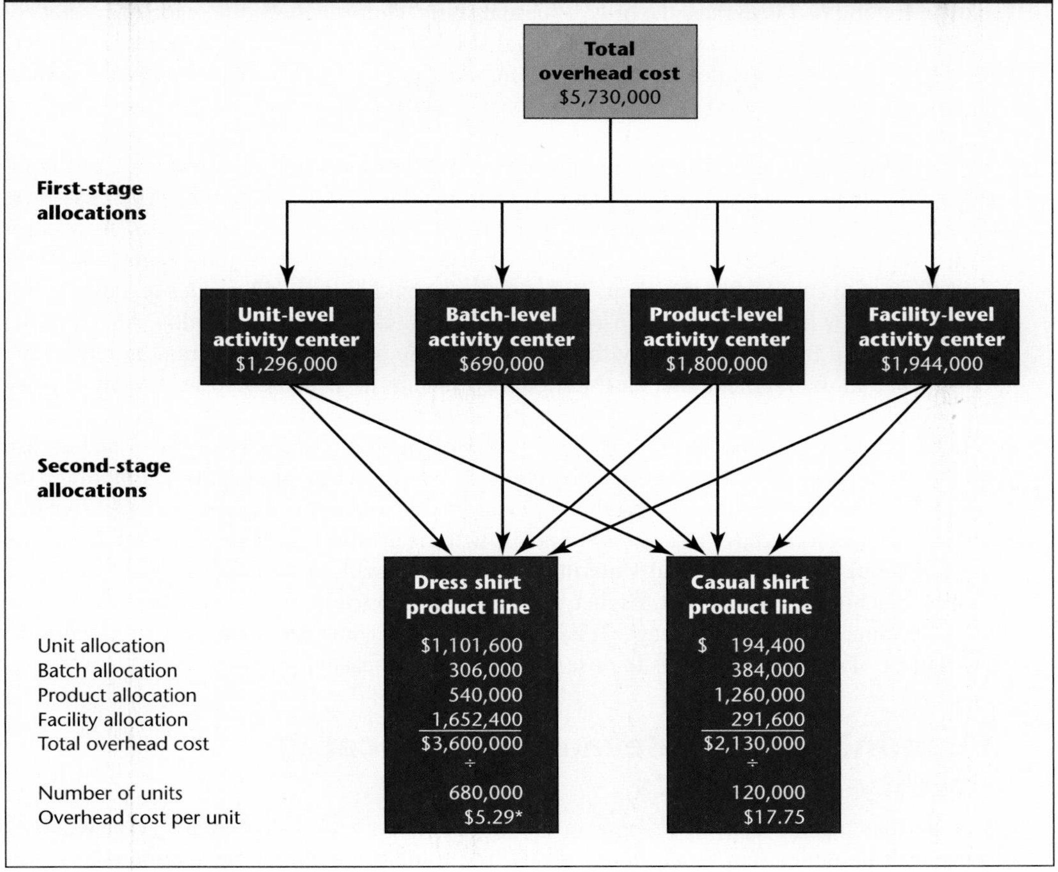

*Rounded to the nearest whole cent.

Exhibit 6–7 *Gross Margins Using Traditional Versus ABC Costing*

	Gross Margins Traditional System		Gross Margins ABC Costing	
	Dress Shirts	**Casual Shirts**	**Dress Shirts**	**Casual Shirts**
Sales price	$31.00	$31.00	$31.00	$31.00
Cost of goods sold				
Materials cost	(8.20)	(8.20)	(8.20)	(8.20)
Labor cost	(6.80)	(6.80)	(6.80)	(6.80)
Overhead	(7.16)	(7.16)	(5.29)	(17.75)
Gross margin	$ 8.84	$ 8.84	$10.71	$ (1.75)

dress and casual shirts are $8.20 and $6.80, respectively. The difference in the margins is attributable to the overhead allocation. Using a traditional companywide overhead rate allocates an equal amount of overhead to each shirt ($5,730,000 ÷ 800,000 units = $7.16 per shirt). In contrast, the ABC approach assigns $5.29 to each dress shirt and $17.75 to each casual shirt. Total overhead cost is $5,730,000 under both approaches. It is the *allocation* of rather than the *amount* of the overhead cost that differs. ABC shows that making a casual shirt costs more than making a dress shirt. After reviewing the data in Exhibit 6–7, Mr. Unterman realized the company was incurring losses on the casual-shirt line. What options does he have?

Under- and Overcosting

LO6 Explain the effect of undercosting or overcosting on profitability.

In using the single companywide overhead rate, Unterman Shirt Company has undercosted its casual line and priced the shirts below cost. The obvious response to the ABC gross margin data in Exhibit 6–7 is to raise the price of casual shirts. Unfortunately, the market may not cooperate. If other companies are selling casual shirts at prices near $31, customers may buy from Unterman's competitors instead of paying a higher price for Unterman's shirts. In a market-driven economy, raising prices may not be a viable option. Unterman may have to adopt a target-pricing strategy.

Target pricing starts with determining the price customers are willing to pay. The company then attempts to produce the product at a low enough cost to sell it at the price customers demand. Exhibits 6–3 and 6–4 indicate that batch-level and product-level costs are significantly higher for casual shirts than for dress shirts. Unterman may be too fashion conscious with respect to casual shirts. Perhaps the company should reduce fashion design costs by focusing on a few traditional styles instead of maintaining a trendsetting position. Also, following established trends is less risky than setting new ones. Retail customers may have more confidence in the marketability of traditional casual shirts, which could lead them to place larger orders, enabling Unterman to reduce its per unit batch costs.

The single companywide overhead rate not only undercosts the casual shirt line but also overcosts the dress shirt line. To the extent that the overhead cost affects the selling price, the dress shirt line is overpriced. Overpricing places the dress shirt business at a competitive disadvantage which can have a snowball effect. If volume declines because of lost market share, sales revenue will decrease and Unterman's fixed costs will be spread over fewer units, resulting in a higher cost per unit. Higher costs encourage price increases, which further aggravate the competitive disadvantage. It is as important for Unterman to consider reducing the sales price of dress shirts as it is to raise the sales price of casual shirts.

Examining the Relevance of Allocated Facility-Level Costs

If Unterman cannot raise the price or lower the cost of its casual shirts, management should consider eliminating the casual shirt product line. As indicated in Chapter 4, elimination decisions require identifying *relevant revenues and costs.* Relevant revenues and costs are those

ANSWERS TO THE *curious* ACCOUNTANT

In 1994, the USPS commissioned **Coopers & Lybrand (C&L),** a large accounting firm, to conduct activity-based cost (ABC) studies of its key revenue collection processes. C&L developed an ABC model for USPS's existing cash and check revenue collection and a similar ABC model for debit and credit card activities. The ABC model identified costs associated with unit, batch, and product activities. *Unit-level activity* was defined as the acceptance and processing of a payment by item. *Batch-level activities* involved the closeout at the end of the day, consolidation, and supervisory review. *Product-level activities* included maintenance for bank accounts and deposit reconciliation for the cash and checks model and terminal maintenance and training for the credit and debit card system. A comparison of the cost of the two activity models revealed that a significant cost savings could be achieved in the long term by implementing a debit and credit card system. Some examples of expected cost savings included a decrease in the per unit transaction cost due to the fact that credit card customers tend to spend more per transaction than do cash customers. In addition, the cost of activities associated with the collection of bad debts falls to virtually zero when debit or credit cards are used and the cost of cash management activities declines. Funds are collected earlier (no check collection float occurs), thereby reducing the need for financing and the resultant interest cost. In summary, C&L projected a negative benefit for a debit and credit card system (due largely to high initial implementation costs) through 1997. Projections showed that from 1998 through 2000, the net benefits of card acceptance would be $5.2 million, $15.6 million, and $28.8 million, respectively. So the USPS started accepting plastic because ABC analysis revealed that implementing a debit and credit card program would save money!

Source: Terrel L. Carter, Ali M. Sedghat, and Thomas D. Williams, "How ABC Changed the Post Office," *Management Accounting,* February 1998, pp. 28–36.

Unterman can *avoid* by eliminating the casual shirt line. The relevant revenue is $31, the sales price of a casual shirt. Which of the ABC–allocated overhead costs can Unterman avoid? Companies can usually eliminate or substantially reduce unit-level, batch-level, and product-level costs by eliminating a product line. *Facility-level costs, however, are usually unavoidable; they are not affected by product eliminations.* Unterman will continue to incur such costs as manufacturing depreciation, security, insurance, and property taxes whether or not it makes casual shirts. *Many companies do not allocate facility-level costs to products for decision-making purposes.* For Unterman, the avoidable overhead cost of a casual shirt is $15.32 (unit-level $1.62 + batch-level $3.20 + product-level $10.50). Assuming direct labor and direct materials costs are avoidable, the total avoidable cost is $30.32 ($8.20 materials + $6.80 labor + $15.32 overhead). Because the avoidable cost is less than the sales price of $31, the analysis suggests Unterman should not eliminate the casual shirt line.

Downstream Costs and Upstream Costs

LO7 Distinguish among manufacturing costs, upstream costs, and downstream costs.

The preceding paragraph analyzed only product costs. Businesses incur **upstream costs** before and **downstream costs** after goods are manufactured. Either upstream or downstream costs may be relevant to product elimination decisions. For example, suppose Unterman pays sales representatives a $2 commission for each shirt sold. Although sales commissions are selling, not product, costs, they are relevant to deciding whether to eliminate the casual-shirt line. Unterman can avoid the commission expense if it sells no casual shirts. Including the sales commission increases the total avoidable cost to $32.32 ($30.32 product costs + $2.00 sales commissions) which is more than the $31 sales price. Unterman would therefore be more profitable if it abandoned the casual-shirt line. Management must also consider upstream costs such as those for research and development. To continue in business, companies must sell products at prices that exceed the *total* cost to develop, make, and sell them.

Employee Attitudes and the Availability of Data

Activity-based costing can lead management to implement cost-cutting measures, including product and product line eliminations, that can result in the loss of jobs. Employees are therefore sometimes uncooperative with management efforts to adopt an ABC system. Companies must help employees recognize that ABC and other **strategic cost management** techniques frequently result in redirecting workers rather than displacing them. Ultimately, jobs depend on the employer's competitive health. The implementation of an ABC system is more likely to succeed when both managers and rank-and-file employees are convinced their own well-being is tied to the company's well-being.

Even when employees cooperate, implementing an ABC system can be difficult. Frequently, the accounting system is not collecting some of the needed data. For example, suppose a manager wants to allocate inspection costs based on the number of hours job inspections take. Inspectors may not record the time spent on individual jobs. Basing the allocation on inspection hours requires inspectors to begin keeping more detailed time records. The accuracy of the allocation then depends on how conscientiously inspectors complete their time reports. Obtaining employee support and accurate data are two of the more challenging obstacles to successfully implementing ABC.

Total Quality Management

LO8 Explain the relationships among the components of quality costs.

Quality is key to a company's ability to obtain and retain customers. What does *quality* mean? It does not always mean the best. A spoon made of silver is of higher quality than a spoon made of plastic, but customers are perfectly willing to use plastic spoons at fast-food restaurants. **Quality** represents the degree to which products or services *conform* to design specifications. The costs companies incur to ensure quality conformance can be classified into four categories: prevention, appraisal, internal failure, and external failure.

Companies incur **prevention costs** to avoid nonconforming products. They incur **appraisal costs** to identify nonconforming products produced in spite of prevention cost expenditures. **Failure costs** result from correcting defects in nonconforming products produced. **Internal failure costs** pertain to correcting defects before goods reach customers; **external failure costs** result from delivering defective goods to customers.

Because prevention and appraisal costs are a function of managerial discretion, they are often called **voluntary costs.** Management chooses how much to spend on these voluntary costs. In contrast, management does not directly control failure costs. The cost of dissatisfied customers may not be measurable, much less controllable. Even though failure costs may not be directly controllable, they are related to voluntary costs. When management spends additional funds on prevention and appraisal controls, failure costs tend to decline. As the level of control increases, quality conformance increases, reducing failure costs. When control activities are reduced, quality conformance decreases and failure cost increases. *Voluntary costs and failure costs move in opposite directions.*

Exhibit 6–8 *Relationships Among Components of Quality Cost*

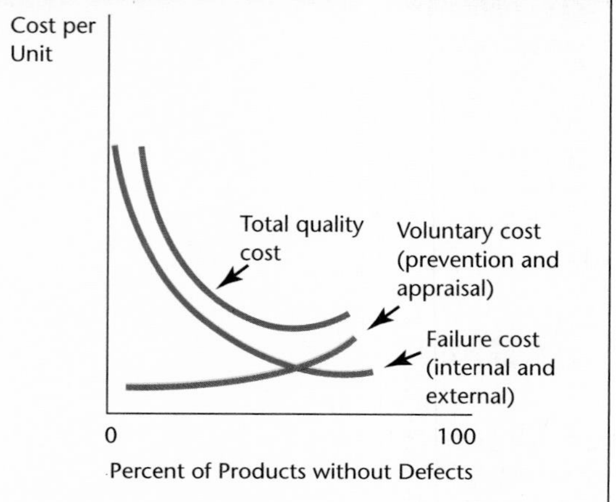

Minimizing Total Quality Cost

Total quality control cost is the sum of voluntary costs plus failure costs. Because voluntary costs and failure costs are negatively correlated, the minimum amount of *total* quality cost is located at the point on a graph where the marginal voluntary expenditures equal the marginal savings on failure cost as shown in Exhibit 6–8.

Exhibit 6–8 indicates that the minimum total quality cost per unit occurs at quality level of less than 100 percent. At very low levels of quality assurance, significant failure costs outweigh any cost savings available by avoiding voluntary costs. In contrast, extremely high levels of quality assurance result in voluntary cost expenditures that are not offset by failure cost savings. Although the goal of zero defects is appealing, it is not a cost-effective strategy. Realistic managers seek to minimize total quality cost rather than to eliminate all defects.

Check Yourself 6–3

Is it wiser to spend money on preventing defects or on correcting failures?

Answer The answer depends on where a company's product falls on the "total quality cost" line (see Exhibit 6–8). If the product falls left of the cost minimization point, spending more on preventing defects would produce proportionately greater failure cost savings. In other words, a company would spend less in total by reducing failure costs through increasing prevention costs. Under these circumstances, it would be wise to incur prevention costs. On the other hand, if the product falls right of the cost minimization point line, the company would spend more to prevent additional defects than it would save by reducing failure costs. Under these circumstances, it makes more sense to pay the failure costs than attempt to avoid them by incurring prevention costs.

Quality Cost Reports

LO9 Prepare and interpret quality cost report information.

Managing quality costs to achieve the highest level of customer satisfaction is known as **total quality management (TQM).** Accountants support TQM by preparing a **quality cost report,** which typically lists the company's quality costs and analyzes horizontally each item as a percentage of the total cost. Data are normally displayed for two or more accounting periods to disclose the effects of changes over time. Exhibit 6–9 shows a quality cost report for Unterman Shirt Company. The company's accountant prepared the report to assess the effects of a quality control campaign the company recently initiated. Review Exhibit 6–9. What is Unterman's quality control strategy? Is it succeeding?

Exhibit 6–9 indicates Unterman is seeking to control quality costs by focusing on appraisal activities. The total expenditures for prevention activities remained unchanged, but expenditures for appraisal activities increased significantly. The results of this strategy are apparent in

Exhibit 6–9 *Quality Cost Report for Unterman Shirt Company*

	2002		2001	
	Amount	**Percentage***	**Amount**	**Percentage***
Prevention costs				
Product design	$ 50,000	6.54%	$ 52,000	6.60%
Preventive equipment (depreciation)	7,000	0.92	7,000	0.89
Trainingcosts	27,000	3.53	25,000	3.17
Promotion and awards	22,000	2.88	22,000	2.79
Total prevention	106,000	13.87	106,000	13.45
Appraisal costs				
Inventory inspection	75,000	9.82	25,000	3.17
Reliability testing	43,000	5.63	15,000	1.90
Testing equipment (depreciation)	20,000	2.62	12,000	1.52
Supplies	12,000	1.57	8,000	1.02
Total appraisal	150,000	19.63	60,000	7.61
Internal failure costs				
Scrap	90,000	11.78	40,000	5.08
Repair and rework	140,000	18.32	110,000	13.96
Downtime	38,000	4.97	20,000	2.54
Reinspection	30,000	3.93	12,000	1.52
Total internal failure	298,000	39.01	182,000	23.10
External failure costs				
Warranty repairs and replacement	120,000	15.71	260,000	32.99
Freight	20,000	2.62	50,000	6.35
Customer relations	40,000	5.24	60,000	7.61
Restocking and packaging	30,000	3.93	70,000	8.88
Total external failure	210,000	27.49	440,000	55.84
Grand total	$764,000	100.00%	$788,000	100.00%

*Percentages do not add exactly because of rounding.

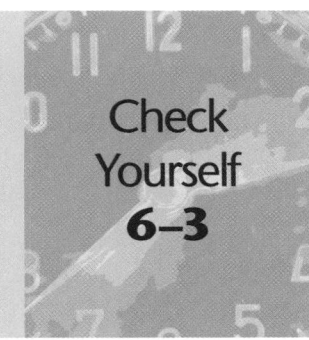

REALITY *bytes*

Does quality pay? It definitely does, according to returns provided in the stock market. The Baldridge Index, which is composed of companies that have received the Malcolm Baldridge National Quality Award, outperformed the **Standard & Poor's (S&P)** 500 stock index by almost 3 to 1. As indicated in Exhibit 6–10, the Baldridge Index provided a 362 percent four-year return as compared to a 148 percent return provided by the S&P 500 index. Because stock prices reflect investor beliefs regarding companies' present and future earnings, these returns provide a clear indication that investors believe that quality enhances profitability.

Exhibit 6–10 *Real-World Reporting Practices*

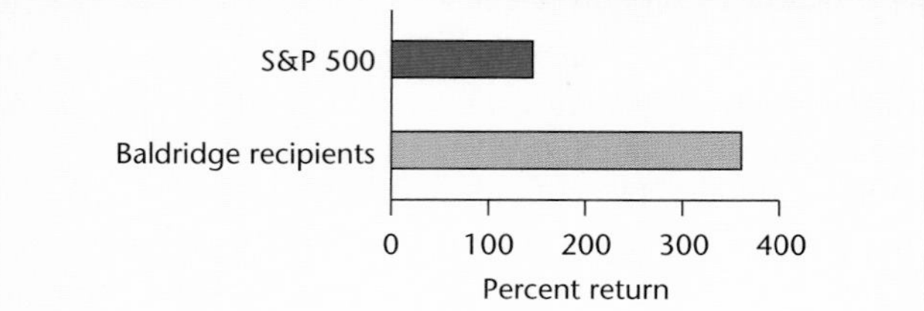

Source: "Quality Claims Its Own Bull Market," *BusinessWeek,* March 16, 1998, p. 113.

the failure cost data. Internal failure costs increased significantly while external failure costs decreased dramatically. The strategy succeeded in lowering total quality costs. The report suggests, however, that more improvement is possible. Notice that 86.13 percent (appraisal 19.63 percent + internal failure 39.01 percent + external failure 27.49 percent) of total quality costs is spent on finding and correcting mistakes. The adage "an ounce of prevention is worth a pound of cure," applied to Unterman, implies spending more on prevention could perhaps eliminate many of the appraisal and failure costs.

a look back

Many traditional cost systems used direct labor hours as the sole base for allocating overhead costs. Labor hours served as an effective *companywide allocation base* because labor was highly correlated with overhead cost incurrence. It made sense to assign more overhead to cost objects that required more labor. Because direct labor was related to production volume, it was frequently called a *volume-based cost driver.* Other volume-based cost drivers included machine hours, number of units, and labor dollars. Companywide, volume-based cost drivers were never perfect measures of overhead consumption. However, misallocation was not a serious problem because overhead costs were relatively small. If a manager misallocated an insignificant cost, it did not matter.

Automation has changed the nature of the manufacturing process. This change may cause significant distortions in the allocation of overhead costs when the allocation base is a companywide, volume-based cost driver. There are two primary reasons for distortions. First, in an automated environment, the same amount of labor (e.g., flipping a switch) may produce a large or a small volume of products. Under these circumstances, labor use is not related to the incurrence of overhead and is not a rational allocation base. Second, the distortions may be significant because overhead costs are much higher relative to the cost of labor and materials. For example, when robots replace people in the production process, depreciation becomes a larger portion of total product cost and labor becomes a smaller portion of the total.

To improve the accuracy of allocations, managerial accountants began to study the wide array of activities required to make a product. Such activities may include acquiring raw materials, materials handling and storage activities, product design activities, legal activities, and traditional production labor activities. Various measures of these activities can be used as bases for numerous overhead allocations related to determining product cost. Using activity measures to allocate overhead costs has become known as *activity-based costing (ABC).* In an ABC system, costs are allocated in a two-stage process. First, activities are organized into *activity centers* and the related costs of performing these activities are combined into *cost pools.* Second, the pooled costs are allocated to designated cost objects using activity-based cost drivers. Implementing ABC is most likely to succeed when employees understand that it will positively affect their fate and that of the company. Without employee cooperation, collecting data necessary for the system's success may be difficult.

Many ABC systems begin by organizing activities into one of four categories. Total *unit-level activity cost* increases each time a unit of product is made and decreases when production volume declines. Unit-level activity costs can be allocated with a base correlated to the level of production (volume-based cost drivers). *Batch-level activities* are related to producing groups of products. Their costs are fixed regardless of the number of units in a batch. Batch-level costs are assigned so that the products requiring the most batches are assigned the most batch costs. *Product-level activities* support a specific product or product line. Product-level costs are frequently assigned to products based on the product's percentage use of product-level activities. *Facility-level activities* are performed for the benefit of the production process as a whole. The allocation of these costs is often arbitrary.

Accurate allocations prevent the distortions of overcosted or undercosted products. Overcosting can cause a product line to be overpriced. Overpriced products may cause a company to lose market share, and the decline in sales revenue will cause profits to fall. When products are underpriced, revenue is less than it could be, and profitability suffers.

Product costs are frequently distinguished from upstream and downstream costs. *Upstream costs* result from activities that occur *before* goods are manufactured. Examples include research and development, product design, and legal work. *Downstream costs* result from activities that occur *after* goods are manufactured. Examples of downstream costs include selling and administrative expenses. Upstream and downstream costs affect pricing decisions and product elimination decisions.

a look forward

The next chapter introduces planning and cost control, including how to prepare budgets and projected (pro forma) financial statements. In addition to quantitative aspects, it illustrates the effect of the budgeting process on human behavior.

SELF-STUDY REVIEW PROBLEM

Adventure Luggage Company makes two types of airline carry-on bags. One bag type designed to meet mass market needs is constructed of durable polyester. The other bag type aimed at the high-end luxury market is made of genuine leather. Sales of the polyester bag have declined recently because of stiff price competition. Indeed, Adventure would have to sell this bag at less than production cost to match the competition. Adventure's president suspects that something is wrong with how the company estimates the bag's cost. He has asked the company's accountant to investigate that possibility. The accountant gathered the following information relevant to estimating the cost of the company's two bag types.

Both bags require the same amount of direct labor. The leather bags have significantly higher materials costs, and they require more inspections and rework because of higher quality standards. Since the leather bags are produced in smaller batches of different colors, they require significantly more setups. Finally, the leather bags generate more legal costs due to patents and more promotion costs because Adventure advertises them more aggressively. Specific cost and activity data follow.

	Polyester Bags	Leather Bags
Per unit direct materials cost	$30	$90
Per unit direct labor cost	2 hours @ $14 per hour	2 hours @ $14 per hour
Annual sales volume	7,000 units	3,000 units

Total annual overhead costs are $872,000. Adventure currently allocates overhead costs using a traditional costing system based on direct labor hours.

To reassess the overhead allocation policy and the resulting product cost estimates, the accountant subdivided the overhead into four categories and gathered information about these cost categories and the activities that caused the company to incur the costs. These data follow.

Category	Estimated Cost	Cost Driver	Amount of Cost Driver		
			Polyester	Leather	Total
Unit level	$480,000	Number of machine hours	20,000	60,000	80,000
Batch level	190,000	Number of machine setups	1,500	3,500	5,000
Product level	152,000	Number of inspections	200	600	800
Facility level	50,000	Equal percentage	50%	50%	100%
Total	$872,000				

Required

a. Determine the total cost and cost per unit for each product line, assuming that Adventure allocates overhead costs to each product line using direct labor hours as a companywide allocation base. Also determine the combined cost of the two product lines.

b. Determine the total cost and cost per unit for each product line, assuming that Adventure allocates overhead costs using an ABC system. Determine the combined cost of the two product lines.

c. Explain why the total combined cost computed in Requirements *a* and *b* is the same. Given that the combined cost is the same using either system, why is an ABC system with many different allocation rates better than a traditional system with a single companywide overhead rate?

Solution to Requirement a

Predetermined Overhead Rate

Polyester		Leather		
2 hr. × 7,000 Units	+	2 hr. × 3,000 Units		
14,000 direct labor hours		6,000 direct labor hours	=	20,000 Hours

Allocation rate = $872,000 ÷ 20,000 hours = $43.60 per direct labor hour

Allocated Overhead Costs

Type of Bag	Allocation Rate	×	Number of Hours	=	Allocated Cost
Polyester	$43.60	×	14,000	=	$610,400
Leather	43.60	×	6,000	=	261,600
Total			20,000		$872,000

Total Cost of Each Product Line and Combined Cost

Type of Bag	Direct Materials*	+	Direct Labor†	+	Allocated Overhead	=	Total
Polyester	$210,000	+	$196,000	+	$610,400	=	$1,016,400
Leather	270,000	+	84,000	+	261,600	=	615,600
Combined totals	$480,000	+	$280,000	+	$872,000	=	$1,632,000

*Direct materials
Polyester $30 × 7,000 units = $210,000
Leather 90 × 3,000 units = 270,000

†Direct labor
Polyester $14 × 14,000 hours = 196,000
Leather 14 × 6,000 hours = 84,000

Cost per Unit Computations Using Traditional Cost System

Type of bag	Total Cost	÷	Units	=	Cost per Unit
Polyester	$1,016,400	÷	7,000	=	$145.20
Leather	615,600	÷	3,000	=	205.20
Combined total	$1,632,000				

Solution to Requirement b

Overhead Cost Allocation Using ABC

	Unit	Batch	Product	Facility	Total
Cost pool	$480,000	$190,000	$152,000	$50,000	$872,000
÷ Cost drivers	Number of machine hours 80,000	Number of setups 5,000	Number of inspections 800	Equally 50%	
= Rate	$6 per machine hour	$38 per setup	$190 per inspection	$25,000	

Overhead Allocation for Polyester Bags

	Unit	Batch	Product	Facility	Total
Weight	20,000	1,500	200	1	
× Rate	$ 6	$ 38	$ 190	$25,000	
Allocation	$120,000	$57,000	$38,000	$25,000	$240,000

Overhead Allocation for Leather Bags

	Unit	Batch	Product	Facility	Total
Weight	60,000	3,500	600	1	
× Rate	$ 6	$ 38	$ 190	$25,000	
Allocation	$360,000	$133,000	$114,000	$25,000	$632,000

Total Cost of Each Product Line and Combined Cost

Type of Bag	Direct Materials	+	Direct Labor	+	Allocated Overhead	=	Total
Polyester	$210,000	+	$196,000	+	$240,000	=	$ 646,000
Leather	270,000	+	84,000	+	632,000	=	986,000
Combined totals	$480,000	+	$280,000	+	$872,000	=	$1,632,000

Cost per Unit Computations Under ABC System

Type of bag	Total Cost	÷	Units	=	Cost per Unit
Polyester	$ 646,000	÷	7,000	=	$ 92.29
Leather	986,000	÷	3,000	=	328.67
Combined total	$1,632,000				

Solution to Requirement c

The allocation method (ABC versus traditional costing) does not affect the total amount of cost to be allocated. Therefore, the total cost is the same using either method. However, the allocation method (ABC versus traditional costing) does affect the cost assigned to each product line. Since the ABC system more accurately traces costs to the products that cause the costs to be incurred, it provides a more accurate estimate of the true cost of making the products. The difference in the cost per unit using ABC versus traditional costing is significant. For example, the cost of the polyester bag was determined to be $145.20 using the traditional allocation method and $92.29 using ABC. This difference could have led Adventure to overprice the polyester bag, thereby causing the decline in sales volume. To the extent that ABC is more accurate, using it will improve pricing and other strategic decisions that significantly affect profitability.

KEY TERMS

Activities *233*
Activity-based cost drivers *231*
Activity-based costing (ABC) *233*
Activity centers *233*
Appraisal costs *242*
Batch-level activities *236*
Companywide allocation rate *230*
Downstream costs *241*
External failure costs *242*
Facility-level activities *237*
Failure costs *242*
Internal failure costs *242*
Prevention costs *242*
Product-level activities *236*
Quality *242*
Quality cost report *243*
Start-up (setup) costs *232*
Strategic cost management *241*
Target pricing *240*
Total quality management (TQM) *243*
Unit-level activities *235*
Upstream costs *241*
Volume-based cost drivers *231*
Voluntary costs *242*

QUESTIONS

1. Why did traditional cost systems base allocations on a single companywide cost driver?
2. Why are labor hours ineffective as a companywide allocation base in many industries today?
3. What is the difference between volume-based cost drivers and activity-based cost drivers?
4. Why do activity-based cost drivers provide more accurate allocations of overhead in an automated manufacturing environment?
5. When would it be appropriate to use volume-based cost drivers in an activity-based cost system?
6. Martinez Manufacturing makes two products, one of which is produced at a significantly higher volume than the other. The low-volume product consumes more of the company's engineering resources because it is technologically complex. Even so, the company's cost accountant chose to allocate engineering department costs based on the number of units produced. How could selecting this allocation base affect a decision about outsourcing engineering services for the low-volume product?
7. Briefly describe the activity-based costing allocation process.
8. Tom Rehr made the following comment: "Facility-level costs should not be allocated to products because they are irrelevant for decision-making purposes." Do you agree or disagree with this statement? Justify your response.
9. To facilitate cost tracing, a company's activities can be subdivided into four hierarchical categories. What are these four categories? Describe them and give at least two examples of each category.
10. Beth Nelson, who owns and runs a small sporting goods store, buys most of her merchandise directly from manufacturers. Ms. Nelson was shocked at the $7.50 charge for a container of three ping-pong balls. She found it hard to believe that it could have cost more than $1.00 to make the balls. When she complained to Jim Wilson, the marketing manager of the manufacturing company, he tried to explain that the cost also included companywide overhead costs. How could companywide overhead affect the cost of ping-pong balls?
11. If each patient in a hospital is considered a cost object, what are examples of unit-, batch-, product- and facility-level costs that would be allocated to this object using an activity-based cost system?
12. Milken Manufacturing has three product lines. The company's new accountant, Marvin LaSance, is responsible for allocating facility-level costs to these product lines. Mr. LaSance is finding the allocation assignment a daunting task. He knows there have been disagreements among the product managers over the allocation of facility costs, and he fears being asked to defend his method of allocation. Why would the allocation of facility-level costs be subject to disagreements?
13. Why would machine hours be an inappropriate allocation base for batch-level costs?
14. Alisa Kamuf's company has reported losses from operations for several years. Industry standards indicate that prices are normally set at 30 percent above manufacturing cost, which Ms. Kamuf has done. Assuming that her other costs are in line with industry norms, how could she continue to lose money while her competitors earn a profit?

15. Issacs Corporation produces two lines of pocket knives. The Arrowsmith product line involves very complex engineering designs; the Starscore product line involves relatively simple designs. Since its introduction, the low-volume Arrowsmith products have gained market share at the expense of the high-volume Starscore products. This pattern of sales has been accompanied by an overall decline in company profits. Why may the existing cost system be inadequate?

16. What is the relationship between activity-based management and just-in-time inventory?

EXERCISES—SERIES A

All Exercises in Series A are available with McGraw-Hill's Homework Manager.

EXERCISE 6–1A *Classifying the Costs of Unit-, Batch-, Product-, or Facility-Level Activities* L.O. 5

Russet Manufacturing is developing an activity-based costing system to improve overhead cost allocation. One of the first steps in developing the system is to classify the costs of performing production activities into activity cost pools.

Required

Using your knowledge of the four categories of activities, classify the cost of each activity in the following list into unit-, batch-, product-, or facility-level cost pools.

Cost Activity	Cost Pool
a. Ordering materials for a specific type of product	
b. Wages of workers moving units of work between work stations	
c. Factorywide electricity	
d. Salary of a manager in charge of a product line	
e. Sales commissions	
f. Engineering product design	
g. Supplies	
h. Wages of maintenance staff	
i. Labeling and packaging	
j. Plant security	

EXERCISE 6–2A *Identifying Appropriate Cost Drivers* L.O. 4

Required

Provide at least one example of an appropriate cost driver (allocation base) for each of the following activities.

a. Lighting is used for production facilities.
b. Materials are unloaded and stored for production.
c. Maintenance is performed on manufacturing equipment.
d. Sales commissions are paid.
e. Direct labor is used to change machine configurations.
f. Production equipment is set up for new production runs.
g. Engineering drawings are produced for design changes.
h. Purchase orders are issued.
i. Products are labeled, packaged, and shipped.
j. Machinists are trained on new computer-controlled machinery.

EXERCISE 6–3A *Classifying Costs and Identifying the Appropriate Cost Driver* L.O. 4, 5

Walton Manufacturing incurred the following costs during 2005 to produce its high-quality precision instruments. The company used an activity-based costing system and identified the following activities.

1. Materials handling.
2. Inventory storage.
3. Inspection of each batch produced.
4. Salaries of receiving clerks.
5. Setup for each batch produced.
6. Insurance on production facilities.
7. Depreciation on manufacturing equipment.

Required

a. Classify each activity as a unit-level, batch-level, product-level, or facility-level activity.

b. Identify an appropriate cost driver (allocation base) for each activity.

L.O. 5 EXERCISE 6–4A *Context-Sensitive Nature of Activity Classification*

Required

Describe a set of circumstances in which the cost of painting could be classified as a unit-level, a batch-level, a product-level, or a facility-level cost.

L.O. 5 EXERCISE 6–5A *Context-Sensitive Nature of Activity Classification*

Milner Company makes two types of circuit boards. One is a high-caliber board designed to accomplish the most demanding tasks; the other is a low-caliber board designed to provide limited service at an affordable price. During its most recent accounting period, Milner incurred $96,000 of inspection cost. When Milner recently established an activity-based costing system, its activities were classified into four categories. Each of the categories and appropriate cost drivers follow.

	Direct Labor Hours	Number of Batches	Number of Inspectors	Number of Square Feet
High caliber	4,000	25	3	40,000
Low caliber	16,000	15	2	60,000
Totals	20,000	40	5	100,000

Required

Allocate the inspection cost between the two products assuming that it is driven by (a) unit-level activities, (b) batch-level activities, (c) product-level activities, or (d) facility-level activities.

L.O. 4 EXERCISE 6–6A *Computing Overhead Rates Based on Different Cost Drivers*

Wang Industries produces two electronic decoders, P and Q. Decoder P is more sophisticated and requires more programming and testing than does Decoder Q. Because of these product differences, the company wants to use activity-based costing to allocate overhead costs. It has identified four activity pools. Relevant information follows.

Activity Pools	Cost Pool Total	Cost Driver
Repair and maintenance on assembly machine	$200,000	Number of units produced
Programming cost	420,000	Number of programming hours
Software inspections	30,000	Number of inspections
Product testing	40,000	Number of tests
Total overhead cost	$649,000	

Expected activity for each product follows.

	Number of Units	Number of Programming Hours	Number of Inspections	Number of Tests
Decoder P	20,000	2,000	190	1,400
Decoder Q	30,000	1,500	60	1,100
Totals	50,000	3,500	250	2,500

Required

a. Compute the overhead rate for each activity pool.

b. Determine the overhead cost allocated to each product.

L.O. 1, 3 EXERCISE 6–7A *Comparing an ABC System With a Traditional Cost System*

Use the information in Exercise 6–6A to complete the following requirements. Assume that before shifting to activity-based costing, Wang Industries allocated all overhead costs based on direct labor hours. Direct labor data pertaining to the two decoders follow.

	Direct Labor Hours
Decoder P	12,000
Decoder Q	18,000
Total	30,000

Required

a. Compute the amount of overhead cost allocated to each decoder when using direct labor hours as the allocation base.

b. Determine the cost per unit for overhead when using direct labor hours as the allocation base and when using ABC.

c. Explain why the per unit overhead cost is lower for the high-volume product when using ABC.

EXERCISE 6–8A *Allocating Costs With Different Cost Drivers*

L.O. 1, 3

Yangoon Company produces commercial gardening equipment. Since production is highly automated, the company allocates its overhead costs to product lines using activity-based costing. The costs and cost drivers associated with the four overhead activity cost pools follow.

	Activities			
	Unit Level	Batch Level	Product Level	Facility Level
Cost	$100,000	$40,000	$20,000	$240,000
Cost driver	2,000 labor hrs.	40 setups	Percentage of use	12,000 units

Production of 800 sets of cutting shears, one of the company's 20 products, took 200 labor hours and six setups and consumed 15 percent of the product-sustaining activities.

Required

a. Had the company used labor hours as a companywide allocation base, how much overhead would it have allocated to the cutting shears?

b. How much overhead is allocated to the cutting shears using activity-based costing?

c. Compute the overhead cost per unit for cutting shears using first activity-based costing and then using direct labor hours for allocation if 800 units are produced. If direct product costs are $50 and the product is priced at 30 percent above cost (rounded to the nearest whole dollar), for what price would the product sell under each allocation system?

d. Assuming that activity-based costing provides a more accurate estimate of cost, indicate whether the cutting shears would be over- or underpriced if direct labor hours are used as an allocation base. Explain how over- or undercosting can affect Sunshine's profitability.

e. Comment on the validity of using the allocated facility-level cost in the pricing decision. Should other costs be considered in a cost-plus-pricing decision? If so, which ones? What costs would you include if you were trying to decide whether to accept a special order?

EXERCISE 6–9A *Allocating Costs With Different Cost Drivers*

L.O. 1, 3

Colombo Publishing identified the following overhead activities, their respective costs, and their cost drivers to produce the three types of textbooks the company publishes.

		Type of Textbook		
Activity (Cost)	Cost Driver	Deluxe	Moderate	Economy
Machine maintenance ($160,000)	Number of machine hours	250	750	1,000
Setups ($400,000)	Number of setups	30	15	5
Packing ($180,000)	Number of cartons	10	30	50
Photo development ($364,000)	Number of pictures	4,000	2,000	1,000

Deluxe textbooks are made with the finest-quality paper, six-color printing, and many photographs. Moderate texts are made with three colors and a few photographs spread throughout each chapter. Economy books are printed in black and white and include pictures only in chapter openings.

Required

a. Colombo currently allocates all overhead costs based on machine hours. The company produced the following number of books during the prior year.

Deluxe	Moderate	Economy
50,000	150,000	200,000

Determine the overhead cost per book for each book type.

b. Determine the overhead cost per book, assuming that the volume-based allocation system described in Requirement *a* is replaced with an activity-based costing system.

c. Explain why the per unit overhead costs determined in Requirements *a* and *b* differ.

L.O. 4

EXERCISE 6–10A *Computing Product Cost With Given Activity Allocation Rates*

Stein Manufacturing produces two modems, one for laptop computers and the other for desktop computers. The production process is automated, and the company has found activity-based costing useful in assigning overhead costs to its products. The company has identified five major activities involved in producing the modems.

Activity	Allocation Base	Allocation Rate
Materials receiving & handling	Cost of material	2% of material cost
Production setup	Number of setups	$100.00 per setup
Assembly	Number of parts	$5.00 per part
Quality inspection	Inspection time	$1.50 per minute
Packing and shipping	Number of orders	$10.00 per order

Activity measures for the two kinds of modems follow.

	Labor Cost	Material Cost	Number of Setups	Number of Parts	Inspection Time	Number of Orders
Laptops	$2,500	$10,000	30	42	7,200 min.	65
Desktops	2,100	15,000	12	24	5,100 min.	20

Required

a. Compute the cost per unit of laptop and desktop modems, assuming that Stein made 300 units of each type of modem.

b. Explain why laptop modems cost more to make even though they have less material cost and are smaller than desktop modems.

L.O. 4

EXERCISE 6–11A *Allocating Facility-Level Cost and a Product Elimination Decision*

Poole Boards produces two kinds of skate boards. Selected unit data for the two boards for the last quarter follow.

	Basco Boards	Shimano Boards
Production costs		
Direct materials	$54	$72
Direct labor	$78	$102
Allocated overhead	$30	$36
Total units produced and sold	2,000	4,000
Total sales revenue	$336,000	$888,000

Poole allocates production overhead using activity-based costing. It allocates delivery expense and sales commissions, which amount to $54,000 per quarter, to the two products equally.

Required

a. Compute the net profit for each product.

b. Assuming that the overhead allocation for Basco boards includes $24,000 of facility-level cost, would you advise Poole to eliminate these boards? (*Hint:* Consider the method used to allocate the delivery and selling expense.)

EXERCISE 6–12A *Quality Cost Components and Relationships*

L.O. 8

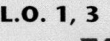

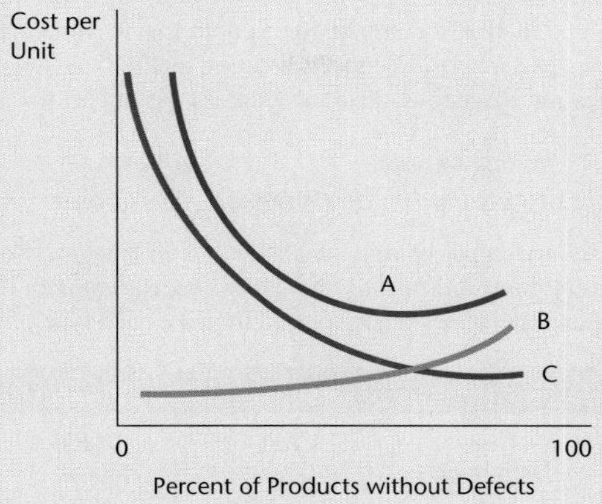

Required

The preceding graph depicts the relationships among the components of total quality cost.

a. Label the lines identified as A, B, and C.

b. Explain the relationships depicted in the graph.

PROBLEMS—SERIES A

All Problems in Series A are available with McGraw-Hill's Homework Manager.

PROBLEM 6–13A *Comparing an ABC System With a Traditional Cost System*

L.O. 1, 3

excel
www.mhhe.com/edmonds3e

Sassar Electronics produces video games in three market categories, commercial, home, and miniature. Sassar has traditionally allocated overhead costs to the three products using the companywide allocation base of direct labor hours. The company recently implemented an ABC system when it installed computer-controlled assembly stations that rendered the traditional costing system ineffective. In implementing the ABC system, the company identified the following activity cost pools and cost drivers.

Category	Total Pooled Cost	Types of Costs	Cost Driver
Unit	$360,000	Indirect labor wages, supplies, depreciation, machine maintenance	Machine hours
Batch	270,000	Materials handling, inventory storage, labor for setups, packaging, labeling and shipping, scheduling	Number of production orders
Product	240,000	Research and development	Time spent by research department
Facility	400,000	Rent, utilities, maintenance, admin. salaries, security	Square footage

Additional data for each of the product lines follow.

	Commercial	Home	Miniature	Total
Direct materials cost	$36.00/unit	$24.00/unit	$30.00/unit	—
Direct labor cost	$14.40/hour	$14.40/hour	$18.00/hour	—
Number of labor hours	6,000	12,000	2,000	20,000
Number of machine hours	10,000	45,000	25,000	80,000
Number of production orders	100	1,000	400	1,500
Research and development time	10%	20%	70%	100%
Number of units	15,000	45,000	14,000	74,000
Square footage	20,000	50,000	30,000	100,000

CHECK FIGURES

b. Cost per unit:
Comerical: $52.89
Home: $41.85
Miniature: $66.32

Required

a. Determine the total cost and cost per unit for each product line, assuming that overhead costs are allocated to each product line using direct labor hours as a companywide allocation base. Also determine the combined cost of all three product lines.

b. Determine the total cost and cost per unit for each product line, assuming that an ABC system is used to allocate overhead costs. Determine the combined cost of all three product lines.

c. Explain why the combined total cost computed in Requirements *a* and *b* is the same amount. Given that the combined cost is the same using either allocation method, why is an ABC system with many different allocation rates more accurate than a traditional system with a single companywide overhead rate?

L.O. 2

PROBLEM 6–14A *Effect of Automation on Overhead Allocation*

CHECK FIGURES
b. Allocated costs:
Seasonal: $24,000
All purpose: $336,000

Dhaka Rug Company makes two types of rugs, seasonal and all purpose. Both types of rugs are handmade, but the seasonal rugs require significantly more labor because of their decorative designs. The annual number of rugs made and the labor hours required to make each type of rug follow.

	Seasonal	All Purpose	Totals
Number of rugs	1,200	2,800	4,000
Number of direct labor hours	150,000	210,000	360,000

Required

a. Assume that annual overhead costs total $288,000. Select the appropriate cost driver and determine the amount of overhead to allocate to each type of rug.

b. Dhaka automates the seasonal rug line resulting in a dramatic decline in labor usage, to make 1,200 rugs in only 15,000 hours. Dhaka continues to make the all-purpose rugs the same way as before. The number of rugs made and the labor hours required to make them after automation follow.

	Seasonal	All Purpose	Totals
Number of rugs	1,200	2,800	4,000
Number of direct labor hours	15,000	210,000	225,000

Overhead costs are expected to increase to $360,000 as a result of the automation. Allocate the increased overhead cost to the two types of rugs using direct labor hours as the allocation base and comment on the appropriateness of the allocation.

L.O. 3, 4

PROBLEM 6–15A *Using Activity-Based Costing to Improve Allocation Accuracy*

CHECK FIGURES
b. Allocated costs:
Seasonal: $199,480
All purpose: 160,520

This problem is an extension of Problem 6–14A, which must be completed first.
Dhaka's accounting staff has disaggregated the $360,000 of overhead costs into the following items.

(1) Inspection costs	$ 32,000
(2) Setup costs	21,600
(3) Engineering costs	32,000
(4) Legal costs related to products	12,000
(5) Materials movement cost per batch	4,800
(6) Salaries of production supervisors	80,000
(7) Fringe benefit costs	16,000
(8) Utilities costs	8,000
(9) Plant manager's salary	48,000
(10) Depreciation on production equipment	72,000
(11) Depreciation on building	16,000
(12) Miscellaneous costs	10,000
(13) Indirect materials costs	5,600
(14) Production employee incentive costs	2,000
Total	$360,000

Required

a. Each of Dhaka's rug lines operates as a department. The all-purpose department occupies 6,000 square feet of floor space, and the seasonal department occupies 12,000 square feet of space. Comment on the validity of allocating the overhead costs by square footage.

b. Assume that the following additional information is available.

(1) Rugs are individually inspected.

(2) Dhaka incurs setup costs each time a new style of seasonal rug is produced. The seasonal rugs were altered nine times during the year. The manual equipment for all-purpose rugs is reset twice each year to ensure accurate weaving. The setup for the technical equipment used to weave seasonal rugs requires more highly skilled workers, but the all-purpose rugs require more manual equipment, thereby resulting in a *per setup* charge that is roughly equal for both types of rugs. Oriental undertook 22 setups during the year, 18 of which applied to seasonal rugs and 4 that applied to all-purpose rugs.

(3) Ninety percent of the product-level costs can be traced to producing seasonal rugs.

(4) Six supervisors oversee the production of all-purpose rugs. Because seasonal rugs are made in an automated department, only two production supervisors are needed.

(5) Each rug requires an equal amount of indirect materials.

(6) Costs associated with production activities are assigned to six activity cost pools: (1) labor-related activities, (2) unit-level activities, (3) batch-level activities, (4) product-level supervisory activities, (5) other product-level activities, and (6) facility-level activities.

Organize the $360,000 of overhead costs into activity center cost pools and allocate the costs to the two types of rugs.

c. Assuming that 90 seasonal and 240 all-purpose rugs were made in January, determine the overhead costs that would be assigned to each of the two rug types for the month of January.

PROBLEM 6–16A *Using Activity-Based Costing to Improve Allocation Accuracy*

L.O. 4

CHECK FIGURES
a. Cost per student:
Computer-Assisted: $327
Classroom: $237

The After School, Inc. (ASI), is a profit-oriented education business. ASI provides remedial training for high school students who have fallen behind in their classroom studies. It charges its students $350 per course. During the previous year, ASI provided instruction for 1,000 students. The income statement for the company follows.

Revenue	$300,000
Cost of instructors	(170,000)
Overhead costs	(85,000)
Net income	$ 45,000

The company president, Dee Stone, indicated in a discussion with the accountant, Gene Johnson, that she was extremely pleased with the growth in the area of computer-assisted instruction. She observed that this department served 200 students using only one part-time instructor. In contrast, the classroom-based instructional department required 32 instructors to teach 800 students. Ms. Stone noted that the per student cost of instruction was dramatically lower for the computer-assisted department. She based her conclusion on the following information.

ASI pays its part-time instructors an average of $5,000 per year. The total cost of instruction and the cost per student are computed as follows.

Type of Instruction	Computer-Assisted	Classroom
Number of instructors (a)	2	32
Number of students (b)	200	800
Total cost (c = a × $5,000)	$10,000	$160,000
Cost per student (c ÷ b)	$50	$200

Assuming that overhead costs were distributed equally across the student population, Ms. Stone concluded that the cost of instructors was the critical variable in the company's capacity to generate profits. Based on her analysis, her strategic plan called for heavily increased use of computer-assisted instruction.

Mr. Johnson was not so sure that computer-assisted instruction should be stressed. After attending a seminar on activity-based costing (ABC), he believed that the allocation of overhead cost could be more closely traced to the different types of learning activities. To facilitate an activity-based analysis, he developed the following information about the costs associated with computer-assisted versus classroom instructional activities. He identified $48,000 of overhead costs that were directly traceable to computer-assisted activities, including the costs of computer hardware, software, and technical assistance. He believed the remaining $37,000 of overhead costs should be allocated to the two instructional activities based on the number of students enrolled in each program.

Required

a. Based on the preceding information, determine the total cost and the cost per student to provide courses through computer-assisted instruction versus classroom instruction.

b. Comment on the validity of stressing growth in the area of computer-assisted instruction.

L.O. 6

PROBLEM 6–17A *Key Activity-Based Costing Concepts*

Agee Paint Company makes paint in many different colors; it charges the same price for all of its paint regardless of the color. Recently, Agee's chief competitor cut the price of its white paint, which normally outsells any other color by a margin of 4 to 1. Agee's marketing manager requested permission to match the competitor's price. When Gene Taylor, Agee's president, discussed the matter with Kay Spencer, the chief accountant, he was told that the competitor's price was below Agee's cost. Mr. Taylor responded, "If that's the case, then there is something wrong with our accounting system. I know the competition wouldn't sell below cost. Prepare a report showing me how you determine our paint cost and get back to me as soon as possible."

The next day, Ms. Spencer returned to Mr. Taylor's office and began by saying, "Determining the cost per gallon is a pretty simple computation. It includes $1.10 of labor, $3.10 of materials, and $4.00 of overhead for a total cost of $8.20 per gallon. The problem is that the competition is selling the stuff for $7.99 per gallon. They've got to be losing money."

Mr. Taylor then asked Ms. Spencer how she determined the overhead cost. She replied, "We take total overhead cost and divide it by total labor hours and then assign it to the products based on the direct labor hours required to make the paint." Mr. Taylor then asked what kinds of costs are included in the total overhead cost. Ms. Spencer said, "It includes the depreciation on the building and equipment, the cost of utilities, supervisory salaries, interest. Just how detailed do you want me to go with this list?"

Mr. Taylor responded, "Keep going, I'll tell you when I've heard enough."

Ms. Spencer continued, "There is the cost of setups. Every time a color is changed, the machines have to be cleaned, the color release valves reset, a trial batch prepared, and color quality tested. Sometimes mistakes occur and the machines must be reset. In addition, purchasing and handling the color ingredients must be accounted for as well as adjustments in the packaging department to change the paint cans and to mark the boxes to show the color change. Then . . . "

Mr. Taylor interrupted, "I think I've heard enough. We sell so much white paint that we run it through a separate production process. White paint is produced continuously. There are no shutdowns and setups. White uses no color ingredients. So why are these costs being assigned to our white paint production?"

Ms. Spencer replied, "Well, sir, these costs are just a part of the big total that is allocated to all of the paint, no matter what color it happens to be."

Mr. Taylor looked disgusted and said, "As I told you yesterday, Ms. Spencer, something is wrong with our accounting system!"

Required

a. Explain what the terms *overcost* and *undercost* mean. Is Agee's white paint over- or undercosted?

b. Explain what the term *companywide overhead rate* means. Is Agee using a companywide overhead rate?

c. Explain how Agee could improve the accuracy of its overhead cost allocations.

L.O. 4, 7

Excel

www.mhhe.com/edmonds3e

CHECK FIGURES

a. Cost per unit:
Tennis Racquet: $14.71
Badminton Racquet: $25.67

PROBLEM 6–18A *Pricing Decisions Made With ABC System Cost Data*

Lendle Sporting Goods Corporation makes two types of racquets, tennis and badminton. The company uses the same facility to make both products even though the processes are quite different. The company has recently converted its cost accounting system to activity-based costing. The following are the cost data that Kay Segrest, the cost accountant, prepared for the third quarter of 2004 (during which Lendle made 70,000 tennis racquets and 30,000 badminton racquets):

Direct Cost	Tennis Racquet (TR)	Badminton Racquet (BR)
Direct materials	$20 per unit	$12 per unit
Direct labor	25 per unit	20 per unit

Category	Estimated Cost	Cost Driver	Amount of Cost Driver
Unit level	$ 750,000	Number of inspection hours	TR: 15,000 hours; BR: 10,000 hours
Batch level	250,000	Number of setups	TR: 80 setups; BR: 45 setups
Product level	150,000	Number of TV commercials	TR: 4; BR: 1
Facility level	650,000	Number of machine hours	TR: 30,000 hours; BR: 35,000 hours
Total	$1,800,000		

Inspectors are paid according to the number of actual hours worked, which is determined by the number of racquets inspected. Engineers who set up equipment for both products are paid monthly salaries.

TV commercial fees are paid at the beginning of the quarter. Facility-level cost includes depreciation of all production equipment.

Required

a. Compute the cost per unit for each product.

b. If management wants to price badminton racquets 30 percent above cost, what price should the company set?

c. The market price of tennis racquets has declined substantially because of new competitors entering the market. Management asks you to determine the minimum cost of producing tennis racquets in the short term. Provide that information.

PROBLEM 6–19A *Target Pricing and Target Costing With ABC*

L.O. 4, 7

CHECK FIGURES
a. Cost per unit:
ZM: $76.84
DS: $29.43

Taylor Cameras, Inc., manufactures two models of cameras. Model ZM has a zoom lens; Model DS has a fixed lens. Hardy uses an activity-based costing system. The following are the relevant cost data for the previous month.

Direct Cost per Unit	Model ZM	Model DS
Direct materials	$32	$10
Direct labor	30	8

Category	Estimated Cost	Cost Driver	Use of Cost Driver
Unit level	$ 27,000	Number of units	ZM: 2,400 units; DS: 9,600 units
Batch level	50,000	Number of setups	ZM: 25 setups; DS: 25 setups
Product level	90,000	Number of TV commercials	ZM: 15; DS: 10
Facility level	300,000	Number of machine hours	ZM: 500 hours; DS: 1,000 hours
Total	$467,000		

Taylor's facility has the capacity to operate 4,500 machine hours per month.

Required

a. Compute the cost per unit for each product.

b. The current market price for products comparable to Model ZM is $146 and for DS is $52. If Taylor sold all of its products at the market prices, what was its profit or loss for the previous month?

c. A market expert believes that Taylor can sell as many cameras as it can produce by pricing Model ZM at $140 and Model DS at $50. Taylor would like to use those estimates as its target prices and have a profit margin of 20 percent of target prices. What is the target cost for each product?

d. Is there any way for the company to reach its target costs?

PROBLEM 6–20A *Cost Management With an ABC System*

L.O. 4

excel
www.mhhe.com/edmonds3e

CHECK FIGURES
a. Cost per unit:
Diamond: $116.80
Gold: $73.08

Munn Chairs, Inc., makes two types of chairs. Model Diamond is a high-end product designed for professional offices. Model Gold is an economical product designed for family use. Judith Munn, the president, is worried about cut-throat price competition in the chairs market. Her company suffered a loss last quarter, an unprecedented event in its history. The company's accountant prepared the following cost data for Ms. Munn.

Direct Cost per Unit	Model Diamond (D)	Model Gold (G)
Direct materials	$22 per unit	$12 per unit
Direct labor	$24/hour × 2 hours production time	$24/hour × 1 hour production time

Category	Estimated Cost	Cost Driver	Use of Cost Driver
Unit level	$ 300,000	Number of units	D: 15,000 units; G: 35,000 units
Batch level	750,000	Number of setups	D: 104 setups; G: 146 setups
Product level	450,000	Number of TV commercials	D: 5; G: 10
Facility level	500,000	Number of machine hours	D: 1,500 hours; G: 3,500 hours
Total	$2,000,000		

The market price for office chairs comparable to Model Diamond is $114 and to Model Gold is $70.

Required

a. Compute the cost per unit for both products.

b. Andrew Ryan, the chief engineer, told Ms. Munn that the company is currently making 150 units of Model Diamond per batch and 245 units of Model Gold per batch. He suggests doubling the batch sizes to cut the number of setups in half, thereby reducing the setup cost by 50 percent. Compute the cost per unit for each product if Ms. Munn adopts his suggestion.

c. Is there any side effect if Ms. Munn increases the production batch size by 100 percent?

L.O. 8, 9

PROBLEM 6–21A *Assessing a Quality Control Strategy*

The following quality cost report came from the records of Ludman Company.

	2006		2005	
	Amount	**Percentage**	**Amount**	**Percentage**
Prevention costs				
Engineering and design	$136,000	13.74%	$ 58,000	3.86%
Training and education	34,000	3.43	12,000	0.80
Depreciation on prevention equipment	58,000	5.86	30,000	1.99
Incentives and awards	88,000	8.89	40,000	2.66
Total prevention	316,000	31.92%	140,000	9.31%
Appraisal costs				
Inventory inspection	50,000	5.05	50,000	3.32
Reliability testing	32,000	3.23	30,000	1.99
Testing equipment (depreciation)	22,000	2.22	24,000	1.60
Supplies	14,000	1.41	16,000	1.06
Total appraisal	118,000	11.92%	120,000	7.98%
Internal failure costs				
Scrap	48,000	4.85	80,000	5.32
Repair and rework	98,000	9.90	220,000	14.63
Downtime	24,000	2.42	40,000	2.66
Reinspection	8,000	0.81	24,000	1.60
Total internal failure	178,000	17.98%	364,000	24.20%
External failure cost				
Warranty repairs and replacement	220,000	22.22	520,000	34.57
Freight	48,000	4.85	100,000	6.65
Customer relations	56,000	5.66	120,000	7.98
Restocking and packaging	54,000	5.45	140,000	9.31
Total external failure	378,000	38.18%	880,000	58.51%
Grand total	$990,000	100.00%	$1,504,000	100.00%

Required

a. Explain the strategy that Ludman Company initiated to control its quality costs.

b. Indicate whether the strategy was successful or unsuccessful in reducing quality costs.

c. Explain how the strategy likely affected customer satisfaction.

EXERCISES—SERIES B

L.O. 5

EXERCISE 6–1B *Classifying the Costs of Unit-, Batch-, Product-, or Facility-Level Activities*

Kenneth Manufacturing is developing an activity-based costing system to improve overhead cost allocation. One of the first steps in developing the system is to classify the costs of performing production activities into activity cost pools.

Required

Using the four-tier cost hierarchy described in the chapter, classify each of the following costs into unit-level, batch-level, product-level, or facility-level cost pools.

Cost Activity	Cost Pool
a. Machine setup cost	
b. Salary of the plant manager's secretary	
c. Factory depreciation	
d. Advertising costs for a particular product	
e. Wages of assembly line workers	
f. Product design costs	
g. Materials requisition costs for a particular work order	
h. Security guard wages	
i. Lubricant for machines	
j. Parts used to make a particular product	

EXERCISE 6–2B *Identifying Appropriate Cost Drivers* — L.O. 4

Required
Provide at least one example of an appropriate cost driver (allocation base) for each of the following activities.

a. Workers move materials from the warehouse to the factory floor.
b. Assembly line machines are operated.
c. Workers count completed goods before moving them to a warehouse.
d. A logistics manager runs a computer program to determine the materials release schedule.
e. Janitors clean the factory floor after workers have left.
f. Mechanics apply lubricant to machines.
g. Engineers design a product production layout.
h. Engineers set up machines to produce a product.
i. The production supervisor completes the paperwork initiating a work order.
j. The production manager prepares materials requisition forms.

EXERCISE 6–3B *Classifying Costs and Identifying the Appropriate Cost Driver* — L.O. 4, 5

Gurosky Corporation, a furniture manufacturer, uses an activity-based costing system. It has identified the following selected activities:

1. Inspecting completed furniture for quality control.
2. Purchasing TV time to advertise a particular product.
3. Incurring property taxes on factory buildings.
4. Incurring paint cost for furniture produced.
5. Setting up machines for a particular batch of production.
6. Inspecting wood prior to using it in production.
7. Packaging completed furniture in boxes for shipment.

Required
a. Classify each activity as a unit-level, batch-level, product-level, or facility-level activity.
b. Identify an appropriate cost driver (allocation base) for each of the activities.

EXERCISE 6–4B *Understanding the Context-Sensitive Nature of Classifying Activities* — L.O. 5

Required
Describe a set of circumstances in which labor cost could be classified as a unit-level, a batch-level, a product-level, or a facility-level cost.

EXERCISE 6–5B *Understanding the Context-Sensitive Nature of Classifying Activities* — L.O. 5

Lyle Company makes two types of cell phones. Handy is a thin, pocket-size cell phone that is easy to carry around. Action is a palm-size phone convenient to hold while the user is talking. During its most recent accounting period, Lyle incurred $300,000 of quality-control costs. Recently Lyle established an activity-based costing system, which involved classifying its activities into four categories. Each of the categories and appropriate cost drivers follow.

	Direct Labor Hours	Number of Batches	Number of Engineers	Number of Square Feet
Handy	26,000	38	10	37,000
Action	24,000	22	5	83,000
Totals	50,000	60	15	120,000

Lyle uses direct labors hours to allocate unit-level activities, number of batches to allocate batch-level activities, number of engineers to allocate product-level activities, and number of square feet to allocate facility-level activities.

Required
Allocate the quality-control cost between the two products, assuming that it is driven by (a) unit-level activities, (b) batch-level activities, (c) product-level activities, and (d) facility-level activities.

L.O. 4

EXERCISE 6–6B *Computing Overhead Rates Based on Different Cost Drivers*

Cordova Industries produces two surge protectors: VC620 with six outlets and PH630 with eight outlets and two telephone line connections. Because of these product differences, the company plans to use activity-based costing to allocate overhead costs. The company has identified four activity pools. Relevant information follows.

Activity Pools	Cost Pool Total	Cost Driver
Machine setup	$240,000	Number of setups
Machine operation	360,000	Number of machine hours
Quality control	60,000	Number of inspections
Packaging	40,000	Number of units
Total overhead cost	$700,000	

Expected activity for each product follows.

	Number of Setups	Number of Machine Hours	Number of Inspections	Number of Units
VC620	48	1,400	78	25,000
PH630	72	2,600	172	15,000
Total	120	4,000	250	40,000

Required
a. Compute the overhead rate for each activity pool.
b. Determine the overhead cost allocated to each product.

L.O. 1, 3

EXERCISE 6–7B *Comparing an ABC System With a Traditional Cost System*

Use the information in Exercise 6–6B to complete the following requirements. Assume that before shifting to activity-based costing, Cordova Industries allocated all overhead costs based on direct labor hours. Direct labor data pertaining to the two surge protectors follow.

	Direct Labor Hours
VC620	16,000
PH630	9,000
Total	25,000

Required
a. Compute the amount of overhead cost allocated to each surge protector when using direct labor hours as the allocation base.
b. Determine the cost per unit for overhead when using direct labor hours as the allocation base and when using ABC.
c. Explain why the per unit overhead cost is lower for the higher-volume product when using ABC.

L.O. 1, 3

EXERCISE 6–8B *Allocating Costs With Different Cost Drivers*

Fritz Sporting Goods, Inc., produces indoor treadmills. The company allocates its overhead costs using activity-based costing. The costs and cost drivers associated with the four overhead activity cost pools follow.

Activities	Unit Level	Batch Level	Product Level	Facility Level
Cost	$1,000,000	$500,000	$300,000	$900,000
Cost driver	12,500 labor hours	50 setups	Percentage of use	15,000 units

Producing 5,000 units of PFT200, one of the company's five products, took 4,000 labor hours, 25 setups, and consumed 30 percent of the product-sustaining activities.

Required

a. Had the company used labor hours as a companywide allocation base, how much overhead would it have allocated to the 5,000 units of PFT200?

b. How much overhead is allocated to the 5,000 PFT200 units using activity-based costing?

c. Compute the overhead cost per unit for PFT200 using activity-based costing and direct labor hours if 5,000 units are produced. If direct product costs are $337 and PFT200 is priced at 20 percent above cost (rounded to the nearest whole dollar), compute the product's selling price under each allocation system.

d. Assuming that activity-based costing provides a more accurate estimate of cost, indicate whether PFT200 would be over- or underpriced if Fritz uses direct labor hours as the allocation base. Explain how over- or undercosting can affect Fritz's profitability.

e. Comment on the validity of using the allocated facility-level cost in the pricing decision. Should other costs be considered in a cost-plus pricing decision? If so, which ones? What costs would you include if you were trying to decide whether to accept a special order?

EXERCISE 6–9B *Allocating Costs With Different Cost Drivers*

L.O. 1, 3

Gosha Shoes Corporation produces three brands of shoes, Brisk, Pro, and Runner. Relevant information about Burns' overhead activities, their respective costs, and their cost drivers follows.

Overhead Costs	Cost Driver	Brisk	Pro	Runner
Fringe benefits ($720,000)	Labor hours	10,000	20,000	20,000
Setups ($400,000)	Number of setups	15	25	10
Packing costs ($80,000)	Number of cartons	200	300	300
Quality control ($600,000)	Number of tests	120	200	80

Required

a. Burns currently allocates all overhead costs based on labor hours. The company produced the following numbers of pairs of shoes during the prior year.

Brisk	Pro	Runner
20,000	30,000	40,000

Determine the overhead cost per pair of shoes for each brand.

b. Determine the overhead cost per pair of shoes for each brand, assuming that the volume-based allocation system described in Requirement *a* is replaced with an activity-based costing system.

c. Explain why the per pair overhead costs determined in Requirements *a* and *b* differ.

EXERCISE 6–10B *Computing Product Cost With Given Activity Allocation Rates*

L.O. 4

Using automated production processes, Fleck Videos produces two kinds of camcorders: N100 is an analog recorder and D200 is a digital recorder. The company has found activity-based costing useful in assigning overhead costs to its products. It has identified the following five major activities involved in producing the camcorders.

Activity	Allocation Base	Allocation Rate
Materials receiving and handling	Cost of materials	3% of materials cost
Production setup	Number of setups	$800 per setup
Assembly	Number of parts	$10 per part
Quality inspection	Inspection time	$25 per minute
Packing and shipping	Number of orders	$80 per order

Activity measures for the two kinds of camcorders follow.

	Labor Cost*	Materials Cost*	Number of Setups	Number of Parts	Inspection Time	Number of Orders
N100	$450,000	$250,000	10	10,000	800 min.	25
D200	300,000	300,000	25	10,000	4,800 min.	50

*Both are direct costs.

Required

a. Compute the cost per unit of N100 and D200, assuming that Fleck made 1,000 units of each type of camcorder.

b. Explain why the D200 digital camcorders cost more to make although their direct costs are less than those for the N100 analog camcorders.

L.O. 4

EXERCISE 6–11B *Allocating Facility-Level Cost and a Product Elimination Decision*

Arrington Corporation produces two types of juice that it packages in cases of 24 cans per case. Selected per case data for the two products for the last month follow.

	Orange Juice	Tomato Juice
Production costs		
Direct material	$5	$4
Direct labor	$2	$3
Allocated overhead	$3	$4
Total cases produced and sold	24,000	14,000
Total sales revenue	$320,000	$189,000

Arrington allocates production overhead using activity-based costing but allocates monthly packaging expense, which amounted to $76,000 last month, to the two products equally.

Required

a. Compute the net profit for each product.

b. Assuming that the overhead allocation for the tomato juice includes $30,000 of facility-level cost, would you advise Arrington to eliminate this product? (*Hint:* Consider the method used to allocate the monthly packaging expense.)

L.O. 8

EXERCISE 6–12B *Applying Concepts of Quality Cost Management*

May Lowery, the president of Fulmar Industries, Inc., was beaming when she was reviewing the company's quality cost report. After she had implemented a quality-control program for three years, the company's defect rate had declined from 20 percent to 3 percent. Mrs. Lowery patted Julian Marbury, the production manager, on his back and said: "You have done a great job! I plan to reward you for your hard work. However, I want the defects to disappear completely before I promote you to the position of executive vice president. So, zero-defect is going to be your personal goal for the coming year." Mr. Marbury responded wearily, "I'm not sure that's really a good idea."

Required

Write a memorandum to the president explaining that zero defect is not a practical policy.

PROBLEMS—SERIES B

L.O. 1, 3

PROBLEM 6–13B *Comparing an ABC System With a Traditional Costing System*

Since its inception, Drake Laboratory, Inc., has produced a single product, Product S109. With the advent of automation, the company added the technological capability to begin producing a second product, Product N227. Because of the success of Product N227, manufacturing has been shifting toward its production. Sales of Product N227 are now 50 percent of the total annual sales of 20,000 units, and the company is optimistic about the new product's future sales growth. One reason the company is excited about the sales potential of its new product is that the new product's gross profit margin is higher than that of Product S109. Management is thrilled with the new product's initial success but concerned about the company's declining profits since the product's introduction. Suspecting a problem with the company's costing system, management hires you to investigate.

In reviewing the company's records, product specifications, and manufacturing processes, you discover the following information.

1. The company is in an extremely competitive industry in which markups are low and accurate estimates of cost are critical to success.
2. Product N227 has complex parts that require more labor, machine time, setups, and inspections than Product S109.
3. Budgeted costs for direct materials and labor follow.

Direct Cost per Unit	Product S109	Product N227
Direct materials	$48	$48
Direct labor	$30/hour × 2 hours production time	$30/hour × 2.8 hours production time

4. The company presently allocates overhead costs to its products based on direct labor hours. After carefully studying the company's overhead, you identify four different categories of overhead costs. Using your knowledge of this company and similar companies in the same industry, you estimate the total costs for each of these categories and identify the most appropriate cost driver for measuring each product's overhead consumption. Detailed information for each cost category follows.

Category	Estimated Cost	Cost Driver	Use of Cost Driver
Unit level	$1,080,000	Number of machine hours	S109: 20,000 hours; N227: 60,000 hours
Batch level	456,000	Number of machine setups	S109: 1,500; N227: 3,500
Product level	360,000	Number of inspections	S109: 200; N227: 600
Facility level	120,000	Equal percentage for products	S109: 50%; N227: 50%
Total	$2,016,000		

Required

a. Determine the predetermined overhead rate the company is using.
b. Compute the amount of overhead the company assigns to each product using this rate.
c. Determine the cost per unit and total cost of each product when overhead is assigned based on direct labor hours.
d. To remain competitive, the company prices its products at only 20 percent above cost. Compute the price for each product with this markup.
e. Compute the overhead rate for each category of activity.
f. Determine the amount of overhead cost, both in total and per unit, that would be assigned to each product if the company switched to activity-based costing.
g. Assuming that prices are adjusted to reflect activity-based costs, determine the revised price for each product.
h. Based on your results for Requirements *f* and *g,* explain why Product N227 costs more to make than previously apparent and why sales prices therefore need to be adjusted.

PROBLEM 6–14B *Using Activity-Based Costing to Improve Allocation Accuracy*

L.O. 1, 3

Owen's Commemoratives makes and sells two types of decorative plates. One plate displays a hand-painted image of Princess Diana; the other plate displays a machine-pressed image of Marilyn Monroe. The Diana plates require 25,000 hours of direct labor to make; the Monroe plates require only 5,000 hours of direct labor. Overhead costs are composed of (1) $140,000 machine-related activity costs including indirect labor, utilities, and depreciation and (2) $100,000 labor-related activity costs including overtime pay, fringe benefits, and payroll taxes.

Required

a. Assuming that Owen's uses direct labor hours as the allocation base, determine the amount of the total $240,000 overhead cost that would be allocated to each type of plate.
b. Explain why using direct labor hours may distort the allocation of overhead cost to the two products.
c. Explain how activity-based costing could improve the accuracy of the overhead cost allocation.

PROBLEM 6–15B *Using Activity-Based Costing to Improve Allocation Accuracy*

L.O. 4

This problem is an extension of Problem 6–14B, which must be completed first.
Assume the same data as in Problem 6–14B with the following additional information. The hours of machine time for processing plates are 1,000 for Diana plates and 2,500 for Monroe plates.

Required

a. Establish two activity centers, one for machine-related activities and the second for labor-related activities. Assign the total overhead costs to the two activity centers.
b. Allocate the machine-related overhead costs to each product based on machine hours.
c. Allocate the labor-related overhead costs to each product based on direct labor hours.
d. Draw a diagram that compares the one-stage allocation method used in Problem 6–14B with the two-stage activity-based costing approach used in this problem.

L.O. 4 PROBLEM 6–16B *Using Activity-Based Costing to Improve Business Decisions*

Parrish CPA and Associates is a local accounting firm specializing in bookkeeping and tax services. The firm has four certified public accountants who supervise 20 clerks. The clerks handle basic bookkeeping jobs and prepare tax return drafts. The CPAs review and approve the bookkeeping jobs and tax returns. Each CPA receives a fixed salary of $8,000 per month; the clerks earn an hourly rate of $18. Because the clerks are paid by the hour and their work hours can be directly traced to individual jobs, their wages are considered direct costs. The CPAs' salaries are not traced to individual jobs and are therefore treated as indirect costs. The firm allocates overhead based on direct labor hours. The following is Parrish's income statement for the previous month.

	Bookkeeping	Tax	Total
Revenues	$60,000	$60,000	$120,000
Direct Expenses	(22,500)*	(22,500)*	(45,000)
Indirect Supervisory Expenses	(16,000)	(16,000)	(32,000)
Net Income	$21,500	$21,500	$43,000

*1,250 clerical hours were used in each category during the previous month.

Nancy Parrish, CPA and chief executive officer, is not sure that the two operations are equally profitable as the income statement indicates. First, she believes that most of the CPAs' time was spent instructing clerks in tax return preparation. The bookkeeping jobs appear to be routine, and most of the clerks can handle them with little supervision. After attending a recent professional development seminar on activity-based costing (ABC), Ms. Parrish believes that the allocation of indirect costs can be more closely traced to different types of services. To facilitate an activity-based analysis, she asked the CPAs to document their work hours on individual jobs for the last week. The results indicate that, on average, 25 percent of the CPAs' hours was spent supervising bookkeeping activities and the remaining 75 percent was spent supervising tax activities.

Required

a. Based on the preceding information, reconstruct the income statement for bookkeeping services, tax services, and the total, assuming that Parrish revises its allocation of indirect supervisory costs based on ABC.

b. Comment on the results and recommend a new business strategy.

L.O. 6 PROBLEM 6–17B *Key Activity-Based Costing Concepts*

Cascade Boot and Shoe Company makes hand-sewn boots and shoes. Cascade uses a companywide overhead rate based on direct labor hours to allocate indirect manufacturing costs to its products. Making a pair of boots normally requires 2.4 hours of direct labor, and making a pair of shoes requires 1.8 hours. The company's shoe division, facing increased competition from international companies that have access to cheap labor, has responded by automating its shoe production. The reengineering process was expensive, requiring the purchase of manufacturing equipment and the restructuring of the plant layout. In addition, utility and maintenance costs increased significantly for operating the new equipment. Even so, labor costs decreased significantly. Now making a pair of shoes requires only 18 minutes of direct labor. As predicted, the labor savings more than offset the increase in overhead cost, thereby reducing the total cost to make a pair of shoes. The company experienced an unexpected side effect, however; according to the company's accounting records, the cost to make a pair of boots increased although the manufacturing process in the boot division was not affected by the reengineering of the shoe division. In other words, the cost of boots increased although Cascade did not change anything about the way it makes them.

Required

a. Explain why the accounting records reflected an increase in the cost to make a pair of boots.

b. Explain how the companywide overhead rate could result in the underpricing of shoes.

c. Explain how activity-based costing could improve the accuracy of overhead cost allocations.

L.O. 4 PROBLEM 6–18B *Pricing Decisions Made With ABC System Cost Data*

Helsinki Furniture Corporation makes two types of dining tables, Elegance for formal dining and Comfort for casual dining, at its single factory. With the economy beginning to experience a recession, Victor Helsinki, the president, is concerned about whether the company can stay in business as market prices fall. At Mr. Helsinki's request, Sue Delan, the controller, prepared cost data for analysis.

Inspectors are paid according to the number of actual hours worked, determined by the number of tables inspected. Engineers who set up equipment for both products are paid monthly salaries. TV commercial fees are paid at the beginning of the quarter.

Direct Cost	Elegance (E)	Comfort (C)
Direct materials	$70 per unit	$43 per unit
Direct labor	$36 per hour × 1.5 hours production time	$36 per hour × 1 hour production time

Category	Estimated Cost	Cost Driver	Use of Cost Driver
Product inspection	$120,000	Number of units	E: 2,500 units; C: 7,500 units
Machine setups	75,000	Number of setups	E: 23 setups; C: 27 setups
Product advertising	210,000	Number of TV commercials	E: 5; C: 9
Facility depreciation	405,000	Number of machine hours	E: 5,000 hours; C: 5,000 hours
Total	$810,000		

Required

a. Compute the cost per unit for each product.

b. If management wants to make 30 percent of cost as a profit margin for Elegance, what price should the company set?

c. The market price of tables in the Comfort class has declined because of the recession. Management asks you to determine the minimum cost of producing Comfort tables in the short term. Provide that information.

PROBLEM 6–19B *Target Pricing and Target Costing With ABC*

L.O. 4, 7

Sanchez Corporation manufactures two models of watches. Model Wonder displays cartoon characters and has simple features designed for kids. Model Marvel has sophisticated features such as dual time zones and an attached calculator. Sanchez's product design team has worked with a cost accountant to prepare a budget for the two products for the next fiscal year as follows.

Direct Cost	Wonder (W)	Marvel (M)
Direct materials	$4 per unit	$10 per unit
Direct labor	$20/hour × 0.2 hour production time	$20/hour × 0.6 hour production time

Category	Estimated Cost	Cost Driver	Use of Cost Driver
Materials handling	$183,000	Number of parts	W: 700,000; M: 520,000
Machine setups	90,000	Number of setups	W: 50; M: 40
Product testing	14,000	Number of units tested	W: 1,000; M: 400
Facility depreciation	180,000	Number of machine hours	W: 3,200; M: 4,000
Total	$467,000		

Wonder watches have 35 parts, and Marvel watches have 65 parts. The budget calls for producing 20,000 units of Wonder and 8,000 units of Marvel. Sanchez tests 5 percent of its products for quality assurance. It sells all its products at market prices.

Required

a. Compute the cost per unit for each product.

b. The current market price for products comparable to Wonder is $18 and for products comparable to Marvel is $55. What will Sanchez's profit or loss for the next year be?

c. Sanchez likes to have a 25 percent profit margin based on the current market price for each product. What is the target cost for each product? What is the total target profit?

d. The president of Sanchez has asked the design team to refine the production design to bring down the product cost. After a series of redesigns, the team recommends a new process that requires purchasing a new machine that costs $200,000 and has five years of useful life and no salvage value. With the new process and the new machine, Sanchez can decrease the number of machine setups to four for each product and cut the cost of materials handling in half. The machine hours used will be 4,500 for Wonder and 6,500 for Marvel. Does this new process enable Sanchez to achieve its target costs?

L.O. 4, 7 PROBLEM 6–20B *Cost Management With an ABC System*

Chase Corporation manufactures two different coffee makers, Professional for commercial use and Home for family use. Bill Ponce, the president, recently received complaints from some members of the board of directors about the company's failure to reach the expected profit of $200,000 per month. Mr. Ponce is, therefore, under great pressure to improve the company's bottom line. Under his direction, Amy Kance, the controller, prepared the following monthly cost data for Mr. Ponce.

Direct Cost	Professional (P)	Home (H)
Direct materials	$21 per unit	$7 per unit
Direct labor	$18 per hour × 0.8 hour production time	$18 per hour × 0.3 hour production time

Category	Estimated Cost	Cost Driver	Use of Cost Driver
Product inspection	$ 60,000	Number of units	P: 15,000 units; H: 45,000 units
Machine setups	15,000	Number of setups	P: 30 setups; H: 45 setups
Product promotion	200,000	Number of TV commercials	P: 10; H: 10
Facility depreciation	295,000	Number of machine hours	P: 7,160 hours; H: 4,640 hours
Total	$570,000		

The market price for coffee makers comparable to Professional is $65 and to Home is $22. The company's administrative expenses amount to $195,000.

Required

a. Compute the cost per unit for both products.

b. Determine the company's profit or loss.

c. Jim Wei, the marketing manager, recommends that the company implement a focused marketing strategy. He argues that advertisements in trade journals would be more effective for the commercial market than on TV. In addition, the cost of journal ads would be only $21,000. He also proposes sending discount coupons to targeted households to reach a broad market base. The coupons program would cost $72,000. Compute the new cost of each product, assuming that Mr. Ponce replaces TV advertising with Mr. Wei's suggestions.

d. Determine the company's profit or loss using the information in Requirement *c*.

L.O. 8, 9 PROBLEM 6–21B *Assessing a Quality Control Strategy*

Mike Annan, the president of Ocean Plastic Company, is a famous cost cutter in the plastics industry. Two years ago, he accepted an offer from Ocean's board of directors to help the company cut costs quickly. In fact, Mr. Annan's compensation package included a year-end bonus tied to the percentage of cost decrease over the preceding year. On February 12, 2006, Mr. Annan received comparative financial information for the two preceding years. He was especially interested in the results of his cost-cutting measures on quality control. The quality report shown on page 000 was extracted from the company's financial information:

Required

a. Explain the strategy that Mr. Annan initiated to control Ocean's costs.

b. Indicate whether the strategy was successful or unsuccessful in reducing quality costs.

c. Explain how the strategy will likely affect the company's business in the long term.

	2005		2004	
	Amount	Percentage	Amount	Percentage
Prevention costs				
Engineering and design	$ 65,000	6.57%	$ 69,000	7.39%
Training and education	26,000	2.63	76,000	8.14
Depreciation on prevention equipment	15,000	1.51	15,000	1.60
Incentives and awards	20,000	2.02	20,000	2.14
Total prevention	126,000	12.73%	180,000	19.27%
Appraisal costs				
Product and materials inspection	33,000	3.33	73,000	7.82
Reliability testing	27,000	2.73	67,000	7.17
Testing equipment (depreciation)	38,000	3.83	38,000	4.07
Supplies	10,000	1.01	16,000	1.71
Total appraisal	108,000	10.90%	194,000	20.77%

continued

	2005		2004	
	Amount	**Percentage**	**Amount**	**Percentage**
Internal failure costs				
Scrap	52,000	5.25	120,000	12.85
Repair and rework	46,000	4.65	150,000	16.06
Downtime	64,000	6.46	40,000	4.28
Reinspection	8,000	0.81	24,000	2.57
Total internal failure	170,000	17.17%	334,000	35.76%
External failure cost				
Warranty repairs and replacement	347,000	35.05	125,000	13.38
Freight	75,000	7.58	31,000	3.32
Customer relations	45,000	4.55	28,000	3.00
Restocking and packaging	119,000	12.02	42,000	4.50
Total external failure	586,000	59.20%	226,000	24.20%
Grand total	$990,000	100.00%	$934,000	100.00%

ANALYZE, THINK, COMMUNICATE

BUSINESS APPLICATION CASE *Using ABC to Improve Product Costing*

ATC 6–1

Dayton Technologies produces component parts for vinyl window manufacturers. The component parts consist of strips of material priced and sold by the linear foot. The material comes in different grades and colors. Dayton recently implemented an ABC system. To evaluate the effectiveness of the new system, Dayton's managerial accountants prepared reports comparing cost data based on ABC allocations and cost data based on traditional costing methods. The traditional costing approach used a single driver (material dollars) as the basis for product costing allocations. The ABC system uses a variety of cost drivers related to the activities required to produce the vinyl materials. The following data about three specific products were included in the reports.

Product	Selling Price per Foot	Feet Produced	ABC Cost per Foot	Traditional Cost per Foot
X	$1.90	552,000	$1.65	$1.22
Y	1.43	500,000	1.31	1.01
Z	1.34	440,000	1.11	0.80

Data Source: N. R. Pemberton, L. Arumugam, and N. Hassan, "From Obstacles to Opportunities," *Management Accounting,* March 1996, pp. 20–27. To facilitate the development of the case, it was necessary to rename the products and to mathematically manipulate some of the original data included in the article, but these changes are cosmetic in nature and do not compromise the results of the comparison.

Required

a. Determine the ABC margin ([selling price − ABC cost] × feet produced) for each product.

b. Determine the traditional margin ([selling price − traditional cost] × feet produced) for each product.

c. Explain why the ABC margins are lower than the traditional margins.

d. Based on the information provided, has traditional costing resulted in over- or undercosting of products X, Y, and Z? Suggest how the over- or undercosting has affected Dayton's profitability.

e. Suggest what action management should take with respect to the discoveries brought to light by the ABC cost analysis. Assume that Dayton normally expects a product to produce a margin of at least 25 percent of the sales price.

GROUP ASSIGNMENT *Using ABC in a Service Business*

ATC 6–2

A dialysis clinic provides two types of treatment for its patients. Hemodialysis (HD), an in-house treatment, requires that patients visit the clinic three times each week for dialysis treatments. Peritoneal dialysis (PD) permits patients to self-administer their treatments at home on a daily basis. On average, the clinic serves 102 HD patients and 62 PD patients. A recent development caused clinic administrators to develop a keen interest in cost measurement for the two separate services. Managed care plans such as HMOs began to pay treatment providers a fixed payment per insured participant regardless of the level of services provided by the clinic. With fixed fee revenues, the clinic was forced to control costs to ensure profitability. As a result, knowing the cost to provide HD versus PD services was critically important for the clinic. It needed accurate cost measurements to answer the following questions. Were both services profitable, or was one service carrying the burden of the other service? Should advertising be directed toward acquiring HD or PD patients? Should the clinic eliminate HMO service?

Management suspected the existing cost allocation system was inaccurate in measuring the true cost of providing the respective services; it had been developed in response to Medicare reporting requirements. It allocated costs between HD and PD based on the ratio of cost to charges (RCC). In other words, RCC allocates indirect costs in proportion to revenues. To illustrate, consider the allocation of $883,280 of indirect nursing services costs, which are allocated to the two treatment groups in relation to the revenue generated by each group. Given that the clinic generated total revenue of $3,006,775, an allocation rate of 0.2937633 per revenue dollar was established ($883,280 ÷ $3,006,775). This rate was multiplied by the proportionate share of revenue generated by each service category to produce the following allocation.

Type of Service	Service Revenue	×	Allocation Rate	=	Allocated Cost
HD	$1,860,287	×	0.2937633	=	$546,484
PD	1,146,488	×	0.2937633	=	336,796
Total	$3,006,775	×	0.2937633	=	$883,280

To better assess the cost of providing each type of service, the clinic initiated an activity-based costing (ABC) system. The ABC approach divided the nursing service cost into four separate cost pools. A separate cost driver (allocation base) was identified for each cost pool. The cost pools and their respective cost drivers follow.

	Total	HD	PD
Nursing services cost pool categories			
RNs	$239,120	?	?
LPNs	404,064	?	?
Nursing administration and support staff	115,168	?	?
Dialysis machine operations (tech. salaries)	124,928	?	?
Total	$883,280	?	?

	Total	HD	PD
Activity cost drivers (corresponding to cost pools)			
Number of RNs	7	5	2
Number of LPNs	19	15	4
Number of treatments (nursing administration)	34,967	14,343	20,624
Number of dialyzer treatments (machine operations)	14,343	14,343	0

Data Source: T. D. West and D. A. West, "Applying ABC to Healthcare," *Management Accounting,* February 1999, pp. 22–33.

Required

a. Organize the class into four sections and divide the sections into groups of four or five students each. Assign Task 1 to the first section of groups, Task 2 to the second section, Task 3 to the third section, and Task 4 to the fourth section.

Group Tasks

(1) Allocate the RN cost pool between the HD and PD service centers.
(2) Allocate the LPN cost pool between the HD and PD service centers.
(3) Allocate the nursing administration and support staff cost pool between the HD and PD service centers.
(4) Allocate the dialysis machine operations cost pool between the HD and PD service centers.

b. Have the class determine the total cost to allocate to the two service centers in the following manner. Select a representative from each section and have the selected person go to the board. Each representative should supply the allocated cost for the cost pool assigned by her respective section. The instructor should total the amounts and compare the ABC cost allocations with those developed through the traditional RCC system.

c. The instructor should lead the class in a discussion that addresses the following questions.
(1) Assuming that the ABC system provides a more accurate measure of cost, which service center (HD or PD) is overcosted by the traditional allocation system and which is undercosted?
(2) What is the potential impact on pricing and profitability for both service centers?
(3) How could management respond to the conditions described in the problem?

RESEARCH ASSIGNMENT *When ABC Does Not Work Well* ATC 6–3

Is ABC the silver bullet? Does it always provide better estimates of product cost? Are ABC results always superior? Does it always improve the fairness of allocation? Will ABC always identify the nonvalue-added activities? The answer to all of these questions is, unfortunately, a definitive no! Read the article "Can ABC Bring Mixed Results?" by S. P. Landry, L. M. Wood, and T. M. Lindquist in the March 1997 edition of *Management Accounting* (pp. 28–33) and complete the following requirements.

Required

a. The article compares the results of implementing an ABC system at two divisions of Hewlett-Packard (HP). Identify the division that reported success with its ABC system.
b. Why was an ABC system established at the Colorado Springs Division?
c. What is the primary difference between the operations of the Colorado Springs Division and the Boise Division? How could this difference impact the implementation of ABC?
d. The article identifies four conditions that caused the failure of ABC at the Colorado Springs Division. What were these conditions?
e. Based on this article, do you believe that its authors have a positive or negative opinion of the capacity of ABC to more accurately measure cost than a traditional system?

WRITING ASSIGNMENT *Assessing a Strategy to Control Quality Cost* ATC 6–4

Lucy Sawyer, who owns and operates Sawyer Toy Company, is a perfectionist. She believes literally in the "zero-defects" approach to quality control. Her favorite saying is, "You can't spend too much on quality." Even so, in 2001 her company experienced an embarrassing breach of quality that required the national recall of a defective product. She vowed never to repeat the experience and instructed her staff to spend whatever it takes to ensure that products are delivered free of defects in 2002. She was somewhat disappointed with the 2002 year-end quality cost report shown here.

	2001	2002
Prevention costs	$120,000	$ 80,000
Appraisal costs	240,000	430,000
Internal failure costs	140,000	560,000
External failure cost	320,000	210,000
Total	$820,000	$1,280,000

Although external failure costs had declined, they remained much higher than expected. The increased inspections had identified defects that were corrected, thereby avoiding another recall; however, the external failure costs were still too high. Ms. Sawyer responded by saying, "We will have to double our efforts." She authorized hiring additional inspectors and instructed her production supervisors to become more vigilant in identifying and correcting errors.

Required

Assume that you are the chief financial officer (CFO) of Sawyer Company. Ms. Sawyer has asked you to review the company's approach to quality control. Prepare a memo to her that evaluates the existing approach, and recommend changes in expenditure patterns that can improve profitability as well as increase the effectiveness of the quality control system.

ETHICAL DILEMMA *Conflicts Between Controlling Cost and Providing Social Responsibility to Patients* ATC 6–5

This case examines potential ethical issues faced by the dialysis clinic described in ATC 6–2. It is, however, an independent case that students may study in conjunction with or separately from ATC 6–2. The dialysis clinic provides two types of treatment for its patients. Hemodialysis (HD), an in-house treatment, requires patients to visit the clinic three times each week. Peritoneal dialysis (PD) permits patients to self-administer their treatments at home on a daily basis. The clinic serves a number of HMO patients under a contract that limits collections from the HMO insurer to a fixed amount per patient. As a result, the clinic's profitability is directly related to its ability to control costs. To illustrate, assume that the clinic is paid a fixed annual fee of $15,000 per HMO patient served. Also assume that the current cost to provide health care averages $14,000 a year per patient, resulting in an average profitability of $1,000 per patient ($15,000 − $14,000). Because the revenue base is fixed, the only way the clinic can increase profitability is to lower its average cost of providing services. If the clinic fails to control costs and the average cost of patient care increases, profitability will decline. A recent ABC study suggests that the cost to provide HD service exceeds the amount of revenue generated from providing that service. The clinic is profitable because PD services generate enough profit to more than make up for losses on HD services.

Required

Respond to each potential scenario described here. Each scenario is independent of the others.

a. Suppose that as a result of the ABC analysis, the chief accountant, a certified management accountant (CMA), recommends that the clinic discontinue treating HD patients referred by the HMO provider. Based on this assumption, answer the following questions.

(1) Assume that the clinic is located in a small town. If it discontinues treating the HD patients, they will be forced to drive 50 miles to the nearest alternative treatment center. Does the clinic have a moral obligation to society to continue to provide HD service although it is not profitable to do so?

(2) The accountant's recommendation places profitability above the needs of HD patients. Does this recommendation violate any of the standards of ethical conduct described in Chapter 1, Exhibit 1–13?

b. Assume that the clinic continues to treat HD patients referred by HMOs. However, to compensate for the loss incurred on these patients, the clinic raises prices charged to non-HMO patients. Is it fair to require non-HMO patients to subsidize services provided to the HMO patients?

c. Suppose that the clinic administrators respond to the ABC data by cutting costs. The clinic overbooks HMO patients to ensure that downtime is avoided when cancellations occur. It reduces the RN nursing staff and assigns some of the technical work to less qualified assistants. Ultimately, an overworked, underqualified nurse's aide makes a mistake, and a patient dies. Who is at fault—the HMO, the accountant who conducted the ABC analysis, or the clinic administrators who responded to the ABC information?

ATC 6–6 SPREADSHEET ASSIGNMENT *Using Excel*

Tameron Corporation produces video games in three market categories: commercial, home video, and miniature handheld. Tameron has traditionally allocated overhead costs to the three product categories using the companywide base of direct labor hours. The company recently switched to an ABC system when it installed computer-controlled assembly stations that rendered the traditional costing system ineffective. In implementing the ABC system, the company identified the cost pools and drivers shown in the following spreadsheet. The activity in each of the three product lines appears in rows 3 to 9. The pooled costs are shown in cells E11 to E15.

Required

a. Construct a spreadsheet like the following one to compute the total cost and cost per unit for each product line. Cells K4 to K9, G12 to I15, E19 to E28, G19 to G28, I19 to I28, and K26 should all be formulas.

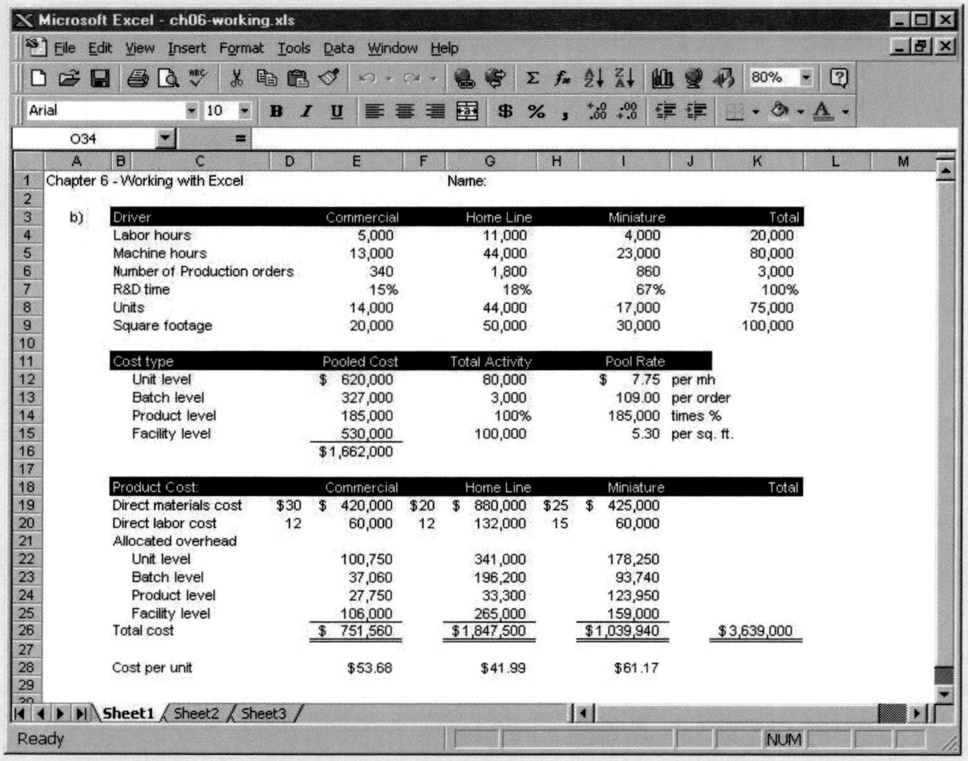

Row	B	C	D	E	F	G	H	I	J	K
3	b)	Driver		Commercial		Home Line		Miniature		Total
4		Labor hours		5,000		11,000		4,000		20,000
5		Machine hours		13,000		44,000		23,000		80,000
6		Number of Production orders		340		1,800		860		3,000
7		R&D time		15%		18%		67%		100%
8		Units		14,000		44,000		17,000		75,000
9		Square footage		20,000		50,000		30,000		100,000
11		Cost type		Pooled Cost		Total Activity		Pool Rate		
12		Unit level		$ 620,000		80,000		$ 7.75	per mh	
13		Batch level		327,000		3,000		109.00	per order	
14		Product level		185,000		100%		185,000	times %	
15		Facility level		530,000		100,000		5.30	per sq. ft.	
16				$1,662,000						
18		Product Cost:		Commercial		Home Line		Miniature		Total
19		Direct materials cost	$30	$ 420,000	$20	$ 880,000	$25	$ 425,000		
20		Direct labor cost	12	60,000	12	132,000	15	60,000		
21		Allocated overhead								
22		Unit level		100,750		341,000		178,250		
23		Batch level		37,060		196,200		93,740		
24		Product level		27,750		33,300		123,950		
25		Facility level		106,000		265,000		159,000		
26		Total cost		$ 751,560		$1,847,500		$1,039,940		$3,639,000
28		Cost per unit		$53.68		$41.99		$61.17		

SPREADSHEET ASSIGNMENT *Mastering Excel*

ATC 6–7

Beasley Company makes three types of exercise machines. Data have been accumulated for four possible overhead drivers. Data for these four possible drivers are shown in rows 3 to 7 of the following spreadsheet.

Required

a. Construct a spreadsheet that will allocate overhead and calculate unit cost for each of these alternative drivers. A screen capture of the spreadsheet and data follows.

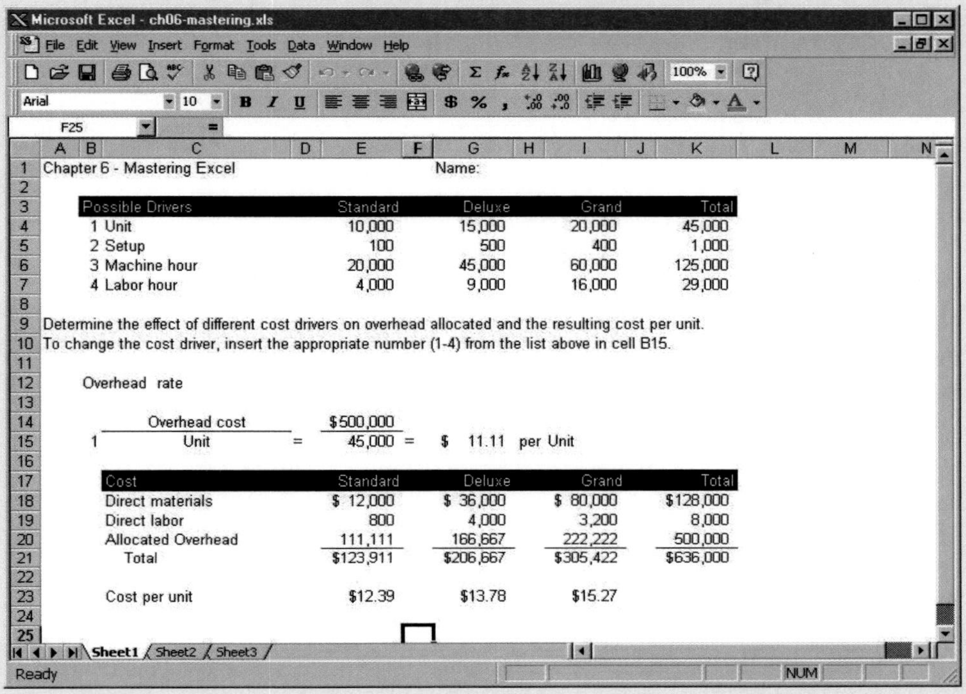

Microsoft Excel - ch06-mastering.xls

Chapter 6 - Mastering Excel   Name:

Possible Drivers	Standard	Deluxe	Grand	Total
1 Unit	10,000	15,000	20,000	45,000
2 Setup	100	500	400	1,000
3 Machine hour	20,000	45,000	60,000	125,000
4 Labor hour	4,000	9,000	16,000	29,000

Determine the effect of different cost drivers on overhead allocated and the resulting cost per unit.
To change the cost driver, insert the appropriate number (1-4) from the list above in cell B15.

Overhead rate

	Overhead cost		$500,000	
1	Unit	=	45,000 =	$ 11.11 per Unit

Cost	Standard	Deluxe	Grand	Total
Direct materials	$ 12,000	$ 36,000	$ 80,000	$128,000
Direct labor	800	4,000	3,200	8,000
Allocated Overhead	111,111	166,667	222,222	500,000
Total	$123,911	$206,667	$305,422	$636,000
Cost per unit	$12.39	$13.78	$15.27	

Spreadsheet Tips

1. This spreadsheet uses a function called *vertical lookup.* This function can pull the appropriate values from a table. The form of this function is =VLOOKUP (value, table, column#). In this example, the table is in cells B4 to K7. Three examples of the use of VLOOKUP follow.
2. Cell C15 is =VLOOKUP (B15, B4:K7, 2). This function operates by using the one (1) in cell B15 to look up a value in the table. Notice that the table is defined as B4: K7 and that the function is looking up the value in the second column, which is Unit.
3. Cell E15 is =VLOOKUP (B15, B4:K7, 10). In this case, the function is looking up the value in the tenth column, which is 45,000. Be sure to count empty columns.
4. Cell E20 is =VLOOKUP (B15, B4:K7, 4)*G15. In this case, the function is looking up the value in the fourth column, which is $10,000. Be sure to count empty columns.
5. Cells I15, G20, and I20 also use the VLOOKUP function.
6. After completing the spreadsheet, you can change the value in cell B15 (1-4) to see the effect of choosing a different driver for overhead.

COMPREHENSIVE PROBLEM

To this point we have assumed the Magnificent Modems produced only one type of modem. Suppose instead we assume the company produces several different kinds of modems. The production process differs for each type of product. Some require more setup time than others, they are produced in different batch sizes, and they require different amounts of indirect labor (supervision). Packaging and delivery to customers also differs for each type of modem. Even so, Magnificent Modems uses a single allocation base (number of units) to allocate overhead costs.

Required

Write a brief memo that explains how Magnificent Modems could benefit from an ABC cost system.

CHAPTER *seven*

PLANNING FOR PROFIT AND COST CONTROL

LEARNING *objectives*

After you have mastered the material in this chapter you will be able to:

1. Describe the budgeting process and the benefits it provides.
2. Explain the relationship between budgeting and human behavior.
3. Prepare a sales budget and related schedule of cash receipts.
4. Prepare an inventory purchases budget and related schedule of cash payments.
5. Prepare a selling and administrative expense budget and related schedule of cash payments.
6. Prepare a cash budget.
7. Prepare a pro forma income statement, balance sheet, and statement of cash flows.

THE *curious* ACCOUNTANT

People in television commercials often say they shop at a particular store because, "my family is on a budget." The truth is, most families do not have a formal budget. What these people mean is that they need to be sure their spending does not exceed their available cash.

When a family expects to spend more money in a given year than it will earn, it must plan on borrowing funds needed to make up the difference. However, even if a family's income for a year will exceed its spending, it may still need to borrow money because the timing of its cash inflows may not match the timing of its cash outflows. Whether a budget is being prepared for a family or a business, those preparing the budget must understand the specific issues facing that entity if potential financial problems are to be anticipated. There is no such thing as a "one size fits all" budget.

The United States Olympic Committee (USOC), like all large organizations, devotes considerable effort to budget planning.

Think about the Olympic Games, and how the USOC generates revenues and incurs expenditures. Can you identify any unusual circumstances facing the USOC that complicate its budgeting efforts? (Answer on page 287.)

CHAPTER *opening*

Planning is crucial to operating a profitable business. Expressing business plans in financial terms is commonly called **budgeting.** *The budgeting process involves coordinating the financial plans of all areas of the business. For example, the production department cannot prepare a manufacturing plan until it knows how many units of product to produce. The number of units to produce depends on the marketing department's sales projection. The marketing department* *cannot project sales volume until it knows what products the company will sell. Product information comes from the research and development department. The point should be clear: a company's* master budget *results from combining numerous specific plans prepared by different departments.*

Master budget preparation is normally supervised by a committee. The budget committee is responsible for settling disputes among various departments over budget matters. The committee also monitors reports on how various segments are progressing toward achieving their budget goals. The budgeting committee is not an accounting committee. It is a high-level committee that normally includes the company president, vice presidents of marketing, purchasing, production and finance, and the controller.

Topic Tackler PLUS 7–1

LO1 Describe the budgeting process and the benefits it provides.

The Planning Process

Planning normally addresses short, intermediate, and long-range time horizons. Short-term plans are more specific than long-term plans. Consider, for example, your decision to attend college. Long-term planning requires considering general questions such as:

- Do I want to go to college?
- How do I expect to benefit from the experience?
- Do I want a broad knowledge base, or am I seeking to learn specific job skills?
- In what field do I want to concentrate my studies?

Many students go to college before answering these questions. They discover the disadvantages of poor planning the hard way. While their friends are graduating, they are starting over in a new major.

Intermediate-range planning usually covers three to five years. In this stage, you consider which college to attend, how to support yourself while in school, and whether to live on or off campus.

Short-term planning focuses on the coming year. In this phase you plan specific courses to take, decide which instructors to choose, schedule part-time work, and join a study group. Short-term plans are specific and detailed. Their preparation may seem tedious, but careful planning generally leads to efficient resource use and high levels of productivity.

Three Levels of Planning for Business Activity

Businesses describe the three levels of planning as *strategic planning, capital budgeting,* and *operations budgeting.* **Strategic planning** involves making long-term decisions such as defining the scope of the business, determining which products to develop or discontinue, and identifying the most profitable market niche. Upper-level management is responsible for these decisions. Strategic plans are descriptive rather than quantitative. Objectives such as "to have the largest share of the market" or "to be the best-quality producer" result from strategic planning. Although strategic planning is an integral component of managing a business, an in-depth discussion of it is beyond the scope of this text.

Capital budgeting focuses on intermediate range planning. It involves such decisions as whether to buy or lease equipment, whether to stimulate sales, or whether to increase the company's asset base. Capital budgeting is discussed in detail in a later chapter.

The central focus of this chapter is the *master budget* which describes short-term objectives in specific amounts of sales targets, production goals, and financing plans. The master budget describes how management intends to achieve its objectives and directs the company's short-term activities.

The master budget normally covers one year. It is frequently divided into quarterly projections and often subdivides quarterly data by month. Effective managers cannot wait until year-end to know whether operations conform to budget targets. Monthly data provide feedback to permit making necessary corrections promptly.

Many companies use **perpetual,** or **continuous, budgeting** covering a 12-month reporting period. As the current month draws to a close, an additional month is added at the end of the budget period, resulting in a continuous 12-month budget. A perpetual budget offers the advantage of keeping management constantly focused on thinking ahead to the next 12 months. The more traditional annual approach to budgeting invites a frenzied stop-and-go mentality, with managers preparing the budget in a year-end rush that is soon forgotten. Changing conditions may not be discussed until the next year-end budget is due. A perpetual budget overcomes these disadvantages.

Advantages of Budgeting

Budgeting is costly and time-consuming. The sacrifices, however, are more than offset by the benefits. Budgeting promotes planning and coordination; it enhances performance measurement and corrective action.

Planning

Almost everyone makes plans. Each morning, most people think about what they will do during the day. Thinking ahead is planning. Most business managers think ahead about how they will direct operations. Unfortunately, planning is frequently as informal as making a few mental notes. Informal planning cannot be effectively communicated. The business manager might know what her objectives are, but neither her superiors nor her subordinates know. Because it serves as a communication tool, budgeting can solve these problems. The budget formalizes and documents managerial plans, clearly communicating objectives to both superiors and subordinates.

Coordination

Sometimes a choice benefits one department at the expense of another. For example, a purchasing agent may order large quantities of raw materials to obtain discounts from suppliers. But excessive quantities of materials pose a storage problem for the inventory supervisor who must manage warehouse costs. The budgeting process forces coordination among departments to promote decisions in the best interests of the company as a whole.

Performance Measurement

Budgets are specific, quantitative representations of management's objectives. Comparing actual results to budget expectations provides a way to evaluate performance. For example, if a company budgets sales of $10 million, it can judge the performance of the sales department against that level. If actual sales exceed $10 million, the company should reward the sales department; if actual sales fall below $10 million, the company should seek an explanation for the shortfall from the sales manager.

Corrective Action

Budgeting provides advance notice of potential shortages, bottlenecks, or other weaknesses in operating plans. For example, a cash budget alerts management to when the company can expect cash shortages during the coming year. The company can make borrowing arrangements well before it needs the money. Without knowing ahead of time, management might be unable to secure necessary financing on short notice, or it may have to pay excessively high interest rates to obtain funds. Budgeting advises managers of potential problems in time for them to carefully devise effective solutions.

Budgeting and Human Behavior

LO2 Explain the relationship between budgeting and human behavior.

Effective budgeting requires genuine sensitivity on the part of upper management to the effect on employees of budget expectations. People are often uncomfortable with budgets. Budgets are constraining. They limit individual freedom in favor of an established plan. Many people find evaluation based on budget expectations stressful. Most students experience a similar fear about testing. Like examinations, budgets represent standards by which performance is evaluated. Employees worry about whether their performance will meet expectations.

The attitudes of high-level managers significantly impact budget effectiveness. Subordinates are keenly aware of management's expectations. If upper-level managers degrade, make fun of, or ignore the budget, subordinates will follow suit. If management uses budgets to humiliate, embarrass, or punish subordinates, employees will resent the treatment and the budgeting process. Upper-level managers must demonstrate that they view the budget as a sincere effort to express realistic goals employees are expected to meet. An honest, open, respectful atmosphere is essential to budgeting success.

Participative budgeting has frequently proved successful in creating a healthy atmosphere. This technique invites participation in the budget process by personnel at all levels of the organization, not just upper-level managers. Information flows from the bottom up as well as from the top down during budget preparation. Because they are directly responsible for meeting budget goals, subordinates can offer more realistic targets. Including them in budget preparation fosters development of a team effort. Participation fosters more cooperation and motivation, and less fear. With participative budgeting, subordinates cannot complain that the budget is management's plan. The budget is instead a self-imposed constraint. Employees can hold no one responsible but themselves if they fail to accomplish the budget objectives they established.

Upper management participates in the process to ensure that employee-generated objectives are consistent with company objectives. Furthermore, if subordinates were granted complete freedom to establish budget standards, they might be tempted to adopt lax standards to ensure they will meet them. Both managers and subordinates must cooperate if the participatory process is to produce an effective budget. If developed carefully, budgets can motivate employees to achieve superior performance. Normal human fears must be overcome, and management must create an honest budget atmosphere.

Topic Tackler PLUS 7–2

The Master Budget

LO1 Describe the budgeting process and the benefits it provides.

The **master budget** is a group of detailed budgets and schedules representing the company's operating and financial plans for a future accounting period. The master budget usually includes (1) *operating budgets,* (2) *capital budgets,* and (3) *pro forma financial statements.* The budgeting process normally begins with preparing the **operating budgets** which focus on detailed operating activities. This chapter illustrates operating budgets for Hampton Hams, a retail sales company that uses (1) a sales budget, (2) an inventory purchases budget, (3) a selling and administrative (S&A) expense budget, and (4) a cash budget.

The sales budget includes a schedule of cash receipts from customers. The inventory purchases and S&A expense budgets include schedules of cash payments for inventory and

Exhibit 7–1 *Information Flows in the Master Budget*

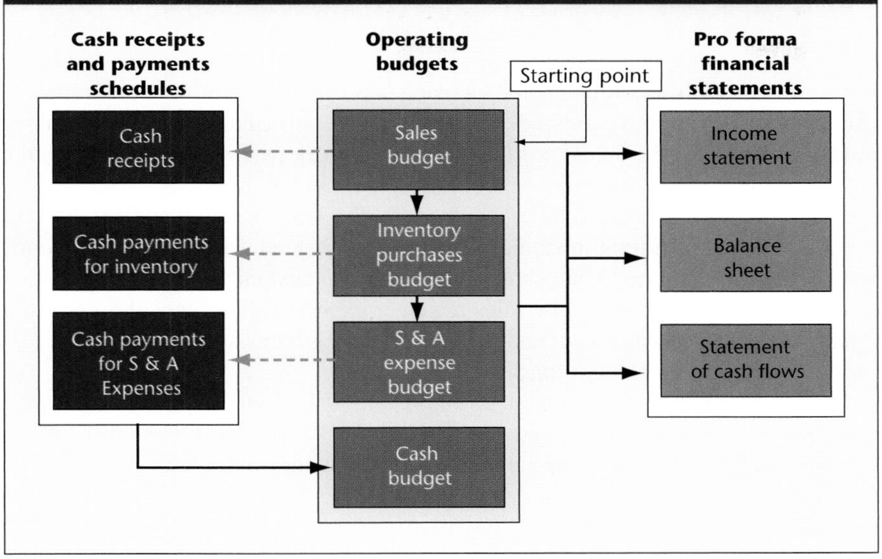

expenses. Preparing the master budget begins with the sales forecast. Based on the sales forecast, the detailed budgets for inventory purchases and operating expenses are developed. The schedules of cash receipts and cash payments provide the foundation for preparing the cash budget.

The **capital budget** describes the company's intermediate-range plans for investments in facilities, equipment, new products, store outlets, and lines of business. The capital budget affects several operating budgets. For example, equipment acquisitions result in additional depreciation expense on the S&A expense budget. The cash flow effects of capital investments influence the cash budget.

The operating budgets are used to prepare *pro forma statements.* **Pro forma financial statements** are based on projected (budgeted) rather than historical information. Hampton Hams prepares a pro forma income statement, balance sheet, and statement of cash flows.

Exhibit 7–1 shows how information flows in a master budget.

Hampton Hams Budgeting Illustration

Hampton Hams (HH), a major corporation, sells cured hams nationwide through retail outlets in shopping malls. By focusing on a single product and standardized operations, the company controls costs stringently. As a result, it offers high-quality hams at competitive prices.

HAMPTON HAMS

Hampton Hams has experienced phenomenal growth during the past five years. It opened two new stores in Indianapolis, Indiana, last month and plans to open a third new store in October. Hampton Hams finances new stores by borrowing on a line of credit arranged with National Bank. National's loan officer has requested monthly budgets for each of the first three months of the new store's operations. The accounting department is preparing the new store's master budget for October, November, and December. The first step is developing a sales budget.

Sales Budget

LO3 Prepare a sales budget and related schedule of cash receipts.

Preparing the master budget begins with the sales forecast. The accuracy of the sales forecast is critical because all the other budgets are derived from the sales budget. Normally, the marketing department coordinates the development of the sales forecast. Sales estimates frequently flow from the bottom up to the higher management levels. Sales personnel prepare sales projections for their products and territories and pass them up the line where they are combined with the estimates of other sales personnel to develop regional and national estimates. Using various information sources, upper-level sales managers adjust the estimates generated by sales personnel. Adjustment information comes from industry periodicals and trade journals, economic analysis, marketing surveys, historical sales figures, and changes in competition. Companies assimilate this data using sophisticated computer programs, statistical techniques, and quantitative methods, or, simply, professional judgment. Regardless of the technique, the senior vice president of sales ultimately develops a sales forecast for which she is held responsible.

To develop the sales forecast for HH's new store, the sales manager studied the sales history of existing stores operating in similar locations. He then adjusted for start-up conditions. October is an opportune time to open a new store because customers will learn the store's location before the holiday season. The sales manager expects significant sales growth in November and December as customers choose the company's hams as the centerpiece for many Thanksgiving and winter holiday dinner tables.

The new store's sales are expected to be $160,000 in October ($40,000 in cash and $120,000 on account). Sales are expected to increase 20 percent per month during November and December. Based on these estimates, the sales manager prepared the sales budget in Exhibit 7–2.

Projected Sales

The sales budget has two sections. Section 1 shows the projected sales for each month. The November sales forecast reflects a 20 percent increase over October sales. For example, November *cash sales* are calculated as $48,000 ($40,000 + [$40,000 × 0.20]) and December *cash sales* as $57,600 ($48,000 + [$48,000 × 0.20]). *Sales on account* are similarly computed.

Schedule of Cash Receipts

Section 2 is a schedule of the cash receipts for the projected sales. This schedule is used later to prepare the cash budget. The accountant has assumed in this schedule that Hampton Hams will collect accounts receivable from credit sales *in full* in the month following the sale. In practice, collections may be spread over several months, and some receivables may become bad debts that are never collected. Regardless of additional complexities, the objective is to estimate the amount and timing of expected cash receipts.

Exhibit 7–2 *Sales Budget*

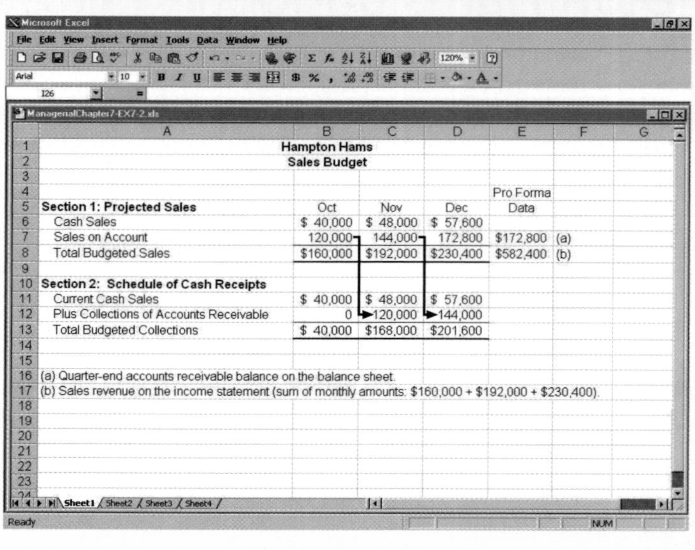

Hampton Hams
Sales Budget

	Oct	Nov	Dec	Pro Forma Data	
Section 1: Projected Sales					
Cash Sales	$ 40,000	$ 48,000	$ 57,600		
Sales on Account	120,000	144,000	172,800	$172,800	(a)
Total Budgeted Sales	$160,000	$192,000	$230,400	$582,400	(b)
Section 2: Schedule of Cash Receipts					
Current Cash Sales	$ 40,000	$ 48,000	$ 57,600		
Plus Collections of Accounts Receivable	0	120,000	144,000		
Total Budgeted Collections	$ 40,000	$168,000	$201,600		

(a) Quarter-end accounts receivable balance on the balance sheet.
(b) Sales revenue on the income statement (sum of monthly amounts: $160,000 + $192,000 + $230,400).

In the HH case, *total cash receipts* are determined by adding the current month's *cash sales* to the cash collected from the previous month's *credit sales* (accounts receivable balance). Cash receipts for each month are determined as follows:

- October receipts are projected to be $40,000. Because the store opens in October, no accounts receivable from September exist to be collected in October. Cash receipts for October equal the amount of October's cash sales.
- November receipts are projected to be $168,000 ($48,000 November cash sales + $120,000 cash collected from October sales on account).
- December receipts are projected to be $201,600 ($57,600 December cash sales + $144,000 cash collected from November sales on account).

Pro Forma Financial Statement Data

The Pro Forma Data column in the sales budget displays two figures HH will report on the quarter-end (December 31) budgeted financial statements. Since HH expects to collect December credit sales in January, the *accounts receivable balance* will be $172,800 on the December 31, 2006 pro forma balance sheet (shown later in Exhibit 7–7).

The $582,400 of *sales revenue* in the Pro Forma Data column will be reported on the budgeted income statement for the quarter (shown later in Exhibit 7–6). The sales revenue

focus on INTERNATIONAL ISSUES

Cash Flow Planning in Bordeaux

The year 2000 was considered the greatest year for wine in the Bordeaux region of France since at least 1982, and the winemakers could look forward to selling their wines for record prices, but there was one catch; these wines would not be released to consumers until late in 2003. The winemakers had incurred most of their costs in 2000 when the vines were being tended and the grapes were being processed into wine. In many industries this would mean the companies would have to finance their inventory for almost four years—not an insignificant cost. The company must finance the inventory by either borrowing the money, which results in out-of-pocket interest expense, or using its own funds. The second option generates an opportunity cost resulting from the interest revenue that could have been earned if these funds were not being used to finance the inventory.

To address this potential cash flow problem, many of the winemakers in Bordeaux offer some of their wines for sale as "futures." That means the wines are purchased and paid for while they are still aging in barrels in France. Selling wine as futures reduces the time inventory must be financed from four years to only one to two years. Of course there are other types of costs in such deals. For one, the wines must be offered at lower prices than they are expected to sell for upon release. The winemakers have obviously decided this cost is less than the cost of financing inventory through borrowed money, or they would not do it.

Companies in other industries use similar techniques to speed up cash flow, such as factoring of accountants receivable. A major reason entities prepare cash budgets is to be sure they will have enough cash on hand to pay bills as they come due. If the budget indicates a temporary cash flow deficit, action must be taken to avoid the problem, and new budgets must be prepared based on these options. Budgeting is not a static process.

represents the sum of October, November, and December sales ($160,000 + $192,000 + $230,400 = $582,400).

Inventory Purchases Budget

LO4 Prepare an inventory purchases budget and related schedule of cash payments.

The inventory purchases budget shows the amount of inventory HH must purchase each month to satisfy the demand projected in the sales budget. The *total inventory needed* each month equals the amount of inventory HH plans to sell that month plus the amount of inventory HH wants on hand at month-end. To the extent that total inventory needed exceeds the inventory on hand at the beginning of the month, HH will need to purchase additional inventory. The amount of inventory to purchase is computed as follows:

Cost of Budgeted Sales	XXX
Plus: Desired Ending Inventory	XXX
Total Inventory Needed	XXX
Less: Beginning Inventory	(XXX)
Required Purchases	XXX

It is HH's policy to maintain an ending inventory equal to 25 percent of the next month's *projected cost of goods sold.* HH's cost of goods sold normally equals 70 percent of *sales.* Using this information and the sales budget, the accounting department prepared the inventory purchases budget shown in Exhibit 7–3.

Section 1 of the inventory purchases budget shows required purchases for each month. HH determined *budgeted cost of goods sold* for October by multiplying October *budgeted sales* by 70 percent ($160,000 × 0.70 = $112,000). Budgeted cost of goods sold for November and December were similarly computed. The October *desired ending inventory* was computed by multiplying November *budgeted cost of goods sold* by 25 percent ($134,400 × 0.25 = $33,600). Desired ending inventory for November is $40,320 ($161,280 × .25). Desired ending inventory for December is based on January projected cost of goods sold (not shown in the exhibit). HH expects ham sales to decline after the winter holidays. Because January projected cost of goods sold is only $140,000, the December desired ending inventory falls to $35,000 ($140,000 × .25).

Exhibit 7–3 *Inventory Purchases Budget*

Hampton Hams
Inventory Purchases Budget

Section 1: Projected Purchases	Oct	Nov	Dec	Pro Forma Data
Budgeted Cost of Goods Sold	$112,000	$134,400	$161,280	$407,680 (a)
Plus Desired Ending Inventory	33,600	40,320	35,000	$35,000 (b)
Total Inventory Needed	145,600	174,720	196,280	
Less Beginning Inventory	0	33,600	40,320	
Required Purchases (on account)	$145,600	$141,120	$155,960	$62,384 (c)
Section 2: Schedule of Cash Payments for Inventory Purchases				
Pay 60% of Current Month Accts Pay	$87,360	$84,672	$93,576	
Pay 40% of Prior Month Accts Pay	0	58,240	56,448	
Total Budgeted Disbursements for Inventory	$87,360	$142,912	$150,024	

(a) Cost of goods sold reported on pro forma income statement:
 (Sum of monthly amounts $112,000 + $134,400 + $161,280 = $407,680).
(b) Ending inventory balance reported on pro forma balance sheet.
(c) Ending accounts payable balance reported on proforma balance sheet ($155,960 x .40)

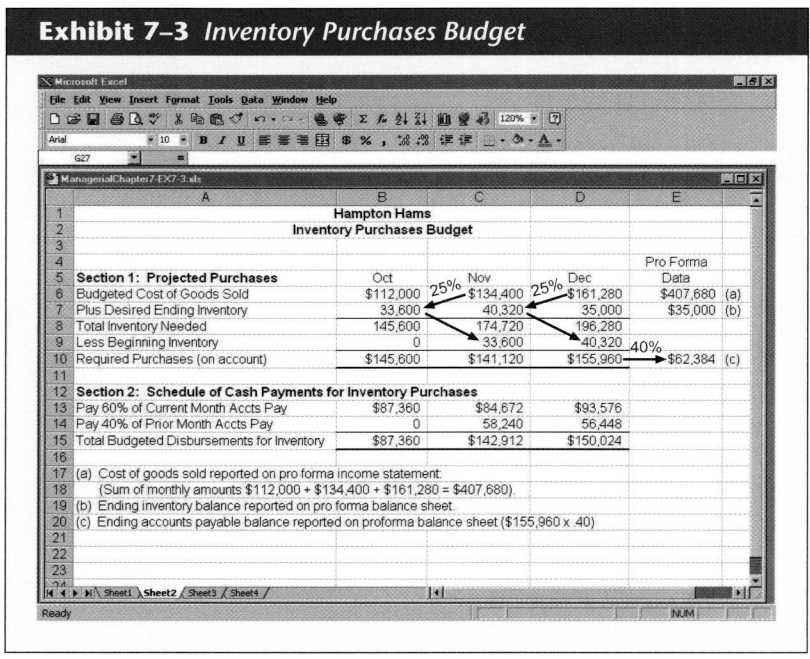

Schedule of Cash Payments for Inventory Purchases

Section 2 is the schedule of cash payments for inventory purchases. HH makes all inventory purchases on account. The supplier requires that HH pay for 60 percent of inventory purchases in the month goods are purchased. HH pays the remaining 40 percent the month after purchase.

Cash payments are projected as follows (amounts are rounded to the nearest whole dollar):

- October cash payments for inventory are $87,360. Because the new store opens in October, no accounts payable balance from September remains to be paid in October. Cash payments for October equal 60 percent of October inventory purchases.
- November cash payments for inventory are $142,912 (40 percent of October purchases + 60 percent of November purchases).
- December cash payments for inventory are $150,024 (40 percent of November purchases + 60 percent of December purchases).

Pro Forma Financial Statement Data

The Pro Forma Data column in the inventory purchases budget displays three figures HH will report on the quarter-end budgeted financial statements. The $407,680 *cost of goods sold* reported on the pro forma income statement (shown later in Exhibit 7–6) is the sum of the monthly cost of goods sold amounts ($112,000 + $134,400 + $161,280 = $407,680).

The $35,000 *ending inventory* as of December 31, 2006, is reported on the pro forma balance sheet (shown later in Exhibit 7–7). December 31 is the last day of both the month of December and the three-month quarter represented by October, November, and December.

The $62,384 of *accounts payable* reported on the pro forma balance sheet (shown later in Exhibit 7–7) represents the 40 percent of December inventory purchases HH will pay for in January ($155,960 × .40).

Main Street Sales Company purchased $80,000 of inventory during June. Purchases are expected to increase by 2 percent per month in each of the next three months. Main Street makes all purchases on account. It normally pays cash to settle 70 percent of its accounts payable during the month of purchase and settles the remaining 30 percent in the month following purchase. Based on this information, determine the accounts payable balance Main Street would report on its July 31 balance sheet.

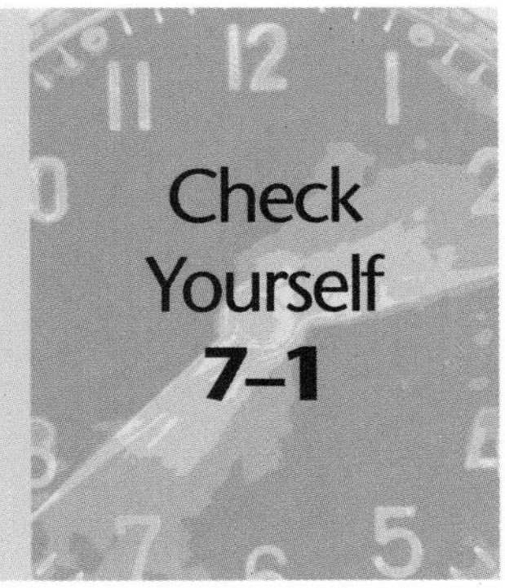

Answer Purchases for the month of July are expected to be $81,600 ($80,000 × 1.02). Main Street will pay 70 percent of the resulting accounts payable in cash during July. The remaining 30 percent represents the expected balance in accounts payable as of July 31. Therefore, the balance would be $24,480 ($81,600 × 0.3).

Selling and Administrative Expense Budget

LO5 Prepare a selling and administrative expense budget and related schedule of cash payments.

Section 1 of Exhibit 7–4 shows the selling and administrative (S&A) expense budget for Hampton Hams' new store. Most of the projected expenses are self-explanatory; depreciation and interest, however, merit comment. The depreciation expense is based on projections in the *capital expenditures budget.* Although not presented in this chapter, the capital budget calls for the cash purchase of $130,000 of store fixtures. The fixtures were purchased on October 1. The supplier allows a thirty-day inspection period. As a result, payment for the fixtures was made at the end of October. The fixtures are expected to have a useful life of 10 years and a $10,000 salvage value. Using the straight-line method, HH estimates annual depreciation expense at $12,000 ([$130,000 − $10,000] ÷ 10). Monthly depreciation expense is $1,000 ($12,000 annual charge ÷ 12 months).

Interest expense is missing from the S&A expense budget. HH cannot estimate interest expense until it completes its borrowing projections. Expected borrowing (financing activities) and related interest expense are shown in the *cash budget.*

Exhibit 7–4 *Selling and Administrative Expense Budget*

	A	B	C	D	E	
1		**Hampton Hams**				
2		**Selling and Administrative (S&A) Expense Budget**				
3					Pro Forma	
4	**Section 1: Projected S&A Expenses**	Oct	Nov	Dec	Data	
5	Salary Expense	$24,000	$24,000	$24,000		
6	Sales Commissions, 2% of Sales	3,200	3,840	4,608	$ 4,608	(a)
7	Supplies Expense, 1% of Sales	1,600	1,920	2,304		
8	Utilities Expense	1,400	1,400	1,400	$ 1,400	(b)
9	Depreciation Expense on Store Fixtures	1,000	1,000	1,000	$ 3,000	(c)
10	Rent Expense	3,600	3,600	3,600		
11	Miscellaneous Expense	900	900	900		
12	Total S&A Expenses before Interest	$35,700	$36,660	$37,812	$110,172	(d)
13						
14	**Section 2: Schedule of Cash Payments for S&A Expenses**					
15	Salary Expense	$24,000	$24,000	$24,000		
16	100% of Prior Month Sales Commissions	0	3,200	3,840		
17	Supplies Expense, 1% of Sales	1,600	1,920	2,304		
18	100% of Prior Month Utilities Expense	0	1,400	1,400		
19	Rent Expense	3,600	3,600	3,600		
20	Miscellaneous Expense	900	900	900		
21	Total Payments for S&A Expenses	$30,100	$35,020	$36,044		
22						
23	(a) Sales commissions payable in January reported on the pro forma balance sheet.					
24	(b) Utiltities payable in January reported on the pro forma balance sheet.					
25	(c) Accumulated depreciation on the pro forma balance sheet: sum of monthly amounts ($1,000 + $1,000 + $1,000 = $3,000).					
26	(d) S&A expense on the pro forma income statement: sum of monthly amounts ($35,700 + $36,660 + $37,812 = $110,172).					

Schedule of Cash Payments for Selling and Administrative Expenses

Section 2 of the S&A expense budget shows the schedule of cash payments. There are several differences between the S&A expenses recognized on the pro forma income statement and the cash payments for S&A expenses. First, Hampton Hams' pays sales commissions and utilities expense the month following their incurrence. Since the store opens in October there are no payments due from September. Cash payments for sales commissions and utilities in October are zero. In November, HH will pay the October expenses for these items and in December it will pay the November sales commissions and utility expenses. Depreciation expense does not affect the cash payments schedule. The cash outflow for the store fixtures occurs when the assets are purchased, not when they are depreciated. The cost of the investment in store fixtures is in the cash budget, not in the cash outflow for S&A expenses.

Pro Forma Financial Statement Data

The Pro Forma Data column of the S&A expense budget displays four figures HH will report on the quarter-end budgeted financial statements. The first and second figures are the sales commissions payable ($4,608) and utilities payable ($1,400) on the pro forma balance sheet in Exhibit 7–7. Because December sales commissions and utilities expense are not paid until January, these amounts represent liabilities as of December 31. The third figure in the column ($3,000) is the amount of accumulated depreciation on the pro forma balance sheet in Exhibit 7–7. Since depreciation accumulates, the $3,000 balance is the sum of the monthly depreciation amounts ($1,000 + $1,000 + $1,000 = $3,000). The final figure in the Pro Forma Data column ($110,172) is the total S&A expenses reported on the pro forma income statement in

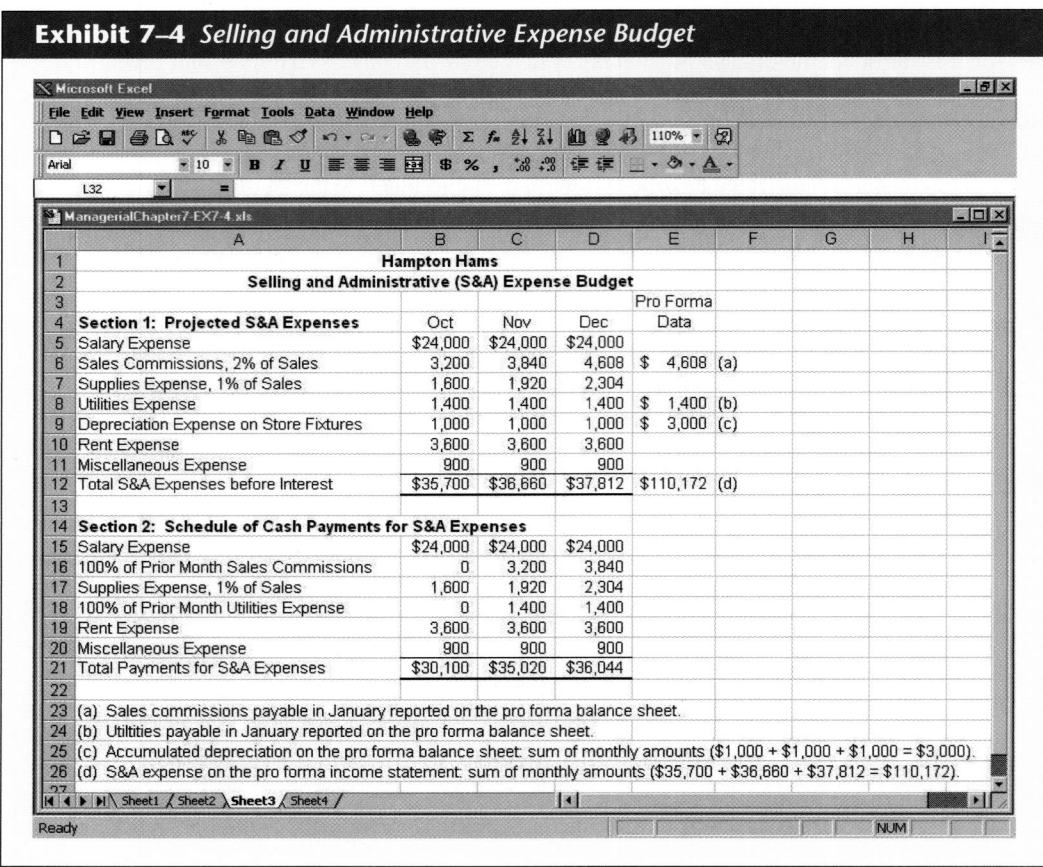

Exhibit 7–6. The total S&A expense is the sum of the monthly amounts ($35,700 + $36,660 + 37,812 = $110,172).

Cash Budget

LO6 Prepare a cash budget.

Little is more important to business success than effective cash management. If a company experiences cash shortages, it will be unable to pay its debts and may be forced into bankruptcy. If excess cash accumulates, a business loses the opportunity to earn investment income or reduce interest costs by repaying debt. Preparing a **cash budget** alerts management to anticipated cash shortages or excess cash balances. Management can plan financing activities, making advance arrangements to cover anticipated shortages by borrowing and planning to repay past borrowings and make appropriate investments when excess cash is expected.

The cash budget is divided into three major sections: (1) a cash receipts section, (2) a cash payments section, and (3) a financing section. Much of the data needed to prepare the cash budget are included in the cash receipts and payments schedules previously discussed; however, further refinements to project financing needs and interest costs are sometimes necessary. The completed cash budget is shown in Exhibit 7–5.

Exhibit 7–5 *Cash Budget*

Hampton Hams
Cash Budget

	Oct	Nov	Dec	Pro Forma Data	
Section 1: Cash Receipts					
Beginning Cash Balance	$0	$ 10,540	$ 10,428		
Add Cash Receipts (Exhibit 7-2)	40,000	168,000	201,600	$409,600	(a)
Total Cash Available	40,000	178,540	212,028		
Section 2: Cash Payments					
For Inventory Purchases (Exhibit 7-3)	87,360	142,912	150,024	$ 380,296	(b)
For S&A Expenses (Exhibit 7-4)	30,100	35,020	36,044	$ 101,164	(c)
For Interest Expense		2,180	2,300	$ 4,480	(d)
For Purchase of Store Fixtures	130,000	0	0	$ 130,000	(e)
Total Budgeted Disbursements	247,460	180,112	188,368		
Section 3: Financing Activities					
Surplus (Shortage)	(207,460)	(1,572)	23,660		
Borrowing (Repayment)	218,000	12,000	(13,000)	$ 217,000	(f)
Ending Cash Balance	$ 10,540	$ 10,428	$ 10,660	$ 10,660	(g)

Pro forma data items (a) through (d) appear in the operating activities section of the pro forma statement of cash flows. Item (d), interest expense, also appears on the pro forma income statement. Each of these items is computed by summing the monthly amounts.

(a) Cash receipts from customers: $40,000 + $168,000 + $201,600 = $409,600.
(b) Cash payments for inventory purchases: $87,360 + $142,912 + $150,024 = $380,296.
(c) Cash payments for S&A Expenses: $30,100 + $35,020 + $36,044 = $101,164.
(d) Cash payments for interest expense: $0 + $2,180 + $2,300 = $4,480.
(e) Investing activities section of the pro forma statement of cash flows.
(f) Financing activities section of the pro forma statements of cash flows ($218,000 +12,000 - $13,000 = $217,000 and liabilities section of the pro forma balance sheet.

Cash Receipts Section

The total cash available (Exhibit 7–5, row 7) is determined by adding the beginning cash balance to the cash receipts from customers. There is no beginning cash balance in October because the new store is opening that month. The November beginning cash balance is the

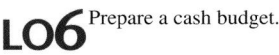

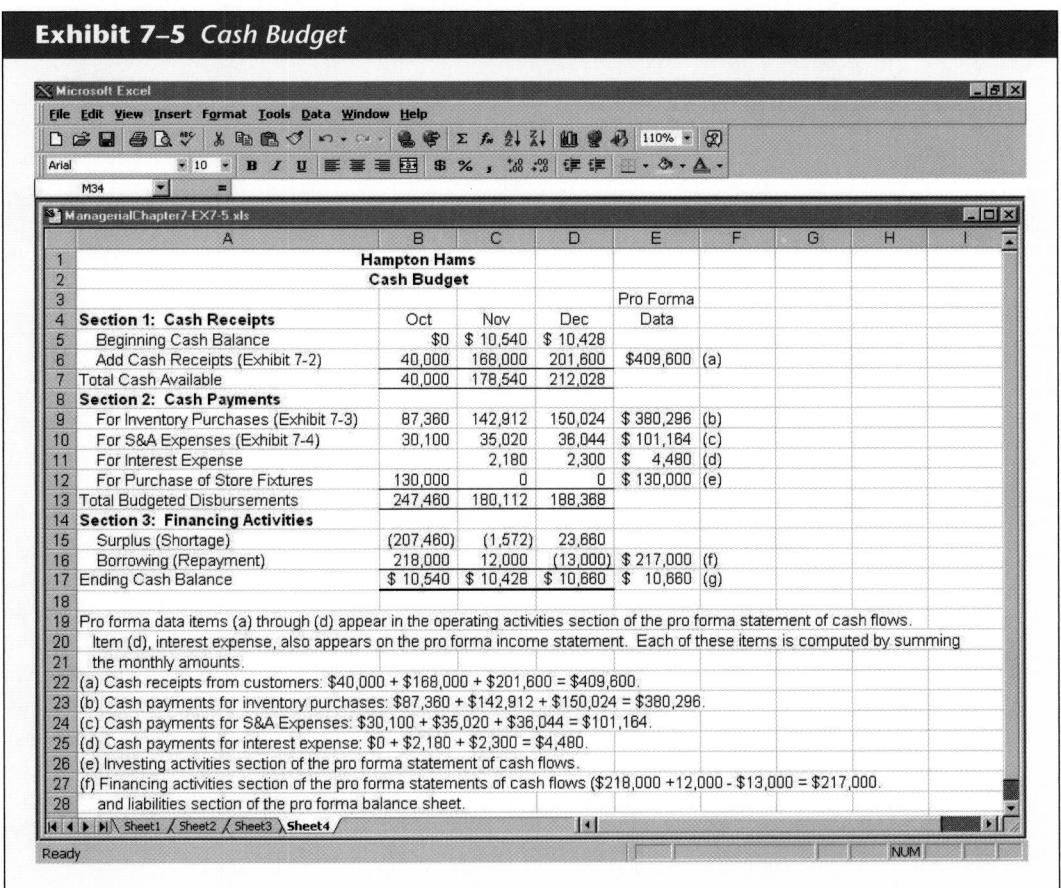

REALITY *bytes*

Budgeting in Governmental Entities

This chapter has presented several reasons organizations should prepare budgets, but for governmental entities, budgets are not simply good planning tools—law requires them. If a manager at a commercial enterprise does not accomplish the budget objectives established for his or her part of the business, the manager may receive a poor performance evaluation. At worst, they may be fired. If managers of governmental agencies spend more than their budgets allow, they may have broken the law. In some cases the manager could be required to personally repay the amount by which the budget was exceeded. Since governmental budgets are enacted by the relevant elected bodies, to violate the budget is to break the law.

Because budgets are so important for governments and are not to be exceeded, government accounting practices require that budgeted amounts be formally entered into the bookkeeping system. As you learned in your first course of accounting, companies do not make formal accounting entries when they order goods; they only make an entry when the goods are received. Governmental accounting systems are different. Each time goods or services are ordered by a government, an "encumbrance" is recorded against the budgeted amount so that agencies do not commit to spend more money than their budgets allow.

October ending cash balance. The December beginning cash balance is the November ending cash balance. Cash receipts from customers comes from the *schedule of cash receipts* in the sales budget (Exhibit 7–2, section 2, row 13).

Cash Payments Section

Cash payments include expected cash outflows for inventory purchases, S&A expenses, interest expense and investments. The cash payments for inventory purchases comes from the *schedule of cash payments for inventory purchases* (Exhibit 7–3, section 2, row 15). The cash payments for S&A expenses comes from the *schedule of cash payments for S&A expenses* (Exhibit 7–4, section 2, row 21).

HH borrows or repays principal and pays interest on the last day of each month. The cash payments for interest are determined by multiplying the loan balance for the month by the monthly interest rate. Since there is no outstanding debt during October, there is no interest payment at the end of October. HH expects outstanding debt of $218,000 during the month of November. The bank charges interest at the rate of 12% per year, or 1% per month. The November interest expense and cash payment for interest is $2,180 ($218,000 × .01). The outstanding loan balance during December is $230,000. The December interest expense and cash payment for interest is $2,300 ($230,000 × .01). Determining the amount to borrow or repay at the end of each month is discussed in more detail in the next section of the text.

Finally, the cash payment for the store fixtures comes from the *capital expenditures budget* (not shown in this chapter).

Financing Section

HH has a line of credit under which it can borrow or repay principal in increments of $1,000 at the end of each month as needed. HH desires to maintain an ending cash balance of at least $10,000 each month. With the $207,460 projected cash shortage in row 15 of the cash budget ($40,000 cash balance in row 7 less $247,460 budgeted cash payments in row 13), HH must borrow $218,000 on October 31 to maintain an ending cash balance of at least $10,000. This $218,000 balance is outstanding during November. On November 30, HH must borrow an additional $12,000 to cover the November projected cash shortage of $1,572 plus the $10,000 desired ending cash balance. HH projects a surplus of $23,660 for the month of December. This surplus will allow HH to repay $13,000 of debt and still maintain the desired $10,000 cash balance.

Pro Forma Financial Statement Data

Figures in the Pro Forma Data column of the cash budget (Exhibit 7–5) are alphabetically referenced. The cash receipts from customers, item (a), and the cash payment items (b), (c), and (d) are reported in the operating activities section of the pro forma statement of cash flows (Exhibit 7–8). The interest expense, item (d), is also reported on the pro forma income statement (Exhibit 7–6). The figures are determined by summing the monthly amounts. The $130,000 purchase of store fixtures, item (e), is reported in the investing activities section of the pro forma statement of cash flows. The $217,000 net borrowings, item (f), is reported in the financing activities section of the pro forma statement of cash flows (Exhibit 7–8) and also as a liability on the pro forma balance sheet (Exhibit 7–7). The $10,660 ending cash balance, item (g), is reported as the ending balance on the pro forma statement of cash flows and as an asset on the pro forma balance sheet.

Astor Company expects to incur the following operating expenses during September: Salary Expense, $25,000; Utility Expense, $1,200; Depreciation Expense, $5,400; and Selling Expense, $14,000. In general, it pays operating expenses in cash in the month in which it incurs them. Based on this information alone, determine the total amount of cash outflow Astor would report in the Operating Activities section of the pro forma statement of cash flows.

Answer Depreciation is not included in cash outflows because companies do not pay cash when they recognize depreciation expense. The total cash outflow is $40,200 ($25,000 + $1,200 + $14,000).

Check Yourself 7–2

Pro Forma Income Statement

LO7 Prepare a pro forma income statement, balance sheet, and statement of cash flows.

Exhibit 7–6 shows the budgeted income statement for Hampton Hams' new store. The figures for this statement come from Exhibits 7–2, 7–3, 7–4, and 7–5. The budgeted income statement provides an advance estimate of the new store's expected profitability. If expected profitability is unsatisfactory, management could decide to abandon the project or modify planned activity. Perhaps HH could lease less costly store space, pay employees a lower rate, or reduce the number of employees hired. The pricing strategy could also be examined for possible changes.

Budgets are usually prepared using spreadsheets or computerized mathematical models that allow managers to easily undertake "what-if " analysis. What if the growth rate differs from expectations? What if interest rates increase or decrease? Exhibits 7–2 through 7–5 in this chapter were prepared using Microsoft Excel. When variables such as growth rate, collection assumptions, or interest rates are changed, the spreadsheet software instantly recalculates the budgets. Although

Exhibit 7–6

HAMPTON HAMS
Pro Forma Income Statement
For the Quarter Ended December 31, 2006

		Data Source
Sales Revenue	$582,400	Exhibit 7–2
Cost of Goods Sold	(407,680)	Exhibit 7–3
Gross Margin	174,720	
Selling and Administrative Expenses	(110,172)	Exhibit 7–4
Operating Income	64,548	
Interest Expense	(4,480)	Exhibit 7–5
Net Income	$ 60,068	

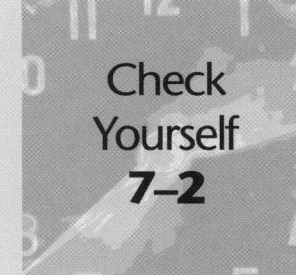

managers remain responsible for data analysis and decision making, computer technology offers powerful tools to assist in those tasks.

Pro Forma Balance Sheet

Most of the figures on the pro forma balance sheet in Exhibit 7–7 have been explained. The new store has no contributed capital because its operations will be financed through debt and retained earnings. The amount of retained earnings equals the amount of net income because no earnings from prior periods exist and no distributions are planned.

Exhibit 7–7

HAMPTON HAMS
Pro Forma Balance Sheet
As of the Quarter Ended December 31, 2006

			Data Source
Assets			
Cash		$ 10,660	Exhibit 7–5
Accounts Receivable		172,800	Exhibit 7–2
Inventory		35,000	Exhibit 7–3
Store Fixtures	$130,000		Exhibit 7–4 Discussion
Accumulated Depreciation	(3,000)		Exhibit 7–4 Discussion
Book Value of Store Fixtures		127,000	
Total Assets		$345,460	
Liabilities			
Accounts Payable		$62,384	Exhibit 7–3
Sales Commissions Payable		4,608	Exhibit 7–4
Utilities Payable		1,400	Exhibit 7–4
Line of Credit Borrowings		217,000	Exhibit 7–5
Equity			
Retained Earnings		60,068	
Total Liabilities and Equity		$345,460	

Pro Forma Statement of Cash Flows

Exhibit 7–8 shows the pro forma statement of cash flows. All information for this statement comes from the cash budget in Exhibit 7–5.

Exhibit 7–8

HAMPTON HAMS
Pro Forma Statement of Cash Flows
For the Quarter Ended December 31, 2006

Cash Flow from Operating Activities		
Cash Receipts from Customers	$409,600	
Cash Payments for Inventory	(380,296)	
Cash Payments for S&A Expenses	(101,164)	
Cash Payments for Interest Expense	(4,480)	
Net Cash Flow for Operating Activities		$(76,340)
Cash Flow from Investing Activities		
Cash Outflow to Purchase Fixtures		(130,000)
Cash Flow from Financing Activities		
Inflow from Borrowing on Line of Credit		217,000
Net Change in Cash		10,660
Plus Beginning Cash Balance		0
Ending Cash Balance		$ 10,660

ANSWERS TO THE *curious* ACCOUNTANT

Budget preparation at the USOC is complicated by the fact that the timing of its revenues does not match the timing of its expenditures. The USOC spends a lot of money helping to train athletes for the United States Olympic team. Training takes place year-round, every year, for many athletes. The USOC's training facilities in Colorado must also be maintained continuously.

Conversely, much of the USOC's revenues are earned in big batches, received every two years. This money comes from fees the USOC receives for the rights to broadcast the Olympic games on television in the United States. Most companies have a one-year budget cycle during which they attempt to anticipate the coming year's revenues and expenses. This model would not work well for the USOC.

Every business, like every family, faces its own set of circumstances. Those individuals responsible for preparing an entity's budget must have a thorough understanding of the environment in which the entity operates. This is the reason the budget process must be participatory if it is to be successful. No one person, or small group, can anticipate all the issues that will face a large organization in the coming budget period; they need input from employees at all levels.

Check Yourself 7–3

How do pro forma financial statements differ from the financial statements presented in a company's annual report to stockholders?

Answer Pro forma financial statements are based on estimates and projections about business events that a company expects to occur in the future. The financial statements presented in a company's annual report to stockholders are based on historical events that occurred prior to the preparation of the statements.

a look back

The planning of financial matters is called *budgeting.* The degree of detail in a company's budget depends on the budget period. Generally, the shorter the time period, the more specific the plans. *Strategic planning* involves long-term plans, such as the overall objectives of the business. Examples of strategic planning include which products to manufacture and sell and which market niches to pursue. Strategic plans are stated in broad, descriptive terms. Capital budgeting deals with intermediate investment planning. *Operations budgeting* focuses on short-term plans and is used to create the master budget.

A budgeting committee is responsible for consolidating numerous departmental budgets into a master budget for the whole company. The *master budget* has detailed objectives stated in specific amounts; it describes how management intends to achieve its objectives. The master budget usually covers one year. Budgeting supports planning, coordination, performance measurement, and corrective action.

Employees may be uncomfortable with budgets, which can be constraining. Budgets set standards by which performance is evaluated. To establish an effective budget system, management should recognize the effect on human behavior of budgeting. Upper-level management must set a positive atmosphere by taking budgets seriously and avoiding using them to humiliate subordinates. One way to create the proper atmosphere is to encourage subordinates' participation in the budgeting process; *participative budgeting* can lead to goals that are more realistic about what can be accomplished and to establish a team effort in trying to reach those goals.

The primary components of the master budget are the *operating budgets,* the *capital budgets,* and the *pro forma financial statements.* The budgeting process begins with preparing the operating budgets, which consist of detailed schedules and budgets prepared by various company departments. The first operating budget to be prepared is the sales budget. The detailed operating budgets for inventory purchases and S&A expenses are based on the projected sales from the sales budget. The information in the schedules of cash receipts (prepared in conjunction with the sales budget) and cash payments (prepared in conjunction with the inventory purchases and S&A expense budgets) is used in preparing the cash budget. The cash budget subtracts cash payments from cash receipts; the resulting cash surplus or shortage determines the company's financing activities.

The capital budget describes the company's long-term plans regarding investments in facilities, equipment, new products, or other lines of business. The information from the capital budget is used as input to several of the operating budgets.

The pro forma financial statements are prepared from information in the operating budgets. The operating budgets for sales, inventory purchases, and S&A expenses contain information that is used to prepare the income statement and balance sheet. The cash budget includes the amount of interest expense reported on the income statement, the ending cash balance, the capital acquisitions reported on the balance sheet, and most of the information included in the statement of cash flows.

a look forward

Once a company has completed its budget, it has defined its plans. Then the plans must be followed. The next chapter investigates the techniques used to evaluate performance. You will learn to compare actual results to budgets, to calculate variances, and to identify the parties who are normally accountable for deviations from expectations. Finally, you will learn about the human impact management must consider in taking corrective action when employees fail to accomplish budget goals.

SELF-STUDY REVIEW PROBLEM

The Getaway Gift Company operates a chain of small gift shops that are located in prime vacation towns. Getaway is considering opening a new store on January 1, 2003. Getaway's president recently attended a business seminar that explained how formal budgets could be useful in judging the new store's likelihood of succeeding. Assume you are the company's accountant. The president has asked you to explain the budgeting process and to provide sample reports that show the new store's operating expectations for the first three months (January, February, and March). Respond to the following specific requirements:

Required

a. List the operating budgets and schedules included in a master budget.

b. Explain the difference between pro forma financial statements and the financial statements presented in a company's annual reports to shareholders.

c. Prepare a sample sales budget and a schedule of expected cash receipts using the following assumptions. Getaway estimates January sales will be $400,000 of which $100,000 will be cash and $300,000 will be credit. The ratio of cash sales to sales on account is expected to remain constant over the three-month period. The company expects sales to increase 10 percent per month. The company expects to collect 100 percent of the accounts receivable generated by credit sales in the month following the sale. Use this information to determine the amount of accounts receivable that Getaway would report on the March 31 pro forma balance sheet and the amount of sales it would report on the first quarter pro forma income statement.

d. Prepare a sample inventory purchases budget using the following assumptions. Cost of goods sold is 60 percent of sales. The company desires to maintain a minimum ending inventory equal to 25 percent of the current month's cost of goods sold. Getaway makes all inventory purchases on account. The company pays 70 percent of accounts payable in the month of purchase. It pays the remaining 30 percent in the following month. Prepare a schedule of expected cash payments for inventory purchases. Use this information to determine the amount of cost of goods sold Getaway would report on the first quarter pro forma income statement and the amounts of ending inventory and accounts payable it would report on the March 31 pro forma balance sheet.

Solution to Requirement a

A master budget would include (1) a sales budget and schedule of cash receipts, (2) an inventory purchases budget and schedule of cash payments for inventory, (3) a general, selling, and administrative expenses budget and a schedule of cash payments related to these expenses, and (4) a cash budget.

Solution to Requirement b

Pro forma statements result from the operating budgets listed in the response to Requirement *a*. Pro forma statements describe the results of expected future events. In contrast, the financial statements presented in a company's annual report reflect the results of events that have actually occurred in the past.

Solution to Requirement c

General Information				
Sales growth rate		**10%**		**Pro Forma Statement Data**
Sales Budget	**January**	**February**	**March**	
Sales				
Cash sales	$100,000	$110,000	$121,000	
Sales on account	300,000	330,000	363,000	$ 363,000*
Total sales	$400,000	$440,000	$484,000	$1,324,000†
Schedule of Cash Receipts				
Current cash sales	$100,000	$110,000	$121,000	
Plus 100% of previous month's credit sales	0	300,000	330,000	
Total budgeted collections	$100,000	$410,000	$451,000	

*Ending accounts receivable balance reported on March 31 pro forma balance sheet.

†Sales revenue reported on first quarter pro forma income statement (sum of monthly sales).

Solution to Requirement d

General information				
Cost of goods sold percentage		**60%**		**Pro Forma Statement Data**
Desired ending inventory percentage of CGS		**25%**		
Inventory Purchases Budget	**January**	**February**	**March**	
Budgeted cost of goods sold	$240,000	$264,000	$290,400	$794,400*
Plus: Desired ending inventory	66,000	72,600	79,860	79,860†
Inventory needed	306,000	336,600	370,260	
Less: Beginning inventory	0	(66,000)	(72,600)	
Required purchases	$306,000	$270,600	$297,660	89,298‡
Schedule of Cash Payments for Inventory Purchases				
70% of current purchases	$214,200	$189,420	$208,362	
30% of prior month's purchases	0	91,800	81,180	
Total budgeted payments for inventory	$214,200	$281,220	$289,542	

*Cost of goods sold reported on first quarter pro forma income statement (sum of monthly amounts).

†Ending inventory balance reported on March 31 pro forma balance sheet.

‡Ending accounts payable balance reported on pro forma balance sheet ($297,660 × 0.3).

KEY TERMS

Budgeting *273*
Capital budget *277*
Capital budgeting *274*
Cash budget *283*
Master budget *276*
Operating budgets *276*
Participative budgeting *276*
Perpetual (continuous) budgeting *275*
Pro forma financial statements *277*
Strategic planning *274*

QUESTIONS

1. Budgets are useful only for small companies that can estimate sales with accuracy. Do you agree with this statement?
2. Why does preparing the master budget require a committee?
3. What are the three levels of planning? Explain each briefly.
4. What is the primary factor that distinguishes the three different levels of planning from each other?
5. What is the advantage of using a perpetual budget instead of the traditional annual budget?

6. What are the advantages of budgeting?
7. How may budgets be used as a measure of performance?
8. Ken Shilov, manager of the marketing department, tells you that "budgeting simply does not work." He says that he made budgets for his employees and when he reprimanded them for failing to accomplish budget goals, he got unfounded excuses. Suggest how Mr. Shilov could encourage employee cooperation.
9. What is a master budget?
10. What is the normal starting point in developing the master budget?
11. How does the level of inventory affect the production budget? Why is it important to manage the level of inventory?
12. What are the components of the cash budget? Describe each.
13. The primary reason for preparing a cash budget is to determine the amount of cash to include on the budgeted balance sheet. Do you agree or disagree with this statement? Explain.
14. What information does the pro forma income statement provide? How does its preparation depend on the operating budgets?
15. How does the pro forma statement of cash flows differ from the cash budget?

EXERCISES—SERIES A

All Exercises in Series A are available with McGraw-Hill's Homework Manager.

L.O. 1, 2

EXERCISE 7–1A *Budget Responsibility*

Janet Pace, the accountant, is a perfectionist. No one can do the job as well as she can. Indeed, she has found budget information provided by the various departments to be worthless. She must change everything they give her. She has to admit that her estimates have not always been accurate, but she shudders to think of what would happen if she used the information supplied by the marketing and operating departments. No one seems to care about accuracy. Indeed, some of the marketing staff have even become insulting. When Ms. Pace confronted one of the salesmen with the fact that he was behind in meeting his budgeted sales forecast, he responded by saying, "They're your numbers. Why don't you go out and make the sales? It's a heck of a lot easier to sit there in your office and make up numbers than it is to get out and get the real work done." Ms. Pace reported the incident, but, of course, nothing was done about it.

Required

Write a short report suggesting how the budgeting process could be improved.

L.O. 3, 7

EXERCISE 7–2A *Preparing the Sales Budget*

Digital Flash, which expects to start operations on January 1, 2005, will sell digital cameras in shopping malls. Digital Flash has budgeted sales as indicated in the following table. The company expects a 10 percent increase in sales per month for February and March. The ratio of cash sales to sales on account will remain stable from January through March.

Sales	January	February	March
Cash sales	$ 40,000	?	?
Sales on account	60,000	?	?
Total budgeted sales	$100,000	?	?

Required

a. Complete the sales budget by filling in the missing amounts.
b. Determine the amount of sales revenue Digital Flash will report on its second quarter pro forma income statement.

L.O. 3, 7

EXERCISE 7–3A *Preparing a Schedule of Cash Receipts*

The budget director of Amy's Florist has prepared the following sales budget. The company had $200,000 in accounts receivable on July 1. Amy's Florist normally collects 100 percent of accounts receivable in the month following the month of sale.

Sales	July	August	September
Sales Budget			
Cash sales	$ 60,000	$ 66,000	$ 72,600
Sales on account	150,000	165,000	181,500
Total budgeted sales	$210,000	$231,000	$254,100
Schedule of Cash Receipts			
Current cash sales	?	?	?
Plus collections from accounts receivable	?	?	?
Total budgeted collections	$260,000	$216,000	$237,600

Required

a. Complete the schedule of cash receipts by filling in the missing amounts.

b. Determine the amount of accounts receivable the company will report on its third quarter pro forma balance sheet.

EXERCISE 7–4A *Preparing Sales Budgets With Different Assumptions* L.O. 3

Stenton Corporation, which has three divisions, is preparing its sales budget. Each division expects a different growth rate because economic conditions vary in different regions of the country. The growth expectations per quarter are 2 percent for East Division, 3 percent for West Division, and 5 percent for South Division.

Division	First Quarter	Second Quarter	Third Quarter	Fourth Quarter
East Division	$300,000	?	?	?
West Division	400,000	?	?	?
South Division	100,000	?	?	?

Required

a. Complete the sales budget by filling in the missing amounts. (Round figures to the nearest dollar.)

b. Determine the amount of sales revenue that the company will report on its quarterly pro forma income statements.

EXERCISE 7–5A *Determining Cash Receipts From Accounts Receivable* L.O. 3

Special Delivery operates a mail-order business that sells clothes designed for frequent travelers. It had sales of $400,000 in December. Because Special Delivery is in the mail-order business, all sales are made on account. The company expects a 25 percent drop in sales for January. The balance in the Accounts Receivable account on December 31 was $80,000 and is budgeted to be $60,000 as of January 31. Special Delivery normally collects accounts receivable in the month following the month of sale.

Required

a. Determine the amount of cash Special Delivery expects to collect from accounts receivable during January.

b. Is it reasonable to assume that sales will decline in January for this type of business? Why or why not?

EXERCISE 7–6A *Using Judgment in Making a Sales Forecast* L.O. 3

Kandy, Inc., is a candy store located in a large shopping mall.

Required

Write a brief memo describing the sales pattern that you would expect Kandy to experience during the year. In which months will sales likely be high? In which months will sales likely be low? Explain why.

EXERCISE 7–7A *Preparing an Inventory Purchases Budget* L.O. 4

Designer Lighting Company sells lamps and other lighting fixtures. The purchasing department manager prepared the following inventory purchases budget. Designer Lighting's policy is to maintain an ending inventory balance equal to 10 percent of the following month's cost of goods sold. April's budgeted cost of goods sold is $90,000.

	January	February	March
Budgeted cost of goods sold	$75,000	$80,000	$86,000
Plus: Desired ending inventory	8,000	?	?
Inventory needed	83,000	?	?
Less: Beginning inventory	16,000	?	?
Required purchases (on account)	$67,000	$80,600	$86,400

Required

a. Complete the inventory purchases budget by filling in the missing amounts.

b. Determine the amount of cost of goods sold the company will report on its first quarter pro forma income statement.

c. Determine the amount of ending inventory the company will report on its pro forma balance sheet at the end of the first quarter.

L.O. 4

EXERCISE 7–8A *Preparing a Schedule of Cash Payments for Inventory Purchases*

Book Warehouse buys books and magazines directly from publishers and distributes them to grocery stores. The wholesaler expects to purchase the following inventory.

	April	May	June
Required purchases (on account)	$60,000	$80,000	$100,000

Book Warehouse's accountant prepared the following schedule of cash payments for inventory purchases. Book Warehouse's suppliers require that 90 percent of purchases on account be paid in the month of purchase; the remaining 10 percent are paid in the month following the month of purchase.

Schedule of Cash Payments for Inventory Purchases			
	April	May	June
Payment for current accounts payable	$54,000	?	?
Payment for previous accounts payable	4,000	?	?
Total budgeted payments for inventory	$58,000	$78,000	$98,000

Required

a. Complete the schedule of cash payments for inventory purchases by filling in the missing amounts.

b. Determine the amount of accounts payable the company will report on its pro forma balance sheet at the end of the second quarter.

L.O. 4

EXERCISE 7–9A *Determining the Amount of Expected Inventory Purchases and Cash Payments*

Jakal Company, which sells electric razors, had $280,000 of cost of goods sold during the month of June. The company projects a 5 percent increase in cost of goods sold during July. The inventory balance as of June 30 is $30,000, and the desired ending inventory balance for July is $25,000. Jakal pays cash to settle 80 percent of its purchases on account during the month of purchase and pays the remaining 20 percent in the month following the purchase. The accounts payable balance as of June 30 was $32,000.

Required

a. Determine the amount of purchases budgeted for July.

b. Determine the amount of cash payments budgeted for inventory purchases in July.

L.O. 5

EXERCISE 7–10A *Preparing a Schedule of Cash Payments for Selling and Administrative Expenses*

The budget director for Shining Window Cleaning Services prepared the following list of expected operating expenses. All expenses requiring cash payments are paid for in the month incurred except salary expense and insurance. Salary is paid in the month following the month in which it is incurred. The insurance premium for six months is paid on October 1. October is the first month of operations; accordingly, there are no beginning account balances.

	October	November	December
Budgeted Operating Expenses			
Equipment lease expense	$ 7,000	$ 7,000	$ 7,000
Salary expense	6,400	6,800	6,900
Cleaning supplies	2,600	2,860	3,146
Insurance expense	1,000	1,000	1,000
Depreciation on computer	1,600	1,600	1,600
Rent	1,800	1,800	1,800
Miscellaneous expenses	600	600	600
Total operating expenses	$21,000	$21,660	$22,046
Schedule of Cash Payments for Operating Expenses			
Equipment lease expense	?	?	?
Prior month's salary expense, 100%	?	?	?
Cleaning supplies	?	?	?
Insurance premium	?	?	?
Depreciation on computer	?	?	?
Rent	?	?	?
Miscellaneous expenses	?	?	?
Total disbursements for operating expenses	$18,000	$18,660	$19,346

Required

a. Complete the schedule of cash payments for operating expenses by filling in the missing amounts.

b. Determine the amount of salaries payable the company will report on its pro forma balance sheet at the end of the fourth quarter.

c. Determine the amount of prepaid insurance the company will report on its pro forma balance sheet at the end of the fourth quarter.

EXERCISE 7–11A *Preparing Inventory Purchases Budgets With Different Assumptions*

L.O. 4

Executive officers of Cary Company are wrestling with their budget for the next year. The following are two different sales estimates provided by two difference sources.

Source of Estimate	First Quarter	Second Quarter	Third Quarter	Fourth Quarter
Sales manager	$400,000	$320,000	$300,000	$480,000
Marketing consultant	500,000	450,000	420,000	630,000

Cary's past experience indicates that cost of goods sold is about 70 percent of sales revenue. The company tries to maintain 10 percent of the next quarter's expected cost of goods sold as the current quarter's ending inventory. This year's ending inventory is $30,000. Next year's ending inventory is budgeted to be $32,000.

Required

a. Prepare an inventory purchases budget using the sales manager's estimate.

b. Prepare an inventory purchases budget using the marketing consultant's estimate.

EXERCISE 7–12A *Determining the Amount of Cash Payments and Pro Forma Statement Data for Selling and Administrative Expenses*

L.O. 5, 7

January budgeted selling and administrative expenses for the retail shoe store that Nell Walker plans to open on January 1, 2006, are as follows: sales commissions, $20,000; rent, $15,000; utilities, $5,000; depreciation, $4,000; and miscellaneous, $2,000. Utilities are paid in the month following their incursion. Other expenses are expected to be paid in cash in the month in which they are incurred.

Required

a. Determine the amount of budgeted cash payments for January selling and administrative expenses.

b. Determine the amount of utilities payable the store will report on the January 31st pro forma balance sheet.

c. Determine the amount of depreciation expense the store will report on the income statement for the year 2006, assuming that monthly depreciation remains the same for the entire year.

L.O. 6, 7

EXERCISE 7–13A *Preparing a Cash Budget*

The accountant for Tricia's Dress Shop prepared the following cash budget. Tricia's desires to maintain a cash cushion of $14,000 at the end of each month. Funds are assumed to be borrowed and repaid on the last day of each month. Interest is charged at the rate of 2 percent per month. The company had a beginning balance in its line-of-credit loan of $50,000.

Cash Budget	July	August	September
Section 1: Cash Receipts			
Beginning cash balance	$ 42,500	$?	$?
Add cash receipts	180,000	200,000	240,600
Total cash available (a)	222,500	?	?
Section 2: Cash Payments			
For inventory purchases	165,526	140,230	174,152
For S&A expenses	54,500	60,560	61,432
For interest expense	0	?	?
Total budgeted disbursements (b)	220,026	?	?
Section 3: Financing Activities			
Surplus (shortage)	2,724	?	?
Borrowing (repayments) (c)	11,526	?	?
Ending Cash Balance (a − b + c)	$ 14,000	$ 14,000	$ 14,000

Required

a. Complete the cash budget by filling in the missing amounts. Round all computations to the nearest whole dollar.

b. Determine the amount of net cash flows from operating activities Tricia's will report on the third quarter pro forma statement of cash flows.

c. Determine the amount of net cash flows from financing activities Tricia's will report on the third quarter pro forma statement of cash flows.

L.O. 6, 7

EXERCISE 7–14A *Determining Amount to Borrow and Pro Forma Statement Balances*

Jane Hesline owns a small restaurant in New York City. Ms. Hesline provided her accountant with the following summary information regarding expectations for the month of June. The balance in accounts receivable as of May 31 is $50,000. Budgeted cash and credit sales for June are $100,000 and $500,000, respectively. Credit sales are made through Visa and MasterCard and are collected rapidly. Ninety percent of credit sales is collected in the month of sale, and the remainder is collected in the following month. Ms. Hesline's suppliers do not extend credit. Consequently, she pays suppliers on the last day of the month. Cash payments for June are expected to be $620,000. Ms. Hesline has a line of credit that enables the restaurant to borrow funds on demand; however, they must be borrowed on the last day of the month. Interest is paid in cash also on the last day of the month. Ms. Hesline desires to maintain a $20,000 cash balance before the interest payment. Her annual interest rate is 9 percent.

Required

a. Compute the amount of funds Ms. Hesline needs to borrow for June.

b. Determine the amount of interest expense the restaurant will report on the June pro forma income statement.

c. What amount will the restaurant report as interest expense on the July pro forma balance sheet?

L.O. 7

EXERCISE 7–15A *Preparing Pro Forma Income Statements With Different Assumptions*

Andy Collum, the controller of Grime Corporation, is trying to prepare a sales budget for the coming year. The income statements for the last four quarters follow.

	First Quarter	Second Quarter	Third Quarter	Fourth Quarter	Total
Sales revenue	$160,000	$180,000	$200,000	$260,000	$800,000
Cost of goods sold	96,000	108,000	120,000	156,000	480,000
Gross profit	64,000	72,000	80,000	104,000	320,000
Selling & admin. expense	16,000	18,000	20,000	26,000	80,000
Net income	$ 48,000	$ 64,000	$ 60,000	$ 78,000	$240,000

Historically, cost of goods sold is about 60 percent of sales revenue. Selling and administrative expenses are about 10 percent of sales revenue.

Tim Grime, the chief executive officer, told Mr. Collum that he expected sales next year to be 10 percent above last year's level. However, Sara Lund, the vice president of sales, told Mr. Collum that she believed sales growth would be only 5 percent.

Required

a. Prepare a pro forma income statement including quarterly budgets for the coming year using Mr. Grime's estimate.
b. Prepare a pro forma income statement including quarterly budgets for the coming year using Ms. Lund's estimate.
c. Explain why two executive officers in the same company could have different estimates of future growth.

PROBLEMS—SERIES A

All Problems in Series A are available with McGraw-Hill's Homework Manager.

PROBLEM 7–16A *Preparing a Sales Budget and Schedule of Cash Receipts*

L.O. 3

excel
www.mhhe.com/edmonds3e

Bedimo Pointers, Inc., expects to begin operations on January 1, 2007; it will operate as a specialty sales company that sells laser pointers over the Internet. Bedimo expects sales in January 2007 to total $100,000 and to increase 10 percent per month in February and March. All sales are on account. Bedimo expects to collect 60 percent of accounts receivable in the month of sale, 30 percent in the month following the sale, and 10 percent in the second month following the sale.

CHECK FIGURES
c. Feb: $96,000
March $115,600

Required

a. Prepare a sales budget for the first quarter of 2007.
b. Determine the amount of sales revenue Bedimo will report on the first 2007 quarterly pro forma income statement.
c. Prepare a cash receipts schedule for the first quarter of 2007.
d. Determine the amount of accounts receivable as of March 31, 2007.

PROBLEM 7–17A *Preparing the Inventory Purchases Budget and Schedule of Cash Payments*

L.O. 4, 7

Stine, Inc., sells fire works. The company's marketing director developed the following cost of goods sold budget for April, May, and June.

CHECK FIGURES
a. May: $71,000
c. June: $76,760

	April	May	June	July
Budgeted cost of goods sold	$60,000	$70,000	$80,000	$86,000

Stine had a beginning inventory balance of $3,600 on April 1 and a beginning balance in accounts payable of $14,800. The company desires to maintain an ending inventory balance equal to 10 percent of the next period's cost of goods sold. Stine makes all purchases on account. The company pays 60 percent of accounts payable in the month of purchase and the remaining 40 percent in the month following purchase.

Required

a. Prepare an inventory purchases budget for April, May, and June.
b. Determine the amount of ending inventory Stine will report on the end-of-quarter pro forma balance sheet.
c. Prepare a schedule of cash payments for inventory for April, May, and June.
d. Determine the balance in accounts payable Stine will report on the end-of-quarter pro forma balance sheet.

PROBLEM 7–18A *Preparing Pro Forma Income Statements With Different Assumptions*

L.O. 7

Top executive officers of Chesnokov Company, a merchandising firm, are preparing the next year's budget. The controller has provided everyone with the current year's projected income statement.

CHECK FIGURE
a. 12.75%

	Current Year
Sales Revenue	$2,000,000
Cost of Goods Sold	1,400,000
Gross Profit	600,000
Selling & Admin. Expenses	260,000
Net Income	$ 340,000

Cost of goods sold is usually 70 percent of sales revenue, and selling and administrative expenses are usually 10 percent of sales plus a fixed cost of $60,000. The president has announced that the company's goal is to increase net income by 15 percent.

Required

The following items are independent of each other.

a. What percentage increase in sales would enable the company to reach its goal? Support your answer with a pro forma income statement.

b. The market may become stagnant next year, and the company does not expect an increase in sales revenue. The production manager believes that an improved production procedure can cut cost of goods sold by 2 percent. What else can the company do to reach its goal? Prepare a pro forma income statement illustrating your proposal.

c. The company decides to escalate its advertising campaign to boost consumer recognition, which will increase selling and administrative expenses to $340,000. With the increased advertising, the company expects sales revenue to increase by 15 percent. Assume that cost of goods sold remains a constant proportion of sales. Can the company reach its goal?

L.O. 5, 6

PROBLEM 7–19A *Preparing a Schedule of Cash Payments for Selling and Administrative Expenses*

CHECK FIGURE
a. Sept: $22,460

Shah is a retail company specializing in men's hats. Its budget director prepared the list of expected operating expenses that follows. All items are paid when incurred except sales commissions and utilities, which are paid in the month following their incursion. July is the first month of operations, so there are no beginning account balances.

	July	August	September
Salary expense	$12,000	$12,000	$12,000
Sales commissions (4 percent of sales)	1,600	1,500	1,800
Supplies expense	360	400	440
Utilities	1,200	1,200	1,200
Depreciation on store equipment	2,600	2,600	2,600
Rent	6,600	6,600	6,600
Miscellaneous	720	720	720
Total S&A expenses before interest	$25,080	$25,020	$25,360

Required

a. Prepare a schedule of cash payments for selling and administrative expenses.

b. Determine the amount of utilities payable as of September 30.

c. Determine the amount of sales commissions payable as of September 30.

L.O. 6

PROBLEM 7–20A *Preparing a Cash Budget*

CHECK FIGURE
Feb cash surplus before financing activities: $7,010

Hoyt Medical Clinic has budgeted the following cash flows.

	January	February	March
Cash receipts	$100,000	$106,000	$126,000
Cash payments			
For inventory purchases	90,000	72,000	85,000
For S&A expenses	31,000	32,000	27,000

Hoyt Medical had a cash balance of $8,000 on January 1. The company desires to maintain a cash cushion of $5,000. Funds are assumed to be borrowed, in increment of $1,000, and repaid on the last day of each month; the interest rate is 1 percent per month. Hoyt pays its vendor on the last day of the month also. The company had a $40,000 beginning balance in its line of credit liability account.

Required

Prepare a cash budget. (Round all computations to the nearest whole dollar.)

PROBLEM 7–21A *Preparing Budgets With Multiple Products*

L.O. 3, 4, 5

excel

www.mhhe.com/edmonds3e

CHECK FIGURES

c. 1st QTR purchases for peaches: $141,120
2nd QTR purchases for oranges: $312,840

Fresh Fruits Corporation wholesales peaches and oranges. Beth Fresh is working with the company's accountant to prepare next year's budget. Ms. Fresh estimates that sales will increase 5 percent annually for peaches and 10 percent for oranges. The current year's sales revenue data follow.

	First Quarter	Second Quarter	Third Quarter	Fourth Quarter	Total
Peaches	$220,000	$240,000	$300,000	$240,000	$1,000,000
Oranges	400,000	450,000	570,000	380,000	1,800,000
Total	$620,000	$690,000	$870,000	$620,000	$2,800,000

Based on the company's past experience, cost of goods sold is usually 60 percent of sales revenue. Company policy is to keep 20 percent of the next period's estimated cost of goods sold as the current period's ending inventory. (*Hint:* Use the cost of goods sold for the first quarter to determine the beginning inventory for the first quarter.)

Required

a. Prepare the company's sales budget for the next year for each quarter by individual product.

b. If the selling and administrative expenses are estimated to be $700,000, prepare the company's budgeted annual income statement.

c. Ms. Fresh estimates next year's ending inventory will be $34,000 for peaches and $56,000 for oranges. Prepare the company's inventory purchases budgets for the next year showing quarterly figures by product.

PROBLEM 7–22A *Preparing a Master Budget for Retail Company With No Beginning Account Balances*

L.O. 3, 4, 5

excel

www.mhhe.com/edmonds3e

CHECK FIGURES

c. Dec. purchases: $113,250

g. Nov. surplus before financing activities: $19,505

Unici Company is a retail company that specializes in selling outdoor camping equipment. The company is considering opening a new store on October 1, 2006. The company president formed a planning committee to prepare a master budget for the first three months of operation. As budget coordinator, you have been assigned the following tasks.

Required

a. October sales are estimated to be $120,000 of which 40 percent will be cash and 60 percent will be credit. The company expects sales to increase at the rate of 25 percent per month. Prepare a sales budget.

b. The company expects to collect 100 percent of the accounts receivable generated by credit sales in the month following the sale. Prepare a schedule of cash receipts.

c. The cost of goods sold is 60 percent of sales. The company desires to maintain a minimum ending inventory equal to 10 percent of the next month's cost of goods sold. Ending inventory of December is expected to be $12,000. Assume that all purchases are made on account. Prepare an inventory purchases budget.

d. The company pays 70 percent of accounts payable in the month of purchase and the remaining 30 percent in the following month. Prepare a cash payments budget for inventory purchases.

e. Budgeted selling and administrative expenses per month follow.

Salary expense (fixed)	$18,000
Sales commissions	5 percent of Sales
Supplies expense	2 percent of Sales
Utilities (fixed)	$1,400
Depreciation on store equipment (fixed)*	$4,000
Rent (fixed)	$4,800
Miscellaneous (fixed)	$1,200

*The capital expenditures budget indicates that Unici will spend $164,000 on October 1 for store fixtures, which are expected to have a $20,000 salvage value and a three-year (36-month) useful life.

Use this information to prepare a selling and administrative expenses budget.

f. Utilities and sales commissions are paid the month after they are incurred; all other expenses are paid in the month in which they are incurred. Prepare a cash payments budget for selling and administrative expenses.

g. Unici borrows funds, in increment of $1,000, and repays them on the last day of the month. The company also pays its vendors on the last day of the month. It pays interest of 1 percent per month in cash on the last day of the month. To be prudent, the company desires to maintain a $12,000 cash cushion. Prepare a cash budget.

h. Prepare a pro forma income statement for the quarter.

i. Prepare a pro forma balance sheet at the end of the quarter.

j. Prepare a pro forma statement of cash flows for the quarter.

L.O. 2 PROBLEM 7–23A *Behavioral Impact of Budgeting*

CHECK FIGURE
a. NI: $945,000
b. NI: $1,035,000

Vanhorn Corporation has three divisions, each operating as a responsibility center. To provide an incentive for divisional executive officers, the company gives divisional management a bonus equal to 20 percent of the excess of actual net income over budgeted net income. The following is Dancy Division's current year's performance.

	Current Year
Sales revenue	$4,500,000
Cost of goods sold	2,700,000
Gross profit	1,800,000
Selling & admin. expenses	900,000
Net income	$ 900,000

The president has just received next year's budget proposal from the vice president in charge of Dancy Division. The proposal budgets a 5 percent increase in sales revenue with an extensive explanation about stiff market competition. The president is puzzled. Dancy has enjoyed revenue growth of around 10 percent for each of the past five years. The president had consistently approved the division's budget proposals based on 5 percent growth in the past. This time, the president wants to show that he is not a fool. "I will impose a 15 percent revenue increase to teach them a lesson!" the president says to himself smugly.

Assume that cost of goods sold and selling and administrative expenses remain stable in proportion to sales.

Required

a. Prepare the budgeted income statement based on Dancy Division's proposal of a 5 percent increase.

b. If growth is actually 10 percent as usual, how much bonus would Dancy Division's executive officers receive if the president had approved the division's proposal?

c. Prepare the budgeted income statement based on the 15 percent increase the president imposed.

d. If the actual results turn out to be a 10 percent increase as usual, how much bonus would Dancy Division's executive officers receive since the president imposed a 15 percent increase?

e. Propose a better budgeting procedure for Vanhorn.

EXERCISES—SERIES B

L.O. 1, 2 EXERCISE 7–1B *Budget Responsibility*

Ken Chaney, the controller of Oxmoore Industries, Inc., is very popular. He is easygoing and does not offend anybody. To develop the company's most recent budget, Mr. Chaney first asked all department managers to prepare their own budgets. He then added together the totals from the department budgets to produce the company budget. When Sally Khatri, Oxmoore's president, reviewed the company budget, she sighed and asked, "Is our company a charitable organization?"

Required

Write a brief memo describing deficiencies in the budgeting process and suggesting improvements.

EXERCISE 7–2B *Preparing a Sales Budget*

L.O. 3, 7

Reese's Restaurant is opening for business in a new shopping center. Casey Mazur, the owner, is preparing a sales budget for the next three months. After consulting friends in the same business, Ms. Mazur estimated July revenues as shown in the following table. She expects revenues to increase 5 percent per month in August and September.

Revenues Budget	July	August	September
Food sales	$20,000	?	?
Beverage and liquor sales	12,000	?	?
Total budgeted revenues	$32,000	?	?

Required

a. Complete the sales budget by filling in the missing amounts.
b. Determine the total amount of revenue Reese's Restaurant will report on its quarterly pro forma income statement.

EXERCISE 7–3B *Preparing a Schedule of Cash Receipts*

L.O. 3, 7

Tilden Imports, Inc., sells goods imported from the Far East. Using the second quarter's sales budget, Sam Wu is trying to complete the schedule of cash receipts for the quarter. The company had accounts receivable of $430,000 on April 1. Tilden Imports normally collects 100 percent of accounts receivable in the month following the month of sale.

Sales	April	May	June
Sales Budget			
Cash sales	$160,000	$176,000	$168,000
Sales on account	480,000	568,000	500,000
Total budgeted sales	$640,000	$744,000	$668,000
Schedule of Cash Receipts			
Current cash sales	?	?	?
Plus: Collections from accounts receivable	?	?	?
Total budgeted collections	$590,000	$656,000	$736,000

Required

a. Help Mr. Wu complete the schedule of cash receipts by filling in the missing amounts.
b. Determine the amount of accounts receivable the company will report on the quarterly pro forma balance sheet.

EXERCISE 7–4B *Preparing Sales Budgets With Different Assumptions*

L.O. 3

Briggs International, Inc., has three subsidiaries, Falcon Trading Company, Ammons Medical Supplies Company, and Ocean Shipping Company. Because the subsidiaries operate in different industries, Briggs's corporate budget for the coming year must reflect the different growth potentials of the individual industries. The growth expectations per quarter for the subsidiaries are 4 percent for Falcon, 1 percent for Ammons, and 3 percent for Ocean.

Subsidiary	Current Quarter Sales	First Quarter	Second Quarter	Third Quarter	Fourth Quarter
Falcon	$250,000	?	?	?	?
Ammons	350,000	?	?	?	?
Ocean	450,000	?	?	?	?

Required

a. Complete the sales budget by filling in the missing amounts. (Round the figures to the nearest dollar.)
b. Determine the amount of sales revenue Briggs will report on the quarterly pro forma income statements.

L.O. 3 **EXERCISE 7–5B** ***Determining Cash Receipts From Accounts Receivable***

Otell Corporation is about to start a business as an agricultural products distributor. Because its customers will all be retailers, Otell will sell its products solely on account. The company expects to collect 60 percent of accounts receivable in the month of sale and the remaining 40 percent in the following month. Otell expects sales revenues of $200,000 in July, the first month of operation, and $250,000 in August.

Required

a. Determine the amount of cash Otell expects to collect in July.
b. Determine the amount of cash Otell expects to collect in August.

L.O. 3 **EXERCISE 7–6B** ***Using Judgment in Making a Sales Forecast***

Merry Greetings Corporation sells greeting cards for various occasions.

Required

Write a brief memo describing the sales pattern that you would expect Merry Greetings to experience during the year. In which months will sales likely be high? Explain why.

L.O. 4 **EXERCISE 7–7B** ***Preparing an Inventory Purchases Budget***

Green Drugstores, Inc., sells prescription drugs, over-the-counter drugs, and some groceries. The purchasing manager prepared the following inventory purchases budget. Green desires to maintain an ending inventory balance equal to 20 percent of the following month's cost of goods sold. April's budgeted cost of goods sold amounts to $50,000.

Inventory Purchases Budget	January	February	March
Budgeted cost of goods sold	$40,000	$35,000	$48,000
Plus: Desired ending inventory	7,000	?	?
Inventory needed	47,000	?	?
Less: Beginning inventory	8,000	?	?
Required purchases (on account)	$39,000	?	?

Required

a. Complete the inventory purchases budget by filling in the missing amounts.
b. Determine the amount of cost of goods sold the company will report on the first quarter pro forma income statement.
c. Determine the amount of ending inventory the company will report on the first quarter pro forma balance sheet.

L.O. 4 **EXERCISE 7–8B** ***Preparing a Schedule of Cash Payments for Inventory Purchases***

Hometown Grocery buys and sells groceries in a community far from any major city. Chuck Portelli, the owner, budgeted the store's purchases as follows:

	October	November	December
Required purchases (on account)	$25,000	$24,000	$32,000

Hometown's suppliers require that 80 percent of accounts payable be paid in the month of purchase. The remaining 20 percent is paid in the month following the month of purchase.

Schedule of Cash Payments for Inventory Purchases

	October	November	December
Payment for current accounts payable	$20,000	?	?
Payment for previous accounts payable	6,000	?	?
Total budgeted payments for inventory	$26,000	?	?

Required

a. Complete the schedule of cash payments for inventory purchases by filling in the missing amounts.

b. Determine the amount of accounts payable Hometown will report on the store's quarterly pro forma balance sheet.

EXERCISE 7–9B *Determining the Amount of Inventory Purchases and Cash Payments* L.O. 4

Duval Oil Corporation, which distributes gasoline products to independent gasoline stations, had \$480,000 of cost of goods sold in January. The company expects a 2.5 percent increase in cost of goods sold during February. The ending inventory balance for January is \$25,000, and the desired ending inventory for February is \$30,000. Duval pays cash to settle 70 percent of its purchases on account during the month of purchase and pays the remaining 30 percent in the month following the purchase. The accounts payable balance as of January 31 was \$35,000.

Required

a. Determine the amount of purchases budgeted for February.

b. Determine the amount of cash payments budgeted for inventory purchases in February.

EXERCISE 7–10B *Preparing a Schedule of Cash Payments for Selling and Administrative Expenses* L.O. 5

The controller for Deluxe Laundry Services prepared the following list of expected operating expenses. All expenses requiring cash payments except salary expense and insurance are paid for in the month incurred. Salary is paid in the month following its incursion. The annual insurance premium is paid in advance on January 1. January is the first month of operations. Accordingly, there are no beginning account balances.

	January	February	March
Budgeted Selling and Administrative Expenses			
Equipment depreciation	\$ 6,000	\$ 6,000	\$ 6,000
Salary expense	2,900	2,700	3,050
Cleaning supplies	1,000	940	1,100
Insurance expense	600	600	600
Equipment maintenance expense	500	500	500
Leases expense	1,600	1,600	1,600
Miscellaneous expenses	400	400	400
Total S&A expenses	\$13,000	\$12,740	\$13,250
Schedule of Cash Payments for Selling and Administrative Expenses			
Equipment depreciation	?	?	?
Prior month's salary expense, 100%	?	?	?
Cleaning supplies	?	?	?
Insurance premium	?	?	?
Equipment maintenance expense	?	?	?
Leases expense	?	?	?
Miscellaneous expenses	?	?	?
Total Payments for S&A expenses	\$10,700	\$ 6,340	\$ 6,300

Required

a. Complete the schedule of cash payments for selling and administrative expenses by filling in the missing amounts.

b. Determine the amount of salaries payable the company will report on its quarterly pro forma balance sheet.

c. Determine the amount of prepaid insurance the company will report on its quarterly pro forma balance sheet.

EXERCISE 7–11B *Preparing Inventory Purchases Budgets With Different Assumptions* L.O. 4

Alice Grant has been at odds with her brother and business partner, Larry, since childhood. The sibling rivalry is not all bad, however; their garden shop, Grant Gardens and Gifts, has been very successful. When the partners met to prepare the coming year's budget, their forecasts were different, naturally. Their sales revenue estimates follow.

Source of Estimate	First Quarter	Second Quarter	Third Quarter	Fourth Quarter
Alice	$360,000	$400,000	$300,000	$420,000
Larry	300,000	320,000	340,000	480,000

Past experience indicates that cost of goods sold is about 60 percent of sales revenue. The company tries to maintain 15 percent of the next quarter's expected cost of goods sold as the current quarter's ending inventory. The ending inventory this year is $25,000. Next year's ending inventory is budgeted to be $35,000.

Required

a. Prepare an inventory purchases budget using Alice's estimate.
b. Prepare an inventory purchases budget using Larry's estimate.

L.O. 5, 7 **EXERCISE 7–12B** ***Determining the Amount of Cash Payments for Selling and Administrative Expenses***

Doug Fleak, managing partner of Fleak Business Consulting, is preparing a budget for January 2004, the first month of business operations. Doug estimates the following monthly selling and administrative expenses: office lease, $5,000; utilities, $1,600; office supplies, $2,400; depreciation, $12,000; referral fees, $5,000; and miscellaneous, $1,000. Referral fees will be paid in the month following the month they are incurred. Other expenses will be paid in the month in which they are incurred.

Required

a. Determine the amount of budgeted cash payments for January selling and administrative expenses.
b. Determine the amount of referral fees payable the firm will report on the January 31 pro forma balance sheet.
c. Determine the amount of office lease expense the company will report on its 2004 pro forma income statement, assuming that the monthly lease expense remains the same throughout the whole year.

L.O. 6, 7 **EXERCISE 7–13B** ***Preparing a Cash Budget***

David Helmi, the accounting manager of Nile Antique Company, is preparing his company's cash budget for the next quarter. Nile desires to maintain a cash cushion of $4,000 at the end of each month. As cash flows fluctuate, the company either borrows or repays funds at the end of a month. It pays interest on borrowed funds at the rate of 1 percent per month. On April 1, Nile owed $30,000 on its line of credit loan.

Cash Budget	July	August	September
Section 1: Cash Receipts			
Beginning cash balance	$ 16,000	$?	$?
Add cash receipts	180,000	192,000	208,000
Total cash available (a)	196,000	?	?
Section 2: Cash Payments			
For inventory purchases	158,000	153,000	171,000
For S&A expenses	37,000	36,000	39,000
For interest expense	0	?	?
Total budgeted disbursements (b)	195,000	?	?
Section 3: Financing Activities			
Surplus (shortage)	1,000	?	?
Borrowing (repayments) (c)	3,000	?	?
Ending Cash Balance (a − b + c)	$ 4,000	$ 4,000	$ 4,000

Required

a. Complete the cash budget by filling in the missing amounts. Round all computations to the nearest whole dollar.
b. Determine the amount of net cash flows from operating activities Nile will report on its quarterly pro forma statement of cash flows.
c. Determine the amount of net cash flows from financing activities Nile will report on its quarterly pro forma statement of cash flows.

EXERCISE 7–14B *Determining Amount to Borrow and Pro Forma Statement Balances*

L.O. 6, 7

Ali Nassar, the president of Ali's Flowers, Inc., has been working with his controller to manage the company's cash position. The controller provided Ali the following data.

Balance of accounts receivable, June 30	$ 40,000
Balance of line of credit, June 30	0
Budgeted cash sales for July	74,000
Budgeted credit sales for July	320,000
Budgeted cash payments for July	400,000

The company typically collects 75 percent of credit sales in the month of sale and the remainder in the month following the sale. Ali's line of credit enables the company to borrow funds readily, with the stipulation that any borrowing must take place on the last day of the month. The company pays its vendors on the last day of the month also. Mr. Nassar likes to maintain a $15,000 cash balance before any interest payments. The annual interest rate is 12 percent.

Required

a. Compute the amount of funds Mr. Nassar needs to borrow on July 31.
b. Determine the amount of interest expense the company will report on the July pro forma income statement.
c. Determine the amount of interest expense the company will report on the August pro forma income statement.

EXERCISE 7–15B *Preparing Pro Forma Income Statements With Different Assumptions*

L.O. 7

Boylan Corporation's budget planning meeting is like a zoo. Todd Owens, the credit manager, is naturally conservative and Jenny Hoover, the marketing manager, is the opposite. They have argued back and forth about the effect of various factors that influence the sales growth rate, such as credit policies and market potential. Based on the following current year data provided by Peggy Sullivan, the controller, Todd expects Boylan's revenues to grow 5 percent each quarter above last year's level; Jenny insists the growth rate will be 8 percent per quarter.

Current Year	First Quarter	Second Quarter	Third Quarter	Fourth Quarter	Total
Sales revenue	$240,000	$200,000	$216,000	$314,000	$970,000
Cost of goods sold	122,000	101,000	106,000	156,000	485,000
Gross margin	118,000	99,000	110,000	158,000	485,000
Selling & admin. expenses	32,000	26,000	26,400	40,600	125,000
Net income	$ 86,000	$ 73,000	$ 83,600	$117,400	$360,000

Historically, cost of goods sold has been about 50 percent of sales revenue. Selling and administrative expenses have been about 12.5 percent of sales revenue.

Required

a. Prepare a pro forma income statement for the coming year using the credit manager's growth estimate.
b. Prepare a pro forma income statement for the coming year using the marketing manager's growth estimate.
c. Explain why two executives in the same company could have different estimates of future growth.

PROBLEMS—SERIES B

PROBLEM 7–16B *Preparing a Sales Budget and Schedule of Cash Receipts*

L.O. 3

Isbell Corporation sells mail-order computers. In December 2005, it has generated $500,000 of sales revenue; the company expects a 20 percent increase in sales in January and 10 percent in February. All sales are on account. Isbell normally collects 80 percent of accounts receivable in the month of sale and 20 percent in the next month.

Required

a. Prepare a sales budget for January and February 2006.
b. Determine the amount of sales revenue Isbell would report on the bimonthly pro forma income statement for January and February 2006.

c. Prepare a cash receipts schedule for January and February 2006.
d. Determine the amount of accounts receivable as of February 28, 2006.

L.O. 4, 7

PROBLEM 7–17B *Preparing the Inventory Purchases Budget and Schedule of Cash Payments*

Rourke Company's purchasing manager, Milton Hayes, is preparing a purchases budget for the next quarter. At his request, Earl Vaiton, the manager of the sales department, forwarded him the following preliminary sales budget.

	October	November	December	January
Budgeted sales	$600,000	$750,000	$900,000	$800,000

For budgeting purposes, Rourke estimates that cost of goods sold is 75 percent of sales. The company desires to maintain an ending inventory balance equal to 20 percent of the next period's cost of goods sold. The September ending inventory is $90,000. Rourke makes all purchases on account and pays 70 percent of accounts payable in the month of purchase and the remaining 30 percent in the following month. The balance of accounts payable at the end of September is $90,000.

Required

a. Prepare an inventory purchases budget for October, November, and December.
b. Determine the amount of ending inventory Rourke will report on the end-of-quarter pro forma balance sheet.
c. Prepare a schedule of cash payments for inventory for October, November, and December.
d. Determine the balance in accounts payable Rourke will report on the end-of-quarter pro forma balance sheet.

L.O. 7

PROBLEM 7–18B *Preparing Pro Forma Income Statements With Different Assumptions*

Arthur Winters, a successful entrepreneur, is reviewing the results of his first year in business. His accountant delivered the following income statement just five minutes ago.

	Current Year
Sales Revenue	$500,000
Cost of Goods Sold	350,000
Gross Profit	150,000
Selling & Admin. Expenses	90,000
Net Income	$ 60,000

Mr. Winters would like net income to increase 20 percent in the next year. This first year, selling and administrative expenses were 10 percent of sales revenue plus $40,000 of fixed expenses.

Required

The following questions are independent of each other.

a. Mr. Winters expects that cost of goods sold and variable selling and administrative expenses will remain stable in proportion to sales next year. The fixed selling and administrative expenses will increase to $68,000. What percentage increase in sales would enable the company to reach Mr. Winters' goal? Prepare a pro forma income statement to illustrate.
b. Market competition may become serious next year, and Mr. Winters does not expect an increase in sales revenue. However, he has developed a good relationship with his supplier, who is willing to give him a volume discount that will decrease cost of goods sold by 3 percent. What else can the company do to reach Mr. Winters' goal? Prepare a pro forma income statement illustrating your proposal.
c. If the company escalates its advertising campaign to boost consumer recognition, the selling and administrative expenses will increase to $150,000. With the increased advertising, the company expects sales revenue to increase by 25 percent. Assume that cost of goods sold remains constant in proportion to sales. Can the company reach Mr. Winters' goal?

L.O. 5

PROBLEM 7–19B *Preparing a Schedule of Cash Payments for Selling and Administrative Expenses*

Perry Travel Services, Inc., has prepared its selling and administrative expenses budget for the next quarter. It pays all expenses when they are incurred except sales commissions, advertising expense, and telephone expense. These three items are paid in the month following the one in which they are incurred. January is the first month of operations, so there are no beginning account balances.

	January	February	March
Salary expense	$10,000	$10,000	$10,000
Sales commissions	700	740	900
Advertising expense	500	500	600
Telephone expense	1,000	1,080	1,100
Depreciation on store equipment	4,000	4,000	4,000
Rent	10,000	10,000	10,000
Miscellaneous	800	800	800
Total S&A expenses before interest	$27,000	$27,120	$27,400

Required

a. Prepare a schedule of cash payments for selling and administrative expenses.
b. Determine the amount of telephone payable as of March 31.
c. Determine the amount of sales commissions payable as of February 28.

PROBLEM 7–20B *Preparing a Cash Budget*

L.O. 6

Mead Company has budgeted the following cash flows:

	April	May	June
Cash receipts	$320,000	$470,000	$624,000
Cash payments			
For inventory purchases	410,000	420,000	464,000
For S&A expenses	80,000	106,000	132,000

Mead had a $36,000 cash balance on April 1. The company desires to maintain a $60,000 cash cushion before paying interest. Funds are assumed to be borrowed, in increment of $1,000, and repaid on the last day of each month; the interest rate is 1.50 percent per month. Mead pays its vendors on the last day of the month also. The company had a $150,000 beginning balance in its line of credit liability account.

Required

Prepare a cash budget.

PROBLEM 7–21B *Preparing Budgets With Multiple Products*

L.O. 3, 4, 5

Leath Enterprises, Inc., has two products, palm-size computers and programmable calculators. Shirley Belvin, the chief executive officer, is working with her staff to prepare next year's budget. Ms. Belvin estimates that sales will increase at an annual rate of 10 percent for palm-size computers and 4 percent for programmable calculators. The current year sales revenue data follow.

	First Quarter	Second Quarter	Third Quarter	Fourth Quarter	Total
Palm-size computers	$500,000	$550,000	$620,000	$ 730,000	$2,400,000
Programmable calculators	250,000	275,000	290,000	325,000	1,140,000
Total	$750,000	$825,000	$910,000	$1,055,000	$3,540,000

Based on the company's past experience, cost of goods sold is usually 75 percent of sales revenue. Company policy is to keep 10 percent of the next period's estimated cost of goods sold as the current period ending inventory.

Required

a. Prepare the company's sales budget for the next year for each quarter by individual products.
b. If the selling and administrative expenses are estimated to be $500,000, prepare the company's budgeted annual income statement for the next year.
c. Ms. Belvin estimates the current year's ending inventory will be $78,000 for computers and $32,000 for calculators and the ending inventory next year will be $88,000 for computers and $42,000 for calculators. Prepare the company's inventory purchases budget for the next year showing quarterly figures by product.

L.O. 3, 4, 5

PROBLEM 7–22B *Preparing a Master Budget for Retail Company With No Beginning Account Balances*

Oversea Gifts Corporation begins business today, December 31, 2004. Sharon Ting, the president, is trying to prepare the company's master budget for the first three months (January, February, and March) of 2005. Since you are her good friend and an accounting student, Ms. Ting asks you to prepare the budget based on the following specifications.

Required

a. January sales are estimated to be $250,000 of which 30 percent will be cash and 70 percent will be credit. The company expects sales to increase at the rate of 10 percent per month. Prepare a sales budget.

b. The company expects to collect 100 percent of the accounts receivable generated by credit sales in the month following the sale. Prepare a schedule of cash receipts.

c. The cost of goods sold is 50 percent of sales. The company desires to maintain a minimum ending inventory equal to 20 percent of the next month cost of goods sold. The ending inventory of March is expected to be $33,000. Assume that all purchases are made on account. Prepare an inventory purchases budget.

d. The company pays 60 percent of accounts payable in the month of purchase and the remaining 40 percent in the following month. Prepare a cash payments budget for inventory purchases.

e. Budgeted selling and administrative expenses per month follow.

Salary expense (fixed)	$25,000
Sales commissions	8 percent of Sales
Supplies expense	4 percent of Sales
Utilities (fixed)	$1,800
Depreciation on store equipment (fixed)*	$5,000
Rent (fixed)	$7,200
Miscellaneous (fixed)	$2,000

*The capital expenditures budget indicates that Oversea will spend $350,000 on January 1 for store fixtures. The fixtures are expected to have a $50,000 salvage value and a five-year (60-month) useful life.

Use this information to prepare a selling and administrative expenses budget.

f. Utilities and sales commissions are paid the month after they are incurred; all other expenses are paid in the month in which they are incurred. Prepare a cash payments budget for selling and administrative expenses.

g. The company borrows funds, in increment of $1,000, and repays them on the last day of the month. It pays interest of 1.5 percent per month in cash on the last day of the month. For safety, the company desires to maintain a $50,000 cash cushion. The company pays its vendors on the last day of the month. Prepare a cash budget.

h. Prepare a pro forma income statement for the quarter.

i. Prepare a pro forma balance sheet at the end of the quarter.

j. Prepare a pro forma statement of cash flows for the quarter.

L.O. 2

PROBLEM 7–23B *Behavioral Impact of Budgeting*

Anita Landy, the director of Mathis Corporation's Mail-Order Division, is preparing the division's budget proposal for next year. The company's president will review the proposal for approval. Ms. Landy estimates the current year final operating results will be as follows.

	Current Year
Sales revenue	$10,000,000
Cost of goods sold	5,680,000
Gross profit	4,320,000
Selling & admin. expenses	1,920,000
Net income	$ 2,400,000

Ms. Landy believes that the cost of goods sold as well as selling and administrative expenses will continue to be stable in proportion to sales revenue.

Mathis has an incentive policy to reward division managers whose performance exceeds their budget. Division directors receive a 10 percent bonus based on the excess of actual net income over the division's budget. For the last two years, Ms. Landy has proposed a 4 percent rate of increase, which proved accurate. However, her honesty and accuracy in forecasting caused her to receive no year-end bonus at all. She is pondering whether she should do something differently this time. If she continues to be honest, she should propose an 8 percent growth rate because of robust market demand. Alternatively, she can propose a 4 percent growth rate as usual and thereby expect to receive some bonus at year-end.

Required

a. Prepare a pro forma income statement, assuming a 4 percent estimated increase.
b. Prepare a pro forma income statement, assuming an 8 percent increase.
c. Assume the president eventually approves the division's proposal with the 4 percent growth rate. If growth actually is 8 percent, how much bonus would Ms. Landy receive?
d. Propose a better budgeting procedure for Mathis Corporation.

ANALYZE, THINK, COMMUNICATE

BUSINESS APPLICATIONS CASE *Preparing and Using Pro Forma Statements*

ATC 7–1

Nancy Chen and Tim Hoffer recently graduated from the same university. After graduation they decided not to seek jobs for established organizations but, rather, to start their own small business. They hoped this would provide more flexibility in their personal lives for a few years. Since both of them enjoyed cooking, they decided on a business selling vegetarian wraps and fruit juices from a street cart near their alma mater.

They bought a small enclosed cart for $3,500 that was set up for selling food. This cost, along with the cost for supplies to get started, a business license, and street vendor license, brought their initial expenditures to $4,500. They used $500 of their personal savings, and they borrowed $4,000 from Nancy's parents. They agreed to pay interest on the outstanding loan balance each month based on an annual rate of 6 percent. They will repay the principal over the next two years as cash becomes available.

After two months in business, September and October, they had average monthly revenues of $5,800 and out-of-pocket costs of $3,600 for ingredients, paper supplies, and so on, but not interest. Tim thinks they should repay some of the money they borrowed, but Nancy thinks they should prepare a set of forecasted financial statements for their first year in business before deciding whether or not to repay any principal on the loan. She remembers a bit about budgeting from a survey of accounting course she took and thinks the results from their first two months in business can be extended over the next 10 months to prepare the budget they need. They estimate the cart will last at least three years, after which they expect to sell it for $500 and move on to something else in their lives. Nancy agrees to prepare a forecasted (pro forma) income statement, balance sheet, and statement of cash flows for their first year in business, which includes the two months already passed.

Required

a. Prepare the annual pro forma financial statements that you would expect Nancy to prepare based on her comments about her expectations for the business. Assume no principal will be repaid on the loan.
b. Review the statements you prepared for the first requirement and prepare a list of reasons why Tim and Nancy's business probably will not match their budgeted statements.

GROUP ASSIGNMENT *Master Budget and Pro Forma Statements*

ATC 7–2

The following trial balance was drawn from the records of Havel Company as of October 1, 2002.

Cash	$ 16,000	
Accounts receivable	60,000	
Inventory	40,000	
Store equipment	200,000	
Accumulated depreciation		$ 76,800
Accounts payable		72,000
Line of credit loan		100,000
Common stock		50,000
Retained earnings		17,200
Totals	$316,000	$316,000

Required

a. Divide the class into groups, each with 4 or 5 students. Organize the groups into three sections. Assign Task 1 to the first section, Task 2 to the second section, and Task 3 to the third section.

Group Tasks

(1) Based on the following information, prepare a sales budget and a schedule of cash receipts for October, November, and December. Sales for October are expected to be $180,000, consisting of $40,000 in cash and $140,000 on credit. The company expects sales to increase at the rate of 10 percent per month. All of accounts receivable is collected in the month following the sale.

(2) Based on the following information, prepare a purchases budget and a schedule of cash payments for inventory purchases for October, November, and December. The inventory balance as of October 1 was $40,000. Cost of goods sold for October is expected to be $72,000. Cost of goods sold is expected to increase by 10 percent per month. The company desires to maintain a minimum ending inventory equal to 20 percent of the current month cost of goods sold. Seventy-five percent of accounts payable is paid in the month that the purchase occurs; the remaining 25 percent is paid in the following month.

(3) Based on the following selling and administrative expenses budgeted for October, prepare a selling and administrative expenses budget for October, November, and December.

Sales commissions (10% increase per month)	$ 7,200
Supplies expense (10% increase per month)	1,800
Utilities (fixed)	2,200
Depreciation on store equipment (fixed)	1,600
Salary expense (fixed)	34,000
Rent (fixed)	6,000
Miscellaneous (fixed)	1,000

Cash payments for sales commissions and utilities are made in the month following the one in which the expense is incurred. Supplies and other operating expenses are paid in cash in the month in which they are incurred.

b. Select a representative from each section. Have the representatives supply the missing information in the following pro forma income statement and balance sheet for the fourth quarter of 2002. The statements are prepared as of December 31, 2002.

Income Statement		
Sales Revenue		$?
Cost of Goods Sold		?
Gross Margin		357,480
Operating Expenses		?
Operating Income		193,290
Interest Expense		(2,530)
Net Income		$190,760
Balance Sheet		
Assets		
Cash		$ 9,760
Accounts Receivable		?
Inventory		?
Store Equipment	$200,000	
Accumulated Depreciation Store Equipment	?	
Book Value of Equipment		118,400
Total Assets		$314,984
Liabilities		
Accounts Payable		?
Utilities Payable		?
Sales Commissions Payable		?
Line of Credit		23,936
Equity		
Common Stock		50,000
Retained Earnings		?
Total Liabilities and Equity		$314,984

c. Indicate whether Havel will need to borrow money during October.

RESEARCH ASSIGNMENT *Simplifying the Budget Process*

ATC 7–3

By their nature, large entities often generate big, complex budgets. There is a danger, however, that budgets can become so detailed and complex that they do not get used after being prepared. In the article, "Streamline Budgeting in the new Millennium: Concentrate on Simplicity and Usefulness, Not Unrealistic Numbers," *Strategic Finance,* December 2001, pp. 45–50, Bruce Neumann provides suggestions for improving the budgeting process. Read this article and complete the following requirements.

Required

a. What are the five steps of budgeting that the author identifies?

b. Briefly explain what the article means by "the Three C's" of motivation for those preparing a budget.

c. The article describes "activity budgeting" as one method for streamlining an entity's budget. Explain the basic concept of activity budgeting.

d. The article describes "global budgeting" as one method for streamlining an entity's budget. Explain the basic concept of global budgeting.

e. Does the author suggest that more budget categories be devoted to fixed-cost categories or variable-cost categories?

WRITING ASSIGNMENT *Continuous Budgeting*

ATC 7–4

HON Company is the largest maker of mid-priced office furniture in the United States and Canada. Its management has expressed dissatisfaction with its *annual* budget system. Fierce competition requires businesses to be flexible and innovative. Unfortunately, building the effects of innovation into an annual budget is difficult because actions and outcomes often are evolutionary. Innovation unfolds as the year progresses. Consequently, HON's management team reached the conclusion that "when production processes undergo continuous change, standards developed annually for static conditions no longer offer meaningful targets for gauging their success."

Required

Assume that you are HON Company's budget director. Write a memo to the management team explaining how the practice of continuous budgeting could overcome the shortcomings of an annual budget process. (For insight, read the article "Continuous Budgeting at the HON Company," *Management Accounting,* January 1996. This article describes HON's real-world experience with a continuous budget system.)

ETHICAL DILEMMA *Bad Budget System or Unethical Behavior?*

ATC 7–5

Clarence Cleaver is the budget director for the Harris County School District. Mr. Cleaver recently sent an urgent E-mail message to Sally Simmons, principal of West Harris County High. The message severely reprimanded Ms. Simmons for failing to spend the funds allocated to her to purchase computer equipment. Ms. Simmons responded that her school already has a sufficient supply of computers; indeed, the computer lab is never filled to capacity and usually is less than half filled. Ms. Simmons suggested that she would rather use the funds for teacher training. She argued that the reason the existing computers are not fully utilized is that the teachers lack sufficient computer literacy necessary to make assignments for their students.

Mr. Cleaver responded that it is not Ms. Simmons' job to decide how the money is to be spent; that is the school board's job. It is the principal's job to spend the money as the board directed. He informed Ms. Simmons that if the money is not spent by the fiscal closing date, the school board would likely reduce next year's budget allotment. To avoid a potential budget cut, Mr. Cleaver reallocated Ms. Simmons' computer funds to Jules Carrington, principal of East Harris County High. Mr. Carrington knows how to buy computers regardless of whether they are needed. Mr. Cleaver's final words were, "Don't blame me if parents of West High students complain that East High has more equipment. If anybody comes to me, I'm telling them that you turned down the money."

Required

a. Do Mr. Cleaver's actions violate the standards of ethical conduct shown in Exhibit 1-13 of Chapter 1?

b. Explain how participative budgeting could improve the allocation of resources for the Harris County School District.

SPREADSHEET ASSIGNMENT *Using Excel*

ATC 7–6

The accountant for Nelly's Dress Shop prepared the fourth quarter, 2004, cash budget that appears on the following spreadsheet. Nelly's has a policy to maintain a minimum cash balance of $14,000 before the interest payment at the end of each month. The shop borrows and repays funds on the first day of the month. The interest rate is 2 percent per month.

Required

a. Construct a spreadsheet to model the cash budget as in the following screen capture. Be sure to use formulas where possible so that any changes to the estimates will be automatically reflected in the spreadsheet.

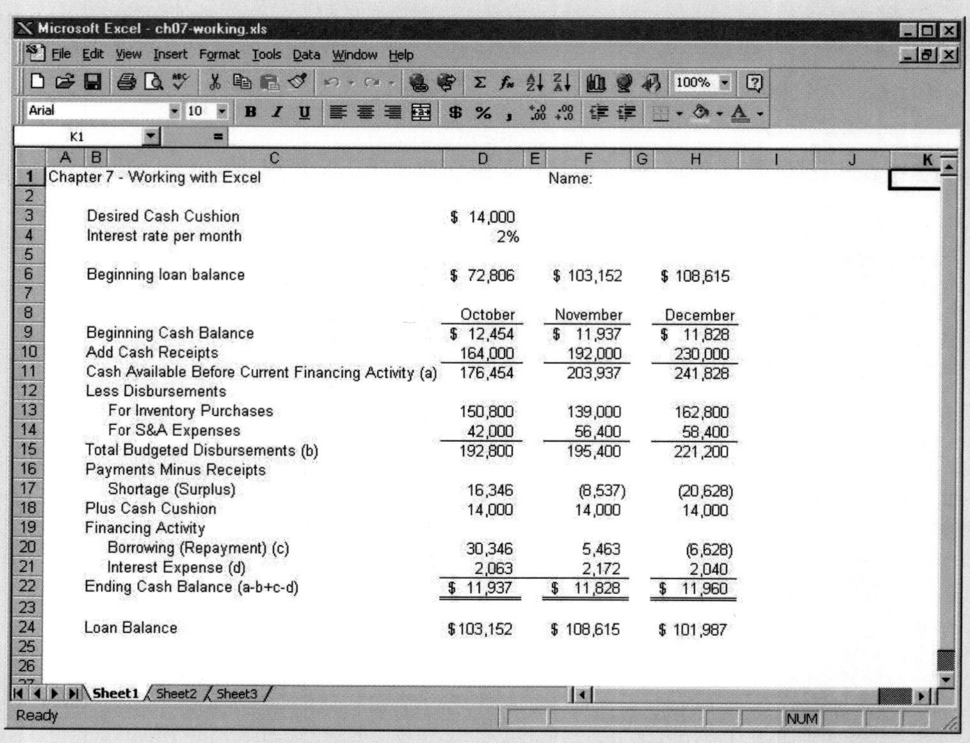

	A	B	C	D	E	F	G	H
1	Chapter 7 - Working with Excel					Name:		
2								
3			Desired Cash Cushion	$ 14,000				
4			Interest rate per month	2%				
5								
6			Beginning loan balance	$ 72,806		$ 103,152		$ 108,615
7								
8				October		November		December
9			Beginning Cash Balance	$ 12,454		$ 11,937		$ 11,828
10			Add Cash Receipts	164,000		192,000		230,000
11			Cash Available Before Current Financing Activity (a)	176,454		203,937		241,828
12			Less Disbursements					
13			For Inventory Purchases	150,800		139,000		162,800
14			For S&A Expenses	42,000		56,400		58,400
15			Total Budgeted Disbursements (b)	192,800		195,400		221,200
16			Payments Minus Receipts					
17			Shortage (Surplus)	16,346		(8,537)		(20,628)
18			Plus Cash Cushion	14,000		14,000		14,000
19			Financing Activity					
20			Borrowing (Repayment) (c)	30,346		5,463		(6,628)
21			Interest Expense (d)	2,063		2,172		2,040
22			Ending Cash Balance (a-b+c-d)	$ 11,937		$ 11,828		$ 11,960
23								
24			Loan Balance	$103,152		$ 108,615		$ 101,987
25								
26								

Spreadsheet Tips

(1) Rows 11, 15, 17, 18, 20 to 22, and 24 should be based on formulas.

(2) Cells F6, H6, F9, and H9 should be based on formulas also. For example, cell F6 should be =D24.

ATC 7–7 SPREADSHEET ASSIGNMENT *Mastering Excel*

Spitzer Company has collected sales forecasts for next year from three people.

Sources of Sales Estimate	First Quarter	Second Quarter	Third Quarter	Fourth Quarter
a. Sales manager	$520,000	$410,000	$370,000	$610,000
b. Marketing consultant	540,000	480,000	400,000	630,000
c. Production manager	460,000	360,000	350,000	580,000

They have estimated that the cost of goods sold is 70 percent of sales. The company tries to maintain 10 percent of next quarter's expected cost of goods sold as the current quarter's ending inventory. The ending inventory of this year is $25,000. For budgeting, the ending inventory of the next year is expected to be $28,000.

Required

a. Construct a spreadsheet that allows the inventory purchases budget to be prepared for each of the preceding estimates.

Spreadsheet Tip

The VLOOKUP function can be used to choose one line of the preceding estimates. See the spreadsheet tips in Chapter 6 for an explanation of VLOOKUP.

COMPREHENSIVE PROBLEM

The management team of Magnificent Modems, Inc. (MMI) wants to investigate the effect of several different growth rates on sales and cash receipts. Cash sales for the month of January are expected to be $10,000. Credit sales for January are expected to be $50,000. MMI collects 100 percent of credit sales in the month following the month of sale. Assume a beginning balance in accounts receivable of $48,000.

Required

Calculate the amount of sales and cash receipts for the months of February and March assuming a growth rate of 1 percent, 2 percent, and 4 percent.

The results at a growth rate of 1 percent are shown as an example.

Sales Budget			
Sales	**Jan**	**Feb**	**Mar**
Cash Sales	$10,000	$10,100	$10,201
Sales on Account	50,000	50,500	51,005
Total Budgeted Sales	$60,000	$60,600	$61,206
Schedule of Cash Receipts			
Current Cash Sales	$10,000	$10,100	$10,201
Plus Collections from Accts. Rec.	48,000	50,000	50,500
Total Budgeted Collections	$58,000	$60,100	$60,701

Use the following forms, assuming a growth rate of 2 percent.

Sales Budget			
Sales	**Jan**	**Feb**	**Mar**
Cash Sales	$10,000		
Sales on Account	50,000		
Total Budgeted Sales	$60,000		
Schedule of Cash Receipts			
Current Cash Sales	$10,000		
Plus Collections from Accts. Rec.	48,000		
Total Budgeted Collections	$58,000		

Use the following forms, assuming a growth rate of 4 percent.

Sales Budget			
Sales	**Jan**	**Feb**	**Mar**
Cash Sales	$10,000		
Sales on Account	50,000		
Total Budgeted Sales	$60,000		
Schedule of Cash Receipts			
Current Cash Sales	$10,000		
Plus Collections from Accts. Rec.	48,000		
Total Budgeted Collections	$58,000		

CHAPTER *eight*

PERFORMANCE EVALUATION

LEARNING *objectives*

After you have mastered the material in this chapter you will be able to:

1 Distinguish between flexible and static budgets.

2 Use spreadsheet software to prepare flexible budgets.

3 Compute revenue and cost variances and interpret whether the variances signal favorable or unfavorable performance.

4 Compute sales volume variances (differences between static and flexible budgets) and explain how volume variances affect fixed and variable costs.

5 Compute and interpret flexible budget variances (differences between flexible budget and actual results).

6 Explain how practical standards can motivate employee performance without negative consequences such as lowballing (the human element).

7 Identify which variances are the most appropriate to investigate.

8 Calculate price and usage variances and identify the parties most likely responsible for them.

THE *curious* ACCOUNTANT

Mr. Flanders sometimes has trouble getting along with the family that lives next door, especially the father. Recalling a line from a Robert Frost poem, "good fences make good neighbors," he decided to build a nice picket fence along his 100-foot property line. He estimated the costs of the boards, nails, paint, and so on, needed to build a 10-foot section of the fence would be $50. After multiplying this by ten, he determined the cost of his 100-foot fence should be $500. He and his sons will do the work themselves, so his only cost will be for materials.

Being compulsive by nature, Flanders kept meticulous records of the amount he spent on materials. Upon completion of the fence, he discovered the actual cost of the fence was $578.

What are two general reasons that may explain why the fence cost more to construct than Mr. Flanders estimated? (Answer on page 323.)

CHAPTER *opening*

Suppose you are a carpenter who builds picnic tables. You normally build 200 tables each year (the planned volume of activity), but because of unexpected customer demand, you are asked to build 225 tables (the actual volume of activity). You work hard and build the tables. Should management chastise you for using more materials, labor, or overhead than you normally use? Should management criticize the sales staff for selling more tables than expected? Of course not. Management must evaluate performance based on the actual volume of activity, not the planned volume of activity. To help management plan and evaluate performance, managerial accountants frequently prepare flexible budgets based on different levels of volume. Flexible budgets flex, or change, when the volume of activity changes.

Preparing Flexible Budgets

8–1

LO1 Distinguish between flexible and static budgets.

A **flexible budget** is an extension of the *master budget* discussed in Chapter 7. The master budget is based solely on the planned volume of activity. The master budget is frequently called a **static budget** because it remains unchanged even if the actual volume of activity differs from the planned volume. Flexible budgets differ from static budgets in that they show expected revenues and costs at a *variety* of volume levels.

To illustrate the differences between static and flexible budgets, consider Melrose Manufacturing Company, a producer of small, high-quality trophies used in award ceremonies. Melrose plans to make and sell 18,000 trophies during 2006. Management's best estimates of the expected sales price and per unit costs for the trophies are called *standard* prices and costs. The standard price and costs for the 18,000 trophies follow.

Per unit sales price and variable costs	
Expected sales price	$80.00
Standard materials cost	12.00
Standard labor cost	16.80
Standard overhead cost	5.60
Standard general, selling, and administrative cost	15.00
Fixed costs	
Manufacturing cost	$201,600
General, selling, and administrative cost	90,000

LO2 Use spreadsheet software to prepare flexible budgets.

Static and flexible budgets use the same per unit *standard* amounts and the same fixed costs. Exhibit 8–1 shows Melrose Manufacturing's static budget in column D of the Excel spreadsheet. The amounts of sales revenue and variable costs in column D come from multiplying the per unit standards in column C by the number of units in cell D4 (planned volume). For example, the sales revenue in cell D7 comes from multiplying the per unit sales price in

Exhibit 8–1 *Static and Flexible Budgets in Excel Spreadsheet*

	Per Unit Standards	Static Budget	Flexible Budgets				
Number of Units		18,000	16,000	17,000	18,000	19,000	20,000
Sales Revenue	$80.00	$1,440,000	$1,280,000	$1,360,000	$1,440,000	$1,520,000	$1,600,000
Variable Manuf. Costs							
Materials	$12.00	216,000	192,000	204,000	216,000	228,000	240,000
Labor	$16.80	302,400	268,800	285,600	302,400	319,200	336,000
Overhead	$5.60	100,800	89,600	95,200	100,800	106,400	112,000
Variable G,S,&A	$15.00	270,000	240,000	255,000	270,000	285,000	300,000
Contribution Margin		550,800	489,600	520,200	550,800	581,400	612,000
Fixed Costs							
Manufacturing		201,600	201,600	201,600	201,600	201,600	201,600
G,S,&A		90,000	90,000	90,000	90,000	90,000	90,000
Net Income		$259,200	$198,000	$228,600	$259,200	$289,800	$320,400

cell C7 by the number of units in cell D4 ($80 × 18,000 units = $1,440,000). The variable costs are similarly computed; the cost per unit amount in column C is multiplied by the planned volume in cell D4.

What if management wants to know the amount net income would be if volume were 16,000, 17,000, 18,000, 19,000, or 20,000 units? Management needs a series of *flexible budgets.* With little effort, an accountant can provide *what-if* information on the Excel spreadsheet. By copying to columns F through J the formulas used to determine the static budget amounts in column D, then changing the volume variables in row 4 to the desired levels, the spreadsheet instantly calculates the alternative flexible budgets in columns F through J.

Management can use the flexible budgets for both planning and performance evaluation. For example, managers may assess whether the company's cash position is adequate by assuming different levels of volume. They may judge if the number of employees, amounts of materials, and equipment and storage facilities are appropriate for a variety of different potential levels of volume. In addition to helping plan, flexible budgets are critical to implementing an effective performance evaluation system.

Check Yourself 8–1

The static (master) budget of Parcel, Inc., called for a production and sales volume of 25,000 units. At that volume, total budgeted fixed costs were $150,000 and total budgeted variable costs were $200,000. Prepare a flexible budget for an expected volume of 26,000 units.

Answer Budgeted fixed costs would remain unchanged at $150,000 because changes in the volume of activity do not affect budgeted fixed costs. Budgeted variable costs would increase to $208,000, computed as follows: Calculate the budgeted variable cost per unit ($200,000 ÷ 25,000 units = $8) and then multiply that variable cost per unit by the expected volume ($8 × 26,000 units = $208,000).

Determining Variances for Performance Evaluation

LO3 Compute revenue and cost variances and interpret whether the variances signal favorable or unfavorable performance.

One means of evaluating managerial performance is to compare *standard* amounts with *actual* results. The differences between the standard and actual amounts are called **variances;** variances can be either **favorable** or **unfavorable.** When actual sales revenue is greater than expected (planned) revenue, a company has a favorable sales variance because maximizing revenue is desirable. When actual sales are less than expected, an unfavorable sales variance exists. Because managers try to minimize costs, favorable cost variances exist when actual costs are *less* than standard costs. Unfavorable cost variances exist when actual costs are *more* than standard costs. These relationships are summarized below.

- When actual sales exceed expected sales, variances are favorable.
- When actual sales are less than expected sales, variances are unfavorable.
- When actual costs exceed standard costs, variances are unfavorable.
- When actual costs are less than standard costs, variances are favorable.

Sales Volume Variances

LO4 Compute sales volume variances (differences between static and flexible budgets) and explain how volume variances affect fixed and variable costs.

The amount of a **sales volume variance** is the difference between the static budget (which is based on planned volume) and a flexible budget based on actual volume. This variance measures management effectiveness in attaining the planned volume of activity. To illustrate, assume Melrose Manufacturing Company actually makes and sells 19,000 trophies during 2006. The planned volume of activity was 18,000 trophies. Exhibit 8–2 shows Melrose's static budget, flexible budget, and volume variances.

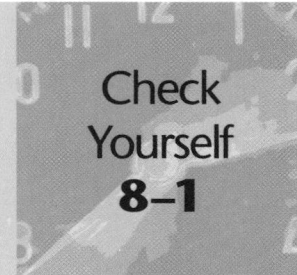

Exhibit 8–2 *Melrose Manufacturing Company's Volume Variances*

	Static Budget	Flexible Budget	Volume Variances	
Number of units	18,000	19,000	1,000	Favorable
Sales revenue	$1,440,000	$1,520,000	$80,000	Favorable
Variable manufacturing costs				
Materials	216,000	228,000	12,000	Unfavorable
Labor	302,400	319,200	16,800	Unfavorable
Overhead	100,800	106,400	5,600	Unfavorable
Variable G, S, & A	270,000	285,000	15,000	Unfavorable
Contribution margin	550,800	581,400	30,600	Favorable
Fixed costs				
Manufacturing	201,600	201,600	0	
G, S, & A	90,000	90,000	0	
Net income	$ 259,200	$ 289,800	$30,600	Favorable

Interpreting the Sales and Variable Cost Volume Variances

Because the static and flexible budgets are based on the same standard sales price and per unit variable costs, the variances are solely attributable to the difference between the planned and actual volume of activity. Marketing managers are usually responsible for the volume variance. Because the sales volume drives production levels, production managers have little control over volume. Exceptions occur; for example, if poor production quality control leads to inferior goods that are difficult to sell, the production manager is responsible. The production manager is responsible for production delays that affect product availability, which may restrict sales volume. Under normal circumstances, however, the marketing campaign determines the volume of sales. Upper-level marketing managers develop the promotional program and create the sales plan; they are in the best position to explain why sales goals are or are not met. When marketing managers refer to **making the numbers,** they usually mean reaching the sales volume in the static (master) budget.

In the case of Melrose Manufacturing Company, the marketing manager not only achieved but also exceeded by 1,000 units the planned volume of sales. Exhibit 8–2 shows the activity variances resulting from the extra volume. At the standard price, the additional volume produces a favorable revenue variance of $80,000 (1,000 units × $80 per unit). The increase in volume also produces unfavorable variable cost variances. The net effect of producing and selling the additional 1,000 units is an increase of $30,600 in the contribution margin, a positive result. These preliminary results suggest that the marketing manager is to be commended. The analysis, however, is incomplete. For example, examining market share could reveal whether the manager won customers from competitors or whether the manager simply reaped the benefit of an unexpected industrywide increase in demand. The increase in sales volume could have been attained by reducing the sales price; the success of that strategy will be analyzed further in a later section of this chapter.

The unfavorable variable cost variances in Exhibit 8–2 are somewhat misleading because variable costs are, by definition, expected to increase as volume increases. In this case the unfavorable cost variances are more than offset by the favorable revenue variance, resulting in a higher contribution margin. The variable cost volume variances could be more appropriately labeled "expected" rather than unfavorable. However, the cost volume variances are described as unfavorable because actual cost is greater than planned cost.

Fixed Cost Considerations

The fixed costs are the same in both the static and flexible budgets. By definition, the budgeted amount of fixed costs remains unchanged regardless of the volume of activity. What insights can management gain by analyzing costs that don't change? Consider the *operating leverage* fixed costs provide. A small increase in sales volume can have a dramatic impact on profitability. Although the 1,000 unit volume variance represents only a 5.6 percent increase in revenue ($80,000 variance ÷ $1,440,000 static budget sales base), it produces an 11.8 percent increase in profitability ($30,600 variance ÷ $259,200 static budget net income base). To understand why profitability increased so dramatically, management should analyze the effect of fixed costs on the higher than expected sales volume.

Companies using a cost-plus pricing strategy must be concerned with differences between the planned and actual volume of activity. Because actual volume is unknown until the end of the year, selling prices must be based on planned volume. At the *planned volume* of activity of 18,000 units, Melrose's fixed cost per unit is expected to be as follows:

Fixed manufacturing cost	$201,600
Fixed G, S, & A cost	90,000
Total fixed cost	$291,600 ÷ 18,000 units = $16.20 per trophy

Based on the *actual volume* of 19,000 units, the fixed cost per unit is actually $15.35 per trophy ($291,600 ÷ 19,000 units). Because Melrose's prices were established using the $16.20 budgeted cost rather than the $15.35 actual cost, the trophies were overpriced, giving competitors a price advantage. Although Melrose sold more trophies than expected, sales volume might have been even greater if the trophies had been competitively priced.

Underpricing (not encountered by Melrose in this example) can also be detrimental. If planned volume is overstated, the estimated fixed cost per unit will be understated and prices will be set too low. When the higher amount of actual costs is subtracted from revenues, actual profits will be lower than expected. To avoid these negative consequences, companies that consider unit cost in pricing decisions must monitor volume variances closely.

The volume variance is *unfavorable* if actual volume is less than planned because cost per unit is higher than expected. Conversely, if actual volume is greater than planned, cost per unit is less than expected, resulting in a *favorable* variance. Both favorable and unfavorable variances can have negative consequences. Managers should strive for the greatest possible degree of accuracy.

Flexible Budget Variances

For performance evaluation, management compares actual results to a flexible budget based on the *actual* volume of activity. Because the actual results and the flexible budget reflect the same volume of activity, any variances result from differences between standard and actual per unit amounts. To illustrate computing and analyzing flexible budget variances, we assume that Melrose's *actual* per unit amounts during 2006 were those shown in the following table. The 2006 per unit *standard* amounts are repeated here for your convenience.

LO5 Compute and interpret flexible budget variances (differences between flexible budget and actual results).

	Standard	Actual
Sales price	$80.00	$78.00
Variable materials cost	12.00	11.78
Variable labor cost	16.80	17.25
Variable overhead cost	5.60	5.75

Actual and budgeted fixed costs are shown in Exhibit 8–3.

Exhibit 8–3 shows Melrose's 2006 flexible budget, actual results, and flexible budget variances. The flexible budget is the same one compared to the static budget in Exhibit 8–2. Recall

Exhibit 8–3 *Flexible Budget Variances for Melrose Manufacturing Company*

	Flexible Budget	Actual Results	Flexible Budget Variances	
Number of units	19,000	19,000	0	
Sales revenue	$1,520,000	$1,482,000	$38,000	Unfavorable
Variable manufacturing costs				
Materials	228,000	223,820	4,180	Favorable
Labor	319,200	327,750	8,550	Unfavorable
Overhead	106,400	109,250	2,850	Unfavorable
Variable G, S, & A	285,000	283,100	1,900	Favorable
Contribution margin	581,400	538,080	43,320	Unfavorable
Fixed costs				
Manufacturing	201,600	210,000	8,400	Unfavorable
G, S, & A	90,000	85,000	5,000	Favorable
Net income	$ 289,800	$ 243,080	$46,720	Unfavorable

the flexible budget amounts come from multiplying the standard per unit amounts by the actual volume of production. For example, the sales revenue in the flexible budget comes from multiplying the standard sales price by the actual volume ($80 × 19,000). The variable costs are similarly computed. The *actual results* are calculated by multiplying the actual per unit sales price and cost figures from the preceding table by the actual volume of activity. For example, the sales revenue in the Actual Results column comes from multiplying the actual sales price by the actual volume ($78 × 19,000 = $1,482,000). The actual cost figures are similarly computed. The differences between the flexible budget figures and the actual results are the **flexible budget variances.**

Calculating the Sales Price Variance

Because both the flexible budget and actual results are based on the actual volume of activity, the flexible budget variance is attributable to sales price, not sales volume. In this case, the actual sales price of $78 per unit is less than the standard price of $80 per unit. Because Melrose sold its product for less than the standard sales price, the **sales price variance** is *unfavorable.* Even though the price variance is unfavorable, however, sales volume was 1,000 units more than expected. It is possible the marketing manager generated the additional volume by reducing the sales price. Whether the combination of lower sales price and higher sales volume is favorable or unfavorable depends on the amount of the unfavorable sales price variance versus the amount of the favorable sales volume variance. The *total* sales variance (price and volume) follows:

Actual sales (19,000 units × $78 per unit)	$1,482,000	
Expected sales (18,000 units × $80 per unit)	1,440,000	
Total sales variance	$ 42,000	Favorable

Alternatively,

Activity variance (i.e., sales volume)	$ 80,000	Favorable
Sales price variance	(38,000)	Unfavorable
Total sales variance	$ 42,000	Favorable

This analysis indicates that reducing the sales price had a favorable impact on *total* revenue. Use caution when interpreting variances as good or bad; in this instance, the unfavorable sales price variance was more than offset by the favorable volume variance. All unfavorable variances are not bad; all favorable variances are not good. Variances signal the need to investigate.

Scott Company's master budget called for a planned sales volume of 30,000 units. Budgeted direct materials cost was $4 per unit. Scott actually produced and sold 32,000 units with an actual materials cost of $131,000. Determine the materials volume variance and identify the organizational unit most likely responsible for this variance. Determine the flexible budget variance and identify the organizational unit most likely responsible for this variance.

Answer The volume (activity) variance is the difference between the expected materials usage at the planned volume of activity and the expected materials usage at the actual volume of activity ([$4 × 30,000 units] − [$4 × 32,000] = $8,000). The variance is unfavorable because expected direct materials cost at actual volume was higher than budgeted direct materials cost at planned volume. The unfavorable variance might not be a bad thing. The variance is due to increased volume, which could be a good thing. The organizational unit most likely responsible for the activity variance is the marketing department.

The flexible budget variance is the difference between the expected materials cost at the actual volume ($4 × 32,000 units = $128,000) and the actual materials cost of $131,000. The $3,000 ($128,000 − $131,000) variance is unfavorable because it cost more than expected to make the 32,000 units. Either the production department or the purchasing department is most likely responsible for this variance.

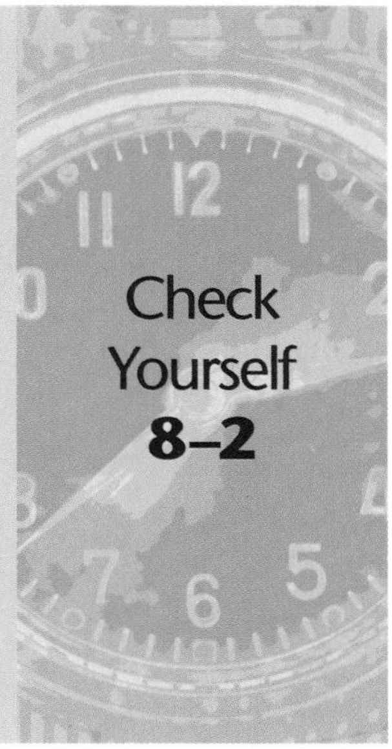

The Human Element Associated with Flexible Budget Variances

LO6 Explain how practical standards can motivate employee performance without negative consequences such as lowballing (the human element).

The flexible budget cost variances offer insight into management efficiency. For example, Melrose Manufacturing Company's favorable materials variance could mean purchasing agents were shrewd in negotiating price concessions, discounts, or delivery terms and therefore reduced the price the company paid for materials. Similarly, production employees may have used materials efficiently, using less than expected. The unfavorable labor variance could mean managers failed to control employee wages or motivate employees to work hard. As with sales variances, cost variances require careful analysis. A favorable variance may, in fact, mask unfavorable conditions. For example, the favorable materials variance might have been caused by paying low prices for inferior goods. Using substandard materials could have required additional labor in the production process, which would explain the unfavorable labor variance. Again, we caution that variances, whether favorable or unfavorable, alert management to investigate further.

In general, variances should not be used to praise or punish managers. The purpose of identifying variances is to help management improve efficiency and productivity. If variances are used to assign rewards and blame, managers are likely to respond by withholding or manipulating information. For example, a manager might manipulate the cost standard for a job by deliberately overstating the amount of materials or labor needed to complete it. The manager's performance will later appear positive when the actual cost of materials or labor is less than the inflated standard. This practice is so common it has a name: **budget slack** is the difference between inflated and realistic standards. Sales staff may play a game called *low-balling* in which they deliberately underestimate the amount of expected sales, anticipating a reward when actual sales subsequently exceed the budget.

Gamesmanship can be reduced if superiors and subordinates participate sincerely in setting mutually agreeable, attainable standards. Once standards are established, the evaluation system that uses them must promote long-term respect among superiors and their subordinates. If standards are used solely for punitive purposes, gamesmanship will rapidly degrade the standard costing system.

Establishing Standards

LO6 Explain how practical standards can motivate employee performance without negative consequences such as lowballing (the human element).

Establishing standards is probably the most difficult part of using a standard cost system. A **standard** represents the amount a price, cost, or quantity *should be* based on certain anticipated circumstances. Consider the complexity of establishing the standard cost to produce a pair of blue jeans. Among other things, managers need to know where they can get the best price for materials, who will pay transportation costs, if cash or volume discounts are available, whether the suppliers with the lowest price can reliably supply the quantities needed on a timely basis, how the material should be cut to conserve time and labor, in what order to sew pieces of material together, the wage rates of the relevant production employees, whether overtime will be needed, and how many pairs of jeans will be produced. Obtaining this information requires the combined experience, judgment, and forecasting ability of all personnel who have responsibility for price and usage decisions. Even when a multitalented group of experienced persons is involved in standard setting, the process involves much trial and error. Revising standards is common even with established systems.

Historical data provide a good starting point for establishing standards. These data must be updated for changes in technology, plant layout, new methods of production, and worker productivity. Frequently, changes of this nature result from initiating a standard cost system. Remember that a *standard* represents what *should be* rather than what *is* or *was*. Engineers often help establish standards, recommending the most efficient way to perform required tasks. The engineers undertake time and motion studies and review material utilization in the process of developing standards. Established practices and policies are frequently changed in response to engineers' reports.

Management must consider behavioral implications when developing standards. Managers, supervisors, purchasing agents, and other affected employees should be consulted for two reasons: (1) their experience and expertise provide invaluable input to standard development and (2) persons who are involved in standard setting are more likely to accept and be motivated to reach the resulting standards. Management should also consider how difficult it should be to achieve standard performance.

Difficulty levels can be described as follows: (1) ideal standards, (2) practical standards, and (3) lax standards.

Ideal standards represent flawless performance; they represent what costs should be under the best possible circumstances. They do not allow for normal materials waste and spoilage or ordinary labor inefficiencies caused by machine down time, cleanups, breaks, or personal needs. Meeting ideal standards is beyond the capabilities of most, if not all, employees. Ideal standards may motivate some individuals to constantly strive for improvement, but unattainable standards discourage most people. When people consistently fail, they become demotivated and stop trying to succeed. In addition, variances associated with ideal standards lose significance. They reflect deviations that are largely beyond employees' control, and they mask true measures of superior or inferior performance, considerably reducing their usefulness.

Practical standards represent reasonable effort; they are attainable for most employees. Practical standards allow for normal levels of inefficiency in materials and labor usage. An average worker performing diligently would be able to achieve standard performance. Practical standards motivate most employees; the feeling of accomplishment attained through earnest effort encourages employees to do their best. Practical standards also produce meaningful variances. Deviations from practical standards usually result from factors employees control. Positive variances normally represent superior performance, and negative variances indicate inferior performance.

Lax standards represent easily attainable goals. Employees can achieve standard performance with minimal effort. Lax standards do not motivate most people; continual success with minimal effort leads to boredom and lackluster performance. In addition, variances lose meaning. Deviations caused by superior or inferior performance are obscured by the built-in slack.

Management must consider employee ability levels when establishing standards. Standards that seasoned workers can attain may represent ideal standards to inexperienced workers. Management should routinely monitor standards and adjust them when it is appropriate to do so.

Need for Standard Costs

As the previous discussion suggests, standard costs are the building blocks for preparing the static and flexible budgets. Standard costs help managers plan and also establish benchmarks against which actual performance can be judged. By highlighting differences between standard (expected) and actual performance, standard costing focuses management attention on the areas of greatest need. Because management talent is a valuable and expensive resource, businesses cannot afford to have managers spend large amounts of time on operations that are functioning normally. Instead, managers should concentrate on areas not performing as expected. In other words, management should attend to the exceptions; this management philosophy is known as **management by exception.**

Standard costing fosters using the management by exception principle. By reviewing performance reports that show differences between actual and standard costs, management can focus its attention on the items that show significant variances. Areas with only minor variances need little or no review.

Selecting Variances to Investigate

LO7 Identify which variances are the most appropriate to investigate.

Managerial judgment, developed through experience, plays a significant role in deciding which variances to investigate. Managers consider the *materiality* of a variance, the *frequency* with which it occurs, their *capacity to control* the variance, and the *characteristics* of the items behind the variance.

Standard costs are estimates. They cannot perfectly predict actual costs. Most business experience minor variances as part of normal operations. Investigating minor variances is not likely to produce useful information. Many companies therefore establish *materiality* guidelines for selecting variances to analyze. They set dollar or percentage thresholds and ignore variances that fall below these limits, investigating material variances only. A **material variance** is one that could influence management decisions. Material variances should be investigated whether they are favorable or unfavorable. As mentioned earlier, a favorable price variance can result from purchasing substandard materials; the quality of the company's products, however, will suffer from the inferior materials and sales will fall.

How *frequently* a variance occurs impacts materiality. A variance of $20,000 may be immaterial in a single month, but if the same variance occurs repeatedly throughout the year, it can become a material $240,000 variance. Variance reports should highlight frequent as well as large variations.

Capacity to control refers to whether management action can influence the variance. If utility rates cause differences between actual and standard overhead costs, management has little control over the resulting variances. Conversely, if actual labor costs exceed standard costs because a supervisor fails to motivate employees, management can take some action. To maximize their value to the firm, managers should concentrate on controllable variances.

The *characteristics* of the items behind the variance may invite management abuse. For example, managers can reduce actual costs in the short term by delaying expenditures for maintenance, research and development, and advertising. Although cost reductions in these areas may produce favorable variances in the current period, they will have a long-term detrimental impact on profitability. Managers under stress may be tempted to focus on short-term benefits. Variances associated with these critical items should be closely analyzed.

The primary advantage of a standard cost system is efficient use of management talent to control costs. Secondary benefits include the following.

1. Standard cost systems quickly alert management to trouble spots. For example, a standard amount of materials may be issued for a particular job. If requisitions of additional materials require supervisory approval, each time a supervisor must grant such approval, she is immediately aware that excess materials are being used and can act before excessive material usage becomes unmanageable.
2. If established and maintained properly, standard cost systems can boost morale and motivate employees. Reward systems can be linked to accomplishments that exceed the established performance standards. Under such circumstances, employees become extremely conscious of the time and materials they use, minimizing waste and reducing costs.
3. Standard cost systems encourage good planning. The failure to plan well leads to overbuying, excessive inventory, wasted time, and so on. A standard cost system forces managers to plan, resulting in more effective operations with less waste.

Flexible Budget Manufacturing Cost Variances

The *manufacturing costs* incurred by Melrose Manufacturing Company in 2006 are summarized here:

	Standard	Actual
Variable materials cost per unit of product	$ 12.00	$ 11.78
Variable labor cost per unit of product	16.80	17.25
Variable overhead cost per unit of product	5.60	5.75
Total per unit variable manufacturing cost (a)	$ 34.40	$ 34.78
Total units produced (b)	19,000	19,000
Total variable manufacturing cost (a × b)	$653,600	$660,820
Fixed manufacturing cost	201,600	210,000
Total manufacturing cost	$855,200	$870,820

ANSWERS TO THE *curious* ACCOUNTANT

As this chapter demonstrates, there are two primary reasons a company spends more or less to produce a product than it estimated it would. First, the company may have paid more or less to purchase the inputs needed to produce the product than it estimated. Second, the company used a greater or lesser quantity of these inputs than expected. In the case of Mr. Flanders's fence, he may have had to pay more for boards, paint, nails, and so on, than he thought he would. Or, he may have used more boards, paint, and nails than he expected. Of course, it could have been a combination of these factors.

If Mr. Flanders were a company in the business of building fences, it would be important for him to determine if the difference between his expected costs and his actual costs was because his estimates were faulty, or because his production process was inefficient. If his estimates were to blame, he would need to revise them so he can charge the proper price to his customers. If his production process is inefficient, he needs to correct it if he is to earn an acceptable level of profit. If his competitors are more efficient than he is, he will eventually be priced out of the market. Standard costs are not only used for preparing budgets, they are also used for evaluating performance.

The total flexible budget manufacturing cost variance is $15,620 ($870,820 − $855,200). Because Melrose actually incurred more cost than expected, this variance is unfavorable. The sum of the individual flexible budget variances for manufacturing costs shown in Exhibit 8–3 equals this variance:

Variable manufacturing cost variances:		
Materials	$ 4,180	Favorable
Labor	8,550	Unfavorable
Overhead	2,850	Unfavorable
Total variable manufacturing cost variances	7,220	Unfavorable
Fixed manufacturing cost variance	8,400	Unfavorable
Total	$15,620	Unfavorable

Exhibit 8–4 shows how to algebraically compute the flexible budget variable manufacturing cost variances.

Exhibit 8–4 *Flexible Budget Variances Calculated Algebraically*

Variable Mfg. Costs	Actual Cost *Per Unit* of Product	−	Standard Cost *Per Unit* of Product	×	Actual Units	=	Flexible Budget Variance
Materials	|$11.78	−	$12.00|	×	19,000	=	$4,180 Favorable
Labor	| 17.25	−	16.80|	×	19,000	=	8,550 Unfavorable
Overhead	| 5.75	−	5.60|	×	19,000	=	2,850 Unfavorable

Note that the difference between the actual and standard cost is expressed as an absolute value. This mathematical notation suggests that the mathematical sign is not useful in interpreting the condition of the variance. To assess the condition of a variance, you must consider the type of variance being analyzed. With respect to cost variances, managers seek to attain actual prices that are lower than standard prices. In this case, the actual price of materials is less than the standard price, so the materials variance is favorable. Since the actual prices for labor and overhead are higher than the standard prices, those variances are unfavorable.

Topic Tackler PLUS 8–2

LO8 Calculate price and usage variances and identify the parties most likely responsible for them.

Price and Usage Variances[1]

For insight into what caused the flexible budget variances, management can analyze them in more detail. Consider the $4,180 favorable flexible budget materials cost variance. This variance indicates that Melrose spent less than expected on materials to make 19,000 trophies. Why? The price per unit of material may have been less than expected (price variance), or the company may have used less material than expected (usage variance). To determine what caused the total favorable variance, Melrose must separate the cost per unit of product into two parts, price per unit of material and quantity of material used.

Calculating Materials Price and Usage Variances

Melrose's accounting records indicate the materials cost per unit of product (trophy) is as follows:

	Actual Data	Standard Data
Price ***per pound*** of material	$ 1.90	$ 2.00
Quantity of materials per unit of product	× 6.2 pounds	× 6.0 pounds
Cost ***per unit*** of product	$11.78	$12.00

Based on this detail, the total quantity of materials is:

	Actual Data	Standard Data
Actual production volume	19,000 Units	19,000 Units
Quantity of materials per unit of product	× 6.2 Pounds	× 6.0 Pounds
Total quantity of materials	117,800 Pounds	114,000 Pounds

Confirm the price and usage components that make up the total flexible budget materials variance, as follows:

Actual Cost		Standard Cost	
Actual quantity used	117,800	Standard quantity	114,000
×	×	×	×
Actual price per pound	$1.90	Standard price per pound	$2.00
	$223,820		$228,000
	Total variance: $4,180 favorable		

To isolate the price and usage variances, insert a Variance Dividing column between the Actual Cost and Standard Cost columns. The Variance Dividing column combines standard and actual data, showing the *standard cost* multiplied by the *actual quantity* of materials purchased and used.[2] Exhibit 8–5 shows the result.

[1] Businesses use various names for price and usage variances. For example, materials price and usage variances are frequently called **price** and **quantity** variances; labor price and usage variances are frequently called **rate** and **efficiency** variances. Regardless of the names, the underlying concepts and computations are the same for all variable price and usage variances.

[2] In practice, raw materials are frequently stored in inventory prior to use. Differences may exist between the amount of materials purchased and the amount of materials used. In such cases, the price variance is based on the quantity of materials *purchased,* and the usage variance is based on the quantity of materials *used.* This text makes the simplifying assumption that the amount of materials purchased equals the amount of materials used during the period.

Exhibit 8–5 *Materials Price and Usage Variances*

Actual Cost		Variance Dividing Data		Standard Cost	
Actual quantity used	117,800	Actual quantity used	117,800	Standard quantity	114,000
×	×	×	×	×	×
Actual price per pound	$1.90	Standard price per pound	$2.00	Standard price per pound	$2.00
	$223,820		$235,600		$228,000

Materials price variance $11,780 favorable

Materials usage variance $7,600 unfavorable

Total variance: $4,180 favorable

Algebraic Solution. The materials price variance (difference between the Actual Cost column and the Variance Dividing column) can be computed algebraically as follows:

$$\begin{aligned} \text{Price variance} &= |\text{Actual price} - \text{Standard price}| \times \text{Actual quantity} \\ &= |\$1.90 - \$2.00| \times 117{,}800 \\ &= \$0.10 \times 117{,}800 \\ &= \$11{,}780 \text{ Favorable} \end{aligned}$$

Since the actual price ($1.90) is less than the standard price ($2.00), the materials price variance is favorable.

The materials usage variance (difference between the Variance Dividing column and the Standard Cost column) also can be determined algebraically, as follows:

$$\begin{aligned} \text{Usage variance} &= |\text{Actual quantity} - \text{Standard quantity}| \times \text{Standard price} \\ &= |117{,}800 - 114{,}000| \times \$2.00 \\ &= 3{,}800 \times \$2.00 \\ &= \$7{,}600 \text{ Unfavorable} \end{aligned}$$

Responsibility for Materials Variances. A purchasing agent is normally responsible for the *favorable price variance.* Management establishes the standard materials cost based on a particular grade of material and assumptions about purchasing terms including volume discounts, cash discounts, transportation costs, and supplier services. A diligent purchasing agent places orders that take advantage of positive trading terms. In such circumstances, the company pays less than standard costs, resulting in a favorable price variance. Investigating the favorable price variance could result in identifying purchasing strategies to share with other purchasing agents. Analyzing favorable as well as unfavorable variances can result in efficiencies that benefit the entire production process.

In spite of a purchasing agent's diligence, unfavorable price variances may still occur. Suppliers may raise prices, poor scheduling by the production department may require more costly rush orders, or a truckers' strike may force the company to use a more expensive delivery system. These conditions are beyond a purchasing agent's control. Management must be careful to identify the real causes of unfavorable variances. False accusations and overreactions lead to resentment that will undermine the productive potential of the standard costing system.

The nature of the *materials usage variance* is readily apparent from the quantity data. Because the actual quantity used was more than the standard quantity, the variance is unfavorable. If management seeks to minimize cost, using more materials than expected is unfavorable. The materials usage variance is largely controlled by the production department. Materials waste caused by inexperienced workers, faulty machinery, negligent processing, or poor planning results in unfavorable usage variances. Unfavorable variances may also be caused by factors beyond the control of the production department. If the purchasing agent

REALITY bytes

Do purchasing agents really make a difference? They certainly do—at least that is the opinion of Inspector General Eleanor Hill, who is in charge of policing waste and fraud at the Department of Defense. Explaining preposterous costs such as a \$76 screw, Ms. Hill told a Senate Armed Services subcommittee that Pentagon buyers failed to obtain volume discounts, neglected to compare prices with competitors, or otherwise failed to pursue aggressive purchasing strategies. Specifically, Ms. Hill said, "Department of Defense procurement approaches were poorly conceived, badly coordinated, and did not result in the government getting good value for the prices paid both for commercial and noncommercial items. We found considerable evidence that the Department of Defense had not yet learned how to be an astute buyer in the commercial marketplace."

Source: John Diamond, "Audits Say Pentagon Continues to Overpay," *USA Today,* March 19, 1998, p. 2A.

buys substandard materials, the inferior materials may lead to more scrap (waste) during production which would be reflected in unfavorable usage variances.

Calculating Labor Variances

Labor variances are calculated using the same general formulas as those used to compute materials price and usage variances. To illustrate, assume the labor cost per unit of product (trophy) for Melrose Manufacturing is as follows:

	Actual Data	Standard Data
Price ***per hour***	\$11.50	\$12.00
Quantity of labor per unit of product	× 1.5 hours	× 1.4 hours
Cost ***per unit*** of product	\$17.25	\$16.80

Based on this detail, the total quantity of labor is:

	Actual Data	Standard Data
Actual production volume	19,000 Units	19,000 Units
Quantity of labor per unit of product	× 1.5 Hours	× 1.4 Hours
Total quantity of labor	28,500 Hours	26,600 Hours

Using this cost and quantity information, the labor price and usage variances are computed in Exhibit 8–6.

Responsibility for Labor Variances. The *labor price variance* is favorable because the actual rate paid for labor is less than the standard rate. The production supervisor is usually responsible for the labor price variance because price variances normally result from labor use rather than underpayment or overpayment of the hourly rate. Because labor costs are usually fixed by contracts, paying more or less than established rates is not likely. However, using semiskilled labor to perform highly skilled tasks or vice versa will produce price variances. Similarly, using unanticipated overtime will cause unfavorable variances. Production department supervisors control which workers are assigned to which tasks and are therefore accountable for the resulting labor price variances.

Exhibit 8–6 *Labor Price and Usage Variances*

Actual Cost		Variance Dividing Data		Standard Cost	
Actual hours used	28,500	Actual hours used (AHrs)	28,500	Standard hours (SHrs)	26,600
×	×	×	×	×	×
Actual price per labor hour (AP)	$11.50	Standard price per labor hour (SP)	$12.00	Standard price per labor hour	$12.00
	$327,750		$342,000		$319,200

Labor price variance $14,250 favorable

Labor usage variance $22,800 unfavorable

Algebraic solution: |AP − SP| × AHrs
|$11.50 − $12.00| × 28,500 = $14,250

Algebraic solution: |AHrs − SHrs| × SP
|28,500 − 26,600| × $12.00 = $22,800

Total variance: $8,550 unfavorable

Labor usage variances measure the productivity of the labor force. Because Melrose used more labor than expected, the labor usage variance is unfavorable. Unsatisfactory labor performance has many causes; low morale or poor supervision are possibilities. Furthermore, machine breakdowns, inferior materials, and poor planning can waste workers' time and reduce productivity. Production department supervisors generally control and are responsible for labor usage variances.

Price and usage variances may be interrelated. Using less skilled employees who earned less but took longer to do the work could have caused both the favorable labor price variance and the unfavorable labor usage variance. As mentioned earlier, management must exercise diligence in determining causes of variances before concluding who should be held responsible for them.

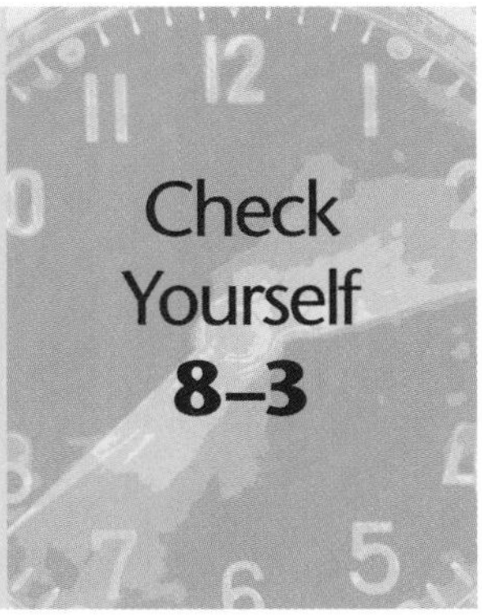

DogHouse, Inc., expected to build 200 dog houses during July. Each dog house was expected to require 2 hours of direct labor. Labor cost was expected to be $10 per hour. The company actually built 220 dog houses using an average of 2.1 labor hours per dog house at an actual labor rate averaging $9.80 per hour. Determine the labor rate and usage variances.

Answer

Labor rate variance = |Actual rate − Standard rate| × Actual quantity
Labor rate variance = |$9.80 − $10.00| × (220 units × 2.1 hours) = $92.40 Favorable

Labor usage variance = |Actual quantity − Standard quantity| × Standard rate
Labor usage variance = |[220 × 2.1] − [220 × 2.0]| × $10 = $220.00 Unfavorable

Variable Overhead Variances

Variable overhead variances are based on the same general formulas used to compute the materials and labor price and usage variances. Unique characteristics of variable overhead costs, however, require special attention. First, variable overhead represents many inputs such as supplies, utilities, and indirect labor. The variable overhead cost pool is normally assigned to products based on a predetermined variable overhead allocation rate. Using a single rate to assign a mixture of different costs complicates variance interpretation. Suppose the actual variable overhead rate is higher than the predetermined rate. Did the company pay more than expected for supplies, utilities, maintenance, or some other input variable? The cost of some variable overhead items may have been higher than expected while others were lower than expected. Similarly, a variable overhead usage variance provides no clue about which overhead inputs were over- or underused. Because meaningful interpretation of the results is difficult, many companies do not calculate price and usage variances for variable overhead costs. We therefore limit coverage of this subject to the total flexible budget variances shown in Exhibit 8–3.

Fixed Overhead Variances

Variable costs can have both price and usage variances. *Fixed overhead costs* can also have price variances. Remember that a *fixed* cost remains the same relative to changes in production *volume*; it does not necessarily remain the same as *expected*. Companies may certainly pay more or less than expected for a fixed cost. For example, a supervisor may receive an unplanned raise, causing actual salary costs to be more than expected. Similarly, a manager may negotiate a reduced rental cost for manufacturing equipment, causing actual rental costs to be less than expected. The difference between the *actual fixed overhead costs* and the *budgeted fixed overhead costs* is the **spending variance.** The spending variance is favorable if the company spent less than expected (actual cost is less than budgeted cost). The variance is unfavorable if the company spent more than expected (actual is more than budget).

Analyzing fixed overhead costs differs from analyzing variable costs because there is no potential usage variance. If Melrose pays $25,000 to rent its manufacturing facility, the company cannot use more or less of this rent no matter how many units of product it makes. Because the rent cost is fixed, however, the *cost per unit* will differ depending on the number of units of product made. The more units Melrose produces, the lower the fixed overhead cost per unit and vice versa. Because the volume of activity affects the cost per unit, companies commonly calculate a volume variance for fixed overhead costs. The **volume variance** is the difference between the *budgeted fixed cost* and the *amount of fixed costs allocated to production.* The amount of fixed costs allocated to production is frequently called *applied fixed cost.*

To illustrate the fixed overhead variances, return to the overhead spending variance for Melrose Manufacturing Company shown in Exhibit 8–3. The spending variance is the difference between the budgeted fixed overhead and the actual fixed overhead (|$201,600 budgeted − $210,000 actual| = $8,400 spending variance). The variance is unfavorable because Melrose actually spent more than expected for fixed overhead costs. Recall there is no fixed overhead usage variance.

To calculate the overhead volume variance, first calculate the predetermined fixed cost overhead rate: divide budgeted fixed costs of $201,600 by planned volume of 18,000 trophies. The predetermined fixed overhead rate is $11.20 per trophy ($201,600 ÷ 18,000 trophies). Since Melrose actually produced 19,000 trophies, it applied (allocated) $212,800 ($11.20 × 19,000 units) of fixed overhead costs to production. The difference between the budgeted fixed overhead and the applied fixed overhead produces a volume variance of $11,200 (|$201,600 budgeted − $212,800 applied| = $11,200 variance). Exhibit 8–7 shows a summary of the fixed overhead variances.

Exhibit 8–7 *Fixed Overhead Spending and Volume Variances for Melrose Manufacturing Company*

Actual Fixed Overhead Cost		**Variance Dividing Data**		**Standard Fixed Overhead Cost**	
Actual fixed cost	$210,000	Budgeted fixed cost	$201,600	Applied fixed cost	$212,800
	Overhead spending variance			Overhead volume variance	
	$8,400 Unfavorable			$11,200 Favorable	

Responsibility for Fixed Overhead Price Variances

There is no way to know who is responsible for the unfavorable fixed overhead spending variance because all of the fixed overhead costs have been pooled together. To improve accountability, significant controllable fixed overhead costs such as supervisory salaries should be tagged for individual analysis. Fixed overhead costs that are not controllable may nevertheless be reported for management oversight. Even if not controllable in the short term, management should stay abreast of fixed costs because they may be controllable in the long term.

The fixed overhead volume variance is favorable because the actual volume of production was greater than the planned volume, resulting in a decreased cost per unit of product. The lower cost per unit does *not* result from reduced spending. Melrose actually spent more than expected on fixed overhead costs. The volume variance is caused by greater utilization of the company's manufacturing facilities. Melrose has benefited from *economies of scale.* As a rule, a company with high fixed costs should produce as high a volume as possible, thereby lowering its cost per unit of production. Of course, this rule assumes products produced can be sold at prevailing prices. An *unfavorable* volume variance alerts management to the underutilization of manufacturing facilities. In summary, a volume variance indicates over- or underutilization of facilities, not over- or underspending.

As previously discussed, production managers are not usually responsible for volume variances. The level of production is normally based on sales volume which is under the control of upper-level marketing managers. Although the volume variance measures the effectiveness of facilities use, the marketing department should be held accountable for volume variances because it is primarily responsible for establishing the volume of activity.

Summary of Manufacturing Cost Variances

To summarize, the total flexible budget variable manufacturing cost variance can be subdivided into materials, labor, and variable overhead variances. These variances can be further subdivided into price and usage variances. Manufacturing fixed cost can be subdivided into spending and volume variances. The *volume variance* is not a cost variance; it shows how volume affects fixed cost *per unit,* but it does not reflect a difference between the *total* amount of actual and expected costs. Exhibit 8–8 summarizes the relationships among the cost variances for Melrose Manufacturing Company. Exhibit 8–9 summarizes the algebraic formulas for the variable and fixed manufacturing cost variances discussed.

General, Selling, and Administrative Cost Variances

Variable general, selling, and administrative (G, S, & A) costs can have *price and usage* variances. For example, suppose Melrose decides to attach a promotional advertising brochure to each trophy it sells. Melrose may pay more or less than expected for each brochure (a price variance). Melrose also could use more or fewer of the brochures than expected (a usage variance). Businesses frequently compute variances for G, S, & A costs such as sales commissions, food and entertainment, postage, and supplies. The same algebraic formulas used to compute variances for variable manufacturing costs apply to computing variable G, S, & A cost variances.

Fixed G, S, & A costs are also subject to variance analysis. As shown in Exhibit 8–3, Melrose Manufacturing incurred a favorable $5,000 G, S, & A fixed cost *spending variance.* This means Melrose actually incurred less fixed G, S, & A cost than expected. A fixed cost *volume variance* could also be computed. Changes in sales volume affect the per unit amounts of fixed G, S, & A costs.

Exhibit 8–8 *Relationships among Manufacturing Cost Variances for Melrose Manufacturing Company*

Total flexible budget manufacturing cost variances
Total variable cost variance
|Actual cost − Standard cost| × Actual units
|$34.78 − $34.40| × 19,000 = $ 7,220 U

Total variable cost variance	7,220 U
Fixed cost variance	8,400 U
Total manufacturing cost variance	$15,620 U

Total flexible budget materials cost variance
|Actual cost − Standard cost| × Actual units
|$11.78 − $12.00| × 19,000 = → $ 4,180 F

- **Materials price variance**
  |Actual price − Standard price| × Actual quantity
  |$1.90 − $2.00| × 117,800 = $11,780 F
- **Materials usage variance**
  |Actual quantity − Standard quantity| × Standard price
  |117,800 − 114,000| × $2.00 = 7,600 U

Total flexible budget labor cost variance
|Actual cost − Standard cost| × Actual units
|$17.25 − $16.80| × 19,000 = → 8,550 U

- **Labor price variance**
  |Actual price − Standard price| × Actual hours
  |$11.50 − $12.00| × 28,500 = 14,250 F
- **Labor usage variance**
  |Actual hours − Standard hours| × Standard price
  |28,500 − 26,600| × $12.00 = 22,800 U

Total flexible budget variable overhead cost variance
|Actual cost − Standard cost| × Actual units
|$5.75 − $5.60| × 19,000 = → 2,850 U → Variable overhead variance 2,850 U

Total variable cost variance	7,220 U	Total variable cost variance	7,220 U
Fixed cost variance	8,400 U	Fixed cost variance	8,400 U
Total manufacturing cost variance	$15,620 U	Total manufacturing cost variance	$15,620 U

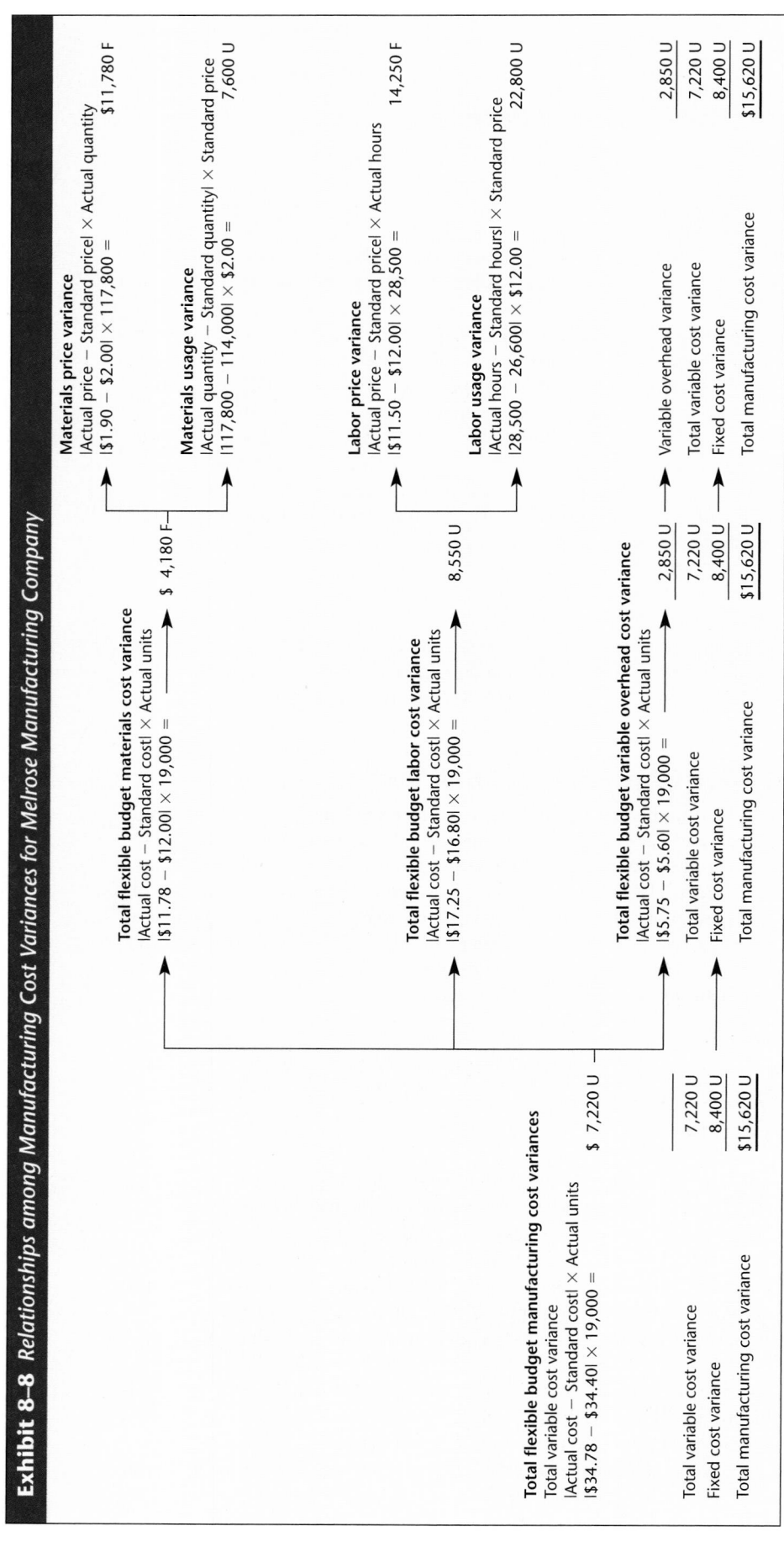

Does variance analysis apply to service companies as well as manufacturers? The answer is a definite yes! Express Oil Change could establish standard rates and times for the labor required to perform specific auto maintenance functions. Similarly, it could establish standards for materials such as oil, filters, and transmission fluid. Also, fixed overhead costs and measures of volume (i.e., number of vehicles serviced) exist. Accordingly, a full range of variances could be computed for the services provided.

Exhibit 8–9 *Algebraic Formulas for Variances*

1. Variable cost variances (materials, labor, and overhead)
   a. Price variance

      |Actual price − Standard price| × Actual quantity

   b. Usage variance

      |Actual quantity − Standard quantity| × Standard price

2. Fixed overhead variances
   a. Fixed overhead spending variance

      |Actual fixed overhead costs − Budgeted fixed overhead costs|

   b. Fixed overhead volume variance

      |Applied fixed overhead costs − Budgeted fixed overhead costs|

Many different individuals are responsible for G, S, & A cost variances. For example, lower level sales personnel are responsible for controlling the price and usage of promotional items. In contrast, upper-level administrative officers are responsible for fixed salary expenses. A full discussion of G, S, & A cost variances is beyond the scope of this text.

a look back

The essential topics of this chapter are the master budget, flexible budgets, and variance analysis. The *master budget* is determined by multiplying the standard sales price and per unit variable costs by the planned volume of activity. The master budget is prepared at the beginning of the accounting period for planning purposes. It is not adjusted to reflect differences between the planned and actual volume of activity. Since this budget remains unchanged regardless of actual volume, it is also called a *static budget. Flexible budgets* differ from static budgets in that they show the estimated amount of revenue and costs expected at different levels of volume. Both static and flexible budgets are based on the same per unit standard amounts and the same fixed costs. The total amounts of revenue and costs in a static budget differ from those in a flexible budget because they are based on different levels of volume. Flexible budgets are used for planning, cost control, and performance evaluation.

The differences between standard (sometimes called *expected* or *estimated*) and actual amounts are called *variances.* Variances are used to evaluate managerial performance and can be either favorable or unfavorable. *Favorable sales variances* occur when actual sales are greater than expected sales. *Unfavorable sales variances* occur when actual sales are less than expected sales. *Favorable cost variances* occur when actual costs are less than expected costs. *Unfavorable cost variances* occur when actual costs are more than expected costs.

Volume variances are caused by the difference between the static and flexible budgets. Since both static and flexible budgets are based on the same standard sales price and costs per unit, the volume variances are attributable solely to differences between the planned and the actual volume of activity. Favorable sales volume variances suggest that the marketing manager has performed well by selling more than was expected. Unfavorable sales volume variances suggest the inverse. Favorable or unfavorable variable cost volume variances are not meaningful for performance evaluation because variable costs are expected to change in proportion to changes in the volume of activity.

Flexible budget variances are computed by taking the difference between the amounts of revenue and variable costs that are expected at the actual volume of activity and the actual amounts of revenue and variable costs incurred at the actual volume of activity. Since the volume of activity is the same for the flexible budget and the actual results, variances are caused by the differences between the standard and actual sales price and per unit costs. Flexible budget variances are used for cost control and performance evaluation.

Flexible budget variances can be subdivided into *price and usage variances.* Price and usage variances for materials and labor can be computed with the following formulas. Variable overhead variances are calculated with the same general formulas; interpreting the results is difficult, however, because of the variety of inputs combined in variable overhead.

$$\text{Price variance} = |\text{Actual price} - \text{Standard price}| \times \text{Actual quantity}$$
$$\text{Usage variance} = |\text{Actual quantity} - \text{Standard quantity}| \times \text{Standard price}$$

The purchasing agent is normally accountable for the material price variance. The production department supervisor is usually responsible for the materials usage variance and the labor price and usage variances.

The fixed overhead cost variance consists of a spending variance and a volume variance computed as follows:

$$\text{Spending OH variance} = \text{Actual fixed OH costs} - \text{Budgeted fixed OH costs}$$
$$\text{OH volume variance} = \text{Budgeted fixed cost} - \text{Applied (allocated) fixed costs}$$

The overhead spending variance is similar to a price variance. Although fixed costs do not change relative to changes in production volume, they may be more or less than expected. For example, a production supervisor's salary will remain unchanged regardless of the volume of activity, but the supervisor may receive a raise resulting in higher than expected fixed costs. The fixed overhead volume variance is favorable if the actual volume of production is greater than the expected volume. A higher volume of production results in a lower fixed cost per unit. The volume variance measures how effectively production facilities are being used.

Management must interpret variances with care. For example, a purchasing agent may produce a favorable price variance by buying inferior materials at a low cost. However, an unfavorable labor usage variance may result because employees have difficulty using the substandard materials. The production supervisor is faced with an unfavorable usage variance for which she is not responsible. In addition, the purchasing agent's undesirable choice produced a favorable price variance. Favorable variances do not necessarily reflect good performance and unfavorable variances do not always suggest poor performance. The underlying causes of variances must be investigated before assigning responsibility for them.

a look forward

Chapter 9 introduces other techniques for evaluating managerial performance. The concept of decentralization and its relationship to responsibility accounting will be covered. You will learn how to calculate and interpret return on investment and residual income. Finally, you will study approaches used to establish the price of products that are transferred between divisions of the same company.

SELF-STUDY REVIEW PROBLEM

Bugout Pesticides, Inc., established the following standard price and costs for a termite control product that it sells to exterminators.

Variable price and cost data (per unit)	Standard	Actual
Sales price	$52.00	$49.00
Materials cost	10.00	10.66
Labor cost	12.00	11.90
Overhead cost	7.00	7.05
General, selling, and administrative (G, S, & A) cost	8.00	7.92
Expected fixed costs (in total)		
Manufacturing	$150,000	$140,000
General, selling, and administrative	60,000	64,000

The 2002 master budget was established at an expected volume of 25,000 units. Actual production and sales volume for the year was 26,000 units.

Required

a. Prepare the pro forma income statement for Bugout's 2002 master budget.
b. Prepare a flexible budget income statement at the actual volume.
c. Determine the sales activity (volume) variances and indicate whether they are favorable or unfavorable. Comment on how Bugout would use the variances to evaluate performance.
d. Determine the flexible budget variances and indicate whether they are favorable or unfavorable.
e. Identify the two variances Bugout is most likely to analyze further. Explain why you chose these two variances. Who is normally responsible for the variances you chose to investigate?
f. Each unit of product was expected to require 4 pounds of material, which has a standard price of $2.50 per pound. Actual materials usage was 4.1 pounds per unit at an actual price of $2.60 per pound. Determine the materials price and usage variances.

Solution to Requirements a, b, and c

Number of units		25,000	26,000	
	Per Unit Standards	Master Budget	Flexible Budget	Activity Variances
Sales revenue	$52	$1,300,000	$1,352,000	$52,000 F
Variable manufacturing costs				
Materials	10	(250,000)	(260,000)	10,000 U
Labor	12	(300,000)	(312,000)	12,000 U
Overhead	7	(175,000)	(182,000)	7,000 U
Variable G, S, & A	8	(200,000)	(208,000)	8,000 U
Contribution margin		375,000	390,000	15,000 F
Fixed costs				
Manufacturing		(150,000)	(150,000)	0
G, S, & A		(60,000)	(60,000)	0
Net income		$ 165,000	$ 180,000	$15,000 F

The sales activity variances are useful in determining how changes in sales volume affect revenues and costs. Since the flexible budget is based on standard prices and costs, the variances do not provide insight into differences between standard prices and costs versus actual prices and costs.

Solution to Requirement d

Number of units		26,000	26,000	
	Actual Unit Price/Cost	Flexible Budget*	Actual Results	Variances
Sales revenue	$49.00	$1,352,000	$1,274,000	$78,000 U
Variable manufacturing costs				
Materials	10.66	(260,000)	(277,160)	17,160 U
Labor	11.90	(312,000)	(309,400)	2,600 F
Overhead	7.05	(182,000)	(183,300)	1,300 U
Variable G, S, & A	7.92	(208,000)	(205,920)	2,080 F
Contribution margin		390,000	298,220	91,780 U
Fixed costs				
Manufacturing		(150,000)	(140,000)	10,000 F
G, S, & A		(60,000)	(64,000)	4,000 U
Net income		$ 180,000	$ 94,220	$85,780 U

*The price and cost data for the flexible budget come from the previous table.

Solution to Requirement e

The management by exception doctrine focuses attention on the sales price variance and the materials variance. The two variances are material in size and are generally under the control of management. Upper- level marketing managers are responsible for the sales price variance. These managers are normally responsible for establishing the sales price. In this case, the actual sales price is less than the planned sales price, resulting in an unfavorable flexible budget variance. Mid-level production supervisors and purchasing agents are normally responsible for the materials cost variance. This variance could have been caused by waste or by paying more for materials than the standard price. Further analysis of the materials cost variance follows in Requirement *f.*

Solution to Requirement f

$$|\text{Actual price} - \text{Standard price}| \times \text{Actual quantity} = \text{Price variance}$$
$$|\$2.60 - \$2.50| \times |4.1 \text{ pounds} \times 26{,}000 \text{ units}| = \$10{,}660 \text{ U}$$

$$|\text{Actual quantity} - \text{Standard quantity}| \times \text{Standard price} = \text{Usage variance}$$
$$|(4.1 \times 26{,}000) - (4.0 \times 26{,}000)| \times \$2.50 = \$6{,}500 \text{ U}$$

The total of the price and usage variances ([$10,660 + $6,500] = $17,160) equals the total materials flexible budget variance computed in Requirement *d.*

KEY TERMS

Budget slack *319*
Favorable variance *315*
Flexible budget *314*
Flexible budget variance *318*
Ideal standard *321*
Labor efficiency variance *324*
Labor rate variance *324*
Lax standard *321*
Making the numbers *316*
Management by exception *321*
Material variance *322*
Materials price variance *324*
Materials quantity variance *324*
Practical standard *321*
Sales volume variance *315*
Sales price variance *318*
Spending variance *328*
Standard *320*
Static budget *314*
Unfavorable variance *315*
Variances *315*
Volume variance *328*

QUESTIONS

1. What is the difference between a static budget and a flexible budget? When is each used?
2. When the operating costs for Bill Smith's production department were released, he was sure that he would be getting a raise. His costs were $20,000 less than the planned cost in the master budget. His supervisor informed him that the results look good but that a more in-depth analysis is necessary before raises can be assigned. What other considerations could Mr. Smith's supervisor be interested in before she rates his performance?
3. When are sales and cost variances favorable and unfavorable?
4. Joan Mason, the marketing manager for a large manufacturing company, believes her unfavorable sales volume variance is the responsibility of the production department. What production circumstances that she does not control could have been responsible for her poor performance?

5. When would variable cost volume variances be expected to be unfavorable? How should unfavorable variable cost volume variances be interpreted?
6. What factors could lead to an increase in sales revenues that would not merit congratulations to the marketing manager?
7. With respect to fixed costs, what are the consequences of the actual volume of activity exceeding the planned volume?
8. How are flexible budget variances determined? What causes these variances?
9. Minnie Divers, the manager of the marketing department for one of the industry's leading retail businesses, has been notified by the accounting department that her department experienced an unfavorable sales volume variance in the preceding period but a favorable sales price variance. Based on these contradictory results, how would you interpret her overall performance as suggested by her variances?
10. What three attributes are necessary for establishing the best standards? What information and considerations should be taken into account when establishing standards?
11. What are the three ranges of difficulty in standard setting? What level of difficulty normally results in superior employee motivation?
12. "So many variances," exclaimed Carl, a production manager with Bonnyville Manufacturing. "How do I determine the variances that need investigation? I can't possibly investigate all of them." Which variances will lead to useful information?
13. What is the primary benefit associated with using a standard cost system?
14. A processing department of Carmine Corporation experienced a high unfavorable materials quantity variance. The plant manager initially commented, "The best way to solve this problem is to fire the supervisor of the processing department." Do you agree? Explain.
15. Sara Anderson says that she is a busy woman with no time to look at favorable variances. Instead, she concentrates solely on the unfavorable ones. She says that favorable variances imply that employees are doing better than expected and need only quick congratulations. In contrast, unfavorable variances indicate that change is needed to get the substandard performance up to par. Do you agree? Explain.
16. What two factors affect the total materials and labor variances?
17. Who is normally responsible for a materials price variance? Identify two factors that may be beyond this individual's control that could cause an unfavorable price variance.
18. John Jamail says that he doesn't understand why companies have labor price variances because most union contracts or other binding agreements set wage rates that do not normally change in the short term. How could rate variances occur even when binding commitments hold the dollar per hour rate constant?
19. Which individuals are normally held responsible for labor usage variances?
20. What is the primary cause of an unfavorable overhead volume variance?
21. What is the primary cause of a favorable overhead spending variance?

EXERCISES—SERIES A

All Exercises in Series A are available with McGraw-Hill's Homework Manager.

EXERCISE 8–1A *Classifying Variances as Favorable or Unfavorable*

L.O. 3

Required

Indicate whether each of the following variances is favorable or unfavorable. The first one has been done as an example.

Item to Classify	Standard	Actual	Type of Variance
Sale volume	40,000 units	42,000 units	Favorable
Sales price	$3.60 per unit	$3.63 per unit	
Materials cost	$2.90 per pound	$3.00 per pound	
Materials usage	91,000 pounds	90,000 pounds	
Labor cost	$10.00 per hour	$9.60 per hour	
Labor usage	61,000 hours	61,800 hours	
Fixed cost spending	$400,000	$390,000	
Fixed cost per unit (volume)	$3.20 per unit	$3.16 per unit	

L.O. 3

EXERCISE 8–2A *Determining Amount and Type (Favorable vs. Unfavorable) of Variance*

Required
Compute variances for the following items and indicate whether each variance is favorable (F) or unfavorable (U).

Item	Budget	Actual	Variance	F or U
Sales revenue	$490,000	$506,000		
Cost of goods sold	$385,000	$360,000		
Material purchases at 5,000 pounds	$275,000	$280,000		
Materials usage	$180,000	$178,000		
Sales price	$500	$489		
Production volume	950 units	900 units		
Wages at 4,000 hours	$60,000	$58,700		
Labor usage at $16 per hour	$96,000	$97,000		
Research and development expense	$22,000	$25,000		
Selling and administrative expenses	$49,000	$40,000		

L.O. 1

EXERCISE 8–3A *Preparing Master and Flexible Budgets*

Burrel Manufacturing Company established the following standard price and cost data.

Sales price	$7.50 per unit
Variable manufacturing cost	3.00 per unit
Fixed manufacturing cost	3,000 total
Fixed selling and administrative cost	1,200 total

Burrel planned to produce and sell 1,100 units. Actual production and sales amounted to 1,200 units.

Required
a. Prepare the pro forma income statement in contribution format that would appear in a master budget.
b. Prepare the pro forma income statement in contribution format that would appear in a flexible budget.

L.O. 4

EXERCISE 8–4A *Determining Sales Volume Variances*

Required
Use the information provided in Exercise 8–3A.

a. Determine the sales volume variances.
b. Classify the variances as favorable (F) or unfavorable (U).
c. Comment on the usefulness of the variances with respect to performance evaluation and identify the member of the management team most likely to be responsible for these variances.
d. Explain why the fixed cost variances are zero.
e. Determine the fixed cost per unit based on planned activity and the fixed cost per unit based on actual activity. Assuming Annapolis uses information in the master budget to price the company's product, comment on how the volume variance could affect the company's profitability.

L.O. 5

EXERCISE 8–5A *Determining Flexible Budget Variances*

Use the standard price and cost data provided in Exercise 8–3A. Assume that the actual sales price is $7.20 per unit and that the actual variable cost is $3.10 per unit. The actual fixed manufacturing cost is $2,850, and the actual selling and administrative expenses are $1,275.

Required
a. Determine the flexible budget variances.
b. Classify the variances as favorable (F) or unfavorable (U).
c. Comment on the usefulness of the variances with respect to performance evaluation and identify the member(s) of the management team who is (are) most likely to be responsible for these variances.

L.O. 5

EXERCISE 8–6A *Using a Flexible Budget to Accommodate Market Uncertainty*

According to its original plan, Katta Consulting Services Company would charge its customers for service at $200 per hour in 2006. The company president expects consulting services provided to customers to reach 40,000 hours at that rate. The marketing manager, however, argues that actual results may range from 35,000 hours to 45,000 hours because of market uncertainty. Katta's standard variable cost is $90 per hour, and its standard fixed cost is $3,000,000.

Required

Develop flexible budgets based on the assumptions of service levels at 35,000 hours, 40,000 hours, and 45,000 hours.

EXERCISE 8–7A *Evaluating a Decision to Increase Sales Volume by Lowering Sales Price*

L.O. 4, 5

Rauch Educational Services had budgeted its training service charge at $80 per hour. The company planned to provide 40,000 hours of training services during 2007. By lowering the service charge to $70 per hour, the company was able to increase the actual number of hours to 42,000.

Required

a. Determine the sales volume variance, and indicate whether it is favorable (F) or unfavorable (U).
b. Determine the flexible budget variance, and indicate whether it is favorable (F) or unfavorable (U).
c. Did lowering the price of training services increase profitability? Explain.

EXERCISE 8–8A *Responsibility for Sales Volume Variance*

L.O. 4

Holbrook Company expected to sell 400,000 of its pagers during 2006. It set the standard sales price for the pager at $30 each. During June, it became obvious that the company would be unable to attain the expected volume of sales. Holbrook's chief competitor, Coker, Inc., had lowered prices and was pulling market share from Holbrook. To be competitive, Holbrook matched Coker's price, lowering its sales price to $28 per pager. Coker responded by lowering its price even further to $24 per pager. In an emergency meeting of key personnel, Holbrook's accountant, Vickie Dees, stated, "Our cost structure simply won't support a sales price in the $24 range." The production manager, Jean Volker, said, "I don't understand why I'm here. The only unfavorable variance on my report is a fixed cost volume variance and that one is not my fault. We can't be making the product if the marketing department isn't selling it."

Required

a. Describe a scenario in which the production manager is responsible for the fixed cost volume variance.
b. Describe a scenario in which the marketing manager is responsible for the fixed cost volume variance.
c. Explain how a decline in sales volume would affect Holbrook's ability to lower its sales price.

EXERCISE 8–9A *Responsibility for Variable Manufacturing Cost Variance*

L.O. 5

Slater Manufacturing Company set its standard variable manufacturing cost at $15 per unit of product. The company planned to make and sell 5,000 units of product during 2005. More specifically, the master budget called for total variable manufacturing cost to be $75,000. Actual production during 2005 was 5,200 units, and actual variable manufacturing costs amounted to $79,040. The production supervisor was asked to explain the variance between budgeted and actual cost ($79,040 − $75,000 = $4,040). The supervisor responded that she was not responsible for the variance that was caused solely by the increase in sales volume controlled by the marketing department.

Required

Do you agree with the production supervisor? Explain.

EXERCISE 8–10A *Calculating the Materials Usage Variance*

L.O. 8

Evelyn Hill is the manager of the Southside Bagel Shop. The corporate office had budgeted her store to sell 4,000 ham sandwiches during the week beginning July 17. Each sandwich was expected to contain 6 ounces of ham. During the week of July 17, the store actually sold 4,500 sandwiches and used 27,450 ounces of ham. The standard cost of ham is $0.25 per ounce. The variance report from company headquarters showed an unfavorable materials usage variance of $650. Ms. Hill thought the variance was too high, but she had no accounting background and did not know how to register a proper objection.

Required

a. Is the variance calculated properly? If not, recalculate it.
b. Provide three independent explanations as to what could have caused the materials price variance that you determined in Requirement *a.*

EXERCISE 8–11A *Determining Materials Price and Usage Variances*

L.O. 8

Cathy's Florals produced a special Mother's Day arrangement that included six roses. The standard and actual costs of the roses used in each arrangement follow.

	Standard	Actual
Average number of roses per arrangement	6.0	6.5
Price per rose	× $0.40	× $0.36
Cost of roses per arrangement	$2.40	$2.34

Cathy's Florals planned to make 760 arrangements but actually made 800.

Required

a. Determine the total flexible budget materials variance and indicate whether it is favorable (F) or unfavorable (U).
b. Determine the materials price variance and indicate whether it is favorable (F) or unfavorable (U).
c. Determine the materials usage variance and indicate whether it is favorable (F) or unfavorable (U).
d. Confirm the accuracy of Requirements *a, b,* and *c* by showing that the sum of the price and usage variances equals the total variance.

L.O. 8 **EXERCISE 8–12A** ***Responsibility for Materials Usage Variance***

Ivy Fruit Basket Company makes baskets of assorted fruit. The standard and actual costs of oranges used in each basket of fruit follow.

	Standard	Actual
Average number of oranges per basket	4.00	4.80
Price per orange	× $0.30	× $0.25
Cost of oranges per basket	$1.20	$1.20

Ivy actually produced 25,000 baskets.

Required

a. Determine the materials price variance and indicate whether it is favorable (F) or unfavorable (U).
b. Determine the materials usage variance and indicate whether it is favorable (F) or unfavorable. (U)
c. Explain why the purchasing agent may have been responsible for the usage variance.

L.O. 8 **EXERCISE 8–13A** ***Responsibility for Labor Price and Usage Variances***

Jolly Manufacturing Company incurred a favorable labor price variance and an unfavorable labor usage variance.

Required

a. Describe a scenario in which the personnel manager is responsible for the unfavorable usage variance.
b. Describe a scenario in which the production manager is responsible for the unfavorable usage variance.

L.O. 8 **EXERCISE 8–14A** ***Calculating and Explaining Labor Price and Usage Variances***

Raman and Sons, a CPA firm, established the following standard labor cost data for completing what the firm referred to as a Class 2 tax return. Raman expected each Class 2 return to require 4.0 hours of labor at a cost of $50 per hour. The firm actually completed 600 returns. Actual labor hours averaged 4.4 hours per return and actual labor cost amounted to $46 per hour.

Required

a. Determine the total labor variance and indicate whether it is favorable (F) or unfavorable (U).
b. Determine the labor price variance and indicate whether it is favorable (F) or unfavorable (U).
c. Determine the labor usage variance and indicate whether it is favorable (F) or unfavorable (U).
d. Explain what could have caused these variances.

L.O. 8 **EXERCISE 8–15A** ***Determining the Standard Labor Price***

Wyman Car Wash, Inc., expected to wash 1,000 cars during the month of August. Washing each car was expected to require 0.20 hours of labor. The company actually used 230 hours of labor to wash 920 cars. The labor usage variance was $368 unfavorable.

Required

a. Determine the standard labor price.
b. If the actual labor rate is $7.50, indicate whether the labor price variance would be favorable (F) or unfavorable (U).

EXERCISE 8–16A *Calculating the Variable Overhead Variance*

L.O. 7, 8

Regan Company established a predetermined variable overhead cost rate at $10.00 per direct labor hour. The actual variable overhead cost rate was $9.60 per hour. The planned level of labor activity was 75,000 hours of labor. The company actually used 77,000 hours of labor.

Required

a. Determine the total flexible budget variable overhead cost variance.

b. Like many companies, Regan has decided not to separate the total variable overhead cost variance into price and usage components. Explain why Regan made this choice.

EXERCISE 8–17A *Determining and Interpreting Fixed Overhead Variances*

L.O. 8

Craig Company established a predetermined fixed overhead cost rate of $30 per unit of product. The company planned to make 9,000 units of product but actually produced only 8,000 units. Actual fixed overhead costs were $280,000.

Required

a. Determine the fixed overhead cost spending variance and indicate whether it is favorable or unfavorable. Explain what this variance means. Identify the manager(s) who is (are) responsible for the variance.

b. Determine the fixed overhead cost volume variance and indicate whether it is favorable or unfavorable. Explain why this variance is important. Identify the manager(s) who is (are) responsible for the variance.

PROBLEMS—SERIES A

All Problems in Series A are available with McGraw-Hill's Homework Manager.

PROBLEM 8–18A *Determining Sales Volume Variances*

L.O. 1, 4

CHECK FIGURES
a. NI = $81,000
b. NI at 29,000 units: $72,000

Tolbert Publications established the following standard price and costs for a hard cover picture book that the company produces.

Standard price and variable costs	
Sales price	$36.00
Materials cost	9.00
Labor cost	4.50
Overhead cost	6.30
General, selling, and administrative costs	7.20
Planned fixed costs	
Manufacturing	$135,000
General, selling, and administrative	54,000

Tolbert planned to make and sell 30,000 copies of the book.

Required

a. Prepare the pro forma income statement that would appear in the master budget.

b. Prepare flexible budget income statements, assuming production volumes of 29,000 and 31,000 units.

c. Determine the sales volume variances, assuming production and sales volume are actually 31,000 units.

d. Indicate whether the variances are favorable (F) or unfavorable (U).

e. Comment on how Irvine could use the variances to evaluate performance.

PROBLEM 8–19A *Determining and Interpreting Flexible Budget Variances*

L.O. 5

CHECK FIGURE
Flexible budget variance of NI: $20,450 U

Use the standard price and cost data supplied in Problem 8–18A. Assume that Tolbert actually produced and sold 31,000 books. The actual sales price and costs incurred follow.

Actual price and variable costs	
Sales price	$35.00
Materials cost	9.20
Labor cost	4.40
Overhead cost	6.35
General, selling, and administrative costs	7.00
Actual fixed costs	
Manufacturing	$120,000
General, selling, and administrative	60,000

Required

a. Determine the flexible budget variances.

b. Indicate whether each variance is favorable (F) or unfavorable (U).

c. Identify the management position responsible for each variance. Explain what could have caused the variance.

L.O. 1

eXcel

www.mhhe.com/edmonds3e

PROBLEM 8–20A *Flexible Budget Planning*

CHECK FIGURES

a. NI = $37,500

c. NI = $28,500

Tommie Okes, the president of Star Computer Services, needs your help. He wonders about the potential effects on the firm's net income if he changes the service rate that the firm charges its customers. The following basic data pertain to fiscal year 2007.

Standard rate and variable costs	
Service rate per hour	$80.00
Labor cost	40.00
Overhead cost	7.20
General, selling, and administrative cost	4.30
Expected fixed costs	
Facility repair	$525,000.00
General, selling, and administrative	150,000.00

Required

a. Prepare the pro forma income statement that would appear in the master budget if the firm expects to provide 30,000 hours of services in 2007.

b. A marketing consultant suggests to Mr. Okes that the service rate may affect the number of service hours that the firm can achieve. According to the consultant's analysis, if Star charges customers $75 per hour, the firm can achieve 38,000 hours of services. Prepare a flexible budget using the consultant's assumption.

c. The same consultant also suggests that if the firm raises its rate to $85 per hour, the number of service hours will decline to 25,000. Prepare a flexible budget using the new assumption.

d. Evaluate the three possible outcomes you determined in Requirements *a, b,* and *c* and recommend a pricing strategy.

L.O. 8

PROBLEM 8–21A *Determining Materials Price and Usage Variances*

CHECK FIGURES

b. $0.27/cap

d. $8,160.60 U

Gibson Fruit Drink Company planned to make 200,000 containers of apple juice. It expected to use two cups of frozen apple concentrate to make each container of juice, thus using 400,000 cups (200,000 containers × 2 cups) of frozen concentrate. The standard price of one cup of apple concentrate is $0.25. Gibson actually paid $110,168.10 to purchase 408,030 cups of concentrate, which was used to make 201,000 containers of apple juice.

Required

a. Are flexible budget materials variances based on the planned volume of activity (200,000 containers) or actual volume of activity (201,000 containers)?

b. Compute the actual price per cup of concentrate.

c. Compute the standard quantity (number of cups of concentrate) required to produce the containers.

d. Compute the materials price variance and indicate whether it is favorable (F) or unfavorable (U).

e. Compute the materials usage variance and indicate whether it is favorable (F) or unfavorable (U).

L.O. 8

PROBLEM 8–22A *Determining Labor Price and Usage Variances*

CHECK FIGURES

c. $616 U

d. $8,800 F

Amy's Doll Company produces handmade dolls. The standard amount of time spent on each doll is 1.5 hours. The standard cost of labor is $8 per hour. The company planned to make 10,000 dolls during the year but actually used 15,400 hours of labor to make 11,000 dolls. The payroll amounted to $123,816.

Required

a. Should labor variances be based on the planned volume of 10,000 dolls or the actual volume of 11,000 dolls?

b. Prepare a table that shows the standard labor price, the actual labor price, the standard labor hours, and the actual labor hours.

c. Compute the labor price variance and indicate whether it is favorable (F) or unfavorable (U).

d. Compute the labor usage variance and indicate whether it is favorable (F) or unfavorable (U).

PROBLEM 8–23A *Computing Fixed Overhead Variances*

L.O. 8

CHECK FIGURE
c. $4,000 F

In addition to other costs, Molton Phone Company planned to incur $212,500 of fixed manufacturing overhead in making 170,000 telephones. Molton actually produced 174,000 telephones, incurring actual overhead costs of $213,500. Molton establishes its predetermined overhead rate based on the planned volume of production (expected number of telephones).

Required

a. Calculate the predetermined overhead rate.
b. Determine the overhead spending variance and indicate whether it is favorable (F) or unfavorable (U).
c. Determine the overhead volume variance and indicate whether it is favorable (F) or unfavorable (U).

PROBLEM 8–24A *Computing Materials, Labor, and Overhead Variances*

L.O. 8

excel
www.mhhe.com/edmonds3e

CHECK FIGURES
d. Price variance: $1,848 F
g. $900 F

The following data were drawn from the records of Walcott Corporation.

Planned volume for year (static budget)	4,000 units
Standard direct materials cost per unit	3 lbs. @ $2.00 per pound
Standard direct labor cost per unit	2 hours @ $4.00 per hour
Total expected fixed overhead costs	$18,000
Actual volume for the year (flexible budget)	4,200 units
Actual direct materials cost per unit	2.9 lbs. @ $2.10 per pound
Actual direct labor cost per unit	2.2 hrs. @ $3.80 per hour
Total actual fixed overhead costs	$17,600

Required

a. Prepare a materials variance information table showing the standard price, the actual price, the standard quantity, and the actual quantity.
b. Calculate the materials price and usage variances. Indicate whether the variances are favorable (F) or unfavorable (U).
c. Prepare a labor variance information table showing the standard rate, the actual rate, the standard hours, and the actual hours.
d. Calculate the labor price and usage variances. Indicate whether the variances are favorable (F) or unfavorable (U).
e. Calculate the predetermined overhead rate, assuming that Walcott uses the number of units as the allocation base.
f. Calculate the overhead spending variance. Indicate whether the variance is favorable (F) or unfavorable (U).
g. Calculate the overhead volume variance. Indicate whether the variance is favorable (F) or unfavorable (U).

PROBLEM 8–25A *Computing Materials, Labor, and Overhead Variances*

L.O. 8

CHECK FIGURES
b. Usage variance: $2,781 U
d. Price variance: $8,916 U

Kingston Manufacturing Company produces a component part of a top secret military communication device. Standard production and cost data for the part, Product X, follow.

Planned production	30,000 units
Per unit direct materials	2 lbs. @ $1.80 per lb.
Per unit direct labor	3 hrs. @ $8.00 per hr.
Total estimated fixed overhead costs	$702,000

Kingston purchased and used 63,345 pounds of material at an average cost of $1.85 per pound. Labor usage amounted to 89,160 hours at an average of $8.10 per hour. Actual production amounted to 30,900 units. Actual fixed overhead costs amounted to $738,000. The company completed and sold all inventory for $1,800,000.

Required

a. Prepare a materials variance information table showing the standard price, the actual price, the standard quantity, and the actual quantity.
b. Calculate the materials price and usage variances. Indicate whether the variances are favorable (F) or unfavorable (U).
c. Prepare a labor variance information table showing the standard price, the actual price, the standard hours, and the actual hours.

d. Calculate the labor price and usage variances. Indicate whether the variances are favorable (F) or unfavorable (U).
e. Calculate the predetermined overhead rate, assuming that Kingston uses the number of units as the allocation base.
f. Calculate the overhead spending and volume variances and indicate whether they are favorable (F) or unfavorable (U).
g. Determine the amount of gross margin Kingston would report on the year-end income statement.

L.O. 8 PROBLEM 8–26A *Computing Variances*

CHECK FIGURES
a. 1,760 lbs
d. $8.60

Kawa Manufacturing Company produces a single product. The following data apply to the standard cost of materials and labor associated with making the product.

Materials quantity per unit	1 pound
Materials price	$5.00 per pound
Labor quantity per unit	2 hours
Labor price	$9.00 per hour

During the year, the company made 1,800 units of product. At the end of the year, the variance accounts had the following balances.

Materials Usage Variance account	$200 Favorable
Materials Price Variance account	$176 Unfavorable
Labor Usage Variance account	$900 Unfavorable
Labor Price Variance account	$1,480 Favorable

Required
a. Determine the actual amount of materials used.
b. Determine the actual price paid per pound for materials.
c. Determine the actual labor hours used.
d. Determine the actual labor price per hour.

L.O. 8 PROBLEM 8–27A *Computing Standard Cost and Analyzing Variances*

excel
www.mhhe.com/edmonds3e

CHECK FIGURES
e. Usage variance: $1,350 F
f. Volume variance: $33,600 U

Ordeck Company manufactures molded candles that are finished by hand. The company developed the following standards for a new line of drip candles.

Amount of direct materials per candle	1.6 pounds
Price of direct materials per pound	$0.75
Quantity of labor per unit	2 hours
Price of direct labor per hour	$6.00/hour
Total budgeted fixed overhead	$168,000

During 2006, Ordeck planned to produce 40,000 drip candles. Production lagged behind expectations, and it actually produced only 32,000 drip candles. At year-end, direct materials purchased and used amounted to 49,400 pounds at a unit price of $0.60 per pound. Direct labor costs were actually $5.75 per hour and 61,400 actual hours were worked to produce the drip candles. Overhead for the year actually amounted to $173,500. Overhead is applied to products using a predetermined overhead rate based on estimated units.

Required
(Round all computations to two decimal places.)

a. Compute the standard cost per candle for direct materials, direct labor, and overhead.
b. Determine the total standard cost for one drip candle.
c. Compute the actual cost per candle for direct materials, direct labor, and overhead.
d. Compute the total actual cost per candle.
e. Compute the price and usage variances for direct materials and direct labor. Identify any variances that Ordeck should investigate. Offer possible cause(s) for the variances.
f. Compute the fixed overhead spending and volume variances. Explain your findings.
g. Although the individual variances (price, usage, and overhead) were large, the standard cost per unit and the actual cost per unit differed by only a few cents. Explain why.

PROBLEM 8–28A *Analyzing Not-for-Profit Entity Variances*

L.O. 1, 3

CHECK FIGURE
b. Variance of surplus: $1,134 U

The Central Accounting Association held its annual public relations luncheon in April 2008. Based on the previous year's results, the organization allocated $21,150 of its operating budget to cover the cost of the luncheon. To ensure that costs would be appropriately controlled, Leigh Dilworth, the treasurer, prepared the following budget for the 2008 luncheon.

The budget for the luncheon was based on the following expectations.

1. The meal cost per person was expected to be $11.80. The cost driver for meals was attendance, which was expected to be 1,400 individuals.
2. Postage was based on $0.37 per invitation and 3,000 invitations were expected to be mailed. The cost driver for postage was number of invitations mailed.
3. The facility charge is $1,000 for a room that will accommodate up to 1,600 people; the charge for one to hold more than 1,600 people is $1,500.
4. A fixed amount was designated for printing, decorations, the speaker's gift, and publicity.

CENTRAL ACCOUNTING ASSOCIATION
Public Relations Luncheon Budget
April 2008

Operating funds allocated	$21,150
Expenses	
Variable costs	
Meals (1,400 × $11.80)	16,520
Postage (3,000 × 0.37)	1,110
Fixed costs	
Facility	1,000
Printing	950
Decorations	840
Speaker's gift	130
Publicity	600
Total expenses	21,150
Budget surplus (deficit)	$ 0

Actual results for the luncheon follow.

CENTRAL ACCOUNTING ASSOCIATION
Actual Results for Public Relations Luncheon
April 2008

Operating funds allocated	$21,150
Expenses	
Variable costs	
Meals (1,620 × $12.50)	20,250
Postage (4,000 × 0.37)	1,480
Fixed costs	
Facility	1,500
Printing	950
Decorations	840
Speaker's gift	130
Publicity	600
Total expenses	25,750
Budget deficit	$(4,600)

Reasons for the differences between the budgeted and actual data follow.

1. The president of the organization, Margaret Church, increased the invitation list to include 1,000 former members. As a result, 4,000 invitations were mailed.
2. Attendance was 1,620 individuals. Because of higher than expected attendance, the luncheon was moved to a larger room, thereby increasing the facility charge to $1,500.
3. At the last minute, Ms. Dilworth decided to add a dessert to the menu, which increased the meal cost to $12.50 per person.
4. Printing, decorations, the speaker's gift, and publicity costs were as budgeted.

Required

a. Prepare a flexible budget and compute the activity variances based on a comparison between the master budget and the flexible budget.

b. Compute flexible budget variances by comparing the flexible budget with the actual results.

c. Ms. Church was extremely upset with the budget deficit. She immediately called Ms. Dilworth to complain about the budget variance for the meal cost. She told Ms. Dilworth that the added dessert caused the meal cost to be $3,730 ($20,250 − $16,520) over budget. She added, "I could expect a couple hundred dollars one way or the other, but a couple thousand is totally unacceptable. At the next meeting of the budget committee, I want you to explain what happened." Assume that you are Ms. Dilworth. What would you tell the members of the budget committee?

d. Since this is a not-for-profit organization, why should anyone be concerned with meeting the budget?

EXERCISES—SERIES B

L.O. 3

EXERCISE 8–1B *Classifying Variances as Favorable or Unfavorable*

Required

Indicate whether each of the following variances is favorable (F) or unfavorable (U). The first one has been done as an example.

Item to Classify	Standard	Actual	Type of Variance
Sales volume	38,000 units	36,750 units	Unfavorable
Sales price	$6.90 per unit	$6.78 per unit	
Materials cost	$2.10 per pound	$2.30 per pound	
Materials usage	102,400 pounds	103,700 pounds	
Labor cost	$8.25 per hour	$8.80 per hour	
Labor usage	56,980 hours	55,790 hours	
Fixed cost spending	$249,000	$244,000	
Fixed cost per unit (volume)	$2.51 per unit	$3.22 per unit	

L.O. 3

EXERCISE 8–2B *Recognizing Favorable vs. Unfavorable Variances*

Compute variances for the following items and indicate whether each variance is favorable (F) or unfavorable (U).

Item	Budget	Actual	Variance	F or U
Sales revenue	$620,000	$650,000		
Cost of goods sold	$450,000	$400,000		
Materials purchases at 10,000 pounds	$260,000	$290,000		
Materials usage	$270,000	$260,000		
Sales price	$550	$560		
Production volume	890 units	900 units		
Wages at 7,600 hours	$91,200	$90,800		
Labor usage	7,600 hours	8,000 hours		
Research and development expense	$81,000	$90,000		
Selling and administrative expenses	$75,000	$71,000		

L.O. 1

EXERCISE 8–3B *Preparing Master and Flexible Budgets*

Lamar Manufacturing Company established-the-following standard price and cost data.

Sales price	$12 per unit
Variable manufacturing cost	8 per unit
Fixed manufacturing cost	40,000 total
Fixed selling and administrative cost	36,000 total

Lamar planned to produce and sell 36,000 units. It actually produced and sold 38,000 units.

Required

a. Prepare the pro forma income statement that would appear in a master budget. Use the contribution margin format.

b. Prepare the pro forma income statement that would appear in a flexible budget. Use the contribution margin format.

EXERCISE 8–4B *Determining Sales Activity (Volume) Variances* L.O. 4

Required

Use the information provided in Exercise 8–3B.

a. Determine the sales volume variances.
b. Classify the variances as favorable or unfavorable.
c. Comment on the usefulness of the variances with respect to performance evaluation and identify the member of the management team most likely to be responsible for these variances.
d. Explain why the fixed cost variances are zero.
e. Determine the fixed cost per unit based on planned activity and the fixed cost per unit based on actual activity. Assuming Lamar uses information in the master budget to price its product, explain how the volume variance could affect the company's profitability.

EXERCISE 8–5B *Determining Flexible Budget Variances* L.O. 5

Use the standard price and cost data provided in Exercise 8–3B. Assume the actual sales price was $11.90 per unit and the actual variable cost was $7.95 per unit. The actual fixed manufacturing cost was $42,000, and the actual selling and administrative expenses were $34,600.

Required

a. Determine the flexible budget variances.
b. Classify the variances as favorable or unfavorable.
c. Comment on the usefulness of the variances with respect to performance evaluation and identify the member(s) of the management team that is (are) most likely to be responsible for these variances.

EXERCISE 8–6B *Using a Flexible Budget to Accommodate Market Uncertainty* L.O. 5

Ritter Cable Installation Services, Inc., is planning to open a new regional office. Based on a market survey Ritter commissioned, the company expects services demand for the new office to be between 30,000 and 40,000 hours annually. The firm normally charges customers $40 per hour for its installation services. Ritter's expects the new office to have a standard variable cost of $25 per hour and standard fixed cost of $550,000 per year.

Required

a. Develop flexible budgets based on 30,000 hours, 35,000 hours, and 40,000 hours of services.
b. Based on the results for Requirement *a,* comment on the likely success of Ritter's new office.

EXERCISE 8–7B *Evaluating a Decision to Increase Sales Volume by Reducing Sales Price* L.O. 4, 5

At the beginning of its most recent accounting period, Sturdy Roof had planned to clean 800 house roofs at an average price of $420 per roof. By reducing the service charge to $390 per roof, the company was able to increase the actual number of roofs cleaned to 900.

Required

a. Determine the sales volume variance and indicate whether it is favorable (F) or unfavorable (U).
b. Determine the flexible budget variance and indicate whether it is favorable (F) or unfavorable (U).
c. Did reducing the price charged for cleaning roofs increase profitability? Explain.

EXERCISE 8–8B *Responsibility for Sales Volume (Activity) Variance* L.O. 4

Dion Manufacturing Company had an excellent year. The company had hired a new marketing director in January. The new director's great motivational appeal had inspired the sales staff, and, as a result, sales were 20 percent higher than expected. In a recent management meeting, the company president, Ken Steele, congratulated the marketing director and then criticized Mr. Cobb, the company's production manager, because of an unfavorable fixed cost spending variance. Mr. Cobb countered that the favorable fixed cost volume variance more than offset the unfavorable fixed cost spending variance. He argued that Mr. Steele should evaluate the two variances in total and that he should be rewarded rather than criticized.

Required

Do you agree with Mr. Cobb's defense of the unfavorable fixed cost spending variance? Explain.

L.O. 5

EXERCISE 8–9B *Assessing Responsibility for a Labor Cost Variance*

Gilliam Technologies Company's 2006 master budget called for using 60,000 hours of labor to produce 180,000 units of software. The standard labor rate for the company's employees is $19 per direct labor hour. Demand exceeded expectations, resulting in production and sales of 210,000 software units. Actual direct labor costs were $661,500. The year-end variance report showed a total unfavorable labor variance of $91,500.

Required
Assume you are the vice president of manufacturing. Should you criticize or praise the production supervisor's performance? Explain

L.O. 8

EXERCISE 8–10B *Calculating the Materials Usage Variance*

Debbie Willis manages the Willis Candy Shop, which was expected to sell 4,000 servings of its trademark candy during July. Each serving was expected to contain 6 ounces of candy. The standard cost of the candy was $0.20 per ounce. The shop actually sold 3,800 servings and actually used 22,100 ounces of candy.

Required

a. Compute the materials usage variance.
b. Explain what could have caused the variance that you computed in Requirement *a.*

L.O. 8

EXERCISE 8–11B *Determining Materials Price and Usage Variances*

Rainbow Company makes paint that it sells in 1-gallon containers to retail home improvement stores. During 2007, the company planned to make 190,000 gallons of paint. It actually produced 198,000 gallons. The standard and actual quantity and cost of the color pigment for 1 gallon of paint follow.

	Standard	Actual
Quantity of materials per gallon	4.0 ounces	4.5 ounces
Price per ounce	× $0.25	× $0.26
Cost per gallon	$1.00	$1.17

Required

a. Determine the total flexible budget materials variance for pigment. Indicate whether the variance is favorable or unfavorable.
b. Determine the materials price variance and indicate whether the variance is favorable (F) or unfavorable (U).
c. Determine the materials usage variance and indicate whether the variance is favorable (F) or unfavorable (U).
d. Confirm your answers to Requirements *a, b,* and *c* by showing that the sum of the price and usage variances equals the total variance.

L.O. 8

EXERCISE 8–12B *Responsibility for Materials Price Variance*

Chilly Delight, Inc., makes ice cream that it sells in 5 gallon containers to retail ice cream parlors. During 2008, the company planned to make 100,000 containers of ice cream. It actually produced 97,000 containers. The actual and standard quantity and cost of sugar per container follow.

	Standard	Actual
Quantity of materials per container	2 pounds	2.1 pounds
Price per pound	× $0.39	× $0.40
Cost per container	$0.78	$0.84

Required

a. Determine the materials price variance and indicate whether the variance is favorable (F) or unfavorable (U).
b. Determine the materials usage variance and indicate whether the variance is favorable (F) or unfavorable (U).
c. Explain how the production manager could have been responsible for the price variance.

EXERCISE 8–13B *Responsibility for Labor Rate and Usage Variance*

L.O. 8

Quincy Manufacturing Company incurred an unfavorable labor rate variance.

Required

a. Describe a scenario in which the personnel manager is responsible for the unfavorable rate variance.
b. Describe a scenario in which the production manager is responsible for the unfavorable rate variance.

EXERCISE 8–14B *Calculating and Explaining Labor Price and Usage Variances*

L.O. 8

Lowder Landscaping Company established the following standard labor cost data to provide complete lawn care service (cutting, edging, trimming, and blowing) for a small lawn. Lowder planned each lawn to require 2 hours of labor at a cost of $12 per hour. The company actually serviced 500 lawns using an average of 1.75 labor hours per lawn. Actual labor costs were $14 per hour.

Required

a. Determine the total labor variance and indicate whether the variance is favorable (F) or unfavorable (U).
b. Determine the labor price variance and indicate whether the variance is favorable (F) or unfavorable (U).
c. Determine the labor usage variance and indicate whether the variance is favorable (F) or unfavorable (U).
d. Explain what could have caused the variances computed in Requirements *b* and *c*.

EXERCISE 8–15B *Determining Standard Labor Hours*

L.O. 8

Hair Styles, Inc., is a hair salon. It planned to provide 120 hair color treatments during December. Each treatment was planned to require 0.5 hours of labor at the standard labor price of $20 per hour. The salon actually provided 125 treatments. The actual labor price averaged $18. The labor price variance was $150 favorable.

Required

a. Determine the actual number of labor hours used per treatment.
b. Indicate whether the labor usage variance would be favorable (F) or unfavorable (U).

EXERCISE 8–16B *Calculating a Variable Overhead Variance*

L.O. 8

Winters Manufacturing Company established a predetermined variable overhead cost rate of $10 per direct labor hour. The actual variable overhead cost rate was $9.50 per direct labor hour. Winters planned to use 150,000 hours of direct labor. It actually used 152,000 hours of direct labor.

Required

a. Determine the total flexible budget variable overhead cost variance.
b. Many companies do not subdivide the total variable overhead cost variance into price and usage components. Under what circumstances would it be appropriate to distinguish between the price and usage components of a variable overhead cost variance? What would be required to accomplish this type of analysis?

EXERCISE 8–17B *Determining and Interpreting Fixed Overhead Variances*

L.O. 8

Pino Manufacturing Company established a predetermined fixed overhead cost rate of $200 per unit of product. The company planned to make 19,000 units of product but actually produced 20,000 units. Actual fixed overhead costs were $4,000,000.

Required

a. Determine the fixed overhead cost spending variance. Indicate whether the variance is favorable (F) or unfavorable (U). Explain what this variance means. Identify the manager(s) who is (are) responsible for the variance.
b. Determine the fixed overhead cost volume variance. Indicate whether the variance is favorable (F) or unfavorable (U). Explain what the designations *favorable* and *unfavorable* mean with respect to the fixed overhead volume variance.

PROBLEMS—SERIES B

L.O. 1, 4

PROBLEM 8–18B *Determining Sales Volume Variances*

Drake Food Corporation developed the following standard price and costs for a refrigerated TV dinner that the company produces.

Standard price and variable costs	
Sales price	$25.96
Materials cost	9.00
Labor cost	2.60
Overhead cost	0.56
General, selling, and administrative costs	4.20
Planned fixed costs	
Manufacturing cost	$500,000
General, selling, and administrative costs	360,000

Drake plans to make and sell 200,000 TV dinners.

Required

a. Prepare the pro forma income statement that would appear in the master budget.
b. Prepare flexible budget income statements, assuming production and sales volumes of 180,000 and 220,000 units.
c. Determine the sales volume variances, assuming production and sales volume are actually 190,000 units.
d. Indicate whether the variances are favorable (F) or unfavorable (U).
e. Comment on how Drake could use the variances to evaluate performance.

L.O. 5

PROBLEM 8–19B *Determining and Interpreting Flexible Budget Variances*

Use the standard price and cost data supplied in Problem 8–18B. Assume that Drake actually produced and sold 216,000 units. The actual sales price and costs incurred follow.

Actual price and variable costs	
Sales price	$25.80
Materials cost	8.80
Labor cost	2.68
Overhead cost	0.56
General, selling, and administrative costs	4.40
Actual fixed costs	
Manufacturing cost	$512,000.00
General, selling, and administrative costs	356,000.00

Required

a. Determine the flexible budget variances.
b. Indicate whether each variance is favorable (F) or unfavorable (U).
c. Identify the management position responsible for each variance. Explain what could have caused the variance.

L.O. 1

PROBLEM 8–20B *Flexible Budget Planning*

Executive officers of Meikung Seafood Processing Company are holding a planning session for fiscal year 2008. They have already established the following standard price and costs for their canned seafood product.

Standard price and variable costs	
Price per can	$3.00
Materials cost	1.05
Labor cost	0.64
Overhead cost	0.10
General, selling, and administrative costs	0.25
Expected fixed costs	
Production facility costs	$215,000.00
General, selling, and administrative costs	180,000.00

Required

a. Prepare the pro forma income statement that would appear in the master budget if the company expects to produce 600,000 cans of seafood in 2008.

b. A marketing consultant suggests to Meikung's president that the product's price may affect the number of cans the company can sell. According to the consultant's analysis, if the firm sets its price at $2.70, it could sell 810,000 cans of seafood. Prepare a flexible budget based on the consultant's suggestion.

c. The same consultant also suggests that if the company raises its price to $3.25 per can, the volume of sales would decline to 400,000. Prepare a flexible budget based on this suggestion.

d. Evaluate the three possible outcomes developed in Requirements *a, b,* and *c* and recommend a pricing strategy.

PROBLEM 8–21B *Determining Materials Price and Usage Variances* — L.O. 8

Hearn Swimsuit Specialties, Inc., makes fashionable women's swimsuits. Its most popular swimsuit, with the Sarong trade name, uses a standard fabric amount of 6 yards of raw material with a standard price of $5.00 per yard. The company planned to produce 100,000 Sarong swimsuits in 2007. At the end of 2007, the company's cost accountant reported that Hearn had used 636,000 square yards of fabric to make 102,000 swimsuits. Actual cost for the raw material was $3,307,200.

Required

a. Are flexible budget material variances based on the planned volume of 100,000 swimsuits or actual volume of 102,000 swimsuits?

b. Compute the actual price per square yard of fabric.

c. Compute the standard quantity (square yards of fabric) required to produce the swimsuits.

d. Compute the materials price variance and indicate whether it is favorable (F) or unfavorable (U).

e. Compute the materials usage variance and indicate whether it is favorable (F) or unfavorable (U).

PROBLEM 8–22B *Determining Labor Price and Usage Variances* — L.O. 8

As noted in Problem 8–21B, Hearn Swimsuit makes swimsuits. In 2007, Hearn produced its most popular swimsuit, the Sarong, for a standard labor price of $30 per hour. The standard amount of labor was 1.0 hour per swimsuit. The company had planned to produce 100,000 Sarong swimsuits. At the end of 2007, the company's cost accountant reported that Hearn had used 107,000 hours of labor to make 102,000 swimsuits. The total labor cost was $3,295,600.

Required

a. Should the labor variances be based on the planned volume of 100,000 swimsuits or on the actual volume of 102,000 swimsuits?

b. Prepare a table that shows the standard labor price, the actual labor price, the standard labor hours, and the actual labor hours.

c. Compute the labor price variance and indicate whether it is favorable (F) or unfavorable (U).

d. Compute the labor usage variance and indicate whether it is favorable (F) or unfavorable (U).

PROBLEM 8–23B *Computing Fixed Overhead Variances* — L.O. 8

Sartin Sporting Goods Co. manufactures baseballs. According to Sartin's 2002 budget, the company planned to incur $300,000 of fixed manufacturing overhead costs to make 200,000 baseballs. Sartin actually produced 187,000 balls, incurring $296,000 of actual fixed manufacturing overhead costs. Sartin establishes its predetermined overhead rate on the basis of the planned volume of production (expected number of baseballs).

Required

a. Calculate the predetermined overhead rate.

b. Determine the overhead spending variance and indicate whether it is favorable (F) or unfavorable (U).

c. Determine the overhead volume variance and indicate whether it is favorable (F) or unfavorable (U).

PROBLEM 8–24B *Computing Materials, Labor, and Overhead Variances* — L.O. 8

Victor Kemp was a new cost accountant at Beck Plastics, Inc. He was assigned to analyze the following data that his predecessor left him.

Planned volume for year (static budget)	10,000 units
Standard direct materials cost per unit	2 lbs. @ $1.50 per pound
Standard direct labor cost per unit	0.5 hours @ $10.00 per hour
Total planned fixed overhead costs	$12,000
Actual volume for the year (flexible budget)	10,800 units
Actual direct materials cost per unit	1.9 lbs. @ $1.60 per pound
Actual direct labor cost per unit	0.6 hrs. @ $8.00 per hour
Total actual fixed overhead costs	$12,400

Required

a. Prepare a materials variance information table showing the standard price, the actual price, the standard quantity, and the actual quantity.

b. Calculate the materials price and quantity variances and indicate whether they are favorable (F) or unfavorable (U).

c. Prepare a labor variance information table showing the standard price, the actual price, the standard hours, and the actual hours.

d. Calculate the labor price and efficiency variances and indicate whether they are favorable (F) or unfavorable (U).

e. Calculate the predetermined overhead rate, assuming that Beck Plastics uses the number of units as the allocation base.

f. Calculate the overhead spending variance and indicate whether it is favorable (F) or unfavorable (U).

g. Calculate the overhead volume variance and indicate whether it is favorable (F) or unfavorable (U).

L.O. 8 **PROBLEM 8–25B** ***Computing Materials, Labor, and Overhead Variances***

Evans Corporation makes mouse pads for computer users. After the first year of operation, Shirley Evans, the president and chief executive officer, was eager to determine the efficiency of the company's operation. In her analysis, she used the following standards provided by her assistant.

Units of planned production	400,000
Per unit direct materials	1 square foot @ $0.25 per square foot
Per unit direct labor	0.2 hrs. @ $7.00 per hr.
Total estimated fixed overhead costs	$200,000

Evans purchased and used 460,000 square feet of material at an average cost of $0.24 per square foot. Labor usage amounted to 79,200 hours at an average of $6.90 per hour. Actual production amounted to 416,000 units. Actual fixed overhead costs amounted to $204,000. The company completed and sold all inventory for $1,414,400.

Required

a. Prepare a materials variance information table showing the standard price, the actual price, the standard quantity, and the actual quantity.

b. Calculate the materials price and usage variances and indicate whether they are favorable (F) or unfavorable (U).

c. Prepare a labor variance information table showing the standard price, the actual price, the standard hours, and the actual hours.

d. Calculate the labor price and efficiency variances and indicate whether they are favorable (F) or unfavorable (U).

e. Calculate the predetermined overhead rate, assuming that Evans uses the number of units as the allocation base.

f. Calculate the overhead spending and volume variances and indicate whether they are favorable (F) or unfavorable (U).

g. Determine the amount of gross margin Evans would report on the year-end income statement.

PROBLEM 8–26B ***Computing Variances*** **L.O. 8**

A fire destroyed most of Omar Products Corporation's records. Sherry Hill, the company's accountant, is trying to piece together the company's operating results from salvaged documents. She discovered the following data.

Standard materials quantity per unit	2.5 pounds
Standard materials price	$2 per pound
Standard labor quantity per unit	0.6 hour
Standard labor price	$12 per hour
Actual number of products produced	8,000 units
Materials price variance	$792 favorable
Materials quantity variance	$400 favorable
Labor price variance	$1,952 unfavorable
Labor usage variance	$960 unfavorable

Required

a. Determine the actual amount of materials used.
b. Determine the actual price per pound paid for materials.
c. Determine the actual labor hours used.
d. Determine the actual labor price per hour.

PROBLEM 8–27B ***Computing Standard Cost and Analyzing Variances*** **L.O. 8**

Nash Manufacturing Company, which makes aluminum alloy wheels for automobiles, recently introduced a new luxury wheel that fits small sports cars. The company developed the following standards for its new product.

Amount of direct materials per wheel	4 pounds
Price of direct materials per pound	$5.50
Quantity of labor per wheel	5.0 hours
Price of direct labor per hour	$8.00/hour
Total budgeted fixed overhead	$336,000

In its first year of operation, Nash planned to produce 3,000 sets of wheels (four wheels per set). Because of unexpected demand, it actually produced 3,600 sets of wheels. By year-end direct materials purchased and used amounted to 60,000 pounds of aluminum at a cost of $351,000. Direct labor costs were actually $8.40 per hour. Actual hours worked were 4.4 hours per wheel. Overhead for the year actually amounted to $360,000. Overhead is applied to products using a predetermined overhead rate based on the total estimated number of wheels to be produced.

Required

(Round all computations to two decimal places.)

a. Compute the standard cost per wheel for direct materials, direct labor, and overhead.
b. Determine the total standard cost per wheel.
c. Compute the actual cost per wheel for direct materials, direct labor, and overhead.
d. Compute the actual cost per wheel.
e. Compute the price and usage variances for direct materials and direct labor. Identify any variances that Nash should investigate. Based on your results, offer a possible explanation for the labor usage variance.
f. Compute the fixed overhead spending and volume variances. Explain your findings.

PROBLEM 8–28B ***Analyzing Not-for-Profit Organization Variances*** **L.O. 3, 4, 5**

The Finance Department of Dothan State University planned to hold its annual distinguished visiting lecturer (DVL) presentation in October 2008. The secretary of the department prepared the following budget based on costs that had been incurred in the past for the DVL presentation.

Finance Department Distinguished Visiting Lecturer Budget October 2008	
Variable costs	
Beverages at break	$ 375
Postage	296
Step costs*	
Printing	500
Facility	250
Fixed costs	
Dinner	200
Speaker's gift	100
Publicity	50
Total costs	$1,771

*Step costs are costs that change abruptly after a defined range of volume (attendance). They do not change proportionately with unit volume increases (i.e., the cost is fixed within a range of activity but changes to a different fixed cost when the volume changes to a new range). For instance, the facility charge is $250 for from 1 to 400 attendees. From 401 to 500 attendees, the next larger room is needed, and the charge is $350. If more than 500 attended, the room size and cost would increase again.

The budget for the presentation was based on the following expectations:

1. Attendance was estimated at 50 faculty from Dothan State and neighboring schools, 125 invited guests from the business community, and 200 students. Beverage charge per attendee would be $1.00. The cost driver for beverages is the number of attendees.
2. Postage was based on $0.37 per invitation; 800 invitations were expected to be mailed to faculty and finance business executives. The cost driver for postage is the number of invitations mailed.
3. Printing cost was expected to be $500 for 800 invitations and envelopes. Additional invitations and envelopes could be purchased in batches of 100 units with each batch costing $50.
4. The DVL presentation was scheduled at a downtown convention center. The facility charge was $250 for a room that has a capacity of 400 persons; the charge for one to hold more than 400 people was $350. The convention center provided refreshments at break except beverages.
5. After the presentation, three Dothan State faculty members planned to take the speaker to dinner. The dinner had been prearranged at a local restaurant for $200 for a three-course dinner.
6. A gift for the speaker was budgeted at $100.
7. Publicity would consist of flyers and posters placed at strategic locations around campus and business offices, articles in the business section of the local newspapers, and announcements made in business classes and school newspapers. Printing for the posters and flyers had been prearranged for $50.
8. The speaker lives in the adjoining state and had agreed to drive to the presentation at his own expense.

The actual results of the presentation follow.

1. Attendance consisted of 450 faculty, business executives, and students.
2. An additional 100 invitations were printed and mailed when the Finance Department decided that selected alumni should also be invited.
3. Based on RSVP responses, the department rented the next size larger room at a cost of $350 for the presentation.
4. The speaker's gift cost was as budgeted.
5. The department chairperson decided to have a four-course dinner, which cost $230.
6. Because of poor planning, the posters and flyers were not distributed as widely as expected. It was decided at the last minute to hire a temporary assistant to make phone calls to alumni. The actual publicity cost was $75.

Required

a. Prepare a flexible budget and compute activity variances based on a comparison between the master budget and the flexible budget. Briefly explain the meaning of the activity variances.

b. Compute flexible budget variances by comparing the flexible budget with the actual results. Briefly explain the meaning of the variable cost flexible budget variances. Discuss the fixed cost variances.

c. Calculate the expected and actual fixed cost per attendee. Discuss the significance of the difference in these amounts.

d. Since the department is a not-for-profit entity, why is it important for it to control the cost of sponsoring the distinguished visiting lecturer presentation?

ANALYZE, THINK, COMMUNICATE

BUSINESS APPLICATIONS CASE *Static Versus Flexible Budget Variances*

ATC 8–1

Vince Jacobs is the manufacturing production supervisor for High-Five Inline Skates Company. Trying to explain why he did not get the year-end bonus that he had expected, he told his wife, "This is the dumbest place I ever worked. Last year the company set up this budget assuming it would sell 200,000 skates. Well, it sold only 190,000. The company lost money and gave me a bonus for not using as much materials and labor as was called for in the budget. This year, the company has the same 200,000 goal and it sells 210,000. The company's making all kinds of money. You'd think I'd get this big fat bonus. Instead, management tells me I used more materials and labor than was budgeted. They say the company would have made a lot more money if I'd stayed within my budget. I guess I gotta wait for another bad year before I get a bonus. Like I said, this is the dumbest place I ever worked."

High-Five Company's master budget and the actual results for the most recent year of operating activity follow.

	Master Budget	Actual Results	Variances	F or U
Number of units	200,000	210,000	10,000	
Sales revenue	$40,000,000	$42,630,000	$2,630,000	F
Variable manufacturing costs				
Materials	(6,000,000)	(6,115,200)	115,200	U
Labor	(5,600,000)	(5,974,500)	374,500	U
Overhead	(2,400,000)	(2,471,700)	71,700	U
Variable general, selling and admin. costs	(7,600,000)	(8,110,200)	510,200	U
Contribution margin	18,400,000	19,958,400	1,558,400	F
Fixed costs				
Manufacturing overhead	(8,150,000)	(8,205,000)	55,000	U
General, selling and admin. costs	(7,200,000)	(7,176,000)	24,000	F
Net income	$ 3,050,000	$ 4,577,400	$1,527,400	F

Required

a. Did High-Five increase unit sales by cutting prices or by using some other strategy?

b. Is Mr. Jacobs correct in his conclusion that something is wrong with the company's performance evaluation process? If so, what do you suggest be done to improve the system?

c. Prepare a flexible budget and recompute the budget variances.

d. Explain what might have caused the fixed costs to be different from the amount budgeted.

e. Assume that the company's material price variance was favorable and its material usage variance was unfavorable. Explain why Mr. Jacobs may not be responsible for these variance. Now, explain why he may have been responsible for the material usage variance.

f. Assume the labor price variance is favorable. Was the labor usage variance favorable or unfavorable?

g. Is the fixed overhead volume variance favorable or unfavorable? Explain the effect of this variance on the cost of each set of inline skates.

GROUP ASSIGNMENT *Variable Price and Usage Variances and Fixed Cost Variances*

ATC 8–2

Kemp Tables, Inc. (KTI), makes picnic tables of 2 × 4 planks of treated pine. It sells the tables to large retail discount stores such as Wal-Mart. After reviewing the following data generated by KTI's chief accountant, Arianne Darwin, the company president, expressed concern that the total manufacturing cost was more than $0.5 million above budget ($7,084,800 − $6,520,000 = $564,800).

	Actual Results	Master Budget
Cost of planks per table	$ 44.10	$ 40.00
Cost of labor per table	26.10	25.50
Total variable manufacturing cost per table (a)	$ 70.20	$ 65.50
Total number of tables produced (b)	82,000	80,000
Total variable manufacturing cost (a × b)	$5,756,400	$5,240,000
Total fixed manufacturing cost	1,328,400	1,280,000
Total manufacturing cost	$7,084,800	$6,520,000

Ms. Darwin asked Conrad Pearson, KTI's chief accountant, to explain what caused the increase in cost. Mr. Pearson responded that things were not as bad as they seemed. He noted that part of the cost variance resulted from making and selling more tables than had been expected. Making more tables naturally causes the cost of materials and labor to be higher. He explained that the flexible budget cost variance was less than $0.5 million. Specifically, he provided the following comparison.

	Actual Results	Flexible Budget
Cost of planks per table	$ 44.10	$ 40.00
Cost of labor per table	26.10	25.50
Total variable manufacturing cost per table (a)	$ 70.20	$ 65.50
Total number of tables produced (b)	82,000	82,000
Total variable manufacturing cost (a × b)	$5,756,400	$5,371,000
Total fixed manufacturing cost	1,328,400	1,280,000
Total manufacturing cost	$7,084,800	$6,651,000

Based on this information, he argued that the relevant variance for performance evaluation was only $433,800 ($7,084,800 − $6,651,000). Ms. Darwin responded, "*Only* $433,800! I consider that a very significant number. By the end of the day, I want a full explanation as to what is causing our costs to increase."

Required

a. Divide the class into groups of four or five students and divide the groups into three sections. Assign Task 1 to the first section, Task 2 to the second section, and Task 3 to the third section.

Group Tasks

1. Based on the following information, determine the total materials cost variance and the price and usage variances. Assuming that the variances are an appropriate indicator of cause, explain what could have caused the variances. Identify the management position responsible.

	Actual Data	Standard Data
Number of planks per table	21	20
Price per plank	× $2.10	× $2.00
Material cost per table	$44.10	$40.00

2. Based on the following information, determine the total labor cost variance and the price and usage variances. Assuming that the variances are an appropriate indicator of cause, explain what could have caused each variance. Identify the management position responsible.

	Actual Data	Standard Data
Number of hours per table	2.9	3.0
Price per hour	× $9.00	× $8.50
Labor cost per table	$26.10	$25.50

3. Determine the amount of the fixed cost spending and volume variances. Explain what could have caused these variances. Based on the volume variance, indicate whether the actual fixed cost per unit would be higher or lower than the budgeted fixed cost per unit.

b. Select a spokesperson from each section to report the amount of the variances computed by the group. Reconcile any differences in the variances reported by the sections. Reconcile the individual variances with the total variance. Specifically, show that the total of the materials, labor, and overhead variances equals the total flexible budget variance ($433,800).

c. Discuss how Ms. Darwin should react to the variance information.

RESEARCH ASSIGNMENT *Nonfinancial Performance Measures*

ATC 8–3

The article "How Nonfinancial Performance Measures Are Used" (*Management Accounting,* February 1998) describes several emerging performance measures that do not rely on financial data. Read this article and complete the following requirements.

Required

a. What are nonfinancial performance measures? Provide several examples.

b. The article describes five categories of nonfinancial performance measures. Identify these categories. Which category do executives consider most important?

c. Can you compute variances for nonfinancial performance measures? Explain.

d. Comment on the extent to which executives use nonfinancial measures.

e. The authors indicate that their study identified three red flags that executives need to address to use nonfinancial performance measures more effectively. Identify and briefly discuss these three red flags.

WRITING ASSIGNMENT *Standard Costing—The Human Factor*

ATC 8–4

Kemp Corporation makes a protein supplement called Power Punch™. Its principal competitor for Power Punch is the protein supplement Superior Strength™, made by Jim Adams Company (JAC). Mr. Adams, a world-renowned weight-lifting champion, founded JAC. The primary market for both products is athletes. Kemp sells Power Punch to wellness stores, which sell it, other supplements, and health foods to the public. In contrast, Superior Strength is advertised in sports magazines and sold through orders generated by the ads.

Mr. Adams's fame is an essential factor in his company's advertising program. He is a dynamic character whose personality motivates people to strive for superior achievement. His demeanor not only stimulates sales but also provides a strong inspirational force for company employees. He is a kind, understanding individual with high expectations who is fond of saying that "mistakes are just opportunities for improvement." Mr. Adams is a strong believer in total quality management.

Mr. Quayle, president of Kemp Corporation, is a stern disciplinarian who believes in teamwork. He takes pride in his company's standard costing system. Managers work as a team to establish standards and then are held accountable for meeting them. Managers who fail to meet expectations are severely chastised, and continued failure leads to dismissal. After several years of rigorous enforcement, managers have fallen in line. Indeed, during the last two years, all managers have met their budget goals.

Even so, costs have risen steadily. These cost increases have been passed on to customers through higher prices. As a result, Power Punch is now priced significantly higher than Superior Strength. In fact, Superior Strength is selling directly to the public at a price that is below the wholesale price that Kemp is charging the wellness stores. The situation has reached a critical juncture. Sales of Power Punch are falling while Superior Strength is experiencing significant growth. Given that industry sales have remained relatively stable, it is obvious that customers are shifting from Power Punch to Superior Strength. Mr. Quayle is perplexed. He wonders how a company with direct market expenses can price its products so low.

Required

a. Explain why JAC has been able to gain a pricing advantage over Kemp.

b. Assume that you are a consultant whom Kemp's board of directors has asked to recommend how to halt the decline in sales of Power Punch. Provide appropriate recommendations.

ETHICAL DILEMMA *Budget Games*

ATC 8–5

Melody Lovelady is the most highly rewarded sales representative at Swift Corporation. Her secret to success is always to understate your abilities. Ms. Lovelady is assigned to a territory in which her customer base is increasing at approximately 25 percent per year. Each year she estimates that her budgeted sales will be 10 percent higher than her previous year's sales. With little effort, she is able to double her budgeted sales growth. At Swift's annual sales meeting, she receives an award and a large bonus. Of course, Ms. Lovelady does not disclose her secret to her colleagues. Indeed, she always talks about how hard it is to continue to top her previous performance. She tells herself if they are dumb enough to fall for this rubbish, I'll milk it for all it's worth.

Required

a. What is the name commonly given to the budget game Ms. Lovelady is playing?

b. Does Ms. Lovelady's behavior violate any of the standards of ethical conduct shown in Exhibit 1–13 of Chapter 1?

c. Recommend how Ms. Lovelady's budget game could be stopped.

ATC 8–6 SPREADSHEET ASSIGNMENT *Using Excel*

Irvine Publications established the following standard price and costs for a hard cover picture book that the company produces.

Standard price and variable costs	
Sales price	$48.00
Materials cost	12.00
Labor cost	6.00
Overhead cost	8.40
General, selling, and administrative costs	9.60
Expected fixed costs	
Manufacturing	$180,000
General, selling, and administrative	72,000

Irvine planned to make and sell 30,000 copies of the book.

Required

Construct a spreadsheet like the one shown in Exhibit 8–1 to illustrate a static budget and a flexible budget for production volumes of 28,000, 29,000, 30,000, 31,000, and 32,000.

ATC 8–7 SPREADSHEET ASSIGNMENT *Mastering Excel*

Wilkin Fruit Drink Company planned to make 400,000 containers of apple juice. It expected to use two cups of frozen apple concentrate to make each container of juice, thus using 800,000 cups (400,000 containers × 2 cups) of frozen concentrate. The standard price of one cup of apple concentrate is $0.25. Actually, Wilkin produced 404,000 containers of apple juice and purchased and used 820,000 cups of concentrate at $0.26 per cup.

Required

a. Construct a spreadsheet template that could be used to calculate price and usage variances. The template should be constructed so that it could be used for any problem in the chapter that refers to price and usage variances by changing the data in the spreadsheet. The screen capture on page 364 represents a template for price and usage variances.

Spreadsheet Tip

(1) The shaded cells can be changed according to the data in each problem. All other cells are formulas based on the numbers in the shaded cells.

(2) The cells that label the variances as F or U (favorable (F) or unfavorable (U)) are based on a function called IF. The IF function is needed because the variance can be either favorable or unfavorable. The formula must determine whether actual expenditures exceed budgeted expenditures to determine whether the variance is unfavorable or favorable. As an example, the formula in cell D13 is =IF(B11>E11,'U','F'). The formula evaluates the expression B11>E11. If this expression is true (B11 is greater than E11), the text U is inserted in cell D13. The IF function can also be used to place formulas or numbers in a cell based on whether an expression is true or false. For example, the formula =IF(B11>E11,B11−E11,E11−B11) would calculate the amount of the variance as a positive number regardless of which amount is larger.

(3) An easier way to make the variance a positive number regardless of whether it is favorable or unfavorable is to use the absolute value function. The format of the formula in cells C13 and F13 would be =ABS(left number − right number).

(4) The lines around the variances are produced by using the borders in Excel (Format, Cells, Border).

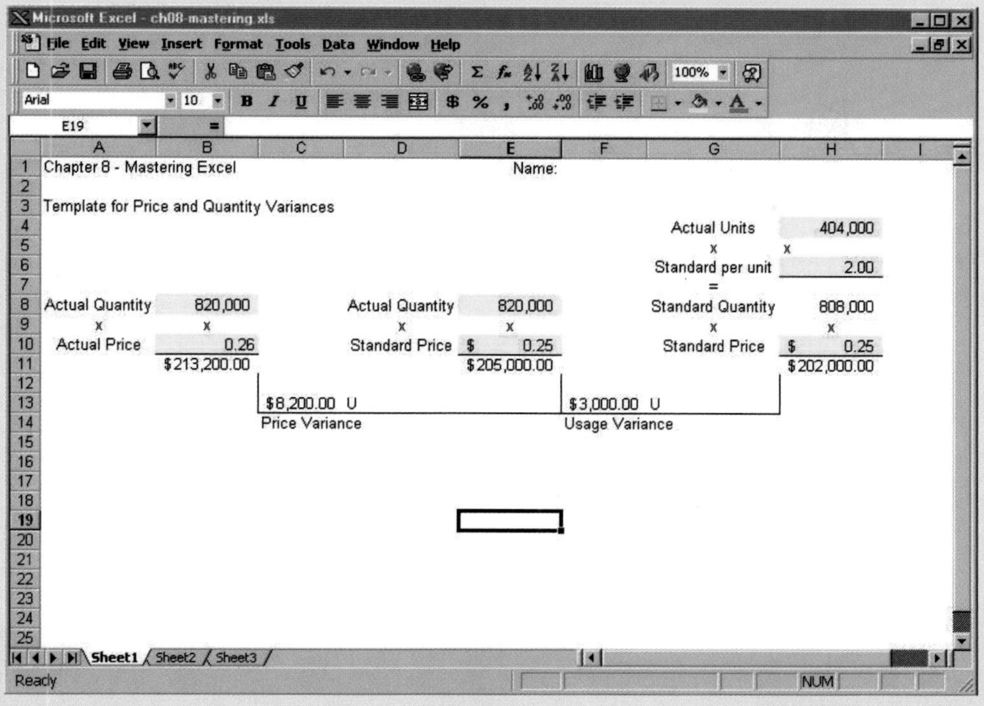

COMPREHENSIVE PROBLEM

The management of Magnificent Modems, Inc. (MMI) is uncertain as to the volume of sales that will exist in 2003. The president of the company asked the chief accountant to prepare flexible budget income statements assuming that sales activity amounts to 3,000 and 6,000 units. The static budget is shown in the following form.

Required

a. Complete the following worksheet to prepare the appropriate flexible budgets.

b. Calculate and show the flexible budget variances for the static budget versus the flexible budget at 6,000 units.

c. Indicate whether each variance is favorable or unfavorable.

Flexible Budget Income Statements

		Static Budget	Flexible Budget	Flexible Budget
Number of Units		5,000	3,000	6,000
	Cost per Unit			
Sales Revenue	$120.00	$600,000		
Variable Manuf. Costs				
Materials	40.00	200,000		
Labor	25.00	125,000		
Overhead	4.00	20,000		
Variable G, S, & A	6.00	30,000		
Contribution Margi		225,000		
Fixed Costs				
Manufacturing Rent		50,000		
Dep. on Manu. Equip.		60,000		
G, S, & A Expenses		71,950		
Dep. On Admin. Equip.		12,000		
Net Income (Loss)		$ 31,050	$(58,950)	$76,050

CHAPTER *nine*

RESPONSIBILITY ACCOUNTING

LEARNING *objectives*

After you have mastered the material in this chapter you will be able to:

1. Describe the concept of decentralization.
2. Describe the differences among cost, profit, and investment centers.
3. Prepare and use responsibility reports.
4. Explain how the management by exception doctrine relates to responsibility reports.
5. Explain the controllability concept.
6. Evaluate investment opportunities using the return on investment technique.
7. Evaluate investment opportunities using the residual income technique.
8. Describe the three common approaches used to establish transfer prices. (Appendix)

THE *curious* ACCOUNTANT

In 1978 Bernie Marcus and Arthur Blank founded **The Home Depot, Inc.**, and their first store opened in 1979. One year later they had four stores, 300 employees, and sales of $22 million. By 2000 there were 1,123 Home Depot stores with 226,000 employees and annual sales of $45.7 billion. Mr. Marcus was the company's CEO during these 20 years of tremendous growth, and he ran the company with a decentralized management style. He wanted store managers to operate individual stores as if they were their owners. Using this strategy, he saw the company's stock price rise from less than $1 per share to over $45 per share (when adjusted for stock splits). In December 2000, Mr. Marcus stepped down as Home Depot's CEO and an outsider, Bob Nardelli, was appointed as his replacement.

Two significant things happened during the first two years of Mr. Nardelli's tenure. First, he began implementing a much more centralized management system, and second, the stock price fell by 51 percent. A few examples of his management changes are: he required stores to hire more part-time employees and fewer full-time employees whether the local manager wanted to or not; he implemented a centralized purchasing system; he required local stores to carry new product lines, such as small appliances, even if the store manager objected. As a result of the change in management style, several long time store managers left the company, and others complained. Despite these problems, Mr. Marcus, who still yielded considerable influence as a major stockholder and member of the board of directors, stood behind Mr. Nardelli and the changes he was implementing.

What could explain why a company that had enjoyed so much success under a decentralized management system would switch to a more centralized system? Why would the architect of the decentralized system that had been so successful support the man who replaced his system? (Answers on page 364.)

CHAPTER *opening*

Walter Keller, a production manager, complained to the accountant, Kelly Oberson, that the budget system failed to control his department's labor cost. Ms. Oberson responded, "people, *not budgets,* control costs." *Budgeting is one of many tools management uses to control business operations. Managers are responsible for using control tools effectively.* ***Responsibility accounting*** *focuses on evaluating the performance of individual managers. For example, expenses controlled by a production department manager are presented in one report and expenses controlled by a marketing department manager are presented in a different report. This chapter discusses the development and use of a responsibility accounting system.*

Decentralization Concept

LO1 Describe the concept of decentralization.

Effective responsibility accounting requires clear lines of authority and responsibility. Divisions of authority and responsibility normally occur as a natural consequence of managing business operations. In a small business, one person can control everything: marketing, production, management, accounting. In contrast, large companies are so complex that authority and control must be divided among many people.

Consider the hiring of employees. A small business usually operates in a limited geographic area. The owner works directly with employees. She knows the job requirements, local wage rates, and the available labor pool. She is in a position to make informed hiring decisions. In contrast, a major corporation may employ thousands of employees throughout the world. The employees may speak different languages and have different social customs. Their jobs may require many different skills and pay a vast array of wage rates. The president of the corporation cannot make informed hiring decisions for the entire company. Instead, he delegates *authority* to a professional personnel manager and holds that manager *responsible* for hiring practices.

Decision-making authority is similarly delegated to individuals responsible for managing specific organization functions such as production, marketing, and accounting. Delegating authority and responsibility is referred to as **decentralization.** Decentralization offers advantages like the following.

1. *Encourages upper-level management to concentrate on strategic decisions.* Because local management makes routine decisions, upper-level management can concentrate on long-term planning, goal setting, and performance evaluation.
2. *Improves the quality of decisions by delegating authority down a chain of command.* Local managers are better informed about local concerns. Furthermore, their proximity to local events allows them to react quickly to changes in local conditions. As a result, local managers can generally make better decisions.
3. *Motivates managers to improve productivity.* The freedom to act coupled with responsibility for the results creates an environment that encourages most individuals to perform at high levels.
4. *Trains lower-level managers for increased responsibilities.* Decision making is a skill. Managers accustomed to making decisions about local issues are generally able to apply their decision-making skills to broader issues when they are promoted to upper management positions.
5. *Improves performance evaluation.* When lines of authority and responsibility are clear, credit or blame can be more accurately assigned.

Organization Chart

Exhibit 9–1 displays a partial organization chart for Panther Holding Company, a decentralized business. The chart shows five levels of authority and responsibility arranged in a hierarchical order from the top down. Other companies may have more or less complex organizational charts, depending on their decentralization needs and philosophy.

Exhibit 9–1 *Organization Chart*

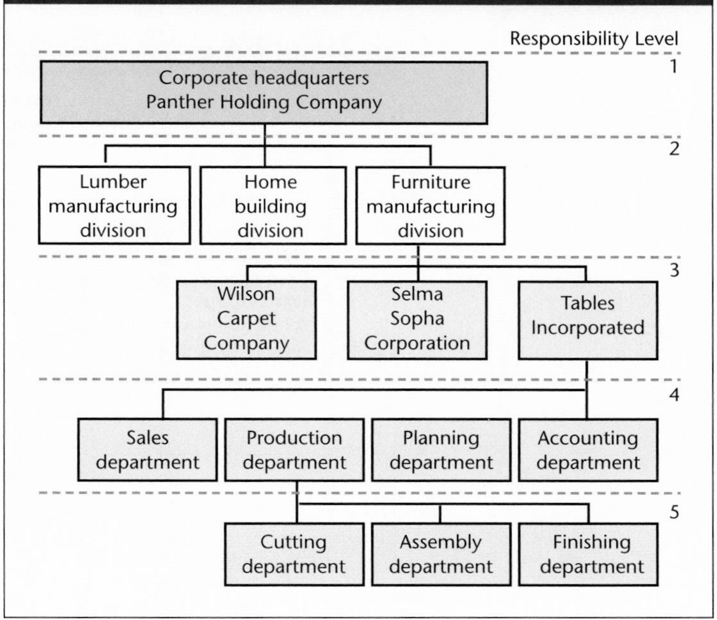

Responsibility Centers

Decentralized businesses are usually subdivided into distinct reporting units called responsibility centers. A **responsibility center** is an organizational unit that controls identifiable revenue or expense items. The unit may be a division, a department, a subdepartment, or even a single machine. For example, a transportation company may identify a semitrailer truck as a responsibility center. The company holds the truck driver responsible for the revenues and expenses associated with operating the truck. Responsibility centers may be divided into three categories: cost, profit, and investment.

A **cost center** is an organizational unit that incurs expenses but does not generate revenue. In the Panther organization chart (Exhibit 9–1), the finishing department and the production department are cost centers. Cost centers normally fall on the lower levels of an organization chart. The manager of a cost center is judged on his ability to keep costs within budget parameters.

LO2 Describe the differences among cost, profit, and investment centers.

A **profit center** differs from a cost center in that it not only incurs costs but also generates revenue. In the Panther organization chart, the companies at the third level (Wilson Carpet Company, Selma Sopha Corporation, and Tables Incorporated) are considered profit centers. The manager of a profit center is judged on his ability to produce revenue in excess of expenses.

Investment center managers are responsible for revenues, expenses, and the investment of capital. Investment centers normally appear at the upper levels of an organization chart. The second-level division managers (managers of the lumber, home, and furniture divisions) in the Panther organization are responsible for investment centers. Managers of investment centers are accountable for assets and liabilities as well as earnings.

Responsibility Reports

A **responsibility report** is prepared for each manager who controls a responsibility center. The report compares the expectations for the manager's responsibility center with the center's actual performance. A typical report lists the items under the manager's control, both the budgeted amount and the actual amount spent for each item, and the differences between budgeted and actual amounts (variances).

LO3 Prepare and use responsibility reports.

Management by Exception and Degree of Summarization

LO4 Explain how the management by exception doctrine relates to responsibility reports.

Responsibility reports are arranged to support using the **management by exception** doctrine. Exhibit 9–2 illustrates a partial set of responsibility reports for Panther Holding Company. From the lower level upward, each successive report includes summary data from the preceding report. For example, the detailed information about the finishing department (a level five responsibility center) is summarized as a single line item ($150 unfavorable variance) in the report for the production department (a level four responsibility center).

Exhibit 9–2 *Responsibility Reports*

PANTHER HOLDING COMPANY
Second Level: Furniture Manufacturing Division
For the Month Ended January 31, 2004

	Budget	Actual	Variance
Controllable expenses			
Administrative division expense	$ 20,400	$ 31,100	$(10,700) U
Company president's salary	9,600	9,200	400 F
Wilson Carpet Company	82,100	78,400	3,700 F
Selma Sopha Corporation	87,200	116,700	(29,500) U
Tables Incorporated	48,600	51,250	(2,650) U
Total	$247,900	$286,650	$(38,750) U

PANTHER HOLDING COMPANY
Third Level: Tables Incorporated
For the Month Ended January 31, 2004

	Budget	Actual	Variance
Controllable expenses			
Administrative division expense	$ 3,000	$ 2,800	$ 200 F
Department managers' salaries	10,000	11,200	(1,200) U
Sales department costs	9,100	8,600	500 F
Production department costs	13,500	13,750	(250) U
Planning department costs	4,800	7,000	(2,200) U
Accounting department costs	8,200	7,900	300 F
Total	$ 48,600	$ 51,250	$ (2,650) U

PANTHER HOLDING COMPANY
Fourth Level: Production Department
For the Month Ended January 31, 2004

	Budget	Actual	Variance
Controllable expenses			
Administrative staff expense	$ 900	$ 1,100	$ (200) U
Supervisory salaries	2,800	2,800	0
Cutting department costs	1,400	1,200	200 F
Assembly department costs	2,800	2,900	(100) U
Finishing department costs	5,600	5,750	(150) U
Total	$ 13,500	$ 13,750	$ (250) U

PANTHER HOLDING COMPANY
Fifth Level: Finishing Department
For the Month Ended January 31, 2004

	Budget	Actual	Variance
Controllable expenses			
Wages expense	$ 3,200	$ 3,000	$ 200 F
Direct materials	1,100	1,400	(300) U
Supplies	400	500	(100) U
Small tools	600	650	(50) U
Other expenses	300	200	100 F
Total	$ 5,600	$ 5,750	$ (150) U

The lack of detailed information may appear to hinder the production manager's ability to control costs. In fact, it has the opposite effect. The supervisor of the finishing department should use her responsibility report to identify and correct problems without bothering the production manager. The production manager should become concerned only when one of his supervisors loses control. The summary data in the production manager's report will adequately advise him of such situations. With this format, managers will concentrate only on significant deviations from expectations (management by exception) because the deviations are highlighted in their responsibility reports.

Applying the management by exception doctrine to the variances in her responsibility report, the division manager of the Furniture Manufacturing Division (second level responsibility center) should concentrate her efforts on two areas. First, the $29,500 unfavorable variance for Selma Sopha Corporation indicates Selma's expenditures are out of line. Second, the $10,700 unfavorable variance for the division manager's own administrative expenses indicates those costs are significantly above budget expectations. The division manager should request detailed reports for these two areas. Other responsibility centers seem to be operating within reason and can be left to their respective managers. This reporting format focuses management's attention on the areas where it is most needed.

The complete responsibility accounting report would also include the first responsibility level, corporate headquarters. At the corporate level, responsibility reports normally include year-to-date income statements to inform management of the company's overall performance. To facilitate decision making, these income statements are normally prepared using the contribution margin format. Exhibit 9–3 shows the January 2004 income statement for Panther Holding Company.

Controllability Concept

LO5 Explain the controllability concept.

The **controllability concept** is crucial to an effective responsibility accounting system. Managers should only be evaluated based on revenues or costs they control. Holding individuals responsible for things they cannot control is demotivating. Isolating control, however, may be difficult, as illustrated in the following case.

Dorothy Pasewark, a buyer for a large department store chain, was criticized when stores could not resell the merchandise she bought at the expected price. Ms. Pasewark countered that the sales staff caused the sluggish sales by not displaying the merchandise properly. The sales staff charged that the merchandise had too little sales potential to justify setting up more enticing displays. The division of influence between the buyer and the sales staff clouds the assignment of responsibility.

Exhibit 9–3 *Panther Income Statement (Contribution Margin Format)*

PANTHER HOLDING COMPANY
Income Statement for Internal Use
For the Month Ended January 31, 2004

	Budget	Actual	Variance	
Sales	$984,300	$962,300	$(22,000)	U
Variable expenses				
Variable product costs	343,100	352,250	(9,150)	U
Variable selling expenses	105,000	98,000	7,000	F
Other variable expenses	42,200	51,100	(8,900)	U
Total variable expenses	490,300	501,350	(11,050)	U
Contribution margin	494,000	460,950	(33,050)	U
Fixed expenses				
Fixed product cost	54,100	62,050	(7,950)	U
Fixed selling expense	148,000	146,100	1,900	F
Other fixed expenses	23,000	25,250	(2,250)	U
Total fixed expenses	225,100	233,400	(8,300)	U
Net income	$268,900	$227,550	$(41,350)	U

ANSWERS TO THE *curious* ACCOUNTANT . . .

The management at **The Home Depot**, along with former CEO Bernie Marcus, understands that the environment in which a business operates changes and successful companies are willing to alter the way they do business to keep up with those changes. For example, in 2000, Home Depot had nine regional purchasing offices that operated independently. Mr. Nardelli consolidated these into one central office. This reduced the cost of ordering inventory—one purchase order is cheaper to process than nine—and it gave the company more power to negotiate lower prices from its suppliers.

One of Mr. Nardelli's changes was to implement a more detailed performance measurement system for each store. Among other things, this system allowed the company to reduce the amount of inventory it carries, thus saving the company the cost of financing that inventory.

The new CEO was willing to admit if a change did not work and to quickly make another change. His requirement to use more part-time employees led to some customer dissatisfaction, so it was revised.

To be fair, the drop in Home Depot's stock price had many causes. The stock price had grown rapidly over the years because the company had grown rapidly. However, the larger a company becomes, the harder it is to maintain a given growth rate. For example, if a company has only ten stores, it can open one new one and realize a ten percent growth rate. If the company has 1,000 stores, it must open 100 new stores to realize a ten percent growth rate. Furthermore, the economy in general was much weaker during 2001 and 2002 than it had been during the 1990s.

Even though Home Depot's stock price fell during Mr. Nardelli's first two years as CEO, its profit margins were up and its cash balance was up. Also, its sales increased by 27 percent from 2000 to 2002, and its earnings were up 42 percent.

Sources: Company disclosures, stock-market data, and Dan Morse, "A Hardware Chain Struggles to Adjust to a New Blueprint," *The Wall Street Journal,* January 17, 2003, pp. A-1 and A-6.

Since the exercise of control may be clouded, managers are usually held responsible for items over which they have *predominant* rather than *absolute* control. At times responsibility accounting may be imperfect. Management must strive to ensure that praise or criticism is administered as fairly as possible.

Qualitative Reporting Features

Responsibility reports should be expressed in simple terms. If they are too complex, managers will ignore them. The reports should include only the budgeted and actual amounts of *controllable* revenues and expenses, with variances highlighted to promote management by exception. Report preparers and report users should communicate regularly to ensure the reports provide relevant information. Furthermore, reports must be timely. A report that presents yesterday's problem is not nearly as useful as one that presents today's problem.

Managerial Performance Measurement

A primary reason for a responsibility accounting system is to evaluate managerial performance. Managers are assigned responsibility for certain cost, profit, or investment centers. They are then evaluated based on how their centers perform relative to specific goals and objectives. The measurement techniques (standard costs and contribution margin format income reporting) used for cost and profit centers have been discussed in previous chapters. The remainder of this chapter discusses performance measures for investment centers.

Topic Tackler PLUS 9–1

Return on Investment

LO6 Evaluate investment opportunities using the return on investment technique.

Society confers wealth, prestige, and power upon those who have control of assets. Unsurprisingly, managers are motivated to increase the amount of assets employed by the investment centers they control. When companies have additional assets available to invest, how do upper-level managers decide which centers should get them? The additional assets are frequently allotted to the managers who demonstrate the greatest potential for increasing the company's wealth. Companies often assess managerial potential by comparing the return on investment ratios of various investment centers. The **return on investment (ROI)** is the ratio of wealth generated (operating income) to the amount invested (operating assets) to generate the wealth. ROI is commonly expressed with the following equation.

$$\text{ROI} = \frac{\text{Operating income}}{\text{Operating assets}}$$

To illustrate using ROI for comparative evaluations, assume Panther Holding Company's corporate (first level) chief financial officer (CFO) determined the ROIs for the company's three divisions (second level investment centers). The CFO used the following accounting data from the records of each division:

	Lumber Manufacturing Division	Home Building Division	Furniture Manufacturing Division
Operating income	$ 60,000	$ 46,080	$ 81,940
Operating assets	300,000	256,000	482,000

The ROI for each division is:

$$\text{Lumber manufacturing:} \quad \frac{\text{Operating income}}{\text{Operating assets}} = \$60{,}000 \div \$300{,}000 = 20\%$$

$$\text{Home building:} \quad \frac{\text{Operating income}}{\text{Operating assets}} = \$46{,}080 \div \$256{,}000 = 18\%$$

$$\text{Furniture manufacturing:} \quad \frac{\text{Operating income}}{\text{Operating assets}} = \$81{,}940 \div \$482{,}000 = 17\%$$

All other things being equal, higher ROIs indicate better performance. In this case the Lumber Manufacturing Division manager is the best performer. Assume Panther obtains additional funding for expanding the company's operations. Which investment center is most likely to receive the additional funds?

If the manager of the Lumber Manufacturing Division convinces the upper level management team that his division would continue to outperform the other two divisions, the Lumber Manufacturing Division would most likely get the additional funding. The manager of the lumber division would then invest the funds in additional operating assets which would in turn increase the division's operating income. As the division prospers, Panther would reward the manager for exceptional performance. Rewarding the manager of the lumber division would likely motivate the other managers to improve their divisional ROIs. Internal competition would improve the performance of the company as a whole.

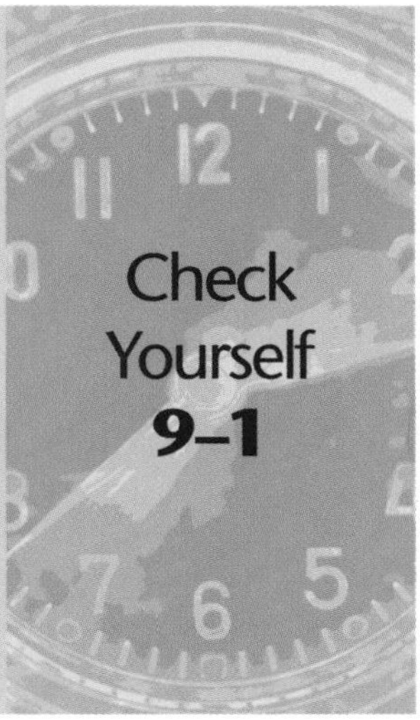

Green View is a lawn services company whose operations are divided into two districts. The District 1 manager controls $12,600,000 of operating assets. District 1 produced $1,512,000 of operating income during the year. The District 2 manager controls $14,200,000 of operating assets. District 2 reported $1,988,000 of operating income for the same period. Use return on investment to determine which manager is performing better.

Answer

District 1

$$\text{ROI} = \text{Operating income} \div \text{Operating assets} = \$1{,}512{,}000 \div \$12{,}600{,}000 = 12\%$$

District 2

$$\text{ROI} = \text{Operating income} \div \text{Operating assets} = \$1{,}988{,}000 \div \$14{,}200{,}000 = 14\%$$

Because the higher ROI indicates the better performance, the District 2 manager is the superior performer. This conclusion is based solely on quantitative results. In real-world practice, companies also consider qualitative factors.

Qualitative Considerations

Why do companies compute ROI using operating income and operating assets instead of using net income and total assets? Suppose Panther's corporate headquarters closes a furniture manufacturing plant because an economic downturn temporarily reduces the demand for furniture. It would be inappropriate to include these nonoperating plant assets in the denominator of the ROI computation. Similarly, if Panther sells the furniture plant and realizes a large gain on the sale, including the gain in the numerator of the ROI formula would distort the result. Since the manager of the Furniture Manufacturing Division does not control closing the plant or selling it, it is unreasonable to include the effects of these decisions in computing the ROI. These items would, however, be included in computing net income and total assets. Most companies use operating income and operating assets to compute ROI because those variables measure performance more accurately.

Measuring Operating Assets

The meaning of ROI results is further complicated by the question of how to *value* operating assets. Suppose Echoles Rental Company's two divisions, Northern and Southern, each rent to customers a vending machine that originally cost $5,000. The vending machines have five-year useful lives and no salvage value. The Northern Division purchased its machine one year ago; the Southern Division purchased its machine three years ago. At the end of the current year, the book values of the two machines are as follows:

	Northern Division's Vending Machine	Southern Division's Vending Machine
Original cost	$5,000	$5,000
Less accumulated depreciation	(1,000)	(3,000)
Book value	$4,000	$2,000

Each machine generates operating income averaging $800 per year. The ROI for each machine this year is as follows:

$$\text{Northern Division:} \quad \frac{\text{Operating income}}{\text{Operating assets}} = \$800 \div \$4{,}000 = 20\%$$

$$\text{Southern Division:} \quad \frac{\text{Operating income}}{\text{Operating assets}} = \$800 \div \$2{,}000 = 40\%$$

Is the manager of the Southern Division outperforming the manager of the Northern Division? No. The only difference between the two divisions is that Southern is using an older asset than Northern. Using book value as the valuation base can distort the ROI and cause severe motivational problems. Managers will consider comparisons between different investment centers unfair because the ROIs do not accurately reflect performance. Furthermore, managers may avoid replacing obsolete equipment because purchasing new equipment would increase the dollar amount of operating assets, reducing the ROI.

Companies may minimize these problems by using original cost instead of book value in the denominator of the ROI formula. In the vending machine example, using original cost produces an ROI of 16 percent ($800 ÷ $5,000). Using original cost, however, may not entirely solve the valuation problem. As a result of inflation and technological advances, comparable equipment purchased at different times will have different costs. Some accountants advocate using *replacement cost* rather than *historical cost* as the valuation base. This solution is seldom used because determining the amount it would cost to replace particular assets is difficult. For example, imagine trying to determine the replacement cost of all the assets in a steel mill that has been operating for years.

Selecting the asset valuation base is a complex matter. In spite of its shortcomings, most companies use book value as the valuation base. Management must consider those shortcomings when using ROI to evaluate performance.

Factors Affecting Return on Investment

Management can gain insight into performance by dividing the ROI formula into two separate ratios as follows:

$$\text{ROI} = \frac{\text{Operating income}}{\text{Sales}} \times \frac{\text{Sales}}{\text{Operating assets}}$$

The first ratio on the right side of the equation is called the margin. The **margin** is a measure of management's ability to control operating expenses relative to the level of sales. In general, high margins indicate superior performance. Management can increase the margin by reducing the level of operating expenses necessary to generate sales. Decreasing operating expenses increases profitability.

The second ratio in the expanded ROI formula is called turnover. **Turnover** is a measure of the amount of operating assets employed to support the achieved level of sales. Operating assets are scarce resources. To maximize profitability, they must be used wisely. Just as excessive expenses decrease profitability, excessive investments in operating assets also limit profitability.

Both the short and expanded versions of the ROI formula produce the same end result. To illustrate, we will use the ROI for the Lumber Manufacturing Division of Panther Holding Company. Recall that the division employed $300,000 of operating assets to produce $60,000 of operating income, resulting in the following ROI:

$$\text{ROI} = \frac{\text{Operating income}}{\text{Operating assets}} = \frac{\$60{,}000}{\$300{,}000} = 20\%$$

Further analysis of the accounting records indicates the Lumber Manufacturing Division had sales of $600,000. The following computation demonstrates that the expanded ROI formula produces the same result as the short formula:

$$\begin{aligned}\text{ROI} &= \text{Margin} \times \text{Turnover}\\ &= \frac{\text{Operating income}}{\text{Sales}} \times \frac{\text{Sales}}{\text{Operating assets}}\\ &= \frac{\$60{,}000}{\$600{,}000} \times \frac{\$600{,}000}{\$300{,}000}\\ &= .10 \times 2\\ &= 20\%\end{aligned}$$

The expanded formula may seem more complicated. It is generally more useful, however, because it helps managers see a variety of strategies to improve ROI. The expanded formula shows that profitability and ROI can be improved in three ways: *by increasing sales, by reducing expenses,* or *by reducing the investment base.* Each of these possibilities is demonstrated using the Lumber Manufacturing Division (LMD) of Panther Holding Company.

1. *Increase ROI by increasing sales.* Because some expenses are fixed, sales can be increased while those expenses are constant. Managers may even be able to reduce variable expenses by increasing productivity as sales increase. As a result, managers can increase their ROIs by increasing sales while limiting growth in expenses. To illustrate, assume the manager of LMD is able to increase sales from $600,000 to $660,000 while controlling expense growth so that net income increases from $60,000 to $72,600. Assuming investment in operating assets remains constant at $300,000, ROI becomes:

$$\begin{aligned}\text{ROI} &= \text{Margin} \times \text{Turnover}\\ &= \frac{\text{Operating income}}{\text{Sales}} \times \frac{\text{Sales}}{\text{Operating assets}}\\ &= \frac{\$72{,}600}{\$660{,}000} \times \frac{\$660{,}000}{\$300{,}000}\\ &= .11 \times 2.2\\ &= 24.2\%\end{aligned}$$

2. *Increase ROI by reducing expenses.* Suppose the manager of LMD takes a different approach. He decides to eliminate waste. By analyzing spending, he is able to cut expenses without affecting sales or the investment in operating assets. As a result of controlling expenses, operating income increases from $60,000 to $72,000. Assume the other variables remain the same as in the original example. ROI becomes:

$$\begin{aligned}\text{ROI} &= \text{Margin} \times \text{Turnover}\\ &= \frac{\text{Operating income}}{\text{Sales}} \times \frac{\text{Sales}}{\text{Operating assets}}\\ &= \frac{\$72{,}000}{\$600{,}000} \times \frac{\$600{,}000}{\$300{,}000}\\ &= 12 \times 2\\ &= 24\%\end{aligned}$$

3. *Increase ROI by reducing the investment base.* Managers who focus too narrowly on income frequently overlook this possibility. Reducing the amount of funds invested in operating assets such as inventory or accounts receivable can increase profitability because the funds released can be invested in other, more productive assets. This effect is reflected in the ROI computation. For example, assume the manager of LMD launches a *just-in-time* inventory system that allows the division to reduce the amount of inventory it carries. The manager also initiates an aggressive campaign to collect receivables which significantly reduces the outstanding receivables balance. As a result of these two initiatives, the assets employed to operate LMD fall from $300,000 to $240,000. All other variables remain the same as in the original example. ROI becomes:

$$\begin{aligned}\text{ROI} &= \text{Margin} \times \text{Turnover}\\ &= \frac{\text{Operating income}}{\text{Sales}} \times \frac{\text{Sales}}{\text{Operating assets}}\\ &= \frac{\$60{,}000}{\$600{,}000} \times \frac{\$600{,}000}{\$240{,}000}\\ &= .10 \times 2.5\\ &= 25\%\end{aligned}$$

The $60,000 of funds released by reducing the operating assets can be returned to headquarters or be reinvested by LMD depending on the opportunities available.

The benefits of increasing the *margin* by increasing sales or reducing expenses are intuitive. They are so obvious that, in their zeal to increase margins, managers for many years overlooked the effect of *turnover.* Growing use of the ROI ratio has alerted managers to the benefits of controlling operating assets as well as expenses. Because ROI blends many aspects of managerial performance into a single ratio that enables comparisons between companies, comparisons between investment centers within companies, and comparisons between different investment opportunities within an investment center, ROI has gained widespread acceptance as a performance measure.

Check Yourself 9–2

What three actions can a manager take to improve ROI?

Answer

1. Increase sales
2. Reduce expenses
3. Reduce the investment base

Residual Income

Suppose Panther Holding Company evaluates the manager of the Lumber Manufacturing Division (LMD) based on his ability to maximize ROI. The corporation's overall ROI is approximately 18 percent. LMD, however, has consistently outperformed the other investment centers. Its ROI is currently 20 percent. Now suppose the manager has an opportunity to invest additional funds in a project likely to earn a 19 percent ROI. Would the manager accept the investment opportunity?

Topic Tackler PLUS 9–2

These circumstances place the manager in an awkward position. The corporation would benefit from the project because the expected ROI of 19 percent is higher than the corporate average ROI of 18 percent. Personally, however, the manager would suffer from accepting the project because it would reduce the division ROI to less than the current 20 percent. The manager is forced to choose between his personal best interests and the best interests of the corporation. When faced with decisions such as these, many managers choose to benefit themselves at the expense of their corporations, a condition described as **suboptimization.**

LO7 Evaluate investment opportunities using the residual income technique.

To avoid *suboptimization,* many businesses base managerial evaluation on **residual income.** This approach measures a manager's ability to maximize earnings above some targeted level. The targeted level of earnings is based on a minimum desired ROI. Residual income is calculated as follows:

$$\text{Residual income} = \text{Operating income} - (\text{Operating assets} \times \text{Desired ROI})$$

To illustrate, recall that LMD currently earns \$60,000 of operating income with the \$300,000 of operating assets it controls. ROI is 20 percent (\$60,000 ÷ \$300,000). Assume Panther's desired ROI is 18 percent. LMD's residual income is therefore:

$$\begin{aligned}\text{Residual income} &= \text{Operating income} - (\text{Operating assets} \times \text{Desired ROI})\\ &= \$60{,}000 - (\$300{,}000 \times .18)\\ &= \$60{,}000 - \$54{,}000\\ &= \$6{,}000\end{aligned}$$

focus on INTERNATIONAL ISSUES

Do Managers in Different Countries Stress the Same Performance Measures?

Companies operating in different countries frequently choose different performance measures to evaluate their managers. For example, although U.S. companies tend to favor some form of return on investment (ROI), Japanese companies tend to emphasize return on sales (ROS) as a primary measure of financial performance.* In general, the Japanese assume a constant sales price, thereby requiring a reduction in cost or an increase in volume to generate an increase in ROS. This approach is consistent with the Japanese orientation toward long-term growth and profitability. In contrast, the majority of U.S. companies focus on ROI, which encourages and emphasizes short-term profitability. U.S. firms were at one time criticized for their emphasis on short-term profitability, but the more entrenched style of Japanese companies has hindered their ability to adapt to changing times. As a result, many Japanese companies have begun to reevaluate their management philosophy and the corresponding measures of performance. Even so, in a world filled with diversity, managers will likely continue to stress performance measures that reflect a variety of social customs.

*Robert S. Kaplan, "Measures for Manufacturing Excellence," *Emerging Practices in Cost Management* in WG&L Corporate Finance Network Database, 1998.

REALITY bytes

In recent years the residual income approach has been refined to produce a new technique called **economic value added (EVA).** EVA was developed and trademarked by the consulting firm Stern Stewart & Co. EVA uses the basic formula behind residual income [Operating income − (Operating assets × Desired ROI)]. EVA, however, uses different definitions of operating income and operating assets. For example, research and development (R&D) costs are classified as operating assets under EVA. In contrast, R&D costs are classified as expenses under traditional accounting. As a result, operating assets and operating income are higher under EVA than they are under the residual income approach. There are more than 100 such differences between EVA and residual income. However, most companies make only a few adjustments when converting from the residual income approach to EVA. Even so, these refinements seem to have had significant benefits. In a recent article in *Fortune* magazine, Shawn Tully concluded "Managers who run their businesses according to the precepts of EVA have hugely increased the value of their companies. Investors who know about EVA, and know which companies are employing it, have grown rich."

Now assume that Panther Holding Company has $50,000 of additional funds available to invest. Because LMD consistently performs at a high level, Panther's corporate management team offers the funds to the LMD manager. The manager believes he could invest the additional $50,000 at a 19 percent rate of return.

If the LMD manager's evaluation is based solely on ROI, he is likely reject the additional funding because investing the funds at 19 percent would lower his overall ROI. If the LMD manager's evaluation is based on residual income, however, he is likely to accept the funds because an additional investment at 19 percent would increase his residual income as follows:

$$\begin{aligned}\text{Operating income} &= \$50{,}000 \times .19\\ &= \$9{,}500\end{aligned}$$

$$\begin{aligned}\text{Residual income} &= \text{Operating income} - (\text{Operating assets} \times \text{Desired ROI})\\ &= \$9{,}500 - (\$50{,}000 \times .18)\\ &= \$9{,}500 - \$9{,}000\\ &= \$500\end{aligned}$$

Accepting the new project would add $500 to LMD's residual income. If the manager of LMD is evaluated based on his ability to maximize residual income, he would benefit by investing in any project that returns an ROI in excess of the desired 18 percent. The reduction in LMD's overall ROI does not enter into the decision. The residual income approach solves the problem of suboptomization.

The primary disadvantage of the residual income approach is that it measures performance in absolute dollars. As a result, a manager's residual income may be larger simply because her investment base is larger rather than because her performance is superior.

To illustrate, return to the example where Panther Holding Company has $50,000 of additional funds to invest. Assume the manager of the Lumber Manufacturing Division (LMD) and the manager of the Furniture Manufacturing Division (FMD) each have investment opportunities expected to earn a 19 percent return. Recall that Panther's desired ROI is 18 percent. If corporate headquarters allots $40,000 of the funds to the manager of LMD and $10,000 to the manager of FMD, the increase in residual income earned by each division is as follows:

$$\text{LMD's Residual income} = (\$40{,}000 \times .19) - (\$40{,}000 \times .18) = \$400$$

$$\text{FMD's Residual income} = (\$10{,}000 \times .19) - (\$10{,}000 \times .18) = \$100$$

Does LMD's higher residual income mean LMD's manager is outperforming FMD's manager? No. It means LMD's manager received more operating assets than FMD's manager received.

Check Yourself 9–3

Young Company's desired rate of return is 14 percent. Christina Fallin, manager of Young's northeastern investment center, controls $12,600,000 of operating assets. During the most recent year, Fallin's district produced operating income of $1,839,600. Determine the amount of the northeastern investment center's residual income.

Answer

Residual income = Operating income − (Operating assets × Desired ROI)

Residual income = $1,839,600 − ($12,600,000 × 0.14) = $75,600

Responsibility Accounting and the Balanced Scorecard

Throughout the text we have discussed many financial measures companies use to evaluate managerial performance. Examples include standard cost systems to evaluate cost center managers; the contribution margin income statement to evaluate profit center managers; and ROI / residual income to evaluate the performance of investment center managers. Many companies may have goals and objectives such as "satisfaction guaranteed" or "we try harder" that are more suitably evaluated using nonfinancial measures. To assess how well they accomplish the full range of their missions, many companies use a *balanced scorecard.*

A **balanced scorecard** includes financial and nonfinancial performance measures. Standard costs, income measures, ROI, and residual income are common financial measures used in a balanced score card. Nonfinancial measures include defect rates, cycle time, on time deliveries, number of new products or innovations, safety measures, and customer satisfaction surveys. Many companies compose their scorecards to highlight leading versus lagging measures. For example, customer satisfaction survey data is a leading indicator of the sales growth which is a lagging measure. The balanced scorecard is a holistic approach to evaluating managerial performance. It is gaining widespread acceptance among world-class companies.

a look back

The practice of delegating authority and responsibility is referred to as *decentralization.* Clear lines of authority and responsibility are essential in establishing a responsibility accounting system. In a responsibility accounting system, segment managers are held accountable for profits based on the amount of control they have over the profits in their segment.

Responsibility reports are used to compare actual results with budgets. The reports should be simple with variances highlighted to promote the *management by exception* doctrine. Individual managers should be held responsible only for those revenues or costs they control. Each manager should receive only summary information about the performance of the responsibility centers under her supervision.

A *responsibility center* is the point in an organization where control over revenue or expense is located. *Cost centers* are segments that incur costs but do not generate revenues. *Profit centers* incur costs and also generate revenues, producing a measurable profit. *Investment centers* incur costs, generate revenues, and use identifiable capital investments.

One of the primary purposes of responsibility accounting is to evaluate managerial performance. Comparing actual results with standards and budgets and calculating *return on investment* are used for this purpose. Because return on investment uses revenues, expenses, and investment, problems with measuring these parameters must be considered. The return on investment can be analyzed in terms of the margin earned on sales as well as the turnover (asset utilization) during the period. The *residual income approach* is sometimes used to avoid *suboptimization,* which occurs when managers choose to reject investment projects that would benefit their company's ROI but would reduce their investment center's ROI. The residual income approach evaluates managers based on their ability to generate earnings above some targeted level of earnings.

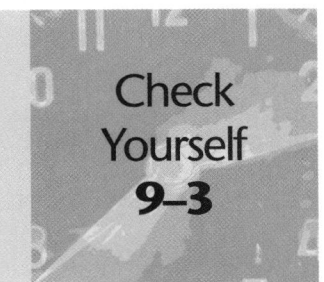

Transfer pricing can affect a division's profitability. A transfer price must be determined when one division sells goods or services to another division within the same company. It is to the advantage of the selling division to obtain the highest price while the purchasing division seeks the lowest price possible. The three most common bases used to establish transfer prices are *market forces, negotiation,* and *cost.*

a look forward

The next chapter expands on the concepts you learned in this chapter. You will see how managers select investment opportunities that will affect their future ROIs. You will learn to use present value techniques that consider the time value of money; specifically, you will learn to compute the net present value and the internal rate of return for potential investment opportunities. You will also learn to use less sophisticated analytical techniques such as payback and the unadjusted rate of return.

APPENDIX

LO8 Describe the three common approaches used to establish transfer prices. (Appendix)

Transfer Pricing

In vertically integrated companies, one division commonly sells goods or services to another division. For example, in the case of Panther Holding Company (Exhibit 9–1), the Lumber Manufacturing Division may sell lumber to the Home Building and Furniture Manufacturing Divisions. When such intercompany sales occur, the price to charge is likely to become a heated issue.

In a decentralized organization, each division is likely to be defined as an investment center. Division managers are held responsible for profitability. When goods are transferred internally, the sales price charged by the selling division becomes a cost to the buying division. The amount of profit included in the **transfer price** will increase the selling division's earnings and decrease the purchasing division's earnings (via increased expenses). The selling division benefits from getting the highest possible price; the purchasing division seeks the possible lowest price. When managers are competitively evaluated based on profitability measures, the transfer price is the subject of considerable controversy.

Companies use three common approaches to establish transfer prices: (1) price based on market forces; (2) price based on negotiation; and (3) price based on cost. Exhibit 9–4 shows some specific measures and the frequency of their use.

Exhibit 9–4 *What Companies Actually Use As Transfer Prices*

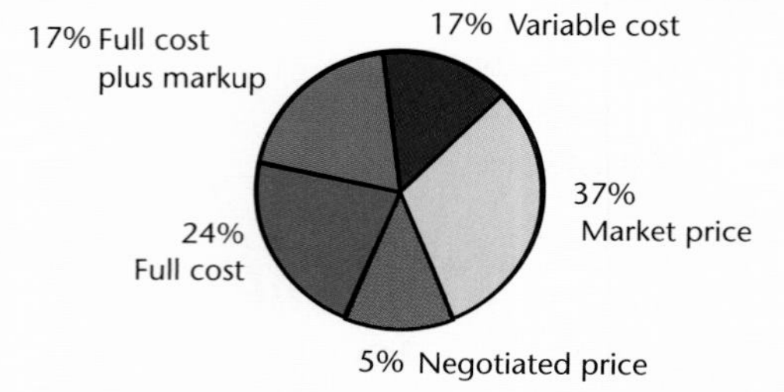

Source: R. Tang, "Transfer Pricing in the 1990s," *Management Accounting,* pp. 22–26.

Market-Based Transfer Prices

The preferred method for establishing transfer prices is to base them on some form of competitive market price. Ideally, selling divisions should be authorized to sell merchandise to outsiders as well as, or in preference to, other divisions. Similarly, purchasing divisions should have the option to buy goods from outsiders if they are able to obtain favorable prices. However, both selling and purchasing divisions would be motivated to deal with each other because of savings in selling, administrative, and transportation costs that arise as a natural result of internal transactions.

Market-based transfer prices are preferable because they promote efficiency and fairness. Market forces coupled with the responsibility for profitability motivate managers to use their resources effectively. For example, Jerry Lowe, the manager of the lumber division, may stop producing the high-quality boards the furniture division uses if he finds it is more profitable to produce low-quality lumber. The furniture division can buy its needed material from outside companies that have chosen to operate in the less-profitable, high-quality market sector. The company as a whole benefits from Mr. Lowe's insight. An additional advantage of using market prices is the sense of fairness associated with them. It is difficult for a manager to complain that the price she is being charged is too high when she has the opportunity to seek a lower price elsewhere. The natural justice of the competitive marketplace is firmly implanted in the psyche of most modern managers.

Negotiated Transfer Prices

In many instances, a necessary product is not available from outside companies or the market price may not be in the best interest of the company as a whole. Sometimes a division makes a unique product that only one of its company's other divisions uses; no external market price is available to use as a base for determining the transfer price. Other times, market-based transfer prices may lead to suboptimization, discussed earlier.

Consider the case of Garms Industries. It operates several relatively autonomous divisions. One division, TrueTrust Motors, Inc., makes small electric motors for use in appliances such as refrigerators,

REALITY bytes

The issue of transfer pricing is mostly relevant to performance evaluation of investment centers and their managers if a company does business in only one country. Transfer prices do not affect the overall profit of the company, because the cost that will be recorded as an expense for the company as a whole is the actual cost incurred to produce it, not its transfer price. However, the situation can be different if the producing division is in one country and the acquiring division is in another. This difference occurs because income tax rates are not the same in all countries.

Assume the Global Tool Company manufactures a product in South Korea for the equivalent of $10. The product is transferred to another segment that operates in the United States where it is ultimately sold for $18. Now, assume the income tax rate is 40 percent in South Korea and 30 percent in the United States. Ignoring all other costs, what amount of taxes will the company pay if the transfer price is set at $10? What amount of taxes will the company pay if the transfer price is set at $18?

If a $10 transfer price is used, then all of the company's $8 per unit profit ($18 − $10) will be recognized in the Unites States. Since the item is assumed to have been "sold" in Korea at an amount equal to its production cost, there will be no profit for the Korean division of the company ($10 − $10 = $0). The United States division will pay $2.40 in taxes ($8 × .30 = $2.40). Conversely, if the transfer price is $18, then all of the profit will be reported in Korea, and $3.20 per unit of taxes will be paid ($8 × .40 = $3.20).

The Internal Revenue Service has rules to prevent companies from setting transfer prices simply for the purpose of reducing taxes, but various companies have been accused of such practices over the years. Remember, it is often impossible to prove exactly what the best transfer price should be. Even though the company in our hypothetical example could not get away with such extreme transfer prices as $10 or $18, it might try to set the price a bit lower than it should be in order to shift more profit to the segment in the United States where the assumed tax rate was lower. Regarding the use of transfer prices to reduce taxes, an article in *BusinessWeek* noted, "Last year, a General Accounting Office study reported that, from 1989 to 1995, an outright majority of corporations, both U.S. and foreign-controlled, paid zero U.S. income taxes."*

*"The Creative Economy," *BusinessWeek,* August 28, 2000, p. 76.

washing machines, and fans. Another Garms division, CleanCo, makes and sells approximately 30,000 vacuum cleaners per year. CleanCo currently purchases the motors used in its vacuums from a company that is not part of Garms Industries. The president of Garms asked the TrueTrust division manager to establish a price at which it could make and sell motors to CleanCo. The manager submitted the following cost and price data.

Variable (unit-level) costs	$45
Per unit fixed cost at a volume of 30,000 units	15
Allocated corporate level facility-sustaining costs	20
Total cost	$80

TrueTrust has enough excess capacity that its existing business will not be affected by a decision to make motors for CleanCo. However, TrueTrust would be required to buy additional equipment and hire a supervisor to make the motors that CleanCo requires.

The TrueTrust manager added a profit margin of $10 per unit and offered to provide motors to CleanCo at a price of $90 per unit. When the offer was presented to the CleanCo division manager, she rejected it. Her division was currently buying motors in the open market for $70 each. Competitive pressures in the vacuum cleaner market would not permit an increase in the sales price of her product.

Accepting TrueTrust's offer would significantly increase CleanCo's costs and reduce the division's profitability.

After studying the cost data, Garms' president concluded the company as a whole would suffer from suboptimization if CleanCo were to continue purchasing motors from a third-party vendor. He noted that the allocated corporate level facility-sustaining costs were not relevant to the transfer pricing decision because they would be incurred regardless of whether TrueTrust made the motors for CleanCo. He recognized that both the variable and fixed costs were relevant because they could be avoided if TrueTrust did not make the motors. Since TrueTrust's avoidable cost of $60 ($45 variable cost + $15 fixed cost) per unit was below the $70 price per unit that CleanCo was currently paying, Garms would save $10 per motor, thereby increasing overall company profitability by $300,000 ($10 cost savings per unit × 30,000 units). The president established a reasonable range for a negotiated transfer price.

If the market price were less than the avoidable cost of production, the supplying division (TrueTrust) and the company as a whole (Garms) would be better off to buy the product than to make it. It would therefore be unreasonable to expect TrueTrust to sell a product for less than its avoidable cost of production, thereby establishing the avoidable cost as the bottom point of the reasonable range for the transfer price. On the other hand, it would be unreasonable to expect an acquiring division (CleanCo) to pay more than the price it is currently paying for motors. As a result, the market price becomes the top point of the reasonable range for the transfer price. The reasonable transfer price range can be expressed as follows:

Market price ≥ Reasonable transfer price ≥ Avoidable product cost

In the case of Garms Industries, the reasonable range of the transfer price for vacuum cleaner motors is between the market price of $70 per unit and the avoidable production cost of $60.[1] Any transfer price within this range would benefit both divisions and the company as a whole. Garms' president encouraged the two division managers to negotiate a transfer price within the reasonable range that would satisfy both parties.

Under the right set of circumstances, a **negotiated transfer price** can be more beneficial than a market-based transfer price. Allowing the managers involved to agree to a negotiated price preserves the notion of fairness. The element of profit remains intact and the evaluation concepts discussed in this chapter can be applied. Negotiated prices may offer many of the same advantages as market prices. They should be the first alternative when a company is unable to use market-based transfer prices.

Suppose the two division managers cannot agree on a negotiated transfer price. Should the president of Garms Industries establish a reasonable price and force the managers to accept it? There is no definitive answer to this question. However, most senior-level executives recognize the motivational importance of maintaining autonomy in a decentralized organization. So long as the negative consequences are not disastrous, division managers are usually permitted to exercise their own judgment. In other words, the long-term benefits derived from autonomous management outweigh the short-term disadvantages of suboptimization.

Cost-Based Transfer Prices

The least desirable transfer price option is a **cost-based transfer price.** To use cost, it must first be determined. Some companies base the transfer price on *variable cost* (a proxy for avoidable cost). Other companies use *full cost* (variable cost plus an allocated portion of fixed cost) as the transfer price. In either case, basing transfer prices on cost removes the profit motive. Without profitability as a goal, the incentive to control cost is diminished. One department's inefficiency is simply passed on to the next department. The result is low companywide profitability. Despite this potential detrimental effect, many companies base transfer prices on cost because cost represents an objective number that is available. When a company uses cost-based transfer prices, *it should use standard rather than actual costs.* Departments will therefore at least be responsible for the variances they generate which will encourage some degree of cost control.

[1] This discussion assumes the supplying division (TrueTrust) has excess capacity. When the supplying division is operating at full capacity and has external buyers, the minimum price for the reasonable transfer price range would include not only the avoidable cost but also an opportunity cost. An opportunity cost exists when the supplying division must forgo the opportunity to profit from sales it could otherwise make to external buyers. On the other hand, if the supplying division has enough capacity to fill both existing orders and the additional orders on which the transfer price is negotiated, the opportunity cost is zero. In other words, the supplying division does not have to give up anything to accept an order from another division. A full discussion of opportunity cost is complex. It is covered in more advanced courses.

SELF-STUDY REVIEW PROBLEM

The following financial statements apply to Hola Division, one of three investment centers operated by Costa Corporation. Costa Corporation has a desired rate of return of 15%. Costa Corporation Headquarters has $80,000 of additional operating assets to assign to the investment centers.

HOLA DIVISION
Income Statement
For the Year Ended December 31, 2006

Sales Revenue	$78,695
Cost of Goods Sold	(50,810)
Gross Margin	27,885
Operating Expenses	
Selling Expenses	(1,200)
Depreciation Expense	(1,125)
Operating Income	25,560
Nonoperating Expense	
Loss on Sale of Land	(3,200)
Net Income	$22,360

HOLA DIVISION
Balance Sheet
As of December 31, 2006

Assets	
Cash	$ 8,089
Accounts Receivable	22,870
Merchandise Inventory	33,460
Equipment Less Acc. Dep.	77,581
Non-Operating Assets	8,250
Total Assets	$150,250
Liabilities	
Accounts Payable	$ 5,000
Notes Payable	58,000
Stockholders' Equity	
Common Stock	55,000
Retained Earnings	32,250
Total Liab. and Stk. Equity	$150,250

Required:

a. Should Costa use operating income or net income to determine the rate of return (ROI) for the Hola investment center? Explain.

b. Should Costa use operating assets or total assets to determine the ROI for the Hola investment center? Explain.

c. Calculate the ROI for Hola.

d. The manager of the Hola division has an opportunity to invest the funds at an ROI of 17 percent. The other two divisions have investment opportunities that yield only 16 percent. The manager of Hola rejects the additional funding. Why would the manager of Hola reject the funds under these circumstances?

e. Calculate the residual income from the investment opportunity available to Hola and explain how residual income could be used to encourage the manager to accept the additional funds.

Solution to Requirement a

Costa should use operating income because net income frequently includes items over which management has no control, such as the loss on sale of land.

Solution to Requirement b

Costa should use operating assets because total assets frequently includes items over which management has no control, such as assets not currently in use.

Solution to Requirement c
ROI = Operating Income / Operating Assets = $25,560 / $142,000 = 18%

Solution to Requirement d
Since the rate of return on the investment opportunity (17 percent) is below the Hola's current ROI (18 percent), accepting the opportunity would decrease Hola's average ROI, which would have a negative effect on the manager's performance evaluation. While it is to the advantage of the company as a whole for Hola to accept the investment opportunity, it will reflect negatively on the manager to do so. This phenomenon is called *suboptomization.*

Solution to Requirement e
Operating income from the investment opportunity is $13,600 ($80,000 × .17)

Residual income = Operating income − (Operating assets × Desired ROI)
Residual income = $13,600 − ($80,000 × .15)
Residual income = $13,600 − $12,000
Residual income = $1,600

Since the investment opportunity would increase Hola's residual income, the acceptance of the opportunity would improve the manager's performance evaluation, thereby motivating the manager to accept it.

KEY TERMS

Balanced scorecard *371*
Controllability concept *363*
Cost-based transfer price *374*
Cost center *361*
Decentralization *360*
Economic value added *370*
Investment center *361*
Management by exception *362*
Margin *367*
Market-based transfer price *372*
Negotiated transfer price *374*
Profit center *361*
Residual income *369*
Responsibility accounting *360*
Responsibility center *361*
Responsibility reports *361*
Return on investment *365*
Suboptimization *369*
Transfer price *372*
Turnover *367*

QUESTIONS

1. Pam Kelly says she has no faith in budgets. Her company, Kelly Manufacturing Corporation, spent thousands of dollars to install a sophisticated budget system. One year later the company's expenses are still out of control. She believes budgets simply do not work. How would you respond to Ms. Kelly's beliefs?
2. All travel expenses incurred by Pure Water Pump Corporation are reported only to John Daniels, the company president. Pure Water is a multinational company with five divisions. Are travel expenses reported following the responsibility accounting concept? Explain.
3. What are five potential advantages of decentralization?
4. Who receives responsibility reports? What do the reports include?
5. How does the concept of predominant as opposed to that of absolute control apply to responsibility accounting?
6. How do responsibility reports promote the management by exception doctrine?
7. What is a responsibility center?
8. What are the three types of responsibility centers? Explain how each differs from the others.
9. Carmen Douglas claims that her company's performance evaluation system is unfair. Her company uses return on investment (ROI) to evaluate performance. Ms. Douglas says that even though her ROI is lower than another manager's, her performance is far superior. Is it possible that Ms. Douglas is correct? Explain your position.
10. What two factors affect the computation of return on investment?
11. What three ways can a manager increase the return on investment?
12. How can a residual income approach to performance evaluation reduce the likelihood of suboptimization?
13. Is it true that the manager with the highest residual income is always the best performer?

14. Why are transfer prices important to managers who are evaluated based on profitability criteria?

15. What are three approaches to establishing transfer prices? List the most desirable approach first and the least desirable last.

16. If cost is the basis for transfer pricing, should actual or standard cost be used? Why?

EXERCISES—SERIES A

All Exercises in Series A are available with McGraw-Hill's Homework Manager.

EXERCISE 9–1A *Organization Chart and Responsibilities* L.O. 1

The production manager is responsible for the assembly, cleaning, and finishing departments. The executive vice president reports directly to the president but is responsible for the activities of the production department, the finance department, and the sales department. The sales manager is responsible for the advertising department.

Required
Arrange this information into an organization chart and indicate the responsibility levels involved.

EXERCISE 9–2A *Responsibility Report* L.O. 5

Grover Department Store is divided into three major departments: Men's Clothing, Women's Clothing, and Home Furnishings. Each of these three departments is supervised by a manager who reports to the general manager. The departments are subdivided into different sections managed by floor supervisors. The Home Furnishings Department has three floor supervisors, one for furniture, one for lamps, and one for housewares. The following items were included in the company's most recent responsibility report.

Travel expenses for the housewares buyer
Seasonal decorations for the furniture section
Revenues for the Home Furnishings Department
Administrative expenses for the Men's Clothing Department
Utility cost allocated to the Home Furnishings Department
Cost of part-time Christmas help for the Women's Department
Delivery expenses for furniture purchases
Salaries for the sales staff in the lamp section
Storewide revenues
Salary of the general manager
Salary of the Men's Clothing Department manager
Allocated companywide advertising expense
Depreciation on the facility

Required
Which items are likely to be the responsibility of the Home Furnishings Department manager?

EXERCISE 9–3A *Organization Chart and Controllable Costs* L.O. 1, 5

Jewel Company has employees with the following job titles.

President of the company
Vice president of marketing
Product manager
Controller
Vice president of manufacturing
Treasurer
Regional sales manager
Personnel manager
Cashier
Vice president of finance
Fringe benefits manager
Board of directors
Production supervisors
Vice president of administration
Sales office manager

Required

a. Design an organization chart using these job titles.

b. Identify some possible controllable costs for the person holding each job title.

L.O. 1, 3

EXERCISE 9–4A *Income Statement for Internal Use*

Geis Company has provided the following 2005 data.

Budget	
Sales	$408,000
Variable product costs	164,000
Variable selling expense	48,000
Other variable expenses	4,000
Fixed product costs	16,800
Fixed selling expense	25,200
Other fixed expenses	2,400
Interest expense	900
Variances	
Sales	8,800 U
Variable product costs	4,000 F
Variable selling expense	2,400 U
Other variable expense	1,200 U
Fixed product costs	240 F
Fixed selling expense	400 F
Other fixed expenses	160 U
Interest expense	100 F

Required

Prepare in good form a budgeted and actual income statement for internal use. Separate operating income from net income in the statements.

L.O. 1, 3

EXERCISE 9–5A *Evaluating a Cost Center Including Flexible Budgeting Concepts*

Herrera Medical Equipment Company makes a blood pressure measuring kit. Cedric Major is the production manager. The production department's static budget and actual results for 2005 follow.

	Static Budget	Actual Results
	20,000 kits	*21,000 kits*
Direct materials	$150,000	$161,700
Direct labor	135,000	138,600
Variable manufacturing overhead	35,000	44,600
Total variable costs	320,000	344,900
Fixed manufacturing cost	180,000	178,000
Total manufacturing cost	$500,000	$522,900

Required

a. Convert the static budget into a flexible budget.
b. Use the flexible budget to evaluate Mr. Major's performance.
c. Explain why Mr. Major's performance evaluation does not include sales revenue and net income.

L.O. 2, 3

EXERCISE 9–6A *Evaluating a Profit Center*

Shelia Parham, the president of Best Toys Corporation, is trying to determine this year's pay raises for the store managers. Best Toys has seven stores in the southwestern United States. Corporate headquarters purchases all toys from different manufacturers globally and distributes them to individual stores. Additionally, headquarters makes decisions regarding location and size of stores. These practices allow Best Toys to receive volume discounts from vendors and to implement coherent marketing strategies. Within a set of general guidelines, store managers have the flexibility to adjust product prices and hire local employees. Ms. Parham is considering three possible performance measures for evaluating the individual stores: cost of goods sold, return on sales (net income divided by sales), and return on investment.

Required

a. Using the concept of controllability, advise Ms. Parham about the best performance measure.
b. Explain how a balanced scorecard can be used to help Ms. Parham.

EXERCISE 9–7A ***Return on Investment*** **L.O. 6**

An investment center of Milton Corporation shows an operating income of $7,200 on total operating assets of $30,000.

Required

Compute the return on investment.

EXERCISE 9–8A ***Return on Investment*** **L.O. 6**

Giddens Company calculated its return on investment as 15 percent. Sales are now $180,000, and the amount of total operating assets is $300,000.

Required

a. If expenses are reduced by $18,000 and sales remain unchanged, what return on investment will result?
b. If both sales and expenses cannot be changed, what change in the amount of operating assets is required to achieve the same result?

EXERCISE 9–9A ***Residual Income*** **L.O. 7**

Tyler Corporation has a desired rate of return of 10 percent. Andy Tan is in charge of one of Tyler's three investment centers. His center controlled operating assets of $3,000,000 that were used to earn $390,000 of operating income.

Required

Compute Mr. Tan's residual income.

EXERCISE 9–10A ***Residual Income*** **L.O. 7**

Brannon Cough Drops operates two divisions. The following information pertains to each division for 2005.

	Division A	Division B
Sales	$180,000	$60,000
Operating income	$ 18,000	$ 9,600
Average operating assets	$ 72,000	$48,000
Company's desired rate of return	20%	20%

Required

a. Compute each division's residual income.
b. Which division increased the company's profitability more?

EXERCISE 9–11A ***Return on Investment and Residual Income*** **L.O. 6, 7**

Required

Supply the missing information in the following table for Haley Company.

Sales	$300,000
ROI	?
Operating assets	?
Operating income	?
Turnover	2
Residual income	?
Margin	0.10
Desired rate of return	18%

EXERCISE 9–12A ***Comparing Return on Investment with Residual Income*** **L.O. 6, 7**

The Spokane Division of Cascade, Inc., has a current ROI of 20 percent. The company target ROI is 15 percent. The Spokane Division has an opportunity to invest $4,000,000 at 18 percent but is reluctant to do so because its ROI will fall to 19.2 percent. The present investment base for the division is $6,000,000.

Required

Demonstrate how Cascade can motivate the Spokane Division to make the investment by using the residual income method.

Appendix

L.O. 8 EXERCISE 9–13A *Transfer Pricing*

Kader Company has two divisions, A and B. Division A manufactures 8,000 units of product per month. The cost per unit is calculated as follows.

Variable costs	$ 8
Fixed costs	24
Total cost	$32

Division B uses the product created by Division A. No outside market for Division A's product exists. The fixed costs incurred by Division A are allocated headquarters-level facility-sustaining costs. The manager of Division A suggests that the product be transferred to Division B at a price of at least $32 per unit. The manager of Division B argues that the same product can be purchased from another company for $19 per unit and requests permission to do so.

Required

a. Should Kader allow the manager of Division B to purchase the product from the outside company for $16 per unit? Explain.

b. Assume you are the president of the company. Write a brief paragraph recommending a resolution of the conflict between the two divisional managers.

L.O. 8 EXERCISE 9–14A *Transfer Pricing and Avoidable Cost*

The Tire Division of Durable Tires Company (DTC) produces a radial all-purpose tire for trucks that it sells wholesale to automotive manufacturers. Per unit sales and cost data for this tire follow.

Selling price	$54
Unit-level variable cost	$36
Corporate-level fixed cost	$15
Manufacturing capacity	30,000 units
Average sales	25,000 units

DTC also has a Trucking Division that provides delivery service for outside independent businesses as well as divisions of DTC. The Trucking Division, which uses approximately 4,000 tires a year, presently buys tires for its trucks from an outside supplier for $51 per tire.

Required

Recommend a transfer price range for the truck tires that would be profitable for both divisions if the Trucking Division purchased the tires internally. Assume that both divisions operate as investment centers.

L.O. 8 EXERCISE 9–15A *Transfer Pricing and Fixed Cost per Unit*

The Saginaw Parts Division of Sims Company plans to set up a facility with the capacity to make 10,000 units annually of an electronic computer part. The avoidable cost of making the part is as follows.

Costs	Total	Cost per Unit
Variable cost	$300,000	$30
Fixed cost	80,000	8 (at capacity)

Required

a. Assume that Sims' Borden Division is currently purchasing 6,000 of the electronic parts each year from an outside supplier at a market price of $50. What would be the financial consequence to Sims if the Saginaw Parts Division makes the part and sells it to the Borden Division? What range of transfer prices would increase the financial performance of both divisions?

b. Suppose that the Borden Division increases production so that it could use 10,000 units of the part made by the Saginaw Parts Division. How would the change in volume affect the range of transfer prices that would financially benefit both divisions?

PROBLEMS—SERIES A

All Problems in Series A are available with McGraw-Hill's Homework Manager.

PROBLEM 9–16A *Determining Controllable Costs*

L.O. 5

John Crew is the manager of the production department of Strong Corporation. Strong incurred the following costs during 2005.

Production department supplies	$ 8,000
Administrative salaries	300,000
Production wages	652,000
Materials used	529,200
Depreciation on manufacturing equipment	361,600
Corporate-level rental expense	240,000
Property taxes	68,600
Sales salaries	286,800

Required

Prepare a list of expenditures that Mr. Crew controls.

PROBLEM 9–17A *Controllability, Responsibility, and Balanced Scorecard*

L.O. 3, 5

Sally Voigt manages the production division of Yates Corporation. Ms. Voigt's responsibility report for the month of August follows.

	Budget	Actual	Variance	
Controllable costs				
Raw materials	$ 60,000	$ 75,000	$15,000	U
Labor	30,000	41,400	10,500	U
Maintenance	6,000	7,200	1,200	U
Supplies	5,100	3,600	1,500	F
Total	$101,100	$127,200	$25,200	U

The budget had called for 7,500 pounds of raw materials at $8 per pound, and 7,500 pounds were used during August; however, the purchasing department paid $10 per pound for the materials. The wage rate used to establish the budget was $30 per hour. On August 1, however, it increased to $36 as the result of an inflation index provision in the union contract. Furthermore, the purchasing department did not provide the materials needed in accordance with the production schedule, which forced Ms. Voigt to use 100 hours of overtime at a $54 rate. The projected 1,000 hours of labor in the budget would have been sufficient had it not been for the 100 hours of overtime. In other words, 1,100 hours of labor were used in August.

Required

a. When confronted with the unfavorable variances in her responsibility report, Ms. Voigt argued that the report was unfair because it held her accountable for materials and labor variances that she did *not* control. Is she correct? Comment specifically on the materials and labor variances.

b. Prepare a responsibility report that reflects the cost items that Ms. Voigt controlled during August.

c. Will the changes in the revised responsibility report require corresponding changes in the financial statements? Explain.

d. Explain how a balanced scorecard may be used to improve the performance evaluation.

PROBLEM 9–18A *Performance Reports and Evaluation*

L.O. 3, 4, 5

eXcel

www.mhhe.com/edmonds3e

Hester Corporation has four divisions: the assembly division, the processing division, the machining division, and the packing division. All four divisions are under the control of the vice president of manufacturing. Each division has a manager and several departments that are directed by supervisors. The chain of command runs downward from vice president to division manager to supervisor. The processing division is composed of the paint and finishing departments. The May responsibility reports for the supervisors of these departments follow.

CHECK FIGURE
a. Total controllable costs: $407,160

	Budgeted*	Actual	Variance	
Paint Department				
Controllable costs				
Raw materials	$28,800	$ 30,000	$1,200	U
Labor	60,000	66,000	6,000	U
Repairs	4,800	3,840	960	F
Maintenance	2,400	2,280	120	F
Total	$96,000	$102,120	$6,120	U
Finishing Department				
Controllable costs				
Raw materials	$22,800	$ 22,560	$ 240	F
Labor	43,200	39,600	3,600	F
Repairs	2,880	3,240	360	U
Maintenance	1,680	2,040	360	U
Total	$70,560	$ 67,440	$3,120	F

*Hester uses flexible budgets for performance evaluation.

Other pertinent cost data for May follow.

	Budgeted*	Actual
Cost data of other divisions		
Assembly	$324,000	$318,240
Machining	282,000	288,480
Packing	421,440	412,920
Other costs associated with		
Processing division manager	240,000	237,600
Vice president of manufacturing	132,000	137,040

*Hester uses flexible budgets for performance evaluation.

Required

a. Prepare a responsibility report for the manager of the processing division.

b. Prepare a responsibility report for the vice president of manufacturing.

c. Explain where the $6,000 unfavorable labor variance in the paint department supervisor's report is included in the vice president's report.

d. Based on the responsibility report prepared in Requirement *a,* explain where the processing division manager should concentrate his attention.

L.O. 2

PROBLEM 9–19A *Different Types of Responsibility Centers*

First National Bank is a large municipal bank with several branch offices. The bank's computer department handles all data processing for bank operations. In addition, the bank sells the computer department's expertise in systems development and excess machine time to several small business firms, serving them as a service bureau.

The bank currently treats the computer department as a cost center. The manager of the computer department prepares a cost budget annually for senior bank officials to approve. Monthly operating reports compare actual and budgeted expenses. Revenues from the department's service bureau activities are treated as other income by the bank and are not reflected on the computer department's operating reports. The costs of serving these clients are included in the computer department reports, however.

The manager of the computer department has proposed that bank management convert the computer department to a profit or investment center.

Required

a. Describe the characteristics that differentiate a cost center, a profit center, and an investment center from each other.

b. Would the manager of the computer department be likely to conduct the operations of the department differently if the department were classified as a profit center or an investment center rather than as a cost center? Explain.

PROBLEM 9–20A *Comparing Return on Investment and Residual Income*

L.O. 6, 7

CHECK FIGURE
c. 18%

Costa Corporation operates three investment centers. The following financial statements apply to the investment center named Hola Division.

HOLA DIVISION
Income Statement
For the Year Ended December 31, 2006

Sales Revenue	$78,695
Cost of Goods Sold	(50,810)
Gross Margin	27,885
Operating Expenses	
Selling Expenses	(1,200)
Depreciation Expense	(1,125)
Operating Income	25,560
Nonoperating Expense	
Gain of Sale of Land	(3,200)
Net Income	$22,360

HOLA DIVISION
Balance Sheet
As of December 31, 2006

Assets	
Cash	$ 8,089
Accounts Receivable	22,870
Merchandise Inventory	33,460
Equipment Less Accum. Dep.	77,581
Non-Operating Assets	8,250
Total Assets	$150,250
Liabilities	
Accounts Payable	$ 5,000
Notes Payable	58,000
Stockholders' Equity	
Common Stock	55,000
Retained Earnings	32,250
Total Liab. and Stk. Equity	$150,250

Required

a. Should operating income or net income be used to determine the rate of return (ROI) for the Hola investment center? Explain your answer.
b. Should operating assets or total assets be used to determine the ROI for the Hola investment center? Explain your answer.
c. Calculate the ROI for Hola.
d. Costa has a desired ROI of 15 percent. Headquarters has $80,000 of funds to assign its investment centers. The manager of the Hola division has an opportunity to invest the funds at an ROI of 17 percent. The other two divisions have investment opportunities that yield only 16 percent. Even so, the manager of Hola rejects the additional funding. Explain why the manager of Hola would reject the funds under these circumstances.
e. Explain how residual income could be used to encourage the manager to accept the additional funds.

PROBLEM 9–21A *Return on Investment*

L.O. 6

www.mhhe.com/edmonds3e

CHECK FIGURES
c. 15%
d. (3) 18.75%

Tipton Corporation's balance sheet indicates that the company has $300,000 invested in operating assets. During 2006, Tipton earned operating income of $45,000 on $600,000 of sales.

Required

a. Compute Tipton's margin for 2006.
b. Compute Tipton's turnover for 2006.
c. Compute Tipton's return on investment for 2006.
d. Recompute Tipton's ROI under each of the following independent assumptions.
  (1) Sales increase from $600,000 to $750,000, thereby resulting in an increase in operating income from $45,000 to $60,000.

(2) Sales remain constant, but Tipton reduces expenses resulting in an increase in operating income from $45,000 to $48,000.

(3) Tipton is able to reduce its invested capital from $300,000 to $240,000 without affecting operating income.

L.O. 6, 7

PROBLEM 9–22A *Comparing Return on Investment and Residual Income*

CHECK FIGURES

b. The ROI would decline to 19.60%.

c. RI would increase by $30,000.

The manager of the Cranston Division of Wynn Manufacturing Corporation is currently producing a 20 percent return on invested capital. Wynn's desired rate of return is 16 percent. The Cranston Division has $6,000,000 of capital invested in operating assets and access to additional funds as needed. The manager is considering a new investment in operating assets that will require a $1,500,000 capital commitment and promises an 18 percent return.

Required

a. Would it be advantageous for Wynn Manufacturing Corporation if the Cranston Division makes the investment under consideration?

b. What effect would the proposed investment have on the Cranston Division's return on investment? Show computations.

c. What effect would the proposed investment have on the Cranston Division's residual income? Show computations.

d. Would return on investment or residual income be the better performance measure for the Cranston Division's manager? Explain.

Appendix

L.O. 8

PROBLEM 9–23A *Transfer Pricing*

CHECK FIGURE

a. The price should range between $18 and $30.

Rankin Radio Corporation is a subsidiary of Gibon Companies. Rankin makes car radios that it sells to retail outlets. It purchases speakers for the radios from outside suppliers for $30 each. Recently, Gibon acquired the Levine Speaker Corporation, which makes car radio speakers that it sells to manufacturers. Levine produces and sells approximately 200,000 speakers per year which represents 70 percent of its operating capacity. At the present volume of activity, each speaker costs $26 to produce. This cost consists of a $18 variable cost component and an $8 fixed cost component. Levine sells the speakers for $32 each. The managers of Rankin and Levine have been asked to consider using Levine's excess capacity to supply Rankin with some of the speakers that it currently purchases from unrelated companies. Both managers are evaluated based on return on investment. Levine's manager suggests that the speakers be supplied at a transfer price of $32 each (the current selling price). On the other hand, Rankin's manager suggests a $26 transfer price, noting that this amount covers total cost and provides Levine a healthy contribution margin.

Required

a. What transfer price would you recommend?

b. Discuss the effect of the intercompany sales on each manager's return on investment.

c. Should Levine be required to use more than excess capacity to provide speakers to Rankin? In other words, should it sell to Rankin some of the 200,000 units that it is currently selling to unrelated companies? Why or why not?

EXERCISES—SERIES B

L.O. 1

EXERCISE 9–1B *Organizational Chart and Responsibilities*

Yesterday Wesson Corporation's board of directors appointed Cheryl Buford as the new president and chief executive officer. This morning, Ms. Buford presented to the board a list of her management team members. The vice presidents are Bill Riggins, regional operations; Dan Nelson, research and development; and Carol Mercer, chief financial officer. Reporting to Mr. Riggins are the directors of American, European, and Asian operations. Reporting to Mr. Nelson are the directors of the Houston, Seattle, and Charlotte laboratories. Reporting to Ms. Mercer are the controller and the treasurer.

Required

Arrange the preceding information into an organization chart and indicate the responsibility levels involved.

EXERCISE 9–2B *Responsibility Report*

L.O. 5

Wesson Corporation divides its operations into three regions: American, European, and Asian. The following items appear in the company's responsibility report.

European director's salary
Revenues of the French branch
Office expenses of the Japanese branch
Corporation president's salary
Asian director's salary
Revenues of the Taiwanese branch
Revenues of the British branch
Office expenses of the French branch
Revenues of the U.S. branch
Administrative expenses of the corporate headquarters
Office expenses of the Taiwanese branch
Office expenses of the Canadian branch
Revenues of the Japanese branch
Revenues of the Canadian branch
Office expenses of the British branch
Office expenses of the U.S. branch
American director's salary

Required
Which items should Wesson include in the responsibility report for the director of Asian operations?

EXERCISE 9–3B *Organizational Chart and Controllable Cost*

L.O. 1, 5

Dan Nelson, Wesson Corporation vice president of research and development, has overall responsibility for employees with the following positions:

Directors of the Houston, Seattle, and Charlotte laboratories
Senior researchers reporting to laboratory directors
A personnel manager in each laboratory
An accounting manager in each laboratory
Research assistants working for senior researchers
Recruiters reporting to a personnel manager
Bookkeepers reporting to an accounting manager

Required
a. Design an organization chart using these job positions.
b. Identify some possible controllable costs for persons holding each of the job positions.

EXERCISE 9–4B *Income Statement for Internal Use*

L.O. 1, 3

Saunders Company has provided the following data for 2006:

Budget	
Sales	$400,000
Variable product costs	120,000
Variable selling expense	39,000
Other variable expenses	8,000
Fixed product costs	56,000
Fixed selling expense	21,000
Other fixed expenses	2,000
Interest expense	1,000
Actual results	
Sales	$414,000
Variable product costs	122,000
Variable selling expense	42,000
Other variable expenses	7,000
Fixed product costs	60,000
Fixed selling expense	19,200
Other fixed expenses	10,000
Interest expense	1,050

Required

a. Prepare in good form a budgeted and actual income statement for internal use. Separate operating income from net income in the statements.

b. Calculate variances and identify them as favorable (F) or unfavorable (U).

L.O. 1

EXERCISE 9–5B *Evaluating a Cost Center (including flexible budgeting concepts)*

Edwin Wingo, president of Wingo Door Products Company, is evaluating the performance of Tim Shirley, the plant manager, for 2005, the last fiscal year. Mr. Wingo is concerned that production costs exceeded budget by over $21,000. He has available the 2005 static budget for the production plant, as well as the actual results, both of which follow:

	Static Budget	Actual Results
	5,000 Doors	5,250 Doors
Direct materials	$200,000	$204,750
Direct labor	85,000	99,750
Variable manufacturing overhead	35,000	34,650
Total variable costs	320,000	339,150
Fixed manufacturing overhead	180,000	178,000
Total manufacturing cost	$500,000	$517,150

Required

a. Convert the static budget into a flexible budget.

b. Use the flexible budget to evaluate Mr. Shirley's performance.

c. Explain why Mr. Shirley's performance evaluation doesn't include sales revenue and net income.

L.O. 2, 5

EXERCISE 9–6B *Evaluating a Profit Center*

Jean Reeder, president of World Travel Company, a travel agency, is seeking a method of evaluating her seven branches. Each branch vice president is authorized to hire employees and devise competitive strategies for the branch territory. Ms. Reeder wonders which of the following three different measures would be most suitable: return on investment, operating income, or return on sales (operating income divided by sales).

Required

a. Using the concept of controllability, advise Ms. Reeder about the best performance measure.

b. Explain how a balanced scorecard can be used for Ms. Reeder.

L.O. 7

EXERCISE 9–7B *Computing Return on Investment*

An Imhof Corporation investment center shows an operating income of $80,000 and an investment in operating assets of $640,000.

Required

Compute the return on investment.

L.O. 6

EXERCISE 9–8B *Return on Investment*

With annual sales of $5,000,000 and operating assets of $2,500,000, Gibbon Company achieved a 10 percent ROI.

Required

a. If Gibbon reduces expenses by $50,000 and sales remain unchanged, what ROI will result?

b. If Gibbon cannot change either sales or expenses, what change in the investment base is required to achieve the same result you calculated for Requirement *a*?

L.O. 7

EXERCISE 9–9B *Computing Residual Income*

Niblett Corporation's desired rate of return is 15 percent. North Division, one of Niblett's five investment centers, earned an operating income of $4,800,000 last year. The division controlled $30,000,000 of operational assets.

Required

Compute North Division's residual income.

EXERCISE 9–10B *Computing Residual Income*

L.O. 7

Quick Oil Change operates two divisions. The following pertains to each division for 2006:

	Houston Division	Dallas Division
Sales	$800,000	$600,000
Operating income	$ 60,000	$ 40,000
Average operating assets	$250,000	$200,000
Company's desired rate of return	15%	15%

Required

a. Compute each division's residual income.

b. Which division increased the company's profitability more?

EXERCISE 9–11B *Supply Missing Information Regarding Return on Investment and Residual Income*

L.O. 6, 7

Required

Supply the missing information in the following table for Tapley Company.

Sales	?
ROI	12%
Investment in operating assets	$500,000
Operating income	?
Turnover	?
Residual income	?
Margin	0.08
Desired rate of return	11%

EXERCISE 9–12B *Contrasting Return on Investment with Residual Income*

L.O. 6, 7

The Boston Division of Massachusetts Garage Doors, Inc., is currently achieving a 16 percent ROI. The company's target ROI is 10 percent. The division has an opportunity to invest in operating assets an additional $600,000 at 13 percent but is reluctant to do so because its ROI will fall to 15.5 percent. The division's present investment in operating assets is $3,000,000.

Required

Explain how management can use the residual income method to motivate the Boston Division to make the investment.

Appendix

EXERCISE 9–13B *Transfer Pricing*

L.O. 6, 7

Welch Company makes household water filtration equipment. The Aquafresh Division manufactures filters. The Sweet Water Division then uses the filters as a component of the final product Welch sells to consumers. The Aquafresh Division has the capacity to produce 8,000 filters per month at the following cost per unit:

Variable costs	$14
Division fixed costs	10
Allocated corporate-level facility-sustaining costs	8
Total cost per filter	$32

Sweet Water currently uses 6,000 Aquafresh filters per month. Jim Sanders, Sweet Water's manager, is not happy with the $32 transfer price charged by Aquafresh. He points out that Sweet Water could purchase the same filters from outside vendors for a market price of only $26. Amy Mead, Aquafresh's manager, refuses to sell the filters to Sweet Water below cost. Mr. Sanders counters that he would be happy to purchase the filters elsewhere. Because Aquafresh does not have other customers for its filters, Ms. Mead appeals to Frank Pell, the president of Welch, for arbitration.

Required

a. Should the president of Welch allow Mr. Sanders to purchase filters from outside vendors for $26 per unit? Explain.

b. Write a brief paragraph describing what Mr. Pell should do to resolve the conflict between the two division managers.

L.O. 8

EXERCISE 9–14B *Transfer Pricing and Avoidable Cost*

Gonzalez Household Equipment Corporation recently acquired two new divisions. The Purdy Division manufactures vacuum cleaner motors. The Oak Mountain Division makes household vacuum cleaners. Each division was formerly an independent company and continues to maintain its own customer base. Purdy Division data pertaining to vacuum cleaner motors follow:

Selling price per motor	$40
Unit-level variable costs per motor	$24
Division-level fixed costs per motor	$6
Corporate-level fixed costs per motor	$4
Manufacturing capacity	54,000 units per year
Average sales	32,000 units per year

The Oak Mountain Division currently buys motors for its vacuum cleaners from an outside supplier at a price of $33 per unit. Oak Mountain uses approximately 20,000 motors per year.

Required

Recommend a transfer price range for the motors that would be profitable for both divisions if the Oak Mountain Division purchased the motors internally. Assume both divisions operate as investment centers.

L.O. 8

EXERCISE 9–15B *Transfer Pricing and Fixed Cost per Unit*

The Murdock Division of Yesso Company currently produces electric fans that desktop computer manufacturers use as cooling components. The Hart Division, which makes laptop computers, has asked the Murdock Division to design and supply 20,000 fans per year for its laptop computers. Hart currently purchases laptop fans from an outside vendor at the price of $28 each. However, Hart is not happy with the vendor's unstable delivery pattern. To accept Hart's order, Murdock would have to purchase additional equipment and modify its plant layout. The additional equipment would enable the company to add 35,000 laptop fans to its annual production. Murdock's avoidable cost of making 20,000 laptop fans follows:

Costs	Total	Per Unit
Variable costs	$200,000	$10
Fixed cost	240,000	12

Required

a. What would be the financial consequence to Yesso Company if the Murdock Division makes the laptop fans and sells them to the Hart Division? What range of transfer prices would increase the financial performance of both divisions?

b. Suppose the Hart Division increases production so that it could use 35,000 Murdock Division laptop fans. How would the change in volume affect the range of transfer prices that would financially benefit both divisions?

PROBLEMS—SERIES B

L.O. 5

PROBLEM 9–16B *Determining Controllable Costs*

At a professional conference just a few days ago, Dick Garrison, the president of Browning Corporation, learned how the concept of controllability relates to performance evaluation. In preparing to put this new knowledge into practice, he reviewed the financial data of the company's sales department.

Salaries of salespeople	$ 560,000
Cost of goods sold	45,000,000
Facility-level corporate costs	820,000
Travel expenses	64,000
Depreciation on equipment	200,000
Salary of the sales manager	120,000
Property taxes	8,000
Telephone expenses	78,000

Required

Help Mr. Garrison prepare a list of expenditures that the sales manager controls.

PROBLEM 9–17B *Controllability, Responsibility, and Balanced Scorecard*

L.O. 3

Patrick Laird, president of Ebitz Corporation, evaluated the performance report of the company's production department. Mr. Laird was confused by some arguments presented by Darlene Rait, the production manager. Some relevant data follow.

Variances	Amount	
Materials usage variance	$200,000	U
Materials price variance	120,000	F
Labor price variance	38,000	F
Labor usage variance	138,000	U
Volume variance	300,000	U

Ms. Rait argues that she had done a great job, noting the favorable materials price variance and labor price variance. She argued that she had had no control over factors causing the unfavorable variances. For example, she argued that the unfavorable materials usage variance was caused by the purchasing department's decision to buy substandard materials that resulted in a substantial amount of spoilage. Moreover, she argued that the unfavorable labor usage variance resulted from the substantial materials spoilage which in turn wasted many labor hours, as did the hiring of underqualified workers by the manager of the personnel department. Finally, she said that the sales department's failure to obtain a sufficient number of customer orders really caused the unfavorable volume variance.

Required

a. What would you do first if you were Patrick Laird?
b. Did Ms. Rait deserve the credit she claimed for the favorable variances? Explain.
c. Was Ms. Rait responsible for the unfavorable variances? Explain.
d. Explain how a balanced scorecard can be used to improve performance evaluation.

PROBLEM 9–18B *Performance Reports and Evaluation*

L.O. 3, 4, 5

The mortgage division of Kemp Financial Services, Inc., is managed by a vice president who supervises three regional operations. Each regional operation has a general manager and several branches directed by branch managers.

The Coleman region has two branches, Cahaba and Garner. The March responsibility reports for the managers of these branches follow.

	Budgeted*	Actual	Variance	
Cahaba Branch				
Controllable costs				
Employee compensation	$288,000	$300,800	$12,800	U
Office supplies	72,000	70,000	2,000	F
Promotions	152,000	128,000	24,000	F
Maintenance	16,000	21,200	5,200	U
Total	$528,000	$520,000	$ 8,000	F
Garner Branch				
Controllable costs				
Employee compensation	$260,000	$250,000	$10,000	F
Office supplies	76,000	84,000	8,000	U
Promotions	144,000	150,000	6,000	U
Maintenance	20,000	19,200	800	F
Total	$500,000	$503,200	$ 3,200	U

*Kemp uses flexible budgets for performance evaluation.

Other pertinent cost data for March follow.

	Budgeted*	Actual
Cost data of other regions		
Helena	$1,400,000	$1,452,000
Alabaster	1,720,000	1,688,000
Other costs controllable by		
Coleman region general manager	280,000	292,000
Vice president of mortgage	384,000	392,000

*Kemp uses flexible budgets for performance evaluation.

Required

a. Prepare a responsibility report for the general manager of the Coleman region.

b. Prepare a responsibility report for the vice president of the mortgage division.

c. Explain where the $24,000 favorable promotions variance in the Cahaba branch manager's report is included in the vice president's report.

d. Based on the responsibility report prepared in Requirement *a,* explain where the Coleman region's general manager should concentrate her attention.

L.O. 2

PROBLEM 9–19B *Different Types of Responsibility Center*

Rosser Industries, Inc., has five different divisions; each is responsible for producing and marketing a particular product line. The electronic division makes cellular telephones, pagers, and modems. The division also buys and sells other electronic products made by outside companies. Each division maintains sufficient working capital for its own operations. The corporate headquarters, however, makes decisions about long-term capital investments.

Required

a. For purposes of performance evaluation, should Rosser classify its electronic division as a cost center, a profit center, or an investment center? Why?

b. Would the manager of the electronic division be likely to conduct the operations of the division differently if the division were classified as a different type of responsibility center than the one you designated in Requirement *a?* Explain.

L.O. 6, 7

PROBLEM 9–20B *Comparing Return on Investment and Residual Income*

Kenton Corporation operates three investment centers. The following financial statements apply to the investment center named Sumter Division.

SUMTER DIVISION
Income Statement
For the Year Ended December 31, 2006

Sales Revenue	$250,975
Cost of Goods Sold	(128,635)
Gross Margin	122,340
Operating Expenses	
Selling Expenses	(13,200)
Administrative Expense	(2,400)
Operating Income	106,740
Nonoperating Expense	
Interest Expense	(6,800)
Net Income	$ 99,940

SUMTER DIVISION
Balance Sheet
As of December 31, 2006

Assets	
Cash	$ 68,360
Accounts Receivable	380,290
Merchandise Inventory	53,750
Equipment Less Accum. Dep.	428,600
Non-Operating Assets	48,000
Total Assets	$979,000
Liabilities	
Accounts Payable	$115,000
Notes Payable	100,000
Stockholders' Equity	
Common Stock	520,000
Retained Earnings	244,000
Total Liab. and Stk. Equity	$979,000

Required

a. Should operating income or net income be used to determine the rate of return (ROI) for the Sumter investment center? Explain your answer.

b. Should operating assets or total assets be used to determine the ROI for the Sumter investment center? Explain your answer.
c. Calculate the ROI for Sumter.
d. Kenton has a desired ROI of 8 percent. Headquarters has $300,000 of funds to assign its investment centers. The manager of the Sumter division has an opportunity to invest the funds at an ROI of 10 percent. The other two divisions have investment opportunities that yield only 9 percent. Even so, the manager of Sumter rejects the additional funding. Explain why the manager of Sumter would reject the funds under these circumstances.
e. Explain how residual income could be used to encourage the manager to accept the additional funds.

PROBLEM 9–21B *Return on Investment*

L.O. 6

Gentry Corporation's balance sheet indicates that the company has $750,000 invested in operating assets. During 2006, Gentry earned $120,000 of operating income on $2,400,000 of sales.

Required

a. Compute Gentry's margin for 2006.
b. Compute Gentry's turnover for 2006.
c. Compute Gentry's return on investment for 2006.
d. Recompute Gentry's ROI under each of the following independent assumptions.
   (1) Sales increase from $2,400,000 to $2,700,000, thereby resulting in an increase in operating income from $120,000 to $141,750.
   (2) Sales remain constant, but Gentry reduces expenses, thereby resulting in an increase in income from $120,000 to $126,000.
   (3) Gentry is able to reduce its operating assets from $750,000 to $720,000 without affecting income.

PROBLEM 9–22B *Comparing Return on Investment and Residual Income*

L.O. 6, 7

Christie House, the manager of Cunny Division, Lockard Corporation, has enjoyed success. Her division's return on investment (ROI) has consistently been 16 percent on a total investment in operating assets of $5,000,000. Valley evaluates its division managers based on ROI. The company's desired ROI is 12 percent. Ms. House is evaluating an opportunity that will require a $1,000,000 investment in additional operating assets and is expected to result in a 13 percent return.

Required

a. Would it be advantageous for Lockard Corporation if Ms. House makes the investment under consideration?
b. What effect will making the proposed investment have on Cunny Division's ROI? Show computations.
c. What effect will making the proposed investment have on Cunny Division's residual income (RI)? Show computations.
d. Would ROI or RI be the better performance measure for Ms. House? Explain.

Appendix

PROBLEM 9–23B *Transfer Pricing*

L.O. 8

Yousuf Electronics Corporation makes a modem that it sells to retail stores for $75 each. The variable cost to produce a modem is $35 each; the total fixed cost is $5,000,000. Yousuf is operating at 80 percent of capacity and is producing 200,000 modems annually. Yousuf's parent company, Marsh Corporation, notified Yousuf's president that another subsidiary company, Kent Technologies, Inc., has begun making computers and can use Yousuf's modem as a part. Kent needs 40,000 modems annually and is able to acquire similar modems in the market for $72 each.

Under instruction from the parent company, the presidents of Yousuf and Kent meet to negotiate a price for the modem. Yousuf insists that its market price is $75 each and will stand firm on that price. Kent, on the other hand, wonders why it should even talk to Yousuf when Kent can get modems at a lower price.

Required

a. What transfer price would you recommend?
b. Discuss the effect of the intercompany sales on each president's return on investment.
c. Should Yousuf be required to use more than excess capacity to provide modems to Kent if Kent's demand increases to 60,000 modems? In other words, should it sell some of the 200,000 modems that it currently sells to unrelated companies to Kent instead? Why or why not?

ANALYZE, THINK, COMMUNICATE

ATC 9–1 BUSINESS APPLICATIONS CASE *Analyzing Segments at Coca-Cola*

The following excerpt is from **Coca-Cola Company's** 2002 annual report filed with the SEC.

Management evaluates the performance of its operating segments separately to individually monitor the different factors affecting financial performance. Segment profit or loss includes substantially all the segment's costs of production, distribution and administration. Our Company typically manages and evaluates equity investments and related income on a segment level. However, we manage certain significant investments, such as our equity interests in Coca-Cola Enterprises, at the Corporate segment. Our Company manages income taxes on a global basis. We manage financial costs, such as exchange gains and losses and interest income and expense, on a global basis at the Corporate segment. Thus, we evaluate segment performance based on profit or loss before income taxes and cumulative effect of accounting change.

Below are selected segment data for Coca-Cola Company for the 2002 and 2001 fiscal years.

	North America	Africa	Europe, Eurasia & Middle East	Latin America	Asia
2002 Fiscal Year					
Net operating revenues	$6,264	$684	$5,262	$2,089	$5,054
Segment income before taxes and effect of accounting change	1,515	187	1,540	1,081	1,848
Identifiable operating assets	4,999	565	4,576	1,205	2,370
2001 Fiscal Year					
Net operating revenues	$5,729	$633	$3,961	$2,181	$4,861
Segment income before taxes and effect of accounting change	1,472	262	1,413	1,279	1,808
Identifiable operating assets	4,738	517	2,292	1,681	2,121

Required

a. Compute the ROI for each of Coke's geographical segments for each fiscal year. Which segment appears to have the best performance during 2002 based on their ROI's? Which segment showed the most improvement from 2001 to 2002?

b. Assuming Coke's management expects a minimum return of 20 percent, calculate the residual income for each segment for each fiscal year. Which segment appears to have the best performance based on their residual incomes? Which segment showed the most improvement from 2001 to 2002?

c. Explain why the segment with the highest ROI is not the segment with the highest residual income.

d. Assume the management of Coke is considering a major expansion effort for the next five years. On which geographic segment would you recommend Coke focus its expansion efforts? Explain the rationale for your answer.

ATC 9–2 GROUP ASSIGNMENT *Return on Investment versus Residual Income*

Bellco, a division of Becker International Corporation, is operated under the direction of Antoin Sedatt. Bellco is an independent investment center with approximately $72,000,000 of assets that generate approximately $8,640,000 in annual net income. Becker International has additional investment capital of $12,000,000 that is available for the division managers to invest. Mr. Sedatt is aware of an investment opportunity that will provide an 11 percent annual net return. Becker International's desired rate of return is 10 percent.

Required

Divide the class into groups of four or five students and then organize the groups into two sections. Assign Task 1 to the first section and Task 2 to the second section.

Group Tasks

1. Assume that Mr. Sedatt's performance is evaluated based on his ability to maximize return on investment (ROI). Compute ROI using the following two assumptions: Bellco retains its current asset size and Bellco accepts and invests the additional $12,000,000 of assets. Determine whether

Mr. Sedatt should accept the opportunity to invest additional funds. Select a spokesperson to present the decision made by the group.

2. Assume that Mr. Sedatt's performance is evaluated based on his ability to maximize residual income. Compute residual income using the following two assumptions: Bellco retains its current asset base and Bellco accepts and invests the additional $12,000,000 of assets. Determine whether Mr. Sedatt should accept the opportunity to invest additional funds. Select a spokesperson to present the decision made by the group.
3. Have a spokesperson from one of the groups in the first section report the two ROIs and the group's recommendation for Mr. Sedatt. Have the groups in this section reach consensus on the ROI and the recommendation.
4. Have a spokesperson from the second section report the two amounts of residual income and disclose the group's recommendation for Mr. Sedatt. Have this section reach consensus on amounts of residual income.
5. Which technique (ROI or residual income) is more likely to result in suboptimization?

RESEARCH ASSIGNMENT *Centralized or Decentralized Management* ACT 9–3

The Curious Accountant story in this chapter related how one company, **The Home Depot**, grew from a small business into a large business in about 20 years. Another company that has experienced explosive growth since its founding in 1971 is **Bed Bath & Beyond, Inc.** Read the article "What's Beyond for Bed Bath & Beyond?" by Nanette Byrnes that appears on pages 46 and 50 of the January 19, 2004, issue of *BusinessWeek* and answer the following questions.

Required

a. Does the management at Bed Bath & Beyond operate using a centralized or decentralized organizational style?

b. Give specific examples from the article to support your conclusion in requirement (a).

c. Some analysts think Bed Bath & Beyond may not be able to maintain its historic growth rate into the future. What are some of their concerns, and how might a centralized or decentralized management style affect these issues?

d. Based on the related article, "Like Father Like Son," that appears next to the Bed Bath & Beyond story, what role do the children of the founders of Bed Bath & Beyond play at the company, and what are the reasons for this?

WRITING ASSIGNMENT *Transfer Pricing* ATC 9–4

Green Lawn Mower, Inc., recently acquired Hallit Engines, a small engine manufacturing company. Green's president believes in decentralization and intends to permit Hallit to continue to operate as an independent entity. However, she has instructed the manager of Green's lawn mower assembly division to investigate the possibility of purchasing engines from Hallit instead of using the current third-party supplier. Hallit has excess capacity. The current full cost to produce each engine is $96. The avoidable cost of making engines is $78 per unit. The assembly division, which currently pays the third party supplier $90 per engine, offers to purchase engines from Hallit at the $90 price. Hallit's president refuses the offer, stating that his company's engines are superior to those the third party supplier provides. Hallit's president believes that the transfer price should be based on the market price for independent customers which is $132 per engine. The manager of the assembly division agrees that Hallit's engines are higher quality than those currently being used but notes that Green's customer base is in the low-end, discount market. Putting more expensive engines on Green mowers would raise the price above the competition and would hurt sales. Green's president tries to negotiate a settlement between the assembly manager and Hallit's president, but the parties are unable to agree on a transfer price.

Required

a. Assuming that Green makes and sells 40,000 lawn mowers per year, what is the cost of suboptimization resulting from the failure to establish a transfer price?

b. Assume that you are a consultant asked by the president of Green to recommend whether a transfer price should be arbitrarily imposed. Write a brief memo that includes your recommendation and your justification for making it.

ETHICAL DILEMMA *Manipulating Return on Investment and Residual Income* ATC 9–5

The October 5, 1998, issue of *Business Week* includes the article "Who Can You Trust?" authored by Sarah Bartlett. Among other dubious accounting practices, the article describes a trick known as the "big bath," which occurs when a company makes huge unwarranted asset write-offs that drastically overstate expenses. Outside auditors (CPAs) permit companies to engage in the practice because the assets being written off are of questionable value. Because the true value of the assets cannot be validated, auditors have little recourse but to accept the valuations suggested by management. Recent examples of questionable write-offs include **Motorola's** $1.8 billion restructuring charge and the multibillion-dollar write-offs for "in-process" research taken by high-tech companies such as **Compaq Computer Corp.** and **WorldCom, Inc.**

Required

a. Why would managers want their companies to take a big bath? (*Hint:* Consider how a big bath affects return on investment and residual income in the years following the write-off.)

b. Annual reports are financial reports issued to the public. The reports are the responsibility of auditors who are CPAs who operate under the ethical standards promulgated by the American Institute of Certified Public Accountants. As a result, attempts to manipulate annual report data are not restricted by the Institute of Management Accountants Standards of Ethical Conduct shown in Exhibit 1-13 of Chapter 1. Do you agree or disagree with this conclusion? Explain your position.

ATC 9–6 SPREADSHEET ASSIGNMENT *Using Excel*

Waldon Corporation's balance sheet shows that the company has $600,000 invested in operating assets. During 2001, Waldon earned $120,000 on $960,000 of sales. The company's desired return on investment (ROI) is 12 percent.

Required

a. Construct a spreadsheet to calculate ROI and residual income using these data. Build the spreadsheet using formulas so that the spreadsheet could be used as a template for any ROI or residual income problem. The following screen capture shows how to construct the template.

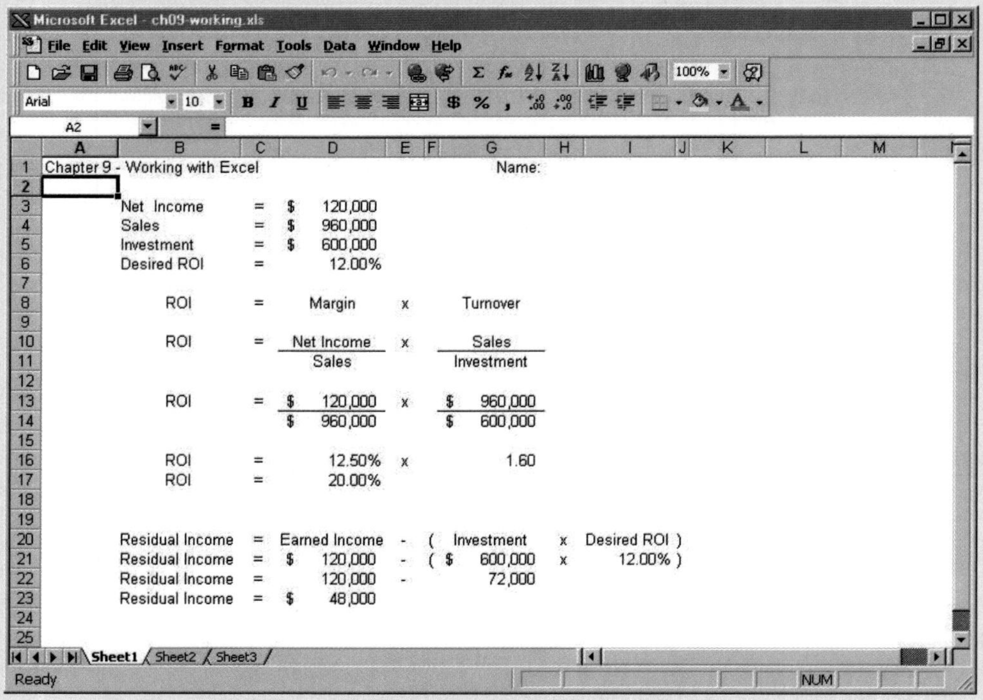

Spreadsheet Tips

(1) The cells below row 12 that show numbers should all be based on formulas. This allows changes in the data rows 3 to 6 to be automatically recalculated.

(2) The parentheses in columns F and J have been entered as text in columns that have a column width of 1.

SPREADSHEET ASSIGNMENT *Mastering Excel*

ATC 9–7

The Pillar Manufacturing Company has three identified levels of authority and responsibility. The organization chart as of December 31, 2004, appears as follows:

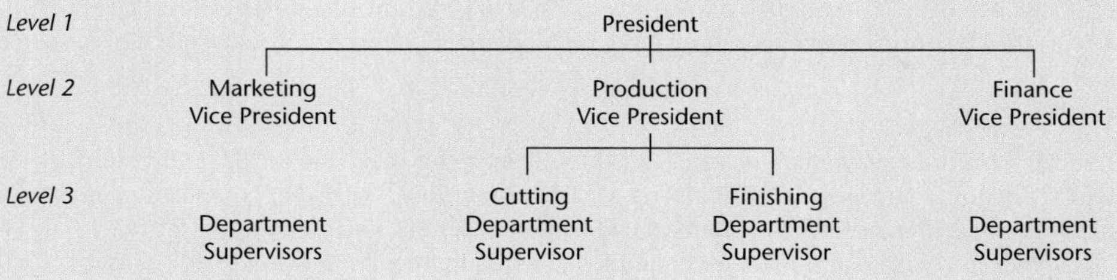

Pertinent expenses for Level 3 follow:

	Budget	Actual
Finishing Department		
Wages expense	$6,240	$6,000
Direct materials	2,300	2,400
Supplies	840	980
Small tools	1,300	1,140
Other	700	820

Pertinent expenses for Level 2 follow:

	Budget	Actual
Production Department		
Administrative expenses	$ 1,200	$ 1,400
Supervisory salaries	5,800	5,200
Cutting Department	6,800	6,420
Finishing Department	11,380	11,340

Pertinent expenses for Level 1 follow:

	Budget	Actual
President's Office Expense		
Supervisory salaries	$ 4,900	$ 5,100
Clerical staff	800	400
Other expenses	600	700
Production Department	25,180	24,360
Marketing Department	8,850	8,300
Finance Department	5,900	6,220

Required

a. Construct a spreadsheet that shows responsibility reports for the finishing department supervisor, the production vice president, and the president.

b. Include formulas in the responsibility reports that illustrate the interrelationships between these reports. For example, changes in the finishing department report should be automatically reflected in the production department report.

Spreadsheet Tip

(1) Use the absolute value function [=ABS(value)] in the formulas that calculate the variances.

COMPREHENSIVE PROBLEM

Assume Magnificent Modems (MM) is a division of Gilmore Business Products (GBP). GBP used ROI as the primary measure of managerial performance. GBP has a desired return on investment (ROI) of 3 percent. The company has $100,000 of investment funds to be assigned to its divisions. The President of MM is aware of an investment opportunity for these funds that is expected to yield an ROI of 3.5 percent.

Required

a. Explain why you believe the President of MM will accept or reject the $100,000 investment opportunity. Support your answer by calculating MM's existing ROI. Base your computation on the information contained in the income statement and balance sheet that you prepared in Chapter 1 (page 47).

b. Name the term used to describe the condition that exists in Requirement *a*. Provide a brief definition of this term.

c. If GBP changes its performance measurement criteria from ROI to residual income (RI), will the new evaluation approach affect the President's decision to accept or reject the $100,000 investment opportunity? Support your answer by calculating MM's residual income for the investment opportunity.

CHAPTER *ten*

PLANNING FOR CAPITAL INVESTMENTS

LEARNING *objectives*

After you have mastered the material in this chapter you will be able to:

1 Explain the time value of money concept and apply it to capital investment decisions.

2 Use present value tables to determine the present value of future cash flows.

3 Use computer software in determining present values.

4 Determine and interpret the net present value of an investment opportunity.

5 Determine the internal rate of return of an investment opportunity.

6 Determine the payback period for an investment opportunity.

7 Determine the unadjusted rate of return for an investment opportunity.

8 Conduct a postaudit of a completed investment.

THE *curious* ACCOUNTANT

Ginger and Fred want to replace the windows in the older house they purchased recently. The company they have talked to about doing the work, RWC, claims that their new windows will reduce Ginger and Fred's heating and cooling costs by around 33 percent. RWC also estimates that they will get back 70 percent of the cost of the new windows when they sell their house, and their real estate agent verifies that this is a good estimate. The new windows will cost $10,000.

The couple gathered the following information to help them make their decision. The heating and cooling costs for Fred and Ginger's house average around $1,800 per year, so they expect to save $600 on these costs per year if they get the new windows. The new windows should also increase the resale value by $7,000 (.70 × $10,000) when they decide to move. They expect to stay in this house for 10 years, so the total savings in energy costs are estimated at $6,000 (10 × $600). These savings, along with the higher resale value, bring the total return on their investment to $13,000 ($6,000 + $7,000).

To pay for the windows they would have to withdraw the money from a mutual fund that has only earned an average annual return of 4 percent over the past few years. They are hesitant about liquidating the mutual fund, but think that spending $10,000 today in order to receive future savings and income of $13,000 seems like a good deal.

Can Fred and Ginger simply compare the $13,000 future cash inflows to the $10,000 cost of the windows in order to decide if replacing them is a good idea? If not, what analysis should they perform in order to make their decision? (Answer on page 413.)

CHAPTER *opening*

The president of EZ Rentals (EZ) is considering expanding the company's rental service business to include LCD projectors that can be used with notebook computers. A marketing study forecasts that renting projectors could generate revenue of $200,000 per year. The possibility of increasing revenue is alluring, but EZ's president has a number of unanswered questions. How much do the projectors cost? What is their expected useful life? Will they have a salvage value? Does EZ have the money to buy them? Does EZ have the technical expertise to support the product? How much will training cost? How long will customer demand last? What if EZ buys the projectors and they become technologically obsolete? How quickly will EZ be able to recover the investment? Are there more profitable ways to invest EZ's funds?

Spending large sums of money that will have long-term effects on company profits makes most managers anxious. What if a cell phone manufacturer spends millions of dollars to build a factory in the United States and its competitors locate their manufacturing facilities in countries that provide cheap labor? The manufacturer's cell phones will be overpriced, but it cannot move overseas because it cannot find a buyer for the factory. What if a pharmaceutical company spends millions of dollars to develop a drug which then fails to receive FDA approval? What if a communications company installs underground cable but satellite transmission steals its market? What if a company buys computer equipment that rapidly becomes technologically obsolete? Although these possibilities may be remote, they can be expensive when they do occur. For example, Wachovia Bank's 1997 annual report discloses a $70 million dollar write-off of computer equipment. This chapter discusses some of the analytical techniques companies use to evaluate major investment opportunities.

Capital Investment Decisions

LO1 Explain the time value of money concept and apply it to capital investment decisions.

Purchases of long-term operational assets are **capital investments.** Capital investments differ from stock and bond investments in an important respect. Investments in stocks and bonds can be sold in organized markets such as the New York Stock Exchange. In contrast, investments in capital assets normally can be recovered only by using those assets. Once a company purchases a capital asset, it is committed to that investment for an extended period of time. If the market turns sour, the company is stuck with the consequences. It may also be unable to seize new opportunities because its capital is committed. Business profitability ultimately hinges, to a large extent, on the quality of a few key capital investment decisions.

A capital investment decision is essentially a decision to exchange current cash outflows for the expectation of receiving future cash inflows. For EZ Rentals, purchasing LCD projectors, cash outflows today, provides the opportunity to collect $200,000 per year in rental revenue, cash inflows in the future. Assuming the projectors have useful lives of four years and no salvage value, how much should EZ be willing to pay for the future cash inflows? If you were EZ's president, would you spend $700,000 today to receive $200,000 each year for the next four years? You would give up $700,000 today for the opportunity to receive $800,000 (4 × $200,000) in the future. What if you collect less than $200,000 per year? If revenue is only $160,000 per year, you would lose $60,000 ($700,000 − [4 × $160,000]). Is $700,000 too much to pay for the opportunity to receive $200,000 per year for four years? If $700,000 is too much, would you spend $600,000? If not, how about $500,000? There is no one right answer to these questions. However, understanding the *time value of money* concept can help you develop a rational response.

Time Value of Money

The **time value of money** concept recognizes that *the present value of a dollar received in the future is less than a dollar.* For example, you may be willing to pay only $0.90 today for a promise to receive $1.00 one year from today. The further into the future the receipt is expected to occur, the smaller is its present value. In other words, one dollar to be received two years from today is worth less than one dollar to be received one year from today. Likewise, one dollar to be received three years from today is less valuable than one dollar to be received two years from today, and so on.

The present value of cash inflows decreases as the time until expected receipt increases for several reasons. First, you could deposit today's dollar in a savings account to earn *interest* that increases its total value. If you wait for your money, you lose the opportunity to earn interest. Second, the expectation of receiving a future dollar carries an element of *risk.* Changed conditions may result in the failure to collect. Finally, *inflation* diminishes the buying power of the dollar. In other words, the longer you must wait to receive a dollar, the less you will be able to buy with it.

When a company invests in capital assets, it sacrifices present dollars in exchange for the opportunity to receive future dollars. Since trading current dollars for future dollars is risky, companies expect compensation before they invest in capital assets. The compensation a company expects is called *return on investment (ROI).* As discussed in Chapter 9, ROI is expressed as a percentage of the investment. For example, the ROI for a $1,000 investment that earns annual income of $100 is 10 percent ($100 ÷ $1,000 = 10%).

Determining the Minimum Rate of Return

To establish the minimum expected *return on investment* before accepting an investment opportunity, most companies consider their cost of capital. To attract capital, companies must provide benefits to their creditors and owners. Creditors expect interest payments; owners expect dividends and increased stock value. Companies that earn lower returns than their cost of capital eventually go bankrupt; they cannot continually pay out more than they collect. *The* **cost of capital** *represents the* **minimum rate of return** *on investments.* Calculating the cost of capital is a complex exercise which is beyond the scope of this text. It is addressed in finance courses. We discuss how management accountants *use* the cost of capital to evaluate investment opportunities. Companies describe the cost of capital in a variety of ways: the *minimum rate of return,* the *desired rate of return,* the *required rate of return,* the *hurdle rate,* the *cutoff rate,* or the *discount rate.* These terms are used interchangeably throughout this chapter.

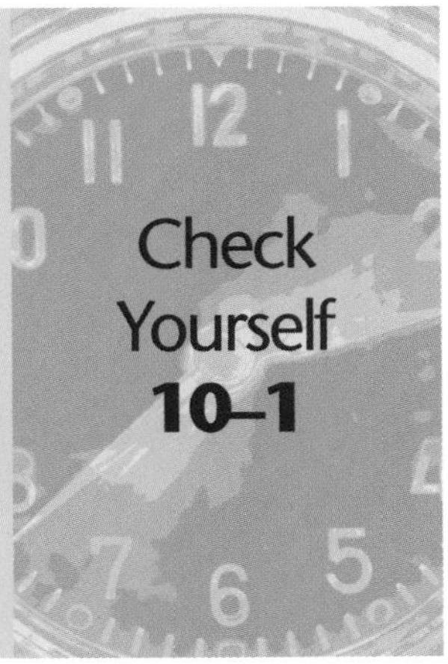

Study the following cash inflow streams expected from two different potential investments.

	Year 1	Year 2	Year 3	Total
Alternative 1	$2,000	$3,000	$4,000	$9,000
Alternative 2	4,000	3,000	2,000	9,000

Based on visual observation alone, which alternative has the higher present value? Why?

Answer Alternative 2 has the higher present value. The size of the discount increases as the length of the time period increases. In other words, a dollar received in year 3 has a lower present value than a dollar received in year 1. Since most of the expected cash inflows from Alternative 2 are received earlier than those from Alternative 1, Alternative 2 has a higher present value even though the total expected cash inflows are the same.

Converting Future Cash Inflows to Their Equivalent Present Values

Given a desired rate of return and the amount of a future cash flow, present value can be determined using algebra. To illustrate, refer to the $200,000 EZ expects to earn the first year it leases LCD projectors.[1] Assuming EZ desires a 12 percent rate of return, what amount of cash would EZ be willing to invest today (present value outflow) to obtain a $200,000 cash inflow at the end of the year (future value)? The answer follows:[2]

$$\begin{aligned} \text{Investment} + (0.12 \times \text{Investment}) &= \text{Future cash inflow} \\ 1.12\ \text{Investment} &= \$200{,}000 \\ \text{Investment} &= \$200{,}000 \div 1.12 \\ \text{Investment} &= \$178{,}571 \end{aligned}$$

If EZ invests $178,571 cash on January 1 and earns a 12 percent return on the investment, EZ will have $200,000 on December 31. An investor who is able to earn a 12 percent return on investment is indifferent between having $178,571 now or receiving $200,000 one year from now. The two options are equal, as shown in the following mathematical proof:

$$\begin{aligned} \text{Investment} + (0.12 \times \text{Investment}) &= \$200{,}000 \\ \$178{,}571 + (0.12 \times \$178{,}571) &= \$200{,}000 \\ \$178{,}571 + 21{,}429 &= \$200{,}000 \\ \$200{,}000 &= \$200{,}000 \end{aligned}$$

LO2 Use present value tables to determine the present value of future cash flows.

Present Value Table for Single-Amount Cash Inflows. The algebra illustrated above is used to convert a one-time future receipt of cash to its present value. One-time receipts of cash are frequently called **single-payment,** or **lump sum,** cash flows. Because EZ desires a 12 percent rate of return, the present value of the first cash inflow is $178,571. We can also determine the present value of a $200,000 single amount (lump sum) at the end of the second, third, and fourth years. Instead of using cumbersome algebraic computations to convert these future values to their present value equivalents, financial analysts frequently use a table of conversion factors to convert future values to their present value equivalents. The table of conversion factors used to convert future values into present values is commonly called a **present value table.**[3] A typical present value table presents columns with different return rates and rows with different periods of time, like Table 1 in the Appendix.

To illustrate using the present value table, locate the conversion factor in Table 1 at the intersection of the 12% column and the one period row. The conversion factor is 0.892857. Multiplying this factor by the $200,000 expected cash inflow yields $178,571 ($200,000 × 0.892857). This is the same value determined algebraically in the previous section of this chapter. The conversion factors in the present value tables simplify converting future values to present values.

The conversion factors for the second, third, and fourth periods are 0.797194, 0.711780, and 0.635518, respectively. These factors are in the 12% column at rows 2, 3, and 4, respectively. Locate these factors in Table 1 of the Appendix. Multiplying the conversion factors by the future cash inflow for each period produces their present value equivalents, shown in Exhibit 10–1. Exhibit 10–1 indicates that investing $607,470 today at a 12 percent rate of return is equivalent to receiving $200,000 per year for four years. Because EZ Rentals desires to earn (at least) a 12 percent rate of return, the company should be willing to pay up to $607,470 to purchase the LCD projectors.

---

[1]The following computations assume the $200,000 cash inflow is received on the last day of each year. In actual practice the timing of cash inflows is less precise and present value computations are recognized to be approximate, not exact.

[2]All computations in this chapter are rounded to the nearest whole dollar.

[3]The present value table is based on the formula $(1 \div [1 + r]^n)$ where r equals the rate of return and n equals the number of periods.

Exhibit 10–1 *Present Value of a $200,000 Cash Inflow to be Received for Four Years*

PV	=	FV	×	Present Value Table Factor	=	Present Value Equivalent
Period 1 PV	=	$200,000	×	0.892857	=	$178,571
Period 2 PV	=	200,000	×	0.797194	=	159,439
Period 3 PV	=	200,000	×	0.711780	=	142,356
Period 4 PV	=	200,000	×	0.635518	=	127,104
Total						$607,470

Present Value Table for Annuities. The algebra described previously for converting equal lump-sum cash inflows to present value equivalents can be further simplified by adding the present value table factors together before multiplying them by the cash inflows. The total of the present value table factors in Exhibit 10–1 is 3.037349 (0.892857 + 0.797194 + 0.711780 + 0.635518). Multiplying this **accumulated conversion factor** by the expected annual cash inflow results in the same present value equivalent of $607,470 ($200,000 × 3.037349). As with lump-sum conversion factors, accumulated conversion factors can be calculated and organized in a table with *columns* for different rates of return and *rows* for different periods of time. Table 2 in the Appendix is a present value table of accumulated conversion factors. Locate the conversion factor at the intersection of the 12% column and the fourth time period row. The factor at this intersection is 3.037349, confirming that the accumulated conversion factors represent the sum of the single-payment conversion factors.

The conversion factors in Table 2 apply to annuities. An **annuity** is a series of cash flows that meets three criteria: (1) equal payment amounts; (2) equal time intervals between payments; and (3) a constant rate of return. For EZ Rentals, the expected cash inflows from renting LCD projectors are all for equivalent amounts ($200,000); the expected intervals between cash inflows are equal lengths of time (one year); and the rate of return for each inflow is constant at 12 percent. The series of expected cash inflows from renting the projectors is therefore an annuity. The present value of an annuity table can be used only if all of these conditions are satisfied.

The present value of an annuity table (Table 2) simplifies converting future cash inflows to their present value equivalents. EZ Rentals can convert the cash inflows as shown in Exhibit 10–1, using four conversion factors, multiplying each conversion factor by the annual cash inflow (four multiplications), and adding the resulting products. In contrast, EZ can recognize that the series of payments is an annuity, which requires multiplying a single conversion factor from Table 2 by the amount of the annuity payment. Regardless of the conversion method, the result is the same (a present value of $607,470). Recall that EZ can also make the conversion using algebra. The table values are derived from algebraic formulas. The present value tables reduce the computations needed to convert future values to present values.

LO3 Use computer software in determining present values.

Software Programs that Calculate Present Values. Software programs offer an even more efficient means of converting future values into present value equivalents. These programs are frequently built into handheld financial calculators and computer spreadsheet programs. As an example, we demonstrate the procedures used in a Microsoft Excel spreadsheet.

An Excel spreadsheet offers a variety of financial functions, one of which converts a future value annuity into its present value equivalent. This present value function uses the syntax *PV(rate,nper,pmt)* in which *rate* is the desired rate of return, *nper* is the number of periods, and *pmt* is the amount of the payment (periodic cash inflow). To convert a future value annuity into its present value equivalent, provide the function with the appropriate amounts for the rate, number of periods, and amount of the annuity (cash inflows) into a spreadsheet cell. Press the Enter key and the present value equivalent appears in the spreadsheet cell.

The power of the spreadsheet to perform computations instantly is extremely useful for answering what-if questions. Exhibit 10–2 demonstrates this power by providing spreadsheet conversions for three different scenarios. The first scenario demonstrates the annuity assumptions

Exhibit 10–2 *Microsoft Excel Spreadsheet Present Value Function*

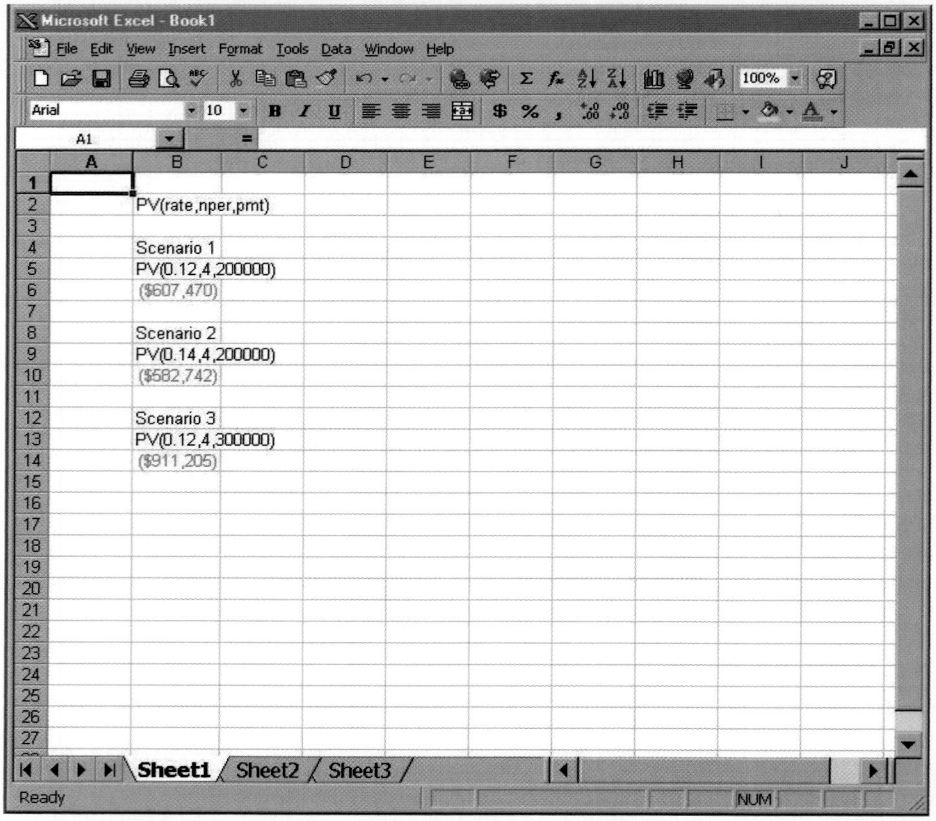

for EZ Rentals, providing the present value equivalent ($607,470) of a four-year cash inflow of $200,000 per year at a 12 percent rate of interest. The present value is a *negative* number. This format indicates that an initial $607,470 *cash outflow* is required to obtain the four-year series of cash inflows. The present value equivalent in Scenario 2 shows the present value if the annuity assumptions reflect a 14 percent, rather than 12 percent, desired rate of return. The present value equivalent in Scenario 3 shows the present value if the annuity assumptions under Scenario 1 are changed to reflect annual cash inflows of $300,000, rather than $200,000. A wide range of scenarios could be readily considered by changing any or all the variables in the spreadsheet function. In each case, the computer does the calculations, giving the manager more time to analyze the data rather than compute it.

Although software is widely used in business practice, the diversity of interfaces used by different calculators and spreadsheet programs makes it unsuitable for textbook presentations. This text uses the present value tables in the Appendix in the text illustrations and the end-of-chapter exercises and problems. If you use software to solve these problems, your answers will be the same. All these tools—formulas, conversion tables, software—are based on the same mathematical principles and will produce the same results.

Ordinary Annuity Assumption. All the conversion methods described above assume the cash inflows occur at the *end* of each accounting period. This distribution pattern is called an **ordinary annuity.**[4] In practice, cash inflows are likely to be received throughout the period, not just at the end. For example, EZ Rentals is likely to collect cash revenue from renting

[4]When equal cash inflows occur at the *beginning* of each accounting period, the distribution is called an *annuity due.* Although some business transactions are structured as annuities due, they are less common than ordinary annuities. This text focuses on the ordinary annuity assumption.

projectors each month rather than in a single lump-sum receipt at the end of each of the four years. Companies frequently use the ordinary annuity assumption in practice because it simplifies time value of money computations. Because capital investment decisions are necessarily based on uncertain projections about future cash inflows, the lives of investment opportunities, and the appropriate rates of return, achieving pinpoint accuracy is impossible. Sacrificing precision for simplicity by using the ordinary annuity assumption is a reasonable trade-off in the decision-making process.

Reinvestment Assumption. The present value computations in the previous sections show that investing $607,470 today at a 12 percent rate of return is equivalent to receiving four individual $200,000 payments at the end of four successive years. Exhibit 10–3 illustrates that a cash inflow of $200,000 per year is equivalent to earning a 12 percent rate of return on a $607,470 investment.[5]

Exhibit 10–3 *Cash Flow Classifications for EZ's Investment in Projectors*

Time Period	(a) Investment Balance During the Year	(b) Annual Cash Inflow	(c) Return on Investment (a × 0.12)	(d) Recovered Investment (b − c)	(e) Year-End Investment Balance (a − d)
1	$607,470	$200,000	$ 72,896	$127,104	$480,366
2	480,366	200,000	57,644	142,356	338,010
3	338,010	200,000	40,561	159,439	178,571
4	178,571	200,000	21,429	178,571	0
Totals		$800,000	$192,530	$607,470	

It is customary to assume that the desired rate of return includes the effects of *compounding*.[6] Saying an investment is "earning the desired rate of return," assumes the cash inflows generated by the investment are reinvested at the desired rate of return. In this case, we are assuming that EZ will reinvest the $200,000 annual cash inflows in other investments that will earn a 12 percent return.

Techniques for Analyzing Capital Investment Proposals

Managers can choose from among numerous analytical techniques to help them make capital investment decisions. Each technique has advantages and disadvantages. A manager may apply more than one technique to a particular proposal to take advantage of more information. Since most companies have computer capabilities that include a variety of standard capital budgeting programs, applying different techniques to the same proposal normally requires little extra effort. Limiting analysis to only one tool could produce biased results. Obtaining more than one perspective offers substantial benefit.

Topic Tackler PLUS 10–1

Net Present Value

LO4 Determine and interpret the net present value of an investment opportunity.

By using the present value conversion techniques described earlier, EZ Rentals' management determined it would be willing to invest $607,470 today (present value) to obtain a four-year, $200,000 future value annuity cash inflow. The $607,470 investment is *not* the cost of the

[5]Exhibit 10–3 is analogous to an amortization table for a long-term note with equal payments of principal and interest.

[6]*Compounding* refers to reinvesting investment proceeds so the total amount of invested capital increases, resulting in even higher returns. For example, assume $100 is invested at a 10 percent compounded annual rate of return. At the end of the first year, the investment yields a $10 return ($100 × 0.10). The $10 return plus any recovered investment is reinvested so that the total amount of invested capital at the beginning of the second year is $110. The return for the second year is $11 ($110 × 0.10). All funds are reinvested so that the return for the third year is $12.10 ([$110 + $11] × 0.10).

LCD projectors, it is the amount EZ is willing to pay for them. The projectors may cost EZ Rentals more or less than their present value. To determine whether EZ should invest in the projectors, management must compare the present value of the future cash inflows ($607,470) to the cost of the projectors (the current cash outflow required to purchase them). Subtracting the cost of the investment from the present value of the future cash inflows determines the **net present value** of the investment opportunity. A positive net present value indicates the investment will yield a rate of return higher than 12 percent. A negative net present value means the return is less than 12 percent.

To illustrate, assume EZ can purchase the projectors for $582,742. Assuming the desired rate of return is 12 percent, EZ should buy them. The net present value of the investment opportunity is computed as follows.

Present value of future cash inflows	$607,470
Cost of investment (required cash outflow)	(582,742)
Net present value	$ 24,728

The positive net present value suggests the investment will earn a rate of return in excess of 12 percent (if cash flows are indeed $200,000 each year). Because the projected rate of return is higher than the desired rate of return, this analysis suggests EZ should accept the investment opportunity.

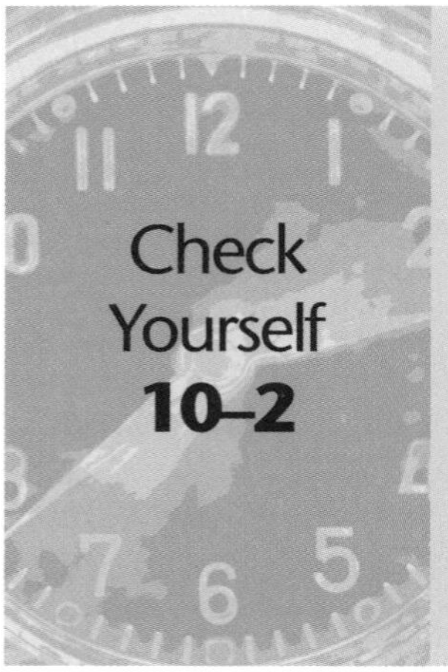

To increase productivity, Wald Corporation is considering the purchase of a new machine that costs $50,000. Wald expects using the machine to increase annual net cash inflows by $12,500 for each of the next five years. Wald desires a minimum annual rate of return of 10 percent on the investment. Determine the net present value of the investment opportunity and recommend whether Wald should acquire the machine.

Answer

Present value of future cash flows = Future cash flow × Table 2 factor ($n = 5, r = 10\%$)

Present value of future cash flows = $12,500 × 3.790787 = $47,385

Net present value = PV of future cash flows − Cost of machine

Net present value = $47,385 − $50,000 = ($2,615)

The negative net present value indicates the investment will yield a rate of return below the desired rate of return. Wald should not acquire the new machine.

Internal Rate of Return

LO5 Determine the internal rate of return of an investment opportunity.

The net present value method indicates EZ's investment in the projectors will provide a return in excess of the desired rate, but it does not provide the actual rate of return to expect from the investment. If EZ's management team wants to know the rate of return to expect from investing in the projectors, it must use the *internal rate of return method.* The **internal rate of return** is the rate at which the present value of cash inflows equals the cash outflows. It is the rate that will produce a zero net present value. For EZ Rentals, the internal rate of return can be determined as follows. First, compute the *present value table factor* for a $200,000 annuity that would yield a $582,742 present value cash outflow (cost of investment).

Present value table factor × $200,000 = $582,742

Present value table factor = $582,742 ÷ $200,000

Present value table factor = 2.91371

Second, since the expected annual cash inflows represent a four-year annuity, scan Table 2 in the Appendix at period $n = 4$. Try to locate the table factor 2.91371. The rate listed at the top of the column in which the factor is located is the internal rate of return. Turn to Table 2 and determine the internal rate of return for EZ Rentals before you read further. The above factor is in the 14 percent column. The difference in the table value (2.913712) and the value computed here (2.91371) is due to truncation. If EZ invests $582,742 in the projectors and they produce a $200,000 annual cash flow for four years, EZ will earn a 14 percent rate of return on the investment.

The *internal rate of return* may be compared with a *desired rate of return* to determine whether to accept or reject a particular investment project. Assuming EZ desires to earn a minimum rate of return of 12 percent, the preceding analysis suggests it should accept the investment opportunity because the internal rate of return (14 percent) is higher than the desired rate of return (12 percent). An internal rate of return below the desired rate suggests management should reject a particular proposal. The desired rate of return is sometimes called the *cutoff rate* or the *hurdle rate.* To be accepted, an investment proposal must provide an internal rate of return higher than the hurdle rate, cutoff rate, or desired rate of return. These terms are merely alternatives for the *cost of capital.* Ultimately, to be accepted, an investment must provide an internal rate of return higher than a company's cost of capital.

Techniques for Measuring Investment Cash Flows

The EZ Rentals example represents a simple capital investment analysis. The investment option involved only one cash outflow and a single annuity inflow. Investment opportunities often involve a greater variety of cash outflows and inflows. The following section of this chapter discusses different types of cash flows encountered in business practice.

Cash Inflows

Cash inflows generated from capital investments come from *four basic sources.* As in the case of EZ Rentals, the most common source of cash inflows is incremental revenue. **Incremental revenue** refers to the *additional* cash inflows from operating activities generated by using additional capital assets. For example, a taxi company expects revenues from taxi fares to increase if it purchases additional taxicabs. Similarly, investing in new apartments should increase rent revenue; opening a new store should result in additional sales revenue.

A second type of cash inflow results from *cost savings.* Decreases in cash outflows have the same beneficial effect as increases in cash inflows. Either way, a firm's cash position improves. For example, purchasing an automated computer system may enable a company to reduce cash outflows for salaries. Similarly, relocating a manufacturing facility closer to its raw materials source can reduce cash outflows for transportation costs.

An investment's *salvage value* provides a third source of cash inflows. Even when one company has finished using an asset, the asset may still be useful to another company. Many assets are sold after a company no longer wishes to use them. The salvage value represents a one-time cash inflow obtained when a company terminates an investment.

Companies can also experience a cash inflow through a *reduction in the amount of* **working capital** needed to support an investment. A certain level of working capital is required to support most business investments. For example, a new retail store outlet requires cash, receivables, and inventory to operate. When an investment is terminated, the decrease in the working capital commitment associated with the investment normally results in a cash inflow.

Cash Outflows

Cash outflows fall into *three primary categories.* One category consists of outflows for the *initial investment.* Managers must be alert to all the cash outflows connected with purchasing a capital asset. The purchase price, transportation costs, installation costs, and training costs are examples of typical cash outflows related to an initial investment.

A second category of cash outflows may result from *increases in operating expenses.* If a company increases output capacity by investing in additional equipment, it may experience higher utility bills, labor costs, and maintenance expenses when it places the equipment into service. These expenditures increase cash outflows.

Third, *increases in working capital* commitments result in cash outflows. Frequently, investments in new assets must be supported by a certain level of working capital. For example, investing in a copy machine requires spending cash to maintain a supply of paper and toner. Managers should treat an increased working capital commitment as a cash outflow in the period the commitment occurs.

Exhibit 10–4 lists the cash inflows and outflows discussed. The list is not exhaustive but does summarize the most common cash flows businesses experience.

Exhibit 10–4 *Typical Cash Flows Associated With Capital Investments*

Inflows	Outflows
1. Incremental revenue	1. Initial investment
2. Cost savings	2. Incremental expenses
3. Salvage values	3. Working capital commitments
4. Recovery of working capital	

Techniques for Comparing Alternative Capital Investment Opportunities

The management of Torres Transfer Company is considering two investment opportunities. One alternative, involving the purchase of new equipment for $80,000, would enable Torres to modernize its maintenance facility. The equipment has an expected useful life of five years and a $4,000 salvage value. It would replace existing equipment that had originally cost $45,000. The existing equipment has a current book value of $15,000 and a trade-in value of $5,000. The old equipment is technologically obsolete but can operate for an additional five years. On the day Torres purchases the new equipment, it would also pay the equipment manufacturer $3,000 for training costs to teach employees to operate the new equipment. The modernization has two primary advantages. One, it will improve management of the small parts inventory. The company's accountant believes that by the end of the first year, the carrying value of the small parts inventory could be reduced by $12,000. Second, the modernization is expected to increase efficiency, resulting in a $21,500 reduction in annual operating expenses.

The other investment alternative available to Torres is purchasing a truck. Adding another truck would enable Torres to expand its delivery area and increase revenue. The truck costs $115,000. It has a useful life of five years and a $30,000 salvage value. Operating the truck will require the company to increase its inventory of supplies, its petty cash account, and its accounts receivable and payable balances. These changes would add $5,000 to the company's working capital base immediately upon buying the truck. The working capital cash outflow is expected to be recovered at the end of the truck's useful life. The truck is expected to produce $69,000 per year in additional revenues. The driver's salary and other operating expenses are expected to be $32,000 per year. A major overhaul costing $20,000 is expected to be required at the end of the third year of operation. Assuming Torres desires to earn a rate of return of 14 percent, which of the two investment alternatives should it choose?

Net Present Value

LO4 Determine and interpret the net present value of an investment opportunity.

Begin the analysis by calculating the net present value of the two investment alternatives. Exhibit 10–5 shows the computations. Study this exhibit. Each alternative is analyzed using three steps. Step 1 requires identifying all cash inflows; some may be annuities, and others may be

Exhibit 10–5 *Net Present Value Analysis*

	Amount	×	Conversion Factor	=	Present Value
Alternative 1: Modernize Maintenance Facility					
Step 1: Cash inflows					
1. Cost savings	$21,500	×	3.433081*	=	$73,811
2. Salvage value	4,000	×	0.519369†	=	2,077
3. Working capital recovery	12,000	×	0.877193‡	=	10,526
Total					$86,414
Step 2: Cash outflows					
1. Cost of equipment ($80,000 cost—$5,000 trade-in)	$75,000	×	1.000000§	=	$75,000
2. Training costs	3,000	×	1.000000§	=	3,000
Total					$78,000
Step 3: Net present value					
Total present value of cash inflows					$86,414
Total present value of cash outflows					(78,000)
Net present value					$ 8,414
Alternative 2: Purchase Delivery Truck					
Step 1: Cash inflows					
1. Incremental revenue	$69,000	×	3.433081*	=	$236,883
2. Salvage value	30,000	×	0.519369†	=	15,581
2. Working capital recovery	5,000	×	0.519369†	=	2,597
Total					$255,061
Step 2: Cash outflows					
1. Cost of truck	$115,000	×	1.000000§	=	$115,000
2. Working capital increase	5,000	×	1.000000§	=	5,000
3. Increased operating expense	32,000	×	3.433081*	=	109,859
4. Major overhaul	20,000	×	0.674972+	=	13,499
Total					$243,358
Step 3: Net present value					
Total present value of cash inflows					$255,061
Total present value of cash outflows					(243,358)
Net present value					$ 11,703

* Present value of annuity table 2, $n = 5$, $r = 14\%$.

† Present value of single payment table 1, $n = 5$, $r = 14\%$.

‡ Present value of single payment table 1, $n = 1$, $r = 14\%$.

§ Present value at beginning of period 1.

+ Present value of single payment table 1, $n = 3$, $r = 14\%$.

lump-sum receipts. In the case of Alternative 1, the cost saving is an annuity, and the inflow from the salvage value is a lump-sum receipt. Once the cash inflows have been identified, the appropriate conversion factors are identified and the cash inflows are converted to their equivalent present values. Step 2 follows the same process to determine the present value of the cash outflows. Step 3 subtracts the present value of the outflows from the present value of the inflows to determine the net present value. The same three-step approach is used to determine the net present value of Alternative 2.

With respect to Alternative 1, the original cost and the book value of the existing equipment are ignored. As indicated in a previous chapter, these measures represent *sunk costs;* they are not relevant to the decision. The concept of relevance applies to long-term capital investment decisions just as it applies to the short-term special decisions that were discussed in Chapter 4. To be relevant to a capital investment decision, costs or revenues must involve different present and future cash flows for each alternative. Since the historical cost of the old equipment does not differ between the alternatives, it is not relevant.

Since the *net present value* of each investment alternative is *positive,* either investment will generate a return in excess of 14 percent. Which investment is the more favorable? The data could mislead a careless manager. Alternative 2 might seem the better choice because it has a greater present value than Alternative 1 ($11,703 vs. $8,414). Net present value, however, is expressed in *absolute dollars*. The net present value of a more costly capital investment can be greater than the net present value of a smaller investment even though the smaller investment earns a higher rate of return.

To compare different size investment alternatives, management can compute a **present value index** by dividing the present value of cash inflows by the present value of cash outflows. *The higher the ratio, the higher the rate of return per dollar invested in the proposed project.* The present value indices for the two alternatives Torres Transfer Company is considering are as follows.

$$\frac{\text{Present value index}}{\text{for Alternative 1}} = \frac{\text{Present value of cash inflows}}{\text{Present value of cash outflows}} = \frac{\$86{,}414}{\$78{,}000} = 1.108$$

$$\frac{\text{Present value index}}{\text{for Alternative 2}} = \frac{\text{Present value of cash inflows}}{\text{Present value of cash outflows}} = \frac{\$255{,}061}{\$243{,}358} = 1.048$$

Management can use the present value indices to rank the investment alternatives. In this case, Alternative 1 yields a higher return than Alternative 2.

Internal Rate of Return

LO5 Determine the internal rate of return of an investment opportunity.

Management can also rank investment alternatives using the internal rate of return for each investment. Generally, *the higher the internal rate of return, the more profitable the investment.* We previously demonstrated how to calculate the internal rate of return for an investment that generates a simple cash inflow annuity. The computations are significantly more complex for investments with uneven cash flows. Recall that the internal rate of return is the rate that produces a zero net present value. Manually computing the rate that produces a zero net present value is a tedious trial-and-error process. You must first estimate the rate of return for a particular investment, then calculate the net present value. If the calculation produces a negative net present value, you try a lower estimated rate of return and recalculate. If this calculation produces a positive net present value, the actual internal rate of return lies between the first and second estimates. Make a third estimate and once again recalculate the net present value, and so on. Eventually you will determine the rate of return that produces a net present value of zero.

Many calculators and spreadsheet programs are designed to make these computations. We illustrate the process with a Microsoft Excel spreadsheet. Excel uses the syntax *IRR(values, guess)* in which *values* refers to cells that specify the cash flows for which you want to calculate the internal rate of return and *guess* is a number you estimate is close to the actual internal rate of return (IRR). The IRRs for the two investment alternatives available to Torres Transfer Company are shown in Exhibit 10–6. Study this exhibit. Excel requires netting cash outflows against cash inflows for each period in which both outflows and inflows are expected. For your convenience, we have labeled the net cash flows in the spreadsheet. Labeling is not necessary to execute the IRR function. The entire function, including values and guess, can be entered into a single cell of the spreadsheet. Persons familiar with spreadsheet programs learn to significantly simplify the input required.

The IRR results in Exhibit 10–6 confirm the ranking determined using the present value index. Alternative 1 (modernize maintenance facility), with an internal rate of return of 18.69 percent, ranks above Alternative 2 (purchase a truck) with an internal rate of return of 17.61 percent, even though Alternative 2 has a higher net present value (see Exhibit 10–5). Alternative 2, however, still may be the better investment option, depending on the amount available to invest. Suppose Torres has $120,000 of available funds to invest. Because Alternative 1 requires an initial investment of only $78,000, $42,000 ($120,000 − $78,000) of capital will not be invested. If Torres has no other investment opportunities for this $42,000, the company would be better off investing the entire $120,000 in Alternative 2 ($115,000 cost of truck + $5,000 working capital increase). Earning 17.61 percent on a $120,000 investment is better than earning 18.69 percent on a $78,000 investment with no return on the remaining $42,000. Management accounting requires exercising judgment when making decisions.

Developing proficiency with present value mathematics is usually the most difficult aspect of capital budgeting for students taking their first managerial accounting course. In real-world companies, the most difficult aspect of capital budgeting is forecasting cash flows for several years into the future. Consider the following capital budgeting project.

In 1965 representatives from the Georgia Power Company visited Ms. Taylor's fifth grade class to tell her students about the Edwin I. Hatch Nuclear Plant that was going to be built nearby. One of the authors of this text was a student in that class.

In 1966 construction began on the first unit of the plant, and the plant started producing electricity in 1975. The next year, 10 years after hearing the presentation in his fifth grade class, the author worked on construction of the second unit of the plant during the summer before his senior year of college. This second unit began operations in 1978.

In its 2002 annual report, the Southern Company, which is now the major owner of the plant, stated that the Hatch plant is expected to operate until 2038, and that decommissioning of the plant will continue until 2042. The cost to construct both units of the plant was $934 million. The estimated cost to dismantle and decommission the plant is over $1 billion.

It seems safe to assume that the students in Ms. Taylor's fifth grade class were not among the first to hear about the power company's plans for the Hatch plant. Thus, we can reasonably conclude that the life of this capital project will be at least 85 years, from around 1960 until 2042.

Try to imagine that you were assigned the task of predicting the cost inflows and outflows for a project that was expected to last 85 years. Clearly, mastering present value mathematics would not be your biggest worry.

Exhibit 10–6 *Microsoft Excel Spreadsheet Internal Rate of Return Function*

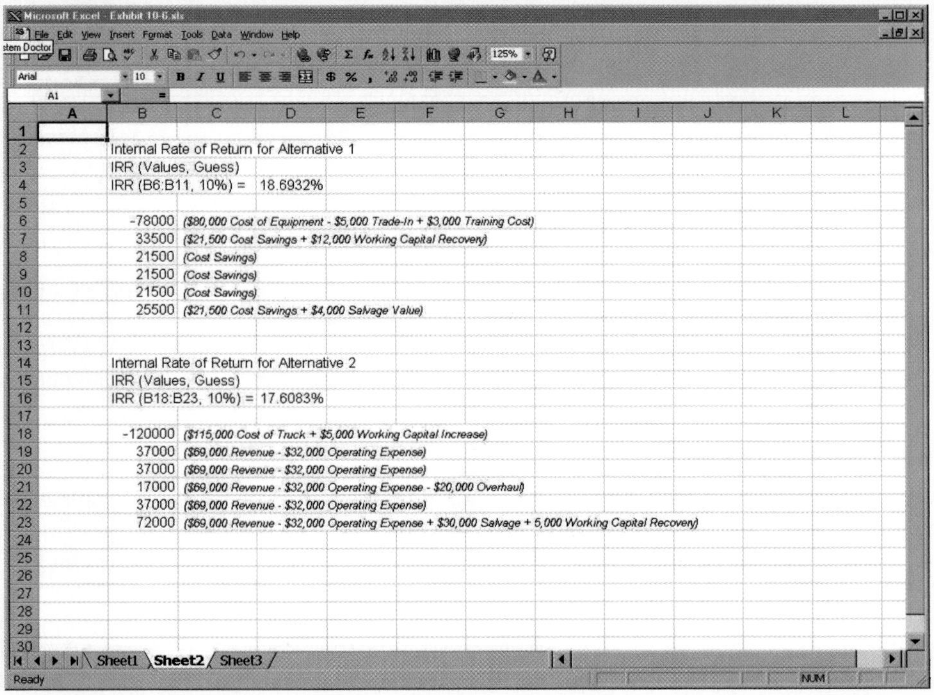

	B	C
2	Internal Rate of Return for Alternative 1	
3	IRR (Values, Guess)	
4	IRR (B6:B11, 10%) = 18.6932%	
6	-78000	($80,000 Cost of Equipment - $5,000 Trade-In + $3,000 Training Cost)
7	33500	($21,500 Cost Savings + $12,000 Working Capital Recovery)
8	21500	(Cost Savings)
9	21500	(Cost Savings)
10	21500	(Cost Savings)
11	25500	($21,500 Cost Savings + $4,000 Salvage Value)
14	Internal Rate of Return for Alternative 2	
15	IRR (Values, Guess)	
16	IRR (B18:B23, 10%) = 17.6083%	
18	-120000	($115,000 Cost of Truck + $5,000 Working Capital Increase)
19	37000	($69,000 Revenue - $32,000 Operating Expense)
20	37000	($69,000 Revenue - $32,000 Operating Expense)
21	17000	($69,000 Revenue - $32,000 Operating Expense - $20,000 Overhaul)
22	37000	($69,000 Revenue - $32,000 Operating Expense)
23	72000	($69,000 Revenue - $32,000 Operating Expense + $30,000 Salvage + 5,000 Working Capital Recovery)

Relevance and the Time Value of Money

Suppose you have the opportunity to invest in one of two capital projects. Both projects require an immediate cash outflow of $6,000 and will produce future cash inflows of $8,000. The only difference between the two projects is the timing of the inflows. The receipt schedule for both projects follows.

	Project 1	Project 2
2001	$3,500	$2,000
2002	3,000	2,000
2003	1,000	2,000
2004	500	2,000
Total	$8,000	$8,000

Because both projects cost the same and produce the same total cash inflows, they may appear to be equal. Whether you select Project 1 or Project 2, you pay $6,000 and receive $8,000. Because of the time value of money, however, Project 1 is preferable to Project 2. To see why, determine the net present value of both projects, assuming a 10 percent desired rate of return.

Computation of Net Present Value for Project 1 and Project 2

Net Present Value for Project 1

Period	Cash Inflow	×	Conversion Factor Table 1, $r = 10\%$	=	Present Value
1	$3,500	×	0.909091	=	$3,182
2	3,000	×	0.826446	=	2,479
3	1,000	×	0.751315	=	751
4	500	×	0.683013	=	342
Present value of future cash inflows					6,754
Present value of cash outflow					(6,000)
Net present value Project 1					$ 754

Net Present Value for Project 2

	Cash Inflow Annuity	×	Conversion Factor Table 2, $r = 10\%$, $n = 4$	
Present value of cash inflow	$2,000	×	3.169865	$6,340
Present value of cash outflow				(6,000)
Net present value Project 2				$ 340

The net present value of Project 1 ($754) exceeds the net present value of Project 2 ($340). The timing as well as the amount of cash flows has a significant impact on capital investment returns. Recall that to be relevant, costs or revenues must differ between alternatives. Differences in the timing of cash flow payments or receipts are also relevant for decision-making purposes.

Tax Considerations

The previous examples have ignored the effect of income taxes on capital investment decisions. Taxes affect the amount of cash flows generated by investments. To illustrate, assume Wu Company purchases an asset that costs $240,000. The asset has a four-year useful life, no salvage value, and is depreciated on a straight-line basis. The asset generates cash revenue of $90,000 per year. Assume Wu's income tax rate is 40 percent. What is the net present value of the asset, assuming Wu's management desires to earn a 10 percent rate of return after taxes? The first step in answering this question is to calculate the annual cash flow generated by the asset, as shown in Exhibit 10–7.

ANSWERS TO THE *curious* ACCOUNTANT

Ginger and Fred should not simply compare $10,000 spent today with $13,000 in energy savings and higher resale value that are to be received in the future. A dollar received in the future is worth less than a dollar spent today because of the time value of money. In order to decide if the replacement windows are worth their cost, today's $10,000 must be compared in common values with the $13,000 that they estimate will be received in the future.

This problem can be solved using the net present value approach that is explained in this chapter. This method calculates the present value of all dollars spent and received, and chooses the option with the highest present value. These computations are shown below. Note that a discount rate of 4 percent is used, because this is the rate that will be lost if the mutual fund is liquidated. This 4 percent is an opportunity cost.

The windows cost more than the present value of their future benefits, so this opportunity has a negative net present value of $404.51 ($10,000.00 − $9,595.49). Therefore, from a strictly financial point of view, Fred and Ginger should not buy the windows. Of course there may be nonquantitative factors in favor of buying the windows that the analysis above did not consider. Perhaps Ginger and Fred believe their new neighbors will like them more if they improve the looks of their house. If Fred and Ginger believe that being liked by their neighbors is worth $404.51, they should go ahead and purchase the windows.

Annual savings in heating and cooling costs	$ 600	
× Present value factor of a 10-year annuity, at 4%	8.110896	
Present value of the annual energy savings		$ 4,866.54
Increase in resale value of the house	7,000	
× Present value factor of $1 in 10 years, at 4%	0.675564	
Present value of the increase in resale value		4,728.95
Total present value of buying the windows		$ 9,595.49
Cost of the new windows, today		$10,000.00

Exhibit 10–7 *Determining Cash Flow from Investment*

	Period 1	Period 2	Period 3	Period 4
Cash revenue	$90,000	$90,000	$90,000	$90,000
Depreciation expense (noncash)	(60,000)	(60,000)	(60,000)	(60,000)
Income before taxes	30,000	30,000	30,000	30,000
Income tax at 40%	(12,000)	(12,000)	(12,000)	(12,000)
Income after tax	18,000	18,000	18,000	18,000
Depreciation add back	60,000	60,000	60,000	60,000
Annual cash inflow	$78,000	$78,000	$78,000	$78,000

Because recognizing depreciation expense does not require a cash payment (cash is paid when assets are purchased, not when depreciation is recognized), depreciation expense must be added back to after-tax income to determine the annual cash inflow. Once the cash flow is determined, the net present value is computed as shown here.

Cash flow annuity	×	Conversion factor Table 2, $r = 10\%$, $n = 4$	=	Present value cash inflows	−	Present value cash outflows	=	Net present value
$78,000	×	3.169865	=	$247,249	−	$240,000	=	$7,249

The depreciation sheltered some of the income from taxation. Income taxes apply to income after deducting depreciation expense. Without depreciation expense, income taxes each year would have been $36,000 ($90,000 × 0.40) instead of $12,000 ($30,000 × 0.40). The $24,000 difference ($36,000 − $12,000) is known as a *depreciation tax shield.* The amount of the depreciation tax shield can also be computed by multiplying the depreciation expense by the tax rate ($60,000 × 0.40 = $24,000).

Because of the time value of money, companies benefit by maximizing the depreciation tax shield early in the life of an asset. For this reason, most companies calculate depreciation expense for tax purposes using the *modified accelerated cost recovery system (MACRS)* permitted by tax law rather than using straight-line depreciation. MACRS recognizes depreciation on an accelerated basis, assigning larger amounts of depreciation in the early years of an asset's useful life. The higher depreciation charges result in lower amounts of taxable income and lower income taxes. In the later years of an asset's useful life, the reverse is true, and lower depreciation charges result in higher taxes. Accelerated depreciation does not allow companies to avoid paying taxes but to delay them. The longer companies can delay paying taxes, the more cash they have available to invest.

Topic Tackler PLUS 10–2

Techniques that Ignore the Time Value of Money

Several techniques for evaluating capital investment proposals ignore the time value of money. Although these techniques are less accurate, they are quick and simple. When investments are small or the returns are expected within a short time, these techniques are likely to result in the same decisions that more sophisticated techniques produce.

Payback Method

LO6 Determine the payback period for an investment opportunity.

The **payback method** is simple to apply and easy to understand. It shows how long it will take to recover the initial cash outflow (the cost) of an investment. The formula for computing the payback period, measured in years, is as follows.

Payback period = Net cost of investment ÷ Annual net cash inflow

To illustrate, assume Winston Cleaners can purchase a new ironing machine that will press shirts in half the time of the one currently used. The new machine costs $100,000 and will reduce labor cost by $40,000 per year over a four-year useful life. The payback period is computed as follows.

Payback period = $100,000 ÷ $40,000 = 2.5 years

Interpreting Payback. Generally, investments with shorter payback periods are considered better. Because the payback method measures only investment recovery, not profitability, however, this conclusion can be invalid when considering investment alternatives. To illustrate, assume Winston Cleaners also has the opportunity to purchase a different machine that costs $100,000 and provides an annual labor savings of $40,000. However, the second machine will last for five instead of four years. The payback period is still 2.5 years ($100,000 ÷ $40,000), but the second machine is a better investment because it improves profitability by providing an additional year of cost savings. The payback analysis does not measure this difference between the alternatives.

Unequal Cash Flows. The preceding illustration assumed Winston's labor cost reduction saved the same amount of cash each year for the life of the new machine. The payback method requires adjustment when cash flow benefits are unequal. Suppose a company purchases a machine for $6,000. The machine will be used erratically and is expected to provide incremental revenue over the next five years as follows.

2001	2002	2003	2004	2005
$3,000	$1,000	$2,000	$1,000	$500

Based on this cash inflow pattern, what is the payback period? There are two acceptable solutions. One accumulates the incremental revenue until the sum equals the amount of the original investment.

Year	Annual Amount	Cumulative Total
2001	$3,000	$3,000
2002	1,000	4,000
2003	2,000	6,000

This approach indicates the payback period is three years.

A second solution uses an averaging concept. The average annual cash inflow is determined. This figure is then used in the denominator of the payback equation. Using the preceding data, the payback period is computed as follows.

1. Compute the average annual cash inflow.

2001	+	2002	+	2003	+	2004	+	2005	=	Total	÷ 5 =	Average
\$3,000	+	\$1,000	+	\$2,000	+	\$1,000	+	\$500	=	\$7,500	÷ 5 =	\$1,500

2. Compute the payback period.

$$\frac{\text{Net cost of}}{\text{investment}} \div \frac{\text{Average annual}}{\text{net cash inflow}} = 6{,}000 \div 1{,}500 = 4 \text{ years}$$

The average method is useful when a company purchases a number of similar assets with differing cash return patterns.

Unadjusted Rate of Return

LO7 Determine the unadjusted rate of return for an investment opportunity.

The **unadjusted rate of return** method is another common evaluation technique. Investment cash flows are not adjusted to reflect the time value of money. The unadjusted rate of return is sometimes called the *simple rate of return.* It is computed as follows.

$$\text{Unadjusted rate of return} = \frac{\text{Average incremental increase in annual net income}}{\text{Net cost of original investment}}$$

To illustrate computing the unadjusted rate of return, assume The Dining Table, Inc., is considering establishing a new restaurant that will require a \$2,000,000 original investment. Management anticipates operating the restaurant for 10 years before significant renovations will be required. The restaurant is expected to provide an average after-tax return of \$280,000 per year. The unadjusted rate of return is computed as follows.

$$\text{Unadjusted rate of return} = \$280{,}000 \div \$2{,}000{,}000 = 14\% \text{ per year}$$

The accuracy of the unadjusted rate of return suffers from the failure to recognize the recovery of invested capital. With respect to a depreciable asset, the capital investment is normally recovered through revenue over the life of the asset. To illustrate, assume we purchase a \$1,000 asset with a two-year life and a zero salvage value. For simplicity, ignore income taxes. Assume the asset produces \$600 of cash revenue per year. The income statement for the first year of operation appears as follows.

Revenue	\$600
Depreciation Expense	(500)
Net Income	\$100

What is the amount of invested capital during the first year? First, a \$1,000 cash outflow was used to purchase the asset (the original investment). Next, we collected \$600 of cash revenue of which \$100 was a *return on investment* (net income) and \$500 was a **recovery of investment.** As a result, \$1,000 was invested in the asset at the beginning of the year and \$500 was invested at the end of the year. Similarly, we will recover an additional \$500 of capital during the second year of operation, leaving zero invested capital at the end of the second year. Given that the cash inflows from revenue are collected somewhat evenly over the life of the investment, the amount of invested capital will range from a beginning balance of \$1,000 to an ending balance of zero. On average, we will have \$500 invested in the asset (the midpoint between \$1,000 and zero). The average investment can be determined by dividing the total original investment by 2 ($1,000 ÷ 2 = $500). The unadjusted rate of return based on average invested capital can be calculated as follows.

$$\frac{\text{Unadjusted rate of return}}{\text{(Based on average investment)}} = \frac{\text{Average incremental increase in annual net income}}{\text{Net cost of original investment} \div 2}$$

$$= \frac{\$100}{\$1{,}000 \div 2} = 20\%$$

To avoid distortions caused by the failure to recognize the recovery of invested capital, the unadjusted rate of return should be based on the *average investment* when working with investments in depreciable assets.

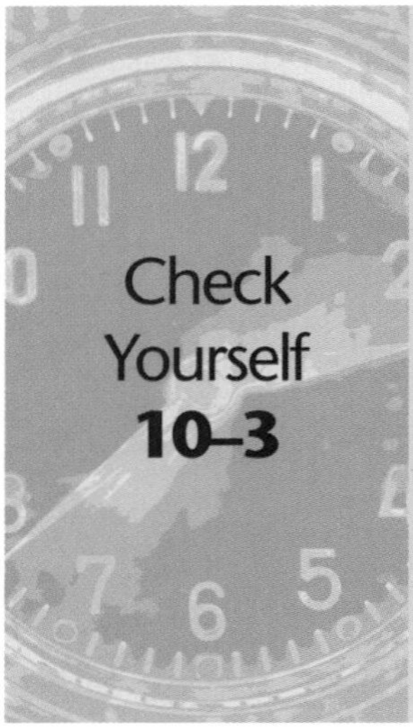

EZ Rentals can purchase a van that costs $24,000. The van has an expected useful life of three years and no salvage value. EZ expects rental revenue from the van to be $12,000 per year. Determine the payback period and the unadjusted rate of return.

Answer

Payback = Cost of the investment ÷ Annual cash inflow

Payback = $24,000 ÷ $12,000 = 2 years

Unadjusted rate of return = Net income ÷ Average cost of the investment

Revenue	$12,000	
Depreciation expense	(8,000)	[$24,000 ÷ 3 years]
Net income	$ 4,000	

Unadjusted rate of return = $4,000 ÷ (24,000 ÷ 2) = 33.33%

Real-World Reporting Practices

In a recent study, researchers found that companies in the forest products industry use discounted cash flow techniques more frequently when the capital project being considered is a long-term timber investment. The use of techniques that ignore the time value of money increased when other shorter-term capital investment projects were being considered. Exhibit 10–8 shows the researchers' findings.

Exhibit 10–8 *Forestry Industry Investments*

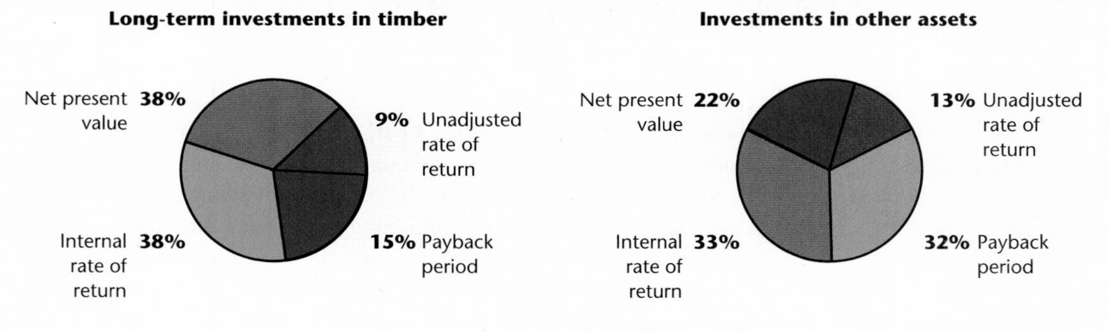

Data Source: J. Bailes, J. Nielsen, and S. Lawton, "How Forest Product Companies Analyze Capital Budgets," *Management Accounting,* October 1998, pp. 24–30.

Postaudits

LO8 Conduct a postaudit of a completed investment.

The analytical techniques for evaluating capital investment proposals depend highly on estimates of future cash flows. Although predictions cannot be perfectly accurate, gross miscalculations can threaten the existence of an organization. For example, optimistic projections of future cash inflows that do not materialize will lead to investments that do not return the cost of capital. Managers must take their projections seriously. A postaudit policy can encourage managers to carefully consider their capital investment decisions. A **postaudit** is conducted at the completion of a capital investment project, using the same analytical technique that was used to justify the original investment. For example, if an internal rate of return was used to justify approving an investment project, the internal rate of return should be computed in the postaudit. In the postaudit computation, *actual* rather than estimated cash flows are used. Postaudits determine whether the expected results were achieved.

Postaudits should focus on continuous improvement rather than punishment. Managers who are chastised for failing to achieve expected results might become overly cautious when asked to provide estimates for future projects. Being too conservative can create problems as serious as those caused by being too optimistic. Managers can err two ways with respect to capital investment decisions. First, a manager might accept a project that should have been rejected. This mistake usually stems from excessively optimistic future cash flow projections. Second, a manager might reject a project that should have been accepted. These missed opportunities are usually the result of underestimating future cash flows. A too cautious manager can become unable to locate enough projects to fully invest the firm's funds.

Idle cash earns no return. If projects continue to outperform expectations, managers are probably estimating future cash flows too conservatively. If projects consistently fail to live up to expectations, managers are probably being too optimistic in their projections of future cash flows. Either way, the company suffers. The goal of a postaudit is to provide feedback that will help managers improve the accuracy of future cash flow projections, maximizing the quality of the firm's capital investments.

a look back

Capital expenditures have a significant, long-term effect on profitability. They usually involve major cash outflows that are recovered through future cash inflows. The most common cash inflows include incremental revenue, operating cost savings, salvage value, and working capital releases. The most common outflows are the initial investment, increases in operating expenses, and working capital commitments.

Several techniques for analyzing the cash flows associated with capital investments are available. The techniques can be divided into two categories: (1) techniques that use time value of money concepts and (2) techniques that ignore the time value of money. Generally, techniques that ignore the time value of money are less accurate but simpler and easier to understand. These techniques include the *payback method* and the *unadjusted rate of return method.*

The techniques that use time value of money concepts are the *net present value method* and the *internal rate of return method.* These methods offer significant improvements in accuracy but are more difficult to understand. They may involve tedious computations and require using experienced judgment. Computer software and programmed calculators that ease the tedious computational burden are readily available to most managers. Furthermore, the superiority of the techniques justifies learning how to use them. These methods should be used when investment expenditures are larger or when cash flows extend over a prolonged time period.

a look forward

The next chapter moves into unexplored territory. It introduces the concept of inventory cost flow. It discusses how costs move through the inventory accounts Raw Materials, Work in Process, and Finished Goods. It presents techniques for assigning overhead costs to inventory as the inventory is produced. It identifies differences in product costing for service and manufacturing companies. Finally, it contrasts two approaches used to value inventory, variable costing versus full-absorption costing.

APPENDIX

Table 1 *Present Value of $1*

n	4%	5%	6%	7%	8%	9%	10%	12%	14%	16%	20%
1	0.961538	0.952381	0.943396	0.934579	0.925926	0.917431	0.909091	0.892857	0.877193	0.862069	0.833333
2	0.924556	0.907029	0.889996	0.873439	0.857339	0.841680	0.826446	0.797194	0.769468	0.743163	0.694444
3	0.888996	0.863838	0.839619	0.816298	0.793832	0.772183	0.751315	0.711780	0.674972	0.640658	0.578704
4	0.854804	0.822702	0.792094	0.762895	0.735030	0.708425	0.683013	0.635518	0.592080	0.552291	0.482253
5	0.821927	0.783526	0.747258	0.712986	0.680583	0.649931	0.620921	0.567427	0.519369	0.476113	0.401878
6	0.790315	0.746215	0.704961	0.666342	0.630170	0.596267	0.564474	0.506631	0.455587	0.410442	0.334898
7	0.759918	0.710681	0.665057	0.622750	0.583490	0.547034	0.513158	0.452349	0.399637	0.353830	0.279082
8	0.730690	0.676839	0.627412	0.582009	0.540269	0.501866	0.466507	0.403883	0.350559	0.305025	0.232568
9	0.702587	0.644609	0.591898	0.543934	0.500249	0.460428	0.424098	0.360610	0.307508	0.262953	0.193807
10	0.675564	0.613913	0.558395	0.508349	0.463193	0.422411	0.385543	0.321973	0.269744	0.226684	0.161506
11	0.649581	0.584679	0.526788	0.475093	0.428883	0.387533	0.350494	0.287476	0.236617	0.195417	0.134588
12	0.624597	0.556837	0.496969	0.444012	0.397114	0.355535	0.318631	0.256675	0.207559	0.168463	0.112157
13	0.600574	0.530321	0.468839	0.414964	0.367698	0.326179	0.289664	0.229174	0.182069	0.145227	0.093464
14	0.577475	0.505068	0.442301	0.387817	0.340461	0.299246	0.263331	0.204620	0.159710	0.125195	0.077887
15	0.555265	0.481017	0.417265	0.362446	0.315242	0.274538	0.239392	0.182696	0.140096	0.107927	0.064905
16	0.533908	0.458112	0.393646	0.338735	0.291890	0.251870	0.217629	0.163122	0.122892	0.093041	0.054088
17	0.513373	0.436297	0.371364	0.316574	0.270269	0.231073	0.197845	0.145644	0.107800	0.080207	0.045073
18	0.493628	0.415521	0.350344	0.295864	0.250249	0.211994	0.179859	0.130040	0.094561	0.069144	0.037561
19	0.474642	0.395734	0.330513	0.276508	0.231712	0.194490	0.163508	0.116107	0.082948	0.059607	0.031301
20	0.456387	0.376889	0.311805	0.258419	0.214548	0.178431	0.148644	0.103667	0.072762	0.051385	0.026084

Table 2 *Present Value of an Annuity of $1*

n	4%	5%	6%	7%	8%	9%	10%	12%	14%	16%	20%
1	0.961538	0.952381	0.943396	0.934579	0.925926	0.917431	0.909091	0.892857	0.877193	0.862069	0.833333
2	1.886095	1.859410	1.83393	1.808018	1.783265	1.759111	1.735537	1.690051	1.646661	1.605232	1.527778
3	2.775091	2.723248	2.673012	2.624316	2.577097	2.531295	2.486852	2.401831	2.321632	2.245890	2.106481
4	3.629895	3.545951	3.465106	3.387211	3.312127	3.239720	3.169865	3.037349	2.913712	2.798181	2.588735
5	4.451822	4.329477	4.212364	4.100197	3.992710	3.889651	3.790787	3.604776	3.433081	3.274294	2.990612
6	5.242137	5.075692	4.917324	4.766540	4.622880	4.485919	4.355261	4.111407	3.888668	3.684736	3.325510
7	6.002055	5.786373	5.582381	5.389289	5.206370	5.032953	4.868419	4.563757	4.288305	4.038565	3.604592
8	6.732745	6.463213	6.209794	5.971299	5.746639	5.534819	5.334926	4.967640	4.638864	4.343591	3.837160
9	7.435332	7.107822	6.801692	6.515232	6.246888	5.995247	5.759024	5.328250	4.946372	4.606544	4.030967
10	8.110896	7.721735	7.360087	7.023582	6.710081	6.417658	6.144567	5.650223	5.216116	4.833227	4.192472
11	8.760477	8.306414	7.886875	7.498674	7.138964	6.805191	6.495061	5.937699	5.452733	5.028644	4.327060
12	9.385074	8.863252	8.383844	7.942686	7.536078	7.160725	6.813692	6.194374	5.660292	5.197107	4.439217
13	9.985648	9.393573	8.852683	8.357651	7.903776	7.486904	7.103356	6.423548	5.842362	5.342334	4.532681
14	10.563123	9.898641	9.294984	8.745468	8.244237	7.786150	7.366687	6.628168	6.002072	5.467529	4.610567
15	11.118387	10.379658	9.712249	9.107914	8.559479	8.060688	7.606080	6.810864	6.142168	5.575456	4.675473
16	11.652296	10.837770	10.105895	9.446649	8.851369	8.312558	7.823709	6.973986	6.265060	5.668497	4.729561
17	12.165669	11.274066	10.477260	9.763223	9.121638	8.543631	8.021553	7.119630	6.372859	5.748704	4.774634
18	12.659297	11.689587	10.827603	10.059087	9.371887	8.755625	8.201412	7.249670	6.467420	5.817848	4.812195
19	13.133939	12.085321	11.158116	10.335595	9.603599	8.905115	8.364920	7.365777	6.550369	5.877455	4.843496
20	13.590326	12.462210	11.469921	10.594014	9.818147	9.128546	8.513564	7.469444	6.623131	5.928841	4.869580

SELF-STUDY REVIEW PROBLEM

The CFO of Advo Corporation is considering two investment opportunities. The expected future cash inflows for each opportunity follow:

	Year 1	Year 2	Year 3	Year 4
Project 1	$144,000	$147,000	$160,000	$178,000
Project 2	204,000	199,000	114,000	112,000

Both investments require an initial payment of $400,000. Advo's desired rate of return is 16 percent.

Required

a. Compute the net present value of each project. Which project should Advo adopt based on the net present value approach?

b. Use the summation method to compute the payback period for each project. Which project should Advo adopt based on the payback approach?

Solution to Requirement a

Project 1	Cash Inflows		Table Factor*		Present Value
Year 1	$144,000	×	0.862069	=	$124,138
Year 2	147,000	×	0.743163	=	109,245
Year 3	160,000	×	0.640658	=	102,505
Year 4	178,000	×	0.552291	=	98,308
PV of cash inflows					434,196
Cost of investment					(400,000)
Net present value					$ 34,196

*Table 1, n = 1 through 4, r = 16%

Project 2	Cash Inflows		Table Factor*		Present Value
Year 1	$204,000	×	0.862069	=	$175,862
Year 2	199,000	×	0.743163	=	147,889
Year 3	114,000	×	0.640658	=	73,035
Year 4	112,000	×	0.552291	=	61,857
PV of cash inflows					458,643
Cost of investment					(400,000)
Net present value					$ 58,643

*Table 1, n = 1 through 4, r = 16%

Advo should adopt Project 2 since it has a greater net present value.

Solution to Requirement b

Cash Inflows	Project 1	Project 2
Year 1	$144,000	$204,000
Year 2	147,000	199,000
Total	$291,000	$403,000

By the end of the second year, Project 2's cash inflows have more than paid for the cost of the investment. In contrast, Project 1 still falls short of investment recovery by $109,000 ($400,000 − $291,000). Advo should adopt Project 2 since it has a shorter payback period.

KEY TERMS

Accumulated conversion factors *403*
Annuity *403*
Capital investments *400*
Cost of capital *401*
Incremental revenue *407*
Internal rate of return *406*
Minimum rate of return *401*
Net present value *406*
Ordinary annuity *404*
Payback method *414*
Postaudit *417*

Present value index *410*
Present value table *402*
Recovery of investment *415*
Single-payment (lump-sum) *402*
Time value of money *401*
Unadjusted rate of return *415*
Working capital *407*

QUESTIONS

1. What is a capital investment? How does it differ from an investment in stocks or bonds?
2. What are three reasons that cash is worth more today than cash to be received in the future?
3. "A dollar today is worth more than a dollar in the future." "The present value of a future dollar is worth less than one dollar." Are these two statements synonymous? Explain.
4. Define the term *return on investment.* How is the return normally expressed? Give an example of a capital investment return.
5. How does a company establish its minimum acceptable rate of return on investments?
6. If you wanted to have $500,000 one year from today and desired to earn a 10 percent return, what amount would you need to invest today? Which amount has more value, the amount today or the $500,000 a year from today?
7. Why are present value tables frequently used to convert future values to present values?
8. Define the term *annuity.* What is one example of an annuity receipt?
9. How can present value "what-if " analysis be enhanced by using software programs?
10. Receiving $100,000 per year for five years is equivalent to investing what amount today at 14 percent? Provide a mathematical formula to solve this problem, assuming use of a present value annuity table to convert the future cash flows to their present value equivalents. Provide the expression for the Excel spreadsheet function that would perform the present value conversion.
11. Maria Espinosa borrowed $15,000 from the bank and agreed to repay the loan at 8 percent annual interest over four years, making payments of $4,529 per year. Because part of the bank's payment from Ms. Espinosa is a recovery of the original investment, what assumption must the bank make to earn its desired 8 percent compounded annual return?
12. Two investment opportunities have positive net present values. Investment A's net present value amounts to $40,000 while B's is only $30,000. Does this mean that A is the better investment opportunity? Explain.
13. What criteria determine whether a project is acceptable under the net present value method?
14. Does the net present value method provide a measure of the rate of return on capital investments?
15. Which is the best capital investment evaluation technique for ranking investment opportunities?
16. Paul Henderson is a manager for Spark Company. He tells you that his company always maximizes profitability by accepting the investment opportunity with the highest internal rate of return. Explain to Mr. Henderson how his company may improve profitability by sometimes selecting investment opportunities with lower internal rates of return.
17. What is the relationship between desired rate of return and internal rate of return?
18. What typical cash inflow and outflow items are associated with capital investments?
19. "I always go for the investment with the shortest payback period." Is this a sound strategy? Why or why not?
20. "The payback method cannot be used if the cash inflows occur in unequal patterns." Do you agree or disagree? Explain.
21. What are the advantages and disadvantages associated with the unadjusted rate of return method for evaluating capital investments?
22. How do capital investments affect profitability?
23. What is a postaudit? How is it useful in capital budgeting?

EXERCISES—SERIES A

All Exercises in Series A are available with McGraw-Hill's Homework Manager.

L.O. 1 **EXERCISE 10–1A** *Identifying Cash Inflows and Outflows*

Required

Indicate which of the following items will result in cash inflows and which will result in cash outflows. The first one is shown as an example.

Item	Type of Cash Flow
a. Incremental revenue	Inflow
b. Initial investment	
c. Salvage values	
d. Recovery of working capital	
e. Incremental expenses	
f. Working capital commitments	
g. Cost savings	

EXERCISE 10–2A *Determining the Present Value of a Lump-Sum Future Cash Receipt* — L.O. 1, 2

Mark Nelson turned 20 years old today. His grandfather established a trust fund that will pay Mr. Nelson $50,000 on his next birthday. Unfortunately, Mr. Nelson needs money today to start his college education, and his father is willing to help. He has agreed to give Mr. Nelson the present value of the future cash inflow, assuming a 10 percent rate of return.

Required

a. Use a present value table to determine the amount of cash that Mr. Nelson's father should give him.
b. Use an algebraic formula to prove that the present value of the trust fund (the amount of cash computed in Requirement *a*) is equal to its $50,000 future value.

EXERCISE 10–3A *Determining the Present Value of a Lump-Sum Future Cash Receipt* — L.O. 1, 2

Ginger Smalley expects to receive a $300,000 cash benefit when she retires five years from today. Ms. Smalley's employer has offered an early retirement incentive by agreeing to pay her $180,000 today if she agrees to retire immediately. Ms. Smalley desires to earn a rate of return of 12 percent.

Required

a. Assuming that the retirement benefit is the only consideration in making the retirement decision, should Ms. Smalley accept her employer's offer?
b. Identify the factors that cause the present value of the retirement benefit to be less than $300,000.

EXERCISE 10–4A *Determining the Present Value of an Annuity* — L.O. 1, 2

The dean of the School of Social Science is trying to decide whether to purchase a copy machine to place in the lobby of the building. The machine would add to student convenience, but the dean feels compelled to earn an 8 percent return on the investment of funds. Estimates of cash inflows from copy machines that have been placed in other university buildings indicate that the copy machine would probably produce incremental cash inflows of approximately $8,000 per year. The machine is expected to have a three-year useful life with a zero salvage value.

Required

a. Use Present Value Table 1 in Appendix A to determine the maximum amount of cash the dean should be willing to pay for a copy machine.
b. Use Present Value Table 2 in Appendix A to determine the maximum amount of cash the dean should be willing to pay for a copy machine.
c. Explain the consistency or lack of consistency in the answers to Requirements *a* and *b*.

EXERCISE 10–5A *Determining Net Present Value* — L.O. 4

Transit Shuttle, Inc., is considering investing in two new vans that are expected to generate cash inflows of $20,000 per year. The vans' purchase price is $65,000. Their expected life and salvage value of each are four years and $15,000, respectively. Transit Shuttle has an average cost of capital of 14 percent.

Required

a. Calculate the net present value of the investment opportunity.
b. Indicate whether the investment opportunity is expected to earn a return that is above or below the cost of capital and whether it should be accepted.

EXERCISE 10–6A *Determining Net Present Value* — L.O. 4

Travis Vintor is seeking part-time employment while he attends school. He is considering purchasing technical equipment that will enable him to start a small training services company that will offer tutorial services over the Internet. Travis expects demand for the service to grow rapidly in the first two years of operation as customers learn about the availability of the Internet assistance. Thereafter, he expects demand to stabilize. The following table presents the expected cash flows.

Year of Operation	Cash Inflow	Cash Outflow
2006	$5,400	$3,600
2007	7,800	4,800
2008	8,400	5,040
2009	8,400	5,040

In addition to these cash flows, Mr. Vintor expects to pay $8,400 for the equipment. He also expects to pay $1,440 for a major overhaul and updating of the equipment at the end of the second year of operation. The equipment is expected to have a $600 salvage value and a four-year useful life. Mr. Vintor desires to earn a rate of return of 8 percent.

Required
(Round computations to the nearest whole penny.)
a. Calculate the net present value of the investment opportunity.
b. Indicate whether the investment opportunity is expected to earn a return that is above or below the desired rate of return and whether it should be accepted.

L.O. 4

EXERCISE 10–7A *Using Present Value Index*

Wrencher Company has a choice of two investment alternatives. The present value of cash inflows and outflows for the first alternative is $60,000 and $56,000, respectively. The present value of cash inflows and outflows for the second alternative is $146,000 and $142,000, respectively.

Required
a. Calculate the net present value of each investment opportunity.
b. Calculate the present value index for each investment opportunity.
c. Indicate which investment will produce the higher rate of return.

L.O. 5

EXERCISE 10–8A *Determining the Internal Rate of Return*

Medina Manufacturing Company has an opportunity to purchase some technologically advanced equipment that will reduce the company's cash outflow for operating expenses by $1,280,000 per year. The cost of the equipment is $6,186,530.56. Medina expects it to have a 10-year useful life and a zero salvage value. The company has established an investment opportunity hurdle rate of 15 percent and uses the straight-line method for depreciation.

Required
a. Calculate the internal rate of return of the investment opportunity.
b. Indicate whether the investment opportunity should be accepted.

L.O. 5

EXERCISE 10–9A *Using the Internal Rate of Return to Compare Investment Opportunities*

Smith and Hough (S&H) is a partnership that owns a small company. It is considering two alternative investment opportunities. The first investment opportunity will have a five-year useful life, will cost $9,335.16, and will generate expected cash inflows of $2,400 per year. The second investment is expected to have a useful life of three years, will cost $6,217.13, and will generate expected cash inflows of $2,500 per year. Assume that S&H has the funds available to accept only one of the opportunities.

Required
a. Calculate the internal rate of return of each investment opportunity.
b. Based on the internal rates of return, which opportunity should S&H select?
c. Discuss other factors that S&H should consider in the investment decision.

L.O. 1, 2

EXERCISE 10–10A *Determining the Cash Flow Annuity With Income Tax Considerations*

To open a new store, Ross Tire Company plans to invest $640,000 in equipment expected to have a four-year useful life and no salvage value. Ross expects the new store to generate annual cash revenues of $840,000 and to incur annual cash operating expenses of $520,000. Ross's average income tax rate is 30 percent. The company uses straight-line depreciation.

Required
Determine the expected annual net cash inflow from operations for each of the first four years after Ross opens the new store.

EXERCISE 10–11A *Evaluating Discounted Cash Flow Techniques* — L.O. 8

Kay Vickery is angry with Gene Libby. He is behind schedule developing supporting material for tomorrow's capital budget committee meeting. When she approached him about his apparent lackadaisical attitude in general and his tardiness in particular, he responded, "I don't see why we do this stuff in the first place. It's all a bunch of estimates. Who knows what future cash flows will really be? I certainly don't. I've been doing this job for five years, and no one has ever checked to see if I even came close at these guesses. I've been waiting for marketing to provide the estimated cash inflows on the projects being considered tomorrow. But, if you want my report now, I'll have it in a couple of hours. I can make up the marketing data as well as they can."

Required

Does Mr. Libby have a point? Is there something wrong with the company's capital budgeting system? Write a brief response explaining how to improve the investment evaluation system.

EXERCISE 10–12A *Determining the Payback Period* — L.O. 6

Cascade Airline Company is considering expanding its territory. The company has the opportunity to purchase one of two different used airplanes. The first airplane is expected to cost $1,800,000; it will enable the company to increase its annual cash inflow by $600,000 per year. The plane is expected to have a useful life of five years and no salvage value. The second plane costs $3,600,000; it will enable the company to increase annual cash flow by $900,000 per year. This plane has an eight-year useful life and a zero salvage value.

Required

a. Determine the payback period for each investment alternative and identify the alternative Cascade should accept if the decision is based on the payback approach.
b. Discuss the shortcomings of using the payback method to evaluate investment opportunities.

EXERCISE 10–13A *Determining the Payback Period With Uneven Cash Flows* — L.O. 6

Shaw Company has an opportunity to purchase a forklift to use in its heavy equipment rental business. The forklift would be leased on an annual basis during its first two years of operation. Thereafter, it would be leased to the general public on demand. Shaw would sell it at the end of the fifth year of its useful life. The expected cash inflows and outflows follow.

Year	Nature of Item	Cash Inflow	Cash Outflow
2008	Purchase price		$48,000
2008	Revenue	$20,000	
2009	Revenue	20,000	
2010	Revenue	14,000	
2010	Major overhaul		6,000
2011	Revenue	12,000	
2012	Revenue	9,600	
2012	Salvage value	6,400	

Required

a. Determine the payback period using the accumulated cash flows approach.
b. Determine the payback period using the average cash flows approach.

EXERCISE 10–14A *Determining the Unadjusted Rate of Return* — L.O. 7

Tharpe Painting Company is considering whether to purchase a new spray paint machine that costs $3,000. The machine is expected to save labor, increasing net income by $450 per year. The effective life of the machine is 15 years according to the manufacturer's estimate.

Required

a. Determine the unadjusted rate of return based on the average cost of the investment.
b. Discuss the shortcomings of using the unadjusted rate of return to evaluate investment opportunities.

EXERCISE 10–15A *Computing the Payback Period and Unadjusted Rate of Return for One Investment Opportunity* — L.O. 6, 7

Padgett Rentals can purchase a van that costs $48,000; it has an expected useful life of three years and no salvage value. Padgett uses straight-line depreciation. Expected revenue is $24,000 per year.

Required

a. Determine the payback period.
b. Determine the unadjusted rate of return based on the average cost of the investment.

PROBLEMS—SERIES A

All Problems in Series A are available with McGraw-Hill's Homework Manager.

L.O. 4

excel

www.mhhe.com/edmonds3e

CHECK FIGURES

a. NPV of the vans investment: $100,811.42
b. NPV index of the trucks investment: 1.126

PROBLEM 10–16A *Using Present Value Techniques to Evaluate Alternative Investment Opportunities*

Parcel Delivery is a small company that transports business packages between Boston and Philadelphia. It operates a fleet of small vans that moves packages to and from a central depot within each city and uses a common carrier to deliver the packages between the depots in the two cities. Parcel recently acquired approximately $4 million of cash capital from its owners, and its president, Roger Makris, is trying to identify the most profitable way to invest these funds.

Nick Wells, the company's operations manager, believes that the money should be used to expand the fleet of city vans at a cost of $720,000. He argues that more vans would enable the company to expand its services into new markets, thereby increasing the revenue base. More specifically, he expects cash inflows to increase by $280,000 per year. The additional vans are expected to have an average useful life of four years and a combined salvage value of $100,000. Operating the vans will require additional working capital of $40,000, which will be recovered at the end of the fourth year.

In contrast, Leigh Young, the company's chief accountant, believes that the funds should be used to purchase large trucks to deliver the packages between the depots in the two cities. The conversion process would produce continuing improvement in operating savings with reductions in cash outflows as the following:

Year 1	Year 2	Year 3	Year 4
$160,000	$320,000	$400,000	$440,000

The large trucks are expected to cost $800,000 and to have a four-year useful life and a $80,000 salvage value. In addition to the purchase price of the trucks, up-front training costs are expected to amount to $16,000. Parcel Delivery's management has established a 16 percent desired rate of return.

Required

a. Determine the net present value of the two investment alternatives.
b. Calculate the present value index for each alternative.
c. Indicate which investment alternative you would recommend. Explain your choice.

L.O. 6, 7

CHECK FIGURES

a. Payback period of the yogurt investment: 1.77 years
Unadjusted rate of return of the cappuccino investment: 52.86%

PROBLEM 10–17A *Using the Payback Period and Unadjusted Rate of Return to Evaluate Alternative Investment Opportunities*

Brice Looney owns a small retail ice cream parlor. He is considering expanding the business and has identified two attractive alternatives. One involves purchasing a machine that would enable Mr. Looney to offer frozen yogurt to customers. The machine would cost $2,700 and has an expected useful life of three years with no salvage value. Additional annual cash revenues and cash operating expenses associated with selling yogurt are expected to be $1,980 and $300, respectively.

Alternatively, Mr. Looney could purchase for $3,360 the equipment necessary to serve cappuccino. That equipment has an expected useful life of four years and no salvage value. Additional annual cash revenues and cash operating expenses associated with selling cappuccino are expected to be $2,760 and $810, respectively.

Income before taxes earned by the ice cream parlor is taxed at an effective rate of 20 percent.

Required

a. Determine the payback period and unadjusted rate of return (use average investment) for each alternative.
b. Indicate which investment alternative you would recommend. Explain your choice.

L.O. 4, 5

PROBLEM 10–18A *Using Net Present Value and Internal Rate of Return to Evaluate Investment Opportunities*

Jane Crawford, the president of Crawford Enterprises, is considering two investment opportunities. Because of limited resources, she will be able to invest in only one of them. Project A is to purchase a machine that will enable factory automation; the machine is expected to have a useful life of four years and no salvage value. Project B supports a training program that will improve the skills of employees operating the current equipment. Initial cash expenditures for Project A are $400,000 and for Project B are $160,000. The annual expected cash inflows are $126,188 for Project A and $52,676 for Project B. Both investments are expected to provide cash flow benefits for the next four years. Crawford Enterprise's cost of capital is 8 percent.

CHECK FIGURES
a. NPV of A: $17,950.68
b. Rate of return of B: 12%

Required

a. Compute the net present value of each project. Which project should be adopted based on the net present value approach?

b. Compute the approximate internal rate of return of each project. Which one should be adopted based on the internal rate of return approach?

c. Compare the net present value approach with the internal rate of return approach. Which method is better in the given circumstances? Why?

PROBLEM 10–19A ***Using Net Present Value and Payback Period to Evaluate Investment Opportunities***

L.O. 4, 6

CHECK FIGURES
a. NPV of #1: $164,189.94
b. Payback period of #2: less than 2 years.

Lowell Cox saved $800,000 during the 25 years that he worked for a major corporation. Now he has retired at the age of 50 and has begun to draw a comfortable pension check every month. He wants to ensure the financial security of his retirement by investing his savings wisely and is currently considering two investment opportunities. Both investments require an initial payment of $600,000. The following table presents the estimated cash inflows for the two alternatives.

	Year 1	Year 2	Year 3	Year 4
Opportunity #1	$178,000	$188,000	$252,000	$324,000
Opportunity #2	328,000	348,000	56,000	48,000

Mr. Cox decides to use his past average return on mutual fund investments as the discount rate; it is 8 percent.

Required

a. Compute the net present value of each opportunity. Which should Mr. Cox adopt based on the net present value approach?

b. Compute the payback period for each project. Which should Mr. Cox adopt based on the payback approach?

c. Compare the net present value approach with the payback approach. Which method is better in the given circumstances?

PROBLEM 10–20A ***Effects of Straight-Line Versus Accelerated Depreciation on an Investment Decision***

L.O. 4, 6, 7

excel
www.mhhe.com/edmonds3e

CHECK FIGURES
a. NPV = $71,810
d. Payback period: 2.32 years

Hilyer Electronics is considering investing in manufacturing equipment expected to cost $184,000. The equipment has an estimated useful life of four years and a salvage value of $24,000. It is expected to produce incremental cash revenues of $96,000 per year. Hilyer has an effective income tax rate of 30 percent and a desired rate of return of 12 percent.

Required

a. Determine the net present value and the present value index of the investment, assuming that Hilyer uses straight-line depreciation for financial and income tax reporting.

b. Determine the net present value and the present value index of the investment, assuming that Hilyer uses double-declining-balance depreciation for financial and income tax reporting.

c. Why do the net present values computed in Requirements *a* and *b* differ?

d. Determine the payback period and unadjusted rate of return (use average investment), assuming that Hilyer uses straight-line depreciation.

e. Determine the payback period and unadjusted rate of return (use average investment), assuming that Hilyer uses double-declining-balance depreciation. (*Note:* Use average annual cash flow when computing the payback period and average annual income when determining the unadjusted rate of return.)

f. Why are there no differences in the payback periods or unadjusted rates of return computed in Requirements *d* and *e*?

L.O. 4

eXcel

www.mhhe.com/edmonds3e

CHECK FIGURE
a. $(46,120.48)

PROBLEM 10–21A *Applying the Net Present Value Approach With and Without Tax Considerations*

Buck Novak, the chief executive officer of Novak Corporation, has assembled his top advisers to evaluate an investment opportunity. The advisers expect the company to pay $400,000 cash at the beginning of the investment and the cash inflow for each of the following four years to be the following.

Year 1	Year 2	Year 3	Year 4
$84,000	$96,000	$120,000	$184,000

Mr. Novak agrees with his advisers that the company should use the discount rate (required rate of return) of 12 percent to compute net present value to evaluate the viability of the proposed project.

Required

a. Compute the net present value of the proposed project. Should Mr. Novak approve the project?

b. Lydia Hollman, one of the advisers, is wary of the cash flow forecast and she points out that the advisers failed to consider that the depreciation on equipment used in this project will be tax deductible. The depreciation is expected to be $80,000 per year for the four-year period. The company's income tax rate is 30 percent per year. Use this information to revise the company's expected cash flow from this project.

c. Compute the net present value of the project based on the revised cash flow forecast. Should Mr. Novak approve the project?

L.O. 5, 7

CHECK FIGURE
b. Internal rate of return: 12%

PROBLEM 10–22A *Comparing Internal Rate of Return With Unadjusted Rate of Return*

Masters Auto Repair, Inc., is evaluating a project to purchase equipment that will not only expand the company's capacity but also improve the quality of its repair services. The board of directors requires all capital investments to meet or exceed the minimum requirement of a 10 percent rate of return. However, the board has not clearly defined the rate of return. The president and controller are pondering two different rates of return: unadjusted rate of return and internal rate of return. The equipment, which costs $400,000, has a life expectancy of five years. The increased net profit per year will be approximately $28,000, and the increased cash inflow per year will be approximately $110,800.

Required

a. If it uses the unadjusted rate of return (use average investment) to evaluate this project, should the company invest in the equipment?

b. If it uses the internal rate of return to evaluate this project, should the company invest in the equipment?

c. Which method is better for this capital investment decision?

L.O. 8

CHECK FIGURE
b. NPV: $(654,174)

PROBLEM 10–23A Postaudit Evaluation

Sean Roberts is reviewing his company's investment in a cement plant. The company paid $15,000,000 five years ago to acquire the plant. Now top management is considering an opportunity to sell it. The president wants to know whether the plant has met original expectations before he decides its fate. The company's discount rate for present value computations is 8 percent. Expected and actual cash flows follow.

	Year 1	Year 2	Year 3	Year 4	Year 5
Expected	$3,300,000	$4,920,000	$4,560,000	$4,980,000	$4,200,000
Actual	2,700,000	3,060,000	4,920,000	3,900,000	3,600,000

Required

a. Compute the net present value of the expected cash flows as of the beginning of the investment.

b. Compute the net present value of the actual cash flows as of the beginning of the investment.

c. What do you conclude from this postaudit?

EXERCISES—SERIES B

L.O. 1

EXERCISE 10–1B *Identifying Cash Inflows and Outflows*

Required

Seth Gunn is considering whether to invest in a dump truck. Mr. Gunn would hire a driver and use the truck to haul trash for customers. He wants to use present value techniques to evaluate the investment opportunity. List sources of potential cash inflows and cash outflows Mr. Gunn could expect if he invests in the truck.

EXERCISE 10–2B *Determining the Present Value of a Lump-Sum Future Cash Receipt* — L.O. 1, 2

One year from today Mary Bray is scheduled to receive a $100,000 payment from a trust fund her father established. She wants to buy a car today but does not have the money. A friend has agreed to give Mary the present value of the $100,000 today if she agrees to give him the full $100,000 when she collects it one year from now. They agree that 8 percent reflects a fair discount rate.

Required

a. You have been asked to determine the present value of the future cash flow. Use a present value table to determine the amount of cash that Mary's friend should give her.

b. Use an algebraic formula to verify the result you determined in Requirement *a.*

EXERCISE 10–3B *Determining the Present Value of a Lump-Sum Future Cash Receipt* — L.O. 1, 2

Kyle Matthews has a terminal illness. His doctors have estimated his remaining life expectancy as three years. Kyle has a $1,500,000 life insurance policy but no close relative to list as the beneficiary. He is considering canceling the policy because he needs the money he is currently paying for the premiums to buy medical supplies. A wealthy close friend has advised Kyle not to cancel the policy. The friend has proposed instead giving Kyle $750,000 to use for his medical needs while keeping the policy in force. In exchange, Kyle would designate the friend as the policy beneficiary. Kyle is reluctant to take the $750,000 because he believes that his friend is offering charity. His friend has tried to convince Kyle that the offer is a legitimate business deal.

Required

a. Determine the present value of the $1,500,000 life insurance benefit. Assume a 10 percent discount rate.

b. Assuming 10 percent represents a fair rate of return, is Kyle's friend offering charity or is he seeking to profit financially from Kyle's misfortune?

EXERCISE 10–4B *Determining the Present Value of an Annuity* — L.O. 1, 2

Andrea James is considering whether to install a drink machine at the gas station she owns. Andrea is convinced that providing a drink machine at the station would increase customer convenience. However, she is not convinced that buying the machine would be a profitable investment. Friends who have installed drink machines at their stations have estimated that she could expect to receive net cash inflows of approximately $4,000 per year from the machine. Andrea believes that she should earn 10 percent on her investments. The drink machine is expected to have a two-year life and zero salvage value.

Required

a. Use Present Value Table 1 to determine the maximum amount of cash Andrea should be willing to pay for a drink machine.

b. Use Present Value Table 2 to determine the maximum amount of cash Andrea should be willing to pay for a drink machine.

c. Explain the consistency or lack of consistency in the answers to Requirement *a* versus Requirement *b.*

EXERCISE 10–5B *Determining the Net Present Value* — L.O. 4

Heidi Kahn, manager of the Grand Music Hall, is considering the opportunity to expand the company's concession revenues. Specifically, she is considering whether to install a popcorn machine. Based on market research, she believes that the machine could produce incremental cash inflows of $1,600 per year. The purchase price of the machine is $5,000. It is expected to have a useful life of three years and a $1,000 salvage value. Ms. Kahn has established a desired rate of return of 16 percent.

Required

a. Calculate the net present value of the investment opportunity.

b. Should the company buy the popcorn machine?

EXERCISE 10–6B *Determining the Net Present Value* — L.O. 4

Marcus Carroll has decided to start a small delivery business to help support himself while attending school. Mr. Carroll expects demand for delivery services to grow steadily as customers discover their availability. Annual cash outflows are expected to increase only slightly because many of the business operating costs are fixed. Cash inflows and outflows expected from operating the delivery business follow:

Year of Operation	Cash Inflow	Cash Outflow
2006	$6,800	$3,200
2007	7,600	3,600
2008	8,400	3,840
2009	9,200	4,000

The used delivery van Mr. Carroll plans to buy is expected to cost $13,200. It has an expected useful life of four years and a salvage value of $2,400. At the end of 2007, Mr. Carroll expects to pay additional costs of approximately $640 for maintenance and new tires. Mr. Carroll's desired rate of return is 12 percent.

Required

(Round computations to the nearest whole penny.)

a. Calculate the net present value of the investment opportunity.

b. Indicate whether the investment opportunity is expected to earn a return above or below the desired rate of return. Should Mr. Carroll start the delivery business?

L.O. 4

EXERCISE 10–7B *Using the Present Value Index*

Two alternative investment opportunities are available to Byron Osborne, president of Osborne Enterprises. For the first alternative, the present value of cash inflows is $266,000, and the present value of cash outflows is $254,000. For the second alternative, the present value of cash inflows is $460,000, and the present value of cash outflows is $446,000.

Required

a. Calculate the net present value of each investment opportunity.

b. Calculate the present value index for each investment opportunity.

c. Indicate which investment will produce the higher rate of return.

L.O. 5

EXERCISE 10–8B *Determining the Internal Rate of Return*

Joel Hodge, CFO of Kleiser Enterprises, is evaluating an opportunity to invest in additional manufacturing equipment that will enable the company to increase its net cash inflows by $600,000 per year. The equipment costs $1,794,367.20. It is expected to have a five-year useful life and a zero salvage value. Kleiser's cost of capital is 18 percent.

Required

a. Calculate the internal rate of return of the investment opportunity.

b. Indicate whether Kleiser should purchase the equipment.

L.O. 5

EXERCISE 10–9B *Using the Internal Rate of Return to Compare Investment Opportunities*

Rachel Allen has two alternative investment opportunities to evaluate. The first opportunity would cost $149,512.23 and generate expected cash inflows of $21,000 per year for 17 years. The second opportunity would cost $136,909.44 and generate expected cash inflows of $18,000 per year for 15 years. Ms. Allen has sufficient funds available to accept only one opportunity.

Required

a. Calculate the internal rate of return of each investment opportunity.

b. Based on the internal rate of return criteria, which opportunity should Ms. Allen select?

c. Identify two other evaluation techniques Ms. Allen could use to compare the investment opportunities.

L.O. 1, 2

EXERCISE 10–10B *Determining a Cash Flow Annuity with Income Tax Considerations*

Rick Howell is considering whether to invest in a computer game machine that he would place in a hotel his brother owns. The machine would cost $14,000 and has an expected useful life of three years and a salvage value of $2,000. Mr. Howell estimates the machine would generate revenue of $7,000 per year and cost $1,200 per year to operate. He uses the straight-line method for depreciation. His income tax rate is 30 percent.

Required

What amount of net cash inflow from operations would Mr. Howell expect for the first year if he invests in the machine?

EXERCISE 10–11B *Evaluating Discounted Cash Flow Techniques* — L.O. 8

Four years ago Valerie Bowen decided to invest in a project. At that time she had projected annual net cash inflows would be $72,000. Over its expected four-year useful life, the project had produced significantly higher cash inflows than anticipated. The actual average annual cash inflow from the project was $84,000. Bowen breathed a sigh of relief. She always worried that projects would not live up to expectations. To avoid this potential disappointment she tried always to underestimate the projected cash inflows of potential investments. She commented, "I prefer pleasant rather than unpleasant surprises." Indeed, no investment approved by Ms. Bowen had ever failed a postaudit review. Her investments consistently exceeded expectations.

Required
Explain the purpose of a postaudit and comment on Ms. Bowen's investment record.

EXERCISE 10–12B *Determining the Payback Period* — L.O. 6

The management team at Nisbett Manufacturing Company has decided to modernize the manufacturing facility. The company can replace an existing, outdated machine with one of two technologically advanced machines. One replacement machine would cost $200,000. Management estimates that it would reduce cash outflows for manufacturing expenses by $80,000 per year. This machine is expected to have an eight-year useful life and a $5,000 salvage value. The other replacement machine would cost $252,000 and would reduce annual cash outflows by an estimated $90,000. This machine has an expected 10–year useful life and a $25,000 salvage value.

Required
a. Determine the payback period for each investment alternative and identify which replacement machine Nisbett should buy if it bases the decision on the payback approach.
b. Discuss the shortcomings of the payback method of evaluating investment opportunities.

EXERCISE 10–13B *Determining the Payback Period With Uneven Cash Flows* — L.O. 6

Mountain Snowmobile Company is considering whether to invest in a particular new snowmobile model. The model is top-of-the-line equipment for which Mountain expects high demand during the first year it is available for rent. However, as the snowmobile ages, it will become less desirable and its rental revenues are expected to decline. The expected cash inflows and outflows follow.

Year	Nature of Cash Flow	Cash Inflow	Cash Outflow
2006	Purchase price	—	$14,000
2006	Revenue	$8,000	—
2007	Revenue	6,000	—
2008	Revenue	5,500	—
2008	Major overhaul	—	2,000
2009	Revenue	3,000	—
2010	Revenue	2,000	—
2010	Salvage value	1,600	—

Required
a. Determine the payback period using the accumulated cash flows approach.
b. Determine the payback period using the average cash flows approach.

EXERCISE 10–14B *Determining the Unadjusted Rate of Return* — L.O. 7

Airport Shuttle Service, Inc., is considering whether to purchase an additional shuttle van. The van would cost $20,000 and have a zero salvage value. It would enable the company to increase net income by $3,350 per year. The manufacturer estimates the van's effective life as five years.

Required
a. Determine the unadjusted rate of return based on the average cost of the investment.
b. What is the shortcoming of using the unadjusted rate of return to evaluate investment opportunities.

EXERCISE 10–15B *Computing the Payback Period and Unadjusted Rate of Return for the Same Investment Opportunity* — L.O. 6, 7

Star Lake Marina (SLM) rents pontoon boats to customers. It has the opportunity to purchase an additional pontoon boat for $36,000; it has an expected useful life of four years and no salvage value. SLM uses straight-line depreciation. Expected rental revenue for the boat is $12,000 per year.

Required

a. Determine the payback period.

b. Determine the unadjusted rate of return based on the average cost of the investment.

c. Assume that the company's desired rate of return is 30 percent. Should SLM purchase the additional boat?

PROBLEMS—SERIES B

L.O. 4 **PROBLEM 10–16B** ***Using Present Value Techniques to Evaluate Alternative Investment Opportunities***

Ruppert Automobile Repair, Inc., currently has three repair shops in Milwaukee. Melvin Ruppert, the president and chief executive officer, is facing a pleasant dilemma: the business has continued to grow rapidly and major shareholders are arguing about different ways to capture more business opportunities. The company requires a 12 percent rate of return for its investment projects and uses the straight-line method of depreciation for all fixed assets.

One group of shareholders wants to open another shop in a newly developed suburban community. This project would require an initial investment of $480,000 to acquire all the necessary equipment, which has a useful life of five years with a salvage value of $160,000. Once the shop begins to operate, another $120,000 of working capital would be required; it would be recovered at the end of the fifth year. The expected net cash inflow from the new shop follows.

Year 1	Year 2	Year 3	Year 4	Year 5
$48,000	$96,000	$152,000	$192,000	$240,000

A second group of shareholders prefers to invest $400,000 to acquire new computerized diagnostic equipment for the existing shops. The equipment is expected to have a useful life of five years with a salvage value of $80,000. Using this state-of-the-art equipment, mechanics would be able to pinpoint automobile problems more quickly and accurately. Consequently, it would allow the existing shops to increase their service capacity and revenue by $120,000 per year. The company would need to train mechanics to use the equipment, which would cost $40,000 at the beginning of the first year.

Required

a. Determine the net present value of the two investment alternatives.

b. Calculate the present value index for each alternative.

c. Indicate which investment alternative you would recommend. Explain your choice.

L.O. 6, 7 **PROBLEM 10–17B** ***Using the Payback Period and Unadjusted Rate of Return to Evaluate Alternative Investment Opportunities***

Alberta and Tony Services is planning a new business venture. With $100,000 of available funds to invest, it is investigating two options. One is to acquire an exclusive contract to operate vending machines in civic and recreation centers in a small suburban city for four years. The contract requires the firm to pay the city $40,000 cash at the beginning. The firm expects the cash revenue from the operation to be $50,000 per year and the cash expenses to be $28,000 per year.

The second option is to operate a printing shop in an office complex. This option would require the company to spend $72,000 for printing equipment that has a useful life of four years with a zero salvage value. The cash revenue is expected to be $85,000 per year and cash expenses are expected to be $47,000 per year. The firm uses the straight-line method of depreciation. Its effective income tax rate is expected to be 20 percent.

Required

a. Determine the payback period and unadjusted rate of return (use average investment) for each alternative.

b. Indicate which investment alternative you would recommend. Explain your choice.

L.O. 4, 5 **PROBLEM 10–18B** ***Using Net Present Value and Internal Rate of Return to Evaluate Investment Opportunities***

Alex Doyle's rich uncle gave him $100,000 cash as a birthday gift for his 40th birthday. Unlike his spoiled cousins who spend money carelessly, Mr. Doyle wants to invest the money for his future retirement. After an extensive search, he is considering one of two investment opportunities. Project 1 would require an immediate cash payment of $88,000; Project 2 needs only a $40,000 cash payment at the beginning. The expected cash inflows are $28,800 per year for Project 1 and $14,000 per year for Project 2. Both projects are expected to provide cash flow benefits for the next four years. Mr. Doyle found that the interest rate for a four-year certificate of deposit is about 7 percent. He decided that this is his required rate of return.

Required

a. Compute the net present value of each project. Which project should Mr. Doyle adopt based on the net present value approach?

b. Compute the approximate internal rate of return of each project. Which project should Mr. Doyle adopt based on the internal rate of return approach?

c. Compare the net present value approach with the internal rate of return approach. Which method is better in the given circumstances?

PROBLEM 10–19B *Using Net Present Value and Payback Period to Evaluate Investment Opportunities*

L.O. 4, 6

Vivian Ogard just won a lottery and received a cash award of $800,000 net of tax. She is 61 years old and would like to retire in four years. Weighing this important fact, she has found two possible investments, both of which require an immediate cash payment of $640,000. The expected cash inflows from the two investment opportunities are as follows.

	Year 1	Year 2	Year 3	Year 4
Opportunity A	$364,800	$208,000	$118,400	$134,400
Opportunity B	91,200	107,200	236,800	540,800

Ms. Ogard decided that her required rate of return should be 10 percent.

Required

a. Compute the net present value of each opportunity. Which should Ms. Ogard choose based on the net present value approach?

b. Compute the payback period for each opportunity. Which should Ms. Ogard choose based on the payback approach?

c. Compare the net present value approach with the payback approach. Which method is better in the given circumstances?

PROBLEM 10–20B *Effects of Straight-Line Versus Accelerated Depreciation on an Investment Decision*

L.O. 4, 6, 7

Gulf Pipe, Inc., decided to spend $80,000 to purchase new state-of-the-art equipment for its manufacturing plant. The equipment has a five-year useful life and a salvage value of $20,000. It is expected to generate additional cash revenue of $32,000 per year. Gulf Pipe's required rate of return is 10 percent; its effective income tax rate is 25 percent.

Required

a. Determine the net present value and the present value index of the investment, assuming that Gulf Pipe uses straight-line depreciation for financial and income tax reporting.

b. Determine the net present value and the present value index of the investment, assuming that Gulf Pipe uses double-declining-balance depreciation for financial and income tax reporting.

c. Why are there differences in the net present values computed in Requirements *a* and *b*?

d. Determine the payback period and unadjusted rate of return (use average investment), assuming that Gulf Pipe uses straight-line depreciation.

e. Determine the payback period and unadjusted rate of return (use average investment), assuming that Gulf Pipe uses double-declining-balance depreciation. (*Note:* Use average annual cash flow when computing the payback period and average annual income when computing the unadjusted rate of return.)

f. Why are there no differences in the payback period or unadjusted rate of return computed in Requirements *d* and *e?*

PROBLEM 10–21B *Applying the Net Present Value Approach With and Without Tax Considerations*

L.O. 4

Jerry Ray, the president of Jerry's Moving Services, Inc., is planning to spend $500,000 for new trucks. He expects the trucks to increase the company's cash inflow as follows.

Year 1	Year 2	Year 3	Year 4
$130,800	$142,572	$155,404	$169,388

The company's policy stipulates that all investments must earn a minimum rate of return of 10 percent.

Required

a. Compute the net present value of the proposed purchase. Should Mr. Ray purchase the trucks?
b. Kim Wells, the controller, is wary of the cash flow forecast and points out that Mr. Ray failed to consider that the depreciation on trucks used in this project will be tax deductible. The depreciation is expected to be $120,000 per year for the four-year period. The company's income tax rate is 30 percent per year. Use this information to revise the company's expected cash flow from this purchase.
c. Compute the net present value of the purchase based on the revised cash flow forecast. Should Mr. Ray purchase the trucks?

L.O. 5, 7

PROBLEM 10–22B *Comparing Internal Rate of Return With Unadjusted Rate of Return*

Elliott Computers, Inc., faces stiff market competition. Top management is considering the replacement of its current production facility. The board of directors requires all capital investments to meet or exceed a 9 percent rate of return. However, the board has not clearly defined the rate of return. The president and controller are pondering two different rates of return: unadjusted rate of return and internal rate of return. To purchase a new facility with a life expectancy of four years, the company must pay $360,000. The increased net profit per year resulting from improved conditions would be approximately $40,000; the increased cash inflow per year would be approximately $110,000.

Required

a. If it uses the unadjusted rate of return (use average investment) to evaluate this project, should the company invest in the new facility?
b. If it uses the internal rate of return to evaluate this project, should the company invest in the new facility?
c. Which method is better for this capital investment decision?

L.O. 8

PROBLEM 10–23B *Postaudit Evaluation*

Derric Pawlik is wondering whether he made the right decision four years ago. As the president of Pawlik Health Care Services, he acquired a hospital specializing in elder care with an initial cash investment of $2,800,000. Mr. Pawlik would like to know whether the hospital's financial performance has met the original investment objective. The company's discount rate (required rate of return) for present value computations is 14 percent. Expected and actual cash flows follow.

	Year 1	Year 2	Year 3	Year 4
Expected	$920,000	$960,000	$1,000,000	$1,200,000
Actual	800,000	760,000	1,280,000	1,400,000

Required

a. Compute the net present value of the expected cash flows as of the beginning of the investment.
b. Compute the net present value of the actual cash flows as of the beginning of the investment.
c. What do you conclude from this postaudit?

ANALYZE, THINK, COMMUNICATE

ATC 10–1

BUSINESS APPLICATIONS CASE *Lottery Winnings Consulting Job*

The February 20, 2004, drawing for the Mergmillions multistate lottery produced one winning ticket. More than a month after the drawing no one had come forward to claim the $239 million prize. Perhaps the winner was simply confused about whether to take the winnings as a lump-sum, immediate payment, or annual payments over the next 26 years.

Assume that you work as a personal financial planner, and that one of your clients held the winning lottery ticket. They face the choice of (1) taking the annual payments of $9,192,308 over the next 26 years ($239 million ÷ 26), or (2) taking an immediate one-time payment of $136 million.

Required

a. Assume you believe you can invest your client's winnings and safely earn an average annual return of 7 percent. Should they take the immediate cash payment or should they take the 26 annual payments? Ignore tax considerations and show the supporting computations used to reach your answer.

b. Assume your client is not convinced you can safely earn an annual rate of 7 percent on their money. What is the minimal annual rate of return you would need to earn for them before they would be better off taking the immediate cash pay out of $136 million rather than the 26 annual payments of $9,192,308? Ignore tax considerations and show the supporting computations used to reach your answer.

(The tables in the Appendix for Chapter 10 end at 20 periods, so the factors for 26 periods are provided below.)

Present Value of $1									
n	4%	5%	6%	7%	8%	9%	10%	12%	14%
26	0.3607	0.2812	0.2198	0.1722	0.1352	0.1064	0.0839	0.0525	0.0331

Present Value of an Annuity of $1									
n	4%	5%	6%	7%	8%	9%	10%	12%	14%
26	15.9828	14.3752	13.0032	11.8258	10.8100	9.9290	9.1609	7.8957	6.9061

GROUP ASSIGNMENT *Net Present Value* — ATC 10–2

Espada Real Estate Investment Company (EREIC) purchases new apartment complexes, establishes a stable group of residents, and then sells the complexes to apartment management companies. The average holding time is three years. EREIC is currently investigating two alternatives.

1. EREIC can purchase Harding Properties for $4,500,000. The complex is expected to produce net cash inflows of $360,000, $502,500, and $865,000 for the first, second, and third years of operation, respectively. The market value of the complex at the end of the third year is expected to be $5,175,000.
2. EREIC can purchase Summit Apartments for $3,450,000. The complex is expected to produce net cash inflows of $290,000, $435,000, and $600,000 for the first, second, and third years of operation, respectively. The market value of the complex at the end of the third year is expected to be $4,050,000.

EREIC has a desired rate of return of 12 percent.

Required

a. Divide the class into groups of four or five students per group and then divide the groups into two sections. Assign Task 1 to the first section and Task 2 to the second section.

Group Tasks

(1) Calculate the net present value and the present value index for Harding Properties.
(2) Calculate the net present value and the present value index for Summit Apartments.

b. Have a spokesperson from one group in the first section report the amounts calculated by the group. Make sure that all groups in the section have the same result. Repeat the process for the second section. Have the class as a whole select the investment opportunity that EREIC should accept given that the objective is to produce the higher rate of return.

c. Assume that EREIC has $4,500,000 to invest and that any funds not invested in real estate properties must be invested in a certificate of deposit earning a 5 percent return. Would this information alter the decision made in Requirement *b*?

d. This requirement is independent of Requirement *c*. Assume there is a 10 percent chance that the Harding project will be annexed by the city of Hoover, which has an outstanding school district. The annexation would likely increase net cash flows by $37,500 per year and would increase the market value at the end of year 3 by $300,000. Would this information change the decision reached in Requirement *b*?

RESEARCH ASSIGNMENT *Real World Capital Budgeting Issues* — ATC 10–3

In recent years companies have devoted considerable time trying to decide if new software systems should be purchased. Vendors trying to sell the systems in question are happy to provide their own analysis to the prospective buyer showing how profitable their system will be. Not surprisingly, buyers are often skeptical of the objectivity of such analysis, and prefer to do their own. "Sizing up Your Payoff," *BusinessWeek,* October 29, 2001, presents anecdotal evidence about problems companies have encountered when evaluating the profitability of proposed software systems. Read this article and complete the following requirements.

Required

a. The focus of the article is on "return on investment" (ROI) analysis. Of the four techniques presented in this chapter for analyzing capital projects, which of them do you think is most closely related to the ROI analysis discussed by the article?

b. Give an example from the article of a company that appears to be using the payback method, at least in part, for capital budgeting decisions.

c. Give an example from the article of a company that appears to be using the internal rate of return method, at least in part, for capital budgeting decisions.

d. Give an example from the article of a company that used a postaudit to evaluate a capital budgeting decision it had made. What were the results of this postaudit?

e. The article discusses a capital project study that Metreo, Inc. undertook before buying a software system. How long did this study take? How many employees were asked to provide input into the analysis?

ATC 10–4 WRITING ASSIGNMENT *Limitations of Capital Investment Techniques*

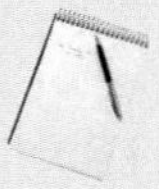

Webb Publishing Company is evaluating two investment opportunities. One is to purchase an Internet company with the capacity to open new marketing channels through which Webb can sell its books. This opportunity offers a high potential for growth but involves significant risk. Indeed, losses are projected for the first three years of operation. The second opportunity is to purchase a printing company that would enable Webb to better control costs by printing its own books. The potential savings are clearly predictable but would make a significant change in the company's long-term profitability.

Required

Write a response discussing the usefulness of capital investment techniques (net present value, internal rate of return, payback, and unadjusted rate of return) in making a choice between these two alternative investment opportunities. Your response should discuss the strengths and weaknesses of capital budgeting techniques in general. Furthermore, it should include a comparison between techniques based on the time value of money versus those that are not.

ATC 10–5 ETHICAL DILEMMA *Postaudit*

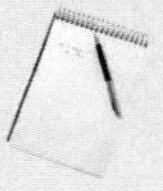

Gaines Company recently initiated a postaudit program. To motivate employees to take the program seriously, Gaines established a bonus program. Managers receive a bonus equal to 10 percent of the amount by which actual net present value exceeds the projected net present value. Victor Holt, manager of the North Western Division, had an investment proposal on his desk when the new system was implemented. The investment opportunity required a $250,000 initial cash outflow and was expected to return cash inflows of $90,000 per year for the next five years. Gaines' desired rate of return is 10 percent. Mr. Holt immediately reduced the estimated cash inflows to $70,000 per year and recommended accepting the project.

Required

a. Assume that actual cash inflows turn out to be $91,000 per year. Determine the amount of Mr. Holt's bonus if the original computation of net present value were based on $90,000 versus $70,000.

b. Is Mr. Holt's behavior in violation of any of the standards of ethical conduct in Exhibit 1-13 of Chapter 1?

c. Speculate about the long-term effect the bonus plan is likely to have on the company.

d. Recommend how to compensate managers in a way that discourages gamesmanship.

ATC 10–6 SPREADSHEET ASSIGNMENT *Using Excel*

Kilby Company is considering the purchase of new automated manufacturing equipment that would cost $150,000. The equipment would save $42,500 in labor costs per year over its six-year life. At the end of the fourth year, the equipment would require an overhaul that would cost $25,000. The equipment would have a $7,500 salvage value at the end of its life. Kilby's cost of capital is 12 percent.

Required

a. Prepare a spreadsheet similar to the one following to calculate net present value, the present value index, and the internal rate of return.

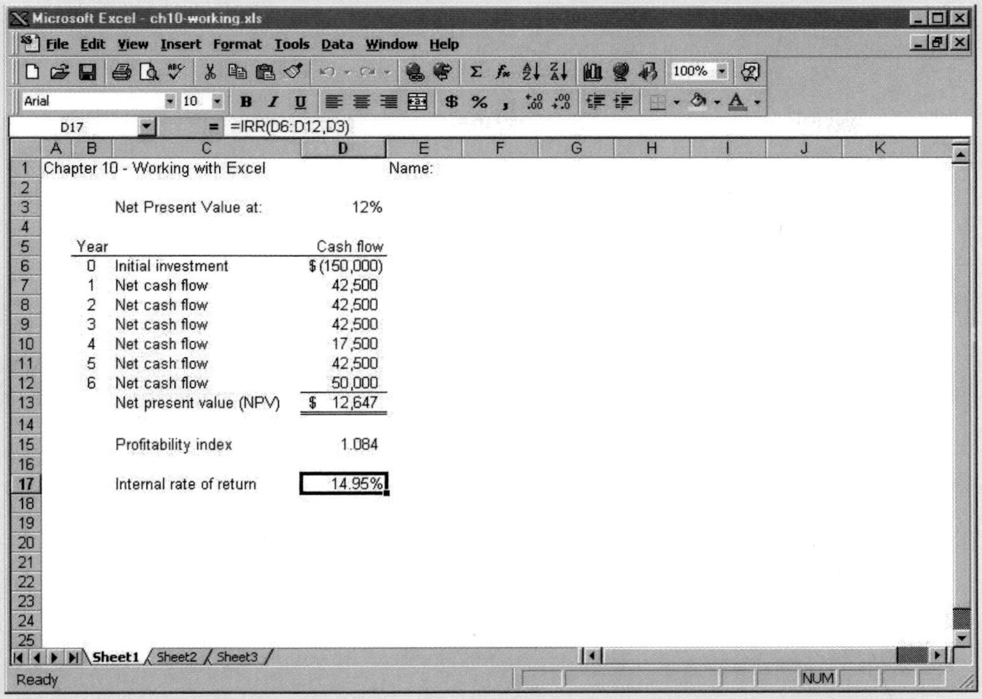

	A	B	C	D	E
1	Chapter 10 - Working with Excel				Name:
2					
3			Net Present Value at:	12%	
4					
5		Year		Cash flow	
6		0	Initial investment	$ (150,000)	
7		1	Net cash flow	42,500	
8		2	Net cash flow	42,500	
9		3	Net cash flow	42,500	
10		4	Net cash flow	17,500	
11		5	Net cash flow	42,500	
12		6	Net cash flow	50,000	
13			Net present value (NPV)	$ 12,647	
14					
15			Profitability index	1.084	
16					
17			Internal rate of return	14.95%	

Spreadsheet Tips

Spreadsheets have built-in financial functions that make net present value and internal rate of return calculations very easy. The formats of these formulas are as follows.

1. *Net Present Value:* = NPV(rate,value1,value2,value3 ... value29) where up to 29 values are allowed. The values must be at the end of the period, and each period must be equal in time (one year, for example). The formula is = NPV(D3,D7,D8,D9,D10,D11,D12) + D6.
2. *Internal Rate of Return:* = IRR(values,guess) where *values* is the range that includes the cash flows (D6 to D12) and *guess* is an estimate of the rate. Use the cost of capital as the guess.
3. *Percentage:* Rather than entering 12% in the formulas, refer to cell D3. This will allow you to change the rate and see the effect on the NPV and present value index.
4. *Present Value Index:* You must construct a formula because no built-in function calculates it.

SPREADSHEET ASSIGNMENT *Mastering Excel* ATC 10–4

ASAP Delivery is a small company that transports business packages between San Francisco and Los Angeles. It operates a fleet of small vans that moves packages to and from a central depot within each city and uses a common carrier to deliver the packages between the depots in the two cities. ASAP recently acquired approximately $4 million of cash capital from its owners, and its president, Alex Cade, is trying to identify the most profitable way to invest these funds.

Phil Duvall, the company's operations manager, believes that the money should be used to expand the fleet of city vans at a cost of $3,600,000. He argues that more vans would enable the company to expand its services into new markets, thereby increasing the revenue base. More specifically, he expects cash inflows to increase by $1,400,000 per year. The additional vans are expected to have an average useful life of four years and a combined salvage value of $500,000. Operating the vans will require additional working capital of $200,000, which will be recovered at the end of the fourth year.

In contrast, Amber Gomez, the company's chief accountant, believes that the funds should be used to purchase large trucks to deliver the packages between the depots in the two cities. The conversion process would produce continuing improvement in operating savings with reductions in cash outflows as the following:

Year 1	Year 2	Year 3	Year 4
$800,000	$1,600,000	$2,000,000	$2,200,000

The large trucks are expected to cost $4,000,000 and to have a four-year useful life and a $400,000 salvage value. In addition to the purchase price of the trucks, up-front training costs are expected to amount to $80,000. ASAP Delivery's management has established a 16 percent desired rate of return.

Required

a. Prepare a spreadsheet similar to the preceding one that calculates the net present value and the present value index for the two investments.

b. Include formulas in your spreadsheet to calculate the internal rate of return for each investment alternative.

COMPREHENSIVE PROBLEM

Magnificent Modems, Inc. (MMI) has several capital investment opportunities. The term, expected cash inflows, and the cost of each opportunity are outlined in the following table. MMI has established a desired rate of return of 16 percent for these investment opportunities.

Opportunity	A	B	C	D
Investment term	4 years	5 years	3 years	5 years
Expected cash inflow	$ 6,000	$ 5,000	$ 8,000	$ 4,800
Cost of investment	$16,000	$15,000	$18,000	$16,000

Required

a. Compute the net present value of each investment opportunity manually using the present value tables. Record your answers in the following table. The results for Investment Opportunity A have been recorded in the table as an example.

Opportunity	A	B	C	D
Cash inflow	$6,000.00	$5,000.00	$8,000.00	$4,800.00
Times present value factor	2.798181			
Present value of cash flows	$16,789.08			
Minus cost of investment	($16,000.00)	($15,000.00)	($18,000.00)	($16,000.00)
Net present value	$789.08			

b. Use Excel spreadsheet software or a financial calculator to determine the net present value and the internal rate of return for each investment opportunity. Record the results in the following table. The results for Investment Opportunity A have been recorded in the following table as an example. Note that the manual computation yields the same net present value amounts as the financial function routines of Excel or a financial calculator.

Opportunity	A	B	C	D
Net present value	$789.08			
Internal rate of return	18.45%			

CHAPTER *eleven*

PRODUCT COSTING IN SERVICE AND MANUFACTURING ENTITIES

LEARNING *objectives*

After you have mastered the material in this chapter you will be able to:

1 Explain the need for service and product cost information.

2 Explain how product costs flow from Raw Materials, to Work in Process, to Finished Goods, and ultimately to Cost of Goods Sold.

3 Distinguish between costing for service and manufacturing entities.

4 Demonstrate, using a horizontal financial statements model, how product cost flows affect financial statements.

5 Explain the need to assign estimated overhead costs to inventory and cost of goods sold during an accounting period.

6 Record applied and actual overhead costs in a Manufacturing Overhead account.

7 Record product costs in T-accounts.

8 Explain the cyclical nature of product cost flows.

9 Explain the relationship between over- or underapplied overhead and variance analysis.

10 Prepare a schedule of cost of goods manufactured and sold.

11 Prepare financial statements for a manufacturing entity.

12 Distinguish between absorption and variable costing.

THE *curious* ACCOUNTANT

Evita Allen wants to buy a set of custom-made dining-room furniture, and she wants it completed in April. Since she is not exactly sure of what she wants her furniture to look like, she ask the furniture maker, Norm, if he will build the table and chairs for "his costs plus 30 percent." The furniture maker says he is not sure if he can agree to that since he will not know how much the furniture costs him to make until the end of the year, and he can't wait that long to get paid.

Evita is confused and asks Norm why he cannot determine the price by simply adding 30 percent to the costs of the materials and wages he uses to make her furniture. Norm explains that his costs include more than just materials and wages. For example, he has to pay the annual rent on his workshop. He admits that his rent is a fixed amount and he knows how much it will be, but he will not know how much of that rent is related to Evita's furniture until he knows how many other jobs he has throughout the year. In other words, if he completes 10 jobs during the year, the cost of Evita's furniture would include 10 percent of his rent, but if he has 20 jobs, then she would be responsible for only 5 percent of his rent.

How can a manufacturer, such as Norm's Furniture Shop, know what price to charge its customers when it does not know the real cost of any one job until the year is over? (Answer on page 449.)

CHAPTER *opening*

Service *and* product costing systems *supply information about the cost of providing services or making products. Organizations need service and product cost information for financial reporting, managerial accounting, and contract negotiations.*

For financial reporting, *companies are required by generally accepted accounting principles (GAAP) to report service and product costs in their published financial statements. For example, product costs for manufacturing companies must be allocated between inventory (reported on the balance sheet) and cost of goods sold (reported on the income statement). Similarly, service companies must match on their income statements the costs of providing services with the revenues generated from the services provided.*

For managerial accounting, *managers need to know the cost of providing services or making products so they can plan company operations. For example, companies could not prepare budgets without knowing the cost of services or products. Service and product costing is also needed for cost control. Managers compare expected costs with actual costs to identify problems that need correcting. Service and product cost information may be used for pricing and other short-term decisions. For example, the cost of a service or product may be used in special order, outsourcing, or product elimination decisions.*

Service and product costing information may be used by governmental agencies to regulate rates for public service entities such as utility companies or hospitals. Service and product costs are also used in determining the amount due on contracts that compensate companies for the costs they incur plus a reasonable profit (cost-plus contracts). For example, many governmental defense contracts are negotiated on a cost-plus basis. Cost-plus pricing may also be used by private companies. For example, many builders of custom homes charge customers based on cost-plus contracts. Cost information is therefore necessary for contract negotiations. *This chapter shows how manufacturing companies determine the cost of the products they make.*

Cost Flow in Manufacturing Companies

LO1 Explain the need for service and product cost information.

In previous chapters, we assumed all inventory started during an accounting period was also completed during that accounting period. All product costs (materials, labor, and manufacturing overhead) were either in inventory or expensed as cost of goods sold. At the end of an accounting period, however, most real-world companies have raw materials on hand, and manufacturing companies are likely to have in inventory items that have been started but are not completed. Most manufacturing companies accumulate product costs in three distinct inventory accounts: (1) **Raw Materials Inventory,** which includes lumber, metals, paints, and chemicals that will be used to make the company's products; (2) **Work in Process Inventory,** which includes partially completed products; and (3) **Finished Goods Inventory,** which includes completed products that are ready for sale.

The cost of materials is first recorded in the Raw Materials Inventory account. The cost of materials placed in production is then transferred from the Raw Materials Inventory account to the Work in Process Inventory account. The costs of labor and overhead are added to the Work in Process Inventory account. The cost of the goods completed during the period is transferred from the Work in Process Inventory account to the Finished Goods Inventory account. The cost of the goods that are sold during the accounting period is transferred from the Finished Goods Inventory account to the Cost of Goods Sold account. The balances that remain in the Raw Materials, Work in Process, and Finished Goods Inventory accounts are reported on the balance sheet. The amount of product cost transferred to the Cost of Goods Sold account is expensed on the income statement. Exhibit 11–1 shows the flow of manufacturing costs through the accounting records.

Exhibit 11–1

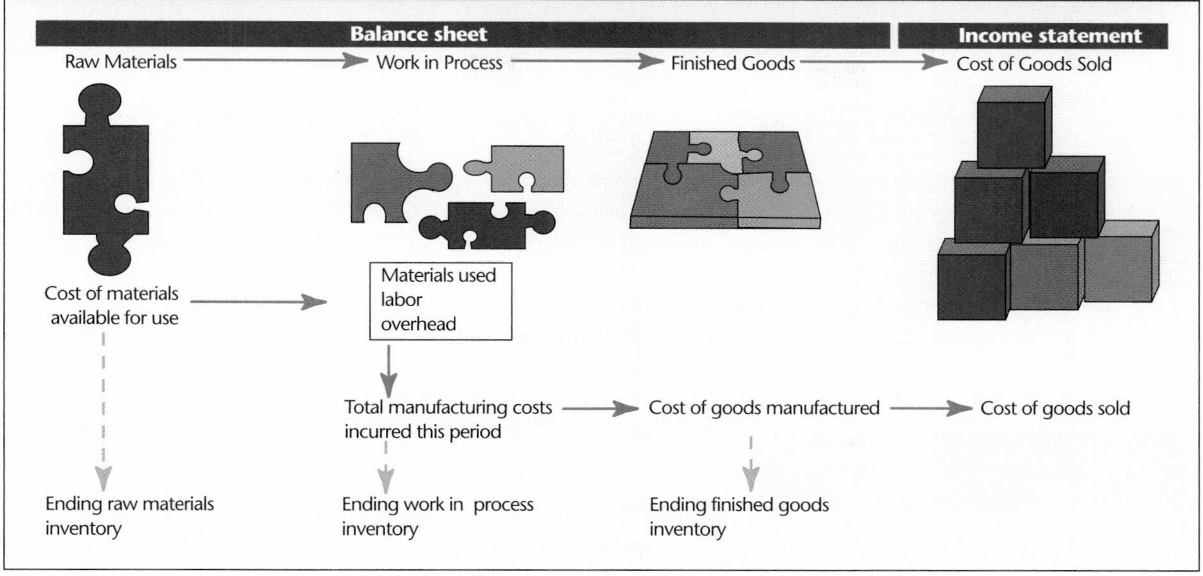

Cost Flow in Service Companies

LO2 Explain how product costs flow from Raw Materials, to Work in Process, to Finished Goods, and ultimately to Cost of Goods Sold.

LO3 Distinguish between costing for service and manufacturing entities.

Like manufacturing companies, many service companies purchase raw materials and transform them through production stages such as work in process, finished goods, and cost of goods sold. For example, a McDonald's hamburger starts with raw materials (meat, bun, and condiments), goes through work in process (is cooked, assembled, and wrapped), becomes a finished product, and is sold to a customer. Why then is McDonald's considered a *service* rather than a *manufacturing* company? The distinguishing feature is that products from McDonald's are consumed immediately. In general, services cannot be stored and sold later. Service companies do not have Work in Process and Finished Goods Inventory accounts for collecting costs before transferring them to a Cost of Goods Sold account. At the end of the day, McDonald's has no work in process or finished goods inventory.

Is a retail company such as Toys "R" Us a service company or a manufacturing company? Because wholesale and retail companies have large inventories, it may seem odd to think of them as service companies. Consider, however, what employees of a wholesale or retail company do. Their efforts cannot be stored and used later. The services of a salesperson are consumed as customers are assisted. Other service organizations include insurance companies, banks, cleaning establishments, airlines, law firms, hospitals, hotels, and governmental agencies.

Even though service companies do not collect costs in inventory accounts for financial reporting purposes, they do accumulate cost information for decision making. For example, a hotel manager needs to know the cost of providing a room to assess whether the pricing policy is appropriate. A private school may compare the expected and actual cost of offering a course to ensure that costs are controlled. Airline executives need to know the cost of serving a specific route to decide whether to maintain or eliminate the route.

Measuring the cost of providing services is just as necessary as measuring the cost of making products whether the cost is collected in an inventory account or charged directly to the income statement.

Topic Tackler PLUS 11-1

LO4 Demonstrate, using a horizontal statements model, how product cost flows affect financial statements.

Manufacturing Cost Flow Illustrated

To illustrate how manufacturing costs flow through ledger accounts, consider Ventra Manufacturing Company, which makes mahogany jewelry boxes that it sells to department stores. The account balances in Exhibit 11–2 were drawn from the company's accounting records as of January 1, 2005.

Ventra Manufacturing's 2005 accounting events are explained here. The effects of the events are summarized in the T-accounts in Exhibit 11–4 on page 449. Study the entries in Exhibit 11–4 as you read the event descriptions in the following section of this chapter. The illustration assumes Ventra determines the cost of making its jewelry boxes on a monthly basis. Accounting events for January are described next.

Exhibit 11–2 *Trial Balance as of January 1, 2005*

Cash	$ 64,500	
Raw Materials Inventory	500	
Work in Process Inventory	0	
Finished Goods Inventory	836	
Manufacturing Equipment	40,000	
Accumulated Depreciation		$ 10,000
Common Stock		76,000
Retained Earnings		19,836
Totals	$105,836	$105,836

Events Affecting Manufacturing Cost Flow in January

Event 1

Ventra Manufacturing paid $26,500 cash to purchase raw materials.

For simplicity, assume Ventra purchased all raw materials needed for the year at the beginning of the year. In practice, materials are usually purchased much more frequently. The effects of the materials purchase on the company's financial statements are shown in the following horizontal financial statements model.[1]

Assets			=	Liabilities	+	Equity	Revenue	−	Expenses	=	Net Income	Cash Flow
Cash	+	Raw Materials Inventory										
(26,500)	+	26,500	=	NA	+	NA	NA	−	NA	=	NA	(26,500) OA

This event is an asset exchange. One asset—cash—decreases, and another asset—raw materials inventory—increases. Neither total assets reported on the balance sheet nor any revenues or expenses on the income statement are affected. Raw materials costs are only one component of total manufacturing (product) costs. The raw materials costs will be included in the cost of goods sold (expense) recognized when completed jewelry boxes are sold to customers. Because Ventra spent cash for a current asset it will use in routine business operations, the cash outflow is classified as an operating activity (OA) on the statement of cash flows.

Event 2

Ventra placed $1,100 of raw materials into production in the process of making jewelry boxes.

This event is also an asset exchange. One asset—raw materials inventory—decreases, and another asset—work in process inventory—increases. Total assets reported on the balance

[1]The horizontal model arranges the major financial statement elements horizontally across a single page. Reading from left to right, balance sheet elements are presented first, followed by income statement elements, and then the statement of cash flows. Cash flow classifications are identified by the letters OA for operating activities, IA for investing activities, and FA for financing activities.

sheet are not affected. Neither the income statement nor the statement of cash flows is affected. The effects on the company's financial statements of using the raw materials follow.

Assets			=	Liabilities	+	Equity	Revenue	−	Expenses	=	Net Income	Cash Flow
Raw Materials Inventory	+	Work in Process Inventory										
(1,100)	+	1,100	=	NA	+	NA	NA	−	NA	=	NA	NA

Ventra's raw materials are *direct* inputs to the production process. They are accounted for using the *perpetual inventory method.* Because the raw materials are traced directly to products, it is easy to match the cost flow with the physical flow. Every time direct raw materials are moved from storage to work in process, their cost is transferred in the accounting records as well.

Event 3
Ventra paid $2,000 cash to purchase production supplies (glue, nails, sandpaper).

This event is also an asset exchange. One asset—cash—decreases, and another asset—production supplies—increases. Total assets reported on the balance sheet are not affected. Net income is not affected. The cash paid for the supplies purchased is reported in the operating activities section of the statement of cash flows. The effects of this event on the company's financial statements follow.

Assets			=	Liabilities	+	Equity	Revenue	−	Expenses	=	Net Income	Cash Flow
Cash	+	Production Supplies										
(2,000)	+	2,000	=	NA	+	NA	NA	−	NA	=	NA	(2,000) OA

The production supplies are recorded in a separate asset account because Ventra finds it more practical to account for them using the *periodic inventory method.* Production supplies are *indirect* inputs. Such small quantities are used on each jewelry box that it is not worth the trouble to track the actual costs as the materials are used. Nobody wants to stop to make a journal entry every time several drops of glue are used. *Instead of recognizing production supplies usage as it occurs (perpetually), Ventra determines at the end of the accounting period (periodically) the cost of supplies used.* The record-keeping procedures for including the cost of production supplies in the flow of manufacturing costs are described in the explanation of the Manufacturing Overhead account described shortly.

Event 4
Ventra paid production workers $1,400 cash.

These wages are *not* classified as salary expense. Because the labor was used to make jewelry boxes, the cost is added to the Work in Process Inventory account. This event is yet another asset exchange. Ventra exchanged cash for the value added by making the inventory. One asset—cash—decreases, and another asset—work in process inventory—increases. Total assets reported on the balance sheet are not affected. The income statement is not affected. The cash outflow is reported in the operating activities section of the statement of cash flows. The effects on the company's financial statements of incurring production labor costs follow.

Assets			=	Liabilities	+	Equity	Revenue	−	Expenses	=	Net Income	Cash Flow
Cash	+	Work in Process Inventory										
(1,400)	+	1,400	=	NA	+	NA	NA	−	NA	=	NA	(1,400) OA

REALITY *bytes*

Like manufacturing companies, service companies must use predetermined overhead rates to make timely decisions, such as determining what price to charge customers. Consider the Engineering and Evaluation (E&E) segment of **National Technical Systems, Inc.**, a large technical services company headquartered in Calabasas, California. In its 2003 fiscal year, the E&E segment generated over $54 million in revenues.

According to the company's 2003 annual report, its E&E segment "provides highly trained technical personnel for product certification, product safety testing, and product evaluation . . . " including " . . . performing structural testing and analysis . . . of large articles such as complete airframes." Fixed pricing is one method the company uses to price its goods.

Since the company has a lot of fixed overhead costs that include, among other things, depreciation of its testing facilities and equipment, it does not know the actual cost of completing a job until the end of the year. However, it cannot wait until then to give the customer a price for a test to be performed in March. How does it determine the price to charge? According to the company's annual report, "At the time the Company enters into a contract that includes multiple tasks, the Company *estimates* the amount of actual labor *and other costs* that will be required to complete each task based on historical experience." (Emphasis supplied.) These cost estimates are used to establish a price to be charged.

Topic Tackler PLUS 11–2

LO5 Explain the need to assign estimated overhead costs to inventory and cost of goods sold during an accounting period.

Flow of Overhead Costs

Assume Ventra made 500 jewelry boxes during January. What is the cost per jewelry box? Why does management need to know this cost? If Ventra uses a cost-plus pricing strategy, management must know the cost per jewelry box to determine what price to charge for each one. Product cost information is also used to control costs and evaluate managerial performance. By comparing current production costs with historical or standard costs, management can evaluate whether performance meets expectations and take appropriate action to ensure the company accomplishes its goals. Ventra has many reasons for needing to know in January the cost of products made in January.

The *direct costs* of making the 500 jewelry boxes in January are $1,100 for materials and $1,400 for labor. The *actual indirect overhead costs* are unknown. Ventra will not know the exact amount of some of these indirect costs until the end of the year. For example, Ventra uses the periodic inventory method to determine the cost of production supplies consumed. The actual cost of supplies consumed is unknown until the end of the year when Ventra counts any unused supplies. Similarly, the actual cost for 2005 of taxes, insurance, landscaping, supervisory bonuses, and other indirect costs may be unknown in January. Ventra cannot delay making managerial decisions until actual cost data become available. Ventra needs information on January 31 that will not be available until December 31. This dilemma is depicted in the following graphic.

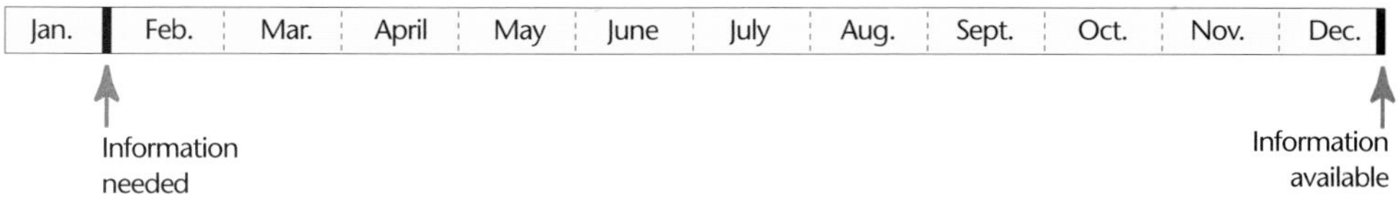

To solve the problem of needing cost information before it is available, Ventra records *estimated costs* in its accounting system *during the accounting period.* To illustrate, assume the accountant estimated Ventra will incur total indirect overhead costs of $40,320 during 2005. This *estimate* of overhead cost includes $1,600 for the cost of production supplies Ventra will use, $10,000 of depreciation cost, and $28,720 of other costs such as supervisory salaries, rent on the manufacturing facility, utilities, and maintenance. How much of the $40,320 *estimated* overhead cost should Ventra allocate to the units produced in January? Ventra must first identify the most appropriate allocation base. Assuming the goods (jewelry boxes) are homogeneous (the jewelry boxes are identical), it makes sense to use number of units as the allocation base, assigning an equal amount of overhead cost to each box.

Suppose Ventra's accountant expected Ventra to produce 12,000 jewelry boxes during the year. Based on this estimate, the allocation rate is $3.36 per unit ($40,320 expected cost ÷ 12,000 units). Because the overhead allocation rate is determined before the actual overhead costs are known, it is called a **predetermined overhead rate.** Using the $3.36 predetermined overhead rate, Ventra allocated $1,680 of overhead cost to the 500 jewelry boxes made in January ($3.36 × 500 boxes).

Manufacturing Overhead Account

LO6 Record applied and actual overhead costs in a Manufacturing Overhead account.

How are overhead costs recorded in the accounting records? Estimated overhead costs are *applied* (assigned) to work in process inventory *at the time goods are produced.* As shown in event 5 below, for January Ventra Manufacturing would apply (transfer) $1,680 of overhead cost to the Work in Process Inventory account. Actual overhead costs may be incurred at different times from when goods are made. For example, Ventra may recognize depreciation or supplies use at year-end. Actual and estimated overhead costs are therefore recorded at different times during the accounting period.

At the time estimated overhead is added (a debit) to the Work in Process Inventory account, a corresponding entry is recorded on the credit side of a *temporary* account called *Manufacturing Overhead.* This credit entry in the Manufacturing Overhead account is **applied overhead.** Think of the **Manufacturing Overhead account** as a temporary asset account. Recognizing estimated overhead can be viewed as an asset exchange transaction. When estimated overhead is recognized, the temporary account, Manufacturing Overhead, decreases and the Work in Process Inventory account increases.

Actual overhead costs are recorded as increases (debits) in the Manufacturing Overhead account. For example, at the end of the year, Ventra will reduce the Production Supplies account and increase the Manufacturing Overhead account by the actual amount of supplies used. The balance in the Production Supplies account will be decreased and the balance in the Manufacturing Overhead account will be increased. When Ventra pays monthly rent cost for the manufacturing facilities, it will increase Manufacturing Overhead and decrease cash. Other actual overhead costs are recorded the same way.

Since differences normally exist between estimated and actual overhead costs, the Manufacturing Overhead account is likely to have a balance at the end of the year. If more overhead has been applied than was actually incurred, the account balance represents the amount of **overapplied overhead.** If less overhead was applied than was incurred, the account balance is **underapplied overhead.** Overapplied overhead means the amount of estimated overhead cost recorded in the Work in Process Inventory account exceeded the actual overhead cost incurred. Underapplied overhead means the amount of estimated overhead cost recorded in the Work in Process Inventory account was less than the actual overhead cost incurred.

Because costs flow from Work in Process Inventory to Finished Goods Inventory and then to Cost of Goods Sold, these accounts will also be overstated or understated relative to actual costs. If the amount of overapplied or underapplied overhead is significant, it must be allocated proportionately at the end of the year to the Work in Process Inventory, Finished Goods Inventory, and Cost of Goods Sold accounts so these accounts will reflect actual, rather than estimated, amounts for financial reporting.

In most cases, over- or underapplied overhead is not significant and companies may allocate it in any convenient manner. In these circumstances, companies normally assign the total amount of the overhead correction directly to Cost of Goods Sold. We have adopted this simplifying practice throughout the text and in the end-of-chapter exercises and problems. Exhibit 11–3 shows the flow of product costs, including actual and applied overhead. To illustrate using a Manufacturing Overhead account, return to Ventra Manufacturing Company.

Exhibit 11–3 *Flow of Product Costs*

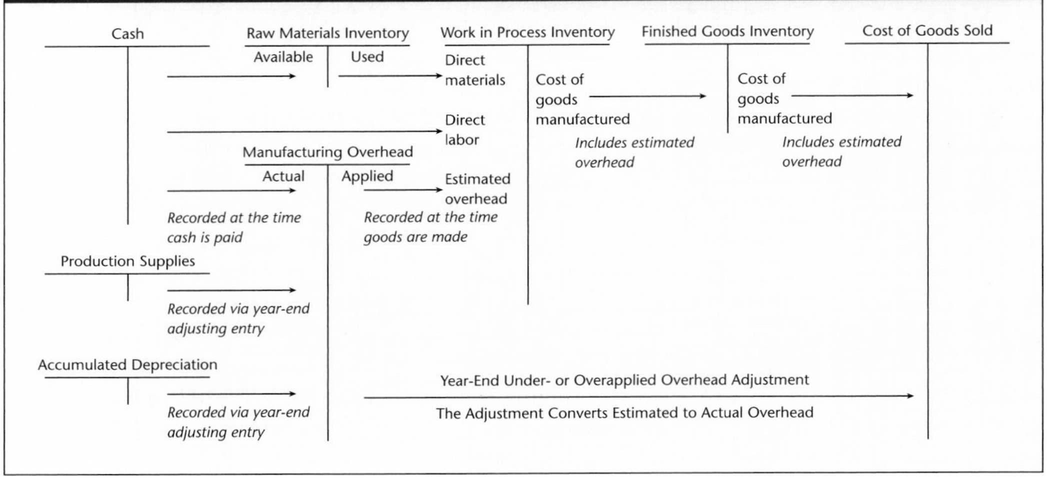

Event 5

Ventra recognized $1,680 of estimated manufacturing overhead costs at the end of January (see previous section entitled Flow of Overhead Costs to review computing this amount).

This event is another asset exchange. Total assets reported on the balance sheet, net income, and cash flow are not affected. The temporary asset account Manufacturing Overhead decreases, and the asset account Work in Process Inventory increases. The effects of this event on the company's financial statements follow.

Assets			=	Liabilities	+	Equity	Revenue	−	Expenses	=	Net Income	Cash Flow
Manufacturing Overhead	+	Work in Process Inventory										
(1,680)	+	1,680	=	NA	+	NA	NA	−	NA	=	NA	NA

Event 6

Ventra transferred the total cost of the 500 jewelry boxes made in January ($1,100 materials + $1,400 labor + $1,680 estimated overhead = $4,180 cost of goods manufactured) from work in process to finished goods.

This event is an asset exchange. Total assets reported on the balance sheet, net income, and cash flow are not affected. The asset account Work in Process Inventory decreases, and the asset account Finished Goods Inventory increases. The effects of this event on the company's financial statements follow.

Assets			=	Liabilities	+	Equity	Revenue	−	Expenses	=	Net Income	Cash Flow
Work in Process Inventory	+	Finished Goods Inventory										
(4,180)	+	4,180	=	NA	+	NA	NA	−	NA	=	NA	NA

Event 7

Ventra transferred the cost of 400 sold jewelry boxes from finished goods inventory to cost of goods sold.

Recall that Ventra made 500 jewelry boxes costing $4,180 during January. Also, the beginning balance in the Finished Goods Inventory account was $836. Assume this balance represented

100 jewelry boxes that had been made in 2004. Therefore, 600 units (100 + 500) of finished goods costing $5,016 ($836 + $4,180) were available for sale. If Ventra sold 400 units, it had 200 units in finished goods inventory at the end of January. The cost of the 600 boxes available ($5,016) must be allocated between the Finished Goods Inventory account and the Cost of Goods Sold account. The allocation is based on the cost per unit of jewelry boxes. Given that 600 boxes cost $5,016, the cost per unit is $8.36 ($5,016 ÷ 600). Based on this cost per unit, Ventra transferred $3,344 ($8.36 × 400 boxes) from finished goods inventory to cost of goods sold, leaving an ending balance of $1,672 ($8.36 × 200 boxes) in the Finished Goods Inventory account.

Transferring cost from finished goods inventory to cost of goods sold is an asset use event. Both total assets and stockholders' equity reported on the balance sheet decrease. The asset finished goods inventory decreases, and the expense cost of goods sold increases, decreasing stockholders' equity (retained earnings). Net income decreases. Recognizing the expense does not affect cash flow. The sales transaction encompasses two events. The following horizontal model shows the effects of the expense recognition. The effects of the corresponding revenue recognition are discussed separately as event 8.

Assets	=	Liabilities	+	Equity	Revenue	−	Expenses	=	Net Income	Cash Flow
Finished Goods Inventory				Retained Earnings						
(3,344)	=	NA	+	(3,344)	NA	−	3,344	=	(3,344)	NA

Knowing the cost per jewelry box is useful for many purposes. For example, the amount of the allocation between the ending Finished Goods Inventory and the Cost of Goods Sold accounts is needed for the financial statements. Ventra must compute the cost per unit data if it wishes to prepare interim (monthly or quarterly) financial reports. The cost per unit for the month of January also could be compared to the cost per unit for the previous accounting period or to standard cost data to evaluate cost control and managerial performance. Finally, the cost per unit data are needed for setting the price under a cost-plus pricing strategy. Assume Ventra desires to earn a gross margin of $5.64 per jewelry box. It would therefore charge $14 ($8.36 cost + $5.64 gross margin) per unit for each jewelry box. When recording the effects of recognizing revenue for the 400 boxes sold, we assume that Ventra charges its customers $14 per unit.

Event 8

Ventra recognized $5,600 ($14 per unit × 400 units) of sales revenue for the cash sale of 400 jewelry boxes.

Recognizing revenue is an asset source transaction. The asset cash increases and stockholders' equity (retained earnings) increases. Net income increases. The cash inflow is reported in the operating activities section of the statement of cash flows. These effects are shown here.

Assets	=	Liabilities	+	Equity	Revenue	−	Expenses	=	Net Income	Cash Flow
5,600	=	NA	+	5,600	5,600	−	NA	=	5,600	5,600 OA

Event 9

Ventra paid $1,200 cash for manufacturing overhead costs including indirect labor, utilities, and rent.

Paying for actual overhead costs is an asset exchange event. Ventra transfers cost from the asset account Cash to the temporary asset account Manufacturing Overhead. Total assets on the balance sheet and net income are unaffected. The cash outflow is reported as a reduction in the operating activities section of the statement of cash flows. These effects follow.

Assets			=	Liabilities	+	Equity	Revenue	−	Expenses	=	Net Income	Cash Flow
Cash	+	Manufacturing Overhead										
(1,200)	+	1,200	=	NA	+	NA	NA	−	NA	=	NA	(1,200) OA

Recall that $1,680 of overhead cost was applied to the January work in process inventory. This amount is significantly more than the $1,200 of actual overhead costs paid for above. These amounts differ because the estimated (applied) overhead includes several costs that have not yet been recognized. For example, the amount of supplies used and depreciation expense are not recognized until Ventra records adjusting entries on December 31. Although these costs are not recognized until December, a portion of them must be included in the cost of products made in January. Otherwise, all of the supplies cost and depreciation cost would be assigned to products made in December.

The manufacturing equipment and supplies are actually used throughout the year. Assigning the total cost of these resources to December alone would overstate the cost of December production and understate the cost of production during other months. Such distortions in measuring product cost could mislead managers making decisions based on the reported costs. By using *estimated* overhead costs during the accounting period, management reduces the distortions using actual monthly costs would create. The difference between actual and estimated overhead is corrected in a *year-end adjusting entry.* Companies do not adjust for these differences on an interim basis.

Check Yourself 11–1

Candy Manufacturing Company had a beginning balance of $24,850 in its Work in Process Inventory account. Candy added the following costs to work in process during the accounting period: direct materials, $32,000; direct labor, $46,000; manufacturing overhead, $39,900. If the ending balance in the Work in Process Inventory account was $22,100, what was the amount of the Cost of Goods Manufactured (cost of goods transferred to Finished Goods Inventory)?

Answer

Beginning work in process inventory	$ 24,850
Manufacturing costs added	
Direct materials	32,000
Direct labor	46,000
Manufacturing overhead	39,900
Total work in process	142,750
Less: Ending work in process inventory	(22,100)
Cost of goods manufactured	$120,650

Summary of January Events

LO7 Record product costs in T-accounts.

Exhibit 11–4 summarizes the events that occurred during January. The upper section of the exhibit illustrates the *physical flow* of the resources used to make the jewelry boxes. The lower section shows the product *cost flow* through Ventra's ledger accounts. The exhibit illustrates Events 1 through 7. Event 8 recognizes the sales revenue, and Event 9 reflects the actual overhead cost incurred in January. The January balances in the Finished Goods Inventory and Cost of Goods Sold accounts include the cost of materials, labor, and an *estimated* amount of overhead. Estimated overhead cost is applied to work in process inventory throughout the year. Actual overhead costs are accumulated in the Manufacturing Overhead account as they are incurred. The accounts are adjusted at year-end to reconcile the difference between the estimated and actual overhead costs.

ANSWERS TO THE *curious* ACCOUNTANT . . .

Obviously, an enterprise such as Norm's Furniture Shop cannot stay in business if it cannot give customers a price for the goods it is selling. As the chapter has explained, manufacturers estimate the manufacturing overhead cost of a job based on a predetermined overhead rate. Although these estimates will not be perfect, they do allow the companies to price their goods before they are manufactured. If the company does not do a reasonably good job of estimating the costs it will incur to complete a job, then it will suffer by either pricing its goods too high, which will cause it to lose business to its competitors, or pricing its goods too low, which will cause it to not make a profit adequate to stay in business.

Exhibit 11–4 *Flow of Product Costs for Ventra Manufacturing Company's January Production*

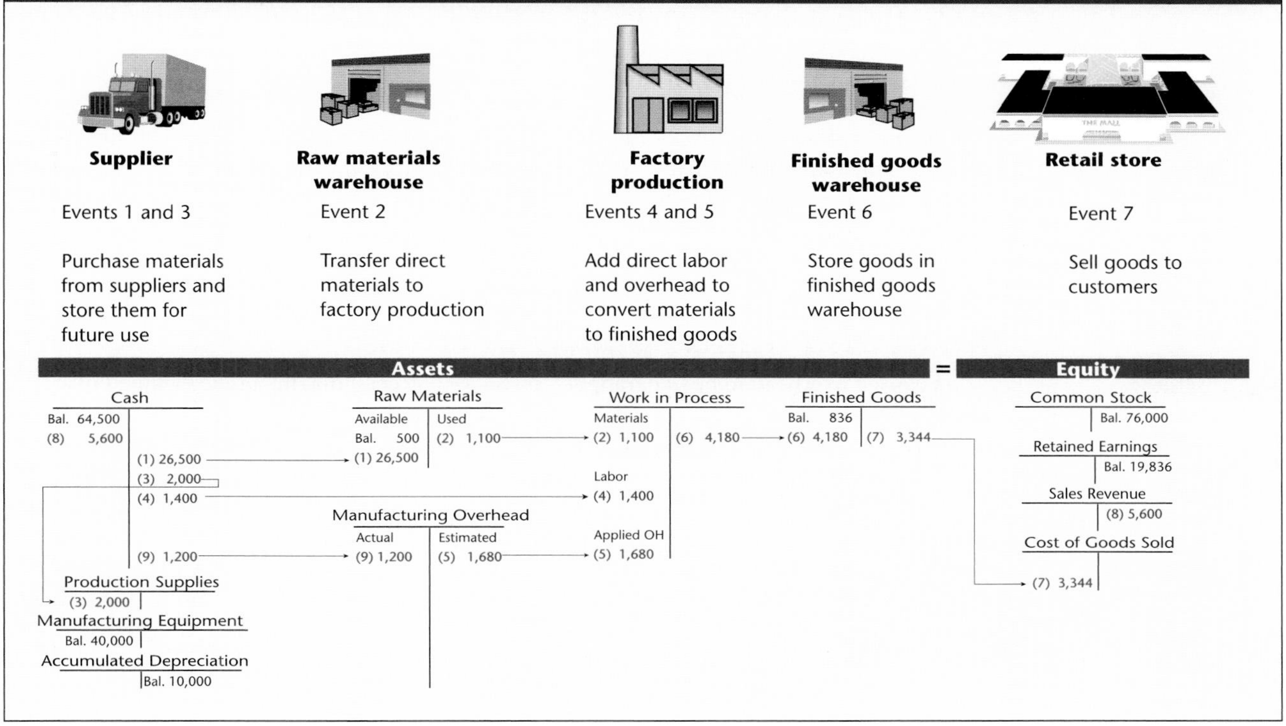

Manufacturing Cost Flow Events for February Through December

LO8 Explain the cyclical nature of product cost flows.

Ventra Manufacturing Company's accounting events for February through December are summarized here. The sequence of events continues from the January activity. Since nine events occurred in January, the first February event is Event 10. The events for the remainder of 2005 follow.

10. Ventra used $24,860 of raw materials.
11. The company paid production workers $31,640 cash.
12. Ventra started production of an additional 11,300 jewelry boxes. Ventra applied overhead of $37,968 (11,300 units × the predetermined overhead rate of $3.36 per unit) to work in process inventory.
13. The company completed 10,300 units and transferred $86,108 of cost of goods manufactured from work in process inventory to finished goods inventory.
14. Ventra sold 9,600 units and recorded $80,256 of cost of goods sold.
15. The company recognized $134,400 of cash revenue for the products sold in Event 14.
16. The company paid $30,500 cash for overhead costs including indirect labor, rent, and utilities.

17. The year-end count of production supplies indicated $300 of supplies were on hand at December 31. Ventra recognized $1,700 ($2,000 supplies available − $300 ending balance) of indirect materials cost for supplies used during the year. This entry reflects year-end recognition of an actual overhead cost.
18. Ventra recognized $10,000 of actual overhead cost for depreciation of manufacturing equipment.
19. The company paid $31,400 cash for general, selling, and administrative expenses.
20. A year-end review of the Manufacturing Overhead account disclosed that overhead cost was underapplied by $3,752. Actual overhead ($43,400) was higher than estimated overhead ($39,648). Because estimated overhead cost passes through the ledger accounts from Work in Process Inventory, to Finished Goods Inventory, and ultimately to Cost of Goods Sold, the balance in the Cost of Goods Sold account is understated. Ventra recorded the adjusting entry to close the Manufacturing Overhead account and increase the balance in the Cost of Goods Sold account.

LO7 Record product costs in T-accounts.

Exhibit 11–5 shows the flow of the 2005 costs through the ledger accounts. The January entries are shown in blue to distinguish them from the entries for the remainder of the year. The product cost flows are highlighted with black arrows. Trace the effects of each transaction to the exhibit before reading further.

Analyzing Underapplied Overhead

LO9 Explain the relationship between over- or underapplied overhead and variance analysis.

What caused overhead to be underapplied by $3,752? Recall that the predetermined overhead rate is based on two estimates, the estimated total overhead cost and the estimated total annual production volume. At the beginning of 2005, Ventra estimated total overhead cost would be $40,320, but actual overhead costs were $43,400, indicating Ventra spent $3,080 more than expected for overhead cost. This $3,080 is a *spending variance.* The remaining $672 of the underapplied overhead ($3,752 − $3,080) results from the difference between the actual and estimated volume of activity; it is called a *volume variance.* Recall that Ventra estimated production volume would be 12,000 units, but actual volume was only 11,800[2] units (500 units made in January + 11,300 units made from February through December). The predetermined overhead rate of $3.36 per unit was applied to 200 fewer units (12,000 units − 11,800 units) than expected, resulting in a volume variance of $672 ($3.36 predetermined overhead rate × 200 units). The combination of the spending and volume variances[3] explains the total underapplied overhead ($3,080 + $672 = $3,752).

Because the actual cost is higher than the expected cost, the spending variance is unfavorable. The volume variance is also unfavorable because actual volume is less than expected, suggesting the manufacturing facilities were not utilized to the extent anticipated. In other words, fixed costs such as depreciation, rent, and supervisory salaries were spread over fewer units of product than expected, thereby increasing the cost per unit of product. If the variances are significant, estimated product costs could have been understated enough to have distorted decisions using the data. For example, products may have been underpriced, adversely affecting profitability. Making estimates as accurately as possible is critically important. Nevertheless, some degree of inaccuracy is inevitable. No one knows precisely what the future will bring. Managers seek to improve decision making. Although managers cannot make exact predictions, the more careful the estimates, the more useful will be the resulting information for timely decision making.

---

[2]There were 11,800 units placed into production. There were 10,800 units completed, leaving an ending work in process inventory balance of 1,000 units.

[3]The predetermined overhead rate in this chapter represents the standard cost and quantity of both variable and fixed inputs. As discussed in Chapter 8, companies may establish separate standards for variable costs and fixed costs. In this chapter, we assume the variable cost variances are insignificant and focus the discussion on the effects of fixed cost variances only.

Exhibit 11–5 *Product Cost Flow for Ventra Manufacturing Company's 2005 Accounting Period*

Cash

Bal. 64,500	(1) 26,500
(8) 5,600	(3) 2,000
(15) 134,400	(4) 1,400
	(11) 31,640
	(9) 1,200
	(16) 30,500
	(19) 31,400
Bal. 79,860	

Raw Materials Inventory

Available	Used
Bal. 500	(2) 1,100
(1) 26,500	(10) 24,860
Bal. 1,040	

Work in Process Inventory

Materials	
(2) 1,100	(6) 4,180
(10) 24,860	(13) 86,108
Labor	
(4) 1,400	
(11) 31,640	
Applied OH	
(5) 1,680	
(12) 37,968	
Bal. 8,360	

Finished Goods Inventory

Bal. 836	(7) 3,344
(6) 4,180	(14) 80,256
(13) 86,108	
Bal. 7,524	

Cost of Goods Sold

(7) 3,344	
(14) 80,256	
(20) 3,752	
Bal. 87,352	

Common Stock

	Bal. 76,000

Retained Earnings

	Bal. 19,836

Sales Revenue

	(8) 5,600
	(15) 134,400

G,S&A Expense

(19) 31,400	

Manufacturing Overhead

Actual	Estimated
(9) 1,200	(5) 1,680
(16) 30,500	(12) 37,968
(17) 1,700	(20) 3,752
(18) 10,000	
Bal. 0	

Production Supplies

(3) 2,000	(17) 1,700
Bal. 300	

Manufacturing Equip.

Bal. 40,000	

Accumulated Depreciation

	Bal. 10,000
	(18) 10,000
	Bal. 20,000

Check Yourself 11–2

At the beginning of the accounting period, Nutrient Manufacturing Company estimated its total manufacturing overhead cost for the coming year would be $124,000. Furthermore, the company expected to use 15,500 direct labor hours during the year. Nutrient actually incurred overhead costs of $128,500 for the year and actually used 15,800 direct labor hours. Nutrient allocates overhead costs to production based on direct labor hours. Would overhead costs be overapplied or underapplied? What effect will closing the overhead account have on cost of goods sold?

Answer

Predetermined overhead rate = Total expected overhead cost ÷ Allocation base
Predetermined overhead rate = $124,000 ÷ 15,500 hours = $8 per direct labor hour

Applied overhead = Predetermined overhead rate × Actual direct labor hours
Applied overhead = $8 × 15,800 = $126,400

Since the applied overhead ($126,400) is less than the actual overhead ($128,500), the overhead is underapplied. Closing the overhead account will increase Cost of Goods Sold by $2,100 ($128,500 − $126,400).

Preparing the Schedule of Cost of Goods Manufactured and Sold

LO10 Prepare a schedule of cost of goods manufactured and sold.

In practice, a general ledger system like that shown in Exhibit 11–5 may capture millions of events. Analyzing operations with such vast numbers of transactions is exceedingly difficult. To help managers analyze manufacturing results, companies summarize the ledger data in a *schedule* that shows the overall cost of goods manufactured and sold. The schedule is an internal document which is not presented with a company's published financial statements. Only the final total on the schedule (cost of goods sold) is disclosed; it is reported on the income statement. Exhibit 11–6 illustrates Ventra's 2005 **schedule of cost of goods manufactured and sold.**

The schedule in Exhibit 11–6 reflects the transaction data in the ledger accounts. Confirm this relationship by comparing the information in the Raw Materials Inventory account in Exhibit 11–5 with the computation of the cost of direct raw materials used in the schedule in Exhibit 11–6. The beginning raw materials inventory, purchases, and ending raw materials inventory amounts in the ledger account agree with the schedule. The schedule, however, presents various amounts in summary form. For example, in the schedule the amount of direct raw materials used is $25,960. In Exhibit 11–5 this same amount is shown as two separate entries ($1,100 + $24,860) in the T-account. Similarly, the $33,040 shown as direct labor in the schedule represents the total of the two amounts ($1,400 + $31,640) of labor cost entered in the Work in Process Inventory account in Exhibit 11–5. In practice, one number in the schedule may represent thousands of individual events captured in the ledger accounts. The schedule simplifies analyzing manufacturing cost flow data for decision-making purposes.

Exhibit 11–6 *Ventra Manufacturing Company*

Schedule of Cost of Goods Manufactured and Sold
For the Year Ended December 31, 2005

Beginning raw materials inventory	$ 500
Plus: Purchases	26,500
Raw materials available for use	27,000
Less: Ending raw materials inventory	(1,040)
Direct raw materials used	25,960
Direct labor	33,040
Overhead (actual overhead cost)	43,400
Total manufacturing costs	102,400
Plus: Beginning work in process inventory	0
Total work in process inventory	102,400
Less: Ending work in process inventory	(8,360)
Cost of goods manufactured	94,040
Plus: Beginning finished goods inventory	836
Cost of goods available for sale	94,876
Less: Ending finished goods inventory	(7,524)
Cost of goods sold	$ 87,352

The schedule of cost of goods manufactured and sold includes the *actual* amount of overhead cost. Data for financial statement reports are summarized at the end of the year when actual cost data are available. Although companies use estimated costs for internal records and decision-making during the year, they use actual historical cost data in this schedule prepared at the end of the year.

LO11 Prepare financial statements for a manufacturing entity.

Financial Statements

The final total on the schedule of cost of goods manufactured and sold is reported as the single line item *cost of goods sold* on the company's income statement. Cost of goods sold is subtracted from sales revenue to determine gross margin. Selling and administrative expenses are subtracted from gross margin to reach net income. Exhibit 11–7 shows Ventra Manufacturing's 2005 income statement; Exhibit 11–8 shows the year-end balance sheet. In Exhibit 11–8 we show the three inventory accounts (Raw Materials, Work in Process, and Finished Goods) separately for teaching purposes. In practice, these accounts are frequently combined and reported as a single amount (Inventories) on the balance sheet. Exhibit 11–9 shows the statement of cash flows. Study each statement, tracing the information from the T-accounts in Exhibit 11–5 to the exhibits to see how companies gather the information they report to the public in their published financial statements.

Exhibit 11–7

Ventra Manufacturing Company
Income Statement
For the Year Ended December 31, 2005

Sales Revenue	$140,000
Cost of Goods Sold	(87,352)
Gross Margin	52,648
Selling and Administrative Expenses	(31,400)
Net Income	$ 21,248

Exhibit 11–8

Ventra Manufacturing Company
Balance Sheet
As of December 31, 2005

Assets	
Cash	$ 79,860
Raw Materials Inventory	1,040
Work in Process Inventory	8,360
Finished Goods Inventory	7,524
Production Supplies	300
Manufacturing Equipment	40,000
Accumulated Depreciation—Manufac. Equip.	(20,000)
Total Assets	$117,084
Stockholders' Equity	
Common Stock	$ 76,000
Retained Earnings	41,084
Total Stockholders' Equity	$117,084

Exhibit 11–9

Ventra Manufacturing Company
Statement of Cash Flows
For the Year Ended December 31, 2005

Cash Flows from Operating Activities	
Inflow from Customers	$140,000
Outflow for Production of Inventory*	(93,240)
Outflow for Selling and Administrative Expenses	(31,400)
Net Inflow from Operating Activities	15,360
Cash Flow from Investing Activities	0
Cash Flow from Financing Activities	0
Net Change in Cash	15,360
Plus: Beginning Cash Balance	64,500
Ending Cash Balance	$ 79,860

*See Cash account in Exhibit 11–5: $26,500 + $2,000 + $1,400 + $31,640 + $1,200 + $30,500 = $93,240.

Motive to Overproduce

Absorption Costing Versus Variable Costing

As discussed previously, managers frequently separate product manufacturing costs into variable and fixed categories based on how the costs behave. For example, the cost of materials, labor, and supplies usually increases and decreases in direct proportion to the number of units produced. Other product costs, such as rent, depreciation, and supervisory salaries are fixed; they remain constant regardless of the number of products made. Generally accepted accounting principles require that *all* product costs, both variable and fixed, be reported as inventory until the products are sold, when the product costs are expensed as cost of goods sold. This practice is called **absorption (full) costing.**[4] To illustrate, assume Hokai Manufacturing Company incurs the following costs to produce 2,000 units of inventory.

[4]Since all manufacturing costs are classified as product costs under absorption costing, absorption costing is also called *full costing*.

LO12 Distinguish between absorption and variable costing.

Inventory Costs	Cost per Unit	×	Units	=	Total
Variable manufacturing costs	$9	×	2,000	=	$18,000
Fixed overhead				=	12,000
Total (full absorption product cost)				=	$30,000

Exhibit 11–10 *Cost per Unit*

Inventory Costs			
Fixed overhead (a)	$12,000	$12,000	$12,000
Number of units (b)	2,000	3,000	4,000
Fixed overhead per unit (a ÷ b)	$ 6	$ 4	$ 3
Variable manufacturing costs	9	9	9
Full absorption product cost per unit	$ 15	$ 13	$ 12

Suppose Hokai sells all 2,000 units of inventory for $20 per unit (sales = 2,000 × $20 = $40,000). Gross margin is therefore $10,000 ($40,000 sales − $30,000 cost of goods sold). What happens to reported profitability if Hokai increases production without also increasing sales? Profitability increases because cost of goods sold decreases. Overproducing spreads the fixed cost over more units, thereby reducing the cost per unit and the amount charged to cost of goods sold. Exhibit 11–10 illustrates this effect; it shows the cost per unit at production levels of 2,000, 3,000, and 4,000 units.

Exhibit 11–11 illustrates for Hokai alternate income statements assuming sales of 2,000 units and production levels of 2,000, 3,000, and 4,000 units.

Exhibit 11–11 *Absorption Costing Income Statements at Different Levels of Production With Sales Held Constant at 2,000 Units*

Level of Production	2,000		3,000		4,000
Sales ($20 per unit × 2,000 units)	$40,000		$40,000		$40,000
Cost of goods sold ($15 × 2,000) =	30,000	($13 × 2,000) =	26,000	($12 × 2,000) =	24,000
Gross margin	$10,000		$14,000		$16,000

Suppose Hokai's management is under pressure to increase profitability but cannot control sales because customers make buying decisions. Management may be tempted to increase reported profitability by increasing production. What is wrong with increasing production without also increasing sales? The problem lies in inventory accumulation. Notice inventory increases by 1,000 units when 3,000 units are produced but only 2,000 are sold. Likewise, inventory rises to 2,000 units when 4,000 are produced but 2,000 are sold. Holding excess inventory entails considerable risks and costs. Inventory is subject to obsolescence, damage, theft, or destruction by fire, weather, or other disasters. Furthermore, holding inventory requires expenditures for warehouse space, employee handling, financing, and insurance coverage. These risks and costs reduce a company's profitability. Overproducing inventory is a poor business practice. To motivate managers to increase profitability without tempting them to overproduce, many companies use *variable costing* for internal reporting.

Variable Costing

Under **variable costing,** inventory includes only *variable* product costs. The income statement is presented using the contribution margin approach, with variable product costs subtracted from sales revenue to determine the contribution margin. Fixed costs are then subtracted from the contribution margin to determine net income.

Fixed manufacturing costs are expensed in the period in which they are incurred (the period in which the resource is used) regardless of when inventory is sold. Using variable costing, increases in production have no effect on the amount of reported profit as shown in the income statements in Exhibit 11–12.

Although managers may still overproduce under variable costing, at least they are not tempted to do so by the lure of reporting higher profits. The variable costing reporting format encourages management to make business decisions that have a more favorable impact on

Exhibit 11–12 *Variable Costing Income Statements at Different Levels of Production With Sales Held Constant at 2,000 Units*

Level of Production	2,000		3,000		4,000
Sales ($20 per unit × 2,000 units)	$40,000		$40,000		$40,000
Variable cost of goods sold ($9 × 2,000) =	(18,000)	($9 × 2,000) =	(18,000)	($9 × 2,000) =	(18,000)
Contribution margin	22,000		22,000		22,000
Fixed manufacturing costs	(12,000)		(12,000)		(12,000)
Net income	$10,000		$10,000		$10,000

long-term profitability. Variable costing can be used only for internal reporting because generally accepted accounting principles prohibit its use in external financial statements.

Check Yourself 11–3

If production exceeds sales, will absorption or variable costing produce the higher amount of net income? Which method (absorption or variable costing) is required for external financial reporting?

Answer Absorption costing produces a higher amount of net income when production exceeds sales. With absorption costing, fixed manufacturing costs are treated as inventory and remain in inventory accounts until the inventory is sold. In contrast, all fixed manufacturing costs are expensed with variable costing. Therefore, with absorption costing, some fixed manufacturing costs will be in inventory rather than in expense accounts, so expenses will be lower and net income will be higher than with variable costing (when production exceeds sales). Generally accepted accounting principles require companies to use absorption costing for external financial reporting purposes.

a look back

Most manufacturing companies accumulate product costs in three inventory accounts. The *Raw Materials Inventory account* is used to accumulate the cost of direct *raw materials* purchased for use in production. The *Work in Process Inventory account* includes the cost of partially completed products. Finally, the *Finished Goods Inventory account* contains the costs of fully completed products that are ready for sale. When direct materials are purchased, their costs are first recorded in raw materials inventory. The costs of the materials used in production are transferred from raw materials inventory to work in process inventory. The cost of direct labor and overhead are added to work in process inventory. As goods are completed, their costs are transferred from work in process inventory to finished goods inventory. When goods are sold, their cost is transferred from finished goods inventory to cost of goods sold. The ending balances in the Raw Materials, Work in Process, and Finished Goods Inventory accounts are reported in the balance sheet. The product cost in the Cost of Goods Sold account is subtracted from sales revenue on the income statement to determine gross margin.

The actual amounts of many indirect overhead costs incurred to make products are unknown until the end of the accounting period. Examples of such costs include the cost of rent, supplies, utilities, indirect materials, and indirect labor. Because many managerial decisions require product cost information before year-end, companies frequently estimate the amount of overhead cost. The estimated overhead costs are assigned to products using a *predetermined overhead rate.*

Actual and applied overhead costs are accumulated in the temporary asset account *Manufacturing Overhead.* Differences between actual and applied overhead result in a balance in the Manufacturing Overhead account at the end of the accounting period. If actual overhead exceeds applied overhead, the account balance represents *underapplied overhead.* If actual overhead is less than applied overhead, the balance represents *overapplied overhead.* If the amount of over- or underapplied overhead is insignificant, it is closed directly to cost of goods sold through a year-end adjusting entry.

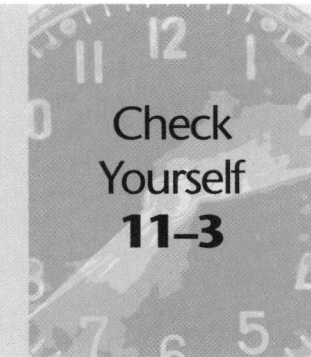

Manufacturing cost information is summarized in a report known as a *schedule of cost of goods manufactured and sold.* This schedule shows how the amount of cost of goods sold reported on the income statement was determined. Actual, rather than applied, overhead cost is used in the schedule.

Generally accepted accounting principles require all product costs (fixed and variable) to be included in inventory until the products are sold. This practice is called *absorption costing.* Results reported under absorption costing may tempt management to increase profitability by producing more units than the company can sell (overproducing). Overproducing spreads fixed costs over more units, reducing the cost per unit and the amount charged to cost of goods sold. Overproducing has the adverse effect of reducing profitability in the long-term by increasing the risks and costs of inventory accumulation. To eliminate the temptation to overproduce, for internal reporting many companies determine product cost using *variable costing.* Under variable costing, only the variable product costs are included in inventory. Fixed product costs are expensed in the period they are incurred, regardless of when products are sold. As a result, overproduction does not decrease the product cost per unit and managers are not tempted to overproduce to increase profitability.

a look forward

Would you use the same product cost system to determine the cost of a bottle of Pepsi as to determine the cost of a stealth bomber? We answer this question in the next chapter, which expands on the basic cost flow concepts introduced in this chapter. You will be introduced to job-order, process, and hybrid cost systems. You will learn to identify the types of services and products that are most appropriate for each type of cost system.

SELF-STUDY REVIEW PROBLEM

Tavia Manufacturing Company's first year of operation is summarized in the following list. All transactions are cash transactions unless otherwise indicated.

1. Acquired cash by issuing common stock.
2. Purchased administrative equipment.
3. Purchased manufacturing equipment.
4. Purchased direct raw materials.
5. Purchased indirect materials (production supplies).
6. Used direct raw materials in making products.
7. Paid direct labor wages to manufacturing workers.
8. Applied overhead costs to Work in Process Inventory.
9. Paid indirect labor salaries (production supervisors).
10. Paid administrative and sales staff salaries.
11. Paid rent and utilities on the manufacturing facilities.
12. Completed work on products.
13. Sold completed inventory for cash. (revenue event only)
14. Recognized cost of goods sold.
15. Recognized depreciation on manufacturing equipment.
16. Recognized depreciation on administrative equipment.
17. Recognized the amount of production supplies that had been used during the year.
18. Closed the Manufacturing Overhead account. Overhead had been underapplied during the year.

Required

a. Use the horizontal statements model to show how each event affects the balance sheet, income statement, and statement of cash flows. Indicate whether the event increases (+), decreases (−), or does not affect (NA) each element of the financial statements. Also designate the classification of cash flows using the letters OA for operating activity, IA for investing activity, and FA for financing activity.

b. Identify the accounts affected by each event and indicate whether they increased or decreased as a result of the event.

Solution to Requirement a

Event No.	Assets	=	Liab.	+	Equity	Rev.	−	Exp.	=	Net Inc.	Cash Flow
1	+		n/a		+	n/a		n/a		n/a	+FA
2	−+		n/a		n/a	n/a		n/a		n/a	− IA
3	−+		n/a		n/a	n/a		n/a		n/a	− IA
4	−+		n/a		n/a	n/a		n/a		n/a	−OA
5	−+		n/a		n/a	n/a		n/a		n/a	−OA
6	−+		n/a		n/a	n/a		n/a		n/a	n/a
7	−+		n/a		n/a	n/a		n/a		n/a	−OA
8	−+		n/a		n/a	n/a		n/a		n/a	n/a
9	−+		n/a		n/a	n/a		n/a		n/a	−OA
10	−		n/a		−	n/a		+		−	−OA
11	−+		n/a		n/a	n/a		n/a		n/a	−OA
12	−+		n/a		n/a	n/a		n/a		n/a	n/a
13	+		n/a		+	+		n/a		+	+OA
14	−		n/a		−	n/a		+		−	n/a
15	−+		n/a		n/a	n/a		n/a		n/a	n/a
16	−		n/a		−	n/a		+		−	n/a
17	−+		n/a		n/a	n/a		n/a		n/a	n/a
18	−		n/a		−	n/a		+		−	n/a

Solution to Requirement b

Event No.	Account Title	Increase/ Decrease	Account Title	Increase/ Decrease
1	Cash	+	Common Stock	+
2	Administrative Equipment	+	Cash	−
3	Manufacturing Equipment	+	Cash	−
4	Raw Materials Inventory	+	Cash	−
5	Production Supplies	+	Cash	−
6	Work in Process Inventory	+	Raw Materials Inventory	−
7	Work in Process Inventory	+	Cash	−
8	Work in Process Inventory	+	Manufacturing Overhead	−
9	Manufacturing Overhead	+	Cash	−
10	Salary Expense	+	Cash	−
11	Manufacturing Overhead	+	Cash	−
12	Finished Goods Inventory	+	Work in Process Inventory	−
13	Cash	+	Sales Revenue	+
14	Cost of Goods Sold	+	Finished Goods Inventory	−
15	Manufacturing Overhead	+	Accumulated Depreciation	+
16	Depreciation Expense	+	Accumulated Depreciation	+
17	Manufacturing Overhead	+	Production Supplies	−
18	Cost of Goods Sold	+	Manufacturing Overhead	−

KEY TERMS

Absorption (full) costing *453*
Applied overhead *445*
Finished goods inventory *440*
Manufacturing overhead account *445*
Overapplied or underapplied overhead *445*
Predetermined overhead rate *445*
Raw materials inventory *440*
Retained earnings *447*
Schedule of cost of goods manufactured and sold *452*
Variable costing *454*
Work in process inventory *440*

QUESTIONS

1. What is the difference between direct and indirect raw materials costs?
2. Direct raw materials were purchased on account, and the costs were subsequently transferred to Work in Process Inventory. How would the transfer affect assets, liabilities, equity, and cash flows?

What is the effect on the income statement? Would your answers change if the materials had originally been purchased for cash?

3. How do manufacturing costs flow through inventory accounts?
4. Goods that cost $2,000 to make were sold for $3,000 on account. How does their sale affect assets, liabilities, and equity? What is the effect on the income statement? What is the effect on the cash flow statement?
5. At the end of the accounting period, an adjusting entry is made for the accrued wages of production workers. How would this entry affect assets, liabilities, and equity? What is the effect on the income statement? What is the effect on the cash flow statement?
6. X Company recorded the payment for utilities used by the manufacturing facility by crediting Cash and debiting Manufacturing Overhead. Why was the debit made to Manufacturing Overhead instead of Work in Process Inventory?
7. Why is the salary of a production worker capitalized while the salary of a marketing manager expensed?
8. Al Carmon says that his company has a difficult time establishing a predetermined overhead rate because the number of units of product produced during a period is difficult to measure. What are two measures of production other than the number of units of product that Mr. Carmon could use to establish a predetermined overhead rate?
9. What do the terms *overapplied overhead* and *underapplied overhead* mean?
10. What are *product costs* and *selling, general, and administrative costs?* Give examples of product costs and of selling, general, and administrative costs.
11. How does the entry to close an insignificant amount of overapplied overhead to the Cost of Goods Sold account affect net income?
12. Why are actual overhead costs not used in determining periodic product cost?
13. Because of seasonal fluctuations, Buresch Corporation has a problem determining the unit cost of its products. For example, high heating costs during the winter months cause the cost per unit to be higher than the per unit cost in the summer months even when the same number of units of product is produced. Suggest how Buresch can improve the computation of per unit cost.
14. What is the purpose of the Manufacturing Overhead account?
15. For what purpose is the schedule of cost of goods manufactured and sold prepared? Do all companies use the statement?
16. How does the variable costing approach differ from the absorption costing approach? Explain the different income statement formats used with each approach.
17. How is profitability affected by increases in productivity under the variable and absorption costing approaches?
18. Under what circumstance is a variable costing statement format used? What potential problem could it eliminate?

EXERCISES—SERIES A

All Exercises in Series A are available with McGraw-Hill's Homework Manager

L.O. 2, 4, 10, 11

EXERCISE 11–1A *Product Cost Flow and Financial Statements*

Weltin Manufacturing Company was started on January 1, 2006. The company was affected by the following events during its first year of operation.

1. Acquired $800 cash from the issue of common stock.
2. Paid $250 cash for direct raw materials.
3. Transferred $200 of direct raw materials to work in process.
4. Paid production employees $300 cash.
5. Paid $150 cash for manufacturing overhead costs.
6. Applied $123 of manufacturing overhead costs to work in process.
7. Completed work on products that cost $500.
8. Sold products that cost $400 for $700 cash.
9. Paid $200 cash for selling and administrative expenses.
10. Made a $25 cash distribution to the owners.
11. Closed the Manufacturing Overhead account.

Required

a. Record these events in a horizontal statements model. Also designate the classification of cash flows using the letters OA for operating activities, IA for investing activities, and FA for financing activities. The first event is shown as an example.

Assets									=	Equity									
Cash	+	MOH	+	Raw M.	+	WIP	+	F. Goods	=	C. Stk.	+	Ret. Ear.	Rev.	−	Exp.	=	Net Inc.	Cash Flow	
800	+	NA	+	NA	+	NA	+	NA	=	800	+	NA	NA	−	NA	=	NA	800	FA

b. Prepare a schedule of cost of goods manufactured and sold.

EXERCISE 11–2A *Recording Events in T-Accounts and Preparing Financial Statements*

L.O. 2, 7, 10, 11

Leimen Manufacturing Company was started on January 1, 2005, when it acquired $2,000 cash from the issue of common stock. During the first year of operation, $800 of direct raw materials was purchased with cash, and $600 of the materials was used to make products. Direct labor costs of $1,000 were paid in cash. Leimen applied $640 of overhead cost to the Work in Process account. Cash payments of $640 were made for actual overhead costs. The company completed products that cost $1,600 and sold goods that had cost $1,200 for $2,000 cash. Selling and administrative expenses of $480 were paid in cash.

Required

a. Open T-accounts and record the events affecting Leimen Manufacturing. Include closing entries.
b. Prepare a schedule of cost of goods manufactured and sold, an income statement, a balance sheet, and a statement of cash flows.
c. Explain the difference between net income and cash flow from operating activities.

EXERCISE 11–3A *Effect of Accounting Events on Financial Statements*

L.O. 4

Required

Use a horizontal statements model to indicate how each of the following independent accounting events affects the elements of the balance sheet, income statement, and statement of cash flows. Indicate whether the event increases (I), decreases (D), or does not affect (NA) each element of the financial statements. Also designate the classification of cash flows using the letters OA for operating activities, IA for investing activities, and FA for financing activities. The first two transactions are shown as examples.

a. Paid cash to purchase raw materials.
b. Recorded cash sales revenue.
c. Paid cash for actual manufacturing overhead cost.
d. Closed the Manufacturing Overhead account when overhead was overapplied.
e. Transferred cost of completed inventory to finished goods.
f. Paid cash for wages of production workers.
g. Paid cash for salaries of selling and administrative personnel.
h. Recorded adjusting entry to recognize amount of manufacturing supplies used (the company uses the periodic inventory method to account for manufacturing supplies).

Event No.	Balance Sheet				Income Statement			Statement of Cash Flow
	Assets =	Liab. −	C. Stk +	Ret Ear.	Rev. −	Exp. =	Net Inc.	
a.	I D	NA	NA	NA	NA	NA	NA	D OA
b.	I	NA	NA	I	I	NA	I	I OA

EXERCISE 11–4A *Preparing Financial Statements*

L.O. 2, 10, 11

Sahag Corporation began fiscal year 2005 with the following balances in its inventory accounts.

Raw Materials	$56,000
Work in Process	84,000
Finished Goods	28,000

During the accounting period, Sahag purchased $240,000 of raw materials and issued $248,000 of materials to the production department. Direct labor costs for the period amounted to $324,000, and factory overhead of $48,000 was applied to Work in Process Inventory. Assume that there was no over- or underapplied overhead. Goods costing $612,000 to produce were completed and transferred to Finished Goods Inventory. Goods costing $602,000 were sold for $800,000 during the period. Selling and administrative expenses amounted to $72,000.

Required

a. Determine the ending balance of each of the three inventory accounts that would appear on the yearend balance sheet.

b. Prepare a schedule of cost of goods manufactured and sold and an income statement.

L.O. 10

EXERCISE 11–5A *Missing Information in a Schedule of Cost of Goods Manufactured*

Required

Supply the missing information on the following schedule of cost of goods manufactured.

PUMA CORPORATION Schedule of Cost of Goods Manufactured For the Year Ended December 31, 2005		
Raw Materials		
Beginning Inventory	$?	
Plus: Purchases	120,000	
Raw Materials Available for Use	148,000	
Minus: Ending Raw Materials Inventory	?	
Cost of Direct Raw Materials Used		$124,000
Direct Labor		?
Manufacturing Overhead		24,000
Total Manufacturing Costs		310,000
Plus: Beginning Work in Process Inventory		?
Total Work in Process during the Period		?
Minus: Ending Work in Process Inventory		46,000
Cost of Goods Manufactured		$306,000

L.O. 10

EXERCISE 11–6A *Cost of Goods Manufactured and Sold*

The following information pertains to Bluegrass Manufacturing Company for March 2005. Assume actual overhead equaled applied overhead.

March 1	
Inventory balances	
Raw materials	$ 95,000
Work in process	120,000
Finished goods	78,000
March 31	
Inventory balances	
Raw materials	$ 60,000
Work in process	145,000
Finished goods	80,000
During March	
Costs of raw materials purchased	$120,000
Costs of direct labor	100,000
Costs of manufacturing overhead	63,000
Sales revenues	310,000

Required

a. Prepare a schedule of cost of goods manufactured and sold.

b. Calculate the amount of gross margin on the income statement.

EXERCISE 11–7A *Calculating Applied Overhead* **L.O. 6, 9**

Stenzil Inc. estimates manufacturing overhead costs for the 2005 accounting period as follows.

Equipment depreciation	$69,000
Supplies	18,000
Materials handling	20,000
Property taxes	16,000
Production setup	24,000
Rent	50,000
Maintenance	23,000
Supervisory salaries	135,000

The company uses a predetermined overhead rate based on machine hours. Estimated hours for labor in 2005 were 125,000 and for machines were 100,000.

Required

a. Calculate the predetermined overhead rate.

b. Determine the amount of manufacturing overhead applied to Work in Process Inventory during the 2005 period if actual machine hours were 120,000.

EXERCISE 11–8A *Treatment of Over- or Underapplied Overhead* **L.O. 5,9**

Beeston Company estimates that its overhead costs for 2007 will be $450,000 and output in units of product will be 300,000 units.

Required

a. Calculate Beeston's predetermined overhead rate based on expected production.

b. If 24,000 units of product were made in March 2007, how much overhead cost would be allocated to the Work in Process Inventory account during the month?

c. If actual overhead costs in March were $35,000, would overhead be overapplied or underapplied and by how much?

EXERCISE 11–9A *Recording Overhead Costs in T-Accounts* **L.O. 6, 9**

Ard Company and Ciza Company both apply overhead to the Work in Process Inventory account using direct labor hours. The following information is available for both companies for the year.

	Ard Company	Ciza Company
Actual manufacturing overhead	$400,000	$800,000
Actual direct labor hours	10,000	12,000
Underapplied overhead		40,000
Overapplied overhead	80,000	

Required

a. Compute the predetermined overhead rate for each company.

b. Using T-accounts, record the entry to close the overapplied or underapplied overhead at the end of the accounting period for each company, assuming the amounts are immaterial.

EXERCISE 11–10A *Treatment of Over- or Underapplied Overhead* **L.O. 6, 9**

Korb Company and Mang Company assign manufacturing overhead to the Work in Process Inventory using direct labor cost. The following information is available for the companies for the year:

	Korb Company	Mang Company
Actual direct labor cost	$580,000	$480,000
Estimated direct labor cost	600,000	400,000
Actual manufacturing overhead cost	224,000	368,000
Estimated manufacturing overhead cost	240,000	320,000

Required

a. Compute the predetermined overhead rate for each company.

b. Determine the amount of overhead cost that would be applied to Work in Process Inventory for each company.

c. Compute the amount of overapplied or underapplied manufacturing overhead cost for each company.

L.O. 6 **EXERCISE 11–11A** *Recording Manufacturing Overhead Costs in T-Accounts*

Parrish Corporation manufactures model airplanes. The company purchased for $375,000 automated production equipment that can make the model parts. The equipment has a $15,000 salvage value and a 10-year useful life.

Required

a. Assuming that the equipment was purchased on March 1, record in T-accounts the adjusting entry that the company would make on December 31 to record depreciation on equipment.
b. n which month would the depreciation costs be assigned to units produced?

L.O. 2, 6, 9 **EXERCISE 11–12A** *Missing Information in T-Accounts*

Ostberg Manufacturing recorded the following amounts in its inventory accounts in 2007.

Raw Materials Inventory

60,000	(a)
16,000	

Work in Process Inventory

	16,000
32,000	
24,000	
(c)	

Finished Goods Inventory

16,000	(d)
2,000	

Cost of Goods Sold

(e)	

Manufacturing Overhead

(b)	24,000
2,000	

Required

Determine the dollar amounts for (a), (b), (c), (d), and (e). Assume that underapplied and overapplied overhead is closed to Cost of Goods Sold.

L.O. 12 **EXERCISE 11–13A** *Variable Costing Versus Absorption Costing*

Hume Company incurred manufacturing overhead cost for the year as follows.

Direct materials	$40/unit
Direct labor	$28/unit
Manufacturing overhead	
Variable	$12/unit
Fixed ($20/unit for 1,500 units)	$30,000
Variable selling & admin. expenses	$ 8,000
Fixed selling & admin. expenses	$16,000

The company produced 1,500 units and sold 1,000 of them at $180 per unit. Assume that the production manager is paid a 2 percent bonus based on the company's net income.

Required

a. Prepare an income statement using absorption costing.
b. Prepare an income statement using variable costing.
c. Determine the manager's bonus using each approach. Which approach would you recommend for internal reporting and why?

L.O. 5 **EXERCISE 11–14A** *Smoothed Unit Cost*

Canty Manufacturing estimated its product costs and volume of production for 2008 by quarter as follows.

	First Quarter	Second Quarter	Third Quarter	Fourth Quarter
Direct raw materials	$ 80,000	$ 40,000	$120,000	$ 60,000
Direct labor	48,000	24,000	72,000	36,000
Manufacturing overhead	80,000	124,000	160,000	92,000
Total production costs	$208,000	$188,000	$352,000	$188,000
Expected units produced	16,000	8,000	24,000	12,000

Canty Company sells a souvenir item at various resorts across the country. Its management uses the product's estimated quarterly cost to determine the selling price of its product. The company expects a large variance in demand for the product between quarters due to its seasonal nature. The company does not expect overhead costs, which are predominately fixed, to vary significantly as to production volume or with amounts for previous years. Prices are established by using a cost-plus-pricing strategy. The company finds variations in short-term unit cost confusing to use. Unit cost variations complicate pricing decisions and many other decisions for which cost is a consideration.

Required

a. Based on estimated total production cost, determine the expected quarterly cost per unit for Canty's product.

b. How could overhead costs be estimated each quarter to solve the company's unit cost problem? Calculate the unit cost per quarter based on your recommendation.

PROBLEMS—SERIES A

All Problems in Series A are available with McGraw-Hill's Homework Manager

PROBLEM 11–15A *Manufacturing Cost Flow Across Three Accounting Cycles*

L.O. 2, 4, 8, 10, 11

CHECK FIGURE
b. Cost of goods sold: $578
NI: $152

The following accounting events affected Estrada Manufacturing Company during its first three years of operation. Assume that all transactions are cash transactions.

Transactions for 2004

1. Started manufacturing company by issuing common stock for $3,000.
2. Purchased $1,200 of direct raw materials.
3. Used $800 of direct raw materials to produce inventory.
4. Paid $400 of direct labor wages to employees to make inventory.
5. Applied $250 of manufacturing overhead cost to Work in Process Inventory.
6. Finished work on inventory that cost $900.
7. Sold goods that cost $600 for $1,100.
8. Paid $370 for selling and administrative expenses.
9. Actual manufacturing cost amounted to $228 for the year.

Transactions for 2005

1. Acquired additional $800 of cash from common stock.
2. Purchased $1,200 of direct raw materials.
3. Used $1,300 of direct raw materials to produce inventory.
4. Paid $600 of direct labor wages to employees to make inventory.
5. Applied $320 of manufacturing overhead cost to Work in Process Inventory.
6. Finished work on inventory that cost $1,800.
7. Sold goods that cost $1,600 for $2,800.
8. Paid $500 for selling and administrative expenses.
9. Actual manufacturing overhead cost amounted to $330 for the year.

Transactions for 2006

1. Paid a cash dividend of $700.
2. Purchased $1,400 of direct raw materials.
3. Used $1,200 of direct raw materials to produce inventory.
4. Paid $440 of direct labor wages to employees to make inventory.
5. Applied $290 of manufacturing overhead cost to work in process.
6. Finished work on inventory that cost $2,000.
7. Sold goods that cost $2,200 for $3,500.
8. Paid $710 for selling and administrative expenses.
9. Annual manufacturing overhead costs were $280 for the year.

Required

a. Record the preceding events in a horizontal statements model. Close overapplied or underapplied overhead to Cost of Goods Sold. Also designate the classification of cash flows using the letters OA for operating activities, IA for investing activities, and FA for financing activities. The first event is shown as an example.

Assets					=	Equity						Cash Flow
Cash	+ MOH	+ Raw M.	+ WIP	+ F. Goods	=	C. Stk.	+ Ret. Ear.	Rev.	− Exp.	= Net Inc.		Cash Flow
3,000	+ NA	+ NA	+ NA	+ NA	=	3,000	+ NA	NA	− NA	= NA		3,000 FA

b. Prepare a schedule of cost of goods manufactured and sold, an income statement, a balance sheet, and a statement of cash flows as of the close of business on December 31, 2004.
c. Close appropriate accounts.
d. Repeat Requirements a through c for years 2005 and 2006.

L.O. 2, 6, 8, 9, 10, 11

PROBLEM 11–16A *Manufacturing Cost Flow for Monthly and Annual Accounting Periods*

CHECK FIGURES
b. Cost of goods sold: $12,198
Total assets: $249,402

Marcia Deavers started Eufala Manufacturing Company to make a universal television remote control device that she had invented. The company's labor force consisted of part-time employees. The following accounting events affected Eufala Manufacturing Company during its first year of operation. (Assume that all transactions are cash transactions unless otherwise stated.)

Transactions for January 2004, First Month of Operation

1. Issued common stock for $3,000.
2. Purchased $420 of direct raw materials and $60 of production supplies.
3. Used $240 of direct raw materials.
4. Used 80 direct labor hours; production workers were paid $9.60 per hour.
5. Expected total overhead costs for the year to be $3,300, and direct labor hours used during the year to be 1,000. Calculate an overhead rate and apply the appropriate amount of overhead costs to Work in Process Inventory.
6. Paid $144 for salaries to administrative and sales staff.
7. Paid $24 for indirect manufacturing labor.
8. Paid $210 for rent and utilities on the manufacturing facilities.
9. Started and completed 100 remote controls; all costs were transferred from the Work in Process Inventory account to the Finished Goods Inventory account.
10. Sold 90 remote controls at a price of $21.60 each.

Transactions for Remainder of 2004

11. Acquired an additional $20,000 by issuing common stock.
12. Purchased $3,900 of direct raw materials and $900 of production supplies.
13. Used $3,000 of direct raw materials.
14. Paid production workers $9.60 per hour for 900 hours of work.
15. Applied the appropriate overhead cost to Work in Process Inventory.
16. Paid $1,560 for salaries of administrative and sales staff.
17. Paid $240 of indirect manufacturing labor cost.
18. Paid $2,400 for rental and utility costs on the manufacturing facilities.
19. Transferred 950 additional remote controls that cost $12.72 each from the Work in Process Inventory account to the Finished Goods Inventory account.
20. Determined that $168 of production supplies was on hand at the end of the accounting period.
21. Sold 850 remote controls for $21.60 each.
22. Determine whether the overhead is over- or underapplied. Close the Manufacturing Overhead account to the Cost of Goods Sold account.
23. Close the revenue and expense accounts.

Required

a. Open T-accounts and post transactions to the accounts.
b. Prepare a schedule of cost of goods manufactured and sold, an income statement, a balance sheet, and a statement of cash flows for 2004.

L.O. 2, 4, 9, 10, 11

PROBLEM 11–17A *Manufacturing Cost Flow for One-Year Period*

CHECK FIGURE
b. NI: $430

Biro Manufacturing started 2005 with the following account balances.

Cash	$ 800
Common Stock	1,600
Retained Earnings	2,400
Raw Materials Inventory	960
Work in Process Inventory	640
Finished Goods Inventory (320 units @$5)	1,600

Transactions during 2005

1. Purchased $2,304 of raw materials with cash.
2. Transferred $3,000 of raw materials to the production department.
3. Incurred and paid cash for 180 hours of direct labor @$12.80 per hour.
4. Applied overhead costs to the Work in Process Inventory account. The predetermined overhead rate is $13.20 per direct labor hour.
5. Incurred actual overhead costs of $2,400 cash.
6. Completed work on 1,200 units for $5.12 per unit.
7. Paid $1,120 in selling and administrative expenses in cash.
8. Sold 1,200 units for $7,680 cash revenue (assume FIFO cost flow).

Biro charges overapplied or underapplied overhead directly to Cost of Goods Sold.

Required

a. Record the preceding events in a horizontal statements model. Also designate the classification of cash flows using the letters OA for operating activities, IA for investing activities, and FA for financing activities. The beginning balances are shown as an example.

Assets									=	Equity				Rev.	−	Exp.	=	Net Inc.	Cash Flow
Cash	+	Raw M.	+	MOH	+	WIP	+	F. Goods	=	C. Stk.	+	Ret. Ear.							
800	+	960	+	NA	+	640	+	1,600	=	1,600	+	2,400		NA	−	NA	=	NA	NA

b. Prepare a schedule of cost of goods manufactured and sold, an income statement, a balance sheet, and a statement of cash flows for 2005.

PROBLEM 11–18A *Manufacturing Cost for One Accounting Cycle*

L.O. 2, 6, 7, 10, 11

excel

www.mhhe.com/edmonds3e

CHECK FIGURE

NI: $3,974

The following trial balance was taken from the records of Maetz Manufacturing Company at the beginning of 2004.

Cash	$ 3,000	
Raw Materials Inventory	750	
Work in Process Inventory	1,200	
Finished Goods Inventory	2,100	
Property, Plant, and Equipment	7,500	
Accumulated Depreciation		$ 3,000
Common Stock		5,400
Retained Earnings		6,150
Total	$14,550	$14,550

Transactions for the Accounting Period

1. Maetz purchased $5,700 of direct raw materials and $300 of indirect raw materials on account. The indirect materials are capitalized in the Production Supplies account. Materials requisitions showed that $5,400 of direct raw materials had been used for production during the period. The use of indirect materials is determined at the end of the year by physically counting the supplies on hand.
2. By the end of the year, $5,250 of the accounts payable had been paid in cash.
3. During the year, direct labor amounted to 950 hours recorded in the Wages Payable account at $10.50 per hour.
4. By the end of the year, $9,000 of wages payable had been paid in cash.
5. At the beginning of the year, the company expected overhead cost for the period to be $6,300 and 1,000 direct labor hours to be worked. Overhead is allocated based on direct labor hours, which, as indicated in Event 3, amounted to 950 for the year.
6. Administrative and sales expenses for the year amounted to $900 paid in cash.
7. Utilities and rent for production facilities amounted to $4,650 paid in cash.
8. Depreciation on the plant and equipment used in production amounted to $1,500.
9. Assume that $12,000 of goods were completed during the year.
10. Assume that $12,750 of finished goods inventory was sold for $18,000 cash.
11. A count of the production supplies revealed a balance of $89 on hand at the end of the year.
12. Any over- or underapplied overhead is considered to be insignificant.

Required

a. Open T-accounts with the beginning balances shown in the preceding list and record all transactions for the year including closing entries in the T-accounts. (*Note:* Open new T-accounts as needed.)

b. Prepare a schedule of cost of goods manufactured and sold, an income statement, a balance sheet, and a statement of cash flows.

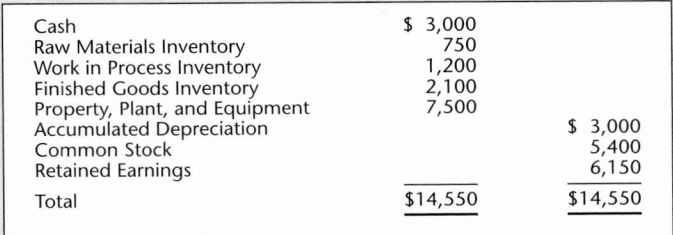

L.O. 2, 6, 7, 8, 9, 10, 11

PROBLEM 11–19A *Manufacturing Cost Flow for Multiple Accounting Cycles*

CHECK FIGURES
b. NI for 2004: $22,860
NI for 2005: $33,040

The following events apply to Sapp Manufacturing Company. Assume that all transactions are cash transactions unless otherwise indicated.

Transactions for the 2004 Accounting Period

1. The company was started on January 1, 2004, when it acquired $162,000 cash by issuing common stock.
2. The company purchased $36,000 of direct raw materials with cash and used $2,430 of these materials to make its products in January.
3. Employees provided 900 hours of labor at $5.70 per hour during January. Wages are paid in cash.
4. The estimated manufacturing overhead costs for 2004 were $64,800. Overhead is applied on the basis of direct labor hours. The company expected to use 12,000 direct labor hours during 2004. Calculate an overhead rate and apply the overhead for January to work in process inventory.
5. The employees completed work on all inventory items started in January. The cost of this production was transferred to the Finished Goods Inventory account. Determine the cost per unit of product produced in January, assuming that a total of 1,800 units of product were started and completed during the month.
6. The company used an additional $31,050 of direct raw materials and 11,500 hours of direct labor at $5.70 per hour during the remainder of 2004. Overhead was allocated on the basis of direct labor hours.
7. The company completed work on inventory items started between February 1 and December 31, and the cost of the completed inventory was transferred to the Finished Goods Inventory account. Determine the cost per unit for goods produced between February 1 and December 31, assuming that 23,000 units of inventory were produced. If the company desires to earn a gross profit of $2.70 per unit, what price per unit must it charge for the merchandise sold?
8. The company sold 22,000 units of inventory for cash at $9.60 per unit. Determine the number of units in ending inventory and the cost per unit incurred for this inventory.
9. Actual manufacturing overhead costs paid in cash were $65,700.
10. The company paid $37,800 cash for selling and administrative expenses.
11. Close the Manufacturing Overhead account.
12. Close the revenue and expense accounts.

Transactions for the 2005 Accounting Period

1. The company purchased $40,500 of direct raw materials with cash and used $2,280 of these materials to make products in January.
2. Employees provided 800 hours of labor at $5.70 per hour during January.
3. On January 1, 2005, Sapp hired a production supervisor at an expected cost of $1,080 cash per month. The company paid cash to purchase $4,500 of manufacturing supplies; it anticipated that $4,140 of these supplies would be used by year end. Other manufacturing overhead costs were expected to total $64,800. Overhead is applied on the basis of direct labor hours. Sapp expected to use 14,000 hours of direct labor during 2005. Based on this information, determine the total expected overhead cost for 2005. Calculate the predetermined overhead rate and apply the overhead cost for the January production.
4. The company recorded a $1,080 cash payment to the production supervisor.
5. The employees completed work on all inventory items started in January. The cost of this production was transferred to the Finished Goods Inventory account. Determine the cost per unit of product produced in January, assuming that 1,600 units of product were started and completed during the month.
6. During February 2005, the company used $2,850 of raw materials and 1,000 hours of labor at $5.70 per hour. Overhead was allocated on the basis of direct labor hours.
7. The company recorded a $1,080 cash payment to the production supervisor for February.
8. The employees completed work on all inventory items started in February; the cost of this production was transferred to the Finished Goods Inventory account. Determine the cost per unit of product produced in February, assuming that 2,000 units of product were started and completed during the month.
9. The company used an additional $34,200 of direct raw materials and 12,000 hours of direct labor at $5.70 per hour during the remainder of 2005. Overhead was allocated on the basis of direct labor hours.
10. The company recorded $10,800 of cash payments to the production supervisor for work performed between March 1 and December 31.
11. The company completed work on inventory items started between March 1 and December 31. The cost of the completed goods was transferred to the Finished Goods Inventory account. Compute the cost per unit of this inventory, assuming that there were 24,000 units of inventory produced.

12. The company sold 26,000 units of product for $9.90 cash per unit. Assume that the company uses the FIFO inventory cost flow method to determine the cost of goods sold.
13. The company paid $38,700 cash for selling and administrative expenses.
14. As of December 31, 2005, $450 of production supplies was on hand.
15. Actual cost of other manufacturing overhead was $63,020 cash.
16. Close the manufacturing overhead account.
17. Close the revenue and expense accounts.

Required

a. Open T-accounts and record the effects of the preceding events.

b. Prepare a schedule of cost of goods manufactured and sold, an income statement, a balance sheet, and a statement of cash flows for both years.

PROBLEM 11–20A *Comprehensive Review Problem*

L.O. 10

CHECK FIGURE

c. Cost per computer with 2,000 units produced: $409.80

During their senior year at Preston College, two business students, John Pickett and Naomi Hayes, began a part-time business making personal computers. They bought the various components from a local supplier and assembled the machines in the basement of a friend's house. Their only cost was $360 for parts; they sold each computer for $630. They were able to make three machines per week and to sell them to fellow students. The activity was appropriately called Pickett Hayes Computers (PHC). The product quality was good, and as graduation approached, orders were coming in much faster than PHC could fill them.

A national CPA firm made Ms. Hayes an attractive offer of employment, and a large electronic company was ready to hire Mr. Pickett. Students and faculty at Preston College, however, encouraged the two to make PHC a full-time venture. The college administration had decided to require all students in the schools of business and engineering to buy their own computers beginning in the coming fall term. It was believed that the quality and price of the PHC machines would attract the college bookstore to sign a contract to buy a minimum of 1,000 units the first year for $540 each. The bookstore sales were likely to reach 2,000 units per year, but the manager would not make an initial commitment beyond 1,000.

The prospect of $540,000 in annual sales for PHC caused the two young entrepreneurs to wonder about the wisdom of accepting their job offers. Before making a decision, they decided to investigate the implications of making PHC a full-time operation. Their study provided the following information relating to the production of their computers.

Components from wholesaler	$ 360 per computer
Assembly labor	15 per hour
Manufacturing space rent	2,250 per month
Utilities	450 per month
Janitorial services	360 per month
Depreciation of equipment	2,880 per year
Labor	2 hours per computer

The two owners expected to devote their time to the sales and administrative aspects of the business.

Required

a. Classify each cost item into the categories of direct materials, direct labor, and manufacturing overhead.

b. Classify each cost item as either variable or fixed.

c. What is the cost per computer if PHC produces 1,000 units per year? What is the cost per unit if PHC produces 2,000 units per year?

d. If the job offers for Mr. Pickett and Ms. Hayes totaled $96,000, would you recommend that they accept the offers or proceed with plans to make PHC a full-time venture?

PROBLEM 11–21A *Absorption Versus Variable Costing*

L.O. 12

excel

www.mhhe.com/edmonds3e

Pace Manufacturing Company makes a product that sells for $27 per unit. Manufacturing costs for the product amount to $10.50 per unit variable, and $30,000 fixed. During the current accounting period, Pace made 4,000 units of the product and sold 3,500 units.

Required

a. Prepare an absorption costing income statement.

b. Prepare a variable costing income statement.

c. Explain why the amount of net income on the absorption costing income statement differs from the amount of net income on the variable costing income statement. Your answer should include the amount of the inventory balance that would exist under the two costing approaches.

CHECK FIGURES

a. NI: $31,500

b. NI: $27,750

L.O. 12

PROBLEM 11–22A *Absorption Versus Variable Costing*

Hardy Glass Company makes stained glass lamps. Each lamp that it sells for $315 per lamp requires $18 of direct materials and $72 of direct labor. Fixed overhead costs are expected to be $202,500 per year. Hardy Glass expects to sell 1,000 lamps during the coming year.

CHECK FIGURES

a. NI when 1,000 lamps where produced: $22,500
b. NI when 1,500 lamps where produced: $22,500

Required

a. Prepare income statements using absorption costing, assuming that Hardy Glass makes 1,000, 1,250, and 1,500 lamps during the year.
b. Prepare income statements using variable costing, assuming that Hardy Glass makes 1,000, 1,250, and 1,500 lamps during the year.
c. Explain why Hardy Glass may produce income statements under both absorption and variable costing formats. Your answer should include an explanation of the advantages and disadvantages associated with the use of the two reporting formats.

L.O. 12

PROBLEM 11–23A *Absorption and Variable Costing*

www.mhhe.com/edmonds3e

Kwan Manufacturing pays its production managers a bonus based on the company's profitability. During the two most recent years, the company maintained the same cost structure to manufacture its products.

CHECK FIGURES

a. NI for 2004: $24,000
d. $138,000

Year	Units Produced	Units Sold
Production and Sales		
2004	4,000	4,000
2005	6,000	4,000
Cost Data		
Direct materials		$15 per unit
Direct labor		$24 per unit
Manufacturing overhead—variable		$12 per unit
Manufacturing overhead—fixed		$108,000
Variable selling & administrative expenses		$9 per unit sold
Fixed selling & administrative expenses		$60,000

(Assume that selling & administrative expenses are associated with goods sold.)

Kwan sells its products for $108 a unit.

Required

a. Prepare income statements based on absorption costing for 2004 and 2005.
b. Since Kwan sold the same number of units in 2004 and 2005, why did net income increase in 2005?
c. Discuss management's possible motivation for increasing production in 2005.
d. Determine the costs of ending inventory for 2005. Comment on the risks and costs associated with the accumulation of inventory.
e. Based on your answers to Requirements *b* and *c,* suggest a different income statement format. Prepare income statements for 2004 and 2005 using your suggested format.

EXERCISES—SERIES B

L.O. 2, 4

EXERCISE 11–1B *Product Cost Flow and Financial Statements*

Wells Manufacturing began business on January 1, 2005. The following events pertain to its first year of operation.

1. Acquired $1,440 cash by issuing common stock.
2. Paid $480 cash for direct raw materials.
3. Transferred $400 of direct raw materials to Work in Process Inventory.
4. Paid production employees $560 cash.
5. Applied $260 of manufacturing overhead costs to Work in Process Inventory.
6. Completed work on products that cost $880.
7. Sold products for $1,280 cash.
8. Recognized cost of goods sold from Event No. 7 of $700.
9. Paid $360 cash for selling and administrative expenses.
10. Paid $280 cash for actual manufacturing overhead costs.

11. Made a $80 cash distribution to owners.
12. Closed the manufacturing overhead account.

Required

a. Record the preceding events in a horizontal statements model. Also designate the classification of cash flows using the letters OA for operating activities, IA for investing activities, and FA for financing activities. The first event is shown as an example.

Assets					=	Equity						
Cash	+ MOH	+ Raw M.	+ WIP	+ F. Goods	=	C. Stk.	+ Ret. Ear.	Rev.	− Exp.	=	Net Inc.	Cash Flow
1,440	+ NA	+ NA	+ NA	+ NA	=	1,440	+ NA	NA	− NA	=	NA	1,440 FA

b. Prepare a schedule of cost of goods manufactured and sold.

EXERCISE 11–2B *Recording Events in T-Accounts and Preparing Financial Statements*

L.O. 2, 7, 10, 11

Zinn Manufacturing Company was started on January 1, 2005, when it acquired $1,600 cash by issuing common stock. During its first year of operation, it purchased $480 of direct raw materials with cash and used $360 of the materials to make products. Zinn paid $640 of direct labor costs in cash. The company applied $464 of overhead costs to Work in Process Inventory. It made cash payments of $464 for actual overhead costs. The company completed products that cost $1,040 to make. It sold goods that had cost $824 to make for $1,360 cash. It paid $320 of selling and administrative expenses in cash.

Required

a. Open the necessary T-accounts and record the 2005 events in the accounts. Include closing entries.
b. Prepare a schedule of cost of goods manufactured and sold, an income statement, a balance sheet, and a statement of cash flows.

EXERCISE 11–3B *Effect of Accounting Events on Financial Statements*

L.O. 4

Required

Use a horizontal statements model to show how each of the following independent accounting events affects the elements of the balance sheet, income statement, and statement of cash flows. Indicate whether the event increases (I), decreases (D), or does not affect (NA) each element of the financial statements. Also designate the classification of cash flows using the letters OA for operating activities, IA for investing activities, and FA for financing activities. The first two transactions are shown as examples.

a. Paid cash to purchase raw materials.
b. Recorded cash sales revenue.
c. Applied overhead to Work in Process Inventory based on the predetermined overhead rate.
d. Closed the manufacturing overhead account when overhead was underapplied.
e. Recognized cost of goods sold.
f. Recognized depreciation expense on manufacturing equipment.
g. Purchased manufacturing supplies on account.
h. Sold fully depreciated manufacturing equipment for the exact amount of its salvage value.

Event No.	Balance Sheet				Income Statement			Statement of Cash Flows
	Assets	= Liab.	− C. Stk	+ Ret Ear.	Rev.	− Exp.	= Net Inc.	
a.	I D	NA	NA	NA	NA	NA	NA	D OA
b.	I	NA	NA	I	I	NA	I	I OA

EXERCISE 11–4B *Preparing Financial Statements*

L.O. 2, 10, 11

Kerr Manufacturing Company started 2005 with the following balances in its inventory accounts: Raw Materials, $5,400; Work in Process, $5,600; Finished Goods, $6,600. During 2005 Kerr purchased $34,000 of raw materials and issued $33,000 of materials to the production department. It incurred $38,000 of direct labor costs and applied manufacturing overhead of $37,400 to Work in Process Inventory. Assume there was no over- or underapplied overhead at the end of the year. Kerr completed goods costing $105,000 to produce and transferred them to finished goods inventory. During the year, Kerr sold goods costing $101,400 for $153,800. Selling and administrative expenses for 2005 were $36,000.

Required

a. Using T-accounts, determine the ending balance Kerr would report for each of the three inventory accounts that would appear on the December 31, 2005, balance sheet.

b. Prepare the 2005 schedule of cost of goods manufactured and the 2005 income statement.

L.O. 10

EXERCISE 11–5B *Missing Information in a Schedule of Cost of Goods Manufactured and Sold*

Required

Supply the missing information on the following schedule of cost of goods manufactured and sold.

HILLIARD CORPORATION Statement of Cost of Goods Manufactured and Sold For the Year Ended December 31, 2006	
Raw Materials	
Beginning Inventory	$ 8,000
Plus: Purchases	?
Raw Materials Available for Use	64,000
Minus: Ending Raw Materials Inventory	?
Cost of Direct Raw Materials Used	58,000
Direct Labor	48,000
Manufacturing Overhead	?
Total Manufacturing Costs	150,000
Plus: Beginning Work in Process Inventory	?
Total Work in Process during the Year	157,200
Minus: Ending Work in Process Inventory	(8,200)
Cost of Goods Manufactured	?
Plus: Beginning Finished Goods Inventory	?
Finished Goods Available For Sale	159,600
Minus: Ending Finished Goods Inventory	?
Cost of Goods Sold	$151,200

L.O. 10

EXERCISE 11–6B *Cost of Goods Manufactured and Sold*

The following information was drawn from the accounting records of Dismuke Manufacturing Company.

	Beginning	Ending
Raw materials inventory	$4,000	$4,600
Work in process inventory	6,200	5,000
Finished goods inventory	6,800	5,800

During the accounting period, Dismuke paid $16,000 to purchase raw materials, $15,000 for direct labor, and $11,000 for overhead costs. Assume that actual overhead equaled applied overhead.

Required

a. Determine the amount of raw materials used.

b. Determine the amount of cost of goods manufactured (the amount transferred from Work in Process Inventory to Finished Goods Inventory).

c. Assuming sales revenue of $76,800, determine the amount of gross margin.

L.O. 6, 9

EXERCISE 11–7B *Calculating Applied Overhead*

Gentry Enterprises' budget included the following estimated costs for the 2007 accounting period.

Depreciation on manufacturing equipment	$17,200
Cost of manufacturing supplies	3,000
Direct labor cost	86,400
Rent on manufacturing facility	7,600
Direct materials cost	74,000
Manufacturing utilities cost	6,000
Maintenance cost for manufacturing facility	5,200
Administrative salaries cost	30,500

The company uses a predetermined overhead rate based on machine hours. It estimated machine hour usage for 2007 would be 30,000 hours.

Required

a. Identify the manufacturing overhead costs Gentry would use to calculate the predetermined overhead rate.
b. Calculate the predetermined overhead rate.
c. Explain why the rate is called "predetermined."
d. Assuming Gentry actually used 29,200 machine hours during 2007, determine the amount of manufacturing overhead it would have applied to Work in Process Inventory during the period.

EXERCISE 11–8B *Treatment of Over- or Underapplied Overhead*

L.O. 5, 9

On January 1, 2006, Bragg Company estimated that its total overhead costs for the coming year would be $139,400 and that it would make 34,000 units of product. Bragg actually produced 34,600 units of product and incurred actual overhead costs of $140,500 during 2006.

Required

a. Calculate Bragg's predetermined overhead rate based on expected costs and production.
b. Determine whether overhead was overapplied or underapplied during 2006.
c. Explain how the entry to close the manufacturing overhead account will affect the Cost of Goods Sold account.

EXERCISE 11–9B *Recording Overhead Costs in a T-Account*

L.O. 6, 9

Zuber Manufacturing Company incurred actual overhead costs of $29,800 during 2006. It uses direct labor dollars as the allocation base for overhead costs. In 2006, actual direct labor costs were $42,000, and overhead costs were underapplied by $400.

Required

a. Calculate the predetermined overhead rate for 2006.
b. Open T-accounts for Manufacturing Overhead and Cost of Goods Sold. Record the overhead costs and the adjusting entry to close Manufacturing Overhead in these accounts.
c. Explain how the entry to close the Manufacturing Overhead account at the end of 2006 would affect the amount of net income reported on the 2006 income statement.

EXERCISE 11–10B *Treatment of Over- or Underapplied Overhead*

L.O. 6, 9

Craig Company and Rowland Company base their predetermined overhead rates on machine hours. The following information pertains to the companies' most recent accounting periods.

	Craig	Rowland
Actual machine hours	12,300	19,500
Estimated machine hours	12,000	20,000
Actual manufacturing overhead costs	$17,000	$34,500
Estimated manufacturing overhead costs	$16,800	$34,800

Required

a. Compute the predetermined overhead rate for each company.
b. Determine the amount of overhead cost that would be applied to work in process for each company and compute the amount of overapplied or underapplied manufacturing overhead cost for each company.
c. Explain how closing the Manufacturing Overhead account would affect the Cost of Goods Sold account for each company.

EXERCISE 11–11B *Recording Manufacturing Overhead Costs*

L.O. 6, 9

Patton Manufacturing Company incurred the following actual manufacturing overhead costs: (1) cash paid for plant supervisor's salary, $116,000, (2) depreciation on manufacturing equipment, $54,000, and (3) manufacturing supplies used, $4,600 (Patton uses the periodic inventory method for manufacturing supplies). Applied overhead amounted to $176,000.

Required

a. Open the appropriate T-accounts and record the manufacturing overhead costs described.
b. Record the entry Patton would make to close the Manufacturing Overhead account to Cost of Goods Sold.

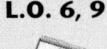

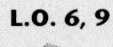

L.O. 6, 9 EXERCISE 11–12B *Missing Information in Inventory T-Accounts*

The following incomplete T-accounts were drawn from the records of Oser Manufacturing Company:

Raw Materials Inventory

25,000	(a)
1,200	

Work in Process Inventory

	52,000
15,600	
(b)	

Finished Goods Inventory

(c)	
5,000	

Cost of Goods Sold

(d)	

Manufacturing Overhead

17,000	(e)
	800

Required

Determine the dollar amounts for (a), (b), (c), (d), and (e). Assume that underapplied and overapplied overhead is closed to Cost of Goods Sold.

L.O. 12 EXERCISE 11–13B *Variable Costing Versus Absorption Costing*

The following information was drawn from the records of Norwood Company:

Variable costs (per unit)		Fixed costs (in total)	
Direct materials	$16	Manufacturing overhead	$48,000
Direct labor	20	Selling and administrative	49,600
Manufacturing overhead	6		
Selling and administrative	14		

During the most recent month Norwood produced 4,000 units of product and sold 3,800 units of product at a sales price of $98 per unit.

Required

a. Prepare an income statement for the month using absorption costing.
b. Prepare an income statement for the month using variable costing.
c. Explain why a company might use one type of income statement for external reporting and a different type for internal reporting.

L.O. 5 EXERCISE 11–14B *Smoothing Unit Cost*

Unit-level (variable) manufacturing costs for Dixon Manufacturing Company amount to $4. Fixed manufacturing costs are $4,500 per month. Production workers provided 800 hours of direct labor in January and 1,400 hours in February. Dixon expects to use 12,000 hours of labor during the year. It actually produced 1,200 units of product in January and 2,100 units of product in February.

Required

a. For each month, determine the total product cost and the per unit product cost, assuming that actual fixed overhead costs are charged to monthly production.
b. Use a predetermined overhead rate based on direct labor hours to allocate the fixed overhead costs to each month's production. For each month, calculate the total product cost and the per unit product cost.
c. Dixon employs a cost-plus-pricing strategy. Would you recommend charging production with actual or allocated fixed overhead costs? Explain.

PROBLEMS—SERIES B

L.O. 2, 4, 6, 8, 10, 11 PROBLEM 11–15B *Manufacturing Cost Flow Across Three Accounting Cycles*

The following accounting events affected Ruff Manufacturing Company during its first three years of operation. Assume that all transactions are cash transactions.

Transactions for 2004

1. Started manufacturing company by issuing common stock for $1,440.
2. Purchased $576 of direct raw materials.
3. Used $432 of direct raw materials to produce inventory.
4. Paid $360 of direct labor wages to employees to make inventory.
5. Applied $360 of manufacturing overhead to Work in Process Inventory.
6. Actual manufacturing overhead costs amounted to $366.
7. Finished work on inventory that cost $648.
8. Sold goods that cost $432 for $576.
9. Paid $36 for selling and administrative expenses.

Transactions for 2005

1. Acquired additional $7200 of cash from issuance of common stock.
2. Purchased $576 of direct raw materials.
3. Used $504 of direct raw materials to produce inventory.
4. Paid $432 of direct labor wages to employees to make inventory.
5. Applied $384 of manufacturing overhead to Work in Process Inventory.
6. Actual manufacturing overhead costs amounted to $378.
7. Finished work on inventory that cost $1,080.
8. Sold goods that cost $1,008 for $1,152.
9. Paid $72 for selling and administrative expenses.

Transactions for 2006

1. Purchased $360 of direct raw materials.
2. Used $576 of direct raw materials to produce inventory.
3. Paid $216 of direct labor wages to employees to make inventory.
4. Applied $300 of manufacturing overhead to Work in Process Inventory.
5. Actual manufacturing overhead costs amounted to $312.
6. Finished work on inventory that cost $1,188.
7. Sold goods that cost $1,296 for $1,584.
8. Paid $144 for selling and administrative expenses.
9. Paid a cash dividend of $288.

Required

a. Record the preceding events in a horizontal statements model. Close overapplied or underapplied overhead to Cost of Goods Sold. Also designate the classification of cash flows using the letters OA for operating activities, IA for investing activities, and FA for financing activities. The first event is shown as an example.

Assets									=	Equity								
Cash	+	**MOH**	+	**Raw M.**	+	**WIP**	+	**F. Goods**	=	**C. Stk.**	+	**Ret. Ear.**	**Rev.**	−	**Exp.**	=	**Net Inc.**	**Cash Flow**
1.440	+	NA	+	NA	+	NA	+	NA	=	1,440	+	NA	NA	−	NA	=	NA	1,440 FA

b. Prepare a schedule of cost of goods manufactured and sold, an income statement, a balance sheet, and a statement of cash flows as of the close of business on December 31, 2004.

c. Close appropriate accounts to the Retained Earnings account.

d. Repeat Requirements *a* through *c* for years 2005 and 2006.

PROBLEM 11–16B *Manufacturing Cost for One Accounting Cycle*

L.O. 2, 6, 7, 10, 11

The following trial balance was taken from the records of Aura Manufacturing Company at the beginning of 2004.

Cash	$ 2,800	
Raw Materials Inventory	200	
Work in Process Inventory	600	
Finished Goods Inventory	400	
Property, Plant, & Equipment	7,000	
Accumulated Depreciation		$ 2,000
Common Stock		4,200
Retained Earnings		4,800
Total	$11,000	$11,000

Transactions for the Accounting Period

1. Aura purchased $4,600 of direct raw materials and $500 of indirect raw materials on account. The indirect materials are capitalized in the Production Supplies account. Materials requisitions showed that $4,000 of direct raw materials had been used for production during the period. The use of indirect materials is determined at the end of the period by physically counting the supplies on hand at the end of the year.
2. By the end of the accounting period, $3,5000 of the accounts payable had been paid in cash.
3. During the year, direct labor amounted to 1,200 hours recorded in the Wages Payable account at $6 per hour.
4. By the end of the accounting period, $6,500 of the Wages Payable account had been paid in cash.
5. At the beginning of the accounting period, the company expected overhead cost for the period to be $5,500 and 1,250 direct labor hours to be worked. Overhead is applied based on direct labor hours, which, as indicated in Event 3, amounted to 1,200 for the year.
6. Administrative and sales expenses for the period amounted to $1,400 paid in cash.
7. Utilities and rent for production facilities amounted to $3,000 paid in cash.
8. Depreciation on the plant and equipment used in production amounted to $2,000.
9. Assume that $15,000 of goods were completed during the period.
10. Assume that $10,000 of finished goods inventory was sold for $14,000 cash.
11. A count of the production supplies revealed a balance of $150 on hand at the end of the accounting period.
12. Any over- or underapplied overhead is considered to be insignificant.

Required

a. Open T-accounts with the beginning balances shown in the preceding list and record all transactions for the period including closing entries in the T-accounts. (*Note:* Open new T-accounts as needed.)

b. Prepare a schedule of cost of goods manufactured and sold, an income statement, a balance sheet, and a statement of cash flows.

L.O. 2, 4, 6, 10, 11

PROBLEM 11–17B *Manufacturing Cost Flow for One-Year Period*

Clifton Manufacturing started 2005 with the following account balances.

Cash	$1,800
Common Stock	1,600
Retained Earnings	600
Raw Materials Inventory	80
Work in Process Inventory	176
Finished Goods Inventory (80 units @ $1.80/unit)	144

Transactions during 2005

1. Purchased $600 of raw materials with cash.
2. Transferred $400 of raw materials to the production department.
3. Incurred and paid cash for 80 hours of direct labor was at $6.00 per hour.
4. Applied overhead costs to the working process inventory. The predetermined overhead rate is $6.00 per direct labor hour.
5. Incurred actual overhead costs of $520 cash.
6. Completed work was on 300 units for $2.88 per unit.
7. Paid $160 in selling and administrative expenses in cash.
8. Sold 200 units for $1,000 cash revenues.

Clifton charges overapplied or underapplied overhead directly to Cost of Goods Sold.

Required

a. Record the preceding events in a horizontal statements model. Also designate the classification of cash flows using the letters OA for operating activities, IA for investing activities, and FA for financing activities. The beginning balances are shown as an example.

Assets					=	Equity					
Cash	+ Raw M. +	MOH	+ WIP +	F. Goods	=	C. Stk.	+ Ret. Ear.	Rev.	− Exp.	= Net Inc.	Cash Flow
1,800 +	80 +	NA	+ 176 +	144	=	1,600	+ 600	NA	− NA	= NA	NA

b. Prepare a schedule of cost of goods manufactured and sold, an income statement, a balance sheet, and a statement of cash flows for 2005.

PROBLEM 11–18B *Manufacturing Cost Flow for Monthly and Annual Accounting Periods* **L.O. 2, 6, 7, 10, 11**

Pratt Manufacturing Company manufactures puzzles that depict the works of famous artists. The company rents a small factory and uses local labor on a part-time basis. The following accounting events affected Pratt during its first year of operation. (Assume that all transactions are cash transactions unless otherwise stated.)

Transactions for First Month of Operation 2005

1. Issued common stock for $25,000.
2. Purchased $4,000 of direct raw materials and $300 of indirect raw materials. Indirect materials are recorded in a Production Supplies account.
3. Used $3,896 of direct raw materials.
4. Used 700 direct labor hours; production workers were paid $6 per hour.
5. Expected total overhead costs for the year to be $16,800 and direct labor hours used during the year to be 9,600. Calculate an overhead rate and apply the appropriate amount of overhead costs to Work in Process.
6. Paid $800 for salaries to administrative and sales staff.
7. Paid $700 for indirect manufacturing labor.
8. Paid $600 for rent and utilities on the manufacturing facilities.
9. Started and completed 956 puzzles; all costs were transferred from the Work in Process Inventory account to the Finished Goods Inventory account.
10. Sold 800 puzzles at a price of $12 each.

Transactions for Remainder of 2005

11. Acquired an additional $200,000 by issuing common stock.
12. Purchased $46,000 of direct raw materials and $4,000 of indirect raw materials.
13. Used $41,050 of direct raw materials.
14. Paid production workers $6 per hour for 9,800 hours of work.
15. Applied the appropriate overhead cost to Work in Process Inventory.
16. Paid $8,800 for salaries of administrative and sales staff.
17. Paid $7,700 for the salary of the production supervisor.
18. Paid $6,600 for rental and utility costs on the manufacturing facilities.
19. Transferred 12,000 additional puzzles that cost $9.75 each from Work in Process Inventory to Finished Goods Inventory accounts.
20. Determined that $2,900 of production supplies was on hand at the end of the accounting period.
21. Sold 8,000 puzzles for $12 each.
22. Determine whether overhead is over- or underapplied. Close the manufacturing overhead account to cost of goods sold.
23. Close the revenue and expense accounts.

Required

a. Open T-accounts and post transactions to the accounts.

b. Prepare a schedule of cost of goods manufactured and sold, an income statement, a balance sheet, and a statement of cash flows for 2005.

PROBLEM 11–19B *Manufacturing Cost Flow for Multiple Accounting Cycles* **L.O. 2, 6, 7, 8, 9, 10, 11**

The following events apply to Gurganes Manufacturing Company. Assume that all transactions are cash transactions unless otherwise indicated.

Transactions for the 2006 Accounting Period

1. The company was started on January 1, 2006, when it acquired $700,000 cash by issuing common stock.
2. The company purchased $300,000 of direct raw materials with cash and used $26,000 of these materials to make its products in January.
3. Employees provided 1,500 hours of labor at $8 per hour during January. Wages are paid in cash.
4. The estimated manufacturing overhead costs for 2006 are $650,000. Overhead is applied on the basis of direct labor costs. The company expected $130,000 of direct labor costs during 2006. Record applied overhead for January.
5. By the end of January, the employees completed work on all inventory items started in January. The cost of this production was transferred to the Finished Goods Inventory account. Determine the cost per unit of product produced in January, assuming that a total of 10,000 units of product were started and completed during the month.

6. The company used an additional $234,000 of direct raw materials and 13,500 hours of direct labor at $8 per hour during the remainder of 2006. Overhead was allocated on the basis of direct labor cost.
7. The company completed work on inventory items started between February 1 and December 31, and the cost of the completed inventory was transferred to the Finished Goods Inventory account. Determine the cost per unit for goods produced between February 1 and December 31, assuming that 90,000 units of inventory were produced. If the company desires to earn a gross profit of $3 per unit, what price per unit must it charge for the merchandise sold?
8. The company sold 60,000 units of inventory for cash at $12.80 per unit. Determine the number of units in ending inventory and the cost per unit of this inventory.
9. Actual manufacturing overhead costs paid in cash were $610,000.
10. The company paid $150,000 cash for selling and administrative expenses.
11. Close the Manufacturing Overhead account.
12. Close the revenue and expense accounts.

Transactions for the 2007 Accounting Period

1. The company acquired $350,000 cash from the owners.
2. The company purchased $200,000 of direct raw materials with cash and used $20,800 of these materials to make products in January.
3. Employees provided 1,200 hours of labor at $8 per hour during January.
4. On January 1, 2007, Gurganes expected the production facilities to cost $1,500 cash per month. The company paid cash to purchase $7,000 of manufacturing supplies, and it anticipated that $7,000 of these supplies would be used by year end. Other manufacturing overhead costs were expected to total $455,000. Overhead is applied on the basis of direct labor costs. Gurganes expects direct labor costs of $80,000 during 2007. Based on this information, determine the total expected overhead cost for 2008. Calculate the predetermined overhead rate and apply the overhead cost for the January production. Also, record the purchase of manufacturing supplies.
5. The company recorded a $1,500 cash payment for production facilities in January.
6. On January, the employees completed work on all inventory items started in January. The cost of this production was transferred to the Finished Goods Inventory account. Determine the cost per unit of product produced in January assuming that a total of 8,000 units of product was started and completed during the month.
7. During February 2007, the company used $15,600 of raw materials and 900 hours of labor at $8 per hour. Overhead was allocated on the basis of direct labor cost.
8. The company recorded a $1,500 cash payment for production facilities in February.
9. In February, the employees completed work on all inventory items started in February; the cost of this production was transferred to the Finished Goods Inventory account. Determine the cost per unit of product produced in February, assuming that 6,000 units of product were started and completed during the month.
10. The company used an additional $143,000 of direct raw materials and 8,250 hours of direct labor at $8 per hour during the remainder of 2007. Overhead was allocated on the basis of direct labor cost.
11. The company recorded $15,000 of cash payments for production facilities for the period between March 1 and December 31.
12. The company completed work on inventory items started between March 1 and December 31. The cost of the completed goods was transferred to the Finished Goods Inventory account. Compute the cost per unit of this inventory, assuming that 55,000 units of inventory were produced.
13. The company sold 90,000 units of product for $14 per unit cash. Assume that the company uses the FIFO inventory cost flow method to determine the cost of goods sold.
14. The company paid $130,000 cash for selling and administrative expenses.
15. As of December 31, 2007, $1,200 of production supplies was on hand.
16. Actual cost of other manufacturing overhead was $461,000 cash.
17. Close the manufacturing overhead account.
18. Close the revenue and expense accounts.

Required

a. Open T-accounts and record the effects of the preceding events.

b. Prepare a schedule of cost of goods manufactured and sold, an income statement, a balance sheet, and a statement of cash flows for both years.

L.O. 10 **PROBLEM 11–20B** *Comprehensive Review Problem*

Lauren Cobb has worked as the plant manager of Sheppard Corporation, a large manufacturing company, for 10 years. The company produces stereo CD players for automotive vehicles and sells them to some of the largest car manufacturers in the country. Ms. Cobb has always toyed with the idea of starting her own car stereo manufacturing business. With her experience and knowledge, she is certain that she can produce a superior stereo at a low cost. Ms. Cobb's business strategy would be to market the product to smaller, more specialized car manufacturers. Her potential market is car manufacturers who sell at a lower volume to discriminating customers. She is confident that she could compete in this market that values low-cost quality production. She would not compete with Sheppard or the other large stereo producers that dominate the market made up of the largest automotive producers.

Ms. Cobb already has firm orders for 800 stereos from several automotive producers. Based on the contacts that she has made working for Sheppard, Ms. Cobb is confident that she can make and sell 2,000 stereos during the first year of operation. However, before making a final decision, she decides to investigate the profitability of starting her own business. Relevant information follows.

Components from wholesaler	$36.00 per stereo
Assembly labor	$8.40 per hour
Rent of manufacturing buildings	$9,600.00 per year
Utilities	$240.00 per month
Sales salaries	$480.00 per month
Depreciation of equipment	$1,600.00 per year
Labor	3 hours per stereo

During the first year, Ms. Cobb expects to be able to produce the stereos with only two production workers and a part-time salesperson to market the product. Ms. Cobb expects to devote her time to the administrative aspects of the business and to provide back-up support in the production work. She has decided not to pay herself a salary but to live off the profits of the business.

Required

a. Classify each cost item into the categories of direct materials, direct labor, and manufacturing overhead.
b. Classify each cost item as either variable or fixed.
c. What is the cost per stereo if Ms. Cobb's company produces 800 units per year? What is the unit cost if the company produces 2,000 units per year?
d. If Ms. Cobb's job presently pays her $12,000 a year, would you recommend that she proceed with the plans to start the new company if she could sell stereos for $96 each?

PROBLEM 11–21B *Absorption versus Variable Costing*

L.O. 12

Carney Manufacturing Company makes a product that sells for $25 per unit. Manufacturing costs for the product amount to $12 per unit variable, and $80,000 fixed. During the current accounting period, Carney made 8,000 units of the product and sold 7,600 units.

Required

a. Prepare an absorption costing income statement.
b. Prepare a variable costing income statement.
c. Explain why the amount of net income on the absorption costing income statement differs from the amount of net income on the variable costing income statement. Your answer should include the amount of the inventory balance that would exist under the two costing approaches.

PROBLEM 11–22B *Absorption versus Variable Costing*

L.O. 12

King Company makes ladderback chairs that it sells for $200 per chair. Each chair requires $28 of direct materials and $72 of direct labor. Fixed overhead costs are expected to be $120,000 per year. King expects to sell 1,500 chairs during the coming year.

Required

a. Prepare income statements using absorption costing, assuming that King makes 1,500, 2,000, and 2,500 chairs during the year.
b. Prepare income statements using variable costing, assuming that King makes 1,500, 2,000, and 2,500 chairs during the year.
c. Explain why King may produce income statements under both absorption and variable costing formats. Your answer should include an explanation of the advantages or disadvantages associated with the use of the two reporting formats.

L.O. 12 PROBLEM 11–23B *Absorption and Variable Costing*

Wofford Manufacturing pays its production managers a bonus based on the company's profitability. During the two most recent years, the company maintained the same cost structure to manufacture its products.

Year	Units Produced	Units Sold
Production and Sales		
2005	4,000	4,000
2006	6,000	4,000
Cost Data		
Direct materials		$8 per unit
Direct labor		$12 per unit
Manufacturing overhead—variable		$4 per unit
Manufacturing overhead—fixed		$72,000
Variable selling & administrative expenses		$4 per unit sold
Fixed selling & administrative expenses		$30,000

(Assume that selling & administrative expenses are associated with goods sold.)

Wofford's sales revenue for both years was $230,000.

Required

a. Prepare income statements based on absorption costing for the years 2005 and 2006.
b. Since Wofford sold the same amount in 2005 and 2006, why did net income increase in 2006?
c. Discuss management's possible motivation for increasing production in 2006.
d. Determine the costs of ending inventory for 2006. Comment on the risks and costs associated with the accumulation of inventory.
e. Based on your answers to Requirements *b* and *c*, suggest a different income statement format and prepare income statements for 2005 and 2006 using your suggested format.

ANALYZE, THINK, COMMUNICATE

ATC 11–1 BUSINESS APPLICATIONS CASE *Predetermined Overhead Rate*

Bytes Storage Company (BSC) makes memory storage chips that it sells to independent computer manufacturers. The average materials cost per set of chips is $3.15, and the average labor cost is $1.25. BSC incurs approximately $5,200,000 of fixed manufacturing overhead costs annually. The marketing department estimated that BSC would sell approximately 700,000 sets of chips during the coming year. Unfortunately, BSC has experienced a steady decline in sales even though the computer industry has had a steady increase in the number of computers sold. The chief accountant, Stella Peng, was overheard saying that when she calculated the predetermined overhead rate, she deliberately lowered the estimated number of chips expected to be sold because she had lost faith in the marketing department's ability to deliver on its estimated sales numbers. Ms. Peng explained, "This way, our actual cost is always below the estimated cost. It is about the only way we continue to make a profit." Indeed, the company had a significant amount of overapplied overhead at the end of each year.

Required

a. Explain how the overapplied overhead affects the determination of year-end net income.
b. Assume that Ms. Peng used 600,000 sets of chips as the estimated sales to calculate the predetermined overhead rate. Determine the difference in expected cost per set of chips she calculated and the cost per set of chips that would result if the marketing department's estimate (700,000 units) had been used.
c. Assuming that BSC uses a cost-plus pricing policy, speculate how Ms. Pengs' behavior could be contributing to the decline in sales.

ATC 11–2 GROUP ASSIGNMENT *Schedule of Cost of Goods Manufactured and Sold*

The following information is from the accounts of Depree Manufacturing Company for 2002.

Required

a. Divide the class into groups of four or five students per group and organize the groups into three sections. Assign Task 1 to the first section of groups, Task 2 to the second section, and Task 3 to the third section.

Group Tasks

(1) The ending balance in the Raw Materials Inventory account was $208,000. During the accounting period, Depree used $2,348,900 of raw materials inventory and purchased $2,200,000 of raw materials. Determine the beginning raw materials inventory balance.

(2) During the accounting period, Depree used $2,348,900 of raw materials inventory and $2,780,200 of direct labor. Actual overhead costs were $3,300,000. Ending work in process inventory amounted to $450,000, and cost of goods manufactured amounted to $8,389,100. Determine the beginning balance in the Work in Process Inventory account.

(3) The cost of goods manufactured was $8,389,100, and the cost of goods sold was $8,419,100. Ending finished goods inventory amounted to $360,000. Determine the beginning balance in the Finished Goods Inventory account.

b. Select a spokesperson from each section. Use input from the three spokespersons to prepare a schedule of cost of goods manufactured and sold. The spokesperson from the first section should provide information for the computation of the cost of raw materials used. The spokesperson from the second section should provide information for the determination of the cost of goods manufactured. The spokesperson from the third section should provide information for the determination of the cost of goods sold.

RESEARCH ASSIGNMENT *Distinction Between Service and Manufacturing Companies* — ATC 11–3

Broadcast.com is an Internet-based company that was highlighted in an article written by Steven V. Brull, which appeared on page 142 of the November 9, 1998, issue of *Business Week*. Read this article and complete the following requirements.

Required

a. Is broadcast.com a service or a manufacturing company? Explain.

b. What type of inventory accounts would you expect broadcast.com to maintain?

c. Identify some cost drivers that would be appropriate for broadcast.com to use when calculating a predetermined overhead rate.

WRITING ASSIGNMENT *Inventory Cost Flow in Manufacturing Environment* — ATC 11–4

Barret Cameron, a student in Professor Wagner's managerial accounting course, asked the following question. "In the first accounting course, the teacher said inventory costs flow on a FIFO, LIFO, or weighted average pattern. Now you are telling us inventory costs flow through raw materials, to work in process, and then to finished goods. Is this manufacturing stuff a new cost flow method or what?"

Required

Assume that you are Professor Wagner. Write a brief memo responding to Mr. Cameron's question.

ETHICAL DILEMMA *Absorption Costing* — ATC 11–5

Cliff Dennis may become a rich man. He is the creative force behind Amazing Drives, a new company. Amazing makes external drives that permit computer users to store large amounts of information on small floppy diskettes. Amazing has experienced tremendous growth since its inception three years ago. Investors have recognized the company's potential, and its stock is currently selling at 60 times projected earnings. More specifically, the company's 2004 earnings forecast shows estimated income to be $0.30 per share and the current market price is $18 per share ($0.30 × 60). Mr. Dennis has stock options permitting him to buy 2,000,000 shares of stock for $12 per share on January 1, 2005. This means that he could earn $6 per share on the options. In other words, he would buy the stock at $12 per share and sell it at $18 per share. As a result, Mr. Dennis would earn $12,000,000 ($6 × 2,000,000 shares).

Unfortunately, weak economies in foreign countries have caused low demand for Amazing's products in international markets. Company insiders are painfully aware that Amazing Drives is going to be unable to meet its projected income numbers. If actual earnings fall short of the projected earnings, the market will manifest its disappointment by discounting the stock price. Mr. Dennis is concerned that the value of his stock options could plummet.

At its inception three years ago, Amazing invested heavily in manufacturing equipment. Indeed, expecting dramatic growth, the company purchased a significant amount of excess capacity. As a result, the company incurs approximately $28,800,000 in fixed manufacturing costs annually. If Amazing continues to produce at its current level, it will make and sell approximately 800,000 drives during 2004. In the face of declining sales, Mr. Dennis has issued a puzzling order to his production manager. Specifically, he has told the production manager to increase production so that 1,200,000 drives will be completed during 2004. Mr. Dennis explained that he believes the economies in foreign countries will surge ahead in 2005 and that he wants Amazing to have the inventory necessary to satisfy the demand.

Required

a. Suppose that actual earnings for 2004 are $0.18 per share. The market becomes disappointed, and the price-earnings ratio falls to 40 times earnings. What is the value of Mr. Dennis' stock options under these circumstances?

b. Determine the impact on income reported in 2004 if production is 800,000 units versus 1,200,000 units.

c. Why would Mr. Dennis order the increase in production?

d. Does Mr. Dennis' behavior violate any of the standards of ethical conduct in Exhibit 1-13 of Chapter 1?

e. Identify the features described in this case that could motivate criminal and ethical misconduct. (It may be helpful to reread the ethics material in Chapter 1 before attempting to satisfy this requirement.)

ATC 11–6 SPREADSHEET ASSIGNMENT *Using Excel*

Manning Cassey Computers (MCC) plans to produce and sell 1,600 computers for $720 each in the next fiscal year. The company's cost data follow.

Components from wholesaler	$480 per computer
Assembly labor	$15 per hour
Manufacturing space rent	$3,000 per month
Utilities	$600 per month
Janitorial services	$480 per month
Depreciation of equipment	$3,840 per year
Labor time per computer	2 hours

Required

a. Construct a spreadsheet to calculate the cost of goods manufactured and the cost per unit for MCC. Use formulas in the schedule so that the cost of goods manufactured will automatically be calculated as you change the number of units sold.

b. Add an abbreviated income statement to your spreadsheet that incorporates the cost from Requirement *a.*

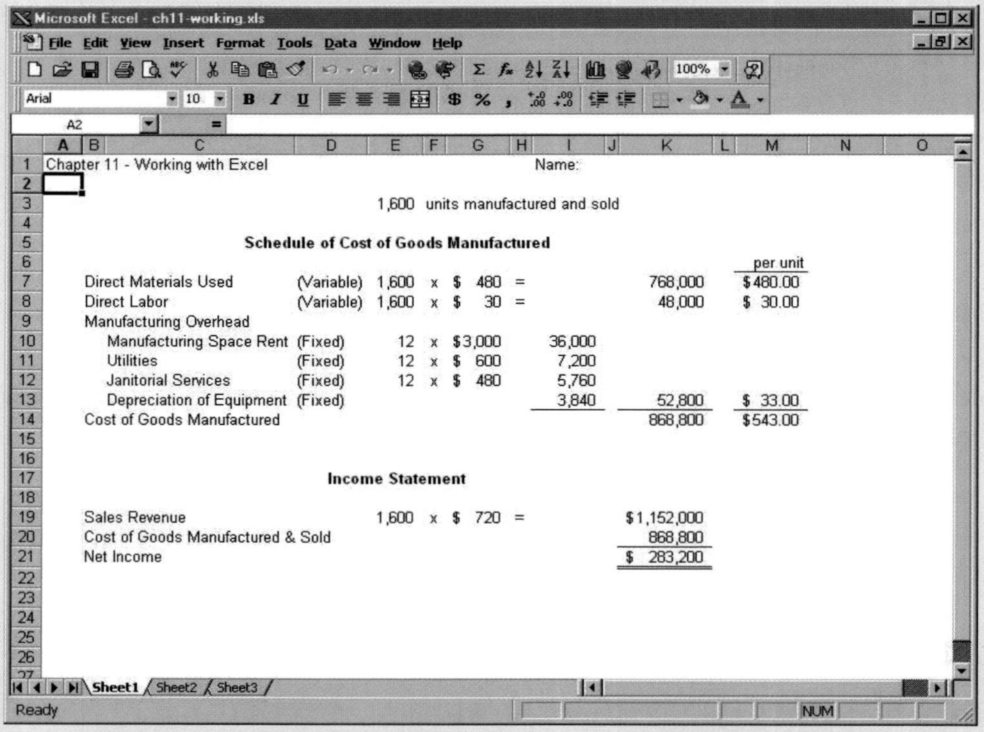

Chapter 11 - Working with Excel — Name:

1,600 units manufactured and sold

Schedule of Cost of Goods Manufactured

						per unit
Direct Materials Used	(Variable)	1,600 x $ 480 =			768,000	$480.00
Direct Labor	(Variable)	1,600 x $ 30 =			48,000	$ 30.00
Manufacturing Overhead						
Manufacturing Space Rent	(Fixed)	12 x $3,000		36,000		
Utilities	(Fixed)	12 x $ 600		7,200		
Janitorial Services	(Fixed)	12 x $ 480		5,760		
Depreciation of Equipment	(Fixed)			3,840	52,800	$ 33.00
Cost of Goods Manufactured					868,800	$543.00

Income Statement

Sales Revenue	1,600 x $ 720 =	$1,152,000
Cost of Goods Manufactured & Sold		868,800
Net Income		$ 283,200

Spreadsheet Tip

1. Build the spreadsheet so that the number of units in cell E3 can be changed and cost of goods manufactured and net income will be recalculated automatically.

SPREADSHEET ASSIGNMENT *Mastering Excel*

ATC 11–7

Stanley Manufacturing Company, which sold 16,000 units of product at $20 per unit, collected the following information regarding three different levels of production.

Inventory Costs			
Fixed overhead	$100,000	$100,000	$100,000
Number of units produced	16,000	20,000	25,000
Fixed overhead per unit	$6.25	$5.00	$4.00
Variable manufacturing costs	$12.00	$12.00	$12.00
Full absorption cost per unit	$18.25	$17.00	$16.00

Required

a. Construct a spreadsheet that includes the preceding data in the top of the spreadsheet. The rows for fixed overhead per unit and full absorption cost per unit should be based on formulas.

b. Include absorption costing income statements at these three levels of production like those in Exhibit 11–11. Use formulas so that the number of units produced in the preceding table can be changed and net income will be recalculated automatically.

c. Include variable costing income statements at these three levels of production like those in Exhibit 11–12. Use formulas so that the number of units produced in the preceding table can be changed and net income will be recalculated automatically.

COMPREHENSIVE PROBLEM

Magnificent Modems, Inc. acquired a subsidiary named Anywhere, Inc. (AI). AI manufactures a wireless modem that enables users to access the Internet through cell phones. The following trial balance was drawn from the accounts of the subsidiary.

Cash	$200,000	
Raw Materials Inventory	4,000	
Work in Process Inventory	6,000	
Finished Goods Inventory	7,000	
Common Stock		$129,000
Retained Earnings		88,000
Totals	$217,000	$217,000

The subsidiary completed the following transactions during 20X2.

1. Paid $60,000 cash for direct raw materials.
2. Transferred $50,000 of direct raw materials to work in process.
3. Paid production employees $80,000 cash.
4. Applied $53,000 of manufacturing overhead costs to work in process.
5. Completed work on products that cost $163,000.
6. Sold products that cost $143,000 for $182,000 cash. Record the recognition of revenue in a row labeled 6a and the cost of goods sold in a row labeled 6b.
7. Paid $20,000 cash for selling and administrative expenses.
8. Actual overhead costs paid in cash amounted to $55,000.
9. Closed the Manufacturing Overhead account. The amount of over- or underapplied overhead was insignificant (immaterial).
10. Made a $5,000 cash distribution to the owners.

Required

a. For Anywhere, Inc., record the events in the financial statements model like the one shown below. In the last column of the model indicate whether the cash inflows or outflows are financing activities (FA), investing activities (IA), or operating activities (OA).

Assets									=	Equity				Rev.	–	Exp.	=	Net Inc.	Cash Flow
Cash	+	MOH	+	Raw M.	+	WIP	+	F. Goods	=	C. Stk.	+	Ret. Ear.							
200,000	+	0	+	4,000	+	6,000	+	7,000	=	129,000	+	88,000		NA	–	NA	=	NA	NA

b. Prepare a schedule of cost of goods manufactured and sold.

c. Prepare an income statement, balance sheet, and statement of cash flows.

CHAPTER *twelve*

JOB-ORDER, PROCESS, AND HYBRID COST SYSTEMS

LEARNING *objectives*

After you have mastered the material in this chapter you will be able to:

1 Distinguish between job-order and process cost systems.

2 Identify how product costs flow through a job-order cost system.

3 Identify how product costs flow through a process cost system.

4 Distinguish between raw materials cost and transferred-in cost.

5 Explain how hybrid accounting systems combine components of job-order and process cost systems.

6 Identify the various forms of documentation used in a job-order cost system.

7 Explain how accounting events in a job-order cost system affect financial statements.

8 Explain how accounting events in a process cost system affect financial statements.

9 Convert partially completed units into equivalent whole units.

THE *curious* ACCOUNTANT

Consider the following two situations:

First, imagine you worked at a company that mills wheat into flour, such as **Pillsbury**, but that your company produced only one product, five-pound bags of whole wheat flour. During the past year, your company incurred manufacturing costs of $32.5 million and it produced 50 million bags of flour.

Next, imagine you worked for a company that constructed houses. All of your activity for the past year has been in one particular subdivision, Estate Homes. Your company incurred construction costs during the past year of $17.8 million, and it built 50 houses from start to finish; however, no two of these houses were the same.

How would you determine the cost of one bag of flour? How would you determine the cost incurred to construct the house on lot 131? Which of the two questions asked above do you think would be the most difficult to answer for a real-world company? (Answers on page 500.)

CHAPTER *opening*

Benchmore Boat Company built five boats during the current year. Each boat has unique characteristics that affect its cost. For example, an 80-foot yacht required more labor and materials than a 30-foot sailboat. Because different boats cost different amounts, Benchmore needs a cost system that traces product costs to individual inventory items (specific boats).

In contrast, Janis Juice Company produced 500,000 cans of apple juice during the same year. Each can of juice is identical to the others. Determining the cost of a boat built by Benchmore requires a different cost system than the system Janis needs to determine the cost of a can of juice. Benchmore needs a cost system that captures the unique cost of each individual inventory item. Janis needs a cost system that distributes costs evenly across total production (number of cans of juice produced during an accounting period).

Cost Systems

The type of product a company produces affects the type of accounting system needed to determine product cost. The two most common types of costing systems are job-order costing and process costing. Some companies use hybrid costing systems that combine features of both job-order and process systems. The following section of the text discusses the types of products most suited to each costing system and the accounting procedures used in each type of costing system.

Cost Systems and Type of Product

LO1 Distinguish between job-order and process cost systems.

Job-order cost systems accumulate costs by individual products. The boats Benchmore builds are suited to job-order costing. Other products for which job-order costing is suitable include movies made by **Walt Disney Productions**, office buildings constructed by **Rust Engineering**, and airplanes made by **Boeing**. Job-order cost systems apply not only to individual inventory items but also to batches of inventory items. For example, **Hernandes Shirt Company** may account for producing a special order of 20,000 shirts sold to the United States Army as a single job. Companies use job-order cost systems when they need to know the costs of individual products or batches of products.

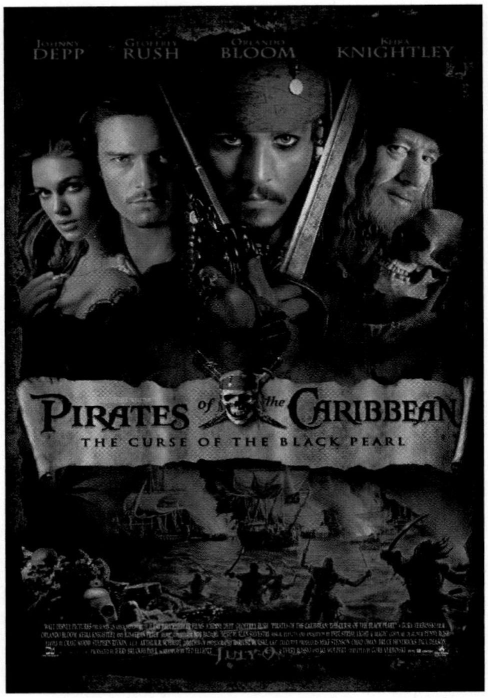

Process cost systems allocate costs evenly to homogeneous products. In addition to beverage companies such as Janis Juice, oil refiners such as **Texaco**, chemical producers such as **Dow Chemical**, food processors such as **General Mills**, and paint manufacturers such as **Sherwin-Williams** use process costing. These companies normally make products in mass quantities using continuous processes. The *per unit product cost* is determined by dividing the *total* product cost by the number of units produced during the accounting period. Process cost systems provide *average* product costs.

To a lesser extent, job-order costing systems also use average costs. It is either not possible or not cost effective to trace costs of indirect materials, indirect labor, utilities, rent, and depreciation directly to particular jobs. Companies normally combine these costs and allocate them to individual products using an average overhead rate based on a common measure of production such as labor hours, machine hours, or square footage. When jobs are produced in batches of a number of similar products, the cost per unit is determined by dividing the total cost of the job by the number of units in the batch. Although more costs are traced to specific products under a job-order system than a process system, *both* systems require *some* form of *cost averaging.*

Job-Order Cost Flow

LO2 Identify how product costs flow through a job-order cost system.

Job-order and process costing systems are patterned after the physical flow of products moving through production. For example, consider how Benchmore Boat Company builds custom boats. Each boat is a separate project. Benchmore starts a project by requisitioning raw materials from materials storage. It assigns specific employees to work on specific boats. Finally,

Exhibit 12–1 *Cost Flow in a Job-Order Cost System*

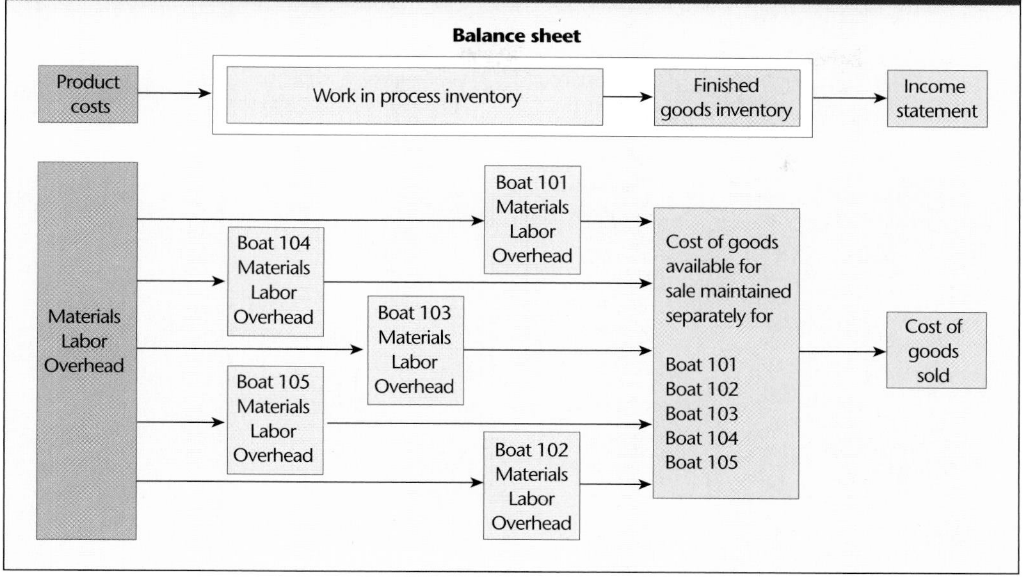

it assigns indirect (overhead) costs to each boat based on the number of direct labor hours required to build the boat.

Benchmore's *job-order cost system* accumulates cost in a manner parallel to physical boat construction. Benchmore assigns each boat a specific job identification number. It records transactions in inventory accounts on a perpetual basis. Product costs are accumulated separately for each job identification number. The costs of each boat move through the Work in Process Inventory account to the Finished Goods Inventory account and finally to the Cost of Goods Sold account as the boat is produced and sold. Exhibit 12–1 shows the flow of product costs for the five boats Benchmore plans to build in 2003. In a job-order system, the amount recorded in the Work in Process Inventory account is the total cost to date of distinct jobs. Each distinct job represents the costs of materials, labor, and overhead accumulated for that specific inventory project. The Work in Process Inventory account is a *control* account supported by numerous *subsidiary* accounts (the records for individual jobs). The Finished Goods Inventory account is also a control account. It is supported by subsidiary accounts in which are recorded the separate costs of each completed, but not yet sold, boat.

Process Cost Flow

LO3 Identify how product costs flow through a process cost system.

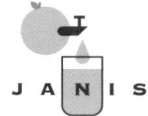

Process cost systems use the same general ledger accounts as job-order cost systems. Product costs flow from Raw Materials Inventory to Work in Process Inventory to Finished Goods Inventory to Cost of Goods Sold. The primary difference between the two systems centers on accounting for the work in process inventory. The physical products move continuously through a series of processing centers. Instead of accumulating product costs by jobs that add up to a single Work in Process Inventory control account, process cost systems accumulate product costs by processing centers, or *departments*. Each department has its own separate Work in Process Inventory account. For example, Janis Juice Company uses three distinct processes to produce cans of apple juice. Raw apples enter the extraction department where juice concentrate is pressed from whole fruit. The concentrate moves to the mixing department where Janis adds water, sugar, food coloring, and preservatives. The resulting juice mixture moves to the packaging department where it is canned and boxed. The materials, labor, and overhead costs incurred as products move through a processing center (department) are charged to that center's Work in Process Inventory account.

Parallel to the physical flow of product through the manufacturing process, cost accumulations pass from one department to the next. The end products of one department become the raw materials of the next department. The costs transferred from one department to the next

Exhibit 12–2 *Cost Flow in a Process Cost System*

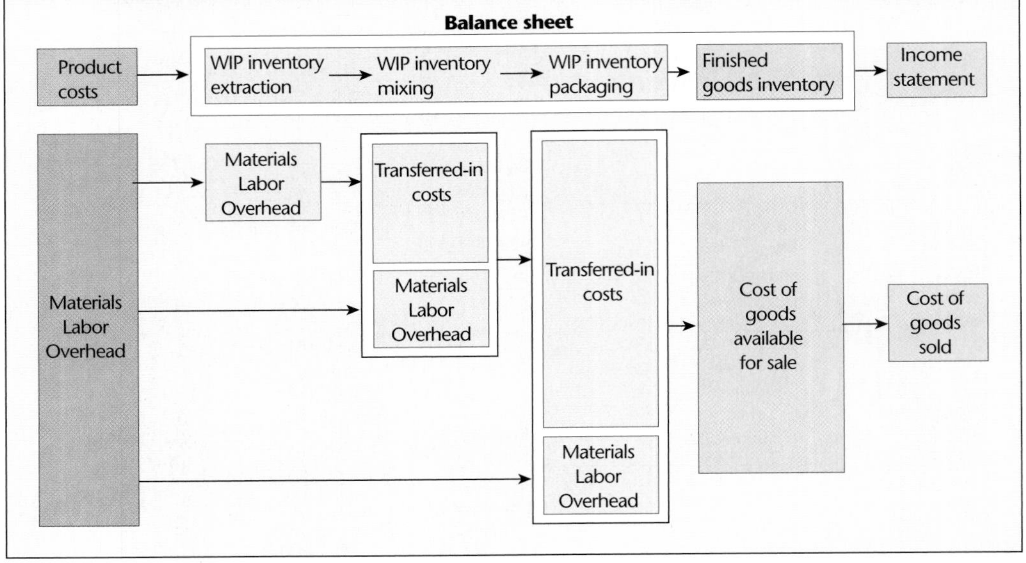

LO4 Distinguish between raw materials cost and transferred-in cost.

are **transferred-in costs.** Transferred-in costs are combined with the additional materials, labor, and overhead costs incurred by each succeeding department. When goods are complete, the total product cost transferred to the Finished Goods Inventory account represents the sum of product costs from all the departments. Exhibit 12–2 illustrates cost flow for the process costing system used by Janis Juice Company. Compare the cost flow patterns in Exhibits 12–1 and 12–2 to clarify the distinction between job-order and process cost systems.

Hybrid Accounting Systems

LO5 Explain how hybrid accounting systems combine components of job-order and process cost systems.

Many companies use **hybrid cost systems.** Hybrid systems combine features of both process and job-order cost systems. For example, Gateway 2000 makes thousands of identical computers using a continuous assembly line that is compatible with process costing. Each unit requires the same amount of labor to assemble a standard set of parts into a finished computer ready for immediate sale. Gateway also builds custom computers with unique features. Customers can order larger monitors, more memory, or faster processors than Gateway's standard model has. Gateway meets these requests by customizing the computers as they move through production. The costs of customized features must be traced to products with a job-order type of system. Gateway charges customers a premium for the custom items.

Documentation in a Job-Order Cost System

LO6 Identify the various forms of documentation used in a job-order cost system.

Topic Tackler PLUS 12–1

In a job-order cost system, product costs for each individual job are accumulated on a **job cost sheet,** also called a *job-order cost sheet* or a *job record.* As each job moves through production, detailed cost information for materials, labor, and overhead is recorded on the job cost sheet. When a job is finished, the job cost sheet summarizes all costs incurred to complete that job.

Two primary source documents, materials requisition forms and work tickets, provide the information recorded on the job cost sheet. Before starting a job, the job supervisor prepares a **materials requisition form** which lists the materials needed to begin work. The materials requisition represents the authorization for raw materials to be released from storage to production. Some companies deliver hard-copy forms to and from the different departments, but most modern businesses deliver requests electronically through a computer network. Whether recorded on paper documents or in electronic files, the information from material requisitions for each job is sent to the accounting department to be summarized on the job cost sheet.

REALITY bytes

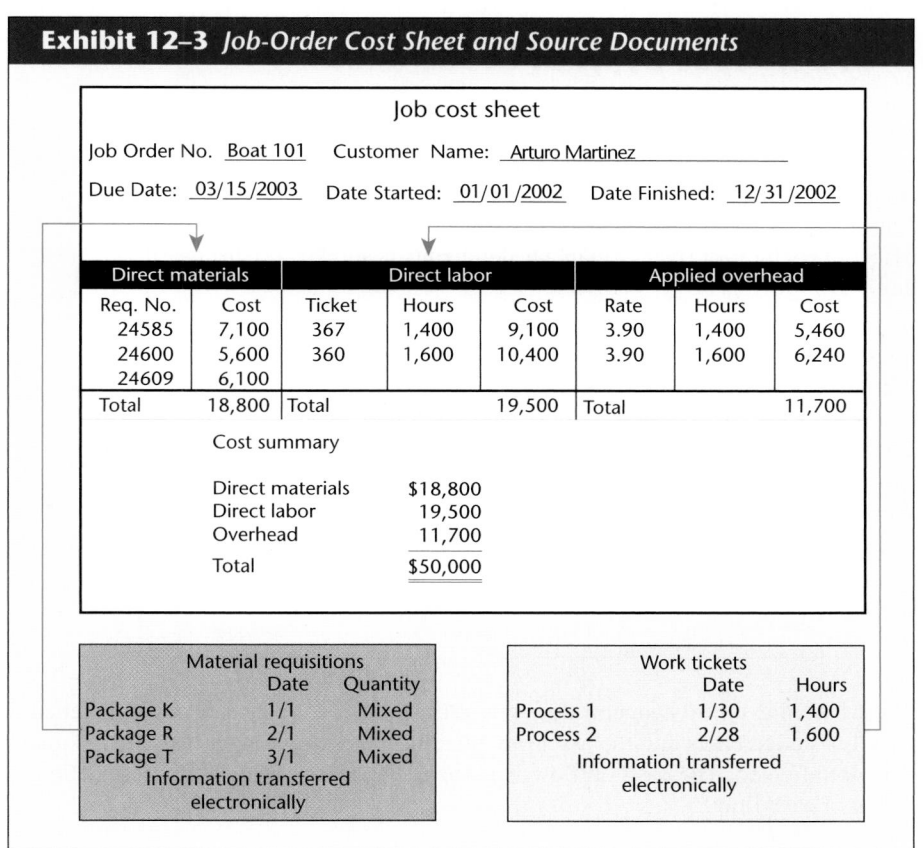

Job-order, process, and hybrid costing systems apply to service businesses as well as manufacturing concerns. Consider a local franchisee of Lawn Doctor who is pricing lawn maintenance contracts for a variety of residential customers. A separate price will be quoted for each lawn, and this price will be based on what the company believes it will cost to maintain that particular lawn. Some customers have larger lawns than others, which cost more to service. Some customers want less lawn care service than others, which costs less. This type service business will use a job-order system.

Now, consider a company in the clothes laundering business. The price the company charges to wash, press, and hang a man's shirt is the same for all shirts because the cost of servicing each shirt, whether large or small, is about the same. This business will use a process cost system to determine the cost of laundering one shirt.

Exhibit 12–3 *Job-Order Cost Sheet and Source Documents*

Job cost sheet

Job Order No. Boat 101 Customer Name: Arturo Martinez

Due Date: 03/15/2003 Date Started: 01/01/2002 Date Finished: 12/31/2002

Direct materials		Direct labor			Applied overhead		
Req. No.	Cost	Ticket	Hours	Cost	Rate	Hours	Cost
24585	7,100	367	1,400	9,100	3.90	1,400	5,460
24600	5,600	360	1,600	10,400	3.90	1,600	6,240
24609	6,100						
Total	18,800	Total		19,500	Total		11,700

Cost summary

Direct materials	$18,800
Direct labor	19,500
Overhead	11,700
Total	$50,000

Material requisitions

	Date	Quantity
Package K	1/1	Mixed
Package R	2/1	Mixed
Package T	3/1	Mixed

Information transferred electronically

Work tickets

	Date	Hours
Process 1	1/30	1,400
Process 2	2/28	1,600

Information transferred electronically

The **work ticket,** sometimes called a *time card,* provides space for the job number, employee identification, and work description. Employees record on the work ticket the amount of time they spend on each job. This information is forwarded to the accounting department. Using wage rate records, the accounting department computes the amount of labor cost and records it on the job cost sheet. The data can be gathered manually or electronically.

Finally, each job cost sheet provides space for applied overhead. Companies maintain job cost sheet records perpetually, adding additional cost data as work on jobs progresses. Using predetermined overhead rates, estimated overhead costs are regularly added to job cost sheets. Exhibit 12–3 illustrates a job cost sheet along with materials requisition forms and work tickets for Benchmore Boat Company's job-order number Boat 101.

Exhibit 12–4

BENCHMORE BOAT COMPANY
Trial Balance
As of January 1, 2003

	Debit	Credit
Cash	$ 73,000	
Raw Materials Inventory	7,000	
Work in Process Inventory	34,000	
Finished Goods Inventory	85,000	
Production Supplies	300	
Manufacturing Equipment	90,000	
Accumulated Depreciation		$ 32,000
Common Stock		200,000
Retained Earnings		57,300
Total	$289,300	$289,300

Exhibit 12–4 ***continued***

Subsidiary Account Balances

Work in Process Inventory		Finished Goods Inventory	
Boat 103	$14,000	Boat 101	$50,000
Boat 104	8,000	Boat 102	35,000
Boat 105	12,000		
Total	$34,000	Total	$85,000

Job-Order Cost System Illustrated

LO7 Explain how accounting events in a job-order cost system affect financial statements.

To illustrate how a job-order cost system works, we follow the operations of Benchmore Boat Company during 2003. Exhibit 12–4 shows the company's 2003 beginning account balances.

Entries for Benchmore's 2003 accounting events, described next, are shown in ledger T-accounts in Exhibit 12–5 on page 494. As you study each event, trace it to the T-accounts. The entries in Exhibit 12–5 are cross-referenced to sequential event numbers. The individual effect of each event on the financial statements is shown and discussed in the following section.

Event 1
Benchmore paid $14,000 cash to purchase raw materials.

The effects of this event on the company's financial statements follow.

Assets			=	Liabilities	+	Equity	Revenue	−	Expenses	=	Net Income	Cash Flow
Cash	+	Raw Materials Inventory										
(14,000)	+	14,000	=	NA	+	NA	NA	−	NA	=	NA	(14,000) OA

Event 1 is an asset exchange; it does not affect total assets reported on the balance sheet. The asset cash decreases and the asset raw materials inventory increases. The income statement is not affected. The cash outflow is reported in the operating activities section of the statement of cash flows.

Event 2
Benchmore used $17,000 of direct raw materials in the process of making boats.

The amounts used for Boat 103, Boat 104, and Boat 105 were $8,000, $3,400, and $5,600, respectively. The effects of this event on the financial statements follow.

Assets			=	Liabilities	+	Equity	Revenue	−	Expenses	=	Net Income	Cash Flow
Raw Materials Inventory	+	Work in Process Inventory										
(17,000)	+	17,000	=	NA	+	NA	NA	−	NA	=	NA	NA

This event is an asset exchange. It does not affect total assets reported on the balance sheet. The asset raw materials inventory decreases and the asset work in process inventory increases. The income statement and the statement of cash flows are not affected. In addition to recording the effects in the Work in Process Inventory control account, Benchmore adjusted the individual job cost sheets to reflect the raw material used on each job, as shown in Exhibit 12–5.

Event 3
Benchmore paid $1,200 cash to purchase production supplies.

The effects of this event on the company's financial statements are shown here.

Assets			=	Liabilities	+	Equity	Revenue	−	Expenses	=	Net Income	Cash Flow
Cash	+	Production Supplies										
(1,200)	+	1,200	=	NA	+	NA	NA	−	NA	=	NA	(1,200) OA

This event is also an asset exchange. It does not affect total assets reported on the balance sheet. One asset, cash, decreases and another asset, production supplies, increases. Purchasing production supplies does not affect the income statement. The cost of supplies is allocated to work in process inventory as part of overhead and is expensed as part of cost of goods sold. The cash outflow for the supplies purchase is reported in the operating activities section of the statement of cash flows.

Event 4
Benchmore paid $8,000 cash to production employees who worked on Boat 103.

The effects of this event on the company's financial statements follow.

Assets			=	Liabilities	+	Equity	Revenue	−	Expenses	=	Net Income	Cash Flow
Cash	+	Work in Process Inventory										
(8,000)	+	8,000	=	NA	+	NA	NA	−	NA	=	NA	(8,000) OA

These wages are *not* salary expense. Because the employees worked to make inventory, the cost of their labor is added to work in process inventory. This event is an asset exchange. The asset cash decreases, and the asset work in process inventory increases. Neither total assets reported on the balance sheet nor any revenues or expenses on the income statement are affected. The cash outflow is reported in the operating activities section of the statement of cash flows. In addition to recording the effects in the Work in Process Inventory control account, Benchmore adjusted the Boat 103 job cost sheet to reflect the labor used on the job. Refer to Exhibit 12–5; the $8,000 labor cost is entered in both the Work in Process Inventory control account and on the job cost sheet for Boat 103.

Event 5
Benchmore applied estimated manufacturing overhead costs of $6,240 to the Boat 103 job.

Production employees completed Boat 103. When the boat was finished, the actual amount of many costs to make it were not then known. During the year, Benchmore sells boats before knowing the exact costs of making them. Although a portion of the total production supplies, depreciation, supervisory salaries, rental cost, and utilities were used while Boat 103 was under construction, the actual cost of these resources is not known until the end of the year. To make timely decisions, such as setting the selling prices for boats, Benchmore must assign estimated overhead costs to boats as they are completed.

To estimate overhead as accurately as possible, Benchmore first reviewed the previous year's actual overhead costs. It adjusted those amounts for expected changes. Assume Benchmore estimated total overhead costs for 2003 would be as follows: production supplies, \$1,400; depreciation, \$4,000; utilities and other indirect costs, \$10,590, for a total of \$15,990 (\$1,400 + \$4,000 + \$10,590).

Benchmore has identified a cause and effect relationship between direct labor time and overhead cost. Boats that require more labor also require more overhead. For example, the more hours production employees work, the more supplies they use. Similarly, more labor hours translates into more equipment use, causing more utilities and depreciation costs. Because of the relationship between labor and indirect costs, Benchmore uses *direct labor hours* as the allocation base for overhead costs. Benchmore estimated it would use a total of 4,100 labor hours during 2003. It established a *predetermined overhead rate* as follows:

$$\text{Predetermined overhead rate} = \text{Total estimated overhead costs} \div \text{Total estimated direct labor hours}$$

$$\text{Predetermined overhead rate} = \$15{,}990 \div 4{,}100$$
$$= \$3.90 \text{ per direct labor hour}$$

Boat 103 required 1,600 actual direct labor hours. Benchmore applied \$6,240 (1,600 hours × \$3.90) of overhead to that job. The effects of the overhead application on the company's financial statements follow.

Assets			=	Liabilities	+	Equity	Revenue	−	Expenses	=	Net Income	Cash Flow
Manufacturing Overhead	+	Work in Process Inventory										
(6,240)	+	6,240	=	NA	+	NA	NA	−	NA	=	NA	NA

The event is an asset exchange. One asset, work in process inventory, increases and a temporary asset, manufacturing overhead, decreases. Applying overhead costs to work in process inventory does not affect the income statement. When finished goods are sold, overhead costs affect the income statement through cost of goods sold. Applying overhead does not affect cash flow either. Cash flow is affected when Benchmore *pays* indirect costs, not when it *applies* them to work in process inventory. The job cost sheet for Boat 103 reflects the applied (estimated) overhead cost. The T-accounts in Exhibit 12–5 also show the overhead application.

Event 6

Benchmore transferred \$36,240 of product costs for completed Boat 103 from work in process inventory to finished goods inventory.

The effects of this transfer on the company's financial statements follow.

Assets			=	Liabilities	+	Equity	Revenue	−	Expenses	=	Net Income	Cash Flow
Work in Process Inventory	+	Finished Goods Inventory										
(36,240)	+	36,240	=	NA	+	NA	NA	−	NA	=	NA	NA

This event is an asset exchange. Benchmore transferred cost from the Work in Process Inventory control account to the Finished Goods Inventory control account. The transfer does not affect total assets reported on the balance sheet, nor does it affect the income statement or the statement of cash flows. The job cost sheet is moved to the finished goods file folder. Exhibit 12–5 illustrates these effects.

Event 7

Benchmore paid \$24,500 cash for selling and administrative expenses.

The effects of this transaction on the financial statements follow.

Assets	=	Liabilities	+	Equity	Revenue	−	Expenses	=	Net Income	Cash Flow
(24,500)	=	NA	+	(24,500)	NA	−	24,500	=	(24,500)	(24,500) OA

This is an asset use transaction. Cash and stockholders' equity (retained earnings) decrease. Recognizing the expense decreases net income. The cash outflow reduces cash flow from operating activities.

Event 8

Benchmore paid $12,000 cash to production employees for work on Boats 104 and 105.

The cost of direct labor used was $5,000 for Boat 104 and $7,000 for Boat 105. These jobs were still incomplete at the end of 2003. The effects of this event on the financial statements follow.

Assets			=	Liabilities	+	Equity	Revenue	−	Expenses	=	Net Income	Cash Flow
Cash	+	Work in Process Inventory										
(12,000)	+	12,000	=	NA	+	NA	NA	−	NA	=	NA	(12,000) OA

This event is an asset exchange. It does not affect total assets reported on the balance sheet. It does not affect the income statement The cash outflow is reported in the operating activities section of the statement of cash flows. In addition to the effects on the Work in Process Inventory control account, Benchmore adjusted the individual job cost sheets to reflect the labor used on each job. Exhibit 12–5 illustrates these effects.

Event 9

Benchmore applied estimated manufacturing overhead costs to the Boat 104 and Boat 105 jobs.

As previously explained, the predetermined overhead rate was $3.90 per direct labor hour (see Event 5). Assume the work described in Event 8 represented 1,000 direct labor hours for Boat 104 and 1,400 direct labor hours for Boat 105. The amount of estimated overhead cost Benchmore applied to the two jobs is calculated as follows:

Job Number	Predetermined Overhead Rate	×	Actual Labor Hours Used	=	Amount of Applied Overhead
Boat 104	$3.90	×	1,000	=	$3,900
Boat 105	3.90	×	1,400	=	5,460
Total					$9,360

The effects on the company's financial statements of applying the overhead follow.

Assets			=	Liabilities	+	Equity	Revenue	−	Expenses	=	Net Income	Cash Flow
Manufacturing Overhead	+	Work in Process Inventory										
(9,360)	+	9,360	=	NA	+	NA	NA	−	NA	=	NA	NA

Applying overhead is an asset exchange. Total assets, net income, and cash flow are not affected. Overhead costs of $3,900 for Boat 104 and $5,460 for Boat 105 are recorded on the job cost sheets. The total, $9,360, is recorded in the Work in Process Inventory control account. Trace these allocations to Exhibit 12–5.

Event 10

Benchmore paid $10,100 cash for utilities and other indirect product costs.

The effects of this event on the financial statements are shown here.

Assets			=	Liabilities	+	Equity	Revenue	−	Expenses	=	Net Income	Cash Flow
Cash	+	Manufacturing Overhead										
(10,100)	+	10,100	=	NA	+	NA	NA	−	NA	=	NA	(10,100) OA

Paying for *actual* overhead costs is an asset exchange. Total assets, net income, and job cost sheets are not affected. The cash outflow is reported in the operating activities section of the statement of cash flows. Recall that estimated overhead costs were previously recorded in work in process inventory and on the job cost sheets (Events 5 and 9).

Event 11

Benchmore recognized $4,000 of actual manufacturing equipment depreciation.

The effects of this event on the financial statements follow.

Assets			=	Liabilities	+	Equity	Revenue	−	Expenses	=	Net Income	Cash Flow
Book Value of Manufacturing Equipment	+	Manufacturing Overhead										
(4,000)	+	4,000	=	NA	+	NA	NA	−	NA	=	NA	NA

Depreciation of manufacturing equipment represents an *actual* indirect product cost (overhead), *not* an expense (even though the *amount* of depreciation is an estimate). Recognizing this depreciation is an asset exchange. The book value of the manufacturing equipment decreases and the Manufacturing Overhead account increases. Neither the total amount of assets reported on the balance sheet, nor the income statement or the statement of cash flows are affected. The job cost sheets are also not affected when *actual* overhead cost (depreciation) is recognized. The inventory accounts and job cost sheets reflect *estimated* overhead.

Event 12

Benchmore counted the production supplies on hand at year-end and recognized actual overhead cost for the supplies used.

During 2003, Benchmore had available for use $1,500 of production supplies ($300 beginning balance + $1,200 supplies purchased). A physical count disclosed there were $400 of supplies on hand at the end of 2003. Benchmore therefore must have used $1,100 of supplies ($1,500 − $400). The effects on the company's financial statements of recognizing supplies used follow:

Assets			=	Liabilities	+	Equity	Revenue	−	Expenses	=	Net Income	Cash Flow
Production Supplies	+	Manufacturing Overhead										
(1,100)	+	1,100	=	NA	+	NA	NA	−	NA	=	NA	NA

The event is an asset exchange. Total assets, net income, and cash flow are not affected. The job cost sheets are not affected. Remember that estimated overhead costs were previously recorded on the job cost sheets.

Event 13
Benchmore sold Boat 101 for $91,000 cash.

The effects of this event on the financial statements follow.

Assets	=	Liabilities	+	Equity	Revenue	−	Expenses	=	Net Income	Cash Flow
91,000	=	NA	+	91,000	91,000	−	NA	=	91,000	91,000 OA

Recognizing revenue from selling inventory is an asset source event. Both assets (cash) and stockholders' equity (retained earnings) increase. Revenue recognition also increases the net income reported on the income statement. The cash inflow is reported in the operating activities section of the statement of cash flows.

Event 14
Benchmore recognized cost of goods sold for Boat 101.

The effects of this event on the financial statements follow.

Assets	=	Liabilities	+	Equity	Revenue	−	Expenses	=	Net Income	Cash Flow
(50,000)	=	NA	+	(50,000)	NA	−	50,000	=	(50,000)	NA

Recognizing cost of goods sold is an asset use transaction. It decreases assets (finished goods inventory) and stockholders' equity (retained earnings). The expense recognition decreases net income, but does not affect cash flow. Benchmore recognized the cash flow impact when it spent cash in the process of building the boat. The job cost sheet for Boat 101 is transferred to the permanent files. The cost sheet is retained because information from it could be useful for estimating costs of future jobs.

Event 15
Benchmore closed the Manufacturing Overhead account, reducing cost of goods sold by $400.

During 2003, Benchmore applied $15,600 of estimated overhead cost to production. Actual overhead costs were $15,200. Overhead was therefore overapplied by $400 ($15,600 − $15,200), meaning too much overhead was transferred to the Work in Process Inventory, Finished Goods Inventory, and Cost of Goods Sold accounts. If the amount of overapplied overhead were significant, Benchmore would have to allocate it proportionately among the inventory and Cost of Goods Sold accounts. In this case, the amount is insignificant and Benchmore assigned it entirely to cost of goods sold. The effects of this event on the company's financial statements follow.

Assets	=	Liabilities	+	Equity	Revenue	−	Expenses	=	Net Income	Cash Flow
400	=	NA	+	400	NA	−	(400)	=	400	NA

Overapplied overhead indicates the estimated cost transferred from the asset accounts to cost of goods sold was too high. The entry to close manufacturing overhead corrects the overstatement. Recording $400 in the overhead account increases total assets. The increase in assets is matched by a decrease in cost of goods sold, which reduces expenses, increases net income, and increases stockholders' equity (retained earnings). Cash flow is not affected. After this adjustment, the total increases in the overhead account (actual costs) equal the total decreases (estimated costs). Manufacturing Overhead is a temporary account. It is closed at year-end and does not appear in the financial statements. Exhibit 12–6 displays Benchmore Boat Company's preclosing trial balance at the end of 2003.

Exhibit 12–5 *Ledger T-Accounts for Benchmore Boat Company*

Cash

Bal.	73,000	(1)	14,000
(13)	91,000	(3)	1,200
		(4)	8,000
		(7)	24,500
		(8)	12,000
		(10)	10,100
Bal.	94,200		

Production Supplies

Bal.	300	(12)	1,100
(3)	1,200		
Bal.	400		

Manufacturing Equipment

Bal.	90,000		

Accumulated Dep.

		Bal.	32,000
		(11)	4,000
		Bal.	36,000

Raw Materials Inventory

Bal.	7,000	(2)	17,000
(1)	14,000		
Bal.	4,000		

Manufacturing Overhead

(10)	10,100	(5)	6,240
(11)	4,000	(9)	9,360
(12)	1,100		
(15)	400		
Bal.	0		

Work in Process Inventory

Bal.	34,000	(6)	36,240
(2)	17,000		
(4)	8,000		
(5)	6,240		
(8)	12,000		
(9)	9,360		
Bal.	50,360		

Finished Goods Inventory

Bal.	85,000	(14)	50,000
(6)	36,240		
Bal.	71,240		

Common Stock

		Bal.	200,000

Retained Earnings

		Bal.	57,300

Sales Revenue

		(13)	91,000

Cost of Goods Sold

(14)	50,000	(15)	400
Bal.	49,600		

Selling and Admin. Exp.

(7)	24,500		

Job Cost Sheets (Subsidiary accounts)

Boat 103

Beginning Balance	14,000
Materials	8,000
Labor	8,000
Overhead	6,240
Product Cost	36,240
To Finish Goods	(36,240)
Ending Balance	0

Boat 104

Beginning Balance	8,000
Materials	3,400
Labor	5,000
Overhead	3,900
Ending Balance	20,300

Boat 105

Beginning Balance	12,000
Materials	5,600
Labor	7,000
Overhead	5,460
Ending Balance	30,060

Boat 101

Balance	50,000
Sold	(50,000)
Balance	0

Boat 102

Balance	35,000
Cost Transferred	0
Balance	35,000

Boat 103

Balance	0
Cost Transferred	36,240
Balance	36,240

Boat 101

Cost Sheet Data Transferred to Permanent Storage

Exhibit 12–6

BENCHMORE BOAT COMPANY
Trial Balance
As of December 31, 2003

	Debit	Credit
Cash	$ 94,200	
Raw Materials Inventory	4,000	
Work in Process Inventory	50,360	
Finished Goods Inventory	71,240	
Production Supplies	400	
Manufacturing Equipment	90,000	
Accumulated Depreciation		$ 36,000
Common Stock		200,000
Retained Earnings		57,300
Sales Revenue		91,000
Cost of Goods Sold	49,600	
Selling and Administrative Expense	24,500	
Total	$384,300	$384,300

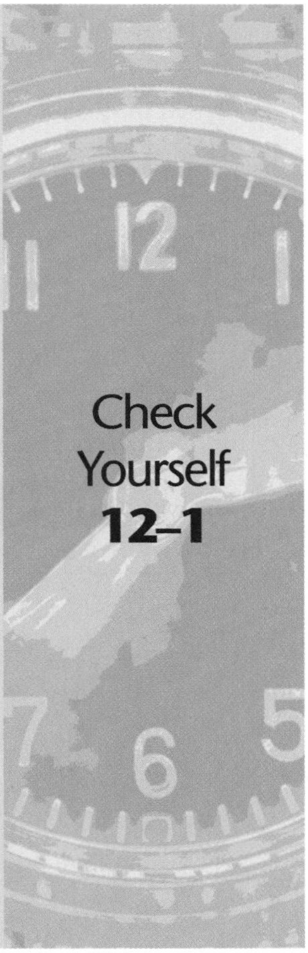

Check Yourself 12–1

Wilson Cabinets makes custom cabinets for home builders. It incurred the following costs during the most recent month.

Inventory	Materials	Labor
Job 1	$4,200	$2,700
Job 2	2,300	5,000
Job 3	1,700	800

Wilson's predetermined overhead rate is $0.80 per direct labor dollar. Actual overhead costs were $7,100. Wilson completed and sold Jobs 1 and 2 during the month, but Job 3 was not complete at month-end. The selling prices for Jobs 1 and 2 were $14,900 and $16,600, respectively. What amount of gross margin would Wilson report on the income statement for the month?

Answer Cost accumulated in the Work in Process account:

Inventory	Materials	Labor	Overhead*	Total
Job 1	$4,200	$2,700	$2,160	$ 9,060
Job 2	2,300	5,000	4,000	11,300
Job 3	1,700	800	640	3,140

*80% of direct labor cost.

Total allocated overhead is $6,800 ($2,160 + $4,000 + $640). Since actual overhead is $7,100, overhead is underapplied by $300 ($7,100 − $6,800).

Sales Revenue ($14,900 + $16,600)	$31,500
Cost of Goods Sold (Job 1, $9,060 + Job 2, $11,300 + Underapplied overhead, $300)	(20,660)
Gross Margin	$10,840

Process Cost System Illustrated

LO8 Explain how accounting events in a process cost system affect financial statements.

In process cost systems, product costs flow through the same general ledger accounts as in job-order cost systems: Raw Materials Inventory, Work in Process Inventory, Finished Goods Inventory, and ultimately Cost of Goods Sold. Accounting for work in process inventory, however, differs between the two systems. Instead of accumulating work in process costs by

Exhibit 12–7

JANIS JUICE COMPANY
Trial Balance
As of January 1, 2003

	Debit	Credit
Cash	$320,000	
Raw Materials—Fruit	7,800	
Raw Materials—Additives	3,100	
Raw Materials—Containers	9,500	
Work in Process—Extraction	22,360	
Work in Process—Mixing	7,960	
Work in Process—Packaging	21,130	
Finished Goods Inventory	20,700	
Common Stock		$180,000
Retained Earnings		232,550
Total	$412,550	$412,550

jobs, process cost systems accumulate product costs by departments. The cost of all goods that move through a processing department during a given accounting period is charged to that department. Work in process subsidiary documents (job cost sheets) are not needed. Process cost systems are easier to use than job-order systems. They do not, however, distinguish the cost of one product from another. Process systems are therefore not appropriate for manufacturers of distinctly different products; they are suited to account for continuous mass production of uniform products. Process cost systems produce the same cost per unit for all products.

To illustrate how a process cost system operates, we analyze the operations of Janis Juice Company during 2003. Recall that Janis uses three distinct processes to produce cans of apple juice. Raw materials (whole apples) enter the *extraction department* where juice concentrate is extracted from whole fruit. The juice extract passes to the *mixing department* where Janis adds water, sugar, food coloring, and preservatives. The juice mixture then moves to the *packaging department* where it is canned and boxed for shipment. Exhibit 12–7 shows the company's 2003 beginning account balances.

The entries for Janis Juice Company's 2003 accounting events, discussed individually in the following sections, are shown in ledger T-accounts in Exhibit 12–9 on page 504. The T-account entries are cross-referenced to sequential event numbers. As you study each event, trace it to the T-accounts.

Event 1
Janis paid $84,000 cash to purchase raw materials.

The effects of this event on the company's financial statements follow.

Assets			=	Liabilities	+	Equity	Revenue	−	Expenses	=	Net Income	Cash Flow
Cash	+	Raw Materials Inventory										
(84,000)	+	84,000	=	NA	+	NA	NA	−	NA	=	NA	(84,000) OA

This event is an asset exchange. Total assets and net income are not affected. The cash outflow is reported in the operating activities section of the statement of cash flows. The total purchase was for $25,000 of whole fruit, $30,000 of additives, and $29,000 of containers. Janis maintains separate inventory accounts for each category of raw material. Trace the entries for this event to the ledger accounts in Exhibit 12–9.

Event 2
Janis processed $26,720 of whole fruit to produce juice extract.

The effects of this event on the financial statements follow.

Assets			=	Liabilities	+	Equity	Revenue	−	Expenses	=	Net Income	Cash Flow
Raw Materials—Fruit	+	WIP—Extraction										
(26,720)	+	26,720	=	NA	+	NA	NA	−	NA	=	NA	NA

This event is an asset exchange. It does not affect total assets, net income, or cash flow. Janis assigns the cost of the materials used to the extraction department rather than to any particular product or batch of products. The extraction department adds the same amount of value to each can of juice.

Event 3

Janis paid $38,000 cash to production employees who worked in the extraction department.

The effects of this event on the financial statements follow.

Assets			=	Liabilities	+	Equity	Revenue	−	Expenses	=	Net Income	Cash Flow
Cash	+	WIP—Extraction										
(38,000)	+	38,000	=	NA	+	NA	NA	−	NA	=	NA	(38,000) OA

This event is also an asset exchange. Production labor cost is not salary expense. Total assets and net income are not affected. The cash outflow is reported in the operating activities section of the statement of cash flows. Like the raw materials, the labor cost is assigned to the department rather than to individual products.

Event 4

Janis applied estimated manufacturing overhead costs to the extraction department work in process inventory.

Janis has identified a relationship between labor dollars and indirect overhead costs. The more labor dollars paid, the more indirect resources consumed. Janis estimated total indirect costs in 2003 would be $96,000 and that it would pay $120,000 to production employees. Using these estimates, Janis established a *predetermined overhead rate* as follows.

$$\text{Predetermined overhead rate} = \text{Total estimated overhead costs} \div \text{Total estimated direct labor dollars}$$

$$\text{Predetermined overhead rate} = \$96{,}000 \div \$120{,}000$$

$$= \$0.80 \text{ per direct labor dollar}$$

Since the extraction department incurred $38,000 of labor cost (see Event 3), Janis applied $30,400 ($38,000 × $0.80) of overhead to that department. The effects of the overhead application on the financial statements follow.

Assets			=	Liabilities	+	Equity	Revenue	−	Expenses	=	Net Income	Cash Flow
Manufacturing Overhead	+	WIP—Extraction										
(30,400)	+	30,400	=	NA	+	NA	NA	−	NA	=	NA	NA

The event is an asset exchange. Total assets, net income, and cash flow are not affected.

Topic Tackler PLUS 12–2

Event 5

Janis finished processing some of the whole fruit and transferred the related cost from the extraction department Work in Process Inventory account to the mixing department Work in Process Inventory account.

LO9 Convert partially completed units in to equivalent whole units.

Total product costs in the extraction department Work in Process Inventory account amounted to $117,480 ($22,360 beginning balance + $26,720 materials + $38,000 labor + $30,400 applied overhead). The beginning inventory represented 100,000 units of product (cans) and the fruit Janis added started an additional 485,000 cans. The amount of fruit placed into production therefore represented 585,000 (100,000 + 485,000) units. Assume the extract transferred to the mixing department represented 500,000 cans of juice. The extraction department therefore had 85,000 (585,000 − 500,000) units in ending inventory that were *started but not completed.*

Janis had to allocate the total $117,480 product cost between the 85,000 partially completed units in ending inventory and the 500,000 completed units it transferred to the mixing department. A rational allocation requires converting the 85,000 partially completed units into *equivalent whole units.* The logic behind **equivalent whole units** relies on basic arithmetic. For example, 2 units that are 50 percent complete are equivalent to 1 whole (100 percent complete) unit (2 × 0.5 = 1). Similarly, 4 units that are 25 percent complete are equivalent to 1 whole unit (4 × 0.25 = 1). Further, 100 units that are 30 percent complete are equivalent to 30 whole units (100 units × 0.30 = 30).

An engineer estimated the 85,000 units in the extraction department's ending inventory were 40 percent complete. The equivalent whole units in ending inventory was therefore 34,000 (85,000 × 0.4). The *total* equivalent units processed by the extraction department during 2003 was 534,000 (500,000 units finished and transferred to the mixing department plus 34,000 equivalent whole units in ending inventory). Janis determined the average **cost per equivalent unit** as follows:

Cost per equivalent unit = Total cost ÷ Number of equivalent whole units
Cost per equivalent unit = $117,480 ÷ 534,000
= $0.22 per equivalent unit

Janis used the *cost per equivalent unit* to allocate the total cost incurred in the extraction department between the amount transferred to the mixing department and the amount in the extraction department's ending work in process inventory as follows.

	Equivalent Units	×	Cost per Unit	Cost to Be Allocated
Transferred-out costs	500,000	×	$0.22	$110,000
Ending inventory	34,000	×	0.22	7,480
Total				$117,480

The effects of transferring $110,000 from the extraction department's work in process inventory to the mixing department's work in process inventory follow.

Assets			=	Liabilities	+	Equity	Revenue	−	Expenses	=	Net Income	Cash Flow
WIP—Extraction	+	WIP—Mixing										
(110,000)	+	110,000	=	NA	+	NA	NA	−	NA	=	NA	NA

This event is an asset exchange. Total assets, net income, and the statement of cash flows are unaffected.

The allocation of costs between units transferred out and ending inventory is frequently summarized in a *cost of production report.* Cost of production reports usually provide details for three categories: the computation of equivalent units; the determination of cost per equivalent unit; and the allocation of total production cost between the units transferred out and the units in ending inventory. Exhibit 12–8 illustrates Janis's 2003 cost of production report for the extraction department.

The method used here to determine equivalent units is the **weighted average method.** The weighted average method does not account for the state of completion of units in *beginning* inventory. Equivalent units are computed for *ending* inventory only. Failing to account for equivalent units in beginning as well as ending inventories can distort the accuracy of the cost assigned to goods transferred out and goods in inventory accounts at the end of the period. Managers frequently tolerate some inaccuracy because the weighted average method is relatively easy to use. If accuracy is of paramount importance, however, a company might use the

Exhibit 12–8

JANIS JUICE COMPANY
Cost of Production Report
Extraction Department
For the Year Ended December 31, 2003

	Actual		Equivalent
Determination of Equivalent Units			
Beginning inventory	100,000		
Units added to production	485,000		
Total	585,000		
Transferred to finished goods	500,000	100% Complete	500,000
Ending inventory	85,000	40% Complete	34,000
Total	585,000		534,000
Determination of Cost per Unit			
Cost accumulation			
Beginning inventory	$ 22,360		
Materials	26,720		
Labor	38,000		
Overhead	30,400		
Total	$117,480		
Divided by	÷		
Equivalent units	534,000		
Cost per equivalent unit (i.e., per can)	$0.22		
Cost Allocation			
To work in process inventory, mixing dept. (500,000 × $0.22)	$110,000		
To ending inventory (34,000 × $0.22)	7,480		
Total	$117,480		

first-in, first-out (FIFO) method. The FIFO method accounts for the degree of completion of both beginning and ending inventories, but it is more complex to apply. Applying the FIFO method in process costing applications is explained in upper-level accounting courses. It is beyond the scope of this text.

Event 6
Janis mixed (used) $24,400 of additives with the extract transferred from the extraction department.

Conceptually, the juice extract transferred from the extraction department is a raw material to the mixing department. The mixing department adds other materials to the juice extract, such as sweetener, food coloring, and preservatives. Although both *transferred-in costs* and *additives* represent raw materials, they are traditionally classified separately. Review the mixing department's Work in Process account in Exhibit 12–9 to see these costs. The effects of using additional materials in the mixing department follow.

Assets			=	Liabilities	+	Equity	Revenue	−	Expenses	=	Net Income	Cash Flow
Raw Materials—Additives	+	WIP—Mixing										
(24,400)	+	24,400	=	NA	+	NA	NA	−	NA	=	NA	NA

This event is an asset exchange. Total assets, net income, and cash flow are not affected.

Event 7
Janis paid $48,000 cash to production employees who worked in the mixing department.

ANSWERS TO THE *curious* ACCOUNTANT

The company that produces flour should use a process costing system. This system is conceptually very simple, especially when there is no beginning or ending work in process inventory. In the situation described in the Curious Accountant, the cost of one bag of whole wheat flour would be calculated by dividing $32.5 million by 50 million bags, yielding a cost per bag of $0.65.

The company that builds houses should use a job-order costing system. This system, as you have seen, requires extensive recordkeeping. The cost of each item of material that goes into a house and the wages of each worker who helps build a house must be tracked to the specific house in question. These costs, along with the appropriate amount of overhead, will constitute the cost of that particular house; it is unlikely that the cost of any two houses will be exactly the same.

The effects of this event on the financial statements follow.

Assets			=	Liabilities	+	Equity	Revenue	−	Expenses	=	Net Income	Cash Flow
Cash	+	WIP—Mixing										
(48,000)	+	48,000	=	NA	+	NA	NA	−	NA	=	NA	(48,000) OA

This is an asset exchange. Total assets and net income are not affected. The cash outflow is reported in the operating activities section of the statement of cash flows.

Event 8
Janis applied estimated manufacturing overhead costs to the mixing department work in process inventory.

Using the *predetermined overhead rate* calculated in Event 4, Janis determined it should apply $38,400 ($48,000 labor × 0.80 overhead rate) of overhead costs to the mixing department's work in process inventory. The effects of the overhead application on the financial statements follow.

Assets			=	Liabilities	+	Equity	Revenue	−	Expenses	=	Net Income	Cash Flow
Manufacturing Overhead	+	WIP—Mixing										
(38,400)	+	38,400	=	NA	+	NA	NA	−	NA	=	NA	NA

The event is an asset exchange. Total assets, net income, and cash flow are not affected.

Event 9
Janis finished mixing some of the juice extract with additives and transferred the related cost from the mixing department Work in Process Inventory account to the packaging department Work in Process Inventory account.

Total product costs in the mixing department were $228,760 ($7,960 beginning balance + $110,000 transferred-in cost + $24,400 materials + $48,000 labor + $38,400 overhead). An engineer estimated that Janis transferred 510,000 units of mixed juice from the mixing department to the packaging department and that the 88,000 units of juice in the mixing department ending inventory were 25 percent complete.

The mixing department ending inventory therefore represented 22,000 (88,000 × 0.25) *equivalent whole units.* The total equivalent whole units produced by the mixing department was 532,000 (510,000 + 22,000). The average *cost per equivalent unit* was therefore $0.43 ($228,760 ÷ 532,000). Janis allocated the total product costs incurred in the mixing department between the amount transferred to the packaging department and the amount in the mixing department's *ending* work in process inventory as follows.

	Equivalent Units	×	Cost per Unit	Cost to Be Allocated
Transferred-out costs	510,000	×	$0.43	$219,300
Ending inventory	22,000	×	0.43	9,460
Total				$228,760

The effects of transferring $219,300 from the mixing department work in process inventory to the packaging department work in process inventory are as follows.

Assets			=	Liabilities	+	Equity	Revenue	−	Expenses	=	Net Income	Cash Flow
WIP— Mixing	+	WIP— Packaging										
(219,300)	+	219,300	=	NA	+	NA	NA	−	NA	=	NA	NA

This event is an asset exchange. Total assets, net income, and the statement of cash flows are unaffected. Find the ending balance in the mixing department's Work in Process Inventory account in Exhibit 12–9. Also find the entry that transfers $219,300 of product cost from the mixing department's Work in Process Inventory account to the packaging department's Work in Process Inventory account.

Event 10

Janis added containers and other packaging materials costing $32,000 to work in process in the packaging department.

The effects of this event on the financial statements follow:

Assets			=	Liabilities	+	Equity	Revenue	−	Expenses	=	Net Income	Cash Flow
Raw Materials— Containers	+	WIP— Packaging										
(32,000)	+	32,000	=	NA	+	NA	NA	−	NA	=	NA	NA

This event is an asset exchange. Total assets, net income, and cash flow are not affected.

Event 11

Janis paid $43,000 cash to production employees who worked in the packaging department.

The effects of this event on the financial statements follow.

Assets			=	Liabilities	+	Equity	Revenue	−	Expenses	=	Net Income	Cash Flow
Cash	+	WIP— Packaging										
(43,000)	+	43,000	=	NA	+	NA	NA	−	NA	=	NA	(43,000) OA

This is an asset exchange. Total assets and net income are not affected. The cash outflow is reported in the operating activities section of the statement of cash flows.

Event 12

Janis applied estimated manufacturing overhead costs to the packaging department work in process inventory.

Using the *predetermined overhead rate* calculated in Event 4, Janis determined it should apply $34,400 ($43,000 labor × 0.80 overhead rate) of overhead costs to the packaging department's work in process inventory. The effects of the overhead application on the financial statements follow.

Assets			=	Liabilities	+	Equity	Revenue	−	Expenses	=	Net Income	Cash Flow
Manufacturing Overhead	+	WIP— Packaging										
(34,400)	+	34,400	=	NA	+	NA	NA	−	NA	=	NA	NA

The event is an asset exchange. Total assets, net income, and cash flow are not affected.

Event 13

Janis finished packaging some of the juice and transferred the related cost from the packaging department Work in Process Inventory account to the Finished Goods Inventory account.

Total product costs in the packaging department were $349,830 ($21,130 beginning balance + $219,300 transferred-in cost + $32,000 materials + $43,000 labor + $34,400 overhead). An engineer estimated that Janis transferred 480,000 units of packaged juice from the packaging department to finished goods inventory and that the 90,000 units of juice in the packaging department ending inventory were 30 percent complete.

The packaging department ending inventory therefore represented 27,000 (90,000 × 0.30) *equivalent whole units.* The total equivalent whole units produced by the packaging department was 507,000 (480,000 + 27,000). The average *cost per equivalent unit* was therefore $0.69 ($349,830 ÷ 507,000). Janis allocated the total product costs incurred in the packaging department between the amount transferred to finished goods inventory and the amount in the packaging department's ending work in process inventory as follows.

	Equivalent Units	×	Cost per Unit	Cost to Be Allocated
Transferred-out costs	480,000	×	$0.69	$331,200
Ending inventory	27,000	×	0.69	18,630
Total				$349,830

The effects of transferring $331,200 from the packaging department work in process inventory to the finished goods inventory follow.

Assets			=	Liabilities	+	Equity	Revenue	−	Expenses	=	Net Income	Cash Flow
WIP— Packaging	+	Finished Goods										
(331,200)	+	331,200	=	NA	+	NA	NA	−	NA	=	NA	NA

This event is an asset exchange. Total assets, net income, and the statement of cash flows are unaffected. Find the ending balance in the packaging department's Work in Process Inventory account in Exhibit 12–9. Also find the entry that transfers $331,200 of product cost from the packaging department's Work in Process Inventory account to the Finished Goods Inventory account.

Event 14

Janis paid $106,330 cash for actual overhead costs.

The effects of this event on the financial statements follow.

Assets			=	Liabilities	+	Equity	Revenue	−	Expenses	=	Net Income	Cash Flow
Cash	+	Manufacturing Overhead										
(106,330)	+	106,330	=	NA	+	NA	NA	−	NA	=	NA	(106,330) OA

Incurring *actual overhead costs* is an asset exchange event. Total assets and net income are not affected. The cash outflow is reported in the operating activities section of the statement of cash flows.

Event 15
Janis sold 490,000 cans of juice for $1 per can.

The effects of this event on the financial statements follow.

Assets	=	Liabilities	+	Equity	Revenue	−	Expenses	=	Net Income	Cash Flow
490,000	=	NA	+	490,000	490,000	−	NA	=	490,000	490,000 OA

Recognizing revenue from the sale of inventory is an asset source event. Assets (cash) and stockholders' equity (retained earnings) both increase, as do revenue and net income reported on the income statement. Since Janis received the revenue in cash, the operating activities section of the statement of cash flows reports the inflow.

Event 16
Janis recognized cost of goods sold for the 490,000 cans of juice sold in Event 15.

The average cost per finished can of juice was $0.69 (see Event 13). Cost of goods sold was therefore $338,100 (490,000 units × $0.69). The effects of this event on the financial statements follow.

Assets	=	Liabilities	+	Equity	Revenue	−	Expenses	=	Net Income	Cash Flow
(338,100)	=	NA	+	(338,100)	NA	−	338,100	=	(338,100)	NA

Recognizing cost of goods sold is an asset use transaction. Both assets (finished goods inventory), and stockholders' equity (retained earnings), decrease. The increase in the expense, cost of goods sold, decreases net income. Cash flow is not affected.

Event 17
Janis paid $78,200 cash for selling and administrative expenses.

The effects of this event on the financial statements follow.

Assets	=	Liabilities	+	Equity	Revenue	−	Expenses	=	Net Income	Cash Flow
(78,200)	=	NA	+	(78,200)	NA	−	78,200	=	(78,200)	(78,200) OA

Recognizing selling and administrative expense is an asset use transaction. It decreases assets (cash) and stockholders' equity (retained earnings). Recognizing the expense decreases net income. The cash outflow is reported as a decrease in the operating activities section of the statement of cash flows.

Event 18
Janis closed the Manufacturing Overhead account and increased the Cost of Goods Sold account by $3,130.

During 2003, Janis applied $103,200 of overhead cost to production. Actual overhead costs were $106,330. Overhead was therefore underapplied by $3,130 ($106,330 − $103,200), indicating that too little overhead was transferred to work in process inventory, finished goods inventory, and cost of goods sold. Janis considered the underapplied amount insignificant and assigned it directly to cost of goods sold. The effects of this event on the financial statements follow.

Assets	=	Liabilities	+	Equity	Revenue	−	Expenses	=	Net Income	Cash Flow
(3,130)	=	NA	+	(3,130)	NA	−	3,130	=	(3,130)	NA

Since underapplied overhead means too little estimated cost was transferred from the asset accounts to the Cost of Goods Sold account, closing the Manufacturing Overhead account to cost of goods sold corrects the understatement. The additional overhead costs of $3,130 increase cost of goods sold and decrease net income. Cash flow is unaffected. After this

Exhibit 12–9 *Ledger T-Accounts for Janis Juice Company*

Cash

Bal.	320,000	(1)	84,000
(15)	490,000	(3)	38,000
		(7)	48,000
		(11)	43,000
		(14)	106,330
		(17)	78,200
Bal.	412,470		

Raw Materials—Fruit

Bal.	7,800	(2)	26,720
(1)	25,000		
Bal.	6,080		

Raw Materials—Additives

Bal.	3,100	(6)	24,400
(1)	30,000		
Bal.	8,700		

Raw Materials—Containers

Bal.	9,500	(10)	32,000
(1)	29,000		
Bal.	6,500		

Manufacturing Overhead

(14)	106,330	(4)	30,400
		(8)	38,400
		(12)	34,400
		(18)	3,130
Bal.	0		

Work in Process—Extraction

Bal.	22,360	(5)	110,000
(2)	26,720		
(3)	38,000		
(4)	30,400		
Bal.	7,480		

Work in Process —Mixing

Bal.	7,960	(9)	219,300
(5)	110,000		
(6)	24,400		
(7)	48,000		
(8)	38,400		
Bal.	9,460		

Work in Process—Packaging

Bal.	21,130	(13)	331,200
(9)	219,300		
(10)	32,000		
(11)	43,000		
(12)	34,400		
Bal.	18,630		

Finished Goods Inventory

Bal.	20,700	(16)	338,100
(13)	331,200		
Bal.	13,800		

Common Stock

		Bal.	180,000

Retained Earnings

		Bal.	232,550

Sales Revenue

		(15)	490,000

Cost of Goods Sold

(16)	338,100		
(18)	3,130		
Bal.	341,230		

Selling and Admin. Exp.

(17)	78,200		

Exhibit 12–10

JANIS JUICE COMPANY
Adjusted Trial Balance
As of December 31, 2003

	Debit	Credit
Cash	$412,470	
Raw Materials—Fruit	6,080	
Raw Materials—Additives	8,700	
Raw Materials—Containers	6,500	
Work in Process—Extraction	7,480	
Work in Process—Mixing	9,460	
Work in Process—Packaging	18,630	
Finished Goods Inventory	13,800	
Common Stock		$180,000
Retained Earnings		232,550
Sales Revenue		490,000
Cost of Goods Sold	341,230	
Selling and Administrative Expenses	78,200	
Total	$902,550	$902,550

adjustment, the total increases in the overhead account (actual costs) equal the total decreases (estimated costs). The ending balance in the Manufacturing Overhead account is zero. Manufacturing overhead is not reported on any financial statement.

Exhibit 12–10 shows the year-end adjusted trial balance for Janis Juice Company.

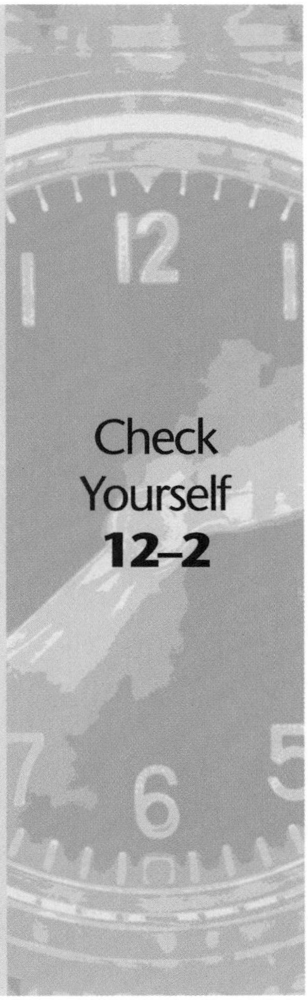

Western Manufacturing Company uses a process cost system. Its products pass through two departments. Beginning inventory in Department I's Work in Process (WIP) account was $5,000. During the month the department added $13,200 of product costs to the WIP account. There were 200 units of product in beginning inventory, and 500 units were started during the month. Ending inventory consisted of 300 units 40 percent complete. Prepare a cost of production report showing the cost of goods transferred from Department I to Department II and the cost of Department I's ending work in process inventory.

Answer

Cost of Production Report

	Actual		Equivalent Units
Determination of Equivalent Units			
Beginning inventory	200		
Units added to production	500		
Total	700		
Transferred to finished goods	400	100% Complete	400
Ending inventory	300	40% Complete	120
Total	700		520
Determination of Cost per Unit			
Cost accumulation			
Beginning inventory	$ 5,000		
Product costs added	13,200		
Total product costs	$18,200		
Divide by	÷		
Equivalent units	520		
Cost per equivalent unit	$ 35		
Cost Allocation			
Transferred to Department II (400 × $35)	$14,000		
Ending WIP Inventory (120 × $35)	4,200		
Total	$18,200		

a look back

Job-order and *process cost systems* represent the two primary methods of accounting for product cost flows in manufacturing companies. In both systems, entries in the accounting records parallel the physical flow of products as they move through production. Job-order cost systems are used by manufacturers that produce distinct products or distinct batches of products. Products suited to job-order systems include buildings, ships, airplanes, and special-order batches. A job-order cost system accumulates costs for individual products or batches of products. Each product or batch has a job identification number. Costs are accumulated separately by job number. A job-order cost system requires detailed accounting information. The total cost of all jobs is accumulated in one Work in Process Inventory control account; details of the cost of materials, labor, and overhead for each job are kept in subsidiary records called *job-order cost sheets*. Process cost systems are used by manufacturers that make homogeneous products in a continuous production process. Products suited to a process cost system include paint, gasoline, and soft drinks. A process cost system accumulates product costs for each processing department (e.g., cutting, processing, assembling, packaging). Because the units are homogeneous, the cost per unit can be determined by dividing the total processing cost by the number of units (cost averaging). Any units that are partially complete at the end of an accounting period must be converted into equivalent whole units prior to determining the average cost per unit. The cost per equivalent whole unit is used to allocate the total processing cost among departments and ending inventories.

a look forward

The remaining two chapters are transitional chapters. Chapter 13 discusses financial statement analysis. Chapter 14 discusses advanced topics relating to the statement of cash flows. Some instructors include these subjects in the financial accounting course, and other instructors cover them in the managerial accounting course.

focus on INTERNATIONAL ISSUES

Job-Order, Process, and Hybrid Cost Systems Cross International Borders

Companies throughout the world use job-order, process, and hybrid cost systems. **Nestlé Group**, a Swiss company, makes chocolate candy bars, among many other products. A homogenous product like candy bars requires the use of a process cost system. In contrast, **Airbus** is an aircraft manufacturing company headquartered in Toulouse, France. When it completes an order for five A320 airplanes for Air New Zealand, the cost of this order will be determined using a job-order cost system.

SELF-STUDY REVIEW PROBLEM 1

Hill Construction Company uses a job-order cost system. The company had three jobs in process at the beginning of the month. The beginning balance in the Work in Process control account was $145,400, made up of $42,400, $65,100, and $37,900 shown on the job cost sheets for Jobs 302, 303, and 304, respectively. During the month, Hill added the following materials and labor costs to each job:

Inventory	Materials	Labor
Job 302	$10,200	$32,000
Job 303	12,400	18,000
Job 304	16,500	10,000
Total	$39,100	$60,000

Overhead cost is applied at the predetermined rate of $0.60 per direct labor dollar. Actual overhead costs for the month were $36,800. Hill completed Job 303 and sold it for $129,000 cash during the month.

Required

a. Determine the balance in the Work in Process account at the end of the month.
b. Explain how the entry to close the Manufacturing Overhead account would affect the Cost of Goods Sold account.
c. Determine the amount of gross margin Hill would report on its income statement for the month.

Solution to Requirement a
Cost accumulated in the Work in Process account:

Inventory	Beg. Bal.	+	Materials	+	Labor	+	Overhead*	=	Total
Job 302	$42,400		$10,200		$32,000		$19,200		$103,800
Job 303	65,100		12,400		18,000		10,800		106,300
Job 304	37,900		16,500		10,000		6,000		70,400

*60% of direct labor cost.

Since Hill has sold Job 303, work in process at the end of the month is the sum of costs assigned to Jobs 302 and 304, $174,200 ($103,800 + $70,400).

Solution to Requirement b
Total applied overhead is $36,000 ($19,200 + $10,800 + $6,000). Since actual overhead is $36,800, overhead is underapplied by $800 ($36,800 − $36,000). Since the overhead is underapplied, cost of goods sold is understated. The entry to close the overhead account would increase the amount of cost of goods sold by $800.

Solution to Requirement c

Sales revenue	$129,000
Cost of goods sold (Job 303, $106,300 + Underapplied Overhead, $800)	(107,100)
Gross margin	$ 21,900

SELF-STUDY REVIEW PROBLEM 2

United Technology Manufacturing Company (UTMC) uses a process cost system. Products pass through two departments. The following information applies to the Assembly Department. Beginning inventory in the department's Work in Process (WIP) account was $18,400. During the month UTMC added $200,273 of product costs to the WIP account. There were 5,700 units of product in the beginning inventory and 45,300 units started during the month. The ending inventory consisted of 4,200 units, which were 30 percent complete.

Required

Prepare a cost of production report for the month.

Solution

Cost of Production Report	Actual		Equivalent Units
Determination of Equivalent Units			
Beginning inventory	5,700		
Units added to production	45,300		
Total	51,000		
Transferred to finished goods	46,800	100% Complete	46,800
Ending inventory	4,200	30% Complete	1,260
Total	51,000		48,060
Determination of Cost per Unit			
Cost accumulation			
Beginning inventory	$ 18,400		
Product costs added	200,273		
Total product costs	$218,673		
Divide by	÷		
Equivalent units	48,060		
Cost per equivalent unit	$ 4.55		
Cost Allocation			
Transferred out (46,800 × $4.55)	$212,940		
Ending WIP inventory (1,260 × $4.55)	5,733		
Total	$218,673		

KEY TERMS

Cost per equivalent unit *498*
Equivalent whole units *498*
First-in, first-out (FIFO) method *499*
Hybrid cost system *486*
Job cost sheet *486*
Job-order cost system *484*
Materials requisition form *486*
Process cost system *484*
Transferred-in costs *486*
Weighted average method *498*
Work ticket *487*

QUESTIONS

1. To what types of products is a job-order cost system best suited? Provide examples.
2. To what types of products is a process cost system best suited? Provide examples.
3. Why do both job-order and process costing require some form of cost averaging?
4. How is the unit cost of a product determined in a process cost system?
5. Ludwig Company, which normally operates a process cost system to account for the cost of the computers that it produces, has received a special order from a corporate client to produce and sell 5,000 computers. Can Ludwig use a job-order cost system to account for the costs associated with the special order even though it uses a process cost system for its normal operations?
6. Which system, a job-order or a process cost system, requires more documentation?
7. How do source documents help accountants operate a cost system?
8. In a job-order cost system, what are the Work in Process Inventory subsidiary records called? What information is included in these subsidiary records?
9. How is indirect labor recorded in ledger accounts? How is this labor eventually assigned to the items produced in a job-order cost system?
10. How is depreciation on manufacturing equipment recorded in ledger accounts? How is this depreciation assigned to the items produced in a job-order cost system and in a process cost system?
11. Why is a process cost system not appropriate for companies that produce items that are distinctly different from one another?

12. The president of Videl Corporation tells you that her company has a difficult time determining the cost per unit of product that it makes. It seems that some units are always partially complete. Counting these units as complete understates the cost per unit because all of the units but only part of the cost is included in the unit cost computation. Conversely, ignoring the number of partially completed products overstates the cost per unit because all of the costs are included but some of the number of units are omitted from the per unit computation. How can Videl obtain a more accurate cost per unit figure?
13. Bindon Furniture Manufacturing has completed its monthly inventory count for dining room chairs and recorded the following information for ending inventory: 600 units 100 percent complete, 300 units 60 percent complete, and 100 units 20 percent complete. The company uses a process cost system to determine unit cost. Why would unit cost be inaccurate if 1,000 units were used to determine unit cost?
14. What is the weighted average method of determining equivalent units? Why is it used? What are its weaknesses?
15. What is the purpose of each of the three primary steps in a process cost system? Describe each.
16. In a process cost system, what does the term *transferred-in costs* mean? How is the amount of transferred-in costs determined?
17. The finishing department is the last of four sequential production departments for Kowalski Graphics, Inc. The company's other production departments are design, layout, and printing. The finishing department incurred the following costs in March 2006: direct materials, $40,000; direct labor, $80,000; applied overhead, $90,000; and transferred-in costs, $120,000. Which department incurred the transferred-in costs? In what month were the transferred-in costs incurred?

EXERCISES—SERIES A

All Exercises in Series A are available with McGraw-Hill's Homework Manager

EXERCISE 12–1A *Matching Products with Appropriate Cost Systems*

L.O. 1

Required

Indicate which cost system (job-order, process, or hybrid) would be most appropriate for the type of product listed in the left-hand column. The first item is shown as an example.

Type of Product	Type of Cost System
a. Apartment building	job order
b. Automobile	
c. Hollywood movie	
d. Concorde aircraft	
e. Personal computer with special features	
f. Coffee table	
g. Plastic storage containers	
h. TV set	
i. Ship	
j. Boom box	
k. House	
l. Custom-made suit	
m. Van with custom features	
n. CPA review course	
o. Shirts	
p. Pots and pans	

EXERCISE 12–2A *Identifying the Appropriate Cost System*

L.O. 1

Extra Space, Inc., makes small aluminum storage bins that it sells through a direct marketing mail-order business. The typical bin measures 6 × 8 feet. The bins are normally used to store garden tools or other small household items. Extra Space customizes bins for special-order customers by adding shelving; occasionally, it makes large bins following the unique specifications of commercial customers.

Required

Recommend the type of cost system (job-order, process, or hybrid) that Extra Space should use. Explain your recommendation.

L.O. 1, 2 **EXERCISE 12–3A** ***Job-Order or Process Cost System and a Pricing Decision***

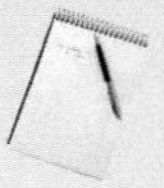

Spence Chang, a tailor in his home country, recently immigrated to the United States. He is interested in starting a business making custom suits for men. Mr. Chang is trying to determine the cost of making a suit so he can set an appropriate selling price. He estimates that his materials cost will range from $50 to $80 per suit. Because he will make the suits himself, he assumes there will be no labor cost. Some suits will require more time than others, but Mr. Chang considers this fact to be irrelevant because he is personally supplying the labor, which costs him nothing. Finally, Mr. Chang knows that he will incur some overhead costs such as rent, utilities, advertising, packaging, delivery, and so on; however, he is uncertain as to the exact cost of these items.

Required

a. Should Mr. Chang use a job-order or a process cost system?

b. How can Mr. Chang determine the cost of suits he makes during the year when he does not know what the total overhead cost will be until the end of the year?

c. Is it appropriate for Mr. Chang to consider labor cost to be zero?

d. With respect to the overhead costs mentioned in the problem, distinguish the *manufacturing overhead* costs from the *selling and administrative* expenses. Comment on whether Mr. Chang should include the selling and administrative expenses in determining the product cost if he uses cost-plus pricing. Comment on whether the selling and administrative expenses should be included in determining the product cost for financial reporting purposes.

L.O. 2, 7 **EXERCISE 12–4A** ***Job-Order Costing in a Manufacturing Company***

Seahawk, Inc., builds sailboats. On January 1, 2004, the company had the following account balances: $40,000 for both cash and common stock. Boat 25 was started on February 10 and finished on May 31. To build the boat, Seahawk had incurred cash costs of $5,100 for labor and $4,350 for materials. During the same period, Seahawk paid $6,600 cash for actual manufacturing overhead costs. The company expects to incur $175,500 of indirect overhead cost during 2004. The overhead is allocated to jobs based on direct labor cost. The expected total labor cost for the year is $135,000.

Seahawk uses a just-in-time inventory management system. Consequently, it does not have raw materials inventory. Raw materials purchases are recorded directly in the Work in Process Inventory account.

Required

a. Use the horizontal financial statements model, as illustrated here, to record Seahawk's manufacturing events. In the Cash Flow column, designate the cash flows as operating activities (OA), investing activities (IA), or financing activities (FA). The first row shows beginning balances.

Assets								=	Equity								
Cash	+	Work in Process	+	Finished Goods	+	Manuf. Overhead		=	Com. Stock	+	Ret. Ear.	Rev.	−	Exp.	=	Net Inc.	Cash Flow
40,000	+	NA	+	NA	+	NA		=	40,000	+	NA	NA	−	NA	=	NA	NA

b. If Seahawk desires to earn a profit equal to 20 percent of cost, for what price should it sell the boat?

c. If the boat is not sold by year end, what amount would appear in the Work in Process Inventory and Finished Goods Inventory on the balance sheet for Boat 25?

d. Is the amount of inventory you calculated in Requirement *c* the actual or the estimated cost of the boat?

e. When is it appropriate to use estimated inventory cost on a year-end balance sheet?

L.O. 2, 7 **EXERCISE 12–5A** ***Job-Order Costing in a Manufacturing Company***

Tanner Special Furniture, Inc., makes custom-order furniture to meet the needs of disabled persons. On January 1, 2005, the company had the following account balances: $28,000 for both cash and common stock. In 2005, Tanner worked on three special orders. The relevant direct operating costs follow.

	Direct Labor	Direct Materials
Job 1	$1,200	$1,600
Job 2	720	560
Job 3	2,880	1,440
Total	$4,800	$3,600

Tanner's predetermined manufacturing overhead rate was $0.25 per direct labor dollar. Actual manufacturing overhead costs amounted to $1,286. Tanner paid cash for all costs. The company completed and delivered Jobs 1 and 2 to customers during the year. Job 3 was incomplete at the end of the year. The company sold Job 1 for $5,280 cash and Job 2 for $2,560 cash. Tanner also paid $1,200 cash for selling and administrative expenses for the year.

Tanner uses a just-in-time inventory management system. Consequently, it does not have raw materials inventory. Raw materials purchases are recorded directly in the Work in Process Inventory account.

Required

a. Record the preceding events in a horizontal statements model. In the Cash Flow column, designate the cash flow as operating activities (OA), investing activities (IA), or financing activities (FA). The first row shows beginning balances.

Assets							=	Equity								
Cash	**+**	**Work in Process**	**+**	**Finished Goods**	**+**	**Manuf. Overhead**	**=**	**Com. Stock**	**+**	**Ret. Ear.**	**Rev.**	**−**	**Exp.**	**=**	**Net Inc.**	**Cash Flow**
28,000	+	NA	+	NA	+	NA	=	28,000	+	NA	NA	−	NA	=	NA	NA

b. Record the entry to close the amount of underapplied or overapplied overhead for the year to Cost of Goods Sold (in the expense category) in the horizontal financial statements model.

c. Determine the gross margin for the year.

EXERCISE 12–6A *Job-Order Costing in a Service Company* L.O. 2, 7

Sertoma Condos, Inc., is a small company owned by Adam Garner. It leases three condos of differing sizes to customers as vacation facilities. Labor costs for each condo consist of maid service and maintenance cost. Other direct operating costs consist of interest and depreciation. The direct operating costs for each condo follow.

	Direct Labor	Other Direct Operating Costs
Condo 1	$ 7,200	$18,000
Condo 2	9,300	21,000
Condo 3	11,250	28,500
Total	$27,750	$67,500

Indirect operating expenses, which amounted to $20,250, are allocated to the condos in proportion to the amount of other direct operating costs incurred for each.

Required

a. Assuming that the amount of rent revenue from Condo 2 is $48,000, what amount of income did it earn?

b. Based on the preceding information, will the company show finished goods inventory on its balance sheet? If so, what is the amount of this inventory? If not, explain why not.

EXERCISE 12–7A *Job-Order Cost System* L.O. 2

The following information applies to Job 730 completed by Ritter Manufacturing Company during October 2005. The amount of labor cost for the job was $67,350. Applied overhead amounted to $96,000. The project was completed and delivered to Lancer Company at a contract price of $285,000. Ritter recognized a gross profit of $51,000 on the project.

Required

Determine the amount of raw materials used to complete Job 730.

EXERCISE 12–8A *Process Cost System—Determine Equivalent Units* L.O. 3

Scott Furniture Company's cutting department had 200 units in its beginning work in process inventory. During the accounting period it began work on 800 units of product and had 400 partially complete units in its ending inventory.

Required

(Each requirement is independent of the others.)

a. Assuming the ending inventory units were 75 percent complete, determine the total number of equivalent whole units (number transferred out plus number in ending inventory) accounted for by the cutting department.
b. Assuming that the total number of equivalent whole units (number transferred out plus number in ending inventory) accounted for by the cutting department was 700, what was the ending inventory percentage of completion?

L.O. 3 EXERCISE 12–9A *Cost Allocation in a Process System*

Accurate Watches, Inc., makes watches. Its assembly department started the accounting period with a beginning inventory balance of $43,000. During the accounting period, the department incurred $82,000 of transferred-in cost, $39,000 of materials cost, $120,000 of labor cost, and $130,800 of applied overhead cost. The department processed 3,050 total equivalent units of product during the accounting period.

Required
(Each requirement is independent of the others.)

a. Assuming that 600 equivalent units of product were in the ending work in process inventory, determine the amount of cost transferred out of the Work in Process Inventory account of the assembly department to the Finished Goods Inventory account. What was the assembly department's cost of ending work in process inventory?
b. Assuming that 2,800 units of product were transferred out of the assembly department's work in process inventory to finished goods inventory, determine the amount of the assembly department's cost of ending work in process inventory. What was the cost of the finished goods inventory transferred out of the assembly department?

L.O. 3 EXERCISE 12–10A *Process Cost System—Determine Equivalent Units and Allocate Costs*

Boulder Ski Company manufactures snow skis. During the most recent accounting period, the company's finishing department transferred 4,200 sets of skis to finished goods. At the end of the accounting period, 450 sets of skis were estimated to be 40 percent complete. Total product costs for the finishing department amounted to $657,000.

Required
a. Determine the cost per equivalent.
b. Determine the cost of the goods transferred out of the finishing department.
c. Determine the cost of the finishing department's ending work in process inventory.

L.O. 3 EXERCISE 12–11A *Process Cost System*

Littrell, Inc., is a cosmetics manufacturer. Its assembly department receives raw cosmetics from the molding department. The assembly department places the raw cosmetics into decorative containers and transfers them to the packaging department. The assembly department's Work in Process Inventory account had a $88,500 balance as of August 1. During August, the department incurred raw materials, labor, and overhead costs amounting to $108,000, $127,500, and $120,000, respectively. The department transferred products that cost $513,000 to the packaging department. The balance in the assembly department's Work in Process Inventory account as of August 31 was $61,500.

Required
Determine the cost of raw cosmetics transferred from the molding department to the assembly department during August.

L.O. 5 EXERCISE 12–12A *Selecting the Appropriate Cost System*

Tony's Car Wash (TCW) offers customers three cleaning options. Under Option 1, only the exterior is cleaned. With Option 2, the exterior and interior are cleaned. Option 3 provides exterior waxing as well as exterior and interior cleaning. TCW completed 4,000 Option 1 cleanings, 5,200 Option 2 cleanings, and 3,200 Option 3 cleanings during 2004. The average cost of completing each cleaning option and the price charged for it are shown here.

	Option 1	Option 2	Option 3
Price charged	$8	$12	$20
Costs of completing task	4	5	15

Required

a. Is TCW a manufacturing or a service company? Explain.
b. Which cost system, job-order or process, is most appropriate for TCW? Why?
c. What is the balance in TCW's Work in Process and Finished Goods Inventory accounts on the December 31 balance sheet?
d. Speculate as to the major costs that TCW incurs to complete a cleaning job.

PROBLEMS—SERIES A

All Problems in Series A are available with McGraw-Hill's Homework Manager.

PROBLEM 12–13A *Job-Order Cost System*

L.O. 2, 7

excel
www.mhhe.com/edmonds3e

CHECK FIGURE
d. COGM: $6,750
NI: $1,500

Holly Manufacturing Corporation was started with the issuance of common stock for $8,000. It purchased $5,000 of raw materials and worked on three job orders during 2004 for which data follow. (Assume that all transactions are for cash unless otherwise indicated.)

	Direct Raw Materials Used	Direct Labor
Job 1	$ 500	$1,000
Job 2	1,000	2,000
Job 3	1,500	1,000
Total	$3,000	$4,000

Factory overhead is applied using a predetermined overhead rate of $0.50 per direct labor dollar. Jobs 2 and 3 were completed during the period and Job 3 was sold for $4,500. Holly paid $200 for selling and administrative expenses. Actual factory overhead was $1,750.

Required

a. Record the preceding events in a horizontal statements model. In the Cash Flow column, designate the cash flows as operating activities (OA), investing activities (IA), or financing activities (FA). The first event for 2004 has been recorded as an example.

Assets									=	Equity								
Cash	+	Raw M.	+	MOH	+	WIP	+	F. Goods	=	C. Stk.	+	Ret. Ear.	Rev.	−	Exp.	=	Net Inc.	Cash Flow
8,000	+	NA	+	NA	+	NA	+	NA	=	8,000	+	NA	NA	−	NA	=	NA	8,000 FA

b. Reconcile all subsidiary accounts with their respective control accounts.
c. Record the closing entry for over- or underapplied manufacturing overhead, assuming that the amount is insignificant. Close revenue and expense accounts.
d. Prepare a schedule of cost of goods manufactured and sold, an income statement, a balance sheet, and a statement of cash flows for 2004.

PROBLEM 12–14A *Job-Order Cost System*

L.O. 2, 7

CHECK FIGURES
d. COGM: $2,140
Total Assets: $6,135

Canto Construction Company began operations on January 1, 2005, when it acquired $6,000 cash from the issuance of common stock. During the year, Canto purchased $2,600 of direct raw materials and used $2,400 of the direct materials. There were 108 hours of direct labor worked at an average rate of $4 per hour paid in cash. The predetermined overhead rate was $2.50 per direct labor hour. The company started construction on three prefabricated buildings. The job cost sheets reflected the following allocations of costs to each building.

	Direct Materials	Direct Labor Hours
Job 1	$ 600	30
Job 2	1,000	50
Job 3	800	28

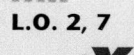

The company paid $80 cash for indirect labor costs. Actual overhead cost paid in cash other than indirect labor was $210. Canto completed Jobs 1 and 2 and sold Job 1 for $1,050 cash. The company incurred $100 of selling and administrative expenses that were paid in cash. Over- or underapplied overhead is closed to Cost of Goods Sold.

Required

a. Record the preceding events in a horizontal statements model. In the Cash Flow column, designate the cash flows as operating activities (OA), investing activities (IA), or financing activities (FA). The first event for 2005 has been recorded as an example.

Assets									=	Equity			Rev.	–	Exp.	=	Net Inc.	Cash Flow
Cash	+	Raw M.	+	MOH	+	WIP	+	F. Goods	=	C. Stk.	+	Ret. Ear.						
6,000	+	NA	+	NA	+	NA	+	NA	=	6,000	+	NA	NA	–	NA	=	NA	6,000 FA

b. Reconcile all subsidiary accounts with their respective control accounts.

c. Record the closing entry for over- or underapplied manufacturing overhead, assuming that the amount is insignificant. Close revenue and expense accounts.

d. Prepare a schedule of cost of goods manufactured and sold, an income statement, a balance sheet, and a statement of cash flows for 2005.

L.O. 3, 8

PROBLEM 12–15A *Process Cost System*

CHECK FIGURES
d. COGS: $27,600
Cash: $45,000

Chairs, Inc., makes rocking chairs. The chairs move through two departments during production. Lumber is cut into chair parts in the cutting department, which transfers the parts to the assembly department for completion. The company sells the unfinished chairs to hobby shops. The following transactions apply to Chairs' operations for its first year, 2006. (Assume that all transactions are for cash unless otherwise stated.)

1. The company was started when it acquired a $75,000 cash contribution from the owners.
2. The company purchased $22,500 of direct raw materials and $600 of indirect materials. Indirect materials are capitalized in the Production Supplies account.
3. Direct materials totaling $9,000 were issued to the cutting department.
4. Labor cost was $42,300. Direct labor for the cutting and assembly departments was $15,000 and $19,500, respectively. Indirect labor costs were $7,800.
5. The predetermined overhead rate was $0.50 per direct labor dollar.
6. Actual overhead costs other than indirect materials and indirect labor were $9,600 for the year.
7. The cutting department transferred $18,000 of inventory to the assembly department.
8. The assembly department transferred $30,000 of inventory to finished goods.
9. The company sold inventory costing $27,000 for $45,000.
10. Selling and administrative expenses were $4,500.
11. A physical count revealed $150 of production supplies on hand at the end of 2006.
12. Assume that over- or underapplied overhead is insignificant.

Required

a. Record the data in T-accounts.

b. Record the closing entry for over- or underapplied manufacturing overhead, assuming that the amount is insignificant.

c. Close the revenue and expense accounts.

d. Prepare a schedule of cost of goods manufactured and sold, an income statement, a balance sheet, and a statement of cash flows for 2006.

L.O. 3, 4, 8

PROBLEM 12–16A *Process Cost System*

CHECK FIGURES
d. NI: $16,350
Cash: $5,025

Use the ending balances from Problem 12–15A as the beginning balances for this problem. The transactions for the second year of operation (2007) are described here. (Assume that all transactions are cash transactions unless otherwise indicated.)

1. The company purchased $30,000 of direct raw materials and $975 of indirect materials.
2. Materials totaling $10,050 were issued to the cutting department.
3. Labor cost was $35,250. Direct labor for the cutting and assembly departments was $16,500 and $15,000, respectively. Indirect labor costs were $3,750. (*Note:* Assume that sufficient cash is available when periodic payments are made. These amounts represent summary data for the entire year and are not presented in exact order of collection and payment.)

4. The predetermined overhead rate was $0.50 per direct labor dollar.
5. Actual overhead costs other than indirect materials and indirect labor for the month were $10,950.
6. The cutting department transferred $22,500 of inventory to the assembly department.
7. The assembly department transferred $45,000 of inventory to finished goods.
8. The company sold inventory costing $25,500 for $48,000.
9. Selling and administrative expenses were $6,300.
10. At the end of 2007, $225 of production supplies was on hand.
11. Assume that over- or underapplied overhead is insignificant.

Required

a. Record the data in T-accounts.
b. Record the closing entry for over- or underapplied manufacturing overhead, assuming that the amount is insignificant.
c. Close the revenue and expense accounts.
d. Prepare a schedule of cost of goods manufactured and sold, an income statement, a balance sheet, and a statement of cash flows for 2007.

PROBLEM 12–17A *Process Cost System Cost of Production Report*

L.O. 3

excel
www.mhhe.com/edmonds3e

CHECK FIGURE
b. $15.60

Hamby Company had 250 units of product in its work in process inventory at the beginning of the period and started 2,000 additional units during the period. At the end of the period, 750 units were in work in process inventory. The ending work in process inventory was estimated to be 60 percent complete. The cost of work in process inventory at the beginning of the period was $3,420, and $27,000 of product costs was added during the period.

Required

Prepare a cost of production report showing the following.

a. The number of equivalent units of production.
b. The product cost per equivalent unit.
c. The total cost allocated between the ending Work in Process Inventory and Finished Goods Inventory accounts.

PROBLEM 12–18A *Determining Inventory Cost Using a Process Cost System*

L.O. 3

CHECK FIGURE
b. $29.50

Mickel Company had 200 units of product in work in process inventory at the beginning of the period. It started 1,400 units during the period and transferred 1,200 units to finished goods inventory. The ending work in process inventory was estimated to be 80 percent complete. Cost data for the period follow.

	Product Costs
Beginning balance	$15,800
Added during period	29,040
Total	$44,840

Required

Prepare a cost of production report showing the following.

a. The number of equivalent units of production.
b. The product cost per equivalent unit.
c. The total cost allocated between ending work in process inventory and finished goods inventory.

PROBLEM 12–19A *Process Cost System*

L.O. 3

CHECK FIGURE
b. $11.00

Slaton Plastic Products, Inc., makes a plastic toy using two departments, parts and assembly. The following data pertain to the parts department's transactions in 2006.

1. The beginning balance in the Work in Process Inventory account was $5,700. This inventory consisted of parts for 2,000 toys. The beginning balances in the Raw Materials Inventory, Production Supplies, and Cash accounts were $64,000, $1,000, and $200,000, respectively.
2. Direct materials costing $52,000 were issued to the parts department. The materials were sufficient to make 10,000 additional toys.
3. Direct labor cost was $47,000, and indirect labor costs are $4,600. All labor costs were paid in cash.

4. The predetermined overhead rate was $0.30 per direct labor dollar.
5. Actual overhead costs other than indirect materials and indirect labor for the year were $9,500, which was paid in cash.
6. The department completed parts work for 9,000 toys. The remaining toy parts were 60 percent complete. The completed parts were transferred to the assembly department.
7. All of the production supplies had been used by the end of 2006.
8. Over- or underapplied overhead was closed to the Cost of Goods Sold account.

Required

a. Determine the number of equivalent units of production.
b. Determine the product cost per equivalent unit.
c. Allocate the total cost between the ending work in process inventory and parts transferred to the assembly department.
d. Record the transactions in a partial set of T-accounts.

L.O. 3

eXcel

www.mhhe.com/edmonds3e

CHECK FIGURE
b. $0.12

PROBLEM 12–20A *Process Cost System*

Royal Cola Corporation produces a new soft drink brand, Sweet Spring, using two production departments, mixing and bottling. Royal's beginning balances and data pertinent to the mixing department's activities for 2005 follow.

Accounts	Beginning Balances
Cash	$ 45,000
Raw Materials Inventory	14,800
Production Supplies	400
Work in Process Inventory (400,000 units)	40,000
Common Stock	100,200

1. Royal Cola issued additional common stock for $54,000 cash.
2. The company purchased raw materials and production supplies for $29,600 and $800, respectively, in cash.
3. The company issued $40,000 of raw materials to the mixing department for the production of 800,000 units of Sweet Spring that were started in 2005. A unit of soft drink is the amount needed to fill a bottle.
4. The mixing department used 2,700 hours of labor during 2005, consisting of 2,500 hours for direct labor and 200 hours for indirect labor. The average wage was $9.60 per hour. All wages were paid in 2005 in cash.
5. The predetermined overhead rate was $1.60 per direct labor hour.
6. Actual overhead costs other than indirect materials and indirect labor for the year amounted to $1,440, which was paid in cash.
7. The mixing department completed 600,000 units of Sweet Spring. The remaining inventory was 50 percent complete.
8. The completed soft drink was transferred to the bottling department.
9. The ending balance in the Production Supplies account was $560.

Required

a. Determine the number of equivalent units of production.
b. Determine the product cost per equivalent unit.
c. Allocate the total cost between the ending work in process inventory and units transferred to the bottling department.
d. Record the transactions in T-accounts.

L.O. 3, 8

CHECK FIGURES
a. Cost/unit: $1.00
b. Cost/unit: $1.60

PROBLEM 12–21A *Process Cost System*

Greene Corporation makes a health beverage named Greene that is manufactured in a two-stage production process. The drink is first created in the Conversion Department where material ingredients (natural juices, supplements, preservatives, etc.) are combined. On July 1, 2005 the company had a sufficient quantity of partially completed beverage mix in the Conversion Department to make 40,000 containers of Greene. This beginning inventory had a cost of $30,000. During July, the company added ingredients necessary to make 160,000 containers of Greene. The cost of these ingredients was $154,000. During July, liquid mix representing 180,000 containers of the beverage was transferred to the Finishing Department. The beverage mix is poured into containers and packaged for shipment in the Finishing

Department. Beverage that remained in the Conversion Department at the end of July was 20 percent complete. At the beginning of July the Finishing Department had 10,000 containers of beverage mix. The cost of this mix was $24,000. The department added $44,000 of manufacturing costs (materials, labor and overhead) during July. During July 120,000 containers of Greene were completed. The ending inventory for this department was 50 percent complete at the end of July.

Required

a. Prepare a Cost of Production Report for the Conversion Department for July.
b. Prepare a Cost of Production Report for the Finishing Department for July.
c. If 100,000 containers of Greene are sold in July for $240,000, determine the company's gross margin for July.

EXERCISES—SERIES B

EXERCISE 12–1B *Matching Products with Appropriate Cost Systems* L.O. 1

Required

Indicate which cost system (job-order, process, or hybrid) would be most appropriate for the type of product listed in the left-hand column. The first item is shown as an example.

Type of Product	Type of Cost System
a. Audit engagement	Job Order
b. Shoes	
c. Treadmill	
d. Textbook	
e. House	
f. Oil	
g. Luxury yacht	
h. Special-order personal computer	
i. Over-the-counter personal computer	
j. Mouse pad for a computer	
k. Aircraft carrier	
l. Makeup sponge	
m. Handheld video game player	
n. Generic coffee mug	
o. Personalized coffee mug	
p. Surgery	

EXERCISE 12–2B *Identifying the Appropriate Cost System* L.O. 1

Cracco Corporation's Valley Plant in Little Rock, Arkansas, produces the company's weed-control chemical solution, Weed Terminator. Production begins with pure water from a controlled stream to which the plant adds different chemicals in the production process. Finally, the plant bottles the resulting chemical solution. The process is highly automated with different computer-controlled maneuvers and testing to ensure the quality of the end product. With only 15 employees, the plant can produce up to 6,000 bottles per day.

Required

Recommend the type of cost system (job-order, process, or hybrid) Valley Plant should use. Explain your recommendation.

EXERCISE 12–3B *Job-Order or Process Costing* L.O. 1, 2

Jocey Smith, an artist, plans to make her living drawing customer portraits at a stand in Underground Atlanta. She will carry her drawing equipment and supplies to work each day in bags. By displaying two of her best hand-drawn portraits on either side of her stand, she expects to attract tourists' attention. Ms. Smith can usually draw a customer's portrait in 30 minutes. Her materials cost is minimal, about $1.60 for a portrait. Her most significant cost will be leasing the stand for $960 per month. She estimates she can replace supplies and worn out equipment for $40 per month. She plans to work 20 days each month from noon to 9:00 P.M. After surveying her planned work environment before beginning the business, she observed that six other artists were providing customer portraits in that section of Underground Atlanta. Their portrait prices ranged from $20 to $36 per portrait. They also offered to frame portraits for customers at $12 per frame. Ms. Smith found that she could obtain comparable frames for $4 each and that properly framing a portrait takes about 10 minutes. The biggest challenge, Ms. Smith observed, was attracting tourists' interest. If she could draw portraits continuously during her workdays, she could earn quite a respectable income. But she noticed several of the artists were reading magazines as she walked by.

Required

a. Should Ms. Smith use a job-order or process cost system for her art business?
b. List the individual types of costs Ms. Smith will likely incur in providing portraits.
c. How could Ms. Smith estimate her overhead rate per portrait when she does not know the number of portraits she will draw in a month?
d. Ms. Smith will not hire any employees. Will she have labor cost? Explain.

L.O. 2, 7

EXERCISE 12–4B *Job-Order Costing in a Manufacturing Company*

Maher Drapery, Inc., specializes in making custom draperies for both commercial and residential customers. It began business on August 1, 2004, by acquiring $40,000 cash through issuing common stock. In August 2004, Ingle accepted drapery orders, Jobs 801 and 802, for two new commercial buildings. The company paid cash for the following costs related to the orders:

Job 801	
Raw materials	$ 7,360
Direct labor (512 hours at $20 per hour)	10,240
Job 802	
Raw materials	5,200
Direct labor (340 hours at $20 per hour)	6,800

During the same month, Ingle paid $14,400 for various indirect costs such as utilities, equipment leases, and factory-related insurance. The company estimated its annual manufacturing overhead cost would be $240,000 and expected to use 20,000 direct labor hours in its first year of operation. It planned to allocate overhead based on direct labor hours. On August 31, 2004, Ingle completed Job 801 and collected the contract price of $28,000. Job 802 was still in process.

Maher uses a just-in-time inventory management system. Consequently, it has no raw materials inventory. Raw materials purchases are recorded directly in the Work in Process Inventory account.

Required

a. Use a horizontal financial statements model as follows to record Maher's accounting events for August 2004. The first event is shown as an example.

Assets							=	Equity								Cash Flow
Cash	+	Work in Process	+	Finished Goods	+	Manuf. Overhead	=	Com. Stock	+	Ret. Ear.	Rev.	−	Exp.	=	Net Inc.	Cash Flow
40,000	+	NA	+	NA	+	NA	=	40,000	+	NA	NA	−	NA	=	NA	40,000 FA

b. What was Ingle's ending inventory on August 31, 2004? Is this amount the actual or the estimated inventory cost?
c. When is it appropriate to use estimated inventory cost on a year-end balance sheet?

L.O. 2, 7

EXERCISE 12–5B *Job-Order Costing in a Manufacturing Company*

McCoy Advertisements, Inc., designs and produces television commercials for clients. On March 1, 2002, the company issued common stock for $48,000 cash. During March, McCoy worked on three jobs. Pertinent data follow.

Special Orders	Materials	Labor
Job 301	$3,600	450 hours @ $32 per hour
Job 302	6,480	360 hours @ $60 per hour
Job 303	5,840	680 hours @ $28 per hour

Actual production overhead cost: $24,080
Predetermined overhead rate: $16 per direct labor hour

McCoy paid these costs in cash. Jobs 301 and 302 were completed and sold for cash to customers during March. Job 303 was incomplete at month end. Job 301 sold for $30,400, and Job 302 sold for $43,200. Lagoon also paid $8,000 cash in March for selling and administrative expenses.

McCoy uses a just-in-time inventory management system. Consequently, it has no raw materials inventory. Raw materials purchases are recorded directly in the Work in Process Inventory account.

Required

a. Use a horizontal financial statements model, as follows, to record McCoy's accounting events for March 2002. The first event is shown as an example.

Assets								=	Equity									
Cash	+	Work in Process	+	Finished Goods	+	Manuf. Overhead	=		Com. Stock	+	Ret. Ear.	Rev.	−	Exp.	=	Net Inc.	Cash Flow	
48,000	+	NA	+	NA	+	NA	=		48,000	+	NA	NA	−	NA	=	NA	48,000 FA	

b. Record the entry to close the amount of underapplied or overapplied manufacturing overhead to Cost of Goods Sold (in the expense category) in the horizontal financial statements model.

c. Determine the gross margin for March.

EXERCISE 12–6B *Job-Order Costing in a Service Company* L.O. 2, 7

Jarman Consulting, Inc., provides financial and estate planning services on a retainer basis for the executive officers of its corporate clients. It incurred the following labor costs on services for three corporate clients during March 2006:

	Direct Labor
Contract 1	$12,000
Contract 2	7,200
Contract 3	28,800
Total	$48,000

Jarman allocated March overhead costs of $21,600 to the contracts based on the amount of direct labor costs incurred on each contract.

Required

a. Assuming the revenue from Contract 3 was $65,600, what amount of income did Jarman earn from this contract?

b. Based on the preceding information, will Jarman report finished goods inventory on its balance sheet for Contract 1? If so, what is the amount of this inventory? If not, explain why not.

EXERCISE 12–7B *Determine Missing Information for a Job Order* L.O. 2

The following information pertains to Job 712 that Dothan Manufacturing Company completed during January 2004. Materials and labor costs for the job were $62,000 and $38,000, respectively. Applied overhead costs were $44,000. Dothan completed and delivered the job to its customer and earned a $50,000 gross profit.

Required

Determine the contract price for the job.

EXERCISE 12–8B *Process Costing: Determining Equivalent Units* L.O. 3

In March 2005, Finkel Corporation's battery plant had 1,500 units in its beginning work in process inventory. During March, the company added 18,000 units to production. At the end of the month, 6,000 units of product were in process.

Required

(Each requirement is independent of the other.)

a. Assuming the ending inventory units were 40 percent complete, determine the total number of equivalent units (number transferred out plus number in ending inventory) processed by the battery plant.

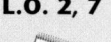

b. Assuming the total number of equivalent units (number transferred out plus number in ending inventory) processed by the battery plant was 15,000, what was the ending inventory percentage of completion?

L.O. 3

EXERCISE 12–9B *Allocating Costs in a Process Costing System*

Osburn Corporation, a manufacturer of diabetic testing kits, started November production with $60,000 in beginning inventory. During the month, the company incurred $336,000 of materials cost and $192,000 of labor cost. It applied $132,000 of overhead cost to inventory. The company processed 18,000 total equivalent units of product.

Required

(Each requirement is independent of the other.)

a. Assuming 3,000 equivalent units of product were in ending work in process inventory, determine the amount of cost transferred from the Work in Process Inventory account to the Finished Goods Inventory account. What was the cost of the ending work in process inventory?

b. Assuming 14,000 equivalent units of product were transferred from work in process inventory to finished goods inventory, determine the cost of the ending work in process inventory. What was the cost of the finished goods inventory transferred from work in process?

L.O. 3

EXERCISE 12–10B *Process Costing: Determining Equivalent Units and Allocating Costs*

Burnside Corporation, which makes suitcases, completed 21,000 suitcases in August 2004. At the end of August, work in process inventory consisted of 3,000 suitcases estimated to be 40 percent complete. Total product costs for August amounted to $666,000.

Required

a. Determine the cost per equivalent unit.

b. Determine the cost of the goods transferred to finished goods.

c. Determine the cost of the ending work in process inventory.

L.O. 3

EXERCISE 12–11B *Process Costing: Supply Missing Information*

Gospel Publications, Inc., produces Bibles in volume. It printed and sold 120,000 Bibles last year. Demand is sufficient to support producing a particular edition continuously throughout the year. For this operation, Gospel uses two departments, printing and binding. The printing department prints all pages and transfers them to the binding department, where it binds the pages into books. The binding department's Work in Process Inventory account had a $60,000 balance on September 1. During September, the binding department incurred raw materials, labor, and overhead costs of $22,000, $76,000, and $142,000, respectively. During the month, the binding department transferred Bibles that cost $720,000 to finished goods. The balance in the binding department's Work in Process Inventory account as of September 30 was $106,000.

Required

Determine the cost of pages transferred from the printing department to the binding department during the month of September.

L.O. 5

EXERCISE 12–12B *Selecting the Appropriate Costing System*

Towns Automotive Specialties, Inc., has a successful market niche. It customizes automobile interiors to fit the various needs of disabled customers. Some customers need special equipment to accommodate disabled drivers. Others need modified entrance and seating arrangements for disabled passengers. Customer vehicles vary according to different brands and models of sedans, minivans, sport utility vehicles, and full-size vans. Towns' engineers interview customers directly to ascertain their special needs. The engineers then propose a design, explaining it and its cost for the customer's approval. Customers have the opportunity to request changes. Once the company and customer agree on an engineering design and its price, they sign a contract, and the customer's vehicle is delivered to Eagan's factory. The factory manager directs mechanics to customize the vehicle according to the engineering design.

Required

a. Is Towns a manufacturing company or a service company? Explain.

b. Which cost system, job-order or process, would be most appropriate for Towns? Why?

c. Does Towns have work in process and finished goods inventories?

d. Should Towns classify engineering design costs as materials, labor, or overhead? Why?

PROBLEMS—SERIES B

PROBLEM 12–13B *Job-Order Cost System* L.O. 2, 7

Chief Corporation was created on January 1, 2006, when it received a stockholder's contribution of $32,000. It purchased $6,320 of raw materials and worked on three job orders during the year. Data about these jobs follow. (Assume all transactions are for cash unless otherwise indicated.)

	Direct Raw Materials Used	Direct Labor
Job 1	$1,680	$2,560
Job 2	1,360	3,840
Job 3	2,560	3,584
Total	$5,600	$9,984

The average wage rate is $12.80 per hour. Manufacturing overhead is applied using a predetermined overhead rate of $6 per direct labor hour. Jobs 1 and 3 were completed during the year, and Job 1 was sold for $7,840. Chief paid $1,120 for selling and administrative expenses. Actual factory overhead was $4,800.

Required

a. Record the preceding events in a horizontal statements model. In the Cash Flow column, designate the cash flows as operating activities (OA), investing activities (IA), or financing activities (FA). The first event for 2006 has been recorded as an example.

Assets									=	Equity								
Cash	+	Raw M.	+	MOH	+	WIP	+	F. Goods	=	C. Stk.	+	Ret. Ear.	Rev.	−	Exp.	=	Net Inc.	Cash Flow
3,200	+	NA	+	NA	+	NA	+	NA	=	3,200	+	NA	NA	−	NA	=	NA	3,200 FA

b. Reconcile all subsidiary accounts with their respective control accounts.

c. Record the closing entry for over- or underapplied manufacturing overhead, assuming that the amount is insignificant. Close revenue and expense accounts.

d. Prepare a schedule of cost of goods manufactured and sold, an income statement, a balance sheet, and a statement of cash flows for 2006.

PROBLEM 12–14B *Job-Order Cost System* L.O. 2, 7

Sayers Roofing Corporation was founded on January 1, 2005, when stockholders contributed $2,800 for common stock. During the year, Sayers purchased $2,400 of direct raw materials and used $2,160 of direct materials. There were 80 hours of direct labor worked at an average rate of $8 per hour paid in cash. The predetermined overhead rate was $6.50 per direct labor hour. The company started three custom roofing jobs. The job cost sheets reflected the following allocations of costs to each.

	Direct Materials	Direct Labor Hours
Roof 1	$800	20
Roof 2	400	12
Roof 3	960	48

The company paid $176 cash for indirect labor costs and $240 cash for production supplies, which were all used during 2005. Actual overhead cost paid in cash other than indirect materials and indirect labor was $144. Sayers completed Roofs 1 and 2 and collected the contract price for Roof 1 of $2,160 cash. The company incurred $496 of selling and administrative expenses that were paid with cash. Over- or underapplied overhead is closed to Cost of Goods Sold.

Required

a. Record the preceding events in a horizontal statements model. In the Cash Flow column, designate the cash flows as operating activities (OA), investing activities (IA), or financing activities (FA). The first event for 2005 has been recorded as an example.

Assets									=	Equity								
Cash	+	Raw M.	+	MOH	+	WIP	+	F. Goods	=	C. Stk.	+	Ret. Ear.	Rev.	−	Exp.	=	Net Inc.	Cash Flow
2,800	+	NA	+	NA	+	NA	+	NA	=	2,800	+	NA	NA	−	NA	=	NA	2,800 FA

b. Reconcile all subsidiary accounts with their respective control accounts.
c. Record the closing entry for over- or underapplied manufacturing overhead, assuming that the amount is insignificant. Close revenue and expense accounts.
d. Prepare a schedule of cost of goods manufactured and sold, an income statement, a balance sheet, and a statement of cash flows for 2005.

L.O. 3, 8

PROBLEM 12–15B *Process Cost System*

Rivera Food Company makes frozen vegetables. Production involves two departments, processing and packaging. Raw materials are cleaned and cut in the processing department and then transferred to the packaging department where they are packaged and frozen. The following transactions apply to Rivera's first year (2004) of operations. (Assume that all transactions are for cash unless otherwise stated.)

1. The company was started when it acquired $64,000 cash from the issue of common stock.
2. Rivera purchased $33,600 of direct raw materials and $6,000 of indirect materials. Indirect materials are capitalized in the Production Supplies account.
3. Direct materials totaling $30,400 were issued to the processing department.
4. Labor cost was $61,600. Direct labor for the processing and packaging departments was $26,000 and $20,400, respectively. Indirect labor costs were $15,200.
5. The predetermined overhead rate was $0.80 per direct labor dollar.
6. Actual overhead costs other than indirect materials and indirect labor were $18,000 for the year.
7. The processing department transferred $48,400 of inventory to the packaging department.
8. The packaging department transferred $56,000 of inventory to finished goods.
9. The company sold inventory costing $50,400 for $94,000.
10. Selling and administrative expenses were $18,800.
11. A physical count revealed $2,400 of production supplies on hand at the end of 2004.
12. Assume that over- or underapplied overhead is insignificant.

Required

a. Record the data in T-accounts.
b. Record the closing entry for over- or underapplied manufacturing overhead, assuming that the amount is insignificant.
c. Close the revenue and expense accounts.
d. Prepare a schedule of cost of goods manufactured and sold, an income statement, a balance sheet, and a statement of cash flows for 2004.

L.O. 3, 4, 8

PROBLEM 12–16B *Process Cost System*

Use the ending balances from Problem 12–15B as the beginning balances for this problem. The transactions for the second year of operation (2005) are described here. (Assume that all transactions are cash transactions unless otherwise indicated.)

1. The company purchased $40,800 of direct raw materials and $7,200 of indirect materials.
2. Materials costing $32,800 were issued to the processing department.
3. Labor cost was $71,600. Direct labor for the processing and packaging departments was $28,800 and $23,600, respectively. Indirect labor costs were $19,200. (*Note:* Assume that sufficient cash is available when periodic payments are made. These amounts represent summary data for the entire year and are not presented in exact order of collection and payment.)
4. The predetermined overhead rate was $0.80 per direct labor dollar.
5. Actual overhead costs other than indirect materials and indirect labor for the year was $20,000.
6. The processing department transferred $100,000 of inventory to the packaging department.
7. The packaging department transferred $140,000 of inventory to finished goods.
8. The company sold inventory costing $136,800 for $260,000.
9. Selling and administrative expenses amounted to $25,600.
10. At the end of the year, $1,600 of production supplies was on hand.
11. Assume that over- or underapplied overhead is insignificant.

Required

a. Record the data in T-accounts.
b. Record the closing entry for over- or underapplied manufacturing overhead, assuming that the amount is insignificant.
c. Close the revenue and expense accounts.
d. Prepare a schedule of cost of goods manufactured and sold, an income statement, a balance sheet, and a statement of cash flows for 2005.

PROBLEM 12–17B *Process Cost System Cost of Production Report*

L.O. 3

At the beginning of 2004, Dozier Company had 1,800 units of product in its work in process inventory, and it started 19,200 additional units of product during the year. At the end of the year, 6,000 units of product were in the work in process inventory. The ending work in process inventory was estimated to be 50 percent complete. The cost of work in process inventory at the beginning of the period was $9,000, and $108,000 of product costs was added during the period.

Required

Prepare a cost of production report showing the following.

a. The number of equivalent units of production.
b. The product cost per equivalent unit.
c. The total cost allocated between the ending Work in Process Inventory and Finished Goods Inventory accounts.

PROBLEM 12–18B *Determining Inventory Cost Using Process Costing*

L.O. 3

Carri Company's beginning work in process inventory consisted of 4,500 units of product on January 1, 2006. During 2006, the company started 24,000 units of product and transferred 23,500 units to finished goods inventory. The ending work in process inventory was estimated to be 30 percent complete. Cost data for 2006 follow.

	Product Costs
Beginning balance	$ 19,000
Added during period	151,000
Total	$170,000

Required

Prepare a cost of production report showing the following.

a. The number of equivalent units of production.
b. The product cost per equivalent unit.
c. The total cost allocated between ending work in process inventory and finished goods inventory.

PROBLEM 12–19B *Process Cost System*

L.O. 3, 8

Lloyd Corporation makes blue jeans. Its process involves two departments, cutting and sewing. The following data pertain to the cutting department's transactions in 2006.

1. The beginning balance in work in process inventory was $8,772. This inventory consisted of fabric for 6,000 pairs of jeans. The beginning balances in raw materials inventory, production supplies, and cash were $45,000, $2,100 and $135,600, respectively.
2. Direct materials costing $28,068 were issued to the cutting department; this amount of materials was sufficient to start work on 15,000 pairs of jeans.
3. Direct labor cost was $33,600, and indirect labor cost was $2,700. All labor costs were paid in cash.
4. The predetermined overhead rate was $0.25 per direct labor dollar.
5. Actual overhead costs other than indirect materials and indirect labor for the year amounted to $3,840, which was paid in cash.
6. The cutting department completed cutting 16,000 pairs of jeans. The remaining jeans were 40 percent complete.
7. The completed units of cut fabric were transferred to the sewing department.
8. All of the production supplies had been used by the end of the year.
9. Over- or underapplied overhead was closed to the Cost of Goods Sold account.

Required

a. Determine the number of equivalent units of production.
b. Determine the product cost per equivalent unit.
c. Allocate the total cost between ending work in process inventory and units transferred to the sewing department.
d. Record the transactions in a partial set of T-accounts.

L.O. 3, 8

PROBLEM 12–20B *Process Cost System*

Vinson Paper Products Corporation produces paper cups using two production departments, printing and forming. Beginning balances and printing department data for 2006 follow.

Accounts	Beginning Balances
Cash	$50,000
Raw Materials	21,000
Production Supplies	1,500
Work in Process Inventory (300,000 units)	18,000
Common Stock	90,500

1. Vinson Paper Products issued additional common stock for $110,000 cash.
2. The company purchased raw materials and production supplies for $40,000 and $3,500, respectively, in cash.
3. The company issued $57,000 of raw materials and $3,600 of production supplies to the printing department for the production of 800,000 paper cups.
4. The printing department used 6,200 hours of labor during 2006, consisting of 5,600 hours for direct labor and 600 hours for indirect labor. The average wage was $5 per hour. All the wages were paid in 2006 in cash.
5. The predetermined overhead rate was $0.50 per direct labor dollar.
6. Actual overhead costs other than indirect materials and indirect labor for the year amounted to $7,400, which was paid in cash.
7. The printing department completed 700,000 paper cups. The remaining cups were 50 percent complete.
8. The completed paper cups were transferred to the forming department.
9. The ending balance in the Production Supplies account was $1,400.

Required

a. Determine the number of equivalent units of production.
b. Determine the product cost per equivalent unit.
c. Allocate the total cost between the ending work in process inventory and units transferred to the forming department.
d. Record the transactions in T-accounts.

L.O. 3, 8

PROBLEM 12–21B *Process Cost System*

Gun Smoke Gifts makes unique western gifts that are sold at souvenir shops. One of the company's more popular products is a ceramic Eagle that is produced in a mass production process that entails two manufacturing stages. In the first production stage ceramic glass is heated and molded into the shape of the Eagle by the Compression Department. Finally, color and artistic detail is applied to the Eagle by the Finishing Department. The company has just hired a new accountant who will be responsible for preparing the Cost of Production Report for June 2006. The accountant is given the following information from which to prepare his report.

Departmental Cost Information for June

	Compression	Finishing
Costs in beginning inventory	$ 3,000	$14,400
Costs added during June:		
Materials	42,000	18,120
Labor	20,000	13,200
Overhead	90,000	62,000

Departmental Product Information for June

	Compression	Finishing
Units in beginning inventory	10,000	3,600
Units started	52,000	46,000
Units in ending inventory	16,000 (25% complete)	9,600 (80% complete)

Required

a. Prepare a Cost of Production Report for the Conversion Department for June.
b. Prepare a Cost of Production Report for the Finishing Department for June.
c. If 24,000 units are sold in July for $160,000, determine the company's gross margin for June.

ANALYZE, THINK, COMMUNICATE

BUSINESS APPLICATION CASE *Comprehensive Job-Order Costing Problem* ATC 12–1

This problem covers concepts that were presented in Chapters 11 and 12 concerning job-order costing systems.

Custom Automobile Restoration Shop (CARS) is a small shop dedicated to high quality restorations of vintage cars. Although it will restore an automobile that a customer already owns, usually the shop buys an old vehicle, restores it, and then sells it in a private party sale or at a classic-car auction. The shop has been in existence for 10 years, but for the sake of simplicity, assume it has no beginning inventories for 2007. Five automobile restoration projects were worked on during 2007. By the end of the year, four of these projects were completed and three of these four were sold.

The following selected data are from CARS' 2007 *budget:*

Advertising	$ 5,000
Direct materials	150,000
Direct labor	130,000
Rent on office space	6,000
Rent on factory space	20,000
Indirect materials	11,000
Maintenance costs for factory equipment	3,000
Utilities costs for office space	1,000
Utilities costs for factory space	2,000
Depreciation on factory equipment	8,000
Machine hours expected to be worked	4,000
Direct labor hours expected to be worked	6,500

The following information relates to production events during 2007.

1. Raw materials were purchased for $155,000.
2. Materials used in production totaled $150,800; $11,500 of these were considered indirect materials costs. The remaining $139,300 of direct materials costs related to individual restoration jobs as follows:

Job Number	Direct Materials Cost
701	$28,200
702	32,100
703	25,800
704	31,700
705	21,500

3. Labor costs incurred for production totaled $133,100. The workers are highly skilled craftsmen who require little supervision. Therefore all of these were considered direct labor costs and related to individual restoration jobs as follows:

Job Number	Direct Labor Cost
701	$30,900
702	29,300
703	22,100
704	36,600
705	14,200

4. Paid factory rent of $18,000.
5. Recorded depreciation on factory equipment of $8,500.

6. Made $2,500 of payments to outside vendors for maintenance of factory equipment.
7. Paid factory utilities costs of $2,400.
8. Applied manufacturing overhead using a predetermined rate of $11.00 per machine hour. The 3,750 machine hours that were used relate to each job as follows:

Job Number	Machine Hours Worked
701	850
702	720
703	870
704	900
705	410

9. Completed all restoration jobs except 705 and transferred the projects to finished goods.
10. Sold three jobs for the following amounts:

Job Number	Sales Price
701	$88,900
702	93,000
703	74,800

11. Closed the Manufacturing Overhead account to transfer any overapplied or underapplied overhead to the Cost of Goods Sold account.

Required

a. Assume CARS had used direct labor hours (versus machine hours) as its cost driver. Compute its predetermined overhead rate.
b. Determine the ending balance in Raw Materials Inventory.
c. Determine the ending balance in Finished Goods Inventory.
d. Determine the ending balance in Work in Process Inventory.
e. Determine the costs of goods manufactured.
f. Determine the amount of cost of goods sold.
g. Determine the amount of gross margin that was earned on Jobs 701, 702, and 703.
h. Determine the amount of overapplied or underapplied overhead the existed at the end of the year.

Hint: Though not required, you might find it helpful to organize the data using a horizontal financial statements model, although it will still be necessary to prepare a job cost sheet for each individual job.

ATC 12–2 GROUP ASSIGNMENT *Job-Order Cost System*

Bowen Bridge Company constructs bridges for the State of Kentucky. During 2003, Bowen started work on three bridges. The cost of materials and labor for each bridge follows.

Special Orders	Materials	Labor
Bridge 305	$407,200	$352,700
Bridge 306	362,300	375,000
Bridge 307	801,700	922,800

The predetermined overhead rate is $1.20 per direct labor dollar. Actual overhead costs were $2,170,800. Bridge 306 was completed for a contract price of $1,357,000 and was turned over to the state. Construction on Bridge 305 was also completed but the state had not yet finished its inspection process. General selling and administrative expenses amounted to $210,000. Over- or underapplied overhead is closed directly to the Cost of Goods Sold account. The company recognizes revenue when it turns over a completed bridge to a customer.

Required

a. Divide the class into groups of four or five students each and organize the groups into three sections. Assign Task 1 to the first section of groups, Task 2 to the second section, and Task 3 to the third section.

Group Tasks

(1) Determine the cost of construction for Bridge 305.

(2) Determine the cost of construction for Bridge 306.
(3) Determine the cost of construction for Bridge 307.

b. Select a spokesperson from each section. Use input from the three spokespersons to prepare an income statement and the asset section of the balance sheet.
c. Does the net income accurately reflect the profitability associated with Bridge 306? Explain.
d. Would converting to a process cost system improve the accuracy of the amount of reported net income? Explain.

RESEARCH ASSIGNMENT *Job-Order or Process Cost System?*

ATC 12–3

The article "Lights! Cameras! . . . Accountants!" (*Management Accounting,* June 1996) describes the product cost system used by **Buena Vista Visual Effects (BVVE)**, which produces special effects used in movies. Some of its credits include the lifelike dinosaurs in *Jurassic Park* and the rapid-fire ping-pong match in *Forrest Gump.* Read this article and complete the following requirements.

Required

a. Does BVVE use a job-order or a process cost system?
b. What type of costs does BVVE include in overhead? Name some of the specific costs included.
c. What predetermined overhead rate does BVVE use?
d. Does BVVE use estimated or actual costs in its product costing system?
e. How often does BVVE prepare variance cost reports? Provide a logical explanation as to why this time span is used.

WRITING ASSIGNMENT *Determining the Proper Cost System*

ATC 12–4

Professor Julia Silverman received the following E-mail message.

"I don't know if you remember me. I am Tim Wallace. I was in your introductory accounting class a couple of years ago. I recently graduated and have just started my first real job. I remember your talking about job-order and process cost systems. I even looked the subject up in the textbook you wrote. In that book, you say that a process cost system is used when a company produces a single, homogeneous, high-volume, low-cost product. Well, the company I am working for makes T-shirts. All of the shirts are the same. They don't cost much, and we make nearly a million of them every year. The only difference in any of the shirts is the label we sew in them. We make the shirts for about 20 different companies. It seems to me that we should be using a process costing system. Even so, our accounting people are using a job-order cost system. Unfortunately, you didn't tell us what to do when the company we work for is screwed up. I need some advice. Should I tell them they are using the wrong accounting system? I know I am new around here, and I don't want to offend anybody, but if your book is right, the company would be better off if it started using a process cost system. Some of these people around here didn't go to college, and I'm afraid they don't know what they are doing. I guess that's why they hired someone with a degree. Am I right about this or what?"

Required

Assume that you are Professor Silverman. Write a return E-mail responding to Mr. Wallace's inquiry.

ETHICAL DILEMMA *Amount of Equivalent Units*

ATC 12–5

René Alverez knew she was in over her head soon after she took the job. Even so, the opportunity for promotion comes along rarely and she believed that she would grow into it. Ms. Alverez is the cost accounting specialist assigned to the finishing department of Standard Tool Company. Bill Sawyer, the manager of the finishing department, knows exactly what he is doing. In each of the three years he has managed the department, the cost per unit of product transferred out of his Work in Process Inventory account has declined. His ability to control cost is highly valued, and it is widely believed that he will be the successor to the plant manager, who is being promoted to manufacturing vice president. One more good year would surely seal the deal for Mr. Sawyer. It was little wonder that Ms. Alverez was uncomfortable in challenging Mr. Sawyer's estimate of the percentage of completion of the department's ending inventory. He contended that the inventory was 60 percent complete, but she believed that it was only about 40 percent complete.

After a brief altercation, Ms. Alverez agreed to sign off on Mr. Sawyer's estimate. The truth was that although she believed she was right, she did not know how to support her position. Besides, Mr. Sawyer was about to be named plant manager, and she felt it unwise to challenge such an important person.

The department had beginning inventory of 5,500 units of product and it started 94,500 units during the period. It transferred out 90,000 units during the period. Total transferred-in and production cost for the period was $902,400. This amount included the cost in beginning inventory plus additional costs incurred during the period. The target (standard) cost per unit is $9.45.

Required

a. Determine the equivalent cost per unit, assuming that the ending inventory is considered to be 40 percent complete.

b. Determine the equivalent cost per unit, assuming that the ending inventory is considered to be 60 percent complete.

c. Comment on Mr. Sawyer's motives for establishing the percentage of completion at 60 percent rather than 40 percent.

d. Assuming that Ms. Alverez is a certified management accountant, would informing the chief accountant of her dispute with Mr. Sawyer violate the confidentiality standards of ethical conduct in Exhibit 1–13 of Chapter 1?

e. Did Ms. Alverez violate any of the standards of ethical conduct in Exhibit 1–13 of Chapter 1? If so, which ones?

ATC 12–6 SPREADSHEET ASSIGNMENT *Using Excel*

Lewis Company had 8,000 units of product in work in process inventory at the beginning of the period and started 16,000 units during the period. At the end of the period, 4,000 units remained in work in process. The ending work in process inventory was estimated to be 40 percent complete. The cost of the units in beginning work in process inventory was $22,080. During the period, $38,400 of product costs were added.

Required

a. Construct a spreadsheet that incorporates the preceding data into a table. The following screen capture is an example.

b. Insert a section into the spreadsheet to calculate total manufacturing costs.

c. Insert a section into the spreadsheet to calculate equivalent units and cost per equivalent unit.

d. Insert a section into the spreadsheet to allocate the manufacturing costs between finished goods and ending work in process.

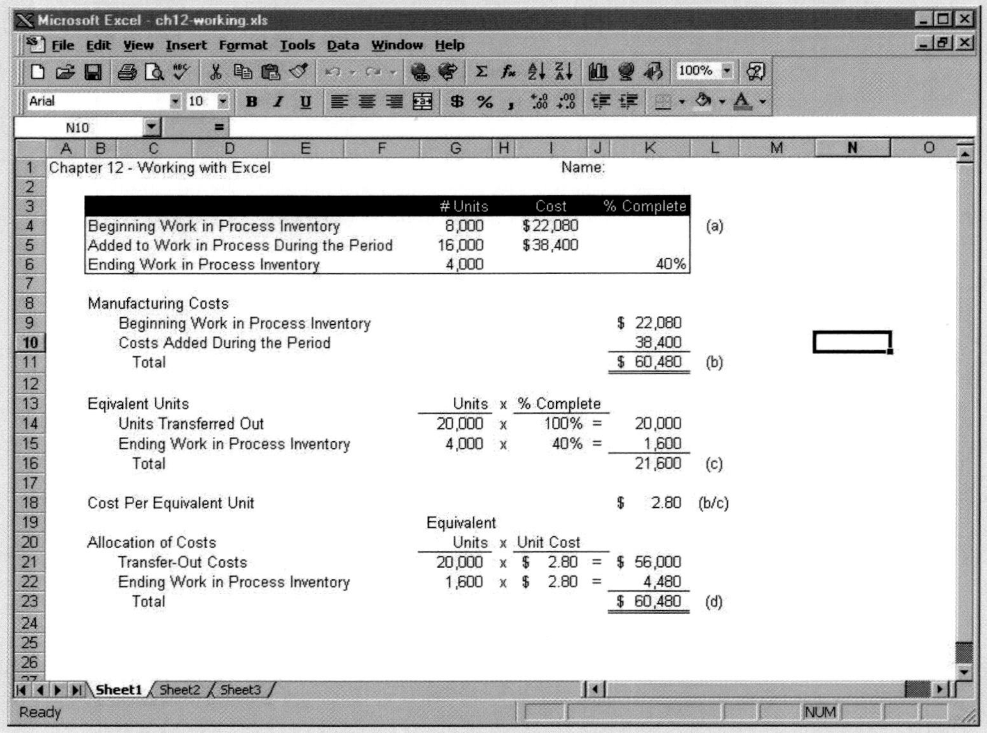

Chapter 12 - Working with Excel				Name:				
	# Units		Cost	% Complete				
Beginning Work in Process Inventory	8,000		$22,080					(a)
Added to Work in Process During the Period	16,000		$38,400					
Ending Work in Process Inventory	4,000			40%				
Manufacturing Costs								
Beginning Work in Process Inventory							$ 22,080	
Costs Added During the Period							38,400	
Total							$ 60,480	(b)
Eqivalent Units	Units	x	% Complete					
Units Transferred Out	20,000	x	100%	=			20,000	
Ending Work in Process Inventory	4,000	x	40%	=			1,600	
Total							21,600	(c)
Cost Per Equivalent Unit							$ 2.80	(b/c)
Allocation of Costs	Equivalent Units	x	Unit Cost					
Transfer-Out Costs	20,000	x	$ 2.80	=			$ 56,000	
Ending Work in Process Inventory	1,600	x	$ 2.80	=			4,480	
Total							$ 60,480	(d)

Spreadsheet Tip

(1) The cells that contain numbers below row 7 should all be formulas to allow changes to the data in rows 3 to 6 that will automatically be reflected in the rest of the spreadsheet.

SPREADSHEET ASSIGNMENT *Mastering Excel*

ATC 12–7

Refer to the job cost sheet in Exhibit 12–3.

Required

Construct a spreadsheet that recreates the job cost sheet in Exhibit 12–3. Use formulas wherever possible, such as in the total row.

Spreadsheet Tips

(1) Center the headings for direct materials, direct labor, and applied overhead across two or three columns by choosing Format and Cells and checking the Merge box under the alignment tab. A shortcut to center these is to click on the Merge and Center icon in the formatting tool bar.

(2) All lines in the job cost sheet can be drawn using Format and Cells and then choosing the border tab.

COMPREHENSIVE PROBLEM

This is a continuation of the comprehensive problem in Chapter 11. During 20X3, Anywhere, Inc. (AI) incurred the following product costs.

Raw materials	$62,000
Labor	89,422
Overhead	58,000

Recall that the 2002 ending balance in the Work in Process (WIP) account was $26,000. Accordingly, this is the beginning WIP balance for 2003. There were 110 units of product in beginning WIP inventory. AI started 1,840 units of product during 2003. Ending WIP inventory consisted of 90 units that were 60 percent complete.

Required

Prepare a cost of production report by filling in the cells that contain question marks.

Equivalent Unit Computations					
	Units		**% Complete**		**Equivalent Units**
Beginning inventory	110				
Units started	1,840				
Total units available for completion	?				
Units in ending inventory	(90)		?		?
Units complete	1,860		100%		?
Total equivalent units					1,914
Cost per Equivalent Unit					
	Cost	÷	**Units**	=	**Cost Per Unit**
Beginning inventory	$26,000				
Raw materials	?				
Labor	?				
Overhead	58,000				
Total product cost	?	÷	1,914	=	?
Allocation of Product Cost					
Cost transferred to finished goods					?
Cost in ending inventory					?
Total product cost					$235,422

CHAPTER *thirteen*

FINANCIAL STATEMENT ANALYSIS

LEARNING *objectives*

After you have mastered the material in this chapter you will be able to:

1. Describe factors associated with communicating useful information.
2. Differentiate between horizontal and vertical analysis.
3. Explain ratio analysis.
4. Calculate ratios for assessing a company's liquidity.
5. Calculate ratios for assessing a company's solvency.
6. Calculate ratios for assessing company management's effectiveness.
7. Calculate ratios for assessing a company's position in the stock market.
8. Identify different forms for presenting analytical data.
9. Explain the limitations of financial statement analysis.

THE *curious* ACCOUNTANT

On February 17, 2004, **Cingular Wireless** agreed to pay $41 billion to acquire **AT&T Wireless Services**. Cingular won a bidding war with Vodafone, a European company that also wanted to acquire AT&T Wireless. The winning bid was $11 billion more than Cingular's original offer.

Cingular Wireless is owned by two regional phone companies, **BellSouth** and **SBC Communications**. Shortly after agreeing to buy AT&T Wireless, BellSouth and SBC announced that as a result of the acquisition, their own net earnings would decline by over $2 billion for 2005 through 2007.

Why would Cingular and its parent companies agree to a deal that would reduce their earnings by so much over the next three years? What type of analysis would these companies use to make this decision? (Answers on page 535.)

CHAPTER *opening*

Expressing financial statement information in the form of ratios enhances its usefulness. Ratios permit comparisons over time and among companies, highlighting similarities, differences, and trends. Proficiency with common financial statement analysis techniques benefits both internal and external users. Before beginning detailed explanations of numerous ratios and percentages, however, we consider factors relevant to communicating useful information.

LO1 Describe factors associated with communicating useful information.

Factors in Communicating Useful Information

The primary objective of accounting is to provide information useful for decision making. To provide information that supports this objective, accountants must consider the intended users, the types of decisions users make with financial statement information, and available means of analyzing the information.

The Users

Users of financial statement information include managers, creditors, stockholders, potential investors, and regulatory agencies. These individuals and organizations use financial statements for different purposes and bring varying levels of sophistication to understanding business activities. For example, investors range from private individuals who know little about financial statements to large investment brokers and institutional investors capable of using complex statistical analysis techniques. At what level of user knowledge should financial statements be aimed? Condensing and reporting complex business transactions at a level easily understood by nonprofessional investors is increasingly difficult. Current reporting standards target users that have a reasonably informed knowledge of business, though that level of sophistication is difficult to define.

The Types of Decisions

Just as the knowledge level of potential users varies, the information needs of users varies, depending on the decision at hand. A supplier considering whether or not to sell goods on account to a particular company wants to evaluate the likelihood of getting paid; a potential investor in that company wants to predict the likelihood of increases in the market value of the company's common stock. Financial statements, however, are designed for general purposes; they are not aimed at any specific user group. Some disclosed information, therefore, may be irrelevant to some users but vital to others. Users must employ different forms of analysis to identify information most relevant to a particular decision.

Financial statements can provide only highly summarized economic information. The costs to a company of providing excessively detailed information would be prohibitive. In addition, too much detail leads to **information overload,** the problem of having so much data that important information becomes obscured by trivial information. Users faced with reams of data may become so frustrated attempting to use it that they lose the value of *key* information that is provided.

Information Analysis

Because of the diversity of users, their different levels of knowledge, the varying information needs for particular decisions, and the general nature of financial statements, a variety of analysis techniques has been developed. In the following sections, we explain several common methods of analysis. The choice of method depends on which technique appears to provide the most relevant information in a given situation.

Topic Tackler PLUS 13–1

LO2 Differentiate between horizontal and vertical analysis.

Methods of Analysis

Financial statement analysis should focus primarily on isolating information useful for making a particular decision. The information required can take many forms but usually involves comparisons, such as comparing changes in the same item for the same company over a number of years, comparing key relationships within the same year, or comparing the operations

Exhibit 13–1

MILAVEC COMPANY
Income Statements and Statements of Retained Earnings
For the Years Ending December 31

	2008	2007
Sales	$900,000	$800,000
Cost of Goods Sold		
Beginning Inventory	43,000	40,000
Purchases	637,000	483,000
Goods Available for Sale	680,000	523,000
Ending Inventory	70,000	43,000
Cost of Goods Sold	610,000	480,000
Gross Margin	290,000	320,000
Operating Expenses	248,000	280,000
Income before Taxes	42,000	40,000
Income Taxes	17,000	18,000
Net Income	25,000	22,000
Plus: Retained Earnings, Beginning Balance	137,000	130,000
Less: Dividends	0	15,000
Retained Earnings, Ending Balance	$162,000	$137,000

Exhibit 13–2

MILAVEC COMPANY
Balance Sheets
As of December 31

	2008	2007
Assets		
Cash	$ 20,000	$ 17,000
Marketable Securities	20,000	22,000
Notes Receivable	4,000	3,000
Accounts Receivable	50,000	56,000
Merchandise Inventory	70,000	43,000
Prepaid Expenses	4,000	4,000
Property, Plant, and Equipment (net)	340,000	310,000
Total Assets	$508,000	$455,000
Liabilities and Stockholders' Equity		
Accounts Payable	$ 40,000	$ 38,000
Salaries Payable	2,000	3,000
Taxes Payable	4,000	2,000
Bonds Payable, 8%	100,000	100,000
Preferred Stock, 6%, $100 par, cumulative	50,000	50,000
Common Stock, $10 Par	150,000	125,000
Retained Earnings	162,000	137,000
Total Liabilities and Stockholders' Equity	$508,000	$455,000

of several different companies in the same industry. This chapter discusses three categories of analysis methods: horizontal, vertical, and ratio. Exhibits 13–1 and 13–2 present comparative financial statements for Milavec Company. We refer to these statements in the examples of analysis techniques.

Horizontal Analysis

Horizontal analysis, also called **trend analysis,** refers to studying the behavior of individual financial statement items over several accounting periods. These periods may be several quarters within the same fiscal year or they may be several different years. The analysis of a given item may focus on trends in the absolute dollar amount of the item or trends in percentages. For example, a user may observe that revenue increased from one period to the next by $42 million (an absolute dollar amount) or that it increased by a percentage such as 15 percent.

Absolute Amounts

The **absolute amounts** of particular financial statement items have many uses. Various national economic statistics, such as gross domestic product and the amount spent to replace productive capacity, are derived by combining absolute amounts reported by businesses. Financial statement users with expertise in particular industries might evaluate amounts reported for research and development costs to judge whether a company is spending excessively or conservatively. Users are particularly concerned with how amounts change over time. For example, a user might compare a pharmaceutical company's revenue before and after the patent expired on one of its drugs.

Comparing only absolute amounts has drawbacks, however, because *materiality* levels differ from company to company or even from year to year for a given company. The **materiality** of information refers to its relative importance. An item is considered material if knowledge of it would influence the decision of a reasonably informed user. Generally accepted accounting principles permit companies to account for *immaterial* items in the most convenient way, regardless of technical accounting rules. For example, companies may expense, rather than capitalize and depreciate, relatively inexpensive long-term assets like pencil sharpeners or waste baskets even if the assets have useful lives of many years. The concept of materiality, which has both quantitative and qualitative aspects, underlies all accounting principles.

It is difficult to judge the materiality of an absolute financial statement amount without considering the size of the company reporting it. For reporting purposes, **Exxon Corporation**'s financial statements are rounded to the nearest million dollars. For Exxon, a $400,000 increase in sales is not material. For a small company, however, $400,000 could represent total sales, a highly material amount. Meaningful comparisons between the two companies' operating performance are impossible using only absolute amounts. Users can surmount these difficulties with percentage analysis.

Percentage Analysis

Percentage analysis involves computing the percentage relationship between two amounts. In horizontal percentage analysis, a financial statement item is expressed as a percentage of the previous balance for the same item. Percentage analysis sidesteps the materiality problems of comparing different size companies by measuring changes in percentages rather than absolute amounts. Each change is converted to a percentage of the base year. Exhibit 13–3 presents a condensed version of Milavec's income statement with horizontal percentages for each item.

Exhibit 13–3

MILAVEC COMPANY
Comparative Income Statements
For the Years Ending December 31

	2008	2007	Percentage Difference
Sales	$900,000	$800,000	+12.5%*
Cost of Goods Sold	610,000	480,000	+27.1
Gross Margin	290,000	320,000	−9.4
Operating Expenses	248,000	280,000	−11.4
Income before Taxes	42,000	40,000	+5.0
Income Taxes	17,000	18,000	−5.6
Net Income	$ 25,000	$ 22,000	+13.6

*($900,000 − $800,000) ÷ $800,000; all changes expressed as percentages of previous totals.

The percentage changes disclose that, even though Milavec's net income increased slightly more than total sales, products may be underpriced. Cost of goods sold increased much more than sales, resulting in a lower gross margin. Users would also want to investigate why operating expenses decreased substantially despite the increase in sales volume.

Whether basing their analyses on absolute amounts, percentages, or ratios, users must avoid drawing overly simplistic conclusions about the reasons for the results. Numerical relationships flag conditions requiring further study. Recall from Chapter 8 that a change which appears favorable on the surface may not necessarily be a good sign. Users must evaluate the underlying reasons for the change.

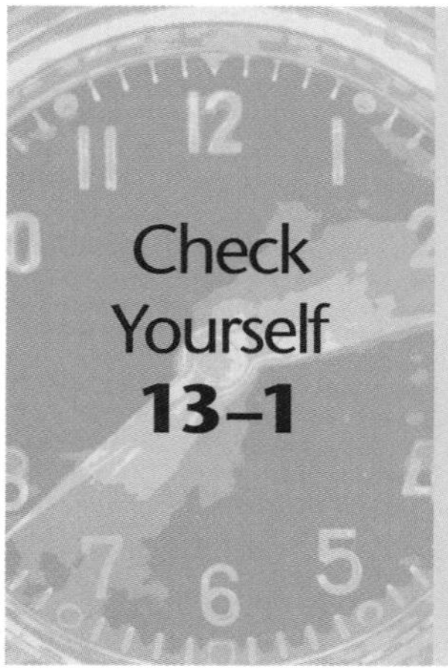

Check Yourself 13–1

The following information was drawn from the annual reports of two retail companies (amounts are shown in millions). One company is an upscale department store; the other is a discount store. Based on this limited information, identify which company is the upscale department store.

	Jenkins Co.	Horn's, Inc.
Sales	$325	$680
Cost of Goods Sold	130	408
Gross Margin	$195	$272

Answer Jenkins' gross margin represents 60 percent ($195 ÷ $325) of sales. Horn's gross margin represents 40 percent ($272 ÷ $680) of sales. Since an upscale department store would have higher margins than a discount store, the data suggest that Jenkins is the upscale department store.

ANSWERS TO THE *curious* ACCOUNTANT

Although BellSouth and SBC expect the acquisition of AT&T Wireless to depress earnings from 2005 through 2007, they believe the acquisition will significantly increase earnings after 2007. They expect to achieve this benefit by reducing capital expenditures and operating costs; one combined company will need less equipment than two separate companies and will not need to spend as much as two companies for such items as marketing and personnel. They estimate these costs savings will range from $1.4 to $2.1 billion annually.

Not all analysts agree with the two companies' forecasts. After studying the same basic information some analysts think competition from rivals such as Verizon may force Cingular to spend more on advertising than it expects in order to keep customers from switching providers. These analysts believe the year or so it takes to implement the merger will give rivals the opportunity to steal existing customers from AT&T Wireless. Additionally, some think Verizon currently has a technically superior network, which may cause Cingular to spend more on equipment than it estimated when bidding for AT&T Wireless. These analysts' think Cingular paid too much for AT&T Wireless.

The point is that financial analysis techniques can help managers make decisions, but cannot guarantee success. When using such tools as ratios and trend analysis, decision makers must understand the businesses being evaluated, and they must make assumptions about future events. Only the future will tell whether Cingular paid too much for AT&T Wireless, but we can be sure that many ratio and capital budgeting computations were made before Cingular decided how much its winning bid would be.

Source: Companies' filings with the SEC and Roger O. Crockett, "How the Cingular Deal Helps Verizon," *BusinessWeek*, March 1, 2004, pp. 36–37.

When comparing more than two periods, analysts use either of two basic approaches: (1) choosing one base year from which to calculate all increases or decreases or (2) calculating each period's percentage change from the preceding figure. For example, assume Milavec's sales for 2005 and 2006 were $600,000 and $750,000, respectively.

	2008	2007	2006	2005
Sales	$900,000	$800,000	$750,000	$600,000
Increase over 2005 sales	50.0%	33.3%	25.0%	—
Increase over preceding year	12.5%	6.7%	25.0%	—

Analysis discloses that Milavec's 2008 sales represented a 50 percent increase over 2005 sales, and a large increase (25 percent) occurred in 2006. From 2006 to 2007, sales increased only 6.7 percent but in the following year increased much more (12.5 percent).

Vertical Analysis

Vertical analysis uses percentages to compare individual components of financial statements to a key statement figure. Horizontal analysis compares items over many time periods; vertical analysis compares many items within the same time period.

Vertical Analysis of the Income Statement

Vertical analysis of an income statement (also called a *common size* income statement) involves converting each income statement component to a percentage of sales. Although vertical analysis suggests examining only one period, it is useful to compare common size income statements for several years. Exhibit 13–4 presents Milavec's income statements, along with vertical percentages, for 2008 and 2007. This analysis discloses that cost of goods sold increased significantly as a percentage of sales. Operating expenses and income taxes, however, decreased in relation to sales. Each of these observations indicates a need for more analysis regarding possible trends for future profits.

Vertical Analysis of the Balance Sheet

Vertical analysis of the balance sheet involves converting each balance sheet component to a percentage of total assets. The vertical analysis of Milavec's balance sheets in Exhibit 13–5

Exhibit 13–4

MILAVEC COMPANY
Vertical Analysis of Comparative Income Statements

	2008		2007	
	Amount	**Percentage of Sales**	**Amount**	**Percentage of Sales**
Sales	$900,000	100.0%	$800,000	100.0%
Cost of Goods Sold	610,000	67.7	480,000	60.0
Gross Margin	290,000	32.3	320,000	40.0
Operating Expenses	248,000	27.6	280,000	35.0
Income before Taxes	42,000	4.7	40,000	5.0
Income Taxes	17,000	1.9	18,000	2.3
Net Income	$ 25,000	2.8%	$ 22,000	2.7%

Exhibit 13–5

MILAVEC COMPANY
Vertical Analysis of Comparative Balance Sheets

	2008	**Percentage of Total**	**2007**	**Percentage of Total**
Assets				
Cash	$ 20,000	3.9%	$ 17,000	3.7%
Marketable Securities	20,000	3.9	22,000	4.8
Notes Receivable	4,000	0.8	3,000	0.7
Accounts Receivable	50,000	9.8	56,000	12.3
Merchandise Inventory	70,000	13.8	43,000	9.5
Prepaid Expenses	4,000	0.8	4,000	0.9
Total Current Assets	168,000	33.0	145,000	31.9
Property, Plant, and Equipment	340,000	67.0	310,000	68.1
Total Assets	$508,000	100.0%	$455,000	100.0%
Liabilities and Stockholders' Equity				
Accounts Payable	$ 40,000	7.9%	$ 38,000	8.3%
Salaries Payable	2,000	0.4	3,000	0.7
Taxes Payable	4,000	0.8	2,000	0.4
Total Current Liabilities	46,000	9.1	43,000	9.4
Bonds Payable, 8%	100,000	19.7	100,000	22.0
Total Liabilities	146,000	28.8	143,000	31.4
Preferred Stock 6%, $100 par	50,000	9.8	50,000	11.0
Common Stock, $10 par	150,000	29.5	125,000	27.5
Retained Earnings	162,000	31.9	137,000	30.1
Total Stockholders' Equity	362,000	71.2	312,000	68.6
Total Liabilities and Stockholders' Equity	$508,000	100.0%	$455,000	100.0%

discloses few large percentage changes from the preceding year. Even small individual percentage changes, however, may represent substantial dollar increases. Inventory, one of the less liquid current assets, has increased 62.8 percent ([$70,000 − $43,000] ÷ $43,000) from 2007 to 2008, which may have unfavorable consequences. Careful analysis requires considering changes in both percentages *and* absolute amounts.

Ratio Analysis

LO3 Explain ratio analysis.

Ratio analysis involves studying various relationships between different items reported in a set of financial statements. For example, net earnings (net income) reported on the income statement may be compared to total assets reported on the balance sheet. Analysts calculate many different ratios for a wide variety of purposes. The remainder of this chapter is devoted to discussing some of the more commonly used ratios.

Objectives of Ratio Analysis

As suggested earlier, various users approach financial statement analysis with many different objectives. Creditors are interested in whether a company will be able to repay its debts on time. Both creditors and stockholders are concerned with how the company is financed, whether through debt, equity, or earnings. Stockholders and potential investors analyze past earnings performance and dividend policy for clues to the future value of their investments. In addition to using internally generated data to analyze operations, company managers find much information prepared for external purposes useful for examining past operations and planning future policies. Although many of these objectives are interrelated, it is convenient to group ratios into categories such as measures of debt-paying ability and measures of profitability.

Measures of Debt-Paying Ability

Liquidity Ratios

LO4 Calculate ratios for assessing a company's liquidity.

Liquidity ratios indicate a company's ability to pay short-term debts. They focus on current assets and current liabilities. The examples in the following section use the financial statement information reported by Milavec Company.

Working Capital

Working capital is current assets minus current liabilities. Current assets include assets most likely to be converted into cash in the current operating period. Current liabilities represent debts that must be satisfied in the current period. Working capital therefore measures the excess funds the company will have available for operations, excluding any new funds it generates during the year. Think of working capital as the cushion against short-term debt-paying problems. Working capital at the end of 2008 and 2007 for Milavec Company was as follows.

	2008	2007
Current assets	$168,000	$145,000
− Current liabilities	46,000	43,000
Working capital	$122,000	$102,000

Milavec's working capital increased dramatically from 2007 to 2008, but the numbers themselves say little. Whether $122,000 is sufficient or not depends on such factors as the industry in which Milavec operates, its size, and the maturity dates of its current obligations. We can see, however, that the increase in working capital is primarily due to the increase in inventories.

Current Ratio

Working capital is an absolute amount. Its usefulness is limited by the materiality difficulties discussed earlier. It is hard to draw meaningful conclusions from comparing Milavec's working capital of $122,000 with another company that also has working capital of $122,000. By expressing the relationship between current assets and current liabilities as a ratio, however, we have a more useful measure of the company's debt-paying ability relative to other companies. The **current ratio,** also called the **working capital ratio,** is calculated as follows.

$$\text{Current ratio} = \frac{\text{Current assets}}{\text{Current liabilities}}$$

To illustrate using the current ratio for comparisons, consider Milavec's current position relative to Laroque's, a larger firm with current assets of $500,000 and current liabilities of $378,000.

	Milavec	Laroque
Current assets (a)	$168,000	$500,000
− Current liabilities (b)	46,000	378,000
Working capital	$122,000	$122,000
Current ratio (a ÷ b)	3.65:1	1.32:1

The current ratio is expressed as the number of dollars of current assets for each dollar of current liabilities. In the above example, both companies have the same amount of working capital. Milavec, however, appears to have a much stronger working capital position. Any conclusions from this analysis must take into account the circumstances of the particular companies; there is no single ideal current ratio that suits all companies. In recent years the average current ratio of the 30 companies that constitute the Dow Jones Industrial Average was around 1.35:1; the individual company ratios, however, ranged from .37:1 to 4.22:1. A current ratio can be too high. Money invested in factories and developing new products is usually more profitable than money held as large cash balances or invested in inventory.

Quick Ratio

The **quick ratio,** also known as the **acid-test ratio,** is a conservative variation of the current ratio. The quick ratio measures a company's *immediate* debt-paying ability. Only cash, receivables, and current marketable securities (*quick assets*) are included in the numerator. Less liquid current assets, such as inventories and prepaid expenses, are omitted. Inventories may take several months to sell; prepaid expenses reduce otherwise necessary expenditures but do not lead eventually to cash receipts. The quick ratio is computed as follows.

$$\text{Quick ratio} = \frac{\text{Quick assets}}{\text{Current liabilities}}$$

Milavec Company's current ratios and quick ratios for 2008 and 2007 follow.

	2008	2007
Current ratio	168,000 ÷ 46,000 3.65:1	145,000 ÷ 43,000 3.37:1
Quick ratio	94,000 ÷ 46,000 2.04:1	98,000 ÷ 43,000 2.28:1

The decrease in the quick ratio from 2007 to 2008 reflects both a decrease in quick assets and an increase in current liabilities. The result indicates that the company is less liquid (has less ability to pay its short-term debt) in 2008 than it was in 2007.

Accounts Receivable Ratios

Offering customers credit plays an enormous role in generating revenue, but it also increases expenses and delays cash receipts. To minimize bad debts expense and collect cash for use in current operations, companies want to collect receivables as quickly as possible without losing customers. Two relationships are often examined to assess a company's collection record: *accounts receivable turnover* and *average days to collect receivables (average collection period).*

Accounts receivable turnover is calculated as follows.

$$\text{Accounts receivable turnover} = \frac{\text{Net credit sales}}{\text{Average accounts receivable}}$$

Net credit sales refers to total sales on account less sales discounts and returns. When most sales are credit sales or when a breakdown of total sales between cash sales and credit sales is not available, the analyst must use total sales in the numerator. The denominator is based on *net accounts receivable* (receivables after subtracting the allowance for doubtful accounts). Since the numerator represents a whole period, it is preferable to use average receivables in the denominator if possible. When comparative statements are available, the average can be based on the beginning and ending balances. Milavec Company's accounts receivable turnover is computed as follows:

	2008	2007
Net sales (assume all on account) (a)	$900,000	$800,000
Beginning receivables (b)	$ 56,000	$ 55,000*
Ending receivables (c)	50,000	56,000
Average receivables (d) = (a + c) ÷ 2	$ 53,000	$ 55,500
Accounts receivable turnover (a ÷ d)	16.98	14.41

*The beginning receivables balance was drawn from the 2006 financial statements, which are not included in the illustration.

The 2008 accounts receivable turnover of 16.98 indicates Milavec collected its average receivables almost 17 times that year. The higher the turnover, the faster the collections. A company can have cash flow problems and lose substantial purchasing power if resources are tied up in receivables for long periods.

Average days to collect receivables is calculated as follows.

$$\text{Average days to collect receivables} = \frac{\text{365 days}}{\text{Accounts receivable turnover}}$$

This ratio offers another way to look at turnover by showing the number of days, on average, it takes to collect a receivable. If receivables were collected 16.98 times in 2008, the average collection period was 21 days, 365 ÷ 16.98 (the number of days in the year divided by accounts receivable turnover). For 2007, it took an average of 25 days (365 ÷ 14.41) to collect a receivable.

Although the collection period improved, no other conclusions can be reached without considering the industry, Milavec's past performance, and the general economic environment. In recent years the average time to collect accounts receivable for the 25 nonfinancial companies that make up the Dow Jones Industrial Average was around 60 days. (Financial firms are excluded because, by the nature of their business, they have very long collection periods.)

Inventory Ratios

A fine line exists between having too much and too little inventory in stock. Too little inventory can result in lost sales and costly production delays. Too much inventory can use needed space, increase financing and insurance costs, and become obsolete. To help analyze how efficiently a company manages inventory, we use two ratios similar to those used in analyzing accounts receivable.

Inventory turnover indicates the number of times, on average, that inventory is totally replaced during the year. The relationship is computed as follows.

$$\text{Inventory turnover} = \frac{\text{Cost of goods sold}}{\text{Average inventory}}$$

The average inventory is usually based on the beginning and ending balances that are shown in the financial statements. Inventory turnover for Milavec was as follows.

	2008	2007
Cost of goods sold (a)	$610,000	$480,000
Beginning inventory (b)	43,000	40,000*
Ending inventory (c)	70,000	43,000
Average inventory (d) = (b + c) ÷ 2	$ 56,500	$ 41,500
Inventory turnover (a ÷ d)	10.80	11.57

*The beginning inventory balance was drawn from the company's 2006 financial statements, which are not included in the illustration.

Generally, a higher turnover indicates that merchandise is being handled more efficiently. Trying to compare firms in different industries, however, can be misleading. Inventory turnover for grocery stores and many retail outlets is high. Because of the nature of the goods being sold, inventory turnover is much lower for appliance and jewelry stores. We look at this issue in more detail when we discuss return on investment.

Average days to sell inventory is determined by dividing the number of days in the year by the inventory turnover as follows.

$$\text{Average days to sell inventory} = \frac{\text{365 days}}{\text{Inventory turnover}}$$

The result approximates the number of days the firm could sell inventory without purchasing more. For Milavec, this figure was 34 days in 2008 (365 ÷ 10.80) and 32 days in 2007 (365 ÷ 11.57). In recent years it took around 30 days, on average, for the companies in the Dow Jones Industrial Average that have inventory to sell their inventory. The time it took individual companies to sell their inventory varied by industry, ranging from 3 days to 55 days.

Solvency Ratios

LO5 Calculate ratios for assessing a company's solvency.

Solvency ratios are used to analyze a company's long-term debt-paying ability and its financing structure. Creditors are concerned with a company's ability to satisfy outstanding obligations. The larger a company's liability percentage, the greater the risk that the company could fall behind or default on debt payments. Stockholders, too, are concerned about a company's solvency. If a company is unable to pay its debts, the owners could lose their investment. Each user group desires that company financing choices minimize its investment risk, whether the investment is in debt or stockholders' equity.

Debt Ratios

The following ratios represent two different ways to express the same relationship. Both are frequently used.

Debt to assets ratio. This ratio measures the percentage of a company's assets that are financed by debt.

Debt to equity ratio. As used in this ratio, *equity* means stockholders' equity. The debt to equity ratio compares creditor financing to owner financing. It is expressed as the dollar amount of liabilities for each dollar of stockholder's equity.

These ratios are calculated as follows.

$$\text{Debt to assets} = \frac{\text{Total liabilities}}{\text{Total assets}}$$

$$\text{Debt to equity} = \frac{\text{Total liabilities}}{\text{Total stockholders' equity}}$$

Applying these formulas to Milavec Company's results produces the following.

	2008	2007
Total liabilities (a)	$146,000	$143,000
Total stockholders' equity (b)	362,000	312,000
Total equities (liabilities + stockholders' equity) (c)	$508,000	$455,000
Debt to assets (a ÷ c)	29%	31%
Debt to equity ratio (a ÷ b)	0.40:1	0.46:1

Each year less than one-third of the company's assets were financed with debt. The amount of liabilities per dollar of stockholders' equity declined by 0.06. It is difficult to judge whether the reduced percentage of liabilities is favorable. In general, a lower level of liabilities provides greater security because the likelihood of bankruptcy is reduced. Perhaps, however, the company is financially strong enough to incur more liabilities and benefit from financial leverage. The 30 companies that make up the Dow Jones Industrial Average report around 64 percent of their assets, on average, are financed through borrowing.

Number of Times Interest Is Earned

This ratio measures the burden a company's interest payments represent. Users often consider times interest is earned along with the debt ratios when evaluating financial risk. The numerator of this ratio uses *earnings before interest and taxes (EBIT),* rather than net earnings, because the amount of earnings *before* interest and income taxes is available for paying interest.

$$\text{Number of times interest is earned} = \frac{\text{Earnings before taxes and interest expense}}{\text{Interest expense}}$$

Dividing EBIT by interest expense indicates how many times the company could have made its interest payments. Obviously, interest is paid only once, but the more times it *could* be paid, the bigger the company's safety net. Although interest is paid from cash, not accrual earnings, it is standard practice to base this ratio on accrual-based EBIT, not a cash-based amount. For Milavec, this calculation is as follows.

	2008	2007
Income before taxes	$42,000	$40,000
Interest expense (b)	8,000	8,000*
Income before taxes and interest (a)	$50,000	$48,000
Times interest earned (a ÷ b)	6.25 times	6 times

*Interest on bonds: $100,000 × .08 = $8,000.

Any expense or dividend payment can be analyzed this way. Another frequently used calculation is the number of times the preferred dividend is earned. In that case, the numerator is net income (after taxes) and the denominator is the amount of the annual preferred dividend.

Selected data for Riverside Corporation and Academy Company follow (amounts are shown in millions).

	Riverside Corporation	Academy Company
Total liabilities (a)	$650	$450
Stockholders' equity (b)	300	400
Total liabilities + stockholders' equity (c)	$950	$850
Interest expense (d)	$ 65	$ 45
Income before taxes (e)	140	130
Income before taxes and interest (f)	$205	$175

Based on this information alone, which company would likely obtain the less favorable interest rate on additional debt financing?

Answer Interest rates vary with risk levels. Companies with less solvency (long-term debt-paying ability) generally must pay higher interest rates to obtain financing. Two solvency measures for the two companies follow. Recall:

$$\text{Total assets} = \text{Liabilities} + \text{Stockholders' equity}$$

continued

Check Yourself 13–2

	Riverside Corporation	Academy Company
Debt to assets ratio (a ÷ c)	68.4%	52.9%
Times interest earned (f ÷ d)	3.15 times	3.89 times

Since Riverside has a higher percentage of debt and a lower times interest earned ratio, the data suggest that Riverside is less solvent than Academy. Riverside would therefore likely have to pay a higher interest rate to obtain additional financing.

Plant Assets to Long-Term Liabilities

Companies often pledge plant assets as collateral for long-term liabilities. Financial statement users may analyze a firm's ability to obtain long-term financing on the strength of its asset base. Effective financial management principles dictate that asset purchases should be financed over a time span about equal to the expected lives of the assets. Short-term assets should be financed with short-term liabilities; the current ratio, introduced earlier, indicates how well a company manages current debt. Long-lived assets should be financed with long-term liabilities, and the *plant assets to long-term liabilities* ratio suggests how well long-term debt is managed. It is calculated as follows.

$$\text{Plant assets to long-term liabilities} = \frac{\text{Net plant assets}}{\text{Long-term liabilities}}$$

For Milavec Company, these ratios follow.

	2008	2007
Net plant assets (a)	$340,000	$310,000
Bonds payable (b)	100,000	100,000
Plant assets to long-term liabilities (a ÷ b)	3.4:1	3.1:1

Measures of Profitability

Profitability refers to a company's ability to generate earnings. Both management and external users desire information about a company's success in generating profits and how these profits are used to reward investors. Some of the many ratios available to measure different aspects of profitability are discussed in the following two sections.

Measures of Managerial Effectiveness

LO6 Calculate ratios for assessing company management's effectiveness.

The most common ratios used to evaluate managerial effectiveness measure what percentage of sales results in earnings and how productive assets are in generating those sales. As mentioned earlier, the *absolute amount* of sales or earnings means little without also considering company size.

Net Margin (or Return on Sales)

Gross margin and *gross profit* are alternate terms for the amount remaining after subtracting the expense cost of goods sold from sales. **Net margin,** sometimes called *operating margin, profit margin,* or the *return on sales ratio,* describes the percent remaining of each sales dollar after subtracting other expenses as well as cost of goods sold. Net margin can be calculated in several ways; some of the more common methods only subtract normal operating expenses or all expenses other than income tax expense. For simplicity, our calculation uses net income (we subtract all expenses). Net income divided by net sales expresses net income (earnings) as a percentage of sales, as follows.

$$\text{Net margin} = \frac{\text{Net income}}{\text{Net sales}}$$

For Milavec Company, the net margins for 2008 and 2007 were as follows.

	2008	2007
Net income (a)	$ 25,000	$ 22,000
Net sales (b)	900,000	800,000
Net margin (a ÷ b)	2.78%	2.75%

Milavec has maintained approximately the same net margin. Obviously, the larger the percentage, the better; a meaningful interpretation, however, requires analyzing the company's history and comparing the net margin to other companies in the same industry. The average net margin for the 30 companies that make up the Dow Jones Industrial Average has been around 10 percent in recent years; some companies, such as Microsoft with 31 percent, have been much higher than the average. Of course, if a company has a net loss, its net margin for that year will be negative.

Asset Turnover Ratio

The **asset turnover ratio** (sometimes called *turnover of assets ratio*) measures how many sales dollars were generated for each dollar of assets invested. As with many ratios used in financial statement analysis, users may define the numerator and denominator of this ratio in different ways. For example, they may use total assets or only include operating assets. Since the numerator represents a whole period, it is preferable to use average assets in the denominator if possible, especially if the amount of assets changed significantly during the year. We use average total assets in our illustration.

$$\text{Asset turnover} = \frac{\text{Net sales}}{\text{Average total assets}}$$

For Milavec, the asset turnover ratios were as follows.

	2008	2007
Net sales (a)	$900,000	$800,000
Beginning assets (b)	$455,000	$420,000*
Ending assets (c)	508,000	455,000
Average assets (d) = (b + c) ÷ 2	$481,500	$437,500
Asset turnover (a ÷ d)	1.87	1.83

*The beginning asset balance was drawn from the 2006 financial statements, which are not included in the illustration.

As with most ratios, the implications of a given asset turnover ratio are affected by other considerations. Asset turnover will be high in an industry that requires only minimal investment to operate, such as real estate sales companies. On the other hand, industries that require large investments in plant and machinery, like the auto industry, are likely to have lower asset turnover ratios. The asset turnover ratios of the companies that make up the Dow Jones Industrial Average have averaged around 0.75 in recent years. This means that annual sales have averaged 75 percent of their assets.

Return on Investment

Return on investment (ROI), also called *return on assets* or *earning power,* is the ratio of wealth generated (net income) to the amount invested (average total assets) to generate the wealth. ROI can be calculated as follows.[1]

$$\text{ROI} = \frac{\text{Net income}}{\text{Average total assets}}$$

For Milavec, ROI was as follows.

2008

$$\$25{,}000 \div \$481{,}500^* = 5.20\%$$

2007

$$\$22{,}000 \div \$437{,}500^* = 5.03\%$$

*The computation of average assets is shown at the bottom of page 543.

In general, higher ROIs suggest better performance. The ROI of the large companies that make up the Dow Jones Industrial Average has averaged around 7 percent in recent years. These data suggest that Milavec is performing below average, and therefore signals a need for further evaluation that would lead to improved performance.

Return on Equity

Return on equity (ROE) is often used to measure the profitability of the stockholders' investment. ROE is usually higher than ROI because of financial leverage. Financial leverage refers to using debt financing to increase the assets available to a business beyond the amount of assets financed by owners. As long as a company's ROI exceeds its cost of borrowing (interest expense), the owners will earn a higher return on their investment in the company by using borrowed money. For example, if a company borrows money at 8 percent and invests it at 10 percent, the owners will enjoy a return that is higher than 10 percent. ROE is computed as follows.

$$\text{ROE} = \frac{\text{Net income}}{\text{Average total stockholders' equity}}$$

If the amount of stockholders' equity changes significantly during the year, it is desirable to use average equity rather than year-end equity in the denominator. The ROE figures for Milavec Company were as follows.

	2008	2007
Net income (a)	$ 25,000	$ 22,000
Preferred stock, 6%, $100 par, cumulative	50,000	50,000
Common stock, $10 par	150,000	125,000
Retained earnings	162,000	137,000
Total stockholders' equity (b)	$362,000	$312,000
ROE (a ÷ b)	6.9%	7.1%

The slight decrease in ROE is due primarily to the increase in common stock. The effect of the increase in total stockholders' equity offsets the effect of the increase in earnings. This information does not disclose whether Milavec had the use of the additional stockholder investment for all or part of the year. If the data are available, calculating a weighted average amount of stockholders' equity provides more meaningful results.

[1] Detailed coverage of the return on investment ratio is provided in Chapter 9. As discussed in that chapter, companies frequently manipulate the formula to improve managerial motivation and performance. For example, instead of using net income, companies frequently use operating income because net income may be affected by items that are not controllable by management such as loss on a plant closing, storm damage, and so on.

We mentioned earlier the companies that make up the Dow Jones Industrial Average had an average ROI of 7 percent. The average ROE for the companies in the Dow was 19 percent, indicating effective use of financial leverage.

Stock Market Ratios

LO7 Calculate ratios for assessing a company's position in the stock market.

Existing and potential investors in a company's stock use many common ratios to analyze and compare the earnings and dividends of different size companies in different industries. Purchasers of stock can profit in two ways: through receiving dividends and through increases in stock value. Investors consider both dividends and overall earnings performance as indicators of the value of the stock they own.

Earnings per Share

Perhaps the most frequently quoted measure of earnings performance is **earnings per share (EPS).** EPS represents an attempt to express a company's annual earnings in one easily understood figure. Investors may appreciate knowing that a large company's net income increased from \$437 million in 2006 to \$493 million in 2007. But, if they also learn that the company's EPS increased from \$2.19 to \$2.47, the increase is easier to understand. When financial analysts cite companies' earnings, they usually speak of EPS, not total net earnings.

EPS differs from *dividends per share.* Rarely would a company distribute all the year's earnings to stockholders. EPS calculations are among the most complex in accounting, and more advanced textbooks devote entire chapters to the subject. At this level, we use the following basic formula.

$$\text{Earnings per share} = \frac{\text{Net earnings available for common stock}}{\text{Average number of outstanding common shares}}$$

EPS pertains to shares of *common stock.* Limiting the numerator to earnings available for common stock eliminates the annual preferred dividend ($0.06 \times \$50{,}000 = \$3{,}000$) from the calculation. Exhibit 13–1 shows that Milavec did not pay the preferred dividends in 2008. Since the preferred stock is cumulative, however, the preferred dividend is in arrears and not available to the common stockholders. The number of common shares outstanding is determined by dividing the book value of the common stock by its par value per share ($\$150{,}000 \div \$10 = 15{,}000$ for 2008 and $\$125{,}000 \div \$10 = 12{,}500$ for 2007). Using these data, Milavec's 2008 EPS is calculated as follows.

$$\frac{\$25{,}000 \text{ (net income)} - \$3{,}000 \text{ (preferred dividend)}}{(15{,}000 + 12{,}500)/2 \text{ (average outstanding common shares)}} = \$1.60 \text{ per share}$$

Investors attribute a great deal of importance to EPS figures. The amounts used in calculating EPS, however, have limitations. Many accounting choices, assumptions, and estimates underlie net income computations, including alternative depreciation methods, different inventory cost flow assumptions, and estimates of future bad debt or warranty expenses, to name only a few. The denominator is also inexact because various factors (discussed in advanced accounting courses) affect the number of shares to include. Numerous opportunities therefore exist to manipulate EPS figures. Prudent investors consider these variables in deciding how much weight to attach to earnings per share.

Book Value

Book value per share is another frequently quoted measure of a share of stock. It is calculated as follows.

$$\text{Book value per share} = \frac{\text{Stockholders' equity} - \text{Preferred rights}}{\text{Outstanding common shares}}$$

Instead of describing the numerator as stockholders' equity, we could have used assets minus liabilities, the algebraic computation of a company's "net worth." Net worth is a misnomer. A company's accounting records reflect book values, not worth. Because assets are recorded at historical costs and different methods are used to transfer asset costs to expense, the book value of assets after deducting liabilities means little if anything. Nevertheless, investors use the term *book value per share* frequently.

Preferred rights represents the amount of money required to satisfy the claims of preferred stockholders. If the preferred stock has a call premium, the call premium amount is subtracted. In our example, we assume the preferred stock can be retired at par. Book value per share for 2008 was therefore as follows.

$$\frac{\$362{,}000 - \$50{,}000}{15{,}000} = \$20.80 \text{ per share}$$

Price-earnings Ratio

The **price-earnings ratio,** or *P/E ratio,* compares the earnings per share of a company to the market price for a share of the company's stock. Assume Avalanche Company and Brushfire Company each report earnings per share of \$3.60. For the same year, Cyclone Company reports EPS of \$4.10. Based on these data alone, Cyclone stock may seem to be the best investment. Suppose, however, that the price for one share of stock in each company is \$43.20, \$36.00, and \$51.25, respectively. Which stock would you buy? Cyclone's stock price is the highest, but so is its EPS. The P/E ratio provides a common base of comparison:

$$\text{Price-earnings ratio} = \frac{\text{Market price per share}}{\text{Earnings per share}}$$

The P/E ratios for the three companies are:

Avalanche	Brushfire	Cyclone
12.0	10.0	12.5

Brushfire might initially seem to be the best buy for your money. Yet there must be some reason that Cyclone's stock is selling at 12½ times earnings. In general, a higher P/E ratio indicates the market is more optimistic about a company's growth potential than it is about a company with a lower P/E ratio. The market price of a company's stock reflects judgments about both the company's current results and expectations about future results. Investors cannot make informed use of these ratios for investment decisions without examining the reasons behind the ratios. In May 2004, the average P/E ratio for the companies in the Dow Jones Industrial Average was around 20.

Dividend Yield

There are two ways to profit from a stock investment. One, investors can sell the stock for more than they paid to purchase it (if the stock price rises). Two, the company that issued the stock can pay cash dividends to the shareholders. Most investors view rising stock prices as the primary reward for investing in stock. The importance of receiving dividends, however, should not be overlooked. Evaluating dividend payments is more complex than simply comparing the dividends per share paid by one company to the dividends per share paid by another company. Receiving a \$1 dividend on a share purchased for \$10 is a much better return than receiving a \$1.50 dividend on stock bought for \$100. Computing the **dividend yield** simplifies comparing dividend payments. Dividend yield measures dividends received as a percentage of a stock's market price.

$$\text{Dividend yield} = \frac{\text{Dividends per share}}{\text{Market price per share}}$$

To illustrate, consider Dragonfly, Inc., and Elk Company. The information for calculating dividend yield follows:

	Dragonfly	Elk
Dividends per share (a)	$ 1.80	$ 3.00
Market price per share (b)	40.00	75.00
Dividend yield (a ÷ b)	4.5%	4.0%

Even though the dividend per share paid by Elk Company is higher, the yield is lower (4.5 percent versus 4.0 percent) because Elk's stock price is so high. The dividend yields for the companies included in the Dow Jones Industrial Average were averaging around 2 percent in May of 2004.

Other Ratios

Investors can also use a wide array of other ratios to analyze profitability. Most **profitability ratios** use the same reasoning. For example, you can calculate the *yield* of a variety of financial investments. Yield represents the percentage the amount received is of the amount invested. The dividend yield explained above could be calculated for either common or preferred stock. Investors could measure the earnings yield by calculating earnings per share as a percentage of market price. Yield on a bond can be calculated the same way: interest received divided by the price of the bond.

The specific ratios presented in this chapter are summarized in Exhibit 13–6.

Presentation of Analytical Relationships

LO8 Identify different forms for presenting analytical data.

To communicate with users, companies present analytical information in endless different ways in annual reports. Although providing diagrams and illustrations in annual reports is not usually required, companies often include various forms of graphs and charts along with the underlying

Exhibit 13–6 *Summary of Key Relationships*

Liquidity Ratios	1. Working capital	Current assets − Current liabilities
	2. Current ratio	Current assets ÷ Current liabilities
	3. Quick (acid-test) ratio	(Current assets − Inventory − Prepaids) ÷ Current liabilities
	4. Accounts receivable turnover	Net credit sales ÷ Average net receivables
	5. Average days to collect receivables	365 ÷ Accounts receivable turnover
	6. Inventory turnover	Cost of goods sold ÷ Average inventory
	7. Average days to sell inventory	365 ÷ Inventory turnover
Solvency Ratios	8. Debt to assets ratio	Total liabilities ÷ Total assets
	9. Debt to equity ratio	Total liabilities ÷ Total stockholders' equity
	10. Number of times interest is earned	Earnings before taxes and interest expense ÷ interest expense
	11. Plant assets to long-term liabilities	Net plant assets ÷ Long-term liabilities
Profitability Ratios	12. Net margin	Net income ÷ Net sales
	13. Asset turnover	Net sales ÷ Average total assets
	14. Return on investment (also: return on assets)	Net income ÷ Average total assets
	15. Return on equity	Net income ÷ Average total stockholders' equity
Stock Market Ratios	16. Earnings per share	Net earnings available for common stock ÷ Average outstanding common shares
	17. Book value per share	(Stockholders' equity − Preferred rights) ÷ Outstanding common shares
	18. Price-earnings ratio	Market price per share ÷ Earnings per share
	19. Dividend yield	Dividends per share ÷ Market price per share

numbers to help users interpret financial statement data more easily. Common types presented include bar charts, pie charts, and line graphs. Exhibits 13–7, 13–8, and 13–9 show examples of these forms.

Exhibit 13–7 *Earnings and Dividends on Common Stock*

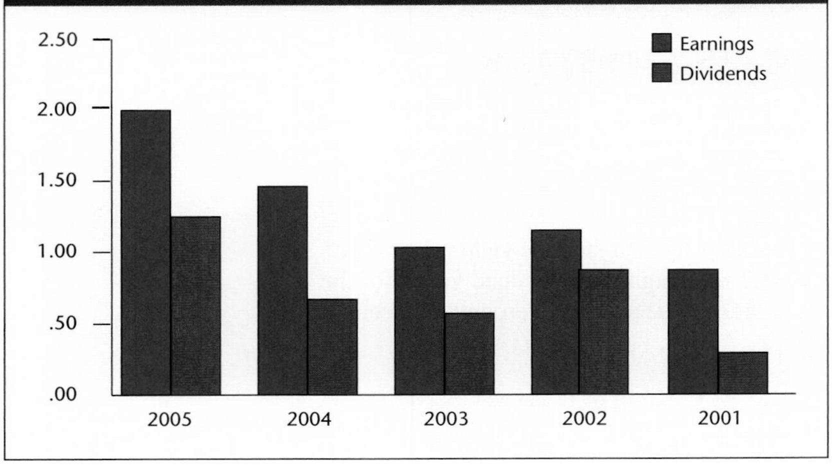

Exhibit 13–8 *Percentage of Sales Dollar*

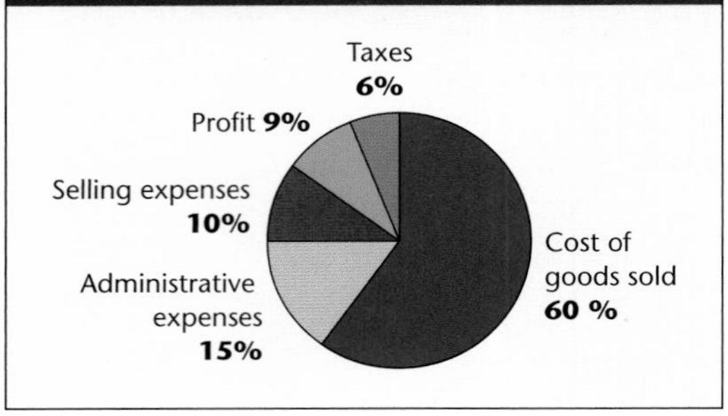

Exhibit 13–9 *Profits by Major Industry Segment*

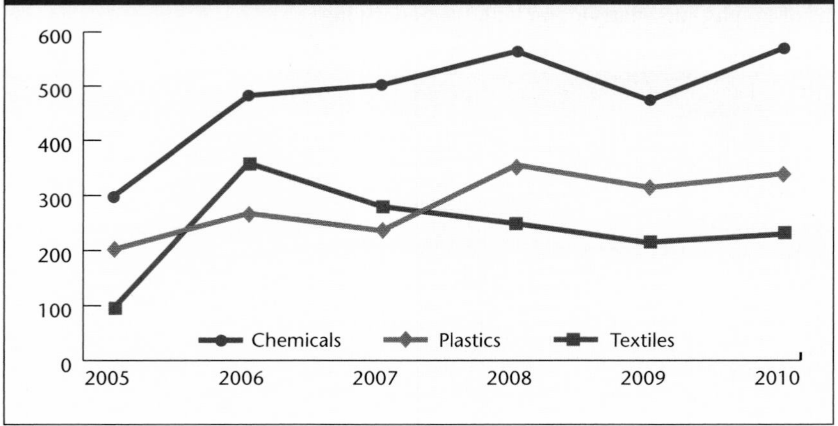

Limitations of Financial Statement Analysis

LO9 Explain the limitations of financial statement analysis.

Analyzing financial statements is analogous to choosing a new car. Each car is different, and prospective buyers must evaluate and weigh a myriad of features: gas mileage, engine size, manufacturer's reputation, color, accessories, and price, to name a few. Just as it is difficult to compare a **Toyota** minivan to a **Ferrari** sports car, so it is difficult to compare a small textile firm to a giant oil company. To make a meaningful assessment, the potential car buyer must focus on key data that can be comparably expressed for each car, such as gas mileage. The superior gas mileage of the minivan may pale in comparison to the thrill of driving the sports car, but the price of buying and operating the sports car may be the characteristic that determines the ultimate choice.

External users can rely on financial statement analysis only as a general guide to the potential of a business. They should resist placing too much weight on any particular figure or trend. Many factors must be considered simultaneously before making any judgments. Furthermore, the analysis techniques discussed in this chapter are all based on historical information. Future events and unanticipated changes in conditions will also influence a company's operating results.

Different Industries

Different industries may be affected by unique social policies, special accounting procedures, or other individual industry attributes. Ratios of companies in different industries are not comparable without considering industry characteristics. A high debt to assets ratio is more acceptable in some industries than others. Even within an industry, a particular business may require more or less working capital than the industry average. If so, the working capital and quick ratios would mean little compared to those of other firms, but may still be useful for trend analysis.

Because of industry-specific factors, most professional analysts specialize in one, or only a few, industries. Financial institutions such as brokerage houses, banks, and insurance companies typically employ financial analysts who specialize in areas such as mineral or oil extraction, chemicals, banking, retail, insurance, bond markets, or automobile manufacturing.

REALITY *bytes*

The most widely recognized source of financial information is a company's annual report. Most companies provide copies of their annual report free of charge. Normally, a person can obtain a copy of the annual report simply by calling the corporate office and asking the receptionist to direct the call to the appropriate department. Another source for public companies registered with the Securities and Exchange Commission is the Edgar database, which can be accessed through the Internet address www.sec.org. Also, many brokerage houses offer free financial information through their Web pages. As an example, we suggest that you try the Internet address www.schwab.com.

Changing Economic Environment

When comparing firms, analysts must be alert to changes in general economic trends from year to year. Significant changes in fuel costs and interest rates in recent years make old rule-of-thumb guidelines for evaluating these factors obsolete. In addition, the presence or absence of inflation affects business prospects.

Accounting Principles

Financial statement analysis is only as reliable as the data on which it is based. Although most firms follow generally accepted accounting principles, a wide variety of acceptable accounting methods is available from which to choose, including different inventory and depreciation methods, different schedules for recognizing revenue, and different ways to account for oil and gas exploration costs. Analyzing statements of companies that seem identical may produce noncomparable ratios if the companies used different accounting methods. Analysts may seek to improve comparability by trying to recast different companies' financial statements as if the same accounting methods had been applied.

Accrual accounting requires the use of many estimates; bad debt expense, warranty expense, asset lives, and salvage value are just a few. The reliability of the resulting financial reports depends on the expertise and integrity of the persons who make the estimates.

The quality and usefulness of accounting information are influenced by underlying accounting concepts. Two particular concepts, *conservatism* and *historical cost,* have a tremendous impact on financial reporting. Conservatism dictates recognizing estimated losses as soon as they occur, but gain recognition is almost always deferred until the gains are actually realized. Conservatism produces a negative bias in financial statements. There are persuasive arguments for the conservatism principle, but users should be alert to distortions it may cause in accounting information.

The pervasive use of the historical cost concept is probably the greatest single cause of distorted financial statement analysis results. The historical cost of an asset does not represent its current value. The asset purchased in 1980 for $10,000 is not comparable in value to the asset purchased in 1995 for $10,000 because of changes in the value of the dollar. Using historical cost produces financial statements that report dollars with differing purchasing power in the same statement. Combining these differing dollar values is akin to adding miles to kilometers. To get the most from analyzing financial statements, users should be cognizant of these limitations.

Check Yourself 13–3

The return on equity for Gup Company is 23.4 percent and for Hunn Company is 17 percent. Does this mean Gup Company is better managed than Hunn Company?

Answer No single ratio can adequately measure management performance. Even analyzing a wide range of ratios provides only limited insight. Any useful interpretation requires the analyst to recognize the limitations of ratio analysis. For example, ratio norms typically differ between industries and may be affected by temporary economic factors. In addition, companies' use of different accounting practices and procedures produces different ratio results even when underlying circumstances are comparable.

a look back

Financial statement analysis involves many factors, among them user characteristics, information needs for particular types of decisions, and how financial information is analyzed. Analytical techniques include *horizontal, vertical,* and *ratio analysis.* Users commonly calculate ratios to measure a company's liquidity, solvency, and profitability. The specific ratios presented in this chapter are summarized in Exhibit 13–6. Although ratios are easy to calculate and provide useful insights into business operations, when interpreting analytical results, users should consider limitations resulting from differing industry characteristics, differing economic conditions, and the fundamental accounting principles used to produce reported financial information.

a look forward

The next chapter presents a detailed explanation of the statement of cash flows. In that chapter, you will learn how to classify cash receipts and payments as financing activities, investing activities, or operating activities. The chapter explains how to use the T-account method to prepare a statement of cash flows and the difference between the direct method of presenting cash flows from operating activities and the indirect method of presenting cash flows from operating activities. The depth and timing of statement of cash flows coverage varies among colleges. Your instructor may or may not cover this chapter.

SELF-STUDY REVIEW PROBLEM

Financial statements for Stallings Company follow.

INCOME STATEMENTS
for the Years Ended December 31

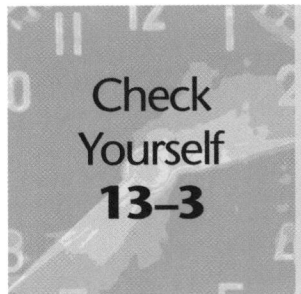

	2009	2008
Revenues		
Net Sales	$315,000	$259,000
Expenses		
Cost of Goods Sold	(189,000)	(154,000)
General, Selling, and Administrative Expenses	(54,000)	(46,000)
Interest Expense	(4,000)	(4,500)
Income Before Taxes	68,000	54,500
Income Tax Expense (40%)	(27,200)	(21,800)
Net Earnings	$ 40,800	$ 32,700

BALANCE SHEETS AS OF DECEMBER 31	2009	2008
Assets		
Current Assets		
Cash	$ 6,500	$ 11,500
Accounts Receivable	51,000	49,000
Inventories	155,000	147,500
Total Current Assets	212,500	208,000
Plant and Equipment (net)	187,500	177,000
Total Assets	$400,000	$385,000
Liabilities and Stockholders' Equity		
Liabilities		
Current Liabilities		
Accounts Payable	$ 60,000	$ 81,500
Other	25,000	22,500
Total Current Liabilities	85,000	104,000
Bonds Payable	100,000	100,000
Total Liabilities	185,000	204,000
Stockholders' Equity		
Common Stock (50,000 shares, $3 par)	150,000	150,000
Paid-In Capital in Excess of Par	20,000	20,000
Retained Earnings	45,000	11,000
Total Stockholders' Equity	215,000	181,000
Total Liabilities and Stockholders' Equity	$400,000	$385,000

Required

a. Use horizontal analysis to determine which expense item increased by the highest percentage from 2008 to 2009.

b. Use vertical analysis to determine whether the inventory balance is a higher percentage of total assets in 2008 or 2009.

c. Calculate the following ratios for 2008 and 2009. When data limitations prohibit computing averages, use year-end balances in your calculations.

(1) Net margin
(2) Return on investment
(3) Return on equity
(4) Earnings per share
(5) Price-earnings ratio (market price per share at the end of 2009 and 2008 was $12.04 and $8.86, respectively)
(6) Book value per share of common stock
(7) Times interest earned
(8) Working capital
(9) Current ratio
(10) Acid-test ratio
(11) Accounts receivable turnover
(12) Inventory turnover
(13) Debt to Equity

Solution to Requirement a

Income tax expense increased by the greatest percentage. Computations follow.

Cost of goods sold ($189,000 − $154,000) ÷ $154,000 = 22.73%
General, selling, and administrative ($54,000 − $46,000) ÷ $46,000 = 17.39%
Interest expense decreased.
Income tax expense ($27,200 − $21,800) ÷ $21,800 = 24.77%

Solution to Requirement b

2008: $147,500 ÷ $385,000 = 38.31%
2009: $155,000 ÷ $400,000 = 38.75%
Inventory is slightly larger relative to total assets in 2009.

Solution to Requirement c

		2009	2008
1.	$\frac{\text{Net income}}{\text{Net sales}}$	$\frac{\$40,800}{\$315,000} = 12.95\%$	$\frac{\$32,700}{\$259,000} = 12.63\%$
2.	$\frac{\text{Net income}}{\text{Average total assets}}$	$\frac{\$40,800}{\$392,500} = 10.39\%$	$\frac{\$32,700}{\$385,000} = 8.49\%$
3.	$\frac{\text{Net income}}{\text{Average total stockholders' equity}}$	$\frac{\$40,800}{\$198,000} = 20.61\%$	$\frac{\$32,700}{\$181,000} = 18.07\%$
4.	$\frac{\text{Net income}}{\text{Average common shares outstanding}}$	$\frac{\$40,800}{50,000} = \$0.816$	$\frac{\$32,700}{50,000} = \$0.654$
5.	$\frac{\text{Market price per share}}{\text{Earnings per share}}$	$\frac{\$12.04}{\$0.816} = 14.75$ times	$\frac{\$8.86}{\$0.654} = 13.55$ times
6.	$\frac{\text{Stockholders' equity} - \text{Preferred rights}}{\text{Outstanding common shares}}$	$\frac{\$215,000}{50,000} = \$4.30$	$\frac{\$181,000}{50,000} = \$3.62$
7.	$\frac{\text{Net income} + \text{Taxes} + \text{Interest expense}}{\text{Interest expense}}$	$\frac{\$40,800 + \$27,200 + \$4,000}{\$4,000} = 18$ times	$\frac{\$32,700 + \$21,800 + \$4,500}{\$4,500} = 13.1$ times
8.	Current assets − Current liabilities	\$212,500 − \$85,000 = \$127,500	\$208,000 − \$104,000 = \$104,000
9.	$\frac{\text{Current assets}}{\text{Current liabilities}}$	$\frac{\$212,500}{\$85,000} = 2.5:1$	$\frac{\$208,000}{\$104,000} = 2:1$
10.	$\frac{\text{Quick assets}}{\text{Current liabilities}}$	$\frac{\$57,500}{\$85,000} = 0.68:1$	$\frac{\$60,500}{\$104,000} = 0.58:1$
11.	$\frac{\text{Net credit sales}}{\text{Average net accounts receivable}}$	$\frac{\$315,000}{\$50,000} = 6.3$ times	$\frac{\$259,000}{\$49,000} = 5.29$ times
12.	$\frac{\text{Cost of goods sold}}{\text{Average inventory}}$	$\frac{\$189,000}{\$151,250} = 1.25$ times	$\frac{\$154,000}{\$147,500} = 1.04$ times
13.	$\frac{\text{Total liabilities}}{\text{Total stockholders' equity}}$	$\frac{\$185,000}{\$215,000} = 86.05\%$	$\frac{\$204,000}{\$181,000} = 112.71\%$

KEY TERMS

Absolute amounts *533*
Accounts receivable turnover *538*
Acid-test ratio *538*
Asset turnover ratio *543*
Average days to collect receivables *539*
Average days to sell inventory *540*
Book value per share *545*
Current ratio *537*
Dividend yield *546*
Earnings per share *545*
Horizontal analysis *533*
Information overload *532*
Inventory turnover *539*
Liquidity ratios *537*
Materiality *533*
Net margin *542*
Percentage analysis *534*
Price-earnings ratio *546*
Profitability ratios *547*
Quick ratio *538*
Ratio analysis *536*
Return on equity *544*
Return on investment *544*
Solvency ratios *540*
Trend analysis *533*
Vertical analysis *535*
Working capital *537*
Working capital ratio *537*

QUESTIONS

1. Why are ratios and trends used in financial analysis?
2. What do the terms *liquidity* and *solvency* mean?
3. What is apparent from a horizontal presentation of financial statement information? A vertical presentation?
4. What is the significance of inventory turnover, and how is it calculated?
5. What is the difference between the current ratio and the quick ratio? What does each measure?
6. Why are absolute amounts of limited use when comparing companies?
7. What is the difference between return on investment and return on equity?
8. Which ratios are used to measure long-term debt-paying ability? How is each calculated?
9. What are some limitations of the earnings per share figure?
10. What is the formula for calculating return on investment (ROI)?

11. What is information overload?
12. What is the price-earnings ratio? Explain the difference between it and the dividend yield.
13. What environmental factors must be considered in analyzing companies?
14. How do accounting principles affect financial statement analysis?

EXERCISES—SERIES A

All Exercises in Series A are available with McGraw-Hill's Homework Manager.

EXERCISE 13–1A *Inventory Turnover* L.O. 4

Selected financial information for Wingo Company for 2007 follows.

Sales	$120,000
Cost of Goods Sold	88,000
Merchandise Inventory	
Beginning of Year	10,000
End of Year	24,000

Required
Assuming that the merchandise inventory buildup was relatively constant, how many times did the merchandise inventory turn over during 2007?

EXERCISE 13–2A *Number of Times Interest Earned* L.O. 5

The following data come from the financial records of Cowser Corporation for 2005.

Sales	$135,000
Interest Expense	4,500
Income Tax Expense	22,500
Net Income	30,000

Required
How many times was interest earned in 2005?

EXERCISE 13–3A *Current Ratio* L.O. 4

Moran Corporation wrote off a $1,000 uncollectible account receivable against the $8,500 balance in its allowance account.

Required
Explain the effect of the write-off on Moran's current ratio.

EXERCISE 13–4A *Working Capital and Current Ratio* L.O. 4

On June 30, 2006, Victor Company's total current assets were $160,000 and its total current liabilities were $100,000. On July 1, 2006, Victor issued a short-term note to a bank for $25,000 cash.

Required
a. Compute Victor's working capital before and after issuing the note.
b. Compute Victor's current ratio before and after issuing the note.

EXERCISE 13–5A *Working Capital and Current Ratio* L.O. 4

On June 30, 2006, Victor Company's total current assets were $160,000 and its total current liabilities were $100,000. On July 1, 2006, Victor issued a long-term note to a bank for $25,000 cash.

Required
a. Compute Victor's working capital before and after issuing the note.
b. Compute Victor's current ratio before and after issuing the note.

L.O. 2

EXERCISE 13–6A *Horizontal Analysis*

Fredrick Corporation reported the following operating results for two consecutive years.

	2005	2004	Percentage Change
Sales	$1,250,000	$1,000,000	
Cost of Goods Sold	750,000	600,000	
Gross Margin	500,000	$ 400,000	
Operating Expenses	300,000	200,000	
Income before Taxes	200,000	$ 200,000	
Income Taxes	61,000	53,000	
Net Income	$ 139,000	$ 147,000	

Required

a. Compute the percentage changes in Fredrick Corporation's income statement components between the two years.

b. Comment on apparent trends revealed by the percentage changes computed in Requirement *a*.

L.O. 2

EXERCISE 13–7A *Vertical Analysis*

Sanchez Company reported the following operating results for two consecutive years.

2004	Amount	Percent of Sales
Sales	$500,000	
Cost of Goods Sold	320,000	
Gross Margin on Sales	180,000	
Operating Expenses	100,000	
Income before Taxes	80,000	
Income Taxes	24,000	
Net Income	$ 56,000	
2005	**Amount**	**Percent of Sales**
Sales	$480,000	
Cost of Goods Sold	307,000	
Gross Margin on Sales	173,000	
Operating Expenses	120,000	
Income before Taxes	53,000	
Income Taxes	16,000	
Net Income	$ 37,000	

Required

Express each income statement component for each of the two years as a percent of sales.

L.O. 2

EXERCISE 13–8A *Ratio Analysis*

The balance sheet for Embry Corporation follows.

Current Assets	$ 750,000
Long-Term Assets (net)	4,250,000
Total Assets	$5,000,000
Current Liabilities	$ 420,000
Long-Term Liabilities	2,460,000
Total Liabilities	2,880,000
Common Stock and Retained Earnings	2,120,000
Total Liabilities and Stockholders' Equity	$5,000,000

Required
Compute the following.

Working capital	______
Current ratio	______
Debt to assets ratio	______
Debt to equity ratio	______

EXERCISE 13–9A *Ratio Analysis*

L.O. 7

During 2006, Ethridge Corporation reported after-tax net income of $3,600,000. During the year, the number of shares of stock outstanding remained constant at 10,000 of $100 par, 9 percent preferred stock and 400,000 shares of common stock. The company's total stockholders' equity is $20,000,000 at December 31, 2006. Ethridge Corporation's common stock was selling at $52 per share at the end of its fiscal year. All dividends for the year have been paid, including $4.80 per share to common stockholders.

Required
Compute the following:

a. Earnings per share
b. Book value per share of common stock
c. Price-earnings ratio
d. Dividend yield

EXERCISE 13–10A *Ratio Analysis*

L.O. 2, 3, 4, 5, 6, 7

Required
Match each of the following ratios with the formula used to compute it.

______	**1.** Working capital	**a.** Net income ÷ Average total stockholders' equity
______	**2.** Current ratio	**b.** Cost of goods sold ÷ Average inventory
______	**3.** Quick ratio	**c.** Current assets − Current liabilities
______	**4.** Accounts receivable turnover	**d.** 365 ÷ Inventory turnover
______	**5.** Average days to collect	**e.** Net income ÷ Average total assets
______	**6.** Inventory turnover	**f.** (Net income − Preferred dividends) ÷ Average outstanding common shares
______	**7.** Average days to sell inventory	**g.** (Current assets − Inventory − Prepaid expenses) ÷ Current liabilities
______	**8.** Debt to assets ratio	**h.** Total liabilities ÷ Total equity
______	**9.** Debt to equity ratio	**i.** 365 ÷ Accounts receivable turnover
______	**10.** Return on investment	**j.** Total liabilities ÷ Total stockholders' equity
______	**11.** Return on equity	**k.** Net credit sales ÷ Average net receivables
______	**12.** Earnings per share	**l.** Current assets ÷ Current liabilities

EXERCISE 13–11A *Horizontal and Vertical Analysis*

L.O. 2

Income statements for Shirley Company for 2005 and 2006 follow.

	2006	2005
Sales	$240,000	$200,000
Cost of Goods Sold	147,900	108,000
Selling Expenses	40,100	22,000
Administrative Expenses	24,000	28,000
Interest Expense	6,000	12,000
Total Expenses	218,000	170,000
Income before Taxes	22,000	30,000
Income Taxes Expense	6,000	8,000
Net Income	$ 16,000	$ 22,000

Required

a. Perform a horizontal analysis, showing the percentage change in each income statement component between 2005 and 2006.

b. Perform a vertical analysis, showing each income statement component as a percent of sales for each year.

L.O. 2, 3, 4, 5, 6, 7

EXERCISE 13–12A *Ratio Analysis*

Compute the specified ratios using Kale Company's balance sheet for 2004.

Assets	
Cash	$ 15,000
Marketable Securities	8,000
Accounts Receivable	13,000
Inventory	11,000
Property and Equipment	170,000
Accumulated Depreciation	(12,500)
Total Assets	$204,500
Equities	
Accounts Payable	$ 8,500
Current Notes Payable	3,500
Mortgage Payable	4,500
Bonds Payable	21,500
Common Stock, $50 Par	110,000
Paid-In Capital in Excess of Par	4,000
Retained Earnings	52,500
Total Liabilities and Stockholders' Equity	$204,500

The average number of common stock shares outstanding during 2004 was 880 shares. Net income for the year was $15,000.

Required

Compute each of the following:

a. Current ratio.
b. Earnings per share.
c. Quick (acid-test) ratio.
d. Return on investment.
e. Return on equity.
f. Debt to equity ratio.

L.O. 4, 5, 6, 7

EXERCISE 13–13A *Comprehensive Analysis*

Required

Indicate the effect of each of the following transactions on (1) the current ratio, (2) working capital, (3) stockholders' equity, (4) book value per share of common stock, (5) retained earnings.

a. Collected account receivable.
b. Wrote off account receivable.
c. Purchased treasury stock.
d. Purchased inventory on account.
e. Declared cash dividend.
f. Sold merchandise on account at a profit.
g. Issued stock dividend.
h. Paid account payable.
i. Sold building at a loss.

L.O. 4, 7

EXERCISE 13–14A *Accounts Receivable Turnover, Inventory Turnover, and Net Margin*

Selected data from Walker Company follow.

Balance Sheet As of December 31		
	2004	2003
Accounts Receivable	$400,000	$376,000
Allowance for Doubtful Accounts	(20,000)	(16,000)
Net Accounts Receivable	$380,000	$360,000
Inventories, Lower of Cost or Market	$480,000	$440,000

Income Statement For the Year Ended December 31		
	2004	2003
Net Credit Sales	$2,000,000	$1,760,000
Net Cash Sales	400,000	320,000
Net Sales	2,400,000	2,080,000
Cost of Goods Sold	1,600,000	1,440,000
Selling, General, & Administrative Expenses	240,000	216,000
Other Expenses	40,000	24,000
Total Operating Expenses	$1,880,000	$1,680,000

Required

Compute the following.

a. The accounts receivable turnover for 2004.
b. The inventory turnover for 2004.
c. The net margin for 2003.

EXERCISE 13–15A *Comprehensive Analysis* L.O. 4, 5

The December 31, 2005, balance sheet for Ivey, Inc., is presented here. These are the only accounts on Ivey's balance sheet. Amounts indicated by question marks (?) can be calculated using the following additional information.

Assets	
Cash	$ 25,000
Accounts Receivable (net)	?
Inventory	?
Property, Plant, and Equipment (net)	294,000
	$432,000
Liabilities and Stockholders' Equity	
Accounts Payable (trade)	$?
Income Taxes Payable (current)	25,000
Long-Term Debt	?
Common Stock	300,000
Retained Earnings	?
	$?
Additional Information	
Current Ratio (at year end)	1.5 to 1.0
Total Liabilities ÷ Total Stockholders' Equity	0.8
Gross Margin Percent	30%
Inventory Turnover (Cost of Goods Sold ÷ Ending Inventory)	10.5 times
Gross Margin for 2002	$315,000

Required
Determine the following.

a. The balance in trade accounts payable as of December 31, 2005.
b. The balance in retained earnings as of December 31, 2005.
c. The balance in the inventory account as of December 31, 2005.

PROBLEMS—SERIES A

All Problems in Series A are available with McGraw-Hill's Homework Manager.

L.O. 2

PROBLEM 13–16A *Vertical Analysis*

CHECK FIGURES
NI of 2006: $36,000
Total Expenses of 2005: $135,000

The following percentages apply to Walden Company for 2005 and 2006.

	2006	2005
Sales	100.0%	100.0%
Cost of Goods Sold	61.0	64.0
Gross Margin	39.0	36.0
Selling and Administrative Expense	26.5	20.5
Interest Expense	2.5	2.0
Total Expenses	29.0	22.5
Income before Taxes	10.0	13.5
Income Tax Expense	5.5	7.0
Net Income	4.5%	6.5%

Required
Assuming that sales were $600,000 in 2005 and $800,000 in 2006, prepare income statements for the two years.

L.O. 5, 6, 7

PROBLEM 13–17A *Ratio Analysis*

excel
www.mhhe.com/edmonds3e

CHECK FIGURES
a. 2004: 12.22 times
e. 2003: 8.5 times

Oxmoore Company's income statement information follows.

	2004	2003
Net Sales	$420,000	$260,000
Income before Interest and Taxes	110,000	85,000
Net Income after Taxes	55,500	63,000
Interest Expense	9,000	8,000
Stockholders' Equity, December 31 (2002: $200,000)	305,000	235,000
Common Stock, par $50, December 31	260,000	230,000

The average number of shares outstanding was 7,800 for 2004 and 6,900 for 2003.

Required
Compute the following ratios for Oxmoore for 2004 and 2003.

a. Number of times interest was earned.
b. Earnings per share based on the average number of shares outstanding.
c. Price-earnings ratio (market prices: 2004, $64 per share; 2003, $78 per share).
d. Return on average equity.
e. Net margin.

L.O. 4

PROBLEM 13–18A *Effect of Transactions on Current Ratio and Working Capital*

Bellaire Manufacturing has a current ratio of 3:1 on December 31, 2003. Indicate whether each of the following transactions would increase (+), decrease (−), or not affect (NA) Bellaire's current ratio and its working capital.

Required

a. Paid cash for a trademark.
b. Wrote off an uncollectible account receivable.
c. Sold equipment for cash.
d. Sold merchandise at a profit (cash).
e. Declared a cash dividend.
f. Purchased inventory on account.
g. Scrapped a fully depreciated machine (no gain or loss).
h. Issued a stock dividend.
i. Purchased a machine with a long-term note.
j. Paid a previously declared cash dividend.
k. Collected accounts receivable.
l. Invested in current marketable securities.

PROBLEM 13–19A *Ratio Analysis*

L.O. 7

Selected data for Faulkner Company for 2005 and additional information on industry averages follow.

CHECK FIGURE
a. Earning per share: $4.38

Earnings (net income)		$ 174,000
Preferred Stock (19,800 shares at $50 par, 4%)		$ 660,000
Common Stock (45,000 shares at $1 par, market value $56)		30,000
Paid-in Capital in Excess of Par—Common		480,000
Retained Earnings		562,500
		1,732,500
Less: Treasury Stock		
Preferred (1,800 shares)	$54,000	
Common (1,800 shares)	24,000	78,000
Total Stockholders' Equity		$1,654,500

Note: Dividends in arrears on preferred stock: $24,000. The preferred stock can be called for $51 per share.

Industry averages	
Earnings per share	$ 5.20
Price-earnings ratio	9.50
Return on equity	11.20%

Required

a. Calculate and compare Faulkner Company's ratios with the industry averages.
b. Discuss factors you would consider in deciding whether to invest in the company.

PROBLEM 13–20A *Supply Missing Balance Sheet Numbers*

L.O. 2

The bookkeeper for Clifford's Country Music Bar went insane and left this incomplete balance sheet. Clifford's working capital is $90,000 and its debt to assets ratio is 40 percent.

CHECK FIGURES
d: $337,500
f: $97,500

Assets	
Current Assets	
Cash	$ 21,000
Accounts Receivable	42,000
Inventory	(A)
Prepaid Expenses	9,000
Total Current Assets	(B)
Long-Term Assets	
Building	(C)
Less: Accumulated Depreciation	(39,000)
Total Long-Term Assets	210,000
Total Assets	$ (D)

Equities	
Liabilities	
Current Liabilities	
Accounts Payable	$ (E)
Notes Payable	12,000
Income Tax Payable	10,500
Total Current Liabilities	37,500
Long-Term Liabilities	
Mortgage Payable	(F)
Total Liabilities	(G)
Stockholders' Equity	
Common Stock	105,000
Retained Earnings	(H)
Total Stockholders' Equity	(I)
Total Liabilities and Stockholders' Equity	$ (J)

Required

Complete the balance sheet by supplying the missing amounts.

L.O. 2, 3, 4, 5, 6, 7

eXcel

www.mhhe.com/edmonds3e

CHECK FIGURES

d. 2005: $0.72

k. 2004: 5.47 times

PROBLEM 13–21A *Ratio Analysis*

The following financial statements apply to Maronge Company.

	2005	2004
Revenues		
Net Sales	$210,000	$175,000
Other Revenues	4,000	5,000
Total Revenues	214,000	180,000
Expenses		
Cost of Goods Sold	126,000	103,500
Selling Expenses	21,000	19,000
General and Administrative Expenses	11,000	10,000
Interest Expense	3,000	3,000
Income Tax Expense (40%)	21,000	18,000
Total Expenses	182,000	153,500
Earnings from Continuing Operations before Extraordinary Items	32,000	27,000
Extraordinary Gain (net of $3,000 tax)	4,000	0
Net Earnings	$ 36,000	$ 27,000
Assets		
Current Assets		
Cash	$ 4,000	$ 8,000
Marketable Securities	1,000	1,000
Accounts Receivable	35,000	32,000
Inventories	100,000	96,000
Prepaid Expenses	3,000	2,000
Total Current Assets	143,000	139,000
Plant and Equipment (net)	105,000	105,000
Intangibles	20,000	0
Total Assets	$268,000	$244,000
Equities		
Liabilities		
Current Liabilities		
Accounts Payable	$ 40,000	$ 54,000
Other	17,000	15,000
Total Current Liabilities	57,000	69,000
Bonds Payable	66,000	67,000
Total Liabilities	123,000	136,000
Stockholders' Equity		
Common Stock ($2 par)	100,000	100,000
Paid-In Capital in Excess of Par	15,000	15,000
Retained Earnings	30,000	(7,000)
Total Stockholders' Equity	145,000	108,000
Total Liabilities and Stockholders' Equity	$268,000	$244,000

Required

Calculate the following ratios for 2004 and 2005. When data limitations prohibit computing averages, use year-end balances in your calculations.

a. Net margin
b. Return on investment
c. Return on equity
d. Earnings per share
e. Price-earnings ratio (market prices at the end of 2004 and 2005 were $5.94 and $4.77, respectively)
f. Book value per share of common stock
g. Times interest earned
h. Working capital
i. Current ratio
j. Quick (acid-test) ratio
k. Accounts receivable turnover
l. Inventory turnover
m. Debt to equity ratio
n. Debt to assets ratio

PROBLEM 13–22A *Horizontal Analysis*

L.O. 2

CHECK FIGURES
Total Assets: +11.6%
Total Liabilities: +14.4%

Financial statements for Pocca Company follow.

POCCA COMPANY
Balance Sheets
As of December 31

	2006	2005
Assets		
Current Assets		
Cash	$ 16,000	$ 12,000
Marketable Securities	20,000	6,000
Accounts Receivable (net)	54,000	46,000
Inventories	135,000	143,000
Prepaid Items	25,000	10,000
Total Current Assets	250,000	217,000
Investments	27,000	20,000
Plant (net)	270,000	255,000
Land	29,000	24,000
Total Assets	$576,000	$516,000
Equities		
Liabilities		
Current Liabilities		
Notes Payable	$ 17,000	$ 6,000
Accounts Payable	113,800	100,000
Salaries Payable	21,000	15,000
Total Current Liabilities	151,800	121,000
Noncurrent Liabilities		
Bonds Payable	100,000	100,000
Other	32,000	27,000
Total Noncurrent Liabilities	132,000	127,000
Total Liabilities	283,800	248,000
Stockholders' Equity		
Preferred Stock, (par value $10, 4% cumulative, non-participating; 7,000 shares authorized and issued no dividends in arrears)	70,000	70,000
Common Stock ($5 par; 50,000 shares authorized; 10,000 shares issued)	50,000	50,000
Paid-In Capital in excess of par—Preferred	10,000	10,000
Paid-In Capital in excess of par—Common	30,000	30,000
Retained Earnings	132,200	108,000
Total Stockholders' Equity	292,200	268,000
Total Liabilities and Stockholders' Equity	$576,000	$516,000

POCCA COMPANY Statements of Income and Retained Earnings For the Years Ended December 31	2006	2005
Revenues		
Sales (net)	$230,000	$210,000
Other Revenues	8,000	5,000
Total Revenues	238,000	215,000
Expenses		
Cost of Goods Sold	120,000	103,000
Selling, General, and Administrative	55,000	50,000
Interest Expense	8,000	7,200
Income Tax Expense (40%)	23,000	22,000
Total Expenses	206,000	182,200
Net Earnings (Net Income)	32,000	32,800
Retained Earnings, January 1	108,000	83,000
Less: Preferred Stock Dividends	2,800	2,800
Common Stock Dividends	5,000	5,000
Retained Earnings, December 31	$132,200	$108,000

Required

Prepare a horizontal analysis of both the balance sheet and income statement.

L.O. 2, 3, 4, 5, 6, 7

www.mhhe.com/edmonds3e

CHECK FIGURES
k. 2006: 2.05:1
p. 2005: $3.00

PROBLEM 13–23A *Ratio Analysis*

Required

Use the financial statements for Pocca Company from Problem 13–22A to calculate the following ratios for 2006 and 2005.

a. Working capital
b. Current ratio
c. Quick ratio
d. Receivables turnover (beginning receivables at January 1, 2005, were $47,000.)
e. Average days to collect accounts receivable
f. Inventory turnover (beginning inventory at January 1, 2005, was $140,000.)
g. Number of days to sell inventory
h. Debt to assets ratio
i. Debt to equity ratio
j. Number of times interest was earned
k. Plant assets to long-term debt
l. Net margin
m. Turnover of assets
n. Return on investment
o. Return on equity
p. Earnings per share
q. Book value per share of common stock
r. Price-earnings ratio (market price per share: 2005, $11.75; 2006, $12.50)
s. Dividend yield on common stock

L.O. 2

www.mhhe.com/edmonds3e

CHECK FIGURE
2006 Retained Earings: 23%

PROBLEM 13–24A *Vertical Analysis*

Required

Use the financial statements for Pocca Company from Problem 13–22A to perform a vertical analysis of both the balance sheets and income statements for 2006 and 2005.

EXERCISES—SERIES B

L.O. 4

EXERCISE 13–1B *Inventory Turnover*

Selected financial information for Hyman Company for 2006 follows.

Sales	$1,100,000
Cost of Goods Sold	960,000
Merchandise Inventory	
Beginning of Year	136,000
End of Year	248,000

Required
Assuming that the merchandise inventory buildup was relatively constant, how many times did the merchandise inventory turn over during 2006?

EXERCISE 13–2B *Number of Times Interest Earned*

L.O. 5

The following data come from the financial records of the Hickel Corporation for 2005.

Sales	$2,000,000
Interest Expense	100,000
Income Tax	280,000
Net Income	520,000

Required
How many times was interest earned in 2005?

EXERCISE 13–3B *Current Ratio*

L.O. 4

Jeter Corporation purchased $200 of merchandise on account.

Required
Explain the effect of the purchase on Jeter's current ratio.

EXERCISE 13–4B *Working Capital and Current Ratio*

L.O. 4

On October 31, 2006, Morey Company's total current assets were $50,000 and its total current liabilities were $20,000. On November 1, 2006, Morey purchased marketable securities for $10,000 cash.

Required
a. Compute Morey's working capital before and after the securities purchase.
b. Compute Morey's current ratio before and after the securities purchase.

EXERCISE 13–5B *Working Capital and Current Ratio*

L.O. 4

On October 31, 2006, Morey Company's total current assets were $50,000 and its total current liabilities were $20,000. On November 1, 2006, Morey bought manufacturing equipment for $10,000 cash.

Required
a. Compute Morey's working capital before and after the equipment purchase.
b. Compute Morey's current ratio before and after the equipment purchase.

EXERCISE 13–6B *Horizontal Analysis*

L.O. 2

Kawai Corporation reported the following operating results for two consecutive years.

	2006	2005	Percentage Change
Sales	$440,000	$400,000	
Cost of Goods Sold	264,000	254,000	
Gross Margin	176,000	146,000	
Operating Expenses	75,000	65,000	
Income before Taxes	101,000	81,000	
Income Taxes	45,000	31,600	
Net Income	$ 56,000	$ 49,400	

Required

a. Compute the percentage changes in Kawai Corporation's income statement components for the two years.
b. Comment on apparent trends revealed by the percentage changes computed in Requirement *a.*

L.O. 2 **EXERCISE 13–7B** ***Vertical Analysis***

Julius Company reported the following operating results for two consecutive years.

2003	Amount	Percentage of Sales
Sales	$100,000	
Cost of Goods Sold	64,000	
Gross Margin	36,000	
Operating Expenses	19,000	
Income before Taxes	17,000	
Income Taxes	5,400	
Net Income	$ 11,600	

2004	Amount	Percentage of Sales
Sales	$128,000	
Cost of Goods Sold	81,600	
Gross Margin	46,400	
Operating Expenses	23,000	
Income before Taxes	23,400	
Income Taxes	6,200	
Net Income	$ 17,200	

Required
Express each income statement component for each of the two years as a percentage of sales.

L.O. 2 **EXERCISE 13–8B** ***Ratio Analysis***

Balance sheet data for the Mathis Corporation follows.

Current Assets	$ 20,000
Long-Term Assets (Net)	140,000
Total Assets	$160,000
Current Liabilities	$ 15,000
Long-Term Liabilities	45,000
Total Liabilities	60,000
Common Stock and Retained Earnings	100,000
Total Liabilities and Stockholders' Equity	$160,000

Required
Compute the following:

a. Working capital
b. Current ratio
c. Liabilities to total assets
d. Debt to assets ratio
e. Debt to equity ratio

L.O. 7 **EXERCISE 13–9B** ***Ratio Analysis***

During 2004, Santini Corporation reported net income after taxes of $192,000. During the year, the number of shares of stock outstanding remained constant at 20,000 shares of $20 par 8 percent preferred stock and 200,000 shares of common stock. The company's total equities at December 31, 2004, were $700,000, which included $128,000 of liabilities. The common stock was selling for $8 per share at the end of the year. All dividends for the year were declared and paid, including $0.72 per share to common stockholders.

Required

Compute the following.

a. Earnings per share
b. Book value per share
c. Price-Earnings ratio
d. Dividend yield

EXERCISE 13–10B *Ratio Analysis*

L.O. 2, 3, 4, 5, 6, 7

Match each of the following ratios with its formula.

______	**1.** Price-Earnings ratio	**a.** Total liabilities ÷ Total stockholders' equity
______	**2.** Dividend yield	**b.** Current assets ÷ Current liabilities
______	**3.** Book value per share	**c.** 365 ÷ Accounts receivable turnover
______	**4.** Plant assets to long-term liabilities	**d.** (Net income − Preferred dividends) ÷ Average outstanding common shares
______	**5.** Times interest is earned	**e.** (Stockholders' equity − Preferred rights) ÷ Outstanding common shares
______	**6.** Earnings per share	**f.** 365 ÷ Inventory turnover
______	**7.** Net margin	**g.** Dividends per share ÷ Market price per share
______	**8.** Debt to equity ratio	**h.** Net plant assets ÷ Long-term liabilities
______	**9.** Current ratio	**i.** Market price per share ÷ Earnings per share
______	**10.** Turnover of assets	**j.** Net income ÷ Net sales
______	**11.** Days to collect A/R	**k.** Net sales ÷ Average total assets
______	**12.** Number of days to sell inventory	**l.** Income before taxes and interest expense ÷ Interest expense

EXERCISE 13–11B *Horizontal and Vertical Analysis*

L.O. 2

Tewalt Company reported the following operating results for 2005 and 2006.

	2006	2005
Sales	$480,000	$432,000
Cost of Goods Sold	252,000	228,000
Selling Expenses	30,000	24,000
Administrative Expenses	54,000	50,000
Interest Expense	8,000	10,000
Total Expenses	344,000	312,000
Income before Taxes	136,000	120,000
Income Taxes Expense	28,000	24,000
Net Income	$108,000	$ 96,000

Required

a. Perform a horizontal analysis, showing the percentage change in each income statement component between 2005 and 2006.

b. Perform a vertical analysis, showing each income statement component as a percent of sales for each year.

EXERCISE 13–12B *Ratio Analysis*

L.O. 2, 3, 4, 5, 6, 7

Compute the specified ratios using the following December 31, 2006, statement of financial position for Clay Company.

Assets	
Cash	$ 32,000
Marketable Securities	9,000
Accounts Receivable	72,800
Inventory	112,200
Property and Equipment	150,000
Accumulated Depreciation	(24,000)
Total Assets	$352,000

Equities	
Accounts Payable	$ 39,200
Current Notes Payable	6,800
Mortgage Payable	62,000
Bonds Payable	42,000
Common Stock	128,000
Retained Earnings	74,000
Total Liabilities and Stockholders' Equity	$352,000

The average number of common shares outstanding during 2006 was 1,500. Net earnings for the year were $48,000.

Required

Compute each of the following:

a. Current ratio
b. Earnings per share
c. Acid-test ratio
d. Return on investment
e. Return on equity
f. Debt to equity ratio

L.O. 4, 5, 6, 7

EXERCISE 13–13B *Comprehensive Analysis*

The following is a list of transactions.

a. Paid cash for short-term marketable securities.
b. Purchased a computer, issuing a short-term note for the purchase price.
c. Purchased factory equipment, issuing a long-term note for the purchase price.
d. Sold merchandise on account at a profit.
e. Paid cash on accounts payable.
f. Received cash from issuing common stock.
g. Sold a factory for cash at a profit.
h. Purchased raw materials on account.
i. Paid cash for property taxes on administrative buildings.

Required

Indicate the effect of each of the preceding transactions on (a) the quick ratio, (b) working capital, (c) stockholders' equity, (d) the debt/equity ratio, (e) retained earnings.

L.O. 4, 7

EXERCISE 13–14B *Accounts Receivable Turnover, Inventory Turnover, and Net Margin*

Selected data from Gilman Company follow.

Balance Sheet Data As of December 31	2004	2003
Accounts Receivable	$640,000	$600,000
Allowance for Doubtful Accounts	(32,000)	(28,000)
Net Accounts Receivable	$608,000	$572,000
Inventories, Lower of Cost or Market	$400,000	$420,000

Income Statement Data Year Ended December 31	2004	2003
Net Credit Sales	$4,000,000	$3,000,000
Net Cash Sales	800,000	600,000
Net Sales	$4,800,000	$3,600,000

continued

Cost of Goods Sold	$2,800,000	$2,200,000
Selling, General, and Administrative Expenses	400,000	280,000
Other Expenses	200,000	160,000
Total Operating Expenses	$3,400,000	$2,640,000

Required

Compute the following.

a. The accounts receivable turnover for 2004.
b. The inventory turnover for 2004.
c. The net margin for 2003.

EXERCISE 13–15B *Comprehensive Analysis* — L.O. 4, 5

December 31, 2005, balance sheet data for Zabel Company follow. All accounts are represented. Amounts indicated by question marks (?) can be calculated using the following additional information.

Assets	
Cash	$ 30,000
Accounts Receivable (net)	?
Inventory	?
Property, Plant, and Equipment (net)	556,000
	$?
Liabilities and Stockholders' Equity	
Accounts Payable (trade)	$ 52,000
Income Taxes Payable (current)	28,000
Long-Term Debt	?
Common Stock	320,000
Retained Earnings	?
	$?
Additional Information	
Quick ratio (at year end)	1.3 to 1
Working Capital	$84,000
Inventory Turnover (Cost of goods sold ÷ Ending Inventory)	12 times
Debt/Equity Ratio	0.8
Gross Margin for 2005	$252,000

Required

Determine the following.

a. The balance in accounts receivable as of December 31, 2005.
b. The turnover of assets for 2005.
c. The balance of long-term debt as of December 31, 2005.
d. The balance in retained earnings as of December 31, 2005.

PROBLEMS—SERIES B

PROBLEM 13–16B *Vertical Analysis* — L.O. 2

Posey Corporation's controller has prepared the following vertical analysis for the president.

	2006	2005
Sales	100.0%	100.0%
Cost of Goods Sold	57.0	54.0
Gross Margin	43.0	46.0
Selling and Administrative Expense	18.0	20.0
Interest Expense	2.8	4.0
Total Expenses	20.8	24.0
Income before Taxes	22.2	22.0
Income Tax Expense	10.0	8.0
Net Income	12.2%	14.0%

Required
Sales were $400,000 in 2005 and $800,000 in 2006. Convert the analysis to income statements for the two years.

L.O. 5, 6, 7 PROBLEM 13–17B *Ratio Analysis*

Information from Gaut Company's financial statements follows.

	2004	2003
Net Sales	$1,440,000	$1,000,000
Income before Interest and Taxes	320,000	260,000
Net Income after Taxes	148,000	96,000
Bond Interest Expense	36,000	24,000
Stockholders' Equity, December 31 (2002: $480,000)	720,000	600,000
Common Stock, Par $24, December 31	420,000	360,000

Average number of shares outstanding was 16,000 for 2004 and 15,000 for 2003.

Required
Compute the following ratios for Gaut Company for 2004 and 2003.

a. Number of times interest was earned.
b. Earnings per share based on the average number of shares outstanding.
c. Price-earnings ratio (market prices: 2004, $60 per share; 2003, $48 per share).
d. Return on average equity.
e. Net margin.

L.O. 4 PROBLEM 13–18B *Effect of Transactions on Current Ratio and Working Capital*

Moreno Company has a current ratio of 2:1 on June 30, 2006. Indicate whether each of the following transactions would increase (+), decrease (−), or not affect (NA) Moreno's current ratio and its working capital.

Required
a. Issued 10-year bonds for $100,000 cash.
b. Paid cash to settle an account payable.
c. Sold merchandise for more than cost.
d. Recognized depreciation on plant equipment.
e. Purchased a machine by issuing a long-term note payable.
f. Purchased merchandise inventory on account.
g. Received customer payment on accounts receivable.
h. Paid cash for federal income tax expense (assume that the expense has not been previously accrued).
i. Declared cash dividend payable in one month.
j. Received cash for interest on a long-term note receivable (assume that interest has not been previously accrued).
k. Received cash from issuing a short-term note payable.
l. Traded a truck for a sedan.

PROBLEM 13–19B *Ratio Analysis*

L.O. 7

Selected data for Taft Company for 2003 and additional information on industry averages follow.

Earnings (net income)		$ 168,000
Preferred Stock (20,000 shares at $28 par, 6%)		$ 560,000
Common Stock (40,500 shares at $8 par, market value $30.40)		324,000
Paid-in Capital in Excess of par—common		360,000
Retained Earnings		480,000
		1,724,000
Less: Treasury Stock		
Preferred (1,000 shares)	$28,800	
Common (500 shares)	12,800	41,600
Total Stockholders' Equity		$1,682,400

Note: Dividends in arrears on preferred stock: $31,920. The preferred stock can be called for $36.80 per share.

Industry averages	
Earnings per share	$2.00
Price-earnings ratio	8.00
Return on equity	7.30%

Required

a. Calculate and compare Taft Company's ratios with the industry averages.

b. Discuss factors you would consider in deciding whether to invest in the company.

PROBLEM 13–20B *Supply Missing Balance Sheet Numbers*

L.O. 2

Agnes Hale discovered a piece of wet and partially burned balance sheet after her office was destroyed by fire. She could recall a current ratio of 1.75 and a debt to assets ratio of 45 percent.

Assets	
Current Assets	
Cash	$ 37,500
Accounts Receivable	(A)
Inventory	63,000
Prepaid Expenses	13,500
Total Current Assets	(B)
Long-Term Assets	
Building	(C)
Less: Accumulated Depreciation	(45,000)
Total Long-Term Assets	270,000
Total Assets	$ (D)
Liabilities and Stockholders' Equity	
Liabilities	
Current Liabilities	
Accounts Payable	$ 63,000
Notes Payable	(E)
Income Tax Payable	27,000
Total Current Liabilities	120,000
Long-Term Liabilities	
Bonds Payable	67,500
Mortgage Payable	(F)
Total Liabilities	(G)
Stockholders' Equity	
Common Stock	135,000
Retained Earnings	(H)
Total Stockholders' Equity	(I)
Total Liabilities and Stockholders' Equity	$ (J)

Required

Complete the balance sheet by supplying the missing amounts.

L.O. 2, 3, 4, 5, 6, 7 **PROBLEM 13–21B** *Ratio Analysis*

The following financial statements apply to Wells Appliances, Inc.

WELLS APPLIANCES, INC.
Balance Sheets
As of December 31

	2006	2005
Assets		
Current Assets		
Cash	$118,000	$ 91,000
Marketable Securities	24,000	18,000
Accounts Receivable (net)	112,000	108,000
Inventories	180,000	192,000
Prepaid Expenses	27,000	14,000
Total Current Assets	461,000	423,000
Investments	120,000	120,000
Plant (net)	260,000	254,000
Other	80,000	74,000
Total Assets	$921,000	$871.000
Equities		
Liabilities		
Current Liabilities		
Notes Payable	$ 20,000	$ 15,000
Accounts Payable	80,000	38,000
Other	66,000	9,000
Total Current Liabilities	166,000	62,000
Noncurrent Liabilities		
Bonds Payable	110,000	210,000
Other	26,000	12,000
Total Noncurrent Liabilities	136,000	222,000
Total Liabilities	302,000	284,000
Stockholders' Equity		
Preferred Stock ($100 par, 4% cumulative, non-participating; $100 liquidating value; 1,000 shares authorized and issued; no dividends in arrears)	100,000	100,000
Common Stock ($10 par; 50,000 shares authorized; 12,000 shares issued)	120,000	120,000
Paid-In Capital in excess of par—Preferred	36,000	36,000
Paid-In Capital in excess of par—Common	120,000	120,000
Retained Earnings	243,000	211,000
Total Stockholders' Equity	619,000	587,000
Total Liabilities and Stockholders' Equity	$921,000	$871,000

WELLS APPLIANCES, INC.
Statements of Income and Retained Earnings
For the Years Ended December 31

	2006	2005
Revenues		
Sales (net)	$240,000	$230,000
Other Revenues	7,000	4,000
Total Revenues	247,000	234,000
Expenses		
Cost of Goods Sold	143,000	130,000
Selling, General, and Administrative	46,000	57,000
Bond Interest Expense	7,000	10,000
Income Tax Expense (40%)	8,000	14,000
Total Expenses	204,000	211,000
Net Earnings (net income)	43,000	23,000
Retained Earnings, January 1	210,000	198,000
Less: Preferred Stock Dividends	4,000	4,000
Common Stock Dividends	6,000	6,000
Retained Earnings, December 31	$243,000	$211,000

Required

Calculate the following ratios for 2006.

a. Working capital
b. Current ratio
c. Quick ratio
d. Accounts receivable turnover
e. Average days to collect accounts receivable
f. Inventory turnover
g. Avg. days to sell inventory
h. Debt to assets ratio
i. Debt to equity ratio
j. Times interest was earned
k. Plant assets to long-term debt
l. Net margin
m. Turnover of assets
n. Return on investment
o. Return on equity
p. Earnings per share
q. Book value
r. Price-earnings ratio (market price: $13.26)
s. Dividend yield on common stock

PROBLEM 13–22B *Ratio Analysis*

L.O. 2, 3, 4, 5, 6, 7

excel

www.mhhe.com/edmonds3e

Galin Company's stock is quoted at $16 per share at December 31, 2006 and 2005. Galin's financial statements follow.

GALIN COMPANY
Balance Sheets
As of December 31
(In thousands)

	2006	2005
Assets		
Current Assets		
Cash	$ 3,000	$ 2,000
Marketable Securities at cost which approximates market	5,000	4,000
Accounts Receivable, net of allowance for doubtful accounts	47,000	44,000
Inventories, lower of cost or market	50,000	60,000
Prepaid Expenses	2,000	1,000
Total Current Assets	107,000	111,000
Property, Plant, and Equipment, net of accumulated depreciation	100,000	105,000
Investments	1,000	1,000
Long-Term Receivables	3,000	2,000
Goodwill and Patents, net of accumulated amortization	2,000	4,000
Other Assets	2,000	3,000
Total Assets	$215,000	$226,000
Liabilities and Stockholders' Equity		
Current Liabilities		
Notes Payable	$ 3,000	$ 5,000
Accounts Payable	12,000	16,000
Accrued Expenses	9,000	11,000
Income Taxes Payable	1,000	1,000
Payments Due within one year	3,000	2,000
Total Current Liabilities	28,000	35,000
Long-Term Debt	50,000	60,000
Deferred Income Taxes	30,000	27,000
Other Liabilities	5,000	4,000
Total Liabilities	113,000	126,000
Stockholders' Equity		
Common Stock, $1 par value; 10,000,000 shares authorized and 5,000,000 shares issued and outstanding	5,000	5,000
5% Cumulative Preferred Stock, par value $100 per share; $100 liquidating value; authorized 25,000 shares; issued and outstanding 20,000 shares	20,000	20,000
Additional Paid-In Capital, common	35,000	35,000
Retained Earnings	42,000	40,000
Total Stockholders' Equity	102,000	100,000
Total Liabilities and Stockholders' Equity	$215,000	$226,000

GALIN COMPANY Statements of Income and Retained Earnings For the Years Ended December 31 (in thousands)	2006	2005
Net Sales	$180,000	$150,000
Expenses		
Cost of Goods Sold	147,000	120,000
Selling, General, and Administrative Expenses	20,000	18,000
Other	2,000	2,000
Total Expenses	169,000	140,000
Income Before Income Taxes	11,000	10,000
Income Taxes	5,000	4,000
Net Income	6,000	6,000
Retained Earnings at Beginning of Period	40,000	38,000
Less: Dividends on Common Stock	3,000	3,000
Dividends on Preferred Stock	1,000	1,000
Retained Earnings at End of Period	$ 42,000	$ 40,000

Required

Based on the preceding information, compute the following for 2006 only.

a. Current ratio
b. Quick (acid-test) ratio
c. Average days to collect accounts receivable, assuming a business year consisting of 300 days and all sales on account
d. Inventory turnover
e. Book value per share of common stock
f. Earnings per share on common stock
g. Price-earnings ratio on common stock
h. Debt to assets ratio
i. Return on investment
j. Return on equity

L.O. 2 **PROBLEM 13–23B** ***Horizontal Analysis***

Required

Use the financial statements for Galin Company from Problem 13–22B to perform a horizontal analysis of both the balance sheet and income statement for 2006 and 2005.

L.O. 2 **PROBLEM 13–24B** ***Vertical Analysis***

Required

Use the financial statements for Galin Company from Problem 13–22B to perform a vertical analysis (based on total assets, total equities, and sales) of both the balance sheets and income statements for 2006 and 2005.

ANALYZE, THINK, COMMUNICATE

ATC 13–1 **BUSINESS APPLICATIONS CASE** ***Analyzing Best Buy Company and Circuit City Stores***

The following information relates to Best Buy and Circuit City Stores, Inc. for their 2003 and 2002 fiscal years.

BEST BUY CO., INC. Selected Financial Information (Amounts in millions, except per share amounts)	March 1, 2003	March 2, 2002
Total current assets	$ 4,867	$ 4,600
Merchandise inventories	2,046	1,875
Property and equipment, net of depreciation	2,062	1,661
Total assets	7,663	7,367
Total current liabilities	3,793	3,705
Total long-term liabilities	1,140	1,141
Total liabilities	4,933	4,846
Total shareholders equity	2,730	2,521
Total liabilities and shareholders equity	7,663	7,367
Revenue	20,946	17,711
Cost of goods sold	15,710	13,941
Gross profit	5,236	3,770
Operating income	1,010	908
Interest expense	30	21
Earnings from continuing operations before income tax expense	1,014	926
Income tax expense	392	356
Earnings from continuing operations	622	570
Net earnings	99	570
Basic earnings per share	$ 0.31	$ 1.80

CIRCUIT CITY STORES, INC. Selected Financial Information (Amounts in millions except per share data)	February 28, 2003	February 28, 2002
Total current assets	$3,103	$3,653
Merchandise inventory	1,410	1,234
Property and equipment, net of depreciation	650	733
Total assets	3,799	4,542
Total current liabilities	1,280	1,641
Total long-term liabilities	178	167
Total liabilities	1,458	1,808
Total stockholders' equity	2,342	2,734
Revenues	9,954	9,518
Cost of sales, buying and warehousing	7,603	7,180
Gross profit	2,350	2,328
Interest expense	1	1
Earnings from continuing operations before income taxes	67	206
Provision for income taxes	25	78
Earnings from continuing operations	42	128
Net earnings	106	219
Basic earnings per share: Continuing operations	$ 0.20	$ 0.62

Required

a. Compute the following ratios for the companies' 2003 fiscal years:

(1) Current ratio.

(2) Average days to sell inventory. (Use average inventory)

(3) Debt to assets ratio.

(4) Return on investment. (Use average assets and use "earnings from continuing operations" rather than "net earnings.")

(5) Gross margin percentage.

(6) Asset turnover. (Use average assets.)

(7) Return on sales. (Use "earnings from continuing operations" rather than "net earnings.")

(8) Plant assets to long-term debt ratio.

b. Which company appears to be more profitable? Explain your answer and identify which of the ratio(s) from Requirement *a* you used to reach your conclusion.

c. Which company appears to have the higher level of financial risk? Explain your answer and identify which of the ratio(s) from Requirement *a* you used to reach your conclusion.

d. Which company appears to be charging higher prices for its goods? Explain your answer and identify which of the ratio(s) from Requirement *a* you used to reach your conclusion.

e. Which company appears to be the more efficient at using its assets? Explain your answer and identify which of the ratio(s) from Requirement a you used to reach your conclusion.

ATC 13–2 GROUP ASSIGNMENT *Ratio Analysis and Logic*

Presented here are selected data from the 10-K reports of four companies for the 1997 fiscal year. The four companies, in alphabetical order, are

BellSouth Corporation, a telephone company that operates in the southeastern United States.
Caterpillar, Inc., a manufacturer of heavy machinery.
Dollar General Corporation, a company that owns Dollar General Stores discount stores.
Tiffany & Company, a company that operates high-end jewelry stores.

The data, presented in the order of the amount of sales, are as follows. Dollar amounts are in millions.

	A	B	C	D
Sales	$20,561	$18,110	$2,627.3	$1,017.6
Cost of goods sold	6,254	13,374	1,885.2	453.4
Net earnings	3,261	1,665	144.6	72.8
Inventory or NA	2,603	632.0	386.4	
Materials and supplies	398	NA	NA	NA
Accounts receivable	4,750	3,331	0	99.5
Total assets	36,301	20,756	914.8	827.1

Required

a. Divide the class into groups of four or five students per group and then organize the groups into four sections. Assign Task 1 to the first section of groups, Task 2 to the second section, Task 3 to the third section, and Task 4 to the fourth section.

Group Tasks

(1) Assume that you represent BellSouth Corporation. Identify the set of financial data (Column A, B, C, or D) that relates to your company.

(2) Assume that you represent Caterpillar, Inc. Identify the set of financial data (Column A, B, C, or D) that relates to your company.

(3) Assume that you represent Dollar General Corporation. Identify the set of financial data (Column A, B, C, or D) that relates to your company.

(4) Assume that you represent Tiffany & Company. Identify the set of financial data (Column A, B, C, or D) that relates to your company.

Hint: Use a gross margin ratio (gross margin ÷ sales), a net margin ratio (net income ÷ sales), and return on assets (net income ÷ total assets) to facilitate identifying the financial data related to your particular company.

b. Select a representative from each section. Have the representatives explain the rationale for the group's selection. The explanation should include a set of ratios that support the group's conclusion.

ATC 13–3 RESEARCH ASSIGNMENT *Different Presentation Formats*

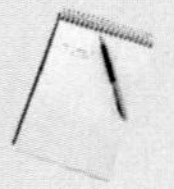

The August 10, 1998, issue of *BusinessWeek* includes the article "**Nokia**" (p. 54). Read this article and complete the following requirements.

Required

a. Comment on the various ways that financial statement information is presented in this article.

b. Does the article focus on horizontal or vertical analysis? Explain why you think the article chose the focus you have identified.

c. Provide some examples of information presented in absolute dollar amounts and in percentages. Explain why a reader may be interested in data that are presented in both absolute and percentage values.

ATC 13–4 WRITING ASSIGNMENT *Interpreting Ratios*

Following are the debt to assets, return on assets, and return on equity ratios for four companies from two different industries. The range of interest rates each company was paying on its long-term debt is provided. Each of these public companies is a leader in its particular industry, and the data are for the fiscal years ending in 1997. All numbers are percentages.

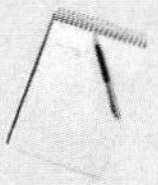

	Debt to Assets*	Return on Assets	Return on Equity	Interest Rates
Banking Industry				
Wachovia Corporation	92	1.0	11.5	5.7–7.0
Wells Fargo & Co.	87	1.2	9.0	6.1–11.0
Home Construction Industry				
Pulte Corporation	62	2.5	6.5	7.0–10.1
Toll Brothers, Inc.	66	5.8	16.9	7.8–10.5

*Debt to assets ratio is defined as total liabilities divided by total assets.

Required

a. Based only on the debt to assets ratios, the banking companies appear to have the most financial risk. Generally, companies that have more financial risk are charged higher interest rates. Write a brief explanation of why the banking companies can borrow money at lower interest rates than the construction companies.

b. Explain why the return on equity ratio for Wachovia is more than 10 times higher than its return on assets ratio, and Pulte's return on equity ratio is less than 3 times higher than its return on assets ratio.

ETHICAL DILEMMA *Making the Ratios Look Good*

ATC 13–5

J. Talbot is the accounting manager for Kolla Waste Disposal Corporation. Kolla is having its worst financial year since its inception. The company is expected to report a net loss. In the midst of such bad news, Ms. Talbot surprised the company president, Mr. Winston, by suggesting that the company write off approximately 25 percent of its garbage trucks. Mr. Winston responded by noting that the trucks could still be operated for another two or three years. Ms. Talbot replied, "We may use them for two or three more years, but you couldn't sell them on the street if you had to. Who wants to buy a bunch of old garbage trucks and besides, it will make next year's financials so sweet. No one will care about the additional write-off this year. We are already showing a loss. Who will care if we lose a little bit more?"

Required

a. How will the write-off affect the following year's return on assets ratio?

b. How will the write-off affect the asset and income growth percentages?

c. Would writing off the garbage trucks violate any of the standards of ethical conduct shown in Exhibit 1–13 of Chapter 1?

SPREADSHEET ASSIGNMENT *Using Excel*

ATC 13–6

Tomkung Corporation's 2003 income statements are presented in the following spreadsheet.

Required

Construct a spreadsheet to conduct horizontal analysis of the income statements for 2003 and 2002.

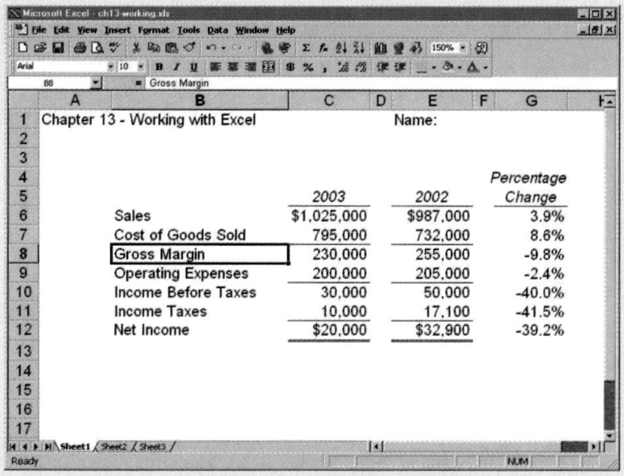

	A	B	C	D	E	F	G
1	Chapter 13 - Working with Excel				Name:		
2							
3							
4							*Percentage*
5			*2003*		*2002*		*Change*
6		Sales	$1,025,000		$987,000		3.9%
7		Cost of Goods Sold	795,000		732,000		8.6%
8		Gross Margin	230,000		255,000		-9.8%
9		Operating Expenses	200,000		205,000		-2.4%
10		Income Before Taxes	30,000		50,000		-40.0%
11		Income Taxes	10,000		17,100		-41.5%
12		Net Income	$20,000		$32,900		-39.2%
13							
14							
15							
16							
17							

ATC 13–7 SPREADSHEET ASSIGNMENT *Mastering Excel*

Refer to the data in ATC 13–6.

Required

Construct a spreadsheet to conduct vertical analysis for both years, 2003 and 2002.

Note:

The chapter supplement that begins on the next page, **Annual Report and Financial Statement Analysis Projects,** includes activities using **The Topps Company, Inc.**, **Harley-Davidson, Inc.**, and general purpose annual reports. You can access their annual reports through their websites www.topps.com and www.harley-davidson.com.

Annual Report and Financial Statement Analysis Projects

Annual Report Project for The Topps Company, Inc. (2003)

Management's Discussion and Analysis

The annual report for The Topps Company, Inc. opens with a letter to the stockholders that describes the company's mission, products and services, customers, past performance, and future prospects. The letter is followed by a section called "Management's Discussion and Analysis" in which management talks about financial results and trends, liquidity, risk factors, and other matters deemed necessary to provide adequate disclosure to users of the report. Read The Topps Company Stockholders' Letter and Management's Discussion and Analysis on pages 1 through 11 to answer questions 1–6.

1. What are the company's two reportable business segments?
2. What were company's goals for each segment in 2003? What specific achievements resulted from these goals?
3. What percentage of the company's total sales came from the Entertainment segment?
4. What effect has inflation had on the company's operations?
5. What is management's view of the company's liquidity status for the foreseeable future? How does the company plan to meet its cash needs?
6. What caused the changes between the company's fiscal year 2003 and 2002 net sales, gross margin, and selling, general and administrative expenses?

Income Statement—Vertical Analysis

7. Using Excel, compute common-size income statements for all three fiscal years. In common-size income statements, net sales is 100% and every other number is a percentage of sales. Attach the spreadsheet to the end of this project.
8. Using the common-size income statements, identify the significant trends.
9. What was the gross margin (gross profit) and the gross margin percentage for fiscal year-end 2003, 2002, and 2001?
10. If the gross margin changed over the three-year period, what caused the change? (The change in the two components of gross margin will reveal what caused any change in the gross margin.)
11. What was the percentage return on sales for fiscal year-end 2003, 2002, and 2001? What do these ratios indicate about Topps?

Income Statement—Horizontal Analysis

12. What were the absolute dollar and the percentage changes in revenues between fiscal 2003 and 2002 and between 2002 and 2001?
13. Describe the trend in revenues. Be specific (e.g., slight/steady/drastic increase or decrease each year, or fluctuating with an initial modest/significant increase or decrease followed by a modest/significant increase or decrease, etc.) to precisely describe the company's situation.

14. What were the absolute dollar and the percentage changes in cost of sales (cost of goods sold) between fiscal 2003 and 2002 and between 2002 and 2001?
15. Describe the trend in cost of goods sold (cost of sales). Be specific (e.g., slight/steady/drastic increase or decrease each year, or fluctuating with an initial modest/significant increase or decrease followed by a modest/significant increase or decrease, etc.) to precisely describe the company's situation.
16. What were the absolute dollar and the percentage changes in selling, general and administrative expenses (operating expenses) between fiscal 2003 and 2002 and between 2002 to 2001?
17. Describe the trend in selling, general and administrative expenses. Be specific (e.g., slight/steady/drastic increase or decrease each year, or fluctuating with an initial modest/significant increase or decrease followed by a modest/significant increase or decrease, etc.) to precisely describe the company's situation.
18. What were the absolute dollar and the percentage changes in net income between fiscal 2003 to 2002 and 2002 to 2001?
19. How would you describe the trend for net income? Be specific (e.g., slight/steady/drastic increase or decrease each year, or fluctuating with an initial modest/significant increase or decrease followed by a modest/significant increase or decrease, etc.) to precisely describe the company's situation. Do you expect the trend to continue?
20. Which items had the largest percentage change between fiscal 2003 and 2001, revenues or expenses (selling, general and administrative expenses and cost of goods sold)?
21. Summarize what is causing the changes in net income from fiscal 2001 to 2002 and 2002 to 2003 based on the percentages computed in questions 12 through 20. Do you expect the trend to continue?

Balance Sheet—Vertical Analysis

22. Using Excel, compute common-size balance sheets at the end of fiscal 2002 and 2003. In common-size balance sheets, total assets is 100% and every other number is a percentage of total assets. Attach the spreadsheet to the end of this project.
23. What percentage were current assets of total assets at the end of fiscal 2003 and 2002?
24. What percentage were long-term assets of total assets at the end of fiscal 2003 and 2002?
25. What percentage was inventory of current assets at the end of fiscal 2003 and 2002?
26. Which current asset had the largest balance at the end of fiscal 2003 and 2002?
27. What percentages were current liabilities of total liabilities and long-term debt of total liabilities at the end of fiscal 2003 and 2002? Comment on the trend and the possible impact on interest expense and net income.

Balance Sheet—Horizontal Analysis

28. What was the absolute dollar and the percentage change between the year-end 2003 and year-end 2002 net accounts receivable balance? Was the change an increase or decrease?
29. What was the absolute dollar and the percentage change between year-end 2003 and year-end 2002 inventory? Was the change an increase or decrease?
30. Compared to year-end 2002, did the amounts reported for the following long-term assets increase or decrease? By how much? Include dollar amounts for each item.

	Year-end 2003	
	Dollar amount	Increase or decrease
Property, plant and equipment, net		
Goodwill, intangibles, and other		
Total long-term assets		

31. What was the amount of the change in the balance in retained earnings between year-end 2003 and 2002? What caused this change?

Balance Sheet—Ratio Analysis

32. Compute the current ratio at the end of fiscal 2003 and 2002. What does this ratio indicate about Topps?
33. Calculate the accounts receivable turnover and the average number of days to collect accounts receivable for fiscal 2003 and 2002. In which year was the turnover and days to collect more favorable?
34. What was the absolute dollar and the percentage change between year-end 2003 and year-end 2002 inventory? Was the change an increase or decrease?
35. Calculate the inventory turnover ratios and the average number of days to sell inventory for fiscal 2003 and 2002. In which year was the turnover and days to sell inventory more favorable?
36. Calculate the ratio of debt to total assets for fiscal year-end 2003 and 2002.
37. Calculate the ratio of stockholders' equity to total assets for fiscal year-end 2003 and 2002. (Recall: 100% Assets = 100% (Liabilities + Stockholders' Equity). Percentages for questions 35 and 36 should total 100% each year.)

Balance Sheet—Stockholders' Equity section

38. Does the company's common stock have a par value? ________ If so, how much was the par value per share? ________
39. How many shares of common stock were issued at the end of fiscal 2003 and 2002?
40. How many shares of treasury stock did the company have at the end of fiscal 2002 and 2003? How were the treasury stock purchases reflected on the statement of cash flows? Include the type of cash flow activity.
41. What percentage of stockholders' equity do the following items represent at year-end?

	2003	2002
Total paid-in capital		
Retained earnings		
Other items		
	100%	100%

Statement of Cash Flows

42. Does the company report cash flows from operating activities using the direct or the indirect method? Describe how you can tell.
43. Did the company pay cash to purchase treasury stock in 2003? If so, what was the amount of the cash outflow?
44. What was the dollar amount of the increase or decrease in cash and cash equivalents for the fiscal years ended 2003, 2002, and 2001?
45. Does the ending balance of cash and cash equivalents agree with the amount reported on the balance sheet?

	2003	2002
Balance Sheet	$	$
Statement of Cash Flows	$	$

46. For each of the following revenue and expense items on the income statement, identify the related current asset or current liability item (working capital item) on the balance sheet.

Revenue or expense item	Related current asset or current liability
Sales	
Cost of sales	
Selling, general and administrative expenses	
Provision for income taxes	

47. Calculate the net increase or decrease in each following working capital items. Do your calculations agree with the amounts reported on the statement of cash flows?

Working capital item	Increase or decrease
Accounts receivable, net	
Inventories	
Income tax receivable	
Prepaid expenses and other current assets	
Accounts payable, accrued expenses and other liabilities, and Income taxes payable	

48. On what statement(s) would you expect to find information regarding the declaration and payment of dividends? Did the company declare or pay dividends in 2003?

Notes to the Financial Statements

49. In your own words briefly summarize two significant accounting policies.
50. How much is the estimated allowance for discounts and doubtful accounts for fiscal 2003?
51. What is the net realizable value of receivables at the end of fiscal 2003?
52. How much is accumulated depreciation and amortization at the end of fiscal 2003? For fiscal 2003, what percent of selling, general and administrative expenses is depreciation and amortization expense?
53. What is the book value of property, plant and equipment at the end of fiscal 2003?
54. How does the company expense goodwill?
55. Identify three different accrued expenses in addition to "other" liabilities.
56. Comment on Topps' long term debt agreement. Name the financial institution extending the credit. What kinds of credit restrictions apply to the long term debt agreement? Identify at least two restrictions. What is the amount of available credit as of March 1, 2003?
57. Identify two kinds of commitments and contingencies.
58. What are the estimated useful lives of the company's depreciable assets?
59. In addition to goodwill, what kinds of intangible assets does the company have? What are their estimated lives?
60. Complete the following schedule contrasting the effect the three inventory cost flow assumptions have on the balance sheet and income statement dollar amounts. Specify for each financial statement the account that is affected by the sale of inventory. Insert the most appropriate term (High, Middle, or Low) to indicate how the specified account would be affected by each of the given cost flow assumptions. Assume an inflationary environment.

	Cost Flow Assumptions		
Account affected	FIFO	AVG	LIFO
1. Balance Sheet:			
2. Income Statement:			

61. What inventory cost flow method does Topps use?
62. Complete the following schedule contrasting the effect the two types of depreciation methods have on the balance sheet and income statement dollar amounts. Specify for each

financial statement the account affected by recording depreciation expense. Designate with an X the method (accelerated or straight-line) that would result in the higher balance in the specified account in the early years of the asset's life.

	Depreciation Methods	
Account affected	**Accelerated**	**Straight-line**
1. Balance Sheet:		
2. Income Statement:		
	(Higher balance early in asset's life)	

63. What method of depreciation does Topps use?

Other Information

64. Topps' financial statements are consolidated. Explain the meaning of the term consolidated. Identify two of the company's subsidiaries. (Hint: You can find the definition of consolidated statements in your textbook. The subsidiary companies are shown on page 33 of the Topps report.)

65. On what exchange is the company's stock traded?

Report of Independent Public Accountants (Auditors)

66. What is the name of the company's independent auditors?

67. Who is responsible for the financial statements?

68. What is the outside auditors' responsibility?

69. What type of opinion did the independent auditors issue on the financial statements (unqualified, qualified, adverse, or disclaimer)? What does this opinion mean?

70. The auditors' report indicates the audit was concerned with material misstatements rather than absolute accuracy in the financial statements. What does "material" mean?

Performance Measures

71. Compute the return on assets ratio (use net income rather than EBIT in the numerator) for fiscal years 2003 and 2002.

72. Compute the return on equity ratio for fiscal years 2003 and 2002.

73. For fiscal 2003, was the return on equity ratio greater than the return on assets ratio? Explain why.

74. What was Topps' basic earnings per share (EPS) for fiscal 2003 and 2002?

75. Given an average market price per share of $9.28 for fiscal 2003 and $10.48 for fiscal 2002, calculate the price-earnings (P/E) ratio. What does the P/E ratio mean?

76. Suggest why the company's stock price fell between fiscal 2003 and 2002 while its P/E ratio increased during the same period.

Annual Report Project for Harley-Davidson, Inc. (2003)

Management's Discussion and Analysis

In addition to financial statements and related footnotes, most corporate annual reports describe the company's mission, products and services, customers, past performance, and future prospects. In Harley-Davidson's annual report this type of information is presented on pages 1 through 35. Annual reports also typically include a section called "Management's Discussion and Analysis (MD&A)" in which management discusses financial results and trends, liquidity, risk factors, and other matters deemed necessary to provide adequate disclosure to users of the reports. Harley-Davidson's MD&A information is included in pages 42 through 56.

1. Read pages 1–11 of the report. What is management's mission for Harley-Davidson?
2. Read the Chairman's letter to shareholders on pages 5 through 8. Assume you own Harley-Davidson stock. Write a brief statement identifying specific details about the company's performance as described by the chairman that impress you favorably or unfavorably. Explain why the items you identify give you a positive or a negative impression.
3. What is the nature of Harley-Davidson's business? What products or services does it produce and sell? *(Hint: footnote 11 on page 88 also provides information pertinent to this question.)*

Income Statement

4. Locate Harley-Davidson's income statements. Are they presented in the single-step or the multi-step format?
5. Use the income statement figures to calculate the percentage growth in net income from 2002 to 2003 and from 2001 to 2002.
6. Is it likely that Harley-Davidson can maintain the rate of net income growth you computed in question 5? *(Hint: The financial performance summary on pages 37 through 42 provides information pertinent to this question.)*
7. Calculate Harley-Davidson's gross margin (profit) percentage for 2002 and 2003.
8. Did Harley-Davidson's gross margin percentage increase or decrease between 2002 and 2003? What caused the change? *(Hint: Information on pages 44 and 45 of the report is pertinent to these questions).*
9. Calculate the percentage change in Harley-Davidson's gross margin (profit) between 2002 and 2003. What caused this change?
10. Use the information in footnote 11 on page 89 of the annual report to answer the following questions.
    a. What percent of income from operations is provided by Motorcycles versus Financial Services for the years 2003, 2002, and 2001 (ignore general corporate expenses)? Identify any trend present in the data.
    b. With respect to income from operations, which segment (Motorcycles or Financial Services) grew more rapidly for the two years between 2001 and 2003?
    c. Do you expect the trends you identified in parts a and b to continue?
11. Based on the information in footnote 11 on page 89 the Financial Services segment had more identifiable assets ($1,821,142) than the Motorcycles segment ($1,778,566). Yet the Financial Services segment has significantly less depreciation ($5,555) than the Motorcycles segment ($191,118). Explain this apparent contradiction.
12. Use the income statement figures on page 57 to calculate the percentage change in Financial Services income and Financial Services expense for the two years between 2001 and 2003.
13. The percentage changes calculated in response to question 12 show that Financial Services income (revenue) grew much faster than Financial Services expense. In fact, between 2001 and 2002, Financial Services expense declined at the same time that income increased. Explain how Harley-Davidson could have significantly increased revenue

while at the same time decreasing expenses. *(Hint: Footnote 3 on page 70 provides information pertinent to this question.)*

Balance Sheet

14. The current asset section of the balance sheets includes the caption "Cash and cash equivalents." What does Harley-Davidson mean by the term "cash equivalents"? *(Hint: cash equivalents are defined in footnote 1 on page 62)*

15. What is the amount of the "At beginning of year" balance of "Cash and cash equivalents" reported on the 2003 statement of cash flows? Where is this amount reported on the consolidated balance sheets?

16. The largest current asset reported on the balance sheets is labeled "Current portion of finance receivables, net." *(Hint: footnote 3 on page 71 and footnote 1 on page 63 provide information pertinent to parts a through d of this question.)*

- **a.** What is the difference between finance receivables and accounts receivable?
- **b.** What do the words "current portion" in the asset description mean?
- **c.** What does the term "net" in the asset description mean?
- **d.** At what point does Harley-Davidson consider finance receivables (retail loans) to be uncollectible?

17. Calculate the percentage change in the current asset "Current portion of finance receivables, net" between year-end 2002 and year-end 2003. Explain the likely reason for the increase or decrease.

18. What is the total net realizable value of all receivables reported on Harley-Davidson's December 31, 2003 balance sheet?

19. Do the balance sheets report any intangible assets? If so, identify them.

20. Read the section of footnote 1 on page 65 that describes product warranty. The footnote reports an ending warranty balance of $30,475. What caption on the balance sheet most likely includes this amount? Do you expect warranty expense to increase or decrease in 2004?

Statement of Cash Flows

21. How does net income compare to cash flows from operating activities for 2003?

22. Does Harley-Davidson report cash flows from operating activities using the direct or the indirect method?

23. In the presentation of cash flows from operating activities, did Harley-Davidson add depreciation expense to net income or subtract it?

24. Does Harley-Davidson have a pattern of paying cash dividends?

25. What percentage of net income did Harley-Davidson pay out in cash dividends during 2003?

26. The percentage computed in question 15 is less than 10%. Provide an explanation for why Harley-Davidson did not pay a greater amount of dividends.

27. In 2003 Harley-Davidson generated nearly $936 million in cash from operating activities. What did the company do with all that cash?

28. What are the two largest items reported in the "Cash flows from investing activities" section of the 2003 statement of cash flows? Do you expect these cash flows to recur regularly?

29. What is the total amount of finance debt reported on the balance sheet at December 31, 2003? What individual components are included in the finance debt category? Identify the interest rates and terms to maturity for each debt component. *(Hint: footnote 3, page 75 provides information pertinent to this question.)*

More on Equity

(Hint: footnote 7 on page 83 provides information pertinent to questions 30–37.)

30. How many shares of common stock was Harley-Davidson authorized to issue as of December 31, 2003?

31. How many shares of common stock had Harley-Davidson issued as of December 31, 2003?
32. How many shares of common stock did Harley-Davidson have outstanding as of December 31, 2003?
33. What is the par value of the common stock as of December 31, 2003?
34. How many shares of preferred stock was Harley-Davidson authorized to issue as of December 31, 2003?
35. How many shares of preferred stock had Harley-Davidson issued as of December 31, 2003?
36. How many shares of preferred stock were outstanding as of December 31, 2003?
37. What is the par value of the preferred stock as of December 31, 2003?
38. What amount of cash did Harley-Davidson spend to purchase treasury stock during 2003?

Report of Independent Auditors

Hint: The report of the independent auditors is presented on page 91 of the annual report. The report of management is presented on page 92. These reports provide information pertinent to questions 39 through 44.

39. Who is responsible for preparing the financial statements?
40. What is the independent auditors' responsibility?
41. What type of opinion did the independent auditors issue on the financial statements (unqualified, qualified, adverse, or disclaimer)? Assume you own shares of Harley-Davidson stock. Does the auditors' opinion indicate the company is a good investment?
42. Who establishes GAAP? Do you trust the organization that establishes accounting standards (GAAP)? Why? Answers to these questions do not appear in the Harley-Davidson annual report. Look for answers in your textbook or do a web search to answer the questions. If you search online, we suggest you begin with the following web site: www.fasb.org.
43. The auditors' report indicates the audit was concerned with material misstatements rather than absolute accuracy in the financial statements. What does "material" mean?
44. Identify the name of the company's independent auditors. Perform a web search to assess the reputation of the audit firm. Assume you own shares of Harley-Davidson stock. Do you feel positive or negative about the audit firm's reputation? Why?

Ratio Analysis

Average ratios computed for the 30 companies that make up the Dow Jones Industrial Average are presented below. The underlying data were drawn from the Compact Disclosure Data Base. Calculate each ratio based on Harley-Davidson's 2003 fiscal year and comment on how Harley-Davidson's ratio compares to the Dow average. Indicate specifically whether Harley-Davidson's ratios are more or less favorable than the Dow average.

Ratio	Dow 30
45. Current ratio	1.34 to 1
46. Average days to collect accounts receivable	241 days for all firms, 61 days for all firms except financial institutions
47. Average days to sell inventory	30 days
48. Debt to assets	.64 to 1
49. Return on equity	19%
50. Price-earnings ratio*	20

*Base your computations for Harley-Davidson on a market price per share of $44.27 and use the basic earnings per common share reported on Harley-Davidson's income statement

Financial Statements Project (Selection of Company to be Decided by Instructor)

Date Due: ________________

Required

Based on the annual report of the company you are reviewing, answer the following questions. If you cannot answer a particular question, briefly explain why. If the question is not applicable to your company's financial statements answer "N/A."

Show all necessary computations in good form. Label all numbers in your computations. If relevant, reference your answers to page(s) in the annual report.

"Current year" means the most recent fiscal year in the company's annual report. "Prior year" means the fiscal year immediately preceding the current year.

1. What products or services does the company sell? Be specific.
2. What do you think the outlook is for these products or services? Why do you think so?
3. By what percentage have sales increased or decreased in each of the last two fiscal years?
4. If the company reported sales by segments, which segment had the largest percentage of total sales? Which segment had the smallest percentage of total sales? **Show computations of the relevant percentages.**
   Largest segment ____________ Percentage of total sales ____________
   Smallest segment ____________ Percentage of total sales ____________
5. What is net income for the current year? ____________________
6. Did the current year's net income increase or decrease since the prior year? By how much? What caused the change?
7. If the company reported earnings by segments, which segment had the largest percentage of total earnings? Which segment had the smallest percentage of total earnings? **Show computations of the relevant percentages.**
   Largest segment ____________ Percentage of total earnings ____________
   Smallest segment ____________ Percentage of total earnings ____________
8. Did the company report any special, unusual, or otherwise nonroutine items in either current or prior year net income? If so, explain the item(s).
9. For the current year, how does net income compare to net cash provided (used) by operating activities?
10. For the current year, what one or two items were most responsible for the difference between net income and net cash provided (used) by operating activities?
11. Did the company pay cash dividends during the current year? If so, how much were they?
12. If the company paid cash dividends, what percentage of net income were the cash dividends? If the company did not pay cash dividends, why do you think it did not?
13. Which of the following is the company's largest asset category: accounts receivable, inventory, or land? What is the amount of that asset category?
14. If the company reported assets by segments, which segment had the largest percentage of total assets? Which segment had the smallest percentage of total assets? **Show computations of the relevant percentages.**
   Largest segment ____________ Percentage of total assets ____________
   Smallest segment ____________ Percentage of total assets ____________
15. How much **cash** did the company invest in property, plant, and equipment during the current year?
16. Which inventory method(s) did the company use?
17. Which depreciation method(s) did the company use?
18. If the company has any intangible assets, what kind are they?
19. Did the company report any contingent liabilities ("contingencies")? If so, briefly explain.
20. Does the company have any preferred stock authorized? If so, how many shares were authorized?

21. Does the company's common stock have a par value? If so, what was it?
22. In what price range was the company's common stock trading during the last quarter of the current year?
23. What was the market price of the company's common stock on DD/MM/Year?
24. Where (on what stock exchange) is the company's stock traded?
25. Who was the company's independent auditor?
26. Develop one question about the company's financial report that you do not know how to answer.
27. Compute the following ratios for the current year and the prior year. Show the appropriate formulas in the first column. Show all supporting computations in the second and third columns.

Ratio	Current Year	Prior Year
Gross Profit Formula:		
Inventory Turnover Formula:		
Current Ratio Formula:		
Debt to Equity Formula:		
Return on Assets Formula:		
Return on Equity Formula:		

CHAPTER *fourteen*

STATEMENT OF CASH FLOWS

LEARNING *objectives*

After you have mastered the material in this chapter, you will be able to:

1 Identify the types of business events that are reported in the three sections of the statement of cash flows.

2 Convert account balances from accrual to cash.

3 Use the T-account method to prepare a statement of cash flows.

4 Explain how the indirect method differs from the direct method in reporting cash flow from operating activities.

5 Explain how the statement of cash flows could mislead decision makers if not interpreted with care.

THE *curious* ACCOUNTANT

Priceline.com began operations in April 1998 and first sold its stock to the public on March 30, 1999. By the end of 2002, the company had cumulative net losses of more than $1.5 billion. Even though its sales grew from $35 million in 1998 to more than $1 billion in 2002, it did not make a profit in any of those years.

How could Priceline.com lose so much money and still be able to pay its bills? (Answer on page 593.)

CHAPTER *opening*

To make informed investment and credit decisions, financial statement users need information to help them assess the amounts, timing, and uncertainty of a company's prospective cash flows. This chapter explains more about the items reported on the statement of cash flows and describes a more practical way to prepare the statement than analyzing every entry in the cash account. As previously shown, the statement of cash flows reports how a company obtained and spent cash during an accounting period. Sources of cash are ***cash inflows,*** *and uses are* ***cash outflows.*** *Cash receipts (inflows) and payments (outflows) are reported as either operating activities, investing activities, or financing activities.*

Topic Tackler PLUS

14–1

LO1 Identify the types of business events that are reported in the three sections of the statement of cash flows.

Operating Activities

Cash inflows and outflows resulting from running (operating) a business are classified as **operating activities.** Items reported as operating activities include:

1. Cash receipts from sales, commissions, fees, and receipts from interest and dividends.
2. Cash payments for inventories, salaries, operating expenses, interest, and taxes.

Gains and *losses* from disposals of long-term operational assets are not shown on the statement of cash flows. The total amount of cash collected from selling long-term assets (including cash associated with gains and losses) is reported in the investing activities section of the statement of cash flows.

Investing Activities

Investing activities always involve assets. Items reported as investing activities include:

1. Cash receipts (inflows) from selling property, plant, equipment, or marketable securities as well as collecting loans.
2. Cash payments (outflows) for purchasing property, plant, equipment, or marketable securities as well as lending to others.

Financing Activities

Financing activities always involve liabilities or equity. Items reported as financing activities include:

1. Cash receipts (inflows) from issuing stock and borrowing money.
2. Cash payments (outflows) to purchase treasury stock, repay debt, and pay dividends.

It is helpful to note that the classification of cash flows is based on the type of activity rather than the type of account. For example, cash flows involving common stock represent investing activities if the company is purchasing or selling its investment in another company's common stock. In contrast, common stock transactions represent financing activities if the company is issuing or buying back its own stock (treasury stock). Similarly, receiving dividends is an operating activity, but paying dividends is a financing activity. Furthermore, lending cash is an investing activity while borrowing cash is a financing activity.

Noncash Investing and Financing Activities

Occasionally, companies engage in significant **noncash investing and financing activities.** For example, a company could issue common stock in exchange for land or acquire a building by accepting a mortgage obligation. Since these types of transactions do not involve exchanging cash, they cannot be reported in the main body of the statement of cash flows. However, the Financial Accounting Standards Board (FASB) has concluded that full and fair reporting requires disclosing all material investing and financing activities whether or not they involve exchanging cash. Companies must therefore include with the statement of cash flows a separate schedule that reports noncash investing and financing activities.

Reporting Format for the Statement of Cash Flows

Cash flows are shown on the statement of cash flows in the following order, (1) operating activities, (2) investing activities, and (3) financing activities. At the end of each category, the difference between the inflows and outflows is presented as a net cash inflow or outflow for the category. These net amounts are combined to determine the net change (increase or

Exhibit 14–1

WESTERN COMPANY
Statement of Cash Flows
For the Year Ended December 31, 2001

Cash Flows from Operating Activities		
Plus: List of Individual Inflows	$XXX	
Less: List of Individual Outflows	(XXX)	
Net Increase (Decrease) from Operating Activities		$XXX
Cash Flows from Investing Activities		
Plus: List of Individual Inflows	XXX	
Less: List of Individual Outflows	(XXX)	
Net Increase (Decrease) from Investing Activities		XXX
Cash Flows from Financing Activities		
Plus: List of Individual Inflows	XXX	
Less: List of Individual Outflows	(XXX)	
Net Increase (Decrease) from Financing Activities		XXX
Net Increase (Decrease) in Cash		XXX
Plus: Beginning Cash Balance		XXX
Ending Cash Balance		$XXX
Schedule of Noncash Investing and Financing Activities		
List of Noncash Transactions		$XXX

decrease) in the company's cash for the period. The net change in cash is combined with the beginning cash balance to determine the ending cash balance. The ending cash balance on the statement of cash flows is the same as the cash balance shown on the balance sheet. The schedule of noncash investing and financing activities is typically presented at the bottom of the statement of cash flows. Exhibit 14–1 outlines this format.

As indicated in Exhibit 14–2, most companies present the statement of cash flows as the last of the four primary financial statements. However, a sizable number of companies present it after the income statement and balance sheet but before the statement of changes in stockholders' equity. Some companies place the statement of cash flows first, before the other three statements.

Exhibit 14–2 *Placement of Statement of Cash Flows Relative to Other Financial Statements*

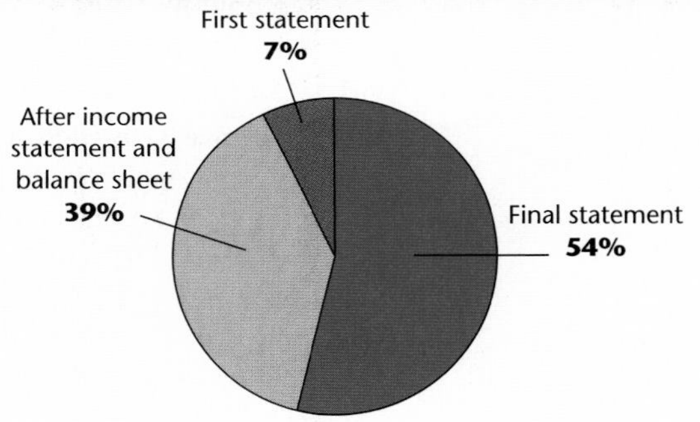

Data source: AICPA, *Accounting Trends and Techniques,* 2002.

Converting from Accrual to Cash-Basis Accounting

The operating activities section of the statement of cash flows is essentially a cash-basis income statement. Since accounting records are normally maintained on an accrual basis, determining the cash flow from operating activities requires converting the accrual based records to cash equivalents.

LO2 Convert account balances from accrual to cash.

Operating Activities

Converting Accruals to Cash

The adjustments to convert **accrual transactions** to cash are explained in the following sections.

Revenue Transactions. The amount of revenue a company recognizes in a given accounting period normally differs from the amount of cash the company collects from customers. The amount of revenue recognized on the income statement can be converted to the amount of cash collected from customers by analyzing the change in the Accounts Receivable balance. For example, assume a company reported on its income statement $500 of sales revenue for the period. Also assume the company's Accounts Receivable balance at the beginning of the period was $100 and at the end of the period was $160 for an increase in receivables of $60 ($160 − $100). These circumstances indicate that $60 of the $500 in sales has not yet been collected from customers. Therefore, the amount of cash collected must have been $440 ($500 revenue − $60 increase in accounts receivable).

LO3 Use the T-account method to prepare a statement of cash flows.

The conclusion that $440 of cash was collected from the revenue transactions can be confirmed using the **T-account method.** This method uses a T-account to analyze the changes in Accounts Receivable for the period. The beginning and ending Accounts Receivable balances are entered in the T-account, in this case, the beginning balance of $100, and the ending balance of $160. Next a $500 debit is posted to the account to reflect the sales on account recognized during the period. The T-account then appears as follows:

	Accounts Receivable	
Beginning Balance	100	
Debit to Record Sales	500	?
Ending Balance	160	

Since adding $500 to the beginning balance of $100 does not produce the ending balance of $160, we know that Accounts Receivable must have been credited for some amount. We can use algebra to determine the amount of the credit in the receivables account ($\$100 + \$500 - x = \$160$; $x = \$440$). Since credits to Accounts Receivable are normally the result of cash collections from customers, the Cash account would have been debited when the receivables account was credited. T-account analysis, therefore, suggests that $440 of cash was collected from revenue generating activities.

Expense Transactions. Accrual accounting requires recognizing expenses when they are incurred, which is frequently before the accounting period when cash is paid for the expenses. Expenses on the income statement that include accrued amounts must be analyzed in conjunction with related balance sheet liabilities in order to determine the amount of cash paid for the expenses during the period. For example, assume a company reports $200 of utilities expense on its income statement. Furthermore, assume the beginning and ending balances of Utilities Payable are $70 and $40, respectively. The company therefore paid not only for the current period's utilities but also paid an additional $30 ($70 − $40) to reduce utility obligations from prior periods. The cash outflow for utility use must have been $230 ($200 expense incurred + $30 reduction in liability).

The T-account method confirms that $230 cash was paid. Enter the beginning and ending balances of Utilities Payable into a T-account. Post a credit of $200 to the account to reflect recognizing the current period's utility expense. The T-account then appears as follows:

Utilities Payable		
	70	Beginning Balance
?	200	Credit to Record Expense
	40	Ending Balance

Algebra dictates that the account must have been debited $230 to produce the $40 ending balance ($\$70 + \$200 - x = \$40$; $x = \$230$). Since debits to payable accounts are normally the result of cash payments, the Cash account would have been credited when Utilities Payable was debited, indicating that cash outflows for utility expenses were $230.

ANSWERS TO THE *curious* ACCOUNTANT

First, it should be remembered that GAAP requires that earnings and losses be computed on an accrual basis. A company can have negative earnings and still have positive cash flows from operating activities. This was not the case at Priceline.com, however. From 1998 through 2001, the company's cash flows from operating activities totaled a negative $94.8 million. Although this is much less than the $1.5 billion cumulative losses the company incurred during the same period, it still does not pay the bills.

Priceline.com, like many new companies, was able to stay in business because of the cash it raised through financing activities. These cash flows were a positive $376.9 million for 1998 through 2001. The company also had some significant noncash transactions. Exhibit 14–3 presents Priceline.com's statement of cash flows from the first four years (1998–2001) of its life.

Exhibit 14–3

PRICELINE.COM INCORPORATED
Statements of Cash Flows
(dollars in thousands)

	Year Ended December 31			
	2001	**2000**	**1999**	**1998**
Operating Activities				
Net loss	$ (7,303)	$(315,145)	$(1,055,090)	$(112,243)
Adjustments to reconcile net loss to net cash used in operating activities:				
Depreciation and amortization	16,578	17,385	5,348	1,860
Provision for uncollectible accounts	18,548	7,354	3,127	581
Warrant costs	—	8,595	1,189,111	67,866
Webhouse warrant	—	189,000	(189,000)	—
Net loss on disposal of fixed assets	17	12,398	—	—
Net loss on sale of equity investments	946	2,558	—	—
Impairment of Myprice loan	—	4,886	—	—
Equity in net income of pricelinemortgage	(551)	—	—	—
Noncash severance	3,076	—	—	—
Enhanced withholding on restricted shares	3,136	—	—	—
Compensation expense arising from deferred stock awards	13,395	1,711	—	—
Changes in assets and liabilities:				
Accounts receivable	(19,768)	7,401	(29,617)	(4,757)
Prepaid expenses and other current assets	699	1,194	(12,043)	(1,922)
Related party receivables	—	(3,484)	—	—
Accounts payable and accrued expenses	(1,501)	45,155	28,470	8,300
Other	824	1,276	(3,331)	112
Net cash used in operating activities	28,096	(19,716)	(63,025)	(40,203)
Investing Activities				
Additions to property and equipment	(9,415)	(37,320)	(27,416)	(6,607)
Proceeds from sales of fixed assets	170	—	—	—
Purchase of convertible notes and warrants of licencees	—	(25,676)	(2,000)	—
Proceeds from sales/maturities of investments	770	31,101	—	—
Funding of restricted cash and bank certificate of deposits	2,646	(4,779)	(8,789)	(680)
Investment in priceline.com europe Ltd.	(14,248)	—	—	—
Cash acquired from acquisition of priceline europe Ltd.	2,779	—	—	—
Investment in marketable securities	(38,878)	(5,000)	(38,771)	—
Net cash used in investing activities	(56,176)	(41,674)	(76,976)	(7,287)
Financing Activities				
Related party payable	—	—	—	(1,072)
Issuance of long-term debt	—	—	—	1,000
Payment of long-term debt	—	—	(1,000)	—
Principal payments under capital lease obligations	—	—	(25)	(22)
Shares reacquired for withholding taxes	(8,716)	—	—	—
Proceeds from sale of common stock, net	49,459	—	208,417	26,495
Proceeds from exercise of stock options and warrants	10,256	14,031	3,399	—
Payment received on stockholder note	—	—	—	250
Issuance of Series A convertible preferred stock	—	—	—	20,000
Issuance of Series B convertible preferred stock	—	—	—	54,415
Net cash provided by financing activities	50,999	14,031	210,791	101,066
Net increase (decrease) in cash and cash equivalents	22,919	(47,359)	70,790	53,576
Cash and cash equivalents, beginning of period	77,024	124,383	53,593	17
Cash and cash equivalents, end of period	$99,943	$ 77,024	$ 124,383	$ 53,593
Supplemental Cash Flow Information				
Cash paid during the period for interest	$ —	$ 4	$ 37	$ 61
Acquisition of priceline.com europe Ltd.—net liabilities assumed	$ 7,896	$ —	$ —	$ —

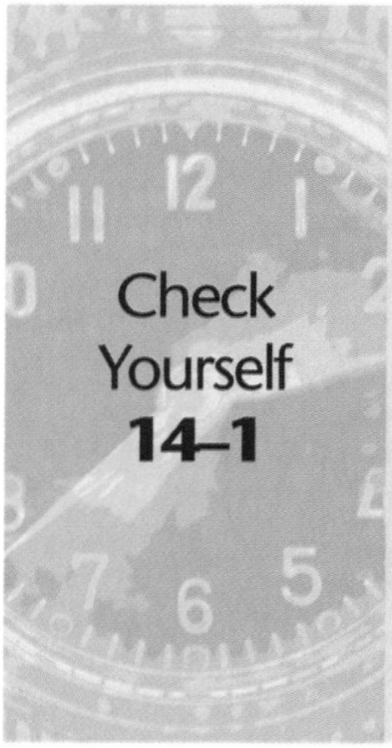

Hammer, Inc., had a beginning balance of $22,400 in its Accounts Receivable account. During the accounting period, Hammer earned $234,700 of revenue on account. The ending balance in the Accounts Receivable account was $18,200. Based on this information alone, determine the amount of cash received from revenue transactions. In what section of the statement of cash flows would this cash flow appear?

Answer

Beginning accounts receivable balance	$ 22,400
Plus: Revenue earned on account during the period	234,700
Receivables available for collection	257,100
Less: Ending accounts receivable balance	(18,200)
Cash collected from receivables (revenue)	$238,900

A $238,900 credit to accounts receivable is required to balance the account. This credit would be offset by a corresponding debit to cash. Cash received from revenue transactions appears in the operating activities section of the statement of cash flows.

Converting Deferrals to Cash

With **deferral transactions,** cash receipts or payments occur before the related revenue or expense is recognized. The following section explains how to convert deferred income and expense items to their cash equivalents.

Revenue Transactions. When a company collects cash from customers before it delivers goods or services, it incurs an obligation (liability) to provide the goods or services at some future date. If the goods or services are provided in a different accounting period from the cash collection, the amount of revenue reported on the income statement will differ from the amount of cash collected. Converting deferred revenue to its cash equivalent requires analyzing the revenue reported on the income statement in conjunction with the liability unearned revenue.

To illustrate, assume revenue of $400 was recognized and Unearned Revenue increased from a beginning balance of $80 to an ending balance of $110. The increase in the liability means that the company received more cash than the amount of revenue it recognized. Not only did the company earn the $400 of revenue reported on the income statement but also it received $30 ($110 − $80) for goods and services to be provided in a future period. Cash receipts from customers was $430 ($400 earned revenue + $30 unearned revenue).

Analyzing the T-account for Unearned Revenue confirms that $430 cash was received. Enter the beginning and ending balances into the Unearned Revenue account. Post a debit of $400 to reflect the revenue earned. The account then appears as follows:

Unearned Revenue

	Debit	Credit	
		80	Beginning Balance
Debit to Recognize Revenue	400	?	
		110	Ending Balance

Use algebra to determine that $430 must have been credited to the account ($\$80 + x - \$400 = \$110$; $x = \$430$). Since credit entries to the Unearned Revenue account are normally the result of cash collections, the T-account analysis indicates that $430 of cash receipts was generated by revenue activities.

Expense Transactions. Companies often pay cash for goods or services before using them. The costs of such goods or services are normally recorded first in asset accounts. The assets are then recognized as expenses in later periods when the goods or services are used. The amount of cash paid for expenses therefore normally differs from the amount of expense recognized in a given period.

Expenses recognized on the income statement can be converted to cash flows by analyzing the changes in relevant asset accounts in conjunction with their corresponding expenses. For example, assume the beginning and ending balances of Prepaid Rent are \$60 and \$80, respectively, and reported rent expense is \$800. These circumstances indicate the company not only paid enough cash for the \$800 of recognized expense but also paid an additional \$20 (\$80 − \$60) to increase the Prepaid Rent account. Therefore, the cash outflow for rent was \$820 (\$800 recognized expense + \$20 prepaid rent).

Analyzing the T-account for Prepaid Rent confirms that \$820 was paid for rent. Enter the beginning and ending balances, then post an \$800 credit to reflect the rent expense. The account then appears as follows:

Prepaid Rent

	Debit	Credit	
Beginning Balance	60		
	?	800	Credit to Recognize Expense
Ending Balance	80		

Use algebra to determine that the account must have been debited for \$820 ($\$60 + x - \$800 = \$80$; $x = \$820$). Since debit entries to the Prepaid Rent account are normally the result of cash payments, the analysis confirms that the cash outflow for rent was \$820.

Investing Activities

Determining cash flow from investing activities also requires analyzing changes in various account balances along with related income statement amounts. For example, assume the beginning and ending balances in the Land account were \$900 and \$300, respectively. Furthermore, assume the income statement recognized a \$200 gain on the sale of land. The \$600 (\$900 − \$300) decrease in book value means land was sold. The gain on the income statement means the land was sold for \$200 more than its book value. This suggests that land was sold for \$800 cash (\$600 decrease in Land account + \$200 Gain). The cash flow amount is different from the gain amount reported on the income statement. The full \$800 cash inflow is reported in the investing activities section of the statement of cash flows. The gain has no effect on the operating activities section of the statement of cash flows.

The \$800 cash inflow from selling land can be confirmed using the T-account method. Analyzing the beginning and ending Land balances indicates that land costing \$600 (\$900 beginning balance – \$300 ending balance) was sold. Because of the \$200 gain (which is closed to Retained Earnings), \$800 cash must have been collected from the sale. The relevant T-accounts appear as follows:

Cash		Land		Retained Earnings	
?		900	600		200
		300			

Financing Activities

Cash flow from financing activities can frequently be determined by simply analyzing the changes in liability and stockholders' equity accounts. For example, an increase in bond liabilities from \$500 to \$800 implies that a company issued new bonds for \$300 cash. The T-account method supports this conclusion. Enter the beginning and ending balances in Bonds Payable as shown:

Bonds Payable

Debit	Credit	
	500	Beginning Balance
	?	
	800	Ending Balance

To have an ending balance of $800, the T-account must have been credited for $300. Since increases in bond liabilities are normally the result of borrowing cash, the analysis suggests $300 of cash inflow must have been derived from issuing bonds.

Other explanations are possible. Some of the company's stockholders may have exchanged their equity securities for debt securities or the company may have incurred the obligation in exchange for some asset (property, plant, or equipment) other than cash. Such transactions would be reported in the schedule of noncash investing and financing activities.

Comprehensive Example Using the T-Account Approach

LO3 Use the T-account method to prepare a statement of cash flows.

The preceding discussion suggests that a statement of cash flows can be prepared by analyzing other financial statements. Beginning and ending asset, liability, and equity account balances can be obtained from two successive balance sheets. Revenues, expenses, gains, and losses can be found on the intervening income statement. Notes to the financial statements may contain information about noncash transactions. Exhibits 14–4 and 14–5 display the balance sheets, income statement, and additional information needed to prepare a statement of cash flows.

Exhibit 14–4

THE NEW SOUTH CORPORATION
Comparative Balance Sheets
As of December 31

	2004	2005
Current Assets		
Cash	$ 400	$ 900
Accounts Receivable	1,200	1,000
Interest Receivable	300	400
Inventory	8,200	8,900
Prepaid Insurance	1,400	1,100
Total Current Assets	11,500	12,300
Long-Term Assets		
Marketable Securities	3,500	5,100
Equipment	4,600	5,400
Less: Accumulated Depreciation	(1,200)	(900)
Land	6,000	8,500
Total Long-Term Assets	12,900	18,100
Total Assets	$24,400	$30,400
Current Liabilities		
Accounts Payable—Inventory Purchases	$ 1,100	$ 800
Salaries Payable	900	1,000
Other Operating Expenses Payable	1,300	1,500
Interest Payable	500	300
Unearned Rent Revenue	1,600	600
Total Current Liabilities	5,400	4,200
Long-Term Liabilities		
Mortgage Payable	0	2,500
Bonds Payable	4,000	1,000
Total Long-Term Liabilities	4,000	3,500
Stockholders' Equity		
Common Stock	8,000	10,000
Retained Earnings	7,000	12,700
Total Stockholders' Equity	15,000	22,700
Total Liabilities and Stockholders' Equity	$24,400	$30,400

Exhibit 14–5

THE NEW SOUTH CORPORATION Income Statement For the Year Ended December 31, 2005		
Sales		$20,600
Cost of Goods Sold		(10,500)
Gross Margin		10,100
Operating Expenses		
Depreciation Expense	$ 800	
Salaries Expense	2,700	
Insurance Expense	600	
Other Operating Expenses	1,400	
Total Operating Expenses		(5,500)
		4,600
Operating Income—Rent Revenue		2,400
Total Operating Income		7,000
Nonoperating Revenue and Expenses		
Interest Revenue	700	
Interest Expense	(400)	
Loss on Sale of Equipment	(100)	
Total Nonoperating Items		200
Net Income		$ 7,200

Additional information
1. The corporation sold equipment for $300 cash. This equipment had an original cost of $1,500 and accumulated depreciation of $1,100 at the time of the sale.
2. The corporation issued a $2,500 mortgage note in exchange for land.
3. There was a $1,500 cash dividend paid during the accounting period.

Preparing a Statement of Cash Flows

Analyzing the financial statements begins by setting up T-accounts for each balance sheet item, entering beginning balances from the 2004 balance sheet (see Exhibit 14–4) and ending balances from the 2005 balance sheet. Enough room is left in the Cash account to separately record cash flows as operating, investing, and financing activities. For convenience, the T-account analysis uses only balance sheet accounts; any entries to revenue, expense, or dividend accounts is posted directly to retained earnings. Exhibit 14–6 displays the full set of T-accounts after all transactions have been analyzed. Each transaction is labeled with a lowercase letter and a number to clarify the details of the analysis. The following section explains each transaction. Trace every transaction from its explanation to Exhibit 14–6.

Cash Flows from Operating Activities

Determining cash flows from operating activities essentially requires converting the accrual-based revenues and expenses reported on the income statement to their cash equivalents. Each income statement amount should be analyzed separately to assess its cash flow consequences.

Cash Receipts from Sales

The first item reported on the income statement is $20,600 of sales revenue. Assuming all sales were on account, the entry to record sales would have debited Accounts Receivable and credited Sales Revenue. Since sales revenue increases retained earnings, the entry posted to the T-accounts is a debit to Accounts Receivable and a credit to Retained Earnings. This entry is labeled (a1) in Exhibit 14–6.

After recording the sales revenue transaction, the cash inflow from sales can be determined by analyzing the Accounts Receivable T-account. Use algebra to determine that $20,800 ($1,200 + $20,600 − x = $1,000; x = $20,800) of receivables must have been collected. The

Exhibit 14–6 *Balance Sheet T-Accounts*

Assets = Liabilities + Equity

Assets

Cash

	Debit	Credit	
Bal.	400		
Operating Activities			
(a2)	20,800	11,500	(b3)
(g2)	1,400	2,600	(d2)
(h2)	600	300	(e2)
		1,200	(f2)
		600	(i2)
Investing Activities			
(k1)	300	1,600	(j1)
		2,300	(l1)
Financing Activities			
(o1)	2,000	3,000	(n1)
		1,500	(p1)
Bal.	900		

Accounts Receivable

	Debit	Credit	
Bal.	1,200	20,800	(a2)
(a1)	20,600		
Bal.	1,000		

Interest Receivable

	Debit	Credit	
Bal.	300	600	(h2)
(h1)	700		
Bal.	400		

Inventory

	Debit	Credit	
Bal.	8,200	10,500	(b1)
(b2)	11,200		
Bal.	8,900		

Prepaid Insurance

	Debit	Credit	
Bal.	1,400	600	(e1)
(e2)	300		
Bal.	1,100		

Marketable Securities

	Debit	Credit	
Bal.	3,500		
(j1)	1,600		
Bal.	5,100		

Equipment

	Debit	Credit	
Bal.	4,600	1,500	(k1)
(l1)	2,300		
Bal.	5,400		

Accumulated Depreciation

	Debit	Credit	
(k1)	1,100	1,200	Bal.
		800	(c1)
		900	Bal.

Land

	Debit	Credit	
Bal.	6,000		
(m1)	2,500		
Bal.	8,500		

Liabilities

Accounts Payable—Inventory

	Debit	Credit	
(b3)	11,500	1,100	Bal.
		11,200	(b2)
		800	Bal.

Salaries Payable

	Debit	Credit	
(d2)	2,600	900	Bal.
		2,700	(d1)
		1,000	Bal.

Other Operating Exp. Payable

	Debit	Credit	
(f2)	1,200	1,300	Bal.
		1,400	(f1)
		1,500	Bal.

Interest Payable

	Debit	Credit	
(i2)	600	500	Bal.
		400	(i1)
		300	Bal.

Unearned Rent Revenue

	Debit	Credit	
(g1)	2,400	1,600	Bal.
		1,400	(g2)
		600	Bal.

Mortgage Payable

	Debit	Credit	
		0	Bal.
		2,500	(m1)
		2,500	Bal.

Bonds Payable

	Debit	Credit	
(n1)	3,000	4,000	Bal.
		1,000	Bal.

Equity

Common Stock

	Debit	Credit	
		8,000	Bal.
		2,000	(o1)
		10,000	Bal.

Retained Earnings

	Debit	Credit	
(b1)	10,500	7,000	Bal.
(c1)	800	20,600	(a1)
(d1)	2,700	2,400	(g1)
(e1)	600	700	(h1)
(f1)	1,400		
(i1)	400		
(k1)	100		
(p1)	1,500		
		12,700	Bal.

cash inflow is recorded with a debit to the Cash account in the operating activities section and a credit to the Accounts Receivable account. This entry is labeled (a2) in Exhibit 14–6.

The analysis is complete when the difference between the beginning and ending balances in an account has been fully explained. In this case, the analysis of Accounts Receivable is complete. However, the analysis of retained earning will not be complete until all revenue, expense, and dividend events have been recorded.

Cash Payments Associated with Cost of Goods Sold (Inventory Purchases)

The next item on the income statement is cost of goods sold.

When analyzing the inventory account, it is helpful to make two simplifying assumptions. First, assume the company maintains perpetual inventory records; second, assume all inventory purchases are made on account. The following analysis uses these two assumptions.

Recording the \$10,500 cost of goods sold (reported on the income statement in Exhibit 14–5) would have required crediting Inventory and debiting Cost of Goods Sold. Since cost of good sold reduces retained earnings, the entry is posted as a debit to Retained Earnings and a credit to Inventory. This entry is labeled (b1) in Exhibit 14–6. Further review of the Inventory account indicates that some inventory must have been purchased. Use algebra to determine that \$11,200 (\$8,200 + x − \$10,500 = \$8,900; x = \$11,200) of inventory must have been purchased. The entry to record the inventory purchase, labeled (b2), involves a debit to Inventory and a credit to Accounts Payable. This entry completes the analysis of the Inventory account.

The Accounts Payable analysis is still incomplete. Use algebra and entry (b2) to determine that Accounts Payable decreased by \$11,500 (\$1,100 + \$11,200 − x = \$800; x = \$11,500), reflecting cash payments that must have been made to reduce the liability. The entry to record this cash outflow, labeled (b3), involves a debit to Accounts Payable and a credit in the operating activities section of the Cash account. The analysis of the Accounts Payable account is now complete.

Noncash Effects of Depreciation

The next item on the income statement is depreciation expense, a noncash charge against revenues. No cash is paid when depreciation expense is recorded. The entry to record depreciation expense (c1) involves a debit to Retained Earnings (depreciation expense) and a credit to Accumulated Depreciation. This entry only partly explains the change in accumulated depreciation. Since cash flow consequences related to long-term assets and their respective contra accounts affect the investing activities section of the statement of cash flows, the analysis of Accumulated Depreciation will be completed in the discussion of investing activities after the analysis of cash flows from operating activities is completed.

Cash Payments for Salaries

The entry to record \$2,700 of salary expense (d1) involves a debit to Retained Earnings (salary expense) and a credit to Salaries Payable. This entry partly explains the change in the Salaries Payable account. Use algebra to determine that Salaries Payable decreased \$2,600 (\$900 + \$2,700 − x = \$1,000; x = \$2,600), reflecting cash paid for salaries. The entry to record the cash outflows for salaries (d2) involves a debit to the Salaries Payable account and a credit to the operating activities section of the Cash account.

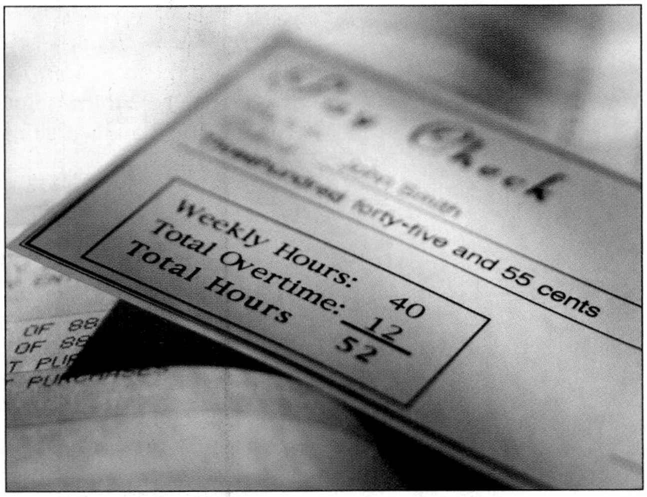

Cash Payments for Insurance

The entry to record \$600 of insurance expense (e1) requires a debit to Retained Earnings (insurance expense) and a credit to Prepaid Insurance. This entry partly explains the change in the Prepaid Insurance account. Use algebra to determine that Prepaid Insurance increased \$300 (\$1,400 + x − \$600 = \$1,100; x = \$300), reflecting cash payments to purchase Prepaid Insurance during the accounting period. The entry to record the cash outflow for the purchase of insurance (e2) involves a debit to the Prepaid Insurance account and a credit to the operating activities section of the Cash account.

Cash Payments for Other Operating Expenses

The \$1,400 of other operating expenses reported on the income statement is recorded in the T-accounts with a debit to Retained Earnings and a credit to the Other Operating Expenses Payable account. This entry (f1) partly explains the change in the Other Operating Expenses

Payable account. Use algebra to determine that the liability decreased by $1,200 ($\$1{,}300 + \$1{,}400 - x = \$1{,}500$; $x = \$1{,}200$), reflecting cash payments for other operating expenses. The entry to record the cash outflow (f2) involves a debit to the Other Operating Expenses Payable account and a credit to the operating activities section of the Cash account.

Cash Receipts for Rent

The entry to record $2,400 of rent revenue (g1) involves a debit to the Unearned Rent Revenue account and a credit to the Retained Earnings account. This entry partly explains the change in the Unearned Rent Revenue account. Use algebra to determine that the account must have been credited for $1,400 ($\$1{,}600 + x - \$2{,}400 = \$600$; $x = \$1{,}400$), reflecting cash received in advance for rent revenue. The entry to record the cash inflow involves a credit to the Unearned Rent Revenue account and a debit to the operating activities section of the Cash account, (g2) in Exhibit 14–6.

Cash Receipts of Interest Revenue

The entry to record $700 of interest revenue (h1) involves a debit to the Interest Receivable account and a credit to Retained Earnings (interest revenue). This entry partly explains the change in the Interest Receivable account. Use algebra to determine that interest receivable must have decreased by $600 ($\$300 + \$700 - x = \$400$; $x = \$600$), reflecting cash collection of interest revenue. The entry to record this cash inflow (h2) involves a credit to Interest Receivable and a debit to the operating activities section of the Cash account.

Cash Payments for Interest Expense

The entry to record $400 of interest expense (i1) involves a debit to Retained Earnings (interest expense) and a credit to Interest Payable. The entry partly explains the change in the Interest Payable account. Use algebra to determine that interest payable decreased by $600 ($\$500 + \$400 - x = \$300$; $x = \$600$), reflecting cash payments of interest obligations. The entry to recognize the cash outflow for interest payments (i2) involves a debit to the Interest Payable account and a credit to the operating activities section of the Cash account.

Noncash Effects of Loss

The loss on sale of equipment does not represent a cash flow. The cash flow represented by the proceeds of the sale is explained shortly in the investing activities discussion. Cash flow from operating activities is not affected by gains or losses on the disposal of long-term assets.

Completion of Analysis of Operating Activities

Since all income statement items have now been analyzed, the conversion of revenues and expenses from accrual to cash for operating activities is complete. The example now moves to cash flows from investing activities.

Check Yourself 14–2

Q Magazine, Inc., reported $234,800 of revenue for the month. At the beginning of the month, its Unearned Revenue account had a balance of $78,000. At the end of the month, the account had a balance of $67,000. Based on this information alone, determine the amount of cash received from revenue.

Answer The Unearned Revenue account decreased by $11,000 ($78,000 − $67,000). This decrease in unearned revenue would have coincided with an increase in revenue that did not involve receiving cash. As a result, $11,000 of the revenue earned had no effect on cash flow during this month. To determine the cash received from revenue, subtract the noncash increase from reported revenue. Cash received from revenue is $223,800 ($234,800 − $11,000).

Cash Flows from Investing Activities

Since investing activities generally involve the acquisition (purchase) or disposal (sale) of long-term assets, determining cash flows from investing activities centers on analyzing balance sheet changes in these asset accounts.

Cash Payments to Purchase Marketable Securities

The first long-term asset reported on the balance sheets, Marketable Securities, increased from \$3,500 at the beginning of the year to \$5,100 at the end of the year. The increase most likely resulted from purchasing additional securities for \$1,600 (\$5,100 − \$3,500). In the absence of evidence to the contrary, it is assumed securities were purchased with cash. The entry to record the purchase (j1) involves a debit to the Marketable Securities account and a credit to the investing activities section of the Cash account. Trace this entry into Exhibit 14–6.

Cash Receipts from Sale of Equipment

The next asset on the balance sheets is Equipment. Previous review of the income statement disclosed a loss on sale of equipment, indicating some equipment was sold during the period. The additional information below the income statement discloses that equipment costing \$1,500 with accumulated depreciation of \$1,100 was sold for \$300. The difference between the \$400 (\$1,500 − \$1,100) book value and the \$300 sales price explains the \$100 loss on the income statement. The cash inflow from the sale, \$300, is unaffected by the original cost, accumulated depreciation, or the amount of the loss. The entry to recognize the cash receipt (k1) involves a debit to the investing activities section of the Cash account, a debit to Retained Earnings (loss), a debit to the Accumulated Depreciation account, and a credit to the Equipment account. Trace this entry into Exhibit 14–6.

Cash Payments to Purchase Equipment

The sale of equipment partly explains the change in the Equipment account. However, further analysis indicates some equipment must have been purchased. Use algebra and entry (k1) to determine that the Equipment account must have increased by \$2,300 (\$4,600 + x − \$1,500 = \$5,400; x = \$2,300), reflecting the purchase of additional equipment. The entry to record the equipment purchase (l1) involves a debit to the Equipment account and a credit to the investing activities section of the Cash account.

Noncash Transaction for Land Acquisition

Land increased from \$6,000 to \$8,500, indicating that land costing \$2,500 (\$8,500 − \$6,000) was acquired during the accounting period. The additional information below the income statement discloses that the corporation issued a mortgage to acquire this land. The entry to record the transaction (m1), a noncash exchange, involves a debit to Land and a credit to Mortgage Payable in Exhibit 14–6. Since the transaction does not affect cash, it is reported in the separate schedule for noncash investing and financing activities included with the statement of cash flows.

Since the changes in all long-term asset accounts have now been explained, the analysis of cash flows from investing activities is complete. The example continues with determining cash flows from financing activities.

Cash Flows from Financing Activities

Since financing activities involve borrowing and repayment transactions and transactions with owners, determining cash flows from financing activities requires analyzing the long-term liability and stockholders' equity sections of the balance sheets. The first long-term liability on the balance sheet is Mortgage Payable. The change in this account was explained previously

REALITY *bytes*

How did Florida Power and Light (FPL) acquire $501 million of property and equipment without spending any cash? Oddly enough, the answer can be found in the company's statement of cash flows. The supplemental schedule of noncash investing and financing activities section of FPL's cash statement shows that it acquired $81 million of equipment by accepting lease obligations and that it acquired $420 million of property by assuming debt. In other words, FPL acquired $501 million ($81 million + $420 million) in property and equipment by agreeing to pay for it later.

in conjunction with analyzing the land account. The financing activity of issuing the mortgage payable is reported along with the investing activity of acquiring land in the separate schedule for noncash transactions.

Cash Repayment for Bond Principal

The Bonds Payable balance decreased from $4,000 to $1,000. In the absence of evidence to the contrary, it is likely that $3,000 ($4,000 − $1,000) cash was paid to reduce bond liabilities. The entry to record the cash outflow (n1) involves a debit to the Bonds Payable account and a credit to the financing activities section of the Cash account.

Cash Receipt from Stock Issue

The Common Stock balance increased from $8,000 to $10,000. It is reasonable to assume the company issued common stock for $2,000 ($10,000 − $8,000) cash. The entry to record this cash inflow (o1) involves a credit to Common Stock and a debit to the financing activities section of the Cash account.

Cash Payments for Dividends

Finally, additional information below the income statement discloses a cash dividend of $1,500. The transaction to record this cash outflow (p1) involves a debit to the Retained Earnings account and a credit to the financing activities section of the Cash account.

Now all income statement items have been accounted for, all changes in balance sheet accounts have been analyzed, and all additional information has been considered. Review the analysis by tracing each entry into the T-accounts in Exhibit 14–6.

Exhibit 14–7

THE NEW SOUTH CORPORATION Statement of Cash Flows For the Year Ended December 31, 2005			
Cash Flows from Operating Activities			
Cash Receipts from			
Sales	$20,800		
Rent	1,400		
Interest	600		
Total Cash Inflows		$22,800	
Cash Payments for			
Inventory Purchases	11,500		
Salaries	2,600		
Insurance	300		
Other Operating Expenses	1,200		
Interest	600		
Total Cash Outflows		(16,200)	
Net Cash Flow from Operating Activities			$6,600
Cash Flows from Investing Activities			
Inflow from Sale of Equipment		300	
Outflow to Purchase Marketable Securities		(1,600)	
Outflow to Purchase Equipment		(2,300)	
Net Cash Flow for Investing Activities			(3,600)
Cash Flows from Financing Activities			
Inflow from Stock Issue		2,000	
Outflow to Repay Debt		(3,000)	
Outflow for Dividends		(1,500)	
Net Cash Flow for Financing Activities			(2,500)
Net Increase in Cash			500
Plus: Beginning Cash Balance			400
Ending Cash Balance			$ 900
Schedule of Noncash Investing and Financing Activities			
Issue of Mortgage for Land			$ 2,500

Presenting Information in the Statement of Cash Flows

To prepare the formal statement of cash flows, the inflows and outflows summarized in the Cash T-account must be appropriately organized and labeled. Cash flows from operating activities are presented first, followed by cash flows from investing activities, and finally, cash flows from financing activities. Noncash investing and financing activities are reported in a separate schedule or in the footnotes. Exhibit 14–7 displays the statement of cash flows and a separate schedule for noncash activities.

Topic Tackler PLUS 14–2

Statement of Cash Flows Presented under the Indirect Method

LO4 Explain how the indirect method differs from the direct method in reporting cash flow from operating activities.

In all previous examples this textbook has illustrated the operating activities section of the statement of cash flows using the **direct method.** Although the direct method is easier to understand and is preferred by the Financial Accounting Standards Board, most companies use an alternative format called the **indirect method.** The amount of net cash flow from operating activities is the same using either method, but the presentation of the operating activities section differs. The indirect method starts with net income as reported on the income statement followed by the adjustments necessary to convert the accrual-based net income figure to a cash-basis equivalent. The conversion process uses three basic rules.

Rule 1: Increases in current assets are deducted from net income, and decreases in current assets are added to net income. For example, an increase in accounts receivable suggests that not all sales were collected in cash. The amount of sales revenue reported on the income statement exceeds the amount of cash collections. The increase in receivables must therefore be subtracted from the amount of net income to convert the net income figure to its cash equivalent. Similarly, a decrease in receivables must be added to the net income figure. Comparable logic holds for all current assets.

Rule 2: Increases in current liabilities are added to net income, and decreases in current liabilities are deducted from net income. The rule for current liabilities is the opposite of the rule for current assets. For example, an increase in accounts payable suggests that not all expenses were paid in cash. A greater amount of expenses was subtracted in determining net income than the amount of cash payments for those expenses. The increase in payables must be added to the amount of net income to convert the net income figure to its cash equivalent. Conversely, decreases in payable accounts are deducted from net income. This logic applies to all current liabilities that are affected by operating activities.

Check Yourself 14-3

The following account balances were drawn from the accounting records of Loeb, Inc.

Account Title	Beginning Balance	Ending Balance
Prepaid Rent	$4,200	$3,000
Interest Payable	2,900	2,650

Loeb reported $7,400 of net income during the accounting period. Based on this information alone, determine the amount of cash flow from operating activities.

Answer Based on Rule 1, the $1,200 decrease ($3,000 − $4,200) in Prepaid Rent (current asset) must be added to net income to determine the amount of cash flow from operating activities. Rule 2 requires that the $250 decrease ($2,650 − $2,900) in Interest Payable (current liability) must be deducted from net income. Accordingly, the cash flow from operating activities is $8,350 ($7,400 + $1,200 − $250). Note that paying interest is defined as an operating activity and should not be confused with dividend payments, which are classified as financing activities.

Rule 3: All noncash expenses and losses are added to net income, and all noncash revenue and gains are subtracted from net income. Some expense and revenue transactions do not have cash consequences. For example, although depreciation is an expense subtracted in determining net income, it does not require a cash payment. The amount of depreciation expense must therefore be added to net income to convert net income to its cash equivalent. Similarly, losses and gains reported on the income statement do not have cash consequences. Net income must be adjusted to remove the effects of losses and gains to convert it to cash flow.

Check Yourself 14-4

Arley Company's income statement reported net income (in millions) of $326 for the year. The income statement included depreciation expense of $45 and a net loss on the sale of disposable assets of $22. Based on this information alone, determine the net cash flow from operating activities.

Answer Based on Rule 3, both the depreciation expense and the loss would have to be added to net income to determine cash flow from operating activities. Net cash flow from operating activities would be $393 ($326 + $45 + $22).

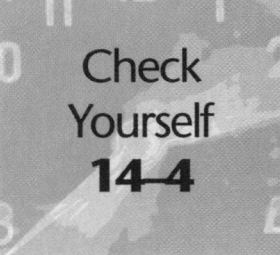

Exhibit 14–8

THE NEW SOUTH CORPORATION
Statement of Cash Flows (Indirect Method)
For the Year Ended December 31, 2005

Cash Flows from Operating Activities		
Net Income	$7,200	
Plus: Decreases in Current Assets and Increases in Current Liabilities		
Decrease in Accounts Receivable	200	
Decrease in Prepaid Insurance	300	
Increase in Salaries Payable	100	
Increase in Other Operating Expenses Payable	200	
Less: Increases in Current Assets and Decreases in Current Liabilities		
Increase in Interest Receivable	(100)	
Increase in Inventory	(700)	
Decrease in Accounts Payable	(300)	
Decrease in Interest Payable	(200)	
Decrease in Unearned Rent Revenue	(1,000)	
Plus: Noncash Charges		
Depreciation Expense	800	
Loss on Sale of Equipment	100	
Net Cash Flow from Operating Activities		$6,600
Cash Flows from Investing Activities		
Inflow from Sale of Equipment	300	
Outflow to Purchase Marketable Securities	(1,600)	
Outflow to Purchase Equipment	(2,300)	
Net Cash Flow for Investing Activities		(3,600)
Cash Flows from Financing Activities		
Inflow from Stock Issue	2,000	
Outflow to Repay Debt	(3,000)	
Outflow for Dividends	(1,500)	
Net Cash Flow for Financing Activities		(2,500)
Net Increase in Cash		500
Plus: Beginning Cash Balance		400
Ending Cash Balance		$ 900
Schedule of Noncash Investing and Financing Activities		
Issue of Mortgage for Land		$2,500

Exhibit 14–8 displays the statement of cash flows with operating activities presented using the indirect method. The statement was constructed by applying the three basic conversion rules to The New South Corporation data from Exhibits 14–4 and 14–5. The only difference between the indirect method (Exhibit 14–8) and the direct method (Exhibit 14–7) is in the presentation of the cash flows from operating activities section. Cash flows from investing and financing activities and the schedule of noncash investing and financing activities are the same for both reporting formats.

THE FINANCIAL ANALYST

LO5 Explain how the statement of cash flows could mislead decision makers if not interpreted with care.

Why are financial analysts interested in the statement of cash flows? Understanding the cash flows of a business is essential because cash is used to pay the bills. A company, especially one experiencing rapid growth, can be short of cash in spite of earning substantial net income. To illustrate, assume you start a computer sales business. You borrow $2,000 and spend the money to purchase two computers for $1,000 each. You sell one of the computers on account for $1,500. If your loan required a payment at this time, you could not make it. Even though you have net income of $500 ($1,500 sales − $1,000 cost of goods sold), you have no cash until you collect the $1,500 account receivable. A business cannot survive without managing cash flow carefully. It is little wonder that financial analysts are keenly interested in cash flow.

Real-World Data

The statement of cash flows frequently provides a picture of business activity that would otherwise be lost in the complexities of accrual accounting. For example, **IBM Corporation's** combined operating losses (before taxes) for 1991, 1992, and 1993 were more than $17.9 *billion*. During this same period, IBM reported "restructuring charges" of more than $24 billion. Restructuring costs relate to reorganizing a company. They may include the costs of closing facilities and losses on asset disposals. Without the restructuring charges, IBM would have reported operating *profits* of about $6 billion (before taxes). Do restructuring charges signal positive or negative changes? Different financial analysts have different opinions about this issue. However, one aspect of IBM's performance during these years is easily understood. The company produced over $21 billion in positive cash flow from operating activities. It had no trouble paying its bills.

Investors consider cash flow information so important that they are willing to pay for it, even when the FASB discourages its use. The FASB *prohibits* companies from disclosing *cash flow per share* in audited financial statements. However, one prominent stock analysis service, ***Value Line Investment Survey***, sells this information to a significant customer base. Clearly, Value Line's customers value information about cash flows.

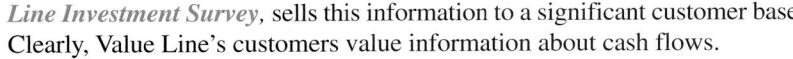

Exhibit 14–9 compares income from operations and cash flow from operating activities for six real-world companies from five different industries for the 2000, 2001, and 2002 fiscal years.

Several things are apparent from Exhibit 14–9. The cash flow from operating activities exceeds income from operations for all of the companies except **Toll Brothers**. Many real-world companies report such a result because depreciation, a noncash expense, is usually significant. The most dramatic example is for **Sprint** in 2001. Even though Sprint reported a *net loss* from operations of approximately $2.3 billion, it generated *positive* cash flow from operating activities of more than $4.5 *billion*. This difference between cash flow from operating activities and operating income helps explain how some companies can have significant losses over a few years and continue to stay in business and pay their bills.

The exhibit shows that cash flow from operating activities can be more stable than operating income. Results for Sprint also demonstrate this clearly. Although the company's earnings were negative in 2000, more negative in 2001, and positive in 2002, its cash flows from operating activities were always positive. Stability is one of the reasons many financial analysts prefer cash flow over earnings as a predictor of future performance.

Exhibit 14–9 *Operating Income versus Cash flow From Operating Activities (Amounts in $000)*

Company		2002	2001	2000
Alaska Airlines	Oper. Income	$ (57,000)	$ (11,800)	$ (14,800)
	Cash Flow Oper. Activities	119,600	202,000	282,900
Southwest Airlines	Oper. Income	240,969	511,147	625,224
	Cash Flow Oper. Activities	520,209	1,484,608	1,298,286
Boeing	Oper. Income	2,319,000	2,826,000	2,128,000
	Cash Flow Oper. Activities	4,375,000	3,894,000	6,226,000
Mattel	Oper. Income	455,042	310,920	170,177
	Cash Flow Oper. Activities	1,156,084	756,793	555,090
Sprint	Oper. Income	468,000	(2,274,000)	(963,000)
	Cash Flow Oper. Activities	6,206,000	4,563,000	4,096,000
Toll Brothers	Oper. Income	219,887	213,673	145,943
	Cash Flow Oper. Activities	(94,105)	(148,379)	(16,863)

Finally, what could explain why Toll Brothers has *less* cash flow from operating activities than operating income? Does the company have a problem? Not necessarily. Toll Brothers is experiencing the kind of growth described earlier for your computer sales business. Its cash is supporting growth in inventory levels. Toll Brothers is one of the nation's largest new-home construction companies. Its growth rates, based on revenue from sales of new homes, for the 2002, 2001, and 2000 fiscal years were 5 percent, 24 percent, and 23 percent, respectively. When Toll Brothers begins to build new homes, it needs more inventory. Increases in inventory *do* affect cash flow from operating activities. Remember, increases in current assets decrease cash flow from operating activities. This condition alone might explain why the company has less cash flow from operating activities than operating income. Is this situation unfavorable? Chapter 6 made the point that, *other things being equal*, it is better to have less inventory. At Toll Brothers, however, other things are not equal. The company has been growing rapidly.

The Toll Brothers situation highlights a potential weakness in the format of the statement of cash flows. Some accountants consider it misleading to classify all increases in long-term assets as *investing activities* and all changes in inventory as affecting cash flow from operating activities. They argue that the increase in inventory at Toll Brothers that results from building more houses should be classified as an investing activity, just as the cost of a new building is. Although inventory is classified as a current asset and buildings are classified as long-term assets, in reality there is a certain level of inventory a company must permanently maintain to stay in business. The GAAP format of the statement of cash flows penalizes cash flow from operating activities for increases in inventory that are really a permanent investment in assets.

Conversely, the same critics might argue that some purchases of long-term assets are not actually *investments* but merely replacements of old, existing property, plant, and equipment. In other words, the *investing activities* section of the statement of cash flows makes no distinction between expenditures that expand the business and those that simply replace old equipment (sometimes called *capital maintenance* expenditures).

Users of the statement of cash flows must exercise the same care interpreting it as when they use the balance sheet or the income statement. Numbers alone are insufficient. Users must evaluate numbers based on knowledge of the particular business and industry they are analyzing.

Accounting information alone cannot guide a businessperson to a sound decision. Making good business decisions requires an understanding of the business in question, the environmental and economic factors affecting the operation of that business, and the accounting concepts on which the financial statements of that business are based.

a look back

Thus far in this text, you have considered many different accounting events that businesses experience. You have been asked to consider the effects these events have on a company's balance sheet, income statement, and statement of cash flows. By now, you should recognize that each financial statement shows a different, but equally important, view of a company's financial situation.

This chapter examined in detail only one financial statement, the statement of cash flows. The chapter provided a more comprehensive discussion of how accrual accounting relates to cash-based accounting. Effective use of financial statements requires understanding not only accrual and cash-based accounting systems but also how they relate to each other. That relationship is why a statement of cash flows can begin with a reconciliation of net income, an accrual measurement, to net cash flow from operating activities, a cash measurement. Finally, this chapter explained how the conventions for classifying cash flows as operating, investing, or financing activities require analysis and understanding to make informed decisions with the financial information.

a look forward

This chapter probably completes your first course in accounting. We sincerely hope that this text has provided you a meaningful learning experience that will serve you well as you progress through your academic training and ultimately, your career. Good luck and best wishes!

SELF-STUDY REVIEW PROBLEM

The following financial statements pertain to Schlemmer Company.

Balance Sheets As of December 31	2003	2004
Cash	$ 2,800	$48,400
Accounts Receivable	1,200	2,200
Inventory	6,000	5,600
Equipment	22,000	18,000
Accumulated Depreciation—Equip.	(17,400)	(13,650)
Land	10,400	17,200
Total Assets	$25,000	$77,750
Accounts Payable	$ 4,200	$ 5,200
Long-Term Debt	6,400	5,600
Common Stock	10,000	19,400
Retained Earnings	4,400	47,550
Total Liabilities and Equity	$25,000	$77,750

Income Statement For the Year Ended December 31, 2004	
Sales Revenue	$67,300
Cost of Goods Sold	(24,100)
Gross Margin	43,200
Depreciation Expense	(1,250)
Operating Income	41,950
Gain on Sale of Equipment	2,900
Loss on Disposal of Land	(100)
Net Income	$44,750

Additional Data

1. During 2004 the company sold equipment for $8,900 that had originally cost $11,000. Accumulated depreciation on this equipment was $5,000 at the time of sale. Also, the company purchased equipment for $7,000.
2. The company sold for $2,500 land that had cost $2,600, resulting in the recognition of a $100 loss. Also, common stock was issued in exchange for land valued at $9,400 at the time of the exchange.
3. The company declared and paid dividends of $1,600.

Required

a. Use T-accounts to analyze the preceding data.
b. Using the direct method, prepare in good form a statement of cash flows for the year ended December 31, 2004.

Solution to Requirement a
Transactions Legend

a1. Revenue, $67,300.
a2. Collection of accounts receivable, $66,300 ($1,200 + $67,300 − $2,200).
b1. Cost of goods sold, $24,100.
b2. Inventory purchases, $23,700 ($5,600 + $24,100 − $6,000).
b3. Payments for inventory purchases, $22,700 ($4,200 + $23,700 − $5,200).
c1. Depreciation expense, $1,250 (noncash).
d1. Sale of equipment, $8,900; cost of equipment sold, $11,000; accumulated depreciation on equipment sold, $5,000.
d2. Purchase of equipment, $7,000.
e1. Sale of land, $2,500; cost of land sold, $2,600.
f1. Issue of stock in exchange for land, $9,400.
g1. Paid dividends, $1,600.
h1. Paid off portion of long-term debt, $800.

SCHLEMMER COMPANY
T-Accounts

Assets = Liabilities + Equity

Assets

Cash

Bal.	2,800		
(a2)	66,300	(b3)	22,700
(d1)	8,900	(d2)	7,000
(e1)	2,500	(g1)	1,600
		(h1)	800
Bal.	48,400		

Accounts Receivable

Bal.	1,200		
(a1)	67,300	(a2)	66,300
Bal.	2,200		

Inventory

Bal.	6,000		
(b2)	23,700	(b1)	24,100
Bal.	5,600		

Equipment

Bal.	22,000		
(d2)	7,000	(d1)	11,000
Bal.	18,000		

Accumulated Depreciation

		Bal.	17,400
(d1)	5,000	(c1)	1,250
		Bal.	13,650

Land

Bal.	10,400		
(f1)	9,400	(e1)	2,600
Bal.	17,200		

Liabilities

Accounts Payable

		Bal.	4,200
(b3)	22,700	(b2)	23,700
		Bal.	5,200

Long-Term Debt

		Bal.	6,400
(h1)	800		
		Bal.	5,600

Equity

Common Stock

		Bal.	10,000
		(f1)	9,400
		Bal.	19,400

Retained Earnings

		Bal.	4,400
(b1)	24,100	(a1)	67,300
(c1)	1,250	(d1)	2,900
(e1)	100		
(g1)	1,600		
		Bal.	47,550

Solution to Requirement b

SCHLEMMER COMPANY
Statement of Cash Flows
For the Year Ended December 31, 2004

Cash Flows from Operating Activities		
Cash Receipts from Customers	$66,300	
Cash Payments for Inventory Purchases	(22,700)	
Net Cash Flow Provided by Operating Activities		$43,600
Cash Flows from Investing Activities		
Inflow from Sale of Equipment	8,900	
Inflow from Sale of Land	2,500	
Outflow to Purchase Equipment	(7,000)	
Net Cash Flow Provided by Investing Activities		4,400
Cash Flows from Financing Activities		
Outflow for Dividends	(1,600)	
Outflow for Repayment of Debt	(800)	
Net Cash Flow Used by Financing Activities		(2,400)
Net Increase in Cash		45,600
Plus: Beginning Cash Balance		2,800
Ending Cash Balance		$48,400
Schedule of Noncash Investing and Financing Activities		
Issued Common Stock for Land		$ 9,400

KEY TERMS

Accrual accounting *592*
Accrual transactions *591*
Cash inflows *589*
Cash outflows *589*
Deferral transactions *594*
Direct method *603*
Expense transactions *592*
Financing activities *590*
Indirect method *603*
Investing activities *590*
Noncash investing and financing activities *590*
Operating activities *590*
Revenue transactions *592*
T-account method *592*

QUESTIONS

1. What is the purpose of the statement of cash flows?

2. What are the three categories of cash flows reported on the cash flow statement? Discuss each and give an example of an inflow and an outflow for each category.

3. What are noncash investing and financing activities? Provide an example. How are such transactions shown on the statement of cash flows?

4. Best Company had beginning accounts receivable of $12,000 and ending accounts receivable of $14,000. If total sales were $110,000, what amount of cash was collected?

5. Best Company's Utilities Payable account had a beginning balance of $3,300 and an ending balance of $5,200. Utilities expense reported on the income statement was $87,000. What was the amount of cash paid for utilities for the period?

6. Best Company had a balance in the Unearned Revenue account of $4,300 at the beginning of the period and an ending balance of $5,700. If the portion of unearned revenue Best recognized as earned during the period was $15,600, what amount of cash did Best collect?

7. Which of the following activities are financing activities?
(a) Payment of accounts payable.
(b) Payment of interest on bonds payable.
(c) Sale of common stock.
(d) Sale of preferred stock at a premium.
(e) Payment of a cash dividend.

8. Does depreciation expense affect net cash flow? Explain.

9. If Best Company sold land that cost $4,200 at a $500 gain, how much cash did it collect from the sale of land?

10. If Best Company sold office equipment that originally cost $7,500 and had $7,200 of accumulated depreciation at a $100 loss, what was the selling price for the office equipment?

11. In which section of the statement of cash flows would the following transactions be reported?
(a) Cash receipt of interest income.
(b) Cash purchase of marketable securities.
(c) Cash purchase of equipment.
(d) Cash sale of merchandise.
(e) Cash sale of common stock.
(f) Payment of interest expense.
(g) Cash proceeds from loan.
(h) Cash payment on bonds payable.
(i) Cash receipt from sale of old equipment.
(j) Cash payment for operating expenses.

12. What is the difference between preparing the statement of cash flows using the direct approach and using the indirect approach?

13. Which method (direct or indirect) of presenting the statement of cash flows is more intuitively logical? Why?

14. What is the major advantage of using the indirect method to present the statement of cash flows?

15. What is the advantage of using the direct method to present the statement of cash flows?

16. How would Best Company report the following transactions on the statement of cash flows?
(a) Purchased new equipment for $46,000 cash.
(b) Sold old equipment for $8,700 cash. The equipment had a book value of $4,900.

17. Can a company report negative net cash flows from operating activities for the year on the statement of cash flows but still have positive net income on the income statement? Explain.

18. Why does the FASB prohibit disclosing cash flow per share in audited financial statements?

EXERCISES—SERIES A

All Exercises in Series A are available with McGraw-Hill's Homework Manager

EXERCISE 14–1A *Classifying Cash Flows into Categories—Direct Method* L.O. 1

Required

Classify each of the following operating activities, investing activities, financing activities, or non cash transactions. (assume the use of the direct method).

a. Paid cash to settle note payable.
b. Sold land for cash.
c. Paid cash to purchase a computer.
d. Paid cash for employee compensation.
e. Received cash interest from a bond investment.
f. Recognized depreciation expense.
g. Acquired cash from issue of common stock.
h. Provided services for cash.
i. Acquired cash by issuing a note payable.
j. Paid cash for interest.
k. Paid cash dividends.

EXERCISE 14–2A *Cash Outflows from Operating Activities—Direct Method* L.O. 1

Required

Which of the following transactions produce cash outflows from operating activities (assume the use of the direct method)?

a. Cash receipt from collecting accounts receivable.
b. Cash receipt from sale of land.
c. Cash payment for dividends.
d. Cash payment to settle an account payable.
e. Cash payment to purchase inventory.
f. Cash payment for equipment.

EXERCISE 14–3A *Using Account Balances to Determine Cash Flows from Operating Activities—Direct Method* L.O. 2

The following account balances are available for Max Company for 2007.

Account Title	Beginning of Year	End of Year
Accounts Receivable	$42,000	$46,000
Interest Receivable	6,000	5,000
Accounts Payable	22,000	26,000
Salaries Payable	12,000	15,000

Other Information for 2007

Sales on Account	$680,000
Interest Income	24,000
Operating Expenses	270,000
Salaries Expense for the Year	172,000

Required

(*Hint:* It may be helpful to assume that all revenues and expenses are on account.)

a. Compute the amount of cash *inflow* from operating activities.
b. Compute the amount of cash *outflow* from operating activities.

L.O. 2

EXERCISE 14–4A *Using Account Balances to Determine Cash Flow from Operating Activities—Direct Method*

The following account balances were available for Theri Enterprises for 2007.

Account Title	Beginning of Year	End of Year
Unearned Revenue	$5,000	$6,500
Prepaid Rent	2,400	1,800

During the year, $68,000 of unearned revenue was recognized as having been earned. Rent expense for the period was $15,000. Theri Enterprises maintains its books on the accrual basis.

Required

Using T-accounts and the preceding information, determine the amount of cash inflow from revenue and cash outflow for rent.

L.O. 2, 3

EXERCISE 14–5A *Using Account Balances to Determine Cash Flow from Investing Activities*

The following account information pertains to Guidry Company for 2005.

Land

	Debit	Credit
Bal.	46,000	56,000
	128,000	
Bal.	118,000	

Marketable Securities

	Debit	Credit
Bal.	82,000	46,000
	120,000	
Bal.	156,000	

The income statement reported a $3,000 loss on the sale of land and a $2,500 gain on the sale of marketable securities.

Required

Prepare the investing activities section of the 2005 statement of cash flows.

L.O. 2, 3

EXERCISE 14–6A *Using Account Balances to Determine Cash Flow from Financing Activities*

The following account balances pertain to Olack, Inc., for 2006.

Bonds Payable

Debit		Credit
	Bal.	220,000
90,000		
	Bal.	130,000

Common Stock

Debit		Credit
	Bal.	280,000
		180,000
	Bal.	460,000

Paid-in Capital in Excess of Par Value

Debit		Credit
	Bal.	90,000
		50,000
	Bal.	140,000

Required

Prepare the financing activities section of the 2006 statement of cash flows.

L.O. 2, 3

EXERCISE 14–7A *Using Account Balances to Determine Cash Outflow for Inventory Purchases*

The following account information pertains to Maze Company, which uses the perpetual inventory method and purchases all inventory on account.

Inventory

	Debit	Credit
Bal.	52,000	
	?	352,000
Bal.	61,000	

Accounts Payable

Debit		Credit
	Bal.	44,000
?		?
	Bal.	41,000

Required

Compute the amount of cash paid for the purchase of inventory.

EXERCISE 14–8A *Using Account Balances to Determine Cash Flow from Operating Activities—Indirect Method*

L.O. 2

Kwon Company presents its statement of cash flows using the indirect method. The following accounts and corresponding balances were drawn from Kwon's accounting records for the period.

Account Titles	Beginning Balances	Ending Balances
Accounts Receivable	$32,000	$28,000
Prepaid Rent	1,500	1,800
Interest Receivable	500	700
Accounts Payable	9,800	8,500
Salaries Payable	3,200	3,600
Unearned Revenue	6,000	4,000

Net income for the period was $52,000.

Required

Using the preceding information, compute the net cash flow from operating activities using the indirect method.

EXERCISE 14–9A *Using Account Balances to Determine Cash Flow from Operating Activities—Direct and Indirect Methods*

L.O. 2, 3, 4

The following account balances are from Marlin Company's accounting records. Assume Marlin had no investing or financing transactions during 2007.

December 31	2006	2007
Cash	$65,000	$107,000
Accounts Receivable	75,000	78,000
Prepaid Rent	900	800
Accounts Payable	33,000	34,000
Utilities Payable	1,200	1,500
Sales Revenue		$272,000
Operating Expenses		(168,000)
Utilities Expense		(36,400)
Rent Expense		(24,000)
Net Income		$ 43,600

Required

a. Prepare the operating activities section of the 2007 statement of cash flows using the direct method.
b. Prepare the operating activities section of the 2007 statement of cash flows using the indirect method.

EXERCISE 14–10A *Interpreting Statement of Cash Flows Information*

L.O. 3, 5

The following selected transactions pertain to Johnston Corporation for 2007.

1. Paid $35,200 cash to purchase delivery equipment.
2. Sold delivery equipment for $3,500. The equipment had originally cost $18,000 and had accumulated depreciation of $12,000.
3. Borrowed $50,000 cash by issuing bonds at face value.
4. Purchased a building that cost $220,000. Paid $50,000 cash and issued a mortgage for the remaining $170,000.
5. Exchanged no-par common stock for machinery valued at $38,700.

Required

a. Prepare the appropriate sections of the 2007 statement of cash flows.
b. Explain how a company could spend more cash on investing activities than it collected from financing activities during the same accounting period.

PROBLEMS—SERIES A

All Problems in Series A are available with McGraw-Hill's Homework Manager

L.O. 1

PROBLEM 14–11A *Classifying Cash Flows*

Required

Classify each of the following as an operating activity (OA), an investing activity (IA), or a financing activity (FA) cash flow, or a noncash transaction (NT).

a. Provided services for cash.
b. Purchased marketable securities with cash.
c. Paid cash for rent.
d. Received interest on note receivable.
e. Paid cash for salaries.
f. Received advance payment for services.
g. Paid a cash dividend.
h. Provided services on account.
i. Purchased office supplies on account.
j. Bought land with cash.
k. Collected cash from accounts receivable.
l. Issued common stock for cash.
m. Repaid principal and interest on a note payable.
n. Declared a stock split.
o. Purchased inventory with cash.
p. Recorded amortization of goodwill.
q. Paid insurance with cash.
r. Issued a note payable in exchange for equipment.
s. Recorded depreciation expense.

L.O. 2, 3

PROBLEM 14–12A *Using Transaction Data to Prepare a Statement of Cash Flows*

CHECK FIGURE
Net Cash Flow from Operating Activities: $(110,775)

Store Company engaged in the following transactions during the 2007 accounting period. The beginning cash balance was $28,600.

1. Credit sales were $250,000. The beginning receivables balance was $87,000 and the ending balance was $103,000.
2. Salaries expense for the period was $56,000. The beginning salaries payable balance was $3,500 and the ending balance was $2,000.
3. Other operating expenses for the period were $125,000. The beginning operating expense payable balance was $4,500 and the ending balance was $8,500.
4. Recorded $19,500 of depreciation expense. The beginning and ending balances in the Accumulated Depreciation account were $14,000 and $33,500, respectively.
5. The Equipment account had beginning and ending balances of $210,000 and $240,000, respectively. The increase was caused by the cash purchase of equipment.
6. The beginning and ending balances in the Notes Payable account were $50,000 and $150,000, respectively. The increase was caused by additional cash borrowing.
7. There was $6,000 of interest expense reported on the income statement. The beginning and ending balances in the Interest Payable account were $1,500 and $1,000, respectively.
8. The beginning and ending Merchandise Inventory account balances were $90,000 and $108,000, respectively. The company sold merchandise with a cost of $156,000 (cost of goods sold for the period was $156,000). The beginning and ending balances of Accounts Payable were $9,500 and $11,500, respectively.
9. The beginning and ending balances of Notes Receivable were $5,000 and $10,000, respectively. The increase resulted from a cash loan to one of the company's employees.
10. The beginning and ending balances of the Common Stock account were $100,000 and $120,000, respectively. The increase was caused by the issue of common stock for cash.
11. Land had beginning and ending balances of $50,000 and $41,000, respectively. Land that cost $9,000 was sold for $12,200, resulting in a gain of $3,200.
12. The tax expense for the period was $7,700. The Taxes Payable account had a $950 beginning balance and an $875 ending balance.

13. The Investments account had beginning and ending balances of $25,000 and $29,000, respectively. The company purchased investments for $18,000 cash during the period, and investments that cost $14,000 were sold for $9,000, resulting in a $5,000 loss.

Required
Convert the preceding information to cash-equivalent data and prepare a statement of cash flows.

PROBLEM 14–13A ***Using Financial Statement Data to Determine Cash Flow from Operating Activities***

L.O. 2, 3

excel
www.mhhe.com/edmonds3e

CHECK FIGURE
a. Net Cash Flow from Operating Activities: $(11,600)

The following account information is available for Park Company for 2004:

Account Title	Beginning of Year	End of Year
Accounts Receivable	$26,000	$24,000
Merchandise Inventory	52,000	56,000
Prepaid Insurance	24,000	20,000
Accounts Payable (Inventory)	20,000	23,000
Salaries Payable	4,200	4,600

Other Information
1. Sales for the period were $180,000.
2. Purchases of merchandise for the period were $90,000.
3. Insurance expense for the period was $42,000.
4. Other operating expenses (all cash) were $30,000.
5. Salary expense was $35,000.

Required
a. Compute the net cash flow from operating activities.
b. Prepare the cash flow from the operating activities section of the statement of cash flows.

PROBLEM 14–14A ***Using Financial Statement Data to Determine Cash Flow from Investing Activities***

L.O. 2, 3

excel
www.mhhe.com/edmonds3e

CHECK FIGURE
a. Net Cash Flow from Investing Activities: $(152,000)

The following information pertaining to investing activities is available for Leach Company for 2005:

Account Title	Beginning of Year	End of Year
Machinery and Equipment	$425,000	$520,000
Marketable Securities	112,000	102,000
Land	90,000	140,000

Other Information for 2005
1. Marketable securities were sold at book value. No gain or loss was recognized.
2. Machinery was purchased for $120,000. Old machinery with a book value of $5,000 (cost of $25,000, accumulated depreciation of $20,000) was sold for $8,000.
3. No land was sold during the year.

Required
a. Compute the net cash flow from investing activities.
b. Prepare the cash flow from investing activities section of the statement of cash flows.

PROBLEM 14–15A ***Using Financial Statement Data to Determine Cash Flow from Financing Activities***

L.O. 2, 3

CHECK FIGURE
a. Net Cash Flow from Financing Activities: $(25,000)

The following information pertaining to financing activities is available for Rebel Company for 2007:

Account Title	Beginning of Year	End of Year
Bonds Payable	$300,000	$210,000
Common Stock	200,000	260,000
Paid-in Capital in Excess of Par	75,000	110,000

Other Information

1. Dividends paid during the period amounted to $30,000.
2. No new funds were borrowed during the period.

Required

a. Compute the net cash flow from financing activities for 2007.
b. Prepare the cash flow from the financing activities section of the statement of cash flows.

L.O. 2, 3

PROBLEM 14–16A *Using Financial Statements to Prepare a Statement of Cash Flows—Direct Method*

CHECK FIGURES
Net Cash Flow from Operating Activities: $18,750
Net Increase in Cash: $21,400

The following financial statements were drawn from the records of Pacific Company.

Balance Sheets
As of December 31

	2006	2007
Assets		
Cash	$ 2,800	$24,200
Accounts Receivable	1,200	2,000
Inventory	6,000	6,400
Equipment	42,000	19,000
Accumulated Depreciation—Equipment	(17,400)	(9,000)
Land	10,400	18,400
Total Assets	$45,000	$61,000
Liabilities and Equity		
Accounts Payable	$ 4,200	$ 2,600
Long-Term Debt	6,400	2,800
Common Stock	10,000	22,000
Retained Earnings	24,400	33,600
Total Liabilities and Equity	$45,000	$61,000

Income Statement
For the Year Ended December 31, 2007

Sales Revenue	$35,700
Cost of Goods Sold	(14,150)
Gross Margin	21,550
Depreciation Expense	(3,600)
Operating Income	17,950
Gain on Sale of Equipment	500
Loss on Disposal of Land	(50)
Net Income	$18,400

Additional Data

1. During 2007, the company sold equipment for $18,500; it had originally cost $30,000. Accumulated depreciation on this equipment was $12,000 at the time of the sale. Also, the company purchased equipment for $7,000 cash.
2. The company sold land that had cost $4,000. This land was sold for $3,950, resulting in the recognition of a $50 loss. Also, common stock was issued in exchange for title to land that was valued at $12,000 at the time of exchange.
3. Paid dividends of $9,200.

Required

Use the T-account method to analyze the data and prepare a statement of cash flows using the direct method.

PROBLEM 14–17A ***Using Financial Statements to Prepare a Statement of Cash Flows—Direct Method***

L.O. 2, 3

CHECK FIGURES
Net Cash Flow from Operating Activities: $86,800
Net Increase in Cash: $95,400

The following financial statements were drawn from the records of Raceway Sports:

Balance Sheets
As of December 31

	2006	2007
Assets		
Cash	$ 28,200	$123,600
Accounts Receivable	66,000	57,000
Inventory	114,000	126,000
Notes Receivable	30,000	0
Equipment	255,000	147,000
Accumulated Depreciation—Equipment	(141,000)	(74,740)
Land	52,500	82,500
Total Assets	$404,700	$461,360
Liabilities and Equity		
Accounts Payable	$ 48,600	$ 42,000
Salaries Payable	24,000	30,000
Utilities Payable	1,200	600
Interest Payable	1,800	0
Note Payable	60,000	0
Common Stock	240,000	300,000
Retained Earnings	29,100	88,760
Total Liabilities and Equity	$404,700	$461,360

Income Statement
For the Year Ended December 31, 2007

Sales Revenue	$580,000
Cost of Goods Sold	(288,000)
Gross Margin	292,000
Operating Expenses	
Salary Expense	(184,000)
Depreciation Expense	(17,740)
Utilities Expense	(12,200)
Operating Income	78,060
Nonoperating Items	
Interest Expense	(3,000)
Gain or (Loss)	(1,800)
Net Income	$ 73,260

Additional Information

1. Sold equipment costing $108,000 with accumulated depreciation of $84,000 for $22,200 cash.
2. Paid a $13,600 cash dividend to owners.

Required

Use the T-account method to analyze the data and prepare a statement of cash flows, using the direct method.

L.O. 2 **PROBLEM 14–18A** *Using Financial Statements to Prepare a Statement of Cash Flows—Indirect Method*

eXcel
www.mhhe.com/edmonds3e

CHECK FIGURES
Net Cash Flow from Operating Activities: $170,200
Net Increase in Cash: $28,200

The comparative balance sheets for Redwood Corporation for 2006 and 2007 follow:

Balance Sheets
As of December 31

	2006	2007
Assets		
Cash	$ 40,600	$ 68,800
Accounts Receivable	22,000	30,000
Merchandise Inventory	176,000	160,000
Prepaid Rent	4,800	2,400
Equipment	288,000	256,000
Accumulated Depreciation	(236,000)	(146,800)
Land	80,000	192,000
Total Assets	$375,400	$562,400
Liabilities		
Accounts Payable (Inventory)	$ 76,000	$ 67,000
Salaries Payable	24,000	28,000
Stockholders' Equity		
Common Stock, $25 Par Value	200,000	250,000
Retained Earnings	75,400	217,400
Total Liabilities and Equity	$375,400	$562,400

Income Statement
For the Year Ended December 31, 2007

Sales	$1,500,000
Cost of Goods Sold	(797,200)
Gross Profit	702,800
Operating Expenses	
Depreciation Expense	(22,800)
Rent Expense	(24,000)
Salaries Expense	(256,000)
Other Operating Expenses	(258,000)
Net Income	$ 142,000

Other Information

1. Purchased land for $112,000.
2. Purchased new equipment for $100,000.
3. Sold old equipment that cost $132,000 with accumulated depreciation of $112,000 for $20,000 cash.
4. Issued common stock for $50,000.

Required

Prepare the statement of cash flows for 2007, using the indirect method.

EXERCISES—SERIES B

L.O. 1 **EXERCISE 14–1B** *Classifying Cash Flows into Categories—Direct Method*

Required

Identify whether the cash flows in the following list should be classified as operating activities, investing activities, or financing activities on the statement of cash flows (assume the use of the direct method).

a. Sold merchandise on account.
b. Paid employee salary.
c. Received cash proceeds from bank loan.
d. Paid dividends.
e. Sold used equipment for cash.

f. Received interest income on a certificate of deposit.
g. Issued stock for cash.
h. Repaid bank loan.
i. Purchased equipment for cash.
j. Paid interest on loan.

EXERCISE 14–2B *Cash Inflows from Operating Activities—Direct Method* L.O. 1

Required
Which of the following transactions produce cash inflows from operating activities (assume the use of the direct method)?

a. Cash payment for utilities expense.
b. Cash payment for equipment.
c. Cash receipt from interest.
d. Cash payment for dividends.
e. Collection of cash from accounts receivable.
f. Provide services for cash.

EXERCISE 14–3B *Using Account Balances to Determine Cash Flow from Operating Activities—Direct Method* L.O. 2

The following account balances are available for Norstom Company for 2002.

Account Title	Beginning of Year	End of Year
Accounts Receivable	$40,000	$46,000
Interest Receivable	5,000	3,000
Accounts Payable	30,000	33,000
Salaries Payable	12,000	10,500

Other Information for 2002

Sales on Account	$275,000
Interest Income	25,000
Operating Expenses	196,000
Salaries Expense for the Year	75,000

Required
(*Hint:* It may be helpful to assume that all revenues and expenses are on account.)

a. Compute the amount of cash *inflow* from operating activities.
b. Compute the amount of cash *outflow* from operating activities.

EXERCISE 14–4B *Using Account Balances to Determine Cash Flow from Operating Activities—Direct Method* L.O. 2

The following account balances were available for Earles Candy Company for 2001:

Account Title	Beginning of Year	End of Year
Unearned Revenue	$18,000	$8,000
Prepaid Rent	2,000	900

During the year, $41,000 of unearned revenue was recognized as having been earned. Rent expense for the period was $8,000. Earles Candy Company maintains its books on the accrual basis.

Required
Using T-accounts and the preceding information, determine the amount of cash inflow from revenue and cash outflow for rent.

L.O. 2, 3 **EXERCISE 14–5B** ***Using Account Balances to Determine Cash Flow from Investing Activities***

The following account information is available for McClung, Inc., for 2005:

Land			
Bal.	20,000	50,000	
	100,000		
Bal.	70,000		

Marketable Securities			
Bal.	75,000	30,000	
	40,000		
Bal.	85,000		

The income statement reported a $9,000 gain on the sale of land and a $1,200 loss on the sale of marketable securities.

Required
Prepare the investing activities section of the statement of cash flows for 2005.

L.O. 2, 3 **EXERCISE 14–6B** ***Using Account Balances to Determine Cash Flow from Financing Activities***

The following account balances were available for Golden Company for 2007:

Mortgage Payable		
	148,000	Bal.
62,000		
	86,000	Bal.

Capital Stock		
	200,000	Bal.
	50,000	
	250,000	Bal.

Paid-in Capital in Excess of Par		
	65,000	Bal.
	30,000	
	95,000	Bal.

Required
Prepare the financing activities section of the statement of cash flows for 2007.

L.O. 2 **EXERCISE 14–7B** ***Using Account Balances to Determine Cash Outflow for Inventory Purchases***

The following account information is available for Sherman Company. The company uses the perpetual inventory method and makes all inventory purchases on account.

Inventory			
Bal.	41,000		
	?	120,000	
Bal.	65,000		

Accounts Payable		
	42,000	Bal.
?	?	
	52,000	Bal.

Required
Compute the amount of cash paid for the purchase of inventory.

L.O. 2 **EXERCISE 14–8B** ***Using Account Balances to Determine Cash Flow from Operating Activities—Indirect Method***

Maple Company presents its statement of cash flows using the indirect method. The following accounts and corresponding balances were drawn from Maple's accounting records.

Account Titles	Beginning Balances	Ending Balances
Accounts Receivable	$30,000	$35,000
Prepaid Rent	2,000	1,200
Interest Receivable	800	400
Accounts Payable	9,000	9,500
Salaries Payable	2,500	2,100
Unearned Revenue	1,200	2,200

Net income for the period was $45,000.

Required
Using the preceding information, compute the net cash flow from operating activities using the indirect method.

EXERCISE 14–9B *Using Account Balances to Determine Cash Flow from Operating Activities—Direct and Indirect Methods*

L.O. 2, 3, 4

The following information is from the accounting records of Mong Company:

	2000	2001
Cash	$ 42,000	$ 88,800
Accounts Receivable	158,000	159,800
Prepaid Rent	3,000	5,600
Accounts Payable	120,000	125,000
Utilities Payable	12,000	8,400
Sales Revenue		$212,000
Operating Expenses		(135,000)
Utilities Expense		(17,200)
Rent Expense		(10,000)
Net Income		$ 49,800

Required
a. Prepare the operating activities section of the 2001 statement of cash flows using the direct method.
b. Prepare the operating activities section of the 2001 statement of cash flows using the indirect method.

EXERCISE 14–10B *Interpreting Statement of Cash Flows Information*

L.O. 3, 5

The following selected transactions pertain to Johnston Company for 2003.

1. Purchased new office equipment for $9,800 cash.
2. Sold old office equipment for $2,000 that originally cost $12,000 and had accumulated depreciation of $11,000.
3. Borrowed $20,000 cash from the bank for six months.
4. Purchased land for $125,000 by paying $50,000 in cash and issuing a note for the balance.
5. Exchanged no-par common stock for an automobile valued at $26,500.

Required
a. Prepare the appropriate sections of the statement of cash flows for 2003.
b. What information does the noncash investing and financing activities section of the statement provide? If this information were omitted, could it affect a decision to invest in a company?

PROBLEMS—SERIES B

PROBLEM 14–11B *Classifying Cash Flows*

L.O. 1

Required
Classify each of the following as an operating activity (OA), an investing activity (IA), or a financing activity (FA) cash flow, or a noncash transaction (NT).

a. Paid cash for operating expenses.
b. Wrote off an uncollectible account receivable using the allowance method.
c. Wrote off an uncollectible account receivable using the direct write-off method.
d. Issued common stock for cash.
e. Declared a stock split.
f. Issued a mortgage to purchase a building.
g. Purchased equipment with cash.
h. Repaid the principal balance on a note payable.
i. Made a cash payment for the balance due in the Dividends Payable account.
j. Received a cash dividend from investment in marketable securities.

k. Purchased supplies on account.
l. Collected cash from accounts receivable.
m. Accrued warranty expense.
n. Borrowed cash by issuing a bond.
o. Loaned cash to a business associate.
p. Paid cash for interest expense.
q. Incurred a loss on the sale of equipment.
r. Wrote down inventory because the year-end physical count was less than the balance in the Inventory account.
s. Paid cash to purchase inventory.

L.O. 2, 3

PROBLEM 14–12B *Using Transaction Data to Prepare a Statement of Cash Flows*

Greenstein Company engaged in the following transactions during 2003. The beginning cash balance was $86,000.

1. Credit sales were $548,000. The beginning receivables balance was $128,000 and the ending balance was $90,000.
2. Salaries expense for 2003 was $232,000. The beginning salaries payable balance was $16,000 and the ending balance was $8,000.
3. Other operating expenses for 2003 were $236,000. The beginning Operating Expense Payable balance was $16,000 and the ending balance was $10,000.
4. Recorded $30,000 of depreciation expense. The beginning and ending balances in the Accumulated Depreciation account were $12,000 and $42,000, respectively.
5. The Equipment account had beginning and ending balances of $44,000 and $56,000, respectively. The increase was caused by the cash purchase of equipment.
6. The beginning and ending balances in the Notes Payable account were $44,000 and $36,000, respectively. The decrease was caused by the cash repayment of debt.
7. There was $4,600 of interest expense reported on the income statement. The beginning and ending balances in the Interest Payable account were $8,400 and $7,500, respectively.
8. The beginning and ending Merchandise Inventory account balances were $22,000 and $29,400, respectively. The company sold merchandise with a cost of $83,600. The beginning and ending balances of Accounts Payable were $8,000 and $6,400, respectively.
9. The beginning and ending balances of Notes Receivable were $100,000 and $60,000, respectively. The decline resulted from the cash collection of a portion of the receivable.
10. The beginning and ending balances of the Common Stock account were $120,000 and $160,000, respectively. The increase was caused by the issue of common stock for cash.
11. Land had beginning and ending balances of $24,000 and $14,000, respectively. Land that cost $10,000 was sold for $6,000, resulting in a loss of $4,000.
12. The tax expense for 2003 was $6,600. The Tax Payable account had a $2,400 beginning balance and a $2,200 ending balance.
13. The Investments account had beginning and ending balances of $20,000 and $60,000, respectively. The company purchased investments for $50,000 cash during 2003, and investments that cost $10,000 were sold for $22,000, resulting in a $12,000 gain.

Required

Convert the preceding information to cash-equivalent data and prepare a statement of cash flows.

L.O. 2, 3

PROBLEM 14–13B *Using Financial Statement Data to Determine Cash Flow from Operating Activities*

The following account information is available for Gables Auto Supplies for 2003:

Account Title	Beginning of Year	End of Year
Accounts Receivable	$ 17,800	$ 21,000
Merchandise Inventory	136,000	142,800
Prepaid Insurance	1,600	1,200
Accounts Payable (Inventory)	18,800	19,600
Salaries Payable	6,400	5,800

Other Information

1. Sales for the period were $248,000.
2. Purchases of merchandise for the period were $186,000.
3. Insurance expense for the period was $8,000.
4. Other operating expenses (all cash) were $27,400.
5. Salary expense was $42,600.

Required

a. Compute the net cash flow from operating activities.
b. Prepare the cash flow from the operating activities section of the statement of cash flows.

PROBLEM 14–14B *Using Financial Statement Data to Determine Cash Flow from Investing Activities* L.O. 2, 3

The following information pertaining to investing activities is available for Tony's Flea Markets, Inc., for 2001.

Account Title	Beginning of Year	End of Year
Trucks and Equipment	$162,000	$170,000
Marketable Securities	66,000	51,200
Land	42,000	34,000

Other Information for 2001

1. Tony's sold marketable securities at book value. No gain or loss was recognized.
2. Trucks were purchased for $40,000. Old trucks with a cost of $32,000 and accumulated depreciation of $24,000 were sold for $11,000.
3. Land that cost $8,000 was sold for $10,000.

Required

a. Compute the net cash flow from investing activities.
b. Prepare the cash flow from the investing activities section of the statement of cash flows.

PROBLEM 14–15B *Using Financial Statement Data to Determine Cash Flow from Financing Activities* L.O. 2, 3

The following information pertaining to financing activities is available for Engineered Components Company for 2002.

Account Title	Beginning of Year	End of Year
Bonds Payable	$170,000	$180,000
Common Stock	210,000	280,000
Paid-in Capital in Excess of Par	84,000	116,000

Other Information

1. Dividends paid during the period amounted to $28,000.
2. Additional funds of $40,000 were borrowed during the period by issuing bonds.

Required

a. Compute the net cash flow from financing activities for 2002.
b. Prepare the cash flow from the financing activities section of the statement of cash flows.

PROBLEM 14–16B *Using Financial Statements to Prepare a Statement of Cash Flows—Direct Method* L.O. 2, 3

The following financial statements were drawn from the records of Healthy Products Co.

Balance Sheets
As of December 31

	2002	2003
Assets		
Cash	$ 1,940	$16,120
Accounts Receivable	2,000	2,400
Inventory	2,600	2,000
Equipment	17,100	13,700
Accumulated Depreciation—Equipment	(12,950)	(11,300)
Land	8,000	13,000
Total Assets	$18,690	$35,920
Liabilities and Equity		
Accounts Payable	$ 2,400	$ 3,600
Long-Term Debt	4,000	3,200
Common Stock	10,000	17,000
Retained Earnings	2,290	12,120
Total Liabilities and Stockholders' Equity	$18,690	$35,920

Income Statement
For the Year Ended December 31, 2003

Sales Revenue	$17,480
Cost of Goods Sold	(6,200)
Gross Margin	11,280
Depreciation Expense	(1,750)
Operating Income	9,530
Gain on Sale of Equipment	1,800
Loss on Disposal of Land	(600)
Net Income	$10,730

Additional Data

1. During 2003, the company sold equipment for $6,800; it had originally cost $8,400. Accumulated depreciation on this equipment was $3,400 at the time of the sale. Also, the company purchased equipment for $5,000 cash.
2. The company sold land that had cost $2,000. This land was sold for $1,400, resulting in the recognition of a $600 loss. Also, common stock was issued in exchange for title to land that was valued at $7,000 at the time of exchange.
3. Paid dividends of $900.

Required

Use the T-account method to analyze the data and prepare a statement of cash flows, using the direct method.

L.O. 2, 3 **PROBLEM 14–17B** ***Using Financial Statements to Prepare a Statement of Cash Flows—Direct Method***

The following financial statements were drawn from the records of Norton Materials, Inc.

Balance Sheets
As of December 31

	2000	2001
Assets		
Cash	$ 14,100	$ 94,300
Accounts Receivable	40,000	36,000
Inventory	64,000	72,000
Notes Receivable	16,000	0
Equipment	170,000	98,000
Accumulated Depreciation—Equipment	(94,000)	(47,800)
Land	30,000	46,000
Total Assets	$240,100	$298,500

continued

	2000	2001
Liabilities and Equity		
Accounts Payable	$ 26,400	$ 24,000
Salaries Payable	10,000	15,000
Utilities Payable	1,400	800
Interest Payable	1,000	0
Note Payable	24,000	0
Common Stock	110,000	150,000
Retained Earnings	67,300	108,700
Total Liabilities and Equity	$240,100	$298,500

Income Statement For the Year Ended December 31, 2001	
Sales Revenue	$300,000
Cost of Goods Sold	(144,000)
Gross Margin	156,000
Operating Expenses	
Salary Expense	(88,000)
Depreciation Expense	(9,800)
Utilities Expense	(6,400)
Operating Income	51,800
Nonoperating Items	
Interest Expense	(2,400)
Loss	(800)
Net Income	$ 48,600

Additional Information

1. Sold equipment costing $72,000 with accumulated depreciation of $56,000 for $15,200 cash.
2. Paid a $7,200 cash dividend to owners.

Required

Use the T-account method to analyze the data and prepare a statement of cash flows, using the direct method.

PROBLEM 14–18B ***Using Financial Statements to Prepare a Statement of Cash Flows—Indirect Method*** **L.O. 2**

The comparative balance sheets for Lind Beauty Products, Inc., for 2002 and 2003 follow:

Balance Sheets As of December 31	2002	2003
Assets		
Cash	$ 48,400	$ 6,300
Accounts Receivable	7,260	10,200
Merchandise Inventory	56,000	45,200
Prepaid Rent	2,140	700
Equipment	144,000	140,000
Accumulated Depreciation	(118,000)	(73,400)
Land	50,000	116,000
Total Assets	$189,800	$245,000
Liabilities and Equity		
Accounts Payable (Inventory)	$ 40,000	$ 37,200
Salaries Payable	10,600	12,200
Stockholders' Equity		
Common Stock, $50 Par Value	120,000	150,000
Retained Earnings	19,200	45,600
Total Liabilities and Equity	$189,800	$245,000

Income Statement For the Year Ended December 31, 2003	
Sales	$480,000
Cost of Goods Sold	(264,000)
Gross Profit	216,000
Operating Expenses	
Depreciation Expense	(11,400)
Rent Expense	(7,000)
Salaries Expense	(95,200)
Other Operating Expenses	(76,000)
Net Income	$ 26,400

Other Information

1. Purchased land for $66,000.
2. Purchased new equipment for $62,000.
3. Sold old equipment that cost $66,000 with accumulated depreciation of $56,000 for $10,000 cash.
4. Issued common stock for $30,000.

Required

Prepare the statement of cash flows for 2003 using the indirect method.

ANALYZE, THINK, COMMUNICATE

ATC 14–1 RESEARCH ASSIGNMENT *Analyzing Cash Flow Information*

On March 19, 2003 the United States military began operations in Iraq. Soon afterwards it was announced that the Halliburton Company and its subsidiaries had been awarded contracts to provide services, such as meals, to service men and women serving there. Complete the requirements below using the 2003 financial statements available on the company's website. Obtain these by following these steps:

- Go to www.halliburton.com.
- Click on the "INVESTOR RELATIONS" link, shown under "COMPANY."
- On this screen, click on the "Annual Report and Proxy" link.
- Next, click on "2003 Annual Report—PDF Version."
- The financial statements are on pages 69 through 72 of the annual report.

Required

a. What were Halliburton's *revenues* in 2001, 2002 and 2003?
b. What was the company's *net income (loss)* in 2001, 2002 and 2003?
c. What was Halliburton's *cash flow from operating activities* in 2003?
d. What was the increase or decrease in the company's cash balance from 2002 to 2003?
e. Using the company's statement of cash flows, explain why this increase or decrease occurred.
f. Do you consider the change in Halliburton's cash position from 2002 to 2003 to be good or bad? Explain your answer.
g. Does it appear that Halliburton's acceptance of the government contracts in 2003 required it to make significant new cash investments?

ATC 14–2 REAL-WORLD CASE *Following the Cash*

Panera Bread Company (Panera) was formerly known as Au Bon Pain Company (ABP). In May 1999, the ABP division of the company was sold to private investors for $72 million, and assumed the new name.

Panera operates retail bakery-cafes under the names Panera Bread and Saint Louis Bread Company. The following table shows the number of these cafes in operation for each of the past five years.

Year	Company Owned	Franchise Owned	Total
2000	90	172	262
1999	81	100	181
1998	70	45	115
1997	57	19	76
1996	52	10	62

Most of Panera's baked goods are distributed to the stores in the form of frozen dough. In March 1998, the company sold its frozen dough production facility to the Bunge Food Corporation for $13 million. Panera agreed to purchase its frozen dough from Bunge for at least the next five years.

Panera's statements of cash flows for 1998, 1999, and 2000 follow.

PANERA BREAD COMPANY
Consolidated Statements of Cash Flows
(Dollars in thousands)

	For the Fiscal Years Ended		
	December 30, 2000	December 25, 1999	December 26, 1998
Cash flows from operations			
Net income (loss)	$ 6,853	$ (629)	$(20,494)
Adjustments to reconcile net income (loss) to net cash provided by operating activities:			
Depreciation and amortization	8,412	6,379	12,667
Amortization of deferred financing costs	88	406	683
Provision for losses on accounts receivable	(111)	93	56
Minority interest	—	(25)	(127)
Tax benefit from exercise of stock options	4,001	—	75
Deferred income taxes	664	42	(6,664)
Loss on early extinguishment of debt	—	382	—
Nonrecurring charge	494	5,545	26,236
Loss on disposal of assets	—	—	735
Changes in operating assets and liabilities:			
Accounts receivable	(308)	(1,596)	15
Inventories	(562)	(65)	212
Prepaid expenses	(543)	(3,560)	(535)
Refundable income taxes	(376)	—	480
Accounts payable	1,861	(3,037)	4,069
Accrued expenses	(645)	769	3,104
Deferred revenue	234	2,011	—
Net cash provided by operating activities	20,062	6,715	20,512
Cash flows from investing activities			
Additions to property and equipment	(20,089)	(15,306)	(21,706)
Proceeds from sale of assets	—	72,163	12,694
Change in cash included in net current liabilities held for sale	—	(466)	(1,305)
Payments received on notes receivable	35	114	240
Increase in intangible assets	—	(50)	(139)
Increase (decrease) in deposits and other	(771)	855	(956)
Increase in notes receivable	—	(30)	(45)
Net cash (used in) provided by investing activities	(20,825)	57,280	(11,217)
Cash flows from financing activities			
Exercise of employee stock options	8,206	96	1,203
Proceeds from long-term debt issuance	765	41,837	75,418
Principal payments on long-term debt	(391)	(106,073)	(84,253)
Purchase of treasury stock	(900)	—	—
Proceeds from issuance of common stock	182	148	268
Common stock issued for employee stock bonus	—	304	—
Increase in deferred financing costs	(24)	(110)	(506)
Decrease in minority interest	—	(121)	(418)
Net cash provided by (used in) financing activities	7,838	(63,919)	(8,288)
Net increase in cash and cash equivalents	7,075	76	1,007
Cash and cash equivalents at beginning of year	1,936	1,860	853
Cash and cash equivalents at end of year	$ 9,011	$ 1,936	$ 1,860
Supplemental cash flow information:			
Cash paid during the year for:			
Interest	$ 85	$ 4,250	$ 5,544
Income taxes	$ 512	$ 241	$ 268

Required

Using the information provided, including a careful analysis of Panera's statements of cash flows, answer the following questions. Be sure to explain the rationale for your answers and present any computations necessary to support them.

a. Was the sale of the frozen dough production facility for $13 million a cash sale? If so, what did Panera do with the cash it received?

b. Was the sale of the ABP division for $72 million a cash sale? If so, what did Panera do with the cash it received?

c. As shown in the preceding table, Panera has expanded its operations in each of the past five years. Approximately how much cash was spent on expansion in 1998, 1999, and 2000, and what were the sources of this cash for each year?

ATC 14–3 GROUP ASSIGNMENT *Preparing a Statement of Cash Flows*

The following financial statements and information are available for Blythe Industries, Inc.

Balance Sheets
As of December 31

	2004	2005
Assets		
Cash	$120,600	$ 160,200
Accounts Receivable	85,000	103,200
Inventory	171,800	186,400
Marketable Securities (Available for Sale)	220,000	284,000
Equipment	490,000	650,000
Accumulated Depreciation	(240,000)	(310,000)
Land	120,000	80,000
Total Assets	$967,400	$1,153,800
Liabilities and Equity		
Liabilities		
Accounts Payable (Inventory)	$ 66,200	$ 36,400
Notes Payable—Long-Term	250,000	230,000
Bonds Payable	100,000	200,000
Total Liabilities	416,200	466,400
Stockholders' Equity		
Common Stock, No Par	200,000	240,000
Preferred Stock, $50 Par	100,000	110,000
Paid-in Capital in Excess of Par—Preferred Stock	26,800	34,400
Total Paid-In Capital	326,800	384,400
Retained Earnings	264,400	333,000
Less: Treasury Stock	(40,000)	(30,000)
Total Stockholders' Equity	551,200	687,400
Total Liabilities and Stockholders' Equity	$967,400	$1,153,800

Income Statement
For the Year Ended December 31, 2005

Sales Revenue		$1,050,000
Cost of Goods Sold		(766,500)
Gross Profit		283,500
Operating Expenses		
Supplies Expense	$20,400	
Salaries Expense	92,000	
Depreciation Expense	90,000	
Total Operating Expenses		(202,400)
Operating Income		81,100
Nonoperating Items		
Interest Expense		(16,000)
Gain from the Sale of Marketable Securities		30,000
Gain from the Sale of Land and Equipment		12,000
Net Income		$ 107,100

Additional Information

1. Sold land that cost $40,000 for $44,000.
2. Sold equipment that cost $30,000 and had accumulated depreciation of $20,000 for $18,000.

3. Purchased new equipment for $190,000.
4. Sold marketable securities that cost $40,000 for $70,000.
5. Purchased new marketable securities for $104,000.
6. Paid $20,000 on the principal of the long-term note.
7. Paid off a $100,000 bond issue and issued new bonds for $200,000.
8. Sold 100 shares of treasury stock at its cost.
9. Issued some new common stock.
10. Issued some new $50 par preferred stock.
11. Paid dividends. (*Note:* The only transactions to affect retained earnings were net income and dividends.)

Required

Organize the class into three sections, and divide each section into groups of three to five students. Assign each section of groups an activity section of the statement of cash flows (operating activities, investing activities, or financing activities).

Group Task

Prepare your assigned portion of the statement of cash flows. Have a representative of your section put your activity section of the statement of cash flows on the board. As each adds its information on the board, the full statement of cash flows will be presented.

Class Discussion

Have the class finish the statement of cash flows by computing the net change in cash. Also have the class answer the following questions:

a. What is the cost per share of the treasury stock?
b. What was the issue price per share of the preferred stock?
c. What was the book value of the equipment sold?

BUSINESS APPLICATIONS CASE *Identifying Different Presentation Formats* ATC 14-4

In *Statement of Financial Accounting Standards No. 95,* the Financial Accounting Standards Board (FASB) recommended but did not require that companies use the direct method. In Appendix B, Paragraphs 106–121, the FASB discussed its reasons for this recommendation.

Required

Obtain a copy of *Standard No. 95* and read Appendix B Paragraphs 106–21. Write a brief response summarizing the issues that the FASB considered and its specific reaction to those issues. Your response should draw heavily on paragraphs 119–121.

WRITING ASSIGNMENT *Explaining Discrepancies between Cash Flow and Operating Income* ATC 14-5

The following selected information was drawn from the records of Fleming Company:

Assets	2005	2006
Accounts Receivable	$ 400,000	$ 840,200
Merchandise Inventory	720,000	1,480,000
Equipment	1,484,000	1,861,200
Accumulated Depreciation	(312,000)	(402,400)

Fleming is experiencing cash flow problems. Despite the fact that it reported significant increases in operating income, operating activities produced a net cash outflow. Recent financial forecasts predict that Fleming will have insufficient cash to pay its current liabilities within three months.

Required

Write a response explaining Fleming's cash shortage. Include a recommendation to remedy the problem.

ETHICAL DILEMMA *Would I Lie to You, Baby?* ATC 14-6

Andy and Jean Crocket are involved in divorce proceedings. When discussing a property settlement, Andy told Jean that he should take over their investment in an apartment complex because she would be unable to absorb the loss that the apartments are generating. Jean was somewhat distrustful and asked Andy to support his contention. He produced the following income statement, which was supported by a CPA's unqualified opinion that the statement was prepared in accordance with generally accepted accounting principles.

CROCKET APARTMENTS Income Statement For the Year Ended December 31, 2003		
Rent Revenue		$ 580,000
Less: Expenses		
Depreciation Expense	$280,000	
Interest Expense	184,000	
Operating Expense	88,000	
Management Fees	56,000	
Total Expenses		(608,000)
Net Loss		$ (28,000)

All revenue is earned on account. Interest and operating expenses are incurred on account. Management fees are paid in cash. The following accounts and balances were drawn from the 2002 and 2003 year-end balance sheets.

Account Title	2002	2003
Rent Receivable	$40,000	$44,000
Interest Payable	12,000	18,000
Accounts Payable (Oper. Exp.)	6,000	4,000

Jean is reluctant to give up the apartments but feels that she must because her present salary is only $40,000 per year. She says that if she takes the apartments, the $28,000 loss would absorb a significant portion of her salary, leaving her only $12,000 with which to support herself. She tells you that while the figures seem to support her husband's arguments, she believes that she is failing to see something. She knows that she and her husband collected a $20,000 distribution from the business on December 1, 2003. Also, $150,000 cash was paid in 2003 to reduce the principal balance on a mortgage that was taken out to finance the purchase of the apartments two years ago. Finally, $24,000 cash was paid during 2003 to purchase a computer system used in the business. She wonders, "If the apartments are losing money, where is my husband getting all the cash to make these payments?"

Required

a. Prepare a statement of cash flows for the 2003 accounting period.
b. Compare the cash flow statement prepared in Requirement *a* with the income statement and provide Jean Crocket with recommendations.
c. Comment on the value of an unqualified audit opinion when using financial statements for decision-making purposes.

ATC 14–7 SPREADSHEET ANALYSIS *Preparing a Statement of Cash Flows Using the Direct Method*

Refer to the information in Problem 14–18A. Solve for the statement of cash flows using the direct method. Instead of using the T-account method, set up the following spreadsheet to work through the analysis. The Debit/Credit entries are very similar to the T-account method except that they are entered onto a spreadsheet. Two distinct differences are as follows:

1. Instead of making entries on row 2 for Cash, cash entries are made beginning on row 24 under the heading Cash Transactions.
2. Entries for Retained Earnings are made on rows 15 through 20 since there are numerous revenue and expense entries to that account.

Required

a. Enter information in Column A.
b. Enter the beginning balance sheet amounts in Column B and ending balances in Column G. Total the debits and credits for each column.
c. To prevent erroneous entries to Cash in row 2, darken the area in Columns C through F.

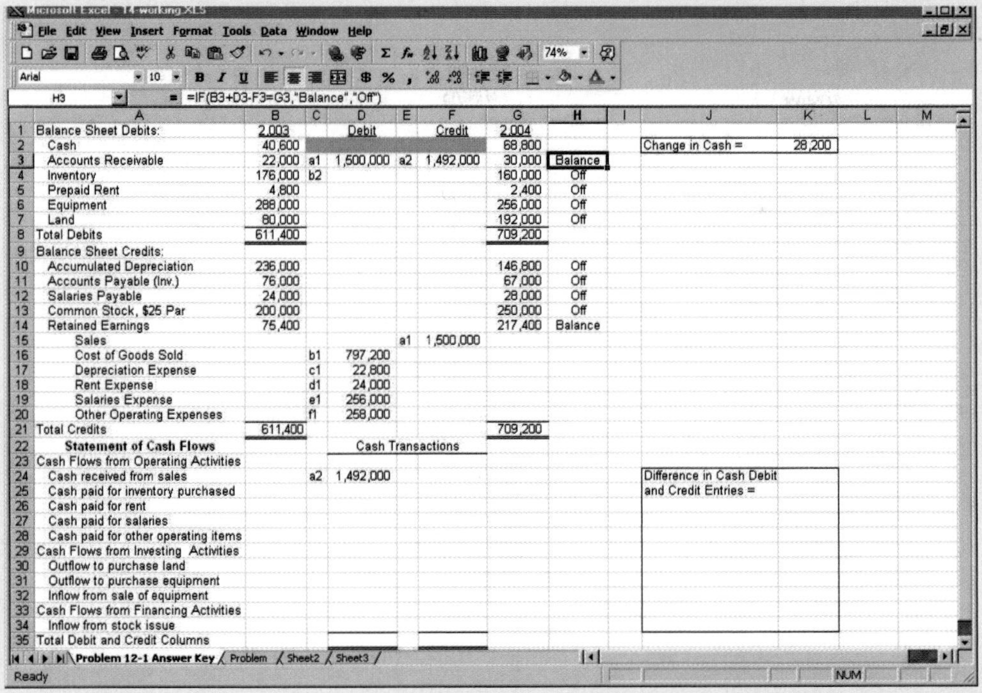

H3: =IF(B3+D3-F3=G3,"Balance","Off")

	A	B	C	D	E	F	G	H	I	J	K
1	Balance Sheet Debits:	2,003		Debit		Credit	2,004				
2	Cash	40,600					68,800			Change in Cash =	28,200
3	Accounts Receivable	22,000	a1	1,500,000	a2	1,492,000	30,000	Balance			
4	Inventory	176,000	b2				160,000	Off			
5	Prepaid Rent	4,800					2,400	Off			
6	Equipment	288,000					256,000	Off			
7	Land	80,000					192,000	Off			
8	Total Debits	611,400					709,200				
9	Balance Sheet Credits:										
10	Accumulated Depreciation	236,000					146,800	Off			
11	Accounts Payable (Inv.)	76,000					67,000	Off			
12	Salaries Payable	24,000					28,000	Off			
13	Common Stock, $25 Par	200,000					250,000	Off			
14	Retained Earnings	75,400					217,400	Balance			
15	Sales				a1	1,500,000					
16	Cost of Goods Sold		b1	797,200							
17	Depreciation Expense		c1	22,800							
18	Rent Expense		d1	24,000							
19	Salaries Expense		e1	256,000							
20	Other Operating Expenses		f1	258,000							
21	Total Credits	611,400					709,200				
22	**Statement of Cash Flows**			Cash Transactions							
23	Cash Flows from Operating Activities										
24	Cash received from sales		a2	1,492,000						Difference in Cash Debit and Credit Entries =	
25	Cash paid for inventory purchased										
26	Cash paid for rent										
27	Cash paid for salaries										
28	Cash paid for other operating items										
29	Cash Flows from Investing Activities										
30	Outflow to purchase land										
31	Outflow to purchase equipment										
32	Inflow from sale of equipment										
33	Cash Flows from Financing Activities										
34	Inflow from stock issue										
35	Total Debit and Credit Columns										

d. In Columns C through F, record entries for the revenue and expenses and then the related conversions to cash flow. The first entry (a1) and (a2) converting Sales to Cash Received from Sales has been provided for you. So has the labeling for the expense entries (b1 through f1).

e. Record the four entries from the Other Information provided in Problem 14–18A. These are investing and financing activities.

f. In Column H, set up the IF function to determine whether the balance sheet accounts are in balance or not ("off"). Cell H3 for Accounts Receivable is provided for you. Cell H3 can be copied to all the balance sheet debit accounts. The balance sheet credit account formulas will differ given the different debit/credit rules for those accounts. The formula for Retained Earnings will need to include rows 14 through 20. *When the word "Balance" is reflected in every balance sheet cell in column H, the spreadsheet analysis is complete.*

g. Total the Debit and Credit columns to ensure that the two columns are equal.

h. As a final check, beginning in cell J2, compute the change in the Cash account by subtracting the beginning balance from the ending balance. The difference will equal $28,200. Also beginning in cell J24, compute the difference in the debit and credit cash entries in rows 24 through 34. The difference should also equal $28,200.

Spreadsheet Tip

(1) Darken cells by highlighting the cells to be darkened. Select Format and then Cells. Click on the tab titled Patterns and choose a color.

SPREADSHEET ANALYSIS *Preparing a Statement of Cash Flows Using the Indirect Method* ATC 14–8

(*Note:* If you completed ATC 14–7, that spreadsheet can be modified to complete this problem.)

Refer to the information in Problem 14–18A. Solve for the statement of cash flows using the indirect method. Instead of using the T-account method, set up the following spreadsheet to work through the analysis. The Debit/Credit entries are very similar to the T-account method except that they are entered onto a spreadsheet. Instead of making entries on row 2 for Cash, Cash Flow entries are made beginning on row 18.

Required

a. Enter information in Column A.

b. Enter the beginning balance sheet amounts in Column B and ending balances in Column G. Total the debits and credits for each column.

c. To prevent erroneous entries to Cash in row 2, darken the area in Columns C through F.

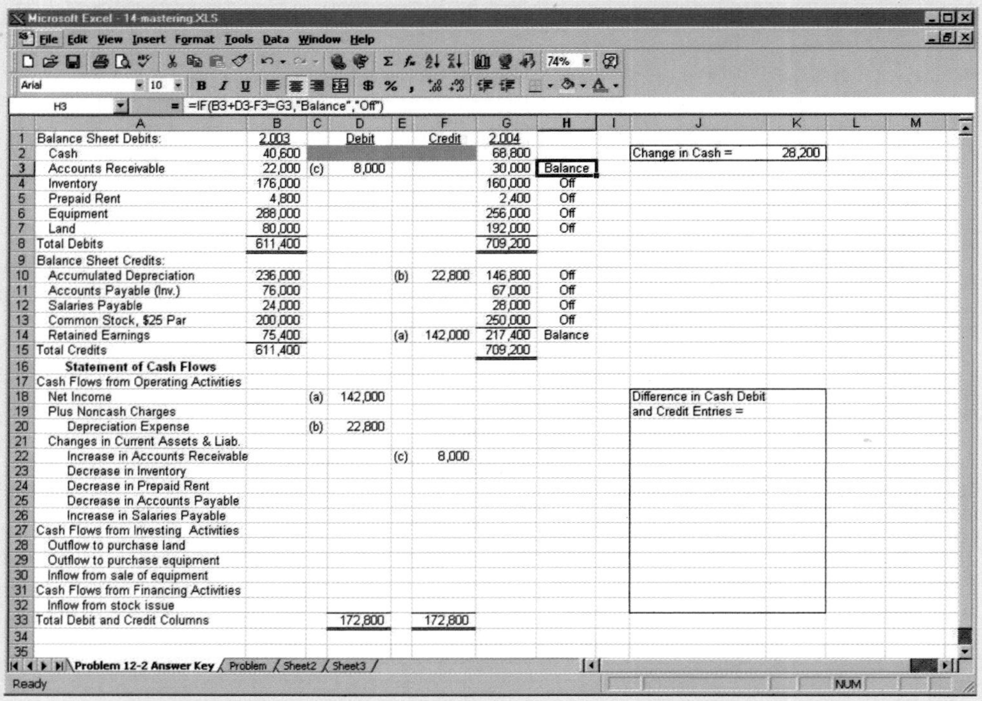

H3 = =IF(B3+D3-F3=G3,"Balance","Off")

	A	B	C	D	E	F	G	H	J	K
1	Balance Sheet Debits:	2,003		Debit		Credit	2,004			
2	Cash	40,600					68,800		Change in Cash =	28,200
3	Accounts Receivable	22,000	(c)	8,000			30,000	Balance		
4	Inventory	176,000					160,000	Off		
5	Prepaid Rent	4,800					2,400	Off		
6	Equipment	288,000					256,000	Off		
7	Land	80,000					192,000	Off		
8	Total Debits	611,400					709,200			
9	Balance Sheet Credits:									
10	Accumulated Depreciation	236,000			(b)	22,800	146,800	Off		
11	Accounts Payable (Inv.)	76,000					67,000	Off		
12	Salaries Payable	24,000					28,000	Off		
13	Common Stock, $25 Par	200,000					250,000	Off		
14	Retained Earnings	75,400			(a)	142,000	217,400	Balance		
15	Total Credits	611,400					709,200			
16	**Statement of Cash Flows**									
17	Cash Flows from Operating Activities									
18	Net Income		(a)	142,000					Difference in Cash Debit and Credit Entries =	
19	Plus Noncash Charges									
20	Depreciation Expense		(b)	22,800						
21	Changes in Current Assets & Liab.									
22	Increase in Accounts Receivable				(c)	8,000				
23	Decrease in Inventory									
24	Decrease in Prepaid Rent									
25	Decrease in Accounts Payable									
26	Increase in Salaries Payable									
27	Cash Flows from Investing Activities									
28	Outflow to purchase land									
29	Outflow to purchase equipment									
30	Inflow from sale of equipment									
31	Cash Flows from Financing Activities									
32	Inflow from stock issue									
33	Total Debit and Credit Columns			172,800		172,800				

d. Record the entry for Net Income. This is entry (a) provided.
e. Record the entry for Depreciation expense. This is entry (b) provided.
f. Record the entries for the changes in current assets and liabilities. The entry for the change in Accounts Receivable has been provided and is referenced as entry (c).
g. Record the four entries from the Other Information provided in Problem 14–18A. These are the investing and financing activities.
h. In Column H set up the IF function to determine whether the balance sheet accounts are in balance or not ("off"). Cell H3 for Accounts Receivable is provided for you. Cell H3 can be copied to all the balance sheet debit accounts. The balance sheet credit account formulas will differ given the different debit/credit rules for those accounts. *When the word "Balance" is reflected in every balance sheet cell in column H, the spreadsheet analysis is complete.*
i. Total the Debit and Credit columns to ensure that the two columns are equal.
j. As a final check, beginning in cell J2, compute the change in the Cash account by subtracting the beginning balance from the ending balance. The difference will equal $28,200. Also beginning in cell J18, compute the difference in the debit and credit cash entries in rows 18 through 32. The difference should also equal $28,200.

absolute amounts Dollar totals reported in accounts on financial reports that can be misleading because they make no reference to the relative size of the company being analyzed. *p. 533*

absorption (full) costing Practice of capitalizing all product costs, including fixed manufacturing costs, in inventory and expensing costs when goods are sold. *p. 453*

accounts receivable turnover Ratio measuring the quality of accounts receivable, calculated by dividing net sales by average net accounts receivable. *p. 538*

accrual accounting Accounting system that recognizes expenses or revenues when they occur regardless of when cash is exchanged. *p. 592*

accumulated conversion factors Factors used to convert a series of future cash inflows into their present value equivalent and that are applicable to cash inflows of equal amounts spread over equal interval time periods and that can be determined by computing the sum of the individual single factors used for each period. *p. 403*

acid-test ratio Measure of immediate debt-paying ability; calculated by dividing very liquid assets (cash, receivables, and marketable securities) by current liabilities. *p. 538*

activities The actions taken by an organization to accomplish its mission. *pp. 18, 233*

activity base Factor that causes changes in variable cost; is usually some measure of volume when used to define cost behavior. *p. 58*

activity-based cost drivers Measures of the use and consumption of activities such as number of setups, percentage of use, and pounds of material delivered; used as allocation bases, the measures can improve the accuracy of allocations in technical and automated business environments in which overhead is no longer driven by volume. *p. 231*

activity-based costing (ABC) A two-stage allocation process that employs a variety of cost drivers. In the first stage, costs associated with specific business activities are allocated or assigned to activity cost pools. The second stage involves allocating these pooled costs to designated cost objects through the use of cost drivers. The cost drivers chosen for each cost pool are drivers that measure the demand placed on that cost pool by the cost object. *p. 233*

activity-based management (ABM) Management of the activities of an organization to add the greatest value by developing products that satisfy the needs of that organization's customers. *p. 19*

activity centers Cost centers organized around operating activities that have similar characteristics; reduce the costs of record keeping by pooling indirect costs in a manner that enables allocations through the use of a common cost driver. *p. 233*

allocation Process of dividing a total cost into parts and apportioning the parts among the relevant cost objects. *p. 186*

allocation base Cost driver that constitutes the basis for the allocation process. *p. 187*

allocation rate Factor used to allocate or assign costs to a cost object; determined by taking the total cost to be allocated and dividing it by the appropriate cost driver. *p. 187*

annuity Equal series of cash flows received over equal intervals of time at a constant rate of return. *p. 403*

applied overhead Amount of overhead costs assigned during the period to work in process using the predetermined overhead rate. *p. 445*

appraisal costs Costs incurred to identify nonconforming products that were not avoided via the prevention cost expenditures. *p. 242*

average cost The total cost of making products divided by the total number of products made. *p. 7*

avoidable costs Future costs that can be avoided by taking a specified course of action. To be avoidable in a decision-making context, costs must differ among the alternatives. For example, if the cost of material used to make two different products is the same for both products, that cost could not be avoided by choosing to produce one product over the other. Therefore, the material's cost would not be an avoidable cost. *p. 137*

batch-level activities Activities (e.g., material handling, production setups) related to the production of groups of products, the cost of which is fixed regardless of the number of units produced; best allocated using cost drivers that measure activity consumption. *p. 236*

batch-level costs The costs associated with producing a batch of products. For example, the cost of setting up machinery to produce 1,000 products is a batch-level cost. The classification of batch-level costs is context sensitive. Postage for one product would be classified as a unit-level cost. In contrast, postage for a large number of products delivered in a single shipment would be classified as a batch-level cost. *p. 138*

benchmarking Identifying the best practices used by world-class competitors. *p. 18*

best practices Practices used by world-class companies. *p. 18*

book value per share Measure of a share of common stock; calculated by dividing stockholders' equity less preferred rights by the number of common shares outstanding. *p. 545*

bottleneck A constraint limiting the capacity of a company to produce or sell its products. An example is a piece of equipment that cannot produce enough component parts to keep employees in the assembly department busy. *p. 152*

break-even point Point where total revenue equals total cost; can be expressed in units or sales dollars. *p. 96*

budget committee Group of individuals responsible for coordinating budgeting activities, normally consisting of upper-level managers including the president; vice presidents of marketing, production, purchasing, and finance; and the controller.

budgeting Form of planning that formalizes a company's goals and objectives in financial terms. *p. 273*

budget slack Difference between inflated and realistic standards. *p. 319*

by-products Products that share common inputs with other joint products but have relatively insignificant market values relative to the other joint products. *p. 198*

capital budget Budget that describes the company's plans regarding investments, new products, or lines of business for the coming year; is used as input to prepare many of the operating budgets and becomes a formal part of the master budget. *p. 277*

capital budgeting Financial planning activities that cover the intermediate range of time such as whether to buy or lease equipment, whether to purchase a particular investment, or whether to increase operating expenses to stimulate sales. *p. 274*

capital investments Expenditures for the purchase of operational assets that involve a long-term commitment of funds that can be critically important to the company's ultimate success; normally recovered through the use of the assets. *p. 400*

cash budget A budget that focuses on cash receipts and payments that are expected to occur in the future. *p. 283*

cash inflows Sources of cash. *p. 589*

cash outflows Uses of cash. *p. 589*

certified suppliers Suppliers who have gained the confidence of the buyer by providing quality goods and services at desirable prices and usually in accordance with strict delivery specifications; frequently provide the buyer with preferred customer status in exchange for guaranteed purchase quantities and prompt payment schedules. *p. 145*

companywide allocation rate Use of direct labor hours or some other measure of volume to allocate all overhead cost to the company's products or other cost objects. *p. 230*

constraints Factors that limit a business's ability to satisfy the demand for its products. *p. 152*

continuous improvement Total quality management (TQM) feature that refers to an ongoing process through which employees learn to eliminate waste, reduce response time, minimize defects, and simplify the design and delivery of products and services to customers. *p. 18*

contribution margin Difference between a company's sales revenue and total variable cost; represents the amount available to cover fixed cost and thereafter to provide a profit. *p. 55*

contribution margin per unit The contribution margin per unit is equal to the sales price per unit minus the variable cost per unit. *p. 96*

contribution margin ratio Result of dividing the contribution margin per unit by the sales price; can be used in cost-volume-profit analysis to determine the amount of the break-even sales volume expressed in dollars or to determine the dollar level of sales required to attain a desired profit. *p. 108*

controllability concept The practice that evaluates a manager only on the revenue and costs under his or her direct control. *p. 363*

cost Amount of resources used to acquire an asset or to produce revenue. *p. 183*

cost accumulation Process of determining the cost of a particular object by accumulating many individual costs into a single total cost. *p. 184*

cost allocation Process of dividing a total cost into parts and assigning the parts to relevant objects. *pp. 12, 185*

cost averaging Method to determine the average cost per unit of a product or service by dividing the total cost by the activity base used in defining the cost; often is more relevant to decision making than actual costs. Pricing, performance evaluation, and control depend most often on average costs. *p. 59*

cost-based transfer price Transfer price based on the historical or standard cost incurred by the supplying segment. *p. 374*

cost behavior How a cost reacts (goes up, down, or remains the same) relative to changes in some measure of activity (e.g., the behavior pattern of the cost of raw materials is to increase as the number of units of product made increases). *p. 57*

cost center Type of responsibility center which incurs costs but does not generate revenue. *p. 361*

cost driver Any factor, usually some measure of activity, that causes cost to be incurred, sometimes referred to as *activity base* or *allocation base*. Examples are labor hours, machine hours, or some other measure of activity whose change causes corresponding changes in the cost object. *p. 184*

cost objects Objects for which managers need to know the cost; can be products, processes, departments, services, activities, and so on. *p. 183*

cost of capital Return paid to investors and creditors for the use of their assets (capital); usually represents a company's minimum rate of return. *p. 401*

cost per equivalent unit Unit cost of product determined by dividing total production costs by the number of equivalent whole units. It is used to allocate product costs between processing departments (compute ending inventory and the amount of costs transferred to the subsequent department). *p. 498*

cost per unit of input Cost of one unit of material, labor, or overhead determined by multiplying the price paid for one unit of material, labor or overhead input by the usage of input for one unit of material, labor or overhead.

cost-plus pricing Pricing strategy that sets the price at cost plus a markup equal to a percentage of the cost. *pp. 6, 96*

cost pool Many individual costs that have been accumulated into a single total for the purposes of allocation. *p. 196*

cost structure Company's cost mix (relative proportion of variable and fixed costs to total cost). When sales change, the size of the corresponding change in net income is directly related to the company's cost structure. Companies with a large percentage of fixed cost to variable costs have more fluctuation in net income with changes in sales. *p. 53*

cost tracing Relating specific costs to the objects that cause their incurrence. *p. 185*

cost-volume-profit (CVP) analysis Analysis that shows the interrelationships among sales prices, volume, fixed, and variable costs; an important tool in determining the break-even point or the most profitable combination of these variables. *p. 96*

current ratio Measure of liquidity; calculated by dividing current assets by current liabilities. *p. 537*

decentralization Practice of delegating authority and responsibility for the operation of business segments. *p. 360*

deferral transactions Accounting transactions in which cash payments or receipts occur before the associated expense or revenue is recognized. *p. 594*

differential costs Costs that differ among alternative business opportunities and are usually relevant information for decision making. Note, however, that not all are relevant. For example, although depreciation may differ between the alternatives, it is not avoidable because it is a sunk cost and therefore not relevant for decision making.

direct cost Cost that is easily traceable to a cost object and for which the sacrifice to trace is small in relation to the information benefits attained. *p. 185*

direct labor Wages paid to production workers whose efforts can be easily and conveniently traced to products. *p. 9*

direct method (1) Allocation method that allocates service center costs directly to operating department cost pools. (2) Method of preparing the statement of cash flows that reports the total cash receipts and cash payments from each of the major categories of activities (collections from customers, payments to suppliers, etc.). *pp. 202, 603*

direct raw materials Costs of raw materials used to make products that can be easily and conveniently traced to those products. *p. 9*

dividend yield Ratio for comparing stock dividends paid in relation to the market price; calculated as dividends per share divided by market price per share. *p. 546*

downstream costs Costs, such as delivery costs and sales commissions, incurred after the manufacturing process is complete. *pp. 17, 241*

earnings per share Measure of the value of a share of common stock in terms of company earnings; calculated as net income available to common stockholders divided by the average number of outstanding common shares. *p. 545*

economies of scale Concept by which the unit cost of production can be reduced by taking advantage of opportunities that become available when an operation's size is increased. Increased size usually results in an increased volume of activity that drives the per unit fixed cost down, resulting in a lower total cost of production.

efficient market hypothesis The proposition that creditors and investors look to the substance of business events regardless of how those events are reported in financial reports.

equation method Cost-volume-profit analysis technique that uses a basic mathematical relationship among sales, variable costs, fixed costs, and desired net income before taxes and provides a solution in terms of units. *p. 109*

equipment replacement decisions Decisions regarding whether existing equipment should be replaced with newer equipment based on identification and comparison of the avoidable costs of the old and new equipment to determine which equipment is more profitable to operate. *p. 149*

equivalent whole units Result of expressing partially completed goods in an equivalent number of fully completed goods. *p. 498*

expense transactions Transactions completed in the process of operating a business that decrease assets or increase liabilities. *p. 592*

external failure costs Costs incurred when defective goods are delivered to customers. *p. 242*

facility-level activities Activities (e.g., paying insurance on the facility, providing plant maintenance, and paying taxes) performed for the benefit of the production process as a whole and whose allocation is arbitrary. *p. 237*

facility-level costs Costs incurred on behalf of the whole company or a segment of the company; not related to any specific product, batch, or unit of production or service and unavoidable unless the entire company or segment is eliminated. *p. 138*

failure costs Costs incurred from the actual occurrence of nonconforming events. *p. 242*

favorable variance Variance that occurs when actual costs are less than standard costs or when actual sales are higher than standard sales. *p. 315*

financial accounting Field of accounting designed to meet the information needs of external users of business information (creditors, investors, governmental agencies, financial analysts, etc.); its objective is to classify and record business events and transactions to facilitate the production of external financial reports (income statement, balance sheet, statement of cash flows, and statement of changes in equity). *p. 4*

Financial Accounting Standards Board (FASB) Private, independent board established by the accounting profession that has been delegated the authority by the SEC to establish most of the accounting rules and regulations for public financial reporting. *p. 5*

financial statement budgets (pro forma statements) Projected financial statements found in the master budget that are based on information contained in the operating budgets.

financing activities Cash inflows and outflows from transactions with investors and creditors (except interest). These cash flows include cash receipts from the issue of stock, borrowing activities, and cash disbursements associated with dividends. *pp. 23, 590*

finished goods End result of the manufacturing process measured by the accumulated cost of raw materials, labor, and overhead. *p. 6*

Finished Goods Inventory Asset account used to accumulate the product costs (direct materials, direct labor, and overhead) associated with completed products that have not yet been sold. *p. 440*

first-in, first-out (FIFO) method Method used to determine equivalent units when accuracy is deemed to be important; accounts for the degree of completion of both beginning and ending inventories but is more complicated than the weighted-average method. *p. 499*

fixed cost Cost that in total remains constant when activity volume changes; varies per unit inversely with changes in the volume of activity. *p. 50*

flexible budgets Budgets that show expected revenues and costs at a variety of different activity levels. *p. 314*

flexible budget variances Differences between budgets based on standard amounts at the actual level of activity and actual results; caused by differences in standard and actual unit cost since the volume of activity is the same. *p. 318*

general, selling, and administrative costs All costs not associated with obtaining or manufacturing a product; in practice are sometimes referred to as *period costs* because they are normally expensed in the period in which the economic sacrifice is incurred. *p. 11*

generally accepted accounting principles (GAAP) Rules and regulations that accountants agree to follow when preparing financial reports for public distribution. *p. 5*

high-low method Method of estimating the fixed and variable components of a mixed cost; determines the variable cost per unit by dividing the difference between the total cost of the high and low points by the difference in the corresponding high and low volumes. The fixed cost component is determined by subtracting the variable cost from the total cost at either the high or low volume. *p. 61*

horizontal analysis Analysis technique that compares amounts of the same item over several time periods. *p. 533*

hybrid cost systems Cost system that blends some of the features of a job-order costing system with some of the features of a process cost system. *p. 486*

ideal standard Highest level of efficiency attainable, based on all input factors interacting perfectly under ideal or optimum conditions. *p. 321*

incremental revenue Additional cash inflows from operations generated by using an additional capital asset. *p. 407*

indirect cost Cost that cannot be easily traced to a cost object and for which the economic sacrifice to trace is not worth the informational benefits. *pp. 11, 185*

indirect method Method of preparing the statement of cash flows that uses the net income from the income statement as a starting point for reporting cash flow from operating activities; adjustments necessary to convert accrual-based net income to a cash-equivalent basis are shown in the operating activities section of the statement of cash flows. *p. 603*

information overload Situation in which presentation of too much information confuses the user of the information. *p. 532*

inputs The resources (material, labor, and overhead) used to make products.

interdepartmental service Service performed by one service department for the benefit of another service department. *p. 203*

internal failure costs Costs incurred when defects are corrected before goods reach the customer. *p. 242*

internal rate of return Rate that will produce a present value of an investment's future cash inflows that equals cash outflows required to acquire the investment; alternatively, the rate that produces in a net present value of zero. *p. 406*

inventory holding costs Costs associated with acquiring and retaining inventory including cost of storage space; lost, stolen, or damaged merchandise; insurance; personnel and management costs; and interest. *p. 19*

inventory turnover Measurement of the volume of sales in relation to inventory levels; calculated as the cost of goods sold divided by average inventory. *p. 539*

investing activities Cash inflows and outflows associated with buying or selling long-term assets Also, cash inflows and outflows associated with lending activities (loans made to others—cash outflows or collections of loans made to others—cash inflows). *pp. 23, 590*

investment center Type of responsibility center for which revenue, expense and capital investments can be measured. *p. 361*

job cost sheet Document used in a job-order cost system to accumulate the materials, labor, and overhead costs of a job through the various stages of production; at job completion, contains a summary of all costs that were incurred to complete that job; also known as *job-order cost sheet* or *job record.* *p. 486*

job-order cost system System used to determine the costs of distinct, one-of-a-kind products. Costs are traced to products that are produced individually (e.g., custom designed building) or produced in batches (e.g., an order for 100 wedding invitations). *p. 484*

joint costs Common costs incurred in the process of making two or more products. *p. 196*

joint product Products derived from joint cost. *p. 196*

just in time (JIT) Inventory flow system that minimizes the amount of inventory on hand by making inventory available for customer consumption on demand, therefore eliminating the need to store inventory. The system reduces explicit holding costs including financing, warehouse storage, supervision, theft, damage, and obsolescence. It also eliminates hidden opportunity costs such as lost revenue due to the lack of availability of inventory. *p. 19*

labor efficiency variance Variance occurring in a standard cost accounting system when the actual amount or quantity of direct labor used differs from the standard amount required. *p. 324*

labor rate variance Variance that occurs when the actual pay rate differs from the standard pay rate for direct labor. *p. 324*

lax standards Easily attainable goals that can be accomplished with minimal effort. *p. 321*

liquidity ratios Measures of short-term debt-paying ability. *p. 537*

low-ball pricing Pricing a product below competitors' price to lure customers away and then raising the price once customers depend on the supplier for the product. *p. 145*

making the numbers Expression that indicates that marketing managers attained the sales volume indicated in the master budget. *p. 316*

management by exception Use of management resources on areas that are not performing in accordance with expectations; a philosophy that directs management to concentrate on areas with significant variances. *pp. 321, 362*

managerial accounting Field of accounting designed to meet the information needs of managers and other individuals working inside the business. It is concerned with information gathering and reporting that adds value to the business. Managerial accounting information is not regulated or made available to the public. *p. 4*

manufacturing overhead Production costs that cannot be traced directly to products. *p. 11*

Manufacturing Overhead account Temporary account used during an accounting period to accumulate the actual overhead costs incurred and the total amount of overhead applied to the Work in Process account. At the end of the period, a debit balance in the account implies that overhead has been underapplied and a credit balance implies that overhead has been overapplied. The account is closed at year end in an adjusting entry to the inventory and Cost of Goods Sold accounts. If the balance is insignificant, it is closed only to Cost of Goods Sold. *p. 445*

margin of safety Difference between break-even sales and budgeted sales expressed in units, dollars, or as a percentage; the amount by which actual sales can fall below budgeted sales before a loss is incurred. *p. 105*

market-based transfer price Transfer price based on the external market price less any savings in cost; the closest approximation to an arm's-length transaction that segments can achieve. *p. 372*

master budget Composition of the numerous separate but interdependent departmental budgets that cover a wide range of operating and financial factors such as sales, production, manufacturing expenses, and administrative expenses. *p. 276*

material variance Variance that would affect decision making. *p. 322*

materiality Characteristic that designates the point at which the knowledge of or lack of information would make a difference in a decision; can be measured in absolute, percentage, quantitative, or qualitative terms. *p. 533*

materials price variance Variance that occurs when actual prices paid for raw materials differ from the standard prices. *p. 324*

materials quantity variance Variance that occurs when the actual amounts of raw materials used to produce a good differ from the standard amounts required to produce that good. *p. 324*

materials requisition A form used to request or order the materials needed to begin a designated job; can be a paper document or an electronic impulse delivered through a computer. Materials requisitioned for a job are summarized by the accounting department on a job cost sheet. *p. 486*

minimum rate of return Minimum amount of profitability required to persuade a company to accept an investment opportunity; also known as *desired rate of return, required rate of return, hurdle rate, cutoff rate,* and *discount rate. p. 401*

mixed costs (semivariable costs) Costs composed of a mixture of fixed and variable components. *p. 61*

most-favored customer status Arrangement by which a supplier and customer achieve mutual benefit by providing each other with favorable treatment that is not extended to other associates. *p. 19*

negotiated transfer price Transfer price established by agreement of both the selling and buying segments of the firm. *p. 374*

net margin Profitability measurement that indicates the percentage of each sales dollar resulting in profit; calculated as net income divided by net sales. *p. 542*

net present value Evaluation technique that uses a desired rate of return to discount future cash flows back to their present value equivalents and then subtracts the cost of the investment from the present value equivalents to determine the net present value. A zero or positive net present value (present value of cash inflows equals or exceeds the present value of cash outflows) implies that the investment opportunity provides an acceptable rate of return. *p. 406*

noncash investing and financing activities Business transactions that do not directly affect cash, such as exchanging stock for land or purchasing property by using a mortgage; are reported as both an inflow and outflow in a separate section of the statement of cash flows. *p. 590*

nonvalue-added activities Tasks undertaken that do not contribute to a product's ability to satisfy customer needs. *p. 19*

number of days' sales in inventory Another way to look at the inventory turnover by converting the inventory turnover ratio into a number of days; calculated by dividing 365 by the inventory turnover ratio.

number of days' sales in receivables (average collection period) Another way to look at the accounts receivable turnover by converting the turnover ratio into a number of days; calculated by dividing 365 days by the turnover ratio.

operating activities Cash inflows and outflows associated with operating the business. These cash flows normally result from revenue and expense transactions including interest. *pp. 22, 590*

operating budgets Budgets prepared by different departments within a company that will become a part of the company's master budget; typically include a sales budget, an inventory purchases budget, a selling and administrative budget, and a cash budget. *p. 276*

operating departments Departments assigned tasks leading to the accomplishment of the organization's objectives. *p. 201*

operating leverage Operating condition in which a percentage change in revenue produces a proportionately larger percentage change in net income; measured by dividing the contribution margin by net income. The higher the proportion of fixed cost to total costs, the greater the operating leverage. *p. 50*

opportunity cost Cost of lost opportunities such as the failure to make sales due to an insufficient supply of inventory. *pp. 21, 139*

ordinary annuity Annuity whose cash inflows occur at the end of each accounting period. *p. 404*

outputs Products that result from processing inputs.

outsourcing The practice of buying goods and services from another company rather than producing them internally. *p. 143*

overapplied or underapplied overhead Result of allocating more or less overhead costs to the Work in Process account than the amount of the actual overhead costs incurred.

overhead Costs associated with producing products that cannot be cost effectively traced to products; includes indirect costs such as indirect materials, indirect labor, utilities, rent, depreciation on manufacturing facilities and equipment, and planning, design, and setup costs related to the manufacture of products. *p. 6*

overhead costs Indirect costs of doing business that cannot be directly traced to a product, department, or process, such as depreciation. *p. 185*

participative budgeting Budget technique that allows subordinates to participate with upper-level managers in setting budget objectives, thereby encouraging cooperation and support in the attainment of the company's goals. *p. 276*

payback method Technique that evaluates investment opportunities by determining the length of time necessary to recover the initial net investment through incremental revenue or cost savings; the shorter the period, the better the investment opportunity. *p. 414*

percentage analysis Analysis of relationships between two different items to draw conclusions or make decisions. *p. 534*

period costs General, selling, and administrative costs that are expensed in the period in which the economic sacrifice is made. *p. 11*

perpetual (continuous) budgeting Continuous budgeting activity normally covering a 12-month time span by replacing the current month's budget at the end of each month with a new budget; keeps management constantly involved in the budget process so that changing conditions are incorporated on a timely bases. *p. 275*

postaudit Repeat calculation using the techniques originally employed to analyze an investment project; accomplished with the use of actual data available at the completion of the investment project so that the actual results can be compared with expected results based on estimated data at the beginning of the project. Its purpose is to provide feedback as to whether the expected results were actually accomplished in improving the accuracy of future analysis. *p. 417*

practical standard Level of efficiency in which the ideal standard has been modified to allow for normal tolerable inefficiencies. *p. 321*

predetermined overhead rate Rate determined by dividing the estimated overhead costs for the period by some measure of estimated total production activity for the period, such as the number of labor hours or machine hours. The base chosen should provide some logical measure of overhead use. The rate is determined before actual costs or activity are known. Throughout the accounting period, the rate is used to allocate overhead costs to the Work in Process Inventory account based on actual production activity. *pp. 196, 445*

present value index Present value of cash inflows divided by the present value of cash outflows. Higher index numbers indicate higher rates of return. *p. 410*

present value table Table that consists of a list of factors to use in converting future values into their present value equivalents; composed of columns that represent different return rates and rows that depict different periods of time. *p. 402*

prestige pricing Pricing strategy that sets the price at a premium (above average markup above cost) under the assumption that people will pay more for the product because of its prestigious brand name, media attention, or some other reason that has piqued the interest of the public. *p. 106*

prevention costs Costs incurred to avoid nonconforming products. *p. 242*

price-earnings ratio Measurement used to compare the values of different stocks in terms of earnings; calculated as market price per share divided by earnings per share. *p. 546*

pro forma financial statements Budgeted financial statements prepared from the information in the master budget. *p. 283*

process cost system System used to determine the costs of homogeneous products, such as chemicals, foods or paints, that distributes costs evenly across total production; determines an average by dividing the total product costs of each production department by the number of units of product made in that department during some designated period of time. The total costs in the last production department include all costs incurred in preceding departments so that the unit cost determined for the last department reflects the final unit cost of the product. *p. 484*

product costs All costs related to obtaining or manufacturing a product intended for sale to customers; are accumulated in inventory accounts and expensed as cost of goods sold at the point of sale. For a manufacturing company, product costs include direct materials, direct labor, and manufacturing overhead. *p. 6*

product costing Classification and accumulation of individual inputs (materials, labor, and overhead) for determining the cost of making a good or providing a service. *p. 6*

product-level activities Activities (e.g., inventory holding cost, engineering developmental costs) that support a specific product or product line and whose allocation is based on the extent to which the activities are used in sustaining the product or product line. *p. 236*

product-level costs Costs incurred to support different kinds of products or services; can be avoided by the elimination of a product line or a type of service. *p. 138*

profit center Type of responsibility center for which both revenues and costs can be indentified. *p. 361*

profitability ratios Measurements of a firm's ability to generate earnings. *p. 547*

qualitative characteristics Nonquantifiable features such as company reputation, welfare of employees, and customer satisfaction that can be affected by certain decisions. *p. 140*

quality The degree to which actual products or services conform to their design specifications. *p. 242*

quality cost report An accountant's report that typically lists the company's quality costs and provides a horizontal analysis showing each item as a percentage of total cost. *p. 243*

quantitative characteristics Numbers in decision making subject to mathematical manipulation, such as the dollar amounts of revenues and expenses. *p. 140*

quick ratio Same as acid-test ratio. *p. 538*

ratio analysis Same as percentage analysis. *p. 536*

raw materials Physical commodities (e.g., wood, metal, paint) used in the manufacturing process. *p. 9*

Raw Materials Inventory Asset account used to accumulate the costs of materials such as lumber, metals, paints, chemicals that will be used to make the company's products. *p. 440*

reciprocal method Allocation method that considers two-way associations between/among service centers (service centers provide to as well as receive services from other service centers); uses simultaneous linear equations, but the resultant cost distributions are difficult to interpret. *p. 205*

reciprocal relationships Two-way associations in which departments provide services to and receive services from one another. *p. 205*

recovery of investment Recovery of the funds used to acquire the original investment. *p. 415*

reengineering Business practices designed by companies to make production and delivery systems more competitive in world markets by eliminating or minimizing waste, errors, and costs. *p. 18*

relevant costs Future-oriented costs that differ between business alternatives; also known as *avoidable costs. p. 137*

relevant information Decision-making information about costs, costs savings, or revenues that have these features: (1) future-oriented information and (2) the information differs between the alternatives; decision specific (information that is relevant in one decision may not be relevant in another decision). *Relevant costs* are referred to as *avoidable costs* and *relevant revenues* are referred to as *differential revenues. p. 136*

relevant range Range of activity over which the definitions of fixed and variable costs apply. *p. 58*

residual income Approach that evaluates managers on their ability to maximize the dollar value of earnings above some targeted level of earnings. *p. 369*

responsibility accounting Accounting system in which the accountability for results is assigned to a segment manager of the firm based on the amount of control or influence the manager possesses over those results. *p. 360*

responsibility center Point in an organization where the control over revenue or expense items is located. *p. 361*

responsibility reports Reports of the performance of various responsibility centers of the firm with respect to controllable items; show the variances that result from comparing budgeted and actual controllable items. *p. 361*

retained earnings Equity account that is the culmination of all earnings retained in the business since inception (all revenues minus all expenses—including cost of goods sold—and distributions for the period added to all past retained earnings). *p. 447*

return on assets The ratio of net income divided by total assets.

return on equity Measure of the profitability of a firm based on earnings generated in relation to stockholders' equity; calculated as net income divided by stockholders' equity. *p. 544*

return on investment Measure of profitability based on the asset base of the firm. It is calculated as net income divided by average total assets. ROI is a product of net margin and asset turnover. *pp. 365, 544*

revenue transactions Transactions completed in the process of operating a business that increase assets or decrease liabilities by providing services or products. *p. 592*

sales volume variance Difference between sales based on a static budget (standard sales price times standard level of activity) and sales based on a flexible budget (standard sales price times actual level of activity). *p. 315*

sales price variance Difference between actual sales and expected sales based on the standard sales price per unit times the actual level of activity. *p. 318*

scattergraph method Method of estimating the variable and fixed components by which cost data are plotted on a graph and a regression line is visually drawn through the points so that the total distance between the data points and the line is minimized. *p. 62*

schedule of cost of goods manufactured and sold Schedule that summarizes the flow of manufacturing product costs; its result, cost of goods sold, is shown as a single line item on the company's income statement. *p. 452*

Securities and Exchange Commission (SEC) Government agency authorized by Congress to establish regulations regarding public reporting practices; requires companies that issue securities to the public to file annual audited financial statements with it. *p. 4*

segment Component part of an organization that is designated as a reporting entity. *p. 146*

sensitivity analysis Spreadsheet analysis that executes "what-if" questions to assess the sensitivity of profits to simultaneous changes in fixed cost, variable cost, and sales volume. *p. 106*

service departments Departments such as quality control, repair and maintenance, personnel, and accounting that provide support to the operating departments. *p. 201*

single-payment (lump-sum) A one-time receipt of cash which can be converted to its present value using a conversion factor. *p. 402*

solvency ratios Measures of a firm's long-term debt-paying ability. *p. 540*

special order decisions Decisions of whether to accept orders from nonregular customers who want to buy goods or services significantly below the normal selling price. If the order's differential revenues exceed its avoidable costs, the order should be accepted. Qualitative features such as the order's effect on the existing customer base if accepted must also be considered. *p. 141*

spending variance Difference between actual fixed overhead costs and budgeted fixed overhead costs. *p. 328*

split-off point Point in the production process where products become separate and identifiable. *p. 196*

standards Per unit price or costs that "should be" based on a certain set of anticipated circumstances; per unit cost standards are composed of price and quantity standards that together provide the per unit cost standard. *p. 320*

start-up (setup) costs The costs associated with the activities of changing machinery, the production configuration, inspection, etc., to prepare for making a new product or a batch of a product. *p. 232*

statement of cash flows A financial statement that describes the sources and uses of cash that occurred during an accounting period. *p. 22*

static budgets Budgets such as the master budget based solely on the level of planned activity; remain constant even when volume of activity changes. *p. 314*

step method Two-step allocation method that considers one-way interdepartmental service center relationships by allocating costs from service centers to service centers as well as from service centers to operating departments; does not consider reciprocal relationships between service centers. *p. 203*

strategic cost management New management techniques that are designed to more accurately measure and control costs. The techniques have been implemented as a response to today's complex automated business environment. These new strategies include efforts to eliminate nonvalue-added activities, more efficient designs for the manufacturing process, and new ways to trace overhead costs to cost objects. *p. 241*

strategic planning Planning activities associated with long-range decisions such as defining the scope of the business, determining which products to develop, deciding whether to discontinue a business segment, and determining which market niche would be most profitable. *p. 274*

suboptimization Situation in which managers act in their own self-interests even though the organization as a whole suffers. *p. 369*

sunk costs Costs that have been incurred in past transactions and therefore are not relevant for decision making. In an equipment replacement decision, the cost of the old machine presently in use is a sunk cost and is not avoidable because it has already been incurred. *p. 136*

T-account method Method of determining net cash flows by analyzing beginning and ending balances on the balance sheet and inferring the period's transactions from the income statement. *p. 592*

target pricing (target costing) Pricing strategy that begins with the determination of a price at which a product will sell and then focuses on the development of that product with a cost structure that will satisfy market demands. *p. 99*

theory of constraints (TOC) Practice used by many businesses to increase profitability by managing bottlenecks or constrained resources by identifying the bottlenecks restricting the operations of the business and then opening them by relaxing the constraints. *p. 153*

time value of money Concept that recognizes the fact that the present value of an opportunity to receive one dollar in the future is less than one dollar because of interest, risk, and inflation factors. *p. 401*

total quality management (TQM) Management philosophy that includes: (1) a continuous systematic problem-solving philosophy that engages personnel at all levels of the organization to eliminate waste, defects, and nonvalue-added activities; and (2) to manage quality costs in a manner that leads to the highest level of customer satisfaction. *pp. 18, 243*

transferred-in costs Costs transferred from one department to the next; combined with the materials, labor, and overhead costs incurred in the department so that when goods are complete, the total product cost of all departments is transferred to the Finished Goods Inventory account. *p. 486*

transfer price Price at which products or services are transferred between divisions or other subunits of an organization. *p. 372*

trend analysis Study of the performance of a business over a period of time. *p. 533*

turnover of assets Measure of sales in relation to assets; calculated as net sales divided by total assets.

unadjusted rate of return Measure of profitability computed by dividing the average incremental increase in annual net income by the average cost of the original investment (original cost ÷ 2). *p. 415*

unfavorable variance Variance that occurs when actual costs exceed standard costs or when actual sales are less than standard sales. *p. 315*

unit-level activities Activities that occur each time a unit of product is made; the costs associated with these activities exhibit a variable cost behavior pattern. *p. 235*

unit-level costs Costs incurred each time a company makes a single product or performs a single service and that can be avoided by eliminating a unit of product or service. Likewise, unit-level costs increase with each additional product produced or service provided. *p. 137*

upstream costs Costs incurred before the manufacturing process begins, for example, research and development costs. *pp. 17, 241*

value-added activity Any unit of work that contributes to a product's ability to satisfy customer needs. *p. 19*

value-added principle The benefits attained (value added) from the process should exceed the cost of the process. *p. 5*

value chain Linked sequence of activities that create value for the customer. *p. 19*

variable cost Cost that in total changes in direct proportion to changes in volume of activity; remains constant per unit when volume of activity changes. *p. 49*

variable costing Product costing system that capitalizes only variable cost in inventory; its income statement subtracts variable costs from revenue to determine contribution margin. Fixed costs, including product cost, are subtracted from the contribution margin to determine net income. In this format the amount of net income is not affected by the volume of production. *p. 454*

variances Differences between standard and actual amounts. *p. 315*

vertical analysis Analysis technique that compares items on financial statements to significant totals. *p. 535*

vertical integration Attainment of control over the entire spectrum of business activity from production to sales; as an example a grocery store that owns farms. *p. 144*

visual fit line Line drawn by visual inspection to minimize the total distance between the data points and the line; used to estimate fixed and variable cost. *p. 62*

volume-based cost drivers Measures of volume such as labor hours, machine hours, or amounts of materials that have a strong correlation with unit-level overhead cost and that make appropriate allocation bases for the allocation of unit-level overhead costs. *p. 231*

volume variance Difference between the budgeted fixed cost and the amount of fixed costs allocated to production. *p. 328*

voluntary costs Prevention and appraisal costs that are a function of managerial discretion. *p. 242*

weighted average method Method often used in a process cost system for determining equivalent units; ignores the state of completion of items in beginning inventory and assumes that items in beginning inventory are complete. *p. 498*

work ticket Mechanism (paper or electronic) used to accumulate the time spent on a job by each employee; sent to the accounting department where wage rates are recorded and labor costs are determined. The amount of labor costs for each ticket is summarized on the appropriate job-order cost sheet; sometimes called a *time card*. *p. 487*

working capital Current assets minus current liabilities. *pp. 407, 537*

working capital ratio Another term for the current ratio; calculated by dividing current assets by current liabilities. *p. 537*

Work in Process Inventory Asset account used to accumulate all product costs (direct materials, direct labor, and overhead) associated with incomplete products in production. *p. 440*

Chapter 1
p. 3 © PhotoLink/Getty. **p. 4** © Amy Etra/PhotoEdit. **p, 16** © Associate Press. **p.18** © Charles Gupton/Stock Boston. **p. 20** Courtesy of Ford Motor Company.

Chapter 2
p. 49 Courtesy of Southwest Airlines. **p. 50** © Alain Benainous/Gamma. **p. 51** © Photo Disc/Getty. **p. 59** © Mark Richards/PhotoEdit. **p. 63** © Corbis.

Chapter 3
p. 95 Jay Silverman Productions/Getty. **p. 100** © Photo Disc/Getty. **p. 103** © JEFF HAYNES/ AFP/Getty Images.

Chapter 4
p. 135 © Photodisc/Getty. **p. 138** © Stephen Mallon/Getty. **p. 140** © Photodisc Red/Getty. **p. 145** © Ryan McVay/Getty Images.

Chapter 5
p. 183 © Jon Feingersh/CORBIS. **p. 184** Cele Seldon. **p. 187** © Digital Vision/Getty. **p. 194** © Digital Vision/Getty.

Chapter 6
p. 229 © David Young-Wolf/PhotoEdit. **p. 230** © Royalty-Free/CORBIS. **p. 234** © Royalty-Free/CORBIS. **p. 244** Courtesy of Malcolm Baldridge National Quality Award Committee.

Chapter 7
p. 273 © Jean-Yves Ruszniewski; TempSport/CORBIS. **p. 275** © Andy Sacks/Tony Stone/Getty. **p. 279** © PhotoLink/PhotoDisc/Getty. **p. 284** © R. Morley/PhotoLink/ Getty Images.

Chapter 8
p. 313 © Peter Gridley/Photographers Choice/Getty. **p. 316** © Royalty-Free/CORBIS. **p. 320** Corbis. **p. 326** Rob Crandall/Stock Boston. **p. 331** © Royalty-Free/CORBIS.

Chapter 9
p. 359 © Michael Newman/PhotoEdit. **p. 361** © Royalty-Free/Corbis. **p. 369** © Brand X Pictures/Getty. **p. 370** © Digital Vision/Getty. **p. 373** © Digital Vision/Getty.

Chapter 10
p. 399 © Beateworks Inc/Brand X Pictures/Getty. **p. 401** © Photo Disc/Getty. **p. 407** © Royalty-Free/CORBIS. **p. 411** © PhotoLink/Getty.

Chapter 11
p. 439 Stickley Furniture, L & L.G. Stickley, Inc. **p. 441** © Royalty-Free/CORBIS. **p. 444** © Allan H Shoemaker/Taxi/Getty.

Chapter 12
p. 483 © PhotoLink/Getty **p. 484** Disney. **p. 487** © Russell Illig/Getty Images. **p. 506** © Syracuse Newspapers/C.W. McKeen/The Image Works.

Chapter 13
p. 531 © TIM SHAFFER/Reuters/ Corbis. **p. 532** © Don Farrall/Getty. **p. 549** © Rachel Epstein/ PhotoEdit. **Chapter 14 p. 589** © Richard Levine. **p. 599** © Steve Cole/Getty. **p. 602** © Royalty-Free/CORBIS. **p. 606** © Susan Van Etten/PhotoEdit.

INDEX

D

E

F

G

H

I

N

O

eInstruction
Partnering with teachers to inspire the next generation

McGraw-Hill Irwin

CPS
Classroom Performance System

What is CPS?

The Classroom Performance System is a revolutionary system that brings ultimate interactivity to the lecture hall or classroom. CPS is a wireless response system that gives you immediate feedback from every student in the class. CPS units include easy-to-use software for creating and delivering questions and assessments to your class. With CPS you can ask subjective and objective questions. Then every student simply responds with their individual, wireless response pad, providing instant results. CPS is the perfect tool for engaging students while gathering important assessment data.

Features and Benefits:

CPS Receiver Unit

- Interactivity–receive instant feedback on what students have learned
- Increased class discussion–anonymous opinion polls can be used to generate debate
- Able to be integrated with PowerPoint slides
- Improved attendance
- Automatically graded testing
- Simple to install, set up, and use
- Low cost
- Reliable technical support

How do I get CPS?

Please contact your McGraw-Hill textbook representative. The keypads are ordered by your bookstore and the enrollment codes needed to incorporate the keypad in your course are packaged with your student's textbook or available online.

The McGraw-Hill Companies